CONTENTS

LEADING and MANAGING in NURSING

SEVENTH EDITION

Patricia S. Yoder-Wise, RN, EdD, NEA-BC, ANEF, FAAN

Professor and Dean Emerita
Texas Tech University Health Sciences Center
Lubbock, Texas

ELSEVIER

ELSEVIER

3251 Riverport Lane
St. Louis, Missouri 63043

Notice

Previous editions copyrighted 2015, 2011, 2007, 2003, 1999, 1995.

International Standard Book Number: 978-0-323-44913-7

Senior Content Strategist: Yvonne Alexopoulos
Content Development Manager: Lisa P. Newton
Senior Content Development Specialist: Tina Kaemmerer
Publishing Services Manager: Julie Eddy
Senior Project Manager: Jodi M. Willard
Design Direction: Brian Salisbury

Printed in Canada.
Last digit is the print number: 9   8   7   6   5   4   3   2   1

Working together
to grow libraries in
developing countries

www.elsevier.com • www.bookaid.org

This book is dedicated to the families and friends who supported all of us who created it, to the faculty who use this book to develop tomorrow's emerging leaders and managers, and to the learners who have the vision and insight to grasp today's reality and mold it into the future of dynamic nursing leadership.
Lead on! ¡Adelante!

CONTRIBUTORS

Joan Benson, BSN, RN, CPN
Manager
Clinical Informatics and Practice
Children's Mercy—Kansas City
Kansas City, Missouri

Kristin K. Benton, BS, BSN, MSN, DNP
Director of Nursing
Nursing
Texas Board of Nursing
Austin, Texas

Amy Boothe, DNP, RN
Instructor
Traditional Undergraduate Program
Texas Tech University Health Sciences Center
Lubbock, Texas

Elizabeth H. Boyd, MSN, BS
Instructor/Site Coordinator
School of Nursing
Texas Tech University Health Sciences Center
Lubbock, Texas

Myra A. Broadway, JD, MS, BSN
Formerly, Executive Director, Maine State Board
   of Nursing
Past President, National Council of State Boards
   of Nursing
Maine Medical Professionals Health Program Advisory
   Committee
USAFR Nurse Corps (Retired Colonel)
Gardiner, Maine

M. Margaret Calacci, MS
Director
Simulation and Learning Resources
Arizona State University College of Nursing
   and Health Innovation
Phoenix, Arizona

Mary Ellen Clyne, PhD
President and Chief Executive Officer
Administration
Clara Maass Medical Center
Belleville, New Jersey

Jeannette T. Crenshaw, DNP, RN, LCCE, IBCLC, NEA-BC, FACCE, FAAN
Associate Professor
School of Nursing
Texas Tech University Health Sciences Center
Lubbock, Texas

Mary Ann T. Donohue-Ryan, PhD, RN, APN, APRN-MH, NEA-BC
Vice President for Patient Care Services
   and Chief Nursing Officer
Administration
Englewood Hospital and Medical Center
Englewood, New Jersey

Michael L. Evans, PhD, MSN, BSN, BA
Dean and Professor
School of Nursing
Texas Tech University Health Sciences Center
Lubbock, Texas

Victoria N. Folse, PhD, APN, PMHCNS-BC, LCPC
Director and Professor; Caroline F. Rupert Endowed
   Chair of Nursing
School of Nursing
Illinois Wesleyan University
Bloomington, Illinois

Jacqueline Gonzalez, DNP, MBA, MSN
Senior Vice President/Chief Nursing Officer
Nicklaus Children's Hospital
Miami, Florida

Debra Hagler, PhD, RN, ACNS-BC, CNE, CHSE, ANEF, FAAN
Clinical Professor
College of Nursing and Health Innovation
Arizona State University
Phoenix, Arizona

Shari Kist, PhD, RN
Missouri Quality Initiative (MOQI) Project Supervisor
Sinclair School of Nursing
University of Missouri—Columbia
Columbia, Missouri

Karren Kowalski, BSN, MSN, PhD
President & CEO
Colorado Center for Nursing Excellence
Denver, Colorado;
Professor
Graduate Program
School of Nursing
Texas Tech University Health Sciences Center
Lubbock, Texas

Mary E. Mancini, RN, MSN, PhD
Senior Associate Dean for Education Innovation
Undergraduate Nursing
University of Texas at Arlington
Arlington, Texas

Maureen Murphy-Ruocco, APN-C, CSN, MSN, EdM, EdD, DPNAP
Senior Fellow, National Academies of Practice
Nurse Consultant/Nurse Practitioner
New York, New York;
Professor and Dean Emerita
Felician University
Lodi and Rutherford, New Jersey

Karen A. Quintana, PhD, APRN, CPNP-PC
Director of Pediatric Nurse Practitioner Studies
Graduate Program, School of Nursing
Texas Tech University Health Sciences Center
Lubbock, Texas

Elaine S. Scott, BSN, MSN, PhD
Chair
Nursing Science
East Carolina University
Greenville, North Carolina

Ashley Sediqzad, RN, BSN
Manager
Clinical Informatics and Practice
Children's Mercy Kansas City
Kansas City, Missouri

Janis Bloedel Smith, DNP, MSN, BSN
Senior Director
Clinical Informatics & Professional Practice
Patient Care Services
Children's Mercy Kansas City
Kansas City, Missouri

Susan Sportsman, PhD
Nurse Consultant
Collaborative Momentum Consulting, LLC
St. Louis, Missouri

Sylvain Trepanier, DNP, MSN, BSN, RN, CENP
Chief Clinical Executive
Administration
Providence St. Joseph Health
Torrance, California

Diane M. Twedell, DNP, MS
Chief Nursing Officer
Mayo Clinic Health System
Southeast Minnesota Region
Austin, Minnesota

Jeffery Watson, DNP, RN-BC, NEA-BC, NE-BC, CRRN
Assistant Professor
School of Nursing
Texas Tech University Health Sciences
    Center
Lubbock, Texas

Jana Wheeler, MSN, RN-BC, CPN
Manager
Clinical Informatics & Practice
Children's Mercy Kansas City
Kansas City, Missouri

Crystal J. Wilkinson, DNP, RN, CNS-CH, CPHQ
Associate Professor
School of Nursing
Texas Tech University Health Sciences Center
Austin, Texas

Patricia S. Yoder-Wise, RN, EdD, NEA-BC, ANEF, FAAN
Professor and Dean Emerita
Texas Tech University Health Sciences Center
Lubbock, Texas

Margarete Lieb Zalon, PhD, RN, ACNS-BC, FAAN
Professor
Nursing
University of Scranton
Scranton, Pennsylvania

REVIEWERS

Karen E. Alexander, PhD, RN, CNOR
Program Director RN-BSN, Assistant Professor
Clinical Heath and Applied Science—Nursing
University of Houston—Clear Lake
Houston, Texas

Vicki Bingham, PhD, RN, CPE
Dean/Associate Professor of Nursing
Robert E. Smith School of Nursing
Delta State University
Cleveland, Mississippi

Deborah Birk, PhD, RN, MHA, NEA-BC
Assistant Professor
Goldfarb School of Nursing
Barnes-Jewish College
St. Louis, Missouri

Barbara B. Blozen, EdD, MA, RN BC, CNL
Associate Professor
New Jersey City University
Jersey City, New Jersey

Joseph Boney, MSN, RN, NEA-BC
Director of Undergraduate Faculty Development/
    Instructor
Rutgers School of Nursing
Accelerated BS in Nursing Program
Newark, New Jersey

Mary T. Boylston, RN, MSN, EdD, AHN-BC
Professor of Nursing
Nursing
Eastern University
St. Davids, Pennsylvania

Jane Campbell, DNP, RN, NE-BC
Professor
School of Nursing
Northern Michigan University
Marquette, Michigan

Holly Johanna Diesel, RN, PhD
Associate Professor
Academic Chair for Accelerated and RN to BSN
    Programs
Department of Nursing
Goldfarb School of Nursing at Barnes-Jewish College
St. Louis, Missouri

Jennifer B. Drexler, RN, MSN, PhDc, CCRN
Clinical Faculty Educator
College of Nursing
University of New Mexico
Albuquerque, New Mexico

Lynn Renee Dykstra, MS, BSN, HPCN, RN
Instructor, Adjunct Faculty
Northern Illinois University
College of Health and Human Sciences, Nursing
DeKalb, Illinois;
Oakton Community College
Division of Science and Health Careers, Nursing
Des Plaines, Illinois

Julie A. Fitzgerald, PhD, RN, CNE
Assistant Professor of Nursing
Ramapo College of New Jersey
Mahwah, New Jersey

Kay E. Gaehle, PhD, RN
Associate Professor of Nursing
Department of Primary Care and Health Systems
Southern Illinois University—Edwardsville
Edwardsville, Illinois

Maria Gillespie, EdD, MSN, BSN, BS, CNE, RN
Assistant Professor
Nursing
University of the Incarnate Word
San Antonio, Texas

Julia Henderson Gist, PhD, RN, CNE
Dean
School of Health Sciences
Arkansas State University Mountain Home
Mountain Home, Arkansas

Stephanie A. Gustman, DNP, MSN, BSN, RN
Assistant Professor
School of Nursing
Ferris State University
Big Rapids, Michigan

Cam A. Hamilton, PhD, MSN, RN, CNE
Assistant Professor
School of Nursing
Auburn University at Montgomery
Montgomery, Alabama

Pamela Gibler Harrison, EdD, RN, CNE
Professor of Nursing
Chair, Pre-Licensure Nursing
Indiana Wesleyan University
Marion, Indiana

Karen L. Hoblet, PhD, MSN, RN, CNL
Licensed RN
Clinical Nurse Leader
Interim Department Chairperson and Associate
    Professor
Interim Director Nurse Educator and Clinical Nurse
    Leader Programs
Advanced Population Care
The University of Toledo College of Nursing
Toledo, Ohio

Janine Dailey Johnson, MSN, RN
Assistant Professor
Nursing
Clarkson College
Omaha, Nebraska

Leo-Felix M. Jurado, PhD, RN, APN, NE-BC,
    CNE, FAAN
Associate Professor
College of Science and Health
William Paterson University of New Jersey
Wayne, New Jersey

Barbara J. Keith, RN, MSN, CNE
Clinical Lecturer
Vera Z. Dwyer College of Health Sciences
Indiana University School of Nursing
South Bend, Indiana

Donnamarie Lovestrand, RN, MSN, CPAN
Faculty, Nursing Programs
Nursing Department
Pennsylvania College of Technology
Williamsport, Pennsylvania

Anne Boulter Lucero, RN, MSN
Assistant Director, Instructor Nursing
Nursing Department
Cabrillo College
Aptos, California

Richard C. Meeks, DNP, RN, COI
Assistant Professor
Graduate Program Coordinator
School of Nursing
Middle Tennessee State University
Murfreesboro, Tennessee

Kereen Forster Mullenbach, MBA, PhD, RN
Associate Professor
Nursing
Radford University School of Nursing
Radford, Virginia

Sue S. Myers, RPN, BSW, MSCTE
Faculty
Psychiatric Nursing and Bachelor of Psychiatric Nursing
    Programs
School of Nursing
Saskatchewan Polytechnic, Parkway Campus
Regina, Saskatchewan

Barbara Pinekenstein, DNP, RN- BC, CPHIMS
Clinical Professor, Richard E. Sinaiko Professor in
    Health Care Leadership
School of Nursing
University of Wisconsin—Madison
Madison, Wisconsin

Dawn M. Pope, MS, RN
Assistant Clinical Professor (retired)
College of Nursing
University of Wisconsin—Oshkosh
Oshkosh, Wisconsin

Cara L. Rigby, DNP, RN, CMSRN
Associate Professor
BSN Program Director
Nursing
The Christ College of Nursing and Health Sciences
Cincinnati, Ohio

Dulce Anne Santacroce, DNP, RN, CCM
Nurse Educator
Nursing
Touro University—Nevada
Henderson, Nevada

Ruth Schumacher, DNP, RN, CNL, CPN
Assistant Professor
Department of Nursing and Health Sciences
Elmhurst College
Elmhurst, Illinois

Kathy S. Sweeney, MSN, RN
Assistant Professor of Nursing
Nursing Education
Kansas Wesleyan University
Salina, Kansas

Denise Robin Zabriskie, DNP, RN, CWOCN, WCC
Assistant Professor
School of Nursing
Touro University Nevada
Henderson, Nevada

ACKNOWLEDGMENTS

As with any publication endeavor, many people other than those whose names appear on the cover make the actual publication possible, including the contributors and the Challenge/Solution authors. These behind-the-scenes people also include the reviewers and the publishing team at Elsevier.

We thank each of the contributors who worked diligently to meet deadlines and content expectations. Their names are listed with the chapters they produced. Without them, this book would be a lot thinner! The nurses who told their fabulous stories related to the various chapters always illustrate the real-world meaning of the importance of the chapter content; their names appear with their stories. Without all of them, this book would be much less interesting! What a fabulous group to work with.

We are indebted to our reviewers, who provided valuable feedback that helped refine the book. Receiving peer review is critical to any successful publication. Now that the book is completed, we know who they are and we thank them!

Jeff Watson took on coordinating the ancillaries, and Shelley Burson coordinated and managed an enormous number of details. Both gently nudged all of us to complete our required tasks in a timely manner.

Special thanks go to our publishing team: Senior Content Strategist Yvonne Alexopoulos, Senior Content Development Specialist Tina Kaemmerer, and Senior Production Manager Jodi Willard.

Even more special thanks go to my husband and best friend, Robert Thomas Wise, who vowed to be minimally disruptive as I sat in my office reading, writing, typing, and talking. He is a man of his word!

This book is designed to stimulate thinking and to encourage continued professional development in the area of leading and managing. When the Institute of Medicine released the report, *The Future of Nursing*, the idea of leadership was clearly a concern for the profession. This book continues its tradition of providing the information that nurses need to assume greater leadership practices and even new management roles. All contributors attempted to provide their best thinking on a given topic so that learners could integrate concepts to form the basis for their contribution to health care. Both the thinking and the complexities will continue to change…and so, hopefully, will you! The passion of nursing and leadership await!

Patricia S. Yoder-Wise, RN, EdD, NEA-BC, ANEF, FAAN
Professor and Dean Emerita
Texas Tech University Health Sciences Center
Lubbock, Texas

PREFACE

The first edition of *Leading and Managing in Nursing* began in a hotel room in New Orleans, Louisiana in January of 1990. Darlene Como, the founding publisher of *Leading and Managing*, and I conceptualized a new way of presenting content about leadership and management: one that might engage learners in valuing the importance of roles that support clinical practice. This new approach included personal stories (The Challenge and The Solution), Literature Perspectives, Research Perspectives, synopses, exercises, and boxes of key information. If you saw that first edition and compared the number of words then compared with the number of words in this edition, you would know the field has grown and become far more complex. Nursing has also grown the field of leadership and management research, and so we have many more citations we can share to make this content both theoretical and practical.

We continue to include everything today's nurses need to know about the basics of leading and managing. The changes with each revision of *Leading and Managing* reflect the intensity with which we know how leading and managing influence nurses in direct and indirect caregiving roles, as well as in other aspects of being a professional nurse in a complex, ever-changing, dynamic healthcare environment.

Nurses throughout the profession serve in various leadership roles. Leading and managing are two essential expectations of all professional nurses and become increasingly important throughout one's career. To lead, manage, and follow successfully, nurses must possess not only knowledge and skills but also a caring and compassionate attitude.

This book results from our continued strong belief in the need for a text that focuses in a distinctive way on the nursing leadership and management issues— both today and in the future. We continue to find that we are not alone in this belief. This edition incorporates reviewers from both service and education to ensure that the text conveys important and timely information to users as they focus on the critical roles of leading, managing, and following. In addition, we took seriously the various comments offered by both educators and learners as I met them in person or heard from them by e-mail.

CONCEPT AND PRACTICE COMBINED

Innovative in both content and presentation, *Leading and Managing in Nursing* merges theory, research, and practical application in key leadership and management areas. Our overriding concern in this edition remains to create a text that, while well-grounded in theory and concept, presents the content in a way that is real. Wherever possible, we use real-world examples from the continuum of today's healthcare settings to illustrate the concepts. Because each chapter contributor synthesizes the designated focus, you will find no lengthy quotations in these chapters. We have made every effort to make the content as engaging, inviting, and interesting as possible. Reflecting our view of the real world of nursing leadership and management today, the following themes pervade the text:

- Every role within nursing has the basic concern for safe, effective care for the people for whom we exist—our clients and patients.
- The focus of health care continues to shift from the hospital to the community at a rapid rate.
- Healthcare consumers and the healthcare workforce are increasingly culturally diverse.
- Today virtually every professional nurse leads, manages, and follows, regardless of title or position.
- Consumer relationships play a central role in the delivery of nursing and health care.
- Communication, collaboration, team-building, and other interpersonal skills form the foundation of effective nursing leadership and management.
- Change continues at a rapid pace in health care and society in general.
- Change must derive from evidence-based practices wherever possible and from thoughtful innovation when no or limited evidence exists.
- Healthcare delivery is highly dependent on the effectiveness of nurses across roles and settings.

DIVERSITY OF PERSPECTIVES

Contributors are recruited from diverse settings, roles, and geographic areas, enabling us to offer a broad perspective on the critical elements of nursing leadership and management roles. To help bridge the gap often found between nursing education and nursing practice, some contributors were recruited from academia, and others were recruited from practice settings. This blend not only contributes to the richness of this text but also conveys a sense of oneness in nursing. The historical "gap" between education and service must become a sense of a continuum, not a chasm.

AUDIENCE

This book is designed for undergraduate learners in nursing leadership and management courses, including those in BSN-completion courses and second-degree programs. In addition, we know that practicing nurses—who had not anticipated formal leadership and management roles in their careers—use this text to capitalize on their own real-life experiences as a way to develop greater understanding about leading and managing and the important role of following. Numerous examples and The Challenge/The Solution in each chapter provide relevance to the real world of nursing.

ORGANIZATION

We have organized this text around issues that are key to the success of professional nurses in today's constantly changing healthcare environment. The content flows from the core concepts (leading, managing, and following; clinical safety; legal considerations; and culture), to knowing yourself (being an effective follower, self-management, conflicts, and power), to knowing the organization (care delivery strategies, staffing), to using your personal and professional skills (technology, delegation, change, and quality), to preparing for the future (personal role transition, self and career management and strategic planning).

Because repetition plays a crucial role in how well learners learn and retain new content, some topics appear in more than one chapter and in more than one section. For example, because problem behavior is so disruptive, it is addressed in several chapters

that focus on conflict, personal/personnel problems, incivility, and self-management. Rather than referring learners to another portion of the text, the key information is provided within the specific chapter.

We also made an effort to express a variety of different views on some topics, as is true in the real world of nursing. This diversity of views in the real world presents a constant challenge to leaders, managers, and followers, who address the critical tasks of creating positive workplaces so that those who provide direct care thrive and continuously improve the patient experience.

DESIGN

The functional full-color design, still distinctive to this text, is used to emphasize and identify the text's many learning strategies, which are featured to enhance learning. Full-color photographs not only add visual interest but also provide visual reinforcement of concepts, such as body language and the changes occurring in contemporary healthcare settings. Figures expand and clarify concepts and activities described in the text graphically.

LEARNING STRATEGIES

The numerous strategies featured in this text are designed both to stimulate learners' interest and to provide constant reinforcement throughout the learning process. Color is used consistently throughout the text to help the reader identify the various chapter elements described in the following sections.

Chapter Opener Elements

- Objectives articulate the chapter's learning intent, typically at the application level or higher.
- Terms to know are listed and appear in color type in each chapter.
- The Challenge presents a contemporary nurse's real-world concern related to the chapter's focus. It is designed to allow us to "hear" a real-life situation. The Challenge ends with a question about what you might do in such a situation.

Elements Within the Chapters

- Exercises stimulate learners to reason critically about how to apply concepts to the workplace and other real-world situations. They provide experiential forcement of key leading, managing, and skills. Exercises are highlighted within a full-color box and are numbered sequentially within each chapter to facilitate their use as assignments or activities. Each chapter is numbered separately so that learners can focus on the concepts inherent in a specific area and educators can readily use chapters to fit their own sequence of presenting information.

- Research Perspectives and Literature Perspectives illustrate the relevance and applicability of current scholarship to practice. Theory Boxes provide a brief description of relevant theory and key concepts.
- Numbered boxes contain lists, tools such as forms and worksheets, and other information relevant to the chapter.
- The vivid full-color chapter opener photographs and other photographs throughout the text help convey each chapter's key message. Figures and tables also expand concepts presented to facilitate a greater grasp of important materials.

End-of-Chapter Elements

- The Solution provides an effective method to handle the real-life situations set forth in The Challenge. It reflects the response of The Challenge author and ends with a question about how that solution would fit for you.
- The Evidence contains either one example of evidence related to the chapter's content or contains a summary of what the literature shows to be evidence related to the topic.
- Reflections provide the learner with the opportunity to reflect on something they've encountered in practice.

- Tips offer practical guidelines for learners to follow in applying some aspect of the information presented in each chapter.
- References provide the learner with a list of key sources for further reading on topics found in the chapter.

COMPLETE TEACHING AND LEARNING PACKAGE

In addition to the text *Leading and Managing in Nursing*, educator resources are provided online through Evolve (http://evolve.elsevier.com/Yoder-Wise/). These resources are designed to help educators present the material in this text and include the following assets:

- Updated **PowerPoint Slides,** with lecture notes where applicable, are provided for each chapter.
- An updated **ExamView Test Bank** includes answers and a rationale.
- An updated **TEACH for Nurses** ties together the chapter resources for the most effective class presentations, with sections dedicated to objectives, instructor and student chapter resources, teaching strategies, application activities and answers, an in-class case study discussion, and answers to the text Exercise boxes.

Student Resources

Learning Resources can also be found online through Evolve (http://evolve.elsevier.com/Yoder-Wise/). These resources provide learners with additional tools for learning and include the following assets:

- NCLEX Review Questions
- Sample Resumes

follower. This chapter is designed to discuss the role and responsibilities of the follower in the team.

7. Managing Self: Stress and Time, 99

This chapter recalls our understanding of stress and applies it to nursing. Almost every point made about what nurses experience could be applied or modified for other groups of professionals. This is important to remember, because any group has the tendency to think of itself as different from others. This chapter also examines the concept of self-management—developing behaviors that enhance rather than duplicate organizational cultures, social contexts, and occupational expectations as a professional nurse. Positive outcomes of effective self-management include better organization of your day, a higher degree of engagement and positivity, and respect for one's needs for daily renewal. Three components of self-management are explored: emotional intelligence, time management, and overall stress management. Methods for managing stress and organizing your time are included. Practical exercises and suggestions for stress management and day-to-day time management are presented so they may be applied to personal and professional situations. Personal and professional growth is a life-long journey, and developing healthy habits can serve you well over your entire career.

8. Communication and Conflict, 123

Effective communication and appropriate conflict-handling strategies are essential in professional nursing practice to ensure positive patient outcomes. This chapter focuses on maximizing the ability of nurse leaders to promote a practice environment characterized by effective interprofessional communication and strategies for conflict resolution.

9. Power, Politics, and Influence, 141

The focus of this chapter is the impact of power and politics on the roles of leaders, managers, and followers and the ways in which leaders and managers use power and politics to be influential. Contemporary concepts of power, empowerment, and types of power exercised by nurses are considered. Key factors important to develop a powerful image and personal and organizational strategies for exercising power are recommended. Finally, the power of nurses to shape health policy by taking action in the arena of legislative politics is explored. Each of these concepts will help the nurse

manager effectively engage in the politics of the workplace and, ultimately, use these skills in the broader healthcare environment.

10. Healthcare Organizations, 159

This chapter presents an overview of healthcare organizations, their characteristics, and their designs. Economic, social, and demographic factors that influence organizational development are discussed. An emphasis is placed on management and leadership responses that professional nurses must consider in planning the delivery of nursing care in the changing environment. Leaders, managers, and followers must be engaged and aware of the changing dynamics if they are to be effective healthcare professionals and advocate for patients, families, and community.

11. Organizational Structures, 176

The key concepts related to organizational structures and information on designing effective structures that reflect the organization's mission, vision, philosophy, and values are the focus of this chapter. This information can be used to help nurse managers and others function in an organization and to design structures that support work processes. An underlying theme is designing organizational structures that will respond to continuous changes in the healthcare environment.

12. Care Delivery Strategies, 193

Nursing care delivery models used to organize care in a variety of healthcare organizations are explored in this chapter. Several historical methods of organizing nursing care—functional nursing, team nursing, and primary nursing (including hybrid forms of these approaches)—are presented. The chapter summarizes an overview of key concepts associated with each care delivery model, including the benefits and disadvantages, with an explanation of the nurse manager's and direct care nurse's role. Also discussed are strategies that influence care delivery, such as differentiated practice, the use of rapid cycle change at the bedside, and transitions models to help patients move through various levels of care. Approaches to case management by nurses are also considered.

13. Staffing and Scheduling, 215

This chapter explores research regarding the relationship between nurse staffing and various nurse and patient outcomes and discusses the interrelationship between the personnel budget and the staffing plan. Measures for evaluating unit productivity and the impact of various staffing and scheduling strategies on overall nursing satisfaction and continuity of patient care are discussed. These key points are critical to nurse managers' ability to deliver safe and effective care in their areas of responsibility while maintaining a high degree of employee satisfaction on the units. Understanding the impact of nurse-sensitive indicators on patient outcomes helps nurse managers control the unit's labor expenses while ensuring safe and effective care. The nurse manager's ability to use this information and communicate about staffing to employees is critical to effectively managing productive services and being a valuable member of the leadership team.

14. Workforce Engagement Through Collective Action and Governance, 237

In the healthcare industry today, organizations must empower and retain highly qualified, knowledgeable nurses to provide their services. The ongoing and projected shortage of qualified nurses provides incentives for healthcare organizations to create work environments that attract and engage the most qualified nursing workforce. Work environments that empower and engage nurses promote nurses having a voice in decisions that impact their professional practice, impact patient outcomes, and increase job satisfaction. Empowerment through shared decision making can also provide leverage for nurses to negotiate pay commensurate with their education and expertise and helps create a healthy work environment. This chapter provides information on how to assess work environments through assessing organizational and governance characteristics, nurse empowerment/engagement strategies, and a variety of collective action and bargaining strategies that can shape nurses' practice.

15. Making Decisions and Solving Problems, 257

This chapter explores the stages of the decision-making and problem-solving processes and describes the analytical tools used in the application of these processes. Strategies for both individual and group (intraprofessional) decision making are addressed.

16. The Impact of Technology, 274

This chapter describes recent technology that allows nurses to effectively and efficiently use data gathered at the point of care. It discusses nurses as knowledge workers who use biomedical and information technology to care for patients. It includes sections on biomedical, information, and knowledge technology with subsections that discuss informatics competencies, information systems hardware, the science of informatics, and patient care safety and quality. Nurses build knowledge for practice by comparing and contrasting not only current patient data with previous data for the same patient but also data across patients with the same diagnosis. Information tools and skills are essential for these decision-making processes now and in the future.

17. Delegating: Authority, Accountability, and Responsibility in Delegation Decisions, 298

Delegation, a multifaceted decision-making process, is a learned nursing leadership behavior achieved by understanding the art of delegation, developing critical thinking and diagnostic reasoning skills, and applying critical judgment to effectively delegate to others in clinical practice. The overall purpose of delegation is to achieve nursing goals and improve person-centered care. This chapter discusses different aspects of delegation including the five rights of delegation, organizational and individual accountability, challenges and barriers to delegation, implementation of effective delegation strategies, and the legal parameters of delegation in professional nursing practice. The emphasis is on the role of registered nurses as delegators.

18. Leading Change, 320

This chapter highlights the increasing changes in health care and describes how all nurses must be change agents. The nature of change and the elements of the change process are reviewed. The theories, conceptual frameworks, and human responses to change are considered in an effort to understand the magnitude of managing the change experience. The roles of both the direct care nurse and the nurse manager in navigating change in the healthcare system are explored. Direct care nurses support change by remaining open to and engaging in new models of care, evidence-based practices, and requirements for ensuring safe and effective patient care. Nurse leaders must anticipate, prepare for, facilitate, oversee, and sustain ch achieve improved outcomes and professional and organizational goals. Avenues for promoting staff empowerment and engagement are examined as proactive change management strategies leaders can use to facilitate rapid, efficient, and almost continuous change.

19. Building Effective Teams, 336

This chapter explains major concepts and presents tools with which to create and maintain a smoothly functioning team. Many important group and team efforts occur in the work setting. Effective teamwork requires that we work together in a smooth and efficient manner, communicate clearly, and develop relationships that produce partnerships. Great team members use behaviors such as establishing a clear purpose, active listening, honesty, compassion, and flexibility. Each individual member of the team commits to participate in conflict resolution and cooperates in order to meet the agreed-upon goals. Leaders who understand the value of building an effective team use skills such as debriefing, acknowledgment, and group agreements to manage issues that can impact team functioning. They support the collaboration of interprofessional team members to provide safe and high-quality care.

20. Managing Costs and Budgets, 358

This chapter focuses on methods of financing health care and specific strategies for managing costs and budgets in healthcare settings—something that has become increasingly important as healthcare delivery evolves. Factors that escalate healthcare costs; sources of healthcare financing; reimbursement methods; cost-containment; promotion of growth, access, and revenues; value-based purchasing (as part of The Patient Protection and Affordable Care Act); and implications for nursing practice are discussed. Various budgets and the budgeting process are explained. In addition to clinical competency and caring practices, understanding the cost and revenue in healthcare delivery and the ethical implications of financial decisions is essential for nurses to contribute fully to the health of patients and populations.

21. Selecting, Developing, and Evaluating Staff, 377

One of the most important roles of a nurse leader is that of interviewing, hiring, and developing employees for an organization. Hiring the right employees is an important part of building a highly functioning team that provides safe and high-quality patient care and staff and patient satisfaction. The role of the nurse leader as a coach who empowers employees to grow as followers and develop their leadership skills in a learning environment is explored. Nursing staff in a patient care area are followers who play an important role in interviewing potential candidates and need to be clear about various role expectations. The nurse leader also plays an important role in staff development and ongoing feedback of an individuals' performance.

22. Person-Centered Care, 385

This chapter provides an overview of concepts related to person-centered care and strategies for its effective delivery. Specifically, the role of nurses in the delivery of person-centered care, factors in the healthcare delivery system driving the development of person-centered care approaches, and strategies that can be used by nurse leaders and followers to enhance the delivery of person-centered care are examined.

23. Managing Quality and Risk, 407

The key concepts and strategies related to quality and risk management are explained in this chapter. All healthcare professionals, including nurses, must be actively involved in the continuous improvement of patient care.

24. Translating Research Into Practice, 428

The importance of research in the development of the scientific basis for nursing practice is described in this chapter. The role of the nurse as a follower, manager, and leader of a healthcare organization in applying research to practice is delineated in the context of demands for the provision of health care based on the best available scientific evidence. This chapter also describes the practical aspects of appraising research, the development of evidence-based practice and practice-based evidence, and the use of large data sets to develop evidence in nursing. Strategies for translating research into practice that can be used by the individual nurse as a follower, leader, and manager in the context of the organization are outlined.

25. Managing Personal and Personnel Problems, 451

The purpose of this chapter is to discuss various personal and personnel problems that a leader must face in all nursing settings. Some specific tips and tools are provided as ways to intervene, coach, correct, and document problem behaviors such as absenteeism, uncooperative employees, emotional problems, or substance abuse. Supportive communication applications are also discussed. The problems and issues discussed are not only the responsibility of nursing leadership but also the responsibility of the entire team, including newly licensed registered nurses. Working on these issues from the perspective of newly licensed registered nurses provides a significant learning experience as these nurses transition into the workplace.

26. Role Transition, 465

As individuals progress through life, they transition through many roles at home, at work, and in relation to other individuals. This chapter focuses on role transition—the process of moving from one role to another. An example of this could be a nurse whose primary role is providing direct patient care (direct care nurse) transitioning to a nurse leader role. Role expectations need to be clearly articulated and determined for successful role transition to occur. The process of role transition and the different phases of this are reviewed.

27. Managing Your Career, 476

Successful people actively manage their careers rather than wait for "lucky breaks." Although trusted others may guide or influence career development, individuals manage their own reputations and careers. Continuous lifelong learning and the ability to demonstrate and document competence are critical elements in effective career management. This chapter provides guidance for creating a successful career in nursing through academic progression, continuing education, certification, and service in professional organizations. In addition, this chapter includes the process of documenting qualifications and accomplishments for use in employment and career transitions.

28. Developing the Role of Leader, 495

The role of leader is vitally important in all healthcare settings. Nurses are present in virtually all settings, and developing the role of leader is very important to quality, safety, and staff productivity. This chapter focuses on leadership and its value in advancing the profession of nursing. Leadership development is explained with examples of how to survive and thrive in a leadership position. The differences between emerging and entrenched workforce generations are explored, and the desired characteristics of a leader for the emerging workforce are described. Leadership in a variety of situations, such as clinical settings, community venues, organizations, and political situations, is described. In addition, this chapter provides an introduction to the opportunities, challenges, and satisfaction of leadership.

29. Developing the Role of Manager, 510

The nurse manager serves as the catalyst for change by exhibiting a multitude of critical skills. Finding a mentor(s) is key in building and learning new skills as a nurse manager. Mentors serve as guides and coaches and share the lessons they have learned, including acute observation, proactivity, and risk-tasking. This chapter provides an overview of important elements that can assist in optimizing the knowledge and competency of the nurse manager. In addition, this chapter addresses items such as the evolution of management theories, managing the complexities of an intergenerational workforce, ensuring a positive workplace culture, mentoring, and the manager's role in handling resources. The importance of the nurse manager's use of dashboards and key performance indicators is demonstrated to ensure positive patient outcomes.

30. The Strategic Planning Process, 530

Today's healthcare landscape is in a state of evolution with a concentrated focus on quality outcomes, patient safety, improved operational efficiencies, new reimbursement models, and demonstrated cost savings. Healthcare organizations must be resilient while navigating this new paradigm. The strategic planning process is one way in which a healthcare organization can chart its course for future success, and nurses are poised to be an integral part of the strategic planning process. The strategic planning process incorporates the same scientific process as the nursing process by: (1) assessing the current state of the organization; (2) conducting a gap analysis to establish a baseline of where the organization needs to be; (3) examining the organization's mission, vision, and values; (4) implementing a plan with benchmark data; and (5) evaluating and continuing to monitor the outcomes of the plan and to revise the plan as needed. Nursing has the ability to create its own strategic plan that aligns with the mission, vision, values, and goals of the organization and that can serve a-basis for a division-, service-, or unit-level strategic plan. Unless all elements in an organization can envision how they fit within the overall strategic plan, it is likely it will not be achieved. This chapter provides an overview of strategic planning and the strategic planning process. Specifically, this chapter will demonstrate how nursing is integral in this strategic journey.

31. Thriving for the Future, 540

As everyone in health care knows, health care is changing so rapidly that keeping up-to-date is an increasing challenge. To be current, we really need to think about the future and what the nature of various changes will do to and for our practice. How we think about the future and the actions we take now shape what health care will be like and what our practice might be. This chapter explores the potential for the future and how the changes we face can be maximized to our benefit—organizationally and personally. The key leadership skills of visioning, forecasting, and innovating are presented. Projections for the future and their implication for nursing are included.

CONTENTS

Leading, Managing, and Following

Shari Kist

LEARNING OUTCOMES

- Describe the evolution of the theoretical basis for leadership and management.
- Evaluate leadership and management theories for appropriateness in health care today.

- Apply concepts of complexity science to healthcare delivery and the evolution of nursing.
- Compare and contrast the actions associated with leading, managing, and following.

KEY TERMS

advanced practice registered nurse (APRN)

clinical process

complexity science

emotional intelligence

followership

leadership

leadership theory

managing

management theory

motivation

process of care

quadruple aim

social networking

values

vision

THE CHALLENGE

The acuity of residents in long-term care [LTC] facilities has increased over time. Today's nursing home residents are similar to hospitalized medical-surgical patients of the past. However, the processes of care in these facilities have not changed to meet the demand. The minimum requirement for physician visits is a 10- to 30-minute visit every other month. A change in the resident's condition generally results in either an emergency department visit or hospitalization—thus the mantra, "when in doubt, send them out." However, hospitalization puts an older person at risk for further decline unrelated to the primary admission diagnoses.

At a particular LTC facility, no systems were in place to prevent transfers. It was not uncommon for multiple residents to be sent to the hospital every week. The solution to any symptom was to add more medications to the resident's drug regimen, often resulting in polypharmacy. Clinical skills of nursing staff were limited, and management

(Continued)

THE CHALLENGE—cont'd

was accustomed to "putting out fires" as opposed to being proactive in having preventive care/conversations with residents and their families. Communication among staff was limited and no active staff education program, beyond new employee education and mandatory in-service classes, was in place. Those in management positions did not make rounds on the nursing units. Additionally, residents and their family members were not having open, honest conversations about the residents' goals for care. In many instances, transfers occurred because goals of care, particularly for end-of-life care, had not been addressed.

What would you do if you were this nurse?
JoAnn Franklin, DNP, RN, GNP-BC, FNP-BC, MHNP, FAANP
Missouri Quality Initiative (MOQI), University of Missouri-Columbia, Columbia, MO; APRN at National Health Care Desloge, Desloge, MO

Angelita Pritchett, MSW, LMSW
MOQI Care Transitions Coach, University of Missouri-Columbia, Columbia, MO

INTRODUCTION

The nursing profession constitutes the backbone of the healthcare system, both in numbers and in span of influence. All too often nurses, especially new graduates, desire to focus on direct patient care, with limited attention to the the healthcare spectrum. However, our complex work environments should stimulate us to look more broadly at the systems affecting how we practice. The skills of leading, managing, and following can be used whether the nurse is providing direct patient care or collaborating with stakeholders of a large healthcare system.

Beyond the expectation to lead, manage, and follow, nurses are also expected to help fulfill health care's quadruple aim. Initially known as the *triple aim* by the Institute for Healthcare Improvement (IHI), the quadruple aim relates to improving access to care, quality of care, cost of care, and work life of the healthcare team (Bodenheimer & Sinsky, 2014) (Fig. 1.1). Nurses who practice in expanded roles, such as advanced practice registered nurses, help improve healthcare access beyond traditional hospitals and ambulatory centers.

Nurses must be vigilant in delivering care that is scientific, state of the art, and sensitive to patients' needs, collectively creating an accessible and cost-effective experience that leaves care providers satisfied with their contributions. Patients want their values and beliefs respected as they partner with the care team. Patients also demand a safe clinical experience, free from medical error and catastrophic events, up to and including death.

Access to care and cost of care must be considered by patients, providers, and payers. Technology, institutional care, supplies, and human resource requirements

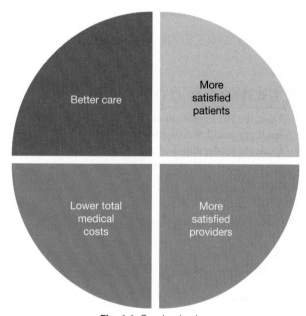

Fig. 1.1 Quadruple aim.

carry a staggering cost burden. How to provide quality care at a reasonable cost is an ongoing discussion at many levels, ranging from the family dinner table to board rooms and Congress.

Providing access to quality, reasonably priced care creates a new level of stress for all members of the healthcare team. Healthcare team members must learn to identify professional burnout and implement strategies that will achieve work–life balance. The expectations of the quadruple aim require that all members of the team function at the highest level possible both as a team member and as an individual. As a discipline, we are called upon to develop expanded roles congruent with societal needs; we influence policy development, and we design and carry out clinical processes to provide safe and high-quality patient- and family-centered experiences in a wide range of settings.

The practice of nursing can be both physically and emotionally demanding. Consistent with the quadruple aim, nurses should actively care for their own physical and emotional well-being and lead initiatives that promote health. Self-care actions for balanced lives with early recognition of burnout can lead to a healthier personal and professional life.

This chapter starts to frame your professional journey, and the chapters that follow add to your professional formation. In this chapter and in subsequent chapters, various perspectives on the concepts of leading (leadership), managing (management), and following (followership) are presented. Leading, managing, and following are not institutionally role-bound concepts—the nurse must lead, manage, and follow within *any* nursing role, from direct care nurse to chief executive nurse, and do so with fluidity among those roles. In the end, nurses with leadership, management, and followership abilities will make better clinical decisions, consider the organizational and societal context of decisions, act as advocates for individuals receiving care, and influence the impact of these decisions on families, the organization, and the society.

THEORY DEVELOPMENT IN LEADING, MANAGING, AND FOLLOWING

Theory has several important functions for the nursing profession. First, theory can be used to guide how the nurse approaches a particular situation. Second, theory can be used to frame a research question and guide a research study. Third, theory directs and sharpens the ability to predict or guide clinical and organizational problem solving and outcomes. Because nursing is a practice discipline, it is possible to focus more effort on the doing rather than the theoretical perspective. However, having a theory-based approach can enhance performance and strengthen the value of the theory.

The theoretical basis for understanding leading, managing, and following originates from multiple disciplines. Early researchers in organizational science noted the differences in the ways some organizations operated. The focus was on traits of individual leaders rather than

characteristics or functioning of the organization. Studies of individual leaders resulted in awareness that some individuals possessed traits that seemed to produce better organizational outcomes. Trait theory, developed from these studies, is still examined as a leadership factor today, even though it holds less influence than some other theories.

Closely tied to this appreciation of traits as one leadership ingredient were observations that a leader could be successful in one environment yet not necessarily in another. The situation at hand and the work environment itself were variables that mattered. Activities being performed were yet another variable that was studied. When the setting required reproducible and repetitive tasks, a charismatic leader may be less effective than in an unpredictable or unstructured situation where the tasks required on-the-spot innovation. Study of these variables advanced knowledge about leading, managing, and following and promoted the development of other theories. These include situational/contingency theory, which examines variables in the external and internal environment, including the nature of the work itself, worker behaviors (individual or group), the predictability or unpredictability of work, and the risk associated with work. Management theories, which address planning, organizing, directing, and controlling aspects of work design, were also included and sometimes were cited as leadership theories. These theories, originating from the mid-1950s, are still relevant today. They continue to evolve and often are combined with other theories to guide professionals into evidence-based organizational practices.

Terms such as leadership theory, *transformational leadership, servant leadership, authentic leadership* management theory, *motivational theory,* and even attempts at followership theories are interrelated and cannot be categorized in a mutually exclusive manner. The theories that leaders, managers, and followers use are drawn from yet another set of theories, some of which are addressed later in this book and include change, conflict, economic, clinical, individual and group interactions, communication, and social networking. The Theory Box on p. 9 is organized as an overview to highlight sets of theoretical works that are commonly referenced for the purpose of demonstrating the variety, approach, and constant evolution of theory development in organizational studies. The complex factors associated with clinical care and organizational functioning explain why no single theory fully addresses the totality of leading, managing, and following.

Using Complex Adaptive Science to Understand Health Care Today

Too often, theories are thought to have evolved from circumstances that do not reflect current practices and are too narrow in scope to be useful. Typically, theory development has been based on assumptions that by reducing something into its component parts, its functioning could be better understood. For example, departments of a healthcare organization, such as laboratory, pharmacy, and dietary, all have leaders and managers. Although they have both responsibility and authority within a department, very often a decision made within the department will have a complex ripple effect on the rest of the organization, and most commonly the nursing department is affected by each of those other departments.

Complexity theory is a nontraditional theory that has emerged over time from the works of physical and social sciences. Complex adaptive science can help us understand health care as it is delivered to patients and families, as well as healthcare systems in general. Complexity science does not refer to the complexity of the decision to be made or to the work environment, but rather to examining how systems adapt and function—where co-creation of ideas and actions unfold in a nonprescriptive manner. Complexity theory can be used by those in leadership and management roles for understanding an organization as well as in planning and executing changes within an organization.

Complexity science promotes the idea that the world is full of patterns that interact and adapt through relationships. These interactive patterns may be missed when one focuses solely on a single part. Complexity scientists pay keen attention to what naturally occurs as patterns in the universe and how these patterns create adaptive change rather than how people create planned or forced change. Stated in nursing terms, nurses care for individual patients who each present a unique challenge. With experience, nurses recognize that patterns of patient behaviors emerge and learn that certain nursing actions lead to effectively managing pain, engaging family members in end-of-life planning discussions, and addressing a host of other issues. Most healthcare team members are very focused on problems and predictable solutions that appear to be linear in nature, which is described as *technical work*. However, if we look more deeply at both disease processes and health care, we realize that both are an interconnected web of physiologic processes and services. Thus a linear solution may not be feasible, and solutions require adaptations that account for a multitude of factors. The application of complexity science is reflected in the elements of evidence-based nursing practice, which includes patient preferences, along with assessment data, research findings, and clinical expertise. Although much work in health care has focused on acute care organizations, complexity science is applicable in other settings, including long-term care, as illustrated in the Research Perspective.

RESEARCH PERSPECTIVE

Resource: Colon-Emeric, C., Toles, M., Cary M. P., Batchelor-Murphy, M., Yap, T., Song, Y., Hall, R., Anderson, A., Burd, A., & Anderson, R. A. (2016). Sustaining complex interventions in long-term-care: A qualitative study of direct care staff and managers. *Implementation Science, 11,* 94.

The aim of this qualitative study was to understand perspectives related to the sustainability of an intervention being tested in a long-term care facility. Complexity science served as the theoretical basis for the intervention portion of the study and thus guided the qualitative study being described here. Fifteen focus groups with 83 participants were conducted. Participants included both managers and direct care staff to get a wide variety of perspectives.

The findings identified that all participants believed the intervention was useful because it would ultimately improve the care of residents. The intervention tested was complex. Some participants, especially those with less education, struggled to grasp the intent and how it could affect their roles in the long-term care facility. Although participants valued the training they received, they expressed concern that sustaining change would be difficult because of staff turnover, lack of leadership support, and lack of culture change.

Implications for Practice
By using the lens of complexity science for this study, nurses can begin to appreciate the numerous factors that come into play when planning, implementing, and evaluating a change in a care process. Being able to sustain a change in behaviors requires that those in administrative roles are supportive, while maintaining a level of accountability for all staff.

In complex adaptive leadership, the goal in responding to patient and organizational problems is to examine a problem through multiple lenses. An adaptive leader understands that systems are ecological—they restore themselves—and that change can happen equally from the bottom up or from the top down. Questioning, observing patterns, and generating new patterns through being involved is how change unfolds. Adaptive leaders appreciate that they have influence and can help shape overall outcomes, with no sense that absolute control is either necessary or possible.

In complexity science, information is not a commodity to be controlled by those in charge. Instead, it is intended to be shared with and interpreted by a wide audience, to provide varying interpretations of the same scenario. Diverse thinking leads to creative problem solving in which multiple individuals are actively engaged, using diverse skills to be part of the solution.

Relationships and communication are central factors in complex adaptive leadership. Poor team communication has been directly linked to preventable medical errors, high staff turnover rates, and low morale. On the other hand, team members who communicate effectively with each other and feel that their voices are heard are likely to provide safe high-quality care, be active team members, and stay with the organization for a period of time. In complexity science, every voice counts and every encounter with patients and families merges to co-create a desired outcome. Co-creation, the idea that a change doesn't belong to one person or group, is critical to moving quality of care and innovation forward.

One of the early references in complexity science and leading and managing identified four concepts:
- Managers must be aware that *employees will self-manage* themselves into work groups. Rather than exerting control, effective managers stimulate creative problem solving. These groups may start as having a single purpose but may be sustained through achieving positive outcomes.
- Managers *must be skillful in providing context.* While keeping a clear vision of the objective to be accomplished, employees can be encouraged to explore and develop solutions to complex problems. Concepts of shared governance and adaptive leadership blend well with the overall aim of safe and effective patient care.
- Managers must *adapt to the changing environment and use influence* where they can have the most

impact. Health care is often procedure driven, yet managers must remain cognizant of the communication and relationships necessary to carry out procedures that create positive outcomes.
- Managers *must address sources of tension and contradiction.* Disagreement and tension may be the result of creative problem solving by the group and are expected when working with diverse groups. Seeking insight and encouraging creativity and communication allow the manager to capitalize on tension for a positive benefit. By addressing this tension, new alliances may be created that contribute to high-quality outcomes (Morgan, 2003).

The ability to do "systems thinking" is a central concept in adaptive leadership because of the broad perspectives needed to understand a situation. The principles of systems thinking theory that we use today were characterized classically by Anderson and Johnson (1997) as:
- *Thinking of the "Big Picture"*: The nurse who looks past an individual assignment and comprehends the needs of all units of the hospital, or who can focus on the needs of all the residents in a long-term care facility, or who can think through the complications of urban emergency department overcrowding is seeing the big picture. Such nurses have the ability to envision the context of their work beyond the immediate tasks.
- *Balancing Short-Term and Long-Term Objectives:* The nurse who recognizes the long-term consequences of actions on the organization or patient, such as the decision of a patient to terminate clinical treatment, can guide thinking about how to balance decision making for quality outcomes.
- *Recognizing the Dynamic, Complex, and Interdependent Nature of Systems:* All things are connected. Patients are connected to families and friends. Together, they are connected to communities and cultures. Communities and cultures make up the fabric of society. The cost of health care is linked to local economies, and local businesses are connected to global industries. Identifying and understanding these relationships helps solve problems with full recognition that small decisions can have a large impact.
- *Using Measurable versus Nonmeasurable Data Systems:* This thinking triggers a "tendency to 'see' only what we measure." If we focus our measuring on morale, working relationships, and teamwork, we

might miss the important signals that only objective statistics can show us. On the other hand, if we consider only numbers (e.g., number of patients seen), we might miss a perspective such as lack of engagement in the workplace.

> **EXERCISE 1.1** Identify a clinical scenario in which a complex problem needs to be addressed. For example, consider how nurses can ensure that drug levels are drawn before and after a medication or how nurses ensure that equipment shared among patients is adequately cleaned and maintained. Who would you include in a team to engage in creative problem solving? How would you go about linking to other key stakeholders if the problem were "bigger than" your immediate contacts? Concentrate on the power of these influencing individuals. What role would the patient and family and community play in co-creating the resolution strategies? How would you encourage nonhierarchical interaction among nurses, patients, families, and others involved in this situation?

LEADING, MANAGING, AND FOLLOWING—DIFFERENT BUT RELATED

Each of these terms—leading, managing, and following—represents a distinct aspect of a nurse's role. Yet the fluidity of a situation may require a change in roles, such as the quietest follower moving into a leadership role when that person's talents are best suited to the situation. Nurses need to appreciate the complexity of the work situation and be prepared to assume different roles and to do so in a fluid manner rather than in only a defined time, role, or situation.

Leading

Leadership can be defined as the use of individual traits and abilities in relationship with others and the ability (often rapidly) to interpret the environment/context where a situation is emerging and enter that situation without the use of a predesigned plan. Leadership is required when the unknown presents itself, necessitating the use of principles to improvise solutions and help others cope, thrive, and function in the situation. Concepts related to leadership are present in nearly all professional disciplines; they are not distinct to nursing and health care. In fact, many of the concepts discussed here originated with other professions and have been adapted for the healthcare environment.

Key traits that leaders possess include (1) articulating a vision for the desired future state; (2) seeing possibilities in the midst of challenging, complex, uncharted, or even dire circumstances; (3) communicating effectively, sometimes powerfully, with others; (4) adapting to new situations and environments; and (5) using experience and knowledge to judge reasonable risks.

Nurses face the unknown every day. New diseases emerge. Natural disasters, such as hurricanes and tornadoes, create havoc, which leaves many people in need of immediate health care. Clinical procedures have to be adapted to a patient's physical and emotional challenges. Each of these requires stepping into the unknown, using principles, showing a commanding presence, and taking risks. Interprofessional educational experiences focus on understanding and communicating with other members of the healthcare team and provide opportunities for the development of leadership skills that can be readily applied in the clinical setting.

Gardner (1990) described tasks of leadership in his seminal book, *On Leadership*. These are still applicable today.

Gardner's Tasks of Leadership

Gardner's leadership tasks are presented in Table 1.1 to demonstrate that leading, managing, and following are relevant for nurses who hold clinical positions, formal management positions, and executive leadership positions. Note that each role represents the interests of the organization, although the focus of attention is different.

Envisioning Goals. Leading requires envisioning goals in partnership with others. At the point of care, leading helps patients envision their life journey when health outcomes are unknown. It might help a patient envision walking again, participating in family events, or changing a lifestyle pattern. In the case of leading peers, the leader envisions an aim while keeping it within the broad purpose of the organization. An effective leader strives to engage those within the organization to embrace a shared vision of a high-performing unit and the process to reach that goal.

Affirming Values. Values are the connecting thoughts and inner driving forces that give purpose, direction, and precedence to life priorities. An organization, through its members, shares collective values that are expressed through its mission, philosophy, and practices. Leaders influence priority setting and decision making as a means to express organizational values.

TABLE 1.1   Gardner's Tasks of Leading/Managing Applied to Practice, Management, and Executive Positions

Gardner's Task	BEHAVIORS		
	Clinical Position	**Management Position**	**Executive Position**
Envisioning goals	Visioning patient outcomes for single patient/families; assisting patients in formulating their vision of future well-being	Creating a vision of how systems support patient care objectives; assisting staff in formulating their professional vision of clinical and organizational performance	Visioning community health and organizational outcomes for aggregates of patient populations to which the organization can respond
Affirming values	Assisting the patient/family to articulate personal values in relation to health problems and to appreciate how these values are reflected in health state	Assisting the staff in interpreting organizational values and strengthening staff members' personal values to more closely align with those of the organization	Assisting other organizational leaders in the expression of community and organizational values; interpreting values to the community and staff
Motivating	Relating to and inspiring patients/families to achieve their vision	Relating to and inspiring staff to achieve the mission of the organization and the vision associated with organizational enhancement	Relating to and inspiring management, staff, and community leaders to achieve desired levels of health and well-being and appropriate use of clinical services
Managing	Executing established procedures while considering appropriateness for the individual patient/family	Assisting the staff with planning, priority setting, and decision making; ensuring that systems work to enhance the staff's ability to meet patient care needs and the objectives of the organization	Assisting other executives and corporate leaders with planning, priority setting, and decision making; ensuring that human and material resources are available to meet health needs
Achieving workable unity	Assisting patients/families to achieve an optimal, yet realistic, health state and quality of life	Collaborating with staff to achieve optimal team functioning to maximize organizational functioning	Guiding multidisciplinary leaders to achieve optimal organizational functioning to benefit patient care delivery
Developing trust	Maintaining honest open communication with patients and families; being honest in role performance	Sharing organizational information openly; being honest in role performance	Representing nursing and executive views openly and honestly; being honest in role performance
Explaining	Teaching and interpreting information to promote patient/family functioning and well-being	Providing information to promote organizational functioning and enhanced services	Communicating organizational information to other leaders within the organization and community.
Serving as a symbol	Representing the nursing profession and the values and beliefs of the organization to patients/families	Representing the values and beliefs of the nursing unit to staff, other departments, professional organizations, and the community at large	Representing the values and beliefs of the organization and patient care services to internal and external constituents

Continued

TABLE 1.1   Gardner's Tasks of Leading/Managing Applied to Practice, Management, and Executive Positions—cont'd

Gardner's Task	BEHAVIORS		
	Clinical Position	**Management Position**	**Executive Position**
Representing the group	Representing nursing and the unit on committees, shared governance councils, and other groups within the organization	Representing nursing on assigned boards, councils, and committees, both internal and external to the organization	Representing the organization and patient care services on assigned boards, councils, committees, and task forces, both internal and external to the organization
Renewing	Providing self-care to maximize one's ability to function as a healthcare team member.	Providing self-care to maximize one's ability to care for function as both a leader and member of the healthcare team.	Providing self-care to maximize one's ability to care for patients, families, staff, and the organization served

Other individuals also use their values to achieve their goals, which are then manifested through behavior.

The word *value* connotes something of worth; intentional actions reflect our values. A leader continuously clarifies and acknowledges the values that draw attention to a problem and develops the resources in human and material terms to solve the problem. Values are powerful forces that promote acceptance of change and drive achievement toward a goal.

Motivating. When values drive our actions, they become a source of motivation. Motivation energizes what we value, personally and professionally, and stimulates growth and movement toward the vision. One task of leadership is communicating organizational values and vision to enhance motivation. Motivators are the reinforcers that keep positive actions alive and sustained, fueling the desire to engage in change. Theories of motivation identify and describe the forces that motivate people. Examples of motivation theory are presented in the Theory Box.

Managing. The ability to manage is an important aspect of organizational functioning, because management requires determining routines and practices that offer structure and stability to others. This is especially true in certain positions of influence within a clinical setting, such as a nurse manager, clinical nurse specialist, or clinical nurse leader, all of whom share responsibility for creating effective structures that support clinical and organizational outcomes. Being effective as a manager requires behaviors different from those associated with effective leadership,

and vice versa. Ideally, those charged with managing are also good leaders and followers, because no organizational position is limited to one exclusive set of behaviors over another. Leaders, managers, and followers who are effective use all three roles to accomplish their goals.

Achieving Workable Unity. Another challenging leadership task is to achieve workable unity between and among the parties being affected by change and to avoid, diminish, or resolve conflict so that vision can be achieved (see Chapters 8 and 18). Conflict resolution skills are essential for leaders. When a dispute occurs because of conflicting values or interests, following the principles of communication and conflict resolution can help facilitate a mutually satisfying resolution.

Developing Trust. A hallmark task of leadership is to behave with consistency so that others believe in and can count on the leader's intentions and direction. Trust develops when leaders establish clear goals and objectives with associated employee behaviors. Inherent in this concept is the behavior of truth telling. Although leaders cannot always share all information, it is unwise to misdirect others in their thinking and actions. Trust, according to Lencioni's (2002) classic work, is the key component of a team. Without trust, the team is dysfunctional. Trustworthiness is reflected in both actions and communications.

Explaining. Leading, managing, and following require a willingness to communicate and explain—again and again. Many of the skills related to patient-centered communication are transferrable to those in leadership roles.

THEORY BOX

Leadership Theories

Theory/Contributor	Key Idea	Application to Practice
Trait Theories Trait theories were first studied from 1900–1950. These theories are sometimes referred to as the Great Man theories, from Aristotle's philosophy extolling the virtue of being "born" with leadership traits. Stogdill (1948) is usually credited as the pioneer in this school of thought.	Leaders have a certain set of physical and emotional characteristics that are crucial for inspiring others toward a common goal. Some theorists believe that traits are innate and cannot be learned; others believe that leadership traits can be developed in each individual.	Self-awareness of traits is useful in self-development (e.g., developing assertiveness) and in seeking employment that matches traits (drive, motivation, integrity, confidence, cognitive ability, and task knowledge).
Style Theories Sometimes referred to as *group and exchange* theories of leadership, style theories were derived in the mid-1950s because of the limitations of trait theory. The key contributors to this renowned research were Shartle (1956), Stogdill (1963), and Likert (1987).	Style theories focus on what leaders do in relational and contextual terms. The achievement of satisfactory performance measures requires supervisors to pursue effective relationships with their subordinates while comprehending the factors in the work environment that influence outcomes.	To understand "style," leaders need to obtain feedback from followers, superiors, and peers, such as through the Managerial Grid Instrument developed by Blake and Mouton (1985). Employee-centered leaders tend to be the leaders most able to achieve effective work environments and productivity.
Situational-Contingency Theories The situational-contingency theorists emerged in the 1960s through the mid-1970s. These theorists believed that leadership effectiveness depends on the relationship among (1) the leader's task at hand, (2) his or her interpersonal skills, and (3) the favorableness of the work situation. Examples of theory development with this expanded perspective include Fiedler's (1967) Contingency Model, Vroom and Yetton's (1973) Normative Decision-Making Model, and House and Mitchell's (1974) Path-Goal theory.	Three factors are critical: (1) the degree of trust and respect between and among leaders and followers, (2) the task structure denoting the clarity of goals and the complexity of problems faced, and (3) the position power in terms of where the leader was able to reward followers and exert influence. Consequently, leaders were viewed as able to adapt their style according to the presenting situation. The Vroom-Yetton model was a problem-solving approach to leadership. Path-Goal theory recognized two contingent variables: (1) the personal characteristics of followers and (2) environmental demands. On the basis of these factors, the leader sets forth clear expectations, eliminates obstacles to goal achievements, motivates and rewards staff, and increases opportunities for follower satisfaction based on effective job performance.	The most important implications for leaders are that these theories consider the challenge of a situation and encourage an adaptive leadership style to complement the issue being faced. In other words, nurses must assess each situation and determine appropriate action based on the people involved.

(Continued)

THEORY BOX—cont'd

Transformational Theories

Transformational theories arose late in the past millennium when globalization and other factors caused organizations to fundamentally reestablish themselves. Many of these attempts were failures, but great attention was given to those leaders who effectively transformed structures, human resources, and profitability balanced with quality. Bass (1990), Bennis and Nanus (2007), and Tichy and Devanna (1997) are commonly associated with the study of transformational theory.

Transformational leadership refers to a process whereby the leader attends to the needs and motives of followers so that the interaction raises each to high levels of motivation and morality. The leader is a role model who inspires followers through displayed optimism, provides intellectual stimulation, and encourages follower creativity.

Transformed organizations are responsive to customer needs, are morally and ethically intact, promote employee development, and encourage self-management. Nurse leaders with transformational characteristics experiment with systems redesign, empower staff, create enthusiasm for practice, and promote scholarship of practice at the patient-side.

Hierarchy of Needs

Maslow is credited with developing a theory of motivation, first published in 1943.

People are motivated by a hierarchy of human needs, beginning with physiologic needs and then progressing to safety, social, esteem, and self-actualizing needs. In this theory, when the need for food, water, air, and other life-sustaining elements is met, the human spirit reaches out to achieve affiliation with others, which promotes the development of self-esteem, competence, achievement, and creativity. Lower-level needs drive behavior before higher-level needs will be addressed.

When this theory is applied to staff, leaders must be aware that the need for safety and security will override the opportunity to be creative and inventive, such as in promoting job change.

Two-Factor Theory

Herzberg (1991) is credited with developing a two-factor theory of motivation, first published in 1968.

Hygiene factors, such as working conditions, salary, status, and security, motivate workers by meeting safety and security needs and avoiding job dissatisfaction. Motivator factors, such as achievement, recognition, and the satisfaction of the work itself, promote job enrichment by creating job satisfaction.

Organizations need both hygiene and motivator factors to recruit and retain staff. Hygiene factors do not create job satisfaction; they simply must be in place for work to be accomplished. If not, these factors will only serve to dissatisfy staff. Transformational leaders use motivator factors liberally to inspire work performance.

Expectancy Theory

Vroom (1994) is credited with developing the expectancy theory of motivation.

Individuals' perceived needs influence their behavior. In the work setting, this motivated behavior is increased if a person perceives a positive

Expectancy is the perceived probability of satisfying a particular need based on experience. Therefore nurses in leadership roles

THEORY BOX—cont'd

	relationship between effort and performance. Motivated behavior is further increased if a positive relationship exists between good performance and outcomes or rewards, particularly when these are valued.	need to provide specific feedback about positive performance.
OB Modification Luthans (2011) is credited with establishing the foundation for Organizational Behavior Modification (OB Mod), based on Skinner's work on operant conditioning.	OB Mod is an operant approach to organizational behavior. OB Mod Performance Analysis follows a three-step *ABC* Model: *A,* antecedent analysis of clear expectations and baseline data collection; *B,* behavioral analysis and determination; and *C,* consequence analysis, including reinforcement strategies.	The leader uses positive reinforcement to motivate followers to repeat constructive behaviors in the workplace. Negative events that demotivate staff are negatively reinforced, and the staff is motivated to avoid certain situations that cause discomfort. Extinction is the purposeful nonreinforcement (ignoring) of negative behaviors. Punishment is used sparingly because the results are unpredictable in supporting the desired behavioral outcome.

The importance of clear and repeated communication cannot be emphasized enough. If instructions are not clear, employees are left to interpret them using their viewpoints. That viewpoint might be consistent with the intended message of the leader, but it may not be. When it is not, both the leader and employee experience frustration, and patient outcomes may be affected. Chapter 8 provides more information on communication. Many organizations offer courses on communicating effectively as a leader; online resources can help hone your explaining and communication skills.

Serving as a Symbol. Every leader has the opportunity to be an ambassador for those he or she represents. Nurses may be symbolically present for patients and families, represent their department at an organizational event, or be involved in community public relations events. Serving as a symbol reflects unity and collective identity.

Representing the Group. More than being present symbolically, many opportunities exist for leaders to represent the group through active participation. Progressive organizations create opportunities for employees to participate in and foster organizational innovation.

Nurses may participate in numerous committees and work groups related to human resources, patient safety, and quality improvement. When nurses offer their "voices" in each of these leadership opportunities, they are representing a group and are thinking beyond personal needs. When decision making is decentralized and layers of management compressed, nurses must demonstrate leadership accountability. A leader treats these newfound opportunities with respect and represents the group's interests with openness and integrity. Ultimately, leaders must understand the organization's objectives and contribute to its mission and purpose. As an example, nurses who speak on behalf of a group should represent an organizational perspective rather than a personal one.

Renewing. Leaders can generate energy within and among others. A true leader attends to the group's energy and does not allow it to lose focus. When changes are made based on a shared vision, they can be made with renewed spirit and purpose. Taking time to celebrate individual accomplishments or creating a "Hall of Honor" to post photos, letters, and other forms of positive feedback renews the spirit of workers.

As identified in the quadruple aim, self-care and avoiding burnout are central to providing high-quality safe care. Leaders must be proponents of self-care for themselves and those they lead. A balanced diet, adequate sleep and exercise, and other wellness-oriented activities are necessary to maintain the perspective, focus, and energy of an effective leader. Gardner (1990) states, "The consideration leaders must never forget is that the key for renewal is the release of human energy and talent" (p. 136). This requires focused energy and personal well-being. The American Nurses' Association has acknowledged this idea of renewal and supports self-care through the Healthy Nurse Healthy Nation Grand Challenge centering around five areas: physical activity, nutrition, rest, quality of life, and safety.

Concepts of complexity science and leadership have been combined into what is known as *generative leadership*. Generative leaders are not satisfied with the status quo; instead they are creative and curious individuals who seek new solutions to old problems (Disch, 2009). Creative solutions evolve from new ways of thinking. Disch (2009) identified three ways to approach developing new solutions: (1) Embrace paradox. Health care is full of paradoxes, that through confronting rather than ignoring a situation, solutions can be developed. (2) Seek ambiguity. By obtaining input from others and accepting that multiple perspectives of any situation exist, leaders can begin to identify broad solutions. (3) Reframe situations. By taking a new perspective on a problem, the solution often becomes more evident.

As you can see, a successful leader must possess the capacity to monitor multiple projects while keeping an eye to the future.

Managing

Managing is the ability to plan, direct, control, and evaluate others in situations where the outcomes are known or preestablished, where one or more ways of performing have been agreed on based on evidence, where feedback and communication is shared to improve clinical processes and outcomes, and where sustained relationships advance consistency of purpose. Traits needed for effective managers include (1) the ability to identify recurring problems and design evidence-based routines to create structure and improve work efficiency, (2) persistent and vigilant behavior in self and others, and (3) communication that maintains esprit de corps in the face of repetitive work tasks. In the workplace,

management is needed to provide structure, a sense of purpose, and safety.

Bleich's Tasks of Management

The ability to manage is very much aligned with how an organization structures its key systems and processes to deliver service. A care delivery system is composed of multiple processes necessary to achieve effective patient care. Some of the key processes relate to medication procurement, ordering, and administration; patient safety practices; patient education; and discharge planning and care coordination. A process of care specifies the desired sequence of steps to achieve clinical standardization, safety, and outcomes. Effective management depends on knowing, adhering to, and improving processes for efficiency and effectiveness. Each person must respect and act on a prescribed role in a process of care. Data-driven outcome measurements provide feedback on the process. Feedback reports provide a basis for improvement programs, which may include coaching and mentoring employees. Rewards for individual and team effectiveness reinforce desired behaviors. Box 1.1 lists Bleich's tasks of management that are essential to effective functioning.

BOX 1.1   Bleich's Tasks of Management

1. Identify systems and processes that require responsibility and accountability, and specify who owns the process.
2. Verify minimum and optimum standards/specifications, and identify roles and individuals responsible to adhere to them.
3. Validate the knowledge, skills, and abilities of available staff engaged in the process; capitalize on strengths; and strengthen areas in need of development.
4. Devise and communicate a comprehensive big-picture plan for the division of work, honoring the complexity and variety of assignments made at an individual level.
5. Eliminate barriers/obstacles to work effectiveness.
6. Measure the equity of workload, and use data to support judgments about efficiency and effectiveness.
7. Offer rewards and recognition to individuals and teams.
8. Recommend ways to improve systems and processes.
9. Use a social network to engage others in decision making and for feedback, when appropriate or relevant.

New nurses typically think of management as it relates to either direct patient care or nursing unit management. You may also be involved in project management. Many efforts in health care are complex and develop over time. Because nurses are often the end users in the rollout of new care processes, it is important that they are involved in the planning and implementation as well. An example of a situation where nurses can contribute greatly to overall project success is planning for implementation of a new electronic health record.

> **EXERCISE 1.2** Examine one structured process in the delivery of patient care from start to finish (e.g., diagnostic laboratory studies). How is the process organized? Describe what steps are involved. How many steps does the process take? Who is responsible for each step in the process? Who has the responsibility and authority for managing the process? What outcome data are available to determine how well the process is working? Are outcomes reviewed on a regular basis?

The tasks of management are designed to enact Gardner's tasks of leadership. For example, although the leader may create a culture of trust, the manager offers rewards that reinforce that value. A professional nurse must have abilities to both lead and manage. Nurses are on the front line when dealing with new and unknown health experiences, which require leadership, and implementing care routines, which must be managed.

Following

Following is a term that can be misinterpreted. Images associated with followers portray passive, uninspired workers waiting for direction. Although that may be accurate for some organizations, following in a high-functioning team is an active, creative role that influences leaders and managers. A healthy definition of followership is that each group member contributes optimally in tandem with other group members to achieve clinical or organizational outcomes. All team members are expected to fully participate, using their knowledge, skills, and experience to help deal with complex clinical and organizational issues. In essence, maximal functioning as a team member exemplifies followership. When in the following role, teamwork is palpable. Each person acts together with purpose and in a rhythm that addresses the aim at hand.

Nurses may demonstrate followership by serving on committees. Even simple activities such as completing readings and reviewing minutes from previous meetings are essential for an organization's success. Traits of followers include acting synergistically with others, being enthusiastic and responsible, speaking and acting with principle and integrity, adding value to the work being accomplished, and questioning decisions and directions that are not congruent with the purpose or values of the group. The effective follower is willing to be led, to share time and talents, to create and innovate solutions, to take direction from the manager and to role model confidence and professionalism. Simultaneously, followers must perform their assigned structured duties, which require critical thinking and decision making. Bleich's tasks associated with followership can be found in Box 1.2.

Followers complement leaders and managers with their skills. Together they work to fill gaps and to build on each other's cognitive, technical, interpersonal, and emotional capabilities. Followers, showing sensitivity to other roles, may offer respite in times of stress. Followers need feedback from others to stay on course. The follower may acquiesce to the skills and abilities of

---

BOX 1.2   Bleich's Tasks of Followership

1. Demonstrate individual accountability while working within the context of organizational systems and processes; do not alter the process for personal gain or shortcuts.
2. Honor and implement care to the standards and specifications required for safe and acceptable care/service.
3. Offer knowledge, skills, and abilities to accomplish the task at hand.
4. Collaborate with leaders and managers; avoid passive-aggressive or nonassertive responses to work assignment.
5. Include evidence-based feedback as part of daily work activities as a self-guide to efficiency and effectiveness and to contribute to outcome measurement.
6. Demonstrate accountability to the team effort.
7. Take reasonable risks as an antidote for fearing change or unknown circumstances.
8. Evaluate the efficiency and effectiveness of systems and processes that affect outcomes of care/service; advocate for well-designed work.
9. Give and receive feedback to others to promote a nurturing and generative culture.

the leader or manager to promote teamwork but is prepared to lead or manage when circumstances demand it.

Leading, Managing, and Following in Action

The relationship between and among followers and leaders and managers is complex. In any given work shift, a nurse may assume all three roles. At the beginning of the shift the nurse may function as a manager to ensure that patient care assignments are distributed, report received, and adequate supplies are ordered. Later, the nurse may lead by inspiring a colleague to discuss end-of-life care with a particularly anxious family. During a facility-wide committee meeting, the nurse may show followership as the group plans to implement a new fall risk assessment.

During a shift, critical clinical events (e.g., cardiac arrest) arise that require a temporary adjustment to maximize the talents and skills of team members. Those team members who are able to nimbly respond to changing situations and roles with little or no fanfare have what is often referred to as emotional intelligence.

> **EXERCISE 1.3** Using the definitions for leading, managing, and following noted previously, observe how work is organized on a clinical unit. What situations occurred that could not be predicted at the onset of the shift? What work followed a routine nature or was driven by protocol? Identify an activity that was driven by principles rather than by formal evidence. Identify an activity that was driven by evidence-based practice or evidence-based organizational practice. Then, notice team functioning. Who led? Who managed? Who followed? Did this happen seamlessly, or were there times when there was tension in efforts?

Emotional Intelligence to Lead, Manage, and Follow

Emotional intelligence is necessary to carry out the expectations of leading, managing, and following. In his classic work, Goleman (2000) refers to emotional intelligence as being characterized by self-awareness, self-regulation, empathy, and social skills that help people harmonize to increase their value in the workplace. Self-awareness and self-regulation are personal skills, whereas empathy and social skills are abilities to manage relationships (Hemens, 2014). These characteristics are essential for direct care nurses as well as those in designated leadership positions (Fig. 1.2). Emotionally

Fig. 1.2 Being empathetic and showing sensitivity to the experiences of others helps nurse leaders develop their emotional intelligence. (© Thinkstock images/iStock/Thinkstock)

intelligent leaders are a common topic of research studies in today's healthcare environment and are critical as our profession adapts to constant change. Delmatoff and Lazarus (2014) described an emotionally and behaviorally intelligent style of leadership. This means that the leader not only possesses emotional intelligence but behaves in an emotionally intelligent manner. Although that may seem obvious, leaders sometimes do not demonstrate emotional intelligence. This is particularly true with those new to leading and managing. A new manager may identify with a leader who does not demonstrate emotional intelligence, so the new manager begins to adopt similar ineffective behaviors. In this instance the new nurse manager fails to demonstrate the very characteristics that likely led to earning the management position.

Emotionally intelligent nurses are credible as leaders, managers, and followers because they possess awareness of the individual, family, or community that is the locus of caregiving, have enhanced organizational skills because they have invested in relationships, and are able to collaborate, show insight into others, and commit to self-growth. When coupled with performing clinical

LITERATURE PERSPECTIVE

Resource: Bisognano, M. (2016). Nursing leadership: New ways to see, *Nurse Leader, 14*(6), 422-426.

The author describes five "lessons" that have occurred in health care over time. The first is new ways to see health care as a system. Hiring the right staff is more than intelligence and competence. It also includes having emotional fortitude and curious spirit. The curious spirit can lead to seeking out the perspective of the patient. Narratives of less than optimal patient experiences provide many opportunities to see, solve, and share in a realtime manner rather than lengthy procedure changes. The second is new ways to see the patient and their support systems. The "What Matters to You" campaign to better identify patient wishes is the epitome of patient-centered care. The third lesson addresses how patients move both within and among healthcare organizations and providers. Testing new models of care within healthcare facilities and homes is central to decreasing the stress and strain of navigating the healthcare system. The fourth lesson is looking at new ways to see and build teams. Currently, it is possible to have five distinct generations, each with their own values, working together. Thus it is essential that employees understand the diverse values and beliefs present in today's workforce. The last lesson is applying new ways to lead. Making decisions based on real-time data allows organizations to nimbly respond to trends. *Exnovation* is defined as ridding the systems of unnecessary processes, meetings, reports, and other duties that take away from the priorities of patient care. The purpose is to develop more efficient and effective clinical care processes.

Implications for Practice

These five lessons provide opportunity for self-reflection on how you can fit into this ever-changing healthcare system.

tasks tied to critical thinking and action, the emotionally intelligent nurse demonstrates the capacity to be a high-performing professional. Employees are tuned in to the emotional intelligence of managers and leaders. The synergy associated with a leader's credibility and capability fuse for success. Without self-reflective skills, growth in emotional intelligence is stymied, work becomes routine, and asynchrony with others results. The Literature Perspective illustrates the importance of emotional intelligence.

> **EXERCISE 1.4** Reflect on the worldview of how family, friends, and others see you. Think about the historical markers that influenced your life perspective. Think about your religious or other belief systems. Review the extent to which others with diverse ideas and beliefs were a part of your life experience. As you journal these thoughts, how do they affect your emotional intelligence? What role can a mentor and continuing education play in advancing your life perspective? Which of the characteristics of emotional intelligence is the most developed and which is the least developed? How might you further enhance your emotional intelligence?

TRADITIONAL AND EMERGING LEADERSHIP AND MANAGEMENT ROLES

The way nurses lead, manage, and follow has changed over time. Formerly, nurses took direction exclusively from physicians or senior nurses such as "head" or "charge" nurses. These formal roles still exist in some places; however, the expectation has shifted from a top-down, order-giving model to one in which shared decision making with collaborative action is the norm. As knowledge expands and the array of treatment interventions available to patients has grown, care delivery has moved far beyond what a command-and-control top-down structure can accommodate in a traditional hierarchical organization. Health care is now delivered in a collaborative and interprofessional manner, such as that reflected in the movement toward primary care or medical homes. In this model of care, providers strive for comprehensive, patient-centered, coordinated, high-quality care (Flieger, 2017). This holistic approach to care delivery requires holistic leadership, emphasizing effective communication and outcomes.

Health care today is an amalgamation of both traditional and dynamic structures. New theories of leadership will emerge to capture the complexity and globalization of health care and changing communication patterns through the influence of the Internet and social media. Professional nurses must be prepared to practice within a system that is both predictable and unpredictable.

Concepts of teamwork and collaborative decision making are critical in a healthcare environment that is dynamic and ever changing. A nurse has great potential to shape those changes. We do not have to have "titles" to be leaders; we just have to be living human beings willing to execute our potentials. In other words, the synchrony of leading, managing, and following is within each of us.

The collective behaviors that reflect leading, managing, and following enhance each other. All interdisciplinary healthcare providers, including professional nurses, experience situations each day in which they must lead, manage, and follow. Some institutional formal positions, such as nurse manager or charge nurse, require an advanced set of attributes and know-how to establish organizational goals and objectives, oversee human resources, provide staff with performance feedback, facilitate change, and manage conflict to meet patient care and organizational requirements.

LEADING, MANAGING, AND FOLLOWING IN A DIVERSE ORGANIZATION

The healthcare industry is going through unparalleled change from the traditional industrial models of the previous century. The culture in most healthcare organizations today is more ethnically diverse; has an expansive educational chasm (from non–high school graduates to doctorally prepared clinicians); has multiple generations of workers with varying values and expectations of the workplace; involves extensive use of technology to support all aspects of the organization; and challenges workers, patients, families, and communities with antibiotic-resistant microorganisms and emerging diseases.

The complexity of the healthcare system is marred with chronic problems, information imbalance (sometimes too much, sometimes not enough), physically and emotionally intense work with little time for reflection, increased consumer and regulatory demands, and fatigue from too many cues and reminders! Upcoming changes may exacerbate these problems.

These and other variables make leading, managing, and following increasingly challenging. A leader must address the needs of the diverse community. Language variations, cultural barriers, and overused electronic communication create opportunities for misunderstanding that could contribute to errors. Followers and leaders of different generations and values can educate each other on the best ways to communicate.

BOX 1.3   Desired Attributes of Leaders, Managers, and Followers

- Use focused energy and stamina to accomplish a vision.
- Use critical-thinking skills in decision making.
- Trust personal intuition and then back up intuition with facts.
- Accept responsibility willingly and follow up on the consequences of actions taken.
- Identify the needs of others.
- Deal with people skillfully: coach, communicate, counsel.
- Demonstrate ease in standard/boundary setting.
- Examine multiple options to accomplish the objective at hand flexibly.
- Be trustworthy and handle information from various sources with respect for the source.
- Motivate others assertively toward the objective at hand.
- Demonstrate competence or be capable of rapid learning in the arena in which change is desired.

The outlook for health care is not all doom and gloom. Our understanding of human behavior allows those in administrative positions to understand characteristics of the workforce better than ever before. As a result, workforce development can be tailored. Although both a gift and a curse, options for technology allow for even greater exchange of information among healthcare team members, patients, and families. Box 1.3 identifies attributes of leaders, managers, and followers, including commonalities. These attributes represent hope for the future.

The importance of teamwork and collaboration is well understood in the healthcare industry. Collaboration requires a set of special conditions between leaders and followers. Among these conditions are the ideas that each voice will be valued in an equitable manner, that power is evenly distributed among the stakeholders, and that conditions allow for innovation.

CONCLUSION

Developing skills and abilities for leading, managing, and following encourages professional nurses to adapt to and accept differences as a positive rather than a negative force in daily work life. Building on gender strengths; generational values, gifts, and talents; cultural diversity; varying educational and experiential perspectives; and a mobile and flexible workforce is rewarding for a leader. It is also rewarding to experience the strength of a good manager and to achieve positive outcomes as a follower and team member.

THE SOLUTION

Complexity science served as the basis for addressing concerns in this LTC setting. A full-time **advanced practice registered nurse (APRN)** was employed in each nursing home to work with nursing staff about the importance of recognizing a change in condition, completing an assessment, and obtaining treatment in the nursing home, rather than transferring to the hospital. Through early illness recognition, the resident could be treated in a proactive manner at the LTC facility, rather than waiting until a significant physical decline occurred that warranted a transfer to the hospital.

Embedding a full-time APRN in the facility resulted in positive outcomes for the residents. The APRN developed relationships with nearly all nursing home staff, no matter their role, and served as an expert clinician and resource. In addition, she volunteered to be on call 24/7 and provided phone support during nonworking hours. The nursing home was primarily staffed with licensed practical nurses and certified nurse assistants, as is typical of most nursing homes. Education was central to enhancing the clinical skills and decision making of the nursing staff. Both formal and roving ongoing education was provided as new staff members were hired and new clinical challenges arose. Role modeling by the APRN enhanced clinical reasoning skills when a resident exhibited a condition change.

Another key feature in the intervention was the use of the Interventions to Reduce Acute Care Transfers (INTERACT) tools. These standardized tools are designed to improve recognition and communication about changes in resident condition. The two main tools used were (1) Stop and Watch and (2) Situation, Background, Assessment, and Recommendation, or SBAR. (**NOTE:** The acronym SBAR is slightly different in the INTERACT model.) The Stop and Watch tool is used to report a subtle change in condition. Any person, including those from dietary, housekeeping, and family members, could fill out a Stop and Watch to alert the nurse of a subtle change in resident condition. This allowed those with the most frequent resident interaction to have a means of communicating what might seem a "bit off" or "different" in a resident. The SBAR tool provided a means for documentation of condition change, as well as guiding critical thinking about a change in status. Nurses completed the SBAR before contacting a provider. Staff reported feeling more confident and empowered in their job performance.

Management of polypharmacy and reduction of antipsychotic medication was led by the APRN in collaboration with staff physicians. Comprehensive, thoughtful medication reviews were conducted on all residents. The original rate of antipsychotic usage of 30.8% was reduced to 3.3%, all of which were for residents with a diagnosis of bipolar disorder. No antipsychotics have been prescribed for residents with only a psychiatric diagnosis of dementia for more than 3 years. Communication regarding medication management as well as condition change has been enhanced through the use of secure, encrypted electronic communication channels.

Site staff have also been active in the education and implementation of advance directives in the facility as well as in the community. Annually, the center hosts advance directive clinics where staff, residents, families, and community members can fill out an advance directive free of charge. Facility representatives also travel to senior centers within the county to provide education and opportunities to enact an advance directive.

Consistent with complexity science, there was no one "magic bullet" that led to the success of the MOQI project at this site. It took a large degree of commitment from staff and providers to be open to a new way of thinking and caring for residents. Care processes and communication channels changed. Monthly quality assurance meetings give actual data demonstrating quality outcomes, which have continued to improve. The change did not occur overnight. It was a gradual change that was nudged and at times pushed by the APRN and the leadership in the home.

Would this be a suitable approach for you? Why?

JoAnn Franklin
Angelita Pritchett

▌REFLECTIONS

Ponder the leadership theories presented here. Does one seem to make more sense to you than another? Consider, for example, what you were doing the last time you were in the clinical area. Does one theory suggest that you were using it as you enacted your role? Identify one way you can incorporate a leadership theoretical perspective into a daily clinical routine.

THE EVIDENCE

What makes a good leader or a good follower? The roles of leader, manager, and follower are different, and each is needed in a successful organization. In fact, the same individual often plays each of the roles in a successful organization. Studies of identity dynamics help explain who wants to lead and who wants to follow and how individuals enact and develop those roles.

Although much of the prior research on leadership considers the perspective of how others see the leader or follower, it is also important to consider how the individuals in those roles see themselves. A multilevel view of identity development includes reflection on intrapersonal, interpersonal, and group identity. Engaging in reflection and identity work can help more fully develop our roles as leaders and followers (Epitropaki, Kark, Mainemelis, & Lord, 2017). Collaboration requires a set of special conditions between leaders and followers. Among these conditions is the idea that each voice will be valued in an equitable manner, that power is evenly distributed among all of the stakeholders, and that conditions exist for innovation to occur.

Organizations often function with effective leaders and managers who preside over work groups with common, short-term goals. When true teamwork is required the work is longer to allow for team relationships to build.

Complexity science does not refer to the complexity of the decision to be made or to the work environment, but rather to examining how systems adapt and function—where co-creation of ideas and actions unfold in a nonprescriptive manner. Social networking is being recognized as a web of relationships that can be tapped and used for communication, problem solving, support, and real-time information, critical to decision making. It is a real tool for individuals to use when leading, managing, or following.

TIPS FOR LEADING, MANAGING, AND FOLLOWING

- Use theories of leadership and management to frame complex problems and guide decision making.
- Understand the situation to be more effective as a manager.
- Acknowledge that situations not well understood are best approached using leadership tasks.
- Lead, manage, and follow as warranted in any role at appropriate times.

REFERENCES

Anderson, V., & Johnson, L. (1997). *Systems thinking basics: From concepts to causal loops.* Waltham, MA: Pegasus Communications.

Bass, B. M. (1990). From transactional to transformational leadership: Learning to share the vision. *Organizational Dynamics, 18,* 19–31.

Bennis, W. G., & Nanus, B. (2007). *Leaders: The strategies for taking charge* (2nd ed.). New York: Harper Business.

Blake, R. R., & Mouton, J. S. (1985). *The managerial grid III.* Houston: Gulf Publishing.

Bodenheimer, T., & Sinsky, C. (2014). From triple aim to quadruple aim: Care of the patient requires care of the provider. *Annals of Family Medicine, 12*(6), 573–576.

Delmatoff, J., & Lazarus, I. R. (2014). The most effective leadership style for the new landscape of healthcare. *Journal of Healthcare Management, 59*(4), 245–249.

Disch, J. (2009). Generative leadership. *Creative Nursing, 15*(4), 172–177.

Epitropaki, O., Kark, R., Mainemelis, C., & Lord, R. C. (2017). Leadership and followership identity processes: A multilevel review. *The Leadership Quarterly, 28*(1), 104–129.

Fiedler, F. A. (1967). *A theory of leadership effectiveness.* New York: McGraw-Hill.

Flieger, S. P. (2017). Implementing the patient-centered medical home in complex adaptive systems: Becoming a relationship-centered patient-centered medical home. *Health Care Management Review, 42*(2), 112–121.

Gardner, J. W. (1990). *On leadership.* New York: Free Press.

Goleman, D. P. (2000). *Working with emotional intelligence.* New York: Bantam Books.

Hemens, M. J. (2014). Emotional intelligence: The sine qua non for effective leadership. *Canadian Journal of Medical Laboratory Science, Winter, 2014,* 14–15.

Herzberg, F. (1991). One more time: How do you motivate employees? In M. J. Ward & S. A. Price (Eds.), *Issues in nursing administration: Selected readings.* St. Louis: Mosby.

House, R. J., & Mitchell, T. R. (1974, Autumn). Path-goal theory of leadership. *Journal of Contemporary Business, 3,* 81–97.

Lencioni, P. M. (2002). *The five dysfunctions of a team: A leadership fable.* San Francisco: Jossey-Bass.

Likert, R. (1987). *New patterns of management.* New York: Garland.

Luthans, F. (2011). *Organizational behavior* (12th ed.). Burr Ridge, IL: McGraw-Hill.

Maslow, A. (1943). A theory of human motivation. *Psychological Review, 50,* 370–396.

Morgan, G. (2003). *Applying complexity science to health and healthcare.* Carlson School of Management: University of Minnesota. http://c.ymcdn.com/sites/www.plexusinstitute. org/resource/collection/6528ED29-9907-4BC7-8D00-8DC907679FED/11261_Plexus_Summit_report_Health_Healthcare.pdf.

Shartle, C. L. (1956). *Executive performance and leadership.* Englewood Cliffs, NJ: Prentice Hall.

Stogdill, R. M. (1948). Personal factors associated with leadership: A survey of the literature. *Journal of Psychology, 25,* 35–71.

Stogdill, R. M. (1963). *Manual for the leader behavior description questionnaire, form XII.* Columbus: The Ohio State University, Bureau of Business Research.

Tichy, N. M., & Devanna, M. A. (1997). *The transformational leader.* New York: John Wiley & Sons.

Vroom, V. H. (1994). *Work and motivation.* New York: John Wiley & Sons.

Vroom, V. H., & Yetton, P. (1973). *Leadership and decision-making.* Pittsburgh, PA: University of Pittsburgh Press.

2

Clinical Safety: The Core of Leading, Managing, and Following

Patricia S. Yoder-Wise

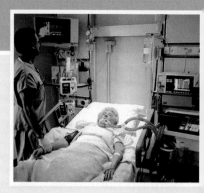

LEARNING OUTCOMES

- Differentiate the key organizations leading patient safety movements in the United States.
- Value the need for leaders, managers, and followers to focus on clinical safety.

- Apply the concepts of today's expectations for how clinical safety is implemented.

KEY TERMS

Agency for Healthcare Research and Quality (AHRQ)

Choosing Wisely

Det Norske Veritas (DNV)

Institute for Healthcare Improvement (IHI)

Magnet Recognition Program®

National Academy of Medicine (NAM) (formerly the Institute of Medicine [IOM])

National Integrated Accreditation for Healthcare Organizations (NIAHO)

National Quality Forum (NQF)

Quality and Safety Education for Nurses (QSEN)

TeamSTEPPS (an AHRQ strategy to promote patient safety)

The Joint Commission (TJC)

THE CHALLENGE

Several years ago, embracing the need to move to evidence-based practice, the nursing department of the hospital I was working in selected a model that we would use. The selection process was admirable, using our collaborative governance structure to make the decision. Several models were presented to the Nursing Practice Council, which was made up of primarily direct-care nurses from each unit of the tertiary care hospital. Pros and cons were weighed, and a decision was made. Voila, our practice was now going to be evidence-based!

Moving from model selection to becoming truly evidence-based was much more challenging for the nurses. Changing practice habits and beliefs requires a lot of education and communication. Nurses on each unit practiced differently from each other, and units had customs of practice that differed from other units. Orthopedic

INTRODUCTION

This book focuses on the concepts of leading and managing effectively. The question is, however, leading for what? No issue is more prominent in the literature or in healthcare organizations than the concern for patient safety and for employee safety, and that is at the core of leading and managing in nursing. Many factors and individuals have influenced the nursing profession's and the public's concern about safety, starting with Florence Nightingale's work in the Crimean War. In the United States, the seminal work, *To Err is Human: Building a Safer Health System* (2000), produced by the Institute of Medicine (IOM) (now known as the National Academy of Medicine [NAM]), shaped much of our thinking about patient safety. This focus fits well with the basic patient advocacy role that nurses have supported over decades. This role has evolved over 175 years, as reflected in a review article in the *American Journal of Nursing* (Kowalski & Anthony, 2017). This is a history befitting nursing, the most trusted profession.

Although less attention has focused on the clinical environment itself, it too has great importance in patient—and provider—safety.

Because the core of concern in any healthcare organization is safety, it also is the core concern for nurses. Safety, and subsequently quality, should drive such aspects of leading and managing as staffing and budgeting decisions, personnel policies and change, information technology, delegation decisions, workplace environment, and personal practices. Another reason to be concerned with preventing patient safety concerns is that at least one study showed that both physicians and nurses who were involved in a patient safety event were more likely to have multiple negative outcomes. Greater risk for burnout, turnover, and "problematic medication use" were three such outcomes (Van Gerven et al., 2016).

Three major driving forces provide the greatest emphasis on quality: the IOM (now NAM), the Agency for Healthcare Research and Quality (AHRQ), and the National Quality Forum (NQF). Many other groups incorporate specific standards and expectations about safety and quality into their respective work. Additionally, specifically focused efforts, such as those of the Quality and Safety Education for Nurses (QSEN) and TeamSTEPPS initiatives, have addressed patient safety issues. No nurse can function today without a focus on patient safety, nor can any nurse leader or manager.

THE CLASSIC REPORTS AND EMERGING SUPPORTS

Several reports are reflective of the efforts to refocus health care to quality, as illustrated in Table 2.1. These reports and the related supporting work form the basis for the continued efforts all healthcare professionals must address to promote safe care.

TABLE 2.1	**Major Forces Influencing Patient Safety**	
Element	**Core Relevance**	**Implications for Leaders and Managers**
Reports		
Institute of Medicine Reports	*To Err is Human* (2000): Defined the number of deaths (n = 98,000) attributed to patient safety issues	Moved safety issues from the incident report level to an integrated patient safety report for the organization. Acknowledged system errors as more common cause of error than individual. Stimulated hospital boards to include reports on quality on agenda.
	Crossing the Quality Chasm (2001): Identified the six major aims in providing health care (see Box 2.1)	Moved care from discipline-centric foci to patient-centered foci. Reinforced the disparities that occur within health care, which, in turn, led to a focus on best practices (and reinforced the need to be patient centered). Addressed issues such as healing environments, evidence-based care, and transparency, which led to a more holistic environment that was built on evidence and that was transparent. Provided substantive support for information technology use. Served as impetus for "pay for quality."
	Health Professions Education: A Bridge to Quality (2003): Addressed the issue of silo education among the health professions in basic and continuing education (Box 2.2)	Attempted to shrink the chasm between education and practice so that interprofessional teams would work more effectively together. Exposed the issue of "silo" education when reality requires collaborative practice. Increased expectation for participation in lifelong learning.
	Keeping Patients Safe: Transforming the Work Environment of Nurses (2004): Identified many past practices that had a negative influence on nurses and thus on patients.	Focused on direct care nurses and supported their involvement in decision making related to their practice. Supported the concept of shared governance. Provided a framework for considering how nurses could determine staffing requirements. Supported public reporting of issues related to unsafe work environments. Moved the Chief Nursing Officer into the Boardroom as a key spokesperson on safety and quality issues.
	Improving the Quality of Health Care for Mental and Substance-Use Conditions (2005): Addressed issues related to this patient population, including those who can be found among a general care population	Provided a focus on mental health needs of patients who were not admitted for the primary reason of mental health issues.
	Preventing Medication Errors (2006): Addressed many of the issues surrounding the use of medications	Validated the complexity of providing medications to patients.
	Future of Nursing: Leading Change, Advancing Health (2010): Identified 8 recommendations based on evidence that the profession must attend to (see Box 2.3)	Created state coalitions focused on improving nursing. Created nursing/community/business coalitions to accomplish the work. Moved the issue of nurses as leaders to a more visible level.

TABLE 2.1   Major Forces Influencing Patient Safety—cont'd

Element	Core Relevance	Implications for Leaders and Managers
Agencies/Organizations		
Agency for Healthcare Research and Quality	Federal agency devoted to improving quality, safety, efficiency, and effectiveness (2008) *www.ahrq.gov*	Provides outcomes research sections as resources for nurses. Created the source of TeamSTEPPS (*http://teamstepps. ahrq.gov/contactus.htm*).
National Quality Forum	Membership-based organization related to quality measurement and reporting *www.nqf.org*	Provides source for Centers for Medicare and Medicaid's never events. Serves as resource for Healthcare Facilities Accreditation Program (a CMS-deemed authority) (uses NQF's Safe Practices). Serves as source of nurse sensitive-care standards.
The Joint Commission	Not-for-profit organization that accredits healthcare organizations internationally *www.jointcommission.org*	Focuses on outcomes that redirected accreditation processes and thus nurses' roles with the process. Changed to unannounced visits and thus changed the way organizations prepare for accreditation. Issues annual patient safety goals. Issues sentinel event announcements.
Det Norske Veritas/National Integrated Accreditation for Healthcare Organizations	Internationally based organization that accredits many fields, including health care *www.dnvaccreditation.com*	Based on an internationally understood set of standards known as ISO (International Organization for Standardization). Visits annually in a consultative manner and thus changed the way accreditation is viewed.
Magnet Recognition Program®	A designation built on, and evolving through, research. Emphasizes outcomes *www.nursecredentialing.org*	Created unified approaches to seek this designation. Redirected focus to outcomes, including data and efforts related to patient safety.
Institute for Healthcare Improvement	Independent, not-for-profit organization Source of rapid cycle testing, bundles and open school to aid practitioners in improving care *www.ihi.org*	Supports rapid cycle change projects designed to improve care rapidly (see the Theory Box on p. 27). Provides Global Trigger Tools.
Quality and Safety Education for Nurses	Comprehensive resource, including references and video modules *www.qsen.org*	Created knowledge, skills, and attitudes for students and graduates related to safety.
Choosing Wisely	Lists of practices for clinicians and patients to question *www.choosingwisely.org*	Provides lists for clinicians, by submitting organization, to question practices. Provides lists by conditions for patients' use in making wise decisions for care.

The Institute of Medicine Reports on Quality

This safety-focused work began with the report *To Err is Human* (IOM, 2000) and rapidly moved to several other reports designed to set aims of health care, to address how professionals were prepared, and to target key areas such as the work environment, mental health and substance use, and medication errors. *Crossing the Quality Chasm* (IOM, 2001) identified six aims of providing health care, which remain relevant to today's practice (Box 2.1). Equally relevant to safety issues is how professionals are prepared, and the report "Health Professions Education: A Bridge to Quality" (IOM, 2003) established expected competencies for all health professions (Box 2.2). Basically, the idea of this report was to shrink the chasm between learning and reality. A commitment to this redirection of learning, to approach reality, is critical for "learning organizations," a term coined by Peter Senge. Thus constant learning is a commitment every healthcare professional and organization must have. Although it is the individual's accountability to maintain competence and participate in learning, a learning organization values and acknowledges learning as a vital element in being effective.

Many nurses think of "Keeping Patients Safe: Transforming the Work Environment of Nurses" (IOM, 2004) as the major impetus behind many changes designed to improve working conditions for nurses. This report identified lack of trust in organizations, lack of readily available resources (such as clinical leaders), and the presence of unsafe equipment, supplies, and practices as contributions to an unsafe work environment. Regrettably, well over a decade later, many of these issues persist in numerous healthcare settings.

Two other related reports in what is called the *Chasm Series* also provide guidance to nursing and were focused on specific, pervasive issues: mental health/substance use and medication errors (IOM, 2005, 2006). Both of these reports fit within the IOM's focus on quality and its attempt to make health care a quality endeavor.

One final report of importance, though it is not focused directly on patient safety, is *The Future of Nursing* (IOM, 2010). The numerous citations of evidence related to education, scope of practice, and leadership clearly indicate that if the eight recommendations (Box 2.3) were fully implemented, the quality of care, including safety, would be enhanced.

Agency for Healthcare Research and Quality

The AHRQ is the primary federal agency devoted to improving quality, safety, efficiency, and effectiveness of health care (Agency for Healthcare Research and Quality [AHRQ], 2018). An example of this agency's

---

BOX 2.1 The Aims of Providing Health Care

- Safe
- Effective
- Patient-centered
- Timely
- Efficient
- Equitable

From Institute of Medicine (IOM). (2001). *Crossing the quality chasm: A new health system for the 21st century.* Washington, DC: National Academy Press.

BOX 2.2 Competencies of Health Professionals

- Provide patient-centered care.
- Work in interdisciplinary teams.
- Employ evidence-based practice.
- Apply quality improvement.
- Utilize informatics.

From Institute of Medicine (IOM). (2003). *Health professions education: A bridge to quality.* Washington, DC: National Academy Press.

BOX 2.3 The Future of Nursing Recommendations

1. Remove scope-of-practice barriers.
2. Expand opportunities for nurse to lead and diffuse collaborative improvement efforts.
3. Implement nurse residency programs.
4. Increase the proportion of nurses with a baccalaureate degree to 80% by 2020.
5. Double the number of nurses with a doctorate by 2020.
6. Ensure that nurses engage in lifelong learning.
7. Prepare and enable nurses to lead change to advance health.
8. Build an infrastructure for the collection and analysis of interprofessional healthcare workforce data.

From Institute of Medicine (IOM). (2010). *The Future of Nursing: Leading Change, Advancing Health.* Washington, DC: National Academies Press.

work is the detailed curriculum for residents in continuing care retirement communities (CCRCs). This tool is designed to help employees promote healthy practices for CCRC residents.

EXERCISE 2.1 Go to *https://www.ahrq.gov/professionals/education/curriculum-tools/stepmanual/index.html* to review the Staying Healthy through Education and Prevention. Note that this site contains an entire curriculum for continuing care retirement communities (CCRCs). Select at least three content areas to determine what healthy older adults should be encouraged to do to stay healthy. After doing that, select one or two local CCRCs and read what they say is available to people who choose to live in those communities. Were you able to determine at least one healthy practice promoted by your local CCRCs?

Most famously, AHRQ's TeamSTEPPS programs are designed to increase attention to safety within healthcare organizations. More recently, the AHRQ issued a report on evidence-based practices, *Making Health Care Safer II* (AHRQ, 2016). This work has focused on various aspects of care such as preoperative checklists, bundles to prevent central line–associated bloodstream infections, interventions to reduce urinary catheter care, hand hygiene, "do not use" abbreviations, barrier precautions to prevent healthcare-associated bloodstream infections, interventions to reduce falls, use of rapid response systems, and simulation exercises in patient safety efforts.

EXERCISE 2.2 Refer to Gardner's Tasks of Leadership in Chapter 1. Create a 3 × 10 grid. Enter Gardner's tasks in the left vertical column. Go to the AHRQ website and find the report on *Making Health Care Safer II*. Select one of the practices and enter one behavior expected of a leader in column two to illustrate each of Gardner's tasks. Then in the third column, enter one behavior expected of a manager to illustrate each task. Finally, reflect on your latest day in the clinical setting. Did you see evidence of the best practices being employed? What leadership and management behaviors were observable?

The National Quality Forum

The **National Quality Forum (NQF)** is a membership-based organization designed to develop and implement a national strategy for healthcare quality measurement and reporting. Through its consensus process, NQF sets standards and endorses measures, which allow for comparison across settings, states, diagnoses, and so forth. The NQF then advises the Centers for Medicare and Medicaid Services (CMS) about measures that can be used to determine payment. These measures can be altered based on emerging evidence and testing of measures, and they form the basis for comparison of quality. As a result, CMS will not pay for certain conditions that result from what might be termed *poor practices* or events that should not have occurred while a patient was under the care of a healthcare professional.

EXERCISE 2.3 The IOM, through its report on *The Future of Nursing*, advocated for having at least 80% of the registered nurse population prepared at the baccalaureate level. Conduct a brief online search regarding the rationale behind this recommendation. Assume that you work in a facility that does not require all staff to hold a bachelor's degree and does not provide support (time off, tuition reimbursement, recognition of educational achievement). How could you use the information you found to change workplace policies and practices to benefit patients and nurses who do not hold a baccalaureate degree in nursing?

In 2016, Press Ganey issued a report on workplace safety and its influence on both nursing and patient outcomes. This report included nurse perceptions about both safety itself and the surveillance capacity. The key findings of the analyses performed were lower rates of missed care, higher rates of job enjoyment, higher overall hospital ratings, and fewer hospital-acquired pressure ulcers. These findings make a business case for attention to the work environment (clinical safety being a major focus of that environment). The Literature Perspective indicates the importance of the workplace on overall safety issues. A study in emergency departments supported the idea of absolute numbers being important as well as the skill and experience mix of the staff for staff to perceive that their workplace can provide safe patient care (Wolf, Perhats, Delao, Clark, & Moon, 2016).

LITERATURE PERSPECTIVE

Resource: Press Ganey. (2016). *2016 Nursing Special Report: The role of workplace safety and surveillance capacity in driving nurse and patient outcomes.* http://www.pressganey.com/resources/white-papers/the-role-of-workplace-safety-and-surveillance-capacity-in-driving-outcomes.

Press Ganey used an integrated, cross-domain analysis approach to consider workplace safety and surveillance capacity. Those elements were significantly associated with several important factors, such as nurse performance and pay-for-performance outcomes. Workplace safety, an environment in which nurses feel safe (both physically and emotionally), was stronger across outcomes than was nurse surveillance, (the monitoring, evaluating, and acting related to patients' changes in conditions).

Implications for Practice
The fourth component of the Quadruple Aim *(http://www.annfammed.org/content/12/6/573.full)* was found to have important influence on many factors, including, by extension, reimbursement percentages. Several strategies are recommended for action, including concurrence with the Safe Patient Handling and Mobility Standards *(http://www.nursingworld.org/nurses-books/safepatient-handling-and-mobility-interprofessional-national-standards-ac/).*

OTHER KEY AGENCIES AND ENDEAVORS

The Joint Commission (TJC) is a not-for-profit organization that accredits healthcare organizations. It has "deemed" status from the CMS, which means that an organization that meets TJC standards is deemed to have met the standards that the CMS sets.

When TJC changed its focus from process to outcomes, it also emphasized patient safety. As a result, TJC issues, with input, annual patient safety goals that are setting-specific; a list of "do-not-use" terms, symbols, and abbreviations; and sentinel events. All of these efforts are directed toward improving patient safety. In addition, with the NQF, TJC sponsors the Eisenberg Award for patient safety to highlight exemplars of quality.

The Det Norske Veritas (DNV) or National Integrated Accreditation for Healthcare Organizations (NIAHO) is an internationally based organization that provides accreditation in various fields, including health care. The accreditation process is based on a set of international standards known as *International Organization for Standardization (ISO).* Organizations are surveyed annually and receive extensive reports that can guide work toward higher quality. Because ISO is relevant to many fields, and it is well recognized in Europe and elsewhere, these standards have high acceptability in global work.

The Magnet Recognition Program® is a national designation built on, and evolving through, research. This program is designed to acknowledge nursing excellence. Through the Magnet Model® (*www.nursecredentialing.org*), organizations must demonstrate how they provide excellence. Five elements comprise the model: transformational leadership; structural empowerment; exemplary professional practice; new knowledge, innovation, and improvements; and empirical quality results. From initial designation to redesignation, greater emphasis is placed on empirical quality results. Magnet®, like other organizations mentioned here, focuses on quality care.

The Institute for Healthcare Improvement (IHI), which merged with the National Patient Safety Foundation in May 2017, is dedicated to rapidly improving care through a variety of mechanisms including rapid cycle change projects. (See the Theory Box for the classic view of rapid cycle change.)

Rapid cycle change is evident in today's intense electronic age. For example, only a few people have the vision and inventiveness that Steve Jobs at Apple did. What makes any product or idea popular is the viral nature with which early adopters grab the product or idea and tell others how valuable this new thing is. As soon as others also adopt the idea or product, it is the new expectation and is already undergoing change so that the "new" idea or product becomes the old one.

Think, for example, how many people worldwide respond when a tragedy occurs. They quickly tweet or

THEORY BOX

Diffusion Theory

Theory/Contributor	Key Idea	Application to Practice
Rogers (2003)	Diffusion is a process of communication about innovation to share information over time and among a group of people. It allows for nonlinear change. More complex change is less likely to be adopted. Early adopters serve as role models.	Engage key leaders in a change to infuse the energy from early adopters. Using Twitter in the hospital culture to engage employees communicates changes quickly. New changes are altered while they are being adopted because new evidence or a better idea emerges.

post and the community responds, often by expressing greater strength and perseverance than previously shown. On April 15, 2013, the famous Boston Marathon was disrupted by bombs at the finish line. The tweets and postings numbered in the millions, and the community refused to let that event change the view of the importance of Boston, its race, or its theme song, Sweet Caroline.

IHI's work, *Transforming Care at the Bedside (TCAB),* has created numerous clinical practice changes for nursing. These small tests of change were designed to be tested quickly so that if failure occurred not many resources nor much time was wasted. Yet the successful ventures spread rapidly to other organizations and became the new practice. The common core of most projects is patient safety. Further, IHI's Global Trigger Tool is one of the most used ways to determine harm to patients (go to *www.ihi.org* and search for Trigger Tools).

A project known as Quality and Safety Education for Nurses (QSEN) serves as a repository for resources related to the knowledge, skills, and attitudes that learners need to develop to serve as safe practitioners. Competencies are identified for both prelicensure and graduate students, and numerous resources are available. In the prelicensure competencies, for example, one element relates directly to leading and managing: teamwork and collaboration. An example of what is expected in communication is shown in the box above.

Research focused on communication found that three subcategories related to communication were critical for

Analyze differences in communication style preferences among patients and families, nurses, and other members of the health team. Describe the impact of one's own communication style on others. Discuss effective strategies for communicating and resolving conflict.	Communicate with team members, adapting one's own style of communicating to needs of the team and situation. Demonstrate commitment to team goals. Solicit input from other team members to improve individual, as well as team, performance. Initiate actions to resolve conflict.	Value teamwork and the relationships upon which it is based. Value different styles of communication used by patients, families, and healthcare providers. Contribute to resolution of conflict and disagreement.

Source: QSEN Institute (n.d.). QSEN Competencies. http://qsen.org/competencies/prelicensure-ksas/#teamwork_collaboration.

safety: fluent information transfer, an open culture of communication, and being actively engaged in collecting information (Kanerva, Kivinen, & Lammintakanen, 2015). Each of these critical elements can be found in numerous exchanges we engage in throughout any work period.

Choosing Wisely is a multidisciplinary approach to helping patients make wise decisions related to various care conditions. Begun by the American Board of Internal Medicine, the Choosing Wisely lists of practices for clinicians and cautions for patients are created by numerous specialty organizations and professional societies. As an example, the American Academy of Nursing adopted this strategy as a major way to influence patients and their health.

> **EXERCISE 2.4** Review the Choosing Wisely website (www.choosingwisely.org) and review back pain tests and treatments. Consider whether the suggestions found at Choosing Wisely reflect your local practices. If not, what are the differences? What ideas do you have about the reason for these differences?

MEANING FOR LEADING AND MANAGING IN NURSING

Many of the approaches to patient safety and, before that, aviation and nuclear energy safety consist of strategies to alert people to safety issues. For example, the use of SBAR (Situation, Background, Assessment, and Recommendation), handoffs, and checklists are designed to decrease omission of important information and practices. These practices aren't designed to limit a professional's distinctive contributions. Rather, they are designed to increase the likelihood of safe practice.

We rely on many sources to enhance safety as much as we can, and the combination of electronic risk assessment tools plus nurses' perceptions would seem to have a good potential for being effective in determining which patients are at risk for harm (Stafos et al., 2017). Although the tools in this study were very useful, they did not assess behavioral or psychosocial issues that could predict whether a patient was at risk. Thus nurses' substantial judgment continues to play a key role in patient safety.

Numerous issues also relate to clinical safety for nurses. Key issues are shift work, sleep disruptions, musculoskeletal injuries, needlesticks, and product allergies. The American Nurses Association has vast resources related to various safety issues for nurses, including fatigue and shift work, mental health, and bullying. These issues can be addressed through activities such as shared governance and clinical safety committees.

Leaders throughout the organization have the obligation to proactively address these issues. Perhaps a place to begin to address safety issues is on a peer basis. Although these types of conversations often are not comfortable, if we have knowledge of someone experiencing a needlestick, appearing sleepy, or engaging in unsafe practices, we each have the opportunity to address, and thus perhaps prevent, a patient safety issue. Lockett et al. (2015) proposed a model, through a research design, that elicited several attributes of an appropriate peer-to-peer accountability approach. These included empowerment to speak up, truth and transparency, reciprocal exchange of information, and respectful communication.

Although the major focus of safety for the people who receive our services has been in hospitals, every other setting where we provide care also has specific concerns related to safety—for both the patient and the nurse. Perhaps the most challenging, however, is the home setting, because most of the issues related to a safe environment are not controlled in the same manner as they are in an institutional setting. As Marrelli (2017) points out, safety issues range from the community and the neighborhood to the individual home environment, and when vulnerable populations, such as children or older adults, are involved, additional precautions come into consideration. If the neighborhood, as an example, is unsafe for clients, it is also unsafe for nurses who enter that neighborhood to provide care.

To think that manager and leader decisions do not affect patient safety is erroneous. Creating a positive environment, ensuring appropriate staffing and equipment, intervening and supporting others in doing so in cases of incivility, and supporting the use of the best evidence in practice all create a safer patient environment. That is, accountability applies to all of us—calling attention to, intervening, or solving threats to clinical safety. Furthermore, with so many organizations focusing on safety (and from multiple perspectives), nurses are challenged to remain clear about what is current and relevant. Conducting a crosswalk, a process of comparison across competencies and standards, may lend clarity (Lyle-Edrosolo & Waxman, 2016). This process is likely too tedious for individuals to perform and is ideally geared for a team within an organization. Additional ideas about a focus on safety are evident in the chapters on change, quality, and translating research into practice.

One of the challenges for nurses in any position, and especially for leaders and managers, is the obligation to have the greatest influence for patient safety. As one cross-sectional study shows, nurse staffing and overtime, which are highly influenced by leaders and managers, are associated with patient safety, the quality of care, and omitted care (Cho et al., 2016) as the Research Perspective shows. The idea of omitted care is further supported as an issue in a study by Jones, Johnstone, and Duke (2016). Basically, the idea of "cutting corners" was studied and found to likely contribute to preventable patient safety issues.

Many frontline nurses are unaware of the work that happens at executive levels on behalf of patient safety. Yet it is equally critical to the organization's overall success in addressing patient safety issues. Seeing the whole picture related to patient safety enhances our potential to solve problems that can lead to harm for patients, nurses, or both. A study of nurse perceptions versus electronic assessment tool scores supports the expectation for nurses to engage actively in assessing for risks (see the second Research Perspective).

RESEARCH PERSPECTIVE

Resource: Cho, E., Lee, N.J., Kim, E.Y., Kim, S., Lee, K., Park, K.O., & Sung, Y.H. (2016). Nurse staffing level and overtime associated with patient safety, quality of care and care left undone in hospitals: A cross-sectional study. *International Journal of Nursing Studies*, 60, 263-271.

This self-report study from South Korea used a common protocol (International Hospital Outcomes Study) in 65 acute care hospitals of 100 beds or more. Fifty-one hospitals and 3037 direct care registered nurses (RNs) participated. Anonymity was maintained by having RNs place responses to questions in a sealed envelope and deposit them into locked boxes. One day was selected to conduct this study, and the response rate was 96.2%. When RNs had a higher number of patients to care for, the odds were

higher for reporting poor/failing patient safety, poor/fair quality of care, and care left undone. When RNs worked overtime, the odds in each of those areas also were reported as higher.

Implications for Practice

Although the percentages of RNs selecting poor or fail responses were higher in South Korea (16.4%) than in the United States (6%), the outcomes seem to reflect what is experienced in other countries, including the United States. Addressing the numbers of patients cared for and the amount of overtime a nurse is expected to provide are two key components a nurse leader must address.

RESEARCH PERSPECTIVE

Resource: Stafos, A., Stark, S., Barbay, K., & Schedler, S. (2017). Identifying hospitalized patients at risk for harm: A comparison of nurse perceptions vs. electronic risk assessment tool scores. *American Journal of Nursing*, 117(4), 26-31.

A nonexperimental correlation study was conducted on three clinical units to compare what nurses perceived of as patients at risk and what electronic tool scores showed. Significant differences were found in the 746 data pairs, which supported the importance of nurses completing risk assessments. The differences were most significant when behavioral or psychosocial factors were involved. These factors were not part of the electronic tools. The findings

also involved situations where the tool indicated risk but nurses did not. This was found in cases where the risk had been identified and was already addressed in the plan for care.

Implications for Practice

Nurses have a crucial role in keeping patients safe through their careful assessment of patients to determine who might be at risk. Until electronic tools assess with great accuracy the behavioral and psychosocial factors, nurses will be key determinants of keeping patients from harm.

CONCLUSION

Creating a culture of safety (IHI, 2018) is everybody's business, and nurses, who are so integral to care, are key players in this important work. Every nurse has the accountability to challenge any act that appears unsafe and to stop actions that do not concur with the patient's best interest. Being proactive is insufficient in itself; examining practices and conditions that support errors is critical, as is sharing knowledge that can redirect care. In this challenging context, nurses continue to provide care and provide the organizational "glue" that supports patient care being accomplished in a safe, effective, and efficient manner. Nurses who serve as leaders and managers have additional opportunities to create conditions where ideas are heard, problems are solved, and the best evidence is used.

THE SOLUTION

One of the guiding principles of the Nursing Practice Council was that it was a direct-care nurse council, with liaison members from the CNS group and nursing administration. It was led by direct-care nurses, and direct-care nurses made the decisions, with input from other stakeholders. The first problem with the Clinical Question Process was that it was being led by a liaison CNS member, violating the guiding principal. The solution was going to have to come from the nurses.

We decided to devote an entire meeting to solving the problem. We broke the 35-member Council into small groups to discuss the following questions:

- Which clinical questions had actually been resolved?
- Which clinical questions could be combined into a single question?
- Which questions were not actually clinical questions at all?
- How would we create a system for the members of the Nursing Practice Council to have more ownership and responsibility over the process and work with the CNSs?
- How would decisions about Clinical Questions be communicated to the Nursing Units and Nursing Policy?

By the end of the meeting, decisions were made that invigorated the Process, moving from unending discussion to decisions and outcomes. The several-page list of questions had been refined into a list that was manageable and trackable. The nurse on the Council from the unit where the question had been submitted would take the lead on the research and discussion in partnership with the CNS and others on the Council who were most interested in that question. Decisions at the time of the meeting would be clear, and methods of communication would be determined, both to nurses on the units and the Nursing Policy Committee.

Would this be a suitable approach for you? Why?

Katheren Koehn

▌ REFLECTIONS

Think about clinical safety from what you have experienced and observed. What will be your biggest challenges in facing issues, and leading solutions, related to clinical safety, and how will you resolve them? What do you know about yourself that will provide you strength to take on issues of clinical safety? What do you need to develop to be more confident in what you can do?

▌ THE EVIDENCE

Numerous studies support various practices to ensure that staffing is adequate, that the clinical environment is free from incivility, that systems are addressed to identify unsafe practices and promote best practices, that nurses have a voice in creating solutions to safe clinical environments, and that using evidence is a high priority.

▌ TIPS FOR CLINICAL SAFETY

- Use the IOM competencies to frame your actions.
- Keep current with the evidence and best practices.
- Use only quality sources, especially for websites.
- Read general nursing literature regarding other organizations' work related to safety.

- Practice hand hygiene.
- Be prepared to intervene in unsafe situations.
- Report faulty equipment (e.g., furniture, monitors, lifts) immediately (Rich & El-Shammaa, 2017).

REFERENCES

Agency for Healthcare Research and Quality (AHRQ). (2018). Making Health Care Safer II: An updated critical analysis of the evidence for patient safety practices. http://www.ahrq.gov/research/findings/evidence-based-reports/ptsafetyuptp.html.

Cho, E., Lee, N. J., Kim, E. Y., Kim, S., Lee, K., Park, K. O., et al. (2016). Nurse staffing level and overtime associated with patient safety, quality of care and care left undone in hospitals: A cross-sectional study. *International Journal of Nursing Studies, 60*, 263–271. https://doi.org/10.1016/j.ijnurstu.2016.05.009.

Institute for Healthcare Improvement. (2018). *Develop a culture of safety.* www.ihi.org/resources/Pages/Changes/DevelopaCultureofSafety.aspx.

Institute of Medicine (IOM). (2000). *To err is human: Building a safer health system.* Washington, DC: National Academy Press.

Institute of Medicine (IOM). (2001). *Crossing the quality chasm: A new health system for the 21st century.* Washington, DC: National Academy Press.

Institute of Medicine (IOM). (2003). *Health professions education: A bridge to quality.* Washington, DC: National Academy Press.

Institute of Medicine (IOM). (2004). *Keeping patients safe: Transforming the work environment of nurses.* Washington, DC: National Academy Press.

Institute of Medicine (IOM). (2005). *Improving the quality of health care for mental and substance-use conditions: Quality Chasm Series.* Washington, DC: National Academy Press.

Institute of Medicine (IOM). (2006). *Preventing medication errors: Quality Chasm Series.* Washington, DC: National Academy Press.

Institute of Medicine (IOM). (2010). *The future of nursing: Leading change, advancing health.* Washington, DC: National Academy Press.

Jones, A., Johnstone, M. J., & Duke, M. (2016). Recognising and responding to 'cutting corners' when providing nursing care: a qualitative study. *Journal of Clinical Nursing, August 2016, 25*(15–16), 2126–2133.

Kanerva, A., Kivinen, T., & Lammintakanen, J. (2015). Communication elements supporting patient safety in psychiatric inpatient care. *Journal of Psychiatric and Mental Health Nursing, 22*(5), 298–305. https://doi.org/10.1111/jpm.12187.

Kowalski, S. L., & Anthony, M. (2017). Nursing's evolving role in patient safety. *American Journal of Nursing, 117*(2), 34–48.

Lockett, J. J., Barkley, L., Stichler, J., Palomo, J., Kik, B., Walker, C., et al. (2015). Defining peer-to-peer accountability from the nurse's perspective. *JONA, 45*, 557–562. https://doi.org/10.1097/NNA.0000000000000263.

Lyle-Edrosolo, G., & Waxman, K. T. (February, 2016). Aligning healthcare safety and quality competencies: Quality and safety education for nurses (QSEN), The Joint Commission, and American Nurses Credentialing Center (ANCC) Magnet® standards crosswalk. *Nurse Leader,* 70–75.

Marrelli, T. M. (2017). *Home care nursing: Surviving in an ever-changing care environment.* Indianapolis, IN: Sigma Theta Tau International.

Rich, S., & El-Shammaa, M. (2017). Medical device reporting: A model for patient safety. *American Nurse Today, 12*(2), 10–12.

Rogers, E. M. (2003). *Diffusion of innovations* (5th ed.). New York: The Free Press.

Stafos, A., Stark, S., Barbay, K., Frost, K., Jacket, D., Peters, L., et al. (2017). Identifying hospitalized patients at risk for harm: A comparison of nurse perceptions vs. electronic risk assessment tool scores. *American Journal of Nursing, 117*(4), 26–31.

Van Gerven, E., Vander Elst, T., Vandenbroeck, S., Dierickx, S., Euwema, M., Sermeus, W., et al. (2016). Increased risk of burnout for physicians and nurses involved in a patient safety incident. *Medical Care, 54*(10), 937–943. https://doi.org/10.1097/MLR.0000000000000582.

Wolf, L. A., Perhats, C., Delao, A. M., Clark, P. R., & Moon, M. D. (2016). On the threshold of safety: A qualitative exploration of nurses' perceptions of factors involved in safe staffing levels in emergency departments. *Journal of Emergency Nursing, 43*(2), 150–157.

3

Legal and Ethical Issues

Myra A. Broadway

LEARNING OUTCOMES

- Examine nurse practice acts, including the legal difference between licensed registered nurses and licensed practical (vocational) nurses.
- Define *unprofessional conduct* according to the state nurse practice act.
- Apply various legal principles, including negligence and malpractice, privacy, confidentiality, reporting statutes, and doctrines that minimize one's liability, when acting in leading and managing roles in nursing practice settings.
- Evaluate informed-consent issues, including patients' rights in research and health literacy, from a nurse manager's perspective.

- Analyze key aspects of employment law and give examples of how these laws benefit professional nursing practice.
- Analyze ethical principles, including autonomy, beneficence, nonmaleficence, veracity, justice, paternalism, fidelity, and respect for others.
- Apply the Code of Ethics for Nurses and the MORAL model from the nurse manager's perspective.
- Discuss moral distress and its implications for nurse managers.
- Analyze the role of institutional ethics committees.
- Analyze decision making when legal and ethical situations overlap, using the Theresa M. Schiavo case as the framework for this analysis.

KEY TERMS

apparent agency
autonomy
beneficence
collective bargaining
confidentiality
corporate liability
emancipated minor
ethics
ethics committee
failure to warn
fidelity
foreseeability
health literacy

indemnification
independent contractor
informed consent
justice
law
liability
liable
licensure
malpractice
moral distress
negligence
nonmaleficence
nurse practice act

paternalism
personal liability
privacy
respect for others
respondeat superior
standard of care
statute
unprofessional conduct
veracity
vicarious liability
whistle-blowing

THE CHALLENGE

In my role as a staff nurse in a busy Level 1 trauma emergency center, staff members were often confronted with questions about family presence during lifesaving techniques. Should the family or other loved ones be allowed to be present during cardiopulmonary resuscitation? Did the presence of family members hinder the ability of staff members to provide appropriate and competent care? Did their presence in some way benefit the patient? Was there a legal right for family members to be present at this time?

Currently the issue of family presence is being addressed on a case-by-case basis. The primary health-care professional has the final say in whether family (1) can be present, (2) are given the option of being present,

or (3) are tactfully escorted to another area of the unit. I continued to be ambivalent, especially when an 18-month-old girl was transported to the emergency center after falling from the family boat into a lake. Cardiopulmonary resuscitation was being given as the child was admitted; her mother was with her and her father was coming with other family members. The mother was escorted to the waiting area, crying, "I want to be with my baby!"

What would you do if you were this nurse?

Acacia Syring, BSN, RN
Staff Nurse Emergency Center, PeaceHealth Southwest Washington Medical Center, Vancouver, Washington

INTRODUCTION

The role of professional nursing continues to expand and incorporate increasingly higher levels of expertise, specialization, autonomy, and accountability from both legal and ethical perspectives. This evolving role continually creates new concerns for nurses, nurse managers, and nurse leaders and a heightened awareness of the interaction of legal and ethical principles. Areas of concern include professional nursing practice, legal issues, ethical principles, labor-management interactions, and employment. Each of these areas is individually addressed in this chapter. Although this chapter emphasizes the perspective of the nurse manager, all nurses benefit from understanding the legal and ethical aspects of managing, if only to understand the guidelines their managers are, or should be, following. Furthermore, all nurses have accountability for their practice and compliance with laws, professional standards, and ethical principles.

PROFESSIONAL NURSING PRACTICE: NURSE PRACTICE ACTS

The scope of nursing practice, those actions and duties that are allowable by the profession, is defined and guided by each state in the nurse practice act. The state nurse practice act is the most important piece of legislation for nursing because it affects all facets of nursing practice. Furthermore, the act is the law within a state or US territory, and state boards of nursing cannot grant

exceptions, waive the act's provisions, or expand practice outside the act's specific provisions.

Nurse practice acts define three categories of nurses: licensed practical or vocational nurses (LPNs and LVNs, respectively), licensed registered nurses (RNs), and advanced practice registered nurses. The various state nurse practice acts set educational and examination requirements, provide for licensing of individuals who have met these requirements, and define the functions of each category of nurse, both in general and in more specific terminology. The nurse practice act must be read to ascertain what actions are allowable for the three categories of nurses. In the few states where separate acts for RNs and LPNs/LVNs exist, the acts must be reviewed at the same time to ensure that all allowable actions are included in one of the two acts and that no overlap exists between the acts. In addition, nurse managers should understand that individual state nurse practice acts may vary among states in defining or delineating nursing practice, especially for advanced nursing roles.

Each practice act also establishes a state board of nursing. The main purpose of state boards of nursing is to ensure enforcement of the act to protect the public. The board enforces the act by regulating those practitioners who come under its provisions and preventing individuals not addressed within the act from practicing nursing. To protect the public, all those who present themselves as nurses must be licensed to practice within the state. The National Council of State Boards of Nursing (NCSBN) is a membership organization consisting of all US state and territorial boards of nursing (except Puerto Rico). NCSBN maintains a database (NURSYS), which enables states to enter and to access current information regarding licensure and discipline of nurses throughout the country. The NCSBN's website features a public portion that allows individuals access to certain nonconfidential information that is valuable to the nurse manager and employer.

The various boards of nursing develop and implement rules and regulations regarding the discipline of nursing and must be read in conjunction with the nurse practice act. Often any changes within the state's definition of nursing practice occur through modifications in the rules and regulations rather than in the act itself. This mandates that nurses and their nurse managers periodically review both the state act and the board of nursing rules and regulations.

Because each state has its own nurse practice act and state courts have jurisdiction for the state, nurses are well advised to understand the provisions of the state's nurse practice act. This is especially true in the areas of diagnosis and treatment; states vary on whether nurses can diagnose and treat or merely assess and evaluate. Thus an acceptable action in one state may be the practice of medicine in another state.

The nurse practice act may state that unprofessional conduct is a violation of the statute. Usually deliberate definition of what constitutes unprofessional conduct is found in rules and regulations. Typical examples of unprofessional conduct include boundary issues; practicing while impaired; violating patient confidentiality; failing to supervise persons to whom nursing functions have been delegated; inaccurate recording, falsifying, or altering a patient or healthcare provider record; and sexual misconduct.

With the advent of the Nurse Licensure Compact (NLC), commonly referred to as "the Compact," the need to know and understand provisions of state nurse practice acts has become even more critical. Multistate licensure permits an RN or LPN/LVN to be licensed in one state and to practice legally in states belonging to the NLC without obtaining additional state licenses. For the purposes of the law, the state nurse practice act that regulates the practice of the RN is the state in which the patient or client resides, not the state in which the nurse holds his or her license. Nurses residing in Compact states who have a Privilege to Practice may care for a patient in another Compact state. For example, a nurse in Compact state A may provide nursing care to a patient in Compact state B via a telephonic nursing advice or triage service program. Many of the nurses practicing under provisions of the Compact work with patients in a variety of states through such electronic capabilities as telenursing, Internet applications, and telecommunications technology such as telephone triage and advice. Others work for agencies or clinics that serve patients across state borders. Many healthcare systems include facilities and practices in more than one jurisdiction. The enhanced Nurse Licensure Compact (eNLC) became effective in most US jurisdictions in 2018 as requirements for a multistate practice privilege changed from the previous NLC in a concerted effort to enable all states to join.

All nurses must know applicable state law and use the nurse practice act for guidance and appropriate action. Nurse managers have this same basic responsibility to apply legal principles in their practice. However, they are also responsible for monitoring the practice of employees under their supervision and for ensuring that personnel maintain current and valid licensure. NCSBN provides the employer the ability to subscribe to its E-Notify program to make nurse managers aware of nurses whose licenses are due for renewal. Subscription to E-Notify also alerts the nurse manager to any discipline the state board may have imposed on the nurse. Unless nurses and nurse managers remain current with the nurse practice act in their state or with nurse practice acts in all states in which nurse managers supervise employees, a potential for liability exists.

EXERCISE 3.1 Review your state's nurse practice act, including rules and regulations that the state board of nursing has promulgated for the profession. You may need to read two acts if RNs and LPNs/LVNs come under different licensing boards. How does your state address advanced practice? How do the definitions of nursing vary for RNs, LPNs/LVNs, and advanced practice registered nurses? Describe why it is vital that the nurse manager understands these distinctions.

NEGLIGENCE AND MALPRACTICE

Nurse managers frequently serve as mentors and consultants for the nurses whom they supervise. Nurse managers must have a full appreciation for this area of the law, because negligence and malpractice continue to be the major causes of action brought against nursing staff members. Managers cannot guide and counsel their employees unless the managers are fully knowledgeable about this area of the law.

Negligence as defined by *Black's Law Dictionary* (2014) is the "failure to use such care as a reasonably prudent and careful person would use under similar circumstances." Negligence applies to both the manager and the direct care nurse. Many experts equate negligence with carelessness, a deviation from the care that a reasonable person would deliver. If managers are careless in their responsibilities, they could be found negligent. The same applies to the direct care nurse.

Malpractice, as defined by *Black's Law Dictionary* (2014), is "professional misconduct or unreasonable lack of skill." Malpractice concerns professional actions and is the failure of a person with professional education and skills to act in a reasonable and prudent manner. Issues of malpractice have become increasingly important to the nurse as the authority, accountability, and autonomy of nurses have increased. The same types of actions may be the basis for either negligence or malpractice, though some actions almost always are seen as malpractice because only the professional person would be performing the action. Specific examples include drawing blood for arterial blood gas analysis via a direct arterial puncture or initiating blood transfusions. Common allegations and/or causes of malpractice or negligence among nurses include the failure to follow standards of care, to use equipment responsibly, to document, to communicate, and to access and monitor patients (Reising, 2012).

Negligence and malpractice have two commonalities. Negligence and malpractice both concern actions that are a result of omission (the failure to do something that the reasonable, prudent person or nurse would have done) or commission (acting in a way that causes injury to the patient). They also concern nonintentional actions; though there is some injury to a patient, the

TABLE 3.1	Elements of Malpractice
Elements	**Examples**
Duty owed the patient	Failure to monitor a patient's response to treatment
Breach of the duty owed	Failure to communicate change in patient status to the primary healthcare provider
Foreseeability	Failure to ensure minimum standards are met
Causation	Failure to provide adequate patient education
Injury	Fractured hip and head concussion after a patient fall
Damages	Additional hospitalization time; future medical and nursing care needs and costs

individual who caused the harm never intended to hurt the patient.

Six elements must be presented in a successful malpractice suit. All of these factors must be shown before the court will find liability against the nurse and/or institution. These six elements are described in Table 3.1.

Elements of Malpractice
Duty Owed the Patient
The first element is duty owed the patient, which involves both the existence of the duty and the nature of the duty. Existence of the duty of care is generally established by showing the valid employment of the nurse within the institution. As the Literature Perspective shows, the concept of duty of care is complex, with many implications. The more difficult part is the nature of the duty, which involves the standard of care that represents the minimum requirements for acceptable practice or the minimum requirements for how one conducts oneself. Standards of care are established by reviewing the institution's policy and procedure manual, the individual's job description, and the practitioner's education and skills, as well as pertinent standards established by professional organizations, journal articles, and standing orders and protocols.

LITERATURE PERSPECTIVE

Resource: Dowie, I. (2017). Legal, ethical and professional aspects of duty of care for nurses. *Nursing Standard, 32*(16-19), 47-52.

The author first points out that duty of care is not unique to professionals, because we all have societal duties of care such as ensuring safety when we drive or walk. Of course, because nurses, among other professionals, have specialized knowledge, they have a higher duty of care in terms of issues related to health. The author reminds us that our duty extends to the control of the environment, such as a spillage on the floor posing a hazard. When nurses leave a unit for a break, and they have sought coverage for their patients by someone who was equally well qualified to provide care, they would not likely be found to have violated the principle of being fair, just, or reasonable. The author cites how in England even not attending to such aspects as personal hygiene can be seen as a neglect of duty of care.

The distinction is made between the legal duty of care, which typically does not apply outside of the employment situation, and the ethical duty of care, which suggests we would respond in emergencies even if we were outside of our workplace and functioning primarily as a citizen. The key to liability is the foreseeability of harm, and in emergency situations that foreseeability is compromised.

Implications for Practice

Two key points can be derived from this article. The first is that the idea of duty of care is not a distinct consideration in the United States. The second, and perhaps more important in today's world, is that we are not legally bound to respond in emergency situations such as disasters; we are ethically expected to respond to the best of our ability.

Several sources may be used to determine the applicable standard of care. The American Nurses Association (ANA), as well as a cadre of specialty nursing organizations, publishes standards for nursing practice. Accreditation standards, such as those published yearly by The Joint Commission (TJC), also assist in establishing the acceptable standard of care for healthcare facilities. In addition, many states have healthcare standards that affect individual institutions and their employees.

Nurse managers are directly responsible for ensuring that standards of care, as written in the hospital policy and procedure manuals, are current and that all nursing staff follow these standards of care. Should a standard of care be revised or changed, nurse managers must ensure that all staff members who are expected to implement this altered standard are apprised of the revised standard. If the new standard entails new skills, staff members must be educated about this revision and acquire the necessary skills before they implement the new standard. For example, if the institution alters a policy regarding a specific skill to be implemented, the nurse manager must first ensure that all nurses who will be performing this skill understand how to perform the skill safely, know possible complications that could occur, and know the most appropriate interventions to take should those complications occur. The nurse manager may work with others, such as clinical nurse educators, in attaining the desired outcomes.

Breach of the Duty of Care Owed the Patient

The second element required in a malpractice case is breach of the duty of care owed the patient. Once the standard of care is established, the breach or falling below the standard of care is relatively easy to show. To determine the appropriate standard of care, expert witnesses give testimony in court on a case-by-case basis, assisting the judge and jury in understanding nursing standards of care. In nursing malpractice suits, nurses serve as expert witnesses. Their testimony helps the judge and jury understand the applicable standards of nursing care (Fig. 3.1).

Opinions of experts attesting to the standard of care may differ depending on whether the injured party is trying to establish the standard of care or whether the defendant nurse's attorney is establishing an acceptable standard of care for the given circumstances. The injured party will attempt to show that the acceptable standard of care is at a much higher level than that shown by the defendant, hospital, and staff. An example appears in Case Example Box 3.1.

Foreseeability

The third element needed for a successful malpractice case, foreseeability, involves the concept that certain events may reasonably be expected to cause specific results. The nurse must have prior knowledge or information that failure to meet a standard of care may result in harm.

Fig. 3.1 Nurse serving as an expert witness.

The challenge is to show what was foreseeable given the facts of the case at the time of the occurrence, not when the case finally comes to court. Some of the more common areas concerning foreseeability are medication errors, patient falls, and failure to enact physician orders. For example, in an older case, *Massey v. Mercy Medical Center (2009)*, a resident known to be at high risk for falls was left unattended standing next to his walker. When he attempted to move forward, he lost his balance and sustained a compression fracture at the level of the twelfth thoracic vertebra. Without difficulty the court could find this was foreseeable.

Causation

The fourth element of a malpractice suit is causation: the nurse's actions or lack of actions directly caused the patient's harm. A direct relationship must exist between the failure to meet the standard of care and the patient's

injury. Merely breaching this standard of care is insufficient to show malpractice; a direct cause-effect factor must be present. For example, *O'Shea v. State of New York* (2007) concerned a patient who sustained an accident in which two fingers were severed while using a power saw. The patient permanently lost the two fingers when the nursing staff failed to follow the order for an immediate orthopedist consultation.

Injury

The resultant injury, the fifth malpractice element, must be physical, not merely psychological or transient. In other words, the patient must incur some physical harm before malpractice will be found against the healthcare provider. Although some specific exceptions exist to the requirement that a physical injury must result, they are extremely limited and usually involve specific relationships, such as the parent–child relationship. Pain and suffering are allowed when they accompany actual physical injuries.

Damages

The injured party must be able to prove damages, the sixth element of malpractice. Damages are vital, because malpractice is nonintentional. Thus the patient must show financial harm before the courts will allow a finding of liability against the defendant nurse and/or hospital. Acceptable damages may be for immediate as well as future medical costs.

A nurse manager must know the applicable standards of care and ensure that all employees of the institution meet or exceed them. The standards must be reviewed periodically to ensure that the staff members remain

---

CASE EXAMPLE BOX 3.1 An older case example, *Sabol v. Richmond Heights General Hospital* (1996), shows the importance of duty to the patient. A patient was admitted to a general acute care hospital for treatment after attempting to commit suicide by drug overdose. While in the acute care facility, the patient became increasingly paranoid and delusional. A nurse sat with the patient and tried to calm him. Restraints were not applied, because the staff feared this would compound the situation by raising the patient's level of paranoia and agitation. The patient jumped out of bed, knocked down the nurse who was in his room, fought his way past two nurses in the hallway, ran off the unit, and jumped from a third-story window, fracturing his arm and sustaining other relatively minor injuries.

Expert witnesses for the patient introduced standards of care pertinent to psychiatric patients, specifically those hospitalized in psychiatric facilities or in acute care hospitals with separate psychiatric units. The court ruled that the nurses in this general acute care situation were not professionally negligent in this patient's care. The court stated that the nurses' actions were consistent with basic professional standards of practice for medical-surgical nurses in an acute care hospital. They did not have, nor were they expected to have, specialized psychiatric nursing training and would not be judged as though they did.

current and attuned to advances in technology and newer ways of performing skills. If standards of care appear outdated or absent, the appropriate committee within the institution should be notified so that timely revisions can be made. Finally, the nurse manager must ensure that all nursing employees meet the standards of care. This may be done by (1) performing or reviewing all performance evaluations for evidence that standards of care are met, (2) reviewing randomly selected patient charts for standards of care documentation, and (3) inquiring of employees what constitutes standards of care and appropriate references for standards of care within the institution.

> **EXERCISE 3.2** You are the nurse manager for a skilled nursing facility that will now accept patients requiring long-term ventilator support. How should you begin to ensure that all the staff in the facility are educated in the care of ventilator-dependent patients, know what complications to anticipate, and know how to respond should these complications arise? Should all staff members be educated in this skill?

Liability: Personal, Vicarious, and Corporate

Personal liability defines each person's responsibility and accountability for individual actions or omissions. Even if others can be shown to be liable for a patient injury, each individual retains personal accountability for his or her actions. The law, though, sometimes allows other parties to be liable for certain causes of negligence. Known as vicarious liability, or substituted liability, the doctrine of respondeat superior (let the master answer) makes employers accountable for the negligence of their employees. The rationale underlying the doctrine is that the employee would not have been in a position to cause the wrongdoing unless hired by the employer, and the injured party would be allowed to suffer a double wrong if the employee was unable to pay damages for the wrongdoings. Nurse managers can best prevent these issues by ensuring that the staff they supervise know and follow hospital policies and procedures and continually deliver safe, competent nursing care or raise issues about policies and procedures through formal channels.

Nurses often believe that the doctrine of vicarious liability shields them from personal liability; the institution may be sued but not the individual nurse or nurses. However, patients injured because of substandard care have the right to sue both the institution and the nurse. This includes potentially suing the direct care nurse's manager if he or she knowingly allowed substandard and unsafe care to be given to a patient. In addition, the institution has the right under indemnification to countersue the nurse for damages paid to an injured patient. The principle of indemnification is applicable when the employer is held liable based solely on the actions of the staff member's negligence and the employer pays monetary damages because of the employee's negligent actions.

Corporate liability holds that the institution has the responsibility and accountability for maintaining an environment that ensures quality healthcare delivery for consumers. Corporate liability issues include negligent hiring and firing issues; failure to maintain safety in the physical environment; and lack of a qualified, competent, and adequate staff. In *Wellstar Health System, Inc., v. Green (2002),* a hospital was held liable to an injured patient for the negligent credentialing of a nurse practitioner. Nurse managers must be aware of trends in court cases and implications for persons in leadership positions, because court outcomes follow precedents. In September 2015 the owner of a peanut butter manufacturing facility in Georgia was sentenced by a federal judge to 28 years in prison for the *Salmonella*-related deaths of nine persons (U.S. vs Parnell, Parnell, Lightest & Wilkerson, 2015.) The essence of the case was the knowledge of the person in a leadership position of the presence of *Salmonella* and his failure to take remedial action. Although this case didn't relate to a healthcare facility, it validated the idea that leaders have accountability for actions within organizations. The literature argues that hospital administration (which may include nurses in leadership positions) are not immune from criminal and civil liability, particularly in situations where hospital-acquired infections (HAIs) cause harm. If defendants have knowledge of the danger and risk posed by HAIs in the facility but take no action to correct the situation, hospital administration may not be immune from civil and criminal prosecution for serious injury and death resulting from HAIs and the failure to take remedial action in light of knowledge of the condition (Ricciardi, 2017).

Nurse managers play a key role in assisting the institution to avoid corporate liability. For example, nurse managers ensure that staff members remain competent and qualified; that personnel within their supervision have current licensure; and that incompetent, illegal, or unethical practices are reported to the proper persons or agencies. Nurse managers also play a pivotal role in whether a nurse remains employed on the unit or is discharged or reassigned.

Perhaps the key to avoiding corporate liability is ensuring that all members of the healthcare team fully collaborate and work with other disciplines to ensure quality, competent health care, regardless of the care setting. Such collaboration is a competency that must be mastered across disciplines.

Causes of Malpractice for Nurse Managers

Nurse managers are charged with maintaining a standard of safe and competent nursing care within the institution. Several potential sources of liability for malpractice among nurse managers may be identified; thus guidelines to prevent or avoid these pitfalls should be developed.

Assignment, Delegation, and Supervision

The field of nursing management involves supervision of various personnel who directly provide nursing care to patients. Supervision is defined as the active process of directing, guiding, and influencing the outcome of an individual's performance of an activity. The nurse manager retains personal liability for the reasonable exercise of assignment, delegation, and supervision activities. The failure to assign, delegate, and supervise within acceptable standards of professional nursing practice may constitute malpractice. In addition, failure to delegate and supervise within acceptable standards may extend to direct corporate liability for the institution.

Delegation, used in nursing practice throughout history, has evolved into a complex, work-enhancing strategy that has the potential for varying levels of legal liability. Before the early 1970s, nurses used delegation to direct the multiple tasks performed by the various levels of staff members in a team-nursing model. Subsequently, the concept of primary nursing and assignment became the desirable nursing model in acute care settings, with the focus on an all-professional staff, requiring little delegation but considerable assignment of duties. By the mid-1990s, a nursing shortage had again shifted the nursing model to a multilevel staff, with the return of the need for delegation. Regardless of the nursing model used, nurse managers must fully understand and implement delegation principles effectively and properly.

Nurse managers need to know certain definitions regarding this area of the law. Delegation involves at least two people, a delegator and a delegatee, with the transfer of authority to perform some type of task or work. A working definition could be that delegation is the transfer of responsibility for the performance of an activity from one individual to another, with the delegator retaining accountability for the outcome. In other words, delegation involves the transfer of responsibility for the performance of tasks and skills without the transfer of accountability for the ultimate outcome. Examples include an RN who delegates patients' personal care tasks to certified nursing assistants who work in a long-term care setting. In delegating these tasks, the RN retains the ultimate accountability and responsibility for ensuring that the delegated tasks are completed in a safe and competent manner.

Typically, delegation involves the tasks and procedures that are given to unlicensed nursing personnel, such as certified nursing aides, orderlies, assistants, attendants, and technicians. However, delegation can also occur with licensed staff members. For example, if one RN has the accountability for an outcome and asks another RN to perform a specific component of the overall function, that is delegation. This is typically the type of delegation that occurs between professional staff members when one member leaves the unit or work area for a meal break.

Delegation is complex because it involves the delegation relationship and communication. It also involves trusting others, because both the delegator and the delegatee have shared accountability for certain tasks and duties. Interventions are needed to improve this relationship and communication effectiveness, which directly affects the quality of competent care delivery. Multiple players, usually with varying degrees of education and experience and different scopes of practice, are involved in the process. Understanding these variances and communicating effectively to the delegatee involve an understanding of competencies and the ability to communicate with all levels of staff personnel.

Assignment is the transfer of both the accountability and the responsibility from one person to another. This is typically what happens between professional staff members. The nurse manager assigns patient care responsibilities to other professional nurses working in the same unit of the institution or community healthcare setting. The level of accountability for the nurse manager who assigns as opposed to delegates is fairly obvious, although some accountability can occur in both instances. The degree of knowledge concerning the skills and competencies of those one supervises is of paramount importance. The doctrine of respondent superior has been extended to include "knew or should have known" as a legal standard in both assigning and delegating tasks to individuals whom one supervises. If it can be shown that the nurse manager assigned or delegated tasks appropriately and had no reason to believe that the nurse to whom tasks were assigned or delegated was not competent to perform the task, the nurse manager potentially has no or minimal personal liability. The converse is also true: if it can be shown that the nurse manager was aware of incompetence in a given employee or that the assigned or delegated task was outside the employee's capabilities, the nurse manager becomes substantially liable for the subsequent injury to a patient.

EXERCISE 3.3 You are the nurse manager on a busy 38-bed surgical postoperative unit. A newly postoperative patient, Mrs. R., requires assistance with feeding, and you note that an unlicensed nursing personnel has been delegated to feed her. Reading Mrs. R.'s care plan, you also note that she is an older adult, has had periods of confusion, and has had difficulty swallowing since her surgery. Determine whether this is the right circumstance for such delegation. What are your next actions and why?

Nurse managers have a duty to ensure that the staff members under their supervision are practicing in a safe and competent manner. The nurse manager must be aware of the staff members' knowledge, skills, and competencies and should know whether they are maintaining their competencies. Knowingly allowing a staff member to function below the acceptable standard of care subjects both the nurse manager and the institution to potential liability. This point is illustrated in Case Example Box 3.2.

As this case illustrates, delegation is both a process and a condition (Potter, Deshields, & Kuhrik, 2010). It is a process of delegating appropriate tasks and activities to others, and it is a condition because a mutual understanding must be held by both the delegator and the delegatee of the specific results expected and the means of attaining those results.

CASE EXAMPLE BOX 3.2 In *Estate of Travaglini v. Ingalls Health* (2009), an 84-year-old patient was admitted to the hospital with general complaints of "not feeling well." At the time of his admission, the physician told the admitting nurse that the patient had dysphagia and must be observed whenever he was eating or trying to swallow liquids. At 10:00 that evening, an aide came to the patient's room and left a sandwich for him to eat. Shortly afterward, the patient's roommate heard the patient choking and summoned help. At autopsy, it was confirmed that he had aspirated the turkey sandwich, and that this was the cause of the cardiopulmonary arrest that killed the patient. Though liability was found against the aide and her supervisor, the court also upheld a verdict of $500,000 against the hospital.

Duty to Orient, Educate, and Evaluate

Most healthcare institutions have continuing education departments to orient nurses who are new to the institution and to supply in-service education addressing new equipment, procedures, and interventions to existing employees. Nurse managers also have a duty to orient, educate, and evaluate. Nurse managers and their representatives are responsible for the daily evaluation of whether nurses are performing safe and competent care. The key to meeting this requirement is reasonableness and is determined by courts on a case-by-case basis. Nurse managers should ensure that they promptly respond to all allegations, whether by patients or staff, of incompetent or questionable nursing care. Nurse managers should thoroughly investigate such allegations, recommend options for correcting the situation, and follow up on recommended options and suggestions.

For example, in *Marinock v. Manor at St Luke's* (2010), the nursing facility had experienced multiple problems with patients falling or being dropped during Hoyer lift transfers because some staff members were unaware of how to properly secure patients in the sling before beginning the transfer. These incidents apparently did not lead to additional training, and subsequently an 82-year-old patient was dropped during a transfer from one bed to another bed, resulting in a femur fracture. The patient's lawsuit resulted in a $310,000 judgment against the facility for failure to properly orient and train its personnel.

EXERCISE 3.4 In a landmark study, the National Academy of Medicine (formerly the Institute of Medicine) (1999) outlined six characteristics for a safe healthcare system, noting that incorporating these six characteristics created a culture of safety. For example, culture focuses on effective systems and teamwork to accomplish the goal of safe, high-quality patient care. Review the National Academy of Medicine report and consider how nurse managers might begin to apply the characteristics of a culture of safety to the facts in the *Marinock v. Manor at St. Luke's* (2010) lawsuit.

Failure to Warn

Another area of potential liability for nurse managers is failure to warn potential employers of staff incompetence or impairment. Information about suspected addictions, violent behavior, and incompetency is of vital importance to subsequent employers. If the institution has sufficient information and suspicion to warrant the discharge of an employee or force a resignation, subsequent employers should be advised of those issues. In addition, the state board of nursing or agency that oversees disciplinary actions of professional and nonprofessional nursing staff should also be notified whenever a cause to dismiss an employee for incompetency or impairment exists unless the employee voluntarily enters a peer assistance program.

One means of supplying this information is through the use of qualified privilege to certain communications. In general, qualified privilege concerns communications made in good faith between persons or entities with a need to know. Most states recognize this privilege and allow previous employers to give factual, objective information to subsequent employers. Note, however, that the previous employee must have listed the nurse manager or institution as a reference before this privilege arises.

Staffing Issues

Three issues arise under the general term *staffing*. These include (1) maintaining adequate numbers of staff members in a time of advancing patient acuity and limited resources; (2) floating staff from one unit to another; and (3) using temporary or "agency" staff to augment the healthcare facility's current staffing. Though each area is addressed separately, common to all three of these staffing issues is the requisite of collaboration among nurse managers in addressing the needs for the entire institution or healthcare agency.

Accreditation standards, such as those of TJC and the Community Health Accreditation Program (CHAP), as well as other state and federal standards, mandate that healthcare institutions provide adequate staffing with qualified personnel. This applies not only to the number of staff but also to the legal status of the staff. For instance, some areas of an institution, such as critical care areas, postanesthesia care areas, and emergency care centers, must have greater percentages of RNs than LPNs/LVNs. Other areas, such as the general nursing areas and some long-term care areas, may have equal or lower percentages of RNs to LPNs/LVNs or nursing assistants. Whether understaffing exists in a given situation depends on the number of patients, care acuity scores, and number and classification of staff. Courts determine whether understaffing existed on an individual case basis.

California was the first state to adopt legislation that mandated fixed nurse-to-patient ratios, passing this historic legislation in 1999. These types of ratios require set nurse-to-patient ratios based solely on numbers of patients within given nursing care areas and do not consider issues such as patient acuity, level of staff preparation, or environmental factors. Though a first step toward beginning to ensure adequate numbers of nurses, many states favor the concept of safe staffing rather than specific nurse-to-patient ratios. Generally, these safe staffing measures call for a committee to develop, oversee, and evaluate a plan for each specific nursing unit and shift based on patient care needs, appropriate skill mix of RNs and other nursing personnel, the physical layout of the unit, and national standards or recommendations regarding nursing staffing. Nurse managers must also know whether their states require public posting of the staffing plan (Safe Nurse Staffing Legislation, March 2008).

As early as 2015 federal legislation was introduced as the Registered Nurse Safe Staffing Act and included such provisions as a required public reporting of staffing information, a procedure for receiving and investigating complaints, and allowing the imposition of civil monetary penalties for each known violation. The proposed legislation also included provision for nurse managers to work with direct care nurses to establish safe staffing based on variable factors. Because staffing has major implications for quality, legislation likely will be introduced and refined over several sessions.

Although the institution is ultimately responsible for staffing issues, nurse managers may also incur liability because they directly oversee numbers of personnel assigned to a given unit. Courts have looked to the constant exercise of professional judgment, rather than reliance on concrete nurse-to-patient ratios, in cases involving staffing issues. Thus nurse managers should exercise sound judgment to ensure patient safety and quality care rather than rely on exact nurse-to-patient ratios. For liability to incur against the nurse manager, it must be shown that a resultant patient injury was directly caused by staffing issues and not by the incompetent or inappropriate actions of an individual staff member. To prevent nurse managers' liability, they must show that sufficient numbers of competent staff were available to meet nursing needs.

Guidelines for nurse managers in inadequate staffing issues include alerting hospital administrators and upper-level managers of concerns. First, however, the nurse manager must do whatever is under his or her control to alleviate the circumstances, such as approving overtime for adequate coverage, reassigning personnel among those areas he or she supervises, and restricting new admissions to the area. Second, nurse managers have a legal duty to notify the chief operating officer, either directly or indirectly, when understaffing endangers patient welfare. One way of notifying the chief operating officer is through formal nursing channels, for example, by notifying the nurse manager's direct supervisor. Upper management must then decide how to alleviate the staffing issue, either on a short-term or a long-term basis. Appropriate measures could be closing a unit or units, restricting elective surgeries, hiring new staff members, or temporarily reassigning personnel from other departments. Once the nurse manager can show that he or she acted appropriately, used sound judgment given the circumstances, and alerted his or her supervisors of the serious nature of the situation, the institution and not the nurse manager becomes potentially liable for staffing issues.

Several states prohibit the use of mandatory overtime by nurses. Generally these laws state that the healthcare facility may not require an employee to work in excess of agreed to, predetermined, and regularly scheduled daily work shifts unless an unforeseeable declared national, state, or municipal emergency or catastrophic event occurs that is unpredicted or unavoidable and that substantially affects or increases the need for healthcare services. In addition, many of these laws define "normal work schedule" as 12 or fewer hours; protect employees from disciplinary action or retribution for refusing to work overtime; and establish monetary penalties for the employer's failure to adhere to the law. Some states also mandate that healthcare facilities are required to have a process for complaints related to patient safety. Note that nothing in these laws negates voluntary overtime.

Floating staff from unit to unit is the second issue that concerns overall staffing. Institutions have a duty to ensure that all areas of the institution are staffed adequately. Units temporarily overstaffed because of low patient census or a lower patient acuity ratio usually float staff to units that are understaffed. Although floating nurses to areas with which they have less familiarity and expertise can increase potential liability for the nurse manager, leaving another area dangerously understaffed can also increase potential liability.

Before floating staff from one area to another, the nurse manager should consider staff expertise, patient-care delivery systems, and patient-care requirements. Nurses should be floated to units as comparable to their own unit as possible. This requires the nurse manager to match the nurse's home unit and float unit as much as possible or to consider negotiating with another nurse manager to cross-float a nurse. For example, a manager might float a critical care nurse to an intermediate care unit and float an intermediate care unit nurse to a general medical-surgical unit. Or the nurse manager might consider floating the general unit nurse to the postpartum unit and floating a postpartum nurse to labor and delivery. Open communications regarding staff limitations and concerns, as well as creative solutions for staffing, can alleviate some of the potential liability involved and create better morale among the floating nurses. A positive option is to cross-train nurses within the institution so that nurses are familiar with two or three areas and can competently float to areas in which they have been cross-trained.

The use of temporary or "agency" personnel has increased liability concerns among nurses and nurse managers. Previously most jurisdictions held that such personnel were considered independent contractors and thus the institution was not liable for their actions, although their primary employment agency did retain potential liability. However, courts have begun to hold the institution liable under the principle of apparent agency. *Apparent authority* or *apparent agency* refers to the doctrine whereby a principal becomes accountable for the actions of his or her agent. Apparent agency is created when a person (agent) holds himself or herself as acting on behalf of the principal; in the instance of the agency nurse, the patient cannot ascertain whether the nurse works directly for the hospital (has a valid employment contract) or is working for a different employer. At law, lack of actual authority is no defense. This principle applies when it can be shown that a reasonable patient believed that the healthcare worker was an employee of the institution. If it appears to the reasonable patient that this worker is an employee of the institution, the law will consider the worker an employee for the purposes of corporate and vicarious liability.

These trends in the law mean that nurse managers must consider the temporary worker's skills, competencies, and knowledge when delegating tasks and supervising the worker's actions. If a manager suspects that the temporary worker is incompetent, he or she must convey this fact to the agency. The nurse manager must also either send the temporary worker home or reassign the worker to other duties and areas. The same screening procedures should be performed with temporary workers as are used with new institutional employees.

Additional areas that nurse managers should stress when using agency or temporary personnel include ensuring that the temporary staff member is given a brief but thorough orientation to institution policies and procedures, is made aware of resource materials within the institution, and is made aware of documentation procedures. Also, nurse managers should assign a resource person to the temporary staff member. This resource person serves in the role of mentor for the agency nurse and serves to prevent potential problems that could arise merely because the agency staff member does not know the institution routine or is unaware of where to turn for assistance. The resource person also serves as a mentor with critical decision making for the agency nurse.

Protective and Reporting Laws

Protective and reporting laws ensure the safety or rights of specific classes of individuals. Most states have reporting laws for suspected child and elder abuse and laws for reporting certain categories of diseases and injuries. Examples of reporting laws include reporting cases of sexually transmitted diseases, abuse of residents in nursing and convalescent homes, and suspected child abuse. Nurse managers are often the individuals who are responsible for ensuring that the correct information

is reported to the correct agencies, thus avoiding potential liability against the institution.

Many states now also have mandatory reporting of incompetent practice, especially through nurse practice acts, medical practice acts, and the National Practitioner Data Bank. In addition, the NCSBN maintains an electronic license verification system called NURSYS that monitors nurses' licensure status in all states and US territories for discipline issues and licensure renewals. State boards submit data to NURSYS regarding disciplinary actions taken by the respective boards. Alerts are then sent to other US jurisdictions in which the nurse is licensed. Special provisions may apply if nurses who struggle with substance abuse or misuse are enrolled in peer assistance programs.

Mandatory reporting of incompetent practitioners is a complex process, involving both legal and ethical concerns. Nurse managers must know what the law requires, when reporting is mandated, to whom the report must be sent, and what the individual institution expects of its nurse managers. When in doubt, seek clarification from the state board of nursing, hospital administration, or state professional nursing association.

INFORMED CONSENT

Informed consent becomes an important concept for nurse managers in three different instances. First, direct care nurses may approach the nurse manager with questions about informed consent; thus the nurse manager becomes a consultant for the direct care nurse. Second, and more often, the nurse manager is queried about patients' rights in research studies that are being conducted in the institution. Third, the issue of medical literacy has implications for the provision of valid informed consent by an ever-growing number of patients.

Remember: informed consent is the authorization by the patient or the patient's legal representative to do something to the patient; it is based on legal capacity, voluntary action, and comprehension. Legal capacity is usually the first requirement and is determined by age and competency. All states have a legal age for adult status defined by statute; generally, this age is 18 years. Competency involves the ability to understand the consequences of actions or the ability to handle personal affairs. State statutes mandate who can serve as the representative for a minor or incompetent adult. The following types of minors may be able to give valid informed consent: emancipated minors, minors seeking treatment for substance abuse or communicable diseases, and pregnant minors.

Voluntary action, the second requirement, means that the patient was not coerced by fraud, duress, or deceit into allowing the procedure or treatment. Comprehension is the third requirement and the most difficult to ascertain. The law states that the patient must be given sufficient information, in terms he or she can reasonably be expected to comprehend, to make an informed choice. Inherent in the doctrine of informed consent is the right of the patient to informed refusal. Patients must clearly understand the possible consequences of their refusal. In recent years, most states have enacted statutes to ensure that a competent adult has the right to refuse care and that the healthcare provider is protected should the adult validly refuse care. This refusal of care is most frequently seen in end-of-life decisions. Box 3.1 lists the information needed for obtaining informed consent.

Nurses often ask about issues concerning informed consent that concern the actual signing of the informed consent document, not the teaching and information that make up informed consent. Many nurses serve as witnesses to the signing of the informed consent document; in this capacity they are attesting only to the voluntary nature of the patient's signature. No duty on the part of the nurse to insist that the patient repeat what has been said or what he or she remembers is present. If the patient asks questions that alert the nurse to the inadequacy of true comprehension on the patient's part or expresses uncertainty while signing the document, the nurse has an obligation to inform the primary healthcare provider and appropriate persons that informed consent has not been obtained.

A separate issue with informed consent concerns a patient who is part of a research study. Federal laws regulate this area, because patients are generally considered to come under the heading of vulnerable populations. Whenever research is involved, such as a drug study or a new procedure, the investigators must disclose the research to the subject or the subject's representative and obtain informed consent. Federal guidelines have been developed that specify the procedures used to review research and the disclosures that must be made to ensure that valid informed consent is obtained.

The federal government mandates the basic elements of information that must be included to meet the standards of informed consent. Elements of informed consent are enumerated in Box 3.2.

BOX 3.1 Information Required for Informed Consent

- An explanation of the treatment or procedure to be performed and the expected results of the treatment or procedure
- Description of the risks involved
- Benefits that are likely to result because of the treatment or procedure
- Options to this course of action, including absence of treatment
- Name of the person(s) performing the treatment/procedure
- Statement that the patient may withdraw his or her consent at any time

---

BOX 3.2 Elements of Informed Consent in Research Studies

- A statement that the study involves research, an explanation of the purposes of the research and the expected duration of the subject's participation, a description of the procedures to be followed, and identification of any procedures that are experimental
- A description of any reasonably foreseeable risks or discomforts to the subject
- A description of any benefits to the subjects or others that may reasonably be expected from the research
- A disclosure of appropriate alternative procedures or courses of treatment, if any, that may be advantageous to the subject
- A statement describing the extent, if any, to which confidentiality of records identifying the subject will be maintained
- For research involving more than minimal research, an explanation as to any compensation and an explanation as to whether any medical treatments are available if injury occurs and, if so, what they consist of or where further information may be obtained
- An explanation of whom to contact for answers to pertinent questions about the research and research subjects' rights and whom to contact in the event of a research-related injury to the subject
- A statement that participation is voluntary, refusal to participate will involve no benefits to which the subject is otherwise entitled, and the subject may discontinue participation at any time without penalty or loss of benefits to which the subject is otherwise entitled

Source: *45 Code of Federal Regulations* (CFR), Sec. 46.116 (1991).

The information given must be in a language that is understandable by the subject or the subject's legal representative. No exculpatory wording may be included, such as a statement that the researcher incurs no liability for the outcomes of the study or any injury to an individual subject. Subjects should be advised of the elements listed in Box 3.3.

Excluded from these strict requirements are studies that use existing data, documents, records, or pathologic and diagnostic specimens, if these sources are publicly available or the information is recorded so that the subjects cannot be identified. Other studies that involve only minimal risks to subjects, such as moderate exercise by healthy adults, may be expedited through the review process (Protection of Human Subjects, 1991, Section 46.110). Nurse managers must verify that staff members understand any research protocol with which their patients are involved.

The advent of the Health Insurance Portability and Accountability Act (HIPAA) of 1996 (Public Law [P. L.] 104-191) affected how health record information can be used in research studies. No separate permission need be secured from the patient to use medical record information if deidentified information is used. Deidentified information is health information that cannot be linked to an individual. Most of the 18 demographic items constituting the protected health information (PHI) must be removed before researchers are permitted to use patient records without obtaining the individual patient's permission to use/disclose PHI. The deidentified data set that is permissible for usage may contain the following demographic factors: gender and age of

individuals and a three-digit ZIP code. Note that all individuals 90 years of age or older are listed as 90 years of age.

To prevent the onerous task of requiring patients who have been discharged from healthcare settings to sign such permission forms, researchers are allowed to submit a request for a waiver. The waiver is a request to forego the authorization requirements based on two conditions: (1) the use and/or disclosure of PHI involves minimal risk to the subject's privacy, and (2) the research cannot be done practically without this waiver. Additional information about HIPAA and confidentiality are covered later in this chapter.

Concerns over the past abuses that have occurred in the area of research with children have led to the adoption of federal guidelines specifically designed to protect children when they are enrolled as research subjects. Before proceeding under these specific guidelines, state and local laws must be reviewed for laws regulating research on human subjects. In 1998 Subpart D: Additional Protections for Children Involved as Subjects in Research was added to the code (Protection of Human Subjects, 1998, 46.401 et seq.). These sections were added to give further protection to children when they are subjects of research studies and to encourage researchers to involve children, where appropriate, in research.

A final issue with informed consent about which nurses and nurse managers should be cognizant concerns health literacy, or the degree to which individuals have the capacity to obtain, process, and understand basic health information, including services needed to make appropriate health decisions. Functional health literacy relates to the person's ability to act on the basic health information received. Comprehending medical jargon is difficult for well-educated Americans; about 12% of American adults are considered proficient in health literacy (Department of Health and Human Services, 2012). Comprehending medical instructions and terms may be impossible for individuals whose first language is not English, who cannot read at greater than a second-grade level, or who have vision or cognitive problems caused by aging or disabilities. These individuals have difficulty following instructions printed on medication labels (both prescription and over-the-counter), interpreting hospital consent forms, and even understanding diagnoses, treatment options, and discharge instructions.

BOX 3.3 Elements of Concern in Research Studies

- Any additional costs that they might incur because of the research
- Potential for any foreseeable risks
- Rights to withdraw at will, with no questions asked or additional incentives given
- Consequences, if any, of withdrawal before the study is completed
- A statement that any significant new findings will be disclosed
- The number of proposed subjects for the study

Source: *45 Code of Federal Regulations* (CFR), Sec. 46.101(b) (1991).

Nurses play a significant role in addressing this growing problem. The first issue to address is awareness of the problem, because many patients and their family members hide the fact that they cannot read or do not understand what healthcare providers are attempting to convey. A second issue involves ensuring that the information and words nurses use to communicate with patients are at a level that the person can comprehend. One means to ensure that patients do understand patient discharge information and medication instructions is to give a patient a bottle of prescription medication and ask him or her to tell you how he or she would take the medication at home.

PRIVACY AND CONFIDENTIALITY

Privacy is the patient's right to protection against unreasonable and unwarranted interference with his or her solitude. This right extends to protection of the person's reputation as well as protection of one's right to be left alone. Within a medical context, the law recognizes the patient's right to protection against (1) appropriation of the patient's name or picture for the institution's sole advantage, (2) intrusion by the institution on the patient's seclusion or affairs, (3) publication of facts that place the patient in a false light, and (4) public disclosure of private facts about the patient by the hospital or staff. Confidentiality is the right to privacy of the health record. Institutions can reduce potential liability in this area by allowing access to patient data, either written or oral, only to those with a "need to know." Persons with a need to know include physicians and nurses caring for the patient, technicians, unit clerks, therapists, social service workers, and patient advocates. Usually this need to know extends to the house staff and consultants. Others wishing to access patient data must first ask the patient for permission to review a record. Administrative staff of the institution can access the patient record for statistical analysis, staffing, and quality-of-care review.

The nurse manager is cautioned to ensure that staff members both understand and abide by rules regarding patient privacy and confidentiality. "Interesting" patients should not be discussed with others, and all information concerning patients should be given only in private and secluded areas. All nurses may need to review the current means of giving reports to oncoming shifts and policies about telephone information. Many institutions have now added to the nursing care plan a place to list persons to whom the patient has allowed information to be given. If the caller identifies himself or herself as one of those listed persons, the nurse can give patient information without violating the patient's privacy rights. Patients are becoming more knowledgeable about their rights in these areas, and some have been willing to take offending staff members to court over such issues. With the advent of social media, nurses must be cautious that their personal posts on Facebook, Twitter, or other platforms do not include pictures and/or information about their patients. This would constitute a violation of the patient's right to privacy and confidentiality. This would also be considered professional misconduct according to the nurse practice act.

The patient's right of access to his or her health record is another confidentiality issue. Although the patient has a right of access, individual states mandate when this right applies. Most states give the right of access only after the health record is completed; thus the patient has the right to review the record after discharge. Some states give the right of access while the patient is hospitalized, and therefore individual state law governs individual nurses' actions. When supervising a patient's review of his or her record, the nurse manager or representative should explain only the entries that the patient questions or about which the patient requests further clarification. The nurse makes a note in the record after the session, indicating that the patient viewed the record and what questions were answered.

Patients also have a right to copies of the record, at their expense. The health record belongs to the institution as a business record, and patients never have the right to retain the original record. This is also true in instances in which a subpoena is obtained to secure an individual's health record for court purposes. A hospital representative will verify that the copy is a "true and valid" copy of the original record.

An issue that is closely related to the health record is that of incident reports or unusual occurrence reports. These reports are mandated by TJC and serve to alert the institution to risk management and quality assurance issues within the setting. As such, incident reports are considered internal documents and thus not discoverable (open for review) by the injured party or attorneys representing the injured party. In most jurisdictions where this question has arisen, however, the courts have held that the incident report was discoverable and thus open to review by both sides of the suit.

Therefore prudent nurse managers complete and have staff members complete incident reports as though they will be open records, omitting any language of liability, such as, "The patient would not have fallen if Jane Jones, RN, had ensured the side rails were in their up and locked position." This document should contain only pertinent observations and care given the patient, such as x-rays that were obtained for a potential broken bone, medication that was given, and consultants who were called to examine the patient. Making any notation of the incident report in the official patient record is inadvisable, because such a notation incorporates the incident report "by reference," and thus can be seen by the injured party or attorneys for the injured party.

PHI is at the crux of the confidentiality aspect of the law. The privacy standards limit how PHI may be used or shared, mandate safeguards for protecting the health information, and shift the control of health information from providers to the patient by giving patients significant rights. Healthcare facilities must provide patients with a documented Notice of Privacy Rights, explaining how PHI will be used or shared with other entities. This document also alerts patients to the process for complaints if they later determine that their information rights have been violated. Nurse managers have the responsibility to ensure that those they supervise uphold these patient rights as dictated by HIPAA and to take corrective actions should these rights not be upheld.

POLICIES AND PROCEDURES

Risk management is a process that identifies, analyzes, and treats potential hazards within a given setting. The object of risk management is to identify potential hazards and eliminate them before anyone is harmed or disabled. Risk management activities include writing policies and procedures, which is a requirement of TJC. These documents set standards of care for the institution and direct practice. They must be clearly stated, well delineated, and based on current practice. Nurse managers should review the policies and procedures frequently for compliance and timeliness. If policies are absent or outdated, the nurse manager must request the appropriate person or committee to either initiate or update the policy.

> **EXERCISE 3.5** You are assigned some risk management activities in the nursing facility where you work. In investigating incident reports filed by staff, you discover that this is the third incident this week in which a patient has fallen while attempting to get out of bed and sit in a chair. How would you begin to address this issue? Decide how you would start a more complete investigation of this issue. For example, is it a facility-wide issue or one that is confined to one unit? Does it affect all shifts or only one? What safety issues are you going to discuss with your staff, and how are you going to discuss these issues? Do these falls involve the same staff member?

EMPLOYMENT LAWS

The federal and individual state governments have enacted laws regulating employment. To be effective and legally correct, nurse managers must be familiar with these laws and how the individual laws affect the institution and labor relations. Many nurse managers have come to fear the legal system because of personal experience or the experiences of colleagues, but much of this concern may be directly attributable to uncertainty with the law or partial knowledge of the law. By understanding and correctly following federal employment laws, nurse managers may actually decrease their potential liability by complying with both federal and state laws. Table 3.2 gives an overview of key federal employment laws.

Equal Employment Opportunity Laws

Several federal laws have been enacted to expand equal employment opportunities by prohibiting discrimination based on gender, age, race, religion, handicap, pregnancy, and national origin. The Equal Employment Opportunity Commission (EEOC) enforces these laws. All states have also enacted statutes that address employment opportunities, and the nurse manager should consider both when hiring and assigning nursing employees.

The most significant legislation affecting equal employment opportunities today is the amended Civil Rights Act of 1964. Section 703(a) of Title VII makes it illegal for an employer "to refuse to hire, discharge an individual, or otherwise to discriminate against an individual, with respect to his compensation, terms, conditions, or privileges of employment because of the individual's race, color, religion, sex, or national origin."

TABLE 3.2   Selected Federal Labor Legislation

Year	Legislation	Primary Purpose of the Legislation
1935	Wagner Act; National Labor Act	Unions, National Labor Relations Board established; unionization rights established
1947	Taft-Hartley Act	Established a more equal balance of power between unions and management
1962	Executive Order 10988	Allowed public employees to join labor unions
1963	Equal Pay Act	Became illegal to pay lower wages based solely on gender
1964	Civil Rights Act	Protected against discrimination based on race, color, creed, national origin, etc.
1967	Age Discrimination in Employment Act	Protected against discrimination based on age
1970	Occupational Safety and Health Act	Established the development and enforcement of standards for occupational health and safety
1974	Wagner Amendments	Allowed nonprofit organizations to unionize and allowed collective bargaining in nursing
1990	Americans With Disabilities Act	Barred discrimination against workers with disabilities in the workplace
1991	Civil Rights Act	Addressed sexual harassment in the workplace
1993	Family and Medical Leave Act	Allowed work leaves based on family and medical needs
1996	Health Insurance Portability and Accountability Act	Provided for the phased introduction of a comprehensive system of mandated health insurance reforms
2010	Patient Protection and Accountability Act	Provided for the phased introduction of a comprehensive system of mandated health insurance reforms
2010	Health Care and Education Reconciliation Act	Amended the Patient Protection and Affordable Care Act to clarify budget resolutions

The Equal Employment Opportunity Act of 1972 also amended Title VII so that it applies to private institutions with 15 or more employees, state and local governments, labor unions, and employment agencies.

The amended Civil Rights Act of 1991 further broadened the issue of sexual harassment in the workplace and supersedes many of the sections of Title VII. Sections of the new legislation define sexual harassment, its elements, and the employer's responsibilities regarding harassment in the workplace, especially prevention and corrective action. The Civil Rights Act of 1991 is enforced by the EEOC. The primary activity of the EEOC is processing complaints of employment discrimination. Three phases comprise processing complaints: investigation, conciliation, and litigation. Investigation focuses on determining whether the employer has violated provisions of Title VII. If the EEOC finds "probable cause," an attempt is made to reach an agreement or conciliation between the EEOC, the complainant, and the employer. If conciliation fails, the EEOC may file suit against the employer in federal court or issue to the complainant the right to sue for discrimination under its auspices, including those relating to staffing practices and sexual harassment in the workplace.

The EEOC defines sexual harassment broadly, and this has generally been upheld in the courts. Nurse managers must realize that it is the duty of employers (management) to prevent employees from sexually harassing other employees. The EEOC issues policies and practices for employers to implement, both to sensitize employees to this problem and to prevent its occurrence. Nurse managers should be aware of these policies and practices and seek guidance in implementing them if sexual harassment occurs in their units.

Employers may seek exceptions to Title VII on a number of premises. For example, employment decisions made on the basis of national origin, religion, and gender (never race or color) are lawful if such decisions are necessary for the normal operation of the business, although the courts have viewed this exception very narrowly. Promotions and layoffs based on bona fide seniority or merit systems are permissible, as are exceptions based on business necessity.

Age Discrimination in Employment Act of 1967

The Age Discrimination in Employment Act of 1967 made discrimination against older men and women by employers, unions, and employment agencies illegal. A 1986 amendment to the law prohibits discrimination against persons older than 40 years. The practical outcome of this act has been that mandatory retirement is no longer allowed in the American workplace.

As with Title VII, some exceptions to this act exist. Reasonable factors other than age may be used when terminations become necessary. Reasonable factors may include a performance evaluation system or certain limited occupational qualifications, such as the tedious physical demands of a specific job.

Americans With Disabilities Act of 1990

The Americans with Disabilities Act (ADA) of 1990 provides protection to persons with disabilities and is the most significant civil rights legislation since the Civil Rights Act of 1964. The purpose of the ADA is to provide a clear and comprehensive national mandate for the elimination of discrimination against individuals with disabilities and to provide clear, strong, consistent, enforceable standards addressing discrimination in the workplace. The ADA is closely related to the Civil Rights Act of 1991 and incorporates the antidiscrimination principles established in Section 504 of the Rehabilitation Act of 1973.

The act has five titles; Table 3.3 depicts the pertinent issues of each title. The ADA has jurisdiction over employers, private and public; employment agencies; labor organizations; and joint labor-management committees. *Disability* is defined broadly. With respect to an individual, a disability is (1) a physical or mental impairment that substantially limits one or more of the major life activities of such individual, (2) a record of such impairment, or (3) an individual being regarded as having such impairment (ADA Amended Act, 2008). The effects of this amended act were to allow the definition of disability to be as broad as possible, and also to

TABLE 3.3 Americans With Disabilities Act of 1990

Title	Provisions
I	Employment: defines the purpose of the act and who is qualified under the act as having a disability
II	Public services: concerns services, programs, and activities of public entities as well as public transportation
III	Public accommodations and services operated by private entities: prohibits discrimination against persons with disabilities in areas of public accommodations, commercial facilities, and public transportation services
IV	Telecommunications: intended to make telephone services accessible to individuals with hearing or speech impairments
V	Miscellaneous provisions: certain insurance matters; incorporation of this act with other federal and state laws

Source: Americans with Disabilities Act of 1990, 42 U.S.C. § 12101 et seq. (1990).

disallow impairments that are transitory (6-month duration or less) and minor. It also allows the definition to include an impairment that is episodic or in remission if the disability substantially limits a major life event when not in remission.

The overall effect of the legislation is that persons with disabilities will not be excluded from job opportunities or adversely affected in any aspect of employment unless they are not qualified or are otherwise unable to perform the job. The ADA thus protects qualified individuals with disabilities in regard to job application procedures, hiring, compensation, advancement, and all other employment matters.

The number of lawsuits filed under the ADA since its enactment is extensive. This is due in part to the fact that to prevent the act from being overly narrow, the determination of qualified individuals is done case by case, and the individual must show (1) that he or she has a physical or mental impairment, (2) that the impairment substantially limits one or more major life activities, and (3) that he or she is still able to perform the essential function of the employment position sought or in which the individual is currently employed.

> **CASE EXAMPLE BOX 3.3** The issue of reasonable accommodations was well illustrated by the court in *Zamudio v. Patia* (1997). The court stated that the employer would be required to inform Ms. Zamudio when a position became available for which the reasonable accommodation she required could be met. She would be allowed to apply, but "as a disabled employee seeking reasonable accommodation she did not have to be given preference over other employees without disabilities who might have better qualifications or more seniority" (*Zamudio v. Patia, 1997,* at 808).

The ADA requires an employer or potential employer to make reasonable accommodations to employ persons with a disability. The law does not mandate that individuals with a disability be hired before fully qualified persons who do not have a disability; it does mandate that those with disabilities not be disqualified merely because of an easily accommodated disability. An example appears in the Case Example Box 3.3.

Moreover, the court will not impose job restructuring on an employer if the person needing accommodation qualifies for other jobs not requiring such accommodation. In *Mauro v. Borgess Medical Center (1995),* the court refused to impose accommodation on the employer hospital merely because the affected employee desired to stay within a certain unit of the institution. In this case an operating surgical technician who tested positive for HIV was offered an equivalent position by the hospital in an area where there would be no patient contact. He refused the transfer, desiring accommodation within the operating arena, and was denied such accommodation by the Michigan court.

The act also provides for essential job functions. These are defined by the ADA as those functions that the person must be able to perform to be qualified for employment positions. Courts have assisted in determining these essential job functions. For example, in *Moschke v. Memorial Medical Center of West Michigan (2003),* the court determined that the ability to take "on-call" work is an essential function of a surgical nurse's job. Such on-call work involves the ability of the surgical nurse to be available when emergency cases or scheduling problems require the staff to work beyond their assigned shifts. In *Laurin v. Providence Hospital and Massachusetts Nurses Association (1998),* the ability to work rotating shifts was held to be an essential job function.

The act specifically excludes the following from the definition of disability: homosexuality and bisexuality, sexual behavioral disorders, gambling addiction, kleptomania, pyromania, and current use of illegal drugs (ADA, 1990). Employers may hold persons with alcohol issues to the same job qualifications and job performance standards as other employees, even if the unsatisfactory behavior or performance is related to alcoholism (ADA, 1990). As with other federal employment laws, the nurse manager should have a thorough understanding of the law as it applies to the institution and his or her specific job description and should know whom to contact within the institution structure for clarification as needed.

Affirmative Action

The policy of affirmative action (AA) differs from the policy of equal employment opportunity (EEO). AA policy enhances employment opportunities of protected groups of people; EEO policy is concerned with implementing employment practices that do not discriminate against or impair the employment opportunities of protected groups. Thus AA can be seen in conjunction with several federal employment laws. For example, in conjunction with the Vietnam Era Veterans' Readjustment Assistance Act of 1974, AA requires that employers with government contracts take steps to enhance the employment opportunities of veterans with disabilities who served during the Vietnam Era.

Equal Pay Act of 1963

The Equal Pay Act of 1963 makes it illegal to pay lower wages to employees of one gender when the jobs (1) require equal skill in experience, training, education, and ability; (2) require equal effort in mental or physical exertion; (3) are of equal responsibility and accountability; and (4) are performed under similar working conditions. Courts have held that unequal pay may be legal if it is based on seniority, merit, incentive systems, or a factor other than gender. The main cases filed under this law in the area of nursing have been by nonprofessionals.

Occupational Safety and Health Act

The Occupational Safety and Health Administration (OSHA) Act of 1970 was enacted to ensure that healthful and safe working conditions would exist in the workplace. Among other provisions, the law requires isolation procedures, placarding areas containing ionizing radiation, proper grounding of electrical equipment, protective storage of flammable and combustible liquids, and the gloving of all personnel when handling bodily fluids. The statute provides that if no federal standard has been established, state statutes prevail. Nurse managers should know the relevant OSHA laws for the institution and their specific area. Frequent review of new additions to the law also must be undertaken, especially in this era of acquired immunodeficiency syndrome (AIDS) and other infectious diseases.

Violence in the workplace is an issue that OSHA continues to address in its rules. Violence is perhaps the greatest hidden health and safety threat in the workplace today, and nurses, as the largest group of healthcare professionals, are most at risk of assault at work. In 1996 OSHA developed voluntary guidelines to protect healthcare workers and consumers. Relatively few states have laws that mandate employers to report incidents of workplace violence, although more states have enacted laws that strengthen or increase penalties for acts of workplace violence. Additionally, TJC created standards that address the incidence and prevention of workplace violence, and the American Nurses Association (ANA) generated a model state bill entitled The Violence Prevention in Health Care Facilities Act (ANA, 2012a).

Another important workplace concern is the issue of safe patient handling, preventing injury to healthcare workers while ensuring that patients are protected as they are transferred or moved in healthcare settings. The ANA (2012b) reported that more than one-third of back injuries in nurses are associated with the handling of patients. Given these data and recognizing that manual patient lifting simply is not safe, the ANA promotes legislation that would require hospitals and other healthcare institutions to develop programs to prevent work-related musculoskeletal disorders and eliminate manual patient lifting. Toward this end, a few states have passed safe patient handling legislation.

In 2012, OSHA initiated its National Emphasis Program (NEP) for nursing and residential care facilities to focus on the workplace hazards that are the most common in the healthcare industry, including ergonomic stressors related to patient lifting. The desire is that this momentum will lead to federal laws that would require mechanical lifting equipment and friction-reducing devices for all healthcare workers, patients, and residents across all healthcare settings. Published in 2015, the "Inspection Guidance for Inpatient Healthcare Settings" memorandum further directs OSHA Regional Administrators and State Plans to focus inspections at these facilities to reduce five primary hazards: musculoskeletal disorders related to patient or resident handling; blood-borne pathogens; workplace violence; tuberculosis; and, slips, trips, and falls.

Family and Medical Leave Act of 1993

The Family and Medical Leave Act of 1993 was passed because of the large numbers of single-parent and two-parent households in which the single parent or both parents are employed full time, placing job security and parenting at odds. The law also supports the growing demands that aging parents are placing on their working children. The act was written in an attempt to balance the demands of the workplace with the demands of the family, allowing employed individuals to take leaves for medical reasons, including the birth or adoption of children and the care of a spouse, child, or parent who has serious health problems. Essentially, the act provides job security for unpaid leave while the employee is caring for a new infant or other family healthcare needs. The act is gender-neutral and allows both men and women the same leave provisions. Medical leave may be taken to care for a spouse, son, daughter, or parent of the employee when that person has a serious medical condition. Employees are also permitted to use medical leave for their own serious health condition.

To be eligible under the act, the employee must have worked for at least 12 months and worked at least 1250 hours during the preceding 12-month period. The employee may take up to 12 weeks of unpaid leave. The act allows the employer to require the employee to use all or part of any paid vacation, personal leave, or sick leave as part of the 12-week family leave. Employees must give the employer 30 days advance notice, or such notice as is practical in emergency cases, before using the medical leave.

On January 28, 2008, President George W. Bush signed the Family and Medical Leave Amended Act of 2008, which became effective January 16, 2009. The amendments permit a spouse, son, daughter, parent, or next of kin to take up to 26 work weeks of leave to care for a member of the U.S. Armed Forces, including a member of the National Guard or Reserves, who is undergoing medical treatment, recuperation, or therapy; is otherwise in outpatient status; or is otherwise on the temporary disability retired list, for a serious injury or illness. In addition, the act permits an employee to take leave for any qualifying exigency arising out of the fact that the spouse or a son, daughter, or parent of the employee is on active duty (or has been notified of an impending call or order to active duty) in the Armed Forces in support of a contingency operation. In 2013 the FMLA was amended to address changes concerning calculating employee eligibility for FMLA leave, military caregiver leave for veterans, qualifying exigency leave for parental care, tracking intermittent or reduced-schedule FMLA leave, and special leave provisions for flight crew employees.

Employment-at-Will and Wrongful Discharge

Historically, the employment relationship has been considered a "free will" relationship. Employees were free to take or not take a job at will, and employers were free to hire, retain, or discharge employees for any reason. Many laws, some federal but predominantly state, have been slowly eroding this at-will employment relationship. Evolving case law provides at least three exceptions to the broad doctrine of employment-at-will.

The first exception is a public policy exception. This exception involves cases in which an employee is discharged in direct conflict with established public policy. Under this exception, an employer may not discharge an employee if it would violate the state's public policy doctrine or a state or federal statute. Some examples include discharging an employee for serving on a jury, reporting employers' illegal actions (better known as whistle-blowing, or the disclosure of information regarding misconduct within a workplace that either is illegal or endangers the welfare of others), and filing a workers' compensation claim. Most states and the District of Columbia recognize public policy as an exception to the at-will rule.

Several recent court cases attest to the number of terminations in healthcare settings that serve as retaliation for the employer. More commonly known as whistle-blowing cases, the healthcare provider in these cases is terminated for one of three distinct reasons: (1) speaking out against unsafe practices, (2) reporting violations of federal laws, or (3) filing lawsuits against employers. Essentially, whistleblower laws state that no employer can discharge,

threaten, or discriminate against an employee regarding compensation, terms, conditions, location, or privileges of employment because the employee in good faith reported or caused to be reported, verbally or in writing, what the employee had a reasonable cause to believe was a violation of a state or federal law, rule, or regulation. Most whistleblowers are internal; that is, they report misconduct to a fellow employee or supervisor within the agency. External whistleblowers are those who report misconduct to outside persons or entities. Examples appear in the Case Example Boxes 3.4 and 3.5.

The second exception to wrongful discharge involves situations in which an implied contract exists. The courts have generally treated employee handbooks, company policies, and oral statements made at the time of employment as "framing the employment relationship" (*Watkins v. Unemployment Compensation Board of Review*, 1997). For example, in *Trombley v. Southwestern Vermont Medical Center* (1999), the court found that the employee handbook outlined the procedure for progressive discipline, mandating that such procedure be followed before a nurse could be terminated for incompetent nursing care.

The third exception to wrongful discharge is a "good faith and fair dealing" exception. The purpose of this exception is to prevent unfair or malicious terminations,

---

CASE EXAMPLE BOX 3.4 *Martell v. Tarpon Springs Hospital* (2010) concerned a hospital surgical nursing supervisor with a spotless 14-year record who was fired 10 days after she voiced a complaint that the hospital administrator had falsified records. In these falsified records, the administrator had personally certified a number of hospital nurses' annual cardiopulmonary resuscitation retraining, which neither he nor anyone else had actually done. During the trial, it was further disclosed that this same administrator had been fired from his previous employments for falsifying time records and for poor performance.

The jury in the case awarded the former nursing supervisor $425,000 as damages for compensation for emotional distress and the fact that her new employment paid less, had fewer benefits, and was less personally satisfying than her former position. The jury also noted that complaining about an illegal action by a superior was expressly protected by the state's whistleblower-protection law and that the hospital had no grounds on which to dismiss her.

CASE EXAMPLE BOX 3.5 Perhaps one of the best-known whistleblower cases involving nurses is what has become known as the Winkler County Nurses Lawsuit (Yoder-Wise, 2010). The case became nationally known after two registered nurses, Anne Mitchell and Vicki Galle, were terminated by the Winkler County Hospital in Kermit, Texas. The nurses first attempted to report a physician's behavior and negligent healthcare practices through designated hospital channels. When the hospital took no action, they reported the physician to the Texas Medical Board for serious misconduct, substandard care, and an inappropriate business partnership with the sheriff of Winkler County.

Although the usual procedure was for the medical board to investigate and keep the complainants' names confidential, the sheriff used the power of his position to learn that the reporting nurses had worked at the hospital for about 20 years and that each nurse was about 50 years old. That information allowed the sheriff to identify the two nurses; he then used his office to confiscate the nurses' computers, where he found the letter to the Texas Medical Board. The nurses were subsequently terminated and indicted on felony charges of misuse of official information, which could have resulted in their imprisonment for 10 years.

The criminal charges against Vicki Galle were dismissed the day before the trial was to occur, though the trial proceeded against Anne Mitchell. The trial lasted less than 4 days, with the jury returning a not guilty verdict. The nurses later filed successful civil lawsuits against the physician, Winkler County, the hospital and its administrator, the sheriff, and the district and county attorneys of Winkler County (*Mitchell & Galle v. Winkler County et al.*, 2010). Their cause of action included violations of their rights of free speech and due process, whistleblower retaliation, and interference with their business relationship, specifically their employment status.

and the courts use the exception sparingly. States also do not favor this exception, and today less than a quarter of the states recognize breach of such implied contracts. Although this exception is rarely seen in nursing, it remains a valid exception to wrongful discharge of an employee.

Nurse managers are urged to know their respective state laws concerning this growing area of the law, particularly in conjunction with whistleblower laws. Managers should review institution documents, especially employee handbooks and recruiting brochures, for unwanted statements implying job security or other unintentional promises. Managers are also cautioned not to say anything during the preemployment negotiations and interviews that might be construed as implying job security or other unintentional promises to the potential employee. To prevent successful suits for retaliation by whistleblowers, nurse managers should carefully monitor the treatment of an employee after a complaint is filed and ensure that performance evaluations are conducted and placed in the appropriate files. The nurse manager should also take steps to correct the whistleblower's complaint or refer the complaint to upper management so that it can effectively be addressed.

Collective Bargaining

Collective bargaining, also called *labor relations,* is the joining together of employees for the purpose of increasing their ability to influence the employer and improve working conditions. Collective bargaining is defined and protected by the National Labor Relations Act of 1935 and its amendments; the National Labor Relations Board (NLRB) oversees the act and those who come under its auspices. The NLRB ensures that employees can choose freely whether they want to be represented by a particular bargaining unit, and it serves to prevent or remedy any violation of the labor laws. Chapter 14 provides further detail regarding collective bargaining and collective action.

PROFESSIONAL NURSING PRACTICE: ETHICS

Ethics is the study of standards of conduct and moral judgment and is an area of professional practice in which nurse managers should have a solid foundation because it is increasingly an issue in clinical practice settings. However, it remains an area in which many nurses feel the most inadequate. This is partially because ethics is much more nebulous than are laws and regulations. In ethics, right and wrong answers are usually not possible, just better or worse answers, and nurses seek mentorship and counseling from nurse managers when they encounter difficult situations. Thus nurse managers must have a deep understanding of ethical principles and their application.

Ethics may be distinguished from the law because ethics is internal to an individual, looks to the ultimate "good" of an individual rather than society as a whole, and concerns the "why" of one's actions. The law, comprising rules and regulations pertinent to society as a whole, is external to oneself and concerns one's actions and conduct. Ethics concerns the individual within society, whereas law concerns society as a whole. Law can be enforced through the courts, statutes, and boards of nursing, whereas ethics is enforced via ethics committees and professional codes.

Today, ethics and legal issues often become entwined, and it may be difficult to separate ethics from legal concerns. Legal principles and doctrines assist the nurse manager in decision making; ethical theories and principles are often involved in those decisions. Thus the nurse manager must be cognizant of both laws and ethics in everyday management concerns, remembering that ethical principles form the essential base of knowledge from which to proceed, rather than giving easy, straightforward answers.

Ethical Principles

Ethical principles, used daily in patient care situations, are equally paramount to the nurse manager. Ethical principles that nurse managers should consider when making decisions include the eight items listed in Box 3.4. Each of the principles is applied daily in clinical practice, though some principles are used a greater degree than others.

The principle of autonomy addresses personal freedom and self-determination, the right to choose what will happen to oneself as well as the accountability for making individual choices. The legal doctrine of informed consent is a direct reflection of this principle. Autonomy involves respect for others' decisions, even if the nurse manager does not agree with the decision chosen. An example could be in the instance of progressive discipline. The employee has the option to meet delineated expectations or accept the consequences of not complying with these delineated expectations.

BOX 3.4 **Ethical Principles**	
• Autonomy	• Justice
• Beneficence	• Paternalism
• Nonmaleficence	• Fidelity
• Veracity	• Respect for others

The principle of beneficence states that the actions one takes should promote good; beneficence is the basic obligation to assist others. Nurse managers use this principle when encouraging employees to seek more challenging clinical experiences or to take on additional responsibilities, such as the position of assistant manager of a specific unit. Progressive discipline incorporates this principle when the employee's positive attributes and qualities are included when developing goals and expected outcomes.

The corollary of beneficence, the principle of nonmaleficence, states that one should do no harm. For a nurse manager following this principle, performance evaluation should emphasize an employee's good qualities and give positive direction for growth. Destroying the employee's self-esteem and self-worth would be considered doing harm under this principle.

Veracity concerns telling the truth and demands that the truth be told completely. Nurse managers employ this principle when they give all the facts of a situation truthfully and then assist employees to make appropriate decisions. For example, when encouraging a staff member to accept a promotion to a position of greater responsibility, both the challenges and the benefits of the position must be discussed.

Justice is the principle of treating all persons equally and fairly. This principle most often arises in times of short supplies or when competition for resources or benefits is occurring. Nurse managers use justice when they decide which staff members to promote or to recommend for professional development opportunities. The staff member's overall performance and skills should be considered rather than who may have seniority or the popular vote of his or her peer group. Justice is also encountered when deciding who should be floated to another unit or service within the institution or which staff member should be moved to a straight day position rather than remaining on a rotating schedule.

The principle of paternalism allows one person to make partial decisions for another and is most frequently deemed to be a negative or undesirable principle. Paternalism, however, may be used to assist persons to make decisions when they do not have sufficient data or expertise. Paternalism becomes undesirable when the entire decision is taken from the employee. Nurse managers use this principle in a positive manner by assisting employees in deciding major career moves and plans, helping the staff member more

LITERATURE PERSPECTIVE

Resource: Hyatt, J. (2017). Recognizing moral disengagement and its impact on patient safety. *Journal of Nursing Regulation, 7*(4), 15-19.

This article focuses on moral disengagement, the process of changing one's moral perceptions to justify actions that are unethical. One of the most common examples of this is when nurses say they were simply following policy; in other words, it is the organization's fault. The author points out that one of the major precursors is dysfunctional or culture issues related to power issues and disruptive actions. In essence, moral disengagement is cognitive dissonance. "Moral disengagement reduces cognitive dissonance by reframing the situation so the person performing the unethical act no longer perceives it as unethical" (p.16).

Several clinical, organizational, and interpersonal examples are provided to illustrate the potential complexity and severity of this problem. Hyatt identifies the process of moving from moral distress, to cognitive dissonance, to moral numbness, to moral disengagement. Three primary mechanisms are at play: shifting blame, reevaluating the gravity of the act, and minimizing the consequences.

Implications for Practice

The complexity of care in many settings contributes to the potential to become disengaged. Knowing how moral distress moves to disengagement allows us to intervene early in our feelings of angst so that we don't threaten patient safety.

---

fully understand all aspects of a possible career change, or, conversely, assisting staff members to comprehend why such a potential change could affect their future growth opportunities within the organization.

Fidelity means keeping one's promises or commitments. Nurse managers abide by this principle when they follow through on any promises they have previously made to employees, such as a promised leave, a certain shift to be worked, or a promotion to a preceptor position within the unit.

Many consider the principle of respect for others as the highest principle. Respect for others acknowledges the right of individuals to make decisions and to live by these decisions. Respect for others also transcends cultural differences, gender issues, and racial concerns and is the first principle enumerated in the American Nurses Association's Code of Ethics for Nurses (2015). Nurse managers positively reinforce this principle daily in their actions with employees, patients, and peers because they serve as leaders and models for staff members and others in the institution.

When nurses disengage from the ethics of the profession and their moral perceptions, patient safety is at risk, as the Literature Perspective shows.

Codes of Ethics

Professional codes of ethics are formal statements that articulate values and beliefs of a given professional, serving as a standard of professional actions and reflecting the ethical principles shared by its members. Professional codes of ethics generally serve the following purposes:

- Inform the public of the minimum standards acceptable for conduct by members of the discipline and assist the public in understanding a discipline's professional responsibilities
- Outline the major ethical considerations of the profession
- Provide to its members guidelines for professional practice
- Serve as a guide for the discipline's self-regulation

The Code of Ethics for Nurses (ANA, 2015) should be the starting point for any nurse faced with an ethical issue. The first American nursing code was adopted in 1950, and it focused on the character of the nurse and the virtues that were essential to the profession. In 1968 the focus shifted to a duty-based ethical focus, and in 2001 the ANA Code of Ethics for Nurses blended these duty-based ethics with a historical focus on character and virtue. In 2015 the revised provisions and interpretive statements were developed with an eye toward the future based on knowledge gained from the past. The Code of Ethics for Nurses (ANA, 2015) has nine points that guide nurses in understanding the extent of their commitment to the patient, themselves, other nurses, and the nursing profession. Further provisions in the code assist nurses in understanding that patients, whether as individuals or as members of families, groups, or communities, are their first obligation and that nurses must not only ensure quality care but also protect the safety of these patients. Nurses and their nurse managers should ensure that the provisions of the code are incorporated into nursing care delivery in all clinical settings. Along with establishing the ethical standard for the disciplines, the nursing code of ethics provides a basis for ethical analysis and decision making in clinical situations.

Ethical Decision-Making Framework

Ethical decision making involves reflection on many factors such as intended outcomes, resources available, professional organizational directives, and likely and unintended consequences.

When making decisions, nurses need to combine all of these elements using an orderly, systematic, and objective method; ethical decision-making models assist in accomplishing this goal.

For most nurses, ethical decision-making models are considered only when complex ethical dilemmas present in clinical settings. In truth, however, nurses use ethical decision-making models each time an ethical situation arises, although the decision-making model may not be acknowledged or fully appreciated. Ethical dilemmas involve situations in which a choice must be made between equally unacceptable options that an individual perceives he or she can accept and reasonably justify on a moral plane or in which there is not a more favorable or appropriate choice that dominates the situation.

Ethical decision making is always a process. To facilitate this process, the nurse manager must use all available resources, including the institutional ethics committee, and communicate with and support all those involved in the process. Some decisions are easier to reach and support than others. Allowing sufficient time for the process contributes to a supportable option being reached.

Moral Distress

Nurses experience stress in clinical practice settings as they are confronted with situations involving ethical dilemmas. Moral distress most often occurs when one is faced with situations in which two ethical principles compete, such as when the nurse is balancing the patient's autonomy issues with attempting to do what the nurse knows is in the patient's best interest. Moral distress may occur also when the nurse manager is balancing a direct care nurse's autonomy with what the nurse manager perceives to be a better solution to an ethical dilemma. Though the dilemmas are stressful,

nurses must make decisions and implement those decisions.

Seen as a major issue in nursing today, moral distress is experienced when nurses cannot provide what they perceive to be best for a given patient. Examples of moral distress include constraints caused by financial pressures, limited patient care resources, disagreements among family members regarding patient interventions, and/or limitations imposed by primary healthcare providers. Moral distress may also be experienced when actions nurses perform violate their personal beliefs.

The impact of moral distress can be quite serious. McAndrew, Leske, and Garcia (2011) reported that moral distress compromises patient care and that moral distress may be manifested in such behaviors as avoiding or withdrawing from patient care situations. Additional behaviors include failure to act as a patient advocate, which often further contributes to patient discomfort and suffering.

Moral distress occurs when professionals cannot carry out what they believe to be ethically appropriate actions. A bibliometric analysis revealed that since 1984, 239 articles were published, with an increase after 2011. Most of them (71%) focused on nursing. Of the 239 articles, 17 empirical studies were systematically analyzed. Moral distress correlated with organizational environment (poor ethical climate and collaboration), professional attitudes (low work satisfaction and engagement), and psychological characteristics (low psychological empowerment and autonomy) (Lamiari, Borghi, & Argentero, 2015).

Nurse managers can best assist nurses experiencing moral distress by remembering that such distress may be lessened through adequate levels of knowledge regarding nursing ethics and its application, acknowledging that such distress does occur, and serving as an advocate for nurses. In this latter role, the nurse manager advocates for improvement in conditions that may directly influence moral distress, such as additional staff during periods of high patient acuity, additional counselors to work with patients' family issues and disputes, and the implementation of in-service education and/or education concerning better communication among all levels of healthcare practitioners. These positive aspects of leadership may significantly reduce the level of moral distress encountered by direct care nurses and greatly increase their job satisfaction. Furthermore, nurses in leadership positions experience moral distress that direct care nurses do not. However, those sources of distress are the same types that direct care nurses experience—those issues simply are seen from a different perspective.

Ethics Committees

With the increasing numbers of ethical dilemmas in patient situations and administrative decisions, healthcare providers are increasingly turning to hospital ethics committees for guidance. Such committees can provide both long-term and short-term assistance. Ethics committees provide structure and guidelines for potential problems, serve as open forums for discussion, and function as true patient advocates by placing the patient at the core of the committee discussions.

To form such a committee, the involved individuals should begin as a bioethical study group so that all potential members can explore ethical principles and theories. The composition of the committee should include nurses, physicians, clergy, clinical social workers, nutritional experts, pharmacists, administrative personnel, and legal experts. Once the committee has become active, individual patients or patients' families and additional representatives of members of the healthcare delivery team may be invited to committee deliberations.

Ethics committees traditionally follow one of three distinct structures, although some institutional committees blend the three structures. The autonomy model facilitates decision making for competent patients. The patient-benefit model uses substituted judgment (what the patient would want for himself or herself if capable of making these issues known) and facilitates decision making for the incompetent patient. The social justice model considers broad social issues and is accountable to the overall institution.

In most settings, the ethics committee already exists, because complex issues divide healthcare workers. In many centers, ethical rounds, conducted weekly or monthly, allow staff members, who may later become involved in ethical decision making, to begin reviewing all the issues and to become more comfortable with ethical issues and their resolution.

Blending Ethical and Legal Issues

Blending legal demands with ethics is a challenge for nursing, and no case better portrays this type of difficult decision making than does the case of Theresa (Terri) M. Schiavo. The Case Example Box 3.6 describes this situation.

Whichever side of the case one supported, the plight of Terri Schiavo created numerous ethical concerns for the nurses caring for her, as well as for the nurse managers in the clinical setting. Issues that created these conflicts ranged from working with feuding family members, to multiple media personnel attempting to cover the story, to constant editorial and news stories invading the privacy of this individual, to masses of people lined at the borders of the hospice center insisting that she be fed, to individual emotions about the correctness of either keeping or removing the feeding tube. One issue remains clear: the nurse managers and nurses caring for this particular patient had a legal obligation to either remove or reinsert the feeding tube based on the prevailing court decision or legislative act. Their individual reflections about the correctness or justice of such court decrees were secondary to the prevailing court orders.

Nurse managers should ensure that nurses whose ethical values differ from court orders are given opportunities to voice their concerns and feelings, mechanisms for requesting reassignment, and time for quiet reflection. Although no deviance can occur from one's legal obligation, the nurse manager must ensure that the emotional and psychological well-being of those he or she supervises are also recognized. Merely acknowledging that such discord can occur and allowing positive means to express this concern may be the best solution in handling these difficult legal and ethical patient situations.

Other Ethical Concerns for Nurses

Other issues of concern involve autonomy and independent practice among nurses, quality of care in home and community settings, and development of nurses as leaders in the healthcare delivery field. Issues that continue to permeate ethical concerns for nurses include the patient's right to refuse health care; issues surrounding death and dying, including the issues of hydration and nutrition for patients in persistent vegetative states; nurses' ability to be patient advocates in today's healthcare structure; and the ability to perform competent,

CASE EXAMPLE BOX 3.6 Ms. Schiavo suffered a cardiac arrest in February 1990, sustaining a period of approximately 11 minutes when she was anoxic. She was resuscitated and, at the insistence of her husband, was intubated, placed on a ventilator, and eventually received a tracheotomy. The cause of her cardiac arrest was determined to be a severe electrolyte imbalance that was directly caused by an eating disorder. In the 6 years preceding the cardiac event, Ms. Schiavo had lost approximately 140 pounds, going from 250 to 110 pounds.

During the first 2 months after her cardiac arrest, Ms. Schiavo was in a coma. She then regained some wakefulness and was eventually diagnosed as being in persistent vegetative state (PVS). She was successfully weaned from the ventilator and was able to swallow her saliva, both reflexive behaviors. However, she was not able to eat food or drink liquids, which is characteristic of PVS. A permanent feeding tube was placed so that she could receive nutrition and hydration.

Throughout the early years of her PVS, there was no challenge to the diagnosis or to the appointment of her husband as her legal guardian. Four years after her cardiac arrest, a successful lawsuit was filed against a fertility physician who failed to detect her electrolyte imbalance. A judgment of $300,000 went to her husband for loss of companionship and $700,000 was placed in a court-managed trust fund to maintain and provide care for Ms. Schiavo.

Sometime after this successful lawsuit, the close family relationship that Ms. Schiavo's husband and her parents had began to erode and the public first became aware of Ms. Schiavo's plight. As her court-appointed guardian noted (Wolfson, 2005): "Thereafter, what is for millions of Americans a profoundly private matter catapulted a close, loving family into an internationally watched blood feud. The end product was a most public death for a very private individual. Theresa was by all accounts a very shy, fun loving, and sweet woman who loved her husband and her parents very much. The family breach and public circus would have been anathema to her" (p. 17).

The court battles regarding the removal or retention of her feeding tube were numerous. There was adequate medical and legal evidence to show that Ms. Schiavo had been correctly diagnosed and that she would not have wanted to be kept alive by artificial means. Laws in the state of Florida, where Ms. Schiavo was a patient, allowed the removal of tubal nutrition and hydration in patients with PVS. The feeding tube was removed and later reinstated after a court order.

In October 2003, there was a second removal of the feeding tube after a higher court overturned the lower court decision that had caused the feeding tube to be reinserted. With this second removal, the Florida legislature passed what has come to be known as Terri's Law. This law gave the Florida governor the right to demand the feeding tube be reinserted and also appoint a special guardian to review the entire case. The special guardian ad litem was appointed in October 2003. Terri's Law was later declared unconstitutional by the Florida Supreme Court, and the US Supreme Court refused to overrule that decision.

In early 2005, during the last weeks of Ms. Schiavo's life, the US Congress attempted to move the issue to the federal rather than Florida state court system. Finally, the Federal District Court in Florida and the 11th Circuit Court of Appeals ruled that there was insufficient evidence to create a new trial, and the US Supreme Court refused to review the findings of these two lower courts (Wolfson, 2005). Ms. Schiavo died on March 31, 2005; she was 41 years old.

---

quality nursing care in health care delivery systems that often reward cost-saving measures rather than quality healthcare delivery. As with ethical dilemmas in patient care, the more expertise and time one has to resolve issues, usually, the better the outcome.

CONCLUSION

In addition to knowing and understanding legal terms and issues related to clinical concerns, formal leaders and managers need to know employment law, union laws, the nursing practice act, and numerous other legal findings. Though each state may have distinctive laws governing being a manager and working in a healthcare organization, the key decisions tested in court or laws that govern all healthcare operations within the United States are ones with which we must all be familiar. Legal and ethical aspects present additional opportunities for nurses to exhibit leadership capabilities.

THE SOLUTION

Staff members and nursing leadership began by working together to understand the varied viewpoints of the healthcare team. We attempted to understand why some of the primary healthcare providers allowed family members to be present and other primary healthcare providers insisted that family members not be present during resuscitation efforts. When asked, primary healthcare providers often noted that the behaviors and attitudes of the family members were a factor in their decision, and that one could not know in advance whether the family members might be hostile or belligerent and thus distract or prevent the healthcare team from being able to provide necessary care. Additionally, no clear hospital policy existed, many of these primary healthcare providers were more comfortable in not having the family members present, and the current practice was to assign a chaplain and social worker to provide supportive services as well as comfort and information to family members when such situations arose. Thus the family members, though not present within the patient's room, were also not alone during this time and had the opportunity to ask questions.

We then looked at the issue from an ethical perspective. For many patients and family members, being present during this crucial time could have many positive effects, thus beneficence and respect for others were the two ethical principles that most clearly seemed to support family presence. Seeing for themselves and understanding that everything possible was being done to save their loved one's life were the most positive outcomes to support family presence. Family members could later have an opportunity to more fully question why certain aspects were performed, and the nursing staff as well as the primary care provider could then explain in more detail answers to the family members' questions.

Viewing the literature about this topic was enlightening. We discovered that this topic has continually been studied, dating back to the early 1980s. These studies almost uniformly noted that family presence did not alter the effectiveness of the healthcare team's interventions, nor did family presence interfere with the duration of resuscitative efforts or selection of medications. Some of the more recent studies addressed the issue of interference by family members and noted that very few family members were aggressive or in conflict with the team's performance and that family members excluded from being present expressed regret at not having been present during resuscitation. Interestingly, some of the reviewed studies continued to question how to best determine which family members should be given the option of viewing resuscitation measures or whether all families should be given this option. At present, we continue to explore possible guidelines concerning family presence during resuscitation, recognizing that such a complex issue cannot be rapidly resolved.

Would this be a suitable approach for you? Why?

Acacia Syring

REFLECTIONS

Consider a situation you may have observed in the clinical area that made you wonder if the action taken was legal or ethical. What triggered that thought for you? What did you think you would have done differently?

THE EVIDENCE

State boards of nursing have worked diligently to uphold high standards of accountability to the public. One example is the enhanced nurse licensure compact agreement. When nurses face ethical or legal concerns, they have resources available through their employment setting, the state board of nursing, and the state professional nursing association.

TIPS FOR INCORPORATING LEGAL AND ETHICAL ISSUES IN PRACTICE SETTINGS

- Read the state nurse practice act, ensuring compliance with the allowable scope of practice.
- Apply legal principles in all healthcare settings.
- Understand and follow state and federal employment laws.
- Follow the Code of Ethics for Nurses (ANA, 2015) in all aspects of healthcare delivery.

- Remember that no right and wrong answers exist in ethical situations, merely better or worse solutions. Consider all aspects and consult with others before proceeding if there are unanswered questions.
- If legal and ethical issues are contradictory, legal aspects are enacted first.

REFERENCES

Age Discrimination in Employment Act of 1967, P.L. 90-202, 29 United States Code 621 (December 15, 1967).

American Nurses Association. (2012a). *Workplace violence.* Available at http://nursingworld.org/workplaceviolence.

American Nurses Association. (2012b). *Safe patient handling.* Available at http://www.anasafepatienthandling.org.

American Nurses Association (ANA). (2015). *Code of ethics for nurses with interpretive statements.* Washington, DC: Author.

Americans with Disabilities Act of 1990, Public Law 101-336, 104 Statutes 327 (July 26, 1990).

Americans with Disabilities Amended Act of 2008, Public Law 110-325 (September 25, 2008).

Black's Law Dictionary. (1979). (5th ed.). St. Paul, MN: West Publishing Company.

Civil Rights Act of 1964, P. L. 88-352, 78 Statutes 241, § 703 et seq. (July 2, 1964).

Civil Rights Act of 1991, P. L. 102-166 (November 21, 1991).

Department of Health and Human Services. (2012). *Quick guide to health literacy: Fact sheet.* U.S. Department of Printing and Engraving Washington, DC: Author.

Equal Employment Opportunity Act of 1972, 78 Statutes 253; 42 U.S.C. 2000e (March 24, 1972).

Equal Pay Act of 1963, P. L. 88-38, 77 Statutes 56 (June 10, 1963).

Family and Medical Leave Act of 1993, P. L. 103-3, 107 Statutes 6 (February 5, 1993).

Family and Medical Leave Amended Act of 2008, P. L. 110-181, 122 Statutes 128 (January 28, 2008).

Health Insurance Portability and Accountability Act of 1996, Public Law 104-191, 100 Statutes 2548, (August 21, 1996).

Lamiari, G., Borghi, L., & Argentero, P. (2015). When healthcare professionals cannot do the right thing: A systematic review of moral distress and its correlates. *Journal of Health Psychology,* July 27, 2015.

Laurin v. Providence Hospital and Massachusetts Nurses Association, 150 F.3d 52 (1st Cir., 1998).

Marinock v. Manor at St. Luke's, 2010 WL 3233125 (Ct. Com. Pl. Luzerne Co., Pennsylvania, January 29, 2010).

Mitchell & Galle v. Winkler County et al., CV 00037-RAJ, Document 42, Winkler County Trail Court, filed April 18, 2010.

Martell v. Tarpon Springs Hospital, 2010 WL 5485106 (Cir. Ct. Pinellas Co., Florida, September 29, 2010).

Massey v. Mercy Medical Center, 180 Cal. App. 4th 690, 103 Cal. Rept. 3d 209 (Cal. App., December 22, 2009).

Mauro v. Borgess Medical Center, 4:94 CV 05 (Mich., 1995).

McAndrew, N. S., Leske, J. S., & Garcia, A. (2011). Influence of moral distress on the professional practice environment during prognostic conflict in critical care. *Journal of Trauma Nursing, 18*(4), 221–230.

Moschke v. Memorial Medical Center of West Michigan, 2003 WL 462374 (Mich. App., February 21, 2003).

National Academy of Medicine (formerly Institute of Medicine). (1999). *To err is human: Building a safer health care system.* Washington, DC: The National Academies Press, Institute of Medicine.

National Labor Relations Act, P. L. 74-198, 49 Statutes 449 (July 5, 1935).

National Safety Council Safety and Health, Understanding OSHA's Special Emphasis Programs, February 4, 2015.

Occupational Safety and Health Administration Act of 1970, P. L. 91-595, 84 Statutes 1590 (December 29, 1970).

O'Shea v. State of New York, WL 1516492 (N.Y. Ct. Cl., January 22, 2007).

Potter, P., Deshields, T., & Kuhrik, M. (2010). Delegation practices between registered nurses and nursing assistive personnel. *Journal of Nursing Management, 18,* 157–165.

Protection of Human Subjects, 45 Code of Federal Regulations, Sec. 46.111, 46.101(b), 46.110, 46.116 (1991).

Protection of Human Subjects, 45 Code of Federal Regulations, Sec. 46.401 et seq. (1998).

Registered Nurse Safe Staffing Act of 2011. United States House Bill 876/United States Senate Bill 58. http://legiscan.com/US/comments/HB876/2011; http://legiscan.com/US/bill/SB58/2011.

Reising, D. L. (2012). Make your nursing care malpractice proof. *American Nurse Today, 7*(1). probability.com.

Ricciardi, C. L. (2015). Hospital administration not immune–criminal and civil liability: A risk for health care administrators. Becker's Hospital Review 2015, ASC Communications.

Sabol v. Richmond Heights General Hospital, 676 N. E.2d 958 (Ohio App. 1996).

Safe Nurse Staffing Legislation, Washington State HB 3123 (March, 2008).

Trombley v. Southwestern Vermont Medical Center, 738 A.2d 103 (Vt., 1999).

U.S. vs Parnell, Parnell, Lightsey & Wilkerson, U.S. District Court for Middle District of GA, 2015.

Vietnam Era Veterans' Readjustment Assistance Act of 1974, 38 United States Code § 4212 (1974).

Watkins v. Unemployment Compensation Board of Review, 689 A.2d 1019 (Pa. Commonwealth, 1997).

Wellstar Health System, Inc. v. Green, WL 31324127 (Ga. App., October 18, 2002).

Wolfson, J. (2005). Erring on the side of Theresa Schiavo: Reflections of the special guardian ad litem. *The Hastings Center Report, 35*(3), 16–19.

Yoder-Wise, P. (2010). More serendipity: The Winkler County trial. *The Journal of Continuing Education in Nursing, 41*(4), 147–148.

Zamudio v. Patia, 956 F. Supp. 803 (N.D. Ill., 1997).

4

Cultural Diversity and Inclusion in Health Care

Karen A. Quintana

LEARNING OUTCOMES

- Describe common characteristics of any culture.
- Evaluate the use of concepts and principles of acculturation, culture, cultural diversity, and cultural sensitivity in leading and managing situations.
- Analyze differences between cross-cultural, transcultural, multicultural, and intracultural concepts; cultural humility; and cultural marginality.

- Evaluate individual and societal factors involved with cultural diversity.
- Value the contributions a diverse workforce can make to the care of people.

KEY TERMS

acculturation
cross-culturalism
cultural competence
cultural diversity
cultural humility

cultural imposition
cultural marginality
cultural sensitivity
culture
ethnicity

ethnocentrism
global
inclusion
multiculturalism
transculturalism

THE CHALLENGE

I work with a large staff of men and women from several cultures, and they have different perspectives about their assignments. Hispanics, Asians, Asian Indians, and Nigerians provide a challenge for me. If I try to address a work issue, such as assignments, some become defensive. Some men feel that they are superior to me. It might be because I am a woman. In contrast, I have noticed that some Asians are more submissive and do better with female-to-female interactions. We frequently have a high patient census in the emergency department. There are times when either the charge nurse or I tell staff members

to complete a task more quickly within their assignment because of the number of patients waiting to be seen in the emergency department. This does not sit well with some staff, who tend to become defensive. For example, a male staff member of one culture felt he was being "overpowered" by the charge nurse from another culture. *What would you do if you were this nurse?*

Sally C. Fernandez, RN, MSN, ANP
*Nurse Manager, Emergency Center, The University of Texas
M.D. Anderson Cancer Center, Houston, Texas*

INTRODUCTION

As our nation grows and evolves within various cultures, the United States of America is swiftly becoming one of the most diverse nations in the world. As a result, leaders and managers need to consider culture as a factor in working with others just as they would consider education, experience, and competence.

Culture influences leadership from two perspectives. One is the way in which we meet patient needs; the other is the way in which we work together in a diverse workforce. Effective leaders can shape the culture of their organization to be accepting of persons from all races, ethnicities, religions, ages, lifestyles, and genders. These interactions of acceptance should involve a minimum of misunderstandings. Multicultural phenomena are cogent for each person, place, and time. Therefore culture-centered leadership provides organizational leaders, such as nurse managers and effective team members, the opportunity to influence cultural differences and similarities among their unit staff and to provide care to a culturally diverse patient population.

CONCEPTS AND PRINCIPLES

What is culture? Does it exhibit certain characteristics? What is cultural diversity, and what do we think of when we refer to cultural sensitivity? Are culture and ethnicity the same? Various authors have different views.

Cultural background stems from one's ethnic background, socioeconomic status, and family rituals, to name three key factors. Ethnicity, according to *The Merriam-Webster Dictionary* (Merriam-Webster, Inc., 2016), is defined as related to groups of people who are "classified" according to common racial, tribal, national, religious, linguistic, or cultural backgrounds. This description differs from what is commonly used to identify racial groups. This broader definition encourages people to think about how diverse the populations in the United States are.

Inherent characteristics of culture are often identified with the following four factors:

1. Culture develops over time and is responsive to its members and their familial and social environments.
2. A culture's members learn it and share it.
3. Culture is essential for survival and acceptance.
4. Culture changes with difficulty.

For the nurse leader or manager, the characteristics of ethnicity and culture are important to keep in mind, because the underlying thread in all of them is that culture and ethnicity of staff and patients have been with them their entire lives. All people view their cultural background as normal; the diversity challenge is for others to also view it as normal and to assimilate it into the existing workforce. Cultural diversity is the term currently used to describe a vast range of cultural differences among individuals or groups, whereas cultural sensitivity describes the affective behaviors in individuals—the capacity to feel, convey, or react to ideas, habits, customs, or traditions unique to a group of people.

Spector (2017) addressed three themes involved with acculturation. (1) *Socialization* refers to growing up or being raised within a culture and taking on the characteristics of that group. All of us are socialized to some culture, and sometimes this change in our identity can be painful. (2) Acculturation refers to adapting to the dominant culture. An example of this might be what a particular society calls a particular food or how healthcare organizations are changing to blame-free environments to encourage safety disclosures. The overall process of acculturation into a new society is extremely difficult and involuntary. "America" has a core culture and numerous subcultures. For example, think how differently people in rural American regions dress from those in urban centers, or how a city looks on a Saturday night versus a Sunday morning. In other words, subcultures expand on how the core culture might be described. "Acculturation also refers to cultural or behavioral assimilation and may be defined as the changes of one's cultural pattern to those of the host society" (Spector, 2017, p. 25). (3) *Assimilation* refers to the change that occurs when nurses move from another country to the United States, or from one part of the country to another. The person becomes similar to the members of a dominant culture. They face different social and nursing practices, and individuals now define themselves as members of the dominant culture. An example of this might be when nurses no longer say they are from their country of origin. They say they are from where they live and practice.

Providing care for a person or people from a culture other than one's own is a dynamic and complex experience. The experience, according to the classic work of Spence (2001, 2004), might involve "prejudice, paradox and possibility" (p. 140). Spence used *prejudice* as conditions that enabled or constrained interpretation based on one's values, attitudes, and actions. By talking with people outside their "circle of familiarity," nurses can enhance their understanding of personally held prejudices.

Prejudices "enable us to make sense of the situations in which we find ourselves, yet they also constrain understanding and limit the capacity to come to new or different ways of understanding. It is this contradiction that makes prejudice paradoxical" (Spence, 2004, p. 163). *Paradox,* although it may seem incongruent with prejudice, describes the dynamic interplay of tensions between individuals or groups. We have the responsibility to acknowledge the "possibility of tension" as a potential for new and different understandings derived from our communication and interpretation. *Possibility* therefore presumes a condition for openness with a person from another culture (Spence, 2004).

EXERCISE 4.1 In a group, discuss the values and beliefs of justice and equality. As a nurse, you may have strong values and beliefs, but you may never have observed their application in health care. Consider language, skin color, dress, and gestures of patients and staff from other cultures. How will you learn and value what differences exist?

Cultural humility helps us explore cultural competency as a process rather than an outcome. Hook, Davis, Owen, Worthington, and Utsey (2013) visualized cultural humility as the "ability to maintain an interpersonal stance that is other-oriented (or open to the other) in relation to aspects of cultural identity that are most important to the [person]" (p. 2). When exploring cultural humility, we find three factors, first described by Tervalon and Murray-Garcia (1998), that help shape the process:

1. A lifelong commitment to self-evaluation and self-critique.
2. Desire to fix power imbalances.
3. Aspiration to develop partnerships with people and groups who advocate for others.

The first factor, a lifelong commitment to self-evaluation and self-critique, looks at our lives as never being finished with learning. The idea of life-long learning is a hallmark of being a professional and, as with clinically based learning, we need to incorporate our newly acquired knowledge into our approach to others. We must remain humble to a point of being able to look at ourselves critically. We need to maintain the desire to learn more.

The second factor holds a desire to fix imbalances where none should exist. The work related to the social determinants of health relates to this factor. This factor acknowledges that everyone brings value to our lives. Everyone holds important information in the big picture. Waters and Asbill (2013) presented the example of the practitioner interviewing a client, and the client's role as the expert of his or her own life, symptoms, and strengths. "The practitioner holds the body of knowledge that the client does not; however, the client also has understanding outside the scope of the practitioner" (p. 2). The practitioner, who is the expert in the scientific knowledge, and the client, the expert in the personal history, must collaborate with each other for successful outcomes. Similarly, the members of a team are each experts in their own lives. The leader's task is to facilitate the sharing of the "how I see it" perspective so that broad considerations are made rather than quick, and often stereotyped, decisions.

The final factor in cultural humility is aspiring to develop partnerships with people and groups who advocate for others. Individuals can create positive change, but groups can have a more profound impact, and a more inclusive perspective, on communities and systems. Change cannot occur on an individual level without the correction of power imbalances within a larger system. "Cultural humility, by definition, is larger than our individual selves—we must advocate for it systemically" (Waters & Asbill, 2013, p. 2).

Cultural marginality is defined as "the resulting sense of being between two cultures or more, living at the edges of each, but rarely at the center" (Bennett, 2014, p. 269). This "betweenness" is a time when managers might perceive disinterest in cultural considerations. This situation might actually reflect cognitive processing of information that is not yet reflected in effective behaviors.

Ethnocentrism classically is defined as "the belief that one's own ways are the best, most superior, or preferred ways to act, believe, or behave" (Leininger, 2002b, p. 50), whereas **cultural imposition** is defined as "the tendency of an individual or group to impose their values, beliefs, and practices on another culture for varied reasons" (Leininger, 2002b, p. 51). Such practices constitute a major concern in nursing and "a largely unrecognized problem as a result of cultural ignorance, blindness, ethnocentric tendencies, biases, racism or other factors" (Leininger, 2002b, p. 51).

Providing quality of life and human care is difficult to accomplish if the nurse does not have knowledge of the recipient's culture as it relates to care. Leininger believed that "culture reflects shared values, beliefs, ideas, and meanings that are learned and that guide human thoughts, decisions, and actions. Cultures have manifest (readily recognized) and implicit (covert and ideal) rules of behavior and expectations. Human cultures have material items or symbols such as artifacts, objects, dress, and actions that have special meaning in a culture" (Leininger, 2002b, p. 48). Leininger (2002b) stated that her views of cultural care are "a synthesized construct that is the foundational basis to understanding and helping people of different cultures in transcultural nursing practices" (p. 48). (See the Theory Box on p. 66). Accordingly, "quality of life" must be addressed from an emic (insider) cultural viewpoint and compared with an etic (outsider) professional's perspective. By comparing these two viewpoints, more meaningful nursing practice interventions will evolve. The same is true for collegial relationships. This comparative analysis will require nurses to include global views in their cultural studies that consider the social and environmental context of different cultures.

EXERCISE 4.2 As a small group activity, assess several clinical settings. Do these settings have programs related to cultural diversity? Why? What are the programs like? If there are no programs, why do you think they have not been implemented?

THEORY

How do leaders, managers, or followers take all of the expanding information on the diversity of healthcare beliefs and practices and give it some organizing structure to provide culturally competent and culturally sensitive care to patients or clients? Historically, Purnell and Paulanka (2008), Campinha-Bacote (1999, 2002), Giger and Davidhizar (2002), and Leininger (2002a) provided an overview of each of their theoretical models to guide healthcare providers for delivering culturally competent and culturally sensitive care in the workplace.

Purnell and Paulanka's (2008) Model for Cultural Competence provides an organizing framework. The model uses a circle with the outer zone representing global society, the second zone representing community, the third zone representing family, and the inner zone representing the person. The interior of the circle is divided into 12 pie-shaped wedges delineating cultural domains

and their concepts (e.g., workplace issues, family roles and organization, spirituality, and healthcare practices). The innermost center circle is black, representing unknown phenomena. Cultural consciousness is expressed in behaviors from "unconsciously incompetent— consciously incompetent—consciously competent to unconsciously competent" (p. 10). The usefulness of this model is derived from its concise structure, applicability to any setting, and wide range of experiences that can foster inductive and deductive thinking when assessing cultural domains. Purnell (2009) described the dominant cultural characteristics of selected ethnocultural groups and a guide for assessing their beliefs and practices. The Purnell Model for Cultural Competence serves as an organizing framework for providing cultural care, which is based on 20 major assumptions. Much of this model can also help us consider how we enact a culturally appropriate workplace.

Campinha-Bacote's (1999, 2002) classic culturally competent model of care identifies five constructs: (1) awareness, (2) knowledge, (3) skill, (4) encounters, and (5) desire. She defined cultural competence as "the process in which the healthcare provider continuously strives to achieve the ability to effectively work within the cultural context of a client (individual, family, or community)" (Campinha-Bacote, 1999, p. 203). Cultural awareness is the self-examination and in-depth exploration of one's own cultural and professional background. It involves the recognition of one's bias, prejudices, and assumptions about the individuals who are different (Campinha-Bacote, 2002). "One's world view can be considered a paradigm or way of viewing the world and phenomena in it" (Campinha-Bacote, 1999, p. 204). Cultural knowledge is the process of seeking and obtaining a sound educational foundation about diverse cultural and ethnic groups. Obtaining cultural information about the patient's health-related beliefs and values will help explain how he or she interprets his or her illness and how it guides his or her thinking, doing, and being (Campinha-Bacote, 2002). The skill of conducting a cultural assessment is learned while assessing one's values, beliefs, and practices to provide culturally competent services. The process of cultural encounters encourages direct engagement in cross-cultural interactions with individuals from other cultures. This process allows the person to validate, negate, or modify his or her existing cultural knowledge. It provides culturally specific knowledge bases from which the individual can develop culturally relevant interventions. Cultural desire requires the intrinsic qualities of motivation and genuine caring of the health-care provider to "want to" engage in becoming culturally competent. Again, these five constructs can help us in our work as professionals interacting to provide quality care.

The Giger and Davidhizar Transcultural Assessment Model identified phenomena to assess provision of care for patients who are of different cultures (2002). Their model includes six cultural phenomena: communication, time, space, social organization, environmental control, and biological variations. Each one is described based on several premises (e.g., culture is a patterned behavioral response that develops over time; is shaped by values, beliefs, norms, and practices; guides our thinking, doing, and being; and implies a dynamic, ever-changing, active or passive process). These phenomena are also appropriate considerations in the workplace.

Leininger's (2002a) central purpose in her theory of transcultural nursing care is "to discover and explain diverse and universal culturally based care factors influencing the health, well-being, illness, or death of individuals or groups" (p. 190). She uses her classic "Sunrise Model" to identify the multifaceted theory and provides five enablers beneficial to "teasing out vague ideas," two of which are the Observation, Participation, and Reflection Enabler and the Researcher's Domain of Inquiry. Nurses can use Leininger's model to provide culturally congruent, safe, and meaningful care to patients or clients of diverse or similar cultures. See the Theory Box for an example of Leininger's work.

NATIONAL AND GLOBAL DIRECTIVES

The American Nurses Association (ANA) has a long and vital history related to ethics, human rights, and numerous efforts to eliminate discriminatory practices against nurses as well as patients. The ANA *Code of Ethics for Nurses with Interpretive Statements*, Provision 8, states, "The nurse collaborates with other health professionals and the public in promoting community, national, and international efforts to meet health needs" (ANA, 2015, p. 47). This provision helps the nurse recognize that health care must be provided to culturally diverse populations in the United States and on all continents of the world. Although a nurse may be inclined to impose his or her own cultural values on others, whether patients or staff, avoiding this imposition affirms the respect and sensitivity for the values and healthcare practices associated with different cultures. This provision is reinforced by the ANA revised position

statement (2016), *The Nurse's Role in Ethics and Human Rights: Protecting and Promoting Individual Worth, Dignity, and Human Rights in Practice Settings*. The value of human rights is placed at the forefront for nurses whose specific actions are to promote and protect the human rights of every individual in all practice care environments.

Similar statements are made with an international emphasis and a specialty emphasis. For example, the International Council of Nurses (ICN)'s *ICN Code of Ethics for Nurses* (2012) states:

> The nurse ensures that the individual receives accurate, sufficient and timely information in a culturally appropriate manner on which to base consent to care and related treatment. The ICN Code of Ethics for Nurses is a guide for action based on social values and needs and was first adopted in 1953. The nurse shares with society the responsibility for initiating and supporting action to meet the health and social needs of the public, in particular those of vulnerable populations. The nurse demonstrates professional values such as respectfulness, responsiveness, compassion, trustworthiness and integrity. (p. 3)

Throughout history, the emphasis and support has been on recipients of care such as patients, but the same attentiveness is needed in the workforce. Patients are aware of how they are treated, and they also see how staff interact with each other.

THEORY BOX

Cultural Care Theory

Theory/ Contributor	Key Ideas	Application to Practice
Leininger (2002a) is credited with developing and advancing a theory of transcultural nursing care since the mid-1950s.	The theory is explicitly focused on the close relationships of culture and care on well-being, health, illness, and death; it is holistic and multidimensional, generic (emic, folk) and professional (etic) care and has a specifically designed research method (ethnonursing).	Care is the essence of nursing, and culturally based care is essential for well-being, health, growth, and survival and for facing handicaps or death.

SPECIAL ISSUES

Health disparities between majority and ethnic minority populations are not new issues and continue to be problematic because they exist for multiple and complex reasons. Causes of disparities in health care include poor education, health behaviors of the minority group, inadequate financial resources, and environmental factors. Disparities in health care that relate to quality of care include provider–patient relationships, actual access to care, treatment regimens that necessarily reflect current evidence, provider bias and discrimination, mistrust of the healthcare system, and refusal of treatment (Baldwin, 2003). Health disparities in ethnic and racial groups are observed in cardiovascular disease, which has a 40% higher incidence in US blacks than in US whites; cancer, which has a 30% higher death rate for all cancers in US blacks than in US whites; and diabetes in Hispanics, who are twice as likely to die of this disease than non-Hispanic whites. Native Americans have a life expectancy that is less than the national average, whereas Asians and Pacific Islanders are considered among the healthiest population groups. However, within the Asian and Pacific Islander population, health outcomes are more diverse. Solutions to health and healthcare disparities among ethnic and racial populations must be accomplished through research to improve care. Consider how these disparities in disease and in healthcare services might affect the healthcare providers in the workplace in relationship to their ethnic or racial group. Increasing healthcare providers' knowledge of such disparities is necessary to more effectively manage and treat diseases related to ethnic and racial minorities, which increasingly might include themselves. Consider also what disparities exist in the workplace. Are all employees treated fairly? Do we value the views of various groups or those of only some groups?

The healthcare system in the United States has consistently focused on individuals and their health problems, but it has failed to recognize the cultural differences, beliefs, symbolisms, and interpretations of illness of some people as a group. As health care moves toward provision of care for populations, culture can have an even greater influence on approaches to care. Often, patients for whom healthcare practitioners provide care are newcomers to health care in the United States. Similarly, new staff are commonly neither acculturated nor assimilated into the cultural values of the dominant culture.

Currently, accessibility to health care in the United States is linked to specific social strata. This challenges nurse leaders, managers, and followers who strive for worth, recognition, and individuality for patients and staff regardless of their ascribed economic and social standing. Beginning nurse leaders, managers, and followers may sense that the knowledge they bring to their job lacks "real-life" experiences that provide the springboard to address staff and patient needs. In reality, although lack of experience may be slightly hampering, it is by no means an obstacle to addressing individualized attention to staff and patients. The key is that if the nurse manager and staff respect people and their needs, economic and social standings become moot points. This challenge will intensify as the implications of the Patient Protection and Affordable Care Act of 2010 and subsequent changes unfold. If nothing else happens, the diversity of insured patients will increase. Even in the culture of the military, where rank carries numerous privileges, respecting people and their needs is a driving force in providing care.

LANGUAGE

Translating a message in one language to another language to ensure equivalence includes maintaining the same meaning of the word or concept. Equivalency is accomplished through interpretation, which extends beyond "word-for-word" translation to explain the meaning of concepts. When providing care to a language-diverse patient, the nurse must realize that the process of translation of illness and disease conditions and treatment is complex and requires certain tasks. Two important tasks are "(a) transferring data from the source language to the target language and (b) maintaining or establishing cross-cultural semantic equivalence" (International Council of Nurses, 2008, p. 5).

The current practice seems to be one of using interpreters rather than translators when speaking with non–English-speaking patients and clients. Why? Purnell and Paulanka (2008) advocate that trained healthcare providers as interpreters can decode words and provide the right meaning of the message. However, the authors also suggest being aware that interpreters might affect the reporting of symptoms, using their own ideas or omitting information. Therefore nurses must allow time for translation and interpretation and clarification of information as needed.

Promotion of culturally competent care with a translator has legal implications in the United States. The legal

LITERATURE PERSPECTIVE

Resource: Gregory, C. (2017). Effective communication for a global workforce. *Nurse Leader, 15*(6), 392-395.

Because of the increasing numbers of foreign-born healthcare workers, how to create clear communication becomes even more critical than it has been. This article addresses accented speech, meaning the sound of English words spoken by someone who speaks English but has a different tonality to speech than found in the United States. A hospital system committed to helping international nurses be better understood in the culture in which they now worked. To achieve this, the system created an educational program ACCENT: A, *accentuate* your unique background; C, *communicate* slowly, clearly, and confidently; C, *communicate* reflectively (repeat back);

E, empathize; N, *narrate* your care; and T, *therapeutic* touch, smile, and other nonverbal cues (p. 394). This approach was integrated into the Studer Group's approach known as *AIDET* (acknowledge, introduce, duration, explanation, and thank you). A key outcome associated with this program is an 8% less turnover rate for nurses who participate in this program.

Implications for Practice
Because the numbers of workers from other parts of the world are likely to increase over the next decades, being proactive about helping with numerous aspects of acculturation is important. Communication clearly is one of those important aspects.

foundation for language access lies in Title VI of the 1964 Civil Rights Act, which states: "No person in the United States, on the ground of race, color, or national origin, be excluded from participation in, be denied the benefit of, or be subjected to discrimination under any program or activity receiving federal financial assistance" (Chen, Youdelman, & Brooks, 2007). The federal government has interpreted and treated language as a proxy for national origin, and language assistance should be pursued. These activities supported by the Civil Rights Act include access to health care. Additionally, once a healthcare provider accepts any federal funds (e.g., Medicaid payments), the provider is responsible for providing language access to all the provider's patients.

One often overlooked need for language competency relates to generational and regional differences. Word choices of millennials, as an example, often differ from those of Gen X or Baby Boomers. In addition, what someone living in Louisiana may call something may differ dramatically from someone from Vermont. Formal translations services for such differences do not exist, so seeking clarity from the person becomes critical.

In many organizations, several nurses typically come from other cultures and languages. As the Literature Perspective shows, deliberate strategies can promote self-esteem with the end goals of cross-cultural understanding and effective patient care.

MEANING OF DIVERSITY IN THE ORGANIZATION

Leading and managing cultural diversity in an organization means managing personal thinking and helping

others think in new ways. Nursing leaders need a workforce that can provide culturally competent care; in essence, not having this can lead to unsafe care. In addition, nursing's goal is to create a workforce that reflects the population it serves. This diversity can occur across roles, including advanced practice registered nurses, managers, and chief nurse executives.

Managing issues that involve culture—whether institutional, ethnic, gender, religious, or any other kind—requires patience, persistence, and much understanding. One way to promote this understanding is through shared stories that have symbolic power.

EXERCISE 4.3 Think of a recent event in a clinical area, such as a project, task force, celebration, or something similar. What meaning did people give the event? Was it viewed as being a symbol of some quality of the workplace, such as its effectiveness, its values and beliefs, or its innovations? Or was it seen as a meaningless gesture? What makes an event relevant and value-centric?

Staff who know what is valuable to patients and to themselves can act accordingly and derive satisfaction from work. Having a clear mission, goals, rewards, and acknowledgment of efforts leads to greater productivity from a culturally diverse staff who aspire to unity and uniqueness. As the Literature Perspective illustrates, leaders have an obligation to create an inclusive culture.

LITERATURE PERSPECTIVE

Resource: Aurilio, L.A. (2017). Creating an inclusive culture for the next generation of nurses. *Nurse Leader, 15*(5), 315-318.

By 2060, over half of the US population will derive from a minority race or ethnic group, and they often have experienced (or are experiencing) health disparities. Nurses who have these diverse backgrounds not only understand the statistics and reports but also, in some cases, the lived experiences. This distinct combination of knowledge and experience creates the opportunity to address health inequities from a different perspective.

An inclusive culture where differences are embraced allows teams to leverage their distinctiveness, which in turn can support creativity and innovation. To create such teams, leaders must identify their personal biases and create respectful environments, to name two key commitments. Box 4.1 identifies 8 key commitments leaders can make to create an inclusive environment.

Implications for Practice

Most of the 8 commitments can be adopted—or adapted—by individuals or teams, even in an environment where leaders have not committed to inclusion. Without these commitments being ingrained in the workplace, nurses (and others) will be ill-prepared to address the needs of patients in the future.

BOX 4.1 Key Commitments to Creating Inclusion

- Identify unconscious biases.
- Understand team differences.
- Create a respectful social environment.
- Provide flexible scheduling.
- Support ongoing professional development.
- Create social support systems.
- Create effective communication systems.
- Empower staff through shared governance.

When assessing staff diversity, the nurse leader or manager can ask these two questions:

- What is the cultural representation of the workforce?
- What type of team-building activities are needed to create a cohesive workforce for effective healthcare delivery?

CULTURAL RELEVANCE IN THE WORKPLACE

Although the literature has addressed multicultural needs of patients, it is sparse in identifying effective methods for nurse managers to use when working with multicultural staff. Differences in education and culture can impede patient care, and uncomfortable situations may emerge from such differences. For example, staff members may be reluctant to admit language problems that hamper their written communication. They may also be reluctant to admit their lack of understanding when interpreting directions. Psychosocial skills may be problematic as well, because non-Westernized countries encourage emotional restraint. Staff may have difficulty addressing issues that relate to private family matters. Non-Asian nurses may have difficulty accepting the intensified family involvement of Asian cultures. The lack of assertiveness and the subservient physician–nurse relationships of some cultures are other issues that provide challenges for nurse managers. Unit-oriented workshops arranged by the nurse manager to address effective assertive techniques and family involvement as it relates to cultural differences are two ways of assisting staff with cultural work situations. Respecting cultural diversity in the team fosters cooperation and supports sound decision making.

Nurse leaders and managers who ascribe to a positive view of culture and its characteristics effectively acknowledge cultural diversity among patients and staff. This includes providing culturally sensitive care to patients while simultaneously balancing a culturally diverse staff. For example, cultural diversity might mean being sensitive to or being able to embrace the emotions of a large multicultural group comprising staff and patients. Unless we understand the differences, we cannot come together and make decisions that are in the best interest of the patient.

Transculturalism sometimes has been considered in a narrow sense as a comparison of health beliefs and practices of people from different countries or geographic regions. However, culture can be construed more broadly to include differences in health beliefs and practices by gender, race, ethnicity, economic status, sexual preference, age, and disability or physical challenge. Thus when concepts of transcultural care are discussed, we should consider differences in health beliefs and practices not only between and among countries but also between and among, for example, races, ethnic groups, genders, and different economic strata. This requires us to consider multiple factors about all individuals. One strategy to initiate discussion about differences is to ask what everyone does on New Year's Day. Every culture marks a new year, even though the date may not be January 1. Asking about family traditions regarding food and activity allows us to gain a perspective that we all may differ, even within a defined culture, yet we all acknowledge starting a new year may have special meaning.

The range of attitudes toward culturally diverse groups can be viewed along a continuum of intensity (Lenburg et al., 1995, p. 4) from hate to contempt to tolerance to respect and ending with celebration/affirmation. Managers need to be aware of this continuum so that they can apply strategies appropriately to the workforce—for example, contempt versus affirmation. Both responses are reflected in employee groups. The goal is to move from acknowledging differences to inclusion.

Variables that may influence the nurse's response may include how the illness is perceived by the culture and the cultural competency of the healthcare provider. If the nurse's culture is different from the patient's, whose cultural perspective dominates? It might not be possible to adapt care totally to the patient's perspective. However, knowing that a difference exists allows for a mutual conversation related to the rationale for care. Similarly, if a workplace dispute occurs, trying to see "the other view" can create new insights into a situation.

To make cultural competence relevant to clinical practice, Engebretson, Mahoney, and Carlson (2008) linked a cultural competency continuum, in which they identified the levels of competence, to values in health care. They cited the levels as cultural destructiveness, cultural incapacity, cultural blindness, cultural precompetence, and proficiency that would be complementary to patient care. The "clinically relevant continuum" included behaviors of maleficence, incompetence, standardization, and outcomes focused (positive health outcomes). A model was developed that integrated the cultural competence continuum with the clinically relevant continuum and the components of evidence-based care; namely, best research practice, clinical expertise, and patients' values and circumstances. The goal was to suggest how to make cultural concerns relevant to clinical practitioners at the level of the patient–provider encounter.

To understand, value, and use diversity, nurse managers need to approach every staff person as an individual. This same strategy works for all of us. Although staff of different cultural groups may be diverse in appearance, values, beliefs, communication patterns, and mannerisms, they have many things in common. Staff members want to be accepted by others and to succeed in their jobs. With fairness and respect, nurse managers should openly support the competencies and contributions of staff members from all cultural groups with a goal of achieving quality patient care. Nurse managers hold the key to allowing the full potential of each person on the staff.

Body movements, eye contact, gestures, verbal tone, and physical closeness when communicating are all part of a person's culture. For the nurse manager, understanding these cultural behaviors is critical in accomplishing effective communication within a diverse workforce population. As if language differences are not challenging enough, add on the slang, idioms, and fads inherent to US culture. It is no surprise that culturally sensitive communication is difficult to achieve. Nurses need to ensure that ineffective communication among staff, with patients, and with others does not lead to misunderstandings and eventual alienation.

Failure to address cultural diversity leads to negative effects on performance and staff interactions. Nurse managers can find many ways to address this issue. For example, in relation to performance, a nurse manager can make sure messages about patient care are received. This might be accomplished by sitting down with a nurse and analyzing a situation to ensure that understanding has occurred. In addition, the nurse manager might use a communication notebook that allows the nurse to slowly "digest" information by writing down communication areas that may be unclear. For effective staff interaction, the nurse manager also can make a special effort to pair mentors and mentees who have different ethnic backgrounds and encourage staff to learn another language, one prominent among the population served. Even a "word a day" approach could alter a team's ability to interact with patients.

EXERCISE 4.4 During one of your group meetings, have everyone share one or two slang words that may have a different meaning for different groups of people. After this meeting, have one in your group post a list of the words and meanings discussed in the meeting. Allow everyone to continue to add slang words that staff members use that may create confusion or misunderstanding. Reviewing the list regularly allows staff to understand phrases and, in some instances, to gain a cultural perspective connected to the phrase.

INDIVIDUAL AND SOCIETAL FACTORS

Nurse managers must work with staff to foster respect of different lifestyles. To do this, nurse managers need to accept three key principles: multiculturalism, which refers to maintaining several different cultures; cross-culturalism, which means mediating between/among cultures; and transculturalism, which denotes bridging significant differences in cultural practices. Each of those principles operates in the workplace. Sometimes we want to keep distinct cultures. For instance, we may advocate for equality unless a particular unit has excellent safety scores. Anyone who wanted to make all cultures alike, and thus increase safety incidents, would be seen as foolish. Healthcare organizations have, as an example, provided various ways to celebrate holy days based on the cultural mix of staff and patients. These practices are designed to acknowledge the individuals who comprise the organization.

When promoting cultural competency within different lifestyles, nurses must also explore the nursing care of the LGBT (or the subsequent group recognitions) patients and staff. LGBT has been an acronym that is typically tied together to suggest homogeneity (Ard & Makadon, 2012). The acronym represents lesbian, gay, bisexual, and transgendered (and subsequent others) and has referred to the behavior, identity, and desire of each group. This broader group has long been addressed as a minority within a wide range of races, ethnicities, ages, and socioeconomic statuses. Often this group has been discriminated against, with healthcare needs not being addressed because of this discrimination. People who define themselves in this gender-identification diverse manner find challenges in accessing culturally competent health services. The T, transgendered, has long held additional subcategories under its name. This adds an additional layer of cultural understanding. For example, in healthcare settings, the term *Male to Female (or MTF) transgendered* is used to describe a person born with male genitalia but who identifies as a female. Female to Male, or FTM, is the reverse. Some people reject the nature of gender and see themselves as neither and commonly are referred to as androgynous.

More nurses and nurse managers must embrace the increasing demographics within this diverse community. This increasing population has seen a history of bias, which has continued to challenge access to care despite the increasing social acceptance. This bias was defined in health care, and until 1973 homosexuality was listed as a disorder in the Diagnostic and Statistical Manual of Mental Disorders (DSM) (National LGBT Health Education Center, 2016). This stigma and discrimination, combined with a lack of access to culturally competent and individualized health care, result in health disparities for the gender-diverse community. Some of these health disparities include higher rates of smoking, depression, anxiety, substance abuse, and violence victimization. The Department of Health and Human Services Healthy People 2020 and the National Academy of Medicine Report both acknowledge these disparities and have asked for steps to address them.

One of the steps in addressing these disparities starts with creating an inclusive environment. Something as simple as changing intake forms can provide a sense of belonging. "As of 2016, HRSA (Health Resources & Services Administration) requires health centers to report sexual orientation and gender identity data in the uniform data system" (The National LGBT Health Education Center, 2016). These forms of data, whether during the history-taking assessment, on paper forms, or electronically, should all pay attention to the sexual orientation and gender identity of the patient.

Providing such culturally competent care and understanding is not limited to patients in the healthcare setting, but also includes the staff within this community. The correct terminology and nonjudgmental support needs to be provided to the nursing staff and healthcare team members. Doing so will facilitate a positive and inclusive work setting. Taking steps to understand the varied cultures will also help clinicians ensure their gender-diverse patients, as well as all of their patients, receive the most positive level of health.

EXERCISE 4.5 Create a group of 4 to 6 people. Ask each group member to write down four to six cultural beliefs that he or she values. When everyone has finished writing, have the group members exchange their lists and discuss why these beliefs are valued. When everyone has had a chance to share lists, have a volunteer compile an all-encompassing list that reflects the values of your workforce. (The key to this exercise is that many of the values are similar or perhaps even identical.)

Cultural differences among groups should not be taken in the context that all members of a certain group or subgroup are indistinguishable. For example, regarding gender differences, women are perceived to have a more participative management style; however, this does not mean that all male managers use an authoritative management model. Likewise, female managers may use multiple sources of information to make decisions, and this does not mean that all male managers make decisions on limited data. Thus the norm for gender recognition should be that women and men be hired, promoted, rewarded, and respected for how successfully they do the job, not for who they are, where they come from, whom they know, or the gender they represent.

In today's workplace, female-male collaboration should provide efficacious models for the future. Gender does not determine response in any given situation. However, men reportedly seem to be better at deciphering what needs to be done, whereas women are better at collaborating and getting others to collaborate in accomplishing a task. Men tend to take neutral, logical, and objective stands on problems, whereas women become involved in how the problems affect people. Women and men bring separate perspectives to resolving problems, which can help them function more effectively as a team on the nursing unit. Men and women must learn to work together and value the contributions of the other and the differences they bring to any situation. Similar kinds of comparisons can be made related to other elements of diversity. Nurses have embraced information related to generational differences and have used religious and ethnic contexts as ways to begin dialogs about values and beliefs (Fig. 4.1).

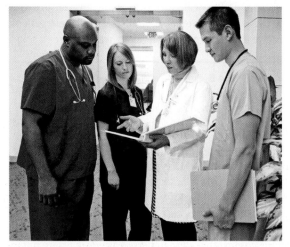

Fig. 4.1 A diverse workforce brings a richness of perspectives to care.

DEALING EFFECTIVELY WITH CULTURAL DIVERSITY

The first individuals in most organizational structures who have to address cultural diversity are the leaders and managers. They have to give unwavering support to embracing diversity in the workplace rather than using a standard cookie-cutter approach. Creating a culturally sensitive work environment involves a long-term vision and financial and healthcare provider commitment. Leaders and managers need to make the strategic decision to design services and programs especially to meet the needs of diverse cultural, ethnic, and racial differences of staff and patients. Policies in healthcare organizations prohibit discrimination based on several aspects. Such policies, however, do not necessarily succeed at promoting a culturally aware environment.

Nurse managers hold the key to making the best use of cultural diversity. Managers have positions of power to begin programs that enrich the diversity among staff. For example, capitalizing on the knowledge that all staff bring to the patient is possible for better quality care outcomes. One method that can be used is to allow staff to verbalize their feelings about particular cultures in relationship to personal beliefs. Another is to have two or three staff members of different ethnic origins present a patient-care conference, giving their views on how they would care for a specific patient's needs based on their own ethnic values.

Mentorship programs should be established so that all staff can expand their knowledge about cultural diversity. Mentors have specific relationships with their mentees. The more closely aligned a mentor is with the mentee (e.g., same gender, age group, ethnicity, and primary language), the more effective the relationship. Programs that address the staff's cultural diversity should not try to make people of different cultures pattern their behavior after the prevailing culture. Nurse managers must carefully select mentors who ascribe to transcultural, rather than ethnocentric, values and beliefs. A much richer staff exists when nurse managers build on the valuable culture of all staff members and when diversity is rewarded. The pacesetter for the cultural norm of the unit is the nurse manager. For example, to demonstrate commitment to cultural diversity, a nurse manager might make a special effort to ensure that US black, Asian American, and Hispanic holidays or other cultural representations on the unit are recognized by the staff. Staff members who are active participants in these programs can then be given positive reinforcement by the nurse manager. These activities promote a better understanding and appreciation of individuals' cultural heritage.

Nurse managers are aware of the increasing shortage of nurses, demanding work environment with its surrounding influences, and statistics indicating that many leave their first professional nursing position by the first year because of job dissatisfaction and level of stress. Nursing workforce projections indicate the registered nurse (RN) shortage will continue at dramatic rates.

This period may be even more challenging for individuals whose culture differs from the predominant unit culture.

Continuing-education programs should help nurses learn about the care of different ethnic groups. Professional organizations related to cultural groups have an opportunity for education within the larger community. Examples of these groups include the National Black Nurses Association, National Hispanic Nurses Association, Philippine Nurses Association of America, Nurse Christian Fellowship, and Association of Jewish Registered Nurses. Some groups may want to develop or sponsor a workshop or conference on cross-cultural nursing for nursing service staff and faculty in schools of nursing who have had limited preparation in cultural care or cultural beliefs in healing.

> **EXERCISE 4.6** Identify a situation in which working with culturally diverse staff had positive or negative outcomes. If a negative outcome resulted, what could you have done to make it a positive one? If a positive outcome resulted, what strategies could you use in another situation?

Muslims are one of the fastest growing populations in the United States and worldwide. For example, Muslim nurses may feel uncomfortable without long sleeves because of their Islamic dress code. Jewish nurses likely would find a pulled pork barbeque an inappropriate celebration. Males may feel awkward participating in a unit baby shower. The point of all of these examples is to think proactively, ask for input, and consider how best to exhibit cultural sensitivity.

Choices, decisions, and behaviors reflect learned beliefs, values, ideals, and preferences. The goal of communication is maintenance or restoration of personal integrity and recognition of worth and respect of individuals or groups.

The two scenarios described in Box 4.2 on p. 74 illustrate how problem-solving communication can promote mutual understanding and respect. The first scenario involves a compromise between staff members and a patient's family, and the second involves a nurse manager and a staff member from a different culture.

> **EXERCISE 4.7** Identify a situation involving a staff member requesting additional days of leave that required a culturally sensitive decision. What religious or ethnic practices did you learn about in regard to this request and decision?

Passages of life that culminate in happy events also can challenge the nurse manager—for example, the quinceañera observed by Hispanic families. This event is the celebration for 15-year-old girls to be introduced into society. A nurse whose daughter is celebrating this event must have time to make plans for this festive celebration. Because of the significance of the celebration and the pride that the parents take in their daughter, inviting "key" staff to the quinceañera is common. Nurse managers who understand and value cultural rituals can help individuals meet their needs and help staff, in general, learn and accept various cultural practices and perspectives.

> **EXERCISE 4.8** Holiday celebrations have cultural significance. Select a specific holiday such as Chinese Lunar New Year (China and Chinatowns) or Araw ng mga Patay (Philippines) or Diwali (India). What is the cultural meaning of the specific holiday? How do staff members of the respective culture celebrate the festive day? Does the nursing unit engage in recognition of special holidays?

IMPLICATIONS IN THE WORKPLACE

Considering culture from a healthcare staff perspective and the nursing workforce perspective is a daunting task, one that can lead to a more solidly aligned service–community relationship. Even if the workforce is not as diverse as one might desire, learning about the cultures of the groups within the workforce is important. Making clear that diversity is valued, in fact celebrated, attracts others to engage in the complexity of care. One way is to make clear how staff are valued as people, not

BOX 4.2   Problem-Solving Communication: Honoring Cultural Attitudes Toward Death and Dying

Scenario 1: Staff and a Patient's Family

What nurses often call interference with the care of a patient commonly reflects family attitudes toward death and dying. Often, Hispanic families rush to the hospital as soon as they hear of a relative's illness. Because most Hispanics believe that death is the passing of an individual to a life that offers tranquility and everlasting happiness, being at the bedside offering prayers and encouragement is the norm rather than the unusual exception. The nurse manager in this situation, herself a non–American-educated nurse manager, had worked extensively at helping her staff understand different cultures. A consensus compromise was worked out between the staff and one such Hispanic family. The family, consisting of three generations, was given the authority to decide what family members could stay at the loved one's side and for how long. By doing this, the family felt they had control of the environment and quickly developed a priority list of family members who could stay no more than 5 minutes at the patient's side. As the family member left the bedside, his or her task was to report the condition of the patient to other family members "camping" in the visitors' lounge. Although their loved one did not survive a massive intracranial hemorrhage, all of the family felt that they were a part of their loved one's "passage of life."

Scenario 2: A Nurse Manager and Another Staff Member

Eastern World cultures that profess Catholicism as their faith celebrate the death of a loved one 40 days after the death. The nurse manager needs to recognize that time off for the nurse involved in this celebration is imperative. Such an occurrence had to be addressed by a nurse manager of Asian descent. The nurse manager quickly realized that the nurse, whose mother died in India, did not ask for any time off to make the necessary burial arrangements but, rather, waited 40 days to celebrate his mother's death. The celebration included formal invitations to a church service, as well as a dinner after the service. One day during early morning rounds, the nurse explained how death is celebrated by Eastern World Catholics. The Bible's description of the Ascension of the Lord into heaven 40 days after his death served as the conceptual framework for the loved one's death. The grieving family believed their loved one's spirit would stay on earth for 40 days. During these 40 days, the family held prayer sessions meant to assist the "spirit" to prepare for its ascension into heaven. When the 40 days have passed, the celebration previously described marks the ascension of the loved one's spirit into heaven.

Because this particular unit truly espoused a multicultural concept, the nurses had no difficulty in allowing the Indian nurse 2 weeks of unplanned vacation so that his mother's "passage of life" celebration could be accomplished in a respectful, dignified manner.

---

as representatives of some group. Showing respect to all patients irrespective of their cultural differences tells the staff that their differences also can be valued. The key is for managers and leaders to attend to the workforce issues with the same zest as they do the patient issues. Cultural differences enrich all of us when we make deliberate efforts to include them in our daily values.

Embracing these differences will also enhance the Quality and Safety Education for Nurses (QSEN) Initiative. The overall goal of the QSEN Initiative is to prepare nurses with the knowledge, skills, and attitudes (KSAs) needed to continuously deliver quality and safe patient care. With this initiative we see the need to respect all patients and staff irrespective of their cultural

differences to empower patient- and family-centered care, which is one of the QSEN initiative competencies. This component recognizes the patient or designee as the source of control and full partner in providing compassionate and coordinated care based on respect for a patient's preferences, values, and needs (American Association of Colleges of Nursing, 2013).

CONCLUSION

Understanding and valuing cultural differences benefits both patients and colleagues. *Culture* is a broad term encompassing many diversities. This broadness both enriches our perspective of diversity and provides a complex challenge. All nurses, regardless of their titles or positions, have a role in improving the workplace and patient care by attending to the implications of culture in health care.

THE SOLUTION

As a nurse manager, I prefer to talk on a one-to-one basis. I had a meeting with the male staff member to learn from him. "What made you upset with the charge nurse when she made your assignment?" In our discussion, he told me, "The charge nurse used words [slang] for which I did not know the meaning ... I did not understand why she said it ... she was trying to overpower me ... I didn't like it ... so I was defensive about it." We talked about being sensitive to cultural communication and the need to understand meanings of words and to ask for immediate clarification when such situations arise with members of two different cultures.

Would this be a suitable approach for you? Why?

Sally C. Fernandez

REFLECTIONS

Consider how many people you know who are different from you in terms of race, ethnicity, gender, age, education, political beliefs, and socioeconomic backgrounds. What knowledge can you transfer to the workplace? What is one goal you could set for achieving a greater understanding of differences and commonalities?

THE EVIDENCE

Numerous studies have demonstrated the importance of understanding and valuing differences in patients' backgrounds to provide high-quality care. Although fewer studies have related to workers in health care, more examples have appeared in recent years that support the value of having an inclusive approach to the workplace culture. Because the culture of the workplace has been shown to be highly influential in people's perception of their work and their intent to stay, being sensitive to what else could be done to enhance the workplace, including inclusion, has potential for positive outcomes.

TIPS FOR INCORPORATING CULTURAL DIVERSITY IN HEALTH CARE

- Listen for differences and seek clarity.
- Value that people follow their perspective of how to act.
- Seek opportunities to experience others' cultures, even from a global perspective.

REFERENCES

American Association of Colleges of Nursing (AACN). (2013). *Quality and Safety Education for Nurses (QSEN) initiative.* Robert Wood Johnson Foundation.

American Nurses Association (ANA). (2015). *Code of ethics for nurses with interpretative statements.* Washington, DC: American Nurses Publishing.

American Nurses Association (ANA). (2016). *Revised Position statement: The nurse's role in ethics and human rights: Protecting and promoting individual worth, dignity, and human rights in practice settings.* American Nurses Association, Inc.

Ard, K. L., & Makadon, H. G. (2012). *Improving the health care of lesbian, gay, bisexual and transgender (LGBT) people: Understanding and eliminating health disparities.* Boston: The National LGBT Health Education Center, The Fenway Institute, Brigham and Women's Hospital, and Harvard Medical School.

Baldwin, D. (2003). Disparities in health and health care: Focusing efforts to eliminate unequal burdens. *Online Journal of Issues in Nursing, 8*(1), 2.

Bennett, J. M. (2014). *Cultural marginality: Identity issues in global leadership training.* In Campinha-Bacote, J. (1999). A model and instrument for addressing cultural competence in health care. *Journal of Nursing Education, 38*(5), 203–207.

Campinha-Bacote, J. (1999). A model and instrument for addressing cultural competence in health care. *Journal of Nursing Education, 38*(5), 203–207.

Campinha-Bacote, J. (2002). The process of cultural competence in a delivery of healthcare services: A model of care. *Journal of Transcultural Nursing, 13*(3), 181–184.

Chen, A. H., Youdelman, M. K., & Brooks, J. (2007). The legal framework for language access in healthcare settings: Title VI and beyond. *Journal of General Internal Medicine, 22*(Suppl. 2), 362–367.

Engebretson, J., Mahoney, J., & Carlson, E. D. (2008). Cultural competence in the era of evidence-based practice. *Journal of Professional Nursing, 24*(3), 172–178.

Giger, J. N., & Davidhizar, R. (2002). The Giger and Davidhizar transcultural assessment model. *Journal of Transcultural Nursing, 13*(3), 185–188.

Hook, J. N., Davis, D. E., Owen, J., Worthington Jr., E. L., & Utsey, S. O. (2013). Cultural humility: Measuring openness to culturally diverse clients. Journal of Counseling Psychology. https://doi.org/10.1037/a0032595.

International Council of Nurses. (2008). *Translation guidelines for International Classification for Nursing Practice (ICNP).* Geneva, Switzerland. www.icn.ch.

International Council of Nurses. (2012). *The ICN code of ethics for nurses* (pp. 1–11). Geneva, Switzerland: ICN-International Council of Nurses.

Leininger, M. (2002a). Cultural care theory: A major contribution to advance transcultural nursing knowledge and practice. *Journal of Transcultural Nursing, 13*(3), 189–192.

Leininger, M. (2002b). Essential transcultural nursing care concepts, principles, examples, and policy statements. In M. Leininger & M. R. McFarland (Eds.), *Transcultural nursing: Concepts, theories, research & practice* (3rd ed). New York: McGraw-Hill Medical Publishing Division.

Lenburg, C. B., Lipson, J. G., Demi, A. S., Blaney, D. R., Stern, P. N., Schultz, P. R., et al. (1995). *Promoting cultural competence in and through nursing education: A critical review and comprehensive plan for action.* Washington, DC: American Academy of Nursing.

Merriam-Webster Inc. (2016). *The Merriam-Webster dictionary.* Springfield, MA: Merriam-Webster.

National LGBT Health Education Center (2016). *Understanding the health needs of LGBT People. A project supported by the Health Resources and Services Administration (HRSA) agreement number U30CS22742.*

Purnell, L. D. (2009). *Guide to culturally competent health care* (2nd ed.). Philadelphia: FA Davis.

Purnell, L. D., & Paulanka, B. J. (2008). *Transcultural health care: A culturally competent approach* (3rd ed.). Philadelphia: FA Davis.

Spector, R. E. (2017). *Cultural diversity in health and illness* (9th ed.). Upper Saddle River, NJ: Pearson Prentice Hall.

Spence, D. (2001). Prejudice, paradox, and possibility: Nursing people from cultures other than one's own. *Journal of Transcultural Nursing, 12*(2), 100–106.

Spence, D. (2004). Prejudice, paradox and possibility: The experience of nursing people from cultures other than one's own. In K. H. Kavanaugh & V. Knowlden (Eds.), *Many voices: Toward caring culture in healthcare and healing.* Madison, WI: The University of Wisconsin Press.

Tervalon, M., & Murray-Garcia, J. (1998). Cultural humility versus cultural competence: A critical distinction in defining physician training outcomes in multicultural education. *Journal of Health Care for the Poor and Underserved, 9*, 117–125.

Waters, A., & Asbill, L. (2013). *Reflections on cultural humility.* American Psychological Association, CYF News.

5

Gaining Personal Insight: The Beginning of Being a Leader

Jeffery Watson, Patricia S. Yoder-Wise

LEARNING OUTCOMES

- Value the need to gain insight into one's self to develop leadership skills.

- Determine how insight into personal talents and abilities can help nurses be effective in their role of nurse and leader.

KEY TERMS

emotional intelligence
formal leadership
informal leader

journaling
personal leadership

reflection
value

THE CHALLENGE

Transitioning to a new nursing specialty involves integrating one's prior knowledge and experience with the essential skills and competencies of the new role. After 9 years of working with critically ill patients in a neurosurgical intensive care unit (ICU), I took a job as a home visiting nurse. I considered myself a very strong nurse with excellent technical skills but quickly realized that home health nursing required a completely different skill set. In the hospital, if I needed supplies, I could easily get them. If I needed to update a physician or clarify orders, they generally responded quickly. Time management was not a problem because most everything we did was on a strict time schedule. I was ready to learn something new and wanted to help people recover from hospitalization in the comfort of their own home.

My first independent visit was to a gentleman with advanced chronic obstructive pulmonary disease (COPD) who was so severely short of breath I was concerned he had been discharged from the hospital too soon. He patted my hand and reassured me that he was having a good day and he only went to the hospital when his breathing "got really bad." Another challenging visit was a person with heart failure who had orders for self-management instruction. His scale was broken and his pantry was mostly bare

(Continued)

except for prepackaged ramen noodles, his preferred meal because they were easy to prepare and stored well between infrequent grocery store visits. Another patient who lived in a high-crime public housing project insisted that he meet me in the parking lot when I arrived and walked me back to my car after I changed his wound dressing. My last scheduled visit of that first week was a routine catheter change. It was only after the patient's cat jumped on the bed and contaminated the sterile field that I realized that was my last Foley insertion kit.

After the first week of home care my confidence was at low ebb. I was aware of social determinants of health but did not realize how people make choices when they can

only afford to fill two of their five hospital discharge prescriptions. I was overwhelmed by the intensity of the patients' needs, the disruption when patients were not home at the time we scheduled, the volume of paperwork, and the chaotic nature of the home environment. I recognized I was a novice again and I was on a learning curve and questioned whether I could succeed as a home care nurse.

What would you do if you were this nurse?

Ellen Martin, PhD, RN, CPHQ
Director of Practice, Texas Nurses Association, Austin, Texas

INTRODUCTION

Approximately 4 million people in the United States are registered nurses. That number seems enormous when we think of the numbers in other healthcare disciplines. In part because we are so large in numbers, we also have additional obligations in health care. One of those obligations is to capitalize on the role of leading and following in any position to the end that quality care is rendered.

Leadership is a journey. It is an iterative process, one that may take twists and turns and always contributes to our learning if we exhibit intentionality in our approach to learning. It begins with being an effective follower, and it never ends. Our task is to continue to develop personally and professionally so that our talents match the tasks we need to address and those evolve over our careers.

Being proactive about learning is a key strategy to developing effective followership and evolving that into effective leadership. That means we have to be mindful of our actions and the motivations behind those actions. As an example, some people think about leadership in terms of power, "being in charge," and fame and glory. When someone exerts leadership from that perspective, he or she may have followers, but they commonly are not really engaged with the mission of the work they are doing. They may even behave very differently depending on the physical presence of the leader. An opposite example can be found when leadership derives from the desire to help others be their best. When leadership is exerted from that perspective, followers are engaged in the mission of their work and they behave

consistently—with or without the formal leader being present.

Our task in leadership is to promote a focus on person- (or population-) centered care with the goal of providing the most accessible, least costly, and highest quality outcomes. To achieve that, we need the vision of each of us contributing something critical to the work at hand. This view of leadership is shared, meaning that one person may hold a title that conveys a position of ultimate authority and yet each person has the potential to step forward and lead the work when that person is the one most capable of a particular element of work.

We can learn leadership through multiple avenues. For example, attending professional association meetings, reading, and connecting with others at a local, state, or national level allow us to learn from others about their development as a leader. This chapter looks at some established tools and strategies that will help us individually even if we are not ready to discuss our leadership journey with someone else.

INFORMAL AND FORMAL LEADERSHIP

When people think of leadership, they typically think of position. Those types of positions have official-sounding titles: president, chief executive, director, etc. That leadership is positional and therefore formal. The assumption is that people in formal leadership roles exert influence over others and that they are "in charge." The other type of leadership is informal. Organizations do not typically have a titled position of Informal Leader, but if we are a member of a team, we know who these people are.

By its very nature, the term informal leaders means that they do not hold formal positions and they do not have official authority for a group (Ross, 2014). Rather, informal leaders are those individuals who influence others because they are engaged with those who listen to and follow the informal leaders. These individuals are often the "behind the scenes" people who motivate others to act. Wise formal leaders acknowledge that they do not have all the answers and thus look to their informal leaders whose talents may differ from their own.

Informal leaders are either the formal leaders' closest allies or their worst fears. When the formal leader and the informal leader(s) are in concordance, great outcomes can be produced. When such does not exist, a lot of energy is expended on working around the other person(s) and creating an appearance of productivity rather than actually being productive.

Although only a small percentage of registered nurses will hold formal leadership positions, all of us are expected to accept the obligation to lead when we are the ones best suited to the work. As a result, all of us have a need to know about how we learn to be better at leading.

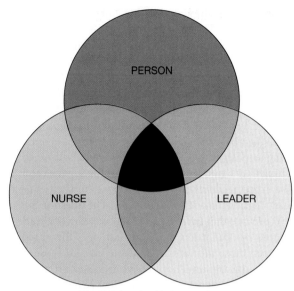

Fig. 5.1 Leadership integration.

EXERCISE 5.1 Consider your recent clinical work. Someone was "in charge." What did you or someone else do to illustrate informal leadership?

EXERCISE 5.2 Review your state's nurse practice act to identify the legal definition of nurse and nursing. What key words suggest leadership expectations?

THE CORE OF LEARNING TO BE A LEADER

Personal leadership is an integration of you, your ideas, and your personhood, into the path you set for your life. It is the ability to lead from your core values and beliefs. Leadership is not a part that you play to fulfill a role responsibility; rather, it is a role responsibility that comes to life because of who you are. Incorporating your unique qualities into to the role of leader is a function of both living and learning. Fig. 5.1 suggests that being a nurse is integral to who we are as individuals and that being a leader overlaps both nurse and person, because we can exert leadership in our personal and professional lives. We are the sum of our life experiences, bringing the fullness of our personhood to the other roles we

fulfill. In this case we are referring to the role of nurse and leader. Sometimes all three elements intersect, indicating that all the roles we assume in life are influenced by all others.

Kouzes and Posner (2012) developed one of the most widely used models for considering leadership (see the Theory Box). Although this model is used widely in other fields, the key for us is that it is used widely in nursing and health care. The five elements of their model begin with *modeling the way*. Basically, that means if we want others to be civil, we must be that way too. *Inspire a shared vision* is an expectation of a formal leader, yet informal leaders contribute to this by

---

THEORY BOX

Theory/ Contributor	Key Ideas	Application to Practice
Kouzes & Posner: The Leadership Challenge (2012)	Model the way Inspire a shared vision Challenge the process Enable others to act Encourage the heart	This approach to leadership provides a view of how to lead and develop others and how to remain personally relevant in leadership

taking such actions as translating a big picture vision to the practicalities faced in the roles of the members of the team. Members of the team, any of whom may exhibit leadership, have the obligation to *challenge the process.* We can all do this by asking questions or posing scenarios to help clarify how something is possible across a wide range of situations. *Enable others to act* refers to how we help others find the conditions that allow them to do their best. Finally, *encourage the heart* is about creating a positive work environment and self-renewal. Think for a moment about the feedback you receive. We expect feedback from those "above" us such as team leader, manager, or clinical director. The question is: Do you provide that same type of feedback to your leader? People in leadership positions are in "the middle" between those they are accountable for and those they are accountable to. They receive feedback from those to whom they report. An opportunity to exert leadership is to provide feedback to those individuals who seldom receive input from those they are accountable for. How powerful you can be if you take this model to heart! And, how do we enhance our current leadership skills? The answer begins with understanding one's self.

At the core of leadership is awareness. Don Miguel Ruiz, in his classic text, *The Four Agreements* (1997), presents a set of agreements we can make with ourselves to enhance personal growth and awareness. These agreements focus on how we present ourselves to self and others and how we act in and interact with the world around us. These four agreements also can serve as core of who we are as leaders (Box 5.1).

The First Agreement: Be Impeccable With Your Word

To *be impeccable with your word* means to maintain principled use of the words we speak about others and ourselves. It means to speak in truth. As leaders, we must use language that reinforces integrity of practice and honors humanity. In other words, leadership is demonstrated when we speak with integrity and when we follow through on our words. Being impeccable with your word is foundational to developing trust and reliability as a leader. Because trust is so critical to the functioning of any group, being true and truthful is highly critical.

EXERCISE 5.3 Think of a situation where someone promised to do something and then did not follow through. Recall how you felt and how your view of that person might have changed. If you pursued a discussion about the lack of follow through, do you recall what the response was and how that affected your thinking about the person?

The Second Agreement: Don't Take Anything Personally

Personalizing every comment or action others make moves you away from the core of who you are. Listening and engaging in discussion are vital leadership skills. However, what others say is reflective of their reality, not yours. You will encounter numerous opinions about you, your work, your ideas, your philosophies, and so forth. Realizing those opinions are not about you but are rather a reflection of the person voicing those views frees you from self-imposed judgment. That said, we also need to acknowledge that some communication may be directed personally. A readily available example can be found in almost any political race. Deliberately destructive communication can also be found in toxic workplaces where incivility is tolerated. Although both examples are personally based, they actually say more about the originator than the target.

EXERCISE 5.4 Recall a situation when you believed your ideas or you yourself were being attacked by someone's statements. What was your reaction? What would your reaction be if you said to yourself: "That statement is that person's response. I wonder what made him feel that way."

BOX 5.1 The Four Agreements

- Be impeccable with your word.
- Don't take anything personally.
- Don't make assumptions.
- Always do your best.

The Third Agreement: Don't Make Assumptions

In conversations, having the willingness to ask clarifying questions provides you the opportunity to avoid making assumptions. Assumptions are created by the imagination when clear communication fails. Personal courage is required to ask deeper questions so you get the information you want and need. Leaders in health care must avoid misunderstandings because of the potential risk to human life. As nurses, we would not assume that a medication authorization was what was intended if it fell outside what we know to be established standards. Why then, as leaders, would we attribute a motivation to someone's behavior without testing our assumption?

> **EXERCISE 5.5** Consider again a time when you were interacting with someone and something they said made you feel uncomfortable, distressed, or angry. Did you seek clarification? If so, what did you say or ask? If not, what could you ask that would facilitate an honest rather than defensive response?

The Fourth Agreement: Always Do Your Best

Numerous factors influence how you feel from day to day and even hour to hour. Yet you can commit to doing your best in each circumstance. In making the commitment to always do your best you acknowledge your humanness. You are able to release any looming self-judgment, because you have put forth your best effort. In other words, you have good days, bad days, and in-between days. On each of those days, and indeed, in varying moments throughout the day, your best will vary. And yet, at the end of the day, you want to be able to say "I did my best." Does that mean we would tolerate "I'm doing my best" (and having a bad day) as rationale for subpar performance? Of course not! And we can use this agreement to enhance a group's performance by acknowledging where we are in our performance. The intent of this agreement is to strive to do our best every day.

> **EXERCISE 5.6** Think of a situation in which everything did not go just as planned. Could you say that despite the situation, you did your best? If not, what would have helped you be able to say you did your best?

GAINING INSIGHT INTO SELF

Many organizations and educational programs address the task of developing leaders. Although we encourage you to explore those and select those that meet your personal needs, our attempt here is to use broad concepts and readily available, and least costly, strategies to help develop your insight into self. You may choose to use each of these strategies or you may choose to use only one or two strategies. The key point is that resources exist to help you understand who you are and that capitalizing on the information those resources provide can help enrich your talents as a leader.

Reflection and Journaling

Developing as a leader comes from knowing and understanding your authentic self (Kouzes & Posner, 2012), and learning from experience is a critical skill in developing your potential for leadership. In the exercises in the previous section, you were practicing the art of reflection about the core of leadership. Reflection, exploring the thoughts you have about your experiences, actions, and reactions, is an active process you can use to strengthen your ongoing professional growth. In his foundational work, Schön (1983) described reflection from two different perspectives: thinking-in-action and thinking-on-action. Thinking-in-action occurs when an individual employs existing knowledge to guide behaviors as a situation develops. Thinking-on-action is a recounting of the situation, inviting self-evaluation (Schön, 1983). We often think-in-action as we provide care. We are not as diligent about thinking-on-action (debrief or reflection). Adding that strategy can create new insights and lead to more effective performance.

Consider a cardiac arrest event in an acute care setting. The decision making occurring in the midst of cardiopulmonary resuscitation (CPR) is an example of thinking-in-action. A post-CPR debriefing, reviewing all aspects of the event, after the fact, is thinking-on-action—giving thoughtful consideration to individual and group performance as well as to any technical issues influencing the outcome. The same type of thinking occurs about leadership when you are in a situation in which you think a patient may be harmed and on the spot you intervene. How you decided to act and what you decided to do are thinking-in-action. After the fact, you consider the many factors leading up to the situation, what else you might have done (or done differently), and what you will do the next time such an event occurs. That is an example of thinking-on-action.

Reflection helps you assess the effect your choices have on both yourself and on those around you. Numerous models have been developed to guide reflection and reflective practice. Fig. 5.2 identifies four basic stages

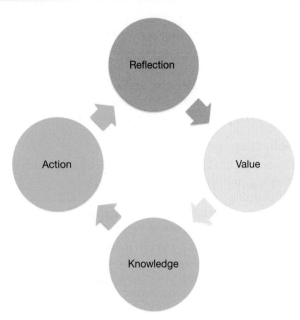

Fig. 5.2 The impact of reflection.

that are common to most reflective practice models: reflection, value, knowledge, and action.

Reflection, the thinking-on-action type, starts when you begin to think about the events of the day. You may choose to take a broad view or focus on a single specific event. The list of questions in Exercise 5.7 is not exhaustive, but you will notice that each experience you have invites other deeply personal questions as you explore the core of who you are as a leader.

> **EXERCISE 5.7** Think of what you did yesterday. You may have been in a clinical setting, or at a religious service, or out to dinner with friends, or at a meeting. As you do so, consider asking questions of yourself to guide the reflection: What happened? Why did I respond the way I did? What precipitated my behavior? Were my values in conflict with others? Did I honor the view of others?

In contemplating and grappling with probing questions, you release yourself to value specific aspects of each experience. Understanding develops about why you felt the way you did in the moment. You have the freedom to study the sources of input that swayed your behavior. You can contemplate different choices that might yield other outcomes. Over time, awareness is raised of your own conduct, and you begin to distinguish more effective patterns for interaction.

Awareness is essential; however, successful leaders go well beyond being aware. Building on self-awareness, leaders cultivate personal insight and new knowledge. A key question at this stage of reflection is: What have I learned about myself and how can I take this knowledge into the future? Leaders embrace new knowledge, making sense of the events of the past and present to develop a plan of action for the future. For example, if you accept that learners learn in different ways, you do not simply tell your team something. You find ways to provide something from the key senses to engage each member in gaining the knowledge you are sharing. You may use a graph to show progress of a new intervention. You may talk with your team about the importance of this work. You might even ask them to manipulate equipment to develop the sensation of a psychomotor skill.

The ultimate goal of reflection is to bolster your leadership acumen. The final stage of the process is action—putting what you have learned into practice. The action stage of reflection is where you test the new knowledge you have gained about yourself. You may discover only incremental improvement toward the desired outcome. If this is the case, you need not worry. With each cycle of reflection you increase your understanding of the leader within. Reflection, as part of leadership development, is a lifelong iterative process. After you act, you recycle through the process again to learn more about what your values are, what knowledge you gained, and what action modifications or replacements you will test next.

A common outcome of reflection in your early stages of development is to focus on what not to do; actively considering what *to do* is equally beneficial and often more reinforcing to us. For example, think about when we started telling people to stop smoking. We did not tell them what to do, just what not to do. As a result, some people who smoked assumed the habit of using chewing tobacco. The point about the harmful effects of tobacco was buried in the focus on what to stop. The incorporation of reflection on a regular basis, however, allows us to move from a narrow thinking of what not to do to the broader thinking about possibilities and what fits with our values.

Reflection occurs through a variety of formats. Writing your thoughts helps make any learning that occurs more concrete (Kouzes & Posner, 2016). Thus journaling, also known as *reflective journaling,* is a method to support the ongoing development of

Fig. 5.3 Keeping a journal allows you to see your personal growth over time. (Copyright © Thinkstock/iStock.)

self-confidence, professional practice, and critical thinking (Fig. 5.3). Journals allow you to retrace your thinking and also to see improvements in your thinking actions.

Because journaling is an individual exercise, you have flexibility to write in your journal at any time. You may choose to use a simple notebook or an e-journal. You might also choose from a variety of guided leadership journals that contain focused themes and questions designed to help direct your thoughts. Box 5.2 describes basic considerations for an individual who is just beginning to journal.

BOX 5.2   Tips for Creating a Personal Journal

1. Determine if you are going to use a hard copy journal or if you are going to do this electronically.
2. Consider how quiet the area might be where you wish to make an entry.
3. Create an entry as soon as possible after an important event so you can remember details, including how you felt.
4. Write in the first person—it is your journal. And don't worry about spelling, etc. Be sure to use abbreviations that are clear to you.
5. Focus on lessons learned. After you make an entry, you need to answer two questions: So what? and What if? "So what" asks whether this was life-changing (or practice-changing) and what you will do. "What if" addresses the idea of alternative thinking so you consider different contexts, players, outcomes, and other ideas.

EXERCISE 5.8 Conduct an Internet search about professional journaling (or reflective journaling) and explore what apps are available to support professional journaling. What rationale for journaling made sense to you? What security was incorporated into any app you explored? Consider how a professional journal might be used to enhance individual leadership skills.

Regardless of the way that you choose to practice reflection, by committing time and energy to this practice you allow yourself an opportunity to grow in clarity around your own beliefs and values and your philosophies about nursing and the core of leadership. You become more adept at integrating the person you are into the professional role of nurse and leader. Reflection is a foundational skill needed to move each of us along the path from individual thought leader to nursing thought leader. Think about it!

Emotional Intelligence

For years, we have focused on test scores, the most common being intelligence tests. Those tests, such as the GRE (Graduate Record Examination) or SAT (Scholastic Assessment Test), are typically used to determine a person's ability to be successful in a graduate program or undergraduate program, respectively. **Emotional intelligence** (EI, or EQ as it is known by some) tests or assessments, however, are typically used by an individual, and to a lesser extent by an organization, to understand what abilities people have in understanding themselves and others. Furthermore, EI can improve and thus is a flexible view of your ability to relate to self and others (Bradberry, n.d.).

Emotional intelligence can be defined as understanding and managing our own emotions with the added social awareness of discerning the emotions of others. Knowing how to identify and use emotions to guide personal behavior and engagement with others is essential for leaders. The core elements of EI, as described in the now classic work, *Emotional Intelligence 2.0* (Bradberry & Greaves, 2009), consist of understanding and then managing yourself (you) and social awareness and how to manage relationships (others). Why is this important to know? Several answers are possible, and one of the most important answers is that people with better EI scores are viewed as more successful. EI is viewed as the basis for numerous skills we use every day as humans, nurses, and leaders. EI is the "single biggest predictor of performance in the workplace and the strongest driver of leadership and personal excellence" (p. 21). Although some of us, at least at some point in our careers, may deny interest in being a leader, who of us wouldn't want to be our personal best? Therefore knowing one's EI would be of great value, and the even better news about EI is that it can be improved.

Being self-aware does not require a process of psychoanalysis. Rather, self-awareness refers to our ability to consider who we are as people. What would we say we do well? What makes us respond with a proverbial "knee jerk" response? What makes us feel confident? Thinking about our "good" and "bad" insights and responses is not geared to categorizing ourselves. It is geared to helping us understand who we are and what we do.

Self-management requires that we act independently for ourselves to strengthen those things we do well and to alter our approach to things we do not do so well. Although we may appreciate someone else pointing out something we need to do differently, our real source of making change is within us. Just knowing how we are is insufficient. We need to determine whether we are going to make adjustments or whether we want to maintain our current state. This aspect of EI is really about aligning ourselves with our goals, and sometimes delaying certain actions or satisfactions to advance toward our goals.

Social awareness now turns the awareness toward others. Think for a moment about Dr. Sheldon Cooper of *The Big Bang Theory* on television. In almost every episode, he is trying to figure out the people around him. He has secured equipment to help him "read people's emotions" and he declares when he understands something is humorous—usually with the intent of garnering concurrence from one of the other members of the cast. Gaining the perspective of another person is what he lacks and what is critically important to working with others. Our observational and listening skills predispose us to being capable of determining what others are experiencing.

Relationship management pulls the first aspects (understanding and managing self and social awareness) together so that you can be effective at responding to people, being clear in expressing your personal assessment of a situation, and creating connections with others that allow you together to be more effective in the work you need to do. Being able to know yourself and others and then manage your own personal reactions allows you to direct energy toward managing a relationship.

EXERCISE 5.9 Conduct an Internet search using the term *emotional intelligence assessments*. What types of assessments are available? Did they identify reliability and validity information? What was the cost range? Were any that seemed useful available online? What could you do with the results of such an assessment?

EXERCISE 5.10 Go to *https://hbr.org/2015/06/quiz-yourself-do-you-lead-with-emotional-intelligence* and complete this online assessment of your E.2. Print or save your results. What did you learn about yourself?

Being able to consider each of these elements and how you can improve your abilities allows for greater success as a leader. Codier and Codier (2017) even suggest that emotional intelligence positively influences patient safety.

Strengths

One of the most widely used self-assessment tools is StrengthsFinder 2.0 (Rath, 2007). Because it has been used worldwide, in numerous cultures, and across all sorts of personal characteristics, this is one of the most tested tools to help people determine their talents for developing strengths. The Research Perspective provides greater detail about the analyses of this tool. If you complete this assessment, you are given your top five strengths, or talents, out of the possible 34 themes. If you complete this assessment with others, you can identify how various themes contribute to the whole of a project or a relationship. Imagine if everyone in your group were deliberative, which is one of the 34 themes. This theme is described as careful, private, and cautious. What would the work look like? Likely, few timelines would be met and very little would be accomplished. However, what was done would have withstood multiple tests of thinking. Now imagine that everyone in your group were competitive. This group would be great to enter into tournaments to represent your organization and, because they are so driven by the need to compete, might dim others' prospects of participating. And we might wonder whether they could ever really reach agreement on a course of action or whether their competitiveness kept them focused on making their own individual points. Fortunately, this tool provides your top five strengths rather than only focusing on one. The authors point out that we can develop any of the strengths; however, our natural tendency is to respond in any given situation with one of our strengths.

RESEARCH PERSPECTIVE

Resource: Asplund, J., Lopez, S.J., Hodges, T, & Harter, J. (2007). *The Clifton's Strengths Finder 2.0 Technical Report: Development and validation.* Princeton, NJ: The Gallup Organization.

  Since the late 20th century, millions of people have used the tool StrengthsFinder (SF) to assess their talents for building certain strengths. This tool has been used worldwide in almost every type of business setting. People of various racial and ethnic backgrounds, living different lifestyles, of various ages and genders have participated in using this tool. Thirty-four themes are assessed via the 177-item online tool. Because all responses enter into the database, the reliability and validity of this tool can be assessed over time. The tool has been subjected to numerous statistical tests and has been found to be reliable and valid.

Implications for Practice
Few people, including nurses, are likely to study the details of this tool. What is valuable for all to know is that the tool is reliable and valid and it is useful in helping people take their talents to a greater potential by focusing on making their strengths their greatest asset.

The key with strengths is to capitalize on those that are *your* talents and to surround yourself with people with other talents that "fill in" the total set of talents needed to accomplish work. No single strength is better than another, except as it relates to some specific activity and goal. You always have to meet the minimum performance expectations for any position in your career. How you will be deemed successful, however, typically derives from practicing and honing your talents so that they become great assets. Leaders need to help others develop their talents to their best potential rather than focusing on those aspects of work that are only acceptable if the goal is to make sure everyone is doing his or her best. As a result, people are focusing on what is positive about themselves and not on what is not among their best talents.

EXERCISE 5.11 Conduct an Internet search using the term *personal strengths assessments*. What types of assessments are available? Did they identify reliability and validity information? What was the cost range? Were any that seemed useful available online? What could you do with the results of such an assessment?

BECOMING AN AUTHENTIC LEADER

Earlier we discussed various leadership theories and models, some of which tend to be more applicable in situations where a person holds a formal title (see Chapter 1). To begin a solid advancement in leadership, one of the most direct models is that developed by George (2003). That model is authentic leadership. Although developing leadership skills is a lifelong journey, being authentic is a good introduction to thinking of oneself as a leader.

  Authentic leadership (Thacker, 2016) focuses on honest relationships (think of Ruiz's statement about being impeccable with your word). How those relationships are formed may be artificial—you are assigned to an organizational task, know none of the people, and have a time frame to accomplish specific goals. In other words, at this point, you are not an organized whole; you are a group. Valuing what each person brings helps others develop trust in you and increases your potential for trusting the others in the group (think of Ruiz's statement about not making assumptions). Exploring with each other what values you hold, how you see the assigned task unfolding, and who has what strengths and talents to contribute to the task are examples of how to build a cohesive team. Yet if we are not authentic in our approach, trust will be at a minimum.

  Being truthful and open is critical to developing as an authentic leader. As George (2003, p. 11) said when he created this view of leadership, "It's being yourself; being the person you were created to be." He goes on to contrast this view of leadership with the idea of creating an image of what a leader is. Thus no matter what list of characteristics you might read, if they are not the real you, trying to adopt those only makes you look fake. That does not mean you should not explore those characteristics or styles. It simply means you will not look as real in leading as you would if you are being the real you. Brooks (2015) refers to these as character strengths. The authentic ones are eulogy virtues; the ones that match

LITERATURE PERSPECTIVE

Resource: Shirey, M.R. (2015). Enhance your self-awareness to be an authentic leader. https://www.americannursetoday.com/enhance-self-awareness-authentic-leader.

Authentic leadership can be assessed by the Authentic Leadership Questionnaire (ALQ) developed by Walumbwa et al. Four scales are used: self-awareness, relational transparency, balanced processing, and internalized moral perspective. Shirey focused on the first element. She identified eight approaches to consider in being better at self-awareness: explore personal strengths and fatal flaws, understand your limitations and seek others to complement you and the team, examine emotional intelligence, observe yourself and engage an observational partner, create down time for daily reflection, dig deep to gain insight, keep a reflective journal, and incorporate time for personal renewal and celebrate milestones.

Implications for Practice

Being self-aware is critical to being an effective leader, especially one who is seen as authentic. Even though the idea of authenticity is being who you are, it is possible to increase skills and abilities in being authentic, and that process begins with being aware of self.

a list of characteristics are resume virtues. The former are the deep virtues you exhibit that you might want said at your funeral; the latter are the virtues that help others see a person–organization fit in a traditional sense.

Being the real you, however, is built on a true caring for others and a desire to help everyone maximize talents so that any group effort is as powerful as possible. As an example, being an authentic leader relies on having a true passion for people and the work in which they engage. Being able to respond to situations in an authentic manner promotes people's personal values. Although this may seem somewhat concerning because some people do not necessarily have values that fit a mission or task, authenticity quickly filters people into those who can achieve a particular goal and those who cannot.

George (2003) developed the concept of authentic leadership having five dimensions: purpose, values, heart, relationships, and self-discipline. The corresponding developments are passion, behavior, compassion, connectedness, and consistency, as Table 5.1 illustrates. Think, as an example, of someone who does not have real compassion. We say that person does not have heart or that person's heart is not in the work.

EXERCISE 5.12 Consider each of the developmental areas listed in Table 5.1 and think of messages we give ourselves (or others) that convey someone is really expert in one of the five dimensions or that ability is lacking. Use the example given for heart and compassion.

So, how does one become better at being an authentic leader? Shirey (2015) offers insight into one key aspect,

TABLE 5.1 Behaviors and Developments of Leading Authentically

Dimensions	Corresponding Developments
Purpose	Passion
Values	Behavior
Heart	Compassion
Relationships	Connectedness
Self-discipline	Consistency

Data from George, B. (2003). *Authentic leadership: Rediscovering the secrets to creating lasting value.* San Francisco, CA: Jossey Bass.

that of self-awareness. The Literature Perspective captures the key points for consideration. If all we developed, as a skill, was awareness of self, think of the potential for further explorations of who we are and the actions we could take to be more—for our patients and ourselves.

CONCLUSION

No matter where anyone is in his or her leadership trajectory, being complacent is not an option. Seeking new insights, using established tools (such as journaling), and wanting to do one's best are lifelong skills that allow each of us to develop our full potential. If leadership is a journey expressed as a skill, each of us has the potential to contribute to the needed changes in health care by starting with a solid knowledge of and value for who we are and what we can become.

THE SOLUTION

Reflecting on that first week as a new home health nurse gave me some important insights. Although I did not feel particularly successful in the beginning, I recognized that I always strive to do my best. I considered how valuable my assessment and critical thinking skills would be in home health for monitoring the health status of people living at home with advanced chronic illnesses. At first, my reflections were focused on the superficial, such as considering each lesson learned the hard way and making a plan to make sure I did not make the same mistakes twice. It was the deeper reflection that allowed me to build on my strengths as a learner and achiever to develop a proactive learning plan to address my knowledge gaps. Beyond learning the tasks and paperwork, reflecting on relational competencies had the most impact on becoming an effective home health nurse.

One breakthrough in self-awareness related to my communication style, which I recognized had to change if I wanted to provide effective patient and family education. In the intensive care unit (ICU) environment, patients and their families are often in crisis, and they are highly dependent on the intense monitoring and frequent interventions provided by the healthcare team. In this context, the norm for patient education involved providing factual information using a directive approach. Although clear and direct communication is helpful in these situations, reflecting on those early encounters in patients' homes made me aware of the ways in which my communication style and assumptions got in the way of therapeutic interactions. Patients and families depend on nurses to provide support and guidance based on nursing knowledge and experience. By engaging the patient and family in a dialogue, rather than a lecture, it became easier to elicit concerns and create a space for them to express concern, such as parts of the treatment plan that would be challenging. The shift to a conversational approach allowed an authentic, collaborative partnership to develop.

Caring for patients and families in their home is deeply personal because it offers a window into the private rhythms of their daily life. Each and every visit is an opportunity to practice deep listening and curiosity about the patient and family perspective on health, illness, and recovery. This is our access to providing truly person-centered care in a way that empowers patients and families to make positive healthcare choices long after discharge from home health services.

Would this be a suitable approach for you? Why?

Ellen Martin

REFLECTIONS

Consider where you want to be in your career in 2 years. What do you need to consider in your personal and professional development? What are one to two first steps you can take to ensure you can reach this career stage?

What do you need to learn about yourself? How will you intentionally use reflection to enhance your leadership skills to be the best nurse possible?

THE EVIDENCE

The successful nurse leader of the future will engage in practices that result in gains in personal insight. Recalling that only a small number of nurses hold official leadership positions, you can and will be called on to lead when a situation calls for one of your strengths. Leadership may find you when you are the only one of a small team and a decision needs to be made.

Leadership is not something that exists outside of you, but rather comes from the core of who you are.

Developing as a leader is rooted in connecting with your most authentic self. Learning to be aware of how you act, react, and respond affords you the opportunity to integrate your full self into the roles of nurse and leader.

In pursuit of authenticity, reflection and journaling are valuable avenues to integrate your work experiences, decisions, and beliefs and values. Using reliable tools that help you identify your strengths will help you find the areas from which you can lead with your authentic self.

TIPS FOR GAINING PERSONAL INSIGHT

- Practice reflection daily.
- Allow what you learn from your reflections to guide your next steps.
- Participate in self-assessments and consider the results.
- Strengthen your strengths.

REFERENCES

Bradberry, R. (ND). Emotional Intelligence-EQ. http://www.forbes.com/sites/travisbradberry/2014/01/09/emotional-intelligence/#4cf302463ecb.

Bradberry, R., & Greaves, J. (2009). *Emotional Intelligence 2.0.* San Diego, CA: TalentSmart.

Brooks, D. (2015). *The road to character.* New York: Random House.

Codier, E., & Codier, D. D. (2017). Could emotional intelligence make patients safer? *American Journal of Nursing,* 117(7), 58-62. https://doi.org/10.1097/01.naj.0000520946.39224.db.

George, B. (2003). *Authentic leadership: Rediscovering the secrets to creating lasting value.* San Francisco: Jossey-Bass.

Kouzes, J. M., & Posner, B. Z. (2012). *The leadership challenge: How to make extraordinary things happen in organizations.* San Francisco: Jossey-Bass.

Kouzes, J. M., & Posner, B. Z. (2016). *Learning leadership: The five fundamentals of becoming an exemplary leader.* San Francisco: Jossey-Bass.

Rath, T. (2007). *StrengthsFinder 2.0.* New York: Gallup Press.

Ross, C. A. (2014). The benefits of informal leadership. *Nurse Leader,* 12(5), 68–70. https://doi.org/10.1016/j.mnl.2014.01.015.

Ruiz, D. M. (1997). *The Four Agreements: A practical guide to personal freedom.* White Plains, NY: Peter Pauper Press.

Schön, D. A. (1983). *The reflective practitioner.* New York: Basic Books.

Shirey, M.R. (2015). Enhance your self-awareness to be an authentic leader. *American Nurse Today, 10*(8), 7. https://www.americannursetoday.com/enhance-self-awareness-authentic-leader.

Thacker, K. (2016). *The art of authenticity: Tools to become and authentic leader and your best self.* Hoboken, NJ: Wiley & Sons.

6

Copyright © Comstock images/iStock/Thinkstock.

Being an Effective Follower

Amy Boothe

LEARNING OUTCOMES

- Envision the goals of the Quadruple Aim in reference to the active follower.
- Understand the difference between Leader, Effective Follower, and Ineffective Follower.
- Define the characteristics and role of the Effective Follower within a healthcare team.
- Compare different theories about followership between nursing and the business world.

KEY TERMS

effective follower
follower
ineffective follower

leader
leader–follower relationship
nursing theories

Quadruple Aim
transformational leadership
model

THE CHALLENGE

I had only been a registered nurse (RN) for a few months when I encountered a situation with a patient that made me question the way his care had been handled by several different disciplines within our healthcare system. This patient was a Hispanic gentleman. I will call him "Mr. A." He was being admitted to our facility for long-term acute care and was on a ventilator. While I was admitting him, I asked his wife all the normal questions and found that she wanted his code status to be do not resuscitate (DNR). I thought it was a little strange because when I received the report, the intensive care unit nurse told me he was a full code, noting that he had just been intubated the day before and placed on the ventilator. I probed, asking the wife more questions to fully appreciate the situation. His wife explained to me that the day before "Mr. A" had begun having more breathing problems. She said that the acute care unit nurse had told her he was getting worse and the oxygen mask was not enough,

they would have to get a machine to help him breathe. The patient's wife agreed and was asked to step out while they worked on him for a few minutes. When the wife returned to the room she was shocked to see they had put a tube down his throat and had him hooked up to a breathing machine. The wife told me she was so upset. (She thought they were going to put him back on the BiPAP machine with the mask that he had been on a few days prior.) She said her husband had told her before he did not want to be placed on any life support machines or have any CPR. She said she questioned the nurse and the nurse told her, "Well it is too late now it has already been done." (It was hard to identify where the communication error occurred between the acute care unit staff and the patient's wife because I was not present for the discussion.) I empathized with the wife's situation and confusion. I explained to her she could change her mind at any time. Even if she had wanted him intubated yesterday and

(Continued)

INTRODUCTION

Following the leader is a concept that is learned at a very early age. Children follow the lead of their parents, schoolchildren follow the leader of the line, adolescents follow whom they perceive is the leader of the group, and adults follow the leaders within their organizations, social groups, and various encounters. This leader and follower concept is mirrored in the workplace as a hierarchy of command. Leaders are said to influence the followers into completing the tasks they are assigned. Educational studies and research projects are plentiful regarding what a leader is, how a leader influences others, what different leadership styles exist, and even what the innate characteristics of a "natural born leader" are. However, very little is known about the follower.

A leader does not have the ability to achieve the vision of the organization alone. A *follower* is defined as being a supporter, who is guided and told what to do. Being a follower is commonly associated with a negative connotation (Malak, 2016). This negative stigma includes words to describe the follower as passive, indecisive, devalued, and the obedient staff within the team. However, this could not be further from the truth. Being a follower does not place the person in a submissive position. The follower has the ability to create influence among other staff and among their leaders (Forbes, 2016); the follower can either advance the leader's goals or divert and limit progress. Within nursing, the follower is often the direct care nurse who is trusted to think critically, ask probing questions about care, and advocate for the patient. Additionally, that probing and advocacy does not turn off in the presence of a patient. Those talents can advance the work of a group

when they are acknowledged and used. This type of independent work is not in any way negative or passive.

RESEARCH ON FOLLOWERSHIP

Literature consistently states the follower plays an important role within the team. Followers are at the bedside more than leaders tend to be, and they gain the trust of patients. In earning this trust, followers are often privy to information that the person in the leadership role does not know, and which may be of significant value in decision making or the plan of care (Malakyan, 2014; Gordon, Rees, Ker, & Cleland, 2015b; Sculli, 2015). Communication opens up the engagement of the leaders and followers and can also increase the trust and influence from and to the leaders and the followers. This open communication increases the confidence and decreases errors and negative outcomes (Gordon et al., 2015b, Malakyan, 2014; Sculli, 2015; Spriggs, 2016).

FOLLOWERSHIP THEORIES

Theories on followership have surfaced within the nursing profession and within the business profession. Nursing has maintained the healthcare hierarchy with limited exploration of the follower/direct care nurse. Within the business world the hierarchy has been challenged by those who have pointed out the importance of what the follower can contribute to the organization's success.

Nursing Theories

One theory on nursing care was developed by *Dorothea Orem* (1980). Orem addressed self-care of patients and described nursing as being needed when patients could not care for themselves or were limited in the care of themselves. Orem's theory described nursing as an action of providing care and educating patients to provide their own care. Orem's theory did not address leadership, but it did address the nurse (follower) as the person who intelligently participates in patient care and educates the patient when needed. Orem places the follower in an active, participatory role within his or her nursing career. The movement from novice nurse to experienced nurse can incorporate this theory into practice and hold the nurse accountable for the needs he or she identifies as lacking within the patient and the care provided.

Patricia Benner (1982) developed the now classic novice-to-expert theory about how nurses progress during their nursing careers. Novice and advanced beginner nurses (followers) rely on what they learned in nursing school to guide their practice, but as they move throughout their careers they also rely on their professional experiences. The leader can play an important role in how novice nurses move throughout the stages of their careers. Being flexible to new ideas through open communication allows nurses to gain even more knowledge by fully experiencing active learning on the job and gaining more experience to develop their expertise in patient care.

Ida Jean Orlando, a nursing theorist, developed a nursing practice model that incorporates both nursing practice and nursing leadership (Orlando, 1961). This theory requires nurses to incorporate their ideas and feelings and to investigate any assumptions they have about the patient. This is a huge step in having nurses (followers) think for themselves. Not only do nurses have instincts about patient care, but also nurses should investigate these instincts to figure out what might be harming or wrong with the patient. This is one of the first types of models that incorporates autonomy and active participation within nursing practice. Orlando called this the *dynamic nurse–patient relationship model* (Orlando, 1961).

Business Theories

Robert E. Kelley decided in 1992 that the world of business needed to pay attention to followers. He stated that leaders do not live or thrive without followers. Kelley's seminal work was to place followers as the central topic with leaders, organizations, peers, and everything else in the periphery. Kelley identified and defined five followership styles by asking questions about the way followers follow. Making use of the different styles, Kelley was able to help organizations understand behaviors and the actions taken by followers (Kelley, 1992).

Ira Chaleff propelled the idea of followership further by describing the courage it takes to become an effective follower within an organization. He strives to bring self-awareness to the ability of followers to courageously question or challenge leaders. Chaleff developed a self-assessment for followers to explain behaviors. The intent of the self-assessment is to identify behaviors among followers to provide reflection. Chaleff stated this is a way to develop followers and help them identify the style of follower they are and move into an effective follower role (Chaleff, 2017). (See the Literature Perspective box.)

Each of these theories contributes to valuing the importance of effective followership. Table 6.1 summarizes these theories.

LITERATURE PERSPECTIVE

Resource: Chaleff, I. (2017). In praise of followership style assessments. *Journal of Leadership Studies, 10*(3), 45-48.

The roles of the leader and follower are not always roles that are solely one person's and static. Most team members will occupy both roles interchangeably or simultaneously within the organizational setting. Chaleff describes the ability to move fluidly into and out of these roles as an area where self-assessment of behaviors should occur. These assessments can be individual, group, or culture. The result will help identify what is needed to know about followers and how they react within their environment.

Implications for Practice

To be effective in any team work, the members of the team (followers) must be as effective at what they do as the leaders are at what they do. Additionally, because leadership is shared and fluid, a leader must be equally capable of transitioning into the role of follower as the follower is in transitioning into the role of leader.

Theorist	Leadership	Followership
Dorothea Orem	Does not address leadership	Participates intelligently in patient care Provides quality care when the patient cannot Educates the patient when needed
Patricia Benner	Plays an important role helping nurses move throughout the stages	Is flexible Is open to new ideas Uses open communication Takes advantage of learning through experience
Ida Jean Orlando	Promotes autonomy Promotes instinctive actions Encourages investigation Listens actively	Incorporates ideas and feelings Engages in instinctive care Investigates assumptions Thinks for self
Robert E Kelley	Defines as nonexistent without followers	Five styles of followers 1. The sheep: passive, do not think for themselves, and no motivation 2. The yes-people: positive, always on the leader's side, look to the leader for thinking and direction, lack vision 3. The alienated: think for themselves, are smart, have negative energy 4. The pragmatics: never the first on board to new ideas; preserve the status quo 5. The star followers: think for themselves, have positive energy, and are active; independently evaluate situations and leadership; offer alternatives to issues; the "go-to" person
Ira Chaleff	Does not address, other than describing the support given by leaders to followers in challenging situations	Does self-assessment Demonstrates courage to speak up Questions leaders Challenges leaders Supports leaders

TABLE 6.1   Theories on Followership

DIFFERENCES BETWEEN LEADING AND FOLLOWING

Leading and following can be visualized within any organization, including and especially within healthcare organizations. However, if we look into the concepts behind each title of leader and follower, we can dive into how they are used within nursing practice. We can see some extreme differences in the characteristics of each one.

Leader

The word leader refers to someone who has the ability to guide people toward a common goal and sets the tone within the unit (Gordon, Rees, Ker, & Cleland,

2015a). Within healthcare organizations and nursing practice, the word *leader* describes a person who does so much more. A leader within this context guides and gives direction to those who are perceived to be subordinate or reliant on them. The leader achieves this level of influence by using active listening and engaging in open communication (Gordon et al., 2015b). The nursing leader does the courageous act of releasing control to create an active learning environment. This release of control allows the leader to share the accountability of decision making with other people within their supervision. Sharing accountability fosters a partnership of trust between leaders and the team members they supervise by inspiring the team members to speak up and voice their opinions and concerns. The leader can handle and adapt to the unknown. Different leadership styles emerge during different crises and everyday situations.

Follower

Followers have the ability to create influence among other staff and their leaders (Forbes, 2016). Within nursing, followers are often the direct care nurse who is trusted to think critically, ask probing questions about care, and advocate for the patient. This type of independent work is not in any way negative or passive. When we think about leadership, we often think only of one element of the equation—the leader. Yet without the follower role, leadership does not actually exist.

Thus the whole process of leadership can be thought of as Fig. 6.1 depicts.

> **EXERCISE 6.1** Name five characteristics of a great leader. Think about a nursing leader you have observed. Does that person match those characteristics? Now, name five characteristics of a great follower. Have you seen a follower exhibit those characteristics? How are the two sets of characteristics similar? How are they different?

Effective Follower

The phrase effective follower identifies an engaged and participating team member who thinks for himself or herself. Effective followers are able to communicate needs and concerns effectively and courageously (Sculli et al., 2015). Effective followers identify the practical aspects of nursing, provide input when needed, and ask questions to clarify. They are positive, and they support the leaders within their organization. Effective followers need leaders who foster professional growth, and in return effective followers can also influence the leader by using intelligent and experience-driven suggestions to solutions about patient care (Sculli et al., 2015). They practice autonomy with decision-making responsibilities and share accountability with their leaders (Mannion, McKimm, & O'Sullivan, 2015). Effective followers are loyal to the organizations and foster partnerships and support leadership in every area of nursing. Followers have the ability to self-manage; have commitment to their organizations; and have competence, focus, and courage (Everett, 2016). The effective follower has the potential to not only influence the leadership but also influence co-workers within the healthcare organization. Positive attitudes can be contagious and increase the morale of the entire unit. Fostering this type of atmosphere will most likely increase productivity and patient outcomes.

Ineffective Follower

The term ineffective followers identifies static team members who rely solely on leadership for all direction and guidance (Malak, 2016). They do not question authority and have a hard time voicing their opinions or concerns because of the traditional hierarchy. The way ineffective followers communicate is through complaining and pointing fingers. They hardly ever offer solutions, only complain about problems. They have no control over their situation and have no loyalty to the healthcare organization in which they work (Forbes, 2016). Ineffective followers are not flexible, and their main concern is just putting in their required number of hours.

Fig. 6.1 The huddle is a brief and precise communication exchange that engages team members to identify any needs or safety issues. (Copyright © Uberimages/iStock/Thinkstock).

> **EXERCISE 6.2** Think of a time when you were involved in a great relationship. What made the relationship great? Was it hierarchical where one person was always the leader and the other was always the follower? Or was it "give and take" depending on the situation? What kind of trust was present? Were you afraid to voice your opinion? Did the other person value your opinion?

LITERATURE PERSPECTIVE

Resource: Malak, R. (2016). A concept analysis of "Follower" within the context of professional nursing. *Nursing Forum 51*(4), 286-294.

The leader and the follower are dynamic and intertwined in the leader–follower relationship. "Followers are practicing more in organizations where governance is shared and the organizational structure is flattened" (p. 286). The effectiveness of the followers and the advancement of the organization, increased trust, and leadership exchange were advanced as outcomes occurring within the leader–follower relationship. This increases the value of engaged and effective followers alongside effective leaders and is increasingly becoming recognized for improved team and organizational performance.

Followers have the expectation for leaders to be "accessible, trustworthy, empathetic, visionary, and to be invested in employee development" (p. 292). "Exemplary and engaged followers are those who show intelligence, commitment, integrity, independence, and courage" (p. 292-293). "Increasing the understanding of the follower and their many levels of impact on nursing practice will help guide how leaders are developed and how engaged followers are cultivated to achieve positive outcomes in all levels of health care" (p. 293).

Implications for Practice
Nurse leaders at every level of the organization need to understand the dynamics of their followers to achieve the aligned vision and goals.

LEADER–FOLLOWER RELATIONSHIP

For a long time within healthcare organizations, the hierarchy of leaders and followers did not permit the development of the leader–follower relationship. The leaders were the source of knowledge and power, and the followers were submissive. This was more like a dictatorship than a true relationship. Fortunately, a shift in thinking occurred away from hierarchies, because the relationship between nursing leaders and followers was defined as circular and not linear, with followers central to leaders, as seen in the Literature Perspective box (Malak, 2016). Simplifying this statement, leaders can become followers and followers can become leaders depending on the situation and expertise and experience of the nurse. With this knowledge, the emphasis on understanding the leader–follower relationship is more important to create a cohesive and productive team.

The relationship between leaders and followers is a true partnership built on trust and accountability. Leaders trust followers to make decisions and speak up about concerns, and followers trust leaders to actively listen and provide guidance and open communication (Forbes, 2016; Gordon et al., 2015b). Communication opens up the engagement, increases the trust, and increases the influence to and from both leaders and followers within this relationship (Malak, 2016).

A cohesive relationship between leaders and followers will reduce skill-based errors because followers are not afraid to ask needed questions, will reduce infection and mortality because the leader will trust the concerns of the followers in detrimental situations, and provide the patients with a better experience (Malak, 2016).

Importance to Nursing Practice
Institute of Medicine/Robert Wood Johnson Foundation Report

Nurses have always contributed to the health and well-being of the populations whom they serve by advocating for improved outcomes. The report conducted by the National Academy of Medicine (formerly known as the Institute of Medicine [IOM]) and the Robert Wood Johnson Foundation (RWJF) expanded the reach of nursing practice to assist with the need from the public for health care. This initiative included ideas such as nurses practicing to the full extent of their training and education and becoming full partners with physicians and other healthcare professionals in redesigning health care (IOM, 2010).

This initiative expands the view of the development of effective followership. Educated and well-trained professionals in nursing with limited experience can feel the weight of the hierarchy ladder on their shoulders. Becoming an effective follower in a learning institution and workforce organization elevates your position and acknowledgment of your skills among your team and gives your voice merit and the ability to be heard. The fact that the National Academy of Medicine is calling for the nursing workforce to be partners with physicians and other healthcare professionals changes the clinical ladder to a clinical round table where all voices can be heard and activated.

TABLE 6.2   How Leaders and Effective Followers Achieve the Quadruple Aim

Quadruple Aim Guidelines	Leader	Effective Follower	Outcomes
1. Enhancing patient experience	Sets the tone on the unit Trusts in the follower's instincts Listens actively to concerns Guides decision making Creates trust	Sees the practical Identifies risks Voices concerns Advocates actively for patients Grows and learns Builds trust	Decreases errors Improves quality of care Improves patient outcomes Engages patients
2. Improving population health	Provides an environment that advocates for high-quality care delivery Uses open communication Encourages participation	Delivers high-quality care to every patient Educates the patient and family Gains the patient's trust to ask questions	Informs populations of patients to return to their communities healthier and more engaged
3. Reducing costs 4. Improving the work life of care providers	Promotes a more productive team Reduces stress by trusting followers Delegates tasks effectively without overloading followers	Commits to increasing productivity Reduces stress by increasing autonomy Commits to the organization Feels accomplished and important because they have a voice	Reduces waste from nonproductive leaders and followers Reduces turnover Increases retention Increases production Results in an effective unit

Quadruple Aim

Nurses in leader or follower roles are expected to fulfill the expectations of the Triple Aim, which the Institute for Healthcare Improvement (IHI) developed in 2008 (Berwick, Nolan, & Whittington, 2008). The Triple Aim's ultimate goal is to improve the health of the communities in which each healthcare organization serves (Bodenheimer & Sinsky, 2014). More recently, the list has increased to include another aim to decrease the incidence of healthcare provider burnout (Bodenheimer & Sinsky, 2014). Guiding healthcare professionals to achieve the quadruple aim will help achieve the goal of improved health while keeping the providers engaged and decreasing turnover. The Quadruple Aim guidelines include the following:

- Enhancing patient experience
- Improving population health
- Reducing costs
- Improving the work life of care providers

The importance of achieving the Quadruple Aim can be emphasized with the engagement of the leader–follower relationship. The outcomes from promoting the leader–follower relationship can be seen in Table 6.2.

A Followership Model

The consensus in the literature is that within the leader and follower relationship, a lot of information is documented about developing and improving the role of the leader. Very little is known about the follower role, but the literature consistently states the follower plays an important role within the team. Identifying the follower as a strength within the relationship has yet to prove the need to actively engage and develop the follower into being an effective member of the team.

Many leadership programs and models have been developed over the years. One model is very close to addressing the leader-follower relationship. This model is the transformational leadership model. Taking this model and transforming it into a followership model (see Box 6.1) illustrates how the follower might be engaged to grow and be effective.

BOX 6.1   Converting the Transformational Leadership Model Into a Followership Model

Leadership Model
- Focuses on leadership
- Acts as a role model
- Influences others
- Demonstrates ethical actions
- Promotes confidence in abilities
- Inspires confidence in followers
- Gives sense of purpose to followers
- Motivates followers
- Communicates well
- Emphasizes the positive
- Values creativity and autonomy
- Involves followers in decision-making process
- Identifies the individual needs of the follower
- Coaches individually
- Mentors

Followership Model
- Focuses on followership
- Acts professionally and ethically
- Influences leaders and colleagues
- Asks intelligent, thought-provoking questions
- Speaks up when concerns arise
- Inspires confidence in the care they provide
- Demonstrates a sense of purpose
- Motivates himself or herself
- Communicates well
- Demonstrates positive behaviors
- Strives for autonomy but knows when to ask for assistance
- Engages in decision-making process
- Identifies the individual needs of the patient and relates them to leadership
- Accepts criticism as a learning opportunity
- Engages in open communication with the mentor
- Transitions into leadership roles when needed
- Advocates for patients
- Commits to evidence-based, quality care
- Engages in lifelong learning
- Demonstrates active membership in shared governance

Based on Choi, S., Goh, C., Adam, M., & Tan, O. (2016). Transformational leadership, empowerment, and job satisfaction: The mediating role of employee empowerment. *Human Resources for Health, 14*(73), 1-14; and Schieltz, M. (2017). Four elements of transformational leadership. *Small Business.* www.smallbusiness.chron.com/four-elements-transformational-leadership-10115.html.

CONCLUSION

Today, what is known about leaders is extensive. Developing the leader, expanding leadership knowledge and expertise, and transforming the individual into a productive leader are all well discussed within the literature. The followers play a very versatile and important role within the leadership–followership team. This is a stated fact among many writings; however, how to engage, motivate, and encourage the follower to become effective has not been well developed. Leaders need followers. Without followers, a leader is simply a team of one.

Followers have a duty and a professional obligation to provide the highest standard of quality care for the patients whom they serve. Followers must step out of the negative shadows and into the positive light and drive leaders within the organization to promote the team as a whole. Followers must participate in the care of their patients, ask questions, voice concerns with intelligent communication, create trust from leadership in their abilities, provide advocacy to the patients, and have courage to make decisions and share them with the leadership team. Being an effective follower is an active role that requires participation. The act of following effectively contributes to the goal of advancing health.

THE SOLUTION

I was assigned to "Mr. A" again the next day. Early in my shift, I observed that his wife was crying. I sat down and offered comfort to her. She was upset because she said she had been attempting to talk with her husband and he was communicating with her that he did want to have the breathing tube and machine by shaking his head yes and no. She said when she would ask him he would shake his head no, he did not want it, and nod yes, he wanted to take it out. I asked her if she had communicated this new information to the physician. She stated, "He is the doctor, he is a man, and in my culture, we do not question the doctor. They know what is best." Later that day the children came to visit. I had another nurse who was a certified interpreter come in and talk to everyone in Spanish to make sure we all understood what could and what would probably happen if they agreed with the patient's wife about extubating the patient. The wife, the children, and most importantly the patient all understood that death was likely if the ventilator was removed because of the severity of his disease. I had a different charge nurse that day so I explained to her the entire situation. She called the physician to come by and talk to the family. Before entering the room, I informed the physician of my conversation with the family members. The interpreter was present for the conversation. After talking to the family, the physician agreed to extubate the patient. I knew that I had done what I was supposed to do, being an effective new nurse and trusting my instincts. I had to have the courage to speak up for the patient, and it was not easy as a new nurse.

There was a lot of miscommunication in this incident. The physician at our facility should have had an interpreter come in with him the first time he talked to the wife. He already knew there had been a miscommunication before at another facility. I got a call from one of my co-workers telling me that his wife had asked them to call me. She got on the phone and thanked me for helping them and that thanks to me her husband had died with dignity and got to enjoy his last hours with a few words, smiles, and a good-bye kiss. Being an effective staff nurse allowed me to trust my instincts, question leadership about the patient's plan of care, and find the courage to speak up and communicate the concerns of the family under my care.

Would this be a suitable approach for you? Why?

Anonymous

REFLECTIONS

Taking on the role of the effective follower is a continuous task. It involves all the characteristics described in this chapter, including active listening, open communication, trusting your own knowledge and instincts, and having the courage to speak up and voice any questions or concerns you may have in any situation. How effective are you as a follower?

Having the courage to take on this active role will improve the morale of the organization, help with increasing patient satisfaction and outcomes, and also provide leaders and peers the opportunity to view you as a "go to" person they can trust. How do you think others perceive you as an effective follower?

THE EVIDENCE

Little research has been completed related to the role of the follower in nursing. The greater emphasis has been placed on the idea that even new graduates are expected to lead, which is often related to intervening for patients as needed. As the idea of being an effective follower at any level grows, more data will be available to inform us about the role and impact of being an effective follower.

■ TIPS ON HOW TO BE AN EFFECTIVE FOLLOWER

- Trust in your knowledge and instincts.
- Do not be afraid to ask questions.
- Have the courage to voice any concerns.
- Be professional.

- Stay up-to-date on evidence-based care.
- Engage in open communication.
- Do not hint and hope.
- Take an active role within your organization.

REFERENCES

Benner, P. (1982). From novice to expert. *American Journal of Nursing, 82*(3), 402–407.

Berwick, D., Nolan, T., & Whittington, J. (2008). The triple aim: Care, cost, and quality. *Health Affiliate, 27*(3), 759–769.

Bodenheimer, T., & Sinsky, C. (2014). From Triple to Quadruple Aim: Care of the patient requires care of the provider. *Annals of Family Medicine, 12*(6), 573–576. https://doi.org/10.1370/afm.1713.

Chaleff, I. (2017). In praise of followership style assessments. *Journal of Leadership Studies, 10*(3), 45–48. https://doi.org/10.1002/jls.21490.

Everett, L. (2016). Academic-practice partnerships: The interdependence between leadership and followership. *Nursing Science Quarterly, 29*(2), 168–172. https://doi.org/10.1177/0894318416630106.

Forbes, M. A. (2016). Followership: A critical shortfall in health leadership. *Internal Medicine Journal,* 637–638. https://doi.org/10.111/imj.12993.

Gordon, L., Rees, C., Ker, J., & Cleland, J. (2015a). Dimensions, discourses and differences: Trainees conceptualizing health care leadership and followership. *Medical Education, 49,* 1248–1262. https://doi.org/10.1111/medu.12832.

Gordon, L., Rees, C., Ker, J., & Cleland, J. (2015b). Leadership and followership in the healthcare workplace: Exploring medical trainees' experiences through narrative inquiry. *BMJ Open, 5,* 1–11. https://doi.org/10.1136/bmjopen-2015-008898.

Institute of Medicine (IOM). (2010). *The future of nursing: Leading change, advancing health.* Washington, DC. *www.nationalacademies.org/hmd/Reports/2010/The-Future-of-Nursing-Leading-Change-Advancing-Health.aspx.*

Kelley, R. E. (1992). *The power of followership: How to create leaders people want to follow and followers who lead themselves.* New York: Doubleday/Currency.

Malak, R. (2016). A concept analysis of "Follower" within the context of professional nursing. *Nursing Forum, 51*(4), 286–294. https://doi.org/10.1111/nuf.12158.

Malakyan, P. (2014). Followership in leadership studies: A case of leader-follower trade approach. *Journal of Leadership Studies, 7,* 6–22. https://doi.org/10.1002/jls.21306.

Mannion, H., McKimm, J., & O'Sullivan, H. (2015). Followership, clinical leadership and social identity. *British Journal of Hospital Medicine, 76*(5), 270–274. https://doi.org/10.12968/hmed.2015.76.5.270.

Orem, D. (1980). *Nursing: Concepts of practice* (2nd ed.). New York: McGraw Hill Company.

Orlando, L. J. (1961). *The dynamic nurse-patient relationship.* New York: Putnam's Sons.

Sculli, G., Fore, A., Sine, D., Paull, D., Tschannen, D., Aebersold, M., et al. (2015). Effective followership: A standardized algorithm to resolve clinical conflicts and improve teamwork. *Clinical Risk Management, 35*(1), 21–30. https://doi.org/10.1002/jhrm.21174.

Spriggs, D. A. (2016). Followership: A critical shortfall in health leadership. *Internal Medicine Journal,* 637–638. https://doi.org/10.111/imj.12993.

7

Managing Self: Stress and Time

Mary Ann T. Donohue-Ryan

LEARNING OUTCOMES

- Define self-management.
- Define emotional intelligence.
- Explore personal and professional stressors.
- Analyze selected strategies to decrease stress.
- Evaluate common barriers to effective time management.
- Critique the strengths and weaknesses of selected time management strategies.
- Evaluate selected strategies to manage time more effectively.
- Assess the manager's role in helping team members manage their time and deal effectively with stress.

KEY TERMS

burnout
coping
delegation
depersonalization
employee assistance program
fatigue

general adaptation syndrome
   (GAS)
information overload
overwork
perfectionism
procrastination

role stress
self-management
self-reflection
time management

THE CHALLENGE

I was a nurse manager for more than 20 years at another facility and was promoted to supervisor and then director of nursing. When I came to this organization, I was administrative supervisor for 2 years. One of the biggest challenges I had in my nursing career was accepting this new position and learning the inpatient environment and covering the entire hospital. Then, after 2 years, I accepted an inpatient nurse manager position. Some of the challenges I faced were narrowing and decentralizing my thought process. I was no longer looking at the organizational picture; I had to refocus my views into just one inpatient unit. I had to focus on my quality indicators, my team members, their accountability, and communication with the patients and the families. Most importantly,

I had to fit everything into an 8-hour day! It was difficult to do this; I didn't have other leaders to assist me. When I was a nursing supervisor, I thought of myself as the liaison to all other leaders throughout the organization. However, when I assumed the nurse manager position, I had trouble with work–life balance. I found myself staying later and later, trying to accomplish everything I needed to do.

What would you do if you were this nurse?

Savitra Sutton, MSN, MBA-HCN, RN
Nurse Manager, Englewood Hospital Medical Center,
Englewood, NJ

INTRODUCTION

What should you do when the skills you have usually deployed in a given situation do not seem to work and things are not going well? What needs changing? Where do you begin? Daniel Goleman (1995, 2017), considered by many to be the seminal author on emotional intelligence (EI), observed that those who are the most successful in organizations are not necessarily more intelligent. Rising stars are distinguished from their peers because they have learned how to master their own emotions as well as their relationships. Such individuals, with average IQs, clearly outpaced those with even the highest IQs when principles are learned and refined over time.

Managing EI, managing stress (or at least our response to it), and managing time when possible are three key strategies for self-management.

EMOTIONAL INTELLIGENCE

EI is a critical leadership competency, and it involves four skills, self-awareness, self-management, social awareness, and relationship management (Goleman, 2017). Briefly, self-awareness relates to how well we perceive our own emotions at the time we are experiencing them. This element is important because our emotions tell us how we are reacting to events and information. If you have an uncomfortable "gut" feeling and do not know what caused that sensation, you may want to practice deliberately thinking about events and information and your reactions so that you gain a better understanding of yourself. Self-management is your response to being self-aware. You either act or not. We all know people who blurt out something about a driver cutting them off on the road. That is an example of an immediate, although not productive, act. Being more self-aware may allow that individual to move from focusing on the other driver to focusing on better application of brakes, having a calm response, and so forth. Social awareness relates to "reading" people. Are they happy, angry, distressed, hurt? The purpose of being socially aware is to gain critical information, so listening and observing are two critical skills. The final element is relationship management. As you might suspect, it relies heavily on your abilities in the other areas. It combines your awareness of self and others in an effort to execute clear communication. Through solid relationship management, even with people we may not like, we can be more effective in reducing personal and sometimes even organizational stress. In times of crises, no matter what the origin is, clear communication is critical to being effective in resolving the issue.

Personal competence includes the skills of self-awareness and self-management (TalentSmart, 2017). Social competence involves the skills of social awareness and relationship management. The good news is that EI can be learned. EI is linked to improved self-performance, employee performance, and organizational performance (Basogul & Ozgur, 2016; TalentSmart, 2017). Emotionally intelligent managers possess greater insight into their staff and manage better because they provide support and guidance, frequent feedback, and, one might infer, a natural give-and-take that results in growth (Spano-Szekely, Griffin, Clavelle, & Fitzpatrick, 2016). Nurse leaders' goals include growth and self-knowledge, learning to balance new as well as formerly held personal and professional objectives, and reorganizing time and activities to reach these goals. The literature suggests that nurses, because we are all human beings, cope with the complex stresses and crises of everyday life as well as unpredictable clinical situations (Scott, 2015). The so-called stress hardiness of nurses and leaders has long been thought to be essential to the survival of the nurse as well as overall staff recruitment and retention, giving rise to a professional alterego—the "supernurse culture" (Steege & Rainbow, 2017). In the past, seasoned nurses would pride themselves on being able to "take it," meaning silently work without openly challenging unfavorable aspects of the workplace, however unacceptable they might be. Those who left nursing, either unable or unwilling to tolerate difficult conditions in the practice setting, were labeled as "weak," "bad nurses," or simply "not a good fit" for the organization. Historically, and even as recently as the mid-2000s, research on stress in the nursing workplace focused on the individual's acceptance of demanding work environments, complex role requirements, and recurring staff shortages instead of proactive problem solving (Shirey, 2006). However, definitive hardiness, as described in the seminal work by Lambert and Lambert (1987), incorporates control, commitment, and challenge as tools in one's personal repertoire to change what cannot easily be changed at the unit- and organization-wide levels. In fact, organizations that make a significant investment in leadership development connect and strengthen social support networks. Even *the perception* of transformational leadership mitigates against the toxic effects of burnout (Shi, Zhang, Xu, Liu, & Miao, 2015).

Leaders in progressive and innovative thinking, called "thought leaders," suggested that the cultivation of stress hardiness produces nurse managers with a leadership style and resilience that actually improves overall working conditions. Fortunately, stress management can be taught and personal hardiness can be acquired, and interventions at all organizational levels exist to mitigate against caregiver burnout and stress (Miller, 2016).

To develop stress hardiness, we must actively improve our skills related to stress management, adaptive coping, healthy communication, and problem solving. The three key strategies presented in this chapter—EI, time management, and stress management—are important ways to support one's talents, energies, and creativity.

UNDERSTANDING STRESS

Time and stress are somewhat a chicken-and-egg phenomenon—trying to "fit everything in," and not having enough time to complete tasks, further contributes to stress. Living a life without a break from stress further erodes efficiency and thus decreases one's ability to contribute to quality outcomes. The key lies in our ability to take charge of our lives and strive to understand ourselves, and manage time and stress, both personally and professionally. Over time, the outcome of skillful self-management is hardiness and an improved ability to accomplish worthwhile goals, infused with our own unique style.

Nurses have learned about the effect of stress on patients and how to provide health teaching to manage its consequences. However, aspiring nurse leaders do not believe that their own skills adequately prepare them for dealing with competing needs and priorities—that is, being able to skillfully manage multiple sources of conflict at the same time. They may feel unprepared and thus reluctant to accept the demands of formal leadership roles (Dyess, Sherman, Pratt, & Chiang-Hanisko, 2016). Stress is defined as the uncomfortable gap between how we would like our life to be and how it actually is. Nurses are not immune to the effects of stress and, in fact, modern nursing is a very stressful occupation. Hospitals care for more and more critically ill patients, which requires advanced knowledge and skill to accomplish highly complex tasks, especially in the critical care setting (Nagel, Towell, Nel, & Foxall, 2016). Nurses need to recognize their unique stressors at home and on the job. The ubiquitous use of the Holmes-Rahe Stress Scale reinforces that everyone experiences stress—the exhilaration of a joyous event, as well as the negative feelings and unpleasant physical symptoms associated with a difficult life situation or even the anticipation of difficulty, such as meeting the parents of a new girlfriend, or taking an examination in a particularly tough subject area. Learning what stress is, its dynamics, and how we individually experience it and determining effective strategies to manage stress are part of the personal and professional maturation of all individuals. Because nurses tend to work in areas and in situations that are extremely stressful, stress management skills must be continuously adapted to new situations and strengthened over time.

DEFINITION OF STRESS

In this chapter, *stress* and *distress* (Selye, 1965) are used interchangeably, although some writers regard stress as neutral and refer to positive attributes or perceptions of stress as *eustress* and negative attributes or perceptions of stress as *distress*. Stress is a consequence or response to an event or stimulus. Stress is not inherently bad. Rather, each individual's interpretation determines whether the event is viewed as positive or threatening. In addition, stress management does not necessarily mean stress reduction or its outright elimination. More than 30 years ago, Kobasa, Maddi, and Kahn (1982) characterized successful stress management as the control of emotions and behaviors, perseverance, and a heightened sense of purpose, along with continuous challenge that is present in the face of stressful events. Stress management is an important nurse manager competency (American Organization of Nurse Executives, 2015), and to what degree leaders incorporate ways to mitigate stress in one's leadership style is tied to employee stress (Fernandez, 2016). Effective stress management has important implications for the workplace because of its link to low absenteeism rates, improved quality, and increased productivity and characteristics associated with workforce flourishing (Schultze & Loi, 2014).

SOURCES OF JOB STRESS

Job stress can be defined as the physical and emotional responses that arise when job requirements do not seem to match the abilities, resources, or needs of the worker. Work-related stress can lead to poor physical and emotional health and injury. Job-related challenges (eustress), which motivate us to learn new skills, master our jobs, and manage new situations, differ from *distress,* which can lead to symptoms from fatigue to exhaustion, feelings of inadequacy and failure, or even complete and total indifference and burnout. For example, if you are involved in an oral interview for a job, you will benefit from a certain amount of stress (eustress). Stress provides the determination to land that new position and gives you the "edge" we all need to help us think quickly and clearly and to express our thoughts in ways that will be appropriate for the interview process. On the way to the interview, however, if your car breaks down or you miss the bus or if a hired driver misinterprets the correct address, these conditions certainly create a negative stress (distress) experience as you realize that you will most certainly be late for the appointment. Certainly, as more is learned about the relationship of stress to physiologic changes, as in its effect on sleep, eating, and social interactions, personal stressors will become even easier to identify. When one looks at job-related stressors, the stressors fall into one of two categories: external (working and living conditions) and internal (worker characteristics).

External Sources

Work-related stressors, such as an ever-increasing workload; rotating shifts; high patient acuity; inadequate or unpredictable staffing; ethical conflicts; dealing with acute illness and death; role ambiguity; constant multi-tasking; work relationships; job insecurity; and the multiple, complex, and continually growing number of nursing responsibilities, have been associated with increased stress, all of which have been reported as stressors (Yu, 2016). Nurses spend more and more time at work, and their managers report 12- to 14-hour days as a normal way of life, with accountability 24 hours a day, 7 days per week. They, like most individuals in management, are tethered to cellphones or other electronic devices that can never be completely "powered down" without ramifications for that missed call, text, or important e-mail. However, some forward-thinking organizations are taking specific actions to avoid this feeling of always "being on."

The needs and expectations of our consumers, patients and families, cannot be underestimated, as they are the reason healthcare organizations exist in the first place. The need to provide safe, effective health care is coupled with the need to provide an outstanding patient and family experience—because every patient has the right to expect it. Patient satisfaction scores are a source of stress, with initiatives linked to survey questions that appear to most closely tie to patient concerns. Recognizing this, many leaders freely provide personal cell and home phone information for their staff, administrators, donors, board members, and people with close ties to the community to allow for immediate communication should a need arise at any time of the day or night.

Role Expectations

Although the distress that results from change takes many forms, two underlying patterns appear to be constant. Often, nurses feel overwhelmed by conflicting expectations to be accountable on many fronts: They are educationally prepared to furnish evidence-based clinical care; to meet their patients' and families' emotional needs; and to be warm, friendly, and supportive to their co-workers. Ultimately, organizations now require nurses to also be knowledgeable about their business unit, possess a keen financial awareness about how they contribute to overall organizational efficiency and cost-effectiveness, and to consistently earn highest marks on their patient satisfaction or experience scores. Because individuals—frontline direct care nurses, nurse managers, and chief nursing executives alike—cannot easily balance caring and clinical expectations with business and administrative expectations, it is completely normal to experience considerable role overload, frustration, chronic fatigue, and distress.

Relationships

Interpersonal relations can buffer stressors or can in themselves become stressors. Outside the work setting, home may represent a refuge for harried nurses; however, stressors at home, when severe, can impair work performance and relationships among staff or even include undesirable patterns that have the potential to invade the workplace and create an unhealthy work environment. When one parent in the home works hours other than daytime hours, for example, children and adolescents are more likely to demonstrate inferior cognitive and behavioral outcomes (Morsy & Rothstein, 2015). Therefore the cycle of work pressure and home pressure can at times seem insurmountable, especially to the nurse who may also be caring for an older parent, sick partner or sibling, or a child with special needs. Added to the mix may be the nurse who attends school to attain a degree, studies for a national board certification, or prepares for clinical ladder advancement—all common requirements of the contemporary work setting.

Changes in healthcare delivery systems, as well as the cycles in the nursing workforce supply and demand, have affected professional nursing in many ways. Some work settings may have a disproportionate representation of Generation X, Generation Y, or Millennials, or perhaps a larger percentage of older nurses, the Baby Boomer Generation. In situations in which the values of one generation of workers clash with those of another, conflict occurs unless the manager becomes aware of how to best maximize the positive behaviors of each generation. The wise leader will adapt to the best attributes of all members of the team (Diesing, 2016).

In geographic areas suffering from staffing shortages, inpatient settings may have minimally safe levels of professional caregivers. Because of the economy and changes in federal financial reimbursement in the form of reduced Medicare payments to US hospitals, strict adherence to unit budgets may result in rigid staffing patterns that are not realistically flexed to actual or perceived patient acuity and case mix index. Consequently, layoffs or early retirement buyouts may occur with the resultant struggle to maintain supportive, collegial relationships that were established over many years of working together. In nationally hard-to-recruit specialties, such as in perioperative and mother–baby areas, organizations have turned to supplemental staffing with agency or "traveling" nurses, thus creating a transient nursing staff for longer than desirable intervals. The practice of "floating" staff, when nurses are reassigned or "floated" to different patient care units, causes nurses to work with unfamiliar staff. They may feel isolated or become unwittingly involved in dysfunctional politics on the unit. *Floating,* by definition, means that nurses work with patients whose requirements for care may be different than the expected, resulting in further stress related to patient safety and professional practice concerns.

Persons in management-level positions may also become stressors. Mixed messages or, worse, multiple initiatives announced at the same time create confusion and stress about what constitutes the real organizational priority. Communication may come only from the top down, with scarce opportunity for nurses to participate in decisions that affect them directly and that they are required to implement without proper training or support. On units or in hospitals without a viable professional governance system of shared decision making, nurses may experience distress. This may arise from feelings of frustration and helplessness in settings without an opportunity to improve the clinical care and work environment with the active participation of the front-line direct care nurse.

Does stress management get any easier when nurses occupy the top job, chief nursing officer (CNO)? All nurses in an organization should care about what the CNO experiences, because that person is the official voice for nursing. One study concluded that although CNOs act with moral courage, they experience moral distress as they contribute to major decisions that affect those within the entire organization and, at the same time, attempt to uphold their moral values and professional responsibilities (see the Research Perspective).

The Position

Upon entering nursing studies in a college or university, most students expect that caring for patients who are chronically or critically ill and their families will be stressful. The current environment in many healthcare agencies, however, is exponentially more complex and is often characterized by overwork, as well as by the stresses inherent in contemporary nursing practice. In some settings, direct care nurses have been expected to work beyond the designated assignment period, constituting mandatory overtime, often with little or no prior notice. Owing to the nature of stress and crisis, some patients and families may escalate in their own threatening behaviors and verbally or physically attack their own caregivers. Several states, in response to legislative efforts and pressure from their constituents, have enacted criminal laws to protect healthcare workers from such violence. Many healthcare institutions have established relationships with local police departments to convey a zero tolerance policy to those who are violent toward their team members (see *www.nursingworld.org/ WorkplaceViolence.aspx*). A zero-tolerance workplace means that acts of violence toward staff are not acceptable and will, in most cases, be prosecuted to the full extent of the law.

Another common stressor for nurses is the paradox of the presence and/or the lack of technology in the workplace. Technology is often anticipated as an assist to the nurse but often turns out to be far different. Therefore

RESEARCH PERSPECTIVE

Resource: Prestia, A., Sherman, R.O., Demezier, C. (2017). Chief nursing officers' experiences with moral distress. *Journal of Nursing Administration, 47*(2), 101-107.

This is a study to qualitatively explore the phenomenon of moral distress in twenty chief nursing officers (CNO). Nurses who function as healthcare executives are required to uphold the tenets and beliefs of their respective profession, which is defined in the American Nurses Associations' (ANA) *Scope and Standards for Nurse Administrators.* The study participants were asked to describe their experiences with moral distress, its effect, and the coping strategies that they used. Content analysis was used to identify themes, consistent with a phenomenologic approach. Moral distress occurred in the areas of salary and compensation; hiring practices; harmful and stressful relationships with peers and hospital presidents; and observations of questionable business practices and other improprieties. Emerging themes were identified that defined the experiences of moral distress. The six themes were (1) lacking psychological safety, (2) feeling a sense

of powerlessness, (3) seeking to maintain moral compass, (4) drawing strength from networking, (5) having moral residue, and (6) living with the consequences. The researchers' conclusion was that this is a rarely discussed aspect of chief nursing officers in acute care settings. Moreover, 8 out of the 20 study participants left their facility as a result of experiencing moral distress.

Implications for Practice
Moral distress is a relentless experience that has the potential to undermine and derail careers. Those who suffer its consequences either deal with it in silence or discover alternatives as they transition out of the disruptive workplace. Networking with other CNOs and within one's professional organizations were described as "invaluable," and of "10-plus" benefit. In conclusion, psychological self-protection and professional discussion about moral distress would support the lives and careers of nursing executives. The descriptions and recommendations may readily apply to nurses in any leadership position.

---

nurses face stress as they attempt to learn and then integrate multiple systems that may lack sufficient interface, which often leads to frustration when they must toggle between multiple screens to complete critical patient documentation. When healthcare software is not designed well to be intuitive to the user, nurses wind up spending more and more time in front of a device instead of their patients. Nurses experience this as a burden because they are, so to speak, constantly feeding *data hungry systems* that were created and put into a production workflow to solve individually focused tasks, such as entering a patient's blood pressure or blood glucose levels, without regard to the comprehensive effect on workflow and without regard for how time consuming computer tasks have become (Patterson et al., 2015; see *http://ncbi.nlm.nih.gov/pubmed/10730596* and *http://ncbi.nlm.nih.gov/pmc/articles/PMC61466*).

Nurses may need to bridge a staggering number of gaps to safely communicate with their internal and external colleagues whose workplaces are technologically different or who have separate and distinct rules about documentation, ordering tests, receiving results, and obtaining outcomes of care—all within the same hospital or setting!

Role stress is an additional stressor for nurses. Viewed as having three components (role ambiguity, role conflict,

and role overload) (Iacobellis, 2015), role stress for new graduates has a positive correlation to burnout. Role stress is particularly acute for new graduates, whose lack of clinical experience and organizational skills, combined with new situations and procedures, may increase feelings of overwhelming stress. Conflict between what was learned in the classroom or limited clinical experience and the actual practice setting compounds the situation and increases stress. This concept has been so historically common in nursing that the phenomenon gave rise to the term "reality shock" in Dr. Marlene Kramer's (1974) seminal work. Unfortunately, transition to practice issues have endured to present day, because academic and practice leaders have not yet managed to completely eradicate its negative effects on successive generations of nurses. However, transition programs have had positive effects on helping new graduates transition.

Gender Roles

Approximately 9.6% of the nation's approximately 4 million licensed registered nurses in the United States are men (Health Resources and Services Administration, 2013). Most nurses are women who go home at the end of their shift to traditional responsibilities, including managing the household and caring for young children and aging parents while they balance their own needs. When added to the already stressful workday of the nurse, the additional responsibilities often contribute to a higher level of distress that may be experienced. Men may have those same experiences, because the "traditional" roles in society have changed to the extent that many men have those same stressors. Thanks to Generation Y's (those born in the 1980s) and Millennials' entry into the workforce, the importance of work–life balance has become increasingly emphasized, but this has not yet entirely translated into improvements in the American workplace, because at 18% (34% of the general workforce), they are underrepresented in the nursing workforce (Whitman, 2017). Owing to vagaries in the economy, spouses, partners, or children may be underemployed or experience sharply reduced work with reduced or nonexistent health benefits. Thus children or even grandchildren may have returned to live at home, and many nurses are shouldering the burden of another full- or part-time job or working overtime for additional income to contribute to overstretched household budgets. Lack of financial security means that in times of severe economic hardships, such as in a national economic recession or regional threats to the local economy, as in a severe hurricane or an industrial plant closing, living from paycheck to paycheck sharply reduces options for self-improvement through career advancement. Financial insecurity may actually curtail career opportunities. For example, some nurses may be too afraid to seek a better position because of concern for not succeeding in a new position, not liking a new job, losing health benefits, or experiencing layoffs in an uncertain economy. The key is to be open to asking for help in managing such stressors so they can be viewed as opportunities rather than setbacks. For example, seeking guidance from others will undoubtedly raise greater awareness and sensitivity to one's patients and management team. The goal is always to maximize our abilities and talents so we can improve the health and lives of others.

Internal Sources

Personal stress "triggers" are events or situations that have an effect on specific individuals. A personal trigger might be a specific event such as the death of a loved one, an automobile accident, losing a job, or getting married or divorced. These events are in addition to daily personal stressors such as working in a noisy environment, experiencing job dissatisfaction, or having a long or difficult daily commute to work. Negative self-talk, pessimistic thinking, self-criticism, and overanalyzing situations can be significant ongoing stressors. These internal sources of stress usually stem from unrealistic self-beliefs (unrealistic expectations, taking things personally, all-or-nothing thinking, exaggerating, or rigid thinking), perfectionism, or a Type A personality.

An individual's ability to deal with stress may be moderated by psychological hardiness, also called *resilience*. According to seminal researchers Lambert, Lambert, and Yamase (2003), psychological hardiness is a composite of commitment, control, and challenge. These form a constellation that (1) dampers the effects of stress by challenging the perception of the situation and (2) decreases the negative impact of a situation by moderating both cognitive appraisal and coping. Nursing resilience is a cultivated characteristic that occurs when individuals strategically use education and other practices in bad situations (Sanders, 2015).

Everyone needs to recognize that the human species require certain basic physiological needs (Maslow, 1943). According to Maslow, these needs govern our understanding of what constitutes homeostasis as well as the polar opposite, such as when we have an appetite for something that ties directly to a specific actual need or something else that is lacking (see the Theory Box). On the other hand, poor and unhealthy lifestyle choices, such as the overuse of caffeine, lack of an exercise schedule, consuming a fat-ridden diet, patterns of inadequate sleep and insufficient leisure time, and drinking alcohol and cigarette smoking, all have a direct effect on the amount of one's stress and have the potential to create a vicious lose-lose cycle. Unfortunately, according to the ANA *Healthy Nurse, Healthy Nation* website, nurses fail nearly every indicator of health compared with the average American (see *http://anahealthynurse.org*). *The Healthy Nurse, Healthy Nation* campaign promotes five constructs: calling to care; priority to self-care; opportunity to role model; responsibility to educate; and authority to advocate (see *http://www.anahealthynurse.org*).

DYNAMICS OF STRESS

Stress in organizations may result from unrealistic or conflicting expectations originating from oneself or others, the pace and magnitude of change, human behavior, individual personality characteristics, the characteristics of the position itself, or the culture of the organization. Other stressors may be unique to certain environments, situations, and persons or groups. Initially, increased stress produces increased performance. However, when stress continues to escalate or remains intense, overall performance suffers. Hans Selye's (1956) mid–20th-century investigations to decode the nature of and reactions to stress have been very influential in our understanding of this human phenomenon. In his classic theory, Selye (1991) described the concept of stress, identified general adaptation syndrome (GAS), and detailed a predictable pattern of response (see the Theory Box and Fig. 7.1). The Theory Box also presents other key theories related to self-manangement.

More recent investigations of the relationship among the brain, the immune system, and health (psychoneuroimmunology) have generated models that challenge Selye's (1956) GAS. Although Selye states that all people respond with a similar set of hormonal and immune responses to any stress, newer thinking, albeit using only male subjects, is that increased stress may connect humans to each other by increasing empathy and prosocial behavior (Tomova et al., 2016).

THEORY BOX

Theories Applicable to Self-Management

Key Contributors	Key Ideas	Application to Practice
Maslow's Hierarchy of Needs: Maslow (1943) identified five need levels of every human.	Although recent research shows the five levels are not always present or in order, it is reasonable that unmet needs motivate most employees most of the time.	Nurse wages should be sufficient to provide shelter and food. Job security and a social environment that rewards and recognizes nurse performance are important.
General Adaptation Syndrome: Selye (1956) is credited with developing this theory.	The "stress response" is an adrenocortical reaction to stressors that is accompanied by psychological changes and physiologic alterations that follow a pattern of fight or flight. The general adaptation syndrome includes an alarm, resistance, and adaptation or exhaustion.	Change, lack of control, and excessive workload are common stressors that evoke psychological and physiologic distress among nurses.
Complex Adaptive Systems: Plsek and Greenhalgh (2001).	This theory of unpredictable interactions between interdependent people and activities emphasizes the importance of innovation and rapid information sharing to improve performance.	Nurse engagement in self-managed groups and teams allows organizations to shape their environment through controlled "experimentation" using the rapid-cycle plan-do-study-act improvement method.
The Pareto Principle: Hafner (2001).	The "Pareto Principle" refers to a universal observation of "vital few, trivial many." Pareto (1848–1923) studied distribution of personal incomes in Italy and observed that 80% of the wealth was controlled by 20% of the population. This concept of disproportion often holds in many areas. Although the exact values of 20% and 80% are not significant, the observation of considerable disproportion is important to remember.	The 80–20 rule can be applied to many aspects of health care today. For example, 80% of healthcare expenditures are on 20% of the population, and 80% of personnel problems come from 20% of the staff. In quality improvement, 80% of improvement can be expected by removing 20% of the causes of unacceptable quality or performance. A nurse can also expect that 80% of patient-care time will be spent working with 20% of his or her patient assignment. This concept may help explain sources of stress when nurses attempt to provide all of the patients in his/her assignment "equal time."

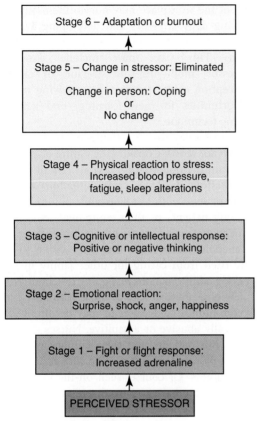

Fig. 7.1 The stress diagram.

Critical of stress research using predominately male subjects, Taylor, Klein, Lewis, Gruenewald, Gurung, and Updegraff (2000) were the first to propose a model of the female stress response, the "tend and befriend," as opposed to the male's "fight or flight" model. The "tend and befriend" response is an estrogen and oxytocin–mediated stress response that is characterized by caring for offspring and befriending those around in times of stress to increase chances of survival.

Most nurses can easily recognize the origins of stress and its symptoms. For example, a healthcare agency may make demands on the nursing staff, such as excessive work, that its nurses regard as beyond their capacity to perform well, or at least in a healthy manner. When they are unable to resolve the problem through overwork, with more staff, or by looking at the situation in another way, nurses may experience decreased job satisfaction, become depressed, and have negative patient outcomes (Steege and Rainbow, 2017). They may also experience headaches, fatigue, inability to concentrate, or other physical symptoms that are associated with a

low level of job performance. If the stress persists, such symptoms may escalate and manifest themselves in medication errors or musculoskeletal or needle-stick injuries. Nurses may attempt to cope by becoming completely apathetic, a sign of **burnout**. Box 7.1 on p. 108 gives physical, mental, and spiritual/emotional signs of overstress in individuals.

A relationship exists between stress and the human immune system and a body of literature that ties unrelenting stress to immune dysregulation. The immune systems of those who are older or already sick are more prone to stress-related immune system changes such as inflammation, delayed wound healing, poor responses to vaccines, and increased susceptibility to infectious disease processes (Gouin, 2011). Physical illnesses linked to stress include visceral adiposity (increase in body fat), type 2 diabetes, cardiovascular disease (hypertension, heart attack, stroke), musculoskeletal disorders, psychological disorders (anxiety, depression), workplace injury, neuromuscular disorders (multiple sclerosis), suicide, cancer, ulcers, asthma, and rheumatoid arthritis. Stress can even cause life-threatening sympathetic stimulation.

MANAGEMENT OF STRESS

Individuals respond to stress by eliciting coping strategies that are a means of dealing with stress to maintain or achieve an improved sense of well-being or perceived work–life balance. Certain strategies may be ineffective because of reliance on excessive alcohol or prescription drug and substance use. Other methods, such as exercise, meditation, or professional counseling, may be quite effective in helping restore a greater sense of well-being and effectiveness. More examples of effective strategies are discussed here.

Workplace Stress Prevention

One effective way to deal with stress is to determine and manage its source. Discovering the origin of stress in patient care may be difficult, because some environments have changed so rapidly that the nursing staff is overwhelmed trying to balance bureaucratic rules and limited resources with the demands of vulnerable human beings for whom they are caring. Labrague, McEnroe-Petitte, Gloe, Tsaras, Arteche, and Maldia (2016), in their study of nurses' stress and burnout, found that positive correlations were identified between the perception of organizational politics and job stress,

BOX 7.1   Signs of Overstress in Individuals

Physical

Physical signs of ill health:
- Increase in flu, colds, accidents
- Change in sleeping habits
- Fatigue

Chronic signs of decreased ability to manage stress:
- Headaches
- Hypertension
- Backaches
- Gastrointestinal problems

Unhealthy coping activities:
- Increased use of drugs and alcohol
- Increased weight
- Smoking
- Crying, yelling, blaming

Mental
- Dread going to work every day
- Rigid thinking and a desire to go by all the rules in all cases; inability to tolerate any changes
- Forgetfulness and anxiety about work to be done; more frequent errors and incidents
- Returning home exhausted and unable to participate in enjoyable activities
- Confusion about duties and roles
- Generalized anxiety
- Decrease in concentration
- Depression
- Anger, irritability, impatience
- Blaming, negotiating

Spiritual
- Sense of being a failure; disappointed in work performance
- Anger and resentment toward patients, colleagues, and managers; overall irritable attitude
- Lack of positive feelings toward others
- Cynicism toward patients, blaming them for their problems
- Excessive worry, insecurity, lowered self-esteem
- Increased family and friend conflict
- Disconnection from family and friends and usual sources of support and love

politics of the workplace may not do them any good. Identifying daily stressors and developing a plan of action for management of the stress includes making a plan. This plan may include eliminating the stressor, modifying the stressor, or changing the perception of the stressor (e.g., viewing mistakes as opportunities for new learning) and using the reframing technique.

Many of the day-to-day activities of nursing can create workplace stress. Consider the nature of acute care nursing and the potential for serious risk of injury to others. Staffing shortages create situations of caring for more patients with less help while pulling, moving, or pushing patients or their equipment. Nurses may have inadequate rest because of rotating shifts or irregular schedules or because they may come to work already tired from caring for other family members or working additional jobs *and* going to school. Nurses routinely give physical care to those who have potentially communicable diseases or may become verbally or physically abusive or assaultive. Nurses are highly engaged with patients and their families who suffer with acute pain and grief associated with either chronic or acute illness. Of course, such on-the-job stressors are often counterbalanced by the rewards of patient appreciation, the joy of seeing a healthy baby born, or seeing firsthand the relief brought by a nursing intervention such as appropriate pain medication or repositioning of an uncomfortable limb. However, given the nature of nursing practice, nurses must be alert to their own signs of stress and be able to develop self-awareness about work-life balance. Each of us has to understand how many hours in a day, how many shifts in a row, and conversely, how many hours or days between shifts is appropriate, all aimed at the goal of understanding what is a reasonable workload. Cultivating healthy lifestyle habits also helps reduce stress. Adequate sleep, a balanced diet, regular exercise, and frequent interactions with friends are excellent stress-buffering habits.

According to Fernandez (2016), the top leadership skills to develop are to (1) model and encourage well-being practices; (2) allow time to disconnect outside of work; (3) train the brain to deal with chaos; (4) emphasize "monotasking" for better focus; (5) be purposeful about "gap" or break time during the day; and (6) exercise empathy and compassion. Practicing these skills can be challenging.

turnover intention, and job burnout. Therefore when in distress, nurses may need to step back and look at the moments that connect them more fully to their purpose and job enjoyment, as attending too much to the

Symptom Management

Unpredictable and uncontrollable change, coupled with immense responsibility and little control over the work environment, produces stress for nurses and other healthcare professionals. Consequently, nurses may develop emotional symptoms such as anxiety, depression, or anger; physical alterations such as fatigue, headache, and insomnia; mental changes such as a decrease in concentration and memory; and behavioral changes such as smoking, drinking, crying, and swearing. The important factor is not the stressor but, rather, how the individual perceives the stressor and what coping mechanisms are available to mediate the hormonal response to the stressor.

Multiple stress-buffering behaviors can be used to reduce the detrimental effects of stress. The stressor-induced changes in the hormonal and immune systems can be modulated by an individual's behavioral coping responses. These coping responses include spending time developing a particular interest such as dancing or playing an instrument, leisure activities with friends and family, taking time for self, drinking water or decaffeinated liquids, positive social support, a strong belief system, a sense of humor, developing realistic expectations, reframing events, regular aerobic exercise, meditation, and the use of yoga for self-care (Alexander, Rollins, Walker, Wong, & Pennings, 2015).

Everyone needs to balance work and leisure in his or her life. Leisure time and stress are inversely proportional. If you find that time for work is more than 60% of awake time or if self-time is less than 10% of awake time, and you find that stress levels increase accordingly, it may be time to take a look at your own work/self-time ratio. Changes should be made to relieve stress, such as decreasing the number of work hours or finding more time for leisure activities. Caffeine is a strong stimulant and, in itself, a stressor. Slowly weaning off caffeine should result in better sleep and more energy. Positive social support can offer validation, encouragement, or advice. By discussing situations with others, one can reduce stress. A great deal of stress comes from our belief systems, which cause stress in two ways. First, behaviors result from them, such as placing work before rest or pleasure. Second, beliefs may also conflict with those of other people, as may happen with patients from different cultures. Articulating beliefs and finding common ground will help reduce anger and stress. Humor is a great stress reducer and laughter a great tension reducer. Other activities may include self-reflection in the form of guided imagery, journaling, or debriefing with a mentor or peer.

A common source of stress is unrealistic expectations. Realistic expectations can make life feel more predictable and more manageable. *Reframing* is changing the way you look at things to make you feel better about them or to obtain a different perspective. For example, an individual who is difficult to deal with may be viewed instead as someone who lacks understanding about how to make an assignment. A situation can be seen in multiple ways, and it is less stressful to take the view that there is always an aspect of our lives (including the rapidly changing health care environment) that is bound to be unpredictable and remain a mystery at times. Plsek and Greenhalgh (2001) observed that according to Complex Adaptive Systems (see the Theory Box), all systems are nested within other systems, and all are in a state of constant interaction. Therefore it would seem that taking one aspect of a situation out of proportion and fretting about it does little to achieve one's overall understanding.

Regular aerobic exercise is a logical method of dissipating the excess energy generated by the stress response. Numerous studies cite the value of such exercise, including stress reduction.

EXERCISE 7.2 This systematic relaxation technique can be used in the middle of a working day, the last thing at night, or at any time you feel tense or anxious. Review the information and strategies at the Mayo Clinic website: *www.mayoclinic.com/health/meditation/HQ01070.* Make a short list of steps to take, and put it in your smartphone or notepad.

Social support in the form of positive work relationships, as well as nurturing family and friends, is an important way to buffer the negative effects of a stressful work environment. Although friendships may be formed with colleagues, the workload and the shifting of staff from one unit to another make it difficult sometimes to establish and maintain close relationships with peers. For many people at work, the time spent with their managers and co-workers represent one of the strongest sources of community in their lives. The Gallup Organization, in its study of more than 80,000 managers to better understand the relationship of great managers to a quality workplace, created the Q-12 survey question: *I have a best friend at work.* Strong friendships with co-workers who will help people get through rough spots positively correlates with employee retention, customer metrics, productivity, and profitability (Miller & Adkins, 2016). Leaders can provide regular recognition feedback, in the form of personal notes that are mailed to their team members' homes; annual Nurses' Week celebrations; or participation in the DAISY Foundation, a not-for-profit organization that formally recognizes the extraordinary contributions of nurses (see the Daisy Foundation website at *http://daisyfoundation.org*). All of these help shape the organization's culture in a way that patients, families, and nurses value.

Young nurses in their first position, those who find themselves in an unfamiliar geographic area, or nurses who switch employers after a long tenure at another hospital all want to anticipate that they will be part of a work group that will furnish emotional support and a sense of belonging to an endeavor that is greater than themselves. Too often, nurses overlook the benefits of active membership in their professional association or specialty associations. Connections established at the beginning of one's career will serve the nurse with an unending lifelong source of enthusiastic colleagues who are as passionate about their individual professional careers as they are about serving their profession. Opportunities to become active members help nurses discover and refine brand-new leadership skills in a warm, comfortable setting. Ongoing mentorship by seasoned nursing leaders from academia, private practice, and organizational sectors is often free for the taking and adds dimension and a valuable perspective to nurses at every level. Such efforts may help nurses cope with workplace demands that seem to exceed their capabilities through mentoring and coaching.

Stress applies to all positions. Direct care nurses may experience stress from a patient's deteriorating condition or lack of ability to function independently. Nurse managers may experience role conflict when they must function as representatives of both the corporate culture and the professional nursing culture. For example, a leader may be stressed about the potential for downsizing or a plan to open a new service or a new unit. The stress (distress) experienced by one group can affect another. The challenge is how to manage individual reactions to stress so that it results in growth rather than inhibiting it and in how to manage the effects of stress on others (see the Research Perspective).

BURNOUT

Sometimes individuals cannot manage stress successfully through their own efforts and require assistance. Examples of behavior related to stress that feels overwhelming are found in Box 7.1 on p. 108. Coping strategies, such as those described previously, may furnish temporary relief or none at all. With this level of distress, one can feel overwhelmed or helpless and may be at greater risk for mental or physical illness. This constellation of emotions is commonly called *burnout*.

The classic view of burnout, a psychological term to describe the effects of prolonged emotional and physical exhaustion and diminished interest caused by an unrelenting workload without relief was described by Maslach and Leiter in 1997. The sources of the stressors may exist in the environment, in the individual, or in the interaction between the individual and the environment. Some stressors, such as employment termination, serious illness or death in the family, or the breakup of a relationship, appear to be universal, whereas other

RESEARCH PERSPECTIVE

Resource: Van Bogaert, P., Peremans, L., Van Heusden, D., Verspuy, M., Kureckova, V., Van de Cruys, Z., & Franck, E. (2017). Predictors of burnout, work engagement and nurse reported job outcomes and quality of care: A mixed method study. *BioMed Central, 16(1),* 1-14.

This is a mixed-method study, using a quantitative approach to retest previously existing models as well as two follow-up qualitative studies to better understand the findings. Workload influenced staff nurses' feelings of stress, negativity, and feelings of failure. Conversely, positive nurse–physician relationships and a supportive, dynamic team seemed to serve as a protective barrier that served nurses well: They balanced their workloads better, served with vigor and determination, and intended to stay within the nursing profession longer when in the presence of management and organizational support.

Implications for Practice

This study seemed to confirm the results of prior studies related to the American Nurses Credentialing Center (ANCC) Magnet® status and demonstrated the effectiveness of a healthy nursing work environment upon key indicators and outcomes.

stressors, such as meeting a work deadline, are more personal. For example, some individuals thrive on goals and timetables, whereas others feel constrained and frustrated and experience distress. Sometimes, stress is experienced when others around the individual have a dominant personality style and the relationships are not complementary to one another. Burnout is not an objective phenomenon as if it were the accumulation of a certain number and type of stressors. How stressors are perceived and how they are mediated by an individual's ability to adapt are crucial variables in determining one's levels of distress.

Nurses who are burned out feel as though their resources are depleted to the point that their well-being is at risk. A self-analysis usually uncovers the characteristics of burnout. First, a feeling of physical, mental, and emotional exhaustion can be recognized. Historically, Greenglass, Burke, and Fiksenbaum (2001) found that emotional exhaustion was directly related to workload. For example, recent graduates may value total, detailed care for individuals and may have little experience in caring for more than two or three patients simultaneously. When confronted with the responsibility of caring for a group of six to eight acutely ill patients, they may have difficulty adapting to the realities of the workplace. Coupled with fear of failure, emotional exhaustion ensues. Emotional exhaustion in turn has a direct effect on levels of cynicism and somatization. A second characteristic of burnout is depersonalization, a state characterized by distancing oneself from the work itself and developing negative attitudes toward work in general (Greenglass et al., 2001). Depersonalization is commonly described as a feeling of being outside one's body,

feeling as if one is a machine or robot, an "unreal" feeling that one is in a dream or that one "is on automatic pilot." Generally, subjective symptoms of unreality make the nurse uneasy and anxious. Others may view this as callousness. Nurses pushed to do too much in too little time may distance themselves from patients as a means of dealing with emotional exhaustion. Also, nurses' personality characteristics may lean too heavily on the caregiving dimension, which often carries over into one's personal life. For example, caregiving individuals may be further challenged by life partners who demand a disproportionate amount of time and energy, either because of physical disabilities or because of latent personality disorders or even alcoholism, so renewal and safe havens are unlikely in such cases.

A decreased sense of professional accomplishment and competence is the third hallmark of burnout. Low professional efficacy has been found to be a function of higher levels of cynicism (Greenglass et al., 2001). *Efficacy* is one's belief in his or her capabilities to organize and execute goal-oriented activities. Nurses are more inclined to take on a task if they believe they can succeed. Lower levels of efficacy can lead nurses to believe tasks are harder than they actually are. This can lead to a sense of failure, perceived helplessness, and eventually crisis. At this point, one's coping skills are no longer effective. Immediate referral to mandated employee assistance program (EAP) counseling and perhaps a medical leave of absence may be recommended. At its best, a healthy peer discussion, whether it is formal or informal, can help to identify when a nurse is troubled. However, assistant nurse managers, nurse managers, or nursing supervisors often have the task of addressing and referring nurses to seek help for themselves, before the stress escalates to a state of personal crisis.

RESOLUTION OF STRESS

Resolution of stress in its early stages can be accomplished through a variety of techniques. Nurses must be able to reach a balance of caring for others and caring for self. Box 7.2 summarizes physical, mental, and emotional and spiritual strategies. When stress rises to unacceptable or even dangerous levels, colleagues can be supportive and perhaps even point out the stress level or recommend appropriate help (Fig. 7.2).

> **EXERCISE 7.3** Using the items in Box 7.2, identify what strategies you most commonly use. Then find at least one strategy you never or rarely use and consider what prevents your using that strategy more effectively.

Social Support

Peers and followers can be supportive and help reduce stress by assisting with problem solving and by presenting different perspectives. Family and friends can provide an affirming, loving perspective and much-needed respite from stress in the form of celebrations around birthdays, graduations, and seasonal holidays. Social isolation increases stress. When nurses find themselves in a never-ending cycle of work, sleep, school, and conflicting calendars with escalating pressures at home, relief must be actively sought. True social support allows us to relax, be playful, have fun, laugh, vent emotions, and enjoy life to the fullest.

Counseling

Persistent, unpleasant feelings; problem behavior; helplessness; and withdrawal during prolonged stress may suggest the need for assistance from a mental health professional. Examples of problem behaviors include tearfulness or angry outbursts over seemingly minor incidents, traffic violations, major or subtle changes in eating and/or sleeping patterns, frequent unwillingness or lack of desire to go to work, chronic complaining and negativity, passive-aggressive behaviors, and even substance abuse. In such cases, the aforementioned coping strategies afford only temporary relief; nurses with this level of distress feel overwhelmed or paralyzed and may believe that they simply cannot go on this

---

BOX 7.2 Stress-Management Strategies

Physical
- Accept physical limitations
- Modify nutrition: moderate carbohydrate, moderate protein, high in fruits and vegetables, low caffeine, low sugar
- Exercise: participate in an enjoyable activity five times a week for 30 minutes
- Make your physical health a priority
- Nurture yourself by taking time for breaks and lunch
- Sleep: get enough in quantity and quality

Mental
- Learn to say "no!"
- Use cognitive restructuring and self-talk
- Use imagery
- Develop hobbies or activities
- Plan vacations
- Learn about the system and how problems are handled
- Learn communication, conflict resolution, and time-management skills
- Take continuing education courses

Emotional/Spiritual
- Relax: use meditation, massage, yoga, or biofeedback
- Seek solace in prayer
- Seek professional counseling
- Participate in support groups
- Participate in networking
- Communicate feelings
- Identify and acquire a mentor
- Ask for feedback and clarification

Fig. 7.2 Peers and followers can be supportive and help reduce stress.

way. In these stressful situations, individuals may feel helpless and see no way out. They may require professional assistance from an advanced practice psychiatric nurse, clinical psychologist, psychiatrist, or another mental health professional.

In some organizations, leaders may refer their peers, subordinates, or themselves to EAPs. EAPs are a source of free, voluntary, confidential, short-term professional counseling and other services for employees either via in-house staff or through a contract with a separate mental health agency. This type of counseling can be effective because the counselors are usually already well aware of organizational issues and stressors in the workplace. Some nurses may have confidentiality concerns when using employer-recommended or employer-provided counseling services. However, mental health professionals are bound by their professional standards of confidentiality. Additionally, it is in the nurse's best interest to sign a release of information, such as when seeking employer accommodation for a certain physical or emotional problem.

Those who seek counseling outside of the workplace may be guided in their selection of mental health professionals by a personal provider (physician or nurse practitioner), a knowledgeable colleague in the human resources department, or the most recent edition of their health insurance referral book. A phone call to the state nurses' association and an inquiry for lists of advanced practice registered nurses in adult psychiatric–mental health practice in your region will often yield significant results. When the problem underlying the distress is ethical or moral, a trained pastoral counselor or spiritual director may be very helpful. Some clergy and mental health professionals are certified in pastoral care or have earned a degree in another discipline such as psychology or spiritual direction counseling. Referrals can be obtained from hospital pastoral care departments or places of worship that affiliate with regional centers where certified counselors are available. When private counseling is being arranged, the health insurance contract should be checked to determine mental health benefits and the payment limitations and types of providers eligible for reimbursement.

Leadership and Management

Although social support and counseling can alter how stressors are perceived, effective leadership that is shared and time management that supports involvement at the level of direct care nurse in the unit can certainly modify or remove stressors. Historically, nurses have had limited formal authority as individuals in most organizations. Shared governance, defined by Tim Porter-O'Grady when he first described the pioneer efforts of Vanderbilt University Medical Center in the 1980s, "is a professional practice model, founded on the cornerstone principles of partnership, equity, accountability and ownership" that embraces the concepts of professional governance (Porter-O'Grady, 2013, 2017). Organizations that implement shared governance systems are either "on the bus or off the bus," according to Dr. Robert Hess, creator of the only measurement tools designed to analyze organizational readiness and level of participation in shared governance activities (Mouro, Tashijian, Bachir, Al-Ruzzeih, & Hess, 2013). In Hess's early study (2011), Magnet® hospitals reported 37%, non-Magnet® hospitals reported 16%, and hospitals pursuing Magnet® designation reported 32% of involvement in shared governance activities that bring policy-making to the nurses whose job it is to implement them. Hess has since observed that although the current conversation is about the inclusion of other professionals, such as pharmacists, physicians, and allied health personnel, professional governance is hardly a new construct (Hess, 2017). It may simply be a good idea whose time has become much more in the here and now. Chief nursing executives and the managerial and administrative groups at which tables they sit continually advocate for nursing resources and certainly influence policy and resource allocation. Nurse managers can and must continue to articulate clinical and workplace issues as they work to control existing environmental stressors on their own units. In addition, managers ought to examine their own behavior as a source of their subordinates' stress via peer review, coaching, and regularly scheduled leadership rounds.

In some cases, a controlling or autocratic style of management is appropriate, such as in emergency or disaster situations and when working with a large percentage of new and inexperienced team members. For the most part, however, professional nurses need, want, and deserve the latitude to direct their activities within their sphere of competence. "Letting go" of autocratic power and learning more about the power in delegating important functions to team members means that the nurse leader trusts the personal integrity and professional competence of the entire team. It does not mean abdicating accountability for achieving accepted standards of patient care and agreed-on outcomes. Such an attitude provides ample opportunity to provide invaluable coaching that has the potential to teach, motivate, and guide others toward reaching their full potential.

Assistance with problem solving is another way to reduce environmental stressors. Nurse leaders may provide technical advice, refer staff to appropriate resources, or mediate conflicts. Often, nurse leaders enable staff to meet the demands of their work more independently by providing time for continuing education and preparation for national board certification. Such nurse leaders make it possible for frontline staff to attend internal and external professional meetings to enhance their clinical competence and exert control over their own workplace.

Another way in which nurse leaders can reduce stress is to be supportive of staff. Support is not equated with being a friend or buddy; rather, it is helping one's peers accomplish good care, develop professionally, and feel valued personally. Leaders can ensure that the expected workload is in line with the nurses' capabilities and resources. They can work to ensure meaningfulness, stimulation, and opportunities for nurses to use their skills. Nurses' roles and responsibilities need to be clearly and publicly defined. Work schedules should be posted as far in advance as possible and should be compatible with what is known about patient safety and respect for their team members' private lives and educational schedules. Encouraging innovation and experimentation, as in self-scheduling, for example, can motivate staff and give them a sense of greater control over their environment. Affirming a good idea, finding resources for further study, or implementing a promising new procedure or proposal by a direct care nurse are all characteristic of supportive leadership. It is possible to be supportive even when things are not necessarily going well. For example, when staff members struggle with their methods of coping with overwork and other stressors, supportive leadership behaviors include helping staff members recognize the need to avoid passive coping strategies that fuel helplessness and lower the standards of care through active, engaged coaching. Nurse leaders must be sensitive to the distress of the nursing staff and acknowledge it without themselves becoming therapists or counselors, which would present a role conflict. Support may involve raising the staff's knowledge of counseling resources and truly getting to know each and every staff member.

Nurse leaders also must be careful to avoid diagnostic labels and to maintain strict confidentiality. This is difficult to do, for example, when a nurse's practice is impaired by alcohol or drug use. Sometimes the staff on the entire unit and even staff on other units may already be aware of the impairment. When distress relates to the personal life of subordinates, managers should focus on the effect of such situations on workplace performance and ask for outside assistance, if necessary, to help the members of the team work through the events. The individual who has produced the stress can then hopefully be welcomed back to the job after recovery in a goal-directed program designed to aid the person in appropriate coping approaches.

In addition, leaders can enhance the workplace by dealing effectively with their own stressors. Maintaining a sense of perspective as well as a sense of humor is important. Some stressors, in fact, can be ignored or minimized by posing three questions:

1. Is this event or situation important? Stressors are not all equally significant. Do not waste energy on minor stressors.
2. Does this stressor affect me or my unit? Although some situations that produce distress are institution-wide and need group action, others target specific units or activities. Do not borrow stressors from another unit. Individuals can "cross-pollinate" stressors by spreading gossip about the misfortunes of other units' team members.
3. Can I change this situation? If not, then find a way to cope with it, or if the situation is intolerable, make plans to change positions or employers. This decision may require gaining added credentials that may produce long-term career benefits or contacting a search firm to simply discover "what's out there."

Keeping stressful situations in perspective can enable nurses to conserve their energies to cope with stressful situations that are important, that are within their domain, or that can be changed or modified.

MANAGEMENT OF TIME

A very close relationship exists between stress management and time management. Time management is one method of stress prevention or reduction. Stress can decrease productivity and lead to poor use of time. Time management can be considered a preventive action to help reduce the elements of stress in a nurse's life.

Everyone has two choices when managing time: organize or "go with the flow." Everyone has only 24 hours in every day, and it is clear that some people make better use of time than others do. *How* people use time makes some people more successful than others. The effective use of time-management skills thus becomes an even more important tool to achieve personal and professional goals. Time management is the appropriate use of tools, techniques, and principles to control time spent on low-priority needs and to ensure that time is invested in activities leading toward achieving desired, high-priority goals. More simply, time management is the ability to spend your time on the things that matter to you and your organization. However, it does take time to plan daily time-management strategies! By setting goals and actively working to reduce time stealers, you will have the extra time to accomplish them. Table 7.1 presents a classification scheme for time-management techniques. Table 7.2 provides ways to make applications of time-management strategies to practice.

The unifying theme is that each activity undertaken should lead to goal attainment and that goal should be the number one priority at that time.

TABLE 7.1 Classification of Time-Management Techniques

Technique	Purpose	Actions
Organization	Promotes efficiency and productivity	Organize and systematize things, tasks, and people. Use basic time-management skills.
Keep focused on goals	Focuses on goal achievement	Assemble a prioritized "to do" list daily, based on goals.
Tool usage	Uses the right tool for planning and preparation	Use tools such as a smartphone.
Time-management plan	Helps refocus, gain control, and use information	Develop a personal time-management plan appropriately.

Goal Setting

The first steps in time management are goal setting and developing a plan to reach the goals. Set goals that are reasonable and achievable. Do not expect to reach long-term goals overnight—*long-term* means just that. Give yourself time to meet the goals. Determine many short-term goals to reach the long-term goal, giving you a frequent sense of goal achievement. Give yourself flexibility. If the path you chose last year is no longer appropriate, change it. Write your goals, date the entry, keep it handy, and refer to it often to give yourself a progress report. Very often, goals are an important discussion point of the annual performance evaluation process. The time for reviewing goals ought not to be the period immediately preceding this year's discussion, yet unfortunately too often this is the case. Savvy nurse leaders will refer to mutually set goals frequently throughout the year and address, encourage, and recognize progress toward achievement during monthly meetings and at specific hallmark times.

Setting Priorities

Once goals are known, priorities are set. They may, however, shift throughout a given period in terms of goal attainment. For example, working on a budget may take precedence at certain times of the year, whereas new staff orientation to a brand-new electronic medical record system is a higher priority at other times. Knowing what your goals and priorities are helps shape the "to do" list. On a nursing unit or as you work in a community setting, you must know your personal goals and current priorities. How you organize work may depend on geographic considerations, patient acuity, or some other schema.

A particular strategy to assist in prioritization suggests that people generally focus on those things that are important and urgent. Clarity is enhanced about priorities by placing the elements of importance and urgency in a grid (Fig. 7.3 on p. 117) or by using the Covey Matrix, also known as the Eisenhower's Urgent-Important Principle (Mueller, 2015).

Typically, we tend to focus on those items in cell A because they are both important and urgent and therefore command our attention. Making shift assignments is an A task because it is both important to the work to be accomplished and commonly urgent, because a time frame is specified during which data about patients and qualifications of staff can be matched. Conversely, if something is neither important nor urgent (cell D), it

TABLE 7.2   Time-Management Applications to Practice

Key Idea	Definition	Application to Practice
Losing track of time	Absorption in one aspect of a task, or even distractions that prevent focus on a task, preventing successful resolution in a time-effective manner	Concentrate on results. Identify common "time stealers" and guard against them. Do not get caught up with the technology such as answering e-mails or responding to instant message alerts. Minimize distractions. Use an alarm or stopwatch feature on your smartphone or other device. Take a class on time management.
Doing too much	Competing priorities that vie for attention	Reduce the number of important projects that are due at the same time. Be realistic and limit major commitments. Give each major activity your undivided attention. Avoid multitasking whenever possible! Make a daily "to do" list and tick them off as each is accomplished. Engage with a supervisor or mentor for advice/guidance on which project needs the most attention.
Learning to say "no" or "not now, please"	Politely declining requests for an additional project or assignment	Agreeing to tasks that are not in alignment with your individual personal/professional priorities may translate into frustration and resentment. Consider whether this task may be easily delegated to another individual. Discuss the request in detail so you may better understand the nature: Is it in alignment with the organization's overall goals or your family's primary needs at this time? Or, is it someone else's "emergency" and they need a favor?
Procrastination	Putting off important tasks because they may not be enjoyable or involve a level of difficulty	Identify the reason for procrastination. Develop a PERT (Program Evaluation and Review Technique) chart or a Gantt chart (see Table 7.3) to help parse out complex assignments. Make that specific task your number one priority for the next opportunity. Select either the least attractive component or the easiest; tackle that part first. Reward yourself after you complete the task.
Complaining/ whining	Expressing dissatisfaction or annoyance	Stop and ask yourself, "What would the ideal resolution be?" and then, take the risk to act on it. Discuss the scenario with a trusted friend/co-worker/mentor or supervisor. Bring potential solutions so that you can move beyond complaining to effective problem solving. Spend time speaking with the parties involved or those with the power to improve the overall situation.

TABLE 7.2   Time-Management Applications to Practice—cont'd

Key Idea	Definition	Application to Practice
		Write yourself a letter describing the situation as well as options for correction. Look for solutions that are very simple or "outside the box" for you.
Perfectionism	The tendency to never completely finish a project or assignment because it is not yet acceptable	Continue to do your best. Find and share feedback with others who have similar assignments or projects or are in situations like yours. Once you receive feedback on your project, move quickly to incorporate it into your final submission and move on to the next assignment.
Interruptions	Avoidable or unavoidable occurrences that distract from one's ability to complete a prioritized task	Set workplace rules to limit lengthy e-mails and other distractions (see Box 7.3). Mentally, dive right back into the immediate task at hand.
Information overload	Proliferation of data that occurs too quickly to be able to interpret the information in an effective manner	Form or join study groups or other forms of knowledge communities. Learn to appreciate podcasts, e-mail capsules of weekly healthcare news, or other professional organizations' and specialty associations' online news summaries.

TABLE 7.3   Sample Gantt Chart

Task	Accountability	Jan	Feb	Mar	Apr	May	June
1. Conduct literature search	Unit clinical nurse specialist	———→					
2. Hold nursing practice committee meeting to review material	Chair, nursing practice committee		X				
3. Create report for the medical staff	Chair, nursing practice committee			————————→			
4. Disseminate findings to nursing and medical staff	Chair, nursing practice committee					————————→	

	IMPORTANT	
	yes	no
URGENT yes	A	C
URGENT no	B	D

Fig. 7.3 Classification of priorities.

may be considered a waste of time, at least in terms of personal goals. An example of a D activity might be reading "junk" e-mail or attention-grabbing department store or vacation advertisements. Even if something is urgent but not important (cell C), it contributes minimally to productivity and goal achievement. An example of a C activity might be responding to a memo that has a specific time line but is not important to goal attainment. The real key to setting priorities is to attend to the B tasks, those that are important but not urgent. Examples of B activities are reviewing the organization's strategic plan or participating on organizational committees.

Organization

A number of simple routines for organization can save many minutes over a day and enhance your efficiency. Keeping a workspace neat or arranging things in an orderly fashion may be a powerful time-management tool. Rather than a system of "pile management," use "file management." Although the historical view was of physical paper

---

BOX 7.3   Tips to Prevent Interruptions and Work More Effectively

- Ask people to put their comments in writing in an e-mail—do not let them catch you "on the run." On the same note, do not use others as you would a Post-it note!
- Let the office or unit secretary know what information you need immediately.
- Conduct a conversation in the hall to help keep it short or in a separate room to keep from being interrupted.
- Be comfortable saying "no" and "not yet."
- When involved in a long procedure or home visit, ask someone else to cover your other responsibilities.
- Break projects into small, manageable pieces.
- Get yourself organized.
- Minimize interruptions—for example, allow voicemail to pick up the phone; shut the door.
- Keep your work surface clear. Have available only those documents needed for the task at hand.
- Keep your manager informed of your goals.
- Plan to accomplish high-priority or difficult tasks early in the day.
- Develop a plan for the day and stick to it. Remember to schedule in some time for interruptions.
- Schedule time to meet regularly throughout the shift with staff members for whom you are responsible.
- Make an effort to round with the night and weekend team; conduct early morning breakfasts so that night staff can meet with you away from their unit.
- Recognize that crises and interruptions are part of the position.
- Be cognizant of your personal time-wasting habits, and try to avoid them.

---

and desk surface, the same concepts apply to a laptop or mobile phone. The following are a few hints:

- Plan where things should go: your desk or your disk
- Keep a clean workspace
- Create a "to do" folder
- Use a "to be filed" folder for any papers
- Schedule time to work your way through the folders

If you don't have a physical desk at work, you typically use something—a designated space, a tablet, a clipboard, or your phone. Consider how to translate this list into a nondesk format.

Determine your priority goals for the next day, and have the materials ready to work on when you start the next day. If you are fortunate to have the resources of a secretary or administrative assistant, even for very limited periods of the day, be sure to discuss with this individual how creative scheduling has the power to either maximize your day or sap your energy and strength to deal with your obligations.

EXERCISE 7.4   Create a goal statement related to some competency you wish to achieve or improve. Using a Gantt chart approach, designate timelines and activities to meet this goal. Print the chart or enter it in your phone to track your progress.

Time Tools

Sometimes, the real problem is that the events of the day become the driving force, rather than a planned schedule. Days may become so tightly scheduled that any little interruption can become a crisis. If you do not plan the day, you may be responding to events rather than prioritized goals. If you think you are a reactor rather than a proactive time user, use a time log to list work-related activities for several days. You may not be able to plan well because you really do not have a good estimate of how long a particular activity actually takes or you do not know how many activities can be accomplished in a given time frame. Ask others around you if *your* lack of planning has a negative impact on *their* work day. The answer may be as unsettling as it is startling: Your work habits may be impacting *their* lives.

As the nurse's role in care management becomes more complex, the need for organizational tools increases. Tracking the care of groups of patients, either as a member of a care team or in a leadership capacity, can be overwhelming. Each nurse must devise a method for tracking care and organizing time, as well as delegating and monitoring care provided by others. Although some nurses depend on a shift flowsheet, many more now have the benefit of computerized information tracking systems. Handheld smartphones or other devices provided by the hospital or bar-code scanners for medication administration are other methods to track information and increase safety and efficiency. The issue of patient confidentiality and organizational privacy cannot be ignored when entering data into any device. Check with your organization's privacy officer and appropriate policies to verify that you are on the right side of managing paper and electronic information.

Managing Information

The first step in managing information is to assess the source. Once you have identified the sources of your data, you have a better idea of how to deal with the information. Track incoming information for a few days. Patterns will begin to emerge and will give clues as to how to deal with it. You can generally predict that, using the Pareto principle, 80% of your incoming data comes from approximately 20% of your sources, and that 80% of useful information comes from 20% of information received (see the Theory Box on p. 106). By developing information-receiving skills, you can quickly interpret the data and convert them to useful information, discarding unneeded data. Initially, you should reduce or eliminate that which is useless. Label files and folders to which e-mail messages can be directed. Delete e-mails, or encourage administrative leaders to endorse systems that automatically archive older messages. Next, monitor the information flow and decide what to do with incoming data. Find and focus on the most important pieces, and then quickly narrow down the specific details you need. Identify resources that are most helpful, and have them readily available. Be able to build the big picture from the masses of data you receive. Finally, recognize when you have enough information to act.

Once you have mastered the receiving end of information, concentrate on your own information-sending skills. Remember, your information is simply another person's data! Try to keep your outflow short; make it a synthesis of the information. Remember, if your e-mail message is more than a few sentences in length, your message probably warrants a phone call or meeting instead. Finally, select the most appropriate mode of communication for your message from the technology available. You may be sending your information in written (memo or report) or verbal (face-to-face or presentation) form or via telephone, webinar or WebEx, voice mail, e-mail, text, Twitter, or fax. Remember, the most important skill is to know when you have said enough. Exercise 7.5 will help you consider how you have dealt with information.

> **EXERCISE 7.5** Think of the last time you were in the clinical area. How often did you record the same piece of data (e.g., a finding in your assessment of the patient)? Remember to include all steps, from your jotting down notes on a piece of paper or entering data into the computer to the final report of the day. What information processing tools could decrease the number of steps?

Delegating

Delegation is a critical component of self-management for nurse managers and care managers. Appropriate delegation not only increases time efficiency but also serves as a means of reducing stress. Delegation is discussed in depth in Chapter 17, but it is also appropriate to discuss briefly as a time-management strategy. Delegation works only when the delegator trusts the delegatee to accomplish the task and to report findings back to the delegator. The delegator wastes time if he or she checks and redoes everything someone else has done. Delegation requires empowerment of the delegatee to accomplish the task. If the nurse does not delegate appropriately, with clear expectations as an opportunity for growth, the delegatee will constantly be asking for assistance or direction. Delegation can also be a means of reducing stress if used appropriately. If the nurse does not understand delegation and does not use it appropriately, it can be a major source of stress as the nurse assumes accountability and responsibility for care administered by others.

CONCLUSION

Self-management is a means to achieve a balance between work and personal life, as well as a way of life to achieve personal goals within self-imposed priorities and deadlines. Time management is clock-oriented; stress management is the control of external and internal stressors. EI allows you to know yourself and others and read situations effectively to respond appropriately.

To achieve a balance in life and minimize stressors, nurses must learn to sit back and see their own personal big picture and examine their personal and professional goals. Personal priorities also must be established. Stressors and coping strategies need to be identified and used. By developing these techniques, nurses can gain a sense of control and become far better nurses, and leaders, in the process.

THE SOLUTION

I knew I couldn't continue at my current pace because I would burn myself out in a short period of time. Most importantly, I knew I couldn't maintain focus on my goals if I was so tired all the time. I decided to set goals for every single day. I put the hours on my calendar for "me" time: There is an hour for my budget, my quality indicators, my paperwork. This served as a constant reminder for me to do what I needed to accomplish. I would print out my daily calendar and I would check it throughout the day so I would actually keep to my deadlines. I do like this method! It keeps me focused and keeps me organized. I find myself meeting deadlines now. I have the time to handle emergencies and unforeseen situations. I tend to stick to my "me" time and excuse myself from any distractions. I say the words, "I have a meeting to go to," when in reality, it is really my own work that I am headed to.

Because the unit was closing, I accepted a nurse manager role in another unit at the hospital. However, this unit was the complete opposite of the one I had led to success. It was way at the bottom in every single metric you could think of! I became focused trying to help my old team during the anticipated closure as best as I knew how: I invited the VP/CNO to come to breakfast frequently on the unit,

along with the bargaining unit and human resources leadership. I constantly checked in with staff to help them apply for posted positions and help some of them transition to new roles in other units. On my new unit, I brought in seasoned assistant nurse managers and encouraged the high-performing staff to apply for the vacancies that were created when the low performers either resigned or were disciplined. In terms of my own stress, I definitely felt I had to get better at taking care of myself. My VP/CNO encouraged me to take days off, and I went on a cruise for a family vacation and celebration. Considering the increased load, I guess I had to! I try to get enough sleep; I try to eat a balanced diet; I take a vitamin daily; I exercise by doing the weighted hula hoop and by enjoying dancing; and I am a spiritual person so I pray and attend religious services.

My family and my nurse leaders are really supportive, and I feel lucky to have people like that around me! I really love my job, and although I miss and mourn for my old unit, I know I can turn this unit around so it can be successful.

Would this be a suitable approach for you? Why?

Savitra Sutton

REFLECTIONS

When you think about stress in your personal life, how would you describe it? What impact does it have on your professional goals? How can you be more personally effective?

THE EVIDENCE

Several studies referenced in this chapter identify stressors we can all experience and how they affect us. Similarly, several stress reducers are offered because they have shown effectiveness in helping people deal with stress.

TIPS FOR SELF-MANAGEMENT

- Make your health a priority and use strategies that keep yourself feeling cared for and in control.
- Make and keep personal physical and mental health appointments.
- Know your personal response to stress and self-evaluate frequently.
- Know what your high-priority goals are and use them to filter decisions.
- Refocus on your priorities whenever you begin to feel overwhelmed.
- Use organizational systems that meet your needs; the simpler, the better.
- Simplify.

REFERENCES

Alexander, G. K., Rollins, K., Walker, D., Wong, L., & Pennings, J. (2015). Yoga for self-care and burnout prevention among nurses. *Workplace Health and Safety, 63*(10), 462–470.

American Organization of Nurse Executives. (2015). *AONE Nurse Manager Competencies.* Chicago: Author. http://www.aone.org/resources/nurse-leader-competencies.shtml.

Basogul, C., & Ozgur, G. (2016). Role of emotional intelligence in conflict management strategies of nurses. *Asian Nursing Research, 10*(2016), 228–233.

Diesing, G. (2016). You've hired a millennial. Now what? *Hospital & Health Networks.* http://www.hhnmag.org.

Dyess, S., Sherman, R., Pratt, B., & Chiang-Hanisko, L. (January 14, 2016). Growing Nurse Leaders: Their Perspectives on Nursing Leadership and Today's Practice Environment. *OJIN: The Online Journal of Issues in Nursing, 21*(1).

Fernandez, R. (2016). Help your team manage stress, anxiety and burnout. *Harvard Business Review.* http://hbr.org.

Goleman, D. (1995). *Emotional intelligence.* New York: Bantam Books.

Goleman, D. (2017). *Emotional self-awareness: A primer.* Florence, MA: More Than Sound LLC.

Gouin, J. P. (2011). Chronic stress, immune dysregulation, and health. *American Journal of Lifestyle Medicine, 5*(6), 476–485.

Greenglass, E., Burke, R., & Fiksenbaum, L. (2001). Workload and burnout in nurses. *Journal of Community and Applied Social Psychology, 11,* 211–215.

Hafner, A. W. (2001). *Pareto's Principle: The 80-20 rule.* www.bsu.edu/libraries/ahafner/awh-th-math-pareto.html.

Health Resources and Services Administration. (2013). Bureau of Health Professionals, National Center for Health Workforce. *The US nursing workforce: Trends in supply and education.* http://bhpr.hrsa.gov/healthworkforce/reports/nursingworkforce/nursingworkforcefullreport.pdf.

Hess, R. (2017). Professional governance: Another new concept? *Journal of Nursing Administration, 47*(1), 1–2.

Hess, R., DesRoches, C., Donelan, K., Norman, L., & Buerhaus, P. (2011). Perceptions of nurses in Magnet® hospitals, non-Magnet hospitals, and hospitals pursuing Magnet status. *Journal of Nursing Administration, 41*(7/8), 315–323.

Iacobellis, F. (2015). The relationship among role stress, structural empowerment and burnout in newly graduated nurses working in acute care hospitals. *Master's Thesis.* http://do.doi.org/doi:10.7282/T3WQ05N0.

Kobasa, S. C., Maddi, S. R., & Kahn, S. (1982). Hardiness and health: A perspective study. *Journal of Personality and Social Psychology, 42*(1), 168–177.

Kramer, M. (1974). *Reality shock: Why nurses leave nursing.* St. Louis: Mosby.

Labrague, L. J., McEnroe-Petitte, D. M., Gloe, D., Tsaras, K., Arteche, D. L., & Maldia, F. (2016). Organizational politics, nurses' stress, burnout levels, turnover intention and job satisfaction. *International Council of Nurses, 67*(2017), 20–28.

Lambert, C. E., & Lambert, V. A. (1987). Hardiness: Its development and relevance to nursing. *Journal of Nursing Scholarship, 19*(2), 92–95.

Lambert, V., Lambert, C., & Yamase, H. (2003). Psychological hardiness, workplace stress and related stress reduction strategies. *Nursing and Health Sciences, 5,* 181–184.

Maslach, C., & Leiter, M. P. (1997). *The truth about burnout: How organizations cause personal stress and what to do about it.* San Francisco: Jossey Bass.

Maslow, A. H. (1943). A theory of human motivation. *Psychological Review, 50,* 370–396.

Miller, E. T. (2016). Preventing burnout. *Rehabilitation Nursing, 41,* 65–66.

Miller, J., & Adkins, A. (2016). Women want close relationships at work. *Gallup Business Journal.* http://businessjournal.gallup.com/content/women-want-close-relationships-at-work.

Morsy, L., & Rothstein, R. (2015). *Parents' non-standard work schedules make adequate child rearing difficult. Economic Policy Institute.* Issue Brief #400. http://epi.org.

Mouro, G., Tashijian, H., Bachir, M., Al-Ruzzeih, H., & Hess, R. (2013). Comparing nurses' perceptions of governance related to hospitals' journeys to excellence status in the Middle East. *Nursing Economics, 31*(4), 184–189.

Mueller, S. (2015). *Stephen Covey's Time Management Matrix Explained.* planetofsuccess.com.

Nagel, Y., Towell, A., Nel, E., & Foxall, F. (2016). The emotional intelligence of registered nurses commencing critical care nursing. *Curationis, 39*(1), 1–7.

Patterson, E., Lowry, S. Z., Ramaiah, M., Gibbons, M. C., Brick, D., Calco, R., et al. (2015). Improving clinical workflow in ambulatory care: Implemented recommendations in an innovation prototype for the veteran's health administration. *Generating Evidence and Methods to Improve Patient Outcomes, 3*(1). Article 11. http://repository.academyhealth.org/egems/vol3/iss2/11.

Plsek, P. E., & Greenhalgh, T. (2001). The challenge of complexity in health care. *British Medical Journal, 323* (7313), 625–628.

Porter-O'Grady, T. (2013). *Shared Governance.* www.mc. vanderbilt.edu/root/vumc.php?site=Shared% 20Governance&doc=23733.

Porter-O'Grady, T. (2017). A response to the question of professional governance versus shared governance. *Journal of Nursing Administration Quarterly, 47*(2), 69–71.

Sanders, E. D. (2015). Nursing resilience: A nursing opportunity. *Nursing Administration Quarterly, 39*(2), 6.

Schultz, N. S., & Loi, N. M. Connections between emotional intelligence and workplace flourishing. *Personality and Individual Differences, 66:*134–139.

Scott, T. (2015). Teaching emotional intelligence. *Emergency Nurse, 23*(3), 5.

Selye, H. (1956). *The stress of life.* New York: McGraw-Hill.

Selye, H. (1965). The stress syndrome. *American Journal of Nursing, 65,* 97–99.

Selye, H. (1991). History and present status of the stress concept. In A. Monat & R. Lazarus (Eds.), *Stress and coping: An anthology* (3rd ed., pp. 21–36). New York: Columbia University Press.

Shi, R., Zhang, S., Xu, H., Liu, X., & Miao, D. (2015). Regulatory focus and burnout in nurses: The mediating effect of perception of transformational leadership. *International Journal of Nursing Practice, 21,* 858–867.

Shirey, M. (2006). Stress and coping in nurse managers: Two decades of research. *Nursing Economic$, 24*(4), 193–211.

Spano-Szekely, L., Quinn Griffin, M. T., Clavelle, J., & Fitzpatrick, J. J. (2016). Emotional intelligence and transformational leadership in nurse managers. *Journal of Nursing Administration, 46*(2), 101–108.

Steege, L. M., & Rainbow, J. G. (2017). Fatigue in hospital nurses – 'Supernurse' culture is a barrier to addressing problems: A qualitative interview study. *International Journal of Nursing Studies, 67*(2017), 20–28.

TalentSmart. (2017). *About emotional intelligence.* www.talentsmart.com/about/emotional-intelligence.php.

Taylor, S. E., Klein, L. C., Lewis, B. P., Gruenewald, T. L., Gurung, R. A., & Updegraff, J. A. (2000). Biobehavioral responses to stress in females: Tend-and-befriend, not fight-or-flight. *Psychological Review, 107,* 411–429.

Tomova, L., Majdandzic, J., Hummer, A., Windischberger, C., Heinrichs, M., & Lamm, C. (2016). Increased neural responses to empathy for pain might explain how acute stress increases prosociality. *Social Cognitive and Affective Neuroscience.* www.sciencedaily.com/releases/2017/04/170411104758.htm.

U.S. Census Bureau. (2013). Male nurses becoming more commonplace. https://www.census.gov/newsroom/press-releases/2013/cb13-32.html.

Whitman, J. (2017). The next generation of leaders: Guiding millennials in the nurse workforce. *Director of Surgical Services Review, 2*(2), 1–3.

Yu, A. (2016). Nurses say stress interferes with caring for their patients. *Shots: Health News from NPR.* npr.org.

Zangaro, G. A., & Soeken, K. L. (2007). A meta-analysis of studies of nurse's job satisfaction. *Research in Nursing & Health, 30,* 445–458.

8

Communication and Conflict

Victoria N. Folse

LEARNING OUTCOMES

- Describe behaviors and techniques that affect communication among members of the healthcare team.
- Use a model of the conflict process to determine the nature and sources of perceived and actual conflict.
- Assess preferred approaches to conflict to be more effective in communicating and resolving future conflict.

- Determine which of the five approaches to conflict is the most appropriate in potential and actual situations.
- Identify conflict management techniques that will prevent lateral violence and bullying from occurring.

KEY TERMS

accommodating
avoiding
bullying
collaborating
competing
compromising
conflict

handoff communication
horizontal violence
incivility
interpersonal conflict
interprofessional communication
intrapersonal conflict
lateral violence

mediation
negotiating
organizational conflict
situation, background, assessment, and recommendation (SBAR)
volatility, uncertainty, complexity, and ambiguity (VUCA)

THE CHALLENGE

After graduating from nursing school, I accepted a job in a Nurse Residency program and was placed on the postanesthesia care unit (PACU). Shortly after finishing my orientation, I was assigned to a two-patient slot, where I received patients straight from the operating room. On this heavy case-load day, I received a patient who was "deep" under anesthesia (meaning a patient at high risk for respiratory spasm) and also sedated on a Precedex drip. Per our PACU protocol, these patients are supposed to be one-to-

one assignments. Because of the high census this day and a shortage of available patient slots, my charge nurse was forced to place another patient in my second slot just minutes after I received this sedated, high-acuity patient. I wasn't sure if I should speak up.

What would you do if you were this nurse?

Shannen R. McCrory, RN, BSN
Staff Nurse, Pediatric Intensive Care Unit,
Vanderbilt Children's Hospital, Nashville, TN

INTRODUCTION

In today's complex practice environment, communicating effectively and resolving conflict are more important than ever to provide optimal patient care and to consistently meet the six competencies identified by Quality and Safety Education for Nurses (QSEN): patient-centered care, teamwork and collaboration, evidence-based practice, quality improvement, safety, and informatics (QSEN Institute, n.d.). To achieve these competencies and to reduce the likelihood of miscommunication that leads to healthcare errors, nurses must communicate with patients and families, fellow nurses, and other members of the healthcare team. Interprofessional communication is effective when healthcare providers communicate with each other and with patients and their families in an open, collaborative, and respectful manner. Conflict is a disagreement in values or beliefs within oneself or between people that causes harm or has the potential to cause harm. Conflict is a catalyst for change and has the ability to produce either detrimental or beneficial effects. Conflict, when used positively, can stimulate stagnant teams and increase productivity (McKibben, 2017). If properly understood and managed, conflict can lead to positive outcomes and practice environments, but if it is left unattended, it can have a negative impact on both the individual and the organization. Good leadership combined with positive team dynamics, effective communication, and successful conflict management practices promotes shared problem solving and acceptance of change (McKibben, 2017). In professional practice environments, unresolved conflict and miscommunication among nurses is a significant issue resulting in job dissatisfaction, absenteeism, and turnover. Effective healthcare team communication may strengthen nurses' engagement within their organizations and improve nurse retention. Patient dissatisfaction is lower in hospitals in which nurses are frustrated and burned out, which signals a problem with quality of care (Stimpfel, Sloane, McHugh, & Aiken, 2016).

Successful organizations are proactive in anticipating the need for interprofessional education about communication, conflict resolution, and teamwork and enact innovative and integrated conflict resolution strategies and communication programs (Turrentine et al., 2016).

Conflict can be desirable at times and can be a strategic tool when addressed appropriately. Some of the first authors on organizational conflict (e.g., Blake & Mouton, 1964; Deutsch, 1973) claimed that a complete resolution of conflict might, in fact, be undesirable, because conflict also stimulates growth, creativity, and change. Seminal work on the concept of organizational conflict management suggested conflict was necessary to achieve organizational goals and cohesiveness of employees, facilitate organizational change, and contribute to creative problem solving and mutual understanding. Moderate levels of conflict contribute to the quality of ideas generated and foster cohesiveness among team members, contributing to an organization's success. An organization without conflict is characterized by no change; in contrast, an optimal level of conflict will generate creativity, a problem-solving atmosphere, a strong team spirit, and motivation of its workers. Conflict in an interdisciplinary team can result in better patient care when collaborative treatment decisions are based on carefully examined and combined expertise. Nursing leaders must focus on healthy work environments to promote effective communication in stressful situations to increase patient safety (André, Frigstad, Nøst, & Sjøvold, 2016).

The complexity of the healthcare environment compounds the impact that ineffective communication, caregiver stress, and unresolved conflict has on patient safety. Conflict is inherent in clinical environments in which nursing responsibilities are driven by patient needs that are complex and frequently changing and in practice settings in which nurses have multiple professional roles. Healthcare providers are exposed to high stress levels from increased demands on a limited and aging workforce, a decrease in available resources, a more acutely ill and underinsured patient population, and a profound period of change in the practice environment. Conflict among healthcare providers is inevitable and is compounded by employee diversity, high nurse-to-patient ratios, pressure to make timely decisions, and status differences. Nurses employed in better care environments report more positive job experiences and fewer concerns about quality care. Interprofessional collaboration has been characterized by effective communication and is a key factor in reducing error and improving patient outcomes (Turrentine et al., 2016). Moreover, hospitals with good nurse–physician relationships are associated with better nurse and patient outcomes, making collaboration and conflict resolution among nurses and physicians crucial in promoting quality of care outcomes (Stimpfel et al., 2016).

An important factor in the successful management of stress and conflict is a better understanding of its context within the practice environment. The diversity of people involved in health care may stimulate conflict, but the shared goal of meeting patient care needs provides a solid foundation for conflict resolution. Because nursing remains a predominately female profession, this may contribute to the use of avoidance and accommodation as primary conflict handling strategies. The stereotypical self-sacrificing behavior seen in avoidance and accommodation is strongly supported by the altruistic nature of nursing. Avoidance may be appropriate during times of high stress, but when overused, avoidance threatens the well-being of nurses and retention within the discipline. To illustrate, a correlation exists for nurses who experience work stress and who use avoidance to handle conflict (Johansen & Cadmus, 2016).

EFFECTIVE COMMUNICATION WITHIN HEALTHCARE SETTINGS

Effective communication between a healthcare provider and other members of the healthcare team promotes optimal patient outcomes. Equally important is making certain the communication that occurs between healthcare providers and patients and families ensures quality care and patient safety and satisfaction. Although the communication within healthcare settings is often complex and chaotic, understanding the basic principles of the communication process is essential (Fig. 8.1). The Joint Commission (TJC, 2017) recognizes that breakdown in communication is the root cause of sentinel events, which are unexpected occurrences that result in death or serious injury. Communication when the patient is handed over from one provider to another or from one setting to another is especially problematic. Not surprisingly, each of the National Patient Safety Goals (see TJC for the current goals) is directly or indirectly related to communication.

> **EXERCISE 8.1** Access The Joint Commission website (https://www.jointcommission.org/standards_information/npsgs.aspx) for the current National Patient Safety Goals. Identify how each goal is affected by communication.

Sender [Encode] → Message → Receiver [Decode]
FEEDBACK [Roles reverse in typical communication exchanges.]

Fig. 8.1 Basic communication model.

Because adverse patient outcomes commonly are a result of communication failures, TJC's National Patient Safety Goals added standardization of handoff communication, the verbal and written exchange of pertinent information during transitions of care. Handoff communication occurs during nurse change-of-shift report, transfer of patients between units or facilities, and reports between departments and between disciplines. Communication is also important when nurses are communicating changes in a patient's condition to other members of the healthcare team. Common language for communicating critical information such as during huddles or rounding can help prevent misunderstandings. Healthcare providers need to allow sufficient time to ask and respond to questions. Reading back information also helps identify any miscommunication and ensures the information received is accurate. Intimidating and disruptive behaviors affect communication and must not be tolerated in healthcare settings, because both employee satisfaction and patient safety can be affected.

Conflicts and miscommunication between nurses and other healthcare providers, including physicians, may be intensified because of the overlapping nature of their professional domains and lack of clarification between roles. Nurses and physicians are prepared differently, and they exhibit differences in communication styles (Foronda, MacWilliams, & McArthur, 2016). Also, when asked to describe relationships with physicians, nurses frequently reported power as a dominant theme, which affects communication and creates conflict. Use of common language, like SBAR, when communicating critical information helps prevent misunderstandings and promotes a culture of quality and safety. SBAR, which stands for situation, background, assessment, and recommendation (Institute for Healthcare Improvement, 2017), has become a best practice for standardizing communication between healthcare providers. The fast pace, frequent interruptions, and stress present in healthcare settings interfere with effective communication (Foronda et al., 2016). The term VUCA describes today's healthcare environment: volatility, uncertainty, complexity, and ambiguity. Each of these elements increases the potential for miscommunication. Clear, complete, and accurate communication among healthcare providers directly affects the quality and safety of care (Lee, Mast, Humbert, Bagnardi, & Richards, 2016). Nurses have a responsibility to provide quality care and thus must serve in leadership roles to ensure effective communication and conflict resolution.

TYPES OF CONFLICT

The recognition that conflict is a part of everyday life suggests that mastering conflict management strategies is essential for overall well-being and personal and professional growth. A need exists to determine the type of conflict present in a specific situation, because the more accurately conflict is defined, the more likely it will be resolved. Conflict occurs in three broad categories and can be intrapersonal, interpersonal, or organizational in nature. A combination of types can also be present in any given conflict.

Intrapersonal conflict occurs within a person when confronted with the need to think or act in a way that seems at odds with one's sense of self. Questions often arise that create a conflict over priorities, ethical standards, and values. When a nurse decides what to do about the future (e.g., "Do I want to accept the job in the city with more cultural opportunities or remain in my hometown and be close to my family?"), conflicts arise between personal and professional priorities. Some issues present a conflict over comfortably maintaining the status quo (e.g., "I know my newest charge nurse likes the autonomy of working nights. Do I really want to ask him to move to days to become a preceptor?"). Taking risks to confront people when needed (e.g., "Would recommending a change in practice that I learned about at a recent conference jeopardize unit governance?") can produce intrapersonal conflict and, because it involves other people, may lead to interpersonal conflict.

Interpersonal conflict is the most common type of conflict and transpires between and among patients, family members, nurses, physicians, and members of other departments. Conflicts occur that focus on a difference of opinion, priority, or approach with others. A manager may be called upon to assist two nurses in resolving a scheduling conflict or issues surrounding patient assignments. Members of healthcare teams often have disputes over the best way to treat particular cases or disagreements over how much information is necessary for patients and families to have about their illness. Yet interpersonal conflict can serve as the impetus for needed change and can strengthen the practice setting.

Organizational conflict arises when discord exists about policies and procedures, personnel codes of conduct, or accepted norms of behavior and patterns of communication. Some organizational conflict is related to hierarchical structure and role differentiation among employees. Nurse managers, as well as their staff, often become embattled in institution-wide conflict concerning staffing patterns and how they affect the quality of care. Complex ethical and moral dilemmas often arise when profitable services are increased and unprofitable ones are downsized or even eliminated.

A major source of organizational conflict stems from strategies that promote more participation and autonomy of direct care nurses. Increasingly, nurses are charged with balancing direct patient care with active involvement in the institutional initiatives surrounding quality patient care. A growing number of standards set by TJC target improving communication and conflict management. Specifically, TJC requires that healthcare organizations have a code of conduct that defines acceptable and inappropriate behaviors and that leaders create and implement a process for managing intimidating and disruptive behaviors that undermine a culture of safety. Standards pertaining to medical staff also include interpersonal skills and professionalism (TJC, 2017). The Magnet Recognition Program® of the American Nurses Credentialing Center (ANCC) identifies effective interdisciplinary relationships as one of the Forces of Magnetism necessary for Magnet® designation (American Nurses Credentialing Center, 2017). Specifically, collaborative working relationships within and among the disciplines are valued, demonstrated through mutual respect, and result in meaningful contributions in the achievement of shared clinical outcomes. Magnet® hospitals must have conflict management strategies in place and use them effectively, when indicated. The following are other "forces" that are particularly germane to communication and conflict in the practice environment:

- Organizational structure (nurses' involvement in shared decision making)
- Management style (nursing leaders who create an environment that supports participation, encourage and value feedback, and demonstrate effective communication with staff)
- Personnel policies and programs (efforts to promote nurse work–life balance)
- Image of nursing (nurses effectively influencing system-wide processes)
- Autonomy (nurses' inclusion in governance leading to job satisfaction, personal fulfillment, and organization success)

EXERCISE 8.2 Recall a situation in which conflict between or among two or more people was apparent. Describe verbal and nonverbal communication and how each person responded. What was the outcome? Was the conflict resolved? Was anything left unresolved?

STAGES OF CONFLICT

The classic view of conflict is that it proceeds through four stages: frustration, conceptualization, action, and outcomes (Thomas, 1992). The ability to resolve conflicts productively depends on understanding this process (Fig. 8.2) and successfully addressing thoughts,

feelings, and behaviors that form barriers to resolution. As one navigates through the stages of conflict, moving into a subsequent stage may lead to a return to and change in a previous stage (Fig. 8.3). To illustrate, the evening shift of a cardiac step-down unit has been asked to pilot a new hand-off protocol for the next 6 weeks, which stimulates intense emotions because the unit is already inadequately staffed (frustration). Two nurses on the unit interpret this conflict as a battle for control with the nurse educator, and a third nurse thinks it is all about professional standards (conceptualization). A nurse leader/manager facilitates a discussion with the three nurses (action); she listens to the concerns and presents evidence about the potential effectiveness of the new hand-off protocol. All agree that the real conflict comes from a difference in goals or priorities (new conceptualization), which leads to less negative emotion and ends with a much clearer understanding of all the issues (diminished frustration). The nurses agree to pilot the

Fig. 8.2 Stages of conflict.

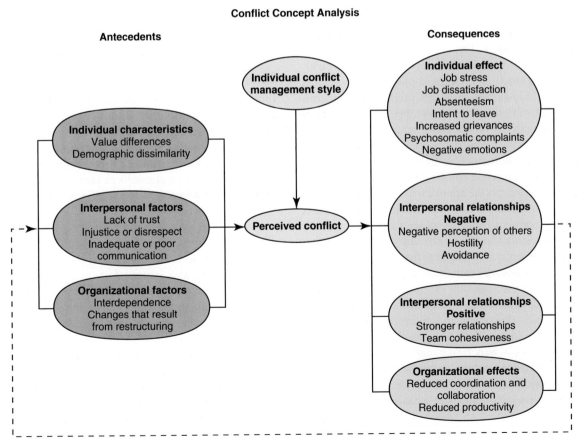

Fig. 8.3 Antecedents and consequences of conflict.

hand-off protocol after their ideas have been incorporated into the plan (outcome).

Frustration

When people or groups perceive that their goals may be blocked, frustration results. This frustration may escalate into stronger emotions, such as anger and deep resignation. For example, a nurse may perceive that a postoperative patient is noncompliant or uncooperative, when in reality the patient is afraid or has a different set of priorities at the start from those of the nurse. At the same time, the patient may view the nurse as controlling and uncaring because the nurse repeatedly asks if the patient has used his incentive spirometer as instructed. When such frustrations occur, it is a cue to stop and clarify the nature and cause of the differences.

Conceptualization

Conflict arises when different interpretations of a situation occur, including a different emphasis on what is important and what is not, and different thoughts about what should occur next. Everyone involved develops an idea of what the conflict is about, and this view may or may not be accurate. This conclusion may be instant or developed over time. Everyone involved has an individual interpretation of what the conflict is and why it is occurring. Most often, these interpretations are dissimilar and involve the person's own perspective, which is based on personal values, beliefs, and culture.

Regardless of its accuracy, conceptualization forms the basis for everyone's reactions to the frustration. The way the individuals perceive and define the conflict has a great deal of influence on the approach to resolution and subsequent outcomes. For example, within the same conflict situation, some individuals may see a conflict between a nurse manager and a direct care nurse as insubordination and become angry at the threat to the leader's role. Others may view it as trivial complaining, voice criticism (e.g., "We've been over this new protocol already; why can't you just adopt the change?"), and withdraw from the situation. Such differences in conceptualizing the issue block its resolution. Thus each person must clarify "the conflict as I see it" and "how it makes me respond" before all the people involved can define the conflict, develop a shared conceptualization, and resolve their differences. The following are questions to consider:

- What is the nature of our differences?
- What are the reasons for those differences?

- Does our leader endorse ideas or behaviors that add to or diminish the conflict?
- Do I need to be mentored by someone, even if that individual is outside my own department or work area, to successfully resolve this conflict?

Action

A behavioral response to a conflict follows the conceptualization. This may include seeking clarification about how another person views the conflict, collecting additional information that informs the issue, or engaging in dialog about the issue. As actions are taken to resolve the conflict, the way that some or all parties conceptualize the conflict may change. Successful resolution commonly stems from identifying a common goal that unites (e.g., quality patient care, good working relations). People are always taking some action regarding the conflict, even if that action is avoiding dealing with it, deliberately delaying action, or choosing to do nothing. The longer ineffective actions continue, though, the more likely people will experience frustration, resistance, or even hostility. The more the actions appropriately match the nature of the conflict, the more likely the conflict will be resolved with desirable results.

Outcomes

Tangible and intangible consequences result from the actions taken and have significant implications for the work setting. Consequences include (1) the conflict being resolved with a revised approach, (2) stagnation of any current movement, or (3) no future movement.

Constructive conflict results in successful resolution, leading to the following outcomes:

- Growth occurs.
- Problems are resolved.
- Groups are unified.
- Productivity is increased.
- Commitment is increased.
- Unsatisfactory resolution is typically destructive and results in the following:
- Negativity, resistance, and increased frustration inhibit movement.
- Resolutions diminish or are absent.
- Groups divide, and relationships weaken.
- Productivity decreases.
- Satisfaction decreases.

Assessing the degree of conflict resolution is useful for improving individual and group skills in resolutions, including more effective communication. Two general outcomes are considered when assessing the degree to which a conflict has been resolved: (1) the degree to which important goals were achieved and (2) the nature of the subsequent relationships among those involved (Box 8.1).

CATEGORIES OF CONFLICT

Categorizing a conflict can further define an appropriate course of action for resolution. Conflicts arise from discrepancies in four areas: facts, goals, approaches, and values. Sources of fact-based conflicts are external written sources and include job descriptions, hospital policies, standards of nursing practice, and TJC mandates. Objective data can be provided to resolve a disagreement generated by discrepancies in information. Goal conflicts often arise from competing priorities (e.g., desire to empower employees vs. control through micromanagement). Frequently, a common goal (e.g., quality patient care) can be identified and used to frame conflict resolution. Even when all agree on a common goal, different ideas about the best approach to achieve that goal may produce conflict. For example, if the unit goal is to reduce costs by 10%, one leader may target overtime hours and another may eliminate the budget for continuing education. Values, opinions, and beliefs are much more personal and thus generate disagreements that can be threatening and adversarial. Because values are subjective, value-based conflicts often remain unresolved. Therefore a need to find a way for

competing values to coexist is necessary for effective communication and conflict management.

MODES OF CONFLICT RESOLUTION

Understanding the way healthcare providers respond to conflict is an essential first step in identifying effective strategies to help nurses constructively handle conflicts in the practice environment. Classically, five distinct approaches can be used in conflict resolution: avoiding, accommodating, competing, compromising, and collaborating (Thomas & Kilman, 1974, 2002). These approaches can be viewed within two dimensions: assertiveness (satisfying one's own concerns) and cooperativeness (satisfying the concerns of others). Most people tend to employ a combined set of actions that are appropriately assertive and cooperative, depending on the nature of the conflict situation (Thomas, 1992). See the conflict self-assessment in Box 8.2.

EXERCISE 8.3 Self-assessment of preferred conflict-handling modes is important. As you read and answer the 30-item conflict survey in Box 8.2, think of how you respond to conflict in professional situations. After completing the survey, tally, total, and reflect on your scores for each of the five approaches. Consider the following questions:
- Which approach do you prefer? Which do you use least?
- What determines whether you respond in a particular manner?
- Considering the reoccurring types of conflicts you have, what are the strengths and weaknesses of your preferred conflict-handling styles?
- Have others offered you feedback about your approach to conflict?

Throughout the rest of this section are descriptions of each approach and related self-assessment and commitment-to-action activities. Use your totals from Box 8.2 to stimulate your thinking about how you do and how you could handle conflict at work. Most important, consider whether your pattern of frequency tends to be consistent or inconsistent with the types of conflicts you face. That is, does your way of dealing with conflict tend to match the situations in which that approach is most useful?

As you read the rest of this section, use this pattern of scores and your reflections to examine the appropriate

BOX 8.2   Conflict Self-Assessment

Directions: Read each of the following statements. Assess yourself in terms of how often you tend to act similarly during conflict at work. Place the number of the most appropriate response in the blank in front of each statement. Put *1* if the behavior is never typical of how you act during a conflict, *2* if it is seldom typical, *3* if it is occasionally typical, *4* if it is frequently typical, or *5* if it is very typical of how you act during conflict.

_____   1. Create new possibilities to address all important concerns.
_____   2. Persuade others to see it and/or do it my way.
_____   3. Work out some sort of give-and-take agreement.
_____   4. Let other people have their way.
_____   5. Wait and let the conflict take care of itself.
_____   6. Find ways that everyone can win.
_____   7. Use whatever power I have to get what I want.
_____   8. Find an agreeable compromise among people involved.
_____   9. Give in so others get what they think is important.
_____ 10. Withdraw from the situation.
_____ 11. Cooperate assertively until everyone's needs are met.
_____ 12. Compete until I either win or lose.
_____ 13. Engage in "give a little and get a little" bargaining.
_____ 14. Let others' needs be met more than my own needs.
_____ 15. Avoid taking any action for as long as I can.
_____ 16. Partner with others to find the most inclusive solution.
_____ 17. Put my foot down assertively for a quick solution.
_____ 18. Negotiate for what all sides value and can live without.
_____ 19. Agree to what others want to create harmony.
_____ 20. Keep as far away from others involved as possible.
_____ 21. Stick with it to get everyone's highest priorities.
_____ 22. Argue and debate over the best way.
_____ 23. Create some middle position everyone agrees to.
_____ 24. Put my priorities below those of other people.
_____ 25. Hope the issue does not come up.
_____ 26. Collaborate with others to achieve our goals together.
_____ 27. Compete with others for scarce resources.
_____ 28. Emphasize compromise and trade-offs.
_____ 29. Cool things down by letting others do it their way.
_____ 30. Change the subject to avoid the fighting.

Conflict Self-Assessment Scoring

Look at the numbers you placed in the blanks on the conflict assessment. Write the number you placed in each blank on the appropriate line below. Add up your total for each column, and enter that total on the appropriate line. The greater your total is for each approach, the more often you tend to use that approach when conflict occurs at work. The lower the score is, the less often you tend to use that approach when conflict occurs at work.

Collaborating	Competing	Compromising	Accommodating	Avoiding
1. _____	2. _____	3. _____	4. _____	5. _____
6. _____	7. _____	8. _____	9. _____	10. _____
11. _____	12. _____	13. _____	14. _____	15. _____
16. _____	17. _____	18. _____	19. _____	20. _____
21. _____	22. _____	23. _____	24. _____	25. _____
26. _____	27. _____	28. _____	29. _____	30. _____
Total _____	Total _____	Total _____	Total _____	Total _____

From Hurst, J.B. (1993). *Conflict self-assessment.* Toledo, OH: Human Resource Development Center, University of Toledo.

uses of each approach, assess your use of each approach more extensively, and commit to new behaviors to increase your future effectiveness.

Avoiding

Avoiding, or withdrawing, is very unassertive and uncooperative, because people who avoid neither pursue their own needs, goals, or concerns immediately nor assist others to pursue theirs. Avoidance as a conflict-management style only ensures that conflict is postponed, and conflict has a tendency to escalate in intensity when ignored. That is not to say that all conflict must be addressed immediately; some issues require considerable reflection, and action should be delayed. The positive side of withdrawing may be postponing an issue until a better time or simply walking away from a "no-win" situation (Box 8.3). The self-assessment in Box 8.4 will help you recognize your own avoidance behaviors and use them more effectively.

Accommodating

When accommodating, people neglect their own needs, goals, and concerns (unassertive) while trying to satisfy those of others (cooperative). This approach has an element of being self-sacrificing and simply obeying orders or serving other people. For example, a co-worker requests you cover her weekends during her children's holiday break. You had hoped to visit friends from college, but you know how important it is for her to have more time with her family, so you agree. Box 8.5 lists some appropriate uses of accommodation.

Individuals who frequently use accommodation may feel disappointment and resentment because they "get nothing in return." This is a built-in by-product

of the overuse of this approach. The self-assessment in Box 8.6 asks you to examine your current use of accommodation and challenges you to think of new ways to use it more effectively.

BOX 8.4 Avoidance: Self-Assessment and Commitment to Action

If You Tend to Use Avoidance Often, Ask Yourself the Following Questions:
1. Do people have difficulty getting my input into and understanding my view?
2. Do I block cooperative efforts to resolve issues?
3. Am I distancing myself from significant others?
4. Are important issues being left unidentified and unresolved?

If You Seldom Use Avoidance, Ask Yourself the Following Questions:
1. Do I find myself overwhelmed by a large number of conflicts and a need to say "no"?
2. Do I assert myself even when things do not matter that much? Do others view me as an aggressor?
3. Do I lack a clear view of what my priorities are?
4. Do I stir up conflicts and fights?

Commitment to Action
What two new behaviors would increase your effective use of avoidance?
1.
2.

BOX 8.3 Appropriate Uses for the Avoiding Approach

1. When facing trivial and/or temporary issues, or when other far more important issues are pressing
2. When there is no chance to obtain what one wants or needs, or when others could resolve the conflict more efficiently and effectively
3. When the potential negative results of initiating and acting on a conflict are much greater than the benefits of its resolution
4. When people need to "cool down," distance themselves, or gather more information

---

BOX 8.5 Appropriate Uses of Accommodation

1. When other people's ideas and solutions appear to be better, or when you have made a mistake
2. When the issue is far more important to the other person or people than it is to you
3. When you see that accommodating now "builds up some important credits" for later issues
4. When you are outmatched and/or losing anyway; when continued competition would only damage the relationships and productivity of the group and jeopardize accomplishing major purpose(s)
5. When preserving harmonious relationships and avoiding defensiveness and hostility are very important
6. When letting others learn from their mistakes and/or increased responsibility is possible without severe damage

---

BOX 8.6 Accommodation: Self-Assessment and Commitment to Action

If You Use Accommodation Often, Ask Yourself the Following Questions:
1. Do I feel that my needs, goals, concerns, and ideas are not being attended to by others?
2. Am I depriving myself of influence, recognition, and respect?
3. When I am in charge, is "discipline" lax?
4. Do I think people are using me?

If You Seldom Use Accommodation, Ask Yourself the Following Questions:
1. Am I building goodwill with others during conflict?
2. Do I admit when I have made a mistake?
3. Do I know when to give in, or do I assert myself at all costs?
4. Am I viewed as unreasonable or insensitive?

Commitment to Action
What two new behaviors would increase your effective use of accommodation?
1.
2.

BOX 8.8 Competing: Self-Assessment and Commitment to Action

If You Use Competing Often, Ask Yourself the Following Questions:
1. Am I surrounded by people who agree with me all the time and who avoid confronting me?
2. Are others afraid to share themselves and their needs for growth with me?
3. Am I out to win at all costs? If so, what are the costs and benefits of competing?
4. What are people saying about me when I am not around?

If You Seldom Compete, Ask Yourself the Following Questions:
1. How often do I avoid taking a strong stand and then feel a sense of powerlessness?
2. Do I avoid taking a stand so that I can escape risk?
3. Am I fearful and unassertive to the point that important decisions are delayed and people suffer?

Commitment to Action
What two new behaviors would increase your effective use of competition?
1.
2.

BOX 8.7 Appropriate Uses of Competing

1. When quick, decisive action is necessary
2. When important, unpopular action needs to be taken, or when trade-offs may result in long-range, continued conflict
3. When an individual or group is right about issues that are vital to group welfare
4. When others have taken advantage of an individual's or group's noncompetitive behavior and now are mobilized to compete about an important topic

---

Competing

When competing, people pursue their own needs and goals at the expense of others. Sometimes people use whatever power, creativeness, or strategies that are available to "win." Competing may also take the form of standing up for your rights or defending important principles, as when opposition to mandatory overtime is voiced (Box 8.7).

People whose primary mode of addressing conflict is through competition often react by feeling threatened, acting defensively or aggressively, or even resorting to cruelty in the form of cutting remarks, deliberate gossip, or hurtful innuendo. Competition within work groups can generate ill will, favor a win-lose stance, and commit people to a stalemate. Such behaviors force people into a corner from which there is no easy or graceful exit. Use Box 8.8 to help you learn to use competing more effectively.

Compromising

Compromising involves both assertiveness and cooperation on the part of everyone and requires maturity and confidence. Negotiating is a learned skill that is developed over time. A give-and-take relationship results in conflict resolution, with the result that each person can meet his or her most important priorities as much of the time as possible. Compromise is very often the exchange of concessions, as it creates a middle ground. This is the preferred means of conflict resolution during union negotiations, in which each side is appeased to some degree. In this mode, nobody gets everything he or she thinks is needed, but a sense of energy exists

---

BOX 8.9   Appropriate Uses of Compromise

1. When two powerful sides are committed strongly to perceived mutually exclusive goals
2. When temporary solutions to complex issues need to be implemented
3. When conflicting goals are "moderately important" and not worth a major confrontation
4. When time pressures people to expedite a workable solution
5. When collaborating and competing fail

BOX 8.10   Negotiation and Compromise Self-Assessment and Commitment to Action

If You Tend to Use Negotiation Often, Ask Yourself the Following Questions:

1. Do I ignore large, important issues while trying to work out creative, practical compromises?
2. Is there a "gamesmanship" in my negotiations?
3. Am I sincerely committed to compromise or negotiated solutions?

If You Seldom Use Negotiation, Ask Yourself the Following Questions:

1. Do I find it difficult to make concessions?
2. Am I often engaged in strong disagreements, or do I withdraw when I see no way to get out?
3. Do I feel embarrassed, sensitive, self-conscious, or pressured to negotiate, compromise, and bargain?

Commitment to Action

What two new behaviors would increase your compromising effectiveness?

1.
2.

---

that is necessary to build important relationships and teams.

Negotiation and compromise are valued approaches. They are chosen when less accommodating or avoiding is appropriate (Box 8.9). Compromising is a blend of both assertive and cooperative behaviors, although it calls for less finely honed skills for each behavior than does collaborating. Compromise supports a balance of power between self and others in the workplace. The compromising mode is a common conflict-handling mode used in nurse–physician interactions. A need exists to strengthen a healthy professional alliance that relies on collaborative practice to ensure favorable patient outcomes. Effective communication with other members of the healthcare team positively influences teamwork and staff satisfaction and improves quality of patient care and safety.

Negotiating is more like trading (e.g., "You can have this if I can have that," as in "I will chair the unit council task force on improving morale if you send me to the hospital's leadership training classes next week so I can have the skills I need to be effective."). Compromise is one of the most effective behaviors used by nurse leaders because it supports a balance of power between themselves and others in the work setting. The self-assessment in Box 8.10 will help you become more aware of your own use of negotiation and compromise and improve it.

Collaborating

Collaborating, although the most time-consuming approach, is the most creative stance. It is both assertive and cooperative, because people work creatively and openly to find the solution that most fully satisfies all important concerns and goals to be achieved. Collaboration involves analyzing situations and

---

BOX 8.11   Appropriate Uses for Collaboration

1. When seeking creative, integrative solutions in which both sides' goals and needs are important, thus developing group commitment and a consensual decision
2. When learning and growing through cooperative problem solving, resulting in greater understanding and empathy
3. When identifying, sharing, and merging vastly different viewpoints
4. When being honest about and working through difficult emotional issues that interfere with morale, productivity, and growth

---

defining the conflict at a higher level where shared goals are identified and commitment to working together is generated (Box 8.11). When nurses use cooperative conflict-management approaches, decision making becomes a collective process in which action plans are mutually understood and implemented. An organizational culture that supports collaborative communication and behavior among nurses and other members of the team, including physicians, is needed to merge the unique strengths of all professions into opportunities to improve patient outcomes (Foronda et al., 2016). For example, when nurses and physicians work together, they can collaborate by asking, "What is the best thing we can do for the patient and family right now?" and "How does each of us fit into the plan of care to meet their needs?" This requires discussion about the plan, how it will be accomplished, and who will make what contributions toward its achievement and proposed outcomes. Use the self-assessment in Box 8.12 to determine your own use of collaboration.

At the onset of conflict, involved collaborating individuals can carefully analyze situations to identify the nature and reasons for conflict and choose an appropriate approach. For example, a conflict arises when a direct care nurse and a charge nurse on a psychiatric unit disagree about how to handle a patient's complaints about the direct care nurse's delay in responding to the patient's requests. At the point that they reach agreement that it is the direct care nurse's responsibility and decision to make, collaboration has occurred. The charge nurse might say, "I

didn't realize your plan of care was to respond to the patient at predetermined intervals or that you told the patient that you would check on her every 30 minutes. I can now inform the patient that I know about and support your approach." Or the direct care nurse and the charge nurse might talk and subsequently agree that the direct care nurse is too emotionally involved with the patient's problems and that it may be time for her to withdraw from providing the care and enlist the support of another nurse, even temporarily. Discussion can result in collaboration aimed at allowing the direct care nurse to withdraw appropriately. Another, less desirable choice could be to compete and let the winner's position stand (e.g., "I'm in charge; I'm going to assign another nurse to this patient to preserve our patient satisfaction scores" or "I know what is best for this patient; I took care of her during her past two admissions").

DIFFERENCES OF CONFLICT-HANDLING STYLES AMONG NURSES

An increased emphasis has been placed on effective communication and appropriate conflict management styles in health care. Avoidance and accommodation are often the predominant choices for direct care nurses, and the prevalent style for nurse managers is frequently compromise, despite the benefits placed on collaboration as an effective strategy for conflict management. Nursing students and new graduates may be unprepared to handle conflict in the practice environment and may experience a number of barriers such as fear of causing conflict. Speaking up as a patient advocate is difficult for novice nurses (Fagan, Parker, & Jackson, 2016). This highlights the need to develop delegation strategies, including conflict-handling skills, to adapt to the evolving professional role. A prevalent conflict management style for nursing students and new nurses is avoidance and accommodation. Nurses who successfully manage disruptive workplace conflict reported a deliberate approach that included delaying confrontation, approaching the colleague calmly, and acknowledging the colleague's point of view. Nurses working in specialty areas may adapt communication and conflict management strategies to respond to diverse patient populations and the unique mix of interprofessional colleagues. See the Research Perspective, which describes the importance of communication with healthcare providers in end-of-life decision making.

BOX 8.12   Collaboration Self-Assessment and Commitment to Action

If You Tend to Collaborate Often, Ask Yourself the Following Questions:
1. Do I spend valuable group time and energy on issues that do not warrant or deserve it?
2. Do I postpone needed action to get consensus and avoid making key decisions?
3. When I initiate collaboration, do others respond in a genuine way, or are there hidden agendas, unspoken hostility, and/or manipulation in the group?

If You Seldom Collaborate, Ask Yourself the Following Questions:
1. Do I ignore opportunities to cooperate, take risks, and creatively confront conflict?
2. Do I tend to be pessimistic, distrusting, withdrawing, and/or competitive?
3. Am I involving others in important decisions, eliciting commitment, and empowering them?

Commitment to Action
What two new behaviors would increase your collaboration effectiveness?
1.
2.

RESEARCH PERSPECTIVE

Resource: Smith-Howell, E.R., Hickman, S.E., Meghani, S. H., Perkins, S.M., & Rawl, S.M. (2016). End-of-life decision making and communication of bereaved family members of African Americans with serious illness. *Journal of Palliative Medicine, 19*(2), 174-182.

Sources of conflict that affect families include end-of-life decisions and communication issues with healthcare providers. Family members who reported higher quality of communication with healthcare providers had lower end-of-life decisional conflict in a novel examination of African American family members' experiences. Previous studies have focused on the communication between the patient and provider, and few have examined African Americans. Good quality of end-of-life communication with healthcare providers was associated with less decisional conflict. African American families whose loved ones received comfort care had less decisional regret than those who received life-prolonging treatment.

Implications for Practice
End-of-life conflict and ineffective communication negatively affect the Quality and Safety Education for Nurses (QSEN) competencies of patient-centered care, teamwork and collaboration, and safety (QSEN Institute, n.d.). Bereaved family members experience barriers to optimal palliative care communication, including discomfort with discussing prognosis, inadequate knowledge, and fear of conflict. Reduced conflict could be achieved when end-of-life decisions are made collaboratively with the patient, physicians, nurses, and the family. Leaders and managers must model and coach nurses in effective conflict-handling strategies and effective communication to favorably impact end-of-life decisions.

THE ROLE OF THE LEADER

Encouraging positive working relationships among healthcare providers requires effective conflict management as part of a healthy working environment. The role of the nurse leader is to create a practice environment that fosters open communication and collaborative practices for achieving mutual goals that enable nurses to use constructive approaches to conflict management. Specifically, leaders must adopt a strategic proactive approach that aligns conflict management approaches with the overall mission of the organization. The training of nurse managers as conflict coaches shows promise in creating a positive practice environment when integrated with other conflict intervention processes. By modeling open communication and acknowledging each team member's viewpoint, the nurse manager can coach staff to independently and effectively resolve future conflicts themselves.

With the aging workforce and current nursing shortage, practice environments must be designed to retain nurses and prevent premature departure from the discipline. How to preserve the wisdom experienced nurses have is a critical challenge. Moreover, nurse leaders need to help challenge the stereotypical gender behavioral expectations and self-esteem issues frequently associated with a female-dominated profession and model effective management and leadership styles. One way to promote a positive work setting is to promote conflict prevention and ensure conflict resolution. The Literature Perspective highlights the results of an integrative review of publications about conflict in healthcare teams. Nurse leaders must provide the best example of advocacy and empowerment to their staff by coaching newer nurses to think strategically about a mode of conflict handling that is appropriate for the situation. Poor communication often creates conflict that jeopardizes patient safety, whereas inadequate leadership appears to be a contributing factor to adverse patient outcomes. Nursing managers need to support their staff's use of effective conflict management strategies by modeling open and honest communication, including staffing decision making, and securing resources whenever possible that meet the staff's need in delivering quality care. Providing education on conflict management could empower nurses to use these newly acquired skills in negotiation and creative problem-solving techniques. One example is nurse leaders using an interprofessional education program designed by the Department of Defense and the Agency for Healthcare Research and Quality (AHRQ) called *TeamSTEPPS* to reduce stress and conflict, because it focuses on evidence-based strategies to enhance teamwork and communication (AHRQ, 2018). Healthcare providers do not always voice concerns about patients and often avoid conflict in clinical settings.

EXERCISE 8.4 Review the educational program Team-STEPPS. Identify two strategies you can incorporate into your practice. State your rationale for selecting those and create an action plan to incorporate those strategies into your practice.

Healthcare leaders and managers who promote effective conflict resolution skills and who discourage the use of avoidance as a strategy have the potential to reduce employee stress and burnout as well as promote higher job satisfaction (Johansen & Cadmus, 2016; Moreland & Apker, 2016). Effective conflict resolution enhances team performance, increases patient safety, and improves patient outcomes (Sexton & Orchard, 2016).

Nurse conflict, stress, burnout, and turnover can be reduced. The nature of the differences, underlying reasons, importance of the issue, strength of feelings, and commitment to shared goals all have to be considered when selecting an approach to resolving conflict. Preferred and previously effective approaches can be considered, but they need to match the situation. Sometimes, a third party may be introduced into a conflict so that mediation can occur. Mediation is a learned skill for which advanced training or certification is available. Principled negotiation can produce mutually acceptable agreements in every type of conflict.

The method involves separating the people from the problem; focusing on interests, not positions; inventing options for mutual gain; and insisting on using objective criteria. The mediator is usually an impartial person who assists each party in the conflict to better hear and understand the other. In society, for example, much focus is on who can control whom and on who is the "winner." The successful individual involved in conflict resolution and negotiation often moves beyond avoidance, accommodation, and compromise. In nursing practice, added difficulty occurs in negotiating conflicts when at least one of the parties is on an unequal or uneven playing field. This disadvantage is made even worse when the other party to the conflict does not even acknowledge the disparities involved.

MANAGING INCIVILITY, LATERAL VIOLENCE, AND BULLYING

Incivility, lateral violence, and bullying in nursing are prevalent in all settings. Incivility is one or more rude, discourteous, or disrespectful actions and can range from gossiping to refusing to assist a co-worker. A significant source of interpersonal conflict in the workplace stems from lateral violence—aggressive and destructive behavior or psychological harassment of nurses against each other. Nurses are particularly vulnerable because

---

LITERATURE PERSPECTIVE

Resource: Almost J., Wolff A.C., Stewart-Pyne A., McCormick L.G., Strachan D., & D'Souza C. (2016). Managing and mitigating conflict in healthcare teams: An integrative review. *Journal of Advanced Nursing, 72*(7), 1490-1505.

An integrative review of publications focusing on conflict within healthcare teams revealed underlying causes and choices of conflict-handling techniques. Sources of conflict originate from individual characteristics, interpersonal factors, and organizational dynamics and include lack of emotional intelligence, certain personality traits, poor work environment, role ambiguity, lack of support from manager and co-workers, and poor communication. The connection between conflict resolution and communication was evident, with support for the role effective communication plays in enhanced problem solving. Team building was essential for enhancing team unity, improving communication, and building mutual respect and trust. Conflict resolution was ineffective when individuals thought their concerns were

devalued or when they were not included in decision making. The organizational impact of negative conflict management includes reduced productivity and ineffective teamwork, which can lead to adverse patient outcomes.

Implications for Practice
Sources of conflict within the practice environment must be anticipated and addressed to enhance organizational effectiveness. Providing quality patient care requires collaborative working relationships punctuated by effective communication and conflict resolution. Healthcare leaders must model and promote conflict management strategies to prevent or resolve conflict within nursing environments to ensure an organizational culture of quality and safety. Nurses should learn effective conflict resolution skills, develop self-awareness, and increase their understanding of conflict through formal education programs.

lateral or horizontal violence involves conflictual behaviors among individuals who consider themselves peers with equal power—but with little power within the system. Bullying is closely related to lateral or horizontal violence, but a real or perceived power differential between the instigator and recipient must be present in bullying. Bullying (defined as repeated, unwanted harmful actions intended to humiliate, offend, and cause distress in the recipient) is a very serious issue that threatens patient safety, nurse safety, and the nursing profession as a whole.

Understanding the sources of intraprofessional conflict in the practice environment is essential. Nurses are in positions to identify and intervene on the part of their colleagues when they see or experience horizontal violence or bullying. With increased awareness and sensitivity, nurses may be better able to monitor themselves and to assist their peers to recognize when they are participating in negative behaviors. Identifying and understanding particular incidences when nurses are most vulnerable and apt to engage in negative behavior (e.g., heavy workload, short staffing) and establishing performance expectations has the potential to reduce lateral violence in the workplace (Thompson & George, 2016). Incorporating workplace civility in nursing orientation programs and modeling professional behaviors provides a foundation to promote a healthy work culture. Nursing students and new graduates often lack the confidence and skill set to prevent interpersonal conflict and must rely on experienced nurse leaders to reduce the likelihood of incivility, horizontal violence, or bullying (Thompson & George, 2016). Nurse educators have a similar responsibility to develop nursing curricula that educate and encourage dialogue about incivility and horizontal violence to increase awareness and communication and conflict resolution skills.

In hostile work environments, the ability to provide quality patient care is compromised. TJC (2017) acknowledges that unresolved conflict and disruptive behavior adversely affect safety and quality of care. The vulnerability of newly licensed nurses as they are socialized within the nursing workforce and deal with interpersonal conflicts is a significant challenge. Lateral violence affects newly licensed nurses' job satisfaction and stress, as well as their perception of whether to remain in their current position and in the profession. Similarly, nursing students are particularly vulnerable

to lateral violence and bullying in the transition to becoming a nurse and may begin to question their long-held belief that nurses are caring and supportive professionals.

Lateral violence may be a response to the practice environment, in which ineffective leadership may exacerbate the problem. Incivility and disruptive behavior that intimidates others and affects morale or staff turnover can be harmful to patient care. It mandates that organizations have a code of conduct that defines acceptable, disruptive, and inappropriate behaviors and that leaders create and implement a process for managing these conflictual situations. One-on-one conflict resolution must be encouraged, but a mechanism for confidential reporting is also necessary. Training on conflict management that includes how to recognize and defend against lateral violence is necessary to ensure a positive professional practice environment. Senior-level leaders and nurse managers are responsible for ensuring appropriate policies are in place to confront negative workplace behaviors, including lateral violence and bullying. The ANA Position Statement on Incivility, Bullying, and Workplace Violence (ANA, 2015) states the nursing profession will not tolerate violence of any type from any source and directs nurses and nurse leaders to collaborate to create a culture of respect.

EXERCISE 8.5 Consider a conflict you would describe as "ongoing" in a clinical setting. Talk to some people who have been around for a while to get their historical perspective on this issue. Then consider the following questions:
- What are their positions and years of experience?
- How are resources, time, and personnel wasted on mismanaging this issue?
- What blocks the effective management of this issue?
- What currently aids in its management?
- What new things and actions would add to its management in the future?

CONCLUSION

Conflict is inevitable within healthcare environments. The major issue of miscommunication and unresolved conflict in nursing is that patients could suffer. Knowing how to respond appropriately in conflictual situations helps the entire healthcare team focus on quality and safety rather than disagreements and disruptions.

Unresolved conflict in the professional practice environment results in negative outcomes for nurses and other healthcare professionals, organizations, and patients. Incivility, bullying, and lateral violence are toxic to the profession through the negative impact on the retention of staff and on detrimental outcomes for patients. Registered nurses must work in an effective and collaborative manner with other members of the healthcare team to enhance retention and eliminate incivility, lateral violence, and bullying from the workplace. Incivility, bullying, lateral violence, and all forms of disruptive behaviors have a negative effect on the retention of nursing staff and the quality and safety of patient care. Nurses must enhance their knowledge and skills in managing conflict and promote workplace policies to eliminate bullying and lateral violence. Nurse leaders must eliminate hostile work environments, workplace intimidation, reality shock for new graduates, and the acceptance of inappropriate professional interactions.

THE SOLUTION

When my charge nurse placed another patient in my second slot, I first confirmed that I would be assigned that patient. I then updated her about my other, high-acuity patient and explained that the patient was still on a Precedex drip and I remained concerned about the potential for respiratory decompensation. My charge nurse acknowledged my concerns but explained that this new patient was ready to come out of the operating room (OR) and that no other postanesthesia care unit (PACU) slots were available. Because I feared for the safety of my current patient as well as for this new patient who was coming out of the OR, I needed to communicate effectively and advocate for my patients. I voiced that I did not feel comfortable caring for both patients and asked if a "help-all" or assistant charge nurse would be able to assist until the patient was stable. A nurse was available to assist with admitting my new patient, but ultimately, I was left with responsibility to care for both. Unfortunately, situations like this happen more frequently than I had expected when I was a nursing student. I continue to advocate for my patients' safety and follow hospital and unit protocols as much as possible; however, it can be hard to speak up when doing so disrupts the flow of a unit, especially as a new graduate. I was fortunate to have an approachable leadership team in the PACU who was always open to input from nurses and other employees. This type of environment allowed me to feel comfortable offering ideas and suggestions so that unsafe patient situations could be reduced.

Would this be a suitable approach for you? Why?

Shannen R. McCrory

REFLECTIONS

Identify how you will use the material from this chapter to promote effective communication and reduce conflict with the patients for whom you provide care as well as with interprofessional co-workers. Write a one-paragraph summary with specific examples. How could you be more effective immediately?

THE EVIDENCE

The literature supports the need to create civil work environments to promote patient safety. Because communication is such a critical element in patient care, all members of any team need to employ effective strategies and to speak up when care can be compromised. Skilled communication contributes to positive patient care.

TIPS FOR EFFECTIVE COMMUNICATION AND ADDRESSING CONFLICT

- Develop common language for critical information for handoff communications and communication of changes in a patient's condition.

- Use a communication tool such as SBAR to standardize communication.

- Use a standardized format for change-of-shift report and handoff communication.
- Use a standardized format for report when patients are transferred to other units or facilities.
- Provide the opportunity for questions and confirmation of understanding of communication.
- Have face-to-face communication when possible.
- Read back all healthcare provider orders or other pertinent information.
- Create a culture of patient safety that has zero tolerance for intimidating and disruptive behavior.
- Work in multidisciplinary teams to develop common language.
- Develop skills in assertive communication and conflict management.
- Recognize that conflict is a necessary and beneficial process typically marked by frustration, different conceptualizations, a variety of approaches to resolving it, and ongoing outcomes.
- Assess the work environment to see what behaviors are endorsed and fostered by the leaders.

Determine whether these behaviors are worthy of imitation.
- Determine any similarities and differences in facts, goals, methods, and values in sorting out the different conceptualizations of a conflict situation.
- Assess the degree of conflict resolution by asking questions about the quality of the decisions (e.g., creativity, practicality, achievement of goals, breakthrough results) and the quality of the relationships (e.g., understanding, willingness to work together, mutual respect, cooperation).
- Remind yourself of your preferences for resolving conflict (e.g., which of the five approaches do you not use often enough and which do you overuse?) and assess each situation to match the best approach for that type of conflict regardless of which is your favorite approach.
- Assist others around you in assessing conflict situations and determining how they can best approach them.

REFERENCES

Agency for Healthcare Research and Quality. (2018). *TeamSTEPPS 2.0.* American Nurses Association. https://www.ahrq.gov/teamstepps/instructor/index.html.

Almost, J., Wolff, A. C., Stewart-Pyne, A., McCormick, L. G., Strachan, D., & D'Souza, C. (2016). Managing and mitigating conflict in healthcare teams: An integrative review. *Journal of Advanced Nursing, 72*(7), 1490–1505.

American Nurses Association. (2015). *ANA Position Statement on Incivility, Bullying, and Workplace Violence.* http://www.nursingworld.org/DocumentVault/Position-Statements/Practice/Position-Statement-on-Incivility-Bullying-and-Workplace-Violence.pdf.

American Nurses Credentialing Center. (2017). *Journey to Magnet Excellence.* http://www.nursecredentialing.org/MagnetJourney.

André, B., Frigstad, S. A., Nøst, T. H., & Sjøvold, E. (2016). Exploring nursing staffs' communication in stressful and non-stressful situations. *Journal of Nursing Management, 24*(2), 175–182.

Blake, R. R., & Mouton, J. S. (1964). *Solving costly organization conflict.* San Francisco: Jossey-Bass.

Deutsch, M. (1973). *The resolution of conflict: Constructive and destructive processes.* New Haven, CT: Yale University Press.

Fagan, A., Parker, V., & Jackson, D. (2016). A concept analysis of undergraduate nursing students speaking up for patient safety in the patient care environment. *Journal of Advanced Nursing, 72*(10), 2346–2357.

Foronda, C., MacWilliams, B., & McArthur, E. (2016). Interprofessional communication in healthcare: An integrative review. *Nurse Education in Practice, 19,* 36–40.

Institute for Healthcare Improvement. (2017). *SBAR communication technique.* http://www.ihi.org/Topics/SBARCommunicationTechnique/Pages/default.aspx.

Johansen, M. L., & Cadmus, E. (2016). Conflict management style, supportive work environments and the experience of work stress in emergency nurses. *Journal of Nursing Management, 24*(2), 211–218.

Lee, J., Mast, M., Humbert, J., Bagnardi, M., & Richards, S. (2016). Teaching handoff communication to nursing students. *Nurse Educator, 41*(4), 189–193.

McKibben, L. (2017). Conflict management: Importance and implications. *British Journal of Nursing, 26*(2), 100–103.

Moreland, J. J., & Apker, J. (2016). Health communication: Conflict and stress in hospital nursing: Improving communicative responses to enduring professional challenges. *Health Communication, 31*(7), 815–823.

QSEN Institute. (n.d.). *QSEN competencies.* http://qsen.org/ competencies/pre-licensure-ksas/.

Sexton, M., & Orchard, C. (2016). Understanding healthcare professionals' self-efficacy to resolve interprofessional conflict. *Journal of Interprofessional Care, 30*(3), 316–323.

Smith-Howell, E. R., Hickman, S. E., Meghani, S. H., Perkins, S. M., & Rawl, S. M. (2016). End-of-life decision making and communication of bereaved family members of African Americans with serious illness. *Journal of Palliative Medicine, 19*(2), 174–182.

Stimpfel, A. W., Sloane, D. M., McHugh, M. D., & Aiken, L. H. (2016). Hospitals known for nursing excellence associated with better hospital experience for patients. *Health Services Research, 51*(3), 1120–1134.

The Joint Commission. (2017). *Summary Data of Sentinel Events Reviewed by the Joint Commission.* https://www .jointcommission.org/sentinel_event_statistics_quarterly/.

Thomas, K. W. (1992). Conflict and conflict management: Reflections and update. *Journal of Organizational Behavior, 13*(3), 265–274.

Thomas, K. W., & Kilmann, R. H. (1974). *Thomas-Kilmann conflict mode instrument.* Tuxedo, NY: Xicom.

Thomas, K. W., & Kilmann, R. H. (2002). *Thomas-Kilmann conflict mode instrument* (revised edition). Mountain View, CA: CPP, Inc.

Thompson, R., & George, L. E. (2016). Preparing new nurses to address bullying: The effect of an online educational module on learner self-efficacy. *MEDSURG Nursing, 25*(6), 412–417.

Turrentine, F. E., Rose, K. M., Hanks, J. B., Lorntz, B., Owen, J. A., Brashers, V. L., et al. (2016). Interprofessional training enhances collaboration between nursing and medical students: A pilot study. *Nurse Education Today, 40,* 33–38.

9

Power, Politics, and Influence

Susan Sportsman

LEARNING OUTCOMES

- Value the concept of power as it relates to leadership and management in nursing.
- Use different types of power in the exercise of nursing leadership.
- Develop a power image for effective nursing leadership.

- Implement appropriate strategies for exercising power to influence the politics of the work setting, professional organizations, legislators, and the development of health policy.

KEY TERMS

coalitions
empowerment
influence

negotiating
policy

politics
power

THE CHALLENGE

Our hospital was trying hard to improve customer service. The emergency department (ED) had been receiving frequent calls that were not relevant to the work of the ED, such as asking how long to cook a turkey and where the closest 24-hour veterinary clinic is. In some cases, in efforts to provide good customer service, the ED staff provided phone numbers (e.g., the Butterball Turkey Talk-Line; the phone number for a 24-hour animal hospital). Often we had to tell callers we could not provide them with the information requested; these responses were met with hostile and even obscene reactions from some callers. Other calls (e.g., calls to determine how much a 20-minute late-night visit to the ED or an x-ray would cost) were also met with hostility at times. Staff requested an in-service class on how to handle such calls while providing

good customer service. Our director provided us with such a program. We learned to deal with verbal hostility with assertive communication.

Shortly after the in-service class, late on a Friday morning, I took a call from a woman who wanted to know how to treat an infected wound on her cat's back. I gave her the name and phone number of the 24-hour animal clinic. The woman responded by screaming obscenities at me, indicating she had taken the cat to a veterinarian and wasn't going to go back. She screamed so loudly that the ED's medical director and other staff heard the woman's tirade. Feeling empowered, I used my new skills to assertively end the conversation. A secretary paged our nursing director to come to the ED while the call was in progress. She arrived just as the call ended. I was debriefed by

(Continued)

the director. The others who overheard the call gave her the same account of the call. I began to write an incident report on the event before my director was paged to go to the office of the vice president (VP) of nursing.

The VP had just gotten off the phone with the chief executive officer (CEO) of the hospital. The woman with the cat called him to accuse me of calling her obscene names and refusing to help her. The director told my VP what I had told her. She emphasized that the caller was the one using obscenities, not me. The VP directed her to suspend me immediately to placate the CEO; my director insisted that I had done nothing wrong and refused to suspend me,

based on the information the others had given her. The VP came to the ED after the director left her office. She then confronted me, threatening to fire me unless I called the woman and apologized. The VP left only when the medical director of the ED insisted that I had used no obscenities and had not responded to the call inappropriately. Badly shaken, I paged the director to come back to the ED as soon as the VP left.

What would you do if you were this nurse?

Anonymous
(A retired emergency department staff nurse)

INTRODUCTION

The profession of nursing developed in the United States at a time when women had limited legal rights (e.g., most were prohibited from voting, and many could not own property). Women were viewed as neither powerful nor political; in the late 19th century *feminine* and *powerful* were practically contradictory terms. During the 20th century, as the status and role of women changed, so did the status and role of nurses. Moving into the 21st century, the economic and social power of women has evolved, as has the power of nurses. This is significant because nursing historically has been and continues to be a discipline composed primarily of women.

In the 21st century, nurses must exercise their power to continue to expand the strong voice of nursing in shaping an evolving healthcare environment. In an era of rapid change with a continuing nursing shortage, healthcare reform offers new opportunities for nurses at the bedside and in the community, for those just entering the profession and those in advanced nursing roles. Nurses must use their collective power to advocate for a preferred future in an evolving healthcare system.

exercise their collective power with the rise of early nursing leaders such as Lillian Wald, Isabel Stewart, Annie Goodrich, Lavinia Dock, M. Adelaide Nutting, Mary Eliza Mahoney, and Isabel Hampton Robb and the development of organizations that evolved into the National League for Nursing (NLN) and the American Nurses Association (ANA).

Today, in an era of expanding nursing roles (e.g., new expectations of registered nurses in primary care, advanced practice nurses, and new roles for graduates of doctor of nursing practice [DNP] programs), nurses must exercise their power to shape the continuing development of the profession of nursing and the future of the healthcare system and manage the efforts of medicine and others to control nursing practice.

The view of the media, politicians, organized medicine, and some healthcare executives and nurses viewed nurses and nursing as powerless began to change dramatically in the 1990s as nurses began to appear more often on local and national news and on talk shows as experts on health care. This trend reflected the changes occurring in the healthcare system, and the effect of these changes on the public at that time.

HISTORY

The word *power* comes from the Latin word *potere*, meaning "to be able." Simply defined, power is the ability to influence others in an effort to achieve goals. Power was once considered almost a taboo in nursing. As previously noted, in nursing's formative years, the exercise of power was considered inappropriate, unladylike, and unprofessional. However, nurses began to

POWER

Power may be defined as the capacity or ability to direct or influence the behavior of others or the course of events. This definition demonstrates the essential nature of power to nursing. Nurses routinely influence patients to improve their health status. When nurses provide health teaching to patients and their families, the goal is to change patient or family behavior to promote optimal health. That is an exercise of power in nursing practice. Coaching other nurses to improve their performances is an exercise of power. Serving as the chief nursing officer of a hospital or health-related corporation that requires managing a multimillion-dollar budget demonstrates another exercise of power. In fact, many nurse managers control budgets larger than many of the businesses in the community. They may also challenge decisions that are not in the best interests of patients, staff, and others.

Having a high-status position in an organization immediately provides stature, but power depends on the ability to accomplish goals from that position. Although some may think that "knowledge is power," acting on that knowledge is where the real power lies. Sharing knowledge expands one's power and, in turn, empowers others, including colleagues and patients, by giving them information or skills that they need to take action in a situation.

EXERCISE 9.1 Recall a recent opportunity in which you observed the work of an expert nurse. Think about that nurse's interactions with patients, family members, nursing students, nursing colleagues, or other professionals. What kinds of power did you observe this nurse using? What did the nurse do that told you, "This is a powerful person"?

In 1959 French and Raven described the five bases of power (legitimate, reward, expert, referent, and coercive), and over time other types of power have been identified (White, 2016). Social scientists, including nurses, have used this theoretical framework to evaluate the sources of power, including the effect of using these types of power in a variety of situations (http://changingminds.org/explanations/power/french-and-raven). The Theory Box provides examples of each type of power in the context of nursing practice.

Nurses can use all of these types of power while implementing a wide range of nursing activities. Nurses who teach patients use expert and information power; they also exercise position power as registered nurses, accorded a certain status by society, by virtue of their education and license. Members of a state nurses' association who lobby members of the state legislature use expert, information, and position power when gaining legislators' support for healthcare legislation. New graduates, employed on probationary status until they demonstrate the initial clinical competencies, may view the nurse manager as exercising position, expert, and either coercive or reward power related to their initial evaluations. Nursing faculty and skilled clinicians exercise expert, position, and information power as students emulate their behavior. Connection power is evident at any social gathering in the workplace. People of high status (e.g., vice presidents, directors, deans) within an organization may be sought out for conversation by those who want to move up the organizational hierarchy.

Influence is the process of using power. Influence can range from the punitive power of coercion to the interactive power of collaboration and cocreation. Coaching a new graduate to complete a complicated nursing procedure successfully demonstrates the ability of the experienced nurse

THEORY BOX

Sources of Power

Key Ideas	Application to Practice
Expert power: Based on one's reputation for expertise and ones' credibility. The knowledge and skills the nurse possesses that are needed by others.	The leader of a state nurses' association (SNA) may have access to the leaders of the state legislature based on the leader's expert power, which has enabled years of work with members of the legislature.
	The SNA president has always delivered on promises of support and provided useful information to legislators on matters of health policy.
Position power: Possessed by virtue of one's position within an organization or status within a group.	The dean of a college of nursing is viewed on campus as powerful, because frequently this dean leads the fastest growing or largest academic unit on campus.

(Continued)

THEORY BOX—cont'd

Sources of Power

Key Ideas	Application to Practice
Information power: Stems from one's possession of selected information that is needed by others.	A direct care nurse demonstrates great skill in teaching patients difficult self-care activities and is sought out by colleagues to help them teach their patients.
Connection power: Gained by association with people who are powerful or who have links to powerful people.	At a National Nurses' Week celebration, nurses take advantage of the opportunity to have extended, informal conversations with those who report to the chief nursing officer.
Referent power: Granted by association with a powerful person.	A senior nursing student asks a well-respected nurse manager to be her preceptor for the senior leadership course. The student wants to work in this agency upon graduation.
Coercive power: Stems from fear of someone's real or perceived fear of another person.	A nurse who lacks confidence in her performance in a new position is worried about an upcoming review with the nursing director.
Reward power: One is perceived as being able to provide rewards or favors.	An instructor is perceived positively by a nursing student who received an A for a clinical course.
Persuasion Power: Based on the ability to influence or convince others to agree with one's opinion or agenda. It involves leading others to a viewpoint with data, facts, and presentation skills.	A nurse is able to persuade an organization to change a policy to better serve a group of patients.
Empowerment: The nurse is a source of shared power to build the exercise of power by others.	The chief nurse executive develops a model of shared governance to enable nurses to have a stronger voice in patient care decisions.

From Mason, D. J., Gardner, D., Outlaw, F. H., & O'Grady, E. T. (2016). *Policy and politics in nursing and health care* (7th ed.). St. Louis: Elsevier.

to influence that orientee. The coach uses expert, positional, and informational power to influence the orientee, not only at that moment but also perhaps over the span of a career. Nurses can use personal, expert, and perceived power while working on the campaigns of legislators who support nursing and healthcare issues.

EMPOWERMENT

Empowerment is a term that has come into common usage in nursing. That term has been used extensively in the nursing literature related to administration and management; it is also highly relevant to the domain of clinical practice. According to the Oxford Dictionary, empowerment is authority or power given to someone to do something or the process of becoming stronger and more confident, especially in controlling one's life and claiming one's rights (https://en.oxforddictionaries.com/definition/empowerment).

Empowerment is consistent with the contemporary view of leadership, a paradigm that is exemplified by behaviors characteristic of all nurse leaders: facilitator, coach, teacher, and collaborator. Nursing leaders, in employment settings or in professional organizations, exercise power in making professional judgments in their daily work.

These leadership skills are also essential to effective followers, as the Research Perspective illustrates. Powerful nurse managers enable nurses to exercise power, influencing them to grow professionally. Powerful nurses support their patients and families so they can participate actively in their own care. Hence these leadership skills can be viewed as an essential component of professional nursing practice whether one is a clinician, an educator, a researcher, or an executive or manager.

RESEARCH PERSPECTIVE

Resource: Saber, D. (2014). Frontline registered nurse job satisfaction and predictors over three decades: A meta-analysis from 1980 to 2009. *Nursing Outlook,* 62(6), 402–414.

The purpose of this study was to comprehensively, quantitatively examine the largest, moderate, and smallest predictors of frontline registered nurse job satisfaction from 1980 to 2009. Task requirements, empowerment, and control were the largest predictors of job satisfaction. Although empowerment was not included in previous job satisfaction meta-analyses, in this study empowerment was a multifaceted predictor of job satisfaction that is predicted to become increasingly important given the escalation of pace and complexity in the workplace (Saber, 2014).

Implication for Practice
Strategies to empower others is key to the successful—and positive—use of power and can be implemented in any arena in which the nurse intends to exert influence.

SHARING POWER

Nurses, including some leaders, may view power as a finite quantity: "If I give you some of my power, I will have less." Empowerment emphasizes the notion that power grows when shared. Envision the exercise of shared power along a spectrum from low to high levels of sharing. As shown in Fig. 9.1, the opposing ends of the spectrum can be characterized by two very different groups of nurses:

- Nurses who view power as finite will avoid cooperation with their colleagues and refuse to share their expertise.
- Nurses who view power as infinite are strong collaborators who gain satisfaction by helping their colleagues expand their expertise and their power base.

Empowered nurses make professional practice possible, creating a culture that satisfies all nurses. Empowered clinicians are essential for effective nursing management, just as empowered managers set the stage for excellence in clinical practice. Encouraging a reticent colleague to be an active participant in committee meetings serves to empower that nurse and to shape practice policy with the institution. Guiding a novice nurse in exercising professional judgment empowers both the senior nurse and the novice clinician. Coaching a patient on how to be more assertive with a physician who is reluctant to answer the patient's questions is another form of empowerment.

> **EXERCISE 9.2** Think about a recent clinical experience in which you empowered a patient. What did you do for and/or with the patient (and family) that was empowering? How did you feel about your own actions in this situation? How did the patient (or family) respond to your efforts?

PERSONAL POWER STRATEGIES

Developing a collection of power strategies or tools is a critical aspect of personal empowerment. These strategies are used in situations that demand the exercise of leadership. Such strategies support one's professional power base and the development of political skills within an organization (Boxes 9.1 and 9.2). These strategies also indicate to others that one is a powerful nurse and a leader. These boxes identify personal power strategies beyond those discussed in this section. These "power tools" have been developed and collected by Karen Kelly during more than 40 years of nursing experience and observation of successful, effective, powerful nurses.

Strategies for Developing a Powerful Image

Consider the words of Lady Margaret Thatcher, former prime minister of Great Britain: "Being powerful is like being a lady. If you have to tell people you are, you aren't." You don't have to wear a sign around your neck to show that you are powerful!

View: Finite_____Infinite

Sharing focus: LOW_____HIGH

Behavior: Avoid Cooperation_____Strong Collaboration

Fig. 9.1 The continuum of shared power.

BOX 9.1   Power Strategies for Nursing Leaders and Aspiring Leaders

Developing a Powerful Image

- Self-confidence
- Body language
- Self-image, including grooming, dress, and speech
- Career commitment and continuing professional education
- Attitudes, beliefs, and values

Additional Personal Power Strategies

- Be honest.
- Be courteous; it makes other people feel good!
- Smile when appropriate; it puts people at ease.
- Accept responsibility for your own mistakes, and then learn from them.
- Be a risk taker.
- Win and lose gracefully.
- Learn to be comfortable with conflict and ambiguity; they are both normal states of the human condition.
- Give credit to others where credit is due.
- Develop the ability to take constructive criticism gracefully; learn to let destructive criticism "roll off your back."
- Use business cards when introducing yourself to new contacts, and collect the business cards of those you meet when networking.
- Follow through on promises.

BOX 9.2   Developing Political Skills

- Build a working relationship with a legislator, such as your state senator or representative or member of the US Congress and the legislative staff members.
- Join and be an active member of your state nurses' association affiliated with the American Nurses Association.
- Join a specialty nursing organization related to your clinical specialty (e.g., critical care, pediatrics) or specialty role in nursing (nurse practitioner, manager).
- Invite a legislator to a professional organization meeting.
- Invite a legislator or staff person from the legislator's office to spend a day with you at work.
- Register to vote, and vote in every election.
- Join your state nurses' association's government relations or legislative committee and political action committee (PAC); join the ANA's PAC.
- Be in touch with your federal and state legislators on nursing and healthcare issues, especially related to specific bills, by writing letters, making telephone calls, or sending e-mails.
- Participate in Nurse Lobby Day and meet with your state legislators.
- Work on a federal or state legislative campaign.
- Visit your US senators and member of Congress if visiting in the Washington, DC area to discuss federal legislation related to nursing and health care, or visit their local offices.
- Get involved in the local group of your political party.
- Run for office at the local, county, state, or congressional level.
- Enhance the image of nursing in all your policy efforts.
- Communicate your message effectively and clearly.
- Develop your expertise in shaping policy.
- Seek appointive positions or elective office to shape policy more effectively.

From Kelly, K. (2015). Power, politics, and influence. In P. Yoder-Wise (Ed.), *Leading and managing in nursing* (6th ed.). St. Louis: Mosby.

The most basic power strategy is the development of a powerful image (Fig. 9.2). If nurses think they are powerful, others will view them as powerful; if they view themselves as powerless, so will others. A sense of self-confidence is a strong foundation in developing one's "power image" and is essential for successful political efforts in the workplace, within the profession, and within the public policy arena. Several key factors contribute to one's power image:

- Self-image: thinking of oneself as powerful and effective
- Grooming and dress: ensuring that clothing, hair, and general appearance are neat, clean, and appropriate to the situation
- Good manners: treating people with courtesy and respect
- Body language: maintaining good posture, using gestures that avoid too much drama, maintaining good eye contact, and being confident in movement
- Speech: using a firm, confident voice; good grammar and diction; an appropriate vocabulary; and strong communication skills

This type of power is known as *presence* (Yoder-Wise & Benton, 2017). Specific strategies can be used to strengthen the ABCs of presence: appearance, behavior/gravitas, and communication. Remember that the good news about appearance is that it isn't about body image or the quality of clothing you wear. Rather, the key to appearance is being clean and well groomed. Behavior, both micro and macro, is important. The former is exhibited by how you treat others and the latter by

Fig. 9.2 Dressing in an appropriate manner helps convey an image of power.

how you spend your time. Communication, in addition to being articulate, focuses on creating messages that inspire and influence others for the good (Yoder-Wise & Benton, 2017).

EXERCISE 9.3 Think about a powerful public figure you admire. What key factors contribute to this person's powerful image? Think about a powerful nurse you have met. Identify this person's key image factors. Think about nurses who work in wrinkled scrubs, whose hair is pulled back haphazardly into ponytails, and who fail to make eye contact with patients or their family members. What kind of power image message do they send?

Concern about a powerful image may seem superficial. However, the impressions we make on people influence the way they view us now and in the future, as well as how they value what we do and say. We get only one chance to make a first impression. Who will be seen as the more competent professional by a patient: the nurse in wrinkled scrubs or the nurse in neat street clothes and a freshly laundered laboratory coat? Who will have a greater positive effect on a member of the

state legislature: the nurse who visits in a sweatshirt and shorts or the nurse in business attire? A powerful image signals to others that one is professionally competent, influential, powerful, and capable of exercising appropriate judgments.

Attitudes and beliefs are also important aspects of a powerful image; they reflect one's values. Believing that power is a positive force in nursing is essential to one's powerful image. A firm belief in nursing's value to society and the centrality of nursing's contribution to the healthcare delivery system is also important. Powerful nurses do not allow the phrase "I'm just a nurse" in their vocabulary. Instead, powerful nurses can enhance the profession by responding to statements of appreciation with the phrase, "I'm a nurse; it's what we do." Behavior reflects one's pride in the profession of nursing. This not only increases a nurse's own power but also helps empower nursing colleagues.

Be Authentic

A critical component of using power effectively is to translate the strategies for developing a powerful image into behaviors that are consistent with your own personality, beliefs, and values. As Kevin Kruse comments in the May 12, 2013, Forbes, Inc., blog, "It surprises me how many leaders attempt to be one way at work, while their 'true' personality emerges outside of work ... And it surprises me when these same leaders seem shocked or confused when their employees don't trust them, don't like them, and can't really wait to work elsewhere."

Table 9.1 synthesizes Kruse's analysis of the theoretical assumptions of the components of the authentic leadership that relate to the use of power and influence.

Make a Commitment to Nursing as a Career

Nursing is a profession, and professions offer careers, not just a series of jobs. Decades ago, nursing marketed itself to recruits as the perfect preparation for marriage and family. Some people still view nurses only as members of an occupation who drop in and out of employment, not as members of a profession with a long-term career commitment. Having a career commitment does not preclude leaving employment temporarily for family, education, or other demands. Having a career commitment means that nurses view themselves first and foremost as members of the discipline of nursing with an obligation to make a contribution to the profession.

TABLE 9.1   Authentic Leadership Characteristics and Behaviors Related to Power and Influence

Characteristics	Description of Behavior
Self-aware and genuine	Self-actualized, aware of strengths, limitations, and emotions. Recognizes that self-actualization is forever ongoing. Behavior is consistent in private and public. Open about mistakes. Does not fear looking weak.
Mission driven and focused on results	Puts the organization ahead of self-interest. Pursues organizational results, not power, money, or ego.
Lead with their heart and their minds	Not afraid to show emotions, vulnerability. Connects with employees. Communicates problems in a direct manner; directness without being cruel.
Focus on the long-term	Concerned about what happens to the organization over the long term. Nurtures individuals and the organization with patience.

Modified from Kruse, K. (2013). *Authentic Leadership.* https://www.forbes.com/sites/kevinkruse/2013/05/12/what-is-authentic-leadership/#2b8d8019def7.

Status as an employee of a particular hospital, home health agency, long-term care facility, or other venue is secondary to one's status as a member of the profession of nursing.

Value Continuing Nursing Education

Valuing education is one of the hallmarks of a profession. The continuing development of one's nursing skills and knowledge is an empowering experience, preparing nurses to make decisions with the support of an expanding body of evidence. Seminars, workshops, and conferences offer opportunities for continued professional growth and empowerment. Seeking advanced nursing degrees or postbaccalaureate or postgraduate certificates is also a powerful growth experience and reflects commitment to the profession. At one time, some nurses sought to get ahead in nursing by seeking education outside of nursing at the baccalaureate and graduate levels.

To develop expertise in nursing, one must be educated in the discipline of nursing. This evolution is now seen in employment policies that specify degrees in nursing as opposed to a generic statement about a bachelor's or master's degree.

Communication Skills

The most basic tool for developing a powerful image is effective communication skills. Communication skills ensure nurses' effective interaction with patients and families. Just as the clinician listens to the patient to collect assessment data, the leader uses listening skills to assess and evaluate. Managers and other leaders who are good listeners develop reputations for being fair and consistent. Listening for recurring themes related to minor issues of staff dissatisfaction in informal conversations can enable a manager to take action before a staff crisis occurs.

Verbal and nonverbal skills are important personal power strategies; the ability to assess these messages is a critical power strategy. Experts in communication estimate that 90% of the messages we communicate to others are nonverbal. When nonverbal and verbal messages are in conflict, the nonverbal message is always more powerful. The basic lessons on the power of nonverbal communication that most nurses learn in an introductory psychiatric nursing course are relevant in all areas of nursing!

Networking

Networking is an important power strategy and political skill. Developing a network involves identifying, valuing, and maintaining relationships with a system of individuals who are sources of information, advice, and support. Networking supports the empowerment of participants through interaction and the refinement of their interpersonal skills. Many nurses have relatively limited networks within the organizations where they are employed. They tend to have lunch or coffee with the people with whom they work most closely. One strategy to expand a workplace network is to have lunch or coffee with someone from another department, including managers from nonnursing departments, at least two or three times a month. Putting this on the calendar reflects the macro level of behavior.

Active participation in nursing organizations is the most effective method of establishing a professional network outside one's place of employment. Although only a minority of nurses actively participate in professional organizations, such participation can propel a nurse into the politics of nursing, including involvement in shaping health policy. State nurses' associations offer excellent opportunities to develop a network that includes nurses from various clinical and functional areas (Haylock, 2016). Membership in specialty organizations, including organizations for nurse managers and executives, provides the opportunity to network with nurses with similar expertise and interests. In addition, membership in civic, volunteer, and special interest groups and participation in educational programs (e.g., formal academic programs and conferences) also provide networking opportunities. Use of social media, like LinkedIn and Twitter, also can expand one's professional network around the globe. Nurses must be cautious to avoid mixing their personal lives and professional lives in social media.

The successful networker identifies a core of networking partners who are particularly skilled, insightful, and eager to support the development of colleagues. These colleagues need to be nurtured through such strategies as sharing information with them that relates to their interests; introducing them to persons who have comparable interests or who are connected with others of influence; staying connected through notes, e-mail, phone calls, social media, or text messages; and meeting them at important events. Successful networkers are not a burden to others in making requests for support, and they do not refuse the support that is provided.

Mentoring

Developing a network provides an opportunity to craft relationships that may progress to mentorship. Mentors are competent, experienced professionals who develop a relationship with less experienced nurses for the purpose of providing advice, support, information, and feedback to encourage the development of that person. Mentoring has long been an important element in the career development of men in business, academia, and selected professions. Mentoring has now become a significant power strategy for women in general and for nurses in particular during the past 30 years. Mentoring provides expanded access to information, power, and career opportunities. Mentors have been a critical asset to novice nurses trying to negotiate workplace and professional politics.

Effective mentoring in nursing benefits both the mentor and the mentee. Mentors benefit by expanding their own professional development and that of their colleagues, improving their own self-awareness, experiencing the intrinsic benefits of teaching another, nurturing their own interpersonal skills, and expanding their political savvy. Mentees receive one-on-one nurturing and coaching from the mentor, gain insight or savvy about the political rules of the organization and learn about organizational culture from an insider, can expand their self-confidence in a supportive relationship, receive career development advice, profit from the mentor's professional network, and have a unique opportunity for individualized professional development.

Mentoring is an empowering experience for both mentors and protégés. The process of seeking out mentors is an exercise in growth for protégés. Mentors sometimes select their protégés; at other times, the reverse is true. Protégés learn new skills from influential mentors and gain self-confidence. Mentors share their influence through the relationship with those they mentor and gain satisfaction by experiencing the evolution of those nurses into experienced nurses.

Goal-Setting

Goal-setting is another power strategy. Every nurse knows about setting goals. Students learn to devise patient care goals or patient outcomes as part of the care-planning process. Nurses may be expected to write annual goals for performance reviews at work. Even a project at home (e.g., painting the bedrooms) may necessitate setting goals (e.g., painting a room every other day of one's vacation). Goals help people know if what was planned was actually accomplished. Likewise, a successful nursing career needs goals to define what one wants to achieve as a nurse. Without such goals, you can wander endlessly through a series of jobs without a real sense of satisfaction. To paraphrase what the Cheshire Cat told Alice during her trip through Wonderland: "Any road will take you there if you don't know where you are going."

Well-defined, long-term goals may be hard to formulate early in a career. For example, few new graduates know specifically that they want to be chief nurse executives, deans, managers, or researchers; yet, eventually, some will choose those career paths. However, developing such a vision early in a career is an important personal power strategy. Once this career vision is developed, the nurse must create opportunities to move toward that vision. Such planning is empowering—

putting the nurse in charge rather than letting a career unfold by chance. Having this sense of vision is consistent with a commitment to a career in nursing, part of developing a power image. This vision is always subject to revision as new opportunities are encountered and new interests, knowledge, and skills are gained. Education and work experiences are tools for achieving the vision of one's career.

Goals may change as circumstances change and life intervenes. Recognizing that this is a normal process of development and an ongoing analysis of the extent to which the goals set still fit the nurse's desired path provides an opportunity for self-reflection critical to personal growth is important.

Developing Expertise

As noted earlier in this chapter, expertise is one of the bases of power. Developing expertise in nursing is an important power strategy. Nursing expertise must not be limited to clinical knowledge. Leadership and communication skills, for example, are essential to the effective exercise of power. Education and practice provide the means for developing such expertise in any domain of nursing—clinical practice, education, research, and management. Developing expertise expands one's power among nursing colleagues, other professional colleagues, and patients. A high level of expertise can make one nearly indispensable within an organization. This is a powerful position to have within any organization, whether it is the workplace or a professional association. A high level of expertise can also lead to a high level of visibility within an organization.

High Visibility

The strategy of high visibility within an organization can begin with volunteering to serve as a member or the chairperson of committees and task forces. High visibility can be nurtured by attending open meetings in the workplace, professional associations, or the community. Even if you are not a member, if meetings deal with local health issues, you must be visible. Review the agendas of these meetings if they are circulated or posted online ahead of time. Use opportunities both before and after meetings to share your expertise and provide valuable information and ideas to members and leaders of such groups. Share your expertise at open meetings when appropriate. Speak up confidently, but have something relevant to say. Be concise and precise; members of

the committee will ask for more information if they need it. Create your own business cards using a computer and sheets of business card stock (purchased in any office supply store) or have them made. Give members of these committees your personal card so that they can contact you later for information.

EXERCISING POWER AND INFLUENCE IN THE WORKPLACE AND OTHER ORGANIZATIONS

To use influence effectively in any organization requires understanding how the system works. Developing organizational savvy includes identifying the real decision makers and those persons who have a high level of influence with the decision makers. Recognize the informal leaders within any organization. An influential senior clinical nurse may have more decision-making power related to direct patient care than the nurse manager. The senior clinical nurse may have more clinical expertise and a greater knowledge about the history of the unit and its personnel than a nurse manager with excellent management and leadership skills who is new to the unit.

For example, the executive assistants of chief nursing officers (CNOs) are usually very powerful people, although they are not always recognized as such. The CNO's assistant has control over information, making decisions about who gets to meet with the nurse executive and when screening incoming and outgoing mail, letting the CNO know when a document needs immediate attention, or placing a memo under a stack of mail for review at a later time.

Collegiality and Collaboration

Nursing does not exist in a vacuum, nor do nurses work in isolation from one another, other professionals, or support personnel. Nurses function within a wide range of organizations, such as schools, hospitals, community health organizations, governments, insurance companies, professional associations, and universities. Nurses are noted for being divided too long over the appropriate educational level for entry into practice. Nurses are also noted for their failure to join nursing organizations that have the potential to be influential in numerous areas, including policy arenas.

Developing a sense of unity requires each nurse to act collaboratively and collegially in the workplace and in other organizations (e.g., professional associations). Collegiality demands that nurses value the accomplishments of nursing colleagues and express a sincere interest in their efforts. Turning to one's colleagues for advice and support empowers them and expands one's own power base at the same time. Unity of purpose does not contradict diversity of thought. One does not have to be a friend to everyone who is a colleague. Collegiality demands mutual respect, not friendship.

Collaboration and collegiality require that nurses work collectively to ensure that the voice of nursing is heard in the workplace and the legislature. Volunteer to serve on committees and task forces in the workplace, not only within the nursing department but also on organization-wide committees. Become an active member of nursing organizations, especially state nursing organizations and specialty organizations consistent with your clinical specialty (e.g., American Association of Critical Care Nurses [AACN]) or functional role (e.g., American Organization of Nurse Executives [AONE] and AACN). If eligible, become a member of a chapter of Sigma Theta Tau International, nursing's honor society. Get involved in the politics of organizations, in the workplace, and in professional associations.

If the workplace uses shared governance or other participatory models, get involved in these councils, committees, task forces, and work groups to share your energy, ideas, and expertise. Many organizations have interdisciplinary committees that bring together nurses, physicians, and other healthcare professionals to improve the quality of professional collaboration and the quality of patient care. Become an active, productive member of such groups within the workplace and in the professional associations and community groups dealing with healthcare issues and problems.

Being committed to nursing does not mean that nurses cannot collaborate effectively with other disciplines. One of the competencies required of all disciplines to provide effective care is to "Engage diverse healthcare professionals who complement one's own professional expertise, as well as associated resources, to develop strategies to meet specific patient care needs" (Interprofessional Education Collaborative, 2016). Nurses have long felt—often correctly—that the profession is under the domination of medicine. To move from that position, nurses must work for autonomy for the profession. This has frequently put us in conflict with organized medicine. Although work still needs to be done to ensure that nurses practice at the full extent of their practice, nurses must recognize the strides that have been made in this area. Nurse competence is sufficiently recognized to be able to practice collaboratively with medicine and other health care professions.

An Empowering Attitude

Recognizing the competencies that nurses bring to care of patients allows nurses to demonstrate a positive and professional attitude about being a nurse to nursing colleagues, patients and their families, other colleagues in the workplace, and the public, including legislators. This attitude facilitates the exercise of power among colleagues while educating others about nurses and nursing. A powerful image is an important aspect of demonstrating this positive professional attitude. The current practice of nurses to identify themselves by first name may only decrease their power image in the eyes of physicians, patients, and others. Physicians are always addressed as "Doctor." When they address others only by their first names, inequality of power and status is evident. The use of first names among colleagues is not inappropriate so long as everyone is playing by the same rules. Managers may want to enhance the empowerment of their staff members by encouraging them to introduce themselves as "Dr.," "Ms.," or "Mr." Arriving at work, appointments, or meetings on time; looking neat and appropriately attired for the work setting or other professional situation; and speaking positively about one's work are examples of how easy it is to demonstrate a positive, powerful, and professional attitude. And calling practitioners of medicine physicians rather than doctors helps reinforce the idea that many other practitioners, including nurses, hold doctoral degrees even though they are not practicing medicine.

Magnet® institutions, as recognized by the American Nurses Credentialing Center (ANCC), are characterized by work environments that empower nurses (ANCC, 2018). Transformational leadership activities have been identified as a critical element of the work culture in Magnet® hospitals, and quality of leadership is one of the "forces of magnetism."

Bullying

Although bullying is described elsewhere in this book, it is an example of ineffective use of power. Such behavior weakens our influence, which provides another reason to address this issue. Despite the recognition of the various positive uses of power in nursing, in the

21st century we also see negative use of power. More than 30 years ago Roberts (1983) addressed the historical evidence of oppressed group behavior among nurses, based on models developed from the study of politically and economically oppressed populations. Oppressed group behavior is apparent when a population is dominated by another group; this population begins to take on the characteristics of the dominant group; and the oppressed population rejects the characteristics of their own group (Roberts, 1983), often bullying and abusing their peers.

Workplace bullying or *lateral violence* is defined as repeated, health-harming mistreatment of one or more persons (the targets) by one or more perpetrators (The Joint Commission [TJC], 2016). Bullying is abusive conduct, and not a powerful strategy, that takes one or more of the following forms:

- Verbal abuse
- Threatening, intimidating, or humiliating (including nonverbal) behaviors
- Work interference or sabotage that prevents work from getting done (Occupational Safety and Health Administration [OSHA], 2016)

According to a TJC report, "Bullying Has No Place in Healthcare," five categories of workplace violence are recognized:

- Threat to professional status (public humiliation)
- Threat to personal standing (name calling, insults, teasing)
- Isolation (withholding information)
- Overwork (impossible deadlines)
- Destabilization (failing to give credit where credit is due)

Each of those has the potential to undermine the power of both the person abused and the abuser. When two or more people find positive ways to interact, their power increases.

In the 21st century, bullying and incivility have become epidemic in both nursing education and clinical settings (Castronovo, Pullizzi, & Evans, 2016). Although this is true of other professions, we can influence our own professions. Of particular concern, bullying and incivility disrupt the healthcare workplace. An OSHA report on workplace violence in health care notes that although 21% of registered nurses and nursing students reported being physically assaulted, more than 50% were verbally abused in a 12-month period. In addition, 12% of emergency nurses experienced physical violence, and 59% experienced verbal abuse during a 7-day period. (OSHA, 2016). Not only is this a problem influencing job satisfaction of staff, but also the problems of bullying and incivility have been linked to patient safety. In the 2012 publication, civility is described as a necessary precursor for a safety culture in which care teams and patients must be treated with respect. TJC recommends the following strategies to reduce bullying:

1. Establish a safety system and culture that does not tolerate bullying behaviors. Make this a core value of all leaders in the organization.
2. Confront bullies and support the targets of bullying.

Furthermore, all healthcare facilities should consider taking the following specific safety actions:

1. Educate all team members on behaviors consistent with the organization's code of conduct.
2. Hold all staff accountable for modeling desirable behaviors.
3. Develop and implement, using an interprofessional group, policies and procedures or processes that address the following:
   a. Bullying
   b. Reducing fear of retaliation
   c. Responding to patients and families who witness bullying
   d. Beginning disciplinary actions (how and when)

In addition, on July 22, 2015, the American Nurses Association developed a new policy statement regarding bullying, which states:

> The nursing profession will no longer tolerate violence of any kind from any source. All registered nurses and employers in all settings, including practice, academia, and research must collaborate to create a culture of respect, free of incivility, bullying, and workplace violence. Best practice strategies based on evidence must be implemented to prevent and mitigate incivility, bullying, and workplace violence; to promote the health, safety, and wellness of registered nurses; and to ensure optimal outcomes across the health care continuum. (Professional Issues Panel on Incivility, Bullying and Workplace Violence, 2015).

To assist in making this statement a reality, the ANA has also developed a web page that provides a wide range of resources from OSHA, the Centers for Disease Control and Prevention, and the Emergency Nurses Association:

http://nursingworld.org/MainMenuCategories/
Workplace Safety/bullyingworkplaceviolence.

Of particular interest on the ANA website is a link to the PACERS website. PACERS (*Passionate about Creative Environment of Respect and CivilitieS*) is a group of nurses who were members of the 2012 RWJ Foundation Executive Nurse Fellowship. This group provided a tool kit that is helpful for combating workplace violence at the individual, institution, community, and policy levels.

Castronovo et al. (2016) suggested that an incentive for institutions to implement strategies to prevent bullying is desirable. They proposed that a measurement pertaining to the level of nurse bullying be factored into the calculation of the value-based incentive payment in the Hospital Value-Based Purchasing (HVBP) program, a Centers for Medicare and Medicaid Service initiative. They further recommended a survey similar to the Hospital Consumer Assessment of Healthcare Providers and Systems (HCAHPS) to measure nurses' perspectives of workplace bullying (Castronovo et al., 2016).

Developing Coalitions

A coalition is a group of individuals or organizations with a common interest who agree to work together toward a common goal. The exercise of power is often directed at creating change. Although an individual can often be effective at exercising power and creating change, creating certain changes within most organizations requires collective action. Coalition building is an effective political strategy for collective action. The Community Tool Box, a service of the Work Group for Community Health and Development at the University of Kansas (2016), provides strategies for developing an effective coalition.

The goals of coalitions often focus on an effort to effect change. The networking among organizations that results in coalition building requires members of one group to reach out to members of other groups. This often occurs at the leadership level and may come through formal mechanisms such as letters that identify an issue or problem—a shared interest—around which a coalition could be built. For example, a state nurses association may invite the leaders of organizations interested in child health (e.g., organizations of pediatric nurses, public health nurses and physicians, elementary school teachers, school nurses, and daycare providers) and consumers (e.g., parents) to discuss collaborative support for a legislative initiative to improve access to immunization programs in urban and rural areas. Such coalitions of professionals and consumers are powerful in influencing public policy related to health care.

Collaboration among groups and individuals with common interests and goals often results in greater success in effecting change and exercising power in the workplace and within other organizations, including legislative bodies. A group of diverse nursing organizations may come together as a coalition to support a modification of the state nursing practice act. Expanding networks in the workplace, as suggested earlier in this chapter, facilitates creating a coalition by developing a pool of candidates for coalition building before they are needed. Effective strategies to prepare for a coalition may include the following:

- Invite people with common goals to lunch or coffee to begin building a coalition around an issue. Discuss this shared interest, and gain the commitment of the individuals.
- Meet informally with members of the committee or task force that is working on this issue. Attend the open meetings of professional groups that share the same interests as the organization to which you belong.
- Share ideas on how to create the desired change most effectively while building coalitions.

Coalition building is an important skill for involvement in legislative politics. Nursing organizations often use coalition building when dealing with state legislatures and Congress. Changes in nurse practice acts to expand opportunities for advanced nursing practice have been accomplished in many states through coalition building. State medical societies or the state agencies that license physicians often oppose such changes. Efforts by a single nursing organization (e.g., a state nurses' association or a nurse practitioners' organization), representing a limited nursing constituency, often lack the clout to overcome opposition by the unified voice of the state's physicians. However, the unified effort of a coalition of nursing organizations, other healthcare organizations, and consumer groups can be powerful in effecting change through legislation.

Negotiating

Negotiating, or bargaining, is a critically important skill for organizational and political power. It is a process of making trade-offs. Children are natural negotiators.

Often, they will initially ask their parents for more than what they are willing to accept in the way of privileges, toys, or activities. The logic is simple to children: Ask for more than is reasonable and negotiate down to what you really want!

Negotiating often works the same way within organizations. People will sometimes ask for more than they want and be willing to accept less. In other situations, both sides will enter negotiations asking for radically different things, but each may be willing to settle for a position that differs markedly from the respective original position. In the simplest forms of bargaining, each participant has something that the other party values: goods, services, or information. At the "bargaining table," each party presents an opening position. The process moves on until they reach a mutually agreeable result or until one or both parties walk away from a failed negotiation.

Bargaining may take many forms. Individuals may negotiate with a supervisor for a more desirable work schedule or with a peer to effect a schedule change so that one can attend an out-of-town conference. A nurse manager may sit at the bargaining table with the department director during budget planning to expand education hours for the nursing unit in the next year's budget. Representatives of a coalition of nursing organizations meeting with a legislator may negotiate with the legislator over sections of a proposed healthcare-related bill in an effort to eliminate or modify those sections not viewed by the nursing coalition as in the best interests of nurses, patients, or the healthcare system. Nurses may bargain with nursing and hospital administration over wages, staffing levels, other working conditions, and the conditions and policies that govern clinical practice. This is called *collective bargaining,* a specific type of negotiating that is regulated by both state and federal labor laws and that usually involves representation by a state nurses association or a nursing or nonnursing labor union (see Collective Action in Chapter 14).

Successful negotiators are well informed about not only their own positions but also those of the opposing side. Negotiators must be able to discuss the pros and cons of both positions. They can assist the other party in recognizing the costs versus the benefits of each position. These skills are also essential to exercising power effectively with the arenas of professional and legislative politics. When lobbying a member of the legislature to support a bill that is desired by nurses, one must understand the position of

those opposed to the bill to respond effectively to questions that the legislator may ask.

Taking Political Action to Influence Policy

In the 1990s Carolyn McCarthy was a licensed practical nurse from New York when a tragedy turned her life upside-down. Her husband was killed and her son injured by a gunman on the Long Island Railroad. She sought the support of her congressman on gun control legislation as a result of her personal tragedy. He refused to support such legislation. She took extraordinary action, changing her party affiliation and then running against the incumbent for his seat in Congress. She served in the US Congress until 2014. There are, of course, other nurses in local politics, state houses, and the US Congress. However, these numbers are few. As a result, the distinct perspective of nursing may not be as visible as it could be if more nurses were elected officials. In 2017 a registered nurse, Erin Murphy, declared her intent to seek the office of governor in Minnesota—a first for Minnesota (and other) nurses!

Running for office at any level of government is important to be sure that the nursing perspective is part of the policy discussion; it is not the only action a nurse might take to participate in policy development. Gaining political skills, like any other skill set, is a developmental process. Some suggested strategies for developing political skills are presented in Box 9.2. Learning one's strengths and areas for improvement requires self-study. The Political Astuteness Inventory (adapted) (Goldwater & Zusy, 1990) is a helpful tool in determining how well prepared you are to influence legislative politics and public policy, especially public policy related to health care (Box 9.3).

Many social, technologic, scientific, and economic trends have shaped nursing's ability to exercise power in the political arena. Although some failures have occurred in moving nurses to autonomous professionals, we also have experienced many successes. For example, in 1988, in response to a nursing shortage, the American Medical Association (AMA) proposed a new category of healthcare worker (the registered care technologist [RCT]). The proposal suggested that the RCT be trained in a hospital and be primarily responsible for carrying out doctors' orders in medication administration, test orders, and discharge plans (Jonas, 2003). Nurses believed that this recommendation, similar to the training of the hospital-based nurse, was not the answer to the nursing shortage.

BOX 9.3 Political Astuteness Inventory

Place a check mark next to those items for which your answer is "yes." Then give yourself 1 point for each "yes." After completing the inventory, compare your total score with the scoring criteria at the end of the inventory.

1. I am registered to vote.
2. I know where my voting precinct is located.
3. I voted in the last general election.
4. I voted in the last two elections.
5. I recognized the names of the majority of the candidates on the ballot and was acquainted with the majority of issues in the last election.
6. I stay abreast of current health issues.
7. I belong to the state professional or student nurse organization.
8. I participate (e.g., as a committee member, officer) in this organization.
9. I attended the most recent meeting of my district/chapter nurses' association.
10. I attended the last state or national convention held by my organization.
11. I am aware of at least two issues discussed and the stands taken at this convention.
12. I read literature published by my state nurses' association, a professional journal/magazine/newsletter, or other literature on a regular basis to stay abreast of current health issues.
13. I know the names of my senators in Washington, DC.
14. I know the name of my representative in Washington, DC.
15. I know the name of the state senator from my district.
16. I know the name of the state representative from my district.
17. I am acquainted with the voting record of at least one of the previously mentioned state or federal representatives in relation to a specific health issue.
18. I am aware of the stand taken by at least one of the previously mentioned state or federal representatives in relation to a specific health issue.
19. I know whom to contact for information about health-related issues at the state or federal level.
20. I know whether my professional organization employs lobbyists at the state or federal level.
21. I know how to contact these lobbyists.
22. I contribute financially to my state and national professional organization's political action committee (PAC).
23. I give information about effectiveness of elected officials to assist the PAC's endorsement process.
24. I actively supported a senator or representative during the last election.
25. I have written to one of my state or national representatives in the last year regarding a health issue.
26. I am personally acquainted with a senator or representative or member of his or her staff.
27. I serve as a resource person for one of my representatives or his or her staff.
28. I know the process by which a bill is introduced in my state legislature.
29. I know which senators or representatives are supportive of nursing.
30. I know which house and senate committees usually deal with health-related issues.
31. I know the committees of which my representatives are members.
32. I know of at least two health issues related to my profession that are currently under discussion.
33. I know of at least two health-related issues that are currently under discussion at the state or national level.
34. I am aware of the composition of the state board that regulates my profession.
35. I know the process whereby one becomes a member of the state board that regulates my profession.
36. I know what DHHS stands for.
37. I have at least a vague notion of the purpose of the DHHS.
38. I am a member of a health board or advisory group to a health organization or agency.
39. I attend public hearings related to health issues.
40. I find myself more interested in political issues now than in the past.

Scoring:
0-9: Totally unaware politically/apathetic
10-19: Slightly more aware of the implications of the politics of nursing/buy-in
20-29: Beginning political astuteness/self-interest to political sophistication
30-40: Politically astute, an asset to nursing/leading the way

Adapted from Goldwater, M., & Zusy, M. J. L. (1990). *Prescription for nurses: Effective political action.* St. Louis: Mosby; with permission by M. Goldwater.

LITERATURE PERSPECTIVE

Resource: Gardner, B., Glickstein, B., Mason, D. (2016). Using the power of media to influence health policy and politics. In D. Mason, D. Gardner, F. Outlaw, & E. O'Grady (Eds.), *Policy and politics in nursing and health care.* St. Louis: Elsevier.

In today's world the power of the media plays a large role in public opinion and policy development. Gardner, Glick, and Mason (2016) describe the integration of traditional and social media as powerful tools for nurses to harness and shape policy and politics. They compare and contrast the media paradigm of the message delivery models as either a "one-to-many" model or a "many-to-many" model. These authors describe steps for effectively using the media to get your message across. Specifically, they provide guidelines to consider in planning a media campaign, including how to do the following:

- Frame the issue of concern
- Develop the message—why would anyone care?
- Identify the target audience; access the media
- Plan for the interviews
- Follow up with the media

They also describe effective ways to use mobile text messaging, blogs, Facebook, Twitter, YouTube, and Flicker.

Implications for Practice

In today's world, nurses must be able to use the media as a strategy to reach the general public regarding policies and positions that have an impact on the health of citizens or the profession. Harnessing traditional and new social media will provide opportunity to shape these policies.

Nurses and nursing organizations responded powerfully. Nursing leaders came together in "summit meetings" to formulate powerful responses to the AMA and implemented a range of actions, including public education and the education of legislators. Even today, after several decades, entering "RCT" into an Internet search results in documentation of responses from various nursing organizations. As a result of this use of power, this new category of worker was not formed.

Nurses have also been influential in healthcare policy at the national level in more recent years. During the Obama administration, after service as chief of staff to North Dakota senators, Mary Wakefield, PhD, RN, FAAN, was appointed the administrator of the Health Resources and Services Administration (HRSA), and her work as well as others in the administration gave the country the regulations associated with the Patient Protection and Affordable Care Act.

The personal power strategies mentioned earlier in this chapter are also important for building one's political power. Nurses can no longer be passive observers of the political world. Political involvement is a professional responsibility, not just a privilege; political advocacy is a mandate. With the rise of the role of media in our lives, we need to be savvy about how we use media to further our work (see the Literature Perspective).

CONCLUSION

Power is played out every day in every setting. Politics are played and often for the good of health care and patients. The abuse of either (power or politics) is what is disheartening; however, recognizing the sources of power and using them effectively is a critical aspect to every nurse's role. The point is that leaders must be influential in positive, effective ways.

THE SOLUTION

The director gave me the rest of the shift off with pay. I decided to use the weekend off to consider whether I should resign. My director went back to the vice president's (VP's) office with my incident report about the phone call and presented it to the VP. She indicated that this was a true and accurate report of the event, now known as the "cat lady call." All the witnesses had signed the report, including the medical director. She calmly told the VP that she understood how the VP was being pressured by the chief executive officer

(CEO) to take some immediate action. But she restated her belief that I handled the situation appropriately and that the caller was not honest with the CEO. She asserted that there would be no apology issued by her or by me. The VP said she would talk to us on Monday, after consulting with the hospital's legal counsel. From experience, we all knew that this meant the VP was considering firing both of us.

On Monday morning, the director received a new incident report. The report noted that the local police had

THE SOLUTION—cont'd

brought an older adult woman into the emergency department (ED) on Saturday night. She was covered with scratches, many of which were infected. She was an animal hoarder and had created a disturbance in her neighborhood that resulted in the police bringing her into the hospital and removing dozens of cats from her home. She kept telling the ED staff that she didn't want to be cared for by the nurse she talked to on Friday. She was our "cat lady caller." She was verbally and physically abusive to the ED staff and the police. She was treated and released to family.

The director gave the VP this incident report, which vindicated me. She asked the VP how she would like to proceed with this issue. The VP's face reddened with embarrassment, and she told the director to apologize to me for her. I had already heard from the night staff about the woman's visit to the ED over the weekend by the time my director came to the ED. She was disappointed that the VP would not apologize to me in person. Because of my director's powerful response to the VP, I remained a hospital employee until my retirement a few years later. The VP's misuse of positional power was blocked by my director's use of personal and informational power. Her support empowered me.

Would this be a suitable approach for you? Why?

Anonymous

REFLECTIONS

The power of nursing in the healthcare delivery system, educational institutions, professional organizations, and state and federal legislatures has certainly increased in the last 30 years, thanks to many nurses and other stakeholders. This work allows novice nurses to use this pioneering work to continue to evolve health care in the United States. What does power mean to you? What circumstances can you envision in your future as a nurse where you might use power strategies?

THE EVIDENCE

The 2011 Institute of Medicine (IOM) study, *The Future of Nursing: Leading Change, Advancing Health,* provides the best evidence of the need for nurses to use their power to influence change.

An interdisciplinary panel reviewed the literature to determine how nursing should move forward to meet the needs of a changing healthcare system. The 2-year initiative was conducted with the Robert Wood Johnson Foundation (RWJF).

The IOM study offers four key messages:

- Nurses should practice to the full extent of their education and training.
- Nurses should achieve higher levels of education and training through an improved education system that promotes seamless academic progression.
- Nurses should be full partners, with physicians and other healthcare professionals, in redesigning health care in the United States.
- Effective workforce planning and policymaking require better data collection and an improved information infrastructure.

These messages and the eight recommendations of the IOM study demand political action from nurses to reshape nursing education and practice to enable nurses to practice to the full extent of their educations. Nurses should have access to a seamless system of educational programs so that they can perform more complex nursing roles and act as full partners in reshaping and leading the healthcare system. Nurses around the country are now participating in state-based work groups to fulfill the recommendations of the IOM study through state action coalitions, working with an initiative of the RWJF and the American Association of Retired Persons called *The Future of Nursing: Campaign for Action.* These action coalitions are working with colleges and universities, state government agencies including state boards of nursing, nursing organizations, other healthcare professions and their organizations, and funding sources. The state coalitions are developing plans to break down the silos in nursing and health care to ensure that nurses can advance their education to fill advanced nursing roles and be a strong voice in shaping a reformed healthcare delivery system.

▌TIPS FOR USING INFLUENCE

- Become an active member of selected nursing organizations, especially one's state nurses' association and a specialty organization (e.g., special role organization or clinical specialty organization).
- Remember that "power" is not a dirty word.
- Develop a powerful personal and professional self-image.

- Invest in your nursing career by continuing your education.
- Make nursing your career, not just a job.
- Develop networking skills.
- Be visible and competent in the organizations in which you work and network.

REFERENCES

American Nurses Credentialing Center. (2018). Magnet Model: Announcing a new model for ANCC's Magnet Recognition Program. https://www.nursingworld.org/organizational-programs/magnet/magnet-model/.

Braun, B., Richle, A., Donofio, K., Hafiz. H. (2012). Improving patient and worker safety: Opportunity for synergy, collaboration, and innovation. https://www.jointcommission.org/assets/1/18/TJC-ImprovingPatientAndWorkerSafety-Monograph.pdf.

Castronovo, M., Pullizzi, A., & Evans, S. (2016). Nursing bullying: A review and a proposed solution. *Nursing Outlook, 63*(3), 208–214.

French, J., & Raven, B. (1959). The basis of social power. In D. Cartwright (Ed.), *Studies in social power* (pp. 150–167). Ann Arbor: University of Michigan Press.

Goldwater, M., & Zusy, M. J. L. (1990). *Prescription for nurses: Effective political action.* St. Louis: Mosby.

Haylock, P. (2016). Professional nursing associations: Operationalizing nursing values. In D. Mason, et al. (Eds.), *Policy and politics in nursing and health care.* (7th ed.). St. Louis: Elsevier.

Institute of Medicine Committee on the Robert Wood Johnson Foundation Initiative on the Future of Nursing. (2011). *The future of nursing: Leading change, advancing health.* Washington, DC: National Academies Press.

Interprofessional Education Collaborative. (2016). *Core competencies for interprofessional collaborative practice: 2016 update.* Washington, DC: Interprofessional Education Collaborative. https://hsc.unm.edu/ipe/resources/ipec-2016-core-competencies.pdf.

Jonas, S. (2003). *An introduction to the U.S. health care system* (5th ed.). New York: Springer.

Kelly, K. (2015). Power, politics, and influence. In P. Yoder-Wise (Ed.), *Leading and managing in nursing* (6th ed., pp. 167–184). St. Louis: Mosby.

Kruse, K. (2013) What is authentic leadership? *Forbes.* https://www.forbes.com/sites/kevinkruse/2013/05/12/what-is-authentic-leadership/.

Mason, D., Gardner, D., Outlaw, F., & O'Grady, E. (2016). *Power & politics in nursing and health care* (7th ed.). St. Louis: Elsevier.

Occupational Safety and Health Administration (OSHA). (2016). Workplace violence in health care: Understanding the challenge. OSHA 3826, 12/2105.

Professional Issues Panel on Incivility, Bullying and Workplace Violence. (2015). American Nurses Association Policy on Incivility, Bullying, and the Workplace. https://www.nursingworld.org/~49baac/globalassets/practiceandpolicy/nursing-excellence/official-policy-statements/ana-wpv-position-statement-2015.pdf.

Roberts, S. (1983). Oppressed group behavior: Implications for nursing. *Advances in Nursing Science, 5*(4), 21–30.

Saber, D. (2014). Frontline registered nurse job satisfaction and predictors over three decades: A meta-analysis from 1980–2009. *Nursing Outcome, 62*(6), 402–414.

The Joint Commission. (2016). Bullying has no place in healthcare. *Quick Safety, 24*(June), 1–4. https://www.jointcommission.org/assets/1/23/Quick_Safety_Issue_24_June_2016.pdf.

University of Kansas. (2016). *The Community Tool Box, a service of the Work Group for Community Health Development.* http://ctb.ku.edua/en/table-of-contents/assessment/promotion-strategies/start-a-coaltion/main.

White, K. (2016). Political analysis and strategies. In D. Mason, D. Gardner, F. Outlaw, & E. O'Grady (Eds.), *Policy & politics in nursing and health care* (7th ed., pp. 80–90). St. Louis: Elsevier.

Yoder-Wise, P., & Benton, K. (2017). The essence of presence and how it enhances a leader's value. *Nurse Leader, 15*(3), 174–178.

Healthcare Organizations

Mary E. Mancini, Kristin K. Benton

LEARNING OUTCOMES

- Identify and compare characteristics that are used to differentiate healthcare organizations.
- Classify healthcare organizations by major types.
- Analyze economic, social, and demographic forces that drive the development of healthcare organizations.

- Describe opportunities for nurse leaders and managers during the evolution of healthcare organizations.

KEY TERMS

accountable care organization
accreditation
care coordination
consolidated systems
deeming authority
fee-for-service
for-profit organization
horizontal integration
independent practice associations (IPAs)

managed care
medical home
networks
preferred provider organizations (PPOs)
primary care
private nonprofit (or not-for-profit) organization
public institution
secondary care

teaching institution
tertiary care
third-party payers
value-based payment
vertical integration

THE CHALLENGE

Although more Americans gained insurance coverage with the passage of the Patient Protection and Affordable Care Act of 2010, many still faced access barriers related to cost of obtaining care. Individuals found themselves making purchase decisions on insurance plans offered on the Health Insurance Marketplace unaware of potential trade-offs between lower monthly premiums and out-of-pocket responsibilities. Some consumers found themselves unable to afford their cost-sharing responsibilities. One such example was a 2-year-old boy with a history of chronic ear infections causing partial hearing loss in need of a myringotomy and adenoidectomy. Although I was able to locate a willing provider and hospital to perform the surgery, the child's mother was told she was responsible for a $7000 deductible before surgery. The mother became anxious and voiced immediately that she could not afford to pay $7000 for her son's procedure and did not understand this was a part of the plan when she enrolled. I knew I had to act quickly to find a resource that would allow the child access to the care he much needed and alleviate his mother's anxiety over her financial responsibilities.

What would you do if you were this nurse?

Alaina M. Wallace, DNP, RN, CCM
Director of Operations, Superior HealthPlan Austin, Texas

INTRODUCTION

Organizations are collections of individuals brought together in a defined environment to achieve a set of predetermined objectives. Healthcare organizations are systems composed of people, institutions, and resources designed to address the healthcare needs of a target population. Economic, social, and demographic factors affect the purpose and structuring of the system, which in turn interact with the mission, philosophy, and structure of healthcare organizations.

Healthcare organizations provide two general types of services: illness care (restorative) and wellness care (preventive). Illness care services help the sick and injured. Wellness care services promote better health as well as illness and accident prevention. In the past, most organizations (e.g., hospitals, clinics, public health departments, community-based organizations, and physicians' offices) focused their attention on illness services. Economic, social, and demographic dynamics have placed emphasis on the development of organizations that strive to achieve the Institute for Healthcare Improvement's Quadruple Aim to improve the patient experience of care, improve population health, and reduce the per capita cost of care and improve the experience of providing care. Contemporary organizations must optimize care delivery to focus on the full spectrum of health, especially wellness and prevention, to meet consumers' needs in more effective ways. Opportunities exist for nurses in roles as designers of these restructured organizations and as healthcare leaders and managers within the organizations. For example, the manner in which chronic and acute illnesses are managed is dramatically different from such a decade ago. Nurses take a much more active and independent role in providing and coordinating these services. Similarly, as population numbers increase and the demand for nurses continue to exceed the supply, we should anticipate more changes in how nurses function within the healthcare system. An increased focus on quality improvement, outcomes measurement, and benchmarking demands that organizations constantly consider their own practices and make appropriate changes, including those related to the organization's culture and the role of nurses within the organization.

Nurses practice in many different types of healthcare organizations. Nursing roles develop in response to the same social, cultural, economic, legislative, and demographic factors that shape the organizations in which they work. As the largest group of healthcare professionals providing direct and indirect care services to individuals, families, and communities, nurses have an obligation to be involved in the development of healthcare, social, regulatory, and economic policies that shape healthcare organizations.

CHARACTERISTICS AND TYPES OF ORGANIZATIONS

Responding to the rapidly changing nature of the economic, social, and demographic environment at the national, state, and local level, the US healthcare system is in a continual state of flux as are the organizations within this system. Organizations either anticipate or respond to these environmental changes and can be classified in a variety of ways. Some classifications include the type of institution, type of services provided, length of services offered, ownership structure, teaching status, and accreditation status. An overview of how these classifications distinguish organizations follows. Currently no official, comprehensive classification system exists, but, as the Literature Perspective identifies, efforts are being made to create one.

Institutional Providers

Acute care hospitals, long-term care facilities, and rehabilitation facilities have traditionally been classified as institutional providers. Major characteristics that differentiate institutional providers as well as other healthcare organizations are (1) types of services provided, (2) length of direct care services provided, (3) ownership, (4) teaching status, and (5) accreditation status.

Types of Services Provided

The type of services offered is a characteristic used to differentiate institutional providers. Services can be classified as either general or special care. Facilities that provide specialty care offer a limited scope of services, such as those targeted to specific disease entities or patient populations. Examples of special care facilities are those providing psychiatric care, burn care, children's care, women's and infants' care, and oncology care. Alternatively, facilities such as general hospitals provide a wide range of services to multiple segments of the population.

Length of Direct Care Services Provided

Another characteristic that is used to differentiate healthcare organizations is the duration of the care

provided. According to the American Hospital Association (AHA, 2017). most hospitals are acute care facilities giving short-term, episodic care. The AHA defined an acute care hospital as a facility in which the average length of stay is less than 30 days. Chronic care or long-term facilities provide services for patients who require care for extended periods in excess of 30 days. Many institutions expand their scope of services through community partnerships not only to provide acute healthcare services but also to address risk factors for chronic disease such as obesity and tobacco use. The term *healthcare network* refers to interconnected units that either are owned by the institution or have cooperative agreements with other institutions to provide a full spectrum of wellness and illness services. The spectrum of care services provided is typically described as primary care (first-access care), secondary care (disease-restorative care), and tertiary care (rehabilitative or long-term care). Table 10.1 describes the continuum of care and the units of healthcare organizations that provide services in the three phases of the continuum.

EXERCISE 10.1 Search online to determine the types and numbers of primary care, secondary care, and tertiary care services available in your community. Table 10.1 provides an example of a format for collecting data.

TABLE 10.1 Continuum of Healthcare Organizations

Type of Care	Purpose	Organization or Unit Providing Services
Primary	• Entry into system • Health maintenance • Chronic care • Treatment of temporary nonincapacitating malfunction	• Ambulatory care centers • Physicians' offices • Preferred provider organizations • Nursing centers • Independent provider organizations • Health maintenance organizations • School health clinics
Secondary	• Prevention of disease complications	• Home health care • Ambulatory care centers • Free standing emergency rooms • Nursing centers
Tertiary	• Rehabilitation • Long-term care	• Home health care • Long-term care facilities • Rehabilitation centers • Skilled nursing facilities • Assisted living programs/retirement centers

Ownership

Ownership is another characteristic used to classify healthcare organizations. Ownership establishes the organization's legal, business, and mission-related imperative. Healthcare organizations have three basic ownership forms: public, private nonprofit, and for-profit. Public institutions provide health services to individuals under the support and/or direction of local, state, or federal government. These organizations answer directly to the sponsoring government agency or boards and are indirectly responsible to elected officials and taxpayers who support them. Examples of these service recipients at the federal level are veterans, members of the military, Native Americans, and inmates of correctional facilities. State-supported organizations may be health service teaching facilities, chronic care facilities, and correctional facilities. Locally supported facilities include county-supported and city-supported facilities. Table 10.2 shows how several common healthcare organizations are classified.

Private nonprofit (or not-for-profit) organizations—often referred to as *voluntary agencies*—are controlled by voluntary boards or trustees and provide care to a mix of paying and charity patients. In these organizations, excess revenue over expenses is redirected into the organization for maintenance and growth rather than returned as dividends to stockholders. Historically, nonprofit organizations have been exempt from paying taxes because they commit to providing an important community service. The owners of such organizations include churches, communities, industries, and special interest groups such as the Shriners. The ownership influences how organizations are structured, what services they provide, and which patients they serve.

For-profit organizations are also referred to as *proprietary* or *investor-owned organizations*. These organizations operate with the specific intent of earning a profit by providing healthcare services to individuals who can afford to pay for these services. Organizations such as private or public insurers who provide healthcare insurance coverage are known as third-party payers.

Accountable care organizations (ACOs) emerged as a result of the Patient Protection and Affordable Care Act of 2010 as a mechanism to meet the challenges of value-based payment models. ACOs coordinate care and chronic disease management and improve the overall quality of care provided to Medicare patients. ACOs are designed as seamless healthcare delivery systems that bring together physicians, hospitals, and other caregivers focused on improving the health of individuals and communities while decreasing costs. These person-centered organizations are designed for the healthcare team and patients to be true partners in caring. Participation in the program is voluntary, and payments to ACOs are tied to achieving explicit healthcare

TABLE 10.2   Characteristics and Types of Healthcare Organizations

Healthcare Organization	Type	Services	Ownership	Financing	Teaching Status	Multiunit
Veterans Administration	Institution	General	Federal	NP	Y	Y
Academic Medical Center	Institution	General	Private	NP	Y	Y
Community General	Institution	General	Private	NP	N	Y
Public Hospital	Institution	General	County	NP	Y	N
Shriners Burn Hospitals	Institution	Specialty	Private	NP	N	N
Prepaid Health Plan	HMO	General	Private	NP-P	N	N
Public Health Department	Community	General	State	NP	N	N
Women's and Infants' Project	Community	Specialty	State	NP	N	N
Geriatric Corporation	Institution	Long term	Private	NP	N	Y
Visiting Nurses Association	Community	Specialty	Private	NP	N	N

HMO, Health maintenance organization; *N,* no; *NP,* nonprofit; *P,* profit; *Y,* yes.

quality goals and outcomes. The Medicare Shared Savings Program is the most prevalent ACO program. More than 33 quality measures are used to determine the percentage of savings that is captured by an ACO. These quality measures are organized in four domains: patient-caregiver experience of care, care coordination, preventive health, and at-risk population health. To maximize the desired outcomes from ACOs, nurses at all levels of the organization, especially the nurse executive, must be well versed in their structure and goals (Dunlap, Green, Cropley, & Estes, 2017).

Ownership can affect efficiency and quality. Although hospital ownership is defined legally, significant differences are found within the three sectors related to teaching status, location, bed size, and corporate affiliation. For-profit hospitals are typically nonteaching, suburban facilities with a small to medium bed capacity and have the ability to access group purchasing cooperatives that lower nonsalary expenses. For-profit hospitals tend to have higher hospital charges and lower wage and salary costs that most likely represent an aggressive approach to maximizing return on investment.

Teaching Status

Teaching status is a characteristic that can differentiate healthcare organizations. The term teaching institution is applied to academic health centers (those directly affiliated with a school of medicine and at least one other health profession school) and affiliated teaching hospitals (those that provide only the clinical portion of a medical school teaching program). Although care is usually more costly at teaching hospitals than at nonteaching hospitals, teaching hospitals are generally able to offer access to state-of-the-art technology and researchers. The higher costs of teaching hospitals have been attributed to the unique missions these institutions tend to pursue, including graduate medical education, biomedical research, and the maintenance of stand-by capacity for highly specialized patient care (Sangli, Kim, Noronha, Ochieng, & Jean, 2016).

Historically, teaching hospitals have received government reimbursement to cover these additional costs. However, intrinsic costs of providing a medical training program are not fully reimbursed by the government. Maintaining a teaching program places a financial burden on hospitals relative to the direct cost of the program and the indirect cost of the inefficiencies surrounding the training process. These inefficiencies include (1) salaries of physicians who supervise students' care delivery and participate in educational programs such as teaching rounds and seminars, (2) duplicated tests or procedures, and (3) delays in processing patients related to the teaching process. Because of the additional costs, few for-profit hospitals sponsor teaching programs. Teaching hospitals are usually located close to their affiliated medical school. They tend to be larger and located in more urban and economically depressed inner-city areas than their nonteaching counterparts. Teaching hospitals therefore tend to exhibit weaker economic performance compared with nonteaching hospitals.

> **EXERCISE 10.2** Return to the data you started in the first exercise and add financial and teaching status information.

Accreditation Status

Another characteristic that can be used to distinguish one organization from another is whether a healthcare organization has been accredited by an external body as having the structure and processes necessary to provide high-quality care. Private organizations play significant roles in establishing standards and ensuring care delivery compliance with standards by accrediting healthcare organizations. Examples are The Joint Commission (TJC) and The National Committee for Quality Assurance (NCQA). TJC provides accreditation programs for ambulatory care, behavioral health care, acute care and critical access hospitals, laboratory services, long-term care, and hospital-based surgery. The NCQA is a nonprofit organization that accredits, certifies, and recognizes a wide variety of healthcare organizations, services, and providers. More information on accrediting organizations is provided in the Accrediting Bodies section later in this chapter.

Consolidated Systems and Networks

Healthcare organizations are being organized into consolidated systems through both the formation of for-profit or not-for-profit multihospital systems and the development of networks of independently owned and operated healthcare organizations. Consolidated systems tend to be organized along five levels. The first level includes the large national hospital companies, most of which are investor owned. The second level involves large voluntary affiliated systems, which provide members with access to capital, political power, management expertise, joint venture opportunities, and links to health insurance services or, as in Canada, to a national healthcare coverage program. The third level involves regional hospital systems that cover a defined geographic area, such as an area of a state. The fourth level involves metropolitan-based systems. The fifth level is composed of the special interest groups that own and operate units organized along religious lines, teaching interests, or related special interests that

drive their activities. This level often crosses over the regional, metropolitan, and national levels already described. Through the creation of multiunit systems, an organization has greater marketing, policy, and contracting potentials.

By 2016, the number of partnerships among healthcare organizations increased in response to the shift from a model driven by quantity of care to one driven by quality, person-centered, value-based care to address population health. Joint ventures are arrangements between two unrelated entities to provide a new or existing service while sharing economic risks and rewards. For example, a hospital system might enter into a joint venture partnership with an existing insurance provider to create a new network product. Although the insurance provider holds the authority to offer the insurance, the financial risks and gains of the new network product are shared among the partners. Theoretically, this sharing of risk and savings encourages cooperation to keep costs controlled and innovate to meet the requirements of a value-based payment model.

Ambulatory-Based Organizations

Many health services are provided on an ambulatory basis. The organizational setting for much of this care has been the group practice or private physician's office. Prepaid group practice plans, referred to as *managed care systems,* combine care delivery with financing and provide comprehensive services for a fixed prepaid fee. A goal of these services is to reduce the cost of expensive acute hospital care by focusing on out-of-hospital preventive care and illness follow-up care.

Since the opening of the first retail clinic in 2001 in Minnesota, the number of retail clinics has increased to approximately 2000 nationwide by 2016. Retail clinics aim to offer convenient care access to patients in retail stores with an aim to also increase store retail business. Although some traditional physician practice–based clinics have expanded access through more flexible scheduling, retail clinics offer walk-in services where patients shop after work and school, including weekends. Retail clinics may offer primary prevention care, health screening and testing, and chronic disease care. Although concerns that sporadic use of retail clinics might contribute to the fragmentation of patient care, patient use continues to grow. A study by Ashwood et al. (2016) found that healthcare spending per capita increased modestly despite predictions that retail clinics would decrease spending by deterring emergency room visits.

Group practice plans take various forms. One form has a centralized administration that directs and pays salaries for physician practice (e.g., health maintenance organizations [HMOs]). The HMO is a configuration of healthcare agencies that provide basic and supplemental health maintenance and treatment services to voluntary enrollees who prepay a fixed periodic fee without regard to the amount of services used. To be federally qualified, an HMO company must offer inpatient and outpatient services, treatment and referral for drug and alcohol problems, laboratory and radiology services, preventive dental services for children younger than 12 years, and preventive healthcare services in addition to physician services.

An HMO plan aims to coordinate all patient care services through an approved primary care provider, who belongs to a provider network. Patients are most often required to obtain referrals from the primary care provider to see a specialist, such as a surgeon. If patients opt to see an out-of-network provider, the HMO will not provide the same level of coverage offered by in-network providers, and in some cases the patient may be responsible to pay 100% of the costs. Although an HMO may limit a patient's choice of providers, patients are usually not required to file individual claims to cover services provided in network.

Independent practice associations (IPAs) (or professional associations [PAs]) are a form of group practice in which physicians in private offices are paid on a fee-for-service basis by a prepaid plan to deliver care to enrolled members. Preferred provider organizations (PPOs) operate similarly to IPAs; contracts are developed with private practice physicians, but fees are discounted from their usual and customary charges. In return, physicians are guaranteed prompt payment.

Advanced practice registered nurses' leadership in managing patients in group practices has contributed greatly to their success. Increasing evidence shows that nurse-run clinics as well as ambulatory care centers can succeed whether they are integrated within a larger medical complex or physically and administratively separate organizations. Examples of freestanding organizations include surgicenters, urgent care centers, imaging centers, and primary care centers (Fig. 10.1). Often, the nurse manager in these facilities is charged with identifying the strategies to maximize the benefits and minimize the risks or challenges inherent in the characteristics of the facility and organization.

Fig. 10.1 Increasingly, care is delivered through freestanding clinics or community or hospital-affiliated services.

EXERCISE 10.3 Again return to the data started in the first exercise and add information about the status of the multiunit systems that are in place.

Other Organizations

Although hospitals, nursing homes, health departments, visiting nurse services, and private physicians' offices have made up the traditional primary service delivery organizations, the critical role being played by other organizations that may be freestanding or units of hospitals or other community organizations cannot be ignored. These include community service organizations, subacute facilities, home health agencies, long-term care facilities, and hospices. In addition, nurse-owned/nurse-organized services and self-help voluntary organizations contribute to the overall service provision.

Community Services

Community services, including public health departments, are focused on the treatment of the community rather than that of the individual. The historical focus of these organizations has been on control of infectious agents and provision of preventive services under the auspices of public health departments. Local, state, and federal governments allocate funds to health departments to provide a variety of necessary services. These funds provide personal health services that include maternal and child care, care for communicable diseases such as acquired immunodeficiency syndrome (AIDS) and tuberculosis, services for children with birth defects, mental health care, and investigation of epidemiology and treatment of bioterrorism threats and attacks such as anthrax. Monies are allocated also for environmental services (e.g., ensuring that food services meet established standards) and for health resources (e.g., control of reproduction, promotion of safer sex, and breast cancer screening programs). Local health departments have been provided some autonomy in determining how to use funds that are not assigned to categorical programs.

School health programs whose funds are also allocated to them by local, state, and federal governments traditionally have been organized to control infectious disease outbreaks; to detect and refer problems that interfere with learning; to treat on-site injuries and illnesses; and to provide basic health education programs. Increasingly, schools are being seen as primary care sites for children.

Day care centers offer services for both adults and children in the community. Day care centers for older adults can provide social interaction, exercise, nutritious meals, and stimulating activities with nurse supervision. These programs give respite to family caregivers and allow adult children the opportunity to work during the day while their parent is being cared for in a safe environment. Day care centers for medically complex children also provide respite to parents while offering children social, cognitive, and emotional stimulation in a safe setting overseen by nurses. This community service helps prevent caregiver burnout and long-term institutionalization by allowing individuals to remain living in their communities.

Visiting nurse associations, which are voluntary organizations, have provided a large amount of the follow-up care for patients after hospitalization and for newborns and their mothers. Some are organized by cities, and others serve entire regions. Some operate for profit; others do not.

Subacute Facilities

As hospitals began to discharge patients earlier in their recuperation, the subacute facility, also known as a *long-term acute care (LTAC) hospital,* emerged as a healthcare

organization. Initially, many of these facilities were old-style nursing homes refurbished with the high-tech equipment necessary to deal with patients who have just come out of surgery or who are still acutely ill and have complex medical needs. Today, many are newly built centers or new businesses that have taken over existing clinical facilities.

Home Health Organizations

Home health organizations have numerous configurations; they may be freestanding or owned by a hospital and may be for-profit or not-for-profit organizations. Professional nurses with expert skills in assessing patients' self-care competencies and in building structures to overcome patients' and families' social and emotional deficits in providing sick and palliative care are needed to meet home care needs. Home care agencies staffed appropriately with adequate numbers of professional nurses have the potential to keep older adults, those with disabilities, and persons with chronic illnesses comfortable and safe at home.

Long-Term Care and Residential Facilities

LTC facilities may also be known as *skilled nursing facilities.* These organizations provide long-term rehabilitation and professional nursing services. In residential facilities, no skilled care is provided, but residents who have special needs are offered safe, sheltered environments in which to live.

Hospice and Palliative Care

The concept of hospice and palliative care was launched at St. Christopher Hospice in London. Hospices can be located on inpatient nursing units, such as the kind commonly found in Canada, the United Kingdom, and Australia, or in the home or residential centers in the community. Hospice care focuses on confirming rather than denying the reality of death and thus provides care that ensures dignity and comfort.

Since its launch in the 1980s, palliative care expanded dramatically to meet unique needs of patients experiencing chronic illness who may not qualify for hospice coverage. Palliative care offers patients of all ages the option of seeking continuing care—symptom control for serious illnesses concurrently with other treatments. A palliative care team, usually comprising a physician, nurse, social worker, and chaplain, works together to address the physical, social, cultural, and spiritual needs of patients and families who are coping with a serious illness.

Most hospitals adopted palliative care after TJC's advanced certification program for hospitals that provide quality palliative care. Although palliative care is offered in some community and long-term care settings, the need for access to palliative care in community settings is currently unmet and expected to grow (Meier & Bowman, 2017).

Nurse-Owned and Nurse-Organized Services

Nursing centers, which are nurse-owned and nurse-operated places where care is provided by nurses, are another form of community-based organizations. Many nursing centers are administered by schools of nursing and serve as a base for faculty practice and research and clinical experience for students. Others are owned and operated by groups of nurses. These centers have a variety of missions. Some focus on care for specific populations, such as people who are homeless, or on care for people with AIDS. Others have taken responsibility for university health services. Some have assumed responsibility for school health programs in the community, and others operate employee wellness programs, hospices, and home care services.

Self-Help and Peer Assistance Voluntary Organizations

Other organizations are the self-help/self-care and peer assistance voluntary organizations. These organizations also come in various forms. They are often composed of and directed by peers who are consumers of healthcare services. Their purpose is most often to enable patients to provide support to each other and raise community consciousness about the nature of a specific physical or emotional disease. AIDS support groups and Alcoholics Anonymous are two examples. Community geriatric organizations, frequently sponsored by healthcare organizations and offering multiple services for promoting wellness and rehabilitation, are increasing rapidly.

Supportive and Ancillary Organizations

Organizations involved in the direct provision of health care are supported by a number of other organizations whose operations have a significant effect on provider organizations, as well as on the overall performance of the health system. These organizations include regulatory organizations; accrediting bodies; third-party financing organizations; pharmaceutical and medical equipment supply corporations; and various professional, educational, and training organizations.

> **EXERCISE 10.4** Identify supportive and ancillary organizations operating in your community. Can you determine whether nurses are playing leadership or frontline roles in those organizations and what functions are incorporated into existing nursing roles?

Regulatory Organizations

Regulatory organizations set standards for the operation of healthcare organizations, ensure compliance with federal and state regulations developed by governmental administrative agencies, and investigate and make judgments regarding complaints brought by consumers of the services and the public. They approve organizations for licensure as providers of health care. Healthcare organizations are regulated by a number of different federal, state, and local agencies to protect the health and safety of the patients and communities they serve. A number of different regulatory agencies monitor functions in healthcare organizations. These include the Centers for Medicare & Medicaid Services (CMS), the U.S. Food and Drug Administration, the Occupational Health and Safety Administration, the U.S. Equal Employment Opportunity Commission, and state licensing boards for various health professions. Regardless of the type of organization in which they work, nurses are often involved in these processes. Therefore all nurses need to be familiar with the regulations that affect their organization.

Established in 1965, Medicare is the country's largest and most influential health insurance program, providing healthcare funding for more than 55 million individuals. This makes the federal government the primary payer of healthcare costs in the United States. The Medicare program is not limited to individuals age 65 years or older. Persons with certain permanent illnesses, such as end-stage renal disease, also receive Medicare health benefits. Because of the size of the Medicare market, the federal government serves as the leading regulator of healthcare services in this country.

Medicare is organized into four parts that recipients may choose from. Medicare Part A, also known as hospital insurance, covers inpatient hospital stays, skilled nursing facility stays, hospice care, and some home health care. Medicare Part B, also known as medical insurance, covers some doctors' services, outpatient care, medical supplies, and primary prevention care. Medicare Part C, or Medicare Advantage Plans, offers recipients the option to enroll in a health plan offered by a private company that contracts with Medicare to coordinate and cover services offered by Parts A and B, often including prescription drug coverage. Medicare Part D covers prescription drug coverage associated with Medicare Parts A and B and most Part C Medicare Advantage Plans.

Medicaid offers government-funded coverage to eligible low-income adults, children, pregnant women, older adults, and people with disabilities. In contrast to Medicare, Medicaid is administered by states, under federal requirements, and is funded by state and federal funding. A state may opt in or opt out to receive federal funding associated with a particular requirement. Families with children dependents who do not meet the income-related eligibility requirement to receive Medicaid but who still cannot afford private coverage may be eligible to receive coverage through the Children's Health Insurance Plan, a joint state and federally funded program.

The CMS administers the Medicare and Medicaid programs. Participation in these programs is regulated by a complex set of rules outlined in a lengthy set of guidelines—the Conditions of Participation (CoP). These guidelines are established to improve quality and protect the health and safety of Medicare and Medicaid beneficiaries by specifying the requirements that organizations must meet to be eligible to receive Medicare and Medicaid reimbursement.

To be in compliance with the CoP, healthcare organizations must meet certain quality assessment and performance improvement requirements. Through its Quality Improvement Organization program (formerly called *Peer Review*), CMS contracts with one organization in each state (typically the state's department of health) to work with healthcare organizations to improve the quality, efficiency, and effectiveness of care provided in that state to Medicare beneficiaries. CMS provides a financial incentive for hospitals to report quality data. These data are used to establish minimum quality standards for healthcare facilities and by patients to help them make decisions about where to seek health care. The program is designed to ensure that healthcare organizations systematically examine the quality of care provided and that they use the data obtained to develop and implement projects that improve quality, enhance patient safety, and reduce medical errors. To help reach these quality goals, CMS sponsors the Medicare Quality

Improvement Community (MedQIC). The MedQIC website contains information and tools to support healthcare providers and organizations in creating community-based approaches to quality improvement.

Nurses are actively involved in CMS patient safety and quality improvement processes. The level of their participation may be as participants in facility-based quality or utilization management activities, or they may be involved as case managers. Nurse case managers can serve in a number of different roles, but they frequently serve as the organization's interface with the physician. In this role, these case managers routinely monitor for appropriate physician documentation of medical necessity and other required CoP elements. In the ambulatory or acute care setting, nurses in the role of case managers typically work with physician advisors to ensure that patient care follows recognized standards and facilitates patient flow to the appropriate setting for care.

Nurses also play key roles in developing, implementing, and evaluating the review processes of these regulatory agencies. As members of healthcare organizations providing both direct and indirect services to patients and as members of or advisors to regulatory agencies, baccalaureate- and graduate-prepared nurses in roles of direct care nurse and nurse managers have active roles in monitoring and improving quality as well as establishing standards and ensuring that organizations comply with standards.

Accrediting Bodies

Accreditation refers to the approval, recognition, or certification by an official review board that an organization has met certain standards. The CMS is responsible for the enforcement of its standards through its certification activities. For a healthcare organization to participate in and receive payment from either Medicare or Medicaid, the organization must be certified as complying with the CoP. One manner that an organization can be recognized as complying with the CoP is through a survey process conducted by a state agency on behalf of the CMS. Alternatively, an organization can be surveyed and accredited by a national accrediting body holding "deeming authority" for CMS. To obtain deeming authority, an accreditation organization must undergo a comprehensive evaluation by CMS to ensure that the standards of the accrediting organization are at least as rigorous as CMS standards. (See Table 10.3 for a list of

TABLE 10.3 Accrediting Organizations With Deeming Authority for Centers for Medicare & Medicaid Services

Accrediting Organization	Services Accredited
Accreditation Association for Ambulatory Health Care (AAAHC)	ASCs
Accreditation Commission for Health Care (ACHC)	HHAs, hospice
American Association for Accreditation of Ambulatory Surgery Facilities (AAAASF)	ASCs, OPTs, RHCs
American Osteopathic Association's Healthcare Facilities Accreditation Program (AOA/HFAP)	ASCs, CAHs, hospitals
Commission on Accreditation of Rehabilitation Facilities (CARF)	Medical rehabilitation programs, behavioral health programs, continuing care retirement centers
Community Health Accreditation Program (CHAP)	HHAs, hospice
Det Norske Veritas Germanischer Lloyd Healthcare, Inc. (DNV GL Healthcare) Accreditation Program	Hospitals, CAHs, ancillary
The Joint Commission (TJC)	ASCs, CAHs, HHAs, hospice, hospitals, psychiatric hospitals

ASC, Ambulatory surgery center; *CAH,* critical access hospital; *HHA,* home health agency; *OPT,* outpatient physical therapy; *RHC,* rural health clinics.
Retrieved from Centers for Medicare and Medicaid Services (2018). CMS-approved accrediting organization contacts for prospective clients. https://www.cms.gov/Medicare/Provider-Enrollment-and-Certification/SurveyCertificationGenInfo/Downloads/Accrediting-Organization-Contacts-for-Prospective-Clients.pdf

organizations with deeming authority.) Healthcare organizations accredited by an organization with CMS deeming authority are therefore deemed as meeting Medicare and Medicaid certification requirements.

Acute care healthcare organizations commonly seek accreditation by the American Osteopathic Association (AOA), TJC, or Det Norske Veritas Germanischer Lloyd Healthcare, Inc. (DNV GL Healthcare). These organizations have been granted deeming authority by CMS. The AOA is a professional association specifically for osteopathic healthcare organizations. The Joint Commission is an independent, not-for-profit organization that accredits more than 15,000 healthcare organizations in the United States and internationally. The explicit mission of TJC is to continuously improve the safety and quality of care provided to the public through the provision of healthcare accreditation and related services that support improvement of performance in healthcare organizations. The DNV GL Healthcare received deeming authority in 2008 and is missioned to accredit organizations that demonstrate high performance and continual improvement.

Third-Party Financing Organizations

Organizations that provide financing for health care comprise another subset of supportive and ancillary organizations. As noted earlier, the government, through CMS, finances a large portion of the population and represents the largest third-party organization involved in healthcare provision. Private health insurance carriers, which account for most of the remaining financing, are composed of not-for-profit and for-profit components. Commercial insurance companies represent the private sector.

Third-party financing organizations have a major effect on the actual delivery of health care. They do so by identifying those procedures, tests, services, or drugs that will be covered under their healthcare insurance programs.

Pharmaceutical and Medical Equipment Supply Organizations

Healthcare expenditures that are allocated to drugs and medical equipment are increasing. Nurses in direct care, manager, and leadership roles are primary users of these products. They play a significant role in healthcare organizations in setting standards for safe and efficient products that meet both consumers' and organizations' needs in a cost-effective manner. Supply organizations often seek nurses as customers and as participants in market surveys for the design of new products, services, and marketing techniques.

Examples of the roles nurses play can be seen by studying organizations that employ nurses to design new products and market them through production and distribution of a newsletter and ongoing continuing education presentations.

INTEGRATION

As the healthcare industry faces continuing and increasing pressure to improve patient safety as well as to be efficient and effective, healthcare organizations are entering into a number of different organizational relationships such as accountable care organizations. Organizations can come together to form affiliations, consortiums, and consolidations that result in multihospital systems and/or multiorganizational arrangements. When organizations that provide similar services come together, the arrangement is referred to as horizontal integration. An example of horizontal integration is a group of acute care facilities that come together to provide coverage for an expanded region. When organizations align to provide a full array or continuum of services, the arrangement is referred to as vertical integration. Organizations brought together in a vertical integration might include an acute care facility, a rehabilitation facility, a home care agency, an ambulatory clinic, and a hospice. Benefits attributed to vertical integration include enhanced coordination of services, efficiency, and customer services. Fig. 10.2 illustrates these approaches to integration.

ACQUISITIONS AND MERGERS

The economic forces of capitated payments and managed care have caused healthcare organizations to reorganize, restructure, and reengineer to decrease waste and economic inefficiency. Many organizations are forming multi-institutional alliances that integrate healthcare systems under a common organizational infrastructure. These alliances are accomplished through acquisitions or mergers. Acquisitions involve one organization directly buying another. Mergers involve combining two or more organizations and their assets to form a new entity. Mergers can also happen within organizations as departments or patient care units come together. People, structure, culture, and political issues or organizational change can be very traumatic and lead to dysfunctional outcomes if they are not managed well.

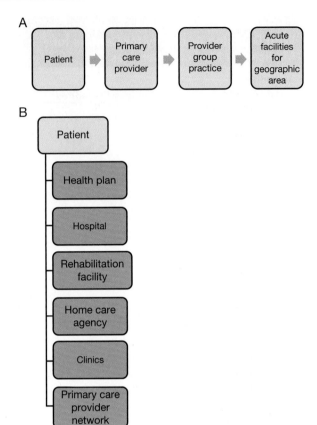

Fig. 10.2 Horizontal (A) and vertical (B) integration of healthcare organizations.

FORCES THAT INFLUENCE HEALTHCARE ORGANIZATIONS

Economic, social, and demographic factors provide the input for future development and act as major forces driving the evolution of healthcare organizations.

Economic Factors

Overall economic conditions as well as decisions surrounding the financing of health care have shaped the supply, configuration, and distribution of healthcare organizations and substantially changed the provision of health care in the United States. The radical restructuring of the healthcare system that is required to reduce the continuing escalation of economic resources into the system and to make health care accessible to all citizens will necessitate ongoing changes in healthcare organizations. As the Literature Perspective points out, nurses have great potential to be engaged with more services and to revamp the approach to care.

LITERATURE PERSPECTIVE

Resource: Morrison, J. (2016). Nursing leadership in ACO payment reform. *Nursing Economic$, 34*(5), 230-235.

Nurses are ideally positioned to demonstrate their leadership competencies as care models founded in value-based versus retrospective fee-for-service payment models become more prevalent. Accountable Care Organizations (ACOs) are provider-led organizations that aim to prevent fragmentation of care, control costs, and achieve high-quality care by offering care services across the continuum while accepting responsibility for costs. In general, when an ACO demonstrates quality outcomes with cost savings, a financial reward is granted through a shared savings model. With 477 ACOs serving almost 9 million Medicare recipients during 2016 and the patient-centered medical home model demonstrating reform in primary care, nurses

can seize these as opportunities to lead with their expertise in such areas as care coordination, wellness and prevention care, and quality improvement. For example, a nurse leader can consult during planning for changes to the electronic health record so that metrics can be easily tracked to demonstrate quality outcomes. Nurses must strive to continue to learn about new care models, understand their potential to improve the healthcare system, advocate for nursing's role, and look toward a future vision of nursing leadership.

Implications for Practice
The opportunities afforded to nursing as a result of healthcare reform are enormous. The challenge lies in our readiness and ability to respond to the opportunities.

Healthcare organizations are being confronted daily with financial pressures associated with caring for uninsured patients, rapidly escalating drug costs, expensive new technology, and spiraling personnel costs (Henry J. Kaiser Family Foundation, 2016). The CMS reported that in 2015, US healthcare spending reached 17.8% of the gross domestic product (GDP).

The complexity of controlling costs remains a major issue driving changes in the healthcare system. Nurses have a major role to play in demonstrating that access to care and quality management are essential components of cost control. With the increasing involvement of industry, business management techniques will assume greater emphasis in healthcare organizations. Nurses will need to lead efforts to redesign roles and restructure healthcare organizations. Nurse leaders and managers will need to go beyond obtaining education in business techniques to gaining skill in adapting that knowledge to meet the specific needs of delivery of cost-effective, quality care. The increasing focus on preparing registered nurses at the levels of master's degrees and doctoral degrees reflects the clear need for practicing nurses, nurse managers, and nurse administrators to be able to work efficiently and effectively in a constantly changing healthcare environment. The evidence section at the end of the chapter describes the role and impact of the clinical nurse leader (CNL).

Social Factors

Increasing consumer attention to disease prevention and promotion of healthful lifestyles is redefining

relationships of healthcare organizations and their patients. Individuals are becoming increasingly active in care planning, implementation, and evaluation and are seeking increased participation with their providers. Demands will be made of healthcare organizations for more personal, responsive, and coordinated care. As such, development of strategies that allow patients to become empowered controllers of their own health status is essential. Responsive structural changes in service delivery will be needed to maintain congruence, with new missions and philosophies developed in response to cultural demands and social changes. Continuous evaluation will be needed to assess cost and quality outcomes related to these changes. Maintaining focus on the quality of care provided as well as access to care will be required so that bottom-line costs do not overshadow quality care provisions. Nursing's history of work with the development of person-centered interactive strategies places nurses in a position to assume leadership roles in this area of organizational development.

Demographic Factors

Geographic dispersion, regional access to care, incomes of the population, aging of the population, and immigration trends are among the demographic factors influencing the design of healthcare organizations. Changing economic and demographic characteristics of many communities are resulting in a larger number of uninsured and underinsured individuals. Geographic isolation often limits access to necessary health services and impedes recruitment of healthcare personnel. Community-based rural health networks that provide primary care links to urban health centers for teaching, consultation, personnel sharing, and the provision of high-tech services are one solution for meeting needs in rural areas. Federal and state funding, which includes incentives for healthcare personnel to work in rural areas, is another approach. Strategic planning by nursing is critical to address community needs.

A major influence exerted on healthcare organizations comes from the aging of the population. By the year 2025, more than 18% of the population is expected to be older than 65 years. The number of "the old-old," those older than 80 years, is increasing dramatically. Although this segment of the population does not necessarily have dependency needs, a need exists for more long-term beds, supportive housing, and community programs. To meet the needs of older adults, new healthcare organizations will continue to evolve and be evaluated, and restructured based on findings. New roles for nurses as leaders and managers of the care of older adults are evolving. An example is the role of advanced practice registered nurses to direct the care of patients who have become members of geriatric care organizations such as retirement centers.

THEORETICAL PERSPECTIVES

Two major views apply to healthcare organizations. One is that organizations evolve in a pleasant manner (systems theory). The other is that change is disruptive and not orderly (chaos theory).

Systems Theory

Systems theory attempts to explain productivity in terms of a unifying whole as opposed to a series of unrelated parts (Thompson, 1967). Systems can be either closed (self-contained) or open (interacting with both internal and external forces). In systems theory, a system is described as comprising four elements: structure, technology, people, and their environment. Systems theorists focus on the interplay among these elements in a framework of (1) inputs—resources such as people, money, or materials; (2) throughputs—the processes that produce a product from the inputs; and (3) outputs—the product of inputs and throughputs.

The theoretical concepts of systems theory have been applied to nursing and to organizations. Systems theory presents an explanation of organizational evolution that is similar to biological evolution. Systems theory produces a model that explains the process of healthcare organization evolution (Fig. 10.3). The survival of the organization, as portrayed throughout this chapter, depends on its evolutionary response to changing environmental forces; it is seen as an open system. The response to environmental changes brings about internal changes, which produce changes that alter environmental conditions. The changes in the environment, in turn, act to bring about changes in the internal operating conditions of the organization.

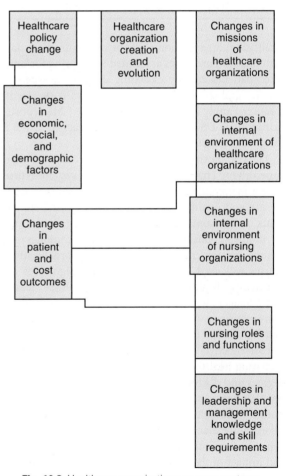

Fig. 10.3 Healthcare organizations as open systems.

This open systems approach to organizational development and effectiveness emphasizes a continual process of adaptation of healthcare organizations to external driving forces and a response to the adaptations by the external environment, which generates continuing inputs for further healthcare organization development. This open system is in contrast to a closed system approach that views a system as being sufficient unto itself and thus untouched by what happens around it.

Chaos Theory

Unfortunately, health care as an industry is not always as predictable and orderly as systems theorists would have us believe. In contrast to the somewhat orderly universe described in systems theory, in which an organization can be viewed in terms of a linear, cause-and-effect model, chaos theory sees the universe as filled with unpredictable and random events (Hawking, 1998). According to the proponents of chaos theory, organizations must be self-organizing and adapt readily to change to survive. Organizations therefore must accept that change is inevitable and unrelenting. When one embraces the tenets of chaos theory, one gives up on any attempt to create a permanent organizational structure. Using creativity and flexibility, successful managers will be those who can tolerate ambiguity, take risks, and experiment with new ideas in response to each day's unique situation or environment. They will not rest on a successful transition or organizational model because they know the environment that it flourished in is fleeting. The successful nurse leaders will be those individuals who are committed to lifelong learning and problem solving. The Theory Box notes key elements of systems and chaos theories.

NURSING ROLE AND FUNCTION CHANGES

Leadership and management roles for nurses are proliferating in healthcare organizations that are developing or evolving in response to environmental driving forces. With a focus on primary care and population medicine, the proportion of nursing positions in the community is increasing, as are various care management positions, clinical nurse leaders, and advanced practice registered nurses. Filling these roles requires knowledge and skills to coordinate the care of patients or communities with

THEORY BOX
Systems and Chaos Theories

Systems theory	• Definition: A system comprises four elements (structure, technology, people, and environment) forming a unified whole
	• Viewed as inputs, throughputs, and outputs
	• Closed systems—self-contained
	• Open systems—interacting with internal and external forces
Chaos theory	• Definition: The universe is chaotic and requires organizations to be self-organizing and adaptive to survive
	• Viewed as unpredictable and random events
	• Constant change resulting in little long-term stability

the many other disciplines and organizational units that are providing the continuum of care. Our society needs nurses who can engage in the political process of policy development, coordinate care across disciplines and settings, use conflict management techniques to create win-win situations for patients and providers in resolving the healthcare system's delivery problems, and use business savvy to market and prepare financial and organizational plans for the delivery of cost-effective care.

Economic, social, and demographic changes are not limited to patients and communities. These shifts are affecting the workplace as well. To be effective, nurse managers and leaders need to consider how these phenomena affect the workplace in the same way they consider it when seeking to address the needs of their patients and the communities they serve. To be efficient and effective, nurse leaders must be not only patient-centered but also employee-centered. Establishing healthy work environments where employee engagement is maximized results in increased job satisfaction and positive patient outcomes.

CONCLUSION

Whether influenced by systems or chaos theory, today's healthcare organizations are in a dynamic state. Nurses must be continuously alert to assessing both the internal and external environment for forces that act as inputs to changes needed in their healthcare organization and for the effects of changes that are made. Awareness of the changing status of healthcare organizations and the ability to play a leading role in creating and evaluating adaptation in response to changing forces will be central functions of nurse leaders and managers in healthcare organizations. Nurses need to develop a foundation of leadership and management knowledge that they can build on through a planned program of continuing education. Even in tumultuous times within the healthcare industry, nursing leaders have demonstrated their ability to strengthen the quality of both their organizations and the practice of nursing. As healthcare organizations continue to undergo transformation, tomorrow's nurses—whether leaders, managers, or followers—need to carry these lessons forward.

THE SOLUTION

I contacted both the provider and the facility that would be performing the surgery to understand what, if any, financial resources were available to help the mother pay the deductible over time. The provider offered no payment plans; however, after contacting the billing department of the facility, I learned that she could set up a payment plan and pay over a series of prearranged payments. For this to work, I had to ensure the deductible went toward the facility charges and not the provider charges. To do this, I coordinated with the health plan claims department to make sure the deductible was directed toward the correct claim and processed accordingly. As nurse leaders, we have to think strategically and creatively for solutions, even if they are outside our comfort zone. Understanding how health insurance works and what we can do to help patients access care are key to providing compassionate and coordinated person-centered care.

Would this be a suitable approach for you? Why?

Alaina M. Wallace

REFLECTIONS

As a nurse, you will have the opportunity to practice within or in collaboration with several types of healthcare organizations. Based on what you have learned about the ownership, governance, structure, and quality focus of contemporary healthcare organizations, with which type of organization do you believe you would prefer to practice? What rationale do you have for that decision?

THE EVIDENCE

The American Association of Colleges of Nursing introduced the role of the master's-prepared CNL in 2004 as a response to the need for more evidence-based, collaborative, cost effective, patient-centered care. The CNL is a master's-prepared registered nurse with competencies in clinical leadership and care environment and clinical outcomes management. Bender, Williams, and Wei (2016) described the characteristics of the CNL to validate a model for CNL practice. The researchers performed a descriptive analysis of survey data from a national sample of CNLs. With 601 respondents representing a 19% response rate, 58% of the respondents reported practicing in a formal CNL role with a high level of accountability to the essential CNL competencies. Most respondents reported practicing in acute care hospital settings. The researchers concluded that although the CNL role is still new, CNLs are practicing in a variety of settings and are expanding at a rate of 64% annually. The CNL continues to hold promise as a nurse with specialized knowledge and competencies to help coordinate patient care and advocate for policies to improve health outcomes.

■ TIPS FOR HEALTHCARE ORGANIZATIONS

- Knowledge of economic, social, and demographic changes is essential to redesigning healthcare organizations to meet society's needs.
- Increasing consolidation of healthcare services that provide all levels of care necessitates the development of communication systems that provide information on patients receiving services at the various points of care in the network.

- Diversified positions will be available for professional nurses in the various organizations that are developing to enhance the provision of care.
- New configurations of healthcare delivery will demand that professional nurses continually acquire new knowledge and skills in leadership and management.

REFERENCES

American Hospital Association. (2017). *AHA hospital statistics* (2017 ed.). Health Forum LLC.

Ashwood, J. S., Gaynor, M., Setodji, C. M., Reid, R. O., Weber, E., & Mehrotra, A. (2016). Retail clinic visits for low-acuity conditions increase utilization and spending. *Health Affairs, 35*(3), 449–455. https://doi.org/10.1377/hlthaff.2015.0995.

Bender, M., Williams, M., & Wei, S. (2016). Diffusion of a nurse-led healthcare innovation. *Journal of Nursing Administration, 46*(7/8), 400–407. https://doi.org/10.1097/NNA.0000000000000365.

Dunlap, C., Green, A., Cropley, S., & Estes, L. J. (2017). Making sense of ACOs: A guide for nurse leaders. *Nurse Leader, 15*(3), 193–198. https://doi.org/10.1016/j.mnl.2017.03.001.

Hawking, S. (1998). *A brief history of time.* London: Bantam Press.

Henry, J., & Kaiser Family Foundation. (2016). *The uninsured: A primer.* http://files.kff.org/attachment/Report-The-Uninsured-A%20Primer-Key-Facts-about-Health-Insurance-and-the-Unisured-in-America-in-the-Era-of-Health-Reform.

Meier, D. E., & Bowman, B. (2017). The changing landscape of palliative care. *Generations, 41*(1), 74–80.

Morrison, J. (2016). Nursing leadership in ACO payment reform. *Nursing Economic$, 34*(5), 230–235.

Sangli, S., Kim, B., Noronha, S., Ochieng, P., & Jean, R. (2016). Outcomes of severe sepsis in patients admitted to teaching hospitals in comparison to non-teaching hospitals. *CHEST Journal, 150*(4_S), 352A.

Thompson, J. D. (1967). *Organization in action.* New York: McGraw-Hill.

11

Organizational Structures

Mary E. Mancini, Kristin K. Benton

LEARNING OUTCOMES

- Analyze the relationships among mission, vision, and philosophy statements and organizational structure.
- Analyze factors that influence the design of an organizational structure.
- Compare and contrast the major types of organizational structures.
- Describe the differences between redesigning, restructuring, and reengineering of organizational systems.

KEY TERMS

accountable care organizations
bureaucracy
chain of command
flat organizational structure
functional structure
hierarchy
hybrid
line function
matrix structure

mission
organization
organizational chart
organizational culture
organizational structure
organizational theory
philosophy
redesign
reengineering

restructuring
service-line structures
shared governance
span of control
staff function
system
systems theory
vision

THE CHALLENGE

I have been a frontline nurse for 2 years and work on a busy 36-bed medical-surgical unit in a community hospital. We primarily care for all of the hospital postoperative patients, but also periodically receive medical, obstetric, and pediatric overflow patients. We are a cohesive team who support each other and genuinely embrace our organizational mission, vision, and core values. Over the past few months the pace of the unit has picked up significantly, and we've received many more overflow patients. We noticed concerning trends, including nurses missing lunch breaks, staying over past shifts to complete charting, and entering late entries more frequently than usual. The nursing shortage in our area of the state makes hiring more nurses an unrealistic remedy to the problem within a reasonable time frame. The stress is increasing, and we have to come up with a creative solution before our team begins to experience burnout and patient safety is threatened.

What would you do if you were this nurse?

Hallie Hurt, RN, BSN
Staff Nurse/Clinical Manager, Midland Memorial Hospital,
Midland, Texas

INTRODUCTION

Since time began, people have organized themselves into groups. The term organization has multiple meanings. It can refer to a business structure designed to support specific business goals and processes, or it can refer to a group of individuals working together to achieve a common purpose. Regardless of how the term is used, learning to determine how an organization accomplishes its work, how to operate productively within an organization, and how to influence organizational processes are essential to a successful professional nursing practice.

Organizational theory (sometimes called *organizational studies*) is the systematic analysis of how organizations and their component parts act and interact. Organizational theory is based largely on the systematic investigation of the effectiveness of specific organizational designs in achieving their purpose. Organizational theory development is a process of creating knowledge to understand the effect of identified factors, such as (1) organizational culture; (2) organizational technology, which is defined as all the work being carried out; and (3) organizational structure or organizational development. A purpose of such work is to determine how organizational effectiveness might be predicted or controlled through the design of the organizational structure.

Specific organizational theories provide insight into areas such as effective organizational structures, motivation of employees, decision making, and leadership. A common framework in health care for analysis and application of organizational theory is systems theory. A system is an interacting collection of components or parts that together make up an integrated whole. The basic tenet of systems theory is that the individual components of any system interact with each other and with their environment. To be effective, nurses need to understand the specific part—role and function—they play within a system and how they interact, influence, and are influenced by other parts of the system. The Theory Box notes key elements of systems theory.

An organization's mission, vision, and philosophy form the foundation for its structure and performance as well as the development of the professional practice models it uses. An organization's mission, or reason for the organization's existence, influences the design of the structure (e.g., to meet the healthcare needs of a designated population, to provide supportive and stabilizing care to an acute care population, or to prepare

---

THEORY BOX

Systems Theory

Definition: A system comprises four elements forming a unified whole:
- Structure
- Technology
- People
- Environment

Viewed as inputs, throughputs, and outputs

Systems may be:
- Closed systems that are self-contained
- Open systems, interacting with internal and external forces

---

patients for a peaceful death). The vision is the articulated goal to which the organization aspires. A vision statement conveys an inspirational view of how the organization wishes to be described at some future time. It suggests how far to strive in all endeavors. Another key factor influencing structure is the organization's philosophy. A philosophy expresses the values and beliefs that members of the organization hold about the nature of their work, about the people to whom they provide service, and about themselves and others providing the services. As demonstrated in The Challenge, mission, vision and core values shape an organization's culture of empowerment to make decisions locally and can impact care improvements.

EXERCISE 11.1 Consider how you might use the information in the Introduction:
1. To analyze an organization that you are considering joining to determine whether it fits your professional goals
2. To assess the functioning of an organization of which you are already a member
3. To make a plan to reengineer the structure or philosophy to better accomplish the mission of the organization

---

MISSION

The mission statement defines the organization's reason or purpose for being. The mission statement identifies the organization's customers (individuals, families, populations, or communities) with an emphasis on improvement of overall health rather than on specific services or treatments offered. It enacts the vision statement. An example of a mission statement for an individual nursing unit appears in Box 11.1. Hospitals' missions are shifting from primarily treatment-oriented to population health improvement; the missions of ambulatory care group practices combine treatment, prevention, and diagnosis-oriented services; long-term care facilities' missions are primarily maintenance and social support–oriented; and the missions of nursing centers are oriented toward promoting optimal health status for a defined group of people. The definition of services to be provided and the implications for technologies and human resources greatly influence the design of the organizational structure—that is, the arrangement of the work group. The mission statements of accountable care organizations (a group of providers and healthcare organizations who are organized to give comprehensive, coordinated care focused on improving patient outcomes) are focused on providing

---

BOX 11.1   Mission, Vision, and Philosophy for a Neurosurgical Unit

Mission Statement

This unit's purpose is to provide high-quality nursing care for neurosurgical patients during the acute phase of their illness that facilitates their progression to the rehabilitation phase. We strive to cultivate a multidisciplinary approach to the care of the neurosurgical patient and provide multiple educational opportunities for the professional development of neurosurgical nurses.

Vision Statement

To be the premier neurosurgical nursing unit in the state.

Philosophy

The philosophy is based on Roy's Adaptation Model and on the American Association of Neurosurgical Nursing conceptual framework.

Patients

We believe

- It is the right of the patients to make informed choices concerning their treatment.
- Patients have a right to high-quality nursing care and opportunities for improving their quality of life, regardless of the potential outcomes of their illness.
- The patient/family/significant other has a right to exercise personal options to participate in care to the extent of individual abilities and needs.

Nursing

We believe

- Neuroscience nursing is a unique area of nursing practice because neurosurgical interventions and/or neurologic dysfunction affect all levels of human existence.
- The goal of the neuroscience nurse is to engage in a therapeutic relationship with his or her patients to facilitate adaptation to changes in physiologic, self-concept, role performance, and interdependent modes.

- The ultimate goal for the neuroscience nurse is to foster internal and external unity of patients to achieve optimal health potentials.

Nurse

We believe

- The nurse is the integral element who coordinates nursing care for the neurosurgical patient using valuable input from all members of the patient care team.
- The nurse has an obligation to assume accountability for maintaining excellence in practice.
- The nurse has three basic rights: human rights, legal rights, and professional rights.
- The nurse has a right to autonomy in providing nursing care based on sound nursing judgment.

Nursing Practice

We believe

- Nursing practice must support and be supported by activities in practice, education, research, and management.
- Insofar as possible, patients must be assigned one nurse who is responsible and accountable for their care throughout their stay on the neurosurgical unit.
- The primary nurse is responsible for consulting and collaborating with other healthcare professionals in planning and delivering patient care.
- The contributions of all members of the nursing team are valuable, and an environment must be created that allows each member to participate fully in the delivery of care in accord with his or her abilities and qualifications.
- The nursing process is the vehicle used by nurses to operationalize nursing practice.
- Data generated in nursing practices must be continually and consistently collected and analyzed for the purpose of managing the quality of nursing practice.

Courtesy Upstate Medical University, University Hospital, Syracuse, NY (W. Painter, J. Van Nest-Kinne).

comprehensive coordinated care to improve the health and well-being of a group of individuals.

Nursing, as a profession providing a service within a healthcare agency, typically formulates its own mission statement that describes its contributions to achieve the agency's mission. The statement should define nursing based on theories that form the basis for the model to be used in guiding the process of nursing care delivery. Nursing's mission statement tells why nursing exists within the context of the organization. The mission should describe nursing's role in achieving the agency's mission and be the guiding framework for decision making. It should be known and understood by other healthcare professionals, by patients and their families, and by the community. It indicates the relationships among nurses and patients, other personnel in the organization, the community, and health and illness. The mission provides direction for the evolving statement of philosophy and the organizational structure. It should be reviewed for accuracy and updated routinely. Various work units that provide specific services such as intensive care, women's health services, or hospice care may also formulate mission statements that detail their specific contributions to the overall organization.

VISION

Vision statements are future-oriented, purposeful statements designed to identify the desired future of an organization. They serve to unify all subsequent statements toward the view of the future and to convey the core message of the mission statement. Typically, vision statements are brief, consisting of only one or two phrases or sentences that reflect the image of how the organization will meet its mission in the future in harmony with its core values and beliefs reflected in the philosophy. An example of a vision statement is provided in Box 11.1.

PHILOSOPHY

A philosophy is a written statement that articulates the values and beliefs about the nature of the work required to accomplish the mission and the nature and rights of both the people being served and those providing the service. A nursing philosophy states the vision of what nursing practice should be within the organization and how it contributes to the health of individuals and communities. For example, the organization's mission statement may incorporate the provision of person-centered care as an organizational purpose. The philosophy statement would then support this purpose through an expression of a belief in the responsibility of nursing staff to act as patient advocates and to provide quality care according to the wishes of the patient, family, and significant others.

Philosophies are evolutionary in that they are shaped both by the social environment and by the

---

LITERATURE PERSPECTIVE

Source: Raso, R. (2016). It's all connected! Patient experience and healthy practice environments. *Nursing Management, 47*(8), 24-29.

The author proposes the goals that healthcare organizations often focus on—such as patient outcomes, patient experience, nurse satisfaction, and a healthy practice environment—are all connected. The connection among these goals is founded in the responsibility and professional obligation for organizations to serve humans, both patients and their employees. The author highlights the similarities of researched themes of needs that must be met to achieve both patient and employee satisfaction. As organizations develop strategies to meet the Quadruple Aim to improve care quality and access, decrease care costs, improve the patient experience, and improve the experience of providing care, the author draws a logical link between meeting needs and improving the experience of both patients and nurses. The shared themes include the need for kindness, caring, autonomy, respect, trust, and communication.

Implications for Practice

Understanding the relationship between patient outcomes and an organization's goals to achieve both patient and nurse satisfaction further reinforces the synergy of the Quadruple Aim of population health. Nurses should seek opportunities to contribute to a healthy working climate and culture highlighting the benefit to the organization's goals when themes of kindness, caring, autonomy, respect, trust, and communication are shared both at the point of care and behind the patient–nurse interface.

stage of development of professionals delivering the service. Nursing staff reflect the values of their time. The values acquired through education are reflected in the nursing philosophy. The Literature Perspective provides a view on the importance of values themes. Philosophies require updating to reflect the extension of rights brought about by such changes. Box 11.1 shows an example of a philosophy developed for a neurosurgical unit.

Values statements may also be used. These statements may simply be a statement of a few words such as *caring* and *excellence.* The values should be reflected in the statement of philosophy and traceable to the vision and mission statements. Perspective reinforces the connectivity of these organizational tools.

EXERCISE 11.2 Obtain a copy of the philosophy of a nursing department. Identify behaviors that you observe on a unit of the department that relate or do not relate to the beliefs and values expressed in the document. Does consistency exist?

ORGANIZATIONAL CULTURE

An organization's mission, vision, and philosophy both shape and reflect organizational culture. Organizational culture is the reflection of the norms or traditions of the organization and is exemplified by behaviors that illustrate values and beliefs. Examples include rituals and customary forms of practice, such as celebrations of promotions, degree attainment, professional performance, weddings, and retirements. Other examples of norms that reflect organizational culture are the characteristics of the people who are recognized as heroes by the organization and the behaviors—either positive or negative—that are accepted or tolerated within the organization.

In organizations, culture is demonstrated in two ways that can be either mutually reinforcing or conflict-producing. Organizational culture is typically expressed in a formal manner via written mission, vision, and philosophy statements; job descriptions; and policies and procedures. Beyond formal documents and verbal descriptions given by administrators and managers, organizational culture is also

represented in the day-to-day experience of staff and patients. To many, it is the lived experience that reflects the true organizational culture. Do the decisions that are made within the organization consistently demonstrate that the organization values its patients and keeps their needs at the forefront? Are the employees treated with trust and respect, or are the words used in recruitment ads simply empty promises with little evidence to back them up? When a lack of congruity exists between the expressed organizational culture and the experienced organizational culture, confusion, frustration, and poor morale often result (Hashish, 2017; Manojlovich & Ketefian, 2016; Moss, Mitchell, & Casey, 2017).

Organizational culture can be effective and promote success and positive outcomes, or it can be ineffective and result in disharmony, dissatisfaction, and poor outcomes for patients, staff, and the organization. A number of workplace variables are influenced by organizational culture. When seeking employment or advancement, nurses need to assess the organization's culture and develop a clear understanding of existing expectations as well as the formal and informal communication patterns. Various techniques and tools are available to assist the nurse in performing a cultural assessment of an organization (Hall, Smith, Mitton, Gibson, & Bryan, 2016; Valentine, Nembhard, & Edmondson, 2015).

Although an organizational culture evolves over time only through the shared experiences of all staff, organizational climate is cultivated and controlled to a degree by leadership behavior. Organizational climate refers to the employees' common beliefs and attitudes about an organization. For example, surveying employees to learn their perceptions regarding mission clarity, satisfaction with salary and benefits, and recognition for quality work are more reflections of the organizational climate than the organizational culture. Culture is more lasting and consequently more challenging to change. With a solid understanding of organizational culture, nurses will be better able to be effective change agents and help transform the organizations in which they work. The Research Perspective presents a study on whether leadership style, the climate of a nursing unit, and the unit safety climate predict safe medication practices.

RESEARCH PERSPECTIVE

Resource: Farag, A., Tullai-McGuinness, S., Anthony, M. K., & Burant, C. (2017). Do leadership style, unit climate, and safety climate contribute to safe medication practices? *Journal of Nursing Administration, 47*(1), 8-15.

This cross-sectional study used survey data from 246 registered nurses working in a hospital to examine relationships among nurse managers' leadership style, nursing unit climate, safety climate, and safe medication practices. The study found that a nurse manager's leadership style combined with a unit climate of warmth and inclusion positively contributed to a safety climate. Safety climate was the common link among leadership styles, a unit climate of warmth, and safe practice. This means nurse managers who foster a warm unit climate where nurses perceive they belong are essential to promote safe nursing practice.

Implications for Practice

Development for new and existing managers should focus on implementing strategies to create a supportive unit climate, not only because it is a caring leadership behavior, but also because it positively affects safe practice. Although nurse managers can act locally within their units to positively impact climate, the underlying culture of the entire organization should have values and beliefs consistent with the climate to increase the chances of sustained improvement.

FACTORS INFLUENCING ORGANIZATIONAL DEVELOPMENT

To be most effective, organizational structures must reflect the organization's mission, vision, philosophy, goals, and objectives. Organizational structure defines how work is organized, where decisions are made, and the authority and responsibility of workers. It provides a map for communication and outlines decision-making paths. As organizations change through acquisitions and mergers, it is essential that structure may change to accomplish revised missions.

Probably the best theory to explain today's nursing organizational development is chaos (complexity, nonlinear, quantum) theory. In essence, chaos theory suggests that lives—and organizations—are web-like. Pulling on one small segment rearranges the web, a new pattern emerges, and yet the whole remains. This theory, applied to healthcare organizations, suggests that differences logically exist between and among various organizations and that the constant environmental forces continue to affect the structure, its functioning, and the services. See the Theory Box in Chapter 10.

Changes in the funding mechanisms for health care can have profound effects on the design of organizational structures. Consumerism, where consumers demand that care be customized to meet their individual needs, is also affecting the structure and processes of health care.

Information from Internet sources and direct-to-consumer advertising are significantly altering the expectation and behaviors of healthcare consumers. For example, Hospital Compare *(www.hospitalcompare.hhs.gov)* is a tool that consumers can use to access a searchable database of information describing how well hospitals care for patients with certain medical and surgical conditions. Access to this information allows consumers to make informed decisions about where they seek their health care. In response to consumer expectations, facilities concentrate on consumer satisfaction and delivery of patient-focused care. Changes in both facility design and care delivery systems are likely to continue as efforts are made to reduce cost while still striving to meet or exceed consumer expectations and improve patient outcomes.

Changes including federal mandates, consumerism, and competition necessitate reengineering healthcare structures. First, redesign is a technique to analyze tasks to improve efficiency (e.g., identifying the most efficient flow of supplies to a nursing unit) and restructuring is a technique to enhance organizational productivity (e.g., identifying the most appropriate type and number of staff members for a particular nursing unit). Reengineering, however, involves a total overhaul of an organizational structure. It is a radical reorganization of the totality of an organization's structure and work processes. In reengineering, fundamentally new organizational expectations and relationships are created.

Regardless of the level of changes made within an organization—redesign, restructuring, or reengineering—staff and patients alike feel the impact. Some of the changes result in improvements, whereas others may not; some of the effects are expected, whereas others are not. Nurse managers, as well as direct care nurses, must be vigilant for both anticipated and unanticipated results of these changes. Nurses need to position themselves to participate in change discussions and evaluations. Ultimately, it is their day-to-day work with their patients that is affected by the decisions made in response to a rapidly changing environment.

EXERCISE 11.3 Arrange to interview a nurse employed in a healthcare agency or use your own experience to identify examples of changes taking place that necessitate reengineering. These may include changes associated with implementation of new reimbursement strategies, development of policies to carry out legislative regulations related to patient confidentiality, or development of chest pain centers. Identify examples of how previous systems of communication and decision making were either adequate or inadequate to cope with these changes.

CHARACTERISTICS OF ORGANIZATIONAL STRUCTURES

The characteristics of different types of organizational structures provide a catalog of options to consider in designing structures that fit specific situations. Knowledge of these characteristics helps leaders, managers, and nursing staff understand the expectations and structures in which they currently function.

Organizational designs are often classified by their characteristics of complexity, formalization, and centralization. *Complexity* concerns the division of labor in an organization, the specialization of that labor, the number of hierarchical levels, and the geographic dispersion of organizational units. *Division of labor* and *specialization* refer to the separation of processes into tasks that are performed by designated people. The horizontal dimension of an organizational chart, the graphic representation of work units and reporting relationships, relates to the division and specialization of labor functions attended by specialists. Hierarchy connotes lines of authority and responsibility. Chain of command is a term used to refer to the hierarchy

and is depicted in vertical dimensions of organizational charts. Hierarchy vests authority in positions on an ascending line away from where work is performed and allows control of work. Staff members are often placed on a bottom level of the organization, and those in authority, who provide control, are placed in higher levels. Span of control refers to the number of subordinates a supervisor manages. For budgetary reasons, span of control is often a major focus for organizational restructuring. Although cost implications are present when a span of control is too narrow, when a span of control becomes too large, supervision becomes less effective.

Geographic dispersion refers to the physical location of units. Units of work may be in one building; in several buildings in one location; spread throughout a city; or in different counties, states, or countries. The more dispersed an organization is, the greater are the demands for creative designs that place decision making related to patient care close to the patient and, consequently, far from corporate headquarters. A similar type of complexity exists in organizations that deliver care at multiple sites in the community; for example, the care delivery sites of an accountable care organization may be at great distances from the corporate office that has overall responsibility for the programs.

Formalization is the degree to which an organization has rules, stated in terms of policies that define a member's function. The amount of formalization varies among institutions. Formalization is often inversely related to the degree of specialization and the number of professionals within the organization.

EXERCISE 11.4 Review a copy of a nursing department's organizational chart and identify the divisions of labor, the hierarchy of authority, and the degree of formalization.

Centralization refers to the location where a decision is made. Decisions are made at the top of a centralized organization. In a decentralized organization, decisions are made at or close to the patient-care level. Highly centralized organizations often delegate *responsibility* (the obligation to perform the task) without the *authority* (the right to act, which is necessary to carry out the responsibility). For example, some hospitals have delegated both the responsibility and the authority for admission decisions to the charge nurse (decentralized), whereas others require the nurse supervisor or chief nurse executive to make such decisions (centralization). As the Center for Medicare & Medicaid Services (CMS) developed guidelines to facilitate the delivery of health care, CMS identified that nonphysicians, including registered nurses, can write orders to admit patients as long as the practice fits with state laws and organizational policies.

BUREAUCRACY

Many organizational theories in use today find their basis in the works of early 21st-century theorists: Max Weber, a German sociologist who developed the basic tenets of bureaucracy (Weber, 1947), and Henri Fayol, a French industrialist who crafted 14 principles of management (Fayol, 1949). Initially, bureaucracy referred to the centralization of authority in administrative bureaus or government departments. The term has come to refer to an inflexible approach to decision making or an agency encumbered by red tape that adds little value to organizational processes.

Bureaucracy is an administrative concept imbedded in how organizations are structured. The concept arose at a time of societal development when services were in short supply, workers' and clients' knowledge bases were limited, and technologies for sharing information were undeveloped. Characteristics of bureaucracy arose out of a need to control workers and were centered on the division of processes into discrete tasks. Weber (1947) proposed that organizations could achieve high levels of productivity and efficiency only by adherence to what he called "bureaucracy." Weber believed that bureaucracy, based on the sociologic concept of rationalization of collective activities, provided the idealized organizational structure. Bureaucratic structures are formal and have a centralized and hierarchical command structure (chain of command). Bureaucratic structures have a clear division of labor, are well articulated, and have commonly accepted expectations for performance. Rules, standards, and protocols ensure uniform actions and limit individualization of services and variance in workers' performance. In bureaucratic organizations, as shown in Fig. 11.1, communication and decisions flow from top to bottom. Although bureaucracy enhances consistency, by nature it limits employee autonomy and thus the potential for innovations and client-centric service.

In developing his 14 principles of management, Fayol (1949) outlined structures and processes that guide how work is accomplished within an organization. Consistent with theories of bureaucracy, his principles of

THEORY BOX

Bureaucracy

Definition: an administrative concept imbedded in how organizations are structured

Characterized by:

- Formality
- Low autonomy
- Hierarchy of authority
- Rule dominated environment
- Division of labor
- Specialization
- Centralized decision making
- High control

Assertions: High control and clear labor division promote efficiency and productivity

Drawbacks: Can lead to frustration and delays due to low autonomy on the front line

management include division of labor or specialization, clear lines of authority, appropriate levels of discipline, unity of direction, equitable treatment of staff, fostering of individual initiative, and promotion of a sense of teamwork and group pride. More than 60 years after they were described, these principles remain the basis of most organizations. Therefore, to be effective organizational leaders and followers, nurses need to be familiar with the theory and concepts of bureaucracy (see the Theory Box).

At the time that bureaucracies were developed, these characteristics promoted efficiency and production. As the knowledge base of the general population and employees grew and technologies developed, the bureaucratic structure no longer fit the evolving situation. Increasingly, employees and consumers functioning in bureaucratic situations complain of red tape, procedural delays, and general frustration.

Regardless of the form an organization takes (acute care hospital, ambulatory setting, accountable care organization, free-standing clinic, etc.), the characteristics of bureaucracy can be present in varying degrees. An organization can demonstrate bureaucratic characteristics in some areas and not in others. For example, nursing staff in intensive care units may be granted autonomy in making and carrying out direct patient care decisions, but they may not be granted a voice in determining work schedules or financial reimbursement systems for hours worked.

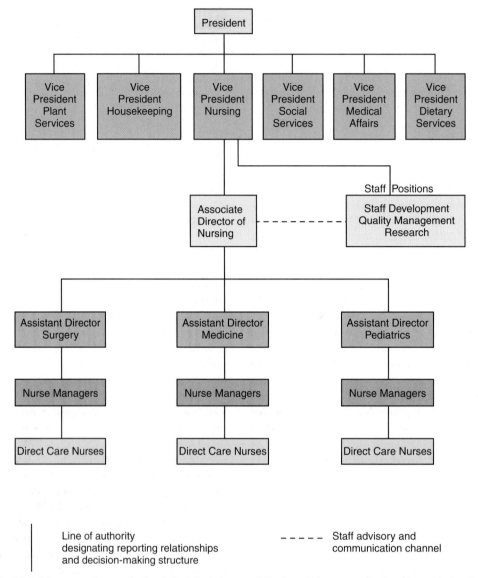

Line of authority
designating reporting relationships
and decision-making structure

— — — — Staff advisory and
communication channel

Fig. 11.1 A bureaucratic organizational chart depicting specialization of labor, centralization, hierarchical authority, and line and staff responsibilities.

Decision making and authority can be described in terms of line and staff functions. Line functions are those that involve direct responsibility for accomplishing the objectives of a nursing department, service, or unit. Line positions may include registered nurses, licensed practical or vocational nurses, and unlicensed assistive (or nursing) personnel who have the responsibility for carrying out all aspects of direct care. Staff functions are those that assist individuals in line positions in accomplishing the primary objectives. In this context, the term *staff positions* should not be confused with specific jobs that include "staff" in their names, such as staff nurse or staff physician. Staff positions include individuals, such as professional or staff development personnel, researchers, and special clinical consultants, who are responsible for supporting line positions through activities of consultation, education, role modeling, and knowledge development, with

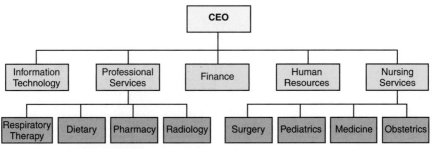

Fig. 11.2 Functional structure. *CEO,* Chief executive officer.

limited or no direct authority for decision making. Line personnel have authority for decision making, whereas personnel in staff positions provide support, advice, and counsel. Organizational charts usually indicate line positions through the use of solid lines and staff positions through broken lines (reminder: in this context, the term *staff [or direct care] position* does not reference titles such as staff nurses). Line structures have a vertical line, designating reporting and decision-making responsibility. The vertical line connects all positions to a centralized authority (see Fig. 11.1).

To make line and staff functions effective, decision-making authority is clearly spelled out in position descriptions. Effectiveness is further ensured by delineating competencies required for the responsibilities, providing methods for determining whether personnel possess these competencies, and providing means of maintaining and developing the competencies.

TYPES OF ORGANIZATIONAL STRUCTURES

In healthcare organizations, several common types of organizational structures exist: functional, service line, matrix, or flat. Nursing organizations often combine characteristics of these structures to form a hybrid structure. Shared governance is an organizing structure designed to meet the changing needs of professional nursing organizations.

Functional Structures

Functional structures arrange departments and services according to specialty. This approach to organizational structure is common in healthcare organizations. Departments providing similar functions report to a common manager or executive (Fig. 11.2). For example, a healthcare organization with a functional structure would have vice presidents for each major function: nursing, finance, human resources, and information technology.

This organizational structure tends to support professional expertise and encourage advancement. It may, however, result in discontinuity of patient care services. Delays in decision making can occur if a silo mentality develops within groups. That is, issues that require communication across functional groups typically must be raised to a senior management level before a decision can be made.

Service-Line Structures

In service-line structures (sometimes called *product lines*), the functions necessary to produce a specific service or product are brought together into an integrated organizational unit under the control of a single manager or executive (Fig. 11.3). For example, a cardiology service line at an acute care hospital might include all professional, technical, and support personnel providing services to the cardiac patient population. The manager or executive in this service line would be responsible for the chest pain evaluation center situated within the emergency department, the coronary care unit, the cardiovascular surgery intensive care unit, the telemetry unit, the cardiac catheterization laboratory, and the outpatient cardiac rehabilitation center. In addition to managing the budget and the facilities for these areas, the manager typically would be responsible for coordinating services for physicians and other providers who care for these patients.

The benefits of a service-line approach to organizational structure include coordination of services, an expedited decision-making process, and clarity of purpose. The limitations of this model can include increased expense associated with duplication of services, loss of professional or technical affiliation, and lack of standardization.

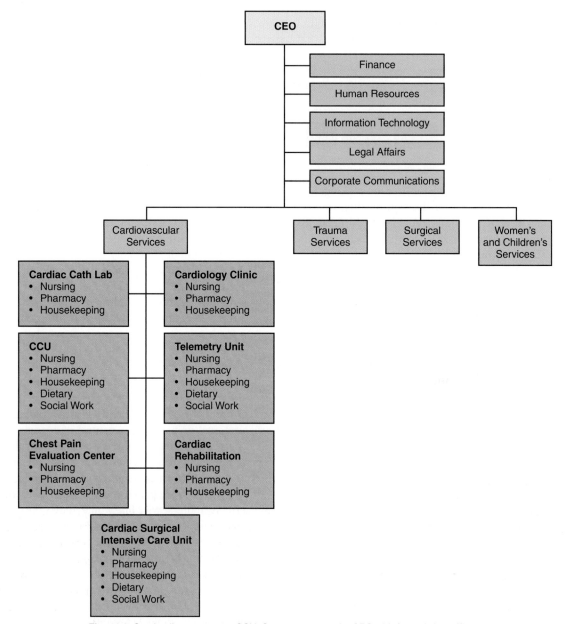

Fig. 11.3 Service-line structure. *CCU,* Coronary care unit; *CEO,* chief executive officer.

Matrix Structures

Matrix structures are complex and designed to reflect both function and service in an integrated organizational structure. In a matrix organization, the manager of a unit responsible for a service reports to both a functional manager and a service or product line manager.

For example, a director of pediatric nursing could report to both a vice president for pediatric services (the service-line manager) and a vice president of nursing (the functional manager) (Fig. 11.4).

The matrix design enables timely response to the forces in the external environment that demand

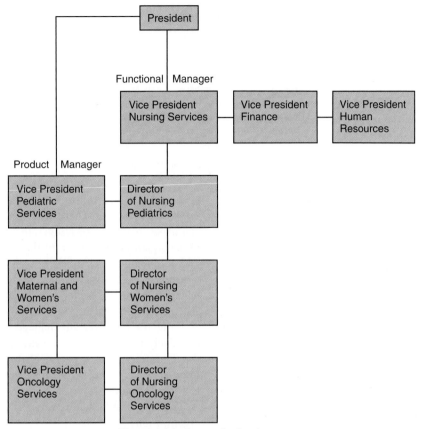

Fig. 11.4 Matrix organizational structure.

continual programming, and it facilitates internal efficiency and effectiveness through the promotion of cooperation among disciplines.

A matrix structure combines both a bureaucratic structure and a flat structure, and teams are used to carry out specific programs or projects. A matrix structure superimposes a horizontal program management over the traditional vertical hierarchy. Personnel from various functional departments are assigned to a specific program or project and become responsible to two supervisors—their functional department head and a program manager. This approach creates an interdisciplinary team.

A line manager and a project manager must function collaboratively in a matrix organization. For example, in nursing, an organization may have a chief nursing executive, a nurse manager, and direct care nurses in the line of authority to accomplish nursing care. In the matrix structure, some of the nurse's time is allocated to project or committee work. Nursing care

is delivered in a teamwork setting or within a collaborative model. The nurse is responsible to a nurse manager for nursing care and to a program or project manager when working within the matrix overlay. Well-developed collaboration and coordination skills are essential to effective functioning in a matrix structure. With the expansion of innovative healthcare organizational designs, the nature of these organizations with their complex interrelationships requires nurses with high levels of knowledge and skill in interprofessional collaborative practice (Delaney, Naegle, Flinter, Pulcini, & Hauenstein, 2016).

One example of the matrix structure is the patient-focused care delivery model. Another example is the program focused on specialty services such as geriatric services, women's services, and cardiovascular services. A matrix model can be designed to cover both comprehensive patient-focused care and a specialty service. Other examples within a healthcare facility include

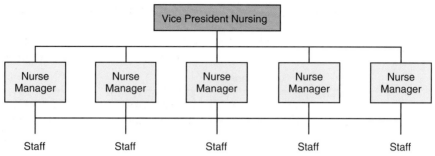

Fig. 11.5 Flat organizational structure.

discharge planning, quality management, and cardio-pulmonary resuscitation teams.

Flat Structures

The primary organizational characteristic of a flat structure is the delegation of decision making to the professionals doing the work. The term *flat* signifies the removal of hierarchical layers, thereby granting authority to act and placing authority at the action level (Fig. 11.5). Decisions regarding work methods, nursing care of individual patients, and conditions under which employees work are made where the work is carried out. In a **flat organizational structure,** decentralized decision making replaces the centralized decision making typical of functional structures. Providing staff with authority to make decisions at the place of interaction with patients is the hallmark of a flat organizational structure. Magnet® hospitals have recognized the benefits of decentralized decision making and its impact on both nursing satisfaction and patient outcomes (Barnes, Rearden, & McHugh, 2016; Kutney-Lee et al., 2016). An example of a flat organizational structure is that at Buurtzorg Netherlands, a home care organization where nurses manage themselves, control their schedules, and operate with few policies or procedures (White, 2016). Office-based practices may also be designed with a flat organizational structure.

Flat organizational structures are less formalized than hierarchical organizations. A decrease in strict adherence to rules and policies allows individualized decisions that fit specific situations and meet the needs created by the increasing demands associated with consumerism, change, and competition. Work supported by the Institute for Healthcare Improvement *(www.ihi.org/IHI/),* as an example, capitalizes on decisions being made at the unit level. The focus of this work is to improve patient safety and outcomes. Therefore nurses on a clinical unit can make changes in real time rather than use the traditional organizational hierarchy that includes committees and administrative channels.

Decentralized structures are not without their challenges, however. These include the potential for inconsistent decision making, loss of growth opportunities, and the need to educate managers to communicate effectively and demonstrate creativity in working within these nontraditional structures. In smaller practice settings, however, these issues may not exist if the staff has some longevity.

The degree of flattening varies from organization to organization. Those that are decentralizing often retain some bureaucratic characteristics. They may at the same time have units that are operating as matrix structures. A **hybrid** structure is one that has characteristics of several different types of structures.

As organizational structures change, some managers are hesitant to relinquish their traditional role in a centralized decision-making process. This reluctance, when combined with recognition of the need to move to a more facilitative role, is partially responsible for the development of hybrid structures. Managers are unsure of what needs to be controlled, how much control is needed, and which mechanisms can replace control. They fear that chaos will ensue without tight managerial control. These fears stem from loss of centralized control because authority, with its concomitant responsibilities, moves to the place of interaction. Registered nurses prepared at a higher educational level develop and use leadership techniques that empower themselves and others to take responsibility for their work and develop skills associated with effective leadership and followership.

The evolutionary development of shared-governance structures in nursing departments demonstrates a type of flat structure being used to replace hierarchical control.

Shared Governance

Shared governance goes beyond participatory management through the creation of organizational structures that facilitate nursing staff having more autonomy to govern their practice. Accountability forms the foundation for designing professional governance models. To be accountable, authority to make decisions concerning all aspects of responsibilities is essential. This need for authority and accountability is particularly important for nurses who treat the wide range of human responses to wellness states and illnesses. Organizations in which professional autonomy is encouraged have demonstrated higher levels of staff satisfaction, enhanced productivity, and improved retention (Fisher, Jabara, Poudrier, Williams, & Wallen, 2016). Theory development and testing related to shared governance in nursing is evolving (Joseph & Bogue, 2016).

The historic early Magnet® hospital study (McClure, Poulin, Sovie, & Wandelt, 1983), which identified characteristics of hospitals successful in recruiting and retaining nurses, found that the major contributing characteristic to success was a nursing department structured to provide nurses the opportunity to be accountable for their own practice. Studies of Magnet® hospitals demonstrate that governance structures that promote nurses' accountability will be effective in recruiting and retaining nursing staff while also meeting consumer demands and remaining competitive. Magnet® characteristics are now accepted as affecting the quality of not only the work environment but also patient care (Kutney-Lee et al., 2016).

Shared or self-governance structures, sometimes referred to as *professional practice models,* go beyond decentralizing and diminishing hierarchies. In an organization that embraces shared governance, the structure's foundation is the professional workplace rather than the organizational hierarchy. Given this foundation, shared governance can be introduced into any organization regardless of the organizational hierarchy. Shared governance vests the necessary levels of authority and accountability for all aspects of the nursing practice in the nurses responsible for the delivery of care.

The management and administrative level serves to coordinate and facilitate the work of the practicing nurses. Mechanisms are designed outside of the traditional hierarchy to provide for the functional areas needed to support professional practice. These functions include areas such as quality management, competency definition and evaluation, and continuing education. Changing nurses' positions from dependent employees to accountable professionals is a prerequisite for the radical redesign of healthcare organizations that is required to create value for patients. This change requires administrators, managers, and staff to abandon traditional notions regarding the division of labor in healthcare organizations. Shared governance structures require new behaviors of all staff, not just new assignments of accountability. The areas of interpersonal relationship development, conflict resolution, and personal acceptance of responsibility for action are of particular importance. Education, experience in group work, and conflict management are essential for successful transitions. Understanding the criteria for Magnet® facilities (American Nurses Credentialing Center, 2012), irrespective of structure, could form the basis for evaluating nursing services.

EMERGING FLUID RELATIONSHIPS

As the continuum of care moves health services outside of institutional parameters, different skill sets, relationships, and behavioral patterns will be required. Healthcare organizations are losing their traditional boundaries. Old boundaries of hierarchy, function, and geography are disappearing. Vertical integration aligns dissimilar but related entities such as hospital, home care agency, rehabilitation center, long-term care facility, insurance provider, and medical office or clinic. For example, some employers are improving access to primary care by providing it in the workplace. On-site primary care clinics ease the challenges of scheduling and transportation for employees and preserve productivity for the organization (Nelson, 2017). New technologies, fast-changing markets, and global competition are revolutionizing relationships in health care, and the roles that people play and the tasks that they perform have become blurred and ambiguous.

Increasingly more nurses are practicing in settings that extend beyond the walls of a single unit or building. Reframing or changing current static organizations into vibrant learning organizations will require significant

Fig. 11.6 Nurses must have the ability to work with other members of the organization to design organizational models for care delivery that meet patient or customer needs and priorities.

customer needs and priorities (Fig. 11.6). Looking at the nature of the work of nursing and proposing innovative models for nursing practice that consider emerging labor-saving assistive technologies and rapidly changing healthcare needs will be critical to successful nursing organizations of the future. Employee participation and learning environments go hand in hand, and work redesign needs to be regarded as a continuous process. Nurses must value their and others' autonomy to deal successfully in these new structures.

CONCLUSION

Highly successful nursing organizations have grasped the importance of a mission, vision, and philosophy that are meaningful to the practice of nursing and reflect those of the organization. Organizations may be structured in various ways to provide service, and no one approach is "best" for all in all circumstances. The culture of the organization derives from these critical documents, and when embedded, they are reflected in the care delivered.

effort. Nurses, whether leaders, managers, or followers, must have the ability to work with other members of the organization and with society at large to design organizational models for care delivery that meet patient and

THE SOLUTION

Through a series of informal conversations on the unit, my team and I brainstormed on how to implement a practical and timely solution to the hectic pace of our unit. We proposed and vetted the idea of offering 4-hour shifts as options for nurses to sign up for during the peak hours of 10 AM and 2 PM, when nurses were most busy and in need of lunch breaks. We proposed this special shift be named the *Power Nurse Shift.* Our organization prides itself on its culture of ownership and shared core values that encourage innovation and finding solutions to challenges at the unit level. We continued to refine our idea of the *Power Nurse Shift,* and formally proposed it to our

leadership for approval. After a quick approval process, we are now using the new shift with positive effects on staff morale and energy levels. Our nurses are now able to take a lunch break and complete nursing care in a more timely manner. I am confident that if our organizational culture of ownership had not been vetted by our frontline nurses, this type of creative solution would not have been a success.

Would this be a suitable approach for you? Why?

Hallie Hurt

▌ REFLECTIONS

By reflecting on your current or past clinical experiences, write a paragraph describing the following elements of the organization and the nursing unit. Were they congruent with each other? Was the philosophy of the nursing unit consistent with your beliefs and values? How and how not? What meanings do these

elements provide to you as you consider your fit with an organization?
• Mission
• Vision
• Philosophy
• Organizational culture

THE EVIDENCE

Every organization has some kind of structure. Often those structures are related to the mission of the organization. Military hospitals are more reflective of the armed services structure, whereas healthcare businesses may be more reflective of start-up businesses. In part the structure reflects the nature of the work and simultaneously supports the nature of the work to be done.

TIPS FOR UNDERSTANDING ORGANIZATIONAL STRUCTURES

- Professional nurses need to understand the mission, vision, philosophy, and structure at the organization and unit level to maximize their contributions to patient care.
- The overall mission of the organization and the mission of the specific unit in which a professional nurse is employed (or seeking employment) provide information concerning the focus of the work and the manner in which it will be accomplished.
- Understanding the organization's and/or the unit's philosophy provides knowledge of the behaviors that are valued in the delivery of care.

- Formal organizational structures describe the expected channels of communication and decision making.
- Matrix organizations typically have more than one person responsible for the work, and therefore it requires understanding both the service and the function.
- For a shared-governance structure to function effectively, the professionals providing the care must put mechanisms in place to promote decision making about patient care.

REFERENCES

American Nurses Credentialing Center. (2012). *Health care organization instructions and application process manual.* Washington, DC: Author.

Barnes, H., Rearden, J., & McHugh, M. D. (2016). Magnet® hospital recognition linked to lower central line-associated bloodstream infection rates. *Research in Nursing & Health, 39*(2), 96–104.

Delaney, K. R., Naegle, M., Flinter, M., Pulcini, J., & Hauenstein, E. J. (2016). Critical workforce issues of registered and advanced practice nurses in integrated care models. *Nursing Outlook, 64*(6), 607–609.

Fayol, H. (1949). *General and industrial management.* London: Pitman.

Fisher, C. A., Jabara, J., Poudrier, L., Williams, T., & Wallen, G. R. (2016). Shared governance: The way to staff satisfaction and retention. *Nursing Management, 47*(11), 14–16.

Hall, W., Smith, N., Mitton, C., Gibson, J., & Bryan, S. (2016). An evaluation tool for assessing performance in priority setting and resource allocation: Multi-site application to identify strengths and weaknesses. *Journal of Health Services Research & Policy, 21*(1), 15–23.

Hashish, E. A. A. (2017). Relationship between ethical work climate and nurses' perception of organizational support, commitment, job satisfaction and turnover intent. *Nursing Ethics, 24*(2), 151–166.

Joseph, M., & Bogue, R. (2016). A theory-based approach to nursing shared governance. *Nursing Outlook, 64*(6), 527–529.

Kutney-Lee, A., Germack, H., Hatfield, L., Kelly, S., Maguire, P., Dierkes, A., et al. (2016). Nurse engagement in shared governance and patient and nurse outcomes. *Journal of Nursing Administration, 46*(11), 605–612.

Manojlovich, M., & Ketefian, S. (2016). The effects of organizational culture on nursing professionalism: Implications for health resource planning. *Canadian Journal of Nursing Research Archive, 33*(4).

McClure, M. L., Poulin, M. A., Sovie, M. D., & Wandelt, M. A. (1983). *Magnet hospitals, attrition and retention of professional nurses.* Kansas City, MO: American Nurses Association.

Moss, S., Mitchell, M., & Casey, V. (2017). Creating a culture of success. *Journal of Nursing Administration, 47*(2), 116–122.

Nelson, K. (2017). Changing health care delivery, one company at a time. *American Journal of Nursing, 117*(4), 19–20.

Valentine, M. A., Nembhard, I. M., & Edmondson, A. C. (2015). Measuring teamwork in health care settings: A review of survey instruments. *Medical Care, 53*(4), e16–e30.

Weber, M. (1947). *The theory of social and economic organization.* Parsons, NY: Free Press.

White, C. (2016). The defining characteristics of the Buurtzorg Nederland Model of home care from the perspective of Buurtzorg nurses. *Inquiry Journal 2016,* 12.

12

Care Delivery Strategies

Susan Sportsman

LEARNING OUTCOMES

- Differentiate the characteristics of nursing care delivery models used in health care.
- Analyze the role of the nurse manager and the direct care nurse in each model.
- Summarize the differentiated nursing practice model and related methods to determine competencies of nurses.
- Consider the impact of the use of rapid cycle change on care delivery in a specific nursing unit.
- Evaluate the effectiveness of transitional care models aimed at reducing unnecessary rehospitalizations.
- Analyze the leadership opportunities for all nurses in care delivery models.

KEY TERMS

advanced generalist
associate nurse
case manager
case method
charge nurse
clinical nurse leader
critical pathway
differentiated nursing practice
expected outcomes
functional model of nursing

Magnet Recognition Program®
nurse navigator
nursing care delivery model
nursing case management
outcome criteria
patient-focused care
patient outcomes
practice partnership model
primary nurse
primary nursing

rapid cycle change
staff mix
Synergy Model
team nursing
total patient care
Transforming Care at the Bedside
unlicensed nursing personnel
variance

THE CHALLENGE

The charge nurses on a newly designed 36-bed hematology-oncology unit were having increased difficulty in making patient assignments because of the layout and design of the 36,000-square-foot unit. In addition, throughout the shift, the nursing staff members were having difficulty remaining engaged with the activities on the unit because of the distance between bedside stations. Also, the layout of the unit made it difficult for a nurse to ask for help when needed.

After occupying the unit for several months and trying a variety of methods to enhance teamwork and communication among the staff, it was apparent that a more formal

(Continued)

process was needed to resolve these problems. The assistant director of nursing was assigned to coordinate the resolution of the problem. What interdisciplinary resource might provide a helpful analysis or workflow process? What considerations could be made?

What would you do if you were this nurse?

Jacqueline Ward, BSN, RN
Assistant Director of Nursing, Texas Children's Hospital,
Houston, Texas

INTRODUCTION

A **nursing care delivery model** is the method used to provide care to patients. Because nursing care is often viewed primarily as a cost rather than a source of revenue, institutions evaluate their method of providing patient care for the purpose of saving money while still providing quality care.

Each nursing care delivery model has advantages and disadvantages, and no single method is ideal. Managers in any organization must examine the organizational goals, the unit objectives, the patient population, staff availability, and the budget when selecting a care delivery model. This chapter explores both the historical methods of organizing nursing care and current organizational strategies that may influence care delivery.

HISTORICAL METHODS OF ORGANIZING NURSING CARE

Historical overviews of the common care models are designed to convey the complexity of how care is currently delivered. This perspective is important, because each of these approaches is still used within the broad range of healthcare organizations. In addition, these models often serve as the foundation for new innovative care delivery models.

Case Method (Total Patient Care)

The premise of the **case method** is that one nurse provides total care for one patient during the entire work period. This method was used in the era of Florence Nightingale when patients received total care in the home. In this approach, the physical, emotional, and technical aspects of care are the responsibility of the assigned registered nurse (RN) (Fig. 12.1). This model is especially useful in the care of complex patients who need active symptom management provided by an RN, such as the

care of a patient in a hospice setting or an intensive care unit. This care delivery model requires the nurse who is assigned to **total patient care** to complete the complex functions of care, such as assessment and teaching the patient and family, as well as the less complex functional aspects of care, such as personal hygiene. Some nurses find satisfaction with this model of care because no aspect of nursing care is delegated to another, thus eliminating the need for supervision of others.

Model Analysis

One advantage for this model of care delivery is that during an 8- or 12-hour shift, the patient receives consistent care from one nurse, who is accountable for the continuity of communication with all healthcare providers and implementing the plan of care. The nurse, patient, and family usually trust one another and can work together toward specific goals. Because the nurse is with the patient during most of the shift, even subtle changes in the patient's status are easily noticed. Usually, the plan of care is patient-centered, comprehensive, continuous,

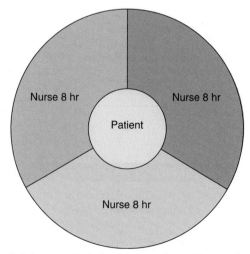

Fig. 12.1 Case method of patient care for an 8-hour shift.

and holistic (Cherry & Jacobs, 2017). However, if the nurse chooses to deliver this care with a task orientation, the holistic perspective is lost. This model of care should not be confused with nursing case management, which is introduced later in the chapter. In today's costly healthcare economy, total patient care provided by an RN is very expensive. Is it realistic to use the highly skilled and extremely knowledgeable professional nurse to provide all the care required in a unit that may have 20 to 30 patients? In times of nursing shortages, there may not be enough resources or nurses to use this model.

Nurse Manager's Role

When using the case method of delivery (total patient care), the manager must consider the expense of the system. He or she must weigh the expense of an RN versus the expense of licensed practical or vocational nurses (LPNs/LVNs) and unlicensed nursing personnel (UNPs) in the context of the outcomes required. UNPs are not licensed as healthcare providers. In various healthcare organizations, they may be called technicians, nurse aides, or certified nursing assistants. When the patient requires 24-hour care, the nurse manager must decide whether the patient should have RN care or RN-supervised care provided by LPNs/LVNs or UNPs.

EXERCISE 12.1 You have recently accepted a position at a home health agency that provides 24-hour care to qualified patients. You are assigned a patient who has care provided by a registered nurse (RN) during the day, a licensed practical or vocational nurse in the evening, and a nursing assistant at night. You are the day RN. You are concerned that the patient is not progressing well, and you suspect that the evening and night shift personnel are not reporting changes in the patient's status. What specific assessments should you make to validate your concerns? How would you justify any change in staffing? What recommendations would you make to the nurse manager, and why? What interventions could the nurse manager perform?

Functional Nursing

The functional model of nursing care delivery became popular during World War II when a severe shortage of nurses in the United States existed. Many nurses joined the armed forces to care for the soldiers. To provide care to patients at home, hospitals began to increase the number of LPNs/LVNs and nurse aides. The functional model of nursing is a method of providing patient care by which each licensed and unlicensed staff member performs specific tasks for a large group of patients. These tasks are in part determined by the scope of practice defined for each type of caregiver. For example, the RN must be responsible for all assessments, although the LPN/LVN and UNPs may collect data that can be used in the assessment. Regarding treatments, an RN may administer all intravenous (IV) medications and do admissions, one LPN/LVN may provide treatments, another LPN/LVN may give all oral medications, one UNP may do all hygiene tasks, and another assistant may take all vital signs. This division of aspects of care is similar to the assembly line system used by manufacturing industries. Just as an autoworker becomes an expert in attaching fenders to a new vehicle, the direct care nurse becomes expert in the tasks expected in functional nursing. A charge nurse coordinates care and assignments and may ultimately be the only person familiar with all the needs of any individual patient (Fig. 12.2).

Model Analysis

Several advantages exist for this model of patient care delivery. First, each person becomes efficient at specific tasks, and much work can be done in a short time. Another advantage is that unskilled workers can be trained to perform one or two specific tasks very well. The organization benefits financially from this model, because care can be delivered to a large number of patients by mixing staff with a fixed number of RNs and a larger number of UNPs. Although financial savings may be the impetus for organizations to choose the functional system of delivering care, the disadvantages may outweigh the savings. A major disadvantage is the fragmentation of care. The physical and technical aspects of care may be met, but the psychological and spiritual needs may be overlooked. Patients become confused by so many different care providers encountered per shift. These different staff members may be so busy with their assigned tasks that they may not have time to communicate with each other about the patient's progress. Because no one care provider sees patient care

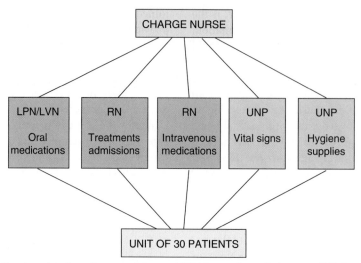

Fig. 12.2 Functional model of nursing care delivery. *LPN,* Licensed practical nurse; *LVN,* licensed vocational nurse; *RN,* registered nurse; *UNP,* unlicensed nursing personnel.

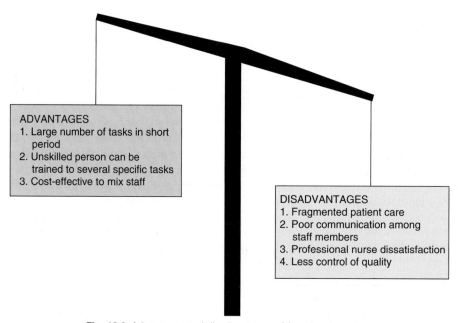

Fig. 12.3 Advantages and disadvantages of functional nursing.

from beginning to end, the patient's response to care is difficult to assess. Critical changes in patient status may go unnoticed. Fragmented care and ineffective communication can lead to patient and family dissatisfaction and frustration (Fig. 12.3). Exercise 12.2 provides an opportunity to consider the implications to patient care when the model does not support a holistic patient perspective.

EXERCISE 12.2 Imagine your mother is a patient at a hospital that uses the functional model of patient care delivery. She just had her knee replaced, and when you ask the nursing assistant for something for pain, she says, "I'll tell the medication nurse." The medication nurse comes to the room and says that your mother's medication is to be administered intravenously, and the IV nurse will need to administer it. The IV nurse is busy starting an IV on another patient and cannot give your mother the medication for at least 10 minutes. This whole communication process has taken 40 minutes, and your mother is still in pain. Discuss your perception of the effectiveness of the functional method of patient care in this situation. How effective do you think communication among staff is when a patient has a problem? What could be done to improve this situation?

EXERCISE 12.3 After 6 months of working on a unit that accommodates patients who have had general surgery, you realize that you are bored and frustrated with the functional model of delivering care. You have been administering all the intravenous medications and pain medications for your assigned patients. You have minimal opportunity to interact with the patients and learn about them, and you cannot be innovative in your care. Discuss strategies you could use to resolve this dissatisfaction with the functional model of nursing care delivery.

Nurse Manager's Role

In the functional model of nursing, the nurse manager must be sensitive to the quality of patient care delivered and the institution's budgetary constraints. Because staff members are responsible only for their specific task, the role of achieving patient outcomes becomes the nurse manager's responsibility. Staff members can view this system as autocratic and may become discontented with the lack of opportunity for input. By using effective management and leadership skills, the nurse manager can improve the staff's perception of their lack of independence. The manager can rotate assignments among staff within legal and organizational contexts to alleviate boredom with repetition. Staff meetings should be conducted frequently. This encourages staff to express concerns and empowers them with the ability to communicate about patient care and unit functions.

Direct Care Nurse's Role

The direct care RN becomes skilled at the tasks that are usually assigned by the charge nurse. Clearly defined policies and procedures are used to complete the physical aspects of care in an efficient and economical manner. However, the functional model of nursing may leave the professional nurse feeling frustrated because of the task-oriented role. Nurses are educated to care for the patient holistically, and providing only a fragment of care to a patient may result in unmet personal and professional expectations of nurses. As a result, this approach often leads to staff dissatisfaction and, ultimately, unacceptable levels of staff turnover.

The functional method of delivering care works well in emergency and disaster situations. Each care provider knows the expectations of the assigned role and completes the tasks quickly and efficiently. Subacute care agencies, extended care facilities, and ambulatory clinics often use the functional model to deliver care.

Team Nursing

After World War II, the nursing shortage continued. Many female nurses who were in the military came home to marry and have children instead of returning to the workforce. Because the functional model received criticism, a new system of team nursing (a modification of functional nursing) was devised to improve patient satisfaction. This type of nursing care delivery remains in use, particularly when reduced reimbursement and nursing shortages have resulted in organizations changing the staff mix and increasing the ratio of unlicensed to licensed personnel.

In team nursing, a team leader, who is an RN, is responsible for coordinating a group of licensed and unlicensed personnel to provide patient care to a small group of patients. The team leader should be a highly skilled leader, manager, and practitioner; he or she assigns each member specific responsibilities according to role, licensure, education, ability, competency, and the complexity of the care required. The members of the team report patient progress according to the plan of care directly to the team leader, who then reports to the charge nurse or unit manager (Fig. 12.4). Each unit typically has several teams, with patient assignments made by each team leader.

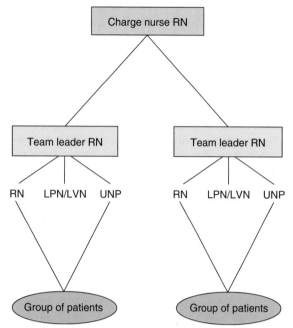

Fig. 12.4 Team nursing. *LPN*, Licensed practical nurse; *LVN*, licensed vocational nurse; *RN*, registered nurse; *UNP*, unlicensed nursing personnel.

Model Analysis

Some advantages of the team method, particularly compared with the functional approach, are improved patient satisfaction, organizational decision making occurring at lower levels, and cost-effectiveness for the agency. Many institutions and community health agencies currently use the team nursing method. Inpatient facilities may view team nursing as a cost-effective system because it works with an expected ratio of unlicensed to licensed personnel. Thus the organization has greater numbers of personnel for a designated amount of money.

The team method of patient care delivery has one major disadvantage, which arises if the team leader has poor leadership skills. The team leader must have excellent communication skills, positive delegation and conflict management abilities, strong clinical skills, and effective decision-making abilities to provide a working "team" environment for the members. The team leader must be sensitive to the needs of the patient and, at the same time, attentive to the needs of the staff providing the direct care. When the team leader is not prepared for this role, the team method becomes a miniature version of the functional method, and the potential for fragmentation of care is high.

> **EXERCISE 12.4** Think of a time when you worked with a group of four to six people to achieve a specific goal or accomplish a task (perhaps in school or at work you were grouped together to complete a project). How did your group achieve the goal? Was one person the organizer or leader? How was the leader selected? Who assigned each member a component, or did you each determine what skills you possessed that would most benefit the group? Did you experience any conflict while working on this project? How did the concepts of group dynamics and leadership skills affect how your group achieved its goal? What similarities do you see between the team nursing system of providing patient care and your group involvement to achieve a goal?

Consider the problems that could arise related to equity of patient assignments, continuity of care, or the holistic patient perspectives when team nursing is used. These issues are addressed in the following sections when nurse manager and direct care nurse roles are discussed.

Nurse Manager's Role

The nurse manager, charge nurse, and team leaders must have management skills to effectively implement the team nursing method of patient care delivery. In addition, the nurse manager must determine which RNs are competent and interested in becoming a charge nurse or team leader. Because the basic education of baccalaureate-prepared RNs emphasizes critical thinking, clinical reasoning, and leadership concepts, they are likely candidates for such roles. The nurse manager should also provide an adequate staff mix and orient team members to the team nursing system by providing continuing education about leadership, management techniques, delegation, and team interaction (see Chapters 1, 13, 18, 19, and 29). By addressing these factors the manager is aiding the teams to function optimally.

The charge nurse functions as a liaison between and among the team leaders and other healthcare providers, because nurse managers are often responsible for more than one unit or have other managerial responsibilities that take them away from the unit. The charge nurse provides support for the teams on a shift-by-shift basis. Appropriate support requires the charge nurse to encourage each team to solve its problems independently.

The team leader plans the care, delegates the work, and follows up with members to evaluate the quality of care for the patients assigned to that team. In the ideal circumstance, the team leader updates the nursing care plans and facilitates patient care conferences. Time constraints during the shift may prevent scheduling daily patient care conferences or prevent some team members attending those that are held. The team leader must also face the challenge of changing team membership on a daily basis. Diverse work schedules and nursing staff shortages may result in daily changes in the staff mix of a team and a daily assignment change for team members. The team leader assigns the professional, technical, and ancillary personnel to the type of patient care they are prepared to deliver. Therefore the team leader must be knowledgeable about the legal and organizational limits of each role.

Direct Care Nurse's Role

Team nursing uses the strengths of each caregiver. Direct care nurses, as members of the team, develop expertise in care delivery. Some members become known for their expertise in the psychomotor aspects of care. If one nurse is skilled at starting IV lines, he or she will start all IV lines for a team of patients. If a nurse is especially skillful at motivating postoperative patients to ambulate, he or she should be assigned to the surgical patients. Under the guidance and supervision of the team leader, the collective efforts of the team become greater than the functions of the individual caregivers.

Primary Nursing

A cultural revolution occurred in the United States during the 1960s. The revolution emphasized individual rights and independence from existing societal restrictions. This revolution also influenced the nursing profession, because nurses were becoming dissatisfied with their lack of autonomy. In addition, the hierarchical nature of communication in team nursing caused further frustration. Institutions were also aware of the declining quality of patient care. The search for autonomy and quality care led to the primary nursing system of patient care delivery as a method to increase RN accountability for patient outcomes.

Primary nursing, an adaptation of the case method or total patient care, was developed by Marie Manthey as a method for organizing patient care delivery in which one RN functions autonomously as the patient's primary nurse throughout the hospital stay (Manthey, Ciske, Robertson, & Harris, 1970). Primary nursing

brought the nurse back to direct patient care. The primary nurse is accountable for the patients' care 24 hours a day from admission through discharge. Conceptually, primary nursing care provides the patient and the family with coordinated, comprehensive, and continuous care. Care is organized using the nursing process. The primary nurse collaborates, communicates, and coordinates all aspects of patient care with other nurses as well as other disciplines. Advocacy, assertiveness, self-awareness, confidence, and direction are desirable leadership attributes for this care delivery model.

The primary nurse, preferably at least baccalaureate-prepared, is held accountable for meeting outcome criteria and communicating with all other healthcare providers about the patient (Fig. 12.5). For example, a patient is admitted to a medical unit with pulmonary edema. His primary nurse admits him and then provides a written plan of care. When his primary nurse is not working, an associate nurse implements the plan. The associate nurse is an RN who has been delegated to provide care to the patient according to the primary nurse's specification. If the patient develops additional complications, the associate nurse notifies the primary nurse, who has 24-hour accountability and responsibility. The associate nurse provides input to the patient's plan of care, and the primary nurse makes the appropriate alterations. The implications of 24-hour accountability for the primary nurse where compensation is not provided for time apart from scheduled work time are considerable. Those include legal, financial, and professional implications.

Model Analysis

In primary nursing, patients and families are typically satisfied with the care they receive because they establish a relationship with the primary nurse and identify the caregiver as "their nurse." Because the patient's primary nurse communicates the plan of care, the patient can move away from the sick role and begin to participate in his or her own recovery. By considering the sociocultural, psychological, and physical needs of the patient and family, the primary nurse can plan the most appropriate care with and for the patient and family.

A professional advantage to the primary nursing method is a decrease in the number of unlicensed personnel. The ideal primary nursing system requires an all-RN staff. The RN can provide total care to the patient, from bed baths to patient education, even both

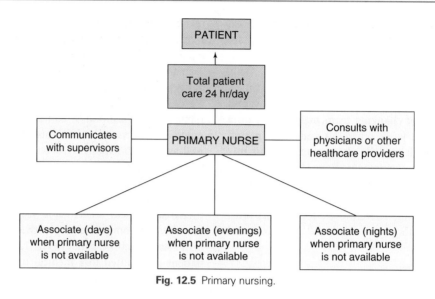

Fig. 12.5 Primary nursing.

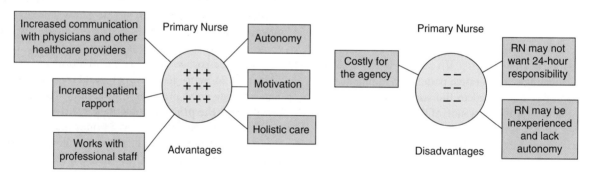

Fig. 12.6 Advantages and disadvantages of primary nursing. *RN,* Registered nurse.

at the same time! Unlicensed personnel are not qualified to provide this level of inclusive care (Fig. 12.6).

A disadvantage of the primary nursing method is that the RN may not have the experience or educational background to provide total care. The agency needs to educate staff for an adequate transition from the previous role to the primary role. One has to ask whether the RN is ready and willing and capable of handling the 24-hour responsibility for patient care. In addition, the nurse practice acts must be evaluated to determine whether primary nurses can be held accountable when they are not physically present.

In times of nursing shortage, primary nursing may not be the model of choice. This model will not be effective if a unit has a large number of part-time RNs who are not available to assume the primary nurse role

(24-hour responsibility). In addition, with the arrival of managed care in the 1990s, patients' hospital stays were shorter than in the 1970s, when primary nursing became popular. Expedited stays make it challenging for primary nurses to adequately provide the depth of care required by primary nursing. If the patient is admitted on Monday and discharged on Wednesday, the primary nurse has a difficult time meeting all patient needs before discharge if he or she is not working on Tuesday. The primary nurse must rely heavily on feedback from associates, which defeats the purpose of primary nursing. In addition, the reduction in reimbursement to hospitals and other organizations associated with managed care caused administrators to consider ways to reduce the cost of care delivery. Because labor costs are the largest expense in care delivery and the nursing staff makes up the largest portion of the labor costs, attention was given to reducing these costs with changes in the model of care delivery.

> **EXERCISE 12.5** Mr. Faulkner is admitted to the medical unit with exacerbated congestive heart failure. Mike Ross, BSN, RN, is Mr. Faulkner's primary nurse and will provide total care to Mr. Faulkner. Mike notes that this is Mr. Faulkner's third admission in 6 months for congestive heart failure–related symptoms. This is the first admission for which Mr. Faulkner has had a primary nurse. What do you think will be different about this admission with Mike providing primary nursing to Mr. Faulkner? Do you think there will be any difference in continuity of care? How involved do you think Mr. Faulkner will be with his own care in the primary nursing system? What will be the effect on the quality of care provided and the resulting patient outcomes?

> **EXERCISE 12.6** Imagine you are a primary nurse at an inpatient psychiatric facility. The patients you are assigned to are usually suicidal. How would you feel about the added responsibility for patients even when you were not at work? Is it realistic to expect the nurse to assume the role of the primary nurse with 24-hour responsibility? How would this responsibility affect your personal life? How would you make decisions about the patients and your home life?

Nurse Manager's Role

The primary nursing system can be modified to meet patient, nursing, and budgetary demands while maintaining the positive components that spawned its conception. The nurse manager who implements this care delivery model experiences some benefits. Primary nursing provides the nurse manager an opportunity to demonstrate leadership capabilities, clinical competencies, and teaching abilities to serve as a role model for professional practice. In addition, the roles of budget controller and unit quality manager remain. The traditional roles of delegation and decision making must be relinquished to the autonomous primary nurse. The nurse manager functions as a role model, advocate, coach, and consultant.

Direct Care Nurse's Role

The primary nurse uses many facets of the professional role—caregiver, advocate, decision maker, teacher, collaborator, care coordinator, and manager. Because primary nurses cannot be present 24 hours a day, they must depend on associate nurses to provide care when they are not available. The associate nurse provides care using the plan of care developed by the primary nurse. Changes to the plan of care can be made by the associate nurse in collaboration with the primary nurse. This model provides consistency among nurses and shifts. To function effectively in this setting, direct care nurses will need experience and opportunities to be mentored in this role. Because it usually is not financially possible for an agency to employ only RNs, true primary nursing rarely exists. Some institutions have modified the primary nursing concept and implemented a partnership model to incorporate their current staff mix.

Primary Nursing Hybrid: Partnership Model

In the practice partnership model (or *coprimary nursing model*) of providing patient care, an RN is paired with an assistant. The partner works with the RN consistently. When the partner is unlicensed, the RN allows the assistant to perform basic nursing functions consistent with the state delegation rules. This frees the RN to provide "semiprimary care" to assigned patients. A partnership between an RN and an LPN/LVN allows the LPN/LVN to take more responsibility, because the scope of practice for an LPN/LVN is greater than that of a UNP. In some settings, the partnership is legitimized with an official contract to formalize the relationship. Rehabilitative care settings often use the partnership model to deliver care.

> **EXERCISE 12.7** You are a primary nurse in a surgical intensive care unit of a small hospital. The unit you work on uses a registered nurse (RN)–licensed practical or vocational nurse (LPN/LVN) partnership to decrease the number of RNs required per shift. You and your partner are assigned four surgical patients. Mr. Jones had a lobectomy 5 hours ago and is on a ventilator; Mrs. Martinez had a quadruple cardiac bypass 14 hours ago; Mr. Wong had a nephrectomy 2 days ago and is receiving continuous peritoneal dialysis; and Mr. Smith has a fractured pelvis and is comatose from a motor vehicle accident 24 hours ago. How would you distribute the staff to provide primary care to these four patients? Do you think it is possible to provide primary care in this situation? What responsibilities would you assume as the primary nurse, and what could you share with the LPN/LVN?

Primary Nursing Hybrid: Patient-Focused, Patient-Centered, or Person-Centered Care

Another view of primary care is the care delivered in a patient-focused care unit. Developed in the late 1980s, the patient-focused care model integrates principles from business and industry. The goals for this model of care included (1) improving patient satisfaction and other patient outcomes, (2) improving worker job satisfaction, and (3) increasing efficiencies and decreasing costs. Flagg (2015) defined patient-centered care as a philosophy, a process, a model, a concept, and a partnership that involves both the patient and healthcare providers, including the nurse, arriving at some form of conclusion about the care of the patient's condition. Original models of a patient-focused care unit included an RN paired with a cross-trained technician who provided patient-side care, including respiratory therapy, phlebotomy, and electrocardiographs. Modifications in this nurse-managed model include team members who provide direct care activities such as recording vital signs, drawing blood, and bathing patients.

Flagg (2015) defined the following as components necessary for the engagement, support, implementation, and sustainment of patient-centered care:

- Leaders must show involvement, support, and buy-in.
- The strategic vision must be defined and operationalized.
- Patients, their family, and other support systems, as well as all involved employees, must be involved.
- Evaluation and feedback processes must be in place.
- Technology that supports communication between patients and healthcare providers must be available.
- The physical environment must support the process.

Nurse Management Role

In a patient-focused care unit, the role and scope of the nurse manager expand. No longer is the individual just a manager of nurses. Now the nurse manager assumes the accountability and responsibility to manage nurses and staff from other, traditionally centralized departments. Because the care is focused on the needs of the patient and not the needs of the department, the role of the manager becomes more sophisticated. The nurse manager orchestrates all the care activities required by the patient and family during the hospitalization.

LEADERSHIP DURING IMPLEMENTATION OF A MODEL OF CARE

The role of the nurse manager in implementing a model of care in a specific organization requires effective management skills. However, developing, implementing, and evaluating a particular model of care also provides significant leadership opportunities for both the nurse manager and the direct provider of care. In Chapter 1, p. 6, leadership is defined as "the use of individual traits and abilities in relationship with others and the ability (often rapidly) to interpret the environment/context" and cope with the situation without a script. This means that regardless of the official title nurses may hold, within their individual work environments they have leadership opportunity to do the following:

- Hold a vision of how things should be—and share that vision with others.
- See possibilities in a very complex situation—and act on them for positive gain.
- Communicate effectively regarding situations in which they find themselves.
- Demonstrate positive adaptive behaviors because of new situations.
- Use their own experience and knowledge to judge a reasonable risk.

ORGANIZATIONAL STRATEGIES INFLUENCING CARE DELIVERY

Over the last 10 to 15 years, additional strategies have been introduced into the healthcare environment, designed to improve patient outcomes regardless of the method of care delivery used. These strategies do not directly influence the nursing care delivery process. Instead, they are designed to provide additional support that patients may need. Nursing case management, differentiated practice, the Magnet hospital® process, and rapid change cycle are examples of these strategies.

Nursing Case Management

Nursing case management (NCM) is the process of coordinating health care by planning, facilitating, and evaluating interventions across levels of care to achieve measurable cost and quality outcomes. Case management was first seen in the early 1900s by social workers and public health nurses working in the public sector to identify and obtain resources for the needy. In the 1960s, insurers began to use NCM as a strategy to manage the needs of complex patients who required coordination over the course of treatment. Acute care hospitals used nurses in this role under the term of *utilization management*, particularly when federal regulations required this service for all Medicare and Medicaid patients.

In the mid-1980s, when acute care hospitals began to be reimbursed based on a certain diagnosis, nursing case management became a popular and effective method to manage shortened lengths of stay for patients while achieving desired patient outcomes and to prevent expensive hospital readmissions. Tufts Medical Center in Boston and Carondelet St. Mary's Hospital in Tucson, Arizona, were leaders in the trend to implement a collaborative system that focuses on comprehensive assessment and intervention and holistic care planning with appropriate referrals to meet the healthcare needs of the patient and the family (Fig. 12.7). The NCM process may be "within the walls" of the hospital or "beyond the walls." The success of NCM models has been demonstrated in all types of healthcare settings, including acute, subacute, and ambulatory settings and long-term care facilities, as well as health insurance companies and the community. Table 12.1 identifies some of the service settings using case management.

The ANA, in congruence with the National Quality Foundation and the Agency for Healthcare Research and Quality, defines care coordination as (1) a function that helps ensure that the patient's needs and preferences are met over time with respect to health services and information sharing across people, functions, and sites and (2) the deliberate organization of patient care activities between two or more participants (including the patient) involved in a patient's care to facilitate the appropriate delivery of healthcare services (Camicia & Chamberlain, 2012).

TABLE 12.1	Nursing Case Management Service Areas
Category	**Service Setting**
Acute	Orthopedics, cardiovascular, critical care, high-risk perinatal, oncology, emergency department
Subacute	Skilled nursing centers, rehabilitation units
Ambulatory	Physicians' offices, clinics
Long-term care	Nursing homes, group homes, assisted-living facilities
Insurance companies	Health maintenance organizations (HMOs), preferred provider organizations (PPOs), workers' compensation, Medicaid, Medicare
Community	Nurse-managed centers, home health agencies, urgent care centers, schools, rural settings

Data from Cohen, E., & Cesta, T. (2004). *Nursing case management from essentials to advanced practice application* (4th ed.). St. Louis: Mosby; Curtis, K., Lien, D., Chan, A., & Morris, R. (2002). The impact of trauma. *The Journal of Trauma*, 53(3), 477–482; and Huber, D. (2010). *Disease management: A guide for case managers.* St. Louis: Elsevier.

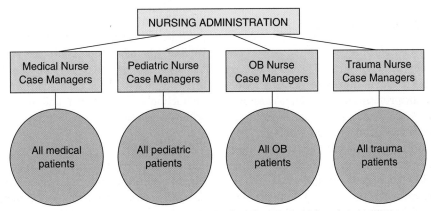

Fig. 12.7 Nursing case management model in which all patients are assigned to a nurse case manager. *OB,* Obstetric.

The Case Management Society of America (CMSA) defines *case management* as a collaborative process of assessment, planning, facilitation, care coordination, evaluation, and advocacy for options and services to meet an individual's and family's comprehensive health needs through communication and available resources to promote quality cost-effective outcomes.

CMSA has identified the standards of practice for case managers regardless of their practice setting. The case manager should

1. Identify and select clients who can most benefit from case management services available in a particular practice setting.
2. Complete a health and psychosocial assessment, taking into account the cultural and linguistic needs of each client.
3. Identify problems or opportunities that would benefit from case management intervention.
4. Identify immediate, short-term, long-term, and ongoing needs, as well as develop appropriate and necessary case management strategies and goals to address those needs.
5. Employ ongoing assessment and documentation to measure the client's response to the plan of care.
6. Maximize the client's health, wellness, safety, adaptation, and self-care through quality case management, client satisfaction, and cost-efficiency.
7. Terminate case management services based on established case closure guidelines. These guidelines may differ in various case management practice settings.
8. Facilitate coordination, communication, and collaboration with the client and other stakeholders to achieve goals and maximize positive client outcomes.
9. Maintain competence in their area(s) of practice by having one of the following:
   • Current, active, and unrestricted licensure or certification in a health or human services discipline that allows the professional to conduct an assessment independently as permitted within the scope of practice of the discipline.
   • In the case of an individual in a state that does not require licensure or certification, the individual must have a baccalaureate or graduate degree in social work or another health or human services field that promotes the physical, psychosocial, and/or vocational well-being of the persons being served. The degree must be from an institution that is fully accredited by a nationally recognized educational accreditation organization, and the individual must have completed a supervised field experience in case management, health, or behavioral health as part of the degree requirement.
10. Adhere to applicable local, state, and federal laws, as well as employer policies, governing all aspects of case management practice, including client privacy and confidentiality rights. It is the responsibility of the case manager to work within the scope of his or her license.
11. Obtain appropriate and informed client consent before case management services are implemented. Case managers should behave and practice ethically, adhering to the tenets of the code of ethics that underlies his or her professional credential (e.g., nursing, social work, rehabilitation counseling, etc.).
12. Advocate for the client at the service delivery, benefits administration, and policy-making levels.
13. Be aware of and responsive to cultural and demographic diversity of the population and specific client profiles.
14. Integrate factors related to quality, safety, access, and cost-effectiveness in assessing, monitoring, and evaluating resources for the client's care.
15. Maintain familiarity with current research findings and be able to apply them, as appropriate, in his or her practice.

Nurses, social workers, and professionals in other disciplines may work as case managers, bringing with them their discipline-specific skills and knowledge. Depending on the facility, several case managers may be needed to coordinate care for all patients, or a case manager may be assigned to a specific high-risk, high-volume, high-cost population (see Fig. 12.7). The case manager may be responsible for coordinating care for up to 20 patients. The case manager must have frequent interaction with the patient and healthcare providers to achieve and evaluate expected outcomes.

Critical Pathways

The tool that case managers use to achieve patient outcomes is a critical pathway. Also referred to as a *multidisciplinary care pathway, integrated care pathway, critical path,* or *collaborative care pathway,* these patient-focused documents describe the clinical standards, necessary interventions, and expected outcomes for the patient throughout the treatment process or hospital stay. These pathways facilitate coordinated and efficient plans to deliver patient care. However, they are not appropriate for all patients and cannot replace professional clinical judgment. If a patient's progress deviates from the normal path, a variance is indicated. A variance is anything that occurs to alter the patient's progress through the normal critical path. The reason(s) for the variance should be analyzed and the care revised to meet the needs of the patients. These reasons may be influenced by patient, provider, or care issues. For example, if a given medication schedule is disrupted because of the patient's absence from the unit, an untoward reaction to the medication, or a change in priority care focus (as in respiratory distress), the progress of the critical pathway is disrupted.

Case management provides a well-coordinated care experience that can improve the care outcome, decrease the length of stay, and use multiple disciplines and services efficiently. Families and patients receive care across a continuum of settings, often from diverse institutions. Nurses who are case managers, referred to as NCMs, often are assigned to patients who have a medical issue that requires coordination of care. Nurses in this role receive a sense of satisfaction knowing that the patient and family received coordinated, quality care in a cost-effective manner across the spectrum of the illness or injury. To implement this approach effectively, interdisciplinary collaboration and coordination and consensus related to patient outcomes and the time frames proposed must be active.

Nurse Manager's Role

The nurse manager has increased demands when leading a case management system. Quality improvement is constantly assessed to ensure that the clinical pathway is appropriate for the diagnosis-related group (DRG) and that case managers are adequately managing their caseloads. Reimbursement for the care delivered is tied to effective planning and care delivery within the case management process. Patient satisfaction is also pertinent to evaluate for quality. If patients are not satisfied with the system, the census may decline. Communication among all systems must be coordinated. Because the NCM works with all departments within a healthcare organization, the nurse manager may need to facilitate interdepartmental communication. Educating the staff of other departments about the NCM's role and responsibilities will increase the effectiveness of the case management process.

Direct Care Nurse's Role

The direct care nurse working with a patient who has a case manager as the coordinator of care provides patient care according to the case manager's specifications and must know the extent of the case manager's role. Effective communication to facilitate care is the responsibility of both the case manager and the staff RN.

Nurse Navigator

A new role, similar in many ways to a case manager, is that of a nurse navigator. This role is sometime referred to as a patient navigator, particularly when disciplines other than nurses fulfill the role. In 1990 Dr. Harold Freeman developed the first nurse navigator role at Harlem Hospital in New York to facilitate diagnosis and treatment for patients with abnormal breast screening results. In 2001 the President's Cancer Panel recommended that funding for community-based programs, such as navigator programs, be increased to provide information, screening, treatment, and supportive care. The Patient Navigator Outreach and Chronic Disease Prevention Act of 2005 authorized federal grants to hire and train navigators (from all disciplines) to help patients with cancer and other serious chronic diseases access screening, diagnosis, treatment, and follow-up care. In 2007, $2.9 million was allocated to this program. Also, in 2006, the Centers for Medicare and Medicaid Services (CMS) funded six demonstration projects to help minority Medicare patients overcome barriers in screening, diagnosis, and treatment (McMurry & Cooper, 2017).

Although a number of navigator programs target care of cancer patients, this role could be implemented when caring for patients with other chronic diseases in a variety of care delivery settings. The Research Perspective illustrates this point.

The term navigator has no single definition. A seminal review of the literature regarding navigators suggests two approaches: (1) the provision of specified services to provide care and (2) removal of barriers to care (Wells et al., 2008). Wells and colleagues (2008) suggest that the role of a navigator, regardless of the professional discipline, is operationalized by providing any service that assists patients in overcoming obstacles from screening to treatment, as well as coping with

RESEARCH PERSPECTIVE

Resource: Seldon, L., McDonough, K., Turner, B., & Simmons, L. Evaluation of a hospital-based pneumonia nurse navigator program. *Journal of Nursing Administration, 46*(12), 654-661.

The purpose of this retrospective, formative evaluation was to evaluate the effectiveness of a hospital-based pneumonia nurse navigator program. The study compared the patient outcomes of patients admitted to a large community hospital from January 2012 to December 2014 with a primary or secondary diagnosis of pneumonia. Several positive results occurred after implementation of the nurse navigator program in this hospital. The core measures of performance were sustained at the 90th percentile 2 years after implementation of the program. Although the average length of stay (ALOS) for patients served by the nurse navigators did not decrease to the established benchmarks, the program did reduce the number and length of extended stays. Variable costs decreased by 4% over the 2 years of the study, whereas net profit per case increased by 5%. The authors concluded that the pneumonia nurse navigator program may improve core measures, reduce ALOS, and increase net revenue, but that further evaluations are necessary to confirm such findings.

Implications for Practice

Nurse navigator programs have the potential to improve outcomes, reduce costs, and increase profits. However, more evaluation of these programs must be conducted to confirm this finding and to determine the internal and external factors, which influence these positive outcomes.

treatment and follow-up. Specifically, navigators are responsible for (1) overcoming health system barriers, (2) providing health education about the disease from prevention to treatment, (3) addressing patient barriers to care, and (4) providing psychosocial support. The navigator role was conceived to reduce patient barriers to care for vulnerable patients who may cope with delays in access, diagnosis, treatment, and/or fragmented and uncoordinated care. As with many roles in health care, a number of disciplines have skills consistent with the navigator role, including nurses, social workers, health educators, and laypeople.

The nurse navigator role has much in common with other healthcare professions and other roles aimed at facilitating patient transitions through the care process. The case manager may be oriented toward care for a variety of conditions, but a navigator is typically focused on a single health condition. In addition, a case manager wants to improve the overall health of a patient for the long term, but a navigator seeks to achieve timely and effective care for the patient for only a defined set of health services. Similarly, patient advocates tend to focus on improving the healthcare system, but the navigator is tasked with removing specific health system barriers particular to an individual patient.

Differentiated Nursing Practice

One of the factors that makes development and implementation of any nursing care delivery model difficult is the variation in competence of nurses based on education and experience. Over the past 50 years, as multiple entry points in nursing (LPN/LVN, associate degree in nursing [ADN], diploma, bachelor of science in nursing [BSN], and advanced generalist master of science in nursing [MSN]) have grown and more is known about the length of time required for a nurse to move from being a novice to competent nurse (as defined in the classic work by Benner [2001]), efforts have been made to document and validate differentiated practice.

Differentiated nursing practice models are models of clinical nursing practice that are defined or differentiated by level of education, expected clinical skills or competencies, job descriptions, pay scales, and participation in decision making. Almost 25 years ago, *A Model for Differentiated Nursing Practice* (American Association of Nurse Executives [AONE], 1994) proposed that the ADN role functions primarily at the bedside in an institutional setting and in less complex patient care situations. Since that time the differentiated nursing practice model has been implemented in acute care inpatient settings, rural community nursing centers, and acute care operating rooms.

As the differentiated practice model gained influence, the time frame for care provided by the ADN has been defined within a shift or limited period, based on activities that provide comfort, physiologic stabilization, or assistance to a peaceful death. The guiding principles of the ADN's work are found in nursing standards, protocols, and pathways.

The BSN role has been conceptualized as operating across time from preadmission to postdischarge. The guiding principles of this role were found in the unusual and often unpredictable response of the patient that goes beyond needs addressed in the standards or pathways. Collaborating with other disciplines and agencies, the BSN nurse intervenes to design and facilitate a comprehensive, well-prepared discharge based on the unique needs of the patient and family. Although differentiated nursing practice is possible to implement in settings where diverse levels of education exist, staffing challenges and staffing mix become major challenges.

The advanced practice registered nurse (APRN) role is based on a Master of Science in nursing (MSN) or doctorate of nursing practice (DNP) competencies. The APRN perspective is supported by in-depth education in physiology, physical assessment, pharmacology, and a broad healthcare systems perspective. The MSN/DNP creates and defines protocols and pathways and assists with development of standards on emerging new healthcare phenomena. The MSN/DNP role is not bound by setting but, instead, provides a continuum of care across all settings, working with the patient and family throughout wellness or illness or until death (AACN, 2009). Differentiated practice outcomes include the opportunity for healthcare delivery organizations to capitalize on the education and experience provided by varied educational programs leading to RN licensure. The RN has the opportunity to practice to his or her potential, taking full advantage of educational preparation. Often, differentiated models of practice are supported by a clinical "ladder" or defined steps for advancement within the organization based on experience in nursing, additional education, specialty certification, or other indicators of professional excellence (AACN, n.d.). In addition, evidence indicates that differentiated practice models foster positive outcomes for job satisfaction, staffing costs, nurse turnover rates, adverse events such as patient falls and medication errors, nursing roles, and patient interventions and outcomes.

As nursing has evolved and environmental factors have influenced the role of a nurse, conflict over the roles of nurses with varied educational backgrounds and philosophy has erupted. These variations have had a significant impact on the success of the delivery system and the satisfaction of the nurse and the patients. These variations are further complicated by the experience and competence of the nurse in the practice arena. Using the Dreyfus model of skill acquisition, Benner (2001) identified five stages of clinical competence for nurses: novice, advanced beginner, competent, proficient, and expert. She suggested that competence is typified by a nurse who has been on the job in the same or similar situations for 2 to 3 years. This would suggest that nurses who are either new graduates or in a new area of clinical practice may require more assistance than those with more experience. A group of nurses who are all at the novice or advanced beginner stage would be less likely than their more experienced counterparts to implement any type of delivery model effectively.

In an effort to clarify the competence level of new graduates, some states, such as Texas, have identified the specific variations in competence among the various educational levels. In addition, many organizations differentiate expectations for recent graduates. These competencies can be used by educational programs for curriculum development and evaluation and by employers to determine the specific roles and responsibilities of these graduates. As practice changes, these competencies are often updated. An example of the use of differentiated practice in both service and education can be found in the Differentiated Educational Competencies from the Texas Board of Nursing (https://www.bon.texas.gov).

EXERCISE 12.8 Go to the Texas Board of Nursing website (https://www.bon.texas.gov) and review the document that outlines the Differentiated Educational Competencies (DECs) presented (https://www.bon.texas.gov/pdfs/differentiated_essential_competencies-2010.pdf). Consider how you might use the DECs if you were a direct care nurse or nurse manager. In what ways would the DECs be helpful? In what ways might they cause confusion?

Role of the Clinical Nurse Leader

In response to a lack of differentiated practice in many worksites and the increased emphasis on patient safety, the American Association of Colleges of Nursing (AACN) developed the clinical nurse leader role in the early 2000s. The clinical nurse leader (CNL), which is a protected title for those who successfully complete the CNL certification examination, is an advanced generalist clinician with education at the master's level, in contrast to APRN, whose designation includes clinical nurse specialists, nurse practitioners, nurse midwives, and nurse anesthetists. The CNL oversees the lateral integration of care for a distinct group of patients and may actively provide direct patient care in complex situations. The CNL uses evidence-based practice to ensure that patients benefit from the latest innovations in care delivery. The CNL is a provider and manager of care at the point of care to individuals and cohorts of patients anywhere health care is delivered. The fundamental aspects of CNL practice are outlined in Box 12.1 and include the following (AACN, 2007):

- Clinical leadership for patient-care practices and delivery, including the design, coordination, and evaluation of care for individuals, families, groups, and populations

---

BOX 12.1   Fundamental Aspects of the Clinical Nurse Leader

- Leadership in the care of the sick in and across all environments
- Design and provision of health promotion and risk reduction services for diverse populations
- Provision of evidence-based practice
- Population-appropriate health care to individuals, clinical groups/units, and communities
- Clinical decision making
- Design and implementation of care plans
- Risk anticipation
- Participation in identification and collection of care outcomes
- Accountability for the evaluation and improvement of point-of-care outcomes
- Mass customization of care
- Client and community advocacy
- Education and information management
- Delegation and oversight of care delivery and outcomes
- Team management and collaboration with other health professional team members
- Development and leverage of human, environmental, and material resources
- Management and use of client-care and information technology
- Lateral integration for specified groups of patients

From American Association of Colleges of Nursing (AACN). (2007). White paper on the education and role of the clinical nurse leader. http://www.aacn.nche.edu/publications/white-papers/ClinicalNurseLeader.pdf.

- Participation in identification and collection of care outcomes
- Accountability for evaluation and improvement of point-of-care outcomes, including the synthesis of data and other evidence to evaluate and achieve optimal outcomes
- Risk anticipation for individuals and cohorts of patients
- Lateral integration of care for individuals and cohorts of patients
- Design and implementation of evidence-based practice(s)
- Team leadership, management, and collaboration with other health professional team members
- Information management or the use of information systems and technologies to improve healthcare outcomes
- Stewardship and leveraging of human, environmental, and material resources
- Advocacy for patients, communities, and the health professional team

Although most of the CNL graduates hold a typical prelicensure program, some CNL programs provide this degree as a master's as an entry into practice degree (Hicks & Rosenberg, 2016).

POSITIVE CARE DELIVERY SYSTEMS

In the search for approaches to improve patient care within the contexts of limited resources, a number of organizations have developed models that guide the practice of nurses in specific situations. In part this is related to the value of case coordination (see the Policy Perspective). Using concepts from the Synergy Model, Magnet Recognition Program®, or rapid cycle change on a clinical unit may also improve the quality of care in a particular unit, regardless of the nursing care delivery model used.

The Synergy Model

Similar to the work of the American Association of Colleges of Nursing in developing the CNL, the American Association of Critical-Care Nurses adopted the Synergy Model as the framework for nursing practice and to guide the certification examination for critical care nurses and clinical nurse specialists. The rationale guiding this model is that the needs or characteristics of patients and families influence and drive the characteristics or competencies of nurses. Synergy results when the needs and characteristics of a patient, clinical unit, or system are matched with a nurse's competencies. The Synergy Model describes the following eight patient characteristics: resiliency, vulnerability, stability, complexity, resource availability, participation in care, participation in decision making, and predictability. The eight nurse competencies are clinical judgment, advocacy and moral agency, caring practices, facilitation of learning, collaboration, systems thinking, response to diversity, and clinical requirement. The American Association of Critical-Care Nurses provides an outline of the ways in which the needs of the patient and the characteristics of the nurse can be evaluated to reach synergy *(https://www.aacn.org/nursing-excellence/aacn-standards/synergy-model)*.

Magnet Recognition Program®

In 1983 the American Academy of Nursing's (AAN) task force on nursing practice in hospitals conducted a study of 163 hospitals to identify and describe variables that created an environment that attracted and retained well-qualified nurses who promoted quality care. Forty-one of these institutions were described as Magnet® hospitals because of their ability to attract and retain professional nurses. In 1990 the American Nurses Credentialing Center, building on the concepts of the 1983 Magnet® hospital study, developed a program that recognized excellence in the nurses' work environment. Prominent in the designation process is the hospital's documentation of the presence of the Forces of Magnetism.

The **Magnet Recognition Program®** is designed for hospitals to achieve recognition of excellent nursing care through a self-nominating, self-appraisal process.

The rigorous self-appraisal process is lengthy, often requiring 2 or more years of preparation. The hospital makes application for Magnet® status, submits documentation to demonstrate its compliance with the Magnet® standards, and hosts a site visit by Magnet® appraisers. When the application process is successful, Magnet® status is awarded for 4 years. For additional information on Magnet® credentialing, see *www.nursecredentialing.org/magnet/index.html*.

Since the mid-1990s, significant research on the effects of Magnet® hospitals on patient outcomes, patient satisfaction, and employee satisfaction has been conducted. For example, McHugh and colleagues (2013) used logistic regression on data from 56 Magnet® hospitals and 508 non-Magnet® hospitals to determine whether Magnet® hospitals have lower risk-adjusted mortality and failure-to-rescue incidents than non-Magnet® hospitals. The researchers found that Magnet® hospitals had significantly better work environments and higher proportions of nurses with bachelor's degrees and specialty certification. These nursing factors explained much of the Magnet® hospital effect on patient outcomes. In addition, patients treated in Magnet® hospitals had 14% lower odds of mortality (odds ratio 0.86; 95% confidence interval, 0.76–0.98; P = 0.02) and 12% lower odds of failure-to-rescue (odds ratio 0.88; 95% confidence interval, 0.77–1.01; P = 0.07) while controlling for nursing factors as well as hospital and patient differences (McHugh et al., 2013).

Rapid Cycle Change

Critical to practice changes, **rapid cycle change** is a process that encourages testing creative change on a small scale while determining potential impact. The process involves four stages—plan, do, study, and act (PDSA). During the *plan phase,* the team had to define the objectives and predict how the identified change would contribute to a design, how the change would occur, and what data collection methods were needed. During the *do phase,* the team had to focus on whether the changed occurred as expected and, if not, what interfered with the plan. In the *study phase,* the team had to determine whether the innovation worked as predicted and what knowledge was gained. The *act phase* required the team to plan the next actions.

The Institute for Healthcare Improvement is a leading proponent of the use of the Model of Improvement, developed by the Associates in Process Improvement, which incorporates rapid cycle change to make changes in a particular clinical arena. Fig. 12.8 provides a pictorial representation of this process.

The rapid cycle change has been used in a variety of innovations within health care. For example, in a 15-month American Organization of Nurse Executives

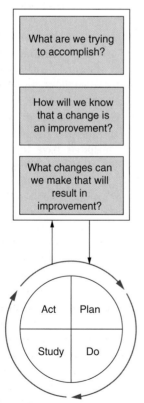

Fig. 12.8 Rapid cycle change. (From Sorenson R, & Iedema R. (2008). *Managing clinical processes in health services.* London: Churchill Livingstone.)

(AONE) collaborative, Transforming Care at the Bedside (TCAB), medical-surgical staff from 67 hospitals used the TCAB process to determine whether participating units successfully implemented recommended change processes, engaged staff, implemented innovations, and generated support from hospital leadership and staff. The broad-based study found that, based on the engagement of staff and the high volume of innovations tested, implemented, and sustained, TCAB appears to be an effective model for organizing and implementing improvements led by front-line staff (Needleman et al., 2016).

The Institute of Health Improvement (IHI) has a number of resources to support transformation. For example, one white paper, *Transforming Care at the Bedside How-to Guide: Engaging Front-Line Staff in Innovation and Quality Improvement,* provides information that (1) describes three key improvement strategies to build improvement capability and engage front-line staff in innovation on medical and surgical units, (2) provides a sequence of steps to build front-line staff's capability in innovation and quality improvement to transform care at the bedside, (3) offers case studies of implementation of TCAB principles, and (4) represents practical tips from TCAB participants (Rutherford et al., 2008).

TRANSITIONAL CARE

As the cost of health care escalated and reimbursement strategies changed, hospital stays shortened and patients transitioned to alternative care, including home, more rapidly than in earlier years. In addition, payers developed approaches to financially penalize providers for hospital readmissions. As a result, organizations need to evaluate how to improve care delivery, as the Literature Perspective illustrates. A review of a number of studies reveals there are serious quality and safety problems after discharge from acute care. Patients may not understand their medication instructions or how to care for themselves. They may not know how to recognize warning signs of health problems or how to follow up. The Agency of Healthcare Research and Quality (AHRQ, 2014) notes that these transitions occur when information about or accountability and responsibility move from one healthcare entity to another. The transition may also occur within one organization because of responsible clinician changes or changes in the patient's age or conditions. A Joint Commission

LITERATURE PERSPECTIVE

Resource: DelBoccio, S., Smith, D., Hicks, M., Low, P., Graves-Rust, J, Volland, J., & Fryda, S. Successes and challenges in patient care transition programming: One hospital's journal. *The Online Journal of Issues in Nursing, 20*(3), Manuscript 2. http://www.nursingworld.org/MainMenuCategories/ANAMarketplace/ANAPeriodicals/OJIN/TableofContents/Vol-20-2015/No3-Sept-2015/Successes-Challenges-in-Patient-Care-Transition-Programming.html.

This article describes the experience of the Indiana University Health North Hospital in their attempt to overcome patient care transition obstacles, and ultimately being designated as a top performer in the Care Transition measures on the Hospital Consumer Assessment of Healthcare Providers and Systems (HCAHPS) Survey. The article describes their strategies to personalize patient outcomes and transition through activation and to improve transition for vulnerable populations.

Implications for Practice

This article illustrates ways in which a hospital can improve the transition process for patients by describing the obstacles to transition and methods to overcome these barriers.

Transitions of Care Report, "Transitions of Care," (2012) categorizes the root causes of ineffective transitions of care as (1) communication breakdowns, (2) patient education breakdowns, and (3) accountability breakdowns. This report suggests the following as important in achieving an effective transition:

- Multidisciplinary communication, collaboration, and coordination—including patient/caregiver education—from admission through transition.
- Clinician involvement and shared accountability during all points of transition. Both sending and receiving clinicians are involved in and accountable for a successful transition.
- Comprehensive planning and risk assessment beginning immediately after admission and throughout hospital stay.
- Standardized transition plans, procedures, and forms.
- Timely follow-up, support, and coordination after the patient leaves a care setting.

INTERPROFESSIONAL EDUCATION AND COLLABORATION

Most of the care models discussed in this chapter address the organization of nursing care. Apart from case management, most of the models do not focus on the impact of interprofessional collaboration (IPC) on the outcomes of patient care, communication, and collaboration, which is increasingly important as the complexity of health care increases. National and international organizations have called for strategies to improve collaboration among health professions to improve the delivery care system. To support these recommendations, calls for interprofessional education (IPE) grew. For example, in 2003 the Committee on the Health Professions Education Summit from the Institute of Medicine (now known as the National Academy of Medicine) recommended that to meet the challenges of the 21st century, health professions should work in interdisciplinary teams (IOM, 2003). In 2006 the World Health Organization (WHO) announced the creation of the WHO Study Group on Interprofessional Education and Collaborative Practice to develop a global strategy to implement IPE and collaborative practices worldwide. In 2010 the WHO and their partners reinforced their commitment to IPE and IPC, stating that these strategies will improve health care across the world (Pinto et al., 2012). In 2011 in the IOM report "The Future of Nursing: Leading Change, Advancing Health," the authors stated that "Nurses should be educated with physicians and other health professions both as students and throughout their careers in lifelong learning opportunities" (p. 2).

The Interprofessional Education Collaborative Expert Panel's Core Competencies for Interprofessional Collaborative Practice: Report of an Expert Panel was published in 2011. Representatives of nursing, medicine, and dentistry envisioned IPC as necessary for safe, high-quality, accessible, patient-centered care. Essential to achieving this goal is the continuous development of interprofessional competencies by health professions students during their educational experience, so when they enter practice, they will be able to interact collaboratively. The competency domains included (1) Values/Ethics for Interprofessional Practice, (2) Roles and Responsibilities, (3) Interprofessional Communication, and (4) Teams and Teamwork.

Given the emphasis on IPC and the multiple reports cited here, the AHRQ developed TeamSTEPPS, an evidence-based set of teamwork tools, aimed at optimizing patient outcomes by improving communication and teamwork skills among the interprofessional team. Specific resources include TeamSTEPPS educational modules for hospital-based, office-based, dental, and long-term care teams. A guide for teamwork with patients with limited English proficiency and a rapid response systems guide, as well as a training guide for using simulation in TeamSTEPPS training, are provided.

Several versions of TeamSTEPPS are available, along with individual modules related to specific audiences, settings, or situations. AHRQ also provides a Readiness Assessment to determine the readiness of a practice environment to implement TeamSTEPPS and webinars to assist in the implementation *(https://www.ahrq.gov/teamstepps/index.html).*

CONCLUSION

Each patient care delivery model has identified strengths and weaknesses. No perfect method for delivering nursing care to groups of patients and their families exists. No one model addresses all needs of the wide range of settings and sizes of healthcare organizations. In addition, in times of local or national emergencies, the typical model of care may be replaced with one designed to best fit the emergency. Regardless of the patient care delivery model used, some characteristics in the practice setting must be present to ensure effective practice. The American Association of Colleges of Nursing's publication "Hallmarks of the Professional Nursing Practice Environment" outlines those characteristics that must be present, including the following:

1. The contributions of nurses' knowledge and expertise to clinical care quality and patient care is recognized. For example, the organization differentiates the practice roles of nurses based on educational preparation, certification, and advanced preparation and use of evidence-based practice.
2. The executive-level nursing leadership is highlighted by, for example, their participation on the governing body and their reporting to the highest level operations or corporate officer.
3. Nurses participate in clinical decision making and the organization of clinical care systems.
4. Clinical advancement programs based on education, certification, and advanced preparation are available, including financial rewards and opportunities for promotion. Longevity is based on education, clinical expertise, and professional contributions. Individuals in nursing leadership/management positions have appropriate education and credentials aligned with their roles and responsibilities.
5. Professional development support for nurses is available.
6. Professional nurses, physicians, and other healthcare professionals practice collaboratively and participate in organizational committees.
7. The organization uses technological advances in clinical care and information systems.

This chapter describes the traditional patient care delivery models that have been used over the past half-century. The complexity of the current healthcare system, the shortage of health professionals, and the pressures to ensure patient safety and cost-effective care have led many organizations to explore optional models to deliver patient care using IPC, in all levels of care.

THE SOLUTION

As an assistant director of nursing, I am responsible for ensuring the delivery of excellent patient care to patients admitted to our hematology-oncology unit. The nurses on the unit were committed to this approach but were faced with communication challenges. Collaborating with other members of the leadership team, receiving feedback from the staff nurses, and seeking out best practices from my peers in the healthcare community produced a solution. We initiated a sit-down report for all nurses called the "huddle" and established a "nurse buddy" system.

The huddle is conducted at the beginning of the shift after each nurse has obtained report from the nurse on the previous shift and has had the opportunity to review each patient's plan of care. The nurses are paged and notified that the huddle will occur. The huddle is facilitated by the charge nurse, who surveys each nurse on his or her workload and the projected times he or she would need assistance with patient care.

The nurse buddy system was initiated to provide the patient-side nurse with an immediate resource—someone other than the charge nurse. These two nurses provide each other with assistance on an as-needed basis. The buddy is assigned at the time all patient assignments are made and is in close proximity.

The feedback is very positive. The charge nurse has a clearer picture of the status of the patients, families, and staff. Because the staff nurses are more engaged, they state that they are involved with the unit's operational needs for the day. Patient care is planned collaboratively so that each nurse is available to the buddy at times of need. Overall, teamwork and communication have been enhanced.

Would this be a suitable approach for you? Why?

Jacqueline Ward

REFLECTIONS

Think of an organizational change that has occurred in a nursing unit where you have worked during your clinical experiences. What were the leadership opportunities for various nurses assigned to that unit? How might you have responded to this change? What ideas do you have to help others see nursing as a revenue producer?

THE EVIDENCE

Each model has strengths and limitations and may be appropriate for one setting or situation and not for another. What matters most in considering care delivery strategies is this: multiple factors influence what the care delivery system can look like. Those factors include physical space, which may dictate how far from one patient to another a group of people can deliver care; preparation of the nursing staff, which can include a limited access to nurses with advanced degrees; licensure laws (including delegation rules), which may require certain conditions; and the inventiveness of leaders and managers to consider what best accomplishes safe, effective care.

TIPS FOR SELECTING A CARE DELIVERY MODEL

- Look at the organization and the population being served when selecting a care delivery model.
- Consider the organizational structure and processes when selecting the care delivery model.
- Any model has advantages and disadvantages; no ideal approach exists.
- Know that every model has specific expectations for both managers and staff.
- Determine whether there are experienced nurses who provide clinical leadership in specific settings.

REFERENCES

Agency for Healthcare Research and Quality. (2014). *Care coordination measures atlas update: What is care coordination?* https://www.ahrq.gov/professionals/prevention-chronic-care/improve/coordination/atlas2014/chapter2.html.

American Association of Colleges of Nursing. (n.d.). Hallmarks of the professional nursing practice environment. http://www.aacnnursing.org/News-Information/Position-Statements-White-Papers/Hallmarks-Practice.

American Association of Colleges of Nursing (AACN). (2007). White paper on the education and role of the clinical nurse leader. http://www.aacn.nche.edu/publications/white-papers/ClinicalNurseLeader.pdf.

American Association of Colleges of Nursing (AACN). (2009). DNP fact sheet. www.aacn.nche.edu/media-relations/fact-sheets/dnp.

American Association of Nursing Executives (AONE). (1994). A model for differentiated nursing practice. *Journal of Nursing Administration, 25*(9), 34–35.

American Nurses Credentialing Center (n.d.). History of the Magnet program. https://www.nursingworld.org/ organizational-programs/magnet/history/.

Benner, P. (2001). *From novice to expert: Excellence and power in clinical nursing practice.* Upper Saddle River, NJ: Prentice Hall.

Camicia, M., et al. (2012) The Value of Nursing Care Coordination. A White Paper of the American Nurses Association. The CNPE Health Policy Work Group-2011-2012. July. http://www.nursingworld.org/ carecoordinationwhitepaper.

Case Management Society of America. *Standards for practice for case management* (4th ed.). Little Rock, AR: Author. http://www.cmsa.org/portals/0/pdf/memberonly/ StandardsOfPractice.pdf

Cherry, B., & Jacobs, S. (2017). *Contemporary nursing: Issues, trends, and management* (7th ed.). St. Louis: Elsevier.

Cohen, E., & Cesta, T. (2004). *Nursing case management from essentials to advanced practice application* (4th ed.). St. Louis: Mosby.

Curtis, K., Lien, D., Chan, A., & Morris, R. (2002). The impact of trauma. *The Journal of Trauma, 53*(3), 477–482.

DelBoccio, S., Smith, D., Hicks, M., Low, P., Graves-Rust, J., Volland, J., et al. (2015). Successes and challenges in patient care transition programming: One hospital's journal. *The Online Journal of Issues in Nursing 20*(3) Manuscript 2. http://www.nursingworld.org/MainMenuCategories/ ANAMarketplace/ANAPeriodicals/OJIN/ TableofContents/Vol-20-2015/No3-Sept-2015/Successes-Challenges-in-Patient-Care-Transition-Programming. html.

Flagg, A. (2015). The role of patient centered care in nursing. *Nursing Clinics, 50*(1), 75–86.

Hicks, F., & Rosenberg, L. (2016). Enacting a vision for a master's entry clinical nurse leader program: Rethinking nursing education. *Journal of Professional Nursing, 32*(1), 41–47.

Huber, D. (2010). *Disease management: A guide for case managers.* St. Louis: Elsevier.

Institute for Healthcare Improvement. (n.d.). How to improve. http://www.ihi.org/resources/Pages/HowtoImprove/ default.aspx.

Institute of Medicine Committee on the Health Professions Education Summit; Greiner, A. C., & Knebel, E., editors. (2003). Washington, DC: National Academies Press.

Institute of Medicine (IOM). (2011). The future of nursing: Leading change, advancing health. *Committee on the*

Robert Wood Johnson Foundation Initiative on the Future of Nursing at the Institute of Medicine; Institute of Medicine. www.nap.edu/catalog/12956.html.

Interprofessional Education Collaborative Expert Panel. (2011). *Core competencies for interprofessional collaborative practice: Report of an expert panel.* Washington, DC: Interprofessional Education Collaborative. https://www. aacom.org/docs/default-source/insideome/ccrpt05-10-11. pdf?sfvrsn=77937f97_2.

Manthey, M., Ciske, K., Robertson, P., & Harris, I. (1970). Primary nursing: A return to the concept of "my nurse" and "my patient." *Nursing Forum, 9,* 65–83.

McHugh, M., Kelly, L., Smith, H., Wu, E., Vanak, J., & Aiken, L. (2013). Lower mortality in magnet hospitals. *Journal of Nursing Administration, 43*(10), S4–S10.

McMurry, A., & Cooper, H. (2017). The nurse navigator: An evolving model of care. *Collegian, 24*(2), 205–212.

Needleman, J., Person, M. L., Upenieks, V. V., Yee, T., Wolstein, J., & Parkerton, M. (2016). Engaging frontline staff in performance improvement: The American Organization of Nurse Executives implementation of transforming care at the bedside collaborative. *Journal of Patient Satisfaction, 42*(2), 61–69.

Pinto, A., Lee, S., Lombardo, S., Salama, M., Ellis, S., Kay, T., et al. (2012). The impact of structured inter-professional education on health care professional students: Perceptions of collaboration in a clinical setting. *Physiotherapy Canada, 64*(2), 145–156.

Rutherford, P., Phillips, J., Coughlan, P., Lee, B., Moen, R., Peck, C., et al. (2008). *Transforming care at the bedside how-to guide: Engaging front-line staff in innovation and quality improvement.* Cambridge, MA: Institute for Healthcare Development. http://www.ihi.org/resources/ Pages/Tools/TCABHowToGuideEngagingStaff.aspx.

Seldon, L., McDonough, K., Turner, B., & Simmons, L. (2016). Evaluation of a hospital-based pneumonia nurse navigator program. *Journal of Nursing Administration, 46*(12), 654–661.

The Joint Commission. (2012). Transitions of care: The need for a more effective approach to continuing patient care. https://www.jointcommission.org/assets/1/18/Hot_ Topics_Transitions_of_Care.pdf.

Wells, K. J., Battaglia, T. A., Dudley, D. J., Garcia, R., Greene, A., Calhoun, E., et al. (2008). Patient navigation: State of the art or is it science? *Cancer, 113*(8), 1999–2010.

13

Staffing and Scheduling

Susan Sportsman

LEARNING OUTCOMES

- Integrate current research into principles to effectively manage nurse staffing.
- Use technology to plan, implement, and evaluate staffing, scheduling, and the effectiveness of a unit's productivity.
- Examine personnel scheduling needs in relation to patients' requirements for continuity of care and positive outcomes, as well as the nurse manager's need to create a schedule that is fair and equitable for all team members.

- Relate floating, mandatory overtime, and the use of supplemental agency staff to nurse satisfaction and patient care outcomes.
- Evaluate the impact of patient and hospital factors, nurse characteristics, nurse staffing, and other organizational factors that influence nurse and patient outcomes.

KEY TERMS

average daily census (ADC)
average length of stay (ALOS)
benefit time
cost center
direct care hours
factor evaluation system
fixed FTEs
fixed staffing
flexible staffing
forecast

full-time equivalents (FTEs)
indirect care hours
labor cost per unit of service
mandatory overtime
nurse-sensitive data
nursing productivity
overtime
patient outcomes
percentage of occupancy
productive time

prototype evaluation system
scheduling
staffing
staffing plan
units of service
variable FTEs
variance report
workload

THE CHALLENGE

The inpatient general surgical units of a large regional medical center have a total of 54 beds, and the surgical trauma intensive care unit (STICU) has 16 beds. The organization was faced with severe capacity constraints as it prepared to begin a master site facility plan that would result in an additional 120 beds over the next 3 years. The lack of a step-down unit for surgical patients was a particular void in service. The coronary care unit (CCU), medical intensive care unit (MICU), and cardiovascular intensive care unit (CVICU) all have step-down units to which they can transfer patients and free up beds for truly critical patients. Beds that were already filled with general surgery patients were targeted to be the step-down unit for the STICU.

The challenge to develop the surgical step-down unit included the identification of the appropriate number of step-down beds needed by considering the volume of patients in STICU that could be transferred to the surgical step-down unit. Admission and discharge criteria for this step-down unit needed to be developed and approved by the medical staff. New equipment needs also had to be identified. The staff competencies necessary to provide appropriate care to these patients had to be considered and education plans developed. In addition, a staffing plan had to be outlined. Communication to the nursing staff was critical—some feared that they would lose their jobs because the critical care staff would assume their positions.

What would you do if you were this nurse?

Mary Ellen Bonczek, BSN, RN, MPA, NEA-BC
Senior Vice President and Chief Nurse Executive, New Hanover Regional Medical Center, Wilmington, North Carolina

INTRODUCTION

An important role of the nurse manager in a healthcare organization is to ensure that sufficient numbers of nurses are available to provide the care needed by patients. However, consistent with one of the components of the Quadruple Aim (Bodenheimer & Sinsky, 2014), to reduce per capita costs, controlling costs associated with the number of nurses on a unit at any given time is also a responsibility of the nurse manager. Because nursing salaries constitute some of the major drivers of labor costs in a healthcare organization, nurse managers are increasingly challenged to tightly manage both staffing and scheduling within their assigned cost centers.

The ANA Principles of Nurse Staffing defines appropriate staffing as "a match of registered nurse expertise with the needs of the recipient of nursing care services in the context of the practice setting and situation. Providing appropriate staffing is achieved by dynamic, multifaceted decision-making processes that must take into account a wide range of variables." (Mensik, 2014). The ANA adopted the principles of safe staffing related to staff and institutions or organizations. These principles addressed issues related to individual and aggregate patient needs, research related to the concept of nursing hours per patient day, unit functions that add to nursing hours, the patient populations and their required competencies, support from management and experienced registered nurses (RNs), and an organizational culture that values RNs' work, a system of documented competencies. From these principles, the following policy statements were crafted:

1. Nurse staffing patterns and the level of care provided should not depend on the type of payor.
2. Evaluation of any staffing system should include quality of work-life outcomes, as well as patient outcomes.
3. Staffing should be based on achieving quality of patient care indices, meeting organizational outcomes and ensuring that the quality of the nurse's work-life is appropriate (American Nurses Association [ANA], 2014).

In general, staffing may be either fixed or flexible. Fixed staffing models are built upon a fixed set of numbers of nurses for a particular unit or shift. The results are an unalterable nurse-to-patient staffing ratio. This approach does not consider the frequent changes within a patient care environment (changes in severity of patient conditions, changes in volume or procedural requirements, etc.) Flexible staffing takes into account these variations. As a result, a flexible staffing plan is more difficult to develop. To be successful, these plans must be created with input from direct care staff (Avalere Health LLC, 2015). Because of the complexity of the staffing process, the requirement is to provide *safe staffing,* in which the availability of appropriate nursing care on a shift-to-shift basis results in patient care needs being met in a hazard-free work environment. However, the ultimate goal is *optimal staffing,* in which the impact of nursing care results in better than average staffing, incorporating evidence-based principles to develop and maintain a flexible staffing plan (Avalere Health LLC, 2015).

Staffing also may be either centralized or decentralized. With centralized staffing, one department is responsible for staffing in all units, including call-in staff, call-off staff, and float staff. With decentralized staffing, unit leaders (nurse managers, charge nurses, etc.) determine the level of staffing needed before and during the shift, depending on multiple factors (Mensik, 2014).

THE STAFFING PROCESS

Over the past 20 years, a significant amount of research has been done in the United States and internationally to evaluate links among nursing staffing, workloads, skill mix, and patient outcomes. Adequate nursing care has been associated with decreased falls, medication errors, hospital acquired infections and mortality rates, as well as enhanced nurse retention and job satisfaction and improved patient satisfaction (Aiken et. al, 2012; Cho, Mark, Knafl, Chang, & Yoon, 2017; Koy, Yunibhand, Angsuroch, & Fisher, 2015). Currently, the exploration of the impact of staffing on patient outcomes has been expanded to the nursing home arena. In a literature review, which examined the relationship between staffing levels in nursing homes and quality of care, Backhaus et al. (2014) found that quality is a difficult concept to capture directly. In an earlier literature review, Spilsbury, Hewitt, Stirk, and Bowman (2011) found that no consistent relationship between nurse staffing and outcomes of care existed. Higher staffing levels were associated with both better and poorer outcomes of care. For example, an increase in staff seemed related to both fewer and more pressure ulcers. Methodologic issues appear to have prevented these studies from demonstrating clear results, highlighting the need for well-designed longitudinal studies to gain better insight into the relationship between nurse staffing and outcomes of care in nursing homes.

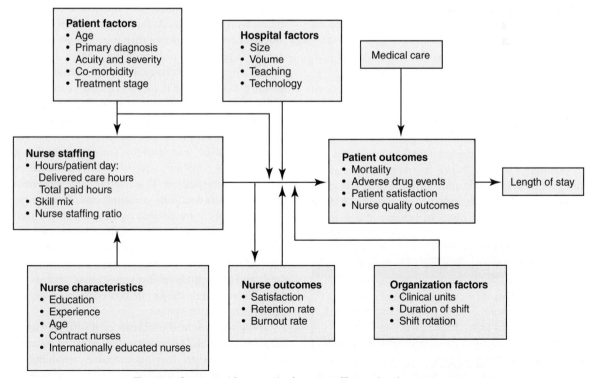

Fig. 13.1 Conceptual framework of nurse staffing and patient outcomes.

Regardless of the setting of research on nursing staffing, having a framework for considering factors that influence the impact of staffing on patient outcomes is helpful. A landmark meta-analysis of the research related to the impact of nursing staffing on patient outcomes sponsored by the Agency for Healthcare Research and Quality (AHRQ) provides the components of such a framework (Fig. 13.1). These factors include the number of patients on the unit and their family situation and needs; their stage of illness; the range of conditions on the unit; the observations, treatments, and interventions needed; and patient satisfaction (Kane, Shamliyan, Mueller, Duval, & Wilt, 2007). This framework can also be used by nurse managers to determine the staffing on their own units (Kane et al., 2007).

Models for Nurse Staffing

Mensik (2014) notes three main models for nurse staffing exist: (1) patient acuity, in which patient characteristics are used to decide the level of staffing; (2) budget-based staffing, in which the number of nurses is determined compared with historical nursing hours per patient days on a unit and on national benchmarks; or (3) a nurse–patient ratio, in which the number of nurses on each unit is designated by policy, based on the type of patients served.

Patient Acuity

The acuity or severity of patients' conditions, influenced by their age, primary diagnosis, comorbidities, severity of illness, treatment stage, socioeconomic status, ability to provide self-care, anticipated length of stay, and family or caregivers to be included in patient education and care planning (Mensik, 2014), is a key component in determining the staffing required for safe care. However, the dynamic nature of patient care often makes it difficult to quantify the care needs of patients at any given time. Thus we need to consider the patient variables in a specific unit as staffing decisions are made. Those variables appear in Box 13.1. Patient classification systems used primarily in acute care settings have been developed in an effort to give nurse managers the tools and language to describe the acuity of patients on their unit. More seriously ill patients receive higher classification scores, indicating that more nursing resources are required to provide patient care. Nurse managers use the classification data to adjust the unit's staffing plan for a given time or to quantify acuity trends over longer periods as they forecast their staffing needs during the budget process.

Patient Classification Types. Two basic types of patient classification systems exist: prototype and factor. A prototype evaluation system, an older approach to evaluating patient characteristics, is considered both subjective and descriptive. Patients are classified into broad categories, and these categories are used to predict patient care needs. The relative intensity measures (RIMs) system is a prototype system. This system classifies patient care needs based on their diagnosis-related group (DRG). The data are then fed to an electronic decision support system that integrates clinical and financial information. A factor evaluation system is considered more objective than a prototype evaluation system. It gives each task, thought process, and patient care activity a time or rating. These associations are then summed to determine the hours of direct care required, or they are weighted for each patient. Each intervention is given a name and a definition and is further specified to incorporate a list of all associated interventional activities. The list of interventions is comprehensive and applicable to inpatient, outpatient, home care, and long-term care patients. Typically, if these systems are used for staffing decisions, organizations use a combination of the two. Some patient types with a single healthcare focus, such as maternal deliveries or outpatient surgical patients, would be appropriately classified with a prototype system. Patients with more complex care needs and a less predictable disease course, such as those with pneumonia or stroke, are more appropriately evaluated with a factor system.

Numerous potential problems exist with patient classification systems. The issue most often raised by administrators relates to the questionable reliability and validity of the data collected through a self-reporting mechanism. Another concern with patient classification

---

BOX 13.1 **Patient Variables Affecting Staffing Decisions**	
Number of patients	Stage of illness
Range of conditions	Family situation and
Observations and interventions	needs
required	Treatment required
Patients' satisfaction	

Modified from Douglas, K. (2010). Ratios—If only it were that easy. *Nursing Economic$*, 28(2), 119-125.

data relates to the inability of the organization to meet the prescribed staffing levels outlined by the patient classification system.

EXERCISE 13.1 Administrators worry that they risk potential liability if they do not follow the staffing recommendations of the patient classification system. If the classification data indicate that six caregivers are needed for the upcoming shift but the organization can provide only five caregivers, what are the potential consequences for the organization if an untoward event occurs?

Concern over the accuracy of biased data and the inability to meet predicted staffing levels outlined by the patient classification systems has caused many healthcare organizations to abandon patient classification as a mechanism for determining appropriate staffing levels. Staff morale is at risk when acuity models indicate one level is necessary and the organization cannot increase staffing to meet those needs. Likewise, staff morale is at risk without acuity models when it is clear to staff that patient needs exceed care capacity.

Budget-Based Staffing

Budget-based staffing requires that the staffing plan be developed in concert with the personnel budget. Mensik (2014) suggests that the number of nursing hours per patient day (HPPD) or nursing hours be divided by the total patient days and then evaluated based on national benchmarks. The total patient days include the average number of patients in a 24-hour period. "Nursing hours" refers to the total number of hours worked by all nurses on that unit for a given time period. These two parameters give a snapshot of overall day or shift, but they do not consider what happens *during* the shift. For example, if several patients are admitted to the unit at one time, or several patients experience untoward events during the shift, the staffing needs may change.

In an effort to address the limitations of the budget-based systems, productivity instruments have been updated, using sophisticated technologies. Based on interviews of nurses on a number of nursing units in three Texas hospitals, Hamilton and Campbell (2011) described the use of productivity instruments, sophisticated technologies that calculate the staffing patterns required on a unit. As previously noted, specific unit productivity is based on assumptions about the number,

type, and acuity of patients projected to be admitted on a unit in the context of the organization's financial goals. The result of the calculations is a staffing matrix, which gives the number of patients expected to be on the unit at midnight of each day projected. The matrix also provides the number of personnel (RNs, licensed vocational nurses [LVNs] or licensed practical nurses [LPNs], unit secretaries, and charge nurses) required to meet the daily demands of the projected number of nurses. The matrix is then used to develop the monthly staffing schedule for the unit.

Every shift provides opportunities to increase or decrease the number of staff on the unit, based on available staff, patient census, and patient acuity level. However, the charge nurse and, ultimately, the nurse manager have the responsibility to meet the goals established by the matrix. If the number of staff required on a shift-by-shift basis exceeds the number budgeted in a given month, an equal reduction at some other time within the month must be made to meet the productivity necessary to meet the targets (projections). In this way, the availability of staff is dictated by the projections for profitability. The productivity of a unit is monitored on a shift-by-shift basis. The charge nurse is expected to complete unit reports, sending them electronically to a number of hospital offices, typically the staffing office, payroll, financial officer, and nursing administration. These reports may include such information as the following:

- Productivity index for the pay period (100% is desirable)
- Amount of overtime
- Amount of supplemental (contract) workers
- Benchmarks against results of peer units
- Actual labor costs (total and per patient day)
- Projected costs (total and per patient day)
- Variance of costs
- Training and orientation costs
- Worked full-time equivalent (FTE) variance compared with target

The nurse manager, and ultimately the nurse executive, are responsible for variances and, as previously discussed, must align the staffing decisions with the financial objectives (Hamilton & Cambell, 2011).

Nurse–Patient Ratio

The recognition that the number of registered nurses providing care to patients is associated with better patient outcomes in acute care leads to a discussion regarding the best model to ensure sufficient staffing. Two major approaches have been put forward. The first requires a specific number of patients cared for by one nurse per shift (mandated nurse–patient ratios). Legislation to mandate specific nurse–patient ratios was initially implemented in California in 1999 and fully implemented in 2004. This law requires that a nurse must care for no more than:

- Six patients in a psychiatric unit
- Five patients in a medical-surgical unit
- Four pediatric patients
- Three patients in a labor and delivery unit
- Two patients in intensive care units (ICUs)

Additionally, in 2014, Massachusetts passed a law specific to ICUs that requires a 1:1 or 1:2 nurse–patient ratio depending on the stability of the patient (Avalere Health LLC, 2015).

In an important, and now classic, evaluation of the nurse–patient ratio policy, Aiken et al. (2010) examined the effects of California's 2004 minimum nurse–patient staff ratio mandate for acute care facilities by comparing patient outcome data and hospital staffing information at hospitals in California, New Jersey, and Pennsylvania. Researchers also surveyed 22,236 hospital nurses in the three states. According to the nurse survey, 88% of the California nurses working in a medical-surgical area reported overseeing only 5 patients, as required by the California law. In contrast, 33% of the Pennsylvania nurses surveyed and 19% of those surveyed in New Jersey reported being responsible for 5 or fewer patients. California nurses cared for 2 fewer patients than nurses in New Jersey and 1.7 fewer patients than nurses in Pennsylvania. The analysis suggested that if California's nurse–patient levels had been instituted in Pennsylvania and New Jersey during the time of the study, the states could have achieved 10.6% and 13.0% fewer deaths, respectively, among general surgical patients. The study also found that California nurses reported higher job satisfaction and the perception that they provided better patient care than did nurses surveyed in Pennsylvania and New Jersey (Aiken et al.,

2010). Two years later, Cook, Gaynor, Stephens, & Taylor (2012) found that when the California hospitals that initially did not meet the California nurse–patient ratio regulations became compliant with the law, the ratio of patients to nurses did decrease. However, these improvements in staffing ratios did not appear to be associated with relative improvements in measured patient safety.

Alternative to the Nurse–Patient Ratio Staffing. The ANA has opted to support the *nurse staffing committee* as the approach to ensure safe staffing. For the last decade, the ANA has advocated for a Registered Nurse Safe Staffing Act. The legislation is based on the ANA Safe Staffing Principles (Box 13.2) and considers the following:

- RN educational preparation, professional certification, and level of clinical experience
- The number and capacity of available healthcare personnel
- Geography of the unit
- Available technology
- Intensity, complexity, and stability of patients (Avalere Health LLC, 2015)

Although the national legislation has yet to be passed, some states have passed legislation designed to require the creation of unit-specific staffing plans and related policies and procedures (CT, IL, NV, OH, OR, TX, WA). In addition, Minnesota requires a Chief Nursing Officer or designee to develop a core staffing plan with input from others. Five states (IL, NJ, NY, RI, and VT) require some type of disclosure and/or reporting of staffing plans (Avalere Health LLC, 2015).

In addition to state regulations, other groups such as accrediting bodies and professional organizations have proposed guidelines for safe standards. For example, The Joint Commission (TJC) requires that adequate nurse staffing be present. TJC works to support performance improvement in healthcare organizations through establishing standards and survey accreditation processes. An institution must provide an adequate number and mix of staff consistent with the hospital's

---

BOX 13.2 **Four Key Points for Staffing**	
1. Patient need	4. Staffing guidelines
2. RN nurse experience	For more specific information, see https://www.nursingworld.org/~4af4f2/globalassets/docs/ana/ethics/principles-of-nurse–staffing–2nd-edition.pdf.
3. Practice environment: ranging from supervisory support to continuing education	

staffing plan to meet the care, treatment, and service needs of the patients. TJC is not prescriptive as to what constitutes "adequate" staffing. However, in response to increasing public concerns about patient care safety and quality, TJC correlates an organization's clinical outcome data with its staffing patterns to determine the effectiveness of the overall staffing plan.

During the TJC accreditation process, the surveyor reviews the staffing plans developed by the nurse manager for any obvious staffing deficiencies— for example, a shift or series of shifts in which the unit staffing plan was not met. The surveyor also interviews direct care nurses outside of the presence of nurse managers to inquire about their perceptions of the units' staffing adequacy. Surveyors may review the staffing effectiveness data for that unit as it compares with any variations from the staffing plan to identify quality-of-care concerns. Nurse managers are well advised to prepare a balanced staffing plan that supports a unit's unique patient care needs and the scrutiny of the TJC survey process. They also should post this staffing plan and the compliance reports for staff to see on a routine basis. In some states, this posting is required.

Organizational policies and clear expectations communicated to staff are essential to manage high and low volume as well as changes in acuity. Proposed personnel budgets and staffing plans that cannot flex up or down when patient acuity or volumes change put the nurse manager in a position in which patient safety may not be maintained and financial obligations cannot be met. In addition, mechanisms must be in place and internally publicized to allow staff to ask for additional help as needed. Patient, staff, and physician satisfaction; service and care improvement; and patient safety improvement are all outcomes of a solid staffing plan. Nurse managers are obligated to consider these variables when preparing the personnel budget.

National Database of Nursing Quality Indicators

An important component in evaluating the effectiveness of staffing is having a process and a structure to ensure that the measurement of outcomes is similar enough so that results can be compared across studies. The National Database of Nursing Quality Indicators (NDNQI) provides an opportunity to monitor staffing effectiveness in a specific nursing service or unit. The

NDNQI, a program developed by the ANA and now operated by the Press Ganey Company, provides a benchmarking report comparing "like" participating organizations and units around the country. This database provides quarterly and annual reporting of structure, process, and outcome indicators to evaluate "nursing-sensitive" measures at the unit level. The NDNQI database was built on the 1994 ANA Patient Safety and Quality Initiative. This initiative involved a series of pilot studies across the United States to identify nurse-sensitive indicators to use in evaluating patient care quality.

The NDNQI is a comprehensive, national nursing database that provides hospitals with nursing unit level comparison on 18 quality indicators that can be used in quality improvement plans to prevent adverse events and improve patient outcomes, such as patient mortality. More than 2000 US hospitals, including 95% of Magnet® recognized facilities (see Chapter 12 for more information on Magnet® status), participate in the NDNQI program to measure nursing quality, improve nurse satisfaction, strengthen the nursing work environment, assess staffing levels, and improve reimbursement under current pay-for-performance policies. Nursing-sensitive structure, process, and outcomes measures monitor relationships between quality indicators and outcomes. Hospitals can benchmark (or compare) their own data against other similar hospitals and participate in the ongoing research on **nurse-sensitive data**. Box 13.3 outlines the nurse-sensitive indicators included in the NDNQI project. The comparison of like-units is very important, because patient acuity and activity, patient care goals, clinical tasks, role expectation, team relations, and social milieu vary by unit and affect the patient outcomes. The measures included in the NDNQI database can be important in making staffing decisions when the accumulated evidence underlying these measures are included. Box 13.4 lists other indictors of staffing effectiveness.

EVALUATION OF EFFECTIVE STAFFING

The most important outcome of effective staffing is the prevention of mortality. The Optimal Nurse Staffing to Improve Quality of Care and Patient Outcomes White Paper (Avalere Health LLC, 2015) summarizes evidence that supports the principle that an increase in nurse–patient ratio leads to a decrease in hospital mortality in ICU, postsurgical, and nonsurgical settings.

BOX 13.3   Nurse-Sensitive Indicators

- Nursing hours per patient day
  - Registered nurses
  - Licensed vocational/practical nurses
  - Unlicensed assistive personnel
- Patient falls, with and without injury
  - Injury level
- Pediatric pain assessment, intervention, reassessment (AIR) cycle
- Pediatric peripheral intravenous infiltration rate
- Pressure ulcers prevalence
  - Hospital acquired
  - Unit acquired
  - Community acquired
- Psychiatric physical/sexual assault rate
- Restraint prevalence
- RN education/certification

- RN satisfaction survey options
  - Job satisfaction scales
  - Job satisfaction scales–short form
  - Practice Environment Scale (PES)
- Skill mix: percent of total nursing hours supplied by agency staff
  - RNs
  - LVN/LPN
- Voluntary nurse turnover
- Nurse vacancy rate
- Healthcare-associated infection
  - Urinary catheter–associated urinary tract infection (UTI)
  - Central line catheter–associated bloodstream infection (CABSI)
  - Ventilator-associated pneumonia (VAP)

LPN, Licensed practical nurse; *LVN,* licensed vocational nurse; *RN,* registered nurse.
Data from National Database of Nursing Quality Indicators (NDNQI): http://www.nursingquality.org/About-NDNQI.

BOX 13.4   Additional Indicators of Staffing Effectiveness

Clinical or Service Indicators	Human Resource Indicators
- Family complaints - Patient complaints - Adverse drug events - Injuries to patients - Postoperative infections - Upper gastrointestinal bleeding - Shock/cardiac arrest - Length of stay	- Overtime - Staff vacancy rate - Staff turnover rate - Understaffing compared with the hospital's staffing plan - Nursing care hours per patient day - Staff injuries on the job - On-call or per diem use - Sick time

---

These studies describe a significant association between mortality and an understaffed shift. In addition, the report identifies three studies that find a positive nurse work environment is associated with a reduction in patient mortality (Avalere Health LLC, 2015).

Hospital readmissions can also be indicative of poor quality care. The Optimal Nurse Staffing to Improve Quality of Care and Patient Outcomes White Paper (Avalere Health LLC, 2015) reviewed relevant research related to nursing staffing and hospital readmissions. The following two key points were highlighted:

- Inadequate staffing was linked to higher rates of readmission.
- Improvement in nursing staffing and nurse work environment can contribute to the prevention of avoidable and costly readmission. The cost of increasing nursing hours could be offset by cost savings from a decrease in unavoidable readmissions (Avalere Health LLC, 2015).

Hospital-Acquired Conditions

The Optimal Nurse Staffing to Improve Quality of Care and Patient Outcomes White Paper (Avalere Health LLC, 2015) defines hospital-acquired conditions (also known as *serious reportable events* and *Never Events*) as preventable events that are, in large measure, a result of failure to follow safety guidelines. This document summarizes evidence that supports nursing's role in the prevention of hospital-acquired conditions, as a result of nurse surveillance. The pertinent evidence is as follows:

Higher RN staffing levels have been shown to do the following (Avalere Health LLC, 2015):

- Reduce patient length of stay
- Decrease avoidable hospital-acquired conditions (HACs)
  - Falls
  - Pressure ulcers
- Decrease odds of patients experiencing the following:
  - Cardiac arrest in the ICU
  - Pneumonia during hospitalization
  - Unplanned extubations
  - Respiratory failure
- Have a positive association between nurse–patient ratios and nurse burnout
- Have a positive association between nurse burnout and the following:
  - Hospital-acquired infections, such as urinary tract infections (UTIs) and surgical site infection
  - Magnet® hospitals have lower rates of patient falls versus non-Magnet® hospitals

Missed Care

The outcome of inadequate staffing may also be missed care. *Missed care* refers to nursing care that is delayed, started but unfinished, or not completed at all. According to the AHRQ, missed care may include the following:

- Delayed or omitted medications or treatments
- Complications such as atelectasis, pressure ulcers, falls, ventilator-associated pneumonia, or other nosocomial infection
- Increased length of stay
- Decreased patient satisfaction

To explore the question of "to what extent are errors of omission (missed or unfinished care) affecting nursing care?" two groups of researchers have developed surveys for direct care nurses to report care that was missed or unfinished during a designated work period. The focus of the surveys is important because they provide the framework for direct care providers to evaluate the factors that influence missed or unfinished care. These surveys are identified in Table 13.1.

In a systematic review of 42 studies sponsored by AHRQ, 55% to 98% of nurse respondents reported missing one or more items of required care during the time of assessment. The activities most frequently missed were those related to emotional and psycho-

logical needs, rather than those related to physiologic needs (however, findings vary depending on the measurement approach). For example, one measurement approach found that ambulation, turning, and mouth care were among the most frequently missed aspects of care. Another approach found surveillance activities were most frequently missed. The most consistent predictors of missed nursing care were staffing levels, the work environment, and teamwork. An example of the research leading to such conclusions can be found in the Research Perspective. Conversely it appears that units with more robust staffing seem to have lower levels of missed care. Although strong evidence is lacking regarding strategies for prevention of missed care, conclusions from this review include the following:

- Missed care is primarily a problem of time pressure and competing demands.
- Organizational and unit culture influences missed nursing care. The organization of nursing work and the support structures may contribute to preventing missed care (AHRQ, 2018).

TABLE 13.1 Surveys Used to Identify Missed or Unfinished Care

Survey	Author	Reference
MISSCARES Survey	Beatrice Kalisch	Kalisch, B. J., & William, R. A. (2009). Development and psychometric testing of a tool to measure missed nursing care. *Journal of Nursing Administration, 39*(5), 211-219.
Perceived Implicit Rationing of Nursing Care (PIRNCA)	Terry Jones	Jones, T. (2014). Validation of the perceived implicit rationing of nursing care (PIRNCA). *Nursing Forum, 49*(29), 77-87.

RESEARCH PERSPECTIVE

Resource: Dabney, B., & Kalisch, B. (2015). Nursing staffing levels and patient-reported missed nursing care. *Journal of Nursing Care Quality, 30*(4), 306-312.

A cross-sectional study of patient reports of missed nursing care was used to conduct a secondary analysis of the relationship between patient reports of missed care and level of nurse staffing. A total of 729 patients on 20 units in two hospitals made up the sample. Patients were asked to respond to the MISSCARE Survey-Patient, which is designed to elicit patient reports of the extent to which nursing care was or was not provided. The analysis found that the timeliness of nursing care was correlated to and predicted by registered nurse (RN) skill mix (defined by the proportion of nursing care hours provided by RNs.) Higher staffing levels of RNs resulted in patient reports of more rapid responses to their needs. These reports were correlated with less missed timeliness. Other nurse staffing variables (nursing hours per patient days and RN hours per patient days) were also correlated to the timeliness of nursing care. However, these variables were not associated with the communication and basic care scales in the survey. These findings are in contrast to previous studies of missed nursing care that show a more consistent relationship between staffing levels and missed care.

Implications for Practice

The findings of this study, which seems to support other research that found higher staffing levels of RNs led to more rapid responses to needs and less missed timeliness, can support the nurse manager's request for sufficient RNs. The conflicting finding that the higher level of RNs does not positively influence appropriate communication, and provision of basic care must be validated in other studies. Nurse managers must continue to evaluate the research in this area to ensure that these patient needs are met.

FACTORS IN STAFFING THAT INFLUENCE PATIENT OUTCOMES

Numerous factors influence staffing, which in turn affects outcomes of the care provided by direct care nurses. Nurse characteristics may include age and education, both the degree held and whether the initial nursing education was in the United States or in a foreign country. The experience of individual nurses, as well as the extent to which the nurse works overtime, or works for a supplemental (agency or contract) agency rather than the clinical setting, may also make a difference in the outcomes. Even the use of nurses from the employer's own float pool may influence patient outcomes.

Education

In a landmark study in 2003, Aiken, Clarke, Cheung, Sloane, and Silber examined whether the proportion of hospital RNs educated at the baccalaureate level or higher was associated with risk-adjusted 30-day mortality and failure to rescue. Using Pennsylvania nurse survey and patient discharge data from 1999 and 2006, the researchers found that a 10-point increase in the percentage of nurses holding a baccalaureate degree in nursing within a hospital was associated with an average reduction of 2.12 deaths for every 1000 patients; and for a subset of patients with complications, they found an average reduction of 7.47 deaths per 1000 patients. They estimated that if all 134 hospitals in the study had increased the percentage of their nurses with baccalaureate degrees by 10 points during the study's time period, some 500 deaths among general, orthopedic, and vascular surgery patients might have been prevented. The findings provide support for efforts to increase the production and employment of baccalaureate nurses.

In 2011, the Institute of Medicine (IOM) (now the National Academies of Medicine), in partnership with the Robert Wood Johnson Foundation, made significant recommendations regarding the future of nursing. One of the recommendations of this study was to increase the proportion of nurses with a baccalaureate degree to 80% by 2020. In making this recommendation, the IOM noted that the level of education required for entry into nursing has been widely debated for more than 40 years. The *Future of Nursing* report recognizes that no conclusive evidence of a causal relationship between the academic degree obtained by RNs and patient outcomes exists despite the groundbreaking work of Aiken et al. (2003). However, the report suggested that an all-BSN workforce would provide a more uniform foundation for the "reconceptualized roles" of nursing in the future. Although a BSN education is not a panacea for all that is to be expected, it does, according to the report, "introduce students to a wider range of competencies in such areas as health policy and health care financing, leadership, quality improvement and systems thinking" (pp. 168-169). Other nurse characteristics that might influence outcomes include "(1) level of clinical experience (i.e., novice to expert), (2) experience with the population services, (3) competency with technology and clinical interventions, (4) language capabilities and cultural competency, and (5) organizational experience" (ANA, 2012).

Overtime

The number of hours per nursing shift a nurse works plays an important role in patient safety, job performance, and satisfaction because of the fatigue that results for most who work more than 40 hours per week. In 2012 Stimpfel, Sloane, and Aiken surveyed nurses in four states and found that more than 80% of the nurses were satisfied with scheduling practices at their hospital, despite the fact that the majority worked 12-hour shifts. However, as the proportion of hospital nurses working shifts of more than 13 hours increased, patients' dissatisfaction with care increased. Furthermore, nurses working shifts of 10 hours or longer were up to 2.5 times more likely than nurses working shorter shifts to experience burnout and job dissatisfaction and expressed an intent to leave the job. Extended shifts that undermine nurses' well-being may result in expensive job turnover and can negatively affect patient care. In 2014 Bae and Fabry completed a systematic review of literature regarding nursing fatigue by evaluating the relationships between nurse work, hours and overtime, and patient outcomes. This review found that there was a strong relationship between working long hours and adverse outcomes. Despite this conclusion, the authors suggested that more evidence around the impact of nurses' work hours on a variety of outcomes is needed.

In 2014, the ANA published the White Paper, "Addressing Nurse Fatigue to Promote Safety and Health: Joint Responsibilities of Registered Nurses and Employers to Reduce Risks." This publication articulates the ANA's position regarding the joint responsibilities of registered nurses and their employers to reduce the risk of nurse fatigue to create and sustain a culture of safety, a healthy work environment, and a work–life balance. Both the nurse and the employer have an ethical responsibility to carefully consider the need for adequate rest and sleep before accepting work assignments.

The specific ANA recommendations included the following:

Employers should do the following (Brown, 2014):

- Involve nurses in designing work schedules that implement a "regular and predictable schedule that allows nurses to plan."
- Stop using mandatory overtime.
- Encourage "frequent, uninterrupted rest breaks during work shifts."
- Adopt official policies that give RNs the "right to accept or reject a work assignment. Policies should indicate that there will be no retaliation or negative consequences for rejecting the assignment."
- Encourage nurses to be proactive about managing their health and rest.

Nurses should do the following:

- Work no more than 40 hours in a 7-day period and limit work shifts to 12 hours in a 24-hour period, including on-call hours worked.

The type of overtime that is required may influence the outcomes. *Requiring* staff to stay on duty after their shift ends to fill staffing vacancies is called mandatory overtime. Mandatory overtime has become a major negotiating point for nurses in unionized settings, and some state nurses associations that use workplace advocacy strategies to improve the work environment in their states have developed legislation that prohibits mandatory overtime. The ANA and other nursing organizations oppose mandatory overtime, because it is seen as a risk to both patients and nurses.

In contrast, *requesting* staff to stay on duty after their shift ends to fill staffing vacancies is called overtime. This differs from mandatory overtime because staff experience no employment consequences when they work overtime. In addition, in a given week, nurses may work in more than one employment setting as a means of increasing their income. Although this practice is an individual decision, tired and overworked nurses are more likely to have compromised decision-making abilities and technical skills because of fatigue. As part of the solution to these negative consequences, ANA recommends legislation to limit the number of hours nurses are *required* to work. A number of states have some legislative restrictions on the use of mandatory overtime for nurses (ANA, 2012). However, these regulations do not address the potential negative consequences from voluntary overtime. Individual nurses must consider their responsibilities for patient safety when voluntarily working overtime.

EXERCISE 13.2 Review a healthcare organization's policies on overtime. Is mandatory overtime covered in the policy? If so, the consequences for failing to work mandatory overtime when requested to do so by a supervisor should be outlined in the policy. How would you respond to a nurse manager who required you to stay on the job after your shift was over? Develop a list of questions you might ask on a job interview relating to use of overtime in the organization. What does the state board of nursing in your state allow regarding mandatory overtime? As a nurse manager, how would you respond to a staffing shortage without mandatory overtime as an option? Develop a list of strategies for eliminating mandatory overtime, if such exists.

SUPPLEMENTAL (AGENCY OR CONTRACT) STAFF AND FLOAT POOLS

Many nurses choose to work for staffing agencies. They may be hired by a nursing unit as an independent contractor for a shift, a week, or longer. Advantages of working for an agency are higher hourly rates of pay, diversity in work assignments, exposure to a variety of work teams, and the ability to travel. Organizations may use supplemental staff to fill temporary staff vacancies. Despite the response to an unexpected vacancy, nurse managers must consider the potential negative aspects of depending on supplemental staff to meet the unit's staffing plan. Patients should be unable to distinguish short-term, supplemental staff from unit staff. In addition, the ability to provide that level of orientation to supplemental agency or contract staff is often difficult. Another strategy that may be used to deal with unanticipated staff vacancies involves "floating" nurses from one clinical unit to another to fill the vacancy. In practice, the use of float nurses may be effective if the nurses are deployed from a centralized flexible staffing pool and they have the competencies to work on the unit to which they are assigned. Nurses willing to work as float nurses are generally experienced nurses who maintain a broad range of clinical

competencies. They often receive added compensation for their willingness to be flexible and to float to a variety of units on short notice.

When an organization does not have the flexibility of a staffing pool, the organization may expect nurses to float across clinical units to fill vacancies. To ensure patient safety and nurse satisfaction, the organization must develop a policy regarding the reassignment of the staff to clinically similar units. If direct care nurses are asked to be reassigned to an area outside of their sphere of clinical competence, they should be asked to support only basic care needs and not assume a complete and independent assignment. This practice should be used only on an emergency basis or with the nurse's agreement, because being required to float is often a "dissatisfier" for nurses and potentially a concern for patient safety.

ORGANIZATIONAL FACTORS THAT AFFECT STAFFING PLANS

Organizational factors include issues such as types of clinical units and the duration of the shift nurses work, as well as the extent to which shifts are rotated. These factors are typically addressed in the structure and philosophy of the nursing service department, organizational staffing policies, organizational supports, and services offered.

Structure and Philosophy of the Nursing Services Department

A nursing philosophy statement outlines the vision, values, and beliefs about the practice of nursing and the provision of patient care within the organization. The philosophy statement is used to guide the practice of nursing in the various nursing units on a daily basis. Nurse managers must propose a staffing plan and a personnel budget that allow consistency between the written philosophy statement and the observable practice of nursing on their units. Nurses feel demoralized when they cannot comply with their nursing philosophy statement or professional values because of problems associated with consistently inadequate staffing. The philosophy statement also guides the establishment of the overall structure of the nursing service department and the staffing models that are used within the organization. The staffing model adopted by the organization plays a major role in determining the mix of professional and assistive staff needed to provide patient care.

Organizational Support Systems

A critical variable that affects the development of the nursing personnel budget is the presence, or absence, of organizational systems that support the nurse in providing care. If the organization has recognized the need to keep the professional nurse at the bedside, support systems to allow that to happen will be evident. Examples of support systems that enhance the nurse's ability to remain on the unit and provide direct care to patients include transporter services, clerical support services, and hospitality services.

However, professional nurses often work in organizations that require them to function in the role of a multipurpose worker, particularly in acute or long-term care. Because nurses in these settings are generally scheduled to work 24 hours a day, 7 days a week, they may be required to provide services for other professionals who provide more limited hours of care to patients. Competent or knowledgeable nurse managers identify what costs are being incurred in the unit as a result of the absence of adequate organizational support systems and develop strategies to put those systems into place or justify the budget accordingly.

Services Offered

When developing a staffing budget, nurse managers must consider the services offered on the unit, as well as organizational plans to provide new or expanded clinical services. For example, a manager of an inpatient surgical unit must consider the potential effect of offering a new surgical procedure to the community. What projections have been made for this market? What is the expected length of stay for patients undergoing this new procedure? What are the national standards for care for this type of patient? A nurse manager will use this information to project added staff to manage these changes in service. Conversely, nurse managers must also be aware of any organizational plans to delete an existing service that their unit supports. For example, if a nurse manager in a home care setting knows that reimbursement for a certain procedure in the

home has declined to the point that this service must be discontinued, allowances for fewer required staffing resources in the coming year must be made.

DEVELOPING A STAFFING BUDGET

Units of service (UOS) are productivity targets, such as nursing HPPD or hours per visit for emergency departments. The UOS multiplied by the volume for a clinical area determines the number of staff needed in a given period. The formula can be adjusted for total paid staff or just for those required for the delivery of direct patient care.

To develop an adequate personnel budget, the amount of work performed by a nursing unit, or cost center, is referred to as its workload. Workload is measured in terms of the UOS defined by the cost center. Nurse managers must understand the nature of the work in their area of responsibility to define the units of service that will be used as their workload statistic and to forecast, or project, the volume of work that will be performed by their cost center during the upcoming year.

Calculation of Full-Time Equivalents

Nurse managers use the unit's forecasted workload to calculate the number of full-time equivalents (FTEs) that will be needed to construct the unit's overall staffing plan. The distinction between an employee in a position and an FTE is important. Chapter 12 describes FTEs and how they are calculated. To achieve a balanced staffing plan, nurse managers must determine the correct combination of full-time and part-time positions that will be needed. Nurse managers must also consider the effect of productive and nonproductive hours when projecting the FTE needs of the unit. Productive time is the paid hours that are actually worked on the unit. Productive hours can be further defined as *direct* or *indirect*. Direct care hours are used to pay for the care of patients. Indirect care hours are used to pay for other required unit activities, such as staff meetings or, in some instances, continuing education attendance. Swiger and Patrician (2016) looked at nursing workload from a concept analysis viewpoint. As the Literature Perspective identifies, workload is a complex idea that requires considerable thought at the organizational and unit level.

LITERATURE PERSPECTIVE

Resource: Swiger, P., & Patrician, P. (2016). Nursing workload in the acute-care setting: A concept analysis of nursing workload. *Nursing Outlook, 64*(3), 244-254.

This article provides a concept analysis of the nursing workforce to understand the complexity of the nurse's workload. Exemplars of nursing work are categorized as direct nursing care, indirect nursing care, and non–patient care work. This analysis provides information regarding factors that provide barriers to the workflow, efficacy, and efficiency of nursing practice.

Direct care is considered physiologic and psychological treatments performed during direct interaction with the patient. Indirect care may include all activities performed on behalf of the patient but not in direct interaction with the patient. This includes management of the unit and interprofessional collaboration. The analysis points out that there are also factors external to the nurse that affect the workload, including patient turnover rate or work interruptions. Complexity compression (the squeeze of additional responsibilities into a work day while still attempting to meet all nursing responsibilities in a shortened amount of available time) is also a barrier. This compression, often called "nursing the organization" rather than nursing the patient, is seen as particularly significant to effective care.

Implications for Practice

This concept analysis provides important information for the nurse manager to use to overcome barriers to good care by the nursing staff. The analysis finds that 75% of the factors that influence nondirect care workload were identified as hospital and unit characteristics. The authors note that other than "poor individual personal work methods," very few factors are within the direct caregivers' control. As a result, requiring the direct care nurse to solve the problems that make their work difficult is not productive. The authors suggest that more accurate assessments of the external components of the nursing workload should be identified as a means of overcoming the barriers nurses face.

The recognition that much of the turbulence of the nurses' work environment is out of the direct care nurses' control is an important principle for nurse managers to use to support direct care nurses. The nurse manager must analyze barriers to care in his or her unit and develop strategies to minimize them so nurses can "nurse patients." The paper provides an example of such a strategy: the development of transportation teams in a hospital to prevent the nursing staff from spending time "hunting" for wheelchairs.

Benefit time (see Chapter 12) includes those hours of benefit time that are paid to an employee for vacation, holiday, personal, or sick time and, in some organizations, for an employee attending orientation or continuing education activities. In most practice settings, nurses must be replaced when they are off duty and accessing their paid benefit time off. Nurse managers must be aware of the average benefit hours required for their unit, or they will understate their FTE needs. This requires nurse managers to consider carefully how to allocate their budgeted FTEs into full-time and part-time positions to meet the staffing requirements for the unit when a portion of the staff is taking paid time off. In addition, looking at the number of employees being paid for any specific day may not reflect the number actually providing care.

So, the nurse manager's role must include competencies in finances, information technology, and automation of staffing and scheduling programs. If healthcare organizations follow the approach of some businesses to increase jobs by creating more part-time positions,

major implications for staffing scheduling will need to be considered.

> **EXERCISE 13.3** Select a hospital-based department and determine the hours of operation. Assess the master scheduling plan and determine how many RNs are needed to ensure that each shift has one RN present. Assuming that a 36-hour work week (three 12-hour shifts) will equal one FTE, convert the required number of registered nurse positions to FTEs. Complete the exercise assuming a 40-hour work week (five 8-hour shifts) and compare the FTE variance.

Distribution of Full-Time Equivalents

Nurse managers must consider a number of variables when they begin the process of distributing FTEs into the unit staffing plan. The staffing plan, which is based on the unit's approved personnel budget *and* the projected staffing needs to ensure patient safety, as previously discussed, serves as a guide for creating the unit's schedules for the upcoming year. Variables that must be considered by managers when creating master staffing plans include the following:

1. The hours of operation of the unit
2. The basic shift length for the unit
3. Known activity patterns for the unit at various times of the day
4. Shift rotation requirements
5. Weekend requirements
6. Personal and professional requirements and requests for time off (e.g., educational schedule, meetings for professional development, opportunities for mentoring and support for models of shared governance as a means of involving staff in the operation of the nursing service)

Each of these variables interrelates with the others, so few "absolutes" are possible. For example, initially one might think that a 24/7 unit might require more staff than a 7 AM to 6 PM area. If the 24/7 unit, however, is providing basic care all day and few activities at night (e.g., a long-term care facility), fewer staff might be needed than for the 7 AM to 6 PM area than if that were, for example, a day surgery unit.

The master staffing plan must consider the distribution of fixed FTEs in the plan. Fixed FTEs are held by those employees who will be scheduled to work, no matter what the volume of activity. These employees generally hold an exempt or salaried position, meaning their compensation does not depend on the unit's workload. Examples of employees who typically hold a fixed FTE include the nurse manager, the clinical nurse specialist, and the education staff.

The manager then distributes the variable FTEs into the staffing plan. Variable FTEs are held by those employees who are scheduled to work based on the workload of the unit. These employees are considered nonexempt or hourly wage employees, meaning their compensation depends on the actual number of hours worked in a given pay period. Examples of employees who typically hold a variable FTE position include direct care nurses, clerical staff, and other ancillary support staff assigned to the unit. Some variable FTEs are those workers who are salaried rather than paid by the hour. For example, a nurse who provides education to the staff on various units may be classified in this manner.

SCHEDULING

Scheduling is a function of implementing the staffing plan by assigning unit personnel to work specific hours and specific days of the week. Scheduling depends on the historical census in a particular unit, as well as its anticipated volume. Schedules may be developed 1 to 3 months in advance, although scheduling for holiday times may be developed 6 to 12 months before the holiday. Although the development of a schedule is generally the responsibility of the nurse manager, direct care nurses can influence the schedule through the unit's shared governance or staffing committees (Menisk, 2014).

The nurse manager is often challenged to take the FTEs that are allotted through the personnel budget, distribute them appropriately, and create a master schedule for the unit that also meets each employee's personal and professional needs. Although completely satisfying each individual staff member is not always possible, a schedule can usually be created that is both fair and balanced from the employee's perspective, while still meeting the patient care needs. Creating a flexible schedule with a variety of scheduling options that leads to work schedule stability for each employee is one mechanism likely to retain staff that is within the control of nurse managers.

Constructing the Schedule

Mechanisms are typically in place within an organization for staff to use in requesting days off and to know when the final schedule will be posted. In addition, most organizations have written policies and procedures that must be followed by nurse managers to ensure compliance with state and federal labor laws relative to scheduling. These policies also aid managers in making scheduling decisions that will be perceived as fair and equitable by all employees. Schedules are usually constructed for a predetermined block of time based on organizational policy—for example, weekly, biweekly, or monthly, typically using the staffing matrix for each unit. The unit schedule may be prepared in a decentralized fashion by nurse managers or by unit staff through a self-scheduling method. In some organizations, centralized staffing coordinators may oversee all of the schedules prepared for the patient care units. Each method of schedule preparation has pros and cons.

Decentralized Scheduling

One decentralized method for preparing the schedule involves nurse managers developing the schedule in isolation from all other units. In this model, the nurse managers approve all schedule changes and actually spend time on a regular basis drafting the staff schedule, considering only the staffing needs of the unit. In other decentralized models, managers do the preliminary work on schedules and then submit them to a centralized staffing office for review and for the addition of any needed supplemental staff. The advantage of a decentralized model is that the accountability for submitting a schedule in alignment with the established staffing plan rests with managers. These individuals are ultimately the ones responsible for maintaining unit productivity in line with the personnel budget, so the incentive to manage the schedule tightly is strong. The negative aspect of this decentralized method relates to the inability of any individual nurse manager to know the "big picture" related to staffing across multiple patient care units. Requests for time off are approved in isolation from all other units, and a real potential with this model is that each manager will make a decision at the unit level that will be felt in aggregate as a "staffing shortage" across multiple units.

Staff Self-Scheduling

A self-scheduling process has the potential to promote staff autonomy and to increase staff accountability. In addition, team communication, problem-solving, and negotiating skills can be enhanced through the self-scheduling process. Successful self-scheduling is achieved when each individual's personal schedule is balanced with the unit's patient care needs. Self-scheduling has become more complicated in the wake of care delivery changes and the decentralization of many activities to the individual patient care units. The professional nursing staff cannot work in isolation of other care members when creating a schedule. Assessing the readiness of support staff to participate in this type of initiative is critical as resource utilization and cost containment continue to be major focal points of concern. Self-scheduling or flexible scheduling needs to be properly managed. Although personal needs of the staff are important to meet, the patient care needs on the unit are the paramount focus for building a schedule. Unit standards for a staffing plan are established, and then a negotiated schedule that results in meeting the needs of staff and patients is the expected and ultimate outcome.

Centralized Scheduling

One benefit to centralized scheduling is that the staffing coordinator is usually aware of the abilities, qualifications, and availability of supplemental personnel who may be needed to complete the schedule. In many organizations, the centralized staffing coordinator is also aware of each unit's personnel budget and any constraints it may impose on the schedule. On the other hand, a disadvantage to centralized staffing is the limited knowledge of the coordinator relative to changing patient acuity needs or other patient-related activities on the unit. Developing a mechanism for the centralized staffing coordinator to share unit-specific knowledge with the respective nurse manager can resolve this disadvantage satisfactorily.

Many organizations have invested in computer software designed to create optimal schedules based on the approved staffing plans for individual units. The centralized staffing coordinator maintains the integrity of the computerized databank for each unit; enters schedule variances daily; generates planning sheets, drafts, and final schedules; and runs any specialized productivity reports requested by nurse managers. Nurse managers review the initial schedule created by the computer, make necessary modifications, and approve the final schedule.

Variables Affecting Staffing Schedules

Nurse managers must consider many variables to create a fair and balanced schedule. Examples of variables nurse managers can anticipate and must consider as they prepare the unit's schedule are found in Box 13.5. Other unanticipated variables can complicate the best-prepared schedule. When faced with call-ins for illness, compassion leaves, jury duty, or an emergent need for a leave of absence (LOA), nurse managers must attempt to fill a shift vacancy on short notice. Requesting staff to add hours over their planned commitment, floating staff from another unit or securing someone from a staffing pool, contracting with agency nursing staff, and seeking overtime are examples of strategies that nurse managers may be compelled to use to ensure safe staffing of their units. However, as discussed, many potential negative consequences are associated with using these strategies.

BOX 13.5   Anticipated Scheduling Variables

- Hours of operation
- Shift rotations
- Weekend rotations
- Approved benefit time for the schedule period—for example, vacations and holidays
- Approved leaves of absence/short-term disability
- Approved seminar, orientation, and continuing education time
- Scheduled meetings for the schedule period
- Current filled positions and current staffing vacancies
- Number of part-time employees

BOX 13.6   Typical Unit Activities Productivity Report Indicators

- Volume statistic: number of units of service for the reporting period
- Capacity statistic: number of beds or blocks of time available for providing services
- Percentage of occupancy: number of occupied beds for the reporting period
- Average daily census (ADC): average number of patients cared for per day for the reporting period
- Average length of stay (ALOS): average number of days that a patient remained in an occupied bed

Formulas for Calculating Volume Statistics

Assume that a 20-bed medical-surgical unit *(capacity statistic)* accrued 566 patient days in June *(volume statistic)*. Ninety-eight of these patients were discharged during the month.

Average Daily Census on This Unit Is 18.9
Formula: patient days for a given time period divided by the number of days in the time period
1. 30 days in June
2. 566 patient days/30 days = ADC of 18.9

Percentage of Occupancy for June Is 95%:
Formula: daily patient census (rounded) divided by the number of beds in the unit
19 patients in a 20-bed unit =
19 patients/20 beds = 95% occupancy

Average Length of Stay for June Is 5.8
Formula: number of patient days divided by the number of discharges
566 patient days/98 patient discharges = 5.8 (rounded)

EXERCISE 13.4 Assume you are going on a job interview. Considering your personal preferred work schedule, what scheduling practices would be most satisfying to you and might lead you to accept employment with the organization? What scheduling practices might cause you to look elsewhere for a job? Develop a list of questions to ask your potential employer regarding scheduling practices in his or her organization.

EVALUATING UNIT STAFFING AND PRODUCTIVITY

Nurse managers are increasingly pressed to justify their staffing decisions to their staff, senior management, and accrediting agencies. The unit activity or production report, which provides a variety of measures of unit workload, can be helpful in such justification. In addition, a review of the extent to which the actual staffing over a specific period matches the staffing plan, particularly coupled with various outcomes over the same period, gives a picture of the productivity and effectiveness of the unit. Although the format of these reports may vary, the kinds of information typically available to nurse managers in an activity report are included in Box 13.6.

In the inpatient setting, the average daily census (ADC) is one measure considered by nurse managers to project the potential workload of the unit. The ADC is a simple measure of the average number of patients being cared for in the available beds on the unit trended over a specific period. The formula for calculating the ADC is found in Box 13.6. If a unit's ADC is trending upward, the nurse manager should propose additional personnel to manage this increase in patient volume. If the ADC is trending downward, the nurse manager should propose the need for fewer resources to manage this downward census trend. In the acute care setting, a unit's ADC can be extremely volatile based on the patterns of admissions, transfers, and discharges on the unit. In a long-term care setting, however, the unit's

ADC may be very stable over prolonged periods. Nurse managers may note census trends based on a particular shift, the day of the week, or the season of the year. The addition of new physicians, the creation of new programs or services, and many other variables may also affect a unit's average daily census. Admissions and discharges increase staffing demands. Nurse managers must maintain a strong grasp on these measures of workload to prepare an adequate staffing plan for their unit.

Another way of assessing a unit's activity level is to calculate the percentage of occupancy. The unit's occupancy rate can be calculated for a specific shift, on a daily basis, or as a monthly or annual statistic. The formula for calculating the percentage of occupancy is also found in Box 13.6. Nurse managers use the percentage of occupancy to develop the unit's staffing plan (Fig. 13.2). Optimal occupancy rates may vary by practice setting. In a long-term care facility, the organization would desire 100% occupancy rates. However, in an acute care facility, 85% occupancy rates would ensure the best potential for patient throughput.

Another measure of unit activity that may be considered by nurse managers is the average length of stay (ALOS), or the average number of days each patient stays in an occupied bed. As reimbursement dollars have decreased, so have lengths of stay. However, the cost of treating the patient has not decreased as dramatically, because patient acuity is greater. Essentially, hospitals need to provide more care in less time for fewer dollars with the same, if not better, outcomes. For this reason, as a unit's ALOS trends downward, the need for staffing resources may not change substantially, or it may actually climb. The formula for calculating the average length of stay is also found in Box 13.6.

The measures just mentioned provide the nurse manager with an understanding of the number of patients who have been admitted to the unit over a period of time. The nurse is then charged with matching the needs of these patients with the appropriate number of staff members. Managers have positions and subsequent budgeted nursing salary dollars in the personnel budget based on the estimated units of service that will be provided in the unit. If managers can provide more care to more patients while spending the same or fewer salary dollars, they have increased their unit productivity. Conversely, if the same or more salary dollars are spent to provide less care to fewer patients, managers have decreased their unit productivity.

Nursing productivity is a formula-driven calculation. UOS multiplied by the volume (patient days or emergency department visits) equals hours available to create direct productive staffing plans. Those hours multiplied by a nonproductive factor (e.g., 1.12) to account for paid time off equals the total hours available for the staffing plan. Getting a ratio of patients to RN is essential. This is then applied to the total hours available, and the support structure (nursing assistants or unit clerks) can be built accordingly. Patient type, scope of service, and acuity and/or classification of the patient are all factors correlated with patient outcomes that drive staffing decisions. Meeting these productivity standards is important to ensure the financial well-being of the organization. However, if the safety needs of the patients are put at risk to achieve this productivity level, the consequences are harmful to patients, staff, and the organization as a whole.

Calculating nursing productivity is challenging for nurse managers, because it is difficult to quantify the efficiency and effectiveness of individual nurses providing care to patients. Individual nurses can vary greatly in their critical-thinking abilities, their skill levels, and their ability to make timely and accurate decisions that affect patient outcomes.

Variance Between Projected and Actual Staff

Organizations can use labor cost or a straight FTE model for comparison of actual with projected staff.

Fig. 13.2 Calculating the percentage of occupancy is essential when developing a unit's staffing plan.

BOX 13.7 Analysis of Labor Costs Per Unit of Service

A manager of a cardiac telemetry unit proposes the following in the personnel budget. These are the unit's productivity targets:

Total patient days: 5840
- ADC = 16
- Staffing plan for ADC of 16:
  - Day shift: 3 RNs and 3 UNP (50% RN skill mix)
  - Evening shift: 3 RNs and 3 UNP (50% RN skill mix)
  - Night shift: 3 RNs and 1 UNP (75% RN skill mix)

Direct care labor costs are also projected by the manager based on the average RN and UNP salaries for this unit
- Target = $139.32 per patient, or $2229.12 per day

The manager actually staffs as follows:
- ADC = 16
- Actual staffing for ADC of 16:
  - Day shift: 4 RNs and 2 UNP (66% RN skill mix)
  - Evening shift: 4 RNs and 2 UNP (66% RN skill mix)
  - Night shift: 3 RNs (100% RN skill mix)
- Direct labor costs for this day = $145.44 per patient, or $2327.04 per day

The manager has incurred a variance:
- Exceed target by $6.12 per patient, or $97.92 for the day

ADC, Average daily census; *RN*, registered nurse; *UNP*, unlicensed nursing personnel.

Labor cost per unit of service is a simple measure that compares budgeted salary costs per budgeted volume of service (productivity target) with actual salary costs per actual volume of service (productivity performance). This measure requires managers to staff according to their staffing plan, because the plan reflects the approved personnel budget. Box 13.7 shows an analysis of labor costs per UOS. Typically, nurse managers must evaluate and explain changes in productivity resulting in a difference between the projected staffing plan and the actual schedule, using a **variance report.** If managers compare the two numbers and the actual productivity performance number is higher than the target, they have spent more money for care than they budgeted. A number of variables may cause the labor costs to be higher than anticipated, such as increased overtime, paying bonus pay for regular staff, using costly agency resources, or a higher-than-anticipated amount of indirect education or orientation time.

If managers compare the two numbers and the actual productivity performance number is lower than the target, they have spent less money for care than they budgeted. Managers must also explain this high degree of productivity. One variable that may cause the labor costs to be lower than anticipated is an increased nonprofessional skill mix or consistently understaffing their unit.

Having a productivity performance number that is either higher or lower than that planned does not represent effective management. Assuming that staffing plans were an accurate reflection of the conditions on the specific units, if managers compare the actual productivity performance with their productivity target and the two numbers match, the managers have probably managed effectively. However, given the dynamic nature of patient care, an ongoing evaluation of the conditions on the unit as well as the extent to which proposed staffing levels are reached or exceeded should be monitored on an ongoing basis. Variance reports provide an opportunity for such evaluation.

EXERCISE 13.5 Assume you are working in the charge nurse role. One of the staff assigned to work with you becomes ill and must go home suddenly, leaving his designated patient assignment to be assumed by someone else. As a charge nurse, what factors would you consider as you determine how to reassign this work to other nurses? If you were a co-worker on the shift, instead of the charge nurse, what effective follower behaviors might you demonstrate to support the charge nurse in this situation? Can you identify behaviors of co-workers that would complicate the staffing situation further?

Impact of Leadership on Productivity

Nurse managers must possess staffing and scheduling skills to prepare a staffing plan that balances organizational directives with unit needs for care and services. Nurse managers must spend time each month evaluating their unit's productivity performance. Yet it is also important that nurse managers improve unit productivity by spending more of their work time coaching and mentoring staff and providing them with clear information and direction related to meeting unit productivity goals. Nurse managers are the chief retention officers and need to perform their duties accordingly.

CONCLUSION

Staffing and scheduling are some of the greatest challenges for a nurse manager. When these functions are performed well, the resulting satisfaction of the unit staff contributes to positive patient outcomes. When they are not performed well, low morale and discontent can result. The manager has various data available to help in planning the staffing patterns for the unit. Success, however, depends on the unit staff and the manager working collaboratively and using effective negotiation strategies to meet the needs for care.

THE SOLUTION

A staff meeting was called to discuss the impact of the transition of a number of beds for surgical trauma intensive care unit (STICU) step-down patients on the inpatient general surgery unit. Information was given to all staff regarding the potential size of the step-down unit and the methods for staffing this unit. Staff members were assured that no jobs would be lost and that appropriate training would be provided to current staff to ensure their competence.

Six beds were determined to be the initial number of step-down beds to be incorporated into the surgical inpatient unit. Staff members were involved in the design of the space from the perspective of identifying which rooms were to be used and what in-room supplies and equipment would be necessary. Continuous pulse oximetry and bedside computers were among the top equipment needs identified.

A staffing plan was established for the step-down unit, and staff members on the general surgery unit were first to be offered the positions. The unit's staffing plan was filled with staff members from the general surgical unit, as well as a related unit. Educational plans were developed, and the STICU nursing staff members were open and welcoming when the new step-down staff rotated and partnered with the STICU staff in the critical care environment. The new step-down staff completed didactic education, and the same STICU nurses provided backup for them when the unit opened.

Continuous discussions were held with the medical staff involved through a champion who was identified within the department of general surgery. Talking points were distributed to the medical staff and the other hospital staff to keep everyone current with the progress. Interdisciplinary teams were developed around the care models and are now engaged in daily patient care conferences to monitor the progress of patients.

The unit has been open for 6 months and is a success. We have no vacant positions, critical care beds are more available, medical staff are pleased with the care delivered, patient satisfaction for this unit is very good, and the staff feel accomplished and proud of their contribution to the overall capacity challenge!

Would this be a suitable approach for you? Why?

Mary Ellen Bonczek, BSN, RN, MPA, NEA-BC

REFLECTIONS

The nurse manager's role in staffing and scheduling a nursing unit requires clinical, legal, regulatory, communication, negotiation, and financial competencies to ensure appropriate outcomes. In preparation for the nurse manager role, what skills will you need to develop to be successful? And because roles are fluid, what do you need to know to be effective as a follower?

THE EVIDENCE

Over several years, numerous studies have been conducted to evaluate the complexities of staffing in hospitals and how staffing affects outcomes. The message is clear that better outcomes are produced when a sufficient staffing level is present and when the staff holds a bachelor's or higher degree.

■ TIPS FOR STAFFING AND SCHEDULING

- Know state laws and voluntary accreditation (professional society and institutional) standards for staffing.
- Evaluate organizational policies for congruence with accreditation and state licensing expectations.
- Integrate ongoing research regarding the impact of various factors on patient outcomes into staffing plans.

- Identify current demands for staff and anticipate externally imposed changes such as services offered and availability of RNs and LPNs/LVNs.
- Value the various responses to short staffing from the manager, staff, and patient perspectives.
- Recognize the complexity of staffing issues and how they relate to staff satisfaction, community perception, budget, and accreditation standards.

REFERENCES

Agency for Healthcare Research and Quality. (2018) *Missed nursing care: Patient safety primer.* https://psnet.ahrq.gov/primers/primer/29/missed-nursing-care.

Aiken, L. H., Clarke, S. P., Cheung, R. B., Sloane, D. M., & Silber, J. H. (2003). Educational levels of hospital nurses and surgical patient mortality. *JAMA: The Journal of the American Medical Association, 290*(12), 1617–1623.

Aiken, L., Sloane, D., Cimiotti, J., Clarke, S., Flynn, L., Seago, J., et al. (2010). Implications of the California nurse staffing mandate for other states. *Health Services Research, 45*(4), 904–921. August.

Aiken, L., et al. (2012) Patient safety, satisfaction, and quality of hospital care: Cross sectional surveys of nurses and patients in 12 countries in Europe and the United States. *British Medical Journal* March 314:e1717.

American Nurses Association. (2012). *Principles for nurse staffing* (2nd ed.). Silver Spring, MD: The Association. https://www.nursingworld.org/~4af4f2/globalassets/docs/ana/ethics/principles-of-nurse–staffing–2nd-edition.pdf.

American Nurses Association. (2014). Addressing nurse fatigue to promote safety and health: Joint responsibilities of registered nurses and employers to reduce risks. https://www.nursingworld.org/~49de63/globalassets/practiceandpolicy/health-and-safety/nurse-fatigue-position-statement-final.pdf.

Avalere Health LLC. (2015). Optimal nurse staffing to improve quality of care and patient outcomes. *American Nurses Association.* September. http://www.nursingworld.org/DocumentVault/NursingPractice/Executive-Summary.pdf.

Backhaus, R., Verbeck, H., van Rossum, E., Capezuti, E., & Hamers, J. (2014). Nurse staffing: Impact on quality of care in nursing home: A systematic review of longitudinal studies. *Journal of American Directors Association, 15*(6), 383–393.

Bae, S. H., & Fabry, D. (2014). Effects of nurse overtime and long hours worked on nursing and patients outcomes. *Nursing Outlook, 62*(2), 138–156.

Bodenheimer, T., & Sinsky, C. (2014). From triple to quadruple aim: Care of the patient requires care of the provider. *Annals of Family Medicine, 12*(6), 573–576. https://doi.org/10.1370/afm.1713.

Brown, T. (2014). ANA releases new position statement on nurse fatigue: News & perspectives. *Medscape.* Thursday, June 8, 2017. http://www.medscape.com/viewarticle/835281.

Cho, S., Mark, B., Knafl, G., Chang, H., & Yoon, H. (2017). Relationships between nurse staffing and patients' experiences, and the mediating effects of missed nursing care. *Journal of Nursing Scholarship, 49*(3), 347–355.

Cook, A., Gaynor, M., Stephens, M., & Taylor, L. (2012). The effect of a hospital nurse staffing mandate on patient health outcomes: Evidence from California's minimum staffing regulations. *Journal of Health Economics, 31*, 340–348.

Dabney, B., & Kalisch, B. (2015). Nursing staffing levels and patient-reported missed nursing care. *Journal of Nursing Care Quality, 30*(4), 306–312.

Hamilton, P., & Campbell, M. (2011). Knowledge for re-forming nursing's future: Standpoint makes a difference. *Advances in Nursing Science, 34*(4), 280–296.

Institute of Medicine (IOM). (2011). *The future of nursing: Leading change, advancing health.* Washington, DC: The National Academies Press.

Jones, T. (2014). Validation of the perceived implicit rationing of nursing care (PIRNCA). *Nursing Forum, 49*(29), 77–79. April-June.

Kalisch, B. J., & Williams, R. A. (2009). Development and psychometric testing of a tool to measures missed nursing care. *Journal of Nursing Administration, 39*(5), 211–219.

Kane, R. L., Shamliyan, T., Mueller, C., Duval, S., & Wilt, T. (2007). *Nursing staffing and quality of patient care: Evidence report/technology assessment No. 151.* (Prepared by the Minnesota Evidence-based Practice Center under Contract No. 290-02-0009.) AHRQ Publication No. 07-E0005. Rockville, MD: Agency for Healthcare Research and Quality.

Koy, V., Yunibhand, J., Angsuroch, Y., & Fisher, M. (2015). Relationship between nursing care quality, nurse staffing, nurse job satisfaction, nurse practice environment and burnout: Literature review. *International Journal of Research in Medical Science, 3*(8), 1825–1831.

Mensik, J. (2014). What every nurse should know about staffing. *American Nurse Today, 9*(2). February. https://www.americannursetoday.com/what-every-nurse-should-know-about-staffing.

Spilsbury, K., Hewitt, C., Stirk, L., & Bowman, C. (2011). The relationship between nurse staffing and quality of care in nursing homes: A systematic review. *International Journal of Nursing Studies, 48*, 732–750.

Stimpfel, A., Sloane, D., & Aiken, L. (2012). The longer the shifts for hospital nurses, the higher the levels of burnout and patient dissatisfaction. *Health Affairs, 31*(11), 2501–2509.

Swiger, P., & Patrician, P. (2016). Nursing workload in the acute-care setting: A concept analysis of nursing workload. *Nursing Outlook, 64*(3), 244–254.

14

Workforce Engagement Through Collective Action and Governance

Crystal J. Wilkinson, Elizabeth H. Boyd

LEARNING OUTCOMES

- Explain the role of nurse empowerment and engagement in creating healthy work environments.
- Evaluate how key characteristics of selected collective action strategies apply in the workplace through shared governance, workplace advocacy, and collective bargaining.
- Evaluate how participation of direct care nurses in decision making relates to job satisfaction and improved patient outcomes.

KEY TERMS

accountability	collective bargaining	responsibility
at-will employee	empowerment	right to work
authority	engagement	shared governance
autonomy	governance	union
bullying	incivility	whistleblower
collective action	organizational justice	workplace advocacy

THE CHALLENGE

The Seton Healthcare Family is a system that includes five major medical centers, a large regional pediatric hospital, two community hospitals, two rural hospitals, one mental health hospital, multiple locations for outpatient medical services, and three primary care clinics for the uninsured and underinsured. Seton is the largest private employer in central Texas, with approximately 12,500 associates. Seton has a rich history of strong leadership that has kept us on the cutting edge of healthcare innovation and quality. As such, Seton was one of the first to implement nursing shared governance, which was instituted in 1996. The culture of shared decision making facilitated an environment where nurses were empowered, motivated, and engaged in taking ownership of decisions that impacted their nursing practice. Seton's nationally recognized shared governance model is composed of nursing colleagues from across sites and specialties to represent nursing and helped us to achieve our third Magnet® designation from the American Nurses Credentialing Center (ANCC) for four of our facilities and Pathway to Excellence designation for five additional sites. By way of shared governance, nurses have positively influenced and provided expert input into many strategies and decisions for clinical practice standards, quality improvement, professional development,

(*Continued*)

THE CHALLENGE—cont'd

and research. Over the almost 20 years since its inception, Seton has benefited from many positive changes in care delivery systems and patient outcomes.

The last few years have been a time of accelerated transformative change within the US healthcare system. Healthcare reform and quality improvement imperatives have caused many organizations to redefine their systems and structures that support the delivery of patient care. Responding to organizational cultural and structural shifts, Seton's executive nursing leaders recognized the need for creative thinking and enhanced interdisciplinary collaboration to drive efficient and patient-centered care. As the life cycle of our shared governance model had matured, participation was declining, and nurses shared concern that their voices were not as strong as they had historically been. The nursing leaders at all levels acknowledged the need to evaluate existing systems in support of greater professional practice accountability and to fully achieve the goal of maintaining nursing's control and ownership for decisions related to prac-

tice. A review of the literature indicated that destabilization of shared governance, especially over time, is to be expected and offers an opportunity for disruptive innovation. A comprehensive evaluation of our entire shared governance framework was needed, so we set out on a new journey to determine how to best modernize our structure to meet the challenges of the times and current needs of the nurses. A Shared Governance Modernization Steering Committee was formed to assess the current committee structures, identify opportunities for improvement, and guide the process for creating change.

What would you do if you were this nurse?

Laura Kidd
Network Nursing Practice, Seton Healthcare Family
Nancy Mastronardi
Manager, Nursing Practice, Seton Healthcare Family
Diana Sellers
Manager, Nursing Practice, Seton Healthcare Family

INTRODUCTION

With a looming nursing shortage and the need to provide high-quality, value-based care, hospitals have a vested interest in attracting and retaining well-educated and engaged nurses. As nurses go about their work, they encounter factors in their workplaces that often make it difficult to do their jobs or to feel safe and respected as professionals. Nurses' concerns about how care is provided and their commitment to patient advocacy can put them in direct conflict with those controlling the work environment. Nurses may also expect or demand a voice in decisions that affect nursing practice. Nurses have many choices of where they want to work but may not have adequate information or experience to assess the work environment or choose an organization with the best fit to help achieve their goals.

NURSES AS KNOWLEDGE WORKERS

Our healthcare system (or lack thereof) is becoming increasingly complex, and healthcare consumers and payers are demanding high-quality care and high performance in nurse-sensitive patient outcomes. In the landmark report, *The Future of Nursing: Leading*

Change, Advancing Health, the National Academy of Medicine (NAM) (formerly known as the Institute of Medicine [IOM]) (2011) called for 80% of US nurses to be prepared at the BSN level (currently 55%) by the year 2020. This recommendation reflects the expectation that nurses are knowledge workers. In his compelling work, Drucker (2011) defined *knowledge workers* as those with advanced formal education who are able to apply theoretical and analytical knowledge. Knowledge workers work with and generate information and new knowledge. As the knowledge content of nursing work increases, the practice of nursing is guided more by science than by procedure. Nurse knowledge workers play a direct, vital role in increasing performance in the organizations where they work. They do this by providing insight and solutions to complex care problems, collecting data, identifying care trends, and using their knowledge to improve care by providing critical input on decision making. Malloch and Porter-O'Grady (2017) suggested that shared governance is a reframing of nursing as knowledge work. The change from producing a physical product to providing a service requiring knowledge has many implications. In the past, employees in manufacturing were treated like interchangeable cogs: when a cog was broken, it was replaced. A large pool

---

BOX 14.1 **American Nurses Association Nurses' Bill of Rights**

The Bill of Rights is designed to delineate the corollary to statements of responsibilities. The latter can be found in numerous documents: state laws, rules and regulations, position descriptions, and professional standards. With responsibilities, certain rights need to be clear. The American Nurses Association identifies that nurses have certain rights that:

- Meet obligations to society and patients
- Meet professional and legal standards
- Allow for ethical practice
- Facilitate advocacy
- Support fair compensation
- Ensure safety
- Address employment conditions

---

of unskilled workers was available to step forward in the steel mill, the coal mine, and the shop floor. In health care, highly skilled nurses are not so easily replaced. With a continued nursing shortage forecasted, practice environments will need to compete to attract and retain highly qualified nurses.

PROFESSIONAL PRACTICE RESPONSIBILITY

Nurses have the right to practice in environments that allow them to act in accordance with professional standards and legally authorized scopes of practice. The nurse practice act of each state governs the practice of nursing and guides nurses and protects the public in performing their duties. Nurses are also guided by the American Nurses Association (ANA) Code of Ethics with Interpretive Statements (ANA, 2015a). The Code of Ethics speaks to the responsibility and accountability of nurses to be advocates for patients and their families, whether it is intervening on their behalf or working with healthcare organizations through decision-making processes. It also means participating in shaping healthcare policy at the institutional, state, or national level. To be able to meet the professional ethical obligations to society, nurses and others must protect the dignity and autonomy of nurses in the workplace. To protect the rights of nurses, the ANA Bill of Rights speaks to several concepts covered in this chapter. The key foci of these rights appear in Box 14.1. This document sets forth seven premises concerning workplace expectations and environments that nurses from across the United States recognize are necessary for sound professional nursing practice. ANA's Code of Ethics (2015a) serves to outline the

ethical obligations and duties of every individual who enters the nursing profession and is an expression of nursing's own understanding of its commitment to society. The ethical standards for the profession helps nurses determine whether their work environments support ethical practice.

EXERCISE 14.1 The ANA Code of Ethics Provision 6 (ANA, 2015a) states that "the nurse, through individual and collective action, establishes, maintains, and improves the moral environment of the work setting and the conditions of employment, conducive to quality health care."

How would you as an individual nurse demonstrate that you are meeting this provision?

If you assumed the role of a manager or a leader, how would you demonstrate meeting the provision?

WORKPLACE ADVOCACY, ENGAGEMENT, AND EMPOWERMENT

Workplace advocacy is an umbrella term that includes an array of activities and strategies undertaken to address the challenges faced by nurses in their practice settings. Healthy workplaces require active participation of all members of the work unit to create conditions where it is safe to speak up, where hazards can be addressed quickly, where incivility is addressed, and where diversity is supported. Workplace advocacy reflects a framework of mutuality, facilitation, protection, and coordination in which nurses control their own practice and is consistent with the goals of the nursing profession. Workplace advocacy activities and strategies focus on career development, employment opportunities, terms and conditions of employment, employment rights and protections, control of practice, labor-management relations, occupational health and safety, and employee assistance. The objective of workplace advocacy is to equip nurses to practice in a rapidly changing environment. Workplace advocacy must be practiced by both staff and leaders to be effective. For example, just as the manager needs an awareness of when a staff member is too tired to work, so too must the staff member acknowledge that condition and make the decision to decline additional work. This idea can be expanded to include a staff member having an awareness of when the leader is also too tired or stressed to be effective. Proactively addressing such issues improves the workplace and supports nurses, which also benefits patients.

Engagement in the workplace is defined as an employee's commitment to the organization's mission, vision, and values. Engagement contributes to the success of an organization while also enhancing an individual's sense of professional and personal satisfaction. Highly engaged nurses go above and beyond what is expected and tie their personal success to the organization's success (Strumwasser & Virkstis, 2015). Trust and autonomy are required for engagement in the workplace. Creating a supportive environment where trust is the core of the work takes effort on the part of all members of the team. Rather than worrying about "am I safe here," all can focus on improving their mutual work. Autonomy, the freedom to make independent decisions consistent within the scope of practice, is also necessary for engagement. When nurses share their individual decisions with each other, they help others move toward more expert practice either through acquiring new knowledge or through challenging the status quo. Autonomy encourages innovation, which may result in processes to improve patient care and reduce cost. To meet current demands in health care, frontline nurses must be engaged (Riley, Dearmon, Mestas, & Buckner, 2016). Engagement is accomplished by leader behaviors that encourage participative decision making, display confidence in employees, and promote autonomy (Riley et al., 2016). Successful engagement can be measured by better patient outcomes and satisfaction with the health care received as well as by improved nurse job satisfaction and better nurse retention. Engagement requires individual and group action.

> **EXERCISE 14.2** Investigate how your organization promotes nurse engagement.
> - How is engagement measured in this organization?
> - Do you believe the engagement strategies are effective?
> - What ideas do you have to improve nurse engagement?

Empowerment in the workplace is defined as sharing power and control through participation in decision making. Empowerment basically translates to supporting nurses and their voice in their own practice. Managers and administrators who empower nurses are promoting autonomy and creating an environment where employees feel safe to take calculated risks, which leads to greater ownership, better patient outcomes, and increased job satisfaction (Wong & Giallonardo, 2013; Dent & Tye, 2016). Nurses who feel empowered to make decisions and implement patient care strategies may perceive that their workplace is safer and more effective (Press Ganey, 2015; Press Gainey, 2016). Engagement and empowerment are linked concepts—you cannot have one without the other. Both promote improved patient outcomes and increased job satisfaction and create a positive work environment for nurses. The concept of ownership further enhances nurses' views of engagement and empowerment (Dent & Tye, 2016).

SHARED GOVERNANCE

Shared governance is an organizational strategy that supports nurses to have ownership, autonomy, and input in their professional practice (American Nurses Credentialing Center, 2014; Brody, Barnes, Ruble, & Sakowski, 2012; Crow & De Bourgh, 2017; Porter-O'Grady, 2009). It derives from a diverse theoretical perspective, as shown in the Theory Box. Since at least 2009, Tim Porter O'Grady, a leader in the development of shared governance models, has described shared governance as a professional practice model based on the principles of partnership, equity, accountability, and ownership (Porter O'Grady, 2009). Shared governance provides nurses an organizational framework to take on greater accountability for decisions that affect their practice. Shared governance provides a way to empower nurses to manage their professional practice. Shared governance positively affects nurse retention and job satisfaction by providing nurses an opportunity to get involved. Increasing involvement improves nurses' daily work, which improves patient outcomes (Kutney-Lee et al., 2015; Ma & Park, 2015; Murray, 2016). Shared governance provides a way for nurses to fulfill their role as the primary professional group that links all aspects of patient care to the organization's mission, vision, and values (Crow and DeBourgh, 2017). The Research Perspective on p. 243 identifies outcomes related to shared governance.

THEORY BOX

Shared Governance: Evolution of a Theory Applicable to Shared Governance

Nursing lacks a general definition of shared governance. No common understanding of the shared governance concept can be described by a specified theory with precepts and propositions. This has contributed to persistent barriers to progress toward increasing the scientific rigor related to shared governance research and building evidence-based knowledge through its systematic study. Joseph and Bogue are currently working to recommend for further testing. Their work is based on years of cumulative information and ideas from content experts who have created a large body of work to draw upon and is described here.

Key Contributors	Key Idea	Application to Practice
Human Resources Perspective McGregor, D. (1960). The human side of enterprise. *Reflections, 2*(1), 6-15. Herzberg, F. (1966). *Work and the Nature of Man.* Cleveland, OH: World.	Championed employees as the organization's most important asset, encouraging organizations to invest in employee motivation and growth.	Initiated the idea that organizations could benefit from employee autonomy, growth, and investment.
Management Perspective/ Structural Power Model Kanter, R. (1977). *Men and Women of the Corporation.* New York: Basic Books. Kanter, R. (1993). *Men and Women of the Corporation* (2nd ed.). New York: Basic Books. Laschinger, H. K., Finegan, J., Shamian, J., & Wilk, P. (2001). Impact of structural and psychological empowerment on job strain in nursing work settings: Expanding Kanter's model. *Journal of Nursing Administration, 31*(5), 260-272.	Provided definition of shared governance as empowerment.	Described the types of actions that express empowerment in practice such as ability of supervisors to give downward control, spreading of formal authority, decentralization, and distribution of decision-making power.
Quality Perspective Deming, W. E. (1986). *Out of crisis.* Cambridge, MA: Massachusetts Institute of Technology Center for Advancement Engineering Study.	Introduced concepts of quality management and propose that an organization's work environment, value, and quality could be improved by empowering the employee to be more productive by solving problems by emphasizing teamwork and leadership.	Created new forms of shared governance that were aligned with organizational quality improvement initiatives.

(Continued)

THEORY BOX — cont'd

Shared Governance: Evolution of a Theory Applicable to Shared Governance

Key Contributors	Key Idea	Application to Practice
Control of Nursing Practice Perspective Hess, R. G. (1989). Measuring nursing governance. *Nursing Research, 47*(1), 35-42.	Described shared governance as including the structure and processes by which organizational participants direct, control, and regulate the many goal-oriented efforts of other members.	Described an accountability-based governance system that shares power, control, and decision-making with the professional nursing staff.
Accountability for Practice Perspective Porter-O'Grady, T. (1995). [Letter to the editor]. *Journal of Nursing Administration, 25*(7/8), 8-9. Porter-O'Grady, T. (2001). Is shared governance still relevant? *Journal of Nursing Administration, 31*(10), 468-473.	Shared governance model where decisions are made at the point of service. Shared governance as a dynamic way of conceptualizing empowerment and building structures to support it.	Encouraged organizations to allow nurse to participate in decision making that affects the practice of nursing and in shaping the work environment where patient care occurs.
Ownership of Nursing Practice Perspective Kramer, M., & Schmalenberg, C. (1988). Magnet hospitals: Part I: Institutions of excellence. *Journal of Nursing Administration, Part II: 18*(1), 13-24; *Part II: 18*(2), 11-19. Kramer, M., & Schmalenberg, C. (2003). Magnet hospital nurses describe control over practice. *Western Journal of Nursing Research, 25*(4), 434-452. Laschinger, H. K., & Havens D. (1996). Staff nurse work empowerment and perceived control over nursing practice. *Journal of Nursing Administration, 26*(9), 27-35.	Professional control over nursing practice (CNP).	Defined CNP in Magnet® hospitals as input, including access to and exchange of information, views and judgments, and decision making on issues of importance (practices, standards, policies, equipment) that affect the nursing profession, the practice of nursing, and the quality of patient care.
Theoretical Perspective Joseph, M. L., & Bouge, R. J. (2016). A theory-based approach to nursing shared governance. *Nursing Outlook, 64*, 339-349.	Theory-based approach to nursing shared governance.	Working to create a theoretical foundation to support systematic study and implementation of shared governance.

At its core, shared governance is shared decision making. With the complexity of today's healthcare systems, shared governance provides a structure to decentralize decision making. To achieve decentralization, most shared governance structures include the establishment of councils that represent various services and departments from within the organization. This provides an avenue for nurses at the unit level to identify problems, develop solutions, and test for improvement (dos Santos et al., 2013; Ma & Park, 2015; Meyers & Costanzo, 2015). In a shared governance model, unit-based improvements can be disseminated and

RESEARCH PERSPECTIVE

Resource: Kutney-Lee, A., Germacke, H. Hatfield, L., Kelley, S. Maguire, P., Dierkes, A., Guidice, M. D. & Aiken, L. H. (2016). Nurse engagement in shared governance and patient and nurse outcomes. *Journal of Nursing Administration, 46*(11), 605-612.

The objective of this study was to examine differences in nurse engagement in shared governance across hospitals and determine the relationship between nurse engagement and patient outcomes. The authors used secondary analysis of linked cross-sectional data from three widely used data sources that provide information on nurse engagement, nurse job outcomes, nurses' perception of quality of care, patient satisfaction, and hospital characteristics. The sample included 20,674 registered nurses working in 425 nonfederal acute care hospitals.

The results indicate that hospitals that provide nurses with the greatest opportunity to be engaged in shared governance are more likely to provide better patient experiences, offer superior quality of care, and have more favorable nurse job outcomes compared with hospitals where nurses are not engaged in institutional decision-making. Magnet® hospitals demonstrated higher levels of nurse engagement than those that had not achieved this recognition.

Implication for Practice

Nurses working at the bedside hold invaluable knowledge of the needs of the hospital's population and can readily identify barriers to care and innovative solutions that improve care and outcomes. These insights are invaluable to hospital administrators and suggest there is a strong business case for including nurses in institutional decision making through shared governance. Nurses who are more engaged also have improved retention, higher job satisfaction, and lower reports of burnout. Shared governance is an attractive transformational leadership strategy based in evidence that can improve patient outcomes, provides an avenue to increased reimbursement, and offers cost savings through nurse job satisfaction and retention.

considered for spread to other units (Gerard, Owens, & Oliver, 2016). A reporting and data management structure is necessary to ensure good communication and demonstrate alignment of goals from the bedside to the boardroom. Implementing a shared governance practice model requires leadership and planning to support staff and demonstrate improved outcomes. Working in a shared governance structure improves the flow of information, stimulates innovation, and reinforces the importance of "us" as a total team.

Effective shared governance strategies include principles and mechanisms for conflict resolution. To have effective conflict resolution, leadership structures should engage nursing staff to provide decision support and input regarding changes in work design at the point of care to improve care delivery systems and work environments. This requires nurses to become adept at conflict resolution, communication, and negotiation to be adequately prepared to address issues that arise.

COLLECTIVE ACTION, COLLECTIVE BARGAINING, AND UNIONIZATION IN NURSING

Collective action is defined as activities that are undertaken by a group of people who have common interests. Minarik and Catramabone (1998) saw collective participation for nurses as having four main purposes: (1) promote the practice of professional nursing, (2) establish and maintain standards of care, (3) allocate resources effectively and efficiently, and (4) create satisfaction and support in the practice environment. When nurses work to achieve Magnet® status, it is the result of collective action. When patient care is delivered in hospitals 24 hours per day, it is the result of the collective action of shifts of nurses. When patients transfer from one specialty clinic to another without disruption of care, it is the result of collective action. The collective action of nurses requires a level of independence during the shift and interdependence among shifts and settings and with other healthcare professionals. Nurses learn quickly to rely on their colleagues but have been less comfortable with formal collectives, such as unions. Understanding power and learning how to use it are essential for nurses to influence practice, work environments, and public policies that affect health. Nurses have identified practice concerns and have joined together through collective action to bring about change in numerous practice settings (Dube, Kaplan, & Thompson, 2016). Organizational governance structures provide the framework for this participation. Collective action can result in an empowered and engaged workforce. When large numbers of nurses in a common setting are engaged in the practice environment, the results are impressive: improved work life, reduced nurse turnover, improved relationships with management, improved patient care, and increased patient satisfaction. Collective action is facilitated by leader behaviors that encourage participative decision making, display confidence in employees, and promote autonomy (Riley, Dearmon, Mestas, & Buckner, 2016).

Collective bargaining is a process of negotiations between employers and a group of employees aimed at reaching agreements to regulate working conditions. Collective bargaining agreements usually address salary, working hours, overtime, training, health and safety, and the right to participate in workplace or organizational decision making that affects, in our case, nursing practice. Although it is possible to engage in collective bargaining without a union, a union model is commonly used when other methods have failed to achieve results. Collective bargaining provides an opportunity for workers to voice their opinion on issues related to their employment and to protect their interest through collective action. In health care, unionization allows for negotiation or bargaining from a position of strength that is in the interest of patients, nurses, and the organization. The goal is to prevent conflict and resolve problems with mutual benefit. In negotiation, failing to reach an agreement can lead to decreased organizational productivity, strikes, lockouts, and deteriorating relations between management and labor.

While seeking to ensure economic and general welfare for nurses, collective bargaining also seeks to keep the interests of both nurses and patients in balance. In the current healthcare environment, nurses may find themselves struggling with the complexity and bureaucratic nature of the large multihospital or multistate organizations that employ them. This creates an inherent tension between the desire for clinical autonomy and the need to work within organizational structures and polices.

Union or At Will

A union is an organization of workers who have come together to achieve common goals such as protecting the integrity of the trade, improving safety standards,

achieving higher pay and benefits such as health care and retirement, increasing the number of employees an employer assigns to complete the work, and better working conditions. Working together in a cooperative, collaborative manner is important for the safety and quality of care, especially when strain occurs between management and nurses (Duncan, Rutkoff, & Spicer, 2017). Nurses have a legal right to bargain. The American Nurses Association (ANA) has long supported the rights of registered nurses to have the freedom of choice regarding how they engage in their work environments. ANA has provided balanced support for both collective bargaining and workplace advocacy depending on the needs of constituent members. ANA has a strong track record of preserving and protecting the inalienable rights and preferences of nurses regarding whether they choose to join a union. The freedom to decide to organize is underscored in the ANA's *Code of Ethics for Nurses With Interpretive Statements* (2015a).

> **EXERCISE 14.3**
> - If you were considering employment at a facility that is unionized, what questions might you want to ask?
> - What does it mean to sign a union card?
> - How might you educate yourself about unions and the collective bargaining process?

Changes in labor laws have had a direct effect on the level of union activity in the healthcare sector (Box 14.2). A 2018 labor statistics report from the U.S. Department of Labor indicates overall union membership of wage and salary workers in the United States is in decline down from 20.1% in 1983, which is the first year of reporting, to 10.7% in 2017. Union coverage for registered nurses (RNs) has not fallen in the same way as it has for the workforce overall. In contrast, the union rate for RNs was stable, holding at about 17% over the past several years (Department for Professional Employees, AFL-CIO, 2016). In part, nurses' union coverage rates have been more stable because of successful organizing drives, enlisting community support, coverage through social media and other electronic media technologies, and the continued growth of health care.

The fear of arbitrary discipline and dismissal may be the catalyst for nurses to seek ways to protect themselves from what are perceived to be capricious actions. The discipline structure provided by a union contract treats

BOX 14.2 **Labor Laws and Unions**

The federal role in labor relations is a dynamic, evolving one. The 1935 Wagner Act (National Labor Relations Act) gave employees the right to self-organize and form unions to bargain collectively. Under this law employees could organize under the terms of the law without fear of being fired for belonging to or participating in a union. The National Labor Relations Board (NLRB) administers the National Labor Relations Act. State laws further define labor law.

Two years later, the American Nurses Association (ANA) included provisions for improving nurses' work and professional lives. The 1947 Taft-Hartley Act placed curbs on some union activity and excluded employees of nonprofit hospitals from coverage. This meant employees and nurses working in nonprofit organizations did not have protections if they participated in unions. The rationale was their services were so essential that organizing activities were a threat to the public's interest. The Labor Management Reporting and Disclosure Act of 1959, also known as the Landrum-Griffin Act, provided greater internal democracy within unions. The 1974 amendments to the Taft-Hartley Act removed the exemption of not-for-profit hospitals, so that employees of these types of organizations have the same rights as industrial workers to join together and form labor unions, and included a 10-day warning period for the intent to strike or picket as a way to protect the public. This exemption was related to the ANA efforts to endorse collective bargaining. While working to secure collective bargaining protections, the ANA struggled with its role in representing nurses who were part of a union and those who were from right-to-work states who did not support unionization. The removal of the exemption for not-for-profit hospitals created a frenzy of activity as traditional industrial unions targeted healthcare facilities.

In a 1991 unanimous opinion, the Supreme Court of the United States upheld the NLRB's ruling that provides for RN-only units. This decision was critical for nursing. At stake was the ability of nurses to control nursing practice and the quality of patient care. Employees, including nurses, must be accorded workplace rights and the protection that allows them to practice. Nurses must have the freedom to do what the profession and their licensure status requires them to do.

Labeling all RNs as supervisors is a second challenge to the right of nurses to organize. RNs monitor and assess patients as a part of their professional practice, not as a statutory supervisor within the definition of the National Labor Relations Act. A 1996 NLRB ruling held that RNs were not statutory supervisors and were protected by federal labor law; the decision was upheld in 1997 by the US Court of Appeals for the Ninth Circuit (Nguyen, 1997). However, a 2001 Supreme Court decision (*National Labor Relations Board v. Kentucky River Community Care, Inc.,* 2001) upheld a lower court's decision to classify RNs as supervisors, though this decision was later appealed.

The most current rules governing the union election process can be found at:

National Labor Relations Board, *www.nlrb.gov/*

Basic Guide to the National Labor Relations Act: *www. nlrb.gov/sites/default/files/attachments/basic-page/node-3024/basicguide.pdf*

all employees in the same manner and may decrease the manager's flexibility in designing or selecting discipline (Box 14.3). Managers of at-will employees have greater latitude in selecting disciplinary measures for specific infractions. State and federal laws do provide a level of protection; however, an at-will employee may be terminated at any time for any reason except discrimination. At-will employees, in essence, work at the will of the employer. Nurses in these positions need to know their rights and accountability. Although whistleblower legislation exists, the current environment in health care places the at-will employee who voices concern about the quality of care in a vulnerable position (Box 14.4). A new social order in the workplace must be based on a spirit of genuine cooperation between management and nurses.

HEALTHY WORK ENVIRONMENTS

What Are Healthy Work Environments?

Many nurses find that working in an environment that does not match their personal values or expectations make it miserable to go to work. Poor job fit is a known contributor to employee turnover. One of the critical factors to evaluate when choosing which organization to work for includes an assessment of the work environment. A healthy work environment is one that supports excellence in nursing practice. In 2006 Shirey described a healthy work environment as "supportive, of the whole human being…patient-focused and…joyful workplaces" (p. 258). She went on to describe the ideal healthy work environment as one where adequate infrastructure to create

BOX 14.3   Due Process

Union contract language requires management to follow "due process" for represented employees. That is, management must provide a written statement outlining disciplinary charges, the penalty, and the reasons for the penalty. Management is required to maintain a record of attempts to counsel the employee. Employees have the right to defend themselves against charges and the opportunity to settle disagreements in a formal grievance hearing. They have the right to have their representative with them during the process. Management must prove that the employee is wrong or in error. Management maintains the record of counseling. The commitment to nursing requires the manager to be clear about the charge. Although all disciplinary charges are important, those directly related to patient care have a more critical dimension. Clarity in describing the situation is important, because it affects patient care, the individual nurse, and nurse colleagues. In a nonunion environment, the burden of proof is generally on the employee.

BOX 14.4   Whistleblowing Protection

Whistleblowers are the "eyes and ears" of the public in critical industries that affect our health, safety, and financial well-being. Objecting to or reporting fraud on shareholders, harm to patients, abusive practices by pharmaceuticals and financial service companies, or the like serves the public interest and should not lead to career damage and job loss. The 1989 Whistleblower Protection Act protects federal workers. The law does not cover the private sector. Some states have specific laws. Whistleblowers need to understand the consequences of action and inaction (Solomon, 2004).

Adapted from Solomon, D. (October 4, 2004). Risk management: For financial whistle-blowers, new shield is an imperfect one. *Wall Street Journal.* https://www.wsj.com/articles/SB109684145991934717.

"sanctuaries of healing" benefits both patients and caregivers (Shirey, 2006). In 2004 the National Academy of Medicine (NAM), formerly known as the Institute of Medicine, published a seminal document, *Keeping Patients Safe: Transforming the Work Environment of Nurses.* The report recommended changes to improve patient outcomes based on the understanding that the environment where nurses work has a profound effect on the safety and quality of care. Since the release of the report, both progress and persistent gaps in improving nurse work environments have resulted (Box 14.5).

Why Is a Healthy Work Environment Important?

In 2008 Don Berwick, the head of the Institute for Healthcare Improvement (IHI), introduced the Triple Aim (Berwick, Nolan, & Whittington, 2008). This conceptual model included three basic elements: improving the quality of care by enhancing patient experience; improving population health; and reducing costs. The model became widely accepted as a compass to optimize health system performance. Yet physicians and other members of the healthcare workforce reported widespread burnout and dissatisfaction as they attempted to meet the goals (Bodenhiemer & Sinsky, 2014). Burnout is associated with lower patient satisfaction and reduced health outcomes that increase costs, which jeopardize the Triple Aim (Bodenhiemer and Sinsky, 2014). Recently the Triple Aim was expanded to the Quadruple Aim (Bodenhiemer & Sinsky, 2014) (Fig. 14.1). The Quadruple Aim added the fourth goal of improving the work life of healthcare providers, acknowledging that significant change in healthcare quality cannot be achieved without addressing the work environment. This fourth element is consistent with nursings' years of documentation stemming from Magnet® organizations.

Characteristics of a Healthy Work Environment
Organizational Justice

Organizations that work to create and maintain healthy work environments have observable common characteristics. One characteristic is organizational justice, which is described as "the extent to which employees are treated with justice in their workplace" (Kuokkanen et al., 2017, p. 350). Three distinct concepts within organizational justice are described by Colquitt and Shaw (2005): distributive, procedural, and interactional justice. Distributive justice is the balance between one's perceived contributions relative to what is received from the organization. Procedural justice is the perceived fairness of the process by which outcomes are derived, and interactional justice is the perceived quality or extent to which people are treated with dignity and respect. Kuokkanen et al. (2017) found that nurses value organizational justice, which is also highly correlated with a sense of empowerment. Organizational justice

BOX 14.5   Benefits of a Healthy Work Environment

The nurse work environment has been shown to be a powerful driver of quality, safety, and experience outcomes in hospitals (Barnes, Rearden, & McHugh, 2016; Copanitsanou, Fotos, & Brokalaki, 2017; Kneflin et al., 2016; Kutney-Lee et al., 2015; Press Ganey, 2015). Recent studies indicate work environments in which nurses believe their physical and psychological safety are a priority have a greater influence than staffing optimization on many of the key indicators of patient safety, quality, satisfaction with care, and reimbursement (Press Ganey, 2016). Hospitals and healthcare systems are beginning to realize that to be competitive in the present consumer-driven, value-based marketplace, they must understand and attend to these environmental influences to achieve their strategic goals.

A significant factor in the achievement of high-quality outcomes is the structure that supports nursing practice within the organization (Day, 2014; Kieft, de Brouwer, Francke, & Delnoij, 2014). The growing body of evidence linking nurse work environments with care outcomes and achievement of organizational goals is helping to create the business case to optimize working conditions for nurses (Aiken, Sloane, Lake, & Cheney, 2014; Kieft, de Brouwer, Francke, & Delnoji, 2014; Ma & Park, 2015; McHugh & Ma, 2014; Roche, Duffield, Aisbett, Diers, & Stasa, 2012; Press Ganey, 2015; Van Bogaert, van Heusden, Timmermans, & Franke, 2014).

Creating an optimal nurse practice environment can be a relatively low-cost strategy to improve patient care (de Brouwer, Fingal, Schoonhoven, Kaljouw, & Van Achterberg, 2017). Nursing leaders have a responsibility to create and maintain healthy work environments. Strong nursing leadership has been highly correlated with positive work environments that have resulted in improved quality of care and nurse retention.

Retention of a highly qualified and engaged nursing staff is a priority for organizations to provide high-quality care and avoid the high cost of turnover (Drennan, Halter, Gale & Harris, 2016). The average cost to a hospital of onboarding a new nurse has been estimated to be anywhere from $36,000 to $57,000 (Becker's Hospital Review, 2017). With national turnover rates of up to 33.5% within the first 2 years of employment, this investment of time and money is substantial (Becker's Hospital Review, 2017).

Even small perceived improvements in nurse work environments can result in increased job engagement through the facilitation of psychological empowerment. For nurse managers wishing to improve nurse engagement and retention, both work environment and psychological empowerment need to be addressed (Fan, Zheng, Lui, & Li, 2016; Kennedy, Hardiker, & Staniland, 2015; Moore & Wang, 2017). Nurse administrators must monitor the work environment constantly for subtle changes that may lead to job dissatisfaction and burnout. They must also work to help nurses have a sense of empowerment and control over their work environment. By examining factors that affect nurses' job satisfaction, organizations can begin to balance retention, cost containment, and patient outcomes.

---

concepts can usually be identified through mission, vision, and value statements that describe the philosophic approach of the organization. Examples of key words that reflect organizational justice include respect, dignity, fairness, compassion, advocacy, and just culture. The overall impression of a healthy work environment is a sense of teamwork and community across disciplines that meets organizational goals and promotes job satisfaction.

Psychological Safety, Shared Decision Making, and Innovation

Another characteristic of a healthy work environment is a strong sense of trust between management and employees. If members of the healthcare team do not feel safe, everyone's safety is compromised (National Patient Safety Foundation, 2013). Organizations that empower employees to participate in shared decision making promote a high degree of ownership that allows for appropriate risk-taking to identify and solve problems and encourages personal and professional growth. Dent and Tye (2016) describe this positive organizational culture of ownership as the *invisible architecture* that creates and sustains a highly engaged and self-empowered workforce (Tye, 2012; Tye & Schwab, 2014). To achieve this high-trust environment, a high degree of psychological safety must exist (Moore & Wang, 2017). Psychological safety is a key factor in healthy work environments that support staff to speak up about problems or concerns without fear of retaliation (Chen, Liao, & Wen, 2014; Malloy and Penprase, 2010). Nurse leaders play an important role in creating and maintaining the psychological work environment by implementing leadership practices consistent with the psychosocial needs of those who work with them. Organizations,

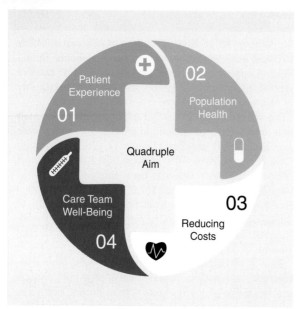

Fig. 14.1 Quadruple Aim. (Data from Bodenheimer, T. & Sinsky, C. [2014]. From triple to quadruple aim: Care of the patient requires care of the provider. *Annals of Family Medicine, 12*[6], 573-576.)

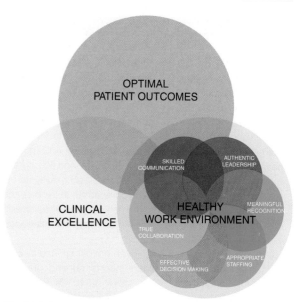

Fig. 14.2 Interdependence of healthy work environment, clinical excellence, and patient outcomes. (From American Association of Critical-Care Nurses. [2016]. *AACN Standards for establishing and sustaining healthy work environments: A journey to excellence* (2nd ed.). Aliso Viejo, CA: American Association of Critical-Care Nurses.)

whether new or well established, must cultivate innovation to be able to survive and thrive.

Adoption of Standards for a Healthy Work Environment

These characteristics of healthy work environments are in alignment with the American Association of Critical Care Nurses (AACN, 2016) standards for establishing and maintaining healthy work environments. The six standards include skilled communication; true collaboration; effective decision making; appropriate staffing; meaningful recognition; and authentic leadership. The standards recognize the links between the quality of the work environment and the impact on nursing care and practice outcomes (Fig. 14.2). Organizations that adopt these standards and actively seek to improve the work environment are attractive to nurses and generally have positive outcomes, as the Research Perspective shows.

Magnet® and Pathway to Excellence® Recognition

The American Nurses Credentialing Center (ANCC, 2014) has endorsed hospitals that provide evidence of

excellence in nursing since 1994 through the Magnet Recognition Program®. The designation indicates that the organization has characteristics that produce improved patient outcomes, attracts and retains nurses, demonstrates exemplary professional practice, and has transformational leadership and evidence-based practices. Through the Magnet® process, hospitals undergo organizational transformation that significantly improves the quality of the nurse work environment. Achieving recognition has also demonstrated marked improvement in patient outcomes (Kutney-Lee et al., 2015) and patient satisfaction (Smith, 2014).

Magnet® hospitals must sustain their standards and demonstrate excellence in patient care outcomes and clinical practice. Magnet® designation is a multiyear commitment; thus it offers a long-term framework for quality improvement efforts and a means for engaging and motivating staff at all levels. The Magnet® brand and its significance is becoming increasingly well known to the public. Approximately 9% of all registered hospitals in the United States have achieved ANCC Magnet Recognition® status (Campaign for Action, 2015). A Magnet® environment is identified

RESEARCH PERSPECTIVE

Resource: Silber, J. H., Rosenbaum, P. R., HcHugh, M. D., Ludwig, J. M, Smith, H. L., Niknam, B. A., Even-Shoshan, O. Fleisher, L. A., Kelz, R. R., & Akien, L. H. (2016). Comparison of the value of nursing work environments in hospitals across different levels of patient risk. *Journal of the American Medical Association, 151*(6), 527-536.

Existing research and literature suggest that hospitals with better nurse work environments provide better quality of care, but less is known about value (cost versus quality). This investigation reviewed and analyzed retrospective Medicare fee-for-service data to determine whether hospitals with excellent nurse work environments (defined as having both a national peer-assisted recognition program and above-average nurse staffing) have better outcomes and value. Thirty-day mortality was the primary quality-related outcome, and value was derived through cost comparisons for higher-quality care. A retrospective matched-cohort design was used, and the study included 25,752 Medicare general surgery patients treated at study hospitals and another 62,882 treated at control hospitals.

The analysis provided considerable evidence that a better nurse work environment is associated with better patient outcomes and had clear-cut value compared with the control hospitals. This is especially true for higher-risk patients.

Implications for Practice
This analysis based on a large data set adds to the evidence that efforts related to improving nurse work environments appear to have a strong correlation to improved patient outcomes and an impact on cost and value. Although causation cannot be linked, the quality and quantity of nursing care likely enables early recognition and management in complex patients and can serve to shorten hospital stays. The success of improved outcomes is heavily reliant on good communication, teamwork, and the skills of front-line nurses and leadership. The consistent message from work environment research to hospital administrations is that efforts that positively affect nurses' daily work such as staffing and sharing in the decision-making process can improve patient care and affect value.

by nurses feeling valued by the organization, having standardized processes, staff empowerment, strong leadership, a sense of community, and strategic planning that reflects the missions and goals of the organization (AACN, 2016).

The ANCC Pathway to Excellence Program® recognizes healthcare and long-term care organizations for positive practice environments for nurses. To qualify, organizations meet practice standards essential to an ideal nursing practice environment similar to those of the Magnet® program. Pathway designation can only be achieved if an organization's nurses validate the data and other evidence submitted, via an independent, confidential survey. This critical element exemplifies the theme of empowering and supporting nurses' voice. Pathway® designated organizations demonstrate respect for nursing contributions, support professional development, and nurture optimal practice environments. Organizations may hold Pathway® and Magnet® designations simultaneously.

> **EXERCISE 14.4** Identify common characteristics of a healthy work environment. From your perspective, which characteristics do you believe are most important? Would your perspective change in a leadership position?

Zero Tolerance for Workplace Violence and Incivility

Violence in health care, whether from persons external or internal to an organization, has been shown to have negative effects: increased job stress, reduced productive work time, decreased morale, increased staff turnover, and loss of trust in the organization and its management (Buttaccio, 2017; Evans, 2017). Not all healthcare workplace violence is of a physical nature; like any other business, the workplace is subject to intradisciplinary and interdisciplinary incivility or bullying. The ANA *Position Statement: Incivility, Bullying and Workplace Violence* (2015b) describes incivility as one or more rude, discourteous, or disrespectful actions that may or may not have a negative intent behind them. Bullying is "repeated, unwanted harmful actions intended to humiliate, offend and cause distress in the recipient" (ANA, 2015b). Workplace violence in any form creates a serious threat to patient safety, nurse safety, and the nursing profession as a whole (Wilson, 2016). Incivility and bullying, whether subtle, covert, or overt, affects every nursing setting from academia to practice (Box 14.6).

For the victims, studies report that bullying can result in psychological symptoms, such as anxiety, sleep problems, depression, burnout, or increased substance use, and can negatively impact job satisfaction and effective engagement (Box 14.7). Any type of violence in health care interferes with optimal job performance and has negative effects on the delivery of high-quality patient care (Evans, 2017; Magnavita, 2016). Data about the incidence of workplace violence is underreported (Kvas & Seljak, 2014), because most victims feel it is part of the job or that reporting will do nothing to change the situation. Workplace violence in nursing is so prevalent (Wolf, Delao, & Perhats, 2014) that all members of the profession must be acquainted with the types and degrees of violence and learn how to manage it.

In 2015, the ANA created a Professional Issues Panel on Incivility, Bullying, and Workplace Violence. The panel revised a previous position statement that charges all registered nurses to "create a culture of respect that is free of incivility, bullying and workplace violence" (para 1). The position statement stresses that any form

---

BOX 14.6   Range of Bullying Behaviors

Overt
- Aggressive behaviors such as shouting or threatening harm
- Being accused of making errors made by someone else
- Nonverbal intimidation
- Eye rolling
- Physical harm

Covert
- Being sabotaged
- Having information or resources withheld that affects performance
- Moving the "goal post" in a person's work without informing them
- Giving confusing or inaccurate information

- Being told tasks were urgent when they were not
- Not responding when a response is called for

Subtle
- Being excluded from activities
- Being gossiped about
- Having opinions ignored
- Assigned unreasonable unpleasant or impossible tasks, targets, or deadlines
- Being humiliated at work
- Having key areas of responsibility removed or replaced with trivial or unpleasant tasks
- Having all decisions challenged
- Being manipulated into taking on roles or tasks that were not in the nurse's best interest

---

BOX 14.7   Negative Impacts of Workplace Violence

For the individual:
- The suffering and humiliation resulting from violence, which usually lead to a lack of motivation, loss of confidence, and reduced self-esteem.
- If the situation persists, consequences such as physical illness; psychological disorders; or tobacco, alcohol, and drug abuse often observed.
- Potential of workplace violence leading to nurses leaving the workforce.

For the workplace:
- Immediate and often long-term disruption to interpersonal relationships, the organization of work, and the overall working environment.
- Deterioration in the quality of service provided.

- Direct costs of legal liabilities.
- Indirect cost of reduced efficiency and productivity.
- Difficulty in recruiting or retaining qualified personnel.
- Loss in company image and a reduction in the number of clients.
- Unemployment and retraining costs for victims who lose or leave their jobs as a result of such violence.
- Disability costs if the working capacities of the victims are impaired by psychological or physical violence at work.
- The need for expensive security measures.

For the community:
- Access to quality health services threatened.

Data from Wilson, J.L. (2016). An exploration of bullying behaviors in nursing: A review of the literature. *British Journal of Nursing, 25*(6), 303-306.

of workplace violence threatens nursing's contract with society (ANA, 2015b) and that any nurses who choose to ignore or fail to report such violence is perpetuating it. Widespread support has been noted from both professional and accrediting organizations to adopt and enforce zero-tolerance policies for bullying behaviors (Plonien, 2016). Violence is not a part of the profession, and nurses deserve to work in a safe working environment. No organization can completely prevent or eliminate workplace violence. Planning effective programs can dramatically reduce the chances of violence or incivility (Fig. 14.3).

Workplace violence is not an isolated, individual problem but a structural, strategic problem rooted in social, economic, organizational, and cultural factors. Consequently interventions should be developed that attack the problem at its roots. This involves all concerned, taking into account the organizational, cultural, and gender dimensions of the problem. Organizational strategies designed to create and sustain new cultural norms are essential (Evans, 2017). This requires sharing a common vision and goals, actively promoting the development of socialization processes, sharing problems, and supporting group problem solving. A clear policy statement should be issued from top management in consultation with stakeholders, recognizing the importance of the fight against workplace violence. The statement should contain a clear definition of violence and an organizational commitment to zero tolerance for any form of violence. Raising awareness about the negative effects of workplace violence can help gain support for planned interventions. The Clark Workplace Civility Index (Clark, 2013) is a tool that can be used to raise awareness and identify strengths and areas for improvement.

Preventive measures designed to improve the work environment, work organization, and interpersonal relationships have been shown to have small effect, and more research is needed, because no one strategy addresses all problems (Escartín, 2016; Gillen, Sinclair, Kernohan, Begley, & Luyben, 2017). When management exemplifies positive attitudes and behaviors in the workplace, the entire organization is likely to follow suit. A management style based on openness, communication, and dialogue can greatly contribute to the diffusion and elimination of workplace violence. Particular attention should be paid to new nurses in their transitional year when they are at highest risk for incivility (Chang & Cho, 2016; D'Ambra & Andrews, 2014).

EXERCISE 14.5 Think about your behavior in the workplace. Have you ever acted in a way that could be described as bullying or incivility? How might you guard against such behaviors? Do you think you would confront a coworker participating in bullying? If you were a manager, how would you handle incivility on your unit?

CONCLUSION

Nurses play a valuable role in the delivery of health care. Attracting and retaining quality nurses is good for patients and good for healthcare organizations. Improved patient outcomes, lower costs, and increased job satisfaction are possible when nurses participate in decision making that shapes their practice and creates positive change in the work environment. Engaging and empowering nurses in the workplace through shared governance, collective action, and collective bargaining is key. Shared governance is an ongoing evolving process that requires continuous support and attention from nurses and nurse leaders. Progress and gains may stall over time and require support and innovation to be productive. True shared governance must have shared participation in decision making. Collective action is when nurses work together to create an impact. An understanding of collective action and the roles of leaders and followers can help the individual nurse navigate in today's complex healthcare organizations. Negotiations may be competitive or collaborative, and

Fig. 14-3 Participating in violence prevention education can prepare staff to deal with situations that contribute to bullying or intimidation.

collaborative negotiations generally have more positive outcomes. Nurses must understand the rules and regulations that apply to workplace and workforce engagement strategies to make informed decisions about where they would like to work. Leaders and managers should facilitate nurse input and create a safe space for nurses to voice their opinions and effect change. Healthy workplace environments require the active participation of all members and can be an avenue for organizations to attract the most qualified workforce. Efforts toward creating healthy work environments benefit everyone involved.

THE SOLUTION

The first step in leading change management is to acknowledge and fully understand the need for change. It was important to our team to engage all stakeholders in developing a shared understanding of the strengths and opportunities for improvement in the current structure. Surveys and multiple focus groups across the system were conducted over the course of several months. Input was received from nurses at all levels on the benefits, challenges, and priorities for the process of shared governance modernization. The results provided clear evidence that nurses at all levels still valued shared governance. Nursing leaders reaffirmed their strong commitment to support and resource shared governance and to explore ways to improve the structure and processes to be highly effective. Through the discovery process, the benefits, challenges, and redesign priorities were identified. Three focus areas for improvement surfaced: (1) developing and integrating site, system, and specialty committees; (2) expanding on the current use of technology; and (3) rethinking committee agendas to encourage strategic discussions and improve clinical nurse input into decision making. The Magnet® program structure and our Catholic social traditions provided the foundation and guiding principles for the redesign work.

Our next step was to review, discuss, and revise the existing shared governance framework in collaboration with nursing leaders. Site- and system-level shared governance structures were redesigned to align with organizational changes and maintain representational membership from all clinical nurses. Four distinct structural entities were solidified to provide for clinical nurse engagement at the unit, site, specialty, and system levels. Consideration was given to membership, coordination, integration, and reporting pathways for each: Unit Practice Councils, Site Advisory Councils, Specialty Coordinating Councils, and the Professional Nursing Congress.

Modernizing an existing shared governance structure in a large network is a complex process that takes time, resilience, and leadership commitment. The process of creating change is just as important as the reason for change itself. The team used a variety of project management tools and techniques to help guide our work, including the development of committee charters, a stakeholder analysis/matrix, and a communication plan. A comprehensive project management plan served as our roadmap and detailed the sequence of milestones, job assignments and roles, and time frames. Taking the time upfront to define each phase in the project was critical, because it allowed us to monitor risk points and communicate progress that moved the plan from concept to implementation.

A phased approach to implementation began with restructuring Unit, Site, and Specialty Councils and concluded with the redesign of the system-level Nursing Congress. Nurses were actively engaged at various points to ensure a full range of viewpoints was considered. For example, nursing leaders and representatives from across the system participated in an intensive, 2-day event charged with developing a strategy and plan to redesign the Nursing Congress as the final step in the modernization of the nursing shared governance framework. Nurses were divided into workgroups with subject matter experts and brainstormed creative solutions for how the Nursing Congress could better meet their needs.

The goals and passion behind Seton's Nursing Shared Governance remain just as strong today as when it was established. Nurses who have been involved in the redesign work have voiced excitement to see many of their innovative ideas come to life. Although there is still work to be done to formalize the changes, nurse participation and engagement is on the rise, and committee members report that their conversations are much more strategic and aligned with other key governance structures. Seton remains committed to shared governance and recognizes that when nurses are given an opportunity to have a voice in how they practice, it increases engagement and positively impacts patient outcomes.

Would this be a suitable solution for you? Why?

Laura Kidd
Nancy Mastronardi
Diana Sellers

REFLECTIONS

How might you become involved in creating a healthier work environment where you are? Respond in a one-paragraph summary.

THE EVIDENCE

The evidence continues to mount to show that people across various work settings who are engaged perform more effectively. Leaders and managers can put strategies in place to facilitate engagement. Yet the peer group often is where engagement is initiated and supported on a day-to-day basis. Acting collectively has great influence when we address issues from the standpoint of benefiting patients and promoting retention of well-qualified staff.

TIPS FOR WORKFORCE ENGAGEMENT AND COLLECTIVE ACTION

- Understand the culture and the organization's approach to any collective action strategy is important for managers and staff.
- Create a list of pros and cons if a decision is being made regarding a unionized approach and include a comparison of various unions, especially in terms of representation of issues currently unresolved.
- Make a personal commitment to stop behaviors that perpetuate incivility or bullying.
- Investigate the AACN Standards for Establishing and Sustaining Healthy Work Environments.

REFERENCES

Aiken, L. H., Sloane, D. M., Lake, E. T., & Cheney, T. (2014). Effects of hospital care environments on patient mortality and nurse outcomes. *Journal of Nursing Administration, 38*(5), 223–229.

American Association of Critical-Care Nurses. (2016). *AACN Standards for establishing and sustaining healthy work environments: A journey to excellence* (2nd ed.). Aliso Viejo, CA: American Association of Critical-Care Nurses. https://www.aacn.org/~/media/aacn-website/nursing-excellence/healthy-work-environment/execsum.pdf?la=en.

American Nurses Association. (2015a). *Code of ethics for nurses with interpretive statements.* Silver Spring, MD: The Association.

American Nurses Association (ANA). (2015b). *Position Statement: Incivility, bullying and workplace violence.* https://www.aorn.org/-/media/.../posstat-endorsed-ana-incivility-bullying-violence.pd.

American Nurses Credentialing Center (ANCC). (2014). *Magnet Recognition Program Overview.* http://www.nursecredentialing.org/Magnet/ProgramOverview/New-Magnet-Model.

Barnes, H., Rearden, J., & McHugh. (2016). Magnet® hospital recognition linked to lower central line-associated bloodstream infection rates. *Research in Nursing and Health, 39,* 96–104.

Becker's Hospital Review. (2017). *Healthcare Retention.* http://www.beckershospitalreview.com/human-ca(50pital-and-risk/infographic-what-s-the-cost-of-nurse-turnover.html.

Berwick, D. M., Nolan, T. W., & Whittington, J. (2008). The triple aim, health and cost. *Health Affairs, 27*(3), 759–769.

Bodenheimer, T., & Sinsky, C. (2014). From triple to quadruple aim: Care of the patient requires care of the provider. *Annals of Family Medicine, 12*(6), 573–576.

Brody, A. A., Barnes, K., Ruble, C., & Sakowski, J. (2012). Evidence-based practice councils: Potential path to staff nurse empowerment and leadership growth. *Journal of Nursing Administration, 42*(1), 28–33. https://doi.org/10.1097/NNA.0b013e31823c17f5.

Buttaccio, J. L. (2017). 3 reasons many nurses are leaving the profession. *RNnetwork,* March 22, 2017. http://www.rnnetwork.com/blog/in-the-news/rnnetwork-nurse-survey/.

Campaign for Action. (2015). *Number of hospitals in the United States with Magnet status.* https://campaignforaction.org/resource/number-hospitals-united-states-magnet-status/.

Chang, H. E., & Cho, S. (2016). Workplace violence and job outcomes of newly licensed nurses. *Asian Nursing Research, 10,* 271–276.

Chen, C., Liao, J., & Wen, P. (2014). Why does formal mentoring matter: The mediating role of psychological safety and the moderation role of power distance orientation in the Chinese context. *International Journal of Human Resource Management, 25,* 1112–1130.

Clark, C. M. (2013). *Creating and sustaining civility in nursing education.* Indianapolis, IN: Sigma Theta Tau International. www.ic4n.org/wp-content/uploads/2015/09/Clark-Workplace-Civility-Index-Revised-Likert.pdf.

Colquitt, J. A., & Shaw, J. C. (2005). How should organizational justice be measured? In J. Greenberg & J. A. Colquitt (Eds.), *Handbook of organizational justice* (pp. 113–152). Mahwah, NJ: Lawrence Erlbaum Associates.

Copanitsanou, P., Fotos, N., & Brokalaki, H. (2017). Effects of work environment on patient and nurse outcomes. *British Journal of Nursing, 26*(3), 172–176.

Crow, G. L., & De Bourgh, G. A. (2017). Shared governance: The infrastructure for innovation. In S. Davidson, D. Weberg, T. Porter-O'Grady, & K. Malloch (Eds.), *Leadership for evidence-based innovation in nursing and health professions* (pp. 401–439). Burlington, MA: Jones & Bartlett Learning.

D'Ambra, A. M., & Andrews, D. R. (2014). Incivility, retention and new graduate nurses: An integrated review of the literature. *Journal of Nursing Management, 22*(6), 735–742. https://doi.org/10.1111/jonm.12060.

Day, H. (2014). Engaging staff to deliver compassionate care and reduce harm. *British Journal of Nursing, 23*(18), 974–980.

De Brouwer, B. J., Fingal, C., Schoonhoven, L., Kaljouw, M. J., & Van Achterberg, T. (2017). Measuring hospital staff nurses perception on quality of the professional practice environment. *Journal of Advanced Nursing, Journal of Advanced Nursing, 73*(10), 2484–2494.

Dent, R., & Tye, J. (2016). Creating a positive culture of ownership. *Nurse Leader,* June, 185-190.

Department for Professional Employees, AFL-CIO. (2016). *Nursing: A profile of the profession.* http://dpeaflcio.org/wp-content/uploads/Nursing-2015.pdf.

dos Santos, J. L., Erdmann, A. L., de Andrade, S. R., de Mello, A. L., de Lima, S., & Pestana, A. (2013). Nursing governance: An integrative review of the literature. *Revista da Escola de Enfermagem da* USP, 47(6), 1414–1421.

Drennan, V. M., Halter, M., Gale, J., & Harris, R. (2016). Retaining nurses in metropolitan areas: Insights from senior nurses and human resource managers. *Journal of Nursing Management, 24,* 1041–1048.

Druker, P. F. (2011). *Post capitalist society.* New York: Routledge.

Dube, A., Kaplan, E., & Thompson, O. (2016). Nurse unions and patient outcomes. *ILR Review, 69*(4), 803–833.

Duncan, D., Rutkoff, J., & Spicer, J. E. (2017). Building diverse partnerships in health care and industry: How organizations must partner to build disruptive futures. In S. Davidson, D. Weberg, T. Porter-O'Grady, & K. Malloch (Eds.), *Leadership for Evidence-Based Innovation in Nursing and Health Professions* (pp. 475–501). Burlington, MA: Jones & Bartlett Learning.

Escartín, J. (2016). Insights into workplace bullying: Psychosocial drivers and effective interventions. *Psychology Research and Behavior Management, 9,* 157–169.

Evans, D. (2017). Categorizing the magnitude and frequency of exposure to uncivil behaviors: A new approach for more meaningful interventions. *Journal of Nursing Scholarship, 49*(2), 214–222.

Fan, Y., Zheng, Q., Liu, S., & Li, Q. (2016). Construction of a new model of job engagement, psychological empowerment and perceived work environment among Chinese registered nurses at four large university hospitals: Implications for nurse managers seeking to enhance nursing retention and quality of care. *Journal of Nursing Management, 24,* 646–655.

Gerard, S. O., Owens, D. L., & Oliver, P. (2016). Nurses' perceptions of shared decision-making process: Quantifying a shared governance culture. *Journal of Nursing Administration, 46*(9), 477–483.

Gillen, P. A., Sinclair, M., Kernohan, W. G., Begley, C. M., & Luyben, A. G. (2017). Interventions for prevention of bullying in the workplace. *Cochrane Database of Systematic Reviews,* 2017, Issue 1.

Joseph, M. L., & Bouge, R. J. (2016). A theory-based approach to nursing shared governance. *Nursing Outlook, 64,* 339–349.

Kennedy, S., Hardiker, N., & Staniland, K. (2015). Empowerment an essential ingredient in the clinical environment: A review of the literature. *Nurse Education Today, 35,* 487–492.

Kieft, R. A., de Brouwer, B. B., Francke, A. L., & Delnoij, D. M. (2014). How nurses and their work environment affect patient experiences of the quality of care: A qualitative study. *BMC Health Services Research, 14,* 249. http://www.biomedcentral.com/1472-6963/14/249.

Kneflin, N., O'Quinn, L., Geigle, G., Mott, B., Nebrig, D., & Mumafo, J. (2016). Direct care nurses on the shared governance journey towards positive patient outcomes. *Journal of Clinical Nursing, 25,* 875–882.

Kuokkanen, L., Leino-Kilpi, H., Katajitso, J., Heponiemi, T., Sinervo, T., & Elovainio, M. (2017). Does organizational justice predict empowerment? Nurses asses their work environment. *Journal of Nursing Scholarship, 46*(5), 349–356.

Kutney-Lee, A., Stimpfel, A., Sloane, D. M., Cimiotti, J. P., Quinn, L. W., & Aiken, L. H. (2015). Changes in patient and nurse outcomes associated with magnet hospital recognition. *Medical Care, 53*(6), 550–557.

Kvas, A., & Seljak, J. (2014). Unreported workplace violence in nursing. *International Nursing Review, 61*, 344–351.

Ma, C., & Park, S. H. (2015). Hospital Magnet status, unit work environment, and pressure ulcers. *Journal of Nursing Scholarship, 47*(6), 565–573.

Magnavita, N. (2016). Workplace violence and occupational stress in healthcare workers: A chicken-and-egg situation – Results of a 6 year study. *Journal of Nursing Scholarship, 46*(5), 366–376.

Malloch, K., & Porter-O'Grady, T. (2017). Assessing your innovation and evidence capacity: Essentials for Organizational infrastructures. In S. Davidson, D. Weberg, T. Porter-O'Grady, & K. Malloch (Eds.), *Leadership for evidence-based innovation in nursing and health professions* (pp. 401–439). Burlington, MA: Jones & Bartlett Learning.

Malloy, T., & Penprase, B. (2010). Nurse leadership style and psychosocial work environment. *Journal of Nursing Management, 18*, 715–725.

McHugh, M. D., & Ma, C. (2014). Wage, work environments and staffing: Effects on nurse outcomes. *Policy, Politics & Nursing Practice, 15*(3-4), 72–80.

Meyers, M. M., & Costanzo, C. (2015). Shared governance in a clinic system. *Nursing Administration Quarterly, 39*(1), 51e57.

Minarik, P., & Catramabone, C. (1998). Collective participation in workforce decision-making. In D. Mason, D. Talbot, & J. Leavitt (Eds.), *Policy and politics for nurses: Action and change in the workplace, government, organizations and community* (3rd ed.). Philadelphia: Saunders.

Moore, J. H., & Wang, Z. (2017). Mentoring top leadership promotes organizational innovativeness through psychological safety and is moderated by cognitive adaptability. *Frontiers in Psychology, 8*(318), 1–10.

Murray, K. (2016). Journey of excellence: Implementing a shared decision-making model. *American Journal of Nursing, 116*(4), 50–56.

National Academy of Medicine. (2004). *Keeping patients safe: Transforming the work environment of nurses*. Washington, DC: National Academies Press.

National Academy of Medicine. (2011). *The future of nursing: Leading change, advancing health*. Washington, DC: National Academies Press.

National Labor Relations Board v. Kentucky River Community Care, Inc. (n.d.). Oyez. https://www.oyez.org/cases/2000/99-1815.

National Patient Safety Foundation. (2013). *Through the eyes of the workforce: Creating joy, meaning, and safer health care*. Boston, MA: Lucian Leape Institute.

Nguyen, B. (1997). Long-awaited Providence ruling upholds right of charge nurses to bargain. *The American Nurse, 29*(1), 14.

Plonien, C. (2016). Bullying in the workplace: A leadership perspective. *American Operating Room Nurses Journal, 103*(1), 107–110.

Porter-O'Grady, T. (Ed.). (2009). *Interdisciplinary shared governance: Integrating practice, transforming health care* (2nd ed.). Sudbury, MA: Jones and Bartlett Publishers.

Press Ganey. (2015). *Nursing special report: The influence of nurse work environment on patient. Payment and nurse: outcomes in acute care settings.*

Press Ganey. (2016). *Nursing special report: The role of workplace safety and surveillance capacity in driving nurse and patient outcomes.*

Riley, B. H., Dearmon, V., Mestas, L., & Buckner, E. B. (2016). Frontline nurse engagement and empowerment: Characteristics and processes for building leadership capacity. *Nursing Administration Quarterly, 40*(4), 325–333.

Roche, M., Duffield, C., Aisbett, C., Diers, D., & Stasa, H. (2012). Nursing work directions in Australia: Does evidence drive the policy? *Collegian, 19*(4), 231–238.

Shirey, M. R. (2006). Authentic leaders creating healthy work environments for nursing practice. *American Journal of Critical Care, 15*(3), 256–267.

Silber, J. H., Rosenbaum, P. R., HcHugh, M. D., Ludwig, J. M, Smith, H. L., Niknam, B. A., et al. (2016). Comparison of the value of nursing work environments in hospitals across different levels of patient risk. *Journal of the American Medical Association, 151*(6), 527–536.

Smith, S. A. (2014). Magnet hospitals: Higher rates of patient satisfaction. *Policy, Politics and Nursing Practice, 15*, 30–41.

Strumwasser, S., & Virkstis, K. (2015). Meaningfully incorporating staff input to enhance frontline engagement. *Journal of Nursing Administration, 45*(5), 179–182.

Tye, J. (2012). *The invisible architecture of your organization.* http://www.valuescoachinc.com/wp-content/uploads/2012/05/The-Invisible-Architecture-of-Your-Organization-.pdf.

Tye, J., & Schwab, D. (2014). *The Florence prescription: From accountability to ownership* (2nd ed.). Solon, OH: Values Coach.

U.S. Department of Labor, Bureau of Labor Statistics (BLS), (n.d.). *Union Members 2017* (News Release, January 19, 2018). https://www.bls.gov/news.release/union2.nr0.htm.

Van Bogaert, P., van Heusden, D., Timmermans, O., & Franck, E. (*2014*). Nurse work engagement impacts job outcome and nurse-assessed quality of care: Model testing with nurse practice environment and nurse work characteristics as predictors. *Frontiers in Psychology,* *5*(1261), 1–11.

Wilson, J. L. (2016). An exploration of bullying behaviors in nursing: A review of the literature. *British Journal of Nursing, 25*(6), 303–306.

Wolf, L. A., Delao, A., & Perhats, C. (2014). Nothing changes, nobody cares: Understanding the experience of emergency nurses physically or verbally assaulted while providing care. *Journal of Emergency Nursing, 40*(4), 305–310. https://doi.org/10.1016/i.jen.2013.11.006.

Wong, C. A., & Giallonardo, L. M. (2013). Authentic leadership and nurse-assessed adverse patient outcomes. *Journal of Nursing Management, 21*(5), 740–752.

15

Making Decisions and Solving Problems

Sylvain Trepanier, Jeannette T. Crenshaw

LEARNING OUTCOMES

- Apply a decision-making model to identify the best options to solve a problem.
- Evaluate the effect of faulty information gathering on a decision-making experience.
- Analyze the decision-making style of a nurse leader or manager.

KEY TERMS

autocratic
clinical judgment
creativity
critical thinking
decision making
optimizing
optimizing decision
problem solving
satisficing
satisficing decision

THE CHALLENGE

Healthcare managers today are faced with numerous and complex issues that pertain to providing quality services for patients within a resource-scarce environment. Stress levels among staff can escalate when problems are not resolved, leading to a decrease in morale, productivity, and quality service. This was the situation I encountered in my previous job as administrator for California Children Services (CCS). When I began my tenure as the new CCS administrator, staff expressed frustration and dissatisfaction with staffing, workload, and team communications. This was evidenced by high staff turnover, lack of teamwork, customer complaints, unmet deadlines for referral and enrollment cycle times, and poor documentation. The team was in crisis, characterized by infighting, blaming, lack of respectful communication, and lack of commitment to program goals and objectives. Because I had not worked as a case manager in this program, it was hard for me to determine how to address the

(Continued)

THE CHALLENGE—cont'd

problems the staff presented to me. I wanted to be fair but thought that I did not have enough information to make immediate changes. My challenge was to lead this team to greater compliance with state-mandated performance measures.

What would you do if you were this nurse?

Vickie Lemmon, RN, MSN
Director of Clinical Strategies, Operations WellPoint, Inc., Ventura, California

INTRODUCTION

Problem solving and decision making are essential skills for effective nursing practice. As one of the contributors to this book often says, "All the easy decisions have already been made." So, the challenges we face often are complex, have critical consequences, require thoughtful consideration, and reflect on us as leaders. These problem-solving and decision-making processes not only are involved in managing and delivering care but also are essential for engaging in planned change. Technological, social, political, and economic changes have dramatically affected health care and nursing. Increased patient acuity, shorter hospital stays, shortage of healthcare providers, increased technology, greater emphasis on quality and patient safety, value-based purchasing, "pay for performance," and the continuing shift from inpatient to ambulatory and home health care are some of the changes that require nurses to make rational and valid decisions and identify solutions to problems precipitated by change. Moreover, increased diversity in patient populations, employment settings, and types of healthcare providers require efficient and effective decision making and problem solving. More emphasis is now placed on recognizing patients as the source of control and as full partners in decision making (shared decision making) and problem solving with interprofessional teams to achieve evidence-based results. The term *VUCA* (volatility, uncertainty, complexity, and ambiguity) creates the context for making decisions and solving problems in health care—and many other fields.

Nurses must possess the basic knowledge and skills required for effective decision making and problem solving. These competencies are especially important for nurses with leadership and management responsibilities.

DIFFERENTIATION OF DECISION MAKING AND PROBLEM SOLVING

Decision making and *problem solving* are not synonymous terms. However, the processes for engaging in decision making and problem solving are similar. Both skills require critical thinking, which is a high-level cognitive process, and both can be improved with practice.

Decision making is a purposeful and goal-directed effort that uses a systematic process to choose among options. Some decisions are not prompted by a problem. The hallmark of any type of decision making is the identification and selection of options or alternatives.

Problem solving, which includes a decision-making step, is focused on trying to resolve an issue that can be viewed as the gap between "what currently is" and "the best available option." Often "what currently is" can be seen as a problem.

Effective decision making and problem solving are based on an individual's ability to think critically. Although critical thinking has been defined in numerous ways, The Critical Thinking Community (2015) defines critical thinking as "the intellectually disciplined process of actively and skillfully conceptualizing, applying, analyzing, synthesizing, and/or evaluating information gathered from, or generated by, observation, experience, reflection, reasoning, or communication, as a guide to belief and action." Effective critical thinkers are self-aware individuals who strive to improve their reasoning abilities by asking "why," "what," or "how." A nurse who questions why a patient is restless is thinking critically. Compare the analytical abilities of a nurse who assumes a patient is restless because of anxiety related to an upcoming procedure with those of a nurse who asks if another explanation could be possible and proceeds to investigate possible causes. Nurse leaders and managers need to assess staff members' ability to think critically and enhance their knowledge and skills through professional development programs, coaching, and role modeling. Establishing a healthy work environment can promote staff members' ability to think critically.

Creativity is essential to generate (or identify) options or solutions. Creative individuals can conceptualize new and innovative approaches to a problem or issue by using flexible and independent thinking.

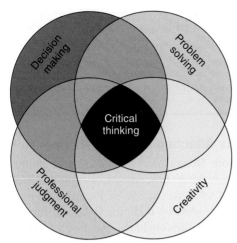

Fig. 15.1 Problem-solving and decision-making model.

BOX 15.1   Decision-Making Format

Objective: _____

Options	Advantages	Disadvantages	Ranking

Add more rows as necessary. Rank the priority of options, with "1" being most preferred. Select the best option.

Implementation plan: _____
_____

Evaluation plan: _____
_____

The model depicted in Fig. 15.1 demonstrates the relationship among concepts such as professional judgment, decision making, problem solving, creativity, and critical thinking. Sound clinical judgment requires critical or reflective thinking. Critical thinking is the concept that interweaves and links the other concepts together. An individual, through the application of critical-thinking skills, engages in decision making and problem solving in an environment that may have the effect of either promoting or inhibiting these skills. The nurse leader and manager have the task to model these skills and promote the use of these skills by others.

DECISION MAKING

The phases of the decision-making process include defining objectives, generating options, identifying advantages and disadvantages of each option, ranking the options, selecting the option most likely to achieve the predefined objectives, implementing the option, and evaluating the result. Box 15.1 contains a form that can be used to complete these steps. The challenge in this work is weighing the advantages and disadvantages.

Poor-quality decision making is likely if objectives are not clearly identified or if objectives are inconsistent with the values of the individual or organization. Lewis Carroll illustrates the essential step of defining the goal, purpose, or objectives in the following excerpt from *Alice's Adventures in Wonderland*:

One day Alice came to a fork in the road and saw a Cheshire Cat in a tree. "Which road do I take?" she asked. His response was a question: "Where do you want to go?" "I don't know," Alice answered. "Then," said the cat, "it doesn't matter."

Decision Models

The decision model that a nurse uses depends on specific circumstances. Is the situation routine and predictable, or complex and uncertain? Is the goal to make a decision that is "just good enough" (conservative) or one that is optimal?

If the situation is fairly routine, nurse leaders and managers can use a normative or prescriptive approach. Agency policy, standard procedures, and analytical tools can be applied to situations that are structured and in which options and outcomes are known.

If the situation is subjective, nonroutine, and unstructured or if outcomes are unknown or unpredictable, the nurse leader and manager may need to take a different approach. In this case a descriptive or behavioral approach is required. More information must be gathered to address the situation effectively. Creativity, experience, and group process are useful in dealing with the unknown. In these situations, nurse leaders must seek expert opinion and involve key stakeholders.

Another strategy is satisficing. With this approach, the decision maker selects an acceptable solution, one that may minimally meet the objective or standard for a decision. This approach allows for quick decisions and may be the most appropriate when lack of time is an issue.

Optimizing is a decision style in which the decision maker selects the option that is best, based on an analysis of the pros and cons associated with each option. A better decision is more likely using this approach, although it takes longer to arrive at a decision.

For example, a young nurse contemplates seeking employment in one of three places: an acute care hospital in the city; a community health organization; or a rural, comprehensive clinic or hospital. A **satisficing decision** might result if the nurse picked the rural hospital because the position provided an adequate salary and benefit package or because the position was closest to home. However, an **optimizing decision** is more likely to occur if the nurse lists the pros and cons of each position being considered, such as salary, benefits, opportunities for advancement, career development, mentorship programs, and career goals.

Decision-Making Styles

In general the various decision-making styles can be categorized in three models: paternalistic, informed, and shared decision making. In the paternalistic style (**autocratic** decision making) managers decide what is best for their team. This style results in more rapid decision making and is appropriate in crisis situations. The informed style offers the staff the ability to make a decision after information has been shared and without the active involvement of the manager. In a shared decision model, the decisions are made through an interactive, deliberate process where the staff and manager may express and discuss options and preferences. Followers are generally more satisfied with a shared decision-making approach. Although this approach takes more time, it is more appropriate when conflict is likely to occur or when the problem is unstructured. The shared decision style has been shown to increase work performance and productivity, decrease employee turnover, and enhance employee satisfaction. Managers need to involve nursing personnel in decisions that affect patient care. One mechanism for doing so is by including nursing representation on various committees or task forces.

Any decision style can be used appropriately or inappropriately. Like the tenets of situational leadership theory, the situation and circumstances should dictate which decision-making style is most appropriate. A Code Blue is not the time for managers to democratically solicit volunteers for chest compressions!

> **EXERCISE 15.1** Interview colleagues about their preferred decision-making style. What barriers or obstacles to effective decision making have your colleagues encountered? What strategies are used to increase the effectiveness of the decisions made? Based on your interview, is the model effective? Why or why not?

Factors Affecting Decision Making

Numerous factors affect individuals and groups in the decision-making process. In a now classic work, Tanner (2006) conducted an extensive review of the literature to develop a clinical judgment model. From her research, she concluded that five principle factors influence decision making. (See the Research Perspective.)

Internal and external factors can influence how a situation is perceived. Internal factors include variables such as the decision maker's physical and emotional state, personal philosophy, biases, values, interests, experience, knowledge, attitudes, and risk-seeking or risk-avoiding behaviors. External factors include environmental conditions, time, and resources. Decision-making options related to external factors are limited when time is short or when the environment is characterized by a "we've always done it this way" attitude.

Values affect all aspects of decision making, from the statement of the problem or issue through the evaluation. Values, which are influenced by an individual's cultural, social, and philosophic background, provide the foundation for one's ethical stance. The steps for engaging in ethical decision making are similar to the steps in other decision-making models. However, in ethical decision making, alternatives or options identified in the decision-making process are evaluated with the use of ethical resources. The resources that can facilitate ethical decision making include institutional policy; principles such as autonomy, nonmaleficence, beneficence, veracity, paternalism, respect, justice, and fidelity; personal judgment; trusted co-workers; institutional ethics committees; and legal precedent. The *Guide to the Code of Ethics for Nurses: Development, Application, and Interpretation* (Fowler, 2015) provides guidance to this model.

Risk-taking is an essential competency for nurse leaders and influences effective decision making and problem solving. The work environment affects whether one is willing to take risks. According to Crenshaw and

RESEARCH PERSPECTIVE

Resource: Tanner, C.A. (2006). Thinking like a nurse: A research-based model of clinical judgment in nursing. *Journal of Nursing Education, 45*(6), 204-211.

Tanner engaged in an extensive review of 200 studies focusing on clinical judgment and clinical decision making to derive a model of clinical judgment that can be used as a framework for instruction. The first review summarized 120 articles and was published in 1998. The 2006 article reviewed an additional 71 studies published since 1998. Based on an analysis of the entire set of articles, Tanner proposed five conclusions, which are listed here. (Refer to the article for detailed explanations of each of the five conclusions.)

The author considers clinical judgment as a "problem-solving activity." She notes that the terms "clinical judgment," "problem solving," "decision making," and "critical thinking" are often used interchangeably. For the purpose of aiding in the development of the model, Tanner (2006) defined *clinical judgment* as actions taken based on the assessment of the patient's needs. Clinical reasoning is the process by which nurses make their judgments (e.g., the decision-making process of selecting the most appropriate option) (p. 204):

- Clinical judgments are more influenced by what nurses bring to the situation than the objective data about a situation.
- Sound clinical judgment rests, to some degree, on knowing the patient and the patient's typical pattern of responses, as well as engaging with the patient and identifying the patient's concerns.
- Clinical judgments are influenced by the context in which a situation occurs and the culture of the nursing care unit.
- Nurses use a variety of reasoning patterns alone or in combination.
- Reflection on practice is often triggered by a breakdown in clinical judgment and is critical for the development of clinical knowledge and improvement in clinical reasoning.

The clinical judgment model involves four steps that are similar to the decision-making and problem-solving steps described in this chapter. The model starts with a phase called "noticing." In this phase, the nurse comes to expect certain responses resulting from knowledge gleaned from similar patient situations, experiences, and knowledge. External factors influence nurses in this phase, such as the complexity of the environment and values and typical practices within the unit culture.

The second phase of the model is "interpreting," during which the nurse understands that a situation requires a response. The nurse uses various reasoning patterns to make sense of the issue and to derive an appropriate action plan.

The third phase is "responding," during which the nurse decides on the best option for handling the situation. This is followed by the fourth phase, "reflecting," during which the nurse assesses the patient's responses to the actions taken.

Tanner emphasized that "reflection-in-action" and "reflection-on-action" are major processes required in the model. Reflection-in-action is real-time reflection on the patient's responses to nursing action with modifications to the plan based on the ongoing assessment. On the other hand, reflection-on-action is a review of the experience, which promotes learning for future similar experiences.

Implications for Practice

Nurse educators and managers can use the clinical judgment model with new and experienced nurses to help them understand more about the thought processes involved in decision making. For example, nurses can be encouraged to maintain reflective journals to record observations and impressions from clinical experiences. In clinical postconferences or professional development meetings, the nurse manager can engage nurses in applying Tanner's five conclusions to their "lived" experiences. The ultimate goal of analyzing their decisions and decision-making processes is to improve clinical judgment, problem-solving, decision-making, and critical-thinking skills.

Yoder-Wise (2013), effective nurse leaders create a work environment that welcomes considered risk taking and encourages employees to share and discuss new and innovative ideas. This type of environment enables effective decision making and problem solving. Certain personality factors, such as self-esteem and self-confidence, also affect whether one is willing to take risks in solving problems or making decisions. Similarly, the work group, peers, and others can influence how decisions are made. For example, are you inclined to make decisions to satisfy people to whom you are accountable or from whom you feel social pressure?

Characteristics of an effective decision maker include courage, a willingness to take considered risks, self-awareness, energy, creativity, sensitivity, and flexibility. Ask yourself, "Do I prefer to let others make the decisions? Am I more comfortable in the role of 'follower' than leader? If so, what might be the reasons? Am I able to assume the role of leader if no leader emerges?"

EXERCISE 15.2 Identify a current or past situation that involved resource allocation, an end-of-life issue, conflict among healthcare providers or with a patient or their family or significant others, or some other ethical dilemma. Describe how internal and external factors influenced the decision options, the option selected, and the outcome.

Group Decision Making

The presence of two primary criteria leads to effective decisions. First, the decision must be of a high quality; that is, it achieves the predefined goals, objectives, and outcomes. Second, those who are responsible for its implementation must accept the decision.

Higher-quality decisions are more likely to result if groups are involved in the decision-making and problem-solving process. With the increased focus on quality and safety, decisions cannot be made alone. When team members are included in the process, they tend to function more productively, and the quality of decisions is generally superior. Taking ownership of both the process and outcome provides a smooth transition. Intraprofessional teams should be used in the decision-making process, especially if the issue, options, or outcome involves other healthcare professionals.

Research findings suggest that groups are more likely to be effective if members are actively involved, the group is cohesive, communication is encouraged, and members demonstrate some understanding of the group process. In deciding to use the group process for decision making, consider group size and composition. If the group is too small, a limited number of options will be generated and fewer points of view expressed. Conversely, if the group is too large, it may lack structure, and consensus becomes more difficult. Homogeneous groups may be more compatible; however, heterogeneous groups may be more successful in problem solving. The most productive groups are those that are moderately cohesive. In other words, divergent thinking is useful to create the best decision.

For groups to be able to work effectively, the group facilitator or leader should carefully select members on the basis of their knowledge and skills in decision making and problem solving. Individuals who are aggressive, authoritarian, or manifest self-serving behaviors tend to decrease the effectiveness of groups.

The nurse leader or manager should provide a non-threatening and positive environment in which group members are encouraged to participate actively. Using tact and diplomacy, the facilitator can minimize the effect of aggressive individuals who may attempt to monopolize the discussion and can encourage more passive individuals to contribute by asking direct, open-ended questions. Providing positive feedback such as "You raised an interesting point," protecting members and their suggestions from attack, and keeping the group focused on a task are strategies that create an environment conducive to problem solving. Table 15.1

TABLE 15.1 **Advantages and Challenges of Group Decision Making**	
Advantages	**Challenges**
• The likelihood of a quality outcome increases when individuals with different knowledge, skills, and resources collaborate to solve a problem or make a decision. • More ideas can be created. • Followers will be more apt to accept the decision because they have an increased sense of ownership and commitment to the decision. • Implementing solutions becomes easier.	• The time required for making group decisions and for achieving consensus may not be appropriate, especially in a time-sensitive situation requiring prompt decisions. • Unequal power among group members may influence the ability to collaborate and may increase the risk of "groupthink" mentality. • Failure of group members to bring up options, explore conflict, or challenge the status quo results in ineffective group functioning and decision outcomes.

summarizes the advantages and challenges related to such group work.

The group leader must establish with the participants what decision procedure will be followed. Will the group strive to achieve consensus, or will the majority prevail? In determining which decision rule to use, the group leader should consider the necessity for quality and acceptance of the decision. Achieving both a high-quality and an acceptable decision is possible, but more time and engagement, and approval from individuals affected by the decision, are required.

Groups will be more committed to an idea if it is achieved by consensus rather than as an outcome of individual decision making or as a majority decision. Consensus requires that all participants agree to go along with the final decision. However, achieving consensus does not mean that the final decision will be all participants' "first choice." When striving for consensus, ask group members if they "can live" with the decision. Achieving consensus requires considerable time. However, consensus leads to both high-quality and high-acceptance decisions and reduces the risk of sabotage.

Majority rule can be used to compromise when 100% agreement cannot be achieved. This method saves time, but the solution may only partially achieve the goals of quality and acceptance. In addition, majority rule carries certain risks. First, if the informal group leaders agree with the minority opinion, they may not support the decision of the majority. Disgruntled members may build coalitions to gain support for their position and block the majority choice. After all, the majority may represent only 51% of the group. In addition, group members may support the position of the formal leader because they fear reprisal or they wish to obtain the leader's approval. In general, as the importance of the decision increases, so does the percentage of group members required to approve and implement it.

To secure the support of the group, the leader should maintain open communication with those affected by the decision and be honest about the advantages and disadvantages of the decision. If possible, the leader should also demonstrate how the advantages outweigh the disadvantages. The leader should also suggest ways the unwanted outcomes can be minimized and be available to assist when necessary. Decisions may result in some group members gaining something valued and some group members losing something valued. Loss should be discussed openly and honestly.

Strategies

Strategies to minimize the problems encountered with group decision making and problem solving include techniques such as brainstorming, nominal group techniques, focus groups, and the Delphi technique.

Brainstorming can be an effective method for generating a large volume of creative options. Often, the premature critiquing of ideas stifles creativity, idea generation, and innovation. When members use inflammatory statements, euphemistically referred to as *killer phrases*, the usual response is for members to stop contributing. Examples of killer phrases are "It will never work," "Administration won't go for it," "What a dumb idea," "It's not in the budget," "If it ain't broke, don't fix it," and "We tried that before."

The hallmark of effective brainstorming is that all ideas are stated without critique or discussion. The group leader or facilitator should encourage people to build on or spin off ideas from those already suggested. One idea may be piggybacked on others. Ideas should not be judged, nor should the relative merits or disadvantages of the ideas be discussed while brainstorming. The goal is to generate ideas, no matter how seemingly unrealistic or absurd. The group leader or facilitator needs to cut off criticism or advocacy and be alert for nonverbal behaviors signaling disapproval or approval. Early support or discouragement of an idea limits this full process of brainstorming. Because the emphasis is on the volume of ideas generated, not necessarily the quality, solutions may be superficial and fail to solve the problem. Group brainstorming also takes longer, and the logistics of getting people together may pose a problem. If the facilitator allows the group to establish the rules for discussion, the aspects that impede open discussion often are eliminated by the group's norms or agreements of participation.

The *nominal group technique* allows group members the opportunity to provide input into the decision-making process. Participants are asked to not talk to each other as they write down their ideas to solve a predefined problem or issue. After a period of silent generation of ideas, generally no more than 10 minutes, each member is asked to share an idea, which is displayed on a flip chart. Comments and elaboration are not allowed during this phase. Each member takes a turn sharing one idea each until all ideas are presented, after which discussion is allowed. Members may "pass" if they have exhausted their list of ideas. During the next step, ideas are clarified, and the merits of each idea are discussed. In the third and final step, each member privately assigns a priority rank to each option. Group members can then place colored stickers on the flip chart next to their first, second, and third choices or they may use pieces of paper to record their choices. The solution chosen is the option that receives the highest ranking by the majority of participants. The advantage of this technique is that it allows equal participation among members and minimizes the influence of dominant personalities. The disadvantages of this method are that it is time-consuming and requires advance preparation. A similar process can be facilitated via the use of web conferencing technologies.

The purpose of *focus groups* is to explore issues and generate information. Focus groups can be used to identify problems or to evaluate the effects of an intervention. The groups meet face-to-face to discuss issues. Under the direction of a moderator or facilitator, participants are able to validate or disagree with ideas expressed. Depending on the purpose of a focus group, an objective individual may facilitate the discussion (e.g., someone other than the manager). Because the interaction is face-to-face, potential disadvantages include the logistics of getting people together, time, and issues related to group dynamics. Nevertheless, if managed effectively, the experience can yield valuable information.

Another group decision-making strategy is the *Delphi technique*. It involves systematically collecting and summarizing opinions and judgments on a particular issue from respondents, such as members of expert panels, through interviews, surveys, or questionnaires. Opinions of the respondents are repeatedly reported back to them with a request to provide more refined opinions and rationales on the issue or matter under consideration. Between each round, the results are tabulated and analyzed so that the findings can be reported to the participants. This allows the participants to reconsider their responses. The goal is to achieve a consensus.

Different variations on the Delphi technique exist. The procedure includes anonymous feedback, multiple rounds, and statistical analyses. One advantage of this technique is the ability to involve a large number of respondents, because the participants do not need to physically convene. Indeed, participants may be located throughout the country or world. Also, the questionnaire or survey requires little time commitment on the part of the participants. This technique may actually save time because it eliminates the off-the-subject digressions typically encountered in face-to-face meetings. In addition, the Delphi technique prevents the negative or unproductive verbal and nonverbal interactions that can occur when groups work together. Although the Delphi technique has its advantages, using it may result in a lower sense of accomplishment and involvement because the participants are detached from the overall process and do not communicate with each other.

Nursing lore places value on actions based on intangible and invisible "gut feeling" responses, referred to as *nursing intuition*. What is nursing intuition? Like critical thinking, many definitions exist. Nursing intuition is a valid form of knowledge (see the Research Perspective that follows). Robert, Tilley, and Petersen (2014) describe the benefits of nursing intuition:

- Holistic
- Complex
- Knowledge-based approach to decision making

RESEARCH PERSPECTIVE

Resource: Cork, L.L. (2014). Nursing intuition as an assessment tool in predicting severity of injury in trauma patients. *Journal of Trauma Nursing, 21*(5), 244-252.

Cork conducted a descriptive, quantitative, cross-sectional study aimed at exploring the validity of nurses' use of intuition to predict the severity of trauma injuries compared with use of a trauma severity tool and its influence on the decision to initiate trauma codes. The study was conducted in a level II trauma–designated rural emergency department and used two distinctive phases to include the assessment of eight charge nurses and a total of 393 retrospective reviews of medical records from June 2010 to May 2012. A t test was performed to determine the probability that the two sets of data had the same means using a two-tailed test

(0.021, alpha 0.05). A Pearson's r correlation coefficient was performed to determine the relationship between the "gut feeling decision" and an assessment trauma tool ($r = 0.992$; $P < 0.001$). The researcher concluded that intuition was a valuable tool and appeared to serve the nurses in this study as effectively as the trauma tool.

Implications for Practice
Helping experienced nurses share with less experienced nurses how they developed their intuition may move the latter group to greater levels of intuition. Providing opportunities to test intuitive thinking with an experienced nurse may also help develop the experiences that contribute to intuition.

Decision-Making Tools

Nurse leaders and managers can use a variety of decision-making tools such as decision grids and Strength, Weakness, Opportunity, Threat (SWOT) analyses in the decision-making process. These tools are most appropriately used when information is available and options are known. To be part of the solution, followers must be a part of making the decisions (Fig. 15.2). Decision grids facilitate the visualization of the options under consideration and allow comparison of options using common criteria. Criteria, which are determined by the decision makers, may include time required, costs, ethical or legal considerations, and equipment needs (Fig. 15.3). The relative advantages and disadvantages should be listed for each option. For example, the manager of a hospital education department is assessing whether it is better to retain the services of an outside consultant to coordinate an advanced cardiac life support (ACLS) course in the hospital, pay the per-person fees to send the staff to another hospital for the training, or train staff in the agency as ACLS instructors to be able to provide the training in-house. The type of information this manager might compile includes a breakdown of the costs for the three options, equipment needs, benefits of each option, the number of nurses needing the course, future training needs, and feasibility of training hospital staff to conduct the course.

A SWOT analysis is commonly used in strategic planning or marketing efforts but can also be used by individuals and groups in decision making. Using the SWOT analysis, the individual or team lists the strengths, weaknesses, opportunities, and threats related to the situation under consideration. Strengths and weaknesses are internal to the individual, group, or organization, whereas the opportunities and threats are external factors (Ojala, 2017). For example, Estella has worked in a medical-surgical unit for 5 years and is considering whether to request a transfer to the intensive care unit (ICU). Box 15.2 is a SWOT analysis outlining potential or actual strengths, weaknesses, opportunities, and threats.

> **EXERCISE 15.3** Examples of decision-making tools include *http://www.mindtools.com*—a commercial website. It provides links to software and other resources. Many of the tools are free to download. Explore the tools in the Toolkit and click on the links to "Decision Making" or "Problem Solving." What could you use to enhance your decision-making and problem-solving abilities?

> **EXERCISE 15.4** Design a decision grid for a current situation you are experiencing. Identify the components you need to explore in the decision-making process, such as cost, time, resources, advantages, and disadvantages, for the various options you are considering.

Fig. 15.2 To be part of the solution, followers must be a part of making the decisions.

Options Under Consideration	Time	Cost	Legal/Ethical Considerations	Equipment Needed

Fig. 15.3 Decision grid.

BOX 15.2 SWOT Analysis

Strengths
- Familiar with the healthcare system
- Clinically competent and has received favorable performance appraisals
- Good communication skills; well-liked by her peers
- Recently completed 12-lead electrocardiogram (ECG) interpretation class

Weaknesses
- Has not attended the critical care class
- Has had a prior unresolved conflict with one of the surgeons who frequently admits to the intensive care unit (ICU)
- Is uncertain whether she wants to work full-time, 12-hour shifts

Opportunities
- Anticipated staff openings in the ICU in the next several months
- Critical care course will be offered in 1 month
- Advanced cardiac life support (ACLS) course is offered four times each year
- A friend who already works in ICU has offered to mentor her

Threats
- Possible bed closures in another critical care unit may result in staff transfers, thus eliminating open positions
- Another medical-surgical nurse is also interested in transferring

---

PROBLEM SOLVING

As Albert Einstein allegedly said, "If I were given one hour to save the planet, I would spend 59 minutes defining the problem and one minute resolving it." Thus the effective leader anticipates problems and develops methods for dealing with them. The leader of group who defines the problem well has the potential to create a solid solution.

Initial Evaluation

Problem solving includes the decision-making process; the trigger for action is the existence of a "problem" or issue. Before attempting to solve a problem, a nurse must ask certain key questions:

1. Is it important?
2. Do I want to do something about it? (e.g., Do I "own" the problem?)
3. Am I qualified to handle it?
4. Do I have the authority to do anything?
5. Do I have the knowledge, interest, time, and resources to deal with it?
6. Can I delegate it to someone else?
7. What benefits will be derived from solving it?

If the answers to questions 1 through 5 are "no," why waste time, resources, and personal energy? At this juncture, a conscious decision is made to ignore the problem, refer or delegate it to others, or consult or collaborate with others to solve it. On the other hand, if the answers are "yes," the nurse leader or manager chooses to accept the problem and assume responsibility for it.

After identifying the problem, nurse leaders and managers must decide whether the problem is within their control and whether it is significant enough to require intervention. Sometimes individuals believe they need to "solve" every problem brought to their attention. Some situations, such as some interpersonal conflicts, are best resolved by the individuals who own the problem. Known as *purposeful inaction,* a "do nothing" approach might be indicated when other persons should resolve problems or when the problem is beyond one's control.

EXERCISE 15.5 Consider the following scenario: Mary complains to the nurse manager that Sam, a fellow nurse, was rude and abrupt with her when passing in the hall. How should the nurse manager handle Mary's complaint? Should the manager discuss the problem with Sam? Should Mary be present during the discussion? What are the possible risks or benefits of such an approach? Alternatively, should the manager assist Mary in developing her communication skills so that Mary can address the problem herself?

EXERCISE 15.6 Using the decision-making format presented in Box 15.1, list other options for this scenario and the advantages and disadvantages of each approach. Rank the options in order of most desirable to least desirable and select the best option. Determine how you would implement and evaluate the chosen option.

Fig. 15.4 The problem-definition process.

Some decisions are "givens" because they are based on firmly established criteria in the institution, which may be based on the traditions, values, doctrines, culture, or policy of the organization. Every manager has to live with mandates from persons higher in the organizational structure. Although managers may not have the authority to control certain situations, they may be able to influence the outcome. For example, because of losses in revenue, administration has decided to eliminate the clinical educator positions in a home health agency and place the responsibility for clinical education with the senior home health nurses. The manager has no control to reverse this decision. Nevertheless, the manager can explore the nurses' fear and concerns regarding this change and facilitate the transition by preparing them for the new role and, as appropriate, share those concerns with those in the decision-making positions.

In these examples, it is a misnomer to refer to the approach as *do nothing,* because there is deliberate

action being made on the part of the manager. This approach should not be confused with the laissez-faire (hands off) approach taken by a manager who chooses to do nothing when intervention is indicated. Rather, in the situation presented here, a conscious decision was made.

Problem-Solving Process

Several models or approaches to problem solving exist. A problem-definition model is illustrated in Fig. 15.4. In this figure, a series of questions is provided to help the nurse leader or manager increase the likelihood of successfully defining a problem by finding the best solution. (See the following Research Perspective.)

Define the Problem, Issue, or Situation

The main principles for diagnosing a problem are (1) know the facts, (2) separate the facts from interpretation, (3) be objective and descriptive, and (4) determine the

RESEARCH PERSPECTIVE

Resource: Llopis, G. (2013). The 4 most effective ways leaders solve problems. *Forbes: Leadership.* https://www.forbes.com/sites/glennllopis/2013/11/04/the-4-most-effective-ways-leaders-solve-problems/#4579c1e4f974

"Problem solving is the essence of what leaders exist to do."[8] Energy should be focused on defining a problem to ensure a suitable solution. In fact, failure to correctly define a problem may result in a team trying to solve the wrong problem. It is critical to ask questions until you get to the root cause of a problem regardless of the politics, self-promotion, power-plays, and ploys that exist in many organizations. Llopis reminds us of the importance of approaching problems "through the lens of opportunity." To ensure successful problem solving, Llopis offers four most effective ways to solve problems: transparent communication, breaking down the silos, open-minded people, and a solid foundational strategy.

Transparent communication requires that everyone's point of view be known and expressed. In other words, speak up and encourage others to do so. Creating a safe environment for everyone is crucial to solving problems. Never assume that others feel comfortable sharing. As the leader of the team you have to seek the feedback of all team members. Organizational silos must be demolished and cannot be allowed. This means that you must include everyone involved in the process in the communication and brainstorming. If silos are allowed, Llopis suggests that decision makers are more likely to encounter self-promoters as opposed to team players. He emphasizes the importance of "getting your hands dirty and solving problems together." Effective communication requires team members to be open-minded. Open-minded people own the problem and aim to fix it together. He reminds us of the importance of articulating a solid strategy. Effective leaders inspire others to rally around the strategy and find common ground to solve any problems they may be facing. In other words, effective leaders are able to connect the dots and make it clear to others what the final destination can look like, the end result, and the outcome. He also reminds us to avoid guessing and to take the required amount of time to step back and analyze the situation and possibilities.

Implications for Practice

Expert clinicians such as clinical nurse specialists, clinical nurse leaders, unit-based nurse managers, and clinical educators can adapt this approach (transparent communication, breaking down the silos, open-minded people, and a solid foundational strategy) in solving problems they have on their units. For example, when you notice that a unit is not producing the expected clinical outcomes, it is important to include all disciplines in the development of an action plan to improve the outcomes. You must include all members (break down the silos). During the meeting transparent communication has to prevail. Remind the members of the team the ultimate purpose, why we do what we do every day (stay connected with the vision, mission, and strategy). Using these four concepts to solve problems has the potential to yield highly innovative solutions to everyday problems.

---

scope of the problem. Nurses need to determine how to establish priorities for solving problems. For example, do you tend to work on the problems that are encountered first, the problems that appear to be the easiest to resolve, the problems that take the shortest amount of time to resolve, or the problems that have the greatest urgency?

The most common cause for failure to resolve problems is the improper identification of the problem or issue; therefore problem recognition and identification are considered the most vital steps. The quality of the outcome depends on accurate identification of the problem, which is likely to recur if the true underlying causes are not targeted. Problem identification is influenced by the information available; by the values, attitudes, and experiences of those involved; and by time. Sufficient time should be allowed for the collection and organization of data. Too often, an inadequate amount of time is allocated for this essential step, resulting in unsatisfactory outcomes. Nurse leaders and managers should remember the power of asking questions. One method is to use the "5 Why" from the Institute for Healthcare Improvement. After answering the first question as to why a problem occurred, ask why again, and so on, until "why" has been asked at least five times. This is particularly helpful for problems that keep resurfacing over time, because "why" gets to the actual root causes of problems.

Differentiating between the actual problem and the symptoms of a problem is crucial. Consider the problem of an inadequately stocked emergency cart from which emergency medications often are missing and equipment often fails to function properly. Individuals charged with resolving this problem may discover that this is symptomatic of the underlying problem, perhaps inadequate staffing or staffing mix. Based on the proper identification of the problem in this scenario, a possible solution might be to assign the task of checking and stocking the emergency cart to the unlicensed personnel in the unit.

In work settings, problems often fall under certain categories that have been described as the *four M's: man*power, *methods, *machines, and *materials. Manpower issues might include inadequate staffing or staffing mix and knowledge or skills deficits. Methods issues could include communication problems or lack of protocols. Machine issues could include lack of equipment or malfunctioning equipment. Last, problems with materials could include inadequate supplies or defective materials. A fishbone diagram, also known as a *cause-and-effect diagram,* is a useful model for categorizing the possible causes of a problem. The diagram graphically displays, in increasing detail, all of the possible causes related to a problem to try to discover its root causes. This tool encourages problem solvers to focus on the content of the problem and not be sidetracked by personal interests, issues, or agendas of team members. A fishbone also creates a snapshot of the collective knowledge of the team and helps build consensus around the problem. The "effect" is generally the problem statement, such as decreased morale, and is placed at the right end of the figure (the "head" of the fish). The major categories of causes are the main bones, and these are supported by smaller bones, which represent issues that contribute to the main causes. An example of a fishbone diagram appears in Fig. 15.5.

EXERCISE 15.7 Using a fishbone diagram (see Fig. 15.5 as a point of reference), identify all the factors (causes) that are at the root of a problem you are currently facing in the workplace. After you have listed as many issues as possible, share the diagram with a colleague. What other issues did you not consider? Where do most of the factors influencing the problem fit: manpower, methods, machines, or materials?

Gather Data

After the general nature of the problem is identified, individuals can focus on gathering and analyzing data

to resolve the issue. Assessment, through the collection of data and information, is done continuously throughout this dynamic process. The data gathered consist of objective (facts) and subjective (feelings) information. Information gathered should be valid, accurate, relevant to the issue, and timely. Moreover, individuals involved in the process must have access to information and adequate resources to make cogent decisions.

Analyze Data

Data are analyzed to further refine the problem statement and identify possible solutions or options. Again, differentiating a problem from the symptoms of a problem is crucial. For example, a nurse manager is dismayed by the latest quality improvement (QI) report indicating nurses are not documenting patient teaching. Is this evidence that patient teaching is not being done? Is lack of documentation the actual problem? Perhaps it is a symptom of the actual problem. On further analysis, the manager may discover nurses do not know how to document patient teaching using the new computerized documentation system. By distinguishing the problem from the symptoms of the problem, a more appropriate solution can be identified and implemented. This example is one where asking the five whys could be effective.

Develop Solutions

The goal of generating options is to identify as many choices as possible. Occasionally, rigid "black and white" thinking hampers the quality of outcomes. A nurse who is unhappy with his or her work situation and can think of only two options—stay or resign—is displaying this type of thinking. That "either/or" thinking limits the possibilities for solutions.

Being flexible, open-minded, and creative—attributes of a critical thinker—is critical to being able to consider a range of possible options. Everyone has preconceived notions and ideas when confronted with certain situations. Although putting these notions on hold and considering other ideas is beneficial, it is difficult to do. However, asking questions such as the following can allow a person to consider other viewpoints:

- Am I jumping to conclusions?
- If I were (insert name of role model), how would I approach the issue?
- How are my beliefs and values affecting my decision?

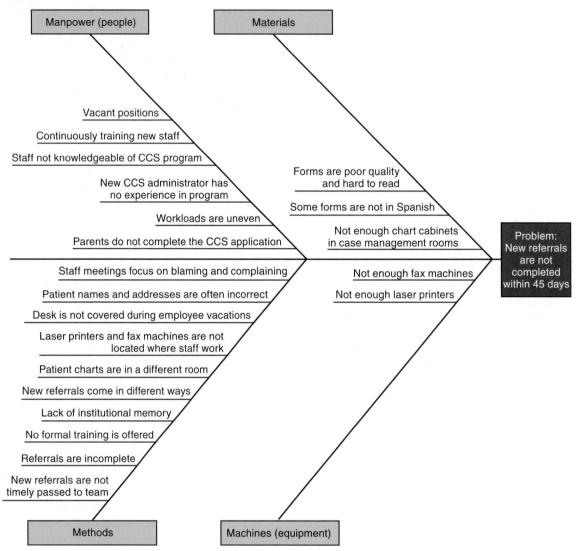

Fig. 15.5 Analysis of root causes of referral problems. *CCS,* California Children Services.

Select a Solution

The decision maker should then objectively weigh each option according to its possible risks and consequences as well as positive outcomes that may be derived. Criteria for evaluation might include variables such as cost-effectiveness, time, and legal or ethical considerations. The options should be ranked in the order in which they are likely to result in the desired goals or objectives. The solution selected should be the one that is most feasible and satisfactory and has the fewest undesirable consequences. Nurses must consider whether they are choosing the solution because it is the best solution or because it is the most expedient. Being able to make cogent decisions based on a thorough assessment of a situation is an important indicator of a nurse's effectiveness.

Implement the Solution

The planned solution is implemented using a defined and often phased strategy. Implementation may include revising policies and procedures, education, and documentation. The nurse leader or manager should remember that the implementation phase requires a contingency plan to deal with negative consequences if they arise and be prepared to implement a "plan B."

Evaluate the Result

Considerable time and energy are usually spent on identifying the problem or issue, generating possible solutions, selecting the best solution, and implementing the solution. However, not enough time is typically allocated for evaluation and follow-up. Therefore establishing early in the process how evaluation and monitoring will take place, who will be responsible for it, when it will take place, and the desired outcome ensures key elements are addressed. The key is to learn from mistakes and use the experiences to help guide future actions. Henry Ford said, "Failure is only the opportunity to begin again more intelligently."

CONCLUSION

Sometimes, individuals and groups do not adopt a structured problem-solving approach because it takes too much time, the process may be boring, stakeholders are too busy to get involved, or participants may perceive that little or no recognition for their participation is likely. Leaders should be cognizant of these potential barriers and should be prepared to prevent or minimize them.

All nurses, whether they are managers, leaders, or followers, need adequate decision-making and problem-solving skills to be effective in their roles. Regardless of the problem-solving approach, the use of a systematic approach will help address issues in an organized and focused manner.

THE SOLUTION

In a previous job, I had used interprofessional process improvement teams that consisted of key stakeholders to initiate process improvement. I chose to try this concept in my current setting. Our team consisted of the public health nurse (PHN) case managers, the California Children Services (CCS) case workers, the billing and claims staff, the CCS medical director, clerical and support staff, and me. I believed that a group approach to these problems would yield the most information and gain the greatest support for any changes that would be made. The team met weekly for an hour. We began by identifying our customers and key stakeholders and their expectations. This was extensive and took a few months to complete. Key stakeholders included the patients (children) and their parents; the providers (physicians and hospitals); pharmacists; vendors; representatives from schools, insurance plans, and other agencies; taxpayers (state and county); and our own team members. The expectations for each stakeholder were listed, discussed for clarity, and recorded. During this exercise, the team learned a great deal about each person's job duties (there were a few surprises) and how each stakeholder's role affected other team members' ability to do their job. As the team began understanding each person's job and issues, they focused less on blaming and more on how to change our processes.

Next, the team brainstormed (divergent thinking) a list of issues. The numerous issues were then grouped according to similarity, and duplicates were eliminated. Multivoting was then used to determine the three highest-priority issues. Our number one problem related to cycle time.

When a client is referred to CCS, determination of eligibility, opening (or denying) the case, and authorizing care are key cycles. Patient care is often coordinated based on the client's eligibility, and delays in service can result when the process is not completed in a timely manner. The reasons for our failure to meet these deadlines seemed overwhelming and beyond our ability to resolve. We needed a method to find the root causes to improve our performance. We chose to use a fishbone diagram, also known as a *cause-and-effect diagram*. Our problem was "New referrals are not completed within 45 days." We categorized our known barriers on the four bones of the fish: manpower, methods, machines, and materials. Once we had identified the factors contributing to our problem, we prioritized them and generated action plans for each major factor. These action plans were extensive and involved implementing training and education programs, redesigning work space for greater efficiency, purchasing more equipment, revising job descriptions, increasing provider outreach activities, and more. Performance data did not improve during the initial year of our process improvement initiative, and I chose not to share it with staff to avoid demoralizing them. My management team and I were taking a leap of faith that our process would eventually result in the desired outcome of meeting the performance metrics.

It took 18 months for CCS to "turn the corner," but once improvement started, it was exponential. The cycle time measure for "referral to case open" was initially 57 days. Two years later, it was 30 days. The cycle time "referral to deny" began at 97 days, and 2 years later was down to

(Continued)

THE SOLUTION—cont'd

39 days. Most important, the cycle time "referral to first authorization" decreased from an initial 189 days to just 49 days! It was at this time that I shared the outcome data with the team. They were ecstatic! I asked the team to list the problems they believed we had solved through our process improvement team's efforts. They listed (1) improved staffing, (2) increased staff morale and decreased turnover (all the positions were now filled), (3) better understanding of the job expectations and the rationale behind those expectations, (4) improved teamwork, and (5) more efficient and effective work space. They have maintained enthusiastic support of the Performance Improvement Team (PIT), and participation remains high. The team is still highly focused on problem solving. I have learned that when assuming leadership of a department in which one has no experience, a structured team approach to information gathering, assessment of data, identification of problems, and implementation of action plans can be highly effective in the resolution of priority problems.

Would this be a suitable approach for you? Why?

Vickie Lemmon

REFLECTIONS

Consider a recurring problem you face. What have you done to try to resolve the issue? What else could you do? Who is a trusted ally who could offer a fresh view of the problem? What are you willing to risk to try a new approach?

THE EVIDENCE

According to Porter-O'Grady and Malloch, authors of *Quantum Leadership* (2015), the three essential components to effective problem solving within organizations are tactical methods, strategic approaches, and cultural changes. Too often, nurse leaders and managers use a "firefighting" approach to problems, which is ineffective and generally causes more problems than it resolves.

Tactical methods for dealing with problems include getting assistance from someone with a fresh perspective, trying something new, and triaging problems (Porter O-Grady & Malloch, 2015). Getting assistance may require sharing some "dirty laundry" outside of the unit or organization, but a new point of view is helpful to bring clarity to a situation. Sometimes nurse leaders and managers rely on specific problem-solving methods out of habit, so a new approach may help resolve a difficult issue. After triaging problems, the urgent and most important can be addressed first.

Strategic approaches include strategies such as prioritizing problems to deal with critical issues first and developing learning scenarios to develop staff to take ownership of problems, and to develop the skills to deal with them independently. This will address the tendency of staff to expect their manager to fix everything for them.

Cultural changes within the organization are necessary to create an environment that supports effective decision making and problem solving. The organization needs to avoid "patching" as a problem-solving approach. Porter-O'Grady and Malloch (2015) describe patching as focusing on the symptoms of a problem instead of the actual issue. They emphasize that deadlines are irrelevant if the methodology used to solve problems is effective. The authors emphasized that firefighting should not be rewarded within the organization.

TIPS FOR DECISION MAKING AND PROBLEM SOLVING

- Seek additional information from other sources, even if they do not support the preferred action.
- Learn how other people approach decision making and problem solving.
- Talk to colleagues and supervisors who you believe are effective problem solvers and decision makers.

- Observe positive role models in action such as clinical nurse specialists, clinical nurse leaders, educators, and managers.
- Review journal articles and relevant sections of textbooks to increase your knowledge base.
- Use new approaches to problem resolution through experimentation, and calculate the risk to self and others.

REFERENCES

Cork, L. L. (2014). Nursing intuition as an assessment tool in predicting severity of injury in trauma patients. *Journal of Trauma Nursing, 21*(5), 244–252.

Crenshaw, J. T., & Yoder-Wise, P. (2013). Creating an environment for innovation: The risk-taking leadership competency. *Nurse Leader, 11*(1), 24–27.

Fowler, M. (2015). *Guide to the code of ethics for nurses: Development, application, and interpretation* (2nd ed.). Silver Springs, MD: American Nurses Association. Institute for Healthcare Improvement. www.ihi.org/IHI/Topics/Improvement/ImprovementMethods/Tools/. Mind Tools. www.mindtools.com/.

Llopis, G. (2013). The 4 most effective ways leaders solve problems. In *Forbes: Leadership.* https://www.forbes.com/sites/glennllopis/2013/11/04/the-4-most-effective-ways-leaders-solve-problems/#458a1f624f97.

Ojala, M. (2017). Locating and creating SWOT analyses. *Online Searcher, 41*(1), 59–62.

Porter-O'Grady, T., & Malloch, K. (2015). *Quantum leadership: Building better partnerships for sustainable health.* Burlington, MA: Jones & Bartlett.

Robert, R. R., Tilley, D. S., & Petersen, S. (2014). A power in clinical nursing practice: Concept analysis on nursing intuition. *MedSurg Nursing, 23*(5), 343–349.

Tanner, C. A. (2006). Thinking like a nurse: A research-based model of clinical judgment in nursing. *Journal of Nursing Education, 45*(6), 204–211.

The Critical Thinking Community. (2015). *Defining critical thinking.* http://www.criticalthinking.org/pages/defining-critical-thinking/410.

16

The Impact of Technology

Joan Benson, Ashley Sediqzad, Jana Wheeler

LEARNING OUTCOMES

- Articulate the role of technologies in patient safety.
- Describe the core components of informatics: data, information, and knowledge.
- Analyze three types of technology for capturing data at the point of care.
- Discuss decision support systems and their impact on patient care.
- Explore the issues of patient safety, ethics, and information security and privacy within information technology.

KEY TERMS

bar-code technology
biomedical technology
clinical decision support
clinical decision support systems
communication technology
computerized provider order
    entry (CPOE)
data

database
electronic health record (EHR)
electronic medical record (EMR)
informatics
information
information technology
knowledge technology
knowledge worker

meaningful use (MU)
QSEN: Quality and Safety
    Education for Nurses
smart card
speech recognition (SR)
telehealth

THE CHALLENGE

The nursing, pharmacy, and information systems teams in our hospital collaborated to implement bar-code medication administration (BCMA) 5 years ago. BCMA "closed the loop" on medication safety by providing an additional layer of safety after the nurse completed the "rights" of medication administration. As time has gone by and technology continues to improve, our teams have several questions to consider:

1. Is our current technology still reliable?
2. What evidence exists in the literature that might affect changes to our BCMA process?
3. Why do we continue to have BCMA work-arounds?
4. How do we train our new staff and provide ongoing training for current staff?

We needed to address these issues.
What would you do if you were this nurse?

Janis B. Smith, DNP, RN-BC
Children's Mercy Kansas City
Senior Director, Clinical Informatics & Professional Practice

INTRODUCTION

Technology surrounds us! Intravenous pumps are "smart," biomedical monitoring is no longer exclusively an intensive care practice, and computers are used at the bank, at the grocery checkout, in our cars, and in almost every other aspect of daily living, including the provision of health care. Health care is both a technology- and an information-intensive business; therefore the success of nurses using biomedical technology, information technology (IT), and knowledge technology will contribute to their personal and professional development and career achievement.

Although information technology abounds in the nursing workplace, students and nurses may not perceive that they are receiving sufficient education about its application in health care, though they report an overall positive attitude toward technology. The Quality and Safety Education for Nurses (QSEN) project identified informatics competency as a necessary component of the knowledge, skills, and attitudes necessary to continuously improve the quality and safety of health care (Drenkard, 2015). Nurses use information and technology daily to communicate and to seek and document knowledge.

The TIGER Initiative, an acronym for Technology Informatics Guiding Education Reform, was formed in 2004 to bring together nursing stakeholders to develop a shared vision, strategies, and specific actions for improving nursing practice, education, and the delivery of patient care through the use of health information technology. The TIGER Informatics Competencies Collaborative (TICC) Team was formed in 2009 to develop informatics recommendations for all practicing nurses and graduating nursing students. The Team created the TIGER Nursing Informatics Competencies Model, which has three parts:

1. Basic computer competencies
2. Information literacy
3. Information management (American Nurses Association, 2015)

Many leaders in health care see technology as a means to facilitate decision making, improve efficacy and efficiency, enhance patient safety and quality, and decrease healthcare costs (Institute of Medicine [IOM], 2000, 2011). If appropriately implemented and fully integrated, technology has the potential to improve the practice environment for nurses, as well as for patients and their families. However, we are also cautioned by patient safety and quality experts that technology is not a panacea (IOM, 2011).

Good decision making for patient care requires good information. Nurses are knowledge workers, who need data and information to provide effective and efficient patient care. According to the American Nurses Association *Nursing Informatics: Practice Scope and Standards of Practice,* "knowledge is information that is synthesized so that relationships are identified and formalized" (2015, p. 2), Data and information must be accurate, reliable, and presented in an actionable form. Technology can facilitate and extend nurses' decision-making abilities and support nurses in numerous ways, including creating a clinical data pool for the conduct of research.

TYPES OF TECHNOLOGIES

As nurses, we commonly use and manage three types of technologies: biomedical technology, information technology, and knowledge technology. Biomedical technology involves the use of equipment in the clinical setting for diagnosis, physiologic monitoring, testing, or administering therapies to patients. Information technology entails recording, processing, and using data and information for the purpose of delivering and documenting patient care. Knowledge technology is the use of expert systems to assist clinicians to make decisions about patient care. In nursing, these systems are designed to mimic the reasoning of nurse experts in making patient care decisions.

Biomedical Technology

Biomedical technology is used for (1) physiologic monitoring, (2) diagnostic testing, (3) intravenous fluid and medication dispensing and administration, and (4) therapeutic treatments.

Physiologic Monitoring

Physiologic monitoring systems measure heart rate, blood pressure, and other vital signs. They also monitor cardiac rhythm; measure and record central venous, pulmonary wedge, intracranial, and intraabdominal pressures; and analyze oxygen and carbon dioxide levels in the blood.

Data about adverse events in hospitalized patients indicate that a majority of physiologic abnormalities are not detected early enough to prevent the event, even when some of the abnormalities are present for hours before the event occurs (Scott, Considine, & Botti, 2015). Patient surveillance systems are designed to provide early warning of a possible impending adverse event. One example is a system that provides wireless monitoring of heart rate, respiratory rate, and attempts by a patient "at risk for falling" to get out of bed unassisted; this monitoring is via a mattress coverlet and bedside monitor.

Innovative technology permits physiologic monitoring and patient surveillance by expert clinicians who may be distant from the patient. The remote or virtual intensive care unit (vICU) is staffed by a dedicated team of experienced critical care nurses, physicians, and pharmacists who use state-of-the-art technology to leverage their expertise and knowledge over a large group of patients in multiple intensive care units (Kleinpell, Barden, Rincon, McCarthy, & Zapatochny Rufo, 2016).

Intracranial pressure (ICP) monitoring systems monitor the cranial pressure in critically ill patients with closed head injuries and postoperative craniotomy patients. The ICP, along with the mean arterial blood pressure, can be used to calculate perfusion pressure. This allows assessment and early therapy as changes occur. When the ICP exceeds a set pressure, some systems allow ventricular drainage. Similarly, monitoring pressure within the bladder has been demonstrated to accurately detect intraabdominal hypertension while measures of maximal and mean intraabdominal pressures and abdominal perfusion pressure are made. Intraabdominal hypertension occurs with abdominal compartment syndrome and other acute abdominal illnesses and has been demonstrated to be independently associated with mortality in these patients (Sugrue, De Waele, Ke Kuelenaer, Roberts, & Malbrain, 2015).

Continuous dysrhythmia monitors and electrocardiograms (ECGs) provide visual representation of electrical activity in the heart and can be used for surveillance and detection of dysrhythmias and for interpretation and diagnosis of the abnormal rhythm. Although not a new technology, these systems have grown increasingly sophisticated. More important, integration with wireless communication technology permits new approaches to triaging alerts to nurses about cardiac rhythm abnormalities. Voice technology and integrated telemetry and nurse paging systems have enhanced our accuracy and timelines in intervening in critical patient situations.

Biomedical devices for physiologic monitoring can be interfaced with clinical information systems. Monitored vital signs and invasive pressure readings are downloaded directly into the patient's electronic medical record, where the nurse confirms their accuracy and affirms the data entry.

Diagnostic Testing

Dysrhythmia systems can also be diagnostic. The computer, after processing and analyzing the ECG, generates a report that is confirmed by a trained professional. ECG tracings can be transmitted over telephone lines from remote sites, such as the patient's home, to the physician's office or clinic. Patients with implantable pacemakers can have their cardiac activity monitored without leaving home.

Other systems for diagnostic testing include blood gas analyzers, pulmonary function systems, and ICP monitors. Contemporary laboratory medicine is virtually all automated. In addition, point-of-care testing devices extend the laboratory's testing capabilities to the patient's bedside or care area. In critical care areas, for example, blood gas, ionized calcium, hemoglobin, and hematocrit values often are measured from unit-based "stat labs." Point-of-care blood glucose monitors can download results of bedside testing into an automated laboratory results system and the patient's electronic record. Results can be communicated quickly and trends analyzed throughout patients' hospital stays and at ongoing ambulatory care visits. Results can calculate the necessary insulin doses based on evidence for tight blood glucose control and evoke electronic orders for administration. This is an example of integrating a diagnostic test result with the appropriate orders-based intervention.

Intravenous Fluid and Medication Administration

Intravenous (IV) fluid and medication distribution and dispensing via automated dispensing cabinets (ADCs) were introduced in the 1980s and are used in a majority of hospitals today. ADCs can decrease the amount of time before a medication is available on patient care units for administration, ensure greater protection of medications (especially controlled substances), and efficiently and accurately capture drug charges. Most importantly, ADCs can reduce the risk of medication errors, but only when safeguards are available and used. In 2008 The Institute for Safe Medication Practices

(ISMP) developed guidelines for safe use of ADCs (Bernier, Yu, Rivard, Atkinson, & Bussières, 2016). The guidelines contain 12 core practices associated with safe ADC use and are available on the ISMP website (*www.ismp.org/Tools/guidelines/ADC/default.asp*). Some ADC machines have the ability to communicate in real time within the electronic health record (EHR), allowing the nurse to see all patient information at the point of care. This closes the loop in the medication process by having all members of the care team using one single patient file and source of truth.

IV smart pumps are used to deliver fluids, blood and blood products, and medications either continuously or intermittently at rates between 0.01 and 999 mL per hour. Twenty-first–century pumps offer safety features, accuracy, advanced pressure monitoring, ease of use, and versatility. These pumps have rate-dependent pressure detection systems, designed to provide an early alert to IV cannula occlusion with real-time display of the patient-side pressure reading in the system. Smart pumps can be programmed to calculate drug doses and medication infusion rates from an internal database or "drug library," as well as to determine the volume and duration of an infusion. Nurses, when programming the smart pump, can receive soft and hard stop alerts to significant programming errors or contradiction based on entered details.

Therapeutic Treatments

Treatments may be administered via implantable infusion pumps that administer medications at a prescribed rate and can be programmed to provide boluses or change doses at set points in time. These pumps are commonly used for hormone regulation, treatment of hypertension, chronic intractable pain, diabetes, venous thrombosis, and cancer chemotherapy.

Therapeutic treatment systems may be used to regulate intake and output, regulate breathing, and assist with the care of the newborn. Intake and output systems are linked to infusion pumps that control arterial pressure, drug therapy, fluid resuscitation, and serum glucose levels. These systems calculate and regulate the IV drip rate.

Increasingly sophisticated mechanical ventilators are used to deliver a prescribed percentage of oxygen and volume of air to the patient's lungs and to provide a set flow rate, inspiratory-to-expiratory time ratio, and various other complex functions with less trauma to lung tissue than was previously possible. Computer-assisted ventilators are electromechanically controlled by a closed-loop feedback system to analyze and control lung volumes and alveolar gases. Ventilators also provide sophisticated, sensitive alarm systems for patient safety.

In the newborn and intensive care nursery, computers monitor the heart and respiratory rates of the babies there. In addition, newborn nursery systems can regulate the temperature of the infant's environment by sensing his or her temperature and the air of the surrounding environment. Alarms can be set to notify the nurse when preset physiologic parameters are exceeded. Computerized systems monitor fetal activity before delivery, linking the ECGs of the mother and baby and the pulse oximetry, blood pressure, and respirations of the mother.

Biomedical technology affects nursing as nurses provide direct care to patients treated with new technologies: monitoring data from new devices, administering therapy with new techniques, and evaluating patients' responses to care and treatment. Nurses must be aware of the latest technologies for monitoring patients' physiologic status, diagnostic testing, drug administration, and therapeutic treatments. Nurses need to identify the data to be collected, the information that might be gained, and the many ways that these data might be used to provide new knowledge (Fig. 16.1). More importantly, nurses must remember that biomedical technology supplements, but does not replace, the skilled observation, assessment, and evaluation of the patient.

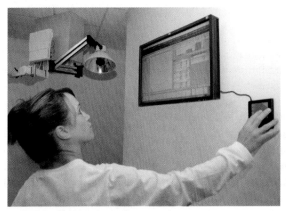

Fig. 16.1 Patient data displayed with computerized systems to provide meaningful information and trends.

Biomedical technology is designed to help keep patients safe and to alert staff of changes in the patient's condition. A Sentinel Event Alert from The Joint Commission (2013a) brought attention to alarm fatigue or alarm desensitization from biomedical technology. The overuse of alarms from infusion pumps, feeding devices, monitors, and ventilators can cause sensory strain. Staff who are overwhelmed by the sheer number of alarms can miss or delay responding, leading to sentinel events or even patient death. Desensitization to the alarms is quickly becoming a national problem (Petersen & Costanzo, 2017).

Nursing leaders must be aware of how these technologies fit into the delivery of patient care and the strategic plan of the organization in which they work. They must have a vision for the future and be ready to suggest solutions that will assist nurses across specialties and settings to improve patient care safety and quality.

EXERCISE 16.1 List the types of biomedical technology available for patient care in your organization. List ways that you currently use the data and information gathered by these systems. How do these help you care for patients? Can you think of other ways to use the technology? Can you think of other ways to use the data or information? For example, data from biomedical devices might be sent directly to the electronic health record, negating the need for transcription of a result into the patient's chart. Nurses spend many hours learning to use biomedical devices and to interpret the data gained from them. Have we come to rely too heavily on technology rather than on our own judgment? You might consider using your computer skills to draw a concept map to illustrate the relationships between the types of biomedical, diagnostic, therapeutic, and information technologies available in healthcare organizations you have worked in.

Information Technology

Health care is an information-intensive and knowledge-intensive enterprise. Information technology can help healthcare providers acquire, manage, analyze, and disseminate both information and knowledge. Health care in the 21st century should be safe, effective, patient-centered, timely, efficient, and equitable (Institute of Medicine [IOM], 2001), and to achieve that we need a comprehensive view. This view isn't new—as a result of information technology, however, it is manageable.

Computers offer the advantage of storing, organizing, retrieving, and communicating digital data with accuracy and speed. Patient care data can be entered once, stored in a database, and then quickly and accurately retrieved many times and in many combinations by healthcare providers and others. A database is a collection of data elements organized and stored together. Data processing is the structuring, organizing, and presenting of data for interpretation as information. For example, vital signs for one patient can be entered into the computer and communicated on a graph; many patients' blood pressure measurements can be compared with the number of doses of antihypertension medication. Vital signs for male patients between the ages of 40 and 50 years can be correlated and used to show relationships with age, ethnicity, weight, presence of comorbid conditions, and so on.

Humans process data continuously, but in an analog form. Computers process data in a digital form. They process data faster and more accurately than humans and provide a method of storage so that data can be retrieved as needed. The Theory Box provides key concepts of information processing, and Box 16.1 describes the development of information management skills from novice to expert.

BOX 16.1   Development of Information Management Skills: Novice to Expert Practice

Novice nurses focus on learning what data to collect, the process of collecting and documenting the data, and how to use this information. They learn what clinical applications are available for use and how to use them. Computer and informatics skills focus on applying concrete concepts.

As nurses grow in expertise, they look for patterns in the data and information. They aggregate data across patient populations to look for similarities and differences in response to interventions. Expert nurses integrate theoretical knowledge with practical knowledge gained from experience.

Expert nurses know the value of personal professional reflection on knowledge and synthesize and evaluate information for discovery and decision making.

THEORY BOX

Information Theory

Key Contributor	Key Ideas	Application to Practice
Locsin (2005): Techno-logical Competency as Caring in Nursing: A Model for Practice	The realities of continuously advancing technologies in health care necessitate that contemporary nursing practice incorporates both the concepts of technology and caring. Nurses practice in environments requiring technological expertise. Technology has transformed the practice of nursing with the coexistence of caring and technology. Competency with technology is demonstrated by registered nurses in skillful, intentional, deliberate, and authentic activities that engage technology in caring for patients and families. Nurses can build a strong connection with patients and families through the competent use of technology.	Nurses at all stages of professional development need to acquire the skills to use technology competently. When nurses are adept in the use of technology they engage it to care for patients. For example, the best online resources for patient/family education can be linked to clinical information systems and accessed when the ideal teaching moment is identified. Nurses can influence patients and families to engage in their own care. Providing patients an electronic copy of their record or making patients aware of a patient portal, enrolling them with a portal account, and teaching them how to use it, are steps toward strengthening patient access to their health information and engagement in their own health care.

Modified from Locsin, R. C. (2005). *Technological competency as caring in nursing: A model for practice.* Indianapolis, IN: Sigma Theta Tau International.

KNOWLEDGE TECHNOLOGY

Knowledge technology consists of systems that generate or process knowledge and provide clinical decision support (CDS). Defined broadly, CDS is a clinical computer system, computer application, or process that helps health professionals make clinical decisions to enhance patient care. The clinical knowledge embedded in computer applications or work processes can range from simple facts and relationships to best practices for managing patients with specific disease states, new medical knowledge from clinical research, and other types of information. Among the most common forms of CDS are drug-dosing calculators—computer-based programs that calculate appropriate doses of medications after a clinician inputs key data (e.g., patient weight or the level of serum creatinine). These calculators are especially useful in managing the administration of medications with a narrow therapeutic index. Allergy alerts, dose range checking, drug-drug interaction, and duplicate order checking are other common applications of CDS.

Clinical (or diagnostic) decision support systems (CDSSs) are interactive computer programs designed to assist health professionals with decision-making tasks by mimicking the inductive or deductive reasoning of a human expert. The basic components of a CDSS include a knowledge base and an *inferencing mechanism* (usually a set of rules derived from the experts and evidence-based practice). The knowledge base contains the knowledge that an expert nurse would apply to data entered about a patient and information to solve a problem. The inference engine controls the application of the knowledge by providing the logic and rules for its use with data from a specific patient. The advent of Watson has helped determine interventions while collecting more data for making decisions.

Box 16.2 illustrates the use of an expert system for determining the maximum dose of pain medication that can safely be given to a patient after an invasive procedure. The knowledge base contains eight items that are to be considered when giving the maximum dose. The inference engine controls the use of the knowledge base by applying logic that an expert nurse would use in making the decision to give the maximum dose. This decision frame states that if pain is severe (A) or a painful procedure is planned (B), and there is an order for pain medication (C) and the time since surgery is less than 48 hours (H) and the time since the last dose is greater than 3 hours (G), and there are no contraindications to the medication (D) or history of allergy (E) or contraindication to the maximum dose (F), then the "decision" would be to give the dose of pain medication. The rules are those that expert nurses would apply in making the decision to give pain medication.

BOX 16.2 Expert Decision Frame for "Give Maximum Dose of Pain Medication"

The Knowledge Base
A. Pain score
B. Invasive procedure scheduled
C. Opiate analgesic ordered
D. Contraindications to the medication
E. History of allergic reaction to opiate analgesics
F. Contraindication to maximum dose of opiate analgesic
G. Time since last dose of opiate analgesic administered
H. Time since surgical procedure

The Inference Engine
Give the maximum dose of pain medication if (A or B) and (C and H < 48 hours and G > 3 hours) and not (D or E or F)
OR
(C and H < 48 hours and G > 4 hours) and not (D or E or F)

EXERCISE 16.2 Mr. Jones's heart rate is 54 beats per minute. Tony is about to give Mr. Jones his scheduled atenolol dose. When Tony scans Mr. Jones's armband and the medication bar codes, the computer warns him that atenolol should not be given to a patient with a heart rate less than 60 beats per minute. What should Tony do?

One of the benefits of CDSSs is that they permit the novice nurse to take advantage of decision-making expertise and judgment of an expert. Nursing leaders must be aware of the usefulness of decision support systems for nursing, because the development of CDS applicable to nursing practices continues to grow (Washington State Nurses Association, 2016). Clinical experts are needed to develop both the knowledge in the database and the logic used to develop the rules for its application to a particular patient in a particular circumstance. Advanced critical thinking skills are needed to develop logic and rules. When these are in place, patient care quality can be standardized and improved.

Medication management has a number of high-risk and high-volume processes. New applications provide support for all aspects of the process, thereby improving safety and efficiency (Box 16.3).

INFORMATION SYSTEMS

A patient information system can be manual or computerized—in fact, we have collected and recorded information about patients and patient care since the dawn of health care. Computer information systems manage large volumes of data, examine data patterns and trends, solve problems, and answer questions. In other words, computers can help translate data into information. Ideally, data are recorded at the point in the care process where they are gathered and are available to healthcare providers when and where they are needed. This is accomplished, in part, by networking computers both within and among organizations to form larger systems. These networked systems might link inpatient care units and other departments, hospitals, clinics, hospice centers, home health agencies, and/or physician practices. Data from all patient encounters with the healthcare system are stored in a central data repository, where they are accessible to authorized users located anywhere in the world. These provide the potential for automated patient records, which contain health data from birth to death.

Adopting the technology necessary to computerize patient care information systems is complex and must be accomplished in stages. The Healthcare Information and Management Systems Society (HIMSS) has described seven stages of adoption—the seventh of which marks achievement of a fully electronic healthcare record. The seven stages of adoption are listed and described in Table 16.1. In 2016 about 31% of US hospitals had achieved stage 6, 4.8% had achieved stage 7, and less than 2% were at stage 0 (HIMSS Analytics, 2017).

Nurses care for patients in acute care, ambulatory, and community settings, as well as in patients' homes. In all settings, nurses focus not only on managing acute illnesses but also on health promotion, maintenance, and education; care coordination and continuity; and monitoring chronic conditions. Ideally, information systems support the work of nurses in all settings.

Communication networks are used to transmit data entered at one computer and received by others in the network. These networks can reduce the clerical functions of nursing. They can provide patient demographic and census data, results from tests, and lists of medications. Nursing policies and procedures can be linked to the network and accessed, when needed, at the point of care. Links can be provided between the patient's

BOX 16.3   Information Technology: Trends in the Medication Management Process

Various information technology (IT) devices and software applications are designed to support the medication management process. Each has unique functionality and targets a specific phase of the medication process.

Computerized Provider Order Entry (CPOE)

- Decision support and clinical warnings (e.g., alerts the provider of allergies, pertinent laboratory data, drug-drug and drug-food interactions)
- Automatic dose calculation
- Link to up-to-date drug reference material
- Automatic order notification
- Standardized formulary-compliant order sets
- Legible, accurate, and complete medication orders
- Decreased variations in practice
- Less time clarifying orders
- Fewer verbal orders
- No manual transcription errors

Electronic Medication Administration Record (e-MAR)

- Integration with clinical documentation (in the electronic record)
- Link to up-to-date drug reference material
- Automatic reminders and alarms for approaching or missed medication administration times
- Prompts for associated tasks or additional documentation requirements
- Alert when cumulative dosing exceeds maximum
- Legible record
- Accessible to multiple users
- Improved accuracy of pharmacokinetic monitoring (administration times are reliable)
- Record matches the pharmacy profile
- Generated reports to track medication errors with visibility of near misses
- Perpetual interface with pharmacy inventory system
- Increase the accuracy of charge capture (at the time of administration vs. when drug is dispensed)

Bar Coding and Radio Frequency Identification (RFID) Scanning

- Medication documentation captured electronically at the time of administration (populates the e-MAR)
- Medication rights verified

- Positive patient identification
- Clinician alerted to discrepancies (e.g., wrong drug, wrong dose, wrong time, wrong patient, expired drug)
- Automatic tracking of medication errors and provides visibility to near misses

"Smart" Infusion Pumps (Medication Infusion Delivery System)

- Reduced need for manual dose/rate calculation
- Institution-defined standardized drug library (drugs, concentrations, dosing parameters)
- Software filter prevention of programming errors/programming within preestablished minimum and maximum limits before infusion can begin
- Device infusion parameter limits based on patient type or care area
- Interface with the patient's pharmacy profile with capabilities to program the pump electronically
- User alerts to pump setting errors, wrong channel selection, and mechanical failures
- Electronic notification to pharmacy when fluids or medications need to be dispensed
- Interface with the patient's e-MAR (accurate documentation of administration times and volumes infused)
- Memory functions for settings and alarms with a retrievable log
- Electronic recording of reprogramming and limited override activity

Automated Dispensing Unit or Cabinet

- Secured drug storage
- Controlled user access—biometric identification
- Interface with the pharmacy profile—access restricted until order reviewed
- Quick access once medication order reviewed by pharmacist
- Ability to monitor controlled substance waste and utilization patterns
- Perpetual interface with pharmacy inventory

Pharmacy Automation and Robotics

- Increased accuracy and speed of dispensing

From Bell, M. J. (2005). Nursing information of tomorrow. *Healthcare Informatics, 22*(2), 74-78; Larrabee, S., & Brown, M. M. (2003). Recognizing the institutional benefits of bar-code point-of-care technology. *Joint Commission Journal on Quality and Safety, 29*(7), 345-353.

TABLE 16.1   Electronic Medical Record Adoption Model

U.S. Electronic Medical Record Adoption Model

Stage	Cumulative Capabilities	% OF ACHIEVEMENT 2016 Q3	% OF ACHIEVEMENT 2016 Q4
Stage 7	Complete EMR, data analytics to improve care	4.6%	4.8%
Stage 6	Physician documentation (templates), full CDSS, closed-loop medication administration	30.5%	30.5%
Stage 5	Full R-PACS	34.5%	34.9%
Stage 4	CPOE, clinical decision support (clinical protocols)	10.1	10.2
Stage 3	Clinical documentation, CDSS (error checking)	14.1	13.9
Stage 2	CDR, Controlled Medical Vocabulary, CDS, HIE capable	2.2	2.3
Stage 1	Ancillaries – Laboratory, Rad, Pharmacy – All Installed	1.7%	1.4%
Stage 0	All Three Ancillaries Not Installed	2.4%	1.9%
		N = 5449	N = 2478

CDR, Clinical data repository; *CDS,* clinical decision support; *CDSS,* clinical documentation support systems; *CPOE,* computerized provider order entry; *HIE,* health information exchange; *R-PACS,* radiology picture archiving and communication system.
From HIMSS Analytics, Healthcare Information and Management Systems Society. 2017 HIMSS Analytics Report. (2017). EMRAM: A strategic roadmap for effective EMR adoption and maturity. http://www.himssanalytics.org/emram.

home, hospital, and/or physician office with computers, handheld technologies, and point-of-care devices. Day-to-day events can be recorded and downloaded into the patient record remotely in community nursing settings or at the point of care in the hospital or clinic.

EXERCISE 16.3 Select a healthcare setting with which you are familiar. What information systems are used? Make a list of the names of these systems and the information they provide. How do they help you in caring for patients or in making management decisions? Think about the communication of data and information among departments. Do the systems communicate with each other? If you do not have computerized systems, think about how data and information are communicated. How might a computer system help you be more efficient?

As an example, assume that an abdominal magnetic resonance imaging (MRI) with contrast has been ordered. In a paper-based system, handwritten requisitions are sent to nutrition services, pharmacy, and the radiology department. With a computerized system, the MRI is ordered and the requests for dietary changes, bowel preparation medications, and the diagnostic study itself are automatically sent to the appropriate departments. Radiology would compare its schedule openings with the patient's schedule and automatically place the date and time for the MRI on the patient's automated plan of care. The images and results of the diagnostic procedure are available online.

Nurses caring for patients in home health care and hospice must complete documentation necessary to meet government and insurance requirements. Computers assist with direct entry of all required data in the correct format. Portable computers are used to download files of the patients to be seen during the day from a main database. During each visit, the computer prompts the nurse for vital signs, assessments, diagnosis, interventions, long-term and short-term goals, and medications based on previous entries in the medical record. Nurses enter any new data, modifications, or nursing information directly. Entries can be transmitted by a telephone line to the main computer at the office or downloaded from the device at the end of the day. This action automatically updates the patient record and any verbal order entry records, home visit reports, federally mandated treatment plans, productivity and quality improvement reports, and other documents for review and signature. Portable and wireless computers have made recording patient care information more efficient and have improved personnel productivity and compliance with necessary documentation. Additionally, the potential for errors and lack of coordination is reduced.

Placing computers or handheld devices "patient-side" permits nurses to enter data once, at the point of care (Fig. 16.2). Documentation of patient assessments and care provided patient-side saves time, gives others more timely access to the data, and decreases the likelihood of forgetting to document vital information. Point-of-care devices and systems that fit with nurses' workflow, personalize patient assessments, and simplify care planning are available. Patient care areas with point-of-care computers have improved the quality of patient care by decreasing errors of omission, providing greater accuracy and completeness of documentation, reducing medication errors, providing more timely responses to patient needs, improving discharge planning and teaching, and facilitating nursing hand-off (Mardis et al., 2016).

Fig. 16.2 Smart phone technology is a platform for widely used mobile clinical applications. (Copyright © Ridofranz/iStock/Thinkstock.)

> **EXERCISE 16.4** Think about the data you gather as you care for a patient through the day. How do you communicate information and knowledge about your patient to others? Does the information system support the way you need this information organized, stored, retrieved, and presented to other healthcare providers? For example, if a patient's pain medication order is about to expire and you want to assess the patient's use and response to the pain medication during the past 24 hours, can the information system generate a graph that compares the time, dose, and pain score for this period? If your assessment is that the medication order needs to be renewed, how do you communicate that message to the prescriber?

Meaningful Use

The potential of electronic health records (EHRs) to benefit caregivers, patients, and their families depends on how they are used. Meaningful use (MU) is the set of standards defined by the Medicare and Medicaid Electronic Health Records (EHR) Incentive Programs that governs the use of EHRs and allows eligible providers and hospitals to earn incentive payments by meeting specific criteria. The goal of MU is to promote the implementation and effective use of EHRs to improve health care in the United States (Kern, Edwards, & Kaushal, 2016). The benefits of the meaningful use of EHRs include the following:

- *Complete and accurate information.* With EHRs, care providers have the information they need to provide the best possible care.
- *Better access to information.* EHRs facilitate greater access to the information needed to diagnose and treat health problems earlier and improve health outcomes for patients. EHRs allow information to be shared among offices, hospitals, and across health systems, which facilitates care coordination.
- *Patient empowerment.* EHRs can empower patients and families to take a more active role in their health. They can receive electronic copies of their healthcare records and share their health information securely over the Internet with their families and care providers.

To achieve MU, eligible providers and hospitals must adopt an EHR that has the technical capabilities to ensure the systems are capable of performing

TABLE 16.2 **Stages of Meaningful Use**		
Stage 1 Criteria Focus	**Stage 2 Criteria Focus**	**Stage 3 Criteria Focus**
Capturing health information electronically in a standardized format	More rigorous health information exchange (HIE)	Improving quality, safety, and efficiency, leading to improved health outcomes
Using that information to track key clinical conditions	Increased requirements for e-prescribing and incorporating laboratory results	Decision support for national high-priority conditions
Communicating that information for care coordination processes	Electronic transmission of patient care summaries across multiple settings	Patient access to self-management tools
Initiating the reporting of clinical quality measures and public health information	More patient-controlled data	Access to comprehensive patient data through patient-centered HIE
Using information to engage patients and their families in their care		Improving population health

Source: https://www.healthit.gov/topic/federal-incentive-programs/meaningful-use. Nursing leaders can learn more about MU at https://www.healthit.gov/.

defined required functions. Thereafter providers and hospitals must use the technology to achieve specific objectives.

The MU objectives and measures evolve over 5 years: Stage 1 is capturing and sharing data via EHRs. Stage 2 is advancing clinical processes with EHRs. Stage 3 is requiring that providers and hospitals use EHRs to demonstrate improved patient outcomes (Table 16.2).

Information Systems Quality and Accreditation

Quality management and measuring patient care efficiency, effectiveness, and outcomes are necessary for accreditation and licensing of healthcare organizations. This is demonstrated by documentation of patient care processes and outcomes. The plan of care outlines what patient care needs to occur, orders are entered to prescribe needed care, and documentation confirms that the care was provided. Computers can capture and aggregate data to demonstrate both the processes of care and the patient outcomes achieved.

The Joint Commission (TJC), an independent, not-for-profit organization, evaluates and provides accreditation and certification to more than 15,000 healthcare organizations and programs in the United States. Accreditation and certification by TJC are recognized nationwide as symbols of an organization's commitment to meeting performance standards focused on improving the quality and safety of patient care.

The *Comprehensive Accreditation Manual for Hospitals* and the manuals for other healthcare programs include a chapter of standards for information management. Planning for information management is the initial focus of the chapter, because a well-planned system meets the internal and external information needs of an organization with efficiency and accuracy. The goals of effective information management are to obtain, manage, and use information to improve patient care processes and patient outcomes, as well as to improve other organizational processes. Planning is also necessary to provide care continuity should an organization's information systems be disrupted or fail. Planning also is necessary to ensure privacy, security, confidentiality, and integrity of data and information.

In the 2013 TJC accreditation manual chapter "The Record of Care, Treatment and Services," standards and recommendations for the components of a complete medical record are provided. It details documentation requirements that include accuracy, authentication, and thorough, timely documentation. Other standards address the requirements for auditing and retaining records (TJC, 2013).

All nurses, including nurse leaders, share responsibility to ensure that cost-effective, high-quality patient care is provided. Nursing administrative databases, containing both clinical and management data, support decision making for these purposes. Administrative databases assist in the development of the organization's information infrastructure, which ultimately allows for links between management decisions (e.g., staffing or nurse–patient ratios), costs, and clinical outcomes.

Selection of a clinical information system and software partner may be one of the most important decisions of a chief nursing officer and the nursing leadership team. Nurse leaders and direct care nurses must be members of the selection team, participate actively, and have a voice in the selection decision. Remember, nurses are knowledge workers who require data, information, and knowledge to deliver effective patient care. The information system must make sense to the people who use it and fit effectively with the processes for providing patient care. Box 16.4 identifies key elements of an ideal clinical information system that can guide the decision making necessary for selecting or developing health information software. Before making a selection, visit organizations already using the software to obtain practical and strategic information. Discussions at site visits include both the utility and performance of the software and the customer service and responsiveness of the vendor.

Information Systems Hardware

Placing the power of computers for both entering and retrieving data at the point of patient care is a major thrust in the move toward increased adoption of clinical information systems. Many hospitals and clinics are using a number of computing devices in the clinical setting—desktop, laptop, or, increasingly, tablet computers; and smart phones—as we learn about both the possibilities and limitations of different hardware solutions. Theoretically, nurses may work best with robust mobile technology. Installing computers on mobile carts, also known as *computers on wheels* or *COWs,* may increase work efficiency and save time. However, if the cart is cumbersome to move around or if concern about infection risk is associated with moving the cart from one room to another, some organizations favor keeping one cart stationed in each patient care room or installing hardwired bedside computers.

Wireless Communication

Wireless (WL) communication is an extension of an existing wired network environment and uses radio-based systems to transmit data signals through the air without any physical connections. Telemetry is a clinical use of WL communication. Nurses can communicate with other healthcare team members, departments, and offices and with patients through the use of pagers, smart phones, and wireless computers. Nurses can send and receive e-mail, clinical data, and other text messages. The Internet can be accessed on these devices.

WL systems are used by emergency medical personnel to request authorization for the treatments or drugs needed in emergency situations. Laboratories use WL technology to transmit laboratory results to physicians; patients awaiting organ transplants are provided with WL pagers so that they can be notified if a donor is found; and parents of critically ill children carry WL pagers when they are away from a phone. Visiting nurses using a home-monitoring system employ WL technology to enter vital signs and other patient-related information. Inpatient nurses can send messages to the admissions department when a patient is being transferred to another unit without having to wait for someone to answer the telephone. Increasingly, whole hospitals use WL technology to deploy their information systems to the point of patient care.

New hardware for patient information systems has both advantages and disadvantages. Portable devices, such as smart phones and tablet computers, are less expensive than placing a stationary computer in each patient room. In addition, each caregiver on a shift can be equipped with a device. Portable, handheld devices

---

BOX 16.4   Elements of the Ideal Hospital Information System

- Data are standardized and use structured terminology.
- The system is reliable—minimal scheduled or unscheduled downtime.
- Applications are integrated across the system.
- Data are collected at the point of care.
- The database is complete, accurate, and easy to query.
- The infrastructure is interconnected and supports accessibility.
- Data are gathered by instrumentation whenever possible so that only minimal data entry is necessary.
- The system has a rapid response time.
- The system is intuitive and reflective of patient care delivery models.
- The location facilitates functionality, security, and support.
- Screen displays can be configured by user preference.
- The system supports outcomes and an evidence-based approach to care delivery.

allow access to information at the point of care, both for retrieval of information and entry of patient data. Disadvantages stem from their size and portability. They have a small display screen, limiting the amount of data that can be viewed on the screen and the size of the font. Portable devices can also be put down and forgotten, dropped and broken, and targeted for theft. Small devices require a convenient and adequate place to store the devices when they are not in use and to charge their batteries, when needed. Finally, WL technology may not operate with the speed necessary to advantage busy healthcare workers in fast-paced environments.

Management of the hardware designed to take advantage of clinical information system software is important. Nursing leaders must make knowledgeable decisions about the type of hardware to use, the education needed to use it effectively, and the proper care and maintenance of the equipment. Important questions to ask include the following: What data and information do we need to gather? When and where should it be gathered? How difficult is the equipment to use? Has the hardware been tested sufficiently to ensure purchase of a dependable product?

Communication Technology

Communication technology is an extension of WL technology that enables hands-free communication among mobile hospital workers. Hospital staff members wear a pendant-like badge around their neck and, by simply pressing a button on the badge, can be connected to the person with whom they wish to speak by stating the name or function of the person.

Voice technology may also enhance the use of computer systems in the future. Speech recognition (SR) is also known as *computer speech recognition*. The term *voice recognition* may also be used to refer to speech recognition but is less accurate. SR converts spoken words to machine-readable input. SR applications in everyday life include voice dialing (e.g., "Call home"), call routing (e.g., "I would like to make a collect call"), and simple data entry (e.g., stating a credit card or account number). In health care, preparation of structured documents, such as a radiology report, is possible. In all these examples, the computer gathers, processes, interprets, and executes audible signals by comparing the spoken words with a template in the system. If the patterns match, recognition occurs and a command is executed by the computer. This allows untrained personnel or those whose hands are busy to enter data in an SR environment without touching the computer. Voice technology will also allow quadriplegic and other physically challenged individuals to function more efficiently when using the computer. SR systems recognize a large number of words but are still immature. The speaker must use staccato-like speech, pausing between each clearly spoken word, and these systems must be programmed for each user so that the system recognizes the user's voice patterns.

Automating the healthcare delivery process is not an easy task. Patient care processes are often not standardized across settings, and most software vendors cannot customize software for each organization. Some current versions of the electronic patient record have merely automated the existing schema of the chart rather than considering how computers could permit data to be viewed or used differently from manual methods. The complexity of decision making about health information systems software and hardware has given rise to the science of informatics.

INFORMATICS

Classically, informatics is "a science that combines a domain science, computer science, information science, and cognitive science" (Hunter, 2001, p. 180). The term *nursing informatics* was probably first used and defined by Scholes and Barber in 1980 in their address to the International Medical Informatics Association (IMIA) at the conference that year in Tokyo. They defined *nursing informatics* as "the application of computer technology to all fields of nursing—nursing services, nurse education, and nursing research" (p. 73).

Nursing informatics is now a thriving subspecialty of nursing that combines nursing knowledge and skills with computer expertise. Like any knowledge-intensive profession, nursing is greatly affected by the explosive growth of both scientific advances and technology. Nurse informatics specialists manage and communicate nursing data and information to improve decision making by consumers, patients, nurses, and other healthcare providers. Nurse informatics specialists formed the American Nursing Informatics Association (ANIA) in the early 1990s to provide networking, education, and information resources that enrich and strengthen the roles of nurses in the field of informatics, including the domains of clinical information, education, and administration decision support. In addition, nursing informatics is represented in the American Medical Informatics Association (AMIA) and the IMIA by working groups that promote the advancement of nursing informatics within the larger interdisciplinary context of health informatics.

The Nursing Informatics Working Group of AMIA defined their practice specialty as "the science and practice (that) integrates nursing, its information and knowledge, with management of information and communication technologies to promote the health of people, families, and communities worldwide" (American Medical Informatics Association, 2017).

Many undergraduate and graduate nursing education programs recognize that it is essential to prepare nurses to practice in a technology-rich environment (National League for Nursing [NLN], 2015). Noting the federal initiatives pushing the adoption of EHRs throughout all healthcare institutions by the year 2014, the NLN recognizes the role of nurse educators in preparing the nursing workforce "to enhance patient care outcomes in a shifting health care environment" (NLN, 2015, p. 4). Certification as a nurse informatics specialist by the American Nurses Credentialing Center (ANCC) requires specific coursework and specific experience and/or continuing education.

Informatics is interdisciplinary, and in its truest form it focuses on the care of patients rather than on a specific discipline (Hannah & Ball, 2011). Although specific bodies of knowledge exist for each healthcare profession (e.g., nursing, dentistry, dietetics, pharmacy, medicine), they interface at the patient. Working with integrated clinical information systems demands interdisciplinary collaboration at a high level.

PATIENT SAFETY

The patient care environment is complex and prone to errors. Nurses have a major role in the quality and safety of health care (Arzouman, 2016). In addition to physical challenges, resource challenges, and interruptions characteristic of nursing work, nurses are challenged by inconsistencies and breakdowns in care communication. Communication and information difficulties are among the most common nursing workplace challenges and are frustrating and potentially dangerous for patients.

Information technology is identified as an essential tool for advancing patient safety (Agboola, Bates, & Kvedar, 2016). Nurses, other health professionals, and patients and families rely increasingly on information technology to communicate, manage information, mitigate error potential, and make informed decisions (Abdrbo, 2015). Health information technology has the potential to improve—or obstruct—work performance, communication, and documentation (Sittig, Ash, & Singh, 2014). Because nurses play a central role in patient care, the extent to which information technology supports or detracts from nurses' work performance may affect nurse-sensitive outcomes (Gomes, Hash, Orsolini, Watkins, & Mazzoccoli, 2016).

Documentation to meet organizational, accreditation, insurance, state, and federal requirements, as well as to provide information needed by other healthcare providers, imposes a heavy demand on nurses' time. Documentation requirements lessen nursing time for direct contact with patients and families.

IMPACT OF CLINICAL INFORMATION SYSTEMS

Clinical information systems that provide access to patient information and provide clinical decision support can reduce errors and inefficiencies (Wang, Zhang, Li & Lin, 2016). Patient information in an electronic clinical information system is organized and legible. Nurses see all of the medications prescribed for a patient in one location; doses are written clearly, and drug names are spelled correctly. The patient problem list shows acute and chronic health conditions and complete allergy information. Abnormal findings are highlighted and can be graphed and compared with interventions. Alerts signal to nurses that critical information has been entered in the electronic record. For example, critical test results signal the need for provider notification and intervention. An alert that a patient is at risk for falling signals the need for additional monitoring and interventions to ensure safety. Nursing reminders to perform pressure area care reduce the incidence of this important hospital-acquired condition.

When standards for care are not being followed, clinical information systems can generate alerts, reminders, or suggestions. Rules remind care providers to perform required care. When documentation is not recorded for medication administration, IV tubing change, or wound care, for example, the system generates a reminder based on rules that have been agreed to by providers. Evidence-based practices are integrated in the process of care as providers are guided to select the most appropriate course of action.

Errors are prevented by eliminating problems stemming from illegible handwriting. Computerized order entry also eliminates the nursing time required for clarification of illegible and incomplete orders. Transcription is no longer required, orders are sent directly to the performing department, and patient care needs are communicated more clearly and quickly to all clinicians. Medication dosing, drug allergy, and drug-drug interaction checking all have a significant impact on patient safety (Creed, 2017).

Impact on Communication

Integrated information systems allow all members of the interdisciplinary patient care team to see pertinent patient information and plan care based on what is currently happening and what should occur in the future. Everyone knows who is responsible for the patient and who needs to communicate about the patient's care. Clinical information systems provide multiple users with simultaneous, real-time access to patient records. Patient care hand-offs are safer when information is not unavailable or lost in the process. Patient care processes are facilitated, and treatment delays are decreased. The patient's care experience is also improved by decreasing redundant data collection by multiple members of the care team.

Impact on Patient Care Documentation

Nurses spend much time documenting patient care activities. Clinical documentation in an electronic information system improves access to patient information and increases documentation efficiency and organization (Wang, Zhang, Li, & Lin, 2016). Redundant documentation is eliminated with an integrated clinical information system, and completeness of nursing documentation has increased with some systems (Richardson et al., 2016).

Impact on Medication Administration Processes

The *Quantros MEDMARX* database includes annual records of medication errors. In 2006 approximately 25% of errors involved some aspect of computer technology as at least one cause of the error. Most errors related to technology involved mislabeled bar codes on medications, mistakes at order entry because of confusing computer screens, or other problems with information management (TJC, 2015). Errors also were related to dispensing devices and human factors, such as failure to scan bar codes or overrides of bar-code warnings.

Computerized provider order entry (CPOE) can be an effective mechanism for improving patient safety. Unintended consequences can occur, however, and new types of errors can be detected (Schwartzberg, Ivanovic, Patel, & Burjonrappa, 2015). Safeguards built into clinical information systems can avert an error, but awareness of the potential for new issues is vital.

Automated medication administration systems that use **bar-code technology** can ensure that the right patient gets the right medication, in the correct dose, by the appropriate route, and at the specified time. However, this new information technology must not impede nurses' care of patients. Faced with urgent or emergent situations with patients, technical difficulties, or poor work redesign, unorthodox and potentially unsafe work-arounds are sometimes invented when the medication administration system is not usable and obstructs patient care (van der Veen, van den Bemt, Bijlsma, de Gier & Taxis, 2017).

Closed-loop electronic prescribing, dispensing, and bar-code patient identification systems reduce prescribing errors and medication adverse events and increase confirmation of patient identity before administration (Fig. 16.3). However, time spent on medication-related tasks increases for physicians, pharmacists, and nurses (Hwang, Yoon, Ahn, Hwang, & Park, 2016).

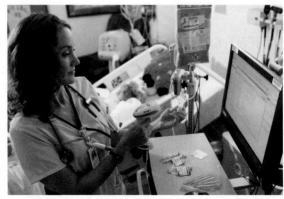

Fig. 16.3 Bar-code medication administration "closes the loop" on medication safety by providing a double-check of the "rights" of medication administration at the point nurses actually give patients their medications.

SAFELY IMPLEMENTING HEALTH INFORMATION TECHNOLOGY

Despite the promise of positive outcomes from clinical information systems, success is not a guarantee. Remaining alert to its limitations and risks is crucial, because new technology and increasing automation make work less transparent and create opportunities for new types of errors (Kai & Lipschultz, 2015). As McBride (2005) eloquently stated more than a decade ago, "Information technology is not a panacea, and will not fulfill its promise unless it is harnessed in support of foundational values. That is why every nurse cannot afford to be unconnected to this transformation, but must take an active role in ensuring that IT is used in service to our profession's values. After all, nurses are knowledge workers" (p. 188).

TJC warns that as health information technology is adopted, users must be mindful of the safety risks and preventable adverse events that implementation can create (TJC, 2015). The report notes that any form of technology can adversely affect patient care safety and quality if it is designed or implemented improperly. TJC suggests 13 actions, which are presented in Table 16.3.

A clinical information system's success or failure is related to the system's "fit" with the organizational culture, the information needs of its users, and users' work processes and practices (Kuziemsky, 2015). Duke University Medical Center informatics experts wrote that they had learned in 1993 that "ongoing planning, adjusting, fitting the technology to the work, and adapting policy formation were more important than the technology itself" (Stead et al., 1993, p. 225). The same is true today!

Relying too heavily on health information technology for communication can reduce teamwork and may negatively affect patient safety and care quality (Saddik & Al-Mansour, 2014). Although improved access and better-organized information can eliminate nurses' locating information for other nurses and physicians, information technology will never eliminate the need for personal communication and teamwork.

Successful development and implementation of nursing information technology depend on nurses working in partnership with organizational leadership, information systems vendors, and systems analysts to create tools that truly benefit nurses. When nurses have the systems and tools needed to provide patient care effectively and efficiently, safety and care quality will follow. Direct-care nurses must work with informatics nurses and information system developers and programmers in system development, implementation, and ongoing improvement. By combining computer and information science with nursing science, the goals of supporting nursing practice and the delivery of high-quality nursing care can be achieved (American Nurses Association, 2015). The Literature Perspective identifies some recommendations related to health information technology (HIT) successes and failures.

LITERATURE PERSPECTIVE

Technology and Nursing Resource Planning

Resource: Welton, J. M., & Harper, E. M. (2016). Measuring nursing value from the electronic health record. *Nursing Informatics, 225,* 63-67.

The potential to use health information technology as a tool to manage effective use of nursing resources is emerging and being tested by leaders in nursing informatics. Leaders must balance nursing staffing and care quality against financial constraints in an era of cost containment.

Little agreement exists about the best approach to achieve nurse–patient ratios that support safe, high-quality nursing care for all patients. A strict ratio may ignore individual patient care needs, whereas attempts to capture details about care needs or derive a formula that precisely predicts care needs and forecasts required staff requirements are very difficult and have not been broadly agreed on.

Welton and Harper (2016) reported findings from a "nursing value expert group" to identify factors that lead to a model that predicts nursing care needs. In the study, a Nursing Care Value Metric was developed to identify how nurses spend their time. The study demonstrated that clinical data from the electronic health record can be extracted in real time and used to calculate the intensity of nursing care required by patients in a given clinical setting.

Implications for Practice

Administering medications, monitoring patients after a procedure, and admitting a new patient for an inpatient stay are a few examples of the need for electronic measurement. Numerous other examples show value in nursing care.

TABLE 16.3 The Joint Commission Recommendations for Safely Implementing Health Information Technology

	Suggested Action
1.	Examine work processes and procedures for risks and inefficiencies. Resolve problems identified before technology implementation. Involve representatives of all disciplines—clinical, clerical, and technical—in the examination and resolution of issues.
2.	Involve clinicians and staff who will use or be affected by the technology, along with information technology (IT) staff with strong clinical backgrounds, in the planning, selection, design, reassessment, and ongoing quality improvement of technology. Involve pharmacists in planning and implementing any technology that involves medication.
3.	Assess your organization's technology needs. Require IT staff to interact with users outside their own facility to learn about real-world capabilities of potential systems from various vendors; conduct field trips; look at integrated systems to minimize the need for interfaces.
4.	Continuously monitor for problems during the introduction of new technology and address issues as quickly as possible to avoid workarounds and errors. Consider an emergent issues desk staffed with project experts and champions to help rapidly resolve problems. Use interdisciplinary problem solving to improve system quality and provide vendor feedback.
5.	Establish training programs for all clinical and operations staff, designed appropriately for each group and focused on how the technology will benefit staff and patients. Do not allow long delays between training and implementation. Provide frequent refresher courses or updates.
6.	Develop and communicate policies delineating staff authorized and responsible for technology implementation, use, oversight, and safety review.
7.	Ensure that all order sets and guidelines are developed, tested, and approved by the Pharmacy and Therapeutics Committee (or equivalent) before implementation.
8.	Develop a graduated system of safety alerts in the new technology to help clinicians determine urgency and relevancy. Review skipped or rejected alerts. Decide which alerts need to be hard stops in the technology and provide supporting documentation.
9.	Develop systems to mitigate potential computerized provider order entry (CPOE) drug errors or adverse events by requiring department and pharmacy review and sign off. Use the Pharmacy and Therapeutics Committee (or equivalent) for oversight and approval of electronic order sets and clinical decision support (CDS) alerts. Ensure proper nomenclature and printed label design, eliminate dangerous abbreviations and dose designations, and ensure electronic medication administration record (e-MAR) acceptance by nurses.
10.	Provide environments that protect staff doing data entry from undue distractions when using the technology.
11.	Maximize the potential of the technology to maximize safety. Continually reassess and enhance safety effectiveness and error detection. Use error-tracking tools, and evaluate events and near-miss events.
12.	Monitor and report errors and near-miss events. Pursue potential system errors or use problems with root cause analysis or other forms of failure-mode analysis. Consider reporting significant issues to external reporting systems.
13.	Reevaluate the applicability of security and confidentiality protocols. Reassess Health Insurance Portability and Accountability Act (HIPAA) compliance periodically to ensure that the addition of technology and the growing responsibilities of IT staff have not introduced new security or compliance risks.

Imagine that a patient you are caring for complains of light-headedness and nausea. When documenting vital signs, you note that the blood pressure measurement is lower than it was the day before. Graphing the values across several days illustrates a steady decline in the readings. Reviewing the medication list, you note he is receiving hydralazine (Apresoline). Processing the data that you have collected, you implement "falls precautions," send a communication order to monitor his blood pressure and other symptoms frequently, and notify the physician if the situation has not changed.

> **EXERCISE 16.5** Think about the data that you gather and document every day: vital signs, intake and output, laboratory and test results, and the patient's responses to care. What data did you automatically combine or reorganize to help you make a decision regarding patient care? How did you use this information to improve your patient's outcome? How and with whom did you communicate the data and information? How did technology combine or organize data?

FUTURE TRENDS AND PROFESSIONAL ISSUES

Biomedical Technology

Devices are becoming smarter every day, and the technology now exists to integrate pump data into the EHR. The nurse validates input from the smart pumps. Integration allows providers to see titration and changes in physiologic parameters, pharmacy to know when a continuous infusion is running low, and a time saver for nurses who no longer have to manually input each data point (Fig. 16.4).

Information Technology

Health care in the United States is expensive and of variable quality. Recognizing that informatics can play an important role in controlling costs and improving quality, the federal government's economic stimulus plan in 2009 earmarked $20 billion for health information technology. However, the money must be spent wisely, not quickly. One consideration suggested was to use the money to move the health information technology industry toward strong, mandated data standards. Data standards are at the foundation of integrated, interoperable information systems that will permit an

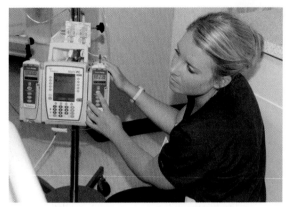

Fig. 16.4 Smart pumps offer integration between the pump and the electronic health record, including auto-pump programming.

emergency department or operating room to transfer data to inpatient hospital units and permit hospitals to send data to a patient's primary care record in the provider's office.

Electronic Patient Care Records

Multiple terms have been used to define electronic patient care records, with overlapping definitions. Both electronic health records (EHR) and electronic medical records (EMR) have gained widespread use, with some health informatics users assigning the term *EHR* to a global concept and *EMR* to a discrete localized record. An EHR refers to an individual patient's medical record in digital format. The EHR is a longitudinal electronic record of patient health information generated across encounters in any care delivery setting. EHR systems coordinate the storage and retrieval of individual records with the aid of computers. The EHR is most often accessed on a computer, often over a network, and may include EMRs from many locations and/or sources. Among the many forms of data often included are patient demographics, health history, progress and procedure notes, health problems, medication and allergy lists (including immunization status), laboratory test results, radiology images and reports, billing records, and advance directives.

Credit card–like devices called smart cards store a limited number of pages of data on a computer chip. The implementation of computer-based health information systems will lead to computer networks that will store health records across local, state, national, and international boundaries. The smart card serves as a

---

BOX 16.5 Smart Cards

1. Patient demographics and photo identification
2. ICE—in case of emergency—contact and other key information
3. Patient medical history: for example, allergies, medications, immunizations, laboratory results
4. Past care encounter summaries, including surgical procedures
5. Patient record locations and electronic address information
6. Ability to upload or download patient information

---

bridge between the clinician terminal and the central repository, making patient information available to the caregiver quickly and cheaply at the point of service because the patients bring it with them. This will help coordinate care; improve quality-of-care decisions; and reduce risk, waste, and duplication of effort. Patients are mobile and consult many practitioners, thereby causing their records to be fragmented. With the electronic smart card, patients, providers, and notes can be brought together in any combination at any place. Box 16.5 provides examples of the types of data that are recorded on smart cards.

Data Privacy and Security

Data protection, systems' security, and patient privacy are concerns with electronic health records. However, patients' rights to privacy of their data must be maintained whether recorded in a manual or automated system. With computerized data, any person with the proper permission may access the information anywhere in the world, and multiple people can do so simultaneously. Data can also be inadvertently sent to the wrong individual or site. Information security and privacy are important concerns as development of electronic health information systems accelerates at the beginning of the 21st century.

A firewall protects the information in the central data repository from access by unauthorized users. It is a network security measure that keeps electronic intruders from accessing an organization's data on its private network while allowing members of the organization to reach the Internet. Organizational policies on the use, security, and accuracy of data must be developed and monitored for compliance.

Telecommunications

Telecommunications and systems technology facilitate clinical oversight of health care via telephone or cable lines, remote monitoring, information links, and the Internet. Telehealth is the use of modern telecommunications and information technologies for the provision of health care to individuals at a distance and the transmission of information to provide that care. This is accomplished by using two-way interactive videoconferencing and high-speed telephone lines, fiber-optic cable, and satellite transmissions. Patients sitting in front of the teleconferencing camera can be diagnosed, treated, monitored, and educated by nurses and physicians. ECGs and radiographs can be viewed and transmitted. Sophisticated electronic stethoscopes and dermascopes allow nurses and physicians to hear heart, lung, and bowel sounds and to look closely at wounds, eyes, ears, and skin. Ready access to expert advice and patient information is available no matter where the patient or information is located. Patients in rural areas and prisons especially benefit from this technology.

CHAMP (cardiac high-acuity monitoring program) is an in-home monitoring system for patients with single ventricle (SV) cardiac disease. Home monitoring is completed using a tablet to input data; the data are stored in a cloud-based secure system and transferred to the EMR daily (Shirali et al., 2016). This secure portal can alert the caregiver team to changes in the patient's condition and allow for quick adjustments to the plan of care. This monitoring program has decreased "at-home mortality from nearly 20% in 2012 to 1% over the past 3 years" (Erikson, Hunt, & Blizzard, 2017, p. 72).

Telecommunication also supports distance learning, which has been possible for some years, with enhanced opportunities to engage learners in online classrooms. With online or "virtual" classrooms, learners from anywhere in the world with computer access can log into a university's or other group's online learning system via the Internet.

Informatics

In 2011, the Healthcare Information and Management Systems Society (HIMSS) identified that just over 90% of American hospitals had implemented some component of an EMR. The American Nurses Association recognized nursing informatics as a specialty nursing practice in 2001. Although more than 8000 nurses are practicing in informatics, many more are needed to achieve widespread development and adoption of effective health information systems (Sensmeier, 2015).

Many opportunities exist to improve the safety, efficiency, and effectiveness of nursing care. The goal of informatics nurses and nursing leaders is to use information technology to ensure that critical information is available to caregivers at the point of care to make health care safer and more effective while improving efficiency. This requires interconnected and integrated healthcare technology across hospitals, healthcare systems, and geographic regions. Standards for data systems that operate efficiently with one another (termed "interoperability") and attention to data security and patient privacy are necessary.

Nurses are working as leaders in several national initiatives to lay the groundwork and guide progress toward the goal of a nationwide health information network. Every nurse can embrace technology to improve nursing practice. Some strategies to accomplish this include (1) involving nurses in every decision about health IT that affects their workflow, (2) investing in training nurses to effectively use technology in their practice, and (3) leveraging opportunities to use IT to enable quality improvement (Sensmeier, 2015).

Knowledge Technology

Technology has the potential to shorten the many years that currently exist between the development of new knowledge for patient care and the application of that knowledge in real-time practice with patients. Increasingly, patient conditions that are directly influenced by nursing care are part of the Centers for Medicare & Medicaid Services (CMS) pay for performance and TJC "Never Events." Having the best knowledge available regarding clinical phenomena is increasingly important. The focus of nursing care includes medication management, activity intolerance, immobility, risk for falls and actual falls, risk for skin impairment and pressure ulcer, anxiety, dementia, sleep, prevention of infection, nutrition, incontinence, dehydration, smoking cessation, pain management, patient and family education, and self-care.

Norma Lang, a nursing informatics leader, has described the challenges of bringing the best evidence for practice to bear against nursing care (Lang, 2008). First, the challenge of synthesizing the knowledge available in a manner that is useful to clinicians is critical. Then, computerized information systems are needed to provide clinical decision support at the point of care. Finally, the computer system must collect good clinical data to promote ongoing knowledge development for nursing care of patients and families. Several "intelligent" clinical information systems are in development. These systems translate nursing knowledge into reference materials that can be accessed at the point of care.

PROFESSIONAL, ETHICAL NURSING PRACTICE AND NEW TECHNOLOGIES

Technology has and will continue to transform the healthcare environment and the practice of nursing. Nurses are professionally obligated to maintain competency with a vast array of technologic devices and systems. Baseline informatics competency is required for all nurses to function in the 21st century.

Because of the increasing ability to preserve human life with biomedical technology, questions about living and dying have become conceptually and ethically complex. Conceptually, it becomes more difficult to define extraordinary treatment and human life because technology has changed our concepts of living and dying. A source of ethical dilemmas is the use of invasive technologic treatment to provide patients with extraordinary means and to prolong life for patients with limited or no decision-making capabilities. Nurses are concerned with individual patient welfare and the effects of technologic intervention on the immediate and long-term quality of life for patients and their families. Patient advocacy remains an important function of the professional nurse.

Safeguarding patients' welfare, privacy, and confidentiality is another obligation of nurses. Security measures are available with computerized information systems, but it is the integrity and ethical principles of system end-users that provide the final safeguard for patient privacy. System users must never share the passwords that allow them access to information in computerized clinical information systems. Each password uniquely identifies a user to the system by name and title, gives approval to carry out certain functions, and provides access to data appropriate to the user. When a nurse signs on to a computer, all data and information that are entered or reviewed can be traced to that password. Every nurse is accountable for all actions taken using his or her password. All nurses must be aware of their responsibilities for the confidentiality and security of the data they gather and for the security of their passwords.

Nurse managers must ensure that policies and procedures for collecting and entering data and the use of security measures (e.g., passwords) are established to maintain confidentiality of patient data and information. They have the responsibility to manage data to effectively lead change. This can be accomplished through documentation audit tools and system compliance reports. Nurse managers must also be knowledgeable patient advocates in the use of technology for patient care by referring ethical questions to the organization's ethics committee.

> **EXERCISE 16.6** Think about the use of the Internet in health care. How do you use it to look up healthcare information? How would you advise a patient to select appropriate sites?

CONCLUSION

Biomedical, information, communication, and knowledge technology will form a bond in the future, linking people and information together in a rapidly changing world of health care. With new technology comes the need for a new set of competencies. Nursing participation in designing this exciting future will ensure that the unique contributions of nurses to patient and family health and illness care are clearly and formally represented.

THE SOLUTION

A systematic review of the literature related to bar-code medication administration (BCMA) informed our teams of the potential for nurses to work around the system when it obstructed the process of getting medications to patients on time.

The literature also demonstrated that hardware reliability does indeed impact nurses' use of the system. If devices don't work, nurses work around them to meet patient care needs! We presented our findings and recommendations to nursing leaders and direct care nurses and, to provide the most reliable hardware, we opted to hardwire computers and attach Bluetooth bar-code scanners at every patient bedside throughout our organization. In addition, patient care areas have a few mobile computers and scanners to use when patients are not in their rooms. Although this was not an inexpensive option, it ensured that hardware would not be a reason for working around

recommended processes for BCMA. Finally, we designed training videos to emphasize work processes that promote best practice and patient safety. These videos are shared with new staff during their orientation period, and experienced staff can access them at any time as a reference to the BCMA process.

Information technology is an essential component of our patient safety program. We report area-specific compliance with BCMA every week to nursing, pharmacy, and informatics leaders who share the information with direct care staff. Most areas comply with work process expectations nearly 95% of the time! More importantly, BCMA has lowered the incidence of adverse drug events in our hospitals and clinics.

Would this be a suitable approach for you? Why?

Janis B. Smith

▮ REFLECTIONS

Have you used more than one information system during your academic preparation in nursing? If yes, what advantages in design and implementation could you detect in one setting or another?

Have you used the same information system in more than one setting? If so, did you detect differences in how the system was designed and implemented in different settings?

If you were to participate on the HIT selection or implementation planning teams in your role as a registered nurse, are you confident you could identify features in the system with potential to either support or threaten patient safety? What do you believe are the most critical?

THE EVIDENCE

Health information technology (HIT) has the potential to reduce healthcare costs, improve efficiency, and enhance patient care safety and quality. HIT is rapidly evolving and changing how we deliver care, while health care reform is simultaneously reshaping the environment in which care is provided. A committee of experts was convened by the Institute of Medicine (now the National Academy of Medicine) in 2011 to review the evidence about the impact of HIT on patient safety and to recommend actions, based on evidence, that safeguard patients in our contemporary technology-rich healthcare environment.

The committee found that specific types of HIT can improve patient safety under the right conditions, but these right conditions may not be easily replicated in all settings. Potential safety benefits and concerns were documented for computerized provider order entry (CPOE), clinical decision support (CDS), bar-code confirmation of patient identity and medications, and patient engagement tools. However if not designed and implemented appropriately, HIT may add a layer of complexity to the already complex delivery of health care and lead to unintended consequences. HIT must be designed, implemented, used, and continuously improved to positively enable health care quality and safety.

Safely functioning HIT provides easy entry and unlimited retrieval of data, has simple and intuitive user interfaces, supports the clinical workflow of all end-users, and permits seamless system interoperability.

TIPS FOR MANAGING INFORMATION AND TECHNOLOGY

- Create a vision for the future.
- Match your vision to the institution's mission and strategic plan.
- Learn what you need to know to fulfill the vision.
- Join initiatives that are moving in the direction of your vision.
- Be prepared to initiate, implement, and support new technology.
- Use an automated dispensing system.
- Use biometric technology.
- Use bar-coding systems/bar-code technology.
- Never stop learning, or you will always be behind.

REFERENCES

Abdrbo, A. A. (2015). Nursing informatics competencies among nursing students and their relationship to patient safety competencies: Knowledge, attitude, and skills. *Computers, Informatics, Nursing CIN, 33*(11), 509–514. https://doi.org/10.1097/CIN.0000000000000197.

Agboola, S. O., Bates, D. W., & Kvedar, J. C. (2016). Digital health and patient safety. *The Journal of the American Medical Association, 315*(16), 1697–1698. https://doi.org/10.1001/jama.2016.2402.

American Medical Informatics Association (AMIA). (2017). *Nursing informatics.* www.amia.org.

American Nurses Association. (2015). *Nursing informatics: Practice scope and standards of practice* (2nd ed.). Silver Spring, MD: Nursesbooks.org.

Arzouman, J. A. (2016). Culture of safety and the role of the Medical-Surgical nurse. *Medsurg Nursing, 25*(2), 75–76.

Bernier, E., Yu, L., Rivard, J., Atkinson, S., & Bussières, J. F. (2016). Compliance of automated dispensing cabinets with guidelines of the Institute for Safe Medication Practices (US): Comparison between 2010 and 2015. *Canadian Journal Hospital Pharmacy, 69*(5), 425–427.

Creed, S. (2017). Avoiding medication errors in general practice. *Practice Nurse, 47*(2), 24–26.

Drenkard, K. N. (2015). The power of alignment: Educating nurses in quality and safety. *Nursing Administration Quarterly, 39*(3), 272–277. https://doi.org/10.1097/NAQ.0000000000000112.

Erikson, L., Hunt, C., & Blizzard, P. (2017). Leveraging technology to improve care and patient outcomes. *American Nurse Today, 12*(9), 71–72.

Gomes, M., Hash, P., Orsolini, L., Watkins, A., & Mazzoccoli, A. (2016). Connecting professional practice and technology at the bedside: Nurses' beliefs about using an electronic health record and their ability to incorporate professional and patient-centered nursing activities in patient care. *Computers, Informatics, Nursing CIN, 34*(12), 578–586.

Hannah, K. J., & Ball, M. J. (2011). *Introduction to nursing informatics* (4th ed.). London; New York: Springer-Verlag.

HIMSS Analytics. (2017). *EMRAM: A strategic roadmap for effective EMR adoption and maturity.* http:/www.himssanalytics.org/emram.

Hunter, K. M. (2001). Nursing informatics theory. In V. K. Saba & K. A. McCormick (Eds.), *Essentials of computers for nurses: Informatics for the new millennium* (pp. 179–190). New York: McGraw-Hill.

Hwang, Y., Yoon, D., Ahn, E. K., Hwang, H., & Park, R. W. (2016). Provider risk factors for medication administration error alerts: analyses of a large-scale closed-loop medication administration system using RFID and barcode. *Pharmacoepidemiology & Drug Safety, 25*(12), 1387–1396. https://doi.org/10.1002/pds.4068.

Institute of Medicine (IOM), Committee on Patient Safety. (2000). *To err is human: Building a safer health care system.* Washington, DC: The National Academies Press.

Institute of Medicine (IOM). (2011). *The future of nursing: Leading change, advancing health.* Washington, DC: National Academy Press.

Institute of Medicine (IOM), Committee on Quality Health Care in America. (July 2001). *Crossing the quality chasm: A new health system for the 21st century.* Washington, DC: National Academy Press.

Kai, S., & Lipschultz, A. (2015). Patient safety and healthcare technology management. *Biomedical Instrumentation & Technology, 49*(1), 60–65.

Kern, L. M., Edwards, A., & Kaushal, R. (2016). The meaningful use of electronic health records and health care utilization. *American Journal of Medical Quality, 31*(4), 301–307. https://doi.org/10.1177/1062860615572439.

Kleinpell, R., Barden, C., Rincon, T., McCarthy, M., & Zapatochny Rufo, R. J. (2016). Assessing the impact of telemedicine on nursing care in intensive care units. *American Journal of Critical Care, 25*(1), 14–20. https://doi.org/10.4037/ajcc2016808.

Kuziemsky, C. E. (2015). Review of social and organizational issues in health information technology. *Health Informatics Research, 21*(3), 152–160. https://doi.org/10.4258/hir.2015.21.3.152.

Lang, N. M. (2008). The promise of simultaneous transformation of practice and research with the use of clinical information systems. *Nursing Outlook, 56,* 232–236.

Locsin, R. C. (2005). *Technological Competency As Caring In Nursing: A Model For Practice.* Indianapolis, IN: Sigma Theta Tau International.

Mardis, T., Mardis, M., Davis, J., Justice, E. M., Holdinsky, S. R., Donnelly, J., et al. (2016). Bedside shift-to-shift handoffs: A systematic review of the literature. *Journal of Nursing Care Quality, 31*(1), 54–60.

McBride, A. (2005). Nursing and the informatics revolution. *Nursing Outlook, 53,* 183–191.

National League for Nursing (NLN). (2015). Position statement: A vision for the changing faculty role: Preparing students for the technological world of health care. www.nln.org.

Petersen, E. M., & Costanzo, C. L. (2017). Assessment of clinical alarms influencing nurses' perceptions of alarm fatigue. *Dimensions of Critical Care Nursing, 36*(1), 36–44.

Richardson, K. J., Sengstack, P., Doucette, J., Hammond, W. E., Schertz, M., Thomspon, J., et al. (2016). *CIN: Computers, Informatics, Nursing, 34*(2), 62–70. https://doi.org/10.1097/CIN. 0000000000000206.

Saddik, B., & Al-Mansour, S. (2014). Does CPOE support nurse-physician communication in the medication order process? A nursing perspective. *Studies in Health Technology and Informatics, 204,* 149–155.

Scholes, M., & Barber, B. (1980). Towards nursing informatics. In D. A. D. Lindberg & S. Kaihara (Eds.), *MEDINFO: 1980* (pp. 7–73). Amsterdam, Netherlands: North-Holland.

Schwartzberg, D., Ivanovic, S., Patel, S., & Burjonrappa, S. C. (2015). We thought we would be perfect: Medication errors before and after the initiation of computerized physician order entry. *Journal of Surgical Research, 198*(1), 108–114.

Scott, B. M., Considine, J., & Botti, M. (2015). Unreported clinical deterioration in emergency department patients: A point prevalence study. *Australasian Emergency Nursing Journal, 18*(1), 33–41. https://doi.org/10.1016/j.aenj.2014.09.002.

Sensmeier, J. (2015). Big data and the future of nursing knowledge. *Nursing Management, 46*(4), 22–27. https://doi.org/10.1097/01.NUMA.0000462365.53035.7d.

Shirali, G., Erikson, L., Apperson, J., Goggin, K., Williams, D., Reid, K., et al. (2016). Harnessing teams and technology to improve outcomes in infants with single ventricle. *Circulation: Cardiovascular Quality and Outcomes, 9*(3), 303–311. https://doi.org/10.1161/circoutcomes.115.002452.

Sittig, D. F., Ash, J. S., & Singh, H. (2014). The SAFER guides: Empowering organizations to improve the safety and effectiveness of electronic health records. *The American Journal of Managed Care, 20*(5), 418–423.

Stead, W. W., Bird, W. P., Califf, R. M., Elchlepp, J. G., Hammond, W. E., & Kinney, T. R. (1993). The IAIMS at Duke University Medical Center: Transition from model testing to implementation. *MD Computing, 10,* 225–230.

Sugrue, M., De Waele, J. J., De Keulenaer, B. L., Roberts, D. J., & Malbrain, M. L. (2015). A user's guide to intra-abdominal pressure measurement. *Anaesthesiology Intensive Therapy, 47*(3), 241–251. https://doi.org/10.5603/AIT.a2015.0025.

The Joint Commission (TJC). (2013). *TJC accreditation manual e-dition.*

The Joint Commission (TJC). (2015). *Sentinel event alert: Safe use of health information technology.* https://www.jointcommission.org/assets/1/6/SEA_54_HIT_4_26_16.pdf.

van der Veen, W., van den Bemt, P., Bijlsma, M., de Gier, H., & Taxis, K. (2017). Association between workarounds and medication administration errors in bar code-assisted medication administration: Protocol of a multicenter study. *JMIR Research Protocols, 6*(4). https://doi.org/10.2196/resprot.7060.

Wang, P., Zhang, H., Li, B., & Lin, K. (2016). Making patient risk visible: Implementation of a nursing document information system to improve patient safety. *Nursing Informatics, 225*, 8–12.

Washington State Nurses Association. (2016). The IOM's "Future of Nursing" report—what's worked, and what hasn't yet been achieved. *Washington Nurse, 45*(4), 7.

Welton, J. M., & Harper, E. M. (2016). Measuring nursing value from the electronic health record. *Nursing Informatics, 225*, 63–67.

17

Delegating: Authority, Accountability, and Responsibility in Delegation Decisions

Maureen Murphy-Ruocco

Copyright © MichaelJung/iStock/Thinkstock

LEARNING OUTCOMES

- Examine the role of the employer or nurse leader, nurse delegator, and delegatee in the delegation process.
- Distinguish between authority, accountability, and responsibility in the delegation process.
- Evaluate how tasks and relationships influence the process of delegation.

- Describe the challenges of delegating to unlicensed nursing personnel (UNP).
- Identify strategies to overcome underdelegation, overdelegation, and improper delegation.
- Comprehend the legal authority of the registered nurse in delegation.

KEY TERMS

accountability
assignment
authority
delegatee
delegation

delegator
individual accountability
nurse practice acts (NPAs)
organizational accountability
responsibility

supervision
unlicensed nursing personnel (UNP)

THE CHALLENGE

Not all emergency trauma care centers are created equally. Trauma centers are classified from Level 1 to 5, with Level 1 being the most equipped to meet the needs of critically ill patients. Emergency medical technicians (EMTs) often transport patients to hospital emergency trauma centers by ambulance, or patients are transported by a family member or friend.

Hospital emergency trauma centers are staffed by physicians, registered professional nurses, radiology technicians, respiratory therapists, emergency technicians, transportation aides, clerks, and secretaries. When a patient arrives at a hospital emergency trauma center, critically injured patients should be immediately triaged by a registered nurse to determine the nature and acuity of the illness or injury. The challenge is to assess the patient's condition and provide emergency health care. If necessary, they must stabilize and transfer the patient to the most appropriate facility.

Recently the emergency trauma department has been expanded and needs to accommodate 15 more patients. To support patient care, the hospital administration hired additional staff, unlicensed nursing personnel (UNP), whose positions were being phased out in their free-standing urgent care center, and employed them as emergency room technicians. The next emergency technician training program will not begin for 2 months. Therefore the new UNPs will be working as emergency room technicians in the emergency department before they are trained.

The emergency department received a call that an explosion at a local chemical plant just occurred. The emergency medical services will be arriving with multiple patients injured in the accident.

What would you do if you were this nurse?

Kathryn King-Dyker, RN, MSN, CSN
*Former Emergency Trauma Nurse, Hackensack University
Medical Center, Hackensack, New Jersey*

INTRODUCTION

The American Nurses Association (ANA) Scope and Standards of Practice, in conjunction with the individual state practice acts, provide guidelines for ethical decision making that operationalizes the definition of nursing, the healthcare system, and the public (ANA, 2015a). To accomplish nursing's goal of providing safe, efficient, and high-quality patient care, registered nurses (RNs) must understand the concept of delegation.

Delegation, an art and skill of professional nursing, is a complex decision-making strategy implemented to improve the work-related performances of individuals employed in healthcare facilities. Delegation requires knowing the level of competence of the individual being delegated to and understanding the concepts of authority, accountability, and responsibility in the delegation process. Learning how to distribute work appropriately builds confidence in others about how to care for groups of patients safely and effectively. Conversely, inappropriate delegation of tasks creates apprehension in others about how to care for the same group of patients. Therefore effective delegation improves person-centered care; however, ineffective delegation can produce negative outcomes.

Many states and jurisdictions have different laws and rules and regulations about delegation. Nurses have the responsibility to know and understand what is permitted in their state nurse practice act (NPA), rules and regulations, and policies (National Council of State Boards of Nursing [NCSBN], 2016). For effective delegation to occur, state NPAs must be clearly understood. Delegation strategies often improve as RNs gain more clinical experience and transition from novice, through advanced beginner, competent, proficient, and expert

(Brenner, 1984). Delegation is the most effective professional leadership and management strategy nurses implement in clinical practice to improve the safety and quality of person-centered care.

HISTORICAL PERSPECTIVE

In the 1970s and 1980s, RNs entered the profession with relatively limited content knowledge and/or clinical experience about delegation and how, what, and when to delegate. During that time, most health care occurred in acute care hospitals, staffed by RNs, licensed practical nurses or licensed vocational nurses (LPNs/LVNs) and unlicensed nursing personnel (UNP), commonly referred to at that time as nurse's aides. Concepts such as "team nursing" permitted LPNs/LVNs and UNPs to function as part of a nursing team, limiting the number of RNs employed on the unit. This allowed for a portion of direct patient care to be provided by LPNs/LVNs and UNPs. Direct patient care included providing physical comforts and basic treatments to patients. As the complexities of patient care delivery increased, the work demands and expectations of RNs became more challenging, creating the need to employ more UNPs to support patient care. Even though in the mid-1990s a shift occurred to a model of primary nursing (all-professional nursing concept), it shifted back to a multi-level nursing model (RNs mixed with LPNs/LVNs and UNPs). At that time, fiscal constraints and new complexities in health care created an urgent need for nurses to learn more about how to use effective delegation skills to deliver safe and effective nursing care. As the healthcare industry began to emphasize community-based care, the need for delegation and supervision of others became even more evident.

During the early part of the 21st century, the ANA and the NCSBN became increasingly concerned about the quality of delegation. Historically, ANA and NCSBN defined delegation slightly differently. ANA's Principles of Delegation by Registered Nurses to Unlicensed Assistive Personnel (UAP) (ANA, 2012) outlines the principles of effective delegation decision-making strategies for clinical nursing practice. Due to the increasing complexities of delegation decisions, ANA and NCSBN collaboratively published a *Joint Statement on Delegation* that had served as guidelines for safe and effective delegation decisions for RNs (ANA & NCSBN, n.d.).

In 2015 the NCSBN Center for Regulatory Excellence funded a group of experts from education, research, and clinical practice to standardize the nursing delegation process. The experts produced delegation guidelines that provide clear direction and standardization of the delegation process, from an organizational perspective and patient care perspective, for safe delegation of nursing responsibilities (NCSBN, 2016). These guidelines do not apply to the transfer of responsibility for care of a patient between licensed healthcare professionals. Nurses are educated to conduct assessments, plan, evaluate, and apply nursing judgment. Nurses need to understand that the "pervasive function of clinical reasoning, nursing judgment, or critical decision making cannot be delegated" (NCSBN, 2016 p. 6).

With ongoing changes in the healthcare environment, limited resources, complexity of patients' chronic conditions, high patient acuity rates, advances in technology, and challenges in the healthcare delivery system, nurses have an even greater demand to be clinically expert in delegation (Mueller & Vogelsmeier, 2015). Today, a comprehensive knowledge base in delegation, diagnostic reasoning, and decision-making skills in clinical practice are essential, because nurses delegate more patient care tasks and activities, while continuing to provide expert nursing care. Because of limited nursing resources, in different regions and in certain facilities, it may be necessary to delegate some responsibilities or assignments beyond the traditional roles, responsibilities, or assignments of a care provider. Thus delegators must understand the delegation process, their state NPA, and the roles and responsibilities of other healthcare providers, including advanced practice registered nurses (APRNs), RNs, LPNs/LVNs, and UNP (NCSBN, 2016). The overarching goal of effective delegation decisions is the protection of the public.

DEFINITIONS

Delegation, a multifaceted decision-making process, has been defined in different ways; however, the definitions have consistent elements. The principles of effective delegation are derived from the corresponding states' NPAs and through an understanding of the key concepts of authority, accountability, and responsibility. Delegation is the "transfer of responsibility for the performance of a task from one individual to another while retaining the accountability for the outcome" (ANA, 2012, p. 6). Responsibility refers to the obligation and dependability to accomplish work. Authority refers to the ability to perform duties in a specific role. The NCSBN defines delegation as "allowing a delegatee to perform a specific nursing skill, activity or procedure that is beyond the delegatee traditional role and not routinely performed" (NCSBN, 2016, p. 6). ANA considers this transfer of responsibility, whereas NCSBN considers it transfer of authority. However, ANA and NCSNB agree that delegation is a process whereby a nurse directs another individual to perform nursing tasks or activities and the nurse retains accountability for total patient care (ANA & NCSBN, n.d.).

Delegation always involves at least two individuals, delegator and delegatee, who engage in open communication to achieve a goal. The terms *delegator* and *delegatee* represent the two key roles enacted in the process of delegation. The delegator is a licensed nurse who delegates nursing responsibilities or allocates a portion of work related to patient care to another individual. The NCSBN (2016) defines a licensed nurse as an APRN, RN, or LPN/LVN. The NCSBN (2016) guidelines can be applied to an APRN delegating to RNs, LPNs/LVNs, and UNPs, or RNs delegating to LPNs/LVNs and/or UNPs. In some NPAs and in certain states and jurisdictions, LPNs/LVNs are also permitted to delegate to UNPs. However, the NCBSN (2016) guidelines reinforce that delegation does not apply to the transfer of responsibility for care of a patient between healthcare providers, such as from an RN to another RN or an LPN/LVN to another LPN/LVN, because this transfer of care for the patient is considered a "handoff" (Agency for Healthcare Research and Quality, 2015).

A delegatee, an individual who is delegated a nursing responsibility by a licensed nurse, is competent to perform the task or activity and must verbally accept the responsibility (NCBSN, 2016). Many delegatees function in a supportive role, and the ANA refers to these individuals as *nursing assistive personnel (NAP)*; however, they are often referred to in the published literature as UNP. Other supportive role titles, used across states, include patient care technicians (PCT), certified nursing assistants (CNA), certified medication assistants (CMAs), and home health aides.

Although licensed nurses do not supervise all assistive personnel, for example, physical therapy technicians, they exchange appropriate information about person-centered care. Regardless of who supervises whom, productive interdisciplinary relationships are essential for collaboration among the disciplines and for the delivery of best practices in health care.

ASSIGNMENT VERSUS DELEGATION

In the workplace, nurses need to differentiate between assignment and delegation. An **assignment** is defined as the "routine care, activities and procedures that are within the authorized scope of practice of the RN or LPN/VN or part of the routine function of the UAP" (NCSBN, 2016, p. 6). The ANA and NCSBN agree that assignment is the distribution of work that each qualified person is responsible for during a given work period. (ANA & NCSBN, n.d.). Once the direct care nurse knows that the routine care, tasks, activities, and procedures were part of his or her basic educational training, he or she can make the assignment. However, the nurse must validate that the assignment was completed and performed correctly. Once an assignment requires a specific type of knowledge or skill, the nurse must consider this a delegation and must validate the competency of the delegatee.

Delegation occurs when delegatees are requested to perform a specific nursing task, activity, or procedure outside their traditional role, have completed additional education and training, and have validated competency in the delegated area (NCSBN, 2016). Validation of competency relates to how safely individuals can perform the delegated task or activity and their role and function in the healthcare facility. The validation of competency applies to the level of the health provider (RN, LPN/LVN, UNP). The licensed nurse, who delegates the responsibility, maintains overall accountability for the patient; however, the delegatee still maintains responsibility for the activity, skill, or procedure. The licensed nurse can never delegate nursing judgment or

critical decision making; however, specific nursing responsibilities can be delegated because of legal authority. When delegating to a licensed nurse, the delegated responsibility must be within the parameters of the delegatee's authorized scope of practice under the NPA (NCSBN, 2016). Delegation is a complex skill that requires critical thinking, clinical judgment, and accountability for care of the client (ANA, 2012).

NCSBN MODEL: AN ORGANIZATIONAL FRAMEWORK FOR DELEGATION

The National Council of State Boards of Nursing (NCSBN) Delegation Model provides an organizing framework for delegation and identifies the roles and responsibilities of the employer or nurse leader; licensed nurse; and delegatee in the delegation process (Fig. 17.1). Delegation commences with the decisions made by the organization at the administrative level and "extends to the staff responsible for delegating, overseeing the process, and performing the responsibilities" (NCSBSN, 2016, p. 5). The NCSBN Delegation Model provides an exceptional graphic that describes the role, function, and collaborative work relationships among those in the role of the employer or nurse leader, licensed nurse, and delegatee.

The responsibilities of the employer/nurse leader include the ability to identify a nurse leader who provides oversight of a delegated task or activity, thorough an assessment process, and is ultimately accountable for a safe healthcare environment. That leader must develop and support a delegation committee, ideally composed of nurse leaders, who determine what tasks and activities can be delegated and to whom and under what circumstances, develop policies and procedures specific to delegation, and standardize the method of care to ensure patient safety. Communication about delegation to licensed nurses and educating them about what tasks and activities can be delegated is essential. On an ongoing basis, the employer or nurse leader must have a procedure to validate the delegatee's knowledge and competence related to the delegated task or activity. The delegation process must be periodically evaluated and documented and resolutions of issues identified to ensure patient safety. For effective delegation, the employer or nurse leader promotes a positive culture and work environment that supports person-centered care.

The licensed nurse's responsibilities include the ability to determine patient needs and conditions, the state

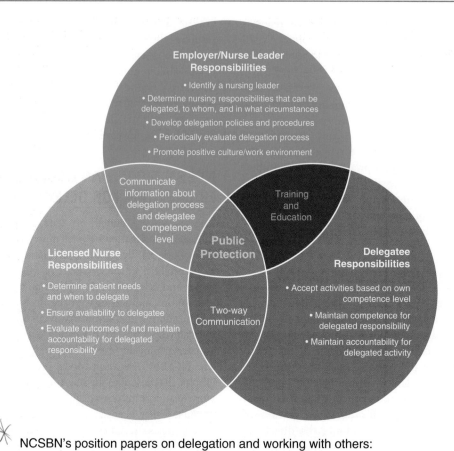

Employer/Nurse Leader Responsibilities

• Identify a nursing leader
• Determine nursing responsibilities that can be delegated, to whom, and in what circumstances
• Develop delegation policies and procedures
• Periodically evaluate delegation process
• Promote positive culture/work environment

Communicate information about delegation process and delegatee competence level

Training and Education

Public Protection

Licensed Nurse Responsibilities

• Determine patient needs and when to delegate
• Ensure availability to delegatee
• Evaluate outcomes of and maintain accountability for delegated responsibility

Two-way Communication

Delegatee Responsibilities

• Accept activities based on own competence level
• Maintain competence for delegated responsibility
• Maintain accountability for delegated activity

NCSBN's position papers on delegation and working with others:

Fig. 17.1 The National Council of State Boards of Nursing (NCSBN) Model and position paper on delegation describes the responsibilities of the employer or nurse leader; licensed nurse; and delegate. (From National Council of State Boards of Nursing. [2016.] National guidelines for nursing delegation. *Journal of Nursing Regulation, 7*[1], 5-14.)

or jurisdiction's provisions for delegation, employer policies and procedures regarding delegating a specific task or activity, and what can and cannot be delegated based on the practice setting. The nurse ensures availability of the delegatee related to the delegated task or activity and communicates with the delegatee to answer questions and provide guidance. If necessary, the nurse assists or completes the delegated responsibility if the patient's condition or other circumstances warrant. After completion of the delegated task or activity, the nurse follows up with the delegatee as well as the patient. The nurse provides feedback about the delegation process, evaluates the delegatee's competency level, and reports any issues to the nurse leader for any needed support or training of the delegatee. The nurse must evaluate outcomes of, and maintain accountability for, the delegated task or activity.

The delegatees' responsibilities include the ability to accept delegated tasks and activities based on their own level of competence and comfort given the patient's condition or circumstances in the practice setting. They must maintain ongoing competence for delegated tasks and activities and attend additional training, when necessary. To ensure continuity of care, they communicate with the licensed nurse in charge of the patient and maintain responsibility for completing delegated tasks and activities. According to the facility policy, they must provide timely and accurate documentation (NCSBN, 2016).

The employer or nurse leader must communicate with the licensed nurse information about the delegation process, provide education and training of employees, and communicate the level of competence of the delegatee. A two-way communication must also be maintained between the licensed nurse and the delegatee to achieve nursing goals. Evidence-based research indicates that successful delegation is influenced by several factors: effective communication, collaborative work relationships, level of competence, and role clarification (NCSBN, 2016). The overall goal of delegation is to achieve quality person-centered care and provide exemplary pubic protection.

EXERCISE 17.1 Interview a nurse leader about his or her role and the support the employer plays in the delegation process. Discuss these findings with a small group of colleagues.

EFFECTIVE COMMUNICATION: AN ESSENTIAL COMPETENCY FOR SUCCESSFUL DELEGATION

Effective communication involves a two-way exchange between the delegator and delegatee. The nurse must provide communication that is clear, concise, timely, and reliable to produce safe and efficient care. Maintaining two-way communication, requesting information from the UNP, and teaching how, when, and what to report are essential. A clear understanding between the delegator and delegatee about a delegated task or activity creates a greater chance of producing a positive outcome. A delay in communicating information can interfere with clinical decision making and have a negative impact on person-centered care. For example,

when a person's health status rapidly changes (e.g., one or more of the patient's vital signs rapidly changes), specific information can lose its value or become irrelevant to the patient's condition. When the reported information is incomplete, it leads to poor clinical judgments that may have adverse effects on person-centered care. A two-way communication and follow-through system established between the delegator and delegatee allows person-centered care to be altered, if necessary, in a timely manner.

Improving lines of communication can occur by appreciating and valuing each other. Healthy work relationships among all personnel, including nurses and UNPs, promote a "synergy between team members," enabling them to work together more effectively. Understanding another individual and developing a trusting relationship are critical components to successful delegation. Trust is developed through the knowledge of one another's capabilities and encouragement of others. Delegating with confidence requires considerable trust between two or more individuals to create an effective team. For example, a UNP who does not concur with the philosophy of the facility (e.g., the goals of hospice care) might have a negative impact on person-centered care. Building on the communication strengths and understanding the communication challenges of the team prove to be an effective strategy for maintaining effective communication. Examples of communication related to delegation appear in Box 17.1.

BOX 17.1 Examples of Communication Related to Delegation

- **Giving information.** This act applies to both the delegator and delegatee. The delegator must provide sufficient information about the patient, situation, delegated tasks, monitoring process and desired outcomes. In turn, the delegatee must report back to the delegator to indicate any deviations from any of those elements.
- **Giving direction.** This is a delegator task. If a delegatee has not performed a task previously or is new to the unit, considerable direction (and additional monitoring) may be expected. The delegator is expected to be as specific as possible in what the performance is to entail, how often reports to the delegator are needed, and what constitutes an immediate concern. With experienced delegatees, the direction may be more generalized (e.g., please check the patient's blood pressure every 2 hours, help the patient out of bed, and check the blood pressure as soon as the patient is sitting in a chair). More detailed direction may be needed for a delegatee to

the extent that various steps are provided for each of the assigned elements.
- **Seeking clarity.** This is a shared task. The delegator is attempting to determine that the delegatee understands what is expected in terms of performance and reporting. The delegatee is attempting to understand the delegator's standards for general statements (e.g., immediately report anything unusual). A repeat-back method can be used by both individuals to be sure clarity is present.
- **Seeking advice.** This is a delegatee task. Examples include finding alternative ways to solicit information from patients or ways to perform a skill when a patient's physical condition prevents a typical approach. To a lesser extent, this can also be used by the delegator to determine how best to support the delegate in performing assigned tasks.

The nurse needs to be an advocate for, and effectively communicate, the needs of the patient to the appropriate members of the healthcare team. Documentation, a form of communication, must be accurate, complete, and provided in a timely manner. It is a legal and ethical responsibly to communicate and document the person-centered care provided.

DELEGATION AND THE DECISION-MAKING PROCESS IN NURSING

To be effective in delegating, nurses must ask a series of questions to determine answers to the points identified in Box 17.2. Once a decision to delegate is made, the nurse confers with the UNP to communicate critical details (Figure 17.2).

Each of the questions in Box 17.2 can guide nurses in deciding if a particular delegation can be achieved while ensuring the best possible patient safety. Organizations often have roles for UNPs that are organization dependent. Just because a particular task could be delegated in a home health situation does not necessarily mean that task can be delegated in a related hospital. Further, just as nurses specialize, so too do UNPs. As care has become more complex, many intensive care units have eliminated LPN/LVNs and use only RNs and UNPs. These UNPs often can receive delegations that would not be appropriate in units that are less intense.

In the provision of nursing care, delegation is built on a foundation that emphasizes professional nursing practice. Delegation is a critical leadership skill that must be learned and implemented effectively to accomplish a nursing goal. During the delegation process, the nurse must perform a critical assessment, make a judgment, and decide whether to delegate. This process can be especially challenging for nurse managers. One strategy for learning how to be an effective delegator

Fig. 17.2 The nurse must confer with the UNP related to any situation involving delegation. Copyright © MichaelJung/iStock/Thinkstock.

is to use some of the concepts learned in the nursing process. Begin with assessment and planning and then proceed with implementation and evaluation.

Assessment and Planning

Assessment begins with selecting a designated nurse leader who has the ability to make a thorough assessment about the facility and who is in a position to develop appropriate staffing models for delegation while maintaining accountability for safe and person-centered care. During assessment, the nurse asks critical questions and evaluates the answers to differentiate what is and is not appropriate to delegate (see Box 17.2).

The nurse must ensure that the laws and rules support their delegation and it is within their scope of practice. The authority to delegate differs across states, so all nurses must verify their jurisdiction's statutes and regulations. Once an assessment of the client's needs is completed, a nurse manager or charge nurse should determine whether the delegating nurse is competent to make delegation decisions. This determination is

---

BOX 17.2 Key Questions to Consider in Delegation

- Do Nurse Practice Act laws, rules, or regulations restrict delegation in a given situation?
- Do organizational policies support delegation in a given situation?
- Does the delegatee have sufficient knowledge and skill to carry out an intended delegation?
- Is the delegator authorized to delegate certain tasks?

- Is the delegator familiar with the KSAs (knowledge, skills, ability) of the delegatee to delegate safely?
- Does the patient's condition influence a normal decision-making process? If so, how?
- Does the delegatee know the untoward signs and symptoms for a specific patient in a specific situation?
- Will supervision be readily available?

usually based on educational level, validated competency, or additional continuing education.

Once the delegating nurse is considered competent, the selection of a delegatee occurs. This step is extremely important because the delegatee's work affects the success of the healthcare team. However, the nurse may or may not have the opportunity to select a particular delegatee for the team.

Before delegating, the nurse must determine whether the task or activity is appropriate to delegate to a UNP. The nurse must determine whether the UNP has the knowledge, skill, and ability to accept the delegation and whether the UNP's ability matches the care needs of the patient. If the nurse believes it is not an appropriate match, no delegation should occur. The direct care nurse must convey a consistent message to the UNP that performing a task or activity is one component of person-centered care. Although the performance of a psychomotor task is essential for providing person-centered care, it is the second component—the nursing process, performed by the nurse—that determines factors for nursing action. The direct care nurse also assesses the situation to determine whether the facility has policies, procedures, and protocols for the delegated tasks or activities. If the policies, procedures, and protocols are not documented, they must be instituted as soon as possible. In addition, appropriate supervision must be available to the delegatee. Box 17.3 reviews elements to consider during assessment and planning in the delegation process.

Implementation and Evaluation
Implementation
During implementation, the delegator allocates work to UNPs and gives them the responsibility to perform the

---

BOX 17.3 Assessment and Planning in the Delegation Process

Assessment

The delegator should:
- Ensure that laws and rules support delegation
- Determine if the task is within the scope of the delegating nurse practice and if he or she is competent to delegate
- Assess the client's needs, stability, health condition, and predictability of the risks and responses
- Assess whether the task is appropriate to delegate to a UNP
- Determine if a specific UNP has the experience and educational background to complete the task safely and effectively
- Consider the type of healthcare facility related to the delegation task/activity
- Determine if the institution's policies and procedures allows for this type of delegation to a UNP
- Assess whether the nurse can provide appropriate guidance, support, and supervision of the delegated task/activity

Planning

The delegator should:
- Identify the delegated task, how it should be accomplished, and the expected outcomes
- Determine the UNP's understanding of the task and expectations

- Alert the UNP to any specific patient conditions, characteristics, or concerns
- Reinforce a willingness to guide and support the delegatee
- Convey expected observations to be reported and recorded
- Specify reporting time frames and/or dates expected
- Specify any specific concerns or emergency situations that warrant prompt reporting
- Validate the delegatee's willingness to accept the responsibility for the delegated task
- Emphasize the importance of timely, accurate, and complete documentation
- Determine any specific patient requirements, characteristics, or concerns to be addressed

The delegatees should:
- Comprehend the delegated task being delegated
- Ask questions and seek clarification regarding the delegation, if needed
- Specify any performance limitations regarding the delegation (e.g., never completed the task before, or completed only once or infrequently)
- Request additional training or supervision if needed
- Affirm an understanding of expectations
- Review the emergency action/communication plan
- Inform the delegator of the inability to accept the task/activity and discomfort with the delegated task/actively

work. When the nurse delegates work, he or she is merely sharing a set of functions to ensure quality outcomes. In essence, sharing work does not negate the nurse's accountability for total person-centered care. The definition of *delegation* emphasizes that patient care itself is not delegated; only a group of tasks or activities is delegated. Thus the final accountability remains with the delegator. For example, requesting the UNP to perform a specific task or activity within a defined set of functions or asking him or her to perform the same tasks as the previous day can be expected. For delegation to be effective, the nurse must understand that sharing activities is essential to benefit person-centered care, and the professional aspects of care may never be delegated. The role of the nurse in providing safe, effective, person-centered care is critical, whether person-centered care is performed by an individual nurse or by other members of the team through the process of delegation. Critical thinking, diagnostic reasoning, and the ability to synthesize information from various sources are what characterize the nurse, a licensed professional, who implements safe and effective nursing care.

The nurse has an essential responsibility for person-centered care and the ability to supervise the UNP by monitoring the performance of the task or activity and ensuring compliance with standards of practice, policies, and procedures. Supervision is the nurse's ability to provide direction, guidance, support, feedback, and evaluation to the UNP for the accomplishment of a delegated nursing task. Delegatees must have the appropriate resources, information, materials, guidance and support, and technology to perform the task or activity successfully (Reyes, 2015). The level of supervision should correlate with the experience of the UNP and the level of complexity of the delegated task or activity. For example, when new skills are being acquired by the UNP, the nurse should provide support, guidance, and oversight of a delegated task or activity.

During supervision a series of questions should be asked by the nurse, such as, "Has the task [activity] been completed?" "What changes were observed with the person?" and "How did the person respond?" Open-ended questions allow the nurse to gain pertinent information from the delegatee about the delegated responsibility. This also allows for the experienced nurse to identify a UNP's verbal or nonverbal clues about how comfortable he or she is with

the task or activity being delegated. For example, a UNP who has functioned in a physician's office for a long time and is not familiar with working under the direction of a nurse may appear concerned about being supervised by a nurse. Initiating a conversation about the nurse's role and function in the facility and why supervision is necessary can eliminate or diminish any negative feelings about being supervised. Similarly, the UNP should feel free to ask questions about tasks and how best to perform them and about the patient's condition and how and when to report relevant information. If the nurse wants the best productive relationship, making certain the UNP knows to ask any question or offer observations about anything will enhance the potential for patient safety. Effective teams communicate specific time frames for meetings to ensure that delegated responsibilities occur within the agreed upon time frame. Specific time frames may include before and after breaks and meals and any time the UNP has any questions or concerns.

It is important to recognize the contributions of the UNP toward person-centered care. UNPs seek the same respect and recognition from nurses that nurses seek from physicians (Lancaster, Kolakowsky-Haper, Kovacich, & Greer-Williams, 2015) (see the Research Perspective). Value and recognition of all members of the healthcare team enhances collegiality and collaboration. Box 17.4 reviews elements to consider during implementation.

Supervision can also vary in different types of healthcare facilities. Some states have different delegation standards, and therefore role confusion among RNs and LPN/LVNs may occur. For example, in long-term care facilities, an LPN/LVN may be responsible for a nursing unit with a registered nurse supervising the patient care. Therefore in long-term care facilities, the roles of RNs and LPNs/LVNs may not be well delineated. This creates an environment in which LPNs/LVNs may be responsible for delegation that exceeds their scope of practice. Variation in NPAs and administrative codes leads to role confusion among LPNs/LVNs regarding their scope of practice, especially as it relates to delegation and supervision of others. This can create a negative impact on the relationship between the RN and the LPN/LVN. Similarly, school nurses who have incorporated assistants may be challenged by working remotely, as noted in the Literature Perspective.

RESEARCH PERSPECTIVE

Resource: Lancaster, G., Kolakowsky-Hayner, S., Kovacich, J., & Greer-Williams, N. (2015). Interdisciplinary communication and collaboration among physician, nurse and unlicensed assistive personnel. *Journal of Nursing Scholarship, 47*(3), 275-284.

Historically, physicians, nurses, and other allied healthcare providers do not have a sufficient amount of experience working as interdisciplinary healthcare teams. This research study explored the potential for an interdisciplinary care model for physicians, nurses, and UAPs in a New York City hospital. The theoretical framework used to guide the study was Malhotra's (1981) phenomenologic orchestra study about how a conductorless orchestra can bring their talents together to produce a cohesive performance. The study used a purposive nonprobability, criterion-based convenience sample, conducted qualitative semistructured interviews, and analyzed the results using a qualitative software program to discover patterns and themes. The study found that physicians perceive themselves as the primary decision maker of patient care, even though they acknowledge the knowledge and expertise of nurses. It also indicated a hierarchical subservient relationship between nurses and UAPs and that even though nurses and physicians work together and consult with each other, UAPs were rarely included in discussions about patient care.

Implications for Practice

To mitigate the hierarchy in health care and to achieve the ultimate goal of person-centered care, physicians, nurses, and UNPs must learn how to communicate and collaborate effectively as members of an interdisciplinary healthcare team. The coordination of care is of utmost importance so interdisciplinary team members are aware of the goals of care, treatments, and interventions. This coordination decreases misunderstandings and conflicts, eliminates fragmentation of care, prevents errors, and enhances patient safety. Just like an orchestra, all members of the interdisciplinary healthcare team bring their own perspectives and talents and promote ongoing communication and collaboration to produce a symphony, enhancing person-centered care. A successful interdisciplinary practice model, like a conductorless orchestra, recognizes all contributions of the interdisciplinary team.

BOX 17.4 Implementation and Evaluation During Delegation

Implementation

The nurse must:

- Review the delegated task, how it should be accomplished, and expected outcomes as implementation begins
- Reinforce any specific patient requirements, characteristics, or concerns
- Provide available resources necessary to complete the task/activity
- Intervene based on the patient's needs and/or complexity of the delegated task on a timely basis
- Supervise the UNP's ability to complete the task/assignment based on education and experience
- Provide appropriate feedback on a timely basis

The delegatee should:

- Complete the delegated task/activity according to established standards
- Ask questions or seek clarification when necessary
- Adhere to specified and agreed upon reporting times
- Report any specific concerns or emergency situations immediately

Evaluation

The nurse reviews if the:

- Task/activity was successfully performed
- Expected client outcome(s) were successfully achieved
- Communication was timely and effective
- Strengths/challenges were identified
- Strengths/challenges created a platform for a quality improvement plan
- Quality improvement plan allowed for addressing concerns/issues and provided constructive feedback for the nurse and UNP
- Quality improvement plan allowed for appropriate training and education
- Team was acknowledged for contributions to safe and effective patient-centered care

LITERATURE PERSPECTIVE

Resource: National Association of School Nurses (NASN). (2015). *Unlicensed assistive personnel in the school setting: Their role in school health services* (Position Statement). Silver Spring, MD: Author

NASN supports delegation in states where laws and regulations allow it in the school setting. An unlicensed assistive personnel (UAP) can be a valuable asset to a school nurse. With advances in health care and technology, children with diabetes, asthma, seizure disorder, life-threatening food allergies, chronic illness, and other rare conditions are an integral part of the school-aged population. The school nurse is accountable for providing care according to the students' Individualized Health Care Plan (IHP) and district policies, including those tasks and activities assigned to the UAP. It is the responsibility of the school nurse to train, educate, validate competency of, monitor, and supervise the UAP. The school nurse is also accountable for documentation of ongoing competency of the UAP and is the only one who can make a delegation decision. School nurses make delegation decisions based on the situation, level of competency, experience, and training of the UAP.

School nurses must educate school administrators, principals, teachers, psychologists, social workers, and other staff members about clinical nursing judgment, legal parameters of their practice, and their accountability for the health care of students. It is important that they under-stand that delegation decisions, made through a nursing decision-making process, are made in the best interest of the students' health and safety. Delegation requires the school nurses to have critical thinking and judgment skills as well as knowledge and expertise in health promotion, disease prevention, and special healthcare issues to make effective delegation decisions.

Implications for Practice

School nurses must make delegation decisions based on the Scope and Standards of Nursing Practice (ANA, 2015a), Scope and of Standards of School Nursing Practice (ANA and NASN, 2011), nurses practice acts (NPAs), state laws, rules and regulation, the five rights of delegation, the students' health care needs, the school practice environment, employer policies and procedures/agency regulations, safety issues, and the level of competence of the UAP. Delegation to a UAP can be a valuable asset to a school nurse, especially when the nurse/student ratio is high. School administrators and others who delegate nursing tasks to nonnurse employees create litigious situations for themselves, the school nurse, and the school district. Therefore only registered nurses can delegate nursing care. School nurses may delegate when they deem it appropriate, but delegation may not be appropriate for all students or in all school settings.

To ensure high-quality care, the Centers for Medicare and Medicaid Services (CMS) mandate that nursing homes employ certified CNAs. CNAs must successfully complete a state-approved program and pass a competency examination to be registered in that state. However, variations in the scope of employment and functions occur across states. Nurses must know the respective state nurse practice acts and understand the delegation standard related to individual job descriptions and function within their states' regulatory guidelines to maintain high-quality patient care and safe clinical practice.

Evaluation

Evaluation is often overlooked in the delegation process. However, it should never be overlooked because it allows time to reflect on delegation decisions. It provides the nurse time to determine whether the delegation was successful and to identify the strengths and challenges related to the delegation decision. Evaluation and constructive reflection allows us to build on the strengths, learn from the challenges, and implement quality measures to improve delegation decisions.

When delegators decrease the amount of direct person-centered care they perform, they automatically increase their supervision of others. The importance of giving clear directions, asking and receiving quality feedback regarding tasks, and having an agreed upon schedule for checkpoints are essential for a well-executed plan. This evaluation plan is influenced by factors such as knowledge of and experience with the delegatee, the number of delegatees and patients for whom the delegator is accountable, the geographic design of the unit, the stability of the patients, and the resources available to the delegatee. Evaluating how the delegatee and patients are doing throughout the work period is critical to work performance and the outcomes of person-centered care.

The delegator should provide constructive feedback to the delegates regarding his or her work-related performance. To convey satisfaction with an individual's performance that is less than satisfactory diminishes the credibility of the nurse. A verbal attack on an individual does not produce effective change and potentially undermines any long-term working relationship. For example, a verbal attack such as, "What is wrong with you today?" is not effective to elicit feedback. The best strategy is to provide open, honest, and constructive feedback, such as, "Let me demonstrate a more effective way to perform the task." Honest feedback about work-related performance and specific strategies for change provide the delegatee a quality improvement plan.

Another concern regarding delegation is when individuals lack the competence to hold their current position. One strategy for managing this issue is to temporarily lower expectations and provide additional support. This strategy allows individuals to build on their strengths, minimize weaknesses, and gain confidence. However, it is essential to examine the effect that lowering expectations for an individual has on other team members. Many questions need to be considered in the decision: Why is one employee held to a standard and another is not? Who becomes responsible for the work that one individual cannot accomplish? Is it fair to compensate an individual for work that does not meet performance expectations? What are the potential liabilities of altering the standards of performance? Because making delegation decisions is a complex process, nurses must understand that delegating to individuals who are not capable of performing safely and effectively and then not intervening creates a high risk for legal liability. Work should not be delegated if the delegator knows the delegatee is not competent to perform the task or activity. In addition to the legal ramifications of poor delegation decisions, ethical considerations should also influence the nurse's decisions. Box 17.4 (p. 307) reviews elements to consider for evaluating delegation decisions.

Nurses always have accountability for assessment, diagnosis, planning, nursing judgment, and evaluation of person-centered care. Evaluation and constructive feedback are essential components for continuous quality improvement and effective nursing management. The ability to make effective delegation decisions and be accountable for providing safe, competent, and effective person-centered care is a critical competency for nurses in the twenty-first century.

> **EXERCISE 17.2** Interview three licensed nurses. Ask them what they believe their responsibilities are in the delegation process. Discuss these responsibilities with a small group of colleagues.

ORGANIZATIONAL AND INDIVIDUAL ACCOUNTABILITY

Organizational accountability is a crucial component of delegation. Highly productive organizations often use a relationship-based leadership model that fosters interdisciplinary communication and collaboration among all members of the healthcare team. This promotes a positive culture and work environment that supports person-centered care that is necessary for effective delegation.

A shared governance model, a framework for organizing nursing care, is often used when hospitals seek Magnet® recognition. A shared governance model, an accountability-based leadership model, fosters structural empowerment, transformational leadership, development of new knowledge, and evidence-based practice improvements and innovations. Successful organizations that achieve Magnet® status, through an extensive evaluation process, usually have supportive work environments and assist healthcare teams to function effectively. Making appropriate decisions depends on how well the organization provides adequate resources, including an appropriate ratio of RNs to LPNs/LVNs and UNP. Chief nursing officers (CNOs) are accountable for establishing systems to assess, monitor, verify, communicate, and evaluate competency requirements related to delegation.

Individual accountability is another component of delegation. The term refers to individuals' abilities to explain their actions and results. Accountability is to be "answerable to oneself and others for one's choices, decisions and actions as measured against standards…" (ANA, 2015a, p. 41) The *Code of Ethics for Nurses with Interpretive Statements* (2015b), is composed of nine provisions and describes the ethical obligations of all nurses. The Code's Provision 4 focuses on the nurse's authority, accountability and responsibility, for nursing practice and how decisions and actions must be consistent with the obligation to promote health and provide high-quality health care (ANA, 2015). Provision 4 also has four interpretive statements related to responsibility and obligations to the patient. The first interpretive statement emphasizes the importance of the role of "authority, accountability, and responsibility" in nursing practice. The second interpretive statement reviews "accountability for nursing judgment, decision making, and actions" and emphasizes that technology is only viewed as an aid to care and cannot be substituted for nursing actions, judgment, and accountability. The third interpretive statement addresses the nurses' responsibilities related to "accountability for nursing judgment, decision making, and actions" and requires nurse executives to empower nurses to actively engage, participate, and contribute to organizational committees and institutional review boards. The fourth interpretive statement addresses the "assignment and delegation of nursing activities or tasks." This statement indicates that nurses cannot delegate nursing assessment and evaluation and emphasizes that employer policies do not release nurses of this responsibility regarding decisions related to assignments or delegation. Legally, nurses have authority, accountability, and responsibility for the quality of care provided to patients in accordance with the scope and standards of practice, nurse practice acts, regulations, and *Codes* (Windland-Brown, Lachman, & Swanson, 2015).

LEGAL AUTHORITY TO DELEGATE

Legal authority, by virtue of the professional nursing license, is the ability to delegate responsibility to complete a task or activity to a competent individual; however, the nurse retains accountability for ensuring that the task is completed by the right person and that person is supervised appropriately.

A critical component of delegation is authority, and the delegated task must comply with the law, such as the state NPA, and comply with the educational preparation and certification of the individual to which the task is delegated. Nurses must be able to articulate their scope of practice and own responsibility for delivery of nursing care congruent with standards of practice and state practice acts (Lucatorto, Thomas, & Siek, 2016). Most state NPAs address the concept of delegation, including some rules and regulations governing when and what tasks can be delegated. State boards of nursing are vested in protecting the public; therefore they regulate the educational preparation and practice of professional nursing.

Nurses must own nursing practice at the individual, organizational, and legislative level (Lucatorto, Thomas, & Siek, 2016).

Legally, delegation is also a complex process. First, the delegator is personally responsible for prudent action. If the delegation task is not performed within acceptable standards, a potential for nursing malpractice emerges. Failure to delegate and supervise within acceptable standards may extend to direct corporate liability for the facility. Whenever care is provided by another individual, rather than a nurse, the accountability for care remains with the delegator even though others provide various aspects of care. This view of professional liability is consistent with the concept that licensure conveys both privilege and expectation. Specific knowledge about nursing and delegation is necessary to make appropriate nursing judgments. The nurse is legally accountable and liable for his or her actions and those of the delegatee. The role of the nurse has evolved over time, so it is essential to maintain current and accurate knowledge about the scope of nursing liability.

EXERCISE 17.3 Review your state's nurse practice act, rules, and regulations. Discuss with two or more colleagues what your state identifies as delegation. Create a written summary related to your conclusions.

LEARNING HOW TO DELEGATE: DIFFERENT STRATEGIES FOR SUCCESS

The Five Rights of Delegation

Using the five rights of delegation, Table 17.1 is a tool that can be used to assist in making effective delegation decisions. Column one includes the five delegation rights, column two includes specific questions to ask before delegating, and a third column that includes a response of "yes" if the answers to the questions are positive and delegation is appropriate. The five rights include how to delegate the right task, under the right circumstances, to the right person, with the right direction and communication, and under the right supervision and evaluation and can assist nurses to make effective delegation decisions. The direct care nurses' communication style influences how the delegatee responds to delegated tasks or activities and influences teamwork and relationships. The fourth right of

TABLE 17.1	**The Five Rights of Delegation**	
Delegation Rights	**The Right Questions (Answer the Following Questions)**	**Yes Responses**
Task	Is the task appropriate to delegate based on the individuals' job description and facility policies and procedures? Is the task legally appropriate to delegate?	Right task
Circumstance	Is the delegation process appropriate to the situation? Is the environment conducive to completing the task safely? Are the equipment and resources available to complete the task? Do staffing ratios demand the use of high-level delegation strategies? Does the delegatee have appropriate supervision to complete the task?	Right circumstances
Person	Is the prospective delegatee a willing and able employee? Does the delegatee have the knowledge and experience to perform the specific task safely? Does the delegatee have the expertise to complete the task safely and effectively in relation to the acuity of the patient?	Right person
Direction/communication	Do the delegator and delegatee understand a common work-related language? (Do terms such *as time frame, patient needs,* and *critical* mean the same to each of them?) Does the delegator provide clear and concise directions for the task? Does the delegatee understand the assignment, directions, limitations, and expected results as they relate to the task? Do the delegator and delegatee know how to maintain open lines of communication for the purpose of questions and feedback? Does the delegatee understand how, what, and when to report to the delegator?	Right direction/communication
Supervision	Is it clear that the delegatee will provide feedback related to the task, when appropriate? Is the delegator able to monitor and evaluate the patient appropriately?	Right supervision

Adapted from American Nurses Association. (2012). *ANA's principles for delegation by registered nurses to unlicensed assistive personnel.* Silver Spring, MD. https://www.nursingworld.org/~4af4f2/globalassets/docs/ana/ethics/principlesofdelegation.pdf; and National Council of State Boards of Nursing (NCSBN). (2016). National guidelines for nursing delegation. *Journal of Nursing Regulation, 7*(1), 5–14. Copyright © 2013, 2017 M. Murphy-Ruocco.

delegation, the "right communication and direction" is the foundation of delegation. High-quality information presented by the direct care nurse in a timely, meaningful, and effective manner and in the right context can significantly shape the quality and safety of patient care.

Assessing Willingness and Readiness for Delegation: Situational Leadership® Model

Hersey's (2006) Situational Leadership® Model, although not originally designed for the process of delegation, is a another valuable tool to determine the willingness and readiness of the delegatee and the type of relationship needed to make the delegation successful. Multiple factors influence the effectiveness of the leader, including an assessment of personality characteristics, the readiness level of the individual as it relates to the type of task and goals to be attained, and specific environmental conditions. Researchers indicate a positive correlation between transformative leadership (TL) and emotional intelligence (EI) exists (Spano-Szekely, Quinn Griffin, Clavelle, & Fitzpatrick, 2016). Transformative leaders need to be able to diagnose the commitment, competence, and performance of others to create partnerships that improve person-centered care. Hersey's model describes two factors that need to be assessed to determine the level of the followers' readiness: ability and willingness. How these factors interact with each other also needs to be considered. Ability relates to knowledge and skills in a specific situation (job readiness). An individual's ability does not change from one moment to the next (Hersey, Blanchard, & Johnson, 2013). Willingness relates to the individual's attitude, confidence, and commitment toward the specific situation (psychological readiness). Willingness, however, can fluctuate from one moment to another (Hersey, Blanchard, & Johnson, 2013). If a delegatee indicates reluctance to perform some work, the delegator must evaluate the situation to determine whether the issue is a knowledge deficit or a psychomotor deficit that interferes with performing the work, or whether the delegatee is bored, anxious, upset, or just unwilling to meet the expectations. Thus if the delegatee is less able or unwilling to perform in a specific situation, the delegator must remain actively engaged in the situation. In theory, the greater the ability and willingness of the delegatee, the more likely the delegator can implement delegation strategies while interacting with individuals in a specific situation. The model also describes the style of the leadership required

of an effective leader and its relationship between task behavior (the amount of guidance) and relationship behavior (the amount of support) needed in the given situation. The model is designed to determine the best approach a leader can use based on the performance readiness of the delegatee.

If the delegatee has limited knowledge and ability to perform a task, the delegator needs to provide more guidance. However, if the relationship is limited (when two or more individuals are unlikely to work together again), the delegator simply "tells" the individual what to do and how to perform. Hersey's Model (2006) describes the leader's behavior as guiding or directing, which is characterized as "telling."

If a situation involves a new task and the relationship is ongoing (two individuals who will usually continue to work together), the delegator explains what to do and how to do it. Hersey's Model (2006) describes the leader's behavior as explaining or persuading, which is characterized as "selling." Logically, if producing outcomes in a given situation is the driving force, the delegator is much less likely to spend the time and effort investing in limited relationships than in established relationships.

If the delegatee has the ability and willingness, but the relationship between the delegator and delegatee is relatively new, they need to establish mutual expectations and conditions of performance. Hersey's model (2006) describes the leader's behavior as encouraging or problem solving, which is characterized as "participating."

If the delegatee has the ability and willingness, the expertise to accomplish the work, and an established relationship, Hersey's Model (2006) describes the leader's behavior as observing or monitoring, which is characterized as "delegating."

Situational Leadership® styles can be observed in real work-related situations. For example, when a new team begins to work together to build a trusting relationship, the delegator must evaluate the ability and willingness of the delegatees. If the ability and willingness is low, the delegator uses the leadership style of telling or selling. If the nature of the relationship is limited, such as a when someone is only going to work for half a day on the unit, the leadership style should be "telling," because it provides a fair amount of guidance but limits the time spent on the interactions. Additionally, if the relationship is developing or ongoing, the delegator needs to understand the delegatee's motivation related to the situation, and the leader's style should be "selling," which takes more time, but leads to a supportive relationship. If the relationship is new or developing, more support is needed and the delegator and delegatee need to interact in a participatory manner. When a delegatee has a high degree of ability and willingness and is familiar with the expected task, little guidance is required. In theory, the greater the ability and willingness of the delegatee, the more likely the delegator can implement delegation strategies while interacting with that individual in a specific situation. In other words, both the amount of guidance (task behavior) and the amount of support (relationship behavior) would be relatively low, which works well for established work relationships. However, delegation can be viewed as a spectrum of behaviors based on the context and needs in a specific situation. To achieve effective outcomes, knowing how to interact with a given delegatee is one of the key challenges for the delegator. The Theory Box illustrates how Hersey's Model applies to nursing. Table 17.2 presents the delegatee's condition, relevance to the delegator, the original terminology, and a clinical exemplar on how to structure communication with the delegatee to achieve a goal.

THEORY BOX

Situational Leadership® Model

Theory	Key Ideas	Application to Practice
Hersey's model (2006) contends that leaders and managers need to behave differently in specific situations.	Nurses must analyze an individual's knowledge and the work-related task before delegating. Nurses make decisions based on this analysis.	Before delegating, the nurse must understand the type of support an individual needs to successfully accomplish the work-related task. Nursing assistive personnel may need a different level of support for different tasks.

TABLE 17.2   Communicating With a Delegatee

Delegatee Condition	Delegator Relevance	Terminology	Clinical Exemplar
Has limited knowledge and ability to perform the task	Requires more guidance	Tell (if the relationship is not going to be ongoing)	"It is important that you take his blood pressure every 15 minutes."
Has ongoing relationship, but a new task is delegated	Requires explanation	Sell	"This is what you need to accomplish; in fact, let me show you what is necessary."
Has willingness and ability, but the relationship is new	Requires that both individuals create mutual expectations and conditions for performance	Participate	"Please tell me how you go about performing this procedure, and I will share with you my expectations about how frequently and under what conditions we need to communicate/report to each other."
Has established relationship and expertise	Little guidance is needed	Delegate	"I know you know what you are doing and when to report. Just remember that I am available to you at any time if an issue or concern arises. Thank you for being part of the team."

Challenges of Delegating to Unlicensed Nursing Personnel

Delegation to UNPs may be challenging, because the educational preparation and job description of a UNP are not consistent across states and need greater public accountability. Some facilities have UNPs with different designation levels, a higher level designation indicating the ability to perform more tasks and activities. The education of a UNP, coupled with facility policies, defines how the UNP may or may not function. Healthcare facilities have descriptors of what tasks may be performed by an individual in a particular position. The job description for a UNP defines the authority for the specific position.

As advances in health care continue, more tasks and activities may need to be delegated to assist nurses in the delivery of quality person-centered care. Even when policies and protocols within facilities indicate an individual may perform a task or activity on behalf of a nurse, the delegatee must be competent to perform the task. Transformative leaders (TLs) create a culture of safety (Merrill, 2015). To assist with the challenges of delegating to UNPs, nurses can use four elements to determine the UNPs' abilities to perform the task or activity. These four elements include safety, critical thinking, stability, and time. One element may play a more important role than the others in different patient care situations. For example, when critical-thinking skills are of utmost importance for person-centered care, other elements may be relatively less important in the delegation decision. Therefore making decisions about to whom to delegate, what to delegate, and when to delegate is a complex process. Safety is a basic physiologic need, and when a patient is unsafe for any reason, delegation may not be appropriate. Exceptions to this rule are usually related to monitoring behaviors of patients (e.g., when patients are placed on suicide precautions). Critical thinking, the intensity and complexity of nurses' decision-making processes, is vital to patient care decisions. For example, simple (straightforward) teaching, such as hand washing, can be performed by UNPs; however, complex (multifaceted) teaching, such as diabetic teaching, cannot be delegated. Stability, the patient's level of strength or steadiness, is also a major factor in making person-centered care decisions. The greater the stability of a patient, the more likely the UNP can provide safe patient care. Time, the intensity and length of the interactions with the patient, is also a significant factor to consider in planning person-centered care. For example, emergency facilities may employ fewer UNPs, because patients are less stable, compared with extended-care and long-term care facilities, where patients are more stable. When the delegatee has the appropriate work and performance abilities, tasks can be delegated. When a delegatee has limited work and performance abilities, tasks can still be delegated, but the delegator must educate, monitor, and evaluate care very closely to ensure quality person-centered care.

With the shortage of nurses and a growing population of patients living at home with chronic conditions and disabilities, nurses must examine their beliefs and attitudes regarding delegation and eliminate any unnecessary challenges to delegating health-related tasks to competent UNPs. With our increasingly complicated healthcare system and the various healthcare providers who care for patients, no one provider can meet all the needs of the patient (Lancaster et al., 2015). At first, this situation may seem overwhelming; however, if patients are in stable condition and the nursing care is somewhat predictable, it may be manageable. When UNPs are well-prepared providers of routine care and the care environment is limited to a designated area, responsibilities are less challenging. If these factors are not consistent, the responsibility for an increased number of patients may become overwhelming. When UNPs render a portion of the care, these factors need to be assessed to determine the appropriateness of the patient care workload and whether it can be managed safely and effectively in each clinical situation. Educating UNPs in how to implement delegated tasks is crucial for positive outcomes. Consumers, nurses, and UNPs must work collaboratively to improve the quality of community living for patients and individuals with disabilities within a broad regulatory framework. Thus nurses must acquire competency skills in critical thinking, clinical practice, organization, leadership, communication, and time management to meet the challenges of delegation decisions. Critical thinking can range from evaluating information or reframing issues to developing creative innovations (Price, 2015).

> **EXERCISE 17.4** Develop a case study in which you must make a delegation decision to a UNP. Use Table 17.2 to practice with colleagues regarding how to delegate a specific task or responsibility for person-centered care.

Challenges Delegating to Diverse Team Members

Delegation, a complex decision-making process, is successful when effective delegation strategies are learned and appropriately used by the nurse. The nurse's crucial challenge is to fully understand the specific skill set and capabilities of each delegatee on the team.

Delegation can be further complicated by other factors such as age, gender, and ethnicity. Younger generations may have a different view of the world and may be more open and flexible regarding change, especially with technology. Gender may also play a role in learning delegation skills. Ethnicity also plays a role in the process of delegation, because individuals from diverse cultures perceive information and their ability to direct others to perform tasks differently. A new leadership framework includes understanding the concept of diversity (Washington, 2015). Cultural background can influence how the delegator is heard or viewed in the delegation process. Different cultures communicate differently. Diverse cultural, educational, and experiential backgrounds also shape the quality, meaning, and clarity of the information communicated between the delegator and the delegatee.

Selecting a delegatee who has the specific skill set for the particular task or activity is a more productive strategy than just selecting a competent individual. When a nurse is a new employee in the workplace, the nurse's ability to make delegation decisions can be difficult, because she or he does not know the capabilities of the delegatee. Working together with the delegatee, as a team, to deliver patient care allows the nurse to assess the delegatee's willingness and ability. Other challenges with teams, especially diverse teams, include the nurse's ability to provide clear and concise directions and expectations, create open and honest lines of communication, provide appropriate resources, ensure that the delegatee knows how to function and understands the time frame. Clear expectations about task accomplishments and making sure the expectations are understood provide a structure for ongoing supervision and evaluation of a delegatee.

If a nurse observes a problem or issue related to delegation but does not have authority specific to the situation and no safety issues, urgency to intervene, or potential negative patient outcomes exist, the nurse can assist other nurses with their delegation decisions by using three strategies: "asking," "offering," and "doing." The first strategy, "asking," begins with questions related to the problem or issue regarding person-centered care. Often, asking questions provides an opportunity to open lines of communication between the delegator and the delegatee and may allow the delegator to examine the situation differently and reassess the situation. The second strategy, "offering," involves making a suggestion that can facilitate the achievement of a desirable person-centered care

outcome. The third strategy, "doing," occurs by demonstrating the specific task or behavior to improve person-centered care.

> **EXERCISE 17.5** Review a delegation decision made by a nurse related to a clinical experience in your practice setting. After reviewing the nurse practice act and professional standards, provide answers with an evidence-based rationale to the following questions:
> 1. Did the nurse make clear what was delegated? Why or why not?
> 2. Were the delegation decisions logical? Why or why not?
> 3. Were the delegation decisions made within legal and ethical parameters?

Barriers to Effective Delegation

Barriers to effective delegation impede the success of the healthcare team. Barriers to delegation can be categorized as underdelegation, overdelegation, and improper delegation (Marquis & Huston, 2017). Underdelegation occurs when nurses do not have the confidence to make an effective delegation decision, lack the time to delegate, choose to complete the responsibility themselves, lack the confidence in the delegatees' abilities to complete the task, or fear a loss of control. Nurses with limited delegation experience can misuse valuable resources, whereas others believe delegation is too time-consuming or requires more energy than doing it themselves. Other nurses may have difficulty trusting others and/or are unable to delegate appropriately because they fear the loss of control. Excessive supervision defeats the purpose of delegation (Reyes, 2015). Fear is the enemy of innovation (Skonnard, 2015). In the ever-changing healthcare setting, knowing and valuing how to be a successful delegator achieves optimum person-centered care outcomes.

Once the delegatee understands the task or activity and is competent to perform the task or activity, any unnecessary interference or micromanaging by the delegator, unless for a safety or ethical concern, can cause the delegatee to lose confidence or become frustrated and erode the trust relationship. Once nurses know delegatees have been trained, educated, and evaluated on a particular task or activity, they usually become more comfortable assigning a task or activities to the delegatees. Developing a working relationship is challenging and complicated (Lancaster et al., 2015). Once the delegatee develops a trusting relationship with the nurse and understands that the ultimate goal of nursing delegation is to maximize person-centered care outcomes, the delegatee becomes more receptive to constructive feedback. This delegation process creates a collaborative and productive work environment. The nurse who trusts, respects, and provides ownership to the delegatee regarding the task or responsibility empowers the delegatee to feel valued, competent, and like an integral part of the healthcare team. Reluctance to give ownership indicates a lack of trust (Skonnard, 2015). Effective delegation decisions do not release power of control but enhance the productivity, accomplishment, and success of the healthcare team.

Overdelegation occurs when the nurse overburdens a delegatee with too many tasks and responsibilities. This occurs when the delegator has difficulty organizing work, has poor time management skills, or lacks self-confidence in performing the task or responsibility. An overburdened and overworked delegatee becomes overwhelmed, experiences employee burnout, and decreases the productivity of the healthcare team. Nurses must develop exemplary organization skills, including time management skills, and foster open communication with the delegatee so that, when necessary, the delegatee can respectfully refuse a task or activity. Nurses must maintain clinical practice skills so that they can be responsive to the needs of the delegatee and serve as a mentor to the delegatee to increase the productivity of the team.

Improper delegation is delegating tasks or responsibilities beyond the delegatee's training or education or assigning a task or responsibility without providing adequate information or data to successfully complete the task or activity. Nurses must determine whether delegates are capable of performing the task or activity according to their job description or whether it requires specialized knowledge and skills that would not be appropriate for their role and function in the facility. Improper delegation can lead to inadequate care for the patient or failure to meet the standards of care and can cause potential harm to patients. This creates a potential for liability for the nurse and the healthcare facility.

EXERCISE 17.6 Interview a nurse and an unlicensed nursing personnel about their perspective regarding barriers to delegation including underdelegation, overdelegation, and improper delegation. Compare and contrast the similarities and differences in the two perspectives and roles.

Building Effective Nurse Delegators and Interprofessional Teams

In a nurse's career, high-quality clinical delegation experiences and engagement with a nursing mentor foster professional self-confidence. The development of leadership skills through mentoring builds nurses' confidence (Eliades, Jakubik, Weese, & Huth, 2017) These experiences advance the nurse's ability to become a successful delegator. Nurses must keep current in delegation decisions by enrolling in continuing education programs to reinforce what, when, and how to effectively delegate. These programs create opportunities for all healthcare professionals to keep current in their fields and adapt to the ever-changing healthcare environment.

Building a cohesive interprofessional healthcare team begins with understanding the individual members of the team, their roles and functions, and their disciplines (Lancaster et al., 2015) Learning with, and understanding the role and responsibilities of, other healthcare professionals creates a respect for the contributions that all healthcare providers make to patient care. Interprofessional collaboration reflects independent and shared decision making, prevents fragmentation of care, and increases the effectiveness of the healthcare team (Lancaster et al., 2015.) Building collaborative staff relationships, based on trust and respect, is necessary for effective delegation and interprofessional team work.

Creating positive, collaborative partnerships between nursing leaders at healthcare facilities and faculty at colleges of nursing can increase experiences in interprofessional practice. This partnership can also support clinical nurses with adjunct faculty appointments at colleges and universities and nursing faculty opportunities to practice in the healthcare facility. This type of partnership assists with maintaining the competency of nurses. Additionally, structured nursing leadership competencies integrated in the curriculum and led by faculty in small group seminars can provide mentoring and the development of leadership skills that socialize students into the role of professional nurse (Denver et al., 2015).

CONCLUSION

Delegation, a multifaceted decision-making process, is a learned skill related to how to make appropriate nursing judgments, achieve nursing goals, and improve person-centered care. Effective delegation skills are essential competencies to practice as a nurse in the 21st century. Multiple factors play a role in the ability of the nurse to delegate effectively. These factors include, but are not limited to, the nurses' educational preparation, demographic area, state practice acts, leadership style, employment area, clinical experience, and self-confidence. The nurse must understand the delegation process, develop critical judgment skills, and effectively use delegation skills to maximize productivity, while providing safe, high-quality, person-centered care.

THE SOLUTION

In a Level I emergency trauma department, the patient acuity is serious and is often changing. The emergency medical service team is arriving with multiple patients injured in an accident at the chemical plant.

The registered professional nurse managing the trauma center must understand the qualifications, experience, and abilities of the nurses assigned patients. The nurses also need to understand the qualifications, experience, and abilities of the emergency technicians to whom they delegate tasks.

The emergency technicians who have been working in the center for a minimum of 1 year can be delegated tasks by the registered nurse. However, the qualifications and experience of the newly employed emergency technicians (unlicensed nursing personnel) were unknown. Because they would not begin the emergency technician training program for another 2 months, one experienced technician and a newly employed emergency technician worked with each registered nurse accountable for patient care. Each technician was directly supervised, observed, and evaluated by her registered nurse.

Each staff member needed to understand what tasks can be delegated and what tasks cannot be delegated.
Would this be a suitable approach for you? Why?

Kathryn King-Dyker

REFLECTIONS

Delegation is a complex process. How comfortable do you feel with delegation? Do you have input on whom to hire to work on the unit? What aspect of delegation do you consider most challenging?

THE EVIDENCE

Effective delegation skills are essential competencies necessary to practice as a registered professional nurse in the 21st century. Multiple factors play a role in the ability of the registered nurse to delegate effectively. These factors include, but are not limited to, the nurses' educational preparation, demographic area, state practice acts, leadership style, employment area, clinical experience, and the individual's self-confidence. When nurses are engaged in a work environment that uses an RN/UNP care model, they gain the clinical experience to effectively use delegation skills. Today, this type of care model supports nurses in providing high-quality, cost-effective health care.

IMPLICATIONS FOR PRACTICE

Nursing research, an instrument to support evidence-based practice, should be used to manage person-centered care. Nursing internships, offered in school, that provide delegation and supervisory experience of UNPs can enhance an individual's clinical experience and confidence, allowing them to learn how to delegate safely and effectively. As registered nurses adapt to the rapidly changing healthcare environment, nurse managers must continue to support nurses with clinical experiences and continued professional education that enhances their leadership skills, allowing them to effectively delegate and supervise others.

TIPS FOR DELEGATING

- Understand the organizational structure, policies, and culture of the facility to make effective delegation decisions.
- Comprehend the job description of individuals before delegating tasks.
- Assess the knowledge, skills, willingness, and readiness of the individual before delegating tasks or activities.
- Use the state NPA and scope and standards of practice to determine how to appropriately delegate tasks and activities.

- Use communication strategies to develop successful delegating skills.
- Use assessment, planning, implementation, and evaluation to determine whether the work-related task and activities can be and/or were successfully delegated.
- Evaluate the effectiveness of delegating tasks and activities to others on a regular basis.

REFERENCES

Agency for Healthcare Research and Quality. (2015). *Patient safety primers: Handoffs and signouts.* www.psnet.ahrq.gov/primer. Aspx?primer ID = 9.

American Nurses Association. (2012). *Principles for Delegation by Registered Nurses to Unlicensed Assistive Personnel (UAP).* Silver Spring, MD: Nursesbooks.org.

American Nurses Association and National Council of State Boards of Nursing. (n.d.) *Joint Statement on delegation.* https://www.ncsbn.org/delegation_joint_statement_NCSBN-ANA.

American Nurses Association (ANA). (2015a). *Nursing: Scope and standards of practice.* Silver Spring, MD: Author.

American Nurses Association (ANA). (2015b). *Code of ethics for nurses with Interpretative statements.* Silver Spring, MD: Author.

Brenner, P. (1954). *From Novice to expert: Excellence and power in clinical nursing practice.* Menlo Park, CA: Addison-Wesley.

Denver, K., Roman, T., Smith, C., Bowllan, N., Dollinger, M., & Blaine, B. (2015). Comparing Professional Values an Authentic Leadership Dimensions in Baccalaureate Nursing Students: A Longitudinal Study. *Journal of Nursing Education, 54*(6).

Eliades, A., Jakubik, Weese, M., & Huth, J. (2017). Mentoring Practice and Mentoring Benefit 6: Equipping for Leadership and Leadership Readiness- an Overview and Application to Practice Using Mentoring Activities. *Pediatric Nursing, 43*(1).

Hersey, P. (2006). *Situational leadership® model.* Escondido, CA: The Center for Leadership Studies, Inc. http://www.situational.com.

Hersey, P., Blanchard, K. H., & Johnson, D. E. (2013). *Management of organizational behavior: leading human resources* (10th ed.). Upper Saddle River, NJ: Pearson.

Lancaster, G., Kolakowsky-Haper, S., Kovacich, J., & Geer-Williams. (2015). Interdisciplinary Communication and Collaboration Among Physicians, Nurses, and Unlicensed Assistive Personnel. *Journal of Nursing Scholarship 47, 3,* 275–284.

Lucatorto, M. A., Thomas, T., & Siek, T. (2016). Registered nurses as caregivers influencing the system as patient advocates. *Journal of Issues in Nursing, 21*(3), 5.

Marquis, B., & Huston, C. (2017). Delegation. In B. Marquis & C. Huston (Eds.), *Leadership Roles and Management Functions in Nursing.* Wolters Kluwer: Philadelphia, PA.

Merrill, K. C. (2015). Leadership style and patient safety: Implications for nurse managers. *Journal of Nursing Administration, 45*(6), 319–324. https://doi.org/10.1097/NNA.0000000000000207.

Mueller, C., & Vogelsmeier, A. (2015). *Effective Delegation: Understanding Responsibly.* Authority and Accountability https://doi.org/10.1016/S2155-825630126-5.

National Association of School Nurses (NASN). (January, 2015). *Unlicensed Assistive Personnel in the School Setting: Their Role in School Health Services (Position Statement).* Silver Spring, MD: Author.

National Council of State Boards of Nursing. (2016). National guidelines for nursing delegation. *Journal of Nursing Regulation, 7*(1), 5–14.

Price, B. (2015). Applying critical thinking. *Nursing Standard, 29*(51), 49–58. https://doi.org/10.7748/ns.29.51.49e10005.

Reyes, S. (2015). *When and how to delegate.* http://tribehr.com/blog/when-and-how-to-delegate/?utm_source=feedburner&utm.medium=feed&utm_campaign=Feed%3A+TribeH+(TribeHR).

Skonnard, A. (2015). *Why you should delegate your hardest decision.* http://www.inc.com/aaron-skonnard/why-you-should-delegate-your-hardest-decisions.html.

Spano-Szekely, L., Quinn Griffin, M. T., Clavelle, J., & Fitzpatrick, J. J. (2016). Emotional intelligence and transformational leadership in nurse managers. *The Journal of Nursing Administration, 46*(2), 101–108. https://doi.org/10.1097/NNA.0000000000000303.

Windland-Brown, J., Lachman, V. D., & Swanson, E. O. (2015). "The new Code of Ethics for Nurses with Interpretative Statements' (2015): Practical clinical application, Part I. *MEDSURG Nursing, 24*(3), 268–271.

Washington, D. (2015). Leading a Multicultural Work Environment: Reflections on the Next Frontier of Nursing Leadership. *Nursing Administration Quarterly, 39*(2), 150–156. April/June.

18

Leading Change

Elaine S. Scott

LEARNING OUTCOMES

- Analyze the nature and types of change in the healthcare system.
- Evaluate theories and conceptual frameworks for understanding and navigating change.
- Examine the use of select functions, principles, and strategies for initiating and managing change.
- Formulate desirable qualities of both direct care nurses and nurse leaders who are effective change agents.
- Explore methods for sustaining change.

KEY TERMS

barriers
change agents
change leaders
change process

chaos theory
complexity theories
facilitators
first-order change

learning organization
planned change
second-order change
unplanned change

THE CHALLENGE

As a nurse manager on a large medical-surgical unit, I often noticed that our nursing assistants did a lot of running around in and out of patients' rooms. They often answered call bells for the same things over and over, all day long. In addition, I saw that the professional nursing staff could not always locate the nursing assistants because they were so spread out over the geographic layout of the unit. Around the same time, patient satisfaction and staff satisfaction had either reached a plateau or remained low. I heard a presentation about hourly rounding and then found some articles explaining how the practice had been introduced in many hospitals across the country. I brought the articles to my staff and introduced the concept to them. The challenge, I told them, is to anticipate patients' needs rather than respond to them as we all had been doing for years. How could I make hourly rounding work on our unit without resistance? Would our patient and staff satisfaction increase? How would the staff adjust to the change?

What would you do if you were this nurse?

Sharon McEvoy, RN
Nurse Manager, Clara Maass Medical Center, Belleville, New Jersey

INTRODUCTION

At no time in history have nurses experienced the amount of change that exists in the current healthcare environment. Advances in technology and nursing science, evolving evidence-based practices, and healthcare regulation and reimbursement are in a state of constant flux. Understanding the nature of change and how to navigate through change is an essential skill for the contemporary nurse. Unless nurses know how to promote changes in the health-seeking behavior of patients, continued decline and negative outcomes may occur. Nurses at the bedside, in clinics, and in patients' homes not only support patients in changing their behavior but also must now foster innovation and promote change in the workplace to adopt best practices, advance patient safety, and improve patient outcomes.

Both nurse leaders and nurses at the bedside must be excellent change managers. Nurse leaders play the role of both coach and coordinator, facilitating the changes needed at a system, unit, or team level (Boyal & Hewsion, 2016). Nurses at the bedside identify and implement needed changes and must be willing to let go of old practice patterns to benefit patients (Dombrowski et al., 2016). During change, nurse leaders keep the delivery of safe and effective care at the center of their attention to ensure that the disruption and chaos of change do not affect patients. By supporting a transparent and evidence-based environment, the nurse leader ensures a culture that will support both patients and staff during the change process (Fuchs & Prouska, 2014). All nurses, in all their roles, are change agents; that means they prepare for, implement, and sustain change.

THE NATURE OF CHANGE

The concept of change is founded on the belief that individuals and organizations are open systems that can be influenced by internal and external variables. Change involves altering the current state of things. Merriam-Webster's (2017) definition of *change* is "to give a different position, course, or direction; to make a shift from one to another." Change can be planned, or it can occur in response to external or internal requirements. For example, as reimbursement methods have changed in health care, health systems have reorganized service delivery, implemented new technology, and created new initiatives such as patient-centered care and transitional care programs. In today's world, change is constant, unavoidable, and pervasive.

Change can happen on a personal level or on an organizational level. Change can be initiated by the individual or the system, or it can be imposed on either. A patient may decide to lose weight and exercise to maintain health. This is an example of a planned change at a personal level. In contrast, when a federal law changes the reimbursement rates for Medicare patients, healthcare organizations may have to alter service delivery to prevent financial losses. This is an example of an organizational change. When a disaster occurs, an unplanned event disrupts both individual and organizational plans. Almost all organizational changes require personal changes for the individuals employed by the organization.

Types of change can be characterized in several ways based on both intensity and cause. Historically, change was thought of as planned change and unplanned change (Lewin, 1951). Planned change is deliberate and organized and has the goal of improvement. Unplanned change is disconcerting, unanticipated, and adaptive. These are also referred to as *first-order change* and *second-order change* (Mannion & Davies, 2016). First-order change is evolutionary, and in healthcare systems, it is often referred to as *continuous improvement*. Most quality improvement programs in healthcare systems are illustrations of first-order change. In this type of change, small, ongoing steps are taken to make things better. First-order change is change that is usually in harmony with the values of persons or systems and thus makes sense to the people involved. Second-order change is revolutionary and episodic and is a large part of what healthcare systems are experiencing today. Second-order change requires radical adjustments in a person or in the structure of a system. This type of change may be unanticipated or expected, but in either case, demonstrative change is required for sustainability.

All changes, whether perceived as positive or negative, large-scale or simple, are scary and generate fear. Some individuals embrace change more readily, whereas others resist even the most minuscule change. Although all change requires interventions for successful implementation, the different types of change necessitate different strategies for successful navigation. Hence the change process is varied depending on whether a change is planned versus unplanned. As change agents, nurses and nurse leaders must understand and be equipped to manage these respective processes.

THE CHANGE PROCESS

Knowledge about the change process is essential for learning to manage it. Central to understanding how to effectively navigate changes in ourselves, patients, and healthcare organizations is the concept of systems. According to Merriam-Webster (2017), a system is a group of interacting, interrelated, or interdependent elements forming a more complex whole. All systems, which can be intricate or simple, have inputs that are collected and processed to develop outputs, or the accomplishment of the goals of the system. Systems have subsystems. For example, an individual is composed of subsystems such as gastrointestinal, cardiovascular, and pulmonary subsystems. A hospital—one example of a healthcare system—includes subsystems such as nursing, dietary, engineering, medicine, and radiology. Systems theory asserts that if one part of the system is changed, then it affects the overall system.

Open systems that function effectively continually exchange feedback among all of the parts to ascertain if the subsystems are healthy and contributing to the goals of the system (Byrne & Callaghan, 2014). If vulnerabilities or weaknesses are present, the system will accommodate to remain stable. Open systems are also influenced by the external environment. Thus healthcare systems and the nurses who work within them are affected by internal factors such as the availability and quality of resources, the levels of staffing, and the processes used to manage patient care. Additionally, external factors such as disease and lifestyle patterns in the community population, healthcare regulation and reimbursement, and the supply of healthcare workers also affect the system. Changes to a system may be anticipated and planned, or they may be sudden and unexpected. Planned change, or first-order change, is about doing what you currently do in a better way (Mannion & Davies, 2016). Second-order change

involves completely disrupting the way things are done by redesigning and reconceptualizing how to do things (Mannion & Davies, 2016).

Planned, First-Order Change

Lewin (1947) was one of the first theorists and scholars to study and illuminate the process of planned change. He postulated that change involves a three-stage process that begins by helping a person, group, or organization release a current behavior or process, move toward the new desired reality, and then sustain that new status. These three steps—unfreezing, moving, and refreezing—can be used to analyze almost any type of change. Sometimes unfreezing involves overcoming inertia, the desire to keep things the same. A patient may realize the need to adopt a low-salt diet after being diagnosed with hypertension, or an organization may acknowledge a need to alter the mix of registered nurses and assistants on a unit to lower the cost of care delivery. This begins the change process, but it takes considerably more effort to actually make the change. Examples of forces of change that are facilitators and barriers are shown in Fig. 18.1. Unfreezing is the step during which individuals and organizations recognize the need to change and begin to get ready to make that change. This is a time of evaluating the benefits and the costs that the change will entail. This evaluation affects the motivation level generated to make the change.

Lewin (1951) called this evaluation *force field analysis*. He described it as the forces or influences that

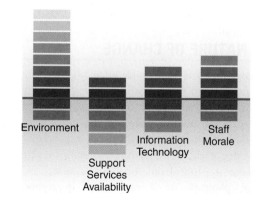

Fig. 18.1 Examples of forces of change: facilitators and barriers.

affect whether change occurs. If more forces favor change—facilitators—then change will be more likely to occur. In contrast, if during this analysis more forces are against the change—barriers—then the change will be less likely to occur. Lewin's force field analysis is simple yet robust in helping nurses understand what it takes to make and sustain a change. This theory is particularly relevant when implementing planned change. Change agents need to know whether individuals see the need to unfreeze. This involves listening and assessing to determine whether all participants in the change have a shared vision for the change. Organizational change is accomplished through individual change, so understanding the power of the status quo is essential. Unless individuals perceive the change will make things better, the resisting forces will limit the success of the change. As in the Challenge, changes in how patients' needs were anticipated on an hourly basis on one unit brought about unfreezing. Unfreezing is a critical step in planned change. During this phase of change we realize what people fear and how we can address those fears.

In the second stage, the moving or changing stage of Lewin's theory, planned interventions and strategies are executed to support the implementation of the change. Commonly used methods include education about the need for the change, vision building to conceptualize and bring life to the change, involving individuals in the process of planning and making the change, and implementing small steps toward the change. Information gained during the analysis of the forces for and against the transition can be used to guide the change agent in making a plan and developing strategies to ensure effective implementation of the change goal. Remembering that a practical first step must be clear can determine the success of a planned change.

The final stage—refreezing—focuses on sustaining the change over a longer period. During this time, the change agent works to reinforce the new, desired behaviors and processes by praising, rewarding, and providing feedback. This phase is commonly undermanaged. Nurse managers must implement systems to ensure that changed behaviors or processes continue, measure the impact of the changes, and provide staff with progress reports and evidence of success. Every nurse has to monitor behaviors during this phase, because slipping back into routines and more comfortable patterns of performance can easily happen without diligence and dedication to the change initiative.

EXERCISE 18.1 Using Lewin's force field analysis concept, identify the facilitators and barriers in the following situation. Using a scale of 1 to 5, rate the potential strength of each in hindering or expediting attainment of the change. Use "+5" for the highest positive strength toward change occurring and "+1" for the weakest. Use "−5" for the greatest negative strength against the change and "−1" for the weakest.

The inpatient psychiatric unit is about to convert 12 of its 20 voluntary beds into short-term care facility (STCF) beds for patients who are involuntarily committed. These beds would coexist with the voluntary beds that are already on the unit. The involuntary beds were transferred from the license of a nearby facility. The talent and the expertise of the former facility were highly desirable to help with the transition to a unit with a higher acuity with sicker patients; therefore 12 of the former facility's nursing staff members were hired. So far, staff's reaction to the merger has been mixed. Individuals from the former facility, although welcomed enthusiastically by the staff from the present unit, were less than enthusiastic. Added to the change was the news that the former facility filed for bankruptcy, leaving the former employees without their retirement pensions and other benefits.

Lewin's work has been the foundation for many change theorists. Lippitt, Watson, and Westley (1958) further developed Lewin's work by considering more of the human factors that are involved in change (see the Theory Box). In particular, Lippitt et al. (1958) created three aspects of the moving phase that further defined what happened to foster change: (1) pushing back on and really clarifying the problem that is requiring the change; (2) examining all of the possible ways to address the problem, developing commitment to one of those plans; and (3) moving individuals from intending to change to actually changing behaviors and processes. Additionally, Lippit et al. (1958) also studied what contributed to the effectiveness of change agents in soliciting change. They found that the relationship the change agent had with the group made a demonstrative difference in accomplishing the change. More recently, Fuchs and Prouska have confirmed this early finding (2014). In addition, Havelock (1973) proposed that change occurred in six phases (see the Theory Box).

Unplanned, Second-Order Change

Though Lewin's theory was designed to describe planned or first-order changes, many scholars think the theory is too simplistic to address how unplanned or second-order change occurs (Ercetin, 2016). Planned change initiatives are still useful in stable situations; however, the magnitude of change in the world today has led to evolution in the thinking about systems, ultimately contributing to the development of complexity theories. These theories address the vast array of non-linear and unpredictable events that occur in the world. Complexity theories alter the traditional systems thinking approach by asserting that system behavior is unpredictable (Byrne & Callaghan, 2014). This type of theory views change as emergent and highly influenced by all individuals and subsystems in an organization. In complexity theories, chaos is viewed as order beneath randomness. Although things may appear chaotic, organizing elements are still beneath them, keeping a careful balance between order and disorder. Complexity theories suggest that change is not episodic but rather an ongoing experience through which a system adjusts and

realigns, recreating itself continuously. This perspective shifts the change experience from a top-down model where leaders design the future and impose it on the system to one where change is systemic, emerging throughout the system, across departments and professions, as an adaptive response fostered by decentralized decision making and collaboration.

Although change can be disruptive, Clayton Christensen suggested that we would deliberately want to create disruption because of the benefits of forward movement. The Literature Perspective provides his and his colleagues' thoughts about disruptive innovation.

Some of the more recent thinking about healthcare systems is framed using complexity theory (Byrne & Callaghan, 2014; Edwards & Porter-O'Grady, 2017). An illustration of this is the Magnet Recognition Program® in the United States. The American Nurses' Credentialing Center (ANCC) awards this status to hospitals that meet or exceed a set of standards designed to measure the quality and effectiveness of nursing in their organizations (ANCC, 2011). Abraham Jerome-D'Emilia, and Begun (2011) characterized this

---

LITERATURE PERSPECTIVE

Resource: Christensen, C. M., Raynor, M. E., & McDonald, R. (2016). What is disruptive innovation? In *The Clayton M Christensen Reader*. Boston MA: Harvard Business Review.

The purpose of this paper was to identify how a theory does not necessarily apply in all cases and how refinements in a theory, if not adopted, tend to negate the value of the theory. The authors define disruption as a process whereby a smaller company with fewer resources is able to successfully challenge established incumbent businesses (p. 158). Typically, the target of the entrant is some segment not currently addressed, whereas the incumbent is typically focused on growing what is already the leader product or service in the organization.

The authors identify that disruptive innovations are either new-market based or at the low end. An analogy in health care might be a distinctive application of the social determinants of health care as a launch of a new service.

The authors point out that disruption is not a thing; it is a process. Furthermore, the business model may be very

different from that which currently exists. This would suggest that proposing a disruption in health care might require a different funding model because so much of how health care is supported is through traditional, established, bureaucratic models. Another key point is that disruption for an incumbent business suggests that the organization has to become bifocused, meaning continuing to maximize the established leading services while attending to the development of a new innovation.

Because this field is relatively young, much remains to be learned about the accuracy of predicting which innovations will be successful and which will not.

Implications for Practice
The strategy of "thinking like the end user" has great potential for innovation. Many end users can tell you what is wrong with something even though they do not know (and maybe do not care about) how to fix the issue. Nurses who are willing to think wildly about possibilities can use disruptive innovation processes to consider new answers to the many questions health care poses.

movement as an "organizational innovation" that fosters "decentralized decision making, relatively flat organizational structures, a participative management culture, and empowered middle managers" (p. 306). Because Magnet® mobilizes an operational framework reflective of the principles derived from complexity theory, it supports a healthcare system in developing and diffusing new ideas, improving nurse satisfaction, and creating better hospital experiences for patients (Stimpfel, Sloane, McHugh, & Aiken, 2016).

Whether change is planned or unplanned, some researchers have estimated that nearly 70% of all change strategies in organizations fail (Ewenstein, Smith, & Sologar, 2015). Organizations and individuals can have well-conceptualized visions and plans for change and still fail to be successful. Central to the effective accomplishment of change is engaging the people affected by the change. This is the major task of the nurse manager functioning as a change agent in the healthcare system. In addition, examining personal resistance against change, poor motivation to adopt new technologies, and evidence-based practice strategies is a critical change management skill all nurses must possess. Many things affect how people react to change. The degree to which the change does not conflict with personal values, the context through which change is brokered in the organization, and the amount of substantive changes individuals must make in their behavior all influence change outcomes.

PEOPLE AND CHANGE

Change, whether proactively initiated at the point of change or imposed from external sources, affects people. Change can be mandated by higher administration, it can originate in any department or unit, or it may begin at the level of direct patient care. Responses to all or part of the change process by individuals and groups may vary from full acceptance and willing participation to outright rejection or even rebellion.

The initial responses to change may be reluctance and resistance. Reluctance and resistance are common when the change threatens personal security. For example, changes in the structure of an organization can result in changes of position for personnel. Eliminating a critical care nurse position and referring that nurse to the only open position as a home health nurse can certainly result in the nurse feeling angry, displaced, and even temporarily incompetent and isolated.

The innovation-decision process (Rogers, 2003; Polster & Villines, 2017) describes the choice of an individual, over time, to accept or reject a new idea for use in practice (see the Theory Box). According to Rogers, the individual's decision-making actions pass through five sequential stages. The decision to not accept the new idea may occur at any stage. However, peer change agents and formal change managers can facilitate movement through these stages by encouraging the use of the idea and providing information about its benefits and disadvantages. This affirms that every nurse, regardless of position, has the power and the responsibility to promote positive change (Sharpe, 2015).

Ideal and common patterns of an individual's behavioral responses to change can facilitate an effective change (Rogers, 2003). These responses and brief descriptions are as follows:

- *Innovators* thrive on change, which may be disruptive to the unit stability.
- *Early adopters* are respected by their peers and thus are sought out for advice and information about innovations and changes.
- *Early majority* prefer doing what has been done in the past but eventually will accept new ideas.
- *Late majority* are openly negative and agree to the change only after most others have accepted the change.
- *Laggards* prefer keeping traditions and openly express their resistance to new ideas.
- *Rejectors* oppose change actively, and may even use sabotage, which can interfere with the overall success of a change process.

One might assume that innovators are the ideal nurse change agent, but all of these perspectives are needed to implement effective change. Often the late majority and laggards have a real reason for rejecting the change. Listening to all the perspectives about change is critical for moving the best change forward successfully. And, as Zuber and Moody (2018) point out, those who wish to be creative and innovative can enhance their success through organizational enablers (see the Research Perspective).

THEORY BOX

Theories for Planned Change

Key Contributors	Key Idea	Application to Practice
Six Phases of Planned Change[a] Havelock (1973) is credited with this planned change model.	Change can be planned, implemented, and evaluated in six sequential stages. The model is advocated for the development of effective change agents and used as a rational problem-solving process. The six stages are as follows: 1. Building a relationship 2. Diagnosing the problem 3. Acquiring relevant resources 4. Choosing the solution 5. Gaining acceptance 6. Stabilizing the innovation and generating self-renewal	Useful for low-level, low-complexity change
Seven Phases of Planned Change[b] Lippitt, Watson, and Westley (1958) are credited with this planned change model.	Change can be planned, implemented, and evaluated in seven sequential phases. Ongoing sensitivity to forces in the change process is essential. The seven phases are as follows: 1. The client system becomes aware of the need for change. 2. The relationship is developed between the client system and change agent. 3. The change problem is defined. 4. The change goals are set and options for achievement are explored. 5. The plan for change is implemented. 6. The change is accepted and stabilized. 7. The change entities redefine their relationships.	Useful for low-level, low-complexity change
Innovation-Decision Process[c] Rogers (2003) is credited with formulating this process.	Change for an individual occurs over five phases when choosing to accept or reject an innovation/idea. Decisions to not accept the new idea may occur at any of the five stages. The change agent can promote acceptance by providing information about benefits and disadvantages and encouragement. The five stages are as follows: 1. Knowledge 2. Persuasion 3. Decision 4. Implementation 5. Confirmation	Useful for individual change

[a]Adapted from Havelock, R. G. (1973). *The change agent's guide to innovation in education.* Englewood Cliffs, NJ: Educational Technology Publications.
[b]Adapted from Lippitt, R., Watson, J., & Westley, B. (1958). *The dynamics of planned change.* New York: Harcourt Brace.
[c]Adapted from Rogers, E. M. (2003). *Diffusion of innovations* (5th ed.). New York: The Free Press.

RESEARCH PERSPECTIVE

Resource: Zuber, C. D., & Moody, L. (2018). Creativity and innovation in health care: Tapping into organizational enablers through human-centered design. *Nursing Administration Quarterly, 42*(1), 62–75.

This grounded-theory, qualitative study was designed to determine what conditions support direct care nurses in being willing to test an innovation. Through a workshop approach, 125 nurses, all of whom were nursing union representatives, provided insight into what were enabling conditions. The researchers found seven enabling themes and then the subsequently stated leadership implications.

1. A personal need for a solution	Pair up challenges with people who have a personal need for the solution.
2. Challenges that have meaningful purpose.	Articulate the bigger vision and purpose.
3. Clarity of goal and control of resources.	Empower staff with clear goals and the ability to control a segment of resources.
4. Active experimentation	Provide time and places for active testing and learning.
5. Experiencing progress quickly and visibly.	Break down innovation efforts into smaller components.
6. Positive encouragement and confidence.	Make time for encouraging feedback and celebrations.
7. The provision of psychological safety.	Support learning that moves the work forward, including perceived failures.

Implications for Practice

Specific strategies can foster efforts to be innovative and creative for nurses in direct care. The value of this is that these nurses often see and experience problems patients need assistance with in managing their care.

Ideally, each of these types of nurses can, in their own way, support implementing needed changes. Whereas late majority and laggards can help illuminate issues with changes, innovators can be used to "test" new ideas in a restricted pilot program so that they are less disruptive and less likely to fail. In this very important sense, the work of the Institute for Healthcare Improvement (IHI) has encouraged organizations to use this approach. The focus of IHI is to accelerate rapid, small tests of change, often at the point of care *(www.ihi.org/)*. Unit-based decision making to change processes and policies revolves around the staff members working on the unit and depends highly on their ongoing adaptation to evolving realities.

For example, one direct care nurse champion of change expressed to her colleagues her frustration with the many interruptions that occurred while preparing and administering medications. The nurse thought this led to an increased likelihood for error. Discussing the problem resulted in the trial of a possible solution: wearing a prominently colored vest that said, "Do not disturb! Medication administration in process." This idea eventually spread to all of the units and resulted in demonstrated reductions in medication errors (Pape, 2013).

All nurses have the capacity to be change agents. Table 18.1 illustrates seven attributes found to

TABLE 18.1 Attributes Characterizing Change Agents

Attribute	Key Points
Commitment to a better way	Excited about designing a better future
Courage to challenge power bases and norms	Closest to the work
Go beyond role, take initiative, think outside the box	Assurance of change happening
Persona	Self-motivated, generate enthusiasm
Caring	Commitment to patients and their welfare
Humility	About the change, not about "me"
Sense of humor	Self-support through challenges

Data from Katzenbach, J. R., Beckett, F., Dichter, S., Feigen, M., Gagnon, C., Hope, Q., & Ling, T. (1996). *Real change leaders.* New York, NY: Random House.

characterize what all change agents possess (Katzenbach et al., 1996). Change agents help others transform by advocating for openness and improvement.

Nurses who act as change agents understand the change process and are committed to growth. These nurses are optimists, have influence with colleagues, know how to build networks, and facilitate communication. The literature often refers to these individuals as change "champions" or "change agents." A literature review on methods for promoting evidence-based practice changes (McCormack et al., 2013) found many forms of change advocacy exist. Change agents may play the roles of "facilitator, knowledge broker, or opinion leader" to advance implementation of best practices by nurses (McCormack et al., 2013, p. 1). Nurses who function as positive change agents within the healthcare system are willing to try new things, stay abreast of new evidence about best practices, and are open to change. See Table 18.2 for an example of a self-assessment related to receptivity to change. These nurses are respected and serve as role models by practicing in accordance with the most current and relevant guidelines (McCormack et al., 2013). Assessment of organizational culture and the readiness of staff and others to engage in making or participating in a change, whether minor or extensive, sets the stage for the selection and use of change strategies (Allen, 2016). An example of the readiness of staff is found in Exercise 18.2. The willingness of the two nurses to learn new skills and the combined talents of the nursing, clinical education, and administrative managerial staff to work together successfully helped achieve the very different nursing and organizational skills required by the new infusion center.

EXERCISE 18.2 Responsibilities for promoting change vary depending on the role a nurse plays in an organization. View this short case study from the perspectives of a manager and a clinical educator. Discuss the responsibilities each nurse would have in transitioning two nurses to staff a new infusion center for a small community hospital and identify the appropriate functions.

Both nurses were long-term employees; one was from the medical-surgical float pool, and the other was the bed coordinator whose position was eliminated because of budget reductions. Ideally, the assistant vice president with oversight for this area will map out in writing (1) the goals of the new infusion program, (2) the activities essential for implementation goals, and (3) a schedule for accomplishing them. The nurse manager and the clinical educator agree to check in with each other daily, as well as to meet weekly for a more formal review of the team's progress. Part of this plan includes the option to alter the plan based on unexpected changes. The two nurses will begin the position in 4 weeks and put the prearranged outline of activities into action.

What would be the nurse manager's responsibility in implementing this change? What would be the clinical educator's responsibility of implementing this change? How could unexpected occurrences, such as the nurse manager extending her medical leave of absence by a few days, require modifying the goal, activities, or time frame of the project (dynamic quality of process)? What feedback from the nurse manager, the clinical educator, and the two nurses transitioning would be important in guiding the overall process?

TABLE 18.2 Self-Assessment: How Receptive Are You to Change and Innovation?

Read the following items. Circle the answer that most closely matches your attitude toward creating and accepting new or different ways.

1. I enjoy learning about new ideas and approaches.	Yes	Depends	No
2. Once I learn about a new idea or approach, I begin to try it right away.	Yes	Depends	No
3. I like to discuss different ways of accomplishing a goal or end result.	Yes	Depends	No
4. I continually seek better ways to improve what I do.	Yes	Depends	No
5. I commonly recognize improved ways of doing things.	Yes	Depends	No
6. I talk over my ideas for change with my peers.	Yes	Depends	No
7. I communicate my ideas for change with my manager.	Yes	Depends	No
8. I discuss my ideas for change with my family.	Yes	Depends	No
9. I volunteer to be at meetings when changes are being discussed.	Yes	Depends	No
10. I encourage others to try new ideas and approaches.	Yes	Depends	No

If you answered "yes" to 8 to 10 of the items, you are probably receptive to creating and experiencing new and different ways of doing things. If you answered "depends" to 5 to 10 of the items, you are probably receptive to change conditionally based on the fit of the change with your preferred ways of doing things. If you answered "no" to 4 to 10 of the items, you are probably not receptive, at least initially, to new ways of doing things. If you answered "yes," "no," and "depends" an approximately equal number of times, you are probably mixed in your receptivity to change based on individual situations.

> **EXERCISE 18.3** Answer the self-assessment questions in Table 18.1 to determine how receptive you are to change.

We do know that the more rapidly change can be incorporated, the more effective the organization is at remaining relevant. Connecting early adopters, such as the unit-based champions, to new ideas and to innovators, such as national peers of an IHI Web-based learning community, keeps them at the cutting edge. When these two groups are supported, an early majority can be recruited to support the change initiative. If as a nurse you realize you are usually a laggard, look to be sure that rejection of new ideas is about some concern with the idea, not with just resisting change. Insight can be gained by using Exercise 18.4.

> **EXERCISE 18.4** Recall a work or personal situation in which a particular individual tried to get you or a group to do something. What rationale supported the decision of whether to cooperate? Was the idea worthwhile from your perception? Was the person making the suggestions known, understood, and trusted? Was the person making the suggestions aware of the real situation—an essential part of carrying out the idea—or had he or she not received official sanctioning to influence activities? Can you see that change agents need specific qualities and abilities to be trusted by others?

CONTEXT AND CHANGE

Although the people who make up an organization have a great impact on change processes, so too does the culture of the organization. Organizational culture and characteristics of the practice environment consistently emerge as variables influencing both the abilities of change agents and the success of efforts to implement change (McCormack et al., 2013). Organizations that are open and aware of community realities and the larger industry and regulatory context in which they operate are more viable, fluid, and responsive to change. Organizations with proactive cultures that promote employee engagement and participation generate environments that embrace change. When the organization values and facilitates development of the deeper aspirations of its members in addition to professional proficiency, it successfully matches organizational learning and personal growth. Today, large nursing organizations that

achieve the designation of Magnet® status are typically those that are flexible, adaptive, and innovative. In smaller and often more rural health systems, designation by the ANCC Pathway to Excellence Program indicates an institution that is open to change and continuous improvement (Bushy, 2009). These types of organizations lead change by instituting programs that capitalize on rapid innovation and improvement of patient safety, patient satisfaction, and nursing work environments (Stimpfel et al., 2016). Health systems with Magnet® status are an excellent illustration of a learning organization.

Senge (2006) first described learning organizations as those entities that emphasize flexibility and responsiveness. Today's complex healthcare entities can best respond and adapt when the organization values learning and development and when members of the organization complete their work with others using a learning approach. Senge, Kleiner, Roberts, Ross, and Smith (1994, p. 11) explained, "If there is one single thing a learning organization does well, it is helping people embrace change. People in learning organizations react more quickly when their environment changes because they know how to anticipate changes that are going to occur … and how to create the kinds of changes they want. Change and learning may not exactly be synonymous, but they are inextricably linked." These organizations have a culture that is open to change and evolution. Senge (2006) described the five disciplines that these organizations value (Box 18.1).

> **BOX 18.1   Five Organizational Disciplines to Support Change and Evolution**
>
> 1. Shared vision—the process of creating a common view about where the organization is going
> 2. Mental models—the practice of helping individuals become aware of how they think, what they value, and how that affects organizational performance
> 3. Personal mastery—the fostering of openness in the face of change by maintaining self-awareness and using reflection
> 4. Team learning—the promotion of teams thinking together, collaborating, and sharing ideas, knowledge, and perspective
> 5. Systems thinking—the development of frameworks that see the organization as a complex entity whose many parts affect outcomes
>
> Modified from Senge, P. (2006). *The fifth discipline.* New York, NY: Doubleday.

The need for nurses and healthcare systems to continuously learn and remain open to changes that improve care has never been greater (Allen, 2016; Harle, Lipori, & Hurley, 2016). Since 2007, the Institute of Medicine (now the Academy of Medicine) has urged organizational change that improves care and reduces costs by creating learning healthcare systems in America (Institute of Medicine, 2012). Learning healthcare systems strive to use the data generated from an electronic record of patient encounters to constantly improve and determine the evidence for what works best (Budrionis & Bellika, 2016). "The essence of a truly learning health care system will be to learn from its daily experience" (Krumholz, 2014, p. 1166). Nurses must understand this drive to constantly improve outcomes and reduce cost so they can work with the interprofessional healthcare team to change practices based on patient and organizational assessments and evaluations. Implementing change in both individual nursing practice and in healthcare organizations is complicated and difficult (Allen, 2016). How much a change initiative deviates from the norms of a culture and of practicing nurses affects the adoption of a change. Box 18.2 highlights six change support strategies leaders can adopt. A concept analysis on leading change determined that it is a "complex process where nurses individually and collectively balance paradoxical priorities to provide operational support, foster relationships, and facilitate organizational learning to achieve improved performance and outcomes and new organizational culture and values" (Nelson-Brantley & Ford, 2016, p. 10).

BOX 18.2   Change Support Strategies

- Promote acceptance of the change by viewing the change as a positive experience.
- Develop skills essential for supporting the change.
- Reduce negative influences and behaviors in the group experiencing the change.
- Mobilize positive peer support for the change.
- Create financial incentives that reward change agents.
- Make structure and process modifications to support the change initiative.

Adapted from Patterson, K., Grenny, J., Maxfield, D., McMillan, R., & Switzler, A. (2011). *Change anything.* New York: Hatchette Book Group.

LEADERSHIP AND CHANGE

Managing change is a major task of all nurse leaders in health care. For leaders to inspire change, they must have intimate knowledge of what matters to the people they manage. Kotter (2012) characterizes this as establishing a sense of urgency, and this involves overcoming complacency. This is especially hard when no crisis is visible, or the crisis seems irrelevant to the people being asked to change (Kotter, 2012). To understand what matters to staff, leaders must listen, establish connection, and build trust. Dialogue is a method that helps accomplish this goal. Dialogue is a special kind of discourse that allows individuals with different perspectives to come together and find common goals. To promote dialogue, leaders must serve as facilitators, promoting the sharing of ideas, fears, and honest reactions to the change proposal. The purpose of dialogue is to understand and learn from one another. Unlike debate, dialogue is not about winning. Its purpose is to discover what has to be understood and considered to give voice to the whole group.

Dialogue can reveal areas where individuals feel inept or overwhelmed, providing the leader with an understanding of what programs need to be developed to increase personal ability to change and what educational initiatives need to be implemented to support change. Although leaders can certainly inspire people to change, ultimately the individual must decide that the change matters. In addition to these personal dimensions that must be addressed to change anything, leaders also need to look at how social systems avert or support change efforts (Allen, 2016). Having a group of change agents and innovators on board to champion an idea builds motivation and can help staff who are less adept at change and also alert the leader to issues that need to be considered as the change is implemented. Working together as an implementation team, this group can keep leaders informed of issues as the change is executed (Allen, 2016).

Finally, leaders must ensure the change is sustainable. Critical to successful, long-term change is ensuring adequate infrastructure, processes, and resources exist to assist nurses in adopting new practices and protocols (Byers, 2015). Kotter (2012) makes clear that change management and change leadership are different. He notes that change management is about keeping the effort to change under control, whereas change

TABLE 18.3   Kotter's Eight-Step Model

Attribute	Principles
Create urgency	Generate open dialogue about external and internal realities affecting the need to change.
Form a powerful coalition	Develop a core group of change advocates who will help build momentum and support individuals through the change experience.
Create a vision for change	Change may involve lots of small alterations, but these must always be connected to a larger, inspiring vision.
Communicate the change vision	People tend to pay attention to what is reinforced, so communicating regularly and consistently is paramount to sustaining the effort.
Remove obstacles	Keep alert for barriers in structure and processes that limit the ability to change; remove them when you find them.
Create short-term wins	Success motivates future success, so create short-term targets and celebrate accomplishing them.
Build on the change	Change is ongoing, so create a culture where continuous improvement is the norm.
Anchor the changes in the culture	Recognize when the change is working, report on the difference it is making, and honor the people who helped make it happen.

leadership is about creating a vision and fostering major organizational transformation. Table 18.3 shows the essence of Kotter's eight-step change model. This model provides an overview of what leaders need to do to foster change. Each step, carefully executed, mobilizes an organization's accomplishment of change (Kotter, 2012). Kotter's model for implementing a change remains relevant and serves as the guide for many successful implementation science initiatives (Woodward, 2016).

Formal leaders in nursing must be effective change leaders or, as Mackoff calls them, "change whisperers" (2014, p. 23). In an increasingly uncertain world, managers and leaders in our profession are challenged to be skilled in using change theory, serving as change agents, and supporting staff during times of change. According to Mackoff (2014, p. 24), direct care nurses, managers, and leaders must remember the 4-A Model of Change Leadership:

- **A**cknowledge thoughts and feelings
- **A**lign with purpose and values
- Create **A**gency with genuine choices
- **A**djust your attitude

The emergence of complex healthcare systems necessitates changing leadership practices that can mobilize the parts without having to direct every activity. This means perceiving leadership as facilitation and support, not just command and control. Empowering nurse leaders have highly engaged nursing staff, ready to work together to embrace continuous change (Reich & Topjan, 2016; Scanlon & Woolforde, 2016). These leaders are always connecting staff with the "why" of what the change is about (Reich & Topjan, 2016). That requires clarifying the purpose and vision of the change (Charlesworth, Jamieson, Davey, & Butler, 2016). These leaders also are fully transparent with nursing staff. They listen to and involve stakeholders and provide repeated messages about the process of the change. Another important action good change leaders take is to provide needed resources that keep nurses evolving at the bedside doing the job they want to do with the latest knowledge on how to best do it (Reich & Topjan, 2016). These leaders know that frontline nurses are critical for successful change implementation (Charlesworth et al., 2016; Scanlon & Woolforde, 2016; Sharpe, 2015). Perhaps the most important thing nurse leaders do is stay inspired so they can motivate and inspire the nurses they lead (Reich & Topjan, 2016).

Today's dynamic environment means that nurse leaders will have less time to plan and that plans must be constantly updated and amended (Fig. 18.2). Nurses are key players in healthcare delivery, and formal leaders must advocate for their inclusion in change planning and implementation (Boyal & Hewsion, 2016). As partners with multiple care providers and pivotal players in open-system organizations, nurses must become adept at interprofessional collaboration and negotiation to

BOX 18.3   Guidelines for Altering the Dominant Logic

Decrease
- Long-term forecasting
- Preplanned strategies
- Emphasis on past successes
- One future vision
- Rigid, permanent structures
- Structural isolation in the workplace
- Stability of leadership
- Standardization
- Insulation from other professions and marketplace
- Marketplace "passivity"
- Expectation of job security

Increase
- Short-term forecasting
- Emergent strategies
- Search for new opportunities
- Multiple scenarios
- Self-organizing, temporary structures
- Structural interdependence in the workplace
- Leadership turnover
- Innovation, experimentation, diversity
- Cooperation and competition
- Marketplace "aggression"
- Self-learning

Modified from Begun, J. W., & White, K. R. (1995). Altering nursing's dominant logic: Guidelines from complex adaptive systems theory. *Complexity and Chaos in Nursing, 2*(1), 10. Used with permission of Angela E. Vicenzi, Editor, *Complexity and Chaos in Nursing.*

Fig. 18.2 Change happens quickly in health care. (Copyright © Ikunl/iStock/Thinkstock.)

BOX 18.4   Classic Principles Characterizing Effective Change Implementation

- Change agents within healthcare organizations use personal, professional, and managerial knowledge and skills to lead change.
- The recipients of change believe they own the change.
- Administrators and other key personnel support the proposed change.
- The recipients of change anticipate benefit from the change.
- The recipients of change participate in identifying the problem warranting a change.
- The change holds interest for the change recipients and other participants.
- Agreement exists within the work group about the benefit of the change.
- The change agents and recipients of change perceive a compatibility of values.
- Trust and empathy exist among the participants of the change process.
- Revision of the change goal and process is negotiable.
- The change process is designed to provide regular feedback to its participants.

Adapted from Harper, C. L. (2007). *Exploring social change* (5th ed.). Englewood Cliffs, NJ: Prentice Hall.

ensure nursing's perspective in change processes. In their classic work, Begun and White (1995) said that nurses had to consider the discipline's dominant logic as a source of structural inertia. Using chaos theory components, they suggested that nursing in certain organizations is too "stuck" and thus too unresponsive and unable to adapt to the influences of rapid change. One way the nurse leader can alter the dominant logic is shown in Box 18.3. Using this methodology, the manager becomes adept at addressing an emergent approach to change that takes place over a long period rather than sporadic and episodic reactions to change. Scenario planning (i.e., raising multiple "what if" questions with many possible optional answers) is an example of the flexibility and creativity urgently needed in nursing

today. Classic elements of effective change implementation can be found in Box 18.4.

Nurse leaders must be able to build relationships with the team and must be aware of the many interdependencies that exist within complex healthcare organizations

(Kraft, Sparr, & Peus, 2016). In this role, a leader serves as a coach, a guide, and a resource. According to Kraft, Sparr, and Peus (2016), good leaders are always working to help employees make sense of the changes they are experiencing. To lead effectively, the leader must be in a relationship with the team, a relationship that fosters trust and promotes openness. Past leadership theories place the leader at the helm, in command of the ship. However, new, emergent leadership theories emphasize collective leadership whereby the person in a formal administrative role serves as a facilitator or a conductor. Today's leader must work to solve process problems with the team and must make process changes as they emerge. Leaders determine the culture by deciding what behaviors are endorsed and what actions are considered unacceptable. Today's healthcare culture must be one that promotes accountability and rewards best practices. Nurse leaders who empower staff to be continuous learners and risk takers build a culture of curiosity and change. Nurse leaders who keep patient care at the center of every decision will advance the ethos of nursing and connect change to something that matters to nurses.

CONCLUSION

Whether delivering direct care, serving as a nurse leader, or providing clinical education, embracing change is the new imperative for nurses. In nursing, we have often resisted change and relied on tradition. Contemporary nursing requires that we celebrate more innovation and diversity, decide to "break the rules" whenever possible to promote improvement, and embrace a spirit of curiosity and adventure as we explore the benefits of change.

THE SOLUTION

The practice of hourly rounding was introduced to the staff—to both the nursing assistants and the professional nurses. We all developed an hourly rounding log, and decided that the unit secretary would announce on the hour for the staff to begin hourly rounding. The nursing staff took to it immediately; the difficulty was coaching the nursing assistants in how to approach patients and anticipate their needs, using a prewritten script. My goal was to make it fun, so I involved other nurse managers to play the role of the patient so the staff could practice. Much focused staff education in the form of didactic lecture material was provided as well. After several months, the change was visible and had an immediate impact on patients and their families. In fact, the chief executive officer of our system, along with the chief nursing officer, visited and thought at first that no patients were on the unit because of the peace and quiet. No more call bells were ringing and no more intercoms were interrupting. My goal in managing this change was to maintain visibility, never lose sight of the goal and its associated requirements, and constantly praise staff for doing a good job of rounding on the patients. Most of my change management strategies had to do with sitting down and asking the staff on all shifts about what worked and what didn't, being approachable, and addressing individual issues of concern before they became unit issues. I also draw the line when needed and have welcomed my assistant vice president when she rounds with one of my staff to coach him or her. If one of the staff is still not performing the essential elements of hourly rounding after 3 to 6 months of intensive education and focus, then I will resort to the discipline process. Overall, I respect the work that the staff do every day, and they know that about me. I think my strategy worked because I introduced hourly rounding first as a philosophy that would make the staff happy and more efficient. In fact, I made it a point not to tell them that hourly rounding was for patient satisfaction specifically, though it certainly has increased since we embraced it.

Would this be a suitable approach for you? Why?

Sharon McEvoy

REFLECTIONS

Throughout your career, you will face many changes and challenges as you work to become highly competent in a given role or field. How can the content in this chapter help you prepare for those changes? What change support strategies are you going to use? How can you approach this as a planned change to promote your success?

THE EVIDENCE

A huge part of change in today's healthcare organizations is promoting the adoption of evidence-based practice. Lusardi (2012) speaks to changing practice at the bedside by reviewing the following common elements of all evidence-based practice models:

1. Identifying a clinical issue
2. Researching the best practices and evidence about that clinical issue
3. Determining the strength of the evidence
4. Developing a proposal for changing clinical practice
5. Implementing the change
6. Evaluating the impact of the change

Lusardi outlines essential elements for success in implementing evidence-based practice initiatives. Adequate resources, strong unit clinical support, administrative directives that reinforce the change, and systems that offer feedback and mentorship of clinical staff during the change must exist.

TIPS FOR LEADING CHANGE

- Whether involved in planned (low-complexity) or nonlinear (high-complexity) change, create a group of outcome/goal scenarios with prospective actions to achieve.
- People cope and adapt better when they assume the role of continuous learner during accelerated change.
- People involved in change may assume the roles of followers or leaders and may emerge from both informal and formal or internal and external sources.
- Creating a detailed plan and rigidly adhering to it reduces opportunities to moderate the inevitable and changing aspects of a change process, especially in an accelerated change environment.
- Building ambiguity and flexibility into a plan and how it is managed promotes responsiveness and movement toward desired outcomes.

REFERENCES

Abraham, J., Jerome-D'Emilia, B., & Begun, J. W. (2011). The diffusion of Magnet hospital recognition. *Health Care Manage Review, 36*(4), 306–314.

Allen, B. (2016). Effective design, implementation and management of change in healthcare. *Nursing Standard, 31*(3), 58–71.

American Nurse Credentialing Center (ANCC). (2011). *Magnet recognition program overview.* Washington, DC: The National Academies Press. http://www.nursecredentialing.org/Magnet/ProgramOverview.

Begun, J. W., & White, K. R. (1995). Altering nursing's dominant logic: Guidelines from complex adaptive systems theory. *Complexity and Chaos in Nursing, 2*(1), 5–15.

Boyal, A., & Hewsion, A. (2016). Exploring senior nurses' experiences of leading organizational change. *Leadership in Health Services, 29*(1), 37–51.

Budrionis, A., & Bellika, J. G. (2016). The learning healthcare system? Where are we now? *Journal of Biomedical Informatics.* https://doi.org/10.1016/j.jbi.2016.09.018.

Bushy, A. (2009). American Nurses Credentialing Center (ANCC) Pathway to Excellence™ Program: Addressing meeting the needs of small and rural. *Online Journal of Rural Nursing and Health Care, 9*(1). https://doi.org/10.14574/ojrnhc.v9i1.96.

Byers, V. (2015). The challenges of leading change in health care delivery from the frontline. *Journal of Nursing Management.* https://doi.org/10.1111/jonm.12342.

Byrne, D., & Callaghan, G. (2014). *Complexity Theory and the Social Sciences: The State of the Art.* New York: Routledge Taylor & Francis Group.

Charlesworth, K., Jamieson, M., Davey, R., & Butler, C. D. (2016). Transformational change in healthcare: An examination of four case studies. *Australian Health Review, 40,* 163–167.

Christensen, C. M., Raynor, M. E., & McDonald, R. (Eds.), (2016). What is disruptive innovation? In *The Clayton M Christensen Reader* (pp. 157–171). Boston MA: Harvard Business Review.

Dombrowski, S. U., Campbell, P., Frost, H., Pollock, A., McLellan, J., MacGillivray, S., et al. (2016). Interventions for sustained healthcare professional behavior change: A protocol for an overview of reviews. *Systematic Reviews, 5*(173), https://doi.org/10.1186s13643-016-0355-9.

Edwards, M. L., & Porter-O'Grady, T. (2017). Advanced practice leadership and innovation. *Nursing Administration Quarterly, 41*(1), 2–3.

Ercetin, S. S. (Ed.). (2016). *Chaos, Complexity, and Leadership.* Switzerland: Springer Publishing.

Ewenstein, B., Smith, W., & Sologar, A. (2015). *Changing change management.* New York: McKinsey & Company. http://www.mckinsey.com/global-themes/leadership/changing-change-management.

Fuchs, S., & Prouska, R. (2014). Creating positive employee change evaluation: The role of different levels of organizational support and change participation. *Journal of Change Management, 14*(3), 361–383.

Harle, C. A., Lipori, G., & Hurley, R. W. (2016). Collecting, integrating, and disseminating patient reported outcomes for research in a learning healthcare system. *eGEMS (Generating Evidence & Methods to improve patient outcomes), 4*(1), article 13. https://doi.org/10.13063/2327-9214.1240.

Havelock, R. (1973). *Change agents guide to innovation in education.* Englewood Cliffs, NJ: Educational Technology Publications.

Institute of Medicine (IOM). (2012). Best care at lower cost: The path to continuously learning health care in America. http://www.nationalacademies.org/hmd/Reports/2012/Best-Care-at-Lower-Cost-The-Path-to-Continuously-Learning-Health-Care-in-America.aspx.

Kotter, J. P. (2012). *Leading change.* Boston, MA: Harvard Business Review Press.

Kraft, A., Sparr, J. L., & Peus, C. (2016). Giving and making sense about change: The back and forth between leaders and employees. *Journal of Business Psychology.* https://doi.org/10.1007/s10869-016-9474-5. https://link.springer.com/article/10.1007/s10869-016-9474-5.

Krumholz, H. M. (2014). Big data and new knowledge in medicine: The thinking, training, and tools needed for a learning health system. *Health Affairs, 33*(7), 1163–1170.

Katzenbach, J. R., Beckett, F., Dichter, S., Feigen, M., Gagnon, C., Hope, Q., et al. (1996). *Real change leaders.* New York: Random House.

Lewin, K. (1947). Frontiers in group dynamics: Concept, method, and reality in social science, social equilibria and social change. *Human Relations, 1*(1), 5–41.

Lewin, K. (1951). *Field theory in social science.* New York: Harper Torchbooks.

Lippitt, R., Watson, J., & Westley, B. (1958). *The dynamics of planned change.* New York: Harcourt Brace.

Lusardi, P. (2012). So you want to change practice: Recognizing practice issues and channeling those ideas. *Critical Care Nurse, 32*(2), 55–64.

Mackoff, B. L. (2014). The practice of change leadership. *Nurse Leader, 12*(6), 23–26.

Mannion, R., & Davies, H. (2016). Culture in health care organizations. In E. Ferlie, K. Montgomery, & A. R. Pedersen (Eds.), *Oxford handbook of health care management.* Oxford: Oxford University Press.

McCormack, B., Rycroft-Malone, J., DeCorby, K., Hutchinson, A. M., Bucknall, T., Kent, B., et al. (2013). A realist review of interventions and strategies to promote evidence-informed healthcare: A focus on change agency. *Implementation Science, 8*(107). https://implementationscience.biomedcentral.com/articles/10.1186/1748-5908-8-107.

Merriam-Webster. (2017). https://www.merriam-webster.com/dictionary/.

Nelson-Brantley, H. V., & Ford, D. J. (2016). Leading change: A concept analysis. *Journal of Advances in Nursing, 73*(4), 834–846.

Pape, T. M. (2013). The effect of a five-part intervention to decrease omitted medications. *Nursing Forum, 48*(3), 211–222.

Polster, D., & Villines, D. (2017). An exploratory descriptive study of registered nurse innovation. *Clinical Nurse Specialist, 31*(1), E1–E9.

Reich, L., & Topjan, D. (June 20, 2016). The effective CNO: 5 skills great nurse leaders use to manage change. In *Hospital & Health Networks.* http://www.hhnmag.com/articles/7419-the-effective-cno-5-skills-great-nurse-leaders-use-to-manage-change.

Rogers, E. M. (2003). *Diffusion of innovations* (5th ed.). New York: The Free Press.

Scanlon, K. A., & Woolforde, L. (2016). Igniting change through an empowered frontline: A unique improvement approach centered on staff engagement, empowerment, and professional development. *Nurse Leader, 14*(1), 38–46.

Senge, P. (2006). *The fifth discipline.* New York: Doubleday.

Senge, P., Kleiner, A., Roberts, C., Ross, R., & Smith, B. (1994). *The 5th discipline fieldbook: Strategies and tools for building a learning organization.* New York: Crown Business.

Sharpe, M. (2015). Engaging front-line nurses to improve the outcomes of patient care, 2006-2013. *Health Affairs, 34*(12), 2196–2201.

Stimpfel, A. W., Sloane, D. M., McHugh, M. D., & Aiken, L. H. (2016). Hospitals known for nursing excellence associated with better hospital experience for patients. *Health Services Research, 51*(3), 1120–1134.

Woodward, S. (2016). Implementing change: Lessons from the patient safety movement. *Journal of Infection Prevention, 17*(2), 79–82.

Zuber, C. D., & Moody, L. (2018). Creativity and innovation in health care: Tapping into organizational enablers through human-centered design. *Nursing Administration Quarterly, 42*(1), 62–75.

19

Building Effective Teams

Karren Kowalski

LEARNING OUTCOMES

- Evaluate the differences between a group and a team.
- Value four key concepts of teams.
- Describe the process of debriefing team functioning.
- Apply the guidelines for acknowledgment to a situation in your clinical setting.
- Compare a setting that uses agreements with your current clinical setting.

- Develop an example of a team that functions synergistically, including the results such a team would produce.
- Discuss the importance of a team to patient safety and quality.

KEY TERMS

acknowledgment
active listening
commitment

dualism
debriefing
group

interprofessional teams
synergy
team

THE CHALLENGE

An extensive "team" of people works together to care for a neonate in a neonatal intensive care unit (NICU). The team includes registered nurses, physicians, respiratory therapists, physical therapists, social workers, neonatal nurse practitioners, and ancillary staff. Occasionally, specialists are consulted for specific cardiac, neurologic, or gastrointestinal problems. These are intermittent "team" members who play a crucial role in the baby's care.

Recently a new group of specialists joined our team. They were identified as a top-notch group who would, by virtue of their expertise and reputation, increase the census and revenues for the hospital. Our team was excited to have this opportunity to grow in an area in which we had infrequent experience. However, integration of these new team members did not go smoothly. Clinical disagreements, communication breakdowns, and

interpersonal conflicts occurred. The experience evolved into mutual distrust and control issues.

As disagreements, insults, and complaints escalated on both sides, the situation came to a defining moment when the director of the specialty group said, "I'm never bringing any of our patients here. I'm sending them to the PICU [pediatric intensive care unit]." The response from the NICU team was, "Fine with us; we don't need you, your patients, or the hassle." It seemed reasonable to not work together because, in fact, functionally we were already not working together. This response was in direct conflict with our belief that we could provide a valuable service and make a difference for both the patients and their families. This posed a dilemma for the staff, but everyone felt the situation was hopeless.

No one believed we could function as a team, and therefore further efforts to work together were futile. We had tried and failed. "Let's just cut our losses and move on." How does one create a team when no one believes it is possible and some believe it is not even necessary?

What would you do if you were this nurse?

Diane Gallagher, RN, MS
*Director, Women's and Children's Services, Rush-Presbyterian–
St. Luke's Medical Center, Chicago, Illinois*

INTRODUCTION

As we experience changes such as cost-cutting and quality and safety issues in health care, teamwork becomes critical. The adage "If we do not all hang together we will all hang separately" was never more true than now as we move through an era in which nursing is accountable for quality patient outcomes that affect reimbursement for care and the institutional financial bottom line. To create finely tuned teams, communication skills (see Chapter 8) must improve. Each team member must focus on improving his or her own skills, as well as supporting other team members, to grow in effective communication. These skills will be increasingly important as teams negotiate an evolving healthcare system that includes rapid change in state and federal payment systems and regulations.

In our society, because of the emphasis placed on the individual and individual achievement, teamwork is the quintessential contradiction. In other words, with all the focus on individuals, we still need individuals to work together in groups to accomplish goals and keep patients safe. In today's world, a nursing unit or team might have representatives from five different generations: The Silent Generation, Baby Boomers, Generation X, Millennials, and Generation Z or iGen (Hampton & Key, 2016). The differences in these generations can be staggering, which is challenging for functioning as a team.

GROUPS AND TEAMS

One definition of group is a number of individuals assembled together or having some unifying relationship. In groups, performance and outcomes are a result of the work of individual group members. Groups could be all the parents in an elementary school, all the members of a specific church, or all the students in a school of nursing, because the members of these various groups are related in some way to one another by definition

of their involvement in a certain endeavor. A team, on the other hand, is a number of individuals collaborating in specific work or activity that focuses on a specific goal or outcome. Not every group is a team, and not every team is effective.

A group of people does not constitute a team. From Lencioni's perspective (2016), a team is a group of people with a high degree of interdependence geared toward the achievement of a goal or a task. Often, we can recognize intuitively when the so-called team is not functioning effectively. We say things such as, "We need to be more like a team" or "I'd like to see more team players around here." Consequently, in the process of defining *team*, effective versus ineffective teams should be considered. Teams are a collective of people who have defined objectives, ongoing positive relationships, effective respectful communication, and a supportive environment. In health care, teams are focused on accomplishing specific tasks and are essential in providing cost-effective, high-quality health care. As resources are expended more prudently, patient care teams must develop clearly defined goals, use creative problem solving, and demonstrate mutual respect and support. Facilities with ineffective teams may not survive the current changes in health care.

> **EXERCISE 19.1** Think of the last team or group in which you participated. Think about what went on in that team or group. Specifically think about what worked for you and what did not work. Use the "Team Assessment Exercise" in Box 19.1 to assess specific aspects of your team. Address each of the identified areas and discover how well your team or group functioned. Think about roles, activities, relationships, and general environment. Consider examples of shared decision making, shared leadership, shared accountability, and shared problem solving. These are the concepts that can be used to evaluate the functioning of almost any team of which you are a member.

BOX 19.1   Team Assessment Exercise: Are We a Team?

Directions: Select a team with which you work. Place a checkmark beside each item that is true of your team. If the statement is not true, place no mark beside the item.

1. The language we use focuses on "we" rather than "you" or "I."
2. When one of us is busy, others try to help.
3. I know I can ask for help from others.
4. Most of us on the team could say what we are trying to accomplish.
5. What we are trying to accomplish on any given work day relates to the mission and vision of nursing and the organization.
6. We treat each other fairly, not necessarily the same.
7. We capitalize on people's strengths to meet the goals of our work.
8. The process for changing policies, procedures, equipment is clear.
9. Meetings are focused on the goals we are trying to achieve.
10. Our outcomes reflect our attention to goals and efforts.
11. Acknowledgment is individual and goal-oriented.
12. Innovation is supported by the team and management.
13. The group makes commitments to each other to ensure goal attainment.
14. Promises are kept.
15. Kindness in communication is evident, especially when bad news is delivered.
16. Individuals can describe their role in the overall work of the group.
17. Other members of the team are seen as trustworthy and valued.
18. The group is cost-effective and time-effective in attaining goals.
19. No member is excluded from the process of decision making.
20. Individuals can speak highly of their team members.

Tally the number of checkmarks and multiply that number by 5. The resultant number is an assessment of how well your team is functioning. The higher the score, the better the functioning.

In a smoothly functioning team, each nurse is responsible for care provided to the patient and for the care provided by the whole team. In thinking about the whole team in a hospital setting, consider such activities as bedside shift handoffs when the teams from both shifts are present and collaborating with one another. Think also of interprofessional rounding when nurses, physicians, pharmacists, physical therapists, case managers, and social workers, to name a few, are present to assess and plan with the patient for the care that is needed. Think about how each of these professional groups communicate respectfully with one another. Huddles also allow nursing staff to focus on how they may best collaborate to provide care for the patient. This interactivity of the team promotes the best possible care for the patient and family while demonstrating the value of nursing (Pappas, 2017).

When a team functions effectively, a significant difference is evident in the entire work atmosphere, the way in which discussions progress, the level of understanding of the team-specific goals and tasks, the willingness of members to listen, the manner in which disagreements are handled, the use of consensus, and the way in which feedback is given and received. The classic work done by McGregor (1960) and the more recent work by England (2013) shed light on some of these significant differences, which are summarized in Table 19.1.

On the other hand, ineffective teams are often dominated by a few members, leaving others bored, resentful, or uninvolved. Leadership tends to be autocratic and rigid, and the team's communication style may be overly stiff and formal. Members tend to be uncomfortable with conflict or disagreement, avoiding and suppressing it rather than using it as a catalyst for change. When criticism is offered, it may be destructive, personal, and hurtful rather than constructive and problem-centered. Team members may begin to hide their feelings of resentment or disagreement, sensing that they are "dangerous." This creates the potential for later eruptions and discord. Similarly, the team avoids examining its own inner workings, or members may wait until after meetings to voice their thoughts and feelings about what went wrong and why.

In contrast, the effective team is characterized by its clarity of purpose, informality and congeniality, commitment, and a high level of participation. The members' ability to listen respectfully to each other and communicate openly helps them handle disagreements in a civilized manner and work through them rather than suppress them. Through ample discussion of

TABLE 19.1 Attributes of Effective and Ineffective Teams

Attribute	Effective Team	Ineffective Team
Goals	Task or objective is understood and supported by team members.	Team interaction fails to clarify the task or objective of group.
Contributions	All team members participate in discussion and comments are pertinent.	A few members dominate the discussion and minimize others' contributions.
Environment	Informal, comfortable, relaxed.	Indifferent, bored, tense.
Leadership	Shared and shifts according to expertise.	Autocratic and remains with the chairperson.
Assignments	Clearly stated, assigned, and accepted.	Unclear and lacks clarity regarding who is doing specific tasks.
Listening	Listen attentively to each member; every idea is heard.	Members do not listen; ideas are ignored, judged, and overridden.
Conflict	Members are comfortable with disagreement with no conflict avoidance.	Disagreements are ignored or suppressed; voting results and minority is disconnected.
Decision making	General agreement reached by consensus.	Actions or voting occurs before examination or resolution of real issues.
Self-evaluation	Conscious of its own process; ongoing evaluation; assesses interferences with team function.	Group avoids any discussion of effectiveness or operation.

Adapted from England, P. *Effective vs ineffective teams*. www.eventus.co.uk/effective-vs-ineffective-teams/.

issues, they reach decisions by consensus. Roles and work assignments are clear, and members share the leadership role, recognizing that each person brings his or her own unique strengths to the group effort. This diversity of styles helps the team adapt to changes and challenges, as does the team's ability and willingness to assess its own strengths and weaknesses and respond to them appropriately. Because of the importance of effective teams, we have seen the movement from the Triple Aim to the Quadruple Aim that incorporates the climate in which care is delivered.

The challenges encountered in today's healthcare systems are prodigious. Patient safety issues are at the forefront. Ongoing rounds of downsizing, budget cuts, declining patient days, reduced payments, and staff layoffs abound. Effective teams participate in effective problem solving, increased creativity, and improved health care. The effects of smoothly functioning teams on patient safety and the creation of a just culture are critically important.

CREATING EFFECTIVE TEAMS

When thinking about teams, consider the power of teamwork and what can be accomplished by a group of people working synergistically. It is helpful to have people who are able to work together in a complementary way. In the classic work of LaFasto and Larson (2001), in which they studied 600 teams and 6000 team members, the two key factors that emerged in the effectiveness of team functioning were great relationships between team members and excellent communication skills. Both of these concepts are complex and worth exploring in more detail. For example, building relationships has two major aspects: behaviors, or what people do with each other; and characteristics, or who they are as human beings.

Building Relationships

Being in relationship is about being connected or related and having mutual dealings, connections, or feelings between two parties. Specific learned behaviors, demonstrated by team members, can accelerate building extraordinary relationships among team members. Occasionally, a team member can shoulder the responsibility for criticism or for what did not work on behalf of the team. Taking the criticism, especially if he or she is not emotionally attached and can remain objective, demonstrates a willingness to go out of the way to support a team member. Thus another team member can have the space to de-escalate and gain control of their

RESEARCH PERSPECTIVE

Resource: Winsborough, D., & Chamorro-Premuzic, T. (2017). Great teams are about personalities, not just skills on teams. *Harvard Business Review*.https://hbr.org/2017/01/great-teams-are-about-personalities-not-just-skills

The authors describe research on assigning teams from several organizations, including Google. The authors' own work suggests that effective teams have a mix of skills and personalities, so it is important to consider the two roles every person plays in a working group: a functional role, based on formal position and technical skill, and a psychological role, based on the type of person one is. For best outcomes, teams should include members with different skills.

Results-oriented: Team members who naturally organize work and take charge tend to be socially self-confident, competitive, and energetic.

Relationship-focused: Team members who naturally focus on relationships, are attuned to others' feelings, and are good at building cohesion tend to be warm, diplomatic, and approachable.

Process and rule followers: Team members who pay attention to details, processes, and rules tend to be reliable, organized, and conscientious.

Innovative and disruptive thinkers: Team members who naturally focus on innovation, anticipate problems, and recognize when the team needs to change tend to be imaginative, curious, and open to new experiences.

Pragmatic: Team members who are practical, hard-headed challengers of ideas and theories tend to be prudent, emotionally stable, and level-headed.

Implications for Practice

As you assign working groups or become part of a group, consider the balance of member characteristics needed to support effective team development.

---

emotions. Such support can go a long way toward developing relationships. Another aspect of building relationships is the ability to "step in" to help without being asked. A subtle difference exists between someone who volunteers help before being asked and someone who agrees to help only after being asked. A true builder of relationships pays close attention to the well-being of others. This is also a demonstration of caring and serendipitously builds stronger relationships.

In building relationships, anticipate the "question under the question." Often team members will ask a more superficial question than the one they really want to ask. A person might ask about an issue that was raised in the last meeting and what is really desired is a deeper understanding and appreciation of his or her contribution to the team.

Be willing to demonstrate thoughtfulness of others by giving unexpected praise or acknowledgment. Take time each day to do something nice for a teammate just because you can. This approach can be coupled with a desire to help, not because you need something from someone, but because you can support or help someone else. Approach relationship building from the perspective of the other person, not about yourself or your needs. In other words, give more than you receive.

Valuing every member of the team can have major positive outcomes. Find something positive about each one and his or her contribution. Every human being is important, as is each job.

Behaviors of Great Team Members

Teams function with varying levels of effectiveness. The interesting part of this is that effectiveness can be created systematically. Truly effective teams are ones in which people work together to produce extraordinary results that could not have been achieved by any one individual. This phenomenon is described as synergy. In the physical sciences, synergy is found in metal alloys. Bronze, the first alloy, was a combination of copper and tin and was found to be much harder and stronger than either copper or tin separately. Because the tensile strength of bronze cannot be predicted by merely adding the tensile strength of tin and of copper, it is far greater than simple addition. Working cooperatively, an effective team produces extraordinary results that no one team member could have achieved alone. To create synergy consistently, certain basic rules must be followed: establish a clear purpose, use active listening, tell the truth, be compassionate, be flexible, commit to resolution, and capitalize on what individuals bring to the team. See the Research Perspective.

Establish a Clear Purpose

Creating a smoothly functioning team requires a clear purpose. Each member of the team must understand the reason the team is together, determine what he or she wishes to accomplish (as delineated by defined goals and objectives), and express his or her belief in both the value and feasibility of the goals and tasks. Teams function best when the members can not only tell others about their purpose but also define and operationalize succinctly the meaning and value of this purpose. Being aware of what each can contribute and expects allows all other members to capitalize on individual talent and support each other in goal attainment.

Use Active Listening

Active listening means that you are completely focused on the individual who is speaking. It means listening without judgment. It means listening to the essence of the conversation so that you can actually repeat to the speaker most of the speaker's intended meaning. It means being 100% present in the communication. This requires the skill of active listening. Examples of how to validate such listening appear in Table 19.2.

Developing a defensive response or argument in your head while the other person is still speaking is not active listening. To listen actively, a person must be absorbing words, posture, tone of voice, and all the queues accompanying the message so that the intent of the communication can be received.

Tell the Truth

To tell the truth means to speak clearly to personal points and perspectives while acknowledging that they are, merely, personal perspectives. If an observation is made about the tone or behavior of a speaker that affects the ability of others to hear the message, feedback can be provided in a way that does not make the speaker wrong. This is accomplished in an objective rather than subjective manner using neither a cynical nor a critical tone of voice or by asking a question for clarification. To be effective, one must own, or be responsible for, personal opinions and attitudes.

Be Compassionate

To be compassionate means to have a sympathetic consciousness of another's distress and a desire to alleviate the distress. Consequently, focusing time and energy on making the other person wrong, especially when your

TABLE 19.2 Active Listening

Use of Active Listening	Examples
To convey interest in what the other person is saying	I see! I get it. I hear what you're saying.
To encourage the individual to expand further on his or her thinking	Yes, go on. Tell us more.
To help the individual clarify the problem in his or her own thinking	Then the problem as you see it is …
To get the individual to hear what he or she has said in the way it sounded to others	This is your decision, then, and the reasons are … If I understand you correctly, you are saying that we should …
To pull out the key ideas from a long statement or discussion	Your major point is … You believe that we should …
To respond to a person's feelings more than to his or her words	You feel strongly that … You do not believe that …
To summarize specific points of agreement and disagreement as a basis for further discussion	We seem to be agreed on the following points … But we seem to need further clarification on these points …
To express a consensus of group feeling	As a result of this discussion, we as a group seem to feel that …

perspective differs from his or hers, is inappropriate. Listening from a caring perspective—one that is focused on understanding the viewpoint of the other person rather than insisting on the "rightness" of one's own point of view—is the goal.

Be Flexible

Flexibility and openness to another person's viewpoint are critical for a team to work well together. No single person has all the right answers. Therefore acknowledging that each person has something to contribute and must be heard is important. Flexibility reflects a willingness to hear another team member's point of view rather than being committed to the "rightness" of a personal point of view.

Commit to Resolution

To commit to resolution means that one can agree to disagree with someone even when that perspective is different. Rather than assuming the person is wrong, this is a commitment to hear his or her perspective, listen to the real message, identify differences, and creatively seek solutions to resolve the areas of differences so a common understanding and shared commitment to the issue can be reached. Both parties need to then agree that they feel heard and agree to the resolution. This differs greatly from compromise and majority vote seen in the democratic process. When compromise exists, acquiescence or relinquishing of a significant portion of what was desired likely occurred. This generally leaves both parties feeling negative about themselves or the agreement. Consequently, most compromises must be reworked at some future date. Working on conflict and its resolution (Box 19.2) is time-consuming but essential to effectively functioning teams (Lencioni, 2016). Commitment to resolution is integral to the needs of the team. One team member may disagree with another team member, but the successful work of the team is at stake in this conflict. Without commitment to resolution for the sake of the team, individuals often have less impetus to seek a common ground or to agree to disagree.

The team is not successful when one team member becomes a self-proclaimed expert who has the "right" answer. Nor is it successful when people fail to speak. Each team member has good ideas, and these need to be shared. They may not be shared, however, when someone feels uncomfortable in the team. It is difficult to speak up and appear wrong or inadequate. The challenge each person faces is to push through discomfort and become a full participant in problem identification and resolution for the overall benefit of the team.

Acknowledge

Part of focusing on people's strengths is being willing to acknowledge peers, faculty, and the other significant people in one's life (Ke Yu, Harter, & Agrawal, 2013). In contrast, many role models focus on correction. Consequently, many of us spend a large portion of our time correcting others rather than appreciating them for all the wonderful things they are. Focusing on strengths rather than on weaknesses is far more productive and leads to excellence. According to the classic work of Gallup about people's strengths as reported by Rath (2007), weaknesses will never be improved to more than average or mediocre. If the focus is on improving our strengths, it is much easier to excel and then to be acknowledged for what we do well. Unfortunately, focusing on weaknesses tends to decrease the appreciation and thus the acknowledgments. Furthermore, we seem to believe that a finite number of acknowledgments exist. This attitude of scarcity of acknowledgments leads to stinginess in acknowledging people. Of course this approach is a bit ridiculous. Acknowledgments are infinite. The more we sincerely give to others and to ourselves, the smoother the team functions. On the other hand, we do not always give acknowledgments in a way they can be received and valued. Box 19.3 can serve as a guide for giving acknowledgments.

BOX 19.2 Aspects of Conflict

Destructive	Constructive
• Diverts energy from more important activities and issues	• Opens up issues of importance, resulting in their clarification
• Destroys the morale of people or reinforces poor self-concepts	• Results in the solution of problems
• Polarizes groups so they increase internal cohesiveness and reduce intergroup cooperation	• Increases the involvement of individuals in issues of importance to them
• Deepens differences in values	• Causes authentic communication to occur
• Produces irresponsible and regrettable behavior such as name-calling and fighting	• Serves as a release for pent-up emotion, anxiety, and stress
	• Helps build cohesiveness among people sharing the conflict, celebrating in its settlement, and learning more about each other
	• Helps individuals grow personally and apply what they learn to future situations

---

EXERCISE 19.2 Within the next 3 days, find three opportunities to acknowledge a peer or acquaintance using the five guidelines for acknowledgment shown in Box 19.3. Use these same guidelines to acknowledge yourself for something you have done well.

BOX 19.3 Guidelines for Acknowledgment

1. Acknowledgments must be specific. The specific behavior or action that is appreciated must be identified in the acknowledgment; for example, "Thank you for taking notes for me when I had to go to the dentist. You identified three key points that needed to be reported."
2. Acknowledgments must be "eye to eye," or personal. Look the person in the eye when you thank him or her. Do not run down the hall and say "Thanks" over your shoulder. Written appreciation also qualifies as "eye to eye."
3. Acknowledgments must be sincere, that is, from the heart. Each of us recognizes insincerity. If you do not truly appreciate a behavior or action, do not say anything.

Insincerity often makes people angry or upset, thus defeating the goal. Further, it discredits the person who is insincere.
4. Acknowledgments are more powerful when they are given in public. Most people receive pleasure from public acknowledgment and remember these occasions for a long time. For people who are shy and may prefer no public acknowledgment, this is an opportunity to work on a personal growth issue with them. Public acknowledgment is an opportunity to communicate what is valued.
5. Acknowledgments need to be timely. The less time that elapses between the event and the acknowledgment, the more powerful and effective it is and the more the acknowledgment is appreciated by the recipient.

BOX 19.4 SBAR Communication

Miscommunication is the most commonly occurring cause of sentinel events and "near misses" in patient care. One of the most popular structured communication systems, created by professionals in the California Kaiser Permanente system, focuses on a method to provide information that honors the system in which practitioners and medical providers learn to glean information and apply it to decision-making trees. SBAR is the system that honors the structured transfer of information.

Situation. The nurse identifies the patient, the physician, the diagnosis, and the location of the patient. The nurse describes the patient situation that has instituted this SBAR communication.

Background. Next the nurse provides background information, which could include information relevant to the current situation, mental status, current vital signs (all of them), chief complaint, pain level, and physical assessment of the patient.

Assessment. The nurse offers an assessment of the chief problem and describes the seriousness of the situation. Any specific changes in the patient's condition should be described.

Recommendation. The nurse can make a request of the physician or suggest specific action such as a medication, laboratory work, or an x-ray examination. The nurse could also request that the physician come and evaluate the patient.

Data from Institute for Healthcare Improvement. (2018). *SBAR tool: Situation-background-assessment-recommendation.* http://www.ihi.org/resources/Pages/Tools/SBARToolkit.aspx.

Communicating Effectively

Communication in the work environment is not only important to creating a healthy work environment that retains nurses, but is essential to reduction of medical errors (American Association of Critical Care Nurses [AACN], 2016). These skills are crucial to smoothly functioning teams. Further discussion of communication skills can be found in Chapter 8. An example of a commonly used tool for effective communication is the Situation, Background, Assessment, Recommendation (SBAR) format in Box 19.4.

For purposes of establishing effective teams, consider some aspects of communication. These skills are essential to clinical practice, to building teams, and to leadership. Because communication consists of both verbal and nonverbal signals, humans are continuously communicating thoughts, ideas, opinions, feelings, and emotions. Once the message is sent, the first impression of the communication usually is lasting. However, it is often an unconscious response or reaction. To become more aware of communication in teams, consider the following model.

Positive Communication Model

Whenever human beings are in distress, unengaged, or disengaged or have an emotional reaction to a situation or the actions of another, a conditioned response is to

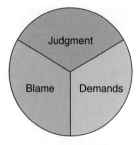

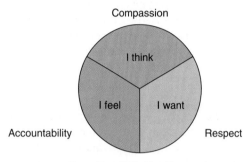

Fig. 19.1 Awareness model: differentiating between unconscious and conscious responses.

and respectful helps clarify what goes on inside each of us.

Everyone needs to feel as though his or her skills, tools, and contributions are needed and valued and that he or she is respected for what personal contributions are offered to the workplace, team, or group. Everyone has weaknesses, and emphasizing these or spending time in ongoing correction is not productive. Rather, focus should be placed on people's strengths, specifically acknowledging and emphasizing what people do well.

EXERCISE 19.3 Think of an example or a recent incident when you were very upset or felt stuck in blame, judgment, and/or demand. You might even write down what you were feeling in that moment, what it was about for you, and what you wanted for yourself. Share the issue or problem situation with someone and practice talking using *I feel, I think,* and *I want* instead of blame, judgment and/or demand.

---

move into one or all of the following: *blame, judgment,* or *demand.* These are depicted in the awareness model found in Fig. 19.1. With effort and practice, it is possible to create a communication interaction that produces a significantly improved outcome.

When an individual is reacting at the feeling level, he or she tends to move unconsciously to blame. By taking accountability for these feelings, one can move out of blame and own one's feelings by stating, "I feel …"

Likewise, when an individual is trapped in distress or reaction at the thinking level, he or she most often turns to judgment. By thinking compassionately, one can dismantle the judgment and state what one thinks in a compassionate way: "I think …"

Finally, when in distress, we make demands that are often unreasonable. By calming yourself, you can find respect for the other human being and make a request for what you want for yourself in a given situation: "I want an effective professional relationship." Wanting the other person to change is pointless because it is unlikely to happen and you don't control the other person.

Most broken relationships are stuck in blame, judgment, and demand. Being accountable, compassionate,

Debriefing

The general definition of **debriefing** is to carefully review upon completion or to question someone about a completed undertaking. The most common use of debriefing in nursing is with the use of simulation. The International Nursing Association for Clinical Simulation and Learning (INACSL, 2016) describes debriefing as a reflection or a conscious consideration of the meaning and implication of an action, which includes the assimilation and understanding of knowledge, skills, and attitudes. Reflection can lead to new interpretations or understanding by participants who can reframe the situation or scenario cognitively as an essential part of learning. The skills of the debriefer are important to ensure the best possible learning outcomes. Debriefing is one example of the process of reflection. Likewise, the exercises in this chapter are an opportunity to practice debriefing and to determine what was learned in the exercise.

KEY CONCEPTS OF TEAMS

In rare instances, a team may produce teamwork spontaneously, like kids in a schoolyard at recess. However, most management teams learn about teamwork because they need and want to work together. This kind of working together requires that they observe how they are together in a group and that they unlearn ingrained self-limiting assumptions about the glory of individual effort and authority that are contrary to cooperation and teamwork. Keys to the concept of team include the following:

- Conflict resolution
- Singleness of mission
- Willingness to cooperate
- Commitment

Conflict Resolution

Realizing that conflict is fundamental to the human experience can be helpful. Conflict is an integral part of all human interaction. Therefore the challenge is to recognize the breakdown in the communication process and to deal appropriately with it (Porter-O'Grady & Malloch, 2017). Conflicts are usually based on attempts to protect a person's self-esteem or to alter perceived inequities in power, because most human beings believe that other people have greater power, and thus these human beings are unlikely to achieve their objectives. For example, when a nurse recognizes upset and reaction between two nursing assistants with whom he or she is working, the following steps can be helpful:

- Identify the triggering event.
- Discover the historical context for each person.
- Assess how interdependent they are on each other.
- Identify the issues, goals, and resources involved in the situation.
- Uncover any previously considered solution.

Assessing the level of working relationship between the conflicted parties is essential, particularly if they work together on a regular basis.

The word *team* is usually reserved for a special type of working together. This working together requires communication in which the members understand how to conduct interpersonal relationships with their peers in thoughtful, supportive, and meaningful ways. Working together requires that team members are able to resolve conflicts among themselves and to do so in ways that enhance rather than inhibit their working together. In addition, team members must be able to trust that they will receive what they need while being able to count on one another to complete tasks related to team functioning and outcomes. To communicate effectively, people must be willing to confront issues and to express openly their ideas and feelings—to use interactive skills to accomplish tasks. In nursing, constructive confrontation has not been a well-used skill. Consequently, if communication patterns are to improve, the onus is on each of us as individuals to change communication patterns. In essence, for things to change, each of us must change.

Singleness of Mission

Every team must have a purpose—that is, a plan, aim, or intention. However, the most successful teams have a mission—some special work or service to which the team is 100% committed. The sense of mission and purpose must be clearly understood and agreed to by all (Lencioni, 2016). The more powerful and visionary the mission is, the more energizing it will be to the team. The more energy and excitement are engendered, the more motivated all members will be to do the necessary work.

Willingness to Cooperate

Just because a group of people has a regular reporting relationship within an organizational chart does not mean the members are a team. Boxes and arrows are not in any way related to the technical and interpersonal coordination or the emotional investment required of a true team. In effective teams, members are required to work together in a respectful, civil manner. Most of us have been involved in organizations in which some people could accomplish assigned tasks but were not successful in their interpersonal relationships. In essence, these employees received a salary for not getting along with a certain person or persons. Some of these employees have not worked cooperatively for years! Organizations can no longer afford to pay people to not work together. Personal friendship or socialization is not required, but cooperation is a necessity. Traditionally, these interpersonal skills were considered "soft" skills and were difficult in coaching people or in holding them accountable. In most organizations, employees can now be terminated for a lack of willingness to work cooperatively with team members.

Commitment

Commitment is a state of being emotionally impelled and is demonstrated when a sense of passion and dedication to a project or event—a mission— exists. Often, this passion looks a little outrageous as people go the extra mile because of their commitment. They do whatever it takes to accomplish the goals or see the project through to completion. Charles Garfield provides an example of commitment when he talks about the team that created the lunar landing module for the first man to walk on the moon. People on the team did all kinds of things that looked odd, including working extended hours and shifts, calling in to see how the project was progressing, and sleeping over at their work stations so as not to be separated from the project—all because each member knew that he or she was a part of something that was much bigger than himself or herself. They were a part of sending a man to the moon, something that human beings had been dreaming about for thousands of years. It was a historic moment, and people were intensely committed to making it happen.

Many people go through their entire lives hating every single day of work. Needless to say, most people who hate their work are not committed. Because we spend an extensive amount of time in the work setting, we must enjoy what we do for both physical and mental well-being. If this is not the case for you, then try to find a different job or profession—one you might love. Life is too short to do something that you hate doing every day. While you are moving into whatever you decide you love doing, commit to yourself to do your best at whatever you are now doing. Be 100% present wherever you are. Do the best work you are capable of doing. This honors you as a human being, and it honors your co-workers and patients.

EXERCISE 19.4 Review the eight questions about exploring commitment in Box 19.5. Spend at least 20 minutes in a quiet place thinking about and writing answers to these eight questions. Pay particular attention to question 7.

ISSUES THAT AFFECT TEAM FUNCTIONING

When individuals come together purposefully to form a team, they spend considerable time in group process or social dynamics, which allows them to advance toward becoming a team and completing a goal. Each person within the emerging team struggles with key issues about cooperation, power, appreciation, agreements, emotions, trust, differences, and feedback that must continually be reevaluated and renegotiated.

"In" Groups and "Out" Groups
Most of us want to be valued and recognized by others as a part of the group, one who "knows" or understands.

BOX 19.5   Exploring Commitment

The key to finding your compelling mission or passion that will lead you to success and peak performance is to ask yourself the right questions. Your answers to these questions will help you understand what you need to know about yourself. Read each question, then think carefully for a few minutes, and answer each question honestly. Do not censor or edit out anything, even if it seems impossible or unrealistic—allow yourself to be surprised. Let your imagination soar.

1. Am I deriving any satisfaction out of the work I am now doing?
2. If they did not reward (praise or pay) me to do what I now do, would I still do it?
3. What is it that I really love to do?
4. What do I want to pursue with my time and energy that is worthwhile?
5. What motivates me to reach out and do my best to excel?
6. What is it that only I can say to the world? What needs to be done that can best be done only by me?
7. If I won $40 million in the lottery tomorrow, how would I live? What would I do each day and for the rest of my life?
8. If I were to write my own obituary right now, what would be my most significant accomplishment? Is that enough?

Repeating this exercise often will give you additional insights and information about what you really want and love to do. If taken seriously, the exercise should help you have an understanding of why you selected this profession and whether you have the stamina to do whatever it takes to make a contribution and to make a difference in the practice of nursing.

Most people want to be at the core of decision making, power, and influence. In other words, they want to be part of the "in" group, and researchers have demonstrated that those who feel "in" cooperate more, work harder and more effectively, and bring enthusiasm to the group. The more we feel we are not a part of the key group, the more "out" we feel and the more we withdraw, work alone, daydream, and engage in self-defeating behaviors. Often, intergroup conflict results when individuals who feel they are "out" and want to be "in" create a schism or a division that prohibits the team from accomplishing its goals.

Dualism

Our society tends to be dualistic in nature. Dualism means that most situations are viewed as right or wrong, black or white. Answers to questions are often reduced to "yes" or "no." As a result, we sometimes forget a broad spectrum of possibilities actually exists. Exercising creativity and exploring numerous possibilities are important. This allows the team to operate at its optimal level.

An extension of this idea of dualism is a person who is a self-proclaimed expert, to whom it is critically important that he or she be right and acknowledged as right and who becomes judgmental of others whose perspectives and opinions differ. Consequently, being able to tell the truth to a team member and to encourage team members to stretch and look at different ways of functioning is vital. This requires strong skills in good negotiation and conflict resolution, something for which few of us have been trained. If self-proclaimed experts think we are judging them, they will not hear the questions, the observations, or the "truth," because the message seems to be making them wrong. Going beyond dualism is critical to the team.

Power and Control

Everybody wants at least some power, and everybody wants to feel he or she is in control. When faced with changes that we cannot influence, we feel impotent and experience a loss of self-esteem. Consequently, we want to feel that we are in control of our immediate environment and that we have enough power and influence to get our needs met. When a situation or an event arises that we cannot handle, we attempt to compensate for it in some way; most of these ways are not productive to smoothly functioning teams. You may have been "right," but the sense of a loss of control or power is very uncomfortable, sometimes resulting in stress and fear. Mature behavior is required to maintain a positive, problem-solving approach.

> **EXERCISE 19.5** Think about a time when you and a small group wanted to change something, such as a scheduled time (a class or meeting), an assignment, or an outcome measure (grading curve of a test or a performance evaluation criterion), and the person "in charge" adamantly refused. How did you feel? What was the response? Did you engage in gossip to make others appear wrong?

Use, Develop, and Be Appreciated for My Skills and Resources

Each member of the team has unique skills and resources to bring to the goals and tasks to be accomplished by the team. The Gallup (2017) research is quite clear in its evaluation of the work environment that one of the most powerful indicators of a successful, supportive work environment can be predicted by the scores from the following question: "At work, do you have the opportunity to do what you do best every day?" When the score is low in this area, team members clearly do not believe their skills are recognized, well used, or appreciated. To accomplish the goal of having each team member believe that his or her skills are recognized, encouraged, and used and his or her growth is encouraged requires a strong, knowledgeable *team leader.* Fewer than 20% of employees feel their strengths are used every day (Wagner & Harter, 2006). When nurses do not believe their skills are used, they are more prone to be in the "out group." This leads to being unengaged and even disengaged in the workplace. This is not supportive of a positive, creative work environment or in developing effective teams.

Group Agreements

One of the most helpful tools available is to have the team members come to an agreement about their relationships with one another. This can take place in various ways. Multiple types of guidelines can even be used to set the context for how people relate. Many hospitals and facilities have service agreements that new employees accept when they are first hired. These are often in the employee handbook and are used to hold people accountable for behaviors. One example of a set of agreements comes from the Colorado Center for Nursing Excellence, the nursing workforce center for the state (Box 19.6). These are called the "Commitment to My Team Members." They have gone through multiple transitions and redesigns, but the basic tenets are essentially the same. People must agree on the goals and mission with which they are involved. They have to reach some understanding of how they will exist together. Tenets or agreements such as "I will respectfully speak promptly with any team member with whom I have a problem" go a long way to avoid gossiping, backbiting, bickering, and misinterpreting others. These team agreements are reviewed regularly (e.g., monthly or quarterly), because this process helps members of

---

BOX 19.6   Commitment to My Team Members

The staff at the Colorado Center for Nursing Excellence developed these agreements in 2010. The staff included both professional and support personnel. These agreements are reviewed at each monthly "all staff meeting." This review serves as a reminder of our agreements, and each person considers these agreements integral to the smooth functioning of the team.

- I accept responsibility for establishing and maintaining healthy interpersonal relationships with every member of this team. I recognize that the words, actions, and attitudes of each of us individually reflect on the whole of the Colorado Center for Nursing Excellence.
- I will respectfully speak promptly with any team member with whom I am having a problem. The only time I will discuss it with another person is when I need assistance in reaching a satisfactory resolution. The goal of a conversation with a trusted colleague is not to complain or triangulate but to gain insight into resolution. I will always remember to "take the mail to the correct address."
- I will establish and maintain a relationship of trust with every member of this team. My relationships with each of you will be equally respectful, regardless of job title, level of educational preparation, or any other differences that may exist.
- I will accept each team member as they are today, forgiving past problems and asking each person to do the same with me.

- I will remember that no one is perfect and that our errors will be accepted as opportunities for forgiveness, growth, and learning.
- Because all members of our team are leaders and followers, we are committed to finding solutions to problems and embracing accountability for the success of the whole organization.

Different projects have different team members as the leader, and the remainder are followers. Sometimes the leader of a specific project is a support person and the followers, both professional staff and support staff, take direction from that person.

- My words, actions, and attitudes make my team members feel appreciated, included, and valued. I will have fun and keep a sense of humor at work.
- As leaders we practice what The Center teaches.

The Center delivers educational offerings on leadership, teaching, quality, and safe patient care and presentations. The common threads exemplified in the above agreements are taught, and each member of the team is expected to demonstrate the behaviors we teach to participants.

- I expect and accept if at any time I do not comply with the above statements my team members will have a confidential conversation with me directly in order to raise awareness and accountability to the above commitments.

From Colorado Center for Nursing Excellence. (n.d.). Commitment to my team members. http://www.coloradonursinfcenter.org/center-staff.

---

the team be accountable for upholding the agreements and receive/give feedback when the agreements have been violated or need to be changed. Without agreement, people have implicit permission to behave in any manner they choose toward one another, including angry, hostile, hurtful, and acting-out behavior.

> **EXERCISE 19.6** Think about a group meeting you attended that did not go well. Identify three examples of group agreements that might have improved the tone and outcomes of the meeting.

Managing Emotions

Probably one of the greatest fears in team-building is that people will become emotional, that they will lose control of themselves or the environment, or that they will appear weakened or vulnerable. Management and leadership are usually more willing to deal with the "thinking" side than the "feeling" side of individuals within the team. The use of a communication tool (Fig. 19.2) can support team members in managing emotions.

Trust

Trust is the basis by which leaders and managers facilitate the activities and the progress of the team. Warrell (2015) believes that trust is not only the core of relationships but also the currency of influence in both the specific workplace and the entire organization. She describes what she believes to be the three core domains of trust: competence, reliability, and sincerity. Competence refers to a specific skill set. For example, you might trust me to teach you about leadership and administration, but you

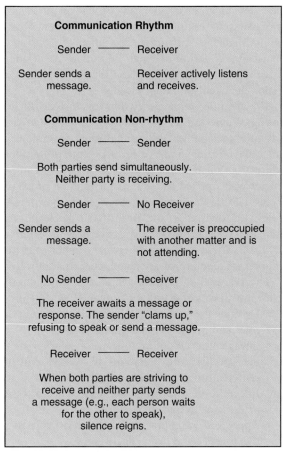

Fig. 19.2 Potential communication rhythms.

would not want me to attempt to take care of you in the critical care unit if that is not my area of expertise (and you shouldn't). From another perspective, when the best clinical nurse is promoted to nurse manager without formal training or preparation for the new role, it would be best to manage expectations until she or he has the skills and resources for that new role.

Reliability relates to counting on a person to manage and honor commitments. A team member may be trusted as competent at a specific task but may have a track record of tardiness or sloppy work, and this prevents you from complete trust. It comes down to: Can your word be trusted?

Sincerity is related to the assessment of someone's integrity, to the fundamental nature of their character. It is the most pivotal in the decision to trust someone and it is the most important aspect of leadership. It is why allegations of impropriety or infidelity in leaders is so devastating. For example, in a marriage, infidelity has a devastating effect, whereas forgetting an anniversary is much less damaging. Likewise, when colleagues talk about you behind your back, it is much more significant than if they are chronically late to meetings. Sincerity also relates to how much someone cares about what you care about, such as a sick or dying relative. Do your colleagues even acknowledge they know about the situation and do they check on you? If the answer is no, trust is eroded. We are supposed to care about those who are part of our workplace "family." When trust erodes, influence, intimacy, and relationships also erode. If this continues in a downward spiral, organizations fail from lack of collaboration, understanding, and effective problem solving, those things which are most closely related to success.

Trust is also a major issue among newly formed teams and their members, and one of the first questions to come up is who can you trust or not trust. Team members model trust through behaviors such as facilitating the establishment of ground rules and agreements by which the team will function and hold team members accountable. Trust is probably the most delicate aspect within relationships and is influenced far more by actions than by words. Therefore what people do is more powerful than what they say. Trust is a fragile thread that can be severed by one act. Once destroyed, trust is more difficult to reestablish than it was to initially create.

Accepting and Celebrating Differences

Every human being is different, with different backgrounds, different skill sets, different strengths, and different approaches. Yet it is not unusual for us to assume that team members are like us. Other team members must understand us and can even see or appreciate our "point of view." If we go into the situation with the awareness that not everyone is like us, we can reach out to other team members. We can always build from one connection to other connections. Appreciating differences may help us capitalize on talents we don't possess or value a behavior or situation from a different perspective. Celebrate the fact that you may complement each other.

Giving and Receiving Feedback

Feedback is like plant fertilizer; it allows human beings to learn and to grow. Feedback may not always feel great, but it can be very good for you. Stone and Heen (2014) have excellent suggestions about how to receive feedback and ask clarifying questions. Many of us are more anxious about receiving feedback than about giving feedback. It is very helpful to attempt to listen to feedback with an openness and to clarify anything that might be unclear. Assume the best of intentions. Work not to be defensive but to search for the pearl—the grain of truth that can support your learning and growing. Any information received can be accepted and incorporated or rejected. It just might be information about a "blind spot" that you may have never seen.

When giving feedback, focus on how you would like to receive it. Remember to ask questions and to focus on growth. Tonality and "how" something is said is of premier importance.

EXERCISE 19.7 Think about the last team project in which you participated. What worked about the team? What did not work about the team? Was there a member who did not carry his or her share of the work? Was there a team member who was a "know it all"? How did you handle the situation? Was there a person on the team who took the lead? How many of the qualities of a good team player do you possess? Be honest. What are areas in which you could improve? What are your strengths; that is, where do you shine?

INTERPROFESSIONAL TEAMS

Interprofessional teams are essential to quality patient care. Nurses, physicians, dietitians, social workers, case managers, pharmacists, and physical therapists, to name a few, must work together to achieve cost-effective care while achieving the highest quality of care in the healthcare setting. This means efforts must be expended to understand the various roles and backgrounds of each profession. At the same time, nurses are frequently leading teams comprising licensed practical/vocational nurses and technicians or assistants of various kinds. Here again, it is critical to understand everyone's role and job description as well as his or her background and identity as an individual. In addition, the collaboration needed in interprofessional teams cannot be created without mutual trust and respect among the members (Maxfield, Grenny, Lavandero, & Groah, 2013).

Core competencies for interprofessional collaborative practice were developed in 2016 by an expert panel of the Interprofessional Education Collaborative consisting of

the following groups: American Association of Colleges of Nursing, American Association of Colleges of Osteopathic Medicine, American Association of Colleges of Pharmacy, American Dental Education Association, Association of American Medical Colleges, and the Association of Schools of Public Health.

The identified competency domains include the following: Values/Ethics for Interprofessional Practice, Roles/Responsibilities, Interprofessional Communication, and Teams and Teamwork (Interprofessional Education Collaborative [IPEC], 2016). These competencies were applied to requests for funding proposals to the Health Resources and Services Administration (HRSA), a division of the Department of Health and Human Services of the US federal government, beginning in 2012. These government grants emphasized the importance of interprofessional practice in healthcare.

The Teams and Teamwork competency includes the following aspects of team functioning (IPEC, 2016):

- Describe the process of team development and the roles and practices of effective teams.
- Engage other health professionals—appropriate to the specific care situation—in shared patient-centered problem-solving.
- Integrate the knowledge and experience of other professions to inform care decisions.
- Apply leadership practices that support collaborative practice and team effectiveness.
- Engage self and others to constructively manage disagreements about values, roles, goals, and actions among healthcare professionals and with patients and families.
- Share accountability with other professions, patients, and communities for outcomes.
- Reflect on individual and team performance for individual as well as team performance improvement.
- Use process improvement strategies to increase the effectiveness of interprofessional teamwork and team-based care.
- Use available evidence to inform effective teamwork and team-based practices.

This work begins with education and transitions to practice and is the wave of the future, even though some practitioners are resistant to adapting traditional roles and responsibilities.

Several additional aspects of interprofessional work are crucial to creating and maintaining these teams.

Coyne (2005) emphasized *the importance of understanding each situation,* which includes clarifying misperceptions and inaccurate information about others within the team, including any assumptions that one professional group is favored over another. *Noticing professional expectations and unwritten processes* and cultures of the various professions within the team is also critical to working together seamlessly. It is helpful for nurses to note how other groups talk and behave and to note the special language they use. *Encourage the different disciplines to learn* from each other. For example, in comparing the different codes of ethics, the many similarities, as opposed to the differences, can create commonalities. Most are focused on the patient.

The team leader must *set a positive tone.* If the leadership expects interprofessional teamwork and verbalizes and models positive and upbeat attitudes, the various disciplines will work together smoothly.

Frequency of interaction of the team members can create ongoing interactions and familiarity with one another. Team members who are in a professional relationship with one another are more apt to work together smoothly. As an example, a weekly patient care meeting in which patients with significant needs or problems are reviewed allows each profession to address issues from a specific area of expertise. *Keep communication open* includes telling the truth in a way that it can be heard and understood. If an aspect of care is governed by regulations, it is helpful when a knowledgeable member of the team speaks to the issue or regulation, always remembering to phrase the information in a way that facilitates hearing and understanding. At all times the interprofessional team must *focus on the patient.* When the deliberations are focused on the delivery of best patient care for the specific patient, mutual respect can be developed, and open sharing of ideas and problem solving occurs.

EXERCISE 19.8 Interprofessional Teams

Identify a problem that you have heard discussed in a healthcare setting—for example, awkward timing of admissions and discharges, running out of supplies, or conflicts in scheduling procedures. Make a list of all of the different professions and support staff who might be involved with that issue in some way and who would need a voice during efforts to improve that situation.

THE VALUE OF TEAM-BUILDING

When things are not going well in an organization and problems need to be resolved, the first intervention people think of is "team-building." Naturally, for teams (a collection of people relying on each other) to be effective, they must function smoothly and communicate effectively to create the best possible work environment. The difficulty is that when organizations are facing difficulties, they generally do not have teams whose members function well together. Team-building and consultants can help; however, to sustain smoothly functioning teams, the leadership is critical.

Regardless of the problem, appropriate assessment of the team is essential (see Exercise 19.1). The success of the team depends on its members and its leadership. Providing feedback in a manner in which it can be heard and growing the team creates value in the team.

A resurgence in team building has occurred. Corporations are once again focused on the importance of teams. Vogt (2017) believes team-building activities are particularly vital to the success of small businesses, and most nursing units or clinics are essentially a small business. Vogt demonstrates that team-building exercises can build trust, ease conflicts, increase collaboration, and increase the effectiveness of communication. She further believes that increasing mutual trust through team-building activities can increase the codependence on one another in the team, thus increasing the efficiency and the productivity. Team building can ease conflicts by supporting team members to know each other better on a personal level, to bond with one another, and to become more comfortable with each other's personalities. Team-building activities can increase collaboration among the team members and increase their awareness of interdependency.

Lencioni (2016) builds a strong case for dealing constructively with building an underlying foundation for teams. He believes that three major components of smoothly functioning teams must be created:

- Mutual trust among the members
- A strong sense of team identity (that the team is unique and worthwhile)
- A sense of team efficacy (that the team performs well and its members are synergistic in their manner of working together)

At the heart of these components are the emotions we often work so hard to keep out of the workplace.

Fig. 19.3 Teams can form strong relationships external to the work environment.

BOX 19.7   Interview Questions for Team Building

1. What do you see as the problems currently facing your team?
2. What are the current strengths of your institution or work group? What are you currently doing well?
3. Does your boss do anything that prevents you from being as effective as you would like to be?
4. Does anybody else in this group do anything that prevents you from being as effective as you would like to be?
5. What would you like to accomplish at your upcoming team-building session? What changes would you be willing to make that would facilitate a smoother-functioning team and accomplishment of the team goals?

However, as human beings, we function the same way in both our work and personal lives. Mutual trust can be developed only when each team member tells the truth about feelings, thoughts, and wants and listens and supports other members of the team to do likewise. Every person yearns to be a part of something bigger than himself or herself—to do something important that makes a difference. Well-functioning teams allow this to happen (Fig. 19.3). Developing such teams can increase nursing job satisfaction and group cohesiveness, decrease nurse turnover rates, and promote patient safety and quality outcomes.

Understandable anxiety exists concerning the safety of being vulnerable and exposed if personal issues are revealed. That is why it is helpful for a team-building facilitator to make a thorough assessment of major issues and the willingness on the part of members to work on issues. One approach is to interview members of the team individually to discover the critical issues. The types of questions that might be asked, found in Box 19.7, provide some sense of the major issues within the team so that the facilitator has a better understanding of how to work with the team.

Because people spend such a large percentage of their time in the work setting, it would be unrealistic to believe that they continually appear in an unemotional and controlled state. Human beings simply do not function that way. What is observed are people's aspirations, their achievements, their hopes, and their social consciousness; they are observed falling in love; falling in hate and anger; winning and losing; and being excited, sad, fearful, anxious, and jealous. Consequently, these "feelings" are important components of organizational life and can undermine work effectiveness. Most of us know of situations in which, because of an emotional disagreement, two individuals have avoided each other for years.

Because of the power of emotions and the inevitability of their presence, their effect on interpersonal relationships, and their influence on productivity, the quality of work, and the safety of patients, emotions should be a high priority when examining the functioning of the team. Fortunately, research addresses the importance of emphasizing the "emotional intelligence" of individuals when working in teams in the classic work by Goleman (2011). Those teams that address these issues are much more successful and create a more positive work environment than those that do not.

Suppressing emotions at work is neither healthy nor constructive for team members. When emotions are handled appropriately within the team, several positive outcomes are possible for the work setting. One creates a sense of internal comfort with the workings of the team and the organization. When stress is lowered and kept at lower levels on average, problems are much more easily resolved. This phenomenon is similar to releasing steam slowly with a steam valve rather than having the gasket blow. Interpersonal relationships on the team are more stable, and people have a sense of closer ties and collegiality when emotions are addressed. Fewer negative relationships or interactions develop, which results in more effective and pleasant working relationships all around.

Work group effectiveness improves when the team is functioning smoothly and emotions and "feelings" are being addressed on a routine basis rather than waiting for a volcanic eruption. The daily routines of frustration and boredom and retreat from the group are likely to

LITERATURE PERSPECTIVE

Resource: Kouzes, J. M., & Posner, B. Z. (2016). *Learning leadership: The five fundamentals of becoming an exemplary leader.* San Francisco: Jossey-Bass, John Wiley & Sons.

The original model focuses on how leaders in all walks of life and all aspects of the workplace mobilize people to get extraordinary things done. Ordinary people such as novice nurses can guide others along pioneering journeys to phenomenal accomplishments. The research and work that Kouzes and Posner have done establish relationships as the core of leading any change or initiative. Five key aspects of establishing and maintaining relationships constitute the heart of this leadership model:

- **Model the Way:** Credibility is the foundation of leadership. It is established by consistently *doing what you say you will do* or by *setting the example* for the other team members.
- **Inspire a Shared Vision:** Imagine exciting and ennobling possibilities, and enlist others in these dreams through positive attitude, excitement, and hard work.

- **Challenge the Process:** Seek innovative ways to change, grow, and improve—experiment and take risks.
- **Enable Others to Act:** Foster collaboration by promoting cooperation and building trust. Create a sense of reciprocity or give and take. Establish a sense of "We're all in this together."
- **Encourage the Heart:** Novice leaders encourage their constituents to carry on. They keep hope and determination alive, recognize contributions, and celebrate victories.

Implications for Practice

When nurses use this model to approach leadership, they can strengthen their skills. Each of these examples provides a way for new, emerging, and established leaders to remain committed to the team with which they work. This model also emphasizes that each of us learn to be leaders and this is a lifelong learning process.

---

undo a team. People who are engaged and have leaders who help them achieve goals are more effective. The skills and tools previously discussed (e.g., speaking supportively) are the basic tools one needs to handle the emotional aspects of the team. Choosing to cope with emotional upset must be a conscious choice, one that requires practice to improve the skill.

THE ROLE OF LEADERSHIP

Teams usually have a leader. In addition, teams function within large organizations that have leaders. Team-building, which can be a costly endeavor in terms of consultation fees as well as work time and team resources, is difficult to undertake and of questionable effectiveness without the approval and the support of the leader. Although very strong teams may be able to educate themselves regarding some of the issues, such as establishing goals and priorities or clarifying their own team process, addressing any kind of relationship issue among team members without a more objective outside party or skilled leader facilitating the process is exceedingly difficult. The Literature Perspective presents the essence of a model for leadership—one that could form the basis for how teams can be built.

Because leadership is such a pivotal part of smoothly functioning teams, it is illuminating to examine leaders more carefully. Truly progressive leaders understand that leadership and followership are not necessarily a set of skills or "putting on a role"; rather, these are qualities of character. Leadership and followership is as much about character and development as it is about education. Leaders realize their capacity for influence, risk taking, and decision making more fully. Team-building is a natural outgrowth. This type of leader understands that the best in a person is tied intimately to the individual's deepest sense of himself or herself—to one's spirit. The efforts of leaders must touch the spiritual aspect in themselves and others. The same could be said for skillful followers. Warren Bennis (2009) once said that leaders simply care about more people. Consequently, this caring manifests itself in doing whatever it takes to improve team functioning. This may imply involving oneself in team building with the team. The risk in such an endeavor is that the team leader is open to being vulnerable, to being judged by others, and to being wrong. However, if the leader has been a role model for the team agreement and has held people accountable to these statements, the team-building exercise will not degenerate into judging and placing blame.

If true leadership is about character development as much as anything, then character development is also beneficial for followers—that is, members of the team. The areas of character development often addressed include communication, particularly those aspects of speaking supportively that enhance understanding the other person's message while avoiding placing blame and justifying. Box 19.8 highlights an example of character development from personal experience, the concept of self-confidence.

Confidence, which loosely translates as faith or belief that one will act in a correct and effective way, is a key aspect of character. Thus it follows that confidence in oneself can be closely tied to self-esteem, which is

---

BOX 19.8   The "Can Do" Brigade: An Army Nurse's Study in Character Development

As life events are reviewed, important or pivotal learning can be identified. One life event that significantly affected me was the year I spent as an Army Nurse Corps officer in South Vietnam. This was the first time I remember an awareness and understanding of confidence in the face of incredible obstacles. I had spent the first 10 months of my nursing career in labor and delivery at Indiana University before volunteering for a guaranteed assignment to Vietnam. I went to Fort Sam Houston for 6 weeks of basic training, where they taught me really important things like how to salute, how to march, and how many men are in a battalion. No one ever asked me if I could start an IV or draw a tube of blood. This was important because Indiana University had the largest medical school class in the United States at that time and nurses did nothing that interfered with medical education. Therefore I had never started an IV or drawn blood. When I arrived in Saigon, they put me in a sedan with another nurse and sent me up to the Third Surgical Hospital, one not unlike the one in *M*A*S*H*. We even had a Major Burns—that was not his name but it was his function. Surgical hospitals receive only battle casualties; their purpose is to stabilize and to transport.

The Third Surgical Hospital was located in the middle of the 173rd Airborne Brigade, whose job it was to defend the Bien Hoa Air Base, where all the sorties in the south were flown during the war. We were stopped at the gate by an MP who stepped up and saluted very snappily. He knew that a staff car must contain either a very-high-ranking officer or, if it was his lucky day, females.

When I was in Vietnam, 500 American women and 500,000 American men were there. The MP looked in the window, saluted snappily, and said "Afternoon, ma'am!" He wanted to know where we were going; he talked to us for a few minutes and assured us that if there was anything he could do for us, we should just give him a call. He saluted us and said, "can do." I didn't understand because I did not know that there are units with very high esprit de corps who attach snappy little sayings at the end of things like salutes, phone conversations, memos, and so forth. The 173rd was the "can do" brigade.

When we got to the hospital and met the chief nurse, she took us down to the mess hall and introduced us to all the doctors and nurses. We were sitting and having coffee when the field phone rang in the kitchen and the mess sergeant yelled out, "Incoming wounded." Everybody got up and started to leave for the preop area. I just sat there until the chief nurse said, "Come on." I said, "You don't understand, I deliver babies." She was not impressed! She took me by the arm and led me to preop.

When we got there, we discovered there were not just a few incoming wounded, there were more than 30, and some were very seriously injured. She immediately told the sergeant to call headquarters battalion of the 173rd Airborne and tell them that the Third Surg needed blood. She turned to me and said, "Lieutenant, you are responsible for drawing 50 units of fresh whole blood." I was shocked! I had never drawn a tube of blood, but I found in the back section of preop a Specialist 4th class who was already setting up "saw horses" and stretchers, putting up IV poles, and hanging plastic blood sets. I started to help, and soon I heard trucks out back. I opened the door and looked outside. There were two huge Army trucks, and kids—17, 18, 19, and 20 years old—were jumping out. They were covered with red mud from the bottom of their boots to the tops of their helmets. I looked at them, and I looked at the clean cement floor, and in an instant, my mother came to me. I put my hand on my hip and said, "Where have you boys been?" One PFC stepped forward and saluted me very snappily and said, "Ma'am, we just came in this afternoon from 30 days in the field, we have been out in the rice paddies chasing the Viet Cong, we have not had a hot meal, and we've not had a shower, but Sergeant Major said the Third Surg needs blood!" He saluted smartly and said, "can do!" They were very clear. After 30 days of chasing and being chased by the Viet Cong, giving a unit of blood was easy. "Can do!" They were confident. They were kids who had looked into the face of death. At that moment, I knew if they *can do,* I Can Do! Life requires confidence. With confidence, you can make your dreams come true!

satisfaction with oneself. The greatest deterrent to self-esteem and self-confidence is fear. Fear is described by some as "false evidence appearing real." Working on self-confidence requires an attitude of belief, of confidence, of I *"can do"* whatever is required.

> False
> Evidence
> Appearing
> Real

Leading the team is clearly not the easiest thing to do, but neither is being an active, fully participating member of the team. Both require taking risks, including being in

a relationship. Being in a team-building experience and hearing those things that have not worked for people in their interactions with peers and the leader can be scary but worthwhile. It requires a focus on personal and professional growth. It requires building character.

CONCLUSION

Whether a nurse is a leader, a manager, or a member of the team, effective performance requires commitment to the group. Forging new relationships and strengthening old ones are typically facilitated by deliberate actions ranging from creating clarity of purpose through holding each other accountable.

THE SOLUTION

The first question that needed to be asked was, "Were we committed to providing the most optimal care for the neonate?" In other words, why would teamwork be important in this situation? What's the vision or mission? After achieving agreement among the neonatal intensive care unit (NICU) team, we strategized on how to create a "team" with the specialists. Making our intent clear was very important. A meeting with the director of the specialty team, the NICU medical director, and nursing leadership was arranged. We discovered that we shared a common goal: to provide the best care possible for the baby. Keeping that goal as the focus, we then identified areas of mutual respect. From there, both sides were willing to listen to each other's concerns. Care guidelines could be identified, as well as areas of responsibility. Ideas on how to improve the communication process were also discussed. A plan based on patient needs, complete with agreements, was implemented.

Were we a team yet? The answer is "no." There was still a little skepticism and reserve. Everyone seemed to have a "wait-and-see" attitude. The first big chance was identified when the specialty group insisted that a patient of

theirs be admitted to the NICU because they believed it was the best place for the baby to be. Another measurable outcome was having the agreements honored. This reinforced to everyone that his or her concerns had been heard and respected. Mutual trust was building, and a collegial relationship began. A year later, it is hard to imagine that this situation ever occurred. There is enthusiasm for this specialty's physicians and their patients. It is certainly a change in attitude.

There are many components to team-building, but the most important component is to be clear about your mission and intentions and to be clear in communication when working with potential team members. The intention to provide the best care possible assisted each one of us to be more open, creative, and trusting. These are all necessary components of team-building. Remember, teams are made up of individuals. Ask yourself if you are willing to accept responsibility for your response and actions. Be the change that you want to see.

Would this be a suitable approach for you? Why?

Diane Gallagher

REFLECTIONS

Consider the following questions, then write a one-paragraph summary. When could you have been more effective as a team member or group leader recently?

What personal behavior could you improve in your next group or team experience?

THE EVIDENCE

TeamSTEPPS is a well-documented, integrated program created through the auspices of the U.S. Department of Health & Human Services Agency for

Healthcare Research and Quality (AHRQ) and the U.S. Department of Defense (DOD) Healthcare Team Coordination Program; it stresses teamwork and communication among physicians, nurses, and other healthcare personnel to increase patient safety (Castner, Foltz-Ramos, Schwartz, & Ceravolo, 2012). Multiple projects and evidence have been accrued regarding the use and implementation of Team-STEPPS, as well as the outcomes produced from this program. The goal is to produce highly effective interdisciplinary teams that achieve the best outcomes for patients. The tools and strategies used include leadership that coordinates the team and initiates planning, problem solving, and process improvement. Also, situation monitoring is used. This tool focuses on the ability of the nurse to actively scan behaviors and actions of co-workers; it also fosters mutual respect and team accountability, which creates a safety net for the team and patient. Specific skills are taught that increase the ability of each team member to support other team members by accurately assessing their workload and helping them. These skills protect the team from work overload that might reduce effectiveness and increase risk to patients. The last skill set focuses on communication that highlights clear, accurate information exchange among team members, including SBAR, Call-out, and Handoff. The TeamSTEPPS teaching manual, including PowerPoint presentations and teaching videos, is available from the DOD Patient Safety Program for minimal cost.

▌ TIPS FOR TEAM BUILDING

- Commit to the purpose of the team.
- Develop team relationships of mutual respect.
- Communicate effectively, and actively listen.
- Create and adhere to team agreements concerning function and process.
- Build trust.

REFERENCES

American Association of Critical Care Nurses. (2016). *AACN standards for establishing and fostering health work environments.* https://www.aacn.org/nursing-excellence/standards/aacn-standards-for-establishing-and-sustaining-healthy-work-environments.

Bennis, W. (2009). *On becoming a leader.* Reading, MA: Addison-Wesley.

Castner, J., Foltz-Ramos, K., Schwartz, D., & Ceravolo, D. (October 2012). A leadership challenge: Staff nurse perceptions after an organizational TeamSTEPPS initiative. *Journal of Nursing Administration, 42*(10), 467–472.

Coyne, C. (2005). Strength in numbers: How team building is improving care in a variety of settings. *PT Magazine of Physical Therapy, 13*(6), 40–51.

England, P. (2013). *Effective vs ineffective teams.* www.eventus.co.uk/effective-vs-ineffective-teams/.

Gallup. (2017). *State of the American workplace.* Washington, DC: Gallup Inc.

Goleman, D. (2011). *The brain & emotional intelligence: New insights.* Northampton, MA: More Than Sound.

Hampton, D., & Key, Y. L. (2016). Generation Z: Emerging force in the workplace. *Voice of Nursing Leadership, 15*(3), 4–15.

International Nursing Association for Clinical Simulation and Learning (INACSL) Standards Committee. (2016). INACSL standards of best practice: Simulation^SM debriefing. *Science Direct, 12*(suppl.), S21–S25. https://www.nursingsimulation.org/article/S1876-1399%2816%2930129-3/fulltext.

Interprofessional Education Collaborative Expert Panel. (2016). *Core competencies for interprofessional collaborative practice: 2016 Update.* Washington, DC: Interprofessional Education Collaborative.

Ke Yu, D., Harter, J., & Agrawal, S. (April 2013). U.S. managers boast best work engagement. *Gallup Economy.* www.gallup.com/poll/162062/managers-boast-best-work-engagement.aspx?utm_source=alert&utm_medium=email&utm_campaign=syndication&utm_content=morelink&utm_term=all%20gallup%20headlines.

Kouzes, J. M., & Posner, B. Z. (2016). *Learning leadership: The five fundamentals of becoming an exemplary leader.* San Francisco: Jossey-Bass, John Wiley & Sons.

LaFasto, F., & Larson, C. (2001). *When teams work best: 6,000 Team members and leaders tell what it takes to succeed.* Thousand Oaks, CA: Sage Publishing.

Lencioni, P. (2016). *The ideal team player: How to recognize and cultivate the three essential virtues.* Hoboken, NJ: Jossey-Bass.

Maxfield, D., Grenny, J., Lavandero, R., & Groah, L. (2013). *Why safety tools and checklists aren't enough to save lives.* April 29. http://www.aacn.org/wd/hwe/docs/the-silent-treatment.pdf.

McGregor, D. (1960). *The human side of enterprise.* New York: McGraw-Hill.

Pappas, S. (2017). From tasks to outcomes: Slowing nursing's value. *Voice of Nursing Leadership, 15*(3), 4–15.

Porter-O'Grady, T., & Malloch, K. (2017). *Quantum leadership: A resource for health care innovation* (6th ed.). Sudbury, MA: Jones & Bartlett.

Rath, T. (2007). *Strengths finder 2.0.* New York: Gallup Press.

Stone, D., & Heen, S. (2014). *Thanks for the feedback: The science & art of receiving feedback well.* New York: Penguin Books.

The International Nursing Association for Clinical Simulation and Learning. https://www.nursingsimulation.org/article/S1876-1399%2816%2930129-3/fulltext.

Vogt, C. (2017). *Importance of team-building activities.* http://smallbusiness.chron.com/importance-teambuilding-activities-40587.html.

Wagner, R., & Harter, J. (2006). *12: The elements of great managing.* New York: Gallup Press.

Warrell, M. (2015). How to build high-trust relationships. *Forbes.* https://www.forbes.com/wites/margiewarrell/2015/08/31/how-to-build-high-trust-relationships/#5eba04ad15cf.

Winsborough, Dave, & Chamorro-Premuzic, Tomas. (2017). Great Teams Are About Personalities, Not Just Skills *On Teams.* In *Harvard Business Review.*

20

Managing Costs and Budgets

Sylvain Trepanier

LEARNING OUTCOMES

- Explain several major factors that are escalating the costs of health care.
- Evaluate different reimbursement methods and their incentives to control costs.
- Differentiate costs, charges, and revenue in relation to a specified unit of service, such as a visit, hospital stay, or procedure.

- Value why all healthcare organizations must make a profit.
- Give examples of cost considerations for nurses.
- Discuss the purpose of and relationships among the operating, cash, and capital budgets.
- Explain the budgeting process.
- Identify variances on monthly expense reports.

KEY TERMS

budget	diagnosis-related group (DRG)	productivity
budgeting process	fixed costs	profit
capital expenditure budget	full-time equivalent (FTE)	prospective payment system
capitation	managed care	providers
case mix	nonproductive hours	revenue
cash budget	observation status	unit of service
charges	operating budget	utilization
contractual allowance	organized delivery system (ODS)	value-based purchasing
cost	payer mix	variable costs
cost-based reimbursement	payers	variance
cost-based system	price	variance analysis
cost center	productive hours	

THE CHALLENGE

Premier Health is an integrated healthcare system based in Dayton, Ohio. The system includes four acute care hospitals (more than 1900 licensed beds) where the primary source of revenue is government payers such as Medicare and Medicaid. Over the last 4 years reimbursement has drastically declined.

Admissions of **"observation-status"** patients were on the rise (more than 40% of total admissions), and the payer mix was not getting any better. The decision for an inpatient hospital admission is rather complex and is based on a provider's judgment of medically necessary hospital care. If the provider expects the patient to stay two or more midnights, an inpatient admission is warranted and offers its own set of rules and reimbursement guidelines. Otherwise, if a provider is not certain that a two or more midnight stays will be necessary, he or she will keep the patient under an observation status, which offers a much lower rate of reimbursement. The traditional inpatient area offers a fixed-cost infrastructure (primarily influenced by the cost of 24/7 nursing care—labor). Therefore if observation-status patients are cared for in a regular inpatient environment, the cost of caring for these patients may very well be higher than the expected reimbursement. In an area of value-based proposition, Premier Health leaders recognized the importance of decreasing the total cost of care to support the decrease in reimbursement, which does not support the current cost structure. The next fiscally

responsible step was to require that variable expenses in hospitals be reduced. Because labor costs are the greatest variable expense in a hospital, such thinking often leads to demands to reduce nursing staff or to substitute lower-paid personnel. As a chief nursing officer at Premier Health, my goal was to maintain a high-quality, high-performance work team that adds value for patients and payers. My challenge was to consider what steps could be taken before reducing staff at Premier Health. How could I decrease my overall cost of care related to observation-status patients, for example?

What would you do if you were this nurse?

Sylvain Trepanier, DNP, RN, CENP, FAAN
Chief Nursing Officer, Premier Health, Dayton, Ohio

INTRODUCTION

Healthcare costs in the United States continue to rise at a rate greater than general inflation. In 2015, for example, Americans spent $3.2 trillion for health care—approximately 17.8% of the gross domestic product (GDP)—and it is expected to rise to 20.1% by 2025 (Centers for Medicare & Medicaid Services [CMS], 2015).

Despite our huge expenditures, major indicators reveal significant health problems in the United States, as well as large disparities in health status related to gender, race, and socioeconomic status (*Healthy People 2020,* 2014). Our infant mortality rate is among the highest of all industrialized nations, and black infants die at more than twice the rate of white infants. Average life expectancy is lower than that in most developed countries, and men have a life expectancy that is 6 years less than that of women. One in eight women will develop breast cancer during her lifetime, with black and Native American women experiencing a much higher death rate than white women. Violence-related injuries are on the rise, and unintentional injuries, such as motor vehicle accidents, are a leading cause of death. Clearly, we are not receiving a high-value return on our healthcare dollar. That said, as of March 2014, 14 (53.9%) of the Health Leading Indicators (HLI) either met target or showed improvements (*Healthy People 2020,* 2014).

The large portion of the GDP that is spent on health care poses problems to the economy in other ways, too. Funds are diverted from needed social programs such as childcare, housing, education, transportation, and the environment. The price of goods and services is increased, and therefore the country's ability to compete in the international marketplace is compromised. As the amount of the GDP devoted to healthcare expenses rises, the more vulnerable the healthcare industry becomes to external influences. This creates a major concern for an industry that already expresses concerns about being overregulated. Nurses must fully understand the cost of health care to ensure the fiscal viability of our healthcare system.

WHAT ESCALATES HEALTHCARE COSTS

Total healthcare costs are a function of the prices and the utilization rates of healthcare services (Costs = Price × Utilization) (Table 20.1). Price is the rate that healthcare providers set for the services they deliver, such as the

TABLE 20.1   Relationship of Price and Utilization Rates to Total Healthcare Costs

Price	× Utilization Rate	= Total Cost	% Change
$1.00	100	$100.00	0%
$1.08[a]	100	$108.00	+8.0%
$1.08	105[b]	$113.40	13.4%
$1.08	110[c]	$118.80	18.8%

[a]8% increase for inflation.
[b]5% more procedures done.
[c]10% more procedures done.

hospital rate or physician fee. *Utilization* refers to the quantity or volume of services provided, such as diagnostic tests provided or number of patient visits.

Price inflation and administrative inefficiency are leading contributors to increasing prices for health services. In recent decades, rises in healthcare prices have dramatically outpaced general inflation. Examples of factors that stimulate price inflation are insurance premiums, medical technology, drug costs, health plan administration, and waste. Administrative inefficiency or waste is primarily a result of the large numbers of clerical personnel whom organizations use to process reimbursement forms from multiple payers. Nearly 15% of healthcare costs are directly related to the financing system in the United States (Jiwani, Himmelstein, Woolhandler, & Kahn, 2014). This single fact indicates why some hospital administrators advocate for the elimination of multiple payers.

Several interrelated factors contribute to increased use of medical services. These include unnecessary care, consumer attitudes, healthcare financing, pharmaceutical usage, and changing population demographics and disease patterns. *Unnecessary care* can be defined as care prescribed that does not contribute to the well-being of a patient. An example is additional laboratory tests that are unrelated to the plan of care. Furthermore, substantial evidence supporting the additional care might not exist. A substantial amount of unnecessary care does not add health benefits for patients.

Our attitudes and behaviors as consumers of health care also contribute to rising costs. In general, we prefer to "be fixed" when something goes wrong rather than practice prevention. When we need "fixing," expensive high-tech services typically are perceived as the best care. Many of us still believe that the physician knows best, so we do not seek much information related to costs and effectiveness of different healthcare options. When we do seek information, it is not readily available or understandable. Also, we are not accustomed to using other, less costly healthcare providers, such as nurse practitioners.

The way health care is financed contributes to rising costs. When health care is reimbursed by third-party payers, consumers are somewhat insulated from personally experiencing the direct effects of high healthcare costs. In most instances, however, consumers do not have many incentives to consider costs when choosing among providers or using services. In addition, the various methods of reimbursement have implications for how providers price and use services.

Evidence of pharmaceutical usage can be seen in advertisements in magazines and on television. No longer do pharmaceutical companies attempt to influence only the prescribers. They go directly to the consumer, who then goes to the prescriber. Because of some typical drug benefit programs, the consumer often is unaware of the total cost of a medication, which may be a "quick fix" (described previously) or a lifestyle enhancement, such as sexual enhancers or skin conditioning.

Changing population demographics also are increasing the volume of health services needed. For example, chronic health problems increase with age, and the number of older adults in America is rising. The fastest growing population is the group aged 85 years and older, and Baby Boomers are moving into their senior years. The growing societal problems of obesity, heart disease, homelessness, drug addiction, and violence increase demands for health services.

HOW HEALTH CARE IS FINANCED

On March 23, 2010, historic healthcare reform was signed into law (The Patient Protection and Affordable Care Act [ACA]). This phased-in legislation includes some features that take effect quickly and others that are delayed for several years. Furthermore, the ACA has been questioned since signed into law and may remain as is, be revised, or be eliminated. However, knowing the essence of the ACA helps us understand what the public views as healthcare support. One of the major benefits of the ACA is access to coverage regardless of the presence of any preexisting conditions. Although the enacted legislation (ACA) does not cover the entire population, a great majority can be covered. According to the Rand Health Reform study, a net increase of 16.9 million Americans obtained healthcare coverage because of the ACA (Carman, Eibner, & Paddock, 2015). This coverage changes how individuals are insured and thus how they are viewed within the system. Multiple demands for nurses, especially those in advanced practice roles, will continue to emerge over the next several years. As all of these changes, including subsequent legislation, unfold, opportunities and challenges exist for the way in which health care will be delivered and paid for, and those changes will alter what nursing does.

Health care is paid for by three major sources: government (Medicare and Medicaid), private health insurance, and out-of-pocket (CMS, 2015). Three-fourths of the government funding is at the federal level. Federal programs include Medicare and health services for members of the military, veterans, Native Americans, and federal prisoners. Medicare, the largest federal program, was established in 1965 and pays for care provided to people 65 years of age and older and some disabled individuals. Medicare coverage is separated in Medicare Part A, B, C, and D. Medicare Part A is an insurance plan for hospital, hospice, home health, and skilled nursing care that is paid for through Social Security taxes. Nursing home care that is mainly custodial is not covered. Medicare Part B is an optional insurance that covers physician services, medical equipment, and diagnostic tests. Part B is funded through federal taxes and monthly premiums paid by the recipients. Medicare Part C is not a separate benefit. Part C is the part that allows private health insurance companies to provide Medicare benefits. These are known as Medicare Advantage Plans. Medicare Part D is the part that provides outpatient drug prescription. These plans change constantly and can be reviewed on www.medicareinteractive.org.

Medicaid, a state-level program financed by federal and state funds, pays for services provided to persons who are medically indigent, blind, or disabled and to children with disabilities. Medicaid, which varies by state, covers nearly 70 million Americans (Kaiser Family Foundation, 2015). The federal government pays between 50% and 83% of total Medicaid costs based on the per capita income of the state. Services funded by Medicaid vary from state to state but must include services provided by hospitals, physicians, laboratories, and radiology departments; prenatal and preventive care; and nursing home and home healthcare services.

Private insurance is the second major source of financing for the healthcare system. Most Americans have private health insurance, which usually is provided by employers through group policies. Individuals can purchase health insurance, but typically the rates are higher and provide minimal coverage. Health insurance that is so intertwined with employment is problematic and contributes to the number of uninsured and underinsured Americans. Many of the uninsured workers are those employed in small businesses that cannot afford to provide group insurance and those that have part-time, seasonal, or service positions.

Individuals also pay directly for health services when they do not have health insurance or when insurance does not cover the service. Costs paid by individuals are called *out-of-pocket expenses* and include deductibles, copayments, and coinsurance. Health insurance benefits often cover limited preventive care and typically do not cover cosmetic surgeries, alternative healthcare therapies, or items such as eyeglasses and nonprescription medications.

HEALTHCARE REIMBURSEMENT

Prices in health care are not set by the same economic equilibrium found in all major industries. For the most part, pricing is highly influenced by the government and the reimbursement plans. For example, both Medicare and Medicaid impose pricing on hospitals, and there is no room for negotiation. Health services researchers do not agree on the exact effects of these reimbursement methods on cost and quality. However, considering these effects is important because changes in payment systems have implications for how care is provided in healthcare organizations. In fact, the government offered a reimbursement payment from a cost-based system, to prospective payment systems, and now a system that pays on performance (pay-for-performance), otherwise known as *value-based purchasing*.

A cost-based system consists of the cost of providing a service plus a markup for profit. Third-party payers often put limitations on what they will pay by establishing usual and customary charges by surveying all providers in a certain area. Usual and customary charges rise over time as providers continually increase their prices. In cost-based reimbursement, all allowable costs are calculated and used as the basis for payment. Each payer (government or insurance company) determines what the allowable costs are for each procedure, visit, or service. Charges and cost-based reimbursement are retrospective payment methods, because the amount of payment is determined after services are delivered. When the reimbursed costs are less than the full charge for the service, a contractual allowance (or discount) exists. Charges and cost-based reimbursement were the predominant payment methods in the 1960s and 1970s but have been largely supplanted by payer fee schedules determined before service delivery.

The prospective payment system is a method in which the third-party payer decides in advance what will be paid for a service or episode of care. If the costs of care are greater than the payment, the provider absorbs the loss. If the costs are less than the payment, the provider makes a profit. In 1983 Medicare implemented a prospective payment system (PPS) for hospital care that uses diagnosis-related groups (DRGs) as the basis for payment.

EXERCISE 20.1 What is the contractual allowance when a hospital charges $800 per day to care for a ventilator-dependent patient and an insurance company reimburses the hospital $685 per day? What is the impact on hospital income (revenue) if this is the reimbursement for 2500 patient-days?

The DRG system is a classification system that groups patients into categories based on the average number of days of hospitalization for specific medical diagnoses, considering factors such as the patient's age, complications, and other illnesses. Payment includes the expected costs for diagnostic tests, various therapies, surgery, and length of stay (LOS). The cost of nursing services is not explicitly calculated. With a few exceptions, DRGs do not adequately reflect the variability of patient intensity or acuity within the DRG. This is problematic for nursing, because the amount of resources (nurses and supplies) used to care for patients are directly related to the patient acuity. Therefore many nurses believe that DRGs are not good predictors of nursing care requirements. In past years, Medicare also began reimbursing home health agencies, nursing homes, and ambulatory care providers through a PPS.

In addition to Medicare, some state Medicaid programs and private insurance companies use a DRG payment system. Although DRGs are not currently used for specialty hospitals (pediatric, psychiatric, and oncology), they are a dominant force in hospital payment. Implementation of a PPS with DRGs resulted in increased patient acuity and decreased LOS in hospitals, along with a greater demand for home care. The need for hospital and community-based nurses also increased.

The pay-for-performance system was introduced in the early 2000s and used a system that reimbursed hospitals, and eventually providers, based on performance and outcomes and not on the cost associated with providing the care. The premise of this payment system is based on quality outcomes. Also referred to as value-based purchasing, it offers rewards and incentives to high-performing organizations. This approach was first used with the passage of the Medicare Prescription Drug, Improvement, and Modernization Act of 2003. This law provided incentives to hospitals that voluntarily submitted data on 10 quality measures.

The pay-for-performance system eventually evolved into the Hospital Value-Based Purchasing Program (HVBPP) established by the Affordable Care Act and became effective in October 2012. The incentives are based on how well a hospital performs on each measure or how much a hospital improves its performance on a measure compared with its performance at baseline. The overall score includes clinical process of care measures and patient experience of care measures. A summary of hospital outcomes affecting HVBPP is offered in Box 20.1.

EXERCISE 20.2 Assume that Medicare reimburses a hospice $70 for home visits. For one particular group of patients, it costs the hospice an average of $98 per day to provide care. What are the implications for the hospice? What options should the hospice nurse manager and nurses consider?

THE CHANGING HEALTHCARE ECONOMIC ENVIRONMENT

Health care is a major public concern, and rapid changes are occurring in an attempt to reduce costs and improve the health and wellness of the nation. As shown in Box 20.2, strategies shaping the evolving healthcare delivery system include managed care, organized delivery systems (ODSs), and competition based on price, patient outcomes, and service quality. These strategies affect both the pricing and use of health services.

EXERCISE 20.3 For each reimbursement method, think about the incentives for healthcare providers (individuals and organizations) regarding their practice patterns. What incentives could change the quantity of services used per patient or the number or types of patients served? Are these incentives efficient? List the incentives. How might each method affect overall healthcare costs? (Think in terms of effect on utilization and price.) What do you think the effect on quality of care might be with each payment method?

BOX 20.1 Hospital Outcomes Affecting Hospital Value-Based Purchasing Program, Fiscal Years 2016-2018

Fiscal Year	Applicable Domains and Weights
2016	Clinical process of care (10%)
	Patient experience of care (25%)
	Outcome (40%)
	Efficiency (25%)
2017	Patient- and caregiver-centered experience of care and care coordination (25%)
	Safety (20%)
	Clinical care, outcomes (25%)
	Clinical care, process (5%)
	Efficiency and cost reduction (25%)
2018	Patient- and caregiver-centered experience of care and care coordination (25%)
	Safety (25%)
	Clinical care (25%)
	Efficiency and cost reduction (25%)

Data from Centers for Medicare & Medicaid Services (CMS). (2015). National health expenditure fact sheet. https://www.cms .gov/research-statistics-data-and-systems/statistics-trends-and-reports/nationalhealthexpenddata/nhe-fact-sheet.html.

BOX 20.2 Healthcare Delivery Reform Strategies

Strategies	Key Features
Managed care	Health plan that includes both service and finance
Organized delivery systems	Networks of organizations; providers and payers
Competition based on price, patient outcomes, and service quality	Basis of cost and quality

Managed care, also known as "managed cost," is a term that brings together the delivery and financing function into one entity, in an attempt to control the cost, utilization, and quality (Medicaid, 2014). A major goal of managed care is to decrease unnecessary services, thereby decreasing costs. Managed care also works to ensure timely and appropriate care. Health maintenance organizations (HMOs) are a type of managed care system in which the primary physician serves as a gatekeeper who determines what services the patient uses.

Because HMOs are paid on a capitated basis, it is to the HMO's advantage to practice prevention and use ambulatory care rather than more expensive hospital care. In other forms of managed care, a nonphysician case manager arranges and authorizes the services provided. Many insurance companies have used case managers for years. Nurses who work in home health and ambulatory settings often communicate with insurance company case managers to plan the care for specific patients. PPOs and point-of-service (POS) plans are other types of managed care plans that give the patient more options than traditional HMOs do for selecting providers and services (Fig. 20.1).

ODSs comprise networks of healthcare organizations, providers, and payers. Typically, this means hospitals, physicians, and insurance companies. The aim of such joint ventures is to develop and market collectively a comprehensive package of healthcare services that will meet most needs of large numbers of consumers. Hospitals, physicians, and payers will share the financial risks of the enterprise. Although hospitals share some risk now with prospective payment, physicians have not generally shared the risk. This risk-sharing is expected to provide incentives to eliminate unnecessary services, use resources more effectively, and improve quality of services.

Competition among healthcare providers increasingly is based on cost and quality outcomes. Decision making

Fig. 20.1 Nurses in ambulatory care settings often work directly with insurance companies to plan patient care.

regarding price and utilization of services is shifting from physicians and hospitals to payers, who are demanding significant discounts or lower prices. Scientific data that demonstrate positive health outcomes and high-quality services are required. Providers who cannot compete based on price, patient outcomes, and service quality will find it difficult to survive as the system evolves.

The Healthcare Economic Environment and Nursing Practice

What does the healthcare economic environment mean for the practicing professional nurse? We must value ourselves as providers and think of our practice within a context of organizational viability and quality of care. To do this, we must always be able to demonstrate and articulate the value contribution of our practice. In other words, it is critical to determine and advertise the *value* of nursing care. Services that add value are of high quality, affect health outcomes positively, and minimize costs. The following content helps develop financial thinking skills and ways to consider how nursing practice adds value for patients by minimizing costs.

Nursing Services as a Source of Revenue

According to Title XVIII of the Social Security Act, an inpatient hospital admission means that a patient was admitted for purposes of receiving care for a period of two midnights or more (CMS, 2017). Furthermore, nursing services resourced by the hospital for care and treatment of inpatients are covered under the law and included in the prospective payment system. Hospitals use a "daily room charge" based on a relative value of the intensity of nursing services rendered. This revenue-generating daily charge should be viewed as the source of revenue for nursing services provided on any given unit. It should be used as a data source to establish the total value contribution of nursing services, include nursing's contribution to the bottom line.

WHY PROFIT IS NECESSARY

Private, nongovernmental healthcare organizations may be either for-profit (FP) or not-for-profit (NFP). This designation refers to the tax status of the organization and specifies how the profit can be used. Profit is the excess income left after all expenses have been paid (Revenues − Expenses = Profit), and many NFP organizations designate their "profit" as excess income. FP organizations pay taxes, and their profits can be distributed to investors and managers. NFP organizations, on the other hand, do not pay taxes and must reinvest all of their profits, commonly called *net income* or *income above expense,* in the organization to better serve the public.

All private healthcare organizations must make a profit to survive. If expenses are greater than revenues, the organization experiences a loss. If revenues equal expenses, the organization breaks even. In both cases, nothing is left over to replace facilities and equipment, expand services, or pay for inflation costs. Some healthcare organizations can survive in the short run without making a profit because they use interest from investments to supplement revenues. The long-term viability of any private healthcare organization, however, depends on consistently making excess income. Box 20.3 presents a simplified example of an income statement from a neighborhood NFP nursing center.

Nurses and nurse managers directly affect an organization's ability to make a profit. Profits can be achieved or improved by decreasing costs or increasing revenues. In tight economic times, many managers think only in terms of cutting costs. Although cost-cutting measures are important, especially to keep prices down so that the organization will be competitive, ways to increase revenues also need to be explored.

BOX 20.3 **Income Statement of Revenues and Expenses From a Neighborhood Nursing Center: Fiscal Year Ending, December 31, 2010**		
Revenues		
Patient revenues	$283,200	
Grant income	$60,000	
Other operating revenues	$24,000	
TOTAL	$367,200	$367,200
Expenses		
Salary costs	$140,400	
Supplies	$64,400	
Other operating expenses (e.g., rent, utilities, administrative services)	$79,900	
TOTAL	$284,700	$284,700
Excess of revenues over expenses [profit][a]		$82,500

[a]Loss would be shown in parentheses ( ) or brackets [ ].

EXERCISE 20.4 Obtain a copy of an itemized patient bill from a healthcare organization and review the charges. What was the source and method of payment? How much of these charges was reimbursed? How much was charged for items you regularly use in clinical care?

COST-CONSCIOUS NURSING PRACTICES

Understanding What Is Required to Remain Financially Sound

Understanding what is required for a department or agency to remain financially sound requires that nurses move beyond thinking about costs for individual patients to thinking about income and expenses and numbers of patients needed to make a profit. In a fee-for-service environment, revenue is earned for every service provided. Therefore increasing the volume of services, such as diagnostic tests and patient visits, increases revenues. In a capitated environment in which one fee is paid for all services provided, increasing the overall number of patients served and decreasing the volume of services used is desirable. With capitation, nurses must strive to accomplish more with each visit to decrease return visits and complications. In today's value-based purchasing environment and reimbursement methodology, nurses need to understand their organization's reimbursement environment, identify how they can influence patient outcomes such as hospital-acquired conditions (HACs) and patient- and caregiver-centered experience of care, and have a strategy for realizing a profit in a specific circumstance.

Knowing Costs and Reimbursement Practices

As direct caregivers and case managers, nurses are constantly involved in determining the type and quantity of resources used for patients. This includes supplies, personnel, and time. Nurses need to know what costs are generated by their decisions and actions. Nurses also need to know what items cost and how they are paid for in an organization so that they can make cost-effective decisions. For example, nurses need to know per-item costs for supplies so that they can appropriately evaluate lower-cost substitutes.

Case management has become a very important role for all acute care organizations. Nurses must partner with case management in reaching organizational goals.

The ideal partnership includes the following contribution by the nursing staff: knowledge of patient goals, expected outcomes, and anticipated discharge date; comprehensive assessment of the patient and family; appropriate and timely interventions when the patient is not progressing as expected; appropriate management of pain, activity, skin integrity, bowel and bladder integrity, and cognition; ongoing patient and family education regarding discharge planning and preventing readmission; and identifying barriers to discharge (Bower, 2013).

In ambulatory and home health settings, nurses must be familiar with the various insurance plans that reimburse the organization. Each plan has different contract rules regarding preauthorization, types of services covered, required vendors, and so on. Although nurses must develop and implement their plans of care with full knowledge of these reimbursement practices, the payer does not totally drive the care. Nurses still advocate for patients in important ways while also working within the cost and contractual constraints. Moreover, when nurses understand the reimbursement practices, they can help patients maximize the resources available to them.

In hospitals, the cost of nursing care usually is not calculated or billed separately to patients; instead, it is part of the general per-diem charge. One major problem with this method is the assumption that all patients consume the same amount of nursing care, and the acuity of the patient is not considered. Another problem with bundling the charges for nursing care with the room rate is that nursing as a clinical service is not perceived by management as generating revenue for the hospital. Rather, nursing is perceived predominantly as an expense to the organization. Although this perception may not matter in a capitated setting in which all provider services are considered a cost, accurate nursing care cost data are needed to negotiate managed care contracts. In addition, patients do not see direct charges and so have no way to understand the monetary value of the services they receive.

EXERCISE 20.5 How was nursing care charged on the bill you obtained? What are the implications for nursing in being perceived as an expense rather than being associated with the revenue stream? Why will this perception be less important in a capitated environment?

Capturing All Charges in a Timely Fashion

Nurses also help contain costs by ensuring that all possible charges are captured. Several large hospitals report more than $1 million a year lost from supplies that were not charged. In hospitals, nurses must know which supplies are charged to patients and which ones are charged to the unit. In addition, the procedures and equipment used need to be accurately documented. In ambulatory and community settings, nurses often need to keep abreast of the codes that are used to bill services. These codes change yearly, and sometimes items are bundled together under one charge and sometimes they are broken down into different charges. Turning in charges in a timely manner is also important, because delayed billing negatively affects cash flow by extending the time before an organization is paid for services provided. This is particularly significant in smaller organizations.

> **EXERCISE 20.6** You used three intravenous (IV) catheters to do a particularly difficult venipuncture. Do you charge the patient for all three catheters? What if you accidentally contaminated one by touching the sheet? How is the catheter paid for if not charged to the patient? Who benefits and who loses when patients are not charged for supplies?

Using Time Efficiently

The adage that time is money is fitting in health care and refers to both the nurse's time and the patient's time. When nurses are organized and efficient in their care delivery and in scheduling and coordinating patients' care, the organization will save money. In a value-based purchasing environment, doing as much as possible during each episode of care is particularly important to decrease repeat visits and unnecessary service utilization. Because LOS is the most important predictor of hospital costs, patients who stay extra days cost the hospital a considerable amount. Decreasing LOS also makes room for other patients, thereby potentially increasing patient volume and hospital revenues. Nurses can become more efficient and effective by evaluating their major work processes and eliminating areas of redundancy and rework. Automated clinical information systems that support integrated practice at the point of care will also increase efficiency and improve patient outcomes.

> **EXERCISE 20.7** The Visiting Nurse Association (VNA) cannot file for reimbursement until all documentation of each visit has been completed. Typically, the paperwork is submitted a week after the visit. When the number of home visits increases rapidly, the paperwork often is not turned in for 2 weeks or more. What are the implications of this routine practice for the agency? Why would the VNA be very vulnerable financially during periods of heavy workload? What are some options for the nurse manager to consider to expedite the paperwork?

Discussing the Cost of Care With Patients

Talking with patients about the cost of care is important, although it may be uncomfortable. Discovering during a clinic visit that a patient cannot afford a specific medication or intervention is preferable to finding out several days later in a follow-up call that the patient has not taken the medication. Such information compels the clinical management team to explore optional treatment plans or to find resources to cover the costs. Talking with patients about costs is important in other ways, too. It involves the patients in the decision-making process and increases the likelihood that treatment plans will be followed. Patients also can make informed choices and better use the resources available to them if they have appropriate information about costs.

> **EXERCISE 20.8** A new patient visits the clinic and is given prescriptions for three medications that will cost about $120 per month. You check her chart and discover that she has Medicare (but not Part D) and no supplemental insurance. How can you determine whether she has the resources to buy this medicine each month and whether she is willing to buy it? If she cannot afford the medications, what are some options?

Evaluating Cost-Effectiveness of New Technologies

Cost-effectiveness is defined as a method to achieve a specific outcome for the least possible cost. The advent of new technologies is presenting dilemmas in managing costs. In the past, if a new piece of equipment was easier to use or benefited the patient in any way, nurses were apt to want to use it for everyone, no matter how much more it cost. Now they are forced to make decisions regarding which patients really need the new equipment and which ones will have good outcomes with the current equipment. Essentially, nurses are analyzing the cost-effectiveness of the new equipment with regard to different types of patients to allocate limited resources. This is a new and sometimes difficult way to think about patient care and at times may not feel like a caring way to make these decisions. However, such decisions conserve resources without jeopardizing patients' health and thus create the possibility of providing additional healthcare services.

EXERCISE 20.9 Last year, a new positive-pressure, needleless system for administering intravenous (IV) antibiotics was introduced. Because the system was so easy to use and convenient for patients, the nurses in the home infusion company where you work ordered it for everyone. Typically, patients get their IV antibiotics four times each day. The minibags and tubing for the regular procedure cost the agency $22 a day. The new system costs $24 per medication administration, or $96 a day. The agency receives the same per-diem (daily) reimbursement for each patient. Discuss the financial implications for the agency if this practice is continued. Generate some optional courses of action for the nurses to consider. How should these options be evaluated? What secondary costs, such as the cost of treating fewer needle-stick injuries, should be included?

Predicting and Using Nursing Resources Efficiently

Because healthcare organizations are service institutions, the largest part of their operating budget typically is for personnel. For hospitals, in particular, nurses are the largest group of employees and often account for most of the personnel budget. Staffing is the major area nurse managers can affect with respect to managing costs, and supply management is the second area. To understand why this is so, understanding the concepts of fixed and variable costs is helpful.

The total fixed costs in a unit are those costs that do not change as the volume of patients changes. In other words, with either a high or a low patient census, expenses related to rent, utilities, loan payments, administrative salaries, and salaries of the minimum number of staff to keep a unit open must be paid. Variable costs are costs that vary in direct proportion to patient volume or acuity. Examples include nursing personnel, supplies,

and medications. Break-even analysis (BEA) is a tool that uses fixed and variable costs for determining the specific volume of patients needed to just break even (Revenue = Expenses) or to realize a profit or loss. BEA can be calculated using this formula:

$$\text{Break-Even Quantity (N)} = \frac{\text{Fixed Costs (FC)}}{\text{Price (P)} - \text{Variable Cost per Patient (VC)}}$$

In hospitals and community health agencies, patient acuity systems are used to help managers predict nursing care requirements (see Chapter 13). These systems differentiate patients according to acuity of illness, functional status, and resource needs. Some nurses do not like these systems because they believe the essence of nursing is not captured. However, we need to remember that these are tools to help managers predict resource needs. Used appropriately, patient acuity systems can help evaluate changing practice patterns and patient acuity levels as well as provide information for budgeting processes.

EXERCISE 20.10 Given the definitions for fixed and variable costs, why do you think nurse managers have the greatest influence over costs through management of staffing and supplies?

Managing staffing and decreasing LOS can achieve the most immediate reductions in costs. Hospitals strive to lower costs so that they will attract new contracts and be attractive as partners in provider networks. Therefore staffing methods and patient care delivery models are being closely scrutinized. Work redesign, a process for changing the way to think about and structure the work of patient care, is the predominant strategy for developing systems that better utilize high-cost professionals and improve service quality. Increased staff retention, patient safety, and positive patient outcomes result from effective work redesign processes.

Using Research to Evaluate Standard Nursing Practices

Nurses use research to restructure their work to ensure they add value for patients. In 2015 MacDonnell et al. studied the impact of implementing advanced nurse practitioner (ANP) roles in an acute care hospital. The study included a sample of 13 ANPs and 23 managers,

---

LITERATURE PERSPECTIVE

Resource: Trepanier, S., & Hilsenbeck, J. (2014). A hospital system approach at decreasing falls with injuries and cost. *Nursing Economic$: The Journal for Health Care Leaders, 32*(3), 135-141.

Falls and fall-related injuries continue to challenge every healthcare organization. Falls are a nurse-sensitive quality outcome. Patient falls are a leading cause of injuries in hospitals, considered to be among the most expensive adverse event, and continue to be a patient safety concern. Researchers analyzed the impact of a standardized fall prevention program across 50 acute care hospitals in 11 states. The implementation of a standardized multifactorial program for adult patients appears to have reduced falls with injuries by 58.3% over a 2-year period, allowing for a potential cost avoidance reduction of $776,064 in 2013 dollars.

Implications for Practice

The findings from this study show that decreasing the variation in care and implementing evidence-based practice has the potential to decrease the overall cost of care. Thus nurses must employ a comprehensive fall prevention program. Such programs should, at a minimum, offer a standardized screening process using a valid and reliable tool, an ability to identify those at risk via visual cues (for example, a complete assessment), the ability to consult a subject matter expert, and the development of a patient-specific plan of care that will include targeted interventions aimed at mitigating the risk factors.

BOX 20.4 Strategies for Cost-Conscious Nursing Practice

1. Understanding what is required to remain financially sound
2. Knowing costs and reimbursement practices
3. Capturing all possible charges in a timely fashion
4. Using time efficiently
5. Discussing the costs of care with patients
6. Partnering with case management in reaching organizational goals
7. Evaluating cost-effectiveness of new technologies
8. Predicting and using nursing resources efficiently
9. Using research to evaluate standard nursing practices

---

consultants, physicians, and members of the healthcare team at large. Using a collective case study design, the authors noted that ANPs positively impacted the patient experience, outcomes, and safety. Box 20.4 summarizes some cost-conscious strategies for nursing practice. Further, the Literature Perspective describes the need for a business case related to outcomes.

BUDGETS

The basic financial document in most healthcare organizations is the budget—a detailed financial plan for carrying out the activities an organization wants to accomplish for a certain period. An organizational budget is a formal plan that is stated in terms of dollars and includes proposed income and expenditures. The budgeting process is an ongoing activity in which plans are made and revenues and expenses are managed to meet or exceed the goals of the plan. The management functions of planning and control are tied together through the budgeting process.

A budget requires managers to plan ahead and to establish explicit program goals and expectations. Changes in medical practices, reimbursement methods, competition, technology, demographics, and regulatory factors must be forecast to anticipate their effects on the organization. Planning encourages evaluation of different options and assists in more cost-effective use of resources.

EXERCISE 20.11 A community nursing organization performs an average of 36 intermittent catheterizations each day. A prepackaged catheterization kit that costs the organization $17 is used. The four items in the kit, when purchased individually, cost the organization a total of $5. What factors should be considered in evaluating the cost-effectiveness of the two sources of supplies?

Types of Budgets

Several types of interrelated budgets are used by well-managed organizations. Major budgets that are discussed in this chapter include the operating budget, the capital budget, and the cash budget. The way these budgets complement and support one another is depicted in Fig. 20.2.

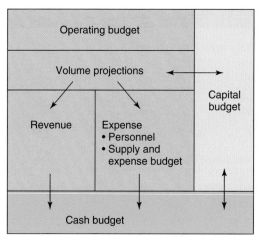

Fig. 20.2 Interrelationships of the operating, capital, and cash budgets.

TABLE 20.2 **Workload Calculation (Total Required Patient Care Hours)**

Patient Acuity Level[a]	Hours of Care Per Patient Day (HPPD)[b]	×	Patient Days[c]	=	Workload[d]
1	3.0		900		2700
2	5.2		3100		16,120
3	8.8		4000		35,200
4	13.0		1600		20,800
5	19.0		400		7600
Total			10,000		82,420

[a]1, Low; 5, high.
[b]Number of hours of care needed based on acuity levels and numbers.
[c]Each day represents a unit of time. For example, 900 patients equals 900 patient-days.
[d]Total number of hours of care needed based on acuity levels and numbers of patient days.

Many organizations also use program, product line, or special purpose budgets. Long-range budgets are used to help managers plan for the future.

Operating Budget

The operating budget is the financial plan for the day-to-day activities of the organization. The expected revenues and expenses generated from daily operations, given a specified volume of patients, are stated. Preparing and monitoring the operating budget, particularly the expense portion, is often the most time-consuming financial function of nurse managers.

The expense part of the operating budget consists of a personnel budget and a supply and expense budget for each cost center. A cost center is an organizational unit for which costs can be identified and managed. The personnel budget is the largest part of the operating budget for most nursing units.

Before the personnel budget can be established, the volume of work predicted for the budget period must be calculated. A unit of service measure appropriate to the work of the unit is used. Units of service may be, for example, patient days, clinic or home visits, hours of service, admissions, deliveries, or treatments. Another factor needed to calculate the workload is the patient acuity mix. The formula for calculating the workload or the required patient care hours for inpatient units is as follows: Workload volume = Hours of care per patient day × Number of patient days (Table 20.2).

In some organizations, the workload is established by the financial office and given to the nurse manager. In other organizations, nurse managers forecast the volume. In both situations, nurse managers should inform administrators about any factors that might affect the accuracy of the forecast, such as changes in physician practice patterns, new treatment modalities, changes in inpatient versus outpatient treatment practices, and changes in technology or equipment.

The next step in preparing the personnel budget is to determine how many staff members will be needed to provide the care. (This topic is discussed in more detail in Chapter 13.) Because some people work full-time and others work part-time, full-time equivalents (FTEs) are used in this step rather than positions. Generally, those costs do not change as the volume of patients changes. One-half of an FTE (0.5 FTE) equates to 20 hours per week. The number of hours per FTE may vary within an organization in relation to staffing plans, so it is important to check agency-specific meaning.

Most organizations use 2080 hours to equal a full-time employee. The 2080 hours paid to an FTE in a year consists of both productive hours and nonproductive hours. Productive hours are paid time that is worked. Nonproductive hours are paid time that is not worked, such as vacation, holiday, orientation, and sick time. Education may be viewed as either depending on the organization's value for learning. Before the number of FTEs

---

BOX 20.5   Productive Hours Calculation

Method 1:   Add All Nonproductive Hours/FTE and Subtract from Paid Hours/FTE
                 Example: Vacation   15 days
                                   Holiday   7 days
                                   Average sick time   4 days
                                   _____
                                   Total   26 days
                 26 × 8^a hours = 208 nonproductive hours/FTE
                 2080 − 208 = 1872 productive hours/FTE

Method 2:   Multiply Paid Hours/FTE by Percentage of Productive Hours/FTE
                 Example: Productive hours = 90%/FTE
                                (1872 productive hours of total 2080 = 90%)
                                2080 × 0.90 = 1872 productive hours/FTE

Total FTE Calculation

Required Patient Care Hours ÷ Productive Hours Per FTE   = Total FTEs Needed
82,420   ÷ 1872   = 44 FTEs

FTE, Full-time equivalent.
^{a}Full-time equivalent. FTE pattern.

needed for the workload can be calculated, the number of productive hours per FTE is determined by subtracting the total number of nonproductive hours per FTE from total paid hours. Alternatively, payroll reports can be reviewed to determine the percentage of paid hours that are productive for each FTE. Finally, the total number of FTEs needed to provide the care is calculated by dividing the total patient care hours required by the number of productive hours per FTE (Box 20.5).

The total number of FTEs calculated by this method represents the number needed to provide care each day of the year. The total FTEs do not reflect the number of positions or the number of people working each day. In fact, the number of positions may be much higher, particularly if many part-time nurses are employed. On any given day, some nurses may be scheduled for their regular day off or vacation and others may be off because of illness. Also, some positions that do not involve direct patient care, such as nurse managers or unit secretaries, may not be replaced during nonproductive time. Only one FTE is budgeted for any position that is not covered with other staff when the employee is off.

EXERCISE 20.12 Change the number of patients at each acuity level listed in Table 20.2, but keep the total number of patients the same. Recalculate the required total workload. Discuss how changes in patient acuity affect nursing resource requirements.

The next step is to prepare a daily staffing plan and to establish positions (see Chapter 13). Once the positions are established, the labor costs that comprise the personnel budget can be calculated. Factors that must be addressed include straight-time hours, overtime hours, differentials and premium pay, raises, and benefits. Differentials and premiums are extra pay for working specific times, such as evening or night shifts and holidays. Benefits usually include health and life insurance, Social Security payments, and retirement plans. Benefits often cost an additional 25% to 30% of a full-time employee's salary. In other words, about one-third of the employee expenses are related to benefits and have to be seriously considered when adding an FTE.

EXERCISE 20.13 If the percentage of productive hours per FTE is 80%, how many worked or productive hours are there per FTE? If total patient care hours are 82,420, how many FTEs will be needed?

The supply and expense budget is often called the *other-than-personnel services (OTPS) expense budget.* This budget includes a variety of items used in daily unit activities, such as medical and office supplies, minor equipment, and books and journals; it also includes orientation, training, and travel. Although different methods are used to calculate the supply and expense budget, the previous year's expenses usually are used as a baseline. This baseline is adjusted for projected patient volume and specific circumstances known to affect expenses, such as predictable personnel turnover, which increases orientation and training expenses. A percentage factor is also added to adjust for inflation.

The final component of the operating budget is the revenue budget. The revenue budget projects the income that the organization will receive for providing patient care. Historically, nurses have not been directly involved with developing the revenue budget, although this is changing. In most hospitals, the revenue budget is established by the financial office and given to nurse managers. The anticipated revenues are calculated according to the price per patient day. Data about the volume and types of patients and reimbursement sources (i.e., the case mix and the payer mix) are necessary to project revenues in any healthcare organization. Even when nurse managers do not participate in developing the revenue budget, learning about the organization's revenue base is essential for good decision making.

Capital Expenditure Budget

The capital expenditure budget reflects expenses related to the purchase of major capital items such as equipment and the physical plant. A capital expenditure must have a useful life of more than 1 year and must exceed a cost level specified by the organization. The minimum cost requirement for capital items in healthcare organizations is usually $300 to $1000, although some organizations have a much higher level. Anything below that minimum is considered a routine operating cost.

Capital expenses are kept separate from the operating budget because their high cost would make the costs of providing patient care appear too high during the year of purchase. To account for capital expenses, the costs of capital items are depreciated. This means that each year, over the useful life of the equipment, a portion of its cost is allocated to the operating budget as an expense. Therefore capital expenditures are subtracted from revenues and, in turn, affect profits.

Organizations usually set aside a fixed amount of money for capital expenditures each year. Complete, well-documented justifications are needed, because the competition for limited resources is stiff. Justifications should be developed using the principle of any business case and should include, at a minimum, projected amount of use; services duplicated or replaced; safety considerations; need for space, personnel, or building renovation; effect on operational revenues and expenses; and contribution to the strategic plan.

Cash Budget

The cash budget is the operating plan for monthly cash receipts and disbursements. Organizational survival depends on paying bills on time. Organizations can be making a profit and still run out of cash. In fact, a profitable trend, such as a rapidly growing census, can induce a cash shortage because of increased expenses in the short run. Major capital expenditures can also cause a temporary cash crisis and so must be staggered in a strategic way. Because cash is the lifeblood of any organization, the cash budget is as important as the operating and capital budgets.

The financial officer prepares the cash budget in large organizations. Understanding the cash budget helps nurse managers discern (1) when constraints on spending are necessary, even when the expenditures are budgeted, and (2) the importance of carefully predicting when budgeted items will be needed.

The Budgeting Process

The steps in the budgeting process are similar in most healthcare organizations, although the budgeting period, budget timetable, and level of manager and employee participation vary. Budgeting is done annually and in relation to the organization's fiscal year. A fiscal year exists for financial purposes and can begin at any point on the calendar. In the title of some financial reports, a phrase similar to "FYE June 30, 2019" appears and means that this report is for the fiscal year ending on the date stated.

Major steps in the budgeting process include gathering information and planning, developing unit budgets, developing the cash budget, negotiating and revising, and using feedback to control budget results and improve future plans. A timetable with specific dates for implementing the budgeting process is developed by each organization. The timetable may be anywhere from 3 to 9 months. The widespread use of computers for budgeting is reducing the time span for budgeting in many organizations. Box 20.6 outlines the budgeting process.

The information-gathering and planning phase provides nurse managers with data essential for developing their individual budgets. This step begins with an

BOX 20.6   Outline of Budgeting Process

1. Gathering information and planning
   - Environmental assessment
   - Mission, goals, and objectives
   - Program priorities
   - Financial objectives
   - Assumptions (employee raises, inflation, volume projections)
2. Developing unit and departmental budgets
   - Operating budgets
   - Capital budgets
3. Developing cash budgets
4. Negotiating and revising
5. Evaluating
   - Analysis of variance
   - Critical performance reports

Modified from Finkler, S. A., Kovner, C. T., & Jones, C. (2012). *Financial management for nurse managers and executives* (4th ed.). St. Louis: Saunders.

environmental assessment that helps the organization understand its position in relation to the entire community. The assessment includes, for example, the changing healthcare needs of the population, influential economic factors such as inflation and unemployment, differences in reimbursement patterns, and patient satisfaction.

Next, the organization's long-term goals and objectives are reassessed in light of the organization's mission and the environmental analysis. This helps all managers situate the budgeting process for their individual units in relation to the whole organization. At this point, programs are prioritized so that resources can be allocated to programs that best help the organization achieve its long-term goals.

Specific, measurable objectives are then established, and the budgets must meet these objectives. The financial objectives might include limiting expenditure increases or making reductions in personnel costs by designated percentages. Nurse managers also set operational objectives for their units that are in concert with the rest of the organization. This is where units or departments interpret what effect the changes in operational activities will have on them. For instance, how will using case managers and care maps for selected patients affect a particular unit? Establishing the unit-level objectives is also a good place for involving direct care nurses in setting the future direction of the unit.

Along with the specific organization- and unit-level operating objectives, managers need the organization-wide assumptions that underpin the budgeting process. Explicit assumptions regarding salary increases, inflation factors, and volume projections for the next fiscal year are essential. With this information in hand, nurse managers can develop the operating and capital budgets for their units. These are usually developed in tandem, because each affects the other. For instance, purchasing a new monitoring system will have implications for the supplies used, staffing, and staff training.

The cash budget is developed after unit and department operating and capital budgets. Then the negotiation and revision process begins in earnest. This is a complex process, because changes in one budget usually require changes in others. Learning to defend and negotiate budgets is an important skill for nurse managers. Nurse managers who successfully negotiate budgets know how costs are allocated and are comfortable speaking about what resources are contained in each budget category. They also can clearly and specifically depict what the effect of not having that resource will be on patient, nurse, or organizational outcomes.

EXERCISE 20.14 If you can interview a nurse manager, ask to review the budgeting process. Ask specifically about the budget timetable, operating objectives, and organizational assumptions. What was the level of involvement for nurse managers and nurses in each step of budget preparation? Is there a budget manual?

The final and ongoing phase of the budgeting process relates to the control function of management. Feedback is obtained regularly so that organizational activities can be adjusted to maintain efficient operations. Variance analysis is the major control process used. A variance is the difference between the projected budget and the actual performance for a particular account. For expenses, a favorable, or positive, variance means that the budgeted amount was greater than the actual amount spent. An unfavorable, or negative, variance means that the budgeted amount was less than the actual amount spent. Positive and negative variances cannot be interpreted as good or bad without further investigation. For example, if fewer supplies were used than were budgeted, this would appear as a positive variance and the unit would save money. This would be good news if it means that supplies were used more efficiently and patient outcomes remained the same or improved. A problem might be suggested, however, if using fewer or less-expensive supplies led to poorer patient outcomes. Or it might mean that exactly the right amount of supplies was used but that the patient census was less than budgeted. To help managers interpret and use variance information better, some institutions use flexible budgets that automatically account for census variances.

EXERCISE 20.15 Examine Table 20.3 and identify major budget variances for the current month. Are they favorable or unfavorable? What additional information would help you explain the variances? What are some possible causes for each variance? Are the causes you identified controllable by the nurse manager? Why or why not? Is a favorable variance on expenses always desirable? Why or why not?

Managing the Unit-Level Budget

How is a unit-based budget managed? At a minimum, nurse managers are responsible for meeting the fiscal goals related to the personnel and the supply and expense part of the operations budget. Typically, monthly reports of operations (see Table 20.3) are sent to nurse managers, who then investigate and explain the underlying cause of variances greater than 5%. Many factors can cause budget variances, including patient census, patient acuity, vacation and benefit time, illness, orientation, staff meetings, workshops, employee mix, salaries, and staffing levels. To accurately interpret budget variances, nurse managers need reliable data about patient census, acuity, and LOS; payroll reports; and unit productivity reports.

Nurse managers can control *some* of the factors that cause variances, but not all. After the causes are determined and if they are controllable by the nurse manager,

TABLE 20.3   Statement of Operations Showing Profit and Loss From a Neighborhood Nursing Center: March 2018

CURRENT MONTH[a]				YEAR-TO-DATE[a]		
Budget	Actual	Variance	Revenues	Budget	Actual	Variance
Patient Revenues						
21,500	22,050	550	Insurance payment	64,500	66,150	1650
1500	1550	50	Donations	4500	4750	250
23,000	23,600	600	Net patient revenues	69,000	70,900	1900
Nonpatient Revenues						
5000	5000	0	Grant income (#138-FG)	15,000	15,000	0
500	500	0	Rent income	1500	1500	0
5500	5500	0	Net nonpatient revenues	16,500	16,500	0
28,500	29,100	600	Net revenues	85,500	87,400	1900
Expenses						
Personnel						
7750	8500	(750)	Managerial/professional	23,250	24,400	(1150)
2000	1800	200	Clerical/technical	6000	5800	200
9750	10,300	(550)	Net salaries and wages	29,250	30,200	(950)
1200	1400	(200)	Benefits	3600	4000	(400)
10,950	11,700	(750)	Net personnel	32,850	34,200	(1350)
Nonpersonnel						
2500	2500	0	Office operating expenses	7500	7500	0
2000	2100	(100)	Supplies and materials	3000	3050	(50)
300	450	(150)	Travel expenses	900	450	450
4800	5050	(250)	Net nonpersonnel	11,400	11,000	400
15,750	16,750	(1000)	Net expenses	44,250	45,200	(950)
Revenues Over/Under Expenses						
3750	3350	(400)	Net income	11,250	11,800	550

[a]Values expressed in 000s.

steps are taken to prevent the variance from occurring in the future. However, even uncontrollable variances that increase expenses might require actions of nurse managers. For example, if supply costs rise drastically because a new technology is being used, the nurse manager might have to look for other areas where the budget can be cut. Information learned from analyzing variances also is used in future budget preparations and management activities.

In addition, nurse managers monitor the productivity of their units. Productivity is the ratio of outputs to inputs; that is, productivity equals output/input. In nursing, outputs are nursing services and are measured by hours of care, number of home visits, and so forth. The inputs are the resources used to provide the services such as personnel hours and supplies. Only decreasing the inputs or increasing the outputs can increase productivity. Hospitals often use hours per patient day (HPPD) as one measure of productivity. For example, if the standard of care in a critical care unit is 12 HPPD, then 360 hours of care are required for 30 patients for 1 day. When 320 hours of care are provided, the productivity rating is 113% (360/320 = 1.13), meaning that the unit was over-productive or very productive. One must consider the quality component into any productivity model related to care. In home health, the number of visits per day per registered nurse is one measure of productivity. If the standard is 5 visits per day but the weekly average was 4.8 visits per day, then productivity was decreased. Variances in productivity are not inherently favorable or unfavorable and thus require investigation and explanation before judgments can be made about them. For example, an explanation of the variance (4.8 visits per day) might include the fact that one visit took twice the amount of time normally spent on a home visit because of patient needs, thus preventing the nurse from making the standard 5 visits per day. The extra time spent on one patient was productive time but not adequately accounted for by this measure of productivity (visits per day).

Although they do not have a direct accountability for the budget, direct care nurses play an important role in meeting budget expectations. Many nurse managers find that routinely sharing the budget and budget-monitoring activities with the whole team fosters an appreciation of the relationship between cost and the mission to deliver high-quality patient care. Providing the team with access to cost and utilization data allows them to identify patterns and participate in selecting appropriate, cost-effective practice options that work for the staff and patients. Managers and staff who work in partnership to understand that cost versus care is a dilemma to manage rather than a problem to solve will develop innovative, cost-conscious nursing practices that produce good outcomes for patients, nurses, and the organization.

CONCLUSION

Managing costs and understanding budgets are important information for nurses in all positions within the organization. The current emphasis on "value" makes knowing what costs are and how to control them important. Being able to understand the basics of a budget helps nurses at all levels in an organization cite the economic impact of decisions related to care. Considering the paramount influence that nurses have on establishing the value contribution, taking actions at the point of care (such as capturing charges in a timely manner) are as important as actions in the manager's office (such as ensuring proper resource allocation) or actions in the executive suite (such as projecting patient volume or changes in delivery). To further develop the value proposition, the importance of engaging the entire team cannot be overstated. Planning significantly impacts the final outcome, which puts nursing in a positive or limited perspective in an organization.

THE SOLUTION

We began by obtaining data on the percentage of admitted patients who were under an observation status compared with others. In partnership with the analytics department we determined the current cost of providing care (using the current model) as well as the reimbursement for observation patients. We quickly noticed that the cost of providing the care far exceeded the reimbursement. We developed a multidisciplinary team in hopes of defining a new model of care of observation patients. First, we identified a new location to cohort observation status patients. In collaboration with the medical staff and case management we determined admission and discharge criteria. We determined that if we provided a case manager and an advanced practice nurse 24/7, we could significantly decrease the length of stay (LOS) and therefore decrease the total cost of care per patient. We launched a pilot unit in one hospital for a period of 180 days. Upon review of our data we noticed a significant reduction in LOS from 57 hours to 24 hours and a significant decrease in cost of care by $300 per patient per day. We launched a similar unit in all hospitals, refined our processes using our lessons learned from the pilot, and within 1 year we decreased the overall cost of care for observation patients by $3.5 million over a period of 12 months.

Would this be a suitable approach for you? Why?

Sylvain Trepanier

REFLECTIONS

Consider a recent "typical" day in the clinical area. Did you consider costs as you provided care to a patient? Were you aware of the financial resources of that patient as part of your decision-making process for discharge planning? What specific activities did you do that led to costs to the patient or organization? Could you have avoided any costs?

THE EVIDENCE

Falls with injuries continues to be a major problem for hospitals across the United States. Furthermore, since 2005, both The Joint Commission and the Centers for Medicare and Medicaid Services deployed programs aimed at decreasing falls with injuries. Therefore many nurse leaders are asked to develop and deploy best practices to decrease falls with injuries. Trepanier and Hilsenbeck (2014) published a study demonstrating the value contribution of implementing an evidence-based standardized protocol in a multihospital system. The program was deployed over a period of 4 months in 50 acute care hospitals (11 states). The authors identified a decrease in falls with injuries of 41% and 31 % over a 2-year period compared with baseline. Using a cost–benefit analysis model, they were able to identify that the program offered cost avoidance of $776,064 for the healthcare system.

TIPS FOR MANAGING COSTS AND BUDGETS

- Know the major changes in the organization and how they might affect the organization's budget.
- Analyze the supplies you use in providing care and what is commonly missing as one way to make recommendations about supply needs.
- Evaluate what each of your patients would find most helpful during the time you will be caring for them.
- Decide which of your actions create costs for the patient or the organization.
- Be aware of how changes in patient acuity and patient census affect staffing requirements and the unit budget.
- Know how charges are generated and how the documentation systems relate to billing.
- Be knowledgeable about the anticipated discharge day and discharge plan, and include the patient and the family in the plan upon admission.
- Examine the upsides and downsides of the cost–care polarity thoughtfully.

REFERENCES

Bower, K. A. (2013). Managing care: The crucial nursing-case management partnership. *Nurse Leader, 10*(6), 26–29.

Carman, K. G., Eibner, C., & Paddock, S. M. (2015). Trends in health insurance enrollment, 2013-15. *Health Affairs, 34*(6), 1–5.

Centers for Medicare & Medicaid Services (CMS). (2017). Medicare Benefit Policy Manual. In *Chapter 1 – Inpatient Hospital Services Covered Under Part A.* https://www.cms.gov/Regulations-and-Guidance/Guidance/Manuals/downloads/bp102c01.pdf.

Centers for Medicare & Medicaid Services. (2015). *Hospital value-based purchasing program.* https://www.cms.gov/Outreach-and-Education/Medicare-Learning-Network-MLN/MLNProducts/Downloads/Hospital_VBPurchasing_Fact_Sheet_ICN907664.pdf.

Healthy People 2020. (2014). https://www.healthypeople.gov/sites/default/files/LHI-ProgressReport-ExecSum_0.pdf.

Jiwani, A., Himmelstein, D., Woolhandler, S., & Kahn, J. G. (2014). Billing and insurance related administrative costs in Unites States health care: Synthesis of micro-costing evidence. *BMC Health Services Research, 14,* 556.

Kaiser Family Foundation. (2015). *Medicaid moving forward.* http://kff.org/health-reform/issue-brief/medicaid-moving-forward/.

Medicaid. (2014). *Managed Care.* https://www.medicaid.gov/medicaid/managed-care/index.html.

Trepanier, S., & Hilsenbeck, J. (2014). A hospital system approach at decreasing falls with injuries and cost. *Nursing Economic$: The Journal for Health Care Leaders, 32*(3), 135–141.

21

Selecting, Developing, and Evaluating Staff

Diane M. Twedell

LEARNING OUTCOMES

- Compare and contrast the various methods of employee performance appraisal.
- Describe the principle that supports behavioral interviewing technique.
- Provide examples of appropriate and inappropriate performance feedback.
- Articulate the importance of a job description in the orientation of a new employee.

KEY TERMS

behavioral interviewing
coaching

empowerment
performance appraisal

position description

THE CHALLENGE

Hiring the right staff for the team is an important responsibility of the nurse manager. Finding a fit upfront makes the orientation, development, and team building on a unit stronger and easier, not to mention the financial investment of a new nurse. I recently took on a nurse manager role in an outpatient specialty clinic and wanted to get started on the right foot with hiring new nursing staff. As a new nurse manager, I wanted to have staff support and buy in for the recruitment process. Staff on the patient care area had never been included in an interview process for new staff. I needed to determine how to empower staff nurses to engage in the interview process and select nurses that were a cultural fit with the patient care area.

What would you do if you were this nurse?

Monica Boege, RN, BSN, MBA
Nurse Manager, Mayo Clinic Health System, Rochester, MN

INTRODUCTION

Healthcare organizations are businesses that are economically driven and emphasize providing the highest-quality care at an affordable price. That said, they also are difficult businesses because they require financial solvency to provide such a personal issue as health care and service for patients. The nurse leader is a key individual whose leadership can directly influence quality, safety, service, and satisfaction for patients and direct care nurses. The nurse leader and manager is really the chief retention officer of a patient care area and has a huge impact on the environment for patient care. The nurse leader, manager, and direct care nurses help shape the environment and learning milieu for new employees. That makes it vital for the entire work unit to understand

377

each individual's role in meeting the goals for quality patient care. Nurses must clearly understand what is expected of their performance, including the ramifications of not meeting those expectations. This can be achieved only when all members of the organization have clearly defined roles and overall objectives.

The ongoing development, mentoring, and coaching of staff must be emphasized. Once a nurse manager has hired the new direct care nurse, the ongoing support mentioned previously is essential. Think of a tree and how it needs ongoing care and feeding; this is similar to the new nurse who requires ongoing development, performance feedback, and coaching to reach optimal growth.

ROLES IN AN ORGANIZATION

All individuals within an organization play a role. This role requires an individual to assume the personal as well as the formal expectations of a specified position. Employees must have clear role expectations and perceive that their contributions are valued. Employees who understand their role and are empowered to succeed in their role have been noted to demonstrate increased personal health, job satisfaction, and individual performance. They are then more likely to be committed to the organization and to provide a higher level of patient care. These principles are applicable to both leaders and followers. A consistent focus on developing staff creates a learning environment directed toward excellence.

Nursing program graduates enter the profession with various levels of educational and life experiences.

The nurse leader plays an integral role in assisting these individuals in the development and acquisition of the complex role as professional nurse. Role development evolves over time and may occur numerous times in a nurse's career. As an example, a registered nurse (RN) who is an expert medical-surgical nurse takes a new position in the operating room as a circulating RN; this is a new role for the nurse. Whenever such a change occurs, the nurse is likely to feel less confident and competent than before, because instead of typical functioning, the nurse is also focused on learning the new role. Refer to the Theory Box for more information on the complexity of taking on a new role.

Position descriptions provide written guidelines detailing the roles and responsibilities of a specific position within the organization. The position description reflects functions and requirements of specific role in an institution. Box 21.1 demonstrates examples of expectations for a nurse in an ambulatory care environment.

BOX 21.1   Excerpts from an Ambulatory Care Nurse Job Description

- Assesses comprehensive data including physical, psychosocial, emotional, and spiritual needs of the patient.
- Involves patient, family, and healthcare team members in formulating a culturally appropriate plan of care.
- Implements plan of care in partnership with patient, family, and healthcare team.

THEORY BOX

Theory/Contributor	Key Ideas	Application to Practices
Dynamics in Organizations Kahn, Wolfe, Quinn, Snoek, & Rosenthal (1964) developed this theory.	Roles within organizations affect an individual's interactions with others. Acquisition of these roles is time-dependent and varies based on individual experiences and value systems. For effective communication to take place, role expectations for performance must be understood by all individuals involved.	The role of the professional nurse is complex. Role acquisition, role clarity, and role performance are enhanced by the use of clear position descriptions and evaluation standards.

Adapted from Kahn, R. L., Wolfe, D. M., Quinn, R. P., Snoek, J. D., & Rosenthal, R. A. (1964). *Occupational stress: Studies in role conflict and ambiguity.* New York: Wiley.

EXERCISE 21.1 Obtain a position description for a registered nurse from an ambulatory care setting and a hospital. Compare them and analyze the general categories. Are specific behaviors outlined? What competencies are different? What competencies are similar?

The position description should reflect current practice guidelines and competency-based requirements. As nursing care models shift to the ambulatory setting, home, and community, nurses must have a clear understanding of the performance that is expected. The nurse is responsible for clearly understanding the roles of the patient care assistant to whom care is delegated. Clear and concise position descriptions for all employees provide the basis for roles in an organization.

SELECTION OF STAFF

The selection of staff is one of the most important functions that nurse managers complete in their daily routines. Nurse managers want the most qualified individual for the position who also fits the culture of the patient care environment and organization. If an applicant values that the needs of the patient come first, and this value is also articulated via the organization, the individual has similar values. Nurse managers need to decide if staff members will be included in the interview process and then provide appropriate education to them about the interview process. Doucette (2016) notes that direct care nurse involvement in the hiring process is linked to positive engagement scores and staff retention.

The nurse manager and the applicant both must prepare for the interview to truly determine whether the individual is a good fit for the organization. The manager's focus before and during the interview is to be prepared and have well–thought-out questions. Identification of the attributes wanted in a direct care nurse can help guide the selection of interview questions. Interview questions should be directed to evaluate values and critical thinking skills. The phrase "the best predictor of future behavior is past behavior" is the premise on which behavioral interviewing is based. Behavioral interviewing requires applicants to provide an example of a situation that they experienced that highlights how they deal with a particular issue. An example of a behavioral interview question could be: *Tell me about a time when you were working in a group and there were problems with other*

individuals who were not doing their fair share. What did you do to maintain a team environment?

The interview should be held in a private location that will not be interrupted. It is helpful to provide the applicant information about the position through an e-mail and attach a copy of the position description for the applicant to review before the interview. Applicants appreciate the opportunity to tour the patient care area either before or after the actual interview. At the conclusion of the interview, the nurse manager should indicate when applicants will hear about their interview result, who will contact them, and how they will be notified. Applicants should be thanked for their time and interest in pursuing a position. Because people typically are on their best behavior during an interview, any concerns should be taken seriously. Those who are involved in interviews have the accountability of sharing such concerns and of answering questions applicants have in the most honest way possible.

Applicants also have responsibilities in the interview process (see Chapter 27 for more details). The applicant should arrive on time and alone and be appropriately dressed in business attire. The applicant should be prepared to answer questions honestly and thoughtfully. The use of behavioral-based interviewing requires the applicant to describe previous situations and how they were handled. They may also be asked to describe why they are interested in working in a specific work area. At the end of the interview, applicants should thank the nurse manager for his or her time and also provide any specific follow-up information the manager has requested. A formal note of appreciation for the interview may be sent by the applicant afterward.

EXERCISE 21.2 You are applying for a position as a primary care registered nurse in a community-based outpatient clinic in a rural community and are invited to an interview. Outline how you will prepare for this interview and what questions you will ask.

DEVELOPING STAFF

Once the interview and offer are completed and an applicant has accepted the position, strategies are used to help the individual acclimate to the organization and new role. Organizations use a variety of approaches, including orientation to the organization, department, and role or new

LITERATURE PERSPECTIVE

Resource: Murray-Parahi, P., DiGiacomo, M., Jackson, D., & Davidson, P. (2016). New graduate registered nurse transition into primary health care roles: An integrative literature review. *Journal of Clinical Nursing, 25,* 3084–3101.

This publication reflects on summarizing the literature available that describes new graduate nurse transition to professional practice within the primary healthcare (PHC) setting. Electronic databases were searched for the terms of *transition, new graduate registered nurse,* and *primary health care.* No articles addressed all key concepts.

An abundance of articles focused on the new graduate registered nurse transition into acute care practice within the hospital, but a gap existed in the literature related to PHC. This is of concern as healthcare reform continues to shift patient care from hospital to community-based care settings.

Implications for Practice

New graduate nurses transitioning to the PHC setting are in a distinct setting where there are fewer resources, less structure, and higher levels of isolation and autonomy. Undergraduate nurses need to have opportunity to have clinical experiences in the PHC, and educators and health service providers need to embrace this practice setting for students. New graduates are already transitioning into this setting, and the larger nursing community needs to help make them successful.

---

graduate residency programs that may provide ongoing support and education for up to a year. General orientation to the organization is usually a structured program for every new employee. It typically includes the mission, vision, values, benefits, safety programs, and other specific topics for the day-to-day operation of the organization. The orientation period must be used efficiently to benefit both the employee and the organization.

Retention of new nursing personnel begins on the day of their hire, because costs for replacement and turnover can be substantial. Factors related to turnover cost include human resource expenses, temporary replacement costs, lost productivity, training, relocation expenses, and terminal pay cuts. Although the cost of turnover may be cited differently, the cost of replacement is high. Nurse managers and educators can play a pivotal role in ongoing development of staff. A watchful eye and recognition of talents displayed by nurses throughout their onboarding and ongoing employment can help retain nurses in an organization. A nurse educator may see that a direct-care nurse is excellent at providing diabetic patient education in a primary care clinic. The nurse educator can recommend the idea of becoming a certified diabetic educator as a development goal.

Orientation is a time for new employees to learn the work environment and the staff. Many institutions use preceptors who are direct care nurses who are strong role models to help orient new staff. A preceptor provides a supportive relationship in a specific work environment to orient or transition staff (Usher, Nolan,

Reser, Owens, & Tollefson, 1999). Clipper and Cherry (2015) note that preceptors play a highly influential role and are responsible for providing a smooth transition.

Preceptors work with orientees to complete a needs assessment to help direct and guide the orientation of the new employee in the clinical setting. An important first step is to determine how a new employee likes to learn. Various learning style assessment tools are available for preceptors to use. When preceptors understand the learning style of new employees, a better focus for implementation of orientation goals is provided. New employees work with preceptors who understand specifically how to address the individualized learning needs. For example, an orientee may learn best by observing a complex dressing change before actually performing it on a patient. Refer to the Literature Perspective for information on orientation and role transition in a primary care environment.

Continued development of the staff is a unique role for the nurse leader. Every member of the nursing team has ongoing needs for continued growth and development. It is key for nurse leaders to get to know their employees and what their interests and career goals are. Formal meetings and everyday interactions with direct care nurses help a nurse leader learn what is important to employees. Specific individual development plans can be determined for each employee.

Empowerment strategies are useful for individual professional development as well as for overall development of staff. Empowerment is a process that

RESEARCH PERSPECTIVE

Resource: Burke, D., & Flanagan, J. (2017). Characteristics of nurse directors that contribute to registered nurse satisfaction. *The Journal of Nursing Administration, 47 (4),* 219–225.

This article focuses on the exploration of registered nurses' (RNs) and Nurse Directors' (NDs) perceptions of leadership on units with high RN satisfaction scores. A qualitative study design using appreciative inquiry was the source of data collection. Interviews were done with direct-care nurses and NDs at a large Magnet® hospital. Nurses were asked, "What do you believe are your NDs strongest leadership qualities that contribute to your job satisfaction?" NDs were asked, "What do you believe are your strongest leadership qualities that contribute to your staff nurses' job satisfaction?" Content analysis indicated that staff nurses and NDs gave similar answers, including empowerment, visibility and authentic presence, passion and vision, role modeling of professional behavior, and clear expectations.

Implications for Practice

Nursing leadership is palpable and recognized by direct care nurses. Nurse leaders who understand what satisfies their staff are able to successfully recruit and retain nurses in the practice environment.

acknowledges the values and judgment of individuals and trusts that their decisions will be the correct ones. For individuals to feel empowered, the environment must be open and they must feel safe to explore and develop their own potential. The organizational environment must encourage individuals to use the freedom of making decisions while retaining the accountability for the consequences of those decisions. Montani, Courcy, Giorgi, and Boilard (2015) shared that nurse leaders who enact empowering practices enable nurses to experience greater competence, meaningfulness, and self-determination. Positive feedback, achievement recognition, and support for new ideas enhance employees' feelings of empowerment and their ability to perform effectively. Refer to the Research Perspective for more about how manager behaviors empower nurses.

EXERCISE 21.3 Describe behaviors demonstrated by a nurse leader that ultimately empower direct care nurses within a patient care area.

PERFORMANCE APPRAISALS

Feedback to employees regarding their performance is one of the strongest rewards an organization can provide. Performance appraisals are individual evaluations of work performance. Ideally, appraisals are conducted on an ongoing basis, not just at the conclusion of a predetermined period. Performance appraisals are generally done annually and also may be required after a scheduled orientation period for new employees. Durcho et al. (2016) noted that "managers should meet with employees more than once a year so they know their expectations and to allow for improvement from both ends" (p. 46).

Performance appraisals can be formal or informal. An informal appraisal might be as simple as immediately praising the individual for performance recognized. A compliment from a family member or patient might be conveyed. Some work areas have a specific bulletin board for thank-you notes from patients and their families. Sometimes a simple "Thank you for all your hard work today!" can be extended from the nurse manager to the staff. The more specific the feedback can be, however, the more influential it is on reinforcing specific performances.

The formal performance appraisal involves written documentation according to specific organizational guidelines. The formal performance appraisal usually involves the use of a standard form or method developed by the organization to measure employee performance. Employees must have a clear understanding of their job description. Providing a new employee a position description is helpful because it can provide a basis for how their performance will be measured. The example in Box 21.2 illustrates an excerpt from a performance appraisal form in which a nurse manager can evaluate a direct care nurse related to health teaching and promotion.

BOX 21.2 Performance Appraisal, Clinical Registered Nurse

Health Teaching and Health Promotion

___a. Uses teaching strategies appropriate to patient's condition and learning needs.

___b. Uses health promotion to support patients and families in developing skills for self-management.

___c. Maintains a safe, clean, and organized environment for patients, families, and staff.

Performance Levels (Enter code in blank.)

AE: Achieves expectations

NFD: Needs further development.

UTA/NA: Unable to assess/not applicable

BOX 21.4 Examples of Goals

1. Obtain specialty certification as a Critical Care Registered Nurse (CCRN) from the American Association of Critical Care Nurses by the end of next January.
2. Participate in shared governance committee as unit representative next year.

Accomplishments (12 Months Later Summary)

1. Successful completion of CCRN examination (see documentation submitted).
2. Participated in every unit council meeting (see attendance records for the unit council meeting) and chaired the documentation task force of the shared governance committee (see e-mail asking me to chair this committee).

BOX 21.3 Key Behaviors for the Performance Appraisal Session

- Provide a quiet, controlled environment, without interruptions.
- Maintain a relaxed but professional atmosphere.
- Put the employee at ease; the overall objective is for the best job to be done.
- Review specific examples for both positive and negative behavior.
- Allow the employee to express opinions, orally and in writing.
- Provide written future plans for training needs and goals.
- Set follow-up dates as necessary to monitor improvements, if cited.
- Show the employee confidence in his or her performance.
- Be sincere and constructive in both praise and criticism.

A performance appraisal is an opportunity for the employee and manager to have a dedicated time together to review how the employee is meeting the performance expectations outlined in the position description. It provides an opportunity to give the employee feedback related to not meeting, meeting, or exceeding expectation. Addressing strengths and areas for improvement related to the employee's performance is important. Specific behaviors by the nurse manager enhance the actual appraisal process. Box 21.3 provides key behaviors for the performance appraisal session.

(See also Chapter 25 on managing personal and personnel problems for more details.)

Ongoing feedback is essential between the nurse manager and the employee. An employee's regular performance appraisal should never be the first time a concern is identified. Feedback is best given as soon as a positive or negative occurrence with the employee happens. For example, if a direct-care nurse demonstrates inappropriate behavior at a patient care area staff meeting, the manager should provide feedback about the behavior as soon as possible after it occurs. Performance appraisals may include self and peer evaluations as well as managerial components.

A critical part of the performance appraisal is the development of goals and career development for the upcoming year. The employee should come to the appraisal prepared to discuss goals to accomplish over the next year. Examples of goals that may be put into an individual nurse's appraisal are noted in Box 21.4.

COACHING

The overall evaluative process can be enhanced if the manager uses the technique of coaching. Coaching is the process that involves the development of individuals within an organization. This coaching process is a personal approach in which the manager and the employee interact on a frequent and regular basis with the ultimate outcome that the employee performs at an optimal level. Coaching can be individual or may involve a team

Fig. 21.1 Coaching can promote team building and optimal performance of the employees. (Copyright © Photodisc/iStock/Thinkstock.)

approach (Fig. 21.1). When implemented in a planned and organized manner, it can promote team building and optimal performance of the employees. Coaching is a learned behavior for the nurse manager, and it takes time and effort to be developed. The rewards for both the employee and the nurse leader are significant; communication is enhanced and the performance appraisal process is an active one between the employee and leader.

CONCLUSION

Selecting new members of a team is critical to success for both the direct care nurse and the nurse manager. Nurse managers and their teams know their individual patient care areas best and are critical to the interview and orientation process. Selecting the right individual for the right reasons makes the development and evaluation of a new member of an organization more productive and successful.

THE SOLUTION

I started by evaluating core beliefs that were essential to my organization and team. I partnered with Human Resources to select focused behavioral interview questions that matched the characteristics and values I prioritized. A scoring rubric was added to each question to help with the evaluation process postinterview. Once I had determined the set of standardized questions that I would use to evaluate each job candidate, I needed to figure out who would bring value to the decision.

I introduced my plan to have staff members sit on the interview panel at a staff meeting. Because this process was new to the group, I wanted to ensure that everyone heard my rationale at the same time to allow for questions and possibly volunteers. I intentionally did not ask for volunteers to speak up at the meeting, but instead I asked that nurses reflect on the plan and if they felt they would be a good evaluator to let me know of their interest.

Several of the natural leaders of the team offered to participate; they were excited about the opportunity to help build the team. I had my eye on two additional nurses who were quiet but consistently role modeled the values that I felt were important to the team. I approached them individually to inquire if they would consider participating because I believed they were great examples of the type of nurses we needed on the team. Both were surprised I

had asked, and one said she was terribly shy. They both considered and decided to join the panel. The shy nurse shared that it would be a great opportunity for her to practice speaking up and to not be afraid. What a great chance to help her build her self-confidence and engage with the team!

This work has resulted in a standing pool of nurses who are selected based on availability to participate in interviews with me. Not all nurses participate in all the interviews; instead the two or three nurses who will be working most consistently during the anticipated interview time are scheduled to participate. The nurses were educated in how to ask appropriate questions, how to use the scoring rubric, and how to probe for additional clarity. The nurses quickly learned these skills and have been positive recruiters for the work area. The nurses enjoy being in the interviews and have been excited to share with the team the announcement of selected candidates. I believe the employees on the panel have taken an interest in welcoming the new hires and have helped the team rally around them. This helps the team in decision making and forward movement of the department.

Would this be a suitable approach for you? Why?

Monica Boege

▌REFLECTIONS

Have you gained a new perspective on the role of the nurse leader while reading this chapter? Explain how you gained appreciation for how the nurse leader affects the environment in a patient care area. How can you use your talents to maximize your performance during interviews to develop a team?

▌THE EVIDENCE

Recruitment and retention of nurses is one of the most important functions that a nurse manager performs. The nurse manager sets the tone for the unit and new employees. An atmosphere of mutual respect, trust, and empowerment is key to nurse retention. Coaching staff is a critical method to develop a high-performance nursing staff. Clear communication, expectations, and accountabilities based on role theory are pivotal to role clarity of new employees.

▌TIPS FOR SELECTING, DEVELOPING, AND EVALUATING STAFF

- Recruitment and retention of the right staff for a patient care area is one of the most important things a nurse leader does.
- Empowerment and career development of direct care nurses are key to helping build a positive work environment and increasing the direct care nurses' intent to stay.
- Clear expectations and accurate position descriptions help new graduate nurses transition into the workforce.

REFERENCES

Burke, D., & Flanagan, J. (2017). Characteristics of nurse directors that contribute to registered nurse satisfaction. *Journal of Nursing Administration, 47*(4), 219–225.

Clipper, B., & Cherry, B. (2015). From transition shock to competent practice: Developing preceptors to support new nurse transition. *Journal of Continuing Education in Nursing, 46*(10), 448–454.

Doucette, J. (2016). Peer interviews: A hiring best practice. *Nursing Management, 47*(2), 56.

Durcho, J., Speroni, K., Jones, R., Daniels, M., Beemer, C., & Daniels, M. (2016). A subjective view: Nurse satisfaction and the review process. *Nursing Management, 47*(2), 40–46.

Montani, F., Courcy, F., Giorgi, G., & Boilard, A. (2015). Enhancing nurses' empowerment: the role of supervisors' empowering management practices. *Journal of Advanced Nursing, 71*(9), 2120–2141.

Murray-Parahi, P., DiGiacomo, M., Jackson, D., & Davidson, P. (2016). New graduate registered nurse transition into primary health care roles: An integrative literature review. *Journal of Clinical Nursing, 25,* 3084–3101.

Usher, K., Nolan, C., Reser, P., Owens, J., & Tollefson, J. (1999). An exploration of the preceptor role: Preceptor's perceptions of benefits, rewards, supports, and commitment to the preceptor role. *Journal of Advanced Nursing, 29,* 507–514.

22

Person-Centered Care

Margarete Lieb Zalon

LEARNING OUTCOMES

- Describe the evolution of person-centered care as a focal point in healthcare delivery.
- Describe factors that affect the importance of person-centered interactions within the healthcare system.
- Evaluate the impact of effective person-centered care in fostering patient engagement.
- Appraise the major responsibilities of nursing in relation to the promotion of person-centered care.

KEY TERMS

advocate
big data
care coordination
cultural and linguistic competence
healthcare provider
health literacy

Internet of everything
Internet of things
learning healthcare system
motivational interviewing
patient activation

patient-centered medical home (PCMH)
patient engagement
patient satisfaction
person-centered care

THE CHALLENGE

Everything we do is about caring—for our patients, our health plan members, our family of physicians and employees, and our communities. It is this *purpose* that galvanizes our patient-centered care approach in every segment of our organization. Nursing, throughout the health system, embraces the importance of a person-centered approach and commits to the ProvenExperience, a program that offers refunds to patients whose expectations weren't met based on kindness and compassion (Burke, 2017). Geisinger has a strong history of delivering high-quality, innovative care and patient-centered care. Nursing is at the heart of Geisinger's commitment to person-centered care.

I received an e-mail from a nurse whose husband had recently been hospitalized for 2 days detailing her concerns about inconsistencies between the medications listed on the computer-generated discharge instructions and discharge prescriptions. Although the nurse indicated that the medical and nursing staff were clear about the changes to be made to the prescriptions, she was concerned about the discrepancies, pointing out that it would be confusing for her husband and for the average person, and potentially dangerous. The first error was noticed by an astute home care nurse who asked why a new prescription was not on the discharge summary yet they had product

(*Continued*)

INTRODUCTION

Person-centered care in healthcare delivery refers to the primacy of patients' needs and perspectives in all the encounters between patients, families, and the people important to them with healthcare providers and all aspects of the healthcare system. It indicates that an individual's values and preferences guide all aspects of health care, that patients and the people important to them and their providers are involved in a dynamic relationship, and that this collaboration informs decision making (American Geriatrics Society, 2016). Principles that can be used to guide person-centered care are (1) treating people with dignity, compassion, and respect; (2) coordination of care; (3) personalization of care; and (4) support of people to develop their strengths and abilities (Health Foundation, 2014) (Fig. 22.1). More specific key elements of person-centered care appear in Box 22.1. Person-centered care reflects the application of humanistic values to encounters between and among patients, families, nurses, and members of the interdisciplinary healthcare team (McCormack, Dewing, & McCance, 2011).

Person-centered care was first popularized in the 1960s by Carl Rogers, a psychotherapist, who focused on the primacy of the person in interpersonal relationships; then it was expanded to care for people with dementia to counteract dehumanizing relationships with caregivers (Evardsson, Fetherstonhaugh, Nay, & Gibson, 2010).

Impetus for the focus on person-centered care is derived from the Institute of Medicine's (IOM) (now the National Academy of Medicine [NAM]) landmark report, *Crossing the Quality Chasm* (2001). The report indicated that one of the six aims for improvement in

the healthcare system was *patient-centered care,* "providing care that is respectful of and responsive to individual patient preferences, needs and values, and ensuring that patient values guide all clinical decisions" (IOM, 2001, p. 3). A narrative review and synthesis of the literature in nursing, medicine, and policy on patient-centered care identified three core themes: patient participation and involvement, the relationship between the patient and healthcare professional, and the context where care is delivered (Kitson, Marshall, Bassett, & Zeitz, 2013). Although patients were not familiar with the term *patient-centered care,* the results of a phenomenologic

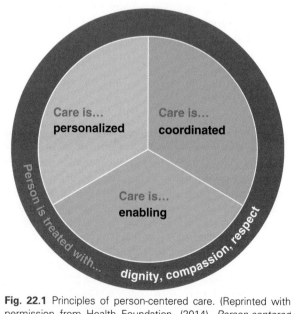

Fig. 22.1 Principles of person-centered care. (Reprinted with permission from Health Foundation. (2014). *Person-centered care made simple: What everyone should know about person-centered care. Quick Guide.* http://www.health.org.uk/sites/health/files/PersonCentredCareMadeSimple.pdf)

BOX 22.1 Essential Elements of Person-Centered Care

- An individualized, goal-oriented care plan based on the person's preferences
- Ongoing review of the person's goals and care plan
- Care supported by an interprofessional team in which the person is an integral team member
- One primary or lead point of contact on the healthcare team
- Active coordination among all healthcare and supportive service providers
- Continual information sharing and integrated communication
- Education and training for providers and, when appropriate, the person and those important to the person
- Performance measurement and quality improvement using feedback from the person and caregivers

From American Geriatrics Society Expert Panel on Person-Centered Care. (2016). Person-centered care: A definition and essential elements. *Journal of the American Geriatrics Society*, *64*(1), 15–18.

study indicated that connectedness, involvement, and attentiveness were what surgical patients wanted from their caregiver (Marshall, Kitson & Zeitz, 2012). These findings illustrate that the inclusion of patients' perspectives is important to the delivery of patient-centered care.

Nurses set the tone for effective staff-patient interaction providing the foundation for person-centered care. Because nurses are the healthcare providers who spend the most time with the patient, and their traditional focus has been on the patient's problems as the patient experiences them, nurses are in an ideal position to lead initiatives designed to deliver person-centered care.

Leaders in healthcare organizations recognize that their facilities are not as person-centered as they might be; that is, they have been built and organized in a manner that best serves the organization and not the recipients of care and their families. Care is compartmentalized, with each department having specialized functions. Patients are transported to departments to receive services. They risk loss of privacy, excessive exposure, increased discomfort and fatigue during transfers, and long periods of waiting. On an average day, a seriously ill patient in a hospital may have encounters with 50 or more staff members. This approach is not person-centered and can be very disruptive for patients. For example, research demonstrates that half of nighttime vital sign checks are performed on low-risk patients (Yoder, Yuen, Churpek,

Arora, & Edelson, 2013). The results of this research indicate that a significant opportunity exists for nurses to implement evidence-based practices to minimize disruptions and improve sleep quality. When possible, services should come to patients and should be as easy, comfortable, pleasant, and effective as possible. Meeting the emotional, psychosocial, and spiritual needs of the patient is important. Care needs to be technologically advanced and compassionate and address what matters to patients.

EXERCISE 22.1 List five examples of practices or situations in your nursing setting that could be more person-centered. (Example: Patients being asked to repeat information several times to different healthcare team members; not sending electronic discharge prescriptions to a pharmacy). For each practice, identify at least two strategies to make it more person-centered. One strategy should focus on what direct care nurses can do to immediately address the situation and the second strategy should focus on what nurse leaders can do to improve the delivery system so that the change can be embedded in practice.

Nursing has a long history of priding itself on the provision of *patient-centered care*. The people nurses regard as patients are at the center of nursing practice and the development of knowledge in nursing: "the person as the center of nursing care has always been the essence of nursing practice" (Fawcett & Clarke, 2016, p. 285). Now, as the focus on care evolves to a broader perspective, the term being used is *person-centered care*. It is reflective of a shifting focus of care that moves beyond an individual episode of illness or a single encounter with a healthcare provider in a clinical setting to a focus on how individuals (family, community, or population) respond to illness while their autonomy is respected.

Nursing's long history of being focused on person-centered care is embodied in the profession's definition of nursing: "Nursing is the protection, promotion, and optimization of health and abilities, prevention of illness and injury, alleviation of suffering through diagnosis and treatment of human response, and advocacy in the care of individuals, families, communities and populations" (American Nurses Association [ANA], 2003).

This definition, or a variation of it, is almost universally included in the registered nurse (RN) practice acts of the states and territories of the United States. Furthermore, the *Code of Ethics for Nurses* holds that the "nurse's primary commitment is to the recipients of nursing health services" with the expectation that the nurse involves patients in planning for care (ANA, 2015, p. 5). Involving patients in their care is a key feature of person-centered care. Involving patients in making decisions about their care demonstrates respect for persons and their right to self-determination. Also integral to person-centered care is the relationship that nurses have with patients, their families, and/or their significant others; the value of caring as an element of that relationship; and nursing's holistic approach to patient care.

We all need health care—friends, neighbors, families, people like us, and people very different from us. People are diverse culturally, ethnically, socially, physically, and psychologically. People are indeed becoming better connoisseurs of health care than they were in the past. People are increasingly making use of healthcare information. They can access their own test results, schedule appointments, monitor key indicators, and communicate with their healthcare providers. However, these services are only available to a small number of people and are not used by all those who have such access. Nurses are in key positions to influence positive outcomes for their patients by using person-centered approaches.

PERSON-CENTERED CARE—WHY NOW?

Person-centered care has captured the interest of healthcare professionals as an overarching strategy to improve health and transform the delivery of health care and is considered a "burgeoning social movement and a mission statement for modern health care" (Sakallaris, Miller, Saper, Krietzer, & Jonas, 2016). This comes at a time of an increased burden of chronic disease around the world. Chronic illness accounted for 68% of global mortality in 2012, with more than 40% considered premature deaths under age 70 years (World Health Organization [WHO], 2014). The WHO has a global target to reduce overall mortality from noncommunicable diseases: cardiovascular diseases, chronic respiratory diseases, alcohol and tobacco use, obesity, diabetes, hypertension, and insufficient physical activity (WHO, 2014). Achieving these global targets requires not only a concerted effort by healthcare professionals, healthcare organizations, and the implementation of sound healthcare policy but also the involvement of the most important person, the recipient of health care.

However, access to health insurance does not necessarily mean that people will take advantage of the available services. Parents in a young family may ensure that their children receive needed care and immunizations, but forgo obtaining preventive health care for themselves.

Coupled with the increase in the number of insured, many of whom are navigating the healthcare system for the first time in their lives, is the aging of the global population. With people living longer, more healthcare services are needed; this includes advanced care planning and end-of-life care.

Healthcare provider relationships with patients have changed. Physicians' typical mode of practice has moved from a single, private enterprise to multigroup practices that also include nurse practitioners, certified nurse-midwives, certified registered nurse anesthetists, clinical nurse specialists, RN first assistants, physician assistants, and other healthcare professionals. Some group practices are incorporated into integrated service models that include health maintenance organizations (HMOs), managed care programs, physician-hospital organizations, accountable care organizations, and patient-centered medical homes (PCMHs).

The nature of these practice settings has changed relationships that patients have with their healthcare providers. When patients visit a group practice, they might not have the option of selecting a specific healthcare provider. Insurers have increasingly restricted provider networks. Rural healthcare consumers have seen local hospitals closed or purchased by large healthcare systems, resulting in the need to develop relationships with new healthcare providers. Patients new to the healthcare system may not know how to navigate it. Others may change their insurance to save on costs, which may result in a change in healthcare providers. They may feel alienated and insecure in unfamiliar circumstances, even if they are receiving the best care. Patients no longer know their healthcare providers as they did in the past, and providers may be less familiar with their patients, resulting in decreased opportunity for the development of mutual respect and trust and continuity of care. Many hospitals use hospitalists instead of patients' own primary care providers, making care coordination after discharge more challenging. Almost half of all hospitalized patients experience a medical error after discharge; these errors can be traced back to communication breakdowns and lack of follow-up (McLeod, 2013).

Coupled with increased numbers of individuals seeking healthcare services, the aging population, and an increase in the number of people living with chronic

TABLE 22.1   Examples of Incentive Programs Designed to Improve Care Efficiency and Effectiveness

Enabling Legislation	Program	Key Features
Patient Protection and Affordable Care Act of 2010	Hospital Readmission Reduction Program (HRRP)	Examines 30-day hospital readmissions for myocardial infarction, heart failure and pneumonia, coronary artery bypass graft surgery, chronic obstructive pulmonary disease (COPD), and total hip and knee replacements.
	Hospital-Acquired Condition Reduction Program (HACRP)	Reduces payment for conditions such as pressure ulcers when they were acquired after admission.
	Hospital Value-Based Purchasing (HVBP)	Medicare payments are adjusted to reward providers for the quality of care provided.
Deficit Reduction Act of 2005	Hospital-Acquired Conditions (Present on Admission Indicator)	Hospitals do not receive additional payment for selected conditions when they were not present on admission.
Medicare Access and Children's Health Insurance Program (CHIP) Reauthorization Act (MACRA) of 2015	Quality Payment Program	Rewards healthcare providers for providing coordinated, comprehensive, and higher-quality care.
	Merit-based Incentive Payment System (MIPS)	
	Advanced Alternative Payment Models (APMs)	

Source: Centers for Medicare & Medicaid Services (CMS), www.cms.gov

diseases, efforts have been made to reduce costs by changing reimbursement mechanisms to provide incentives to improve the efficiency and effectiveness of care. Examples of these efforts are listed in Table 22.1.

The use of technology, with the internet of things, meaning the interconnectedness of various devices with a computer embedded in ordinary objects we use every day such as smartphones, sensors, self-monitoring devices, and electronic health records, has changed the way people interact with the healthcare system and has also changed how healthcare providers interact with patients, their families, groups, and communities. Further transformation is taking place with the internet of everything, which goes beyond the connectivity of things to the connectivity among people, data, processes, and devices. Healthcare systems are becoming learning healthcare systems by using the vast volumes of data to improve patient care. Specifically, a learning health system is one that aligns science, informatics, incentives, and culture for "continuous improvement and innovation, with best practices seamlessly embedded in the delivery process," capturing new knowledge as care is delivered (IOM, 2011). This means that the healthcare data that are being collected are continuously analyzed and improvements are made based on the information garnered from those data. People are increasing their use of self-monitoring technologies, such as physical activity monitors. We are learning that changing behavior requires more than monitoring and that we can use social processes (e.g., social media) guided by a healthcare professional to monitor change. Thus we will see new roles for nurses and other professionals to integrate the use of data with improved self-care, management of illness, and health promotion.

In addition, equitable access to health information and improved communication are key strategies identified in Healthy People 2020 to improving population health outcomes and health quality and to achieving health equity (US Department of Health and Human Services, 2010). The myriad factors described here together have created significant pressures to improve care as it is experienced by individuals, families, groups, and populations.

INITIATIVES TO DELIVER PERSON-CENTERED CARE

Increased emphasis on person-centered care has been facilitated by the efforts to optimize the performance of healthcare systems by improving the experience of care (which includes quality and satisfaction), improving population health while reducing cost, otherwise known as the Institute for Healthcare Improvement's (IHI) "Triple Aim" (IHI, n.d.). Bodenheimer and Sinsky (2014) make the case for expanding the Triple Aim to the "Quadruple Aim" with the inclusion of a focus on improving the work life of healthcare providers to improve outcomes by promoting positive engagement of the workforce. In addition, changes in reimbursement for healthcare services, initiatives that affect the delivery of person-centered care, include the development of innovative models of care, the use of PCMHs, and the use of big data.

Innovative models of care have been developed to fulfill specialized needs for health care and to address system problems—for example, a company providing pediatric day health services for children with complex healthcare needs, or another composed of nurse practitioners providing pediatric urgent care after pediatrician offices are closed. Nurses have developed solutions that can reduce discharge medication errors, thereby facilitating successful transition to home and potentially reducing hospital readmissions (Ruggiero, Smith, Copeland, & Boxer, 2015). The American Academy of Nursing's (AAN) Edgerunner program highlights nurse-developed innovative models of care with demonstrated improved health outcomes. For example, Brenda Reiss-Brennan, PhD, APRN, developed a model that integrates mental health into primary care settings in Utah by managing depression, substance abuse, and other mental health conditions along with other chronic conditions (Reiss-Brennan, et al., 2016; AAN, 2015). The overall goal of Reiss-Brennan's model is to involve patients and their families in their own care by enhancing self-management.

The patient-centered medical home (PCMH) is a delivery model that facilitates care integration across settings. PCMHs focus on improved access, patient-provider relationships, care coordination, and comprehensive patient-centered care in primary care settings (Aktan, 2016). Because the Affordable Care Act (ACA) has provisions supporting their development, PCMHs have proliferated across the country. PCMHs might be called *healthcare homes* to focus on the primacy of the individual and demonstrate respect for the individual's autonomy. Although PCMHs have been particularly successful in addressing specific disease outcomes and costs, one area that continues to be a challenge is making improvements in the experience of care (Sakallaris et al., 2016). Some healthcare systems have created teams of individuals, often led by a nurse, who are charged with addressing patient concerns related to the experience of care. Nurses are well suited to be team members and leaders of PCMHs because of their holistic approach and ability to establish positive relationships with their patients. The addition of 20 million more people with insurance across the country has resulted in policy discussions related to preparing RNs to assume a more substantial role in primary care settings that is in greater alignment with their educational preparation (Josiah Macy Jr. Foundation, 2016). Thus it is likely that RNs will assume more responsibilities in these settings and more responsibilities for ensuring a person-centered approach.

Increasingly competitive healthcare markets experience greater application of data sharing and access to electronic health records, and the use of advanced analytic tools to identify trends and provide decision-making support is occurring. "Big data" analytics using very large patient data sets generated by healthcare systems are being used to harness huge amounts of information to analyze trends and gain new insights into the nature of illness, behaviors, and the processes of care. New services are being created that include self-monitoring with technology in the home, videoconferencing, text messaging and instant messaging with healthcare providers and clinical staff, and the proliferation of walk-in clinics staffed by nurse practitioners at convenient locations such as schools and stores.

These changes require healthcare organization leaders to focus on building relationships with patients who are more knowledgeable and demanding. Nurses, because of their unique perspective and focus on a holistic approach, can play an important role in helping organizations to become more person-centered.

CHALLENGES IN THE DELIVERY OF PERSON-CENTERED CARE

Healthcare organizations face numerous challenges in making their care processes more person-centered.

These include health literacy, diversity, patient satisfaction, and access to care.

Health Literacy

People rely on information from a variety of sources to make healthcare decisions. The relationships that consumers develop with their healthcare providers, including nurses, are important in helping them navigate the healthcare system (Fig. 22.2). However, nearly half of American adults—that is, 90 million people—have difficulty in understanding and using health information (IOM, 2004). Health literacy is defined as the "degree to which individuals have the capacity to obtain, process and understand basic health information and services needed to make appropriate health decisions" (US Department of Health and Human Services, 2010). Health literacy includes reading and understanding text, using quantitative information, and being able to speak and listen effectively. Furthermore, health literacy may include understanding disease, using technology, social interaction motivation, and self-efficacy (Berkman et al., 2011). More people from populations with traditionally higher rates of low health literacy received health insurance coverage with the implementation of the ACA. As a result, health literacy took on new importance.

Understanding consumers' health-literacy needs goes beyond reading ability assessment. Factors ranging from global aging and climate change to medical and technologic advances influence people's ability to access health information. We know that people with low health literacy are less likely to get preventive health care. When they do enter the healthcare system, they are sicker and have more complex needs. Thus

Fig. 22.2 Education empowers consumers to exercise self-determination.

promoting health literacy involves education, consideration of the context, and sociocultural factors. One strategy to promote health literacy is to use a Health Care Literate model, which means weaving health literacy strategies into care by assuming that patients do not understand their health conditions or what to do about them, and then subsequently assessing patients' understanding (Koh, Brach, Harris & Parchman, 2013). For example, a nurse who is an expert clinician in a specialty practice, when diagnosed with a serious chronic illness, may not have the appropriate background to make informed healthcare decisions. Healthcare systems focusing on health literacy support people in understanding information about their health and how to use their services.

Diversity

Nursing practice involves interacting with consumers who are culturally, economically, and socially diverse. Diversity encompasses more than differences in nationality or ethnicity and may include a variety of ways that patients are different from their healthcare providers. Nurses are responsible for assisting patients in accessing and participating in the healthcare system; they also ensure that patients are treated fairly and equitably. Some patients enter the healthcare system much like immigrants entering a foreign country. Patients who enter a system with a set of values, beliefs, and language unlike their own may experience culture shock. Patients who speak little or no English and those who have low health literacy are vulnerable to poor health outcomes. Nurses need to recognize the culture of their work setting, realizing that it may differ markedly from the culture of the patient, and move beyond ethnocentrism to provide culturally competent care.

Race and ethnicity, as factors in influencing the delivery of health care and the quality of health outcomes, are a serious concern; some healthcare providers may erroneously assume that members of a particular group have the same beliefs, attitudes, and values about health, when in fact extraordinary diversity exists. The Census Bureau predicts that by 2040, more than half the US population will be composed of ethnic minorities. As of 2016, 21.6% of US residents age 5 years and older speak a language other than English at home (US Census Bureau, 2017). Diversity refers not just to race or ethnicity but also to age, gender, socioeconomic status, religion, sexual orientation, physical characteristics, disability, and viewpoints. Thus cultural competence will play an increasingly important role in the relationships that nurses have with patients, families, and communities. An organization that creates a culture of mutual respect, recognizing the contributions of all its employees, thereby addressing the fourth aim (of the Quadruple Aim) of improving employee work life, will be much more effective in providing culturally competent health care.

The classic definition of cultural and linguistic competence means bringing together congruent attitudes, behaviors, and policies within an organization in such a way that allows people to work effectively in cross-cultural situations (Cross, Bazron, Dennis, & Isaacs, 1989). It involves understanding a culture and the community and respecting its values, beliefs, and practices. The National Standards for Culturally and Linguistically Appropriate Services (CLAS) in Health and Health Care focuses on services being responsive to diverse cultural health beliefs and practices, preferred languages, health literacy, and other communication needs (Office of Minority Health, 2018). The CLAS includes standards for cultural competence, language access, and organizational support (Office of Minority Health, n.d. a). When CLAS are provided, they have the potential to reduce health disparities and achieve health equity (Office of Minority Health, n.d. b).

Patients often hesitate in asking for help with language skills. Some healthcare agencies include an assessment of a patient's ability to learn, but the lack of assessment criteria may hinder nurses' efforts to institute appropriate teaching. The US Census language-screening questions can be used. The person is asked if a language other than English is spoken at home, and if the answer is "yes," the person is asked to rate how well he or she speaks English: very well, well, not well, or not at all (Shin & Kominski, 2010). Hospital length of stay is significantly longer for patients with limited English proficiency when professional interpreters are not used on admission, or both admission and discharge (Lindholm, Hargraves, Ferguson, & Reed, 2012). Of course, some patients who speak English as their primary language may have equally challenging difficulties because of their limited grasp of standard English, which is what healthcare providers commonly use.

Nurse managers can make a commitment to culturally and linguistically appropriate care highly visible to their staff by advocating for ongoing education to meet the unique needs of their patient population and access language services for patients with limited English proficiency.

> **EXERCISE 22.2** A patient does not speak English and is a member of an immigrant group that is not well represented in your community. Using the CLAS standards, identify four strategies that a culturally competent nurse can use to ensure that the patient receives high-quality care.

Patient Satisfaction

Patient satisfaction, or how satisfied people are with the health care they received, has become increasingly important because it is used to gauge a person's experience of care, an important component of person-centered care. A person's relationships with healthcare providers and healthcare organizations are routinely and systematically evaluated, particularly as pay-for-performance models of care are implemented. Nurses spend a great deal of time with patients and their families. These encounters are generally personal and intensely meaningful. Nurses are in a distinct position to influence and promote positive relationships. The nurse manager can set the tone for effective patient-staff interactions that are centered on the patient.

Understanding how patients determine their satisfaction can only enhance the abilities of nurse leaders and followers in their efforts to improve relationships to impact health outcomes.

Patient satisfaction ratings, along with measurable healthcare outcomes, are important data used by healthcare organizations to improve quality care and maintain a competitive edge. Nurses, because of their 24-hour accountability for patient care, are integral to attaining high patient satisfaction ratings. Standard-setting organizations, such as the National Quality Forum (NQF), have patient satisfaction questions included in their outcome measures designed to assess the patient experience of care. The Centers for Medicare & Medicaid (CMS) and the Agency on Healthcare Research and Quality (AHRQ) developed a tool, the Hospital Consumer Assessment of Healthcare Providers and Systems (HCAHPS), which measures patient perceptions of the quality of hospital care. A hospital's HCAHPS performance is included in the calculation of its Medicare reimbursement as part of Hospital-Value-Based Purchasing Program (CMS, 2017).

Much of a patient's satisfaction with care is dependent on the nursing care that is received. In addition to questions that are related to nursing, the HCAHPS includes questions related to a global rating of the hospital, physician care, and the environment. HCAHPS reports are available on the Hospital Compare website, allowing the public to make meaningful comparisons and creating incentives for hospitals to improve quality. Comparative data for Medicare- and Medicaid-certified nursing homes are available on the Nursing Home Compare website. Despite the availability of publicly reported data, patients and their families also go to websites such as YELP for information about hospitals and patient experiences. A majority of YELP topics were found to be correlated with positive or negative hospital reviews, which were focused on patient- and caregiver-centered experiences but not measured with the HCAPHS (Ranard et al., 2016). Measuring patient satisfaction is an evolving science; nurses do not always accurately gauge what factors are most important to patients. Satisfaction measures are often skewed in a positive direction with scores clustered at the top of the scale. Sometimes these factors make it difficult to interpret results and make improvements.

EXERCISE 22.3 Go to the HCAHPS Survey website *(http://www.hcahpsonline.org/surveyinstrument.aspx)* and identify which questions are affected by (1) nursing care, (2) good team communication, (3) care coordination, and (4) effective transition to home or another care setting. Go to the Hospital Compare website *(www. hospitalcompare.gov)* and examine a hospital's HCAHPS scores. Determine whether the hospital's reimbursement was affected by the overall HCAHPS score and discuss the implications.

Nurses have a responsibility to exercise critical thinking and decision-making skills with respect to patient satisfaction with nursing care. For example, patients who have had major surgery may not want to cough and deep breathe because it is painful, yet we know that failure to do so can result in pneumonia. Nurses are responsible for (1) advocating for their patients, (2) ensuring pain relief, (3) correcting patient misconceptions, and (4) implementing pain management strategies consistent with established standards. This may be more complicated as concerns are raised about appropriate pain management in the context of concerns about prevention of opioid addiction. Patient satisfaction ratings may be low if nurses have not attended to the "hotel amenities." Nurses may become frustrated because they want to focus on delivering high-quality nursing care. The use of patient satisfaction measures and similar tools illustrate how important it is for nurses to explain their roles and the purpose of the care being provided. Reviewing and analyzing patient satisfaction survey ratings are invaluable tools. Managers need to share the results of such surveys with their staff, examine the context of the results, and plan with their staff members how meaningful improvements can be made.

Because patient satisfaction ratings are publicly available and they affect the bottom line, some healthcare organizations use scripting to provide standardized responses for rounding and other events. Some nurses dislike these scripts because they limit critical thinking and professional judgment and make them feel like they are being treated as incompetent. Others indicate scripting provides consistency and assurance to patients by providing tools for handling difficult situations. Strategies used to enhance person-centered care can also positively affect patient satisfaction ratings. These include keeping patients at the front and center of decision-making processes by (1) including first and last name and position title with introductions, (2) asking patients about their most-important concerns, (3) discussing approaches to care with patients, and (4) incorporating patient values and cultural preferences into care.

Access to Care

Access to care is an important component of person-centered care. Care cannot be person-centered if people don't have access to care or if they struggle to get the care that is needed. If people are at the center of care, (1) quality is assumed to be improved, (2) people will receive care when needed, (3) people will take a more active role in their care, and (4) pressures on health and social services will be reduced (Health Innovation Network, n.d.). Access to health care is more than just having health insurance; it is having "timely use of personal health services to achieve the best health outcomes" (IOM, 1993, p. 8). Access to health care includes (1) entry to the healthcare system, (2) access to sites where services are delivered, (3) having providers who meet patients' needs, and (4) patients being able to develop relationships of mutual respect and trust with their providers (Agency for Healthcare Research and Quality [AHRQ], 2011).

Significant healthcare disparities manifest in the United States in numerous ways. For example, African American and Hispanic populations are less likely to have employer-sponsored health insurance, and people with Medicaid insurance may use facilities that are underresourced. Interventions that can be used to reduce disparities include team care, patient navigation, cultural tailoring, collaboration with families and community members, interactive skills-based training, and increasing the diversity of the healthcare workforce. These interventions are all focused on improving the nature of healthcare delivery, particularly relationships with patients and their families.

A major concern in the delivery of health care is unequal treatment because of racial-cultural discrimination. Minorities and women have been significantly underrepresented in health-related research, resulting in less information for decision making. People who lack economic means by being uninsured, underinsured, or undocumented often become powerless in the healthcare delivery system. They are at the mercy or will of those who control power and money. These people may be denied access to care, or if they achieve access they may not receive equal care. As the implementation of the ACA unfolded, states that did not expand Medicaid under the ACA have the highest uninsured and poverty rates in the country, and thus a concern about the equity of care available to new Medicaid enrollees exists (Adepoju, Preston, & Gonzales, 2015).

EXERCISE 22.4 An African American nurse who has worked on the unit for 20 years comes to you very upset telling you that the husband of a patient told her to get out the room, that he didn't want any blacks taking care of his wife. How would you handle this situation? Do patients have a right to refuse care from certain staff members? What resources are available to you to address this problem?

Another access to care issue is the plight of some 60 million people who live in rural areas across the United States. It might take several hours of travel to reach a healthcare provider or hospital. The hospital might not have the specialty services that are available in urban areas. Rural hospitals are closing and many more are at risk of closure, particularly in states that have not expanded Medicaid. This is because these hospitals may

be in more financial difficulty because of the costs of uncompensated care impacting their bottom line (Kaufman, Reiter, Pink, & Holmes, 2016). Thus patients may not only have to travel farther for services but also may be burdened by having to travel several hours home after discharge. If a hospital closes, other associated services may close as well, such as pharmacies and home health agencies.

Equitable access to health information and improved communication are key strategies identified in Healthy People 2020 to improve population health outcomes and healthcare quality and to achieve healthcare equity. One strategy used to enhance access to care is the use of technology such as videoconferencing and access to patient portals where individuals can track their own health information. Many adults use technology to track their own health indicators or that of a loved one. However, individuals with low health literacy are less likely to use fitness and nutrition applications, activity trackers, and patient portals (Mackert, Maby-Flynn, Champlin, Donovan, & Pounders, 2016). These patterns of access to technology and health information affect the nature of the relationship between patients and their healthcare providers, including nurses.

Nurses are in positions to be guardians of the rights of individuals and their families. Nurses act as the primary person to be alert to circumstances that may prevent a successful outcome for the patient and to intervene on the patient's behalf. Nurses are in positions to address the issues of cultural, ethnic, and racial sensitivity. The nurse is concerned with addressing the individualized needs and wants of the patient.

EXERCISE 22.5 You are a nurse in a busy gynecologic-obstetric practice. You notice that a young woman who appears to be Hispanic has been waiting for some time to be addressed by the receptionist. An older Caucasian woman walks up to the desk, and the receptionist immediately addresses her. As it turns out, the older woman, a nurse, was the mother-in-law of the younger woman and had just been parking her car. She was accompanying her daughter-in-law to the office for her first prenatal visit. She complains, raising a concern that the staff will not treat her daughter-in-law professionally. Consider what you might say to the young woman and her mother-in-law and what you would do if you were this nurse. How would you address the issue with the receptionist?

PATIENT ENGAGEMENT

Healthcare organizations, including healthcare systems and insurers, are using a variety of strategies to improve health outcomes, services, and the experience of care. Foremost in the repertoire of initiatives is the focus on patient engagement. The nature of patient engagement implies that getting patients engaged is as simple as getting a prescription filled and taking the medicine, which cures the problem. Patient engagement is a broad concept that includes patient activation (understanding one's own role in the care process and having the knowledge, skills, and confidence to take on that role), the interventions designed to increase it, and the behavior that results from it (Hibbard, Greene & Overton, 2013)

The potential of patient engagement has been recognized with reform initiatives under the ACA. Nurses are well prepared to implement strategies that foster patient engagement because they are educated in establishing productive relationships with patients and their families and are willing to see them as at the center of care and as partners in managing their health.

When patients are engaged, they are empowered to take an active role in the management of their health. The Literature Perspective describes the essential features of patient engagement.

Specific behaviors that are necessary for patients to experience the benefits of the healthcare services available have been identified in an Engagement Behavior Framework and are listed in Box 22.2 (Center for Advancing Health, n.d.). The broad range of behaviors in this framework indicates that considerable opportunities avail nurses to become involved in assisting individuals and their families at multiple points of contact within the healthcare system.

BOX 22.2 Engagement Behavior Framework

1. Find good health care.
2. Communicate with health professionals.
3. Organize health care.
4. Pay for health care.
5. Make good treatment decisions.
6. Participate in treatment.
7. Promote health.
8. Get preventive health care.
9. Plan for the end of life.
10. Seek health knowledge.

From Center for Advancing Health (n.d.). *Engagement behavior framework.* http://www.cfah.org/engagement/research/engagement-behavior-framework

---

LITERATURE PERSPECTIVE

Resource: Higgins, T., Larson, E., & Schnall, R. (2017). Unraveling the meaning of patient engagement: A concept analysis. *Patient Education and Counseling, 100*(1), 30–36.

Patient engagement is a term that is widely used in the literature and has received increased visibility in the healthcare literature related to patient-centered medical homes, comparative effectiveness research, technology use, chronic care management, patient safety, and control of healthcare costs without a common definition. In addition, federal reimbursement is available for the use of technology to enhance patient engagement. A concept analysis of patient engagement as it is used in scientific literature in health care identified four key interrelated attributes: personalization, commitment, access, and therapeutic alliance. *Personalization* refers to adapting care to the individual needs of patients. *Access* refers to the patient's ability to obtain information and assistance to receive high-quality care. *Commitment* refers to fostering the empowerment of patients. *Therapeutic alliance* refers to

the quality of relationships with patients. Based on this concept analysis, patient engagement is defined as the "desire and capability to actively choose to participate in care in a way uniquely appropriate to the individual, in cooperation with a healthcare provider or institutions for the purposes of maximizing outcomes or improving experiences of care" (p. 30). Patient engagement is multifaceted, involving processes, behaviors, and the environment that affect the extent of an individual's involvement in care.

Implications for Practice

Further research is needed to fully comprehend the complexity of patient engagement. However, including all four key elements, personalization, access, commitment, and therapeutic alliance, is likely to enhance patient involvement in care. Nurses and nurse managers have expertise in each of these areas and thus are critical to successful patient engagement.

NURSES IN THE DELIVERY OF PERSON-CENTERED CARE

Nursing has a long history of providing person-centered care from Nightingale, who indicated that nursing was designed to "put the patient in the best conditions for nature to act upon him" (1859/2010, p. 191). Nurses are valued for the ability to deliver person-centered care because of their educational preparation and training that focuses on the person.

Nurses face numerous challenges in the delivery of person-centered care. Patients discharged from hospitals may understand their discharge plan, but quite often they are not asked about barriers to implementing the plan and are not offered guidance in addressing those barriers (Greysen et al., 2017). Nurses in acute care settings have limited time to provide complex discharge instructions. Because of reimbursement constraints, home health nurses may not be permitted to make the necessary number of visits to enable patients to successfully manage a chronic illness. Regardless, RNs and advanced practice registered nurses (APRNs) are in ideal positions to provide person-centered care through the oversight of healthcare delivery and facilitation of communication across systems.

Central to the delivery of person-centered care is the development of trusting relationships. Nurses are readily able to develop trusting relationships. They use the nursing process in focusing care on patients' needs and advance knowledge through research, which again focused on patient needs. Nurses are also ideally suited for facilitating care coordination, which focuses on patients as they traverse different components of the healthcare system.

Nurses are held in high regard by patients and members of the public who view nurses as knowledgeable, worthy of respect, concerned for others, honest, caring, confidential, friendly, hardworking, and especially trustworthy. Nurses have for many years topped the list in the Gallup poll of the public's ratings of honesty and ethical standards of various professions, with a great majority of Americans believing nurses' honesty and ethical standards are "high" or "very high" (Norman, 2016). Nurses, because of their favored status with the public, occupy positions of influence and can foster and promote successful relationships across healthcare settings. Trust is an important component of relationships with patients, families, and persons important to them. Trust is influenced by healthcare providers' competence and interpersonal skills. Clinical competence, demonstrated compassion and goodwill, patient advocacy, and addressing patient needs are components of the nurse-patient relationship that affect trust (Rutherford, 2014). Nurses must be sensitive to the needs of patients to establish trusting relationships. These relationships need to extend to how nurses work together as a team. Nurse leaders and managers can facilitate a culture that fosters trusting working relationships. Research has demonstrated that when nurse supervisors are willing to come to the defense of their nursing staff and are consistent in their promotion of the quality of working relationships, nurse retention is positively impacted (Rodwell, McWilliams, & Gulyas, 2017).

Nursing diagnoses, interventions, and outcomes are standardized nursing terminologies that provide additional support for the distinctive role of nurses in the delivery of person-centered care as members of the collaborative, multidisciplinary team. Standardized nursing terminologies describe patient problems (in terms of where the patient is at a specific point in time) that nurses have responsibility for diagnosing, treating, and measuring patient outcomes, reflecting the expert clinical judgment of nurses. For example, although an individual may have a medical diagnosis of type 2 diabetes mellitus, determining that a patient has a lack of knowledge of medication regimen (an International Classification for Nursing Practice® term, [International Council of Nurses, n.d.]) facilitates the development of an individualized goal-oriented care plan based on the patients' preferences. With only knowing the medical diagnosis, the patient may be at home, needing guidance about diabetes self-management, or be in the hospital with hyperosmolar hyperglycemia nonketotic coma. Nursing diagnoses support the identification of patient outcomes and the implementation of nursing interventions. Thus including standardized international nursing terminologies (noting that many are evidence-based) in electronic health records is key to providing a more precise understanding of what exactly is happening with patients and their progress in meeting their goals for health care.

Likewise, nursing research largely focuses on persons, families, groups and communities, responses to illness, and the testing of interventions to promote health and prevent disease to support the practice of nursing. Nurses focus on systematically analyzing the evidence from numerous research studies to provide a more solid foundation for practice (see Chapter 24).

Professional Practice

Numerous strategies can be used by nurses to deliver person-centered care. A professional practice model such as the Careful Nursing Philosophy and Professional Practice Model (Careful Nursing), because it is centered on the patient as a unitary or holistic person, is a useful guide for nurse leaders and followers. Careful Nursing practice is guided by three philosophic principles: the nature and inherent dignity of the human person, Infinite Transcendent Reality in life processes, and health as human flourishing (Meehan, 2017). The *Code of Ethics for Nurses* specifies that respect for the inherent dignity, worth, and unique attributes and human rights of every person is a fundamental principle underlying nursing practice (ANA, 2015). As human persons, we have unique biophysical and psychospiritual characteristics. The Infinite Transcendent Reality principle is concerned with patients' and nurses' spirituality however spirituality is understood by them. Health is conceptualized as human flourishing and key to achieving full human potential. Four dimensions constitute the professional practice model: (1) the therapeutic milieu, (2) practice competence and excellence, (3) management of practice and influence in health systems, and (4) professional authority (Meehan, 2017). Underpinning each of these dimensions are operational concepts that illustrate how each of the dimensions is translated into care for individuals, their families, and communities (Fig. 22.3).

Although all of nursing care can be described as person-centered care, strategies that can be used by nurse leaders and followers related to safe and restorative

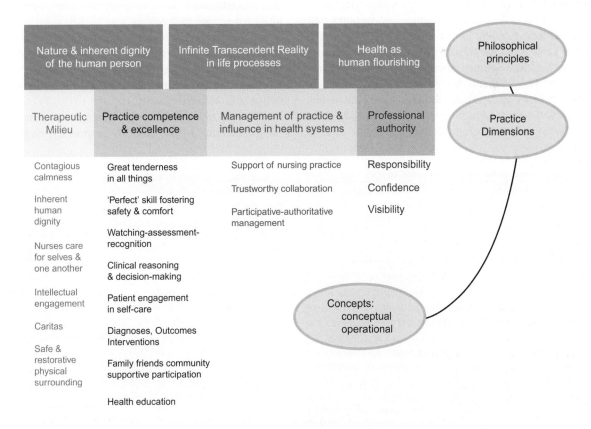

Fig. 22.3 Careful Nursing philosophical principles, and practice dimensions with their concepts.©

physical surroundings, health education, trustworthy collaboration, and visibility are illustrated here.

Providing safe and restorative surroundings, a component of a therapeutic milieu, can be enhanced by frontline nurse and nurse leader advocacy for individuals and their families. The definition of nursing includes advocacy in the care of individuals, families, communities, and populations. Nurses, in accordance with the *Code of Ethics for Nurses,* have the responsibility to promote, advocate, and protect the health, safety, and rights of patients (ANA, 2015). An **advocate** is one who does the following:

- Defends or promotes the rights of others
- Changes systems to meet the needs of others
- Empowers and promotes self-determination in others
- Promotes autonomy of diverse cultures and social groups
- Ensures respect, equity, and dignity for others

The advocate role requires the nurse to perceive and be comfortable with conflict and then mediate, negotiate, clarify, explain, and intervene. The nurse can advocate by being a liaison between and among individuals, their families, and the healthcare system. The nurse's role is to interpret the processes and procedures of the healthcare organization for patients and their families. The role also includes negotiating changes when patients and families differ in their values and beliefs. One way to advocate for patients is to allow them to make choices and participate in their care in accordance with their preferences. Being sensitive to patient preferences and expectations is illustrated in the Research Perspective.

Surroundings that are safe can be restorative. Future nurses and nurse leaders are being prepared under the umbrella of the Quality and Safety Education for Nurses (QSEN) initiative so they gain the necessary knowledge, skills, and attitudes (KSAs) to improve quality and safety for patients. This approach is expanded to include systems thinking (Dolansky & Moore, 2013), with calls to expand these initiatives, by aligning academic programs with healthcare organizations so that all nurses benefit from this comprehensive approach to address quality and safety (Drenkard, 2015). Promoting safety involves followers being advocates by speaking up about safety issues and nurse leaders creating environments that encourage staff to speak up about safety issues. Conducting timeouts in the operating room setting with care to ensure that the right procedure is being done on the right patient and empowering nurses to speak up about breaches in infection control during central-line insertion procedures are just two examples of how opportunities for nurses to speak up and be advocates can be structurally embedded in institutional policies, thus supporting nurses in the delivery of care. Similarly, using evidence to change nursing practice is necessary to be recognized for excellence in nursing by obtaining designation as a Magnet® facility.

However, more challenging are the situations in which the policies may not be so clear, or in which no policy

---

RESEARCH PERSPECTIVE

Resource: Whitty, J. A., Spinks, J., Bucknall, T., Tobiano, G., & Chaboyer, W. (2017, November 2). Patient and nurse preferences for implementation of bedside handover. Findings from a discrete choice experiment. *Health Expectations, 20*(4), 742–750. https://doi.org/10.1111/hex.12513

This study examined medical patients' (N = 401) and nurses' (N = 200) preferences regarding bedside handover—specifically, invitations to patients, invitations to family members or caregivers, number of nurses present, patient involvement, information content, and privacy.

Factors that were most important to patients were being able to hear what was said, being asked to participate, being able to speak up, having a care plan in place, and family member presence. Patients preferred for two nurses to be present (the nurse leaving and the nurse starting) rather than the entire nursing team. Nurses did not consider having a family member present to be important and preferred to hand over sensitive information without the patient present. Patients were not as concerned as nurses about breaches in privacy.

Implications for Practice

Nurses may need additional education on assessing patient preferences, strategies for incorporating family members into bedside handovers, and communication of information patients consider to be sensitive without compromising confidentiality. Individualizing the handover process is a strategy that can also support patient engagement and thus foster stronger consumer relationships.

exists. An unsafe situation can never be person-centered. Here the nurse must act as an advocate to promote safety to support the delivery of person-centered care. Understanding nursing's role and that all nurses are leaders regardless of whether one has a formal title in a managerial role is critical to providing a person-centered environment. For example, one of the worst public health crises in the country occurred when health department officials in Nevada found that up to 63,000 patients had a potential exposure to hepatitis C because of poor infection control practices at a chain of endoscopy clinics (Leary & Diers, 2013). Despite the poor infection control practices that had to be going on for an extended time, only one nurse complained to authorities. Although this example clearly had major implications for many people, day-to-day opportunities to promote safety may be subtle, requiring a more nuanced approach to promote a safe environment. In one hospital desiring to increase reports of safety issues, nurses on clinical units were asked to identify behaviors of the senior leadership that would help in promoting a safety culture; these were identified to be communication, access, and visibility (O'Connor & Carlson, 2016). Subsequently, after a concerted effort to act upon the clinical nurses' recommendations, the number of risk and near-risk safety reports were increased, enabling the leaders to make changes to improve safety.

The restorative function of sleep and how sleep is disrupted in hospitalized patients illustrates another opportunity for nurses to assume a leadership role in examining practices surrounding nighttime nursing care activities. Sleep disruptions in critical care settings, hospital units, long-term care settings, and the home are all areas where nurses can make a difference with the deployment of interventions designed to enhance sleep and/or diminish disruptions. Nurses face challenges between or among adhering to institutional or unit protocols, minimizing interruptions, and having a lack of clear consensus on sleep-promoting interventions (Hopper, Fried, & Pisani, 2015). These interventions may be as simple as grouping tasks together, such as taking vital signs at the same time medication is administered or when answering a call light. Likewise, in the home setting, decreasing daytime sleep may facilitate sleep at night. Nurse leaders can be alert to these kinds of opportunities to focus on patients' needs in improving care in their practice settings.

Health education, as a component of practice competence and excellence, can be enhanced with the use of motivational interviewing. Teaching is a core role of RNs and APRNs regardless of the setting. Motivational interviewing (MI) is an evidence-based strategy that is an important tool in the repertoire of the savvy nurse and nurse leader. It goes hand-in-hand with health teaching because it provides patients the opportunity to become involved in their care while recognizing and affirming their autonomy in making choices. Health education needs to move beyond just providing patients and their families with information. Motivational interviewing can be used any time people need help with making lifestyle changes.

The central feature of motivational interviewing is using intrinsic motivation to change behavior. Intrinsic motivation refers to what is rewarding to the individual. For example, losing weight is important because it will make it easier to engage in activities with one's children, as opposed to getting a monetary incentive to stop smoking. This is consistent with person-centered care in that it focuses behavior change on what is most important to individuals and their families. MI was first developed as a brief person-centered counseling strategy to help people make behavioral changes when dealing with drug and alcohol addictions and subsequently expanded to include helping people manage chronic conditions (Rollnick, Miller & Butler, 2009). MI has four guiding principles known by the acronym, RULE. See Table 22.2 for the guiding principles of MI, rationale for their use and application strategies. These principles are coupled with core communication strategies of asking the person to find out about his or her goals, informing the person about options and what might be helpful, and listening to what the person wants, offering help in accordance with the person's wishes (Rollnick, Miller, & Butler, 2009, p. 33). MI has been demonstrated to be an effective strategy used by nurses for behavior change in a wide variety of populations. Some healthcare organizations and insurers employ nurse coaches who are experts in MI and the needs of specific populations and who support people in achieving goals to improve outcomes.

All frontline nurses and nurse leaders have responsibility for the management of practice and influence in the healthcare system. Trustworthy collaboration is illustrated by the role of nurses in care coordination. Care coordination is an information-rich, patient-centric endeavor that seeks to deliver the right care to the right patient at the right time and uses strategies such as case management, transitional care, disease

TABLE 22.2   Motivational Interviewing: Guiding Principles, Rationales, and Strategies

Principle	Rationale	Strategies
Resisting the righting reflex	People experience ambivalence about the change. Being told what to do results in resistance.	Encourage talking about the value of positive behaviors.
Understanding motivations	People's reasons for change are more important to them.	Ask why making a change would be important.
Listening	Listening takes the guess work out understanding a person's preferences.	Encourage thinking aloud about the change.
Empowering the person	Active involvement improves outcomes.	Help figure out how to make changes.

Adapted from Rollnick, S., Miller, W. R., & Butler, C. (2009). *Motivational interviewing in health care.* New York: Guilford Press.

management, and health technology while providing support to patients and providers (National Quality Forum, 2010). Care coordination is an important factor in the delivery of quality care and requires a strong relationship between the nurse and the patient. Frontline nurses and nurse leaders can facilitate care coordination by working with case managers and members of the multidisciplinary healthcare team. Nurses in care coordinator roles are influential advocates for vulnerable populations who are at high risk for less-than-desired care in a complicated healthcare system. These groups typically have included those who receive no care and need it the most, such as persons who are homeless, uninsured, or underinsured; persons who have opioid addictions; children living in poverty; migrant workers; and people with acquired immunodeficiency syndrome (AIDS). Some healthcare organizations capitalize on the care coordination abilities of nurses by creating "navigator" or case management roles designed to assist patients with accessing the resources of a healthcare system or complex decision needs. Effective use of RNs in all practice settings can result in better care coordination, quality, safety, and efficiency, thus enhancing the delivery of person-centered care.

Professional authority refers to nurses being experts in the delivery of care. It can manifest in numerous ways that are reflective of taking responsibility for care and ownership of nursing practice. One strategy is for frontline nurses to give voice to their actions by being visible in explaining who they are and what they are doing, reflecting the authority they have over their practice. It does not mean being authoritative with patients, but rather describing who they are and what they are doing that reflects the knowledge, competencies, and compassion that are critical to nursing practice. For example, instead of being silent and working behind the scenes, nurses need to give voice to their practice, explaining the value of the care that is provided (e.g., encouraging coughing and deep breathing to prevent pneumonia). Being silent about what we do as nurses means that the fourth aim of the Quadruple Aim, improving the work life of healthcare providers, will never be recognized as important for nurses.

Visibility and Authority

Making nursing visible and demonstrating authority over their own practice can be achieved with how nurses communicate to the public about what they do and how they describe themselves to the public. Historically nurses use very traditional language to describe what they do: care and compassion. Giving voice so that the substantive contributions of nursing to the outcomes of patient care are not minimized includes taking responsibility for one's actions and describing one's actions in a manner that reflects the expertise of the nurse. Frontline nurses can do this every single day. For example, many nurses are reluctant to use their last names in their encounters with patients, turning over their badges so their names are not revealed. From the perspective of the person receiving care, this can be perceived as impersonal, rude, or dangerous, because the nurse may be performing a skill that requires intimacy and personal knowledge. In much of our society, people who introduce themselves with only their first name are very often in service occupations (e.g., waiters, housekeepers).

Providing the people we interact with in the healthcare system with first and last names and title signals that we are willing to be accountable for our actions and take responsibility for following up with concerns while providing needed reassurance. Introductions in our society normally include a handshake, so in the absence of infection control concerns, a handshake should be included. These practices should also be extended to how team members communicate with each other. If professionals of different disciplines in a healthcare setting are on a first-name basis with each other, then that practice should be continued when having discussions with patients and their families. This puts everyone on equal footing. When contacting other members of the healthcare team or contacting patients from a primary care office or performing callbacks for follow-up of care, using first and last names and title is a safe strategy.

EXERCISE 22.7 Think of how many times you have seen a letter from a patient acknowledging the excellence of the nursing care provided by Susan, Ann, and other nurses who are not named. How might nurses' reactions to these letters be different if the patients knew their nurses' names?

The second part of giving voice to nursing is describing nursing care so that it clearly communicates that nurses are knowledgeable and skillful (Buresh & Gordon, 2013). Although a patient may think that the nurse is just idly chatting about the weather or television programs in a patient room, he or she may not understand that the nurse has monitored intravenous fluids, checked outputs of catheters and drains, and assessed for evidence of dyspnea, all in the space of a few minutes; or in a clinic setting, the patient may not realize the nurse has determined whether additional teaching is necessary, or whether a new symptom needs to be brought to a healthcare provider's attention. See Box 22.3 for strategies to enhance the visibility of nursing practice.

Nurse leaders can also enhance professional authority by increasing the visibility of nursing practice through active participation at policy tables both within an organization and in the community. Nurses must lead and actively contribute to decisions being made about nursing practice, patient care, and its documentation using standardized nursing terminologies. Nurses should not just be at policy tables as a token representative of

---

BOX 22.3   Giving Visibility to Nursing Practice

1. Provide a complete introduction to patients, including full name, your role, and purpose of the interaction.
2. Ask the patient about his or her most important concerns.
3. Explain why you are doing assessments, the results of assessments, and the purpose of related interventions.
4. Describe how your interventions will affect outcomes for your patients.
5. Link your interventions to nursing research and/or evidence-based practice.
6. Describe how the judgments you make require consultation or discussion with other health professionals.
7. Regularly participate in team rounds to communicate important findings and patient concerns.
8. Ask patients and families if they have anything additional to share on on team rounds.
9. Follow up on patient concerns and communicate the plan for follow-up to patients and/or their families.
10. Validate with patients that their concerns have been addressed.
11. Include patients and families when planning for transitions of care.

---

nursing whose only role is to implement policies developed by others, but as an expert whose contributions are valued by the organization. Nurses can build on the QSEN competencies learned in school by expanding their focus from individual patients and their families to a systems approach (Phillips, Stalter, Dolansky, & Lopez, 2016). These approaches are illustrated in Table 22.3. Frontline nurses can begin their involvement in policy by volunteering to be on a healthcare agency's committee, joining a professional association, or volunteering for a community organization. These provide valuable experience in articulating the viewpoints of nurses and collaborating with members of other healthcare disciplines and representatives of the community.

Being person-centered also means moving beyond one's traditional focus on direct patient care by ensuring person-centered care is integral to the services provided by healthcare organizations. This can be accomplished by taking part in nursing governance and leadership opportunities within one's own healthcare organization and moving beyond the healthcare organization to

TABLE 22.3　Continuous Systems Thinking for QSEN Domains

QSEN Competency	Personal Effort/ Individual Care			Systems Thinking/ System Care
Patient-Centered Care	Document the presence and extent of my patients' pain.	Use common definitions, terms, and rating scales in documenting my patients' pain.	Formulate pain management plans with my patients, their families, and other healthcare professionals.	Participate in medical record reviews of our unit's pain management documentation.
Evidence-Based Practice	Differentiate clinical opinion from research and evidence summaries.	Discuss conflicting evidence in the literature with my colleagues.	Question the rationale for routine care approaches on my unit that are not evidence based.	Participate in writing unit-level standards of practice that are evidence based.
Teamwork and Collaboration	Ensure that my patients are ready for discharge by making sure they have their prescriptions.	Formulate discharge plan with my patients, their families, and other healthcare professionals.	Solicit input from other team members to improve my team performance.	Participate in improving the discharge process through team meetings to structure communication during a patient's hospital stay.
Safety	Wash my hands at the appropriate times in the care of my patients.	Get patients and families to participate in the campaign to reduce infection by washing hands.	Observe other nurses' handwashing technique and provide feedback.	Study the workarounds on my unit and create a cause-and-effect diagram to summarize why nurses do not wash their hands.
Quality Improvement	Ensure that I care for central lines using evidence-based practice.	Have a peer watch my central line dressing change so that I can improve my performance.	Review the data for our unit's central line infection rates.	Participate in a quality improvement project to improve compliance with central line bundle on our unit.
Informatics	Protect the confidentiality of my patients' protected health information in the electronic health record (EHR).	Attend in-service training updates to learn about new laws regarding health information protection.	Help design patient information flyers describing the patients' and families' rights to confidentiality of information in the EHR.	Participate in an agency-wide committee to update the agency EHR system.

Reprinted with permission from Dolansky, M. A., & Moore, S. M. (2013). Quality and Safety Education for Nurses (QSEN): The key is systems thinking. *OJIN: The Online Journal of Issues in Nursing, 18*(3):1. https://doi.org/10.3912/OJIN.Vol18No03Man01.

organizations providing support services in one's community. Nurse leaders can broaden their circle of involvement and improve the health of communities by volunteering to join a board. Nurse leaders bring not only their experiences in person-centered care but also their expertise in communication, quality improvement, patient engagement, and decision making, which demonstrates the value of nursing to the mission of healthcare organizations. Nurses can join a national effort to increase the number of nurses on boards, the Nurses on Boards Coalition (NOBC), which is designed to improve the health of communities (NOBC, 2016). Although joining a hospital board may seem daunting, joining the board of a local affiliate of a national healthcare organization or the board of a local affiliate of a professional association provides an opportunity to demonstrate the nursing perspective and the value of person-centered care. Board service provides the opportunity to learn about the kinds of support services that may be offered to people in the community while having the opportunity to increase nursing's visibility by sharing information about nurses and how nursing care improves health.

EXERCISE 22.8 Find out if a nurse is on the board of a local hospital. Is there a nurse on the board of the city or county health department? Ask a nurse leader about his or her involvement in committees, community boards, or professional associations and what strategies are used to focus on person-centered approaches to the delivery of services. Ask a direct care nurse about community involvement.

SYNTHESIS AND APPLICATION

Nurses are critically positioned to provide leadership in person-centered care. Understanding paradigm shifts in health care and the need to be responsive to the needs of individual, families, groups, communities, and populations will position nurses to fully participate in shaping health care in the future.

Nurse leaders influence the quality of care delivered by frontline staff, setting the tone for the implementation of the organization's mission and focus in the delivery of person-centered care. They must believe in and model a philosophy of care that is focused on the person. Careful Nursing as a practice model provides guidance on how the nurse interacts with persons and their families or caregiver and gives credence to the essential knowledge and competencies nurses need to provide safe, evidence-based nursing care.

Nurse leaders, when they are visible to frontline nurses, are in a unique position to not only model a person-centered approach for followers but also find solutions that enhance the quality of care. This can be accomplished by understanding the types of problems and their nature as experienced by patients and their families as well as the barriers faced by frontline nurses in delivering person-centered care. Being successful in facilitating the delivery of person-centered care requires openness and flexibility.

CONCLUSION

Health care is changing rapidly, as have the roles of frontline nurses and nurse leaders. The movement of health care into the home, community, clinic, and myriad outpatient settings has placed a new perspective on how to scale up for the volume of care while maintaining quality. Harnessing the motivations of patients and their families to engage them in the self-management of their health has the potential to enhance outcomes while reducing costs. Nurses, with their holistic approach and focus on the person and his or her needs, are a pivotal and powerful resource in the delivery of health care. Likewise, providing frontline nurses with the support and tools to engage in advocacy early in their careers has the potential to reap rewards as they apply the competencies learned in direct care to more complex situations and leadership roles.

THE SOLUTION

Recognizing the concern posed to be a patient safety concern, the nurse leader must leverage multiple resources in the pursuit of a patient-centered resolution. First, we connected the patient and family with our patient advocate to establish a consistent, single point of contact. Once the patient advocate contacted the patient's wife for a discussion, we leveraged the nursing process to evaluate the concern. We gathered the appropriate team members from various departments, including information technology, physicians, pharmacists, and direct care nurses, to assess the concerns and provide an explanation for the outcome. One of the most important diagnoses to make is whether the failure was caused by failure of a process or failure to follow an established process. In this specific case, the team determined the root cause to be a process failure. With that in mind, a workflow redesign was undertaken inclusive of redesign of the electronic medical record to enable reliable flow of information from order to discharge instructions to prescription. Although the resolution of the concern was primarily tactical and workflow, maintaining an open line of communication while the health system navigated the resolution process was important. This was accomplished by first acknowledging the concern and then closing the loop with the patient by sharing details about the problem's resolution.

Would this be a suitable approach for you? Why?

Angelo Venditti

REFLECTIONS

Think of a recent challenging interaction with a patient and/or a family member. What might you do differently to enhance person-centered care the next time that you encounter a similar situation?

Identify one action that you took to advocate for a patient at an individual level. What actions can you take to translate that advocacy to promoting a safe environment at the systems level?

THE EVIDENCE

Nurse researchers are examining patient perceptions of person-centered care. A metasynthesis of qualitative studies of indigenous peoples' experiences and perceptions of hospitalizations for acute care indicate the consistent emergence of three themes: strangers in a strange land, encountering dysfunctional interactions, and suffering stereotypes and assumptions indicating that indigenous peoples' experiences are negative

(Mbuzi, Fulbrook, & Jessup, 2017). Similarly, a systematic review of factors that affect patients' experience in nurse-led clinics indicates that person-centered care has a significant impact on patients' experiences (Jakimowicz, Stirling, & Duddle, 2015). These studies provide evidence for a focus on improving relationships to enhance person-centered care.

TIPS FOR COMPETENT PERSON-CENTERED CARE

- Facilitate professionals' influence over their practice.
- Give staff opportunities to learn new and varied skills.
- Provide recognition and reward for success and support and consolation for lack of success.

- Foster motivation and belief in the importance of everyone and the value of his or her contribution.

REFERENCES

Adepoju, O. E., Preston, M. A., & Gonzales, G. (2015). Health care disparities in the post-Affordable Care Act era. *American Journal of Public Health*, *105*(Suppl 5), S665–S667. https://doi.org/10.2105/AJPH.2015.302611.

Agency for Healthcare Research and Quality. (2011). *National healthcare quality report. Chapter 9. Access to health care.* https://www.ahrq.gov/research/findings/nhqrdr/nhqr11/chap9.html.

Aktan, N. M. (2016). Transforming nursing practice: The patient-centered medical home. *The American Nurse Today*, *11*(8). https://www.americannursetoday.com/transforming-nursing-practice-patient-centered-medical-home/.

American Academy of Nursing. (2015). *Patient-centered/holistic care.* http://www.aannet.org/initiatives/edge-runners/patientcentered-holisticcare.

American Geriatrics Society Expert Panel on Person-Centered Care. (2016). Person-centered care: A definition and essential elements. *Journal of the American Geriatrics Society*, *64*(1), 15–18. https://doi.org/10.1111/jgs.13866.

American Nurses Association (ANA). (2015). *Code of ethics for nurses with interpretive statements.* Silver Spring, MD: Nursesbooks.org.

American Nurses Association (ANA). (2003). *Nursing's social policy statement* (2nd ed.). Silver Spring, MD: Nursesbooks.org.

Berkman, N. D., Sheridan, S. L., Donahue, K. E., Halpern, D. J., Viera, A., Crotty, A., et al. (2011). *Health literacy interventions and outcomes: An updated systematic review. Evidence Report/Technology Assessments, No. 199.* Rockville, MD: Agency for Healthcare Research and Quality.

Bodenheimer, T., & Sinsky, C. (2014). From triple to quadruple aim: Care of the patient requires care of the provider. *Annals of Family Medicine*, *12*(6), 573–576. https://doi.org/10.1370/afm.1713.

Buresh, B., & Gordon, S. (2013). *From silence to voice: What nurses know and must communicate to the public* (3rd ed.). Ithaca, NY: Cornell University Press.

Burke, G. F. (2017, January 12). Geisinger's refund promise: Where things stand after one year. *NEJM Catalyst.* http://catalyst.nejm.org/geisinger-refund-promise-one-year/

Center for Advancing Health. (n.d.). *Engagement behavior framework.* http://www.cfah.org/engagement/research/engagement-behavior-framework.

Centers for Medicare and Medicaid Services. (2017). *HCAHPS Fact Sheet.* http://hcahpsonline.org/globalassets/hcahps/facts/hcahps_fact_sheet_november_2017.pdf.

Cross, T., Bazron, B. Dennis, K., & Isaacs, M. (1989). *Towards a culturally competent system of care (Volume I).* Washington, DC: Georgetown University Center for Child and Human Development, CASSP Technical Assistance Center.

Dolansky, M. A., & Moore, S. M. (2013). Quality and Safety Education for Nurses (QSEN): The key is systems thinking. *OJIN: The Online Journal of Issues in Nursing, 18*(3), 1.

Drenkard, K. (2015). The power of alignment: Educating nurses in quality and safety. *Nursing Administration Quarterly, 39*(3), 272–277. https://doi.org/10.1097/NAQ.0000000000000112.

Evardsson, D., Fetherstonhaugh, D., Nay, R., & Gibson, S. (2010). Development and initial testing of the Person-centered Care Assessment Tool (P-CAT). *International Psychogeriatrics, 22*(1), 101–108. https://doi.org/10.1017/S1041610209990688.

Fawcett, J., & Clarke, P. N. (2016). Nursing knowledge driving person-centered care. *Nursing Science Quarterly, 29*(4), 285–287. https://doi.org/10.1177/0894318416661110.

Greysen, S. R., Harrison, J. D., Kripalani, S., Vasilevskis, E., Robinson, E., Metlay, J., et al. (2017). Understanding patient-centred readmission factors: A multi-site mixed-methods study. *BMJ Quality & Safety, 26*(1), 33–41. https://doi.org/10.1136/bmjqs-2015-004570.

Health Foundation. (2014). *Person-centred care made simple: What everyone should know about person-centred care. Quick Guide.* http://www.health.org.uk/sites/health/files/PersonCentredCareMadeSimple.pdf.

Health Innovation Network. (n.d.). *What is person-centred care and why is it important?* www.hin-southlondon.org.

Hibbard, J. H., Greene, J., & Overton, V. (2013). Patients with lower activation associated with higher costs: Delivery systems should know their patients' scores. *Health Affairs, 32*(2), 216–222. https://doi.org/10.1377/hlthaff.2012.1064.

Hopper, K., Fried, T. K., & Pisani, M. A. (2015). Health care worker attitudes and identified barriers to patient sleep in the medical intensive care unit. *Heart Lung, 44*(2), 95–99. https://doi.org/10.1016/j.hrtlng.2015.01.011.

Institute for Healthcare Improvement. (n.d.). *The IHI Triple Aim Initiative.* http://www.ihi.org/Engage/Initiatives/TripleAim/Pages/default.aspx.

Institute of Medicine. (2004). *Health literacy: A prescription to end confusion.* Washington, DC: The National Academies Press. https://doi.org/10.17226/10883.

Institute of Medicine, Committee on Monitoring Access to Personal Health Care Services. (1993). *Access to health care in America.* Washington, DC: National Academies Press.

Institute of Medicine, Committee on Quality of Health Care in America. (2001). *Crossing the quality chasm: A new system for health in the 21st century.* Washington, DC: National Academies Press.

Institute of Medicine, Roundtable on Value and Science-Driven Health Care. (2011). *The learning health system and its innovation collaboratives. Update Report.* Washington, DC: National Academies Press.

International Council of Nurses. (n. d.). *International Classification for Nursing Practice (ICNP)®.* http://www.icn.ch/what-we-do/international-classification-for-nursing-practice-icnpr/.

Jakimowicz, S., Stirling, C., & Duddle, M. (2015). An investigation of factors that impact patients' subjevtive experience of nurse-led clinics: A qualitative systematic review. *Journal of Clinical Nursing, 24*(1–2), 19–33. https://doi.org/10.1111/jocn.12676.

Josiah Macy Jr. Foundation. (2016, June). *Registered nurses: Partners in transforming primary care.* Recommendations from the Macy Foundation Conference on Preparing Registered Nurses for enhanced roles in primary care. http://macyfoundation.org/publications/publication/conference-summary-registered-nurses-partners-in-transforming-primary-care.

Kaufman, B. G., Reiter, K., Pink, G. H., & Holmes, G. (2016). Medicaid expansion affects rural and urban hospitals differently. *Health Affairs, 35*(9), 1665–1672. https://doi.org/10.1377/hlthaff.2016.0357.

Kitson, A., Marshall, A., Bassett, K., & Zeitz, K. (2013). What are core elements of patient-centered care? A narrative review and synthesis of the literature from health policy, medicine and nursing. *Journal of Advanced Nursing, 69*(1), 4–15. https://doi.org/10.1111/j.1365-2648.2012.06064.x.

Koh, H. K., Brach, C., Harris, L. M., & Parchman, M. L. (2013). A proposed 'health literate care model' would constitute a systems approach to improving patients' engagement in care. *Health Affairs, 32*(2), 357–367. https://doi.org/10.1377/hlthaff.2012.1205.

Leary, E., & Diers, D. (2013). The silence of the unblown whistle: The Nevada hepatitis C public health crisis. *Yale Journal of Biology and Medicine, 86*(1), 79–87.

Lindholm, M., Hargraves, J. L., Ferguson, W. J., & Reed, G. (2012). Professional language interpretation and inpatient length of stay and readmission rates. *Journal of General Internal Medicine, 27*(10), 1294–1299. https://doi.org/10.1007/s11606-012-2041-5.

Mackert, M., Mabry-Flynn, A., Champlin, S., Donovan, E. E. & Pounders, K. (2016). Health literacy and health information technology adoption: The potential for a new digital divide. *Journal of Medical Internet Research, 18*(10), e264.

Marshall, A., Kitson, A., & Zeitz, K. (2012). Patients' view of patient-centered care: A phenomenological case study in one surgical unit. *Journal of Advanced Nursing, 68*(12), 2664–2673. https://doi.org/10.1111/j.1365-2648.2012.05965.x.

Mbuzi, V., Fulbrook, P., & Jessup, M. (2017). Indigenous peoples' experiences and perceptions of hospitalisation for acute care: A metasynthesis of qualitative studies. *International Journal of Nursing Studies, 71*, 39–49. https://doi.org/10.1016/j.ijnurstu.2017.03.003.

McCormack, B., Dewing, J., & McCance, T. (2011). Developing person-centered care: Addressing contextual challenges through practice development. *OJIN: The Online Journal of Issues in Nursing, 16*(2). https://doi.org/10.3912/OJIN.Vol16No02Man0.

McLeod, L. (2013). Patient transitions form inpatient to outpatient: Where are the risks? Can we address them? *Journal of Healthcare Risk Management, 32*(3), 13–19. https://doi.org/10.1002/jhrm.21101.

Meehan, T. C. (2017). *Careful nursing philosophy and professional practice model. Summary.* http://www.carefulnursing.ie/go/overview/summary.

National Quality Forum (2010, October). *Care coordination. Quality. connections.* www.qualityforum.org/Publications/2010/10/Quality_Connections__Care_Coordination.aspx.

Nightingale, F. (1859/2010). *Notes on nursing: what it is and what it is not.* Cambridge: Cambridge University Press.

Norman, J. (2016, December 19). *Americans rate healthcare providers high on honesty, ethics.* http://www.gallup.com/poll/200057/americans-rate-healthcare-providers-high-honesty-ethics.aspx?version=print.

Nurses on Boards Coalition. (2016). *10,000 nurses by 2020: to improve the health of communities nationwide.* http://www.nursesonboardscoalition.org.

O'Connor, S., & Carlson, E. (2016). Safety culture and senior leadership behavior: Using negative safety ratings to align clinical staff and senior leadership. *Journal of Nursing Administration, 46*(4), 215–220. https://doi.org/10.1097/NNA.0000000000000330.

Office of Minority Health. (2018). *The national CLAS standards.* https://minorityhealth.hhs.gov/omh/browse.aspx?lvl=2&lvlid=53.

Office of Minority Health. (n. d. a). *National standards for culturally and linguistically appropriate services (CLAS) in health and health care.* https://www.thinkculturalhealth.hhs.gov/assets/pdfs/EnhancedNationalCLASStandards.pdf.

Office of Minority Health. (n. d. b). *What is CLAS?* https://www.thinkculturalhealth.hhs.gov/clas/what-is-clas.

Phillips, J. M, Stalter, A. M., Dolansky, M. & Lopez, G. M. (2016). Fostering future leadership in quality and safety in health care through systems thinking. *Journal of*

Professional Nursing, 32(1), 15–24. doi.org/10.1016/j.profnurs.2015.06.003.

Ranard, B. L., Werner, R. M., Antanavicius, T., Schwartz, H. A., Smith, R. J., Meisel, Z. F.,. et al. (2016). Yelp reviews of hospital care can supplement and inform traditional surveys of the patient experience of care. *Health Affairs, 35*(4), 697–705. https://doi.org/10.1377/hlthaff.2015.1030.

Reiss-Brennan, B., Brunisholz, K. D., Dredge, C., Briot, P., Grazier, K., Wilcox, A., et al. (2016). Association of integrated team-based care with health care quality, utilization, and cost. *JAMA, 316*(8), 826–834. https://doi.org/10.1001/jama.2016.11232.

Rodwell, J., McWilliams, J., & Gulyas, A. (2017). The impact of characteristics of nurses' relationships with their supervisor, engagement and trust, on performance behaviours and intent to quit. *Journal of Advanced Nursing, 73*(1), 190–200. https://doi.org/10.1111/jan.13102.

Rollnick, S., Miller, W. R., & Butler, C. (2009). *Motivational interviewing in health care.* New York: Guilford Press.

Ruggiero, J., Smith, J., Copeland, J., & Boxer, B. (2015). Discharge time out: An innovative nurse-driven protocol for medication reconciliation. *Medsurg Nursing, 24*(3), 165–172.

Rutherford, M. M. (2014). The value of trust to nursing. *Nursing Economic$, 32*(6), 283–287. 327. quiz 289.

Sakallaris, B. R., Miller, W. L., Saper, R., Kreitzer, M. J., & Jonas, W. (2016). Meeting the challenge of a more person-centered futures for US health. *Global Advances in Health and Medicine, 5*(1), 51–60. https://doi.org/10.7453/gahmj.2015.085.

Shin, H. B., & Kominski, R. A. (2010). Language use in the United States: 2007. *American Community Survey Reports, ACS-12.* Washington, DC: U. S. Census Bureau. https://www.hsdl.org/?abstract&did=4153.

U.S. Census Bureau. (2017). New American Community Survey statistics for income, poverty and health insurance available for states and local areas. https://www.census.gov/newsroom/press-releases/2017/acs-single-year.html?CID=CBSM+ACS16.

U.S. Department of Health and Human Services. (2010). *Healthy People 2020: Health communication and health information technology.* http://www.healthypeople.gov/2020/topicsobjectives2020/overview.aspx?topicid=18.

Yoder, J. C., Yuen, T. C., Churpek, M. M., Arora, V. M., & Edelson, D. P. (2013). A prospective study of nighttime vital sign monitoring. *JAMA Internal Medicine, 173*(16), 1554–1555. https://doi.org/10.1001/jamainternmed.2013.7791.

World Health Organization. (2014). Global status report on noncommunicable diseases. (2014). Geneva: Author. http://www.who.int/nmh/publications/ncd-status-report-2014/en/.

23

Managing Quality and Risk

Victoria N. Folse

LEARNING OUTCOMES

- Apply quality management principles to clinical situations.
- Use the six steps of the quality improvement process.
- Practice using select quality improvement strategies to do the following:
  - Identify customer expectations.
  - Diagram clinical procedures.
- Develop standards and outcomes.
- Evaluate outcomes.
- Incorporate roles of leaders, managers, and followers to create a quality management culture of continuous readiness.
- Apply risk management strategies to an agency's quality management program.

KEY TERMS

accountability measure
always event
benchmarking
continuous quality improvement (CQI)
culture of safety
failure mode and effects analysis (FMEA)
handoff communication

high reliability organization
near miss
never event
nursing-sensitive indicator
performance improvement (PI)
quality assurance (QA)
quality improvement (QI)
quality management (QM)
risk management

root-cause analysis
sentinel event
situation, background, assessment, recommendation (SBAR)
teach-back
total quality management (TQM)
value-based payment/purchasing

THE CHALLENGE

Managing quality and reducing risk are central to patient care. The National Database of Nursing Quality Indicators (NDNQI) gives each unit within a healthcare institution a report card on certain indicators that measure healthcare performance. Examples of those indicators for my unit include incidence of falls, catheter-associated urinary tract infections (CAUTI), and central-line–associated bloodstream infections (CLABSI). Through audits, my unit found nurses were not recognizing patients who were high fall risks. We have patient beds that, when plugged in, alarm to the unit when a high–fall-risk patient gets up without assistance. Although we label high–fall-risk patients with

(Continued)

THE CHALLENGE—cont'd

yellow socks, a sign on the door, and an armband, we had a high incidence of falls on our unit, causing injury to our patients. We also found that patients were at a higher risk of infection when their central line or urinary catheter was inadvertently placed for too long or was not properly assessed. As a unit, we needed a solution to identify these risk indicators within our patient population as well as a tool to assist in decreasing these preventable events.

What would you do if you were this nurse?

Abigail Hertz, RN, BSN
Staff Nurse, Spine Center, Vanderbilt University Medical Center,
Nashville, TN

INTRODUCTION

Healthcare agencies and health professionals strive to provide the highest quality, safest, most efficient, and most cost-effective care possible. The philosophy of quality management and the process of quality improvement must shape the entire healthcare culture and provide specific skills for assessment, measurement, and evaluation of patient care. The goal of an organization committed to quality care is a comprehensive, systematic approach that prevents errors or identifies and corrects errors so that adverse events are decreased and safety and quality outcomes are maximized. Leadership must acknowledge safety challenges and allocate resources at the patient care and unit levels to identify and reduce risks. Managers must enhance work environments to support higher-quality care, less patient risk, and more satisfied nurses.

QUALITY MANAGEMENT IN HEALTH CARE

Healthcare systems that demand quality recognize that survival and competitiveness are built on improved patient outcomes. Success depends on a philosophy that permeates the organization and values a continuous process of improvement. Patient safety and risk management are essential to integrate into broader quality initiatives. The Institute of Medicine (now the National Academy of Medicine) brought the issue of medical errors to the forefront of healthcare awareness in 2000 with its landmark report, *To Err is Human: Building a Safer Health System.* Since then, several key organizations, including the Agency for Healthcare Research and Quality (AHRQ), the National Quality Forum (NQF), the Institute for Healthcare Improvement (IHI), The Joint Commission (TJC), and Quality and Safety Education for Nurses (QSEN), have taken lead roles in promoting quality and safety in health care. Nurses must be prepared to continuously improve the quality and safety of healthcare

systems within which they work, and they must focus on the six competencies identified by QSEN: patient-centered care, teamwork and collaboration, evidence-based practice, quality improvement, safety, and informatics (QSEN Institute, 2014). Quality necessitates maintaining safety in patient care, with a continual focus on clinical excellence from the entire interprofessional team. Patient safety is a key component of quality improvement and clinical governance. Moreover, the prevention of adverse events is paramount to improved patient outcomes (Aiken, Clarke, Sloane, Lake, & Cheney, 2008).

The terms quality management (QM), quality improvement (QI), performance improvement (PI), total quality management (TQM), and continuous quality improvement (CQI) are often used interchangeably in health care, and the terminology continues to evolve. Safety goals are often blended with quality programs and include a culture of safety that is a blame-free environment that encourages employees to report errors and prevent situations that threaten safety so quality can be assured. The Joint Commission's designation of high-reliability organizations signals healthcare organizations that achieve the highest quality and safety standards through organizational effectiveness, efficiency, customer satisfaction, compliance, organizational culture, and documentation.

In this chapter, *QM* refers to an overarching philosophy that defines a healthcare culture emphasizing customer satisfaction, innovation, and employee involvement. Similarly, *QI* refers to an ongoing process of innovative improvements, prevention of error, and development of staff that is used by institutions that adopt the QM philosophy. Nurses maintain a unique role in QM and QI because of the direct patient care provided at the bedside 24 hours a day and because they have an understanding of a patient's day-to-day issues. Nurses are responsible for early warning monitoring, and they have direct knowledge of patients' conditions and changes (McHugh et al., 2016). Active involvement of nurses in patient care improvement efforts (e.g., safe delivery of care during off-peak hours like nights and weekends, as well as during times of low staffing, high census, or high acuity; or interprofessional adverse events) promotes quality and safety of patient care and also positively affects job satisfaction and improves the work environment (McHugh et al., 2016).

BENEFITS OF QUALITY MANAGEMENT

Healthcare systems that use a comprehensive QM program experience many organizational benefits. First, greater efficiency and proactive planning may overcome some of the resource constraints, including limited reimbursement imposed by prospective payment plans and key staff shortages. Second, successful malpractice suits could be reduced with quality care because QM is based on the philosophy that actions should be right the first time and that improvement is always possible. Third, job satisfaction could be enhanced, because QM involves everyone on the improvement team and encourages everyone to contribute. This style of participative management makes employees feel valued as team members who are empowered to make a difference in quality and safety initiatives.

PLANNING FOR QUALITY MANAGEMENT

Interprofessional planning is integral to the quest for quality. Issues are examined from various perspectives using a systematic process. Planning takes time and money; however, the price of poor planning can be very expensive. Costs of inadequate planning might involve correcting a patient care error, resulting in extended length of stay and added procedures. In turn, this increases the risk of liability for what was originally done, it risks a negative public image, and it magnifies employee frustration and promotes turnover. The costs of errors and ineffective nursing actions are avoidable costs. Value-based purchasing initiatives have been initiated in response to escalating healthcare costs and concerns about quality and safety in health care (Stimpfel, Sloane, McHugh, & Aiken, 2016). Value-based payment/purchasing programs (e.g., Centers for Medicare & Medicaid Services [CMS]; UnitedHealth Group) reward or incentivize high-performing organizations whose outcomes are consistent with quality of care standards and reduce reimbursement for poor performers. Thirty-day readmission, for example, is an accountability metric for hospital performance. Thus hospital leaders are greatly concerned when a patient requires readmission soon after discharge, because this can signal an issue with the care received and can result in the hospital losing money.

EVOLUTION OF QUALITY MANAGEMENT

Non-healthcare industries have excelled in focusing on process improvement as part of their core operating strategies. Several models for quality improvement exist in health care and include Lean Sigma and Six Sigma, Failure Mode and Effects Analysis, and Root Cause Analysis. Numerous business management philosophies have been expanded and modified for use in healthcare organizations. For example, Lean Sigma and Six Sigma, data-driven approaches targeting a nearly error-free environment, empower employees to improve processes and outcomes (Deblois & Lepanto, 2016). As healthcare organizations "go lean," nurses are challenged to eliminate unnecessary steps and reduce wasted processes (saving time and money) to improve quality and the patient experience. Lean and Six Sigma management techniques are most effective with improving quality and efficiency in settings in which processes are linear, like operating rooms, emergency departments, and intensive care units (Deblois & Lepanto, 2016). To achieve this, Six Sigma uses a five-step methodology known as *DMAIC,* which stands for *d*efine opportunities, *m*easure performance, *a*nalyze opportunity, *i*mprove performance, and *c*ontrol performance to improve existing processes. Parallels to the nursing process steps of assessment, diagnosis, planning, implementation, and evaluation can be seen in DMAIC and other QI processes. Different types of quality improvement methodology can be combined to improve outcomes.

In health care, emphasis is placed on the areas of patient safety and patient and employee satisfaction. The role of the leader or manager in this TQM method is to enable the team, remove barriers, and instill accountability. One of the most widely used evidence-based teamwork systems to improve communication and teamwork skills to improve patient safety within organizations is the AHRQ Team Strategies and Tools to Enhance Performance and Patient Safety (TeamSTEPPS and TeamSTEPPS 2.0). Teamwork is one of the key safety initiatives that can transform a healthcare culture. Team training is modified for primary care office–based teams as well as for nursing homes and other long-term care settings. A customized Team-STEPPS plan is available to train staff in teamwork skills to work with patients who have difficulty communicating in English (AHRQ, 2016a).

Within healthcare systems, QI combines the assessment of *structure* (e.g., adequacy of staffing, effectiveness of computerized charting, or availability of unit-based medication delivery systems), *process* (e.g., timeliness and thoroughness of documentation, adherence to critical pathways or care maps), and *outcome* (e.g., patient falls, hospital-acquired infection rates, or patient and nurse satisfaction) standards. These three factors are usually considered interrelated, and comprehensive quality improvement initiatives actively involve direct care providers to improve quality and safety. The Literature Perspective presents an opportunity for nurses, including new graduates, to be engaged in shared governance to improve patient and nurse outcomes.

Recognizing the relationship between quality patient care and nursing excellence, the American Academy of Nursing undertook an initiative that resulted in the distinction known as *Magnet®*. The American Nurses Credentialing Center (ANCC) created a process called the *Magnet Recognition Program®*, which recognizes healthcare organizations for quality patient care, nursing excellence, and innovations in professional nursing practice. The term *Magnet®* was chosen to describe a hospital that attracts and retains nurses even in times of nursing shortages. Magnet® hospital research has examined the characteristics of hospital systems that impede or facilitate professional practice in nursing and also promote quality patient outcomes. Common organizational characteristics of Magnet® hospitals include structure factors (e.g., decentralized organizational structure, participative management style, and influential nurse executives) and process factors (e.g., professional autonomy and decision making, ongoing professional development/education, active quality improvement initiatives). ANCC Magnet® designated hospitals and other high-reliability organizations in the United States and abroad generally have lower burnout rates, have higher levels of job satisfaction, and provide higher levels of quality care, resulting in greater levels of patient satisfaction (Stimpfel et al., 2016). This work was the forerunner of the fourth component of the Quadruple Aim.

QUALITY MANAGEMENT PRINCIPLES

The combination of QI ideas from theory and research is sometimes referred to as *TQM* or, more simply, *QM*. The basic principles of QM are summarized in Box 23.1 and are developed further in the next section of this chapter.

LITERATURE PERSPECTIVE

Resources: Kutney-Lee, A., Germack, H., Hatfield, L., Kelly, S., Maguire, P., Dierkes, A., Del Guidice, M., Aiken, L. H. (2016). Nurse engagement in shared governance and patient and nurse outcomes. *JONA: The Journal of Nursing Administration, 46*(11), 605–612.

Because many new graduates work on units where the patient population is extremely complex and levels of staffing are variable, it is critical to understand and mitigate the factors that affect quality and risk. Levels of engagement, including involvement in shared governance like unit safety councils, vary widely across institutions. Nurses engaged in shared governance and quality improvement initiatives allow dialogue about improving interprofessional communication and collaboration and provide opportunities to identify the resources, including evidence-based practice standards, needed to promote favorable nurse and patient outcomes.

Implications for Practice

Shared governance is an opportunity to empower bedside nurses in institutional decision making. Higher levels of engagement were associated with better Hospital Consumer Assessment of Healthcare Providers and Systems (HCAHPS) scores, signaling overall patient satisfaction. In agencies with greater levels of engagement, nurses reported greater job satisfaction and better ratings for quality and safety. A practice environment that encourages nurse engagement promotes optimal nurse and patient outcomes. Improving nurse engagement in shared governance may serve as a transformational leadership strategy that will translate into an improved patient experience and may generate improved reimbursement.

culture that values quality freely make suggestions for improvement and innovation in patient care.

EXERCISE 23.1 Reflect on something that can be improved in one of your clinical settings or in your professional practice environment. Define the problem, using as many specific facts as possible. List the advantages to the staff, patients, and agency of improving this problem. Describe several possible solutions to the problem. Decide whom you could contact about these suggestions.

Structure

When decisions are made closest to where they have an effect, people are more satisfied, decisions are more practical, and quality is enhanced. Every organization has some form of hierarchy. When decisions are made remotely from the point of implementation, they may be theoretically correct yet cumbersome, impractical, or costly to execute. Flat, democratic organizations promote decisions being made closest to where they will be implemented.

Shared Commitment

Leaders, managers, and followers must be committed to QI. Top-level leaders and managers retain the ultimate responsibility for QM but must involve the entire organization in the QI process. Although some healthcare organizations have achieved significant QI results without system-wide support, total organizational involvement is necessary for a culture transformation. If all members of the healthcare team are to be actively involved in QI, clear delineation of roles within a nonthreatening environment must be established (Table 23.1).

To work effectively in a democratic, quality-focused corporate environment, nurses and other healthcare workers must accept QM and QI as an integral part of their roles. Nurses have a direct impact on patient safety and healthcare outcomes and must follow evidence-based guidelines to meet nursing-sensitive outcome indicators. Nursing must be recognized and empowered to mobilize performance improvement knowledge and practice measures throughout the organization. When a separate department controls quality activities, healthcare managers and workers often relinquish responsibility and commitment for quality control to these quality specialists. Employees working in an organizational

Goal

The goal of QM is to improve the system, not to assign blame. Managers strive to provide a system in which workers can function effectively. To encourage commitment to QI, nurse managers must clearly articulate the organization's mission and goals. All levels of employees, from nursing assistants to hospital administrators, must be educated about QI strategies.

Communication should flow freely within the organization. When healthcare professionals understand each other's roles and can effectively communicate and work together, patients are more likely to receive safe, quality care. Because QM stresses improving the system, detection of employees' errors is not stressed; if errors occur, reeducation of staff is emphasized rather than imposition of punitive measures. When patient safety indicators are used to examine hospital performance, the focus of error analysis shifts from the individual provider to the level of the healthcare system. The use of an electronic health record can improve the quality of health care by increasing time efficiency and adherence to guidelines as well as reducing medication errors and adverse drug events (Campanella et al., 2016). Reducing medication errors through improved hand-off communication (e.g., SBAR) and increased use of technology (e.g., electronic health record, barcode scanning) is needed to address time pressures, work overload, and conflicting demands of nurses, including unlicensed nursing personnel. Improving the practice environment will favorably affect quality and risk variables in all healthcare settings.

Focus

QI focuses on outcomes. Patient outcomes are statements that describe the results of health care. They are specific and measurable and describe patients' behavior. Outcome statements may be based on patients' needs,

TABLE 23.1   Roles and Responsibilities in a Quality Improvement Plan

Role of Senior Leader	Role of Nurse Manager	Role of Follower/Staff (e.g., Direct Care Nurse)
Leads culture transformation	Is accountable for quality and safety indicator performance within areas of responsibility	Follows policies, procedures, and protocols to ensure quality and safe patient care
Sets priorities for house-wide activities, staffing effectiveness, and patient health outcomes	Communicates performance priorities and targets to staff	Remains current in the literature on quality and safety specific to nursing
Builds infrastructure, provides resources, and removes barriers for improvement	Meets regularly with staff to monitor progress and help with improvement work	Promotes evidence-based practice standards
Defines procedures for immediate response to errors involving care, treatment, or services and contains risk	Uses data to measure effectiveness of improvement	Communicates with and educates peers immediately if they are observed not following quality and safety standards
Assesses management and staff knowledge of quality management process regularly, and provides education as needed	Works with staff to develop and implement action plans for improvement of measures that do not meet target	Reports quality and safety issues to supervisor/manager
Implements and monitors systems for internal and external reporting of information	Provides time for unit staff to participate in quality improvement measures	Invests in the process by continually asking self, "What makes this indicator important to measure?" "What has been done to improve it?" "What can I do to improve it?"
Defines and provides support system for staff who have been involved in a sentinel event	Observes staff directly and coaches as needed	Participates actively in the quality improvement activities
Empowers nursing leaders and direct care providers to implement and evaluate improvement efforts	Consults quality management team (e.g., Six Sigma) or risk management team as appropriate	Provides insight as a direct care provider
Removes barriers and ensures resources are adequate	Writes and submits to senior leaders periodic action plan including performance measures and plans for improvement	Generates ideas for unit quality improvement efforts
Rewards high-performing teams	Shares information and benchmarks with other units and departments to improve organization's performance	Serves as role model for other direct care providers

ethical and legal standards of practice, or other standardized data systems. Healthcare organizations that implement nursing-sensitive performance measures value nurses and have a strong commitment to patient care quality and workforce sustainability. This commitment is even more critical because CMS and some private insurers no longer reimburse hospitals for the costs of additional care required for hospital-acquired injuries and reduce reimbursement for preventable complications. Pay-for-performance strategies, including value-based payment, has the potential to reduce negative health outcomes.

Decisions

Decisions must be based on data. The use of statistical tools enables nurse managers to make objective decisions about QI activities. Collecting data without a preconceived idea is critical to making quality decisions. Quality information must be gathered and analyzed without bias before improvement suggestions and recommendations are made.

CUSTOMERS

Customers define quality. Successful organizations measure the factors that are most important to customers and focus their energies on enhancing quality in these areas. As patients become more sophisticated and view themselves as "consumers" who can take their business elsewhere, they want input into treatment decisions. Although typical patients may not be knowledgeable about a specific treatment, they know if they were satisfied with their experience with the healthcare provider.

Every nurse and healthcare agency has internal and external customers. Internal customers are people or units within an organization who receive products or services. A nurse working on a hospital unit could describe patients, nurses on the other shifts, and other hospital departments as internal customers. External customers are people or groups outside the organization who receive products or services. For nurses, these external customers may include patients' families, physicians, managed care organizations, and the community at large. Some customers (e.g., physicians, patient families) could be either internal or external customers depending on the actual care environment. Managers and direct care nurses need to identify their internal and external customers.

> **EXERCISE 23.2** For 1 week, list every person with whom you interact in your professional role. The internal customers are those people who work for or receive care in your organization. External customers come from outside the organization. What is the best method to obtain feedback from each of these customers?

Public reporting of quality and risk data is changing the way customers make decisions about health care and is intended to improve care through easily accessed information. Accredited hospitals are required to collect and report data on performance for core quality indicators,

> **BOX 23.2 Accountability Measures**
>
> - Inpatient psychiatric services
> - VTE (venous thromboembolism) care
> - Stroke care
> - Perinatal care
> - Immunization
> - Tobacco treatment
> - Substance use
>

called accountability measures, that produce the greatest positive impact on patient outcomes and for which organizations are held to standards of performance (Box 23.2). These data are made publicly available by The Joint Commission (TJC, 2016a) and through Hospital Compare (Centers for Medicare & Medicaid Services [CMS], 2016a). These data allow customers to (1) find information on how well hospitals care for patients with certain medical conditions or surgical procedures, and (2) access patient survey results about the care received during a recent hospital stay. This information allows customers to compare the quality of care in more than 4000 Medicare-certified hospitals. Patient satisfaction information on Hospital Compare is part of the Consumer Assessment of Healthcare Providers and Systems (CAHPS) Hospital Survey, known as *HCAHPS*. HCAHPS is a national, standardized, publicly reported survey of patient perspectives and satisfaction on care they experience during a hospital stay, including communication with physicians, communication with nurses, responsiveness of hospital staff, pain management, communication about medicines, discharge information, cleanliness of the hospital environment, and quietness of the hospital environment (CMS, 2016b). In addition to Hospital Compare, websites for Physician Compare, Nursing Home Compare, and Home Health Compare provide transparency for consumers. Consumer satisfaction of health care can also be assessed through the use of questionnaires, interviews, focus group discussions, or observation. Patients' perspectives should be a key component of any quality improvement initiative. However, patients cannot always adequately assess the competence of clinical performance, and therefore patient feedback and patient satisfaction surveys must serve as only one data source for QI initiatives.

THE QUALITY IMPROVEMENT PROCESS

QI involves continual analysis and evaluation of products and services to prevent errors and to achieve customer satisfaction. As the term suggests, the work of continuous QI never stops, because products and services can always be improved.

The QI process is a structured series of steps designed to plan, implement, and evaluate changes in healthcare activities. Many models of the QI process exist, including Six Sigma DMAIC, but most parallel the nursing process and all contain steps similar to those listed in Box 23.3. The six steps can easily be applied to clinical situations. In the following example, staff at a community clinic use the QI process to handle patient complaints about excessive wait times. An example of the process follows:

A community clinic receives a number of complaints from patients about waiting up to 2 hours for scheduled appointments to see a licensed practitioner. The clinic secretary and direct care nurses suggest to the clinic manager that scheduling clinic appointments be investigated by the QI committee, which is composed of the clinic secretary, two clinic nurses, one physician, and one nurse practitioner. The clinic manager agrees to the staff's suggestion and assigns the problem to the QI committee. At their next meeting, the QI committee uses a flowchart to describe the scheduling process from the time a patient calls to make an appointment until the patient sees a physician or nurse practitioner in the examining room. Next, the committee members decide to gather and analyze data about the important parts of the process: the number of calls for appointments, the number of patients seen in a day, the number of cancelled or missed

appointments, and the average time each patient spends in the waiting room. The committee discovers that too many appointments are scheduled because many patients miss appointments. This overbooking often results in long waiting times for the patients who do arrive on time. The QI committee also gathers information on clinic waiting times from the literature and through interviews with patients and colleagues. A measurable outcome is written: "Patients will wait no longer than 30 minutes to be seen by a licensed practitioner." After a discussion of options, the team recommends that appointments be scheduled at more reasonable intervals, that patients receive notification of appointments by mail and by phone, and that all clinic patients be educated about the importance of keeping scheduled appointments. The committee communicates its suggestions for throughput improvement to the manager and staff and monitors the results of the implementation of their improvement suggestions. Within 3 months, the average waiting room time per patient decreases to 90 minutes, and the number of missed patient appointments decreases by 20%. Because the desired outcome has not been met, the QI committee will continue the QI process.

Identify Consumers' Needs

The QI process begins with the selection of a clinical activity for review. Theoretically, any and all aspects of clinical care could be improved through the QI process. However, QI efforts should be concentrated on changes to patient care that will have the greatest effect. To determine which clinical activities are most important, nurse managers or direct care nurses may interview or survey patients about their healthcare experiences or may review unmet quality standards. The results of the research study in the Research Perspective give direction to promoting a positive practice environment.

Assemble a Team

Once an activity is selected for possible improvement, an interprofessional team implements the QI process. QI team members should represent a cross section of workers who are involved with the problem. To maximize success, team members may need to be educated about their roles before starting the QI process.

To develop effective unit-based quality councils, the workplace environment must promote teamwork. Some departments within healthcare facilities are more open

---

BOX 23.3   Steps in the Quality Improvement Process

1. Identify needs most important to the consumer of healthcare services.
2. Assemble an interprofessional team to review the identified consumer needs and services.
3. Collect data to measure the current status of these services.
4. Establish measurable outcomes and quality indicators.
5. Select and implement a plan to meet the outcomes.
6. Collect data to evaluate the implementation of the plan and the achievement of outcomes.

RESEARCH PERSPECTIVE

Resources: McHugh, M. D., Rochman, M. F., Sloane, D. M., Berg, R. A., Mancini, M. E., Merchant, R. M., & Aiken, L. H. (2016). Better nurse staffing and nurse work environments associated with increased survival of in-hospital cardiac arrest patients. *Med Care, 54*(1), 74–80; Stimpfel, A.W., Sloane, D. M., McHugh, M. D., & Aiken, L. H. (2016). Hospitals known for nursing excellence associated with better hospital experience for patients. *Health Services Research,* 51(3), 1120–1134.

The quality of the practice environment has a tremendous impact on nurse and patient outcomes. Patient outcomes are better in hospitals with good work environments, yet general clinical units can be underresourced at times, even in high-performing organizations. Many new graduates work on a medical-surgical unit, in which patient-to-nurse ratios are higher than most specialty units and are more variable from shift to shift. Nearly half of all in-hospital cardiac arrests occur on medical-surgical units, making the practice environment on general units particularly important. Improvement in work culture requires a change in interprofessional culture and an investment in nursing resources.

Implications for Practice

Better nurse staffing and nurse work environments are associated with increased survival of in-hospital cardiac arrest patients. Positive patient care environments and decreased patient-to-nurse ratios on medical-surgical units

are associated with better survival rates. Improving work conditions holds promise for preventing deaths, including cardiac arrests.

A strong correlation has been established between nurse practice environments and patient and nurse outcomes. The effects of nurse practice environments on nurse and patient outcomes, including nurse job satisfaction, burnout, intent to leave, and reports of quality of care such as mortality and failure to rescue patients have been established. Patients had a significantly lower risk of death and failure to rescue in hospitals with better care environments, the best nurse staffing levels, and the most highly educated nurses.

Nurse managers and leaders have several options for improving nurse retention and patient outcomes, including improving RN staffing, moving to a more educated nurse workforce, facilitating a positive care environment, and promoting nurse engagement through shared governance. Hospitals whose practice environment includes investment in development of staff, quality management, and good nurse-physician relations (e.g., Magnet® designation) are associated with better nurse and patient outcomes. Nurse managers who promote an empowered workplace and facilitate teamwork support higher-quality care, less patient risk, and more satisfied nurses. Investment in a baccalaureate-educated workforce and specialty certification has great potential to improve quality and reduce risk.

---

to teamwork than are others. Nursing leadership students as well as nurse leaders and managers can use Exercise 23.3 to decide whether their clinical unit is ready for a unit-based QI team.

EXERCISE 23.3 Ask yourself the following questions about the unit or department:

1. Is communication between nurses and other professionals promoted? If so, how?
2. Could the interprofessional communication process be improved in any way? If so, how?
3. Does your system encourage nurses to act as a team? If so, how?
4. Are other disciplines or departments included in team activities? In what manner?
5. Can the team focus be improved in any way? In what ways?

Collect Data

After the interprofessional team forms, the group collects data to measure the current status of the activity, service, or procedure under review. Various data tools, including flowcharts, line graphs, histograms, Pareto charts, and fishbone diagrams, may be used to analyze and present this information. The use of empirical tools to organize QI data is an essential part of the QI process. Many newly licensed registered nurses lack formal training in the use of QI tools and lack sufficient knowledge, concepts, and tools required to fully participate in QI initiatives. QI skills of direct care providers are necessary to identify gaps between current care and best practice and to design, implement, test, and evaluate changes through shared governance (Kutney-Lee et al., 2016)

A detailed flowchart is used to describe complex tasks. The flowchart is a data tool that uses boxes and directional arrows to diagram all the steps of a process or procedure in the proper sequence. Sometimes, just diagramming a patient care process in detail reveals gaps and opportunities for improvement. The flowchart in Fig. 23.1 depicts the process of a home health agency receiving a new patient referral.

Line graphs present data by showing the connection among variables. The dependent variable is usually plotted on the vertical scale, and the independent variable is usually plotted on the horizontal scale. In QI, this technique is often used to show the trend of a particular activity over time, and the result may be called a *trend chart*. The line graph in Fig. 23.2 illustrates the number of referrals a home health agency receives during a year.

The histogram in Fig. 23.3 illustrates the number of home health referrals that come from five different referral sources during a selected year. A histogram is a bar chart that shows the frequency of events.

A bar chart that identifies the major causes or components of a particular quality control problem is called a *Pareto chart*. It differs from a regular bar graph in that the highest frequencies of occurrence of a factor are designated in the bar at the left, with the other factors appearing in descending order. Used often in QI, the Pareto chart helps the QI team determine priorities, allowing the most significant problem to be addressed first. The Pareto chart in Fig. 23.4 demonstrates that, on a medical-surgical unit over a 1-month period, omission of vital signs was the most common type of documentation error.

The fishbone diagram is an effective method of summarizing a brainstorming session. A specific problem or outcome is written on the horizontal line. All possible causes of the problem or strategies to meet the outcome are written in a fishbone pattern. Fig. 23.5 uses a fishbone diagram to present possible causes of patients' complaints about extended waits for clinic appointments.

Although QI teams should be able to use these basic statistical tools, analysis that is more complex is sometimes necessary. In this situation, a statistical expert could be included on the QI team, or the team may consult a statistician.

Establish Outcomes

After analyzing the data, the team next sets a goal for improvement. This goal can be established in a number of ways but always involves a standard of practice and a measurable patient-care outcome or nursing-sensitive

outcome. Nursing-sensitive indicators depend on the quantity or quality of nursing care and reflect the structure, process, and outcomes of nursing care. The structure of nursing care is indicated by the supply of nursing staff, the skill level of the nursing staff, and the education and certification of nursing staff. Process indicators measure aspects of nursing care such as assessment, intervention, and registered nurse (RN) job satisfaction. Patient outcomes that are determined to be nursing sensitive are those that improve if there is a greater quantity or quality of nursing care (e.g., pressure ulcers, falls, intravenous [IV] infiltrations). Some patient outcomes are more highly related to other aspects of institutional care, such as medical decisions and institutional policies (e.g., frequency of primary cesarean sections, cardiac failure) and are not considered nursing sensitive. The interprofessional team should use accepted standards of care and practice whenever possible. Clinical practice guidelines and standards should reflect evidence-based practice and should be updated as new research emerges. Sources that establish these standards include the following:

1. American Nurses Association (ANA) standards of nursing practice
2. State nurse practice acts
3. Accrediting bodies such as TJC or recognition bodies such as the American Nurses Credentialing Center (ANCC)
4. Governmental bodies such as the AHRQ, the CMS, the Centers for Disease Control and Prevention (CDC) Division of Healthcare Quality Promotion (DHQP), and the National Institute for Occupational Safety and Health (NIOSH)
5. Healthcare advisory groups such as the National Academy of Medicine (formerly known as the Institute of Medicine), the NQF, and QSEN
6. Nationally recognized professional organizations
7. Nursing research/evidence-based, best practice standards
8. Internal policies and procedures
9. Internal or external performance measurement data such as patient satisfaction surveys, employee opinion surveys, safety assessment surveys, and patient or employee rounding

Although individual healthcare organizations may have unique patient needs related to their specific population or environment, many targeted outcomes are similar. One way to evaluate the quality of outcomes

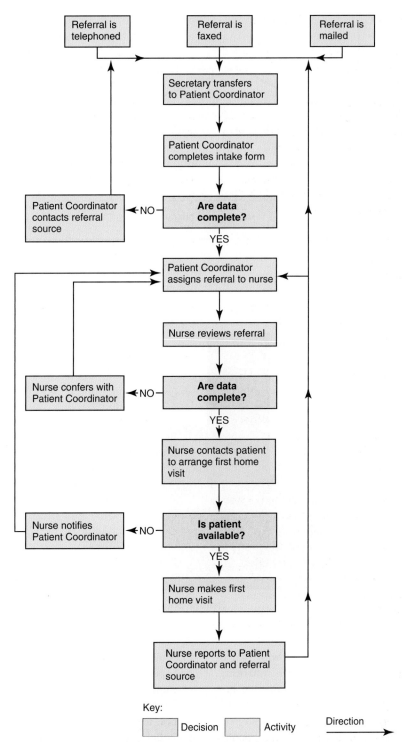

Fig. 23.1 Steps in a flowchart diagramming the process of a new patient referral, starting with the time a home health referral is made and ending with the first home visit.

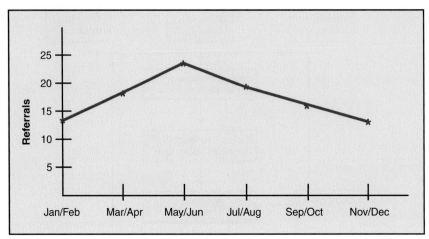

Fig. 23.2 Line graph depicting the number of home health referrals received during 1 year (trend chart).

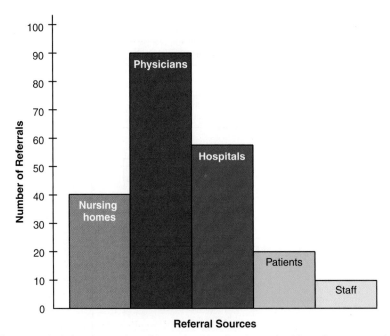

Fig. 23.3 Histogram depicting the number of home health referrals received from five sources during 1 year.

is to compare one agency's performance with that of similar organizations. In a process called benchmarking, a widespread search is conducted to identify the best performance against which to measure others. Through this process of comparing the best practices with your practice and process, your organization learns to identify desired standards of quality performance. Available data include all reported hospital-acquired infection rates in other institutions as well as specific data, such as postoperative infection rates in adult surgical intensive care units of similar-size institutions.

However, recent mandates to publicly disclose outcomes, including nosocomial infection rates, highlight potential issues with disclosure of data. Specifically, simply reporting hospital infection rates is not enough to promote hand hygiene practices and may do little

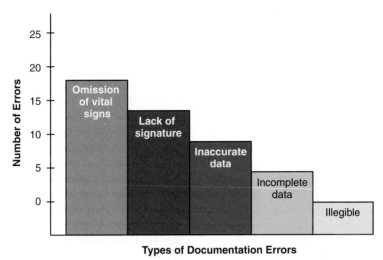

Fig. 23.4 Pareto chart presenting major types of documentation errors that occurred on a medical-surgical unit over a 1-month period.

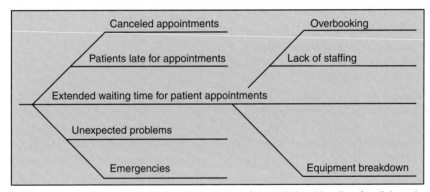

Fig. 23.5 Fishbone diagram showing possible causes of extended waiting time for clinic patients.

to improve outcomes and reduce hospital-acquired infections. Unfortunately, the usefulness of the information from other institutions continues to be hampered by differences in terminology and methodology, including use of present-on-admission data. Information technology plays a vital role in QI by increasing the efficiency of data entry and analysis. A consistent information system that trends high-risk procedures and systematic errors would provide a useful database regarding outcomes of care and resource allocation. The NQF is designed to standardize measures so that true comparisons can be made.

The National Database of Nursing Quality Indicators (NDNQI) is a national nursing quality measurement program that provides hospitals with unit-level performance reports with comparisons with regional, state, and national percentile rankings (Press Ganey, 2015). All indicator data are collected and reported at the nursing unit level, which is valuable for unit-based patient safety and quality improvement initiatives. For example, a report could answer the question, "How is my hospital unit doing relative to the same unit type in peer hospitals?" NDNQI's nursing-sensitive indicators reflect the structure, process, and outcomes of nursing care. NDNQI's mission is to aid the nursing provider in patient safety and quality improvement efforts by providing research-based national comparative data on nursing care and the relationship to patient outcomes. Many of the NDNQI indicators are NQF-endorsed measures and are part of NQF's nursing-sensitive measure set (e.g., falls with injuries, nosocomial infections, restraint prevalence, nursing hours per patient day, staff mix). However, the NDNQI allows additional comparisons of indicators such as nurse job satisfaction, RN education, and certification with adverse patient events such as pressure ulcers, psychiatric patient assaults, and pediatric intravenous infiltration rates. A high-quality work environment, as evidenced by reported job enjoyment and intent to stay, positively affects NDNQI key performance indicators such as patient safety, patient experiences, nurse outcomes, and hospital payment programs (Buhlman, 2016). Nursing has been a leader in the information system field by developing standardized nursing classification systems. The availability of standardized nursing data enables the study of health problems across populations, settings, and caregivers. Consistent use of standardized language enhances the process of QI and also demonstrates the contributions of nursing to lawmakers, healthcare policymakers, and the public.

Although NDNQI is nursing specific, the AHRQ (2016b) reports quality indicators that measure hospital quality and safety performance across disciplines and at the systems level. The AHRQ includes Patient Safety Indicators, a set of hospital-level indicators of safety-related adverse events, as well as Inpatient Quality Indicators and Pediatric Quality Indicators, sets of hospital-level measures of quality for patients.

Three leading nursing classification systems have been identified: The North American Nursing Diagnosis Association International's (NANDA-I) nomenclature (Herdman & Kamitsura, 2014); the Nursing Intervention Classification (NIC) system (Bulechek, Butcher, & Dochtermann, 2013); and the Nursing Outcomes Classification (NOC) system (Moorhead, Johnson, Maas, & Swanson, 2013). The use of standardized nursing terminologies like NANDA-I, NIC, and NOC provides a means of collecting and analyzing nursing data and evaluating nursing-sensitive outcomes.

Each classification system focuses on one component of the nursing process. Nursing diagnoses can be labeled using NANDA-I. These diagnosis labels represent clinical judgments about actual or potential health problems. Each diagnosis contains a definition, major and minor defining characteristics, and related factors. Accurate nursing diagnoses guide the selection of nursing interventions to achieve the desired treatment effects, determine nursing-sensitive outcomes, and ensure patient safety (Herdman & Kamitsura, 2014).

The NIC system consists of interventions that represent both general and specialty nursing practice. Each intervention includes a label, a definition, and a set of activities that nurses perform to carry it out. For example, pain management is defined and specific activities are listed to alleviate pain or reduce the pain to a level that is acceptable to the patient (Bulechek et al., 2013).

The NOC system consists of outcomes that focus on the patient and include patient states, behavior, and perceptions that are sensitive to nursing interventions. Each outcome includes a definition, a five-point scale for rating outcome status over time, and a set of specific indicators to be used in rating the outcomes (Moorhead et al., 2013). Clinical testing for validation and refinement has occurred in various settings, and the standardization of terms continues to develop to reflect current knowledge and changes in nurses' roles and the structure of healthcare systems. The consistency of terms is essential in providing a large database across healthcare settings to predict resource requirements and establish outcomes of care.

Select Plans

The team discusses various strategies and plans to meet the new outcome. One plan is selected for implementation, and the process of change begins. Because QM stresses improving the system rather than assigning blame to employees, change strategies emphasize open communication and education of workers affected by the new standard and outcome. QI is impossible without continual education of all managers and followers.

Policies and procedures may need to be written or rewritten during the QI process. Policies should be reviewed frequently and updated so that they reflect best practice standards and do not become barriers to innovation. Communication about the change or improvement is essential (Fig. 23.6).

Evaluate

As the plan is implemented, the team continues to gather and evaluate data to document that the new outcomes are being met. If an outcome is not met, revisions in the implementation plan are needed. Sometimes improvement in one part of a system presents new problems. For example, nurses implemented screening for suicide risk in adolescents and adults presenting to the emergency department. A result of this improvement in care was a greatly increased number of referrals for

Fig. 23.6 Diagramming a patient-care process in detail can reveal gaps and opportunities for improvement. (Copyright © Wavebreakmedia/iStock/Thinkstock.)

counseling, which overwhelmed the existing hospital and community resources. The interprofessional team may need to reassemble periodically to handle the inevitable obstacles that develop with the implementation of any new process or procedure. Furthermore, individuals outside the organization (external customers) may need to be included in the process. The example that follows also illustrates this idea.

> A hospital is implementing a pneumatic tube system to dispense medications. An interprofessional team is assembled to discuss the process from various viewpoints: pharmacy, nursing, pneumatic tube operation managers, aides who take the medications from the pneumatic tube to the patient medication drawers, administrators, and physicians. The tube system is implemented. A nurse on one unit realizes that several patients do not have their morning medications in their medication drawers. The nurse borrows medications from another patient's drawer and orders the rest of the medications "stat" from pharmacy. Other nurses on that unit and other units have the same problem and are taking the same or similar actions. Several problems are occurring—some of the medications are being given late, nurses waste precious time searching other medication drawers, the pharmacy charges extra for the stat medications and is overwhelmed with stat requests, and the situation increases the nurses' frustration level. In some cases, patients suffer because of late administration of medications. QM principles would encourage the nurses to report the problems to the nurse manager or appropriate team member. Further, the patients' charges likely increase the hospital bill. The

pneumatic tube team could compile data such as frequency of missing medications, timing of medication orders, and nursing units involved. The problems are analyzed with a system perspective to solve the late medication problem effectively.

In some organizations, when a change is implemented successfully, the QI team disbands. One of the crucial tasks of the nurse manager is to publicize and reward the success of each QI team. The nurse manager must also evaluate the work of the team and the ability of individual team members to work together effectively.

Some organizations that have used the QM philosophy for several years establish permanent QI teams or committees. These QI teams do not disband after implementing one project or idea, but rather may meet regularly to focus on improvements in specific areas of patient care. The use of permanent QI teams or the adoption of a culture driven by QM can provide continuity and prevent duplication of efforts within the quality teams.

QM organizations stress system-level change and the evaluation of outcomes. However, in recent years, the need for process and performance improvement, including individual performance appraisal, has reemerged within healthcare organizations. Peer review and self-evaluation are performance assessment methods that fit within the QM philosophy.

In addition to using QI to improve overall team performance, any nurse can use the six steps of the QI process to self-evaluate and improve individual performance. For example, a nurse on a medical unit who wants to improve documentation skills might study past entries on patient records; review current institution policies, professional standards, and literature related to documentation; set specific performance improvement goals after consultation with the nurse manager and expert colleagues; devise strategies and a timeline for achieving performance goals; and, after implementing the strategies, review documentation entries to see whether self-improvement goals have been met.

QUALITY ASSURANCE

Although QI is a comprehensive process to prevent problems, total abandonment of periodic inspection would be naïve. One method used to monitor health care is **quality assurance (QA)** programs, which ensure conformity to a standard. QA focuses on clinical aspects of the provider's care, often in response to an identified problem. Many QA activities focus on process standards (e.g., documentation, adherence to practice standards). The focus may be asking questions such as "Did the nurse document the response to the pain medication within the required time period?" instead of "Did the patient receive adequate pain relief postoperatively?" In contrast, QI may examine process, structure, and outcome standards. The similarities and differences between QA and QI are summarized in Table 23.2.

One of the methods most often used in QA is chart review or chart auditing. Chart audits may be conducted using the records of active or discharged patients. Charts are selected randomly and reviewed by qualified healthcare professionals. In an internal audit, staff members from the same hospital or agency that generated the records examine the data. External auditors are qualified professionals from outside the organization who conduct the review. An audit tool containing specific criteria based on standards of care is applied to each chart under review. For example, auditors might compare documentation related to use of restraints for medical-surgical purposes with the criterion "Licensed independent practitioner evaluates patient in person within 4 hours of application." Auditors note compliance or lack of compliance with each audit criterion and report a summary of these findings to the appropriate manager or committee for corrective action.

Because the focus of the chart audit is on detecting errors and determining the person responsible for them, many staff members tend to view QA negatively. The nurse manager must reinforce that QA is not intended to be punitive but instead is an opportunity to improve patient care at the unit level. For example, to reinforce the importance of documentation, providing the standard of care for documentation and assisting the RN in reviewing several charts is an appropriate educational tool to reinforce policies and procedures or standards regarding documentation. The manager has the responsibility to communicate the importance of daily QA activities and how unit-based monitoring ties into the overall quality improvement program. Moreover, many institutions incorporate both the participation in and the results of QA into annual performance appraisals or clinical ladders.

RISK MANAGEMENT

Every year, The Joint Commission creates specific goals for specific settings. Begun as safety goals for hospitals, these statements have expanded to other settings such as critical access hospitals and to clinical specialties such as behavioral health. These goals are based on an analysis of issues pertinent to the specific focus. Box 23.4 identifies two examples of goals for hospitals.

QM and risk management are related concepts and emphasize the achievement of quality-outcome standards and the prevention of patient-care problems. Risk management also attempts to analyze problems and minimize losses after an adverse event occurs. These

---

TABLE 23.2 Comparison of Traditional Quality Assurance and Quality Improvement Processes

	Quality Assurance (QA) Process	Quality Improvement (QI) Process
Goal	To improve quality	To improve quality
Focus	Discovery and correction of errors	Prevention of errors
Major tasks	Inspection of nursing activities Chart audits	Review of nursing activities Innovation Professional development
Quality team	QA personnel or department personnel	Interprofessional team
Outcomes	Set by QA team with input from staff	Set by QI team with input from staff and patients

---

BOX 23.4 Examples of National Patient Safety Goals for Hospitals

- Improve the accuracy of patient identification.
- Apply the Universal Protocol for preventing wrong site, wrong procedure, and wrong person to all surgical and nonsurgical invasive procedures.

Copyright © The Joint Commission, 2018. Reprinted with permission.

losses include incurring financial loss as a result of malpractice or absorbing the cost of an extended length of stay for the patient, negative public relations, and employee dissatisfaction. Moreover, the inclusion of safety standards in TJC guidelines further emphasizes the importance of risk management. Specific goals exist for hospitals, ambulatory, behavioral health, critical access hospital, and home care settings. For example, an additional goal of reducing the risk of patient harm resulting from falls applies to home care settings. The TJC website carries the most up-to-date patient safety goals for all patient care settings.

The risk management department has several functions, which include the following:

- Defining situations that place the system at some financial risk, such as medication errors or patient falls
- Determining the frequency of occurrence of those situations
- Intervening and investigating identified events
- Identifying potential risks or opportunities to improve care

Each individual nurse is a risk manager and has the responsibility to identify and report unusual occurrences and potential risks. Active involvement in quality and risk management by direct caregivers, however, is a challenge complicated by staffing issues and increased demands on the nurse. Increased nursing staffing in hospitals is associated with better care outcomes. Consistent evidence shows that an increase in RN-to-patient ratios is associated with a reduction in hospital-related mortality, failure to rescue, and other nursing-sensitive outcomes, as well as reduced length of stay. Similarly, favorable patient care environments, including lower patient-to-nurse ratios and adequate nurse staffing, are associated with lower rates of serious complications or adverse events (McHugh et al., 2016). Another barrier to improving patient safety is fear of punishment, which inhibits people from acknowledging, reporting, or discussing errors. One way to minimize errors is to monitor threats to patient safety continually and to recognize that individual errors often reflect organizational and system failures. For example, targeting nurse-to-patient load and work schedules, including 12-hour shifts and overtime, can reduce potential errors from human factors such as fatigue, stress, and distractions. Rotating shifts may have a negative effect on nurses' stress levels and job performance, and working longer hours may have

a negative effect on patient outcomes (Stimpfel et al., 2016).

Both risk management and QM deal with changing behavior, prevention, focus on the customer, and attention to outcomes. The following clinical examples illustrate how QM and risk management complement each other. First, the implementation of lift teams reduces employee injuries associated with lifting heavy or fully dependent patients and simultaneously, for the patient, decreases adverse events associated with difficult transfers. The implementation of lift teams reflects managing both quality and risk. Second, adherence to the universal safety verification known as "time out" before the beginning of a surgical procedure ensures perioperative safety within a TQM framework. A third example, the use of teach-back, ensures quality teaching and health literacy learning has occurred and that risks are minimized by asking patients to explain in their own words what they need to know or do. Asking a question like, "Please tell me, what will you do to take care of yourself when you get home?" provides the nurse with an opportunity to check understanding and reteach information if needed (Minnesota Health Literacy Partnership, 2016). Although nursing managers would prefer that all staff intrinsically embrace risk management practices aimed at patient and staff safety, accountability for safety can be one aspect of performance evaluations. Active involvement of staff in risk management activities is key to prevention of adverse events. Nurse managers should conduct safety rounds and praise employees for using safe practice as part of best practice standards. This philosophy reinforces that risk management not only benefits the patient but also works to keep individual employees safe in the workplace.

Adverse-event reduction is a key strategy for reducing healthcare mortality and morbidity, because patients who suffer adverse events are more likely to die or suffer permanent disability. Nurses have always played a pivotal role in the prevention of adverse events and can reduce negative outcomes with a focus on accurate assessment, early identification, and correction of potentially adverse situations. Also, adherence to best practice standards and ensuring quality standards for high-risk/high-volume practices (e.g., restraint use, medication reconciliation) can reduce adverse events. The NQF and CMS define never events as errors in medical care that are clearly identifiable, preventable, and serious in their consequences for patients and that indicate a real problem in the safety and credibility of a healthcare facility. Examples of never events (or events that should never happen) include surgery on the wrong body part, a foreign body left in a patient after surgery, mismatched blood transfusion, major medication error, severe pressure ulcer acquired in the hospital, and preventable postoperative deaths. Now that many third-party payers are following the CMS lead in withholding payment for preventable complications of care, no member of the healthcare team can fail to recognize the implications of quality care in their organization's overall success. In contrast to never events, always events should occur 100% of the time and include healthcare actions such as hand hygiene and accurate patient identification.

A comprehensive quality and risk program would proactively identify and reduce risks to patient safety through completion of a **failure mode and effects analysis (FMEA)** on select high-risk situations as advanced by TJC. FMEA is a systematic, proactive method for evaluating a process to identify where and how it might fail and to assess the relative impact of different failures to identify the parts of the process that are most in need of change. Nurses should be able to recognize near misses and sentinel events and participate with an interprofessional team in the **root-cause analysis.** A **sentinel event** is a serious, unexpected occurrence involving death or severe physical or psychological harm, such as inpatient suicide, infant abduction, or wrong-site surgery. Similarly, a **near miss** is an unplanned event that did not result in injury, illness, or damage but had the potential to do so. A near miss highlights an imminent problem that must be corrected and can provide useful lessons in terms of risk analysis and reduction. TJC calls for voluntary self-reporting of sentinel events by both inpatient institutions and home health agencies and announce sentinel events via news releases when the events apply to other organizations. See Box 23.5 for the most common sentinel events reported in the healthcare arena. After a sentinel event is identified, a root-cause analysis is performed by a team that includes those directly involved in the event and those in leadership positions. A root-cause analysis is very similar to the QI process described in this chapter except that the root-cause analysis is a retrospective review of an incident to identify the sequence of events with the goal of identifying the root causes. The root-cause analysis leads to the development of specific risk reduction strategies, and in certain situations the plan must be reported to TJC.

> ### BOX 23.5 Most Common Healthcare Sentinel Events (2005-2016)
>
> - Wrong patient, wrong site, wrong procedure
> - Unintended retention of foreign body
> - Delay in treatment
> - Suicide
> - Operative/postoperative complications
> - Fall
> - Medication error
> - Criminal event
> - Perinatal death/injury
> - Medical equipment related
>
> Copyright © The Joint Commission, 2018. Reprinted with permission.

Whereas reporting to TJC illustrates external reporting to regulatory or accrediting agencies, an internal method of communicating risks or adverse events is through electronic safety reporting systems or through incident reporting. Incident reports are kept separate from the patient's medical record and should serve as a means of communicating an incident that caused or could have caused harm to patients, family members, visitors, or employees. Aggregated incident reports should be used to improve quality of care and decrease future risk. Trending data can illuminate systems issues that need to be modified to reduce risk and achieve quality patient care. Although an incident report may not be warranted for a unit-specific problem or an interdepartmental issue in which no adverse event occurred (e.g., delay in diagnosis or treatment), communication at the appropriate chain of command is essential to improve quality. Nurse managers are often responsible for investigating and remedying each identified hazard, which can result in safety being approached in a reactionary and overly narrow way. An effective approach to developing high reliability in healthcare quality and patient safety must also use a systems perspective that allows the manager to look beyond the individual nurse and focus on the entire practice environment.

Evaluating Risks

In gathering data about unusual occurrences, the risk management team may involve perspectives from numerous disciplines to discover underlying problems that a single discipline might miss. Risk managers also use multiple data sources, data collection techniques, and perspectives to collect and interpret the data. Quantitative methods such as questionnaire or records of medication administration can be combined with qualitative methods such as open-ended question interviews. Actionable plans for reducing the incidence of common preventable adverse events such as medication administration errors (wrong patient, time, dose, drug, or mode of delivery) could result from assessment and analysis of both quantitative and qualitative data. Quality and risk strategies aimed at targeting high-volume and high-risk occurrences are essential. Moreover, accountability for quality efforts to third-party payers, including the federal government, on programs such as pay-for-performance, in which healthcare systems receive additional payment incentives if specific quality targets are achieved, and public reporting, in which quality data are made available for comparison, has significant implications for nurses. Opportunities include participation on quality improvement teams, data collection, and involvement in the implementation of quality initiatives.

However, recognizing errors does not always translate into reporting errors. The lack of agreement as to what constitutes error influences the willingness of healthcare professionals to report errors and subsequently affects whether they develop strategies that could reduce future risk. A lack of consensus exists regarding whether patients and families should be informed about healthcare errors.

EXERCISE 23.4 Describe an error that occurred in the agency where you practice that resulted in harm to the patient and one that did not. If you cannot access information about an error, use one of the sentinel events cited in Box 23.5 as an example to consider.

What would you suggest to prevent a reoccurrence? Decide under what circumstances you would inform the patient and family and under what circumstances you would withhold the information.

Approaches to patient safety and risk management require healthcare providers to challenge their attitudes that errors are an unfortunate but inevitable part of patient care. Diminished resources and challenges in the work environment have the potential to compromise communication among providers and to contribute to an environment in which unsafe practices are overlooked or excused. For example, communication errors between nurses and other healthcare providers may result from hurried exchanges in crowded hallways or in the midst of a busy nursing station. Breakdown in communication among healthcare professionals is the most common cause of serious injuries and death in healthcare settings. Not surprisingly, each of the National Patient Safety Goals is directly or indirectly related to communication. Use of common language when communicating critical information helps prevent misunderstandings and creates a culture of quality and safety. SBAR has become a best practice

THE SOLUTION

My unit board created a tool to be used every day to aid in stopping these preventable events from happening. To reduce falls, the tool directs a nurse to label the patients who are a higher fall risk and put a check mark if they have all of the following: a yellow armband, yellow socks, a yellow sign on the front of the door, and an alarmed bed plugged into the wall. The emphasis on patient safety, including educating the patient and family to recognize high fall risk and to call for help, is also stressed. When addressing CAUTIs, the tool signaled when a StatLock was in place and whether the catheter was needed or ordered by a provider. With CLABSIs, we addressed the date and time on the dressing; whether the dressing was clean, dry, and intact; and whether the central line

was still needed. This tool was filled out each day on every patient. As a unit, our number of falls decreased from an average of 4 to 5 a month before the tool was used to 0 to 1 per month after implementing the tool. The tool also assisted in removal of urinary catheters and central lines earlier, preventing the possibility of infection. We also could more easily identify the patients whose central line dressing needed to be changed. The implementation of this tool has allowed our unit to improve our NDNQI scores, and most importantly improve patient safety and outcomes.

Would this be a suitable approach for you? Why?

Abigail Hertz

for standardizing communication between health care providers. SBAR stands for situation, background, assessment, and recommendation (Institute for Healthcare Improvement, 2017). Because adverse patient outcomes commonly are a result of communication failures, The Joint Commission's National Patient Goals added standardization of handoff communication, the verbal and written exchange of pertinent information during transitions of care. A team approach to quality and risk management is needed to promote optimal outcomes. Nurses have a responsibility to provide quality care and thus must serve in leadership roles to ensure a culture of integrated QM and risk management.

CONCLUSION

QM is critical to patient safety. As organizations addressed system errors, having organized quality and safety programs became even more important. Being able to address both clinical and system issues of risk contributes to improved quality. Everyone in an organization is accountable for quality, and nurses play a crucial role in QI, QM, and QA.

■ REFLECTIONS

What issues related to quality have you seen in a clinical setting? Were you comfortable with the actions taken to improve care? How will you use the material from this chapter to promote quality and reduce risk with the patients for whom you provide care? Write a one-paragraph summary with a specific example.

■ THE EVIDENCE

A growing body of literature exists that links the hospital practice environment with safety and quality of care. A strong correlation has been established between practice environments and nurse outcomes, including nurse job satisfaction, burnout, and intent to leave, as well as patient outcomes, including mortality and failure to rescue. Increased nurse staffing is associated with reduced patient mortality, reduced failure to rescue, and decreased length of stay. Nurses report more positive job experiences and fewer concerns about quality care, whereas patients had a significantly lower risk of death and failure to rescue in hospitals with better care environments, the best nurse staffing levels, and the most highly educated nurses.

Nurse specialty certification and baccalaureate education have consistently been associated with better patient outcomes. Staffing levels are an important predictor of nurse-assessed risks including nursing-sensitive outcomes. Empowering nurses and adequately resourcing practice environments to support patient care enhances job satisfaction and nursing retention.

Nurse managers and leaders have several options for improving nurse retention and patient outcomes, including improving RN staffing, moving to a more educated nurse workforce, and facilitating a positive care environment. Hospitals with practice environments that include investment in development of staff, QM, and good nurse-physician relations (e.g., Magnet® designation) are associated with better nurse and patient outcomes. Nurse managers who promote an empowered workplace and facilitate teamwork support higher-quality care, less patient risk, and more satisfied nurses. Investment in a baccalaureate-educated workforce and specialty certification has great potential to improve quality and reduce risk.

■ TIPS FOR QUALITY MANAGEMENT

- QM is based on data; anything measured and recorded can be improved.
- Concentrate QI energies on factors that are most important to patient quality and safety.
- Working together to prevent problems is more effective than fixing problems after they occur.

REFERENCES

Agency for Healthcare Research and Quality. (2016a). *TeamSTEPPS 2.0.* https://www.ahrq.gov/teamstepps/index.html.

Agency for Healthcare Research and Quality. (2016b). *Quality Indicators.* https://qualityindicators.ahrq.gov/.

Aiken, L., Clarke, S. P., Sloane, D. M., Lake, E. T., & Cheney, T. (2008). Effects of hospital care environment on patient mortality and nurse outcomes. *Journal of Nursing Administration, 38*(5), 223–229.

Buhlman, N. (2016). How nurses' work environment influences key performance indicators. *American Nurse Today, 11*(3), 54–55.

Bulechek, G. M., Butcher, H. K., & Dochtermann, J. M. (2013). *Nursing interventions classification (NIC)* (6th ed.). St. Louis, MO: Elsevier.

Campanella, P., Lovato, E., Marone, C., Fallacara, L., Mancuso, A., Ricciardi, W., et al. (2016). The impact of electronic health records on healthcare quality: A systematic review and meta-analysis. *European Journal of Public Health, 26*(1), 60–64.

Centers for Medicare & Medicaid Services. (2016a). *Hospital compare.* https://www.cms.gov/medicare/quality-initiatives-patient-assessment-instruments/hospitalqualityinits/hospitalcompare.html. http://medicare.gov/hospitalcompare/.

Centers for Medicare & Medicaid Services. (2016b). *Hospital consumer assessment of healthcare providers and systems survey.* www.hcahpsonline.org/home.aspx.

Deblois, S., & Lepanto, L. (2016). Lean and Six Sigma in acute care: A systematic review of reviews. *International Journal of Health Care Quality Assurance, 29*(2), 192–208.

Herdman, T. H., & Kamitsura, S. (2014). *NANDA international: Nursing diagnoses: Definitions and classifications 2015–2017.* Oxford: Wiley-Blackwell.

Institute for Healthcare Improvement. (2017). *SBAR communication technique.* http://www.ihi.org/Topics/SBARCommunicationTechnique/Pages/default.aspxASituationalBriefingModel.aspx.

Institute of Medicine. (2000). *To err is human: Building a safer health system.* Washington, DC: National Academies Press.

Kutney-Lee, A., Germack, H., Hatfield, L., Kelly, S., Maguire, P., Dierkes, A., et al. (2016). Nurse engagement in shared governance and patient and nurse outcomes. *JONA: The Journal of Nursing Administration, 46*(11), 605–612. https://doi.org/10.1097/NNA.0000000000000412.

McHugh, M. D., Rochman, M. F., Sloane, D. M., Berg, R. A., Mancini, M. E., Merchant, R. M., et al. (2016). Better nurse staffing and nurse work environments associated with increased survival of in-hospital cardiac arrest patients. *Med Care, 54*(1), 74–80.

Minnesota Health Literacy Partnership. (2016). *Health literacy toolkit.* http://healthliteracymn.org/sites/default/files/images/files/Health%20Literacy%20Toolkit.pdf.

Moorhead, S., Johnson, M., Maas, M., & Swanson, E. (2013). *Nursing outcomes classification (NOC)* (5th ed.). St. Louis, MO: Elsevier.

Press Ganey. (2015). *National database of nursing quality indicators.* http://www.pressganey.com/solutions/clinical-quality/nursing-quality.

QSEN Institute. (2014). *Competencies.* http://qsen.org/competencies/pre-licensure-ksas/.

Stimpfel, A. W., Sloane, D. M., McHugh, M. D., & Aiken, L. H. (2016). Hospitals known for nursing excellence associated with better hospital experience for patients. *Health Services Research, 51*(3), 1120–1134. https://doi.org/10.1111/1475-6773.12357.

The Joint Commission. (2016a). *Accountability measures for 2016.* https://www.jointcommission.org/assets/1/18/accountability_measures_list_2016.pdf.

The Joint Commission. (2016b). *2017 National patient safety goals.* https://www.jointcommission.org/assets/1/6/2017_NPSG_HAP_ER.pdf.

24

Translating Research Into Practice

Margarete Lieb Zalon

LEARNING OUTCOMES

- Value the nurse's obligation to use research evidence in practice.
- Analyze differences among research, evidence-based practice, practice-based evidence, comparative effectiveness research, outcomes research, and quality improvement.
- Formulate a clinical question that can be searched in the literature.

- Identify resources for critically appraising evidence.
- Describe the potential of "big data" in a connected healthcare system.
- Assess organizational barriers and facilitators for the translation of research into practice.
- Identify strategies for translating research into practice within the context of an organization.

KEY TERMS

big data
bundle
clinical guidelines
comparative effectiveness research (CER)
effectiveness
efficacy
evidence-based practice (EBP)
external validity
GRADE system
journal club

implementation science
internal validity
meta-analysis
outcomes
participatory action research (PAR)
patient-centered outcomes research
practice-based evidence (PBE)
practice-based research networks (PBRN)

randomized controlled trial (RCT)
reliability
research
systematic review
translating research into practice (TRIP)
translation science
validity

THE CHALLENGE

Surgical site infection (SSI) rates had increased significantly at our hospital. Literature reviews found that several evidence-based interventions existed that we could implement to help decrease these rates. We also identified specific interventions for patients undergoing hysterectomies and colon surgery. We believed, along with the staff, that we were using these interventions, but clearly we had

more work to do to reduce our infection rates. Nurses who graduated in more recent years seemed to have an easier time in grasping the concept of translating research evidence into practice. When I asked them if it is hard to put this information into practice, they would give me a look of confusion and say, "Isn't this what we are supposed to do?" Incorporating these practices seemed to be a harder challenge for those nurses who went to school years ago, not having had evidence-based practice included in their education. Nursing leadership met and decided that an intraprofessional approach would be best, with the focus on basic techniques, especially asepsis. We decided that the best way to monitor this would be through observational audits, but were concerned about the staff's reaction to the audits.

What would you do if you were this nurse?

Megan Lamoreux, BSN, RN, CNOR
Clinical Nurse Educator, Geisinger Wyoming Valley Medical Center, Wilkes-Barre, PA

INTRODUCTION

If you or a loved one required nursing care, you would want that care to be based on the best research evidence available. For example, if a family member needed to be on a ventilator, you would want to be sure that the nurses providing the care were using best practices to prevent ventilator-associated pneumonia and assessing for delirium, a common complication with serious life-altering consequences. You would want to know that communication is good among nurses and physicians on the clinical unit where your family member has been placed because you know that research demonstrates that teamwork and collaboration lead to lower mortality and fewer errors. If that family member also had a central venous catheter, you would want to be sure that the nurse who removes that catheter is using an established procedure that minimizes the risk for introducing an air embolism into the circulation. And, when that family member is discharged, you would want to know that the nurses are using well-tested strategies to help that person transition to home, recover from his or her illness, and manage that illness. As a follower, leader, and manager, you should be concerned about incorporating research evidence not only into clinical practices but also into the management of systems of care. The challenge is how to (1) find the best research evidence; (2) incorporate the best evidence into practice in a meaningful manner; and (3) motivate nurses, nursing leadership, and organizational leadership to care about using evidence in practice amid all the other challenges faced in delivering high-quality nursing care.

Research is an integral part of professional practice. Research is the "diligent, systematic inquiry or investigation to validate and refine existing knowledge and generate new knowledge" (Gray, Grove, & Sutherland, 2016, p. 1). Nurses, as professionals, have an obligation to society that involves rights and responsibilities as well as a mechanism for accountability. These obligations are outlined in *Nursing's Social Policy Statement: The Essence of the Profession* developed by the American Nurses Association (ANA, 2010) and includes: "To refine and expand nursing's knowledge base, nurses use theories that fit with professional nursing's values of health and health care that are relevant to professional nursing practice. Nurses apply research findings and implement the best evidence into their practice ..." (p. 13).

The *Code of Ethics for Nurses* (ANA, 2015, p. 27) directs that the "nurse, in all roles and settings, advances the profession through research and scholarly inquiry, professional standards development, and the generation of both nursing and health policy." Globally, the International Council of Nurses (ICN) has a Research Network that promotes nursing research, advances nursing knowledge, and improves nursing practice quality to facilitate the exchange of ideas, experience, and expertise (ICN, 2015).

Nursing research is designed to refine and expand the scientific foundation for nursing. Nursing practice draws on nursing science and the physical, economic, biomedical, behavioral, and social sciences (ANA, 2010). The National Institute of Nursing Research (NINR), a part of the National Institutes of Health, in its strategic plan focuses on supporting the development of nursing science that has the greatest impact for the most people: symptom science, wellness, self-management of chronic illness, and end-of-life and palliative care (NINR, 2016). This focus recognizes the relationship between biological processes and behavior. Thus nurses need to apply findings of nursing research and research conducted by members of other disciplines that have relevance for their own practice. Increasingly nurse researchers are members of teams who bring together members of different disciplines to answer complex research questions to advance nursing practice and health care.

Evidence-based practice (EBP) is derived from the widely used definition of evidence-based medicine: the integration of the best research evidence with clinical expertise and the patient's unique values and circumstances in making decisions about the care of individual patients (Straus, Richardson, Glasziou, & Haynes, 2011). Use of the word "practice" denotes the use of evidence by all healthcare practitioners, including nurses. In EBP, clinicians drive the search for solutions to clinical problems based on the best available evidence, which is then translated into practice. EBP is a broader, more encompassing view of using research in practice and is focused on searching for, appraising, and synthesizing the best evidence to address a clinical practice problem.

The translation of evidence into practice involves all healthcare disciplines, and the integration of research with practice in a timely fashion is essential for quality health care. Tremendous variation exists in the lag time between the publication of research findings and integration of the results into practice. Some researchers estimate the lag time may be as long as 17 years (Hanney, et al., 2015). Even if the time lag from publication to the use of findings were dramatically reduced, the gap is still measured in years, not months. We might believe that once a research study is published in a journal, clinicians read it immediately and then clinicians and/or policymakers use it to improve practice. Typically, that is not the case. For example, for more than 20 years, the National Institutes of Child Health and Human Development (NICHD) implemented a public health campaign to prevent Sudden Infant Death Syndrome (SIDS) by educating the public about the importance of placing infants on their back to sleep. Recently the campaign has been renamed "Safe to Sleep," which includes the importance of the infant sleeping in the same room in his or her own space. Despite the extensive campaign that included both physicians and nurses, a study of the advice given to new mothers indicated that 50% of new mothers received no advice on where infants should sleep, and 20% of mothers did not receive recommendations on breastfeeding or placing infants to sleep on their backs (Eisenberg et al., 2015). Specifically, only 52.7% of mothers reported receiving sleep position advice consistent with EBP recommendations; 21.3% received advice inconsistent with EBP recommendations, and 25.9% reported receiving no advice from nurses, with similar results reported for physicians. Considering the number of practitioners who may have contact with a mother before her discharge

with a new baby, clearly additional interprofessional work is needed. EBP has the dual purpose of promoting the use of effective strategies to improve health outcomes and helping healthcare providers stop recommending ineffective, unsafe, or harmful strategies.

Research provides the foundation for nursing practice improvement. Examples include preoperative teaching, pain management, child development assessment, falls prevention, pressure-ulcer risk detection, incontinence care, transitional care, and family-centered care in critical care units. Research needs to be systematically evaluated to determine which interventions should be implemented to improve care outcomes. Practices that were once considered the standard of care may quickly become outdated. Some practices may have been carried out for many years without their scientific basis or effectiveness ever being examined. The latest research findings need to be incorporated into procedures using an evidence-based model when they are being updated by an organization.

> **EXERCISE 24.1** Identify a common activity that is part of your nursing practice and determine whether any research supports the intervention or nursing care activity.

Nursing research designs can be categorized in several ways, such as basic versus applied, qualitative versus quantitative, cross-sectional versus longitudinal, experimental versus descriptive, and retrospective versus prospective. Regardless of the design, some research is ready for implementation, and some research may not warrant a change in practice. Readiness for implementation may be influenced by the strength of the research, which is determined by study design, sample size, ease of implementation, and the beliefs and values of clinicians.

The quality of care and the quality of the outcomes of care can be dramatically improved with the implementation of practices derived from a systematic evaluation of research evidence. Patients, those entrusted to our care, are deserving of practices that are based on the best available evidence. Examining the evidence for a specific practice generally needs to go beyond examining the results of a single study. At times, a single well-designed study might be adequate for recommending and implementing a practice change. However, developing an EBP requires the development of a clearly written clinical question and a more thorough search of the literature, the review of single studies, meta-analyses, metasyntheses, critically appraised topics, systematic reviews, and clinical guidelines.

Evidence must be appraised and placed in the context of patient, family, and community values. Nurse managers and leaders may not necessarily be the ones conducting research, evaluating research evidence, or developing evidence-based guidelines, but they will be facilitating the application of research findings in practice. The end results of care are known as the *outcomes* of care. These are important to a public that wants to know what is best and what was improved. Outcomes of care may include whether a new mother received the correct advice about safe sleep practices, whether a person with diabetes is able to maintain a hemoglobin A1c value that is less than 6.5, or whether a critically ill patient develops a central line–associated bloodstream infection (CLABSI). Improving the outcomes of care involves different approaches such as identifying EBPs, comparative effectiveness research, participatory action research, practice-based evidence, and quality improvement. It also requires understanding how innovations are incorporated into practice, identifying appropriate strategies for translating research into practice, and sustaining the practice improvement. Frontline nurses and nurse leaders face many decisions along the way to effectively implement evidence derived from research into daily care practices.

FROM USING RESEARCH TO EVIDENCE-BASED PRACTICE

Individual nurses may apply research findings to their own practice. However, nurses' broader responsibility to society includes activating the change process in translating research into practice. Research use can be in a variety of forms: enlightenment, implementation of a research-based protocol, or the widespread adoption of standards based on research findings. Ultimately, multiple factors influence how a research finding is adopted, translated into practice, and sustained.

The movement to use research in practice paralleled the development of original nursing research. In the 1970s, three major projects facilitated research utilization: The Western Institute of Commission on Higher Education in Nursing (WICHEN), Conduct and Utilization of Research in Nursing (CURN), and the Nursing Child Assessment Satellite Training (NCAST). These projects used research findings to improve practice. This in turn spawned the growth of many demonstration projects to use research as well as research studies identifying factors that facilitated or created barriers to research utilization. The NCAST programs developed by Kathryn Barnard, PhD, RN, FAAN, a nurse researcher at the University of Washington, used assessments of mother-infant feeding behaviors to promote positive parent-child interactions and enhance the development of cognitive and language abilities which are still in use today (NCAST, 2017). Subsequently, nurse researchers developed models to guide nurses in the steps of the research utilization process. Researchers also identified barriers to nursing research utilization: those within the nurse, the nature of the research, administrators, and the healthcare organization. Research, even when ready for implementation, was not necessarily readily embraced. At times, a new practice was not implemented until the costs of the practice were factored in and the research was demonstrated to have an impact on the bottom line of a healthcare organization.

DEVELOPMENT OF EVIDENCE-BASED PRACTICE

The EBP movement is derived from the work of Archie Cochrane, who described the lack of knowledge about healthcare treatment effects and advocated for using proven treatments. Subsequently, the Cochrane Collaboration was established at Oxford University in 1993. About that time, Gordon Guyatt and his colleagues at McMaster University authored a series of articles in the *Journal of the American Medical Association (JAMA)* known as the *Users' Guides to the Medical Literature*, providing detailed steps for the analysis of different types of research studies.

In the 1990s, the focus changed to finding a research-based solution to clinical problems, not only in nursing but also in medicine and other disciplines. Healthcare organizations began to be more systematic in using research and evaluating patient outcomes. Federal government agencies provide support for EBP and research. See Table 24.1 for EBP resources under the auspices of federal agencies and other organizations. Global initiatives for the EBP have been established around the world, some of which include centers for evidence-based nursing. Resources for learning EBP as well as repositories for EBP reviews and/or guidelines are included in Table 24.2.

TABLE 24.1	Selected Programs and Resources Supporting Evidence-Based Practice		
Agency or Organization	**Program or Resource**	**Description**	**Website**
Agency for Healthcare Research and Quality (AHRQ)	Evidence-based Practice Center (EPC)	Develops evidence reports and technology assessments that are common, expensive, and/or significant for Medicare/Medicaid populations	https://www.ahrq.gov/research/findings/evidence-based-reports/overview/index.html
	Effective Healthcare Program	Sponsors systematic reviews and translation and dissemination of research. Includes comparative effectiveness reviews, effectiveness reviews, and technical briefs on patient-centered outcomes.	http://effectivehealthcare.ahrq.gov/
	Practice-Based Research Networks (PBRNs)	Supports AHRQ in providing support to primary care PBRNs doing clinical and health services research	http://pbrn.ahrq.gov
Centers for Disease Control and Prevention (CDC)	Advisory Committee for Immunization Practices (ACIP)	Medical and public health experts who develop recommendations on the use of vaccines in the US civilian population	https://www.cdc.gov/vaccines/acip
	Guidelines and Recommendations	Guidelines and recommendations developed by the CDC	https://stacks.cdc.gov/
Patient-Centered Outcomes Research Institute (PCORI)	Clinical Effectiveness Research (CER)	Funds and manages CER research to compare outcomes of 2 or more options for people with a particular health problem	http://www.pcori.org/about-us/our-programs/clinical-effectiveness-research-cer
	Healthcare Delivery and Disparities Research	Compares patient-centered approaches to improve the equitability, effectiveness, and efficiency of care	https://www.pcori.org/about-us/our-programs/healthcare-delivery-and-disparities-research
US Preventive Services Task Force (USPSTF)	Independent, volunteer panel of national experts in prevention and evidence-based medicine	Makes evidence-based recommendations about clinical preventive services	https://www.uspreventiveservicestaskforce.org/

The EBP movement has grown exponentially with scientific publications, establishment of collaboration centers, resources on the Internet, and grants focused specifically on translating research into practice, including resources devoted to nursing. The Joanna Briggs Institute (JBI), based in Australia, has a network of nursing collaborating centers and evidence-based synthesis and utilization groups around the world. These centers have teams of researchers critically appraising evidence and disseminating evidence-based protocols. The JBI also provides training programs in conducting systematic reviews, many of which are available from its collaborating centers. Nursing organizations have developed evidence-based standards of practice, clinical guidelines, and EBP toolkits, many of which are publicly available on their websites (Table 24.3). In addition, nurses are also members of interdisciplinary groups involved in guideline development. Many of these guidelines are available through the some of the resources listed in Table 24.2.

TABLE 24.2 Resources for Evidence-Based Health Care

Organization	Website
Centre for Evidence-Based Medicine (CEBM)	www.cebm.net
Centre for Reviews and Dissemination (CRD)	www.york.ac.uk/inst/crd
The Cochrane Collaboration	www.cochrane.org
Guidelines International Network	www.g-i-n.net
The Joanna Briggs Institute (JBI)	joannabriggs.org
The Johns Hopkins Center for Evidence-Based Practice	http://www.hopkinsmedicine.org/evidence-based-practice
Improvement Science Research Network	isrn.net
Knowledge Translation Canada (KT Canada)	ktcanada.org
National Institute for Health and Care Excellence (NICE)	www.nice.org.uk
National Health and Medical Research Council (NHMRC)	www.nhmrc.gov.au
The Ohio State University Center for Transdisciplinary Evidence-based Practice (CTEP)	https://ctep-ebp.com/
The Sarah Cole Hirsch Institute at the Frances Payne Bolton School of Nursing	https://case.edu/nursing/research/centers-of-excellence/sarah-cole-hirsh-institute
Scottish Intercollegiate Guidelines Network (SIGN)	www.sign.ac.uk

TABLE 24.3 Nursing Organization Resources for Evidence-Based Practice

Organization	Website
American Association of Critical-Care Nurses (AACN)	www.aacn.org
American Association of Neuroscience Nurses (AANN)	www.aann.org
American College of Nurse Midwives (ACNM)	www.acnm.org
American Nephrology Nurses Association (ANNA)	www.annanurse.org
Association for Radiologic and Imaging Nursing (ARIN)	www.arinursing.org
American Society of PeriAnesthesia Nurses (ASPAN)	www.aspan.org
Association of PeriOperative Registered Nurses (AORN)	www.aorn.org
Association of Rehabilitation Nurses (ARN)	www.rehabnurse.org
Association of Women's Health, Obstetric and Neonatal Nursing (AWOHNN)	www.awhonn.org
Emergency Nurses Association (ENA)	www.ena.org
Infusion Nurses Society (INS)	www.ins1.org
National Association of School Nurses (NASN)	www.nasn.org
Oncology Nursing Society (ONS)	www.ons.org
Registered Nurses Association of Ontario (RNAO)	www.rnao.ca
Wound and Ostomy Continence Nurses Society™ (WOCN Society)	www.wocn.org

Researchers and clinicians collaborate to address specific practice problems and advance health care. Health maintenance organizations are monitoring provider practices for patients' adherence to screening guidelines. Voluntary organizations providing support services for individuals not covered by health insurance are expecting that the agencies they fund provide evidence for the outcomes of their projects to more effectively meet community needs. Societal factors, such as the rising cost of health care, quality improvement initiatives, and the pressures to avoid errors, have resulted in an increased emphasis on research as a basis for practice decisions. In the midst of an exponentially expanding

RESEARCH PERSPECTIVE

Resource: Melnyk, B. M., Gallagher-Ford, L., Thomas, B. K., Troseth, M., Wyngarden, K., & Szalacha, L. (2016). A study of chief nurse executives indicates low-prioritization of evidence-based practice and shortcomings in hospital performance metrics across the United States. *Worldviews on Evidence-Based Practice, 13*(1), 6–14. https://doi.org/10.1111/wvn.12133.

Melnyk et al. surveyed 276 chief nurse executives (CNEs) (or chief nursing officers [CNOs]) regarding their beliefs about evidence-based practice (EBP) and its implementation, perceptions of the EBP culture at their hospital, their top priorities, their budget for EBP, and hospital metrics (e.g., Centers for Medicare and Medicaid [CMS] Core Measures and the National Database of Nursing Quality [NDNQI] measures). Less than half of the nurses were baccalaureate-prepared at more than two-thirds of the hospitals. Approximately one-fifth of the respondents were CNEs at hospitals with Magnet® designation. Approximately one-third of the hospitals were below national benchmarks for NDNQI measures (falls, falls with injury, pressure ulcers, restraints, nursing care hours, RN education, and RN certification). More than 40% were below national rates for CMS core measures (catheter-associated urinary tract infections, pressure ulcers, vascular-associated infections, falls and trauma, and manifestations of poor glycemic control). The CNEs placed a high value on EBP, but 48% indicated they were unsure of how to measure patient outcomes and almost 60% thought that EBP was either not practiced at all or somewhat practiced in their hospitals. Top priorities for the CNEs were quality, safety, and meeting benchmarks. EBP was rated the least important of nine categories. Nearly three-fourths of the respondents indicated that fiscal resources were either used not at all or somewhat to support EBP.

Implications for Practice

The results indicate that CNEs and CNOs recognize the value of EBP, but they themselves need additional education on (1) EBP, (2) how EBP can be linked to quality and safety in their organizations, and (3) how EBP has the potential to improve national metrics for nursing care quality. Organizational and financial resources for EBP need to be provided so EBP becomes part of the organizational culture. CNEs and CNOs have an important role in embedding EBP into the processes for the improvement of quality and safety in their organization.

Nursing research exists on a continuum, and not all research is ready for, or of a quality that is appropriate for, implementation; nor is it necessarily ready for implementation in all practice settings. However, the quality of care and the quality of the outcomes of care can be dramatically improved with the implementation of evidence-based nursing practices. Nurses are heeding the call to develop evidence-based practices. Frontline nurses and nurse leaders have a critical responsibility in promoting the use of the best evidence for practice.

---

scientific knowledge base, healthcare professionals are increasingly called upon to use evidence in practice. Since 2003, The National Academy of Medicine (formerly Institute of Medicine [IOM]) (Greiner & Knebel, 2003) has indicated that all healthcare professionals should be educated in EBP and be able to do the following:

- Know where and how to find the best possible sources of evidence.
- Formulate clear clinical questions.
- Search for relevant answers to those questions from the best possible sources, including those that evaluate or appraise evidence for its usefulness with respect to a particular patient or population.
- Determine when and how to integrate those findings into practice.

EBP is included in the Quality, Safety, and Education for Nurses (QSEN) project, which identifies the knowledge, skills, and attitudes needed by nurses to improve the quality and safety of healthcare systems (QSEN Institute,

2014). Research-based competencies for EBP are being integrated into healthcare systems by including them in clinical ladders and job descriptions for nurse educators and clinical nurse specialists (Melnyk & Gallagher-Ford, 2015). Frontline nurses and nurse leaders need to participate in an organization's EBP initiatives. The need for nurse leaders to set the tone for the implementation of EBP in healthcare organizations is illustrated in the results of a survey conducted by Melnyk and her colleagues (2016) in the Research Perspective.

EXERCISE 24.2 Select a practice guideline topic appropriate for implementation in your clinical setting. Select two guidelines on the same topic and determine which one might be more useful in your practice setting. Identify as many strategies as possible for disseminating the guideline's key points to direct care nurses at a clinical agency. Compare your list of strategies with that of a colleague.

COMPARATIVE EFFECTIVENESS RESEARCH

Although clinicians are concerned with identifying the best evidence for a practice, very often the benefits of a practice are unclear (Fig. 24.1). Comparing intervention effectiveness can aid in determining which intervention is the best one to use for a patient population. Comparative effectiveness research (CER) examines the evidence for the effectiveness, benefits, and harms of treatment options such as drugs, medical devices, diagnostic tests, surgeries and procedures, or ways to deliver health care (Agency on Healthcare Research and Quality [AHRQ], n.d.). To understand CER, one needs to understand the difference between efficacy and effectiveness. Efficacy is when an intervention or treatment is tested in a rigorously designed research study such as a traditional randomized controlled trial (RCT). Careful attention is paid to internal validity, with carefully selecting the sample and consistency in delivering the intervention or treatment to determine whether it works. Once efficacy has been established, the next step is to test effectiveness—that is, determining what happens when the intervention is delivered in the real world of practice with variations in the setting and delivery of the intervention. CER, although it compares similar interventions, may also be considered part of research dissemination and implementation science. Many RCTs are considered CER studies because different interventions or doses of the intervention (e.g., number of treatments, or length of treatment) are compared. An example of CER in nursing is an RCT study comparing three levels of peer coaching to

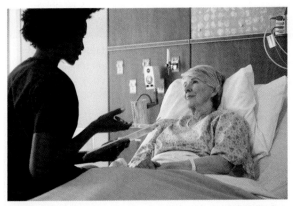

Fig. 24.1 The purpose of gathering and analyzing evidence is to improve patient care. (Copyright © monkeybusinessimages/iStock/Thinkstock.)

increase hepatitis A and B vaccine uptake in individuals who were homeless parolees being released from prison (Nyamathi et al., 2015). This study compared intensive peer coaching and nurse case management, intensive peer coaching with minimal nurse involvement, and usual care and found no differences in the vaccine completion rates, which ranged from 71.8% to 75.4%. However, the researchers were able to identify risk factors associated with noncompletion, indicating that an approach tailored to individual needs might be more suitable. Although RCTs are commonly used in CER studies, many other designs can be used. These include large-scale observational studies, quasi-experimental (no randomization or double-blinding) studies and meta-analyses, and studies that mine data in electronic health records (EHRs).

PRACTICE-BASED EVIDENCE

With the growth of large databases, the use of electronic health records, and sophisticated statistical techniques, examining practices in real-world situations and comparing the effectiveness of interventions is enhanced. Clinicians face challenges in achieving comparable outcomes to RCTs in trying to translate research into practice. Clinicians may also be faced with situations that lack definitive information about a course of action. Practice-based evidence (PBE) is a research methodology that can help inform practice decisions by examining outcomes in the real world. In clinical practice, patients may not be similar, and the application of an intervention may have multiple variations. In PBE, the focus is on external validity. It answers the question of whether similar outcomes can be achieved in broader populations, in different settings, with different clinicians, and, most likely, limited resources (Vaidya et al., 2017). Quite often, PBE studies use observational designs comparing interventions on multiple outcomes in very large samples with study participants whose characteristics and care settings are diverse, mirroring real-world practice. PBE designs need be inclusive of stakeholders and a participatory approach that includes stakeholders in designing the research questions. As an example, this methodology was used in developing a protocol for the prevention of CLABSI in a pediatric oncology unit where the children are typically excluded from RCTs because of their higher risk for CLABSIs (Linder, Gerdy, Abouzelof, & Wilson, 2016). A comprehensive analysis of research reports, their own data, and current practice standards led to the development of structured protocols, which when implemented led to a significant reduction in CLABSI rates.

Big data analytics is a method that can be used in PBE designs. It involves using technology to analyze large data sets to examine patterns and identify new relationships that in turn can be used to make improvements in health care. Big data involves not only large volumes of data but also great variety in the data, velocity (e.g., the data processing needs to occur close to when data are acquired), and veracity (figuring out what are the true data) (Bellazzi, 2014). Nurse researchers are beginning to use data science, drawing on multiple data sources in a variety of settings for not only the creation of new knowledge but also prediction and the evaluation of care practices (Westra et al., 2016). Nurse researchers must be involved in the use of big data for health promotion, chronic care, symptom management, and care coordination; they should also incorporate system data such as that from the Nursing Minimum Data Set (a classification system for essential nursing data) (Westra et al., 2016). Nurses, when documenting their practice, generate large quantities of data that can be harnessed for making predictions about who might respond best to a certain intervention and identifying the most promising interventions to be used for a patient with certain characteristics.

Big data analytics will be coupled with Connected Health (or C-health), which involves people using electronic devices, sensors, activity monitors, and other devices for remote patient monitoring. This generates vast amounts of data to be merged with data from more traditional healthcare sources. Nurses will need to understand how to use these data to provide individualized care for patients. The potential of using big data analytics for translation of research into practice is highlighted by the work of Topaz and Pruinelli (2017) in the Literature Perspective.

The promise of big data analytics linking personal and population data to make continuous improvement in the delivery of health care is the basis for what is known as a continuously learning healthcare system. The complexity and amount of data have increased exponentially, as has computing power. Learning healthcare systems use information from every interaction to continuously develop knowledge, provide feedback to patients and clinicians, and apply the best evidence to improve care (IOM, 2015). Learning healthcare systems provide real-time access to knowledge, digital capture of the care experience, engaged and empowered patients, incentives for continuous improvement, transparency (making information available), strong leadership, and a supportive learning environment (IOM, 2013, p. 159). For example, in a learning healthcare system, potential errors in medication administration or handoffs could be identified so that system improvements can be made more quickly. Frontline nurses and nurse leaders will play an integral role in the development of learning health systems. In turn, they will function in a care environment that provides them with evidence-based resources to be more effective in delivering care.

LITERATURE PERSPECTIVE

Resource: Topaz, M., & Pruinelli, L. (2017). Big data and nursing: Implications for the future. *Studies in Health Technology and Informatics, 232*, 165–171.

The authors describe the skills and competencies of nurses, nurse educators, and nurse scientists for using big data. These skills include (1) mining narrative and structured data to find patterns in care and outcomes, (2) visualizing data, and (3) integrating nurse-sensitive data with artificial intelligence for clinical decision support. The use of standardized nursing terminology would facilitate the use of big data analytics. The development of artificial intelligence systems in health care and data visualization will provide nurses with additional information for making decisions. Direct care nurses need to understand how to extract and use data to provide direction for clinical practice, quality improvement, and decision making as well as communicate with multidisciplinary teams.

Implications for Practice
Big data analytics have tremendous potential for the use of evidence in practice. For example, big data can be used to provide trend analysis to support decision making and demonstrate nursing's value. Currently, the use of big data analytics in nursing is limited. Direct care nurses and nurse leaders need to understand the nature of big data so that they can facilitate its use to improve patient outcomes.

PARTICIPATORY ACTION RESEARCH

Participatory action research (PAR), sometimes also called community-based participatory research (CBAR), involves members from the community being studied, usually as part of an advisory board for a research project, to identify and refine (1) research questions, (2) strategies for engaging community members, and (3) potential challenges in carrying out the research project. The Patient-Centered Outcomes Research Institute (PCORI) recognizes the vital contributions of community stakeholders by including them in making decisions about grant awards so that the research funded is relevant to the community of interest (PCORI, 2017). The use of PAR is common in public health and community settings, but it is increasingly being expanded to other healthcare settings. For example, PAR was used to harness the expertise of key stakeholders to facilitate system-level changes in state prisons to provide end-of-life care (Penrod, Loeb, Ladonne, & Martin, 2016). The process of PAR included ongoing engagement of insiders (frontline prison staff involved in the delivery of end-of-life care) who had the potential to be change agents and academic researchers to develop and manage research. Guiding principles for the collaboration included developing an active partnership, fostering coownership of the project, and building system change on local knowledge.

QUALITY IMPROVEMENT

Quality improvement uses an organization's data to improve both processes (how things are done) and outcomes, whereas evidence-based practice uses the best available evidence along with patient preferences to make clinical decisions, and research focuses on developing new knowledge. Quite often these activities may overlap. For example, it is important to use validated tools to collect data for a quality improvement activity. Or, when beginning a new project, it may be critical to collect data beforehand so that you will know whether the results had an impact. The National Database of Nursing Quality Indicators (NDNQI), established by the ANA and now owned by Press Ganey, is used to collect data on nursing structures, processes, and outcomes, providing a comprehensive assessment of an organization's nursing care quality. NDNQI includes data on nurse-sensitive outcomes such as falls, nosocomial infections, and pressure ulcers. Nurse-sensitive outcomes are directly related to the quality of nursing care, in contrast to those outcomes that are more dependent on a multidisciplinary team effort. These measures also include nurse satisfaction and staffing. Hospitals receive unit-level data as well as benchmark comparisons with similar hospitals. This enables the staff to design practice improvement projects with standardized outcomes measures. These projects often use EBP as a foundation for their quality improvement activities. For example, researchers at one hospital used NDNQI data and found a significant relationship between teamwork and NDNQI outcomes such as pressure ulcers, falls, and catheter-associated urinary tract infections (Rahn, 2016). Physician specialty and other healthcare disciplinary organizations also collect quality indicators for specific procedures such as coronary artery bypass graft surgery and joint replacement to provide their members with benchmark data. The U.S. Department of Veterans Affairs' Quality Enhancement Research Initiative (QUERI) is designed to use research evidence to improve practice. A variety of strategies, very often incorporating different types of research activities, is used to make practice improvements to enhance patient care.

EVALUATING EVIDENCE

Frontline nurses and nurse leaders are being called upon to take an active role in evaluating evidence. Evidence is best evaluated using a systematic process. EBP steps are illustrated in Box 24.1. The first steps are creating a spirit of inquiry and identifying the problem so that the relevant information can be obtained. Clinical questions should be put into the widely used PICOT format of patient, intervention, comparison intervention or group, outcome, and time to facilitate searching for the appropriate evidence. Questions to be asked in developing a PICOT question are illustrated in Table 24.4. Identifying the question is often the most challenging step. Different strategies can be used to identify practice problems. One might conduct a survey of staff members or use a focus group methodology. Conducting a staff survey would necessitate that staff members have sufficient knowledge of research and EBP to understand what is desired. The data from surveys or focus groups, or even informal interviews with staff, can be examined along with patient outcome data to address relevant practice problems. Collaboration between nurses and members

BOX 24.1   Steps of Evidence-Based Inquiry

0. Cultivate a spirit of inquiry.
1. Ask the burning clinical question in PICOT (patient, intervention, comparison, outcome, and time frame) format.
2. Search for and collect the most relevant best evidence.
3. Appraise the evidence (i.e., rapid critical appraisal, evaluation, and synthesis).
4. Integrate the best evidence with one's clinical expertise and patient preferences and values in making a practice decision or change.
5. Evaluate outcomes of the practice design or change based on evidence.
6. Disseminate the outcomes of the EBP (evidence-based practice) decision or change.

From Melnyk, B. M., & Fineout-Overholt, E. (2015). Making the case for evidence-based practice and cultivating a spirit of inquiry. In Melnyk, B. M., & Fineout-Overholt, E. (Eds.), *Evidence-based practice in nursing and healthcare: A guide to best practice* (3rd ed.). Philadelphia: Lippincott, Williams & Wilkins.

of pertinent disciplines will enhance the success of an evidence-based project by early involvement in the project design and conception. When designing the PICOT question, additional consideration should be given to adding a digital component, making it into a PICOT-D question (Elias, Polancich, Jones, & Colvin, 2015). This would include determining what data are to be used, the location of the data, data stewards (for permission to use the data), and format for extracting the data. Once the clinical question has been identified, writing it down will help in moving on to the next step of gathering evidence. Examples of questions to be asked using the PICOT-D format are illustrated in Table 24.4.

EXERCISE 24.3 Develop a clinical question using the PICOT (*patient*, *intervention* [*interest*], *comparison*, *outcome*, and *time*) format. Do a search in PubMed with the key PICOT terms. Identify two potential sources of data that could be used to answer the clinical question.

Searching for evidence is accomplished with using databases effectively. Some databases contain preprocessed evidence, that which has been synthesized and/or summarized, such as systematic reviews of evidence, in addition to citations for original single studies. Commonly used databases are listed in Table 24.5. Obtaining a librarian's assistance to navigate the databases is

TABLE 24.4   Asking the Right Question: The PICOT-D Format

Patient population	What is the patient population or the setting? This could be adults, children, or neonates with a certain health problem; or home, hospital, primary care, schools.
Intervention/ Interest Area	What is the intervention? This can be an intervention or a specific area of interest (e.g., electronic monitoring of self-care or postoperative complications).
Comparison	What is a comparison intervention? This might be a treatment or the absence of a risk factor (e.g., using social networks or group classes for diabetes self-management).
Outcome	What are the results? Measuring results can be accomplished with different methods. Sometimes several methods are used to measure a single outcome. Examples may include complication rates, satisfaction, a nursing diagnosis, a nursing quality indicator, or completion of a rehabilitation program.
Time	What is the time frame for this intervention? Is time a relevant factor for this evaluation? For example, 1 week after discharge from a hospital, or 3 months later.
Digital	What data will be used? Where are the data located? What is the format for data extraction? Who are the data stewards from whom permission to use the data is needed? Examples of these might be readmission and chief nursing informatics officer.

invaluable, because identifying the correct search terms and taking advantage of new database features facilitates successful searching. Tracking search terms used provides consistency when using multiple databases. Preprocessed evidence can be found in the evidence-based resources listed in Tables 24.2 and 24.3. An

TABLE 24.5 **Commonly Used Databases and Search Platforms**	
CINAHL: Cumulative Index to Nursing and Allied Health Literature www.ebscohost.com/cinahl	A comprehensive nursing and allied health abstract database that includes some full-text material such as state nursing journals, nurse practice acts, research instruments, government publications, and patient education material from 1982 to the present.
Clinical Trials clinicaltrials.gov	Registry of publicly and privately supported clinical trials with human participants from around the world.
Cochrane Library www.cochranelibary.org Cochrane Database of Systematic Reviews (CDSR) Cochrane Central Register of Controlled Trials (CENTRAL) Database of Reviews of Effects (DARE) Cochrane Methodology Register (CMR) Health Technology Assessment Database (HTA) NHS Economic Evaluation Database	Six databases with different types of evidence and a 7th about Cochrane workgroups
EMBASE www.elsevier.com/solutions/embase-biomedical-research	Database for biomedical and pharmaceutical studies.
EBSCO www.ebscohost.com	A search platform vendor for a variety of databases, including CINAHL and MEDLINE.
MEDLINE http://www.nlm.nih.gov/databases	The largest component within PubMed, indexing over 5600 journals according to Medical Subject Headings (MeSH). Available through PubMed.
OVID www.ovid.com	A search platform for a variety of databases related to science, medicine, and health care.
PsycINFO http://www.apa.org/pubs/databases/psycinfo/	Abstract database of psychology and the behavioral and social science research literature from the 1800s to the present.
PubMed www.ncbi.nlm.nih.gov/pubmed	The abstract database of the National Library of Medicine, providing access to over 26 million citations from the 1950s to the present. Includes ahead-of-print citations for articles.
PubMed Central https://www.ncbi.nlm.nih.gov/pmc/	Repository of full-text articles by participating publishers and authors complying with the NIH Public Access Policy. Linked with PubMed.
UpToDate www.uptodate.com/	Clinical decision resource for evidence-based practice.

exhaustive and systematic review of multiple databases is necessary to obtain the latest and best evidence.

Evidence for a practice problem can come from a single research study, an integrative review of the literature, a meta-analysis, a metasynthesis, a clinically appraised topic, a clinical guideline, or a systematic review. A hierarchy of evidence that ranges from opinion at the lowest level to systematic reviews at the peak is illustrated in Fig. 24.2. However, keep in mind that the hierarchy is fluid. With the increased capacity to use large data sets for PBE and data analytics for analysis of real-time data, observational data may provide powerful evidence for practice recommendations. No single established method of rating evidence is best for all situations. An evidence hierarchy can be used to compare the strength of the evidence when deciding which intervention might

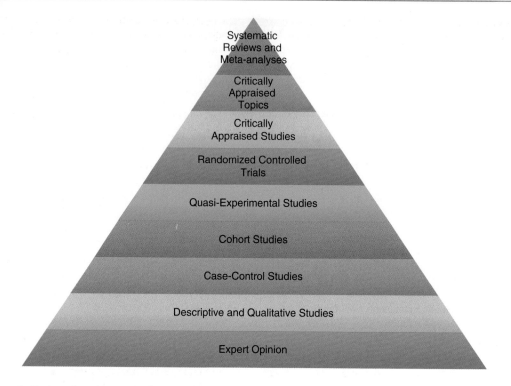

Systematic Review: Appraises evidence thoroughly in accordance with established standards and criteria

Meta-analysis: Synthesizes evidence using quantitative methods

Critically Appraised Topic: Evidence syntheses or clinical guidelines

Critically Appraised Study: Systematic appraisal of a single study

Randomized Controlled Trials: Experimental studies that include randomization and double-blinding

Quasi-Experimental Studies: Well-designed studies without randomization and/or blinding

Cohort Studies: Prospectively examine a population for a disease, outcome, or risk factor

Case-Control Studies: Compare people with a condition (cases) and those who do not have the condition (controls)

Descriptive Studies: Examine patterns occurring in a population

Qualitative Studies: Gain understanding of a phenomenon; develop theory

Expert Opinion: Opinions of authorities or experts in the field

Fig. 24.2 Hierarchy of evidence.

be the best. Researchers examining evidence and developing guidelines use a variety of different rating systems that include a hierarchy and key quality domains.

Ultimately, when appraising multiple sources of evidence, nurses need to make decisions about the strength of the evidence and its application to a patient population. Once the evidence is located, an appropriate and systematic method for rating or appraising the evidence is used along with analysis of its applicability to a clinical situation. Appraisal tools exist for evaluating different types of evidence from a single qualitative study,

qualitative metasyntheses, descriptive studies, randomized clinical trials, and clinical guidelines to systematic reviews. These tools generally include a series of steps for evaluating the quality of the research that is specific to the study design, type of review or guideline, and a strategy for determining the applicability of the evidence to one's practice.

Much of the EBP literature has been devoted to evaluating randomized controlled trials (RCT). These include at least two groups and the random assignment of study participants to one group or another, either by a coin toss or by some other strategy, to test a treatment's effectiveness. Generally, it is preferable that such studies are double-blinded, meaning that the participants and those who are evaluating the outcomes do not know who has received the treatment. Although this design is generally considered the gold standard in terms of ranking individual studies, one needs to consider the quality of the study rather than merely the design. The number of RCTs conducted in nursing has been limited. In certain clinical trials, blinding recipients to interventions may be difficult to accomplish, as when delivering an intervention involving interaction with study participants. RCTs are not always an appropriate design for answering a research question, and implementing RCTs may not be possible for all the research questions that need to be answered. Hence it is important that the appraisal method must examine the rigor or quality of the research in accordance with standards for that type of study.

Consensus on checklists or guides for evaluating different types of research reports have been established by professional societies and interdisciplinary groups. See Box 24.2 for selected checklist resources for types of studies and guidelines that can assist in the evaluation of evidence for nursing practice. Use of these guides ensures that components critical to the evaluation of the strength of evidence are included in the appraisal process.

BOX 24.2   Online Resources for Appraisal Checklists and Guides

Checklist Compilations
- CASP, Critical Appraisal Skills Programme Checklists: http://www.casp-uk.net/casp-tools-checklists
- EQUATOR Network, Enhancing the QUAlity and Transparency Of health Research: http://www.equator-network.org/

Internet Resources for Appraisal of Specific Research Designs
- AGREE, Advancing the Science of Practice Guidelines: www.agreetrust.org
- CONSORT, Consolidated Standards of Reporting Trials: http://www.consort-statement.org/
- PRISMA, Preferred Reporting Items for Systematic Reviews and Meta-Analyses: http://www.prisma-statement.org/
- SQUIRE, Standards for Quality Improvement Reporting Excellence: http://www.squire-statement.org/
- STROBE, Strengthening the Reporting of Observational Studies in Epidemiology: strobe-statement.org

---

Checklists are usually designed so that the presence or absence of a critical component of the research is noted. It is then necessary to make a judgment about the strength of the evidence. For this, a system of grading evidence is used. The Grading of Recommendations Assessment, Development and Evaluation (GRADE) system, developed by a consensus, is a widely used and well-established system to evaluate evidence (Neumann et al., 2016). The GRADE system evaluates evidence on a scale of high, moderate, low, and very low to indicate the degree of certainty about the evidence that supports a recommendation. Professional groups use a grading system for the evidence when formulating practice recommendations that will be used in clinical guidelines. It is useful not only to grade the evidence in making practice recommendations, but also to examine the process used to grade evidence, especially when two organizations have seemingly contradictory recommendations for clinical practice.

First, all the research evidence needs to be examined, regardless of the studies included in the analysis, the types of study designs, their results, and appraisal systems used to evaluate them. Then, questions need to be answered about the validity, reliability, and the applicability of the findings. *Validity* answers the question of whether the results are true, that the study measured what it was supposed to measure because it was well designed (internal validity). *Reliability* answers the question of whether the similar results would be obtained if the study were to be repeated, such as if the instruments used to measure the outcomes were reliable. Finally, if the validity and reliability questions are answered, then it is possible to answer the applicability question: whether the study results can be applied to a patient population. Are the patients sufficiently like those in most of the studies examined? Is it feasible to make a practice change in a particular setting? What are the consequences of not making such a change?

Once the evidence is appraised, the new practice recommendation needs to be integrated with clinical expertise and the preferences and values of patients, families, and communities in making the change. For example, in evaluating a research-based protocol for teaching oncology patients about preparing for a bone marrow transplant, the amount and type of information that would be desired by the patient need to be considered. In this instance a qualitative research study might provide guidance for decision making. For certain types of interventions, the inclusion of patient preferences might not be appropriate, as in the example of implementing a protocol to reduce ventilator-associated pneumonia. However, frontline nurses need to be involved in planning the details. Determining patient preferences depends on the nature of the intervention or change that is proposed.

The sheer quantity and complexity of information available illustrates the importance of frontline nurses and nurse leaders collaborating with nurse researchers. See Box 24.3 for an example of an academic-service partnership to promote the use of evidence in practice. Frontline nurses and nurse leaders bring their clinical expertise, their assessment of clinically relevant questions, and their understanding of the patient population. Nurse researchers bring their capacity to appraise evidence to facilitate its application to the clinical setting. Together, practitioners and researchers can forge a partnership to develop an evidence-based solution to a clinical practice problem, which can then be systematically evaluated and disseminated to the wider community.

> **EXERCISE 24.4** Locate a research column in a clinical nursing journal. Identify one study that has implications for your practice. Retrieve the original article to learn more about the patient population, details of the study design, results, and methods of measuring the outcome.

Translation research and implementation science is known as translation science, the science of translating research into practice (TRIP). Translation science is a research area focused on testing interventions that are designed to facilitate the use of evidence to improve patient outcomes and population health and to determine what strategies work in a setting and why (Titler, 2014). It is often used interchangeably with implementation science, which focuses on studying methods to facilitate the integration of research findings and evidence into healthcare policy and practice (Fogarty International Center, n.d.). Numerous other terms are

---

BOX 24.3 Collaboration in Developing an Evidence-Based Protocol for Kangaroo Care

Clinician Perspective

We discovered there was interest in, but not common practice of, kangaroo care for premature babies. Many of the staff members in our facilities have a wealth of clinical experience. However, they really did not have the chance to learn about evidence-based practice in school. The students came to us to talk about our needs. When they finished their work, they presented their findings about the evidence for kangaroo care and thermoregulation at our regional perinatal center nursing leadership retreat. Initially, they were intimidated about presenting to a group of such experienced nurses. However, it was rewarding to see them become more confident about their work.

Since the student presentation, we have had an upsurge of interest in providing kangaroo care. It has helped us in overcoming resistance to its use. We are now working on how to most effectively implement kangaroo care, because it takes concerted work and staff time to teach and prepare the parents. One of our hospitals is using the poster developed by the students as a training tool. I enjoyed working with the students in a way that produced a tangible outcome for everyone involved. Learning how to conduct research for evidence-based practice gave the students a skill that they will have as new nurses and can offer as a complement to their more experienced nursing colleagues as they begin their professional careers.

Sally Girvin, MPH, BS, RN, NP
Coordinator, New York Presbyterian Regional Perinatal Centers, New York

Student Perspective

The eight of us who worked on this project were in the middle of our accelerated nursing program when it was assigned to us. We had to come up with an answerable clinical question, but because of our lack of clinical experience, we had only a vague idea of what to ask. We were able to develop our question after we talked with Sally and listened to her needs. We had spent some time in the neonatal intensive care unit and realized how hard it would be for the already busy nurses to take on this project. As students, we had the time.

When we went to the retreat to present our project, we thought no one would be interested in what we had done, that it might not be applicable, or that we had discovered something they already knew. The response was incredible. Our presentation created open debate. Some hospitals had kangaroo-care policies, some did not, some had them and did not follow them, and some people were unsure what they had in place. It really prompted people to look at their practices. It was a great experience to work with Sally and her colleagues and to see that what we did had an influence on policy. It was an experience that we can take with us wherever we go.

Elizabeth K. Kelly, BS, RN
Student at Columbia University School of Nursing, New York, when this project was developed

used, including *knowledge translation, knowledge uptake, knowledge exchange,* and *research utilization,* depending on the context and region of the world. Research is translated into practice on a continuum of diffusion-dissemination-implementation: Diffusion is an unfocused and passive adoption of new practices; dissemination is actively spreading new practices with specific strategies, and implementation is integrating practices into the care delivery processes of a clinical setting (Nilson, 2015).

EXERCISE 24.5 Review the Challenge at the beginning of the chapter and identify practices that would promote the translation of research findings into practice. Compare your strategies with those described in the Solution at the end of this chapter. What strategies do you think would be the most effective in sustaining the improvement over time?

Translating research into practice so that it becomes embedded in care processes involves careful planning and understanding the dynamics of the organization and commitment to seeing through all the intermediate steps. Frontline nurses and nurse leaders not only need to pay careful attention to the development of a clinical protocol or an evidence-based guideline but also must address the implementation process. When planning to translate a research finding into practice, considering what types of strategies have been most successful in implementing a practice in one's organization is important. For example, although results of a study protocol used in a randomized controlled trial to decrease ventilator-associated events may have significantly improved patient outcomes, those same results may not be as dramatic when the protocol is implemented at institutions with varying resources and degrees of commitment to implementing the protocol. Even when a practice has changed, it might not be diffused to all settings. For example, teaching nursing students how to administer an intramuscular injection in the dorsogluteal site has largely disappeared from fundamentals textbooks, but nurses in practice for many years might not be aware of the change. Some pharmaceutical companies still include the dorsogluteal site as a recommended location in the product literature for medications administered by the intramuscular route, and some healthcare agencies may still include the site in their procedure manuals. Therefore it is important to not only embed the use of evidence into a practice setting but also disseminate information about the EBP.

Strategies for TRIP can include using opinion leaders, educational programs, observations of behavior, auditing records, reminder systems, and incentives. It is necessary to determine how often and for how long a strategy should be used within an organizational context. Preventing falls in hospitals is a perennial challenge. EBP fall prevention interventions targeting specific fall risk factors were implemented in three community hospitals. A falls prevention **bundle,** which groups several evidence-based practices into a standard protocol, was used along with a TRIP intervention designed to increase the bundle's uptake (Titler et al., 2016). The intervention used a partnership to foster engagement and ownership of interventions. The evidence-based fall prevention practices were adopted with a significant reduction in fall rates, but not fall injuries, indicating additional efforts are needed.

Academic detailing is a popular TRIP strategy. It has been widely used by the pharmaceutical industry to change prescribing behaviors. Clinicians trained in using adult learning principles and active engagement are employed to have a face-to-face discussion of the EBP with healthcare providers. Information is presented in a compelling manner with easily understood graphics and statistics. Choosing Wisely® is a program of the ABIM Foundation (a charitable arm of the American Board of Internal Medicine) designed to reduce unnecessary medical tests, treatments, and procedures. Professional societies representing different professional groups have identified questionable interventions and practices. Two examples of nursing practices identified as questionable include waking hospitalized patients at night when not clinically indicated and using restraints on hospitalized older adult patients (Choosing Wisely, 2017).

ORGANIZATIONAL STRATEGIES TO EMBED EVIDENCE-BASED PRACTICE INTO ORGANIZATIONS

The next challenge in TRIP is embedding EBP practices into organizational systems and processes (Fralick, Kesselheim, & Avorn, 2017). Frontline nurses and nurse leaders need to work as partners in implementing EBPs and TRIP. Frontline nurses bring knowledge of current clinical issues, and nurse leaders bring knowledge of the organization in identifying how EBPs can be embedded into the organization. The partnership between frontline nurses and nurse leaders needs to be extended to the executive level, interdisciplinary groups, and to the organization's stakeholders. For example, implementing a fall risk reduction program will not be successful without physician involvement, because physicians will need to be involved in reducing modifiable fall risk factors related to patient medications. Physical therapists are invaluable team members for a patient mobility program. Partnering with researchers can accelerate the TRIP process and facilitate presenting evidence in a convincing manner. For example, in deciding whether it is best for nurses or parents to administer preprocedure sedation, the evidence for safety issues related to unmonitored or parent-administered sedation when a child is being transported to a procedure in the back seat of a car can be presented. Providing key organizational decision makers with evidence regarding the safety of practices is critical for decision making.

Integrating best evidence into practice can be facilitated by using a framework to understand complex interactions between clinicians and organizational leaders within the context of an organization's environment. The integrated *Promoting Action on Research Implementation in Health Services* (i-PARIHS) framework focuses on the role of individuals in facilitating the innovation process (Kitson & Harvey, 2016). Successful implementation of an EBP depends on the quality and type of evidence (the innovation), the characteristics of the setting (the context), and how the evidence is introduced or facilitated in the setting (impact on the recipients). Key features of the i-PARIHS framework include the following:

- Focusing on the leadership role of the facilitator in guiding implementation
- Using a variety of knowledge sources including research, clinical experience, patient preferences, and local information to develop the evidence
- Recognizing some contexts are more conducive to successful implementation (e.g., transformational leaders, learning organization, monitoring, feedback and evaluation)
- Focusing on the individuals adopting the practice through negotiation, shared understanding of knowledge, and a team effort

The facilitator role enables groups to work together in achieving common goals. The complex factors that need to be considered by facilitators and activities that they carry out are illustrated in Fig. 24.3. Initially, facilitators focus on the nature of the innovation itself, and then move the focus outward to the individuals who will be involved in implementing the innovation, the local

context, and then the organizational context. Finally, the facilitator focuses on the external environment, examining regulatory and policy issues and interorganization relationships and networks. The I-PARIHS framework can be used to understand what is most successful in implementing a practice change. Using the i-PARIHS framework, some of the questions that can be asked by nurses tasked with implementing an EBP include the following:

- How complex is the practice change? Does it require many steps to implement?
- How extensive is the education and preparation that nurses and members of other disciplines need for implementation?
- What type of support is provided by nurse leaders, both formal and informal?
- Are frontline nurses routinely included when proposed changes are planned?
- What other resources are needed: staffing, financial, information technology?
- How will you know when you are successful? How will outcomes be measured?
- Can outcomes be measured without adding to the workload of the nurses?
- How will the results of the project be disseminated to key decision makers and stakeholders?
- Does the change have implications beyond the immediate practice setting? Will it be necessary to change policies, standards, and regulations?

Sustaining EBP in an organization requires leadership support, organizational capacity for EBP, and the capacity to implement a specific EBP (Scaccia et al., 2015). Successful implementation of EBP also includes integrating expectations for participation in EBP into job descriptions and recognition for EBP successes. Hospitals with Magnet Recognition® seek to provide an organizational environment that facilitates the implementation of EBP to improve quality.

> **EXERCISE 21.6** Using the information in Fig. 24.2 and the sample questions that should be asked using the I-PARIHS framework, assess the capacity of your agency to implement an evidence-based practice. Identify one strategy to address a specific barrier to implementation.

The adoption of EBPs and TRIP ultimately depend on a complex interaction of individual and organizational factors. Steps to implement an EBP change and TRIP are illustrated in Box 24.4. Nurse leaders are increasingly called

Facilitator focus and activity

What the facilitator looks at
What the facilitator does

Characteristics of the innovation

Underlying knowledge sources
Clarity
Degree of fit (compatibility or contestability)
Degree of novelty
Likely boundaries
Trialability
Relative advantage

Problem identification
Acquiring/appraising evidence
Baseline context & boundary assessment
Stakeholder mapping

Recipients

Motivation
Values & beliefs
Clinical consensus
Local opinion leaders
Existing data sources
Skills and knowledge
Time and resources
Learning environment
Collaboration and teamwork
Power & authority
Professional boundaries & networks

Goal setting
Consensus building
Audit & feedback
Improvement methods
Project management
Change management
Team building
Conflict management & resolution
Barriers/boundary assessment
Boundary spanning

Outer context

Policy drivers & priorities
Incentives & mandates
Regulatory frameworks
Environmental (in)stability
Inter-organizational networks & relationships

Political awareness & influence
Communication
Marketing
Networking
Boundary spanning
Sustainability & spread

Inner context: local level

Formal & informal leadership support
Culture
Past experience of change
Mechanisms for embedding change
Evaluation & feedback processes

Local context assessment
Communication & feedback
Networking
Boundary assessment & spanning
Negotiating & influencing
Policies & procedures
Structuring learning

Inner context: organizational level

Organizational priorities
Structure
Leadership & senior management support
Systems & processes
Culture
History of innovation & change
Absorptive capacity

Stakeholder engagement
Communication & feedback
Marketing & presentation
Networking
Boundary spanning
Negotiating & influencing
Policies & procedures

Fig. 24.3 The Promoting Action on Research Implementation in Health Services integrated framework (i-PARIHS framework): facilitation as the activity ingredient. (From *Implementing evidence-based practice in healthcare: A facilitation guide,* G. Harvey & A. Kitson. Copyright [© 2015] and Routledge. Reproduced by permission of Taylor & Francis Books, United Kingdom.)

upon to support individual nurses, implement strategies to enhance frontline nurses' use of evidence, and create an organizational infrastructure that promotes EBP.

ISSUES FOR NURSE LEADERS AND MANAGERS

Issues faced by nurse leaders and managers include lack of resources, limited staff expertise with respect to EBP, lack of knowledge about nursing research, and limited time for planning. Not all organizations can hire a full-time nurse researcher. Some organizations may not employ clinical nurse specialists. This is shortsighted in view of the potential benefits of improved patient outcomes and cost savings because of a reduction in adverse outcomes. However, this resource limitation is a reality faced in many organizations. Therefore partnering with

nurse researchers at a university could be invaluable. New graduates can partner with experienced nurses, thus demonstrating leadership skills and strengthening mentorship bonds. Faculty can partner with staff in a facility to provide consultation for a specific patient care problem, and agencies can partner together to address a specific practice problem.

Collaboration is critical to ensuring the success of TRIP. Collaboration can occur not only within an organization but also through practice-based research networks (PBRN) and data warehousing. Originally formed to address primary care research issues, PBRNs are being used in large healthcare organizations because they can integrate systems across multiple practice sites. Primary care PBRNs can register with AHRQ. PBRNs have also been established to serve the needs of advanced practice registered nurses, school nurses, dentists, long-term care

BOX 24.4   Steps in Implementing an Evidence-Based Practice Change and Translating Research Into Practice

1. Create an EBP team to develop and refine the PICOT question, evaluate the evidence, determine the change in practice, and develop a preliminary plan.
2. Identify stakeholders at the unit and organizational level.
3. Complete an environmental assessment of barriers and facilitators.
4. Develop a plan for minimizing barriers and enhancing facilitators.
5. Identify resources needed for implementation (e.g., staffing, information technology, data, publicity).
6. Refine the implementation plan.
7. Obtain necessary approvals (administrative, institutional review board).
8. Educate key stakeholders about the plan.
9. Implement the project.
10. Evaluate the outcomes.
11. Disseminate the results of the project to key stakeholders.

facilities, federally qualified health centers, and rural health care centers. The PBRNs share data to analyze common problems and make improvements in quality. Five large health systems, the Mayo Clinic, Geisinger, Kaiser Permanente, Intermountain Healthcare, and GroupHealth Cooperative, created the Care Connectivity Consortium to share information across systems from their data warehouses. Not only do these networks provide health information exchange for the benefit of individual patients who travel to different regions of the country, but they also facilitate answering research questions that require large samples. Frontline nurses and nurse leaders working in these settings can take advantage of these resources to obtain evidence that has immediate relevance for practice.

Nurses' preparation for EBP is an organizational issue. Many nurses might not have had research or statistics courses in their basic nursing education or had those courses many years ago. Even if nurses had research courses, they might not be familiar with the steps for developing EBP and TRIP. New frontline nurses prepared with a bachelor's or higher degree have had research courses and more recent experience with EBP; therefore they are ideally suited to mentor more experienced nurses. A new nurse could assist in developing capacity for evaluating evidence by starting a

monthly journal club. This involves reading a relevant research article and discussing how it might be applied to practice. Although nursing has general and specialty nursing research journals, *Evidence-Based Nursing, Worldviews on Evidence-Based Nursing,* and the *JBI Database of Systematic Reviews and Implementation Reports* are specifically devoted to EBP. *Implementation Science* is a journal devoted specifically to strategies for TRIP. Journal club discussions can be used to identify clinical practice problems. Healthcare system and university librarians can assist with gathering information and identifying articles.

The outcomes of TRIP initiatives need to be evaluated. It is preferable to collect outcome data before protocol implementation to have a subsequent basis for comparison. When implementing a protocol on one unit, consideration should also be given to the impact of staff casually talking with the staff of other units. This might create competition, making it difficult to interpret the impact of the protocol. It is also important to consider whether the implementation of an EBP project might be considered a research project. Considerable variation exists among institutions in the interpretation of what projects fall under the purview of the Institutional Review Board (IRB). Therefore consulting with the organization's IRB and/or quality improvement oversight committee early in the planning phase is critical. This ensures that ethical considerations have been addressed before implementation.

Nurses, other healthcare professionals, and the public might not be familiar with EBP. Publicizing positive outcomes of EBP efforts helps stimulate interests. When EBP is publicized in the media or through news alerts, to colleagues in nursing and other disciplines, key organizational decision makers and stakeholders need to be alerted.

Joining a professional association and signing up for alerts from key agencies provide nurses with access to the latest news, research, and standards that affect EBP. Research evidence has a much better chance of being implemented if key stakeholders can understand its relevance. It may be necessary to introduce important concepts in small increments. For example, a first step might be incorporating research into the revision of procedures and agency guidelines as they are reviewed. Subsequently, nurses and key stakeholders can be asked to identify clinical practice problems that create challenges in providing care to develop an EBP. Multiple strategies are needed for TRIP; they are also needed to change a culture to one that is driven by research and evidence-based standards for practice. Finally, if one should have the opportunity to implement an EBP, as much consideration needs to be given to planning for implementation using the change process as protocol development (see Chapter 18). Planning should include a thorough and frank discussion of how to minimize the barriers and maximize the facilitators of TRIP. Strategies to sustain the adoption of the practice over time need to be considered. Although the implementation of EBP is a very complex process, the increased emphasis on the use of sound evidence creates an exciting opportunity for frontline nurses and nurse leaders to demonstrate the value of nursing in improving patient care and healthcare outcomes.

CONCLUSION

Nurses are accountable to their patients to provide the best care possible. This means that nurses must translate research into practice. Numerous approaches to do so are possible. The challenge lies in more rapidly incorporating solid evidence into practice so that patients may benefit from that translation sooner than the current translation time.

THE SOLUTION

The main challenge, as always, is getting buy-in from all parties, including staff, physicians, and others. We had to make sure everyone understood that this would not lead to anything punitive, nor were we just giving them extra work, but rather giving them the tools they needed for the best patient outcomes. We took the idea of the audits and the proposed process for them to our Unit Council for feedback about the proposed changes.

Observational audits were conducted over a period of 2 years and included four main parts. First was aseptic technique, which included those who scrubbed following policy, watching for possible contamination of the sterile field, appropriate surgical skin prep, and any excessive movement during the procedure. Second, counts were observed at the end of a case and during handoffs to ensure they were performed per policy. The third part concerned preparation for the case and included staff having all supplies and instruments, positioning devices, and anticipating the needs of the entire team. Lastly, we observed the universal protocol to ensure the timeout and all the components, including infection control practices, were being performed correctly and that staff were comfortable stopping the line when necessary. At first, staff thought we would be punitive if we found them doing something that was not best practice. But, after we started, staff would come to us suggesting specific things that we should examine, such as skin preparation on multiple surgical sites or recommending surgical team members for further coaching. We encouraged staff to bring any issues, good or bad, or recommended changes back to the Unit Council.

Two other intraprofessional groups were also formed for specific specialty areas that had significantly higher infection rates. Both implemented several interventions found in literature reviews along with direct observation of those procedures to see if there were any breaks in sterile technique.

Since implementing these interventions, we have successfully and significantly decreased our SSI rates across the board, with zero infections for three types of surgeries. This was achieved by using a multifaceted approach and engaging all of those on the surgical team. Presently, we are overhauling these audits to continue the success we have shown so far. With continued observation, we hope to see even more consistently below–national average SSI rates, but rates as close to zero as possible.

Would this be a suitable approach for you? Why?

Megan Lamoreux

REFLECTIONS

Think of a clinical practice problem on your unit where there is considerable variation in the nursing care provided, resulting in different outcomes for patients. To help you identify such a practice problem, think about when you have asked yourself, "Why are we doing this?" or "Why are we doing it this way?" Practices to consider are those that have (1) high volume, (2) important clinical outcomes, (3) significant adverse effects, (4) reporting requirements for quality improvement or regulatory agencies, and/or (5) serious financial implications. What strategies might you use to bring this clinical practice problem to the attention of your colleagues and/or leadership? Does the problem include other disciplines? If so, what can you do to engage them in seeking solutions?

THE EVIDENCE

Nurses' readiness for implementing EBP is important to the success of such programs. Numerous studies have been conducted across the globe to assess nurses' EBP competencies and their willingness to adopt EBPs. An integrative review of 37 primary research studies on nurses' readiness for EBP indicated that nurses' attitudes toward EBP were positive (Saunders & Vehviläinen-Julkunen, 2016). However, nurses indicated that they did not have the knowledge and skills for using EBP, nor did they use best evidence in their practice. Although most of the studies had small sample sizes, with low response rates, the results of this review indicate that additional work is needed in preparing the nursing workforce for using EBP.

TIPS FOR DEVELOPING SKILL IN USING EVIDENCE AND TRANSLATING RESEARCH INTO PRACTICE

- Make a personal commitment to read articles reporting on research, EBP, and TRIP projects.
- Complete an online tutorial in EBP.
- Use your clinical experiences to develop relevant clinical questions.
- Obtain assistance from librarians, researchers, advanced practice registered nurses, and nurse leaders.
- Use the Patient, Intervention, Comparison, Outcome, and Time (PICOT) format to search for evidence on a clinical practice problem.

- Learn about your organization's sources of data that may be used to measure outcomes of care.
- Use a journal club to encourage your colleagues to join you in learning about EBP and evaluating research evidence.
- Examine EBP resources on a professional association's website.
- Volunteer to take part in a project that is focused on translating research into practice.
- Identify facilitators and barriers to translating research into practice in your setting and strategies to mitigate them.

REFERENCES

Agency on Healthcare Research and Quality. (AHRQ). (n.d.). *What is comparative effectiveness research.* http://effectivehealthcare.ahrq.gov/index.cfm/what-is-comparative-effectiveness-research1/.

American Nurses Association (ANA). (n.d.). *National Database of Nursing Quality Indicators.* Silver Spring, MD: Author.

American Nurses Association (ANA). (2010). *Nursing's social policy statement: The essence of the profession.* Silver Spring, MD: Nursesbooks.org.

American Nurses Association (ANA). (2015). *Code of ethics for nurses with interpretive statements.* Silver Spring, MD: Nursesbooks.org.

Bellazzi, R. (2014). Big data and biomedical informatics: A challenging opportunity. *Yearbook of Medical Informatics 2014, 9*(1), 14–20.

Choosing Wisely®. (2017). *Clinician lists.* http://www.choosingwisely.org/clinician-lists/.

Eisenberg, S. R., Bair-Merritt, M. H., Colson, E. R., Heeren, T. C., Geller, N. L., & Corwin, M. J. (2015). Maternal report of advice received for infant care. *Pediatrics, 136*(2), e315–e322. https://doi.org/10.1542/peds.2015-0551.

Elias, B. L., Polancich, S., Jones, C., & Conroy, S. (2015). Evolving the PICOT method for the digital age: The PICOT-D. *Journal of Nursing Education, 54*(10), 594–599. https://doi.org/10.3928/01484834-20150916-09.

Fogarty International Center. (n.d.). *Implementation science information and resources.* https://www.fic.nih.gov/researchtopics/pages/implementationscience.aspx.

Fralick, M., Kesselheim, A., & Avorn, J. (2017). Applying academic detailing and process change to promote Choosing Wisely. *JAMA Internal Medicine, 177*(2), 282. https://doi.org/10.1001/jamainternmed.2016.8503.

Gray, J., Grove, S., & Sutherland, S. (2016). Burns and Grove's. In *The Practice of Nursing Research: Appraisal, synthesis, and generation of evidence* (8th ed.). Philadelphia: Elsevier-Saunders.

Greiner, A. C., & Knebel, E. (Eds.). (2003). Board on Health Care Services, Committee on the Health Professions Summit, Institute of Medicine. In *Health professions education: A bridge to quality.* Washington, DC: National Academies Press.

Hanney, S. R., Castle-Clarke, S., Grant, J., Guthrie, S., Henshall, C., Mestre-Ferrandiz, J., et al. (2015). How long does biomedical research take? Studying the time taken between biomedical and health research and its translation into products, policy, and practice. *Health Research and Policy Systems, 13*(1). https://doi.org/10.1186/1478-4505-13-1.

Institute of Medicine (IOM). (2013). *Best care at lower cost: The path to continuously learning health care in America.* Washington, DC: The National Academies Press.

Institute of Medicine (IOM). (2015). *Integrating research and practice: Health system leaders working toward high-value care: Workshop summary.* Washington, DC: The National Academies Press.

International Council of Nurses (ICN). (2015). *Research network.* http://www.icn.ch/networks/research-network/.

Kitson, A. L., & Harvey, G. (2016). Methods to succeed in effective knowledge translation. *Journal of Nursing Scholarship, 48*(3), 294–302. https://doi.org/10.1111/jnu.12206.

Linder, L. A., Gerdy, C., Abouzelof, R., & Wilson, A. (2016). Using practice-based evidence to improve supportive care practices to reduce central line-associated bloodstream infections in a pediatric oncology unit. *Journal of Pediatric Oncology Nursing, 34*(3), 185–195. https://doi.org/10.1177/1043454216676838.

Melnyk, B. M., & Fineout-Overholt, E. (2015). Making the case for evidence-based practice and cultivating a spirit of inquiry. In B. M. Melnyk & E. Fineout-Overholt (Eds.), *Evidence-based practice in nursing and healthcare: A guide to best practice* (3rd ed., p. 10). Philadelphia: Lippincott, Williams & Wilkins.

Melnyk, B. M., & Gallagher-Ford, L. (2015). Implementing the new essential evidence-based practice competencies in real-world clinical and academic settings: Moving from evidence to action in improving healthcare quality and patient outcomes. *Worldviews on Evidence-Based Nursing, 12*(2), 67–69. https://doi.org/10.1111/wvn.12089.

Melnyk, B. M., Gallagher-Ford, L., Thomas, B. K., Troseth, M., Wyngarden, K., & Szalacha, L. (2016). A study of chief nurse executives indicates low-prioritization of evidence-based practice and shortcomings in hospital performance metrics across the United States. *Worldviews on Evidence-Based Nursing, 13*(1), 6–14. https://doi.org/10.1111/wvn.12133.

National Institute of Nursing Research (NINR). (2016). *NINR strategic plan: Advancing science, improving lives.* https://www.ninr.nih.gov/aboutninr/ninr-mission-and-strategic-plan.

NCAST. (2017). *NCAST Programs: Promoting nurturing environments for young children.* www.ncast.org.

Neumann, I., Santesso, N., Aki, E. A., Rind, D. M., Vandvik, P. O., Alonso-Coello, P., et al. (2016). A guide for health professionals to interpret and use recommendations in guidelines developed with the GRADE approach. *Journal of Clinical Epidemiology, 72*, 45–55. https://doi.org/10.1016/j.jclinepi.2015.11.017.

Nilson, P. (2015, April 21). Making sense of implementation theories, models and frameworks. *Implementation Science, 10*(53). https://doi.org/10.1186/s13012-015-0242-0.

Nyamathi, A., Salem, B. E., Zhang, S., Farabee, D., Hall, B. H., Khaliliford, F., & Leake, B. (2015). Nursing case management, peer coaching, Hepatitis A and B vaccine completion among homeless men recently released on parole: randomized clinical trial. *Nursing Research, 64*(3), 177–189. https://doi.org/10.1097/NNR.0000000000000083.

Patient-Centered Outcomes Research Institute. (2017). *Patient-Centered Outcomes Research Institute.* About us www.pcori.org.

Penrod, J., Loeb, S. J., Ladonne, R. A., & Martin, L. M. (2016). Empowering change agents in hierarchical organizations. Participatory action research in prisons. *Research in Nursing and Health, 39*(3), 142–153. https://doi.org/10.1002/nur.21716.

QSEN Institute. (2014). *Competencies.* http://qsen.org/competencies/.

Rahn, D. J. (2016). Transformational teamwork: Exploring the impact of nursing teamwork on nurse-sensitive quality indicators. *Journal of Nursing Care Quality, 31*(3), 262–268. https://doi.org/10.1097/NCQ.0000000000000173.

Saunders, H., & Vehviläinen-Julkunen, K. (2016). The state of readiness for evidence-based practice among nurses: An integrative review. *International Journal of Nursing Studies, 56*, 128–140. https://doi.org/10.1016/j.ijnurstu.2015.10.018.

Scaccia, J. P., Cook, B. S., Lamont, A., Wandersman, A., Castellow, J., Katz, J., & Beidas, R. S. (2015). A practical implementation science heuristic for organizational readiness: $R = MC^2$. *Journal of Community Psychology, 43*(4), 484–501. https://doi.org/10.1002/jcop.21698.

Straus, S. E., Richardson, W. S., Glasziou, P., & Haynes, R. B. (2011). *Evidence-based medicine: How to practice and teach EBM* (4th ed.). Edinburgh: Churchill Livingstone.

Titler, M. G. (2014). Overview of evidence-based practice and implementation science. *Nursing Clinics of North America, 49*(3), 269–274. https://doi.org/10.1016/j.cnur.2014.05.001.

Titler, M. G., Conlon, P., Reynolds, M. A., Ripley, R., Tsodikov, A., Wilson, D. S., & Montie, M. (2016). The effect of a translating research into practice intervention to promote use of evidence-based fall prevention interventions in hospitalized adults: A prospective pre-post implementation study in the U. S. *Applied Nursing Research, 31*, 52–59. https://doi.org/10.1016/j.apnr.2015.12.004.

Topaz, M., & Pruinelli, L. (2017). Big data and nursing: Implications for the future. *Studies in Health Technology and Informatics, 232*, 165–171. https://doi.org/10.3233/978-1-61499-738-2-165.

U.S. Department of Veterans Affairs. (n.d.). *QUERI-Quality Enhancement Research Initiative.* www.queri.research. va.gov/.

Vaidya, N., Thota, A. B., Proia, K. K., Jamieson, S., Mercer, S. L., Elder, R. W., et al. (2017). Practice-based evidence in community guide systematic reviews. *American Journal of Public Health, 107*(3), 413–420. https://doi.org/10.2105/AJPH.2016.303583.

Westra, B. L., Sylvia, M., Weinfurter, E. F., Pruinelli, L., Park, J. L., Dodd, D., et al. (2016). Big data science: A literature review of nursing research exemplars. *Nursing Outlook, 65*(5), 549–561. https://doi.org/10.1016/j.outlook.2016.11.021.

25

Managing Personal and Personnel Problems

Karren Kowalski

LEARNING OUTCOMES

- Differentiate common personal/personnel problems.
- Relate role concepts to clarification of personnel problems.
- Examine strategies useful for approaching specific personnel problems.
- Prepare specific guidelines for documenting performance problems.
- Value the leadership aspects of the role of the novice nurse.

KEY TERMS

absenteeism
chemically dependent

nonpunitive discipline
progressive discipline

role strain
role stress

THE CHALLENGE

I work in a hospital that uses a float pool of well-prepared staff who are ready to be assigned to various areas so that the appropriate level of care can be provided. As you might expect, these nurses, especially when new to the hospital, are not always familiar with all of the aspects of every unit. One of the nurses employed at the hospital in the resource float pool was floated one day to the surgical unit. During her shift, she cared for a patient, who, while unattended, fell out of bed. The nurse manager of the float pool was asked to determine what happened.

What would you do if you were this nurse?

Kathleen Bradley, RN, MSN, NE-BC
Director of Professional Resources, Porter Adventist Hospital, Denver, Colorado

INTRODUCTION

As a novice nurse, the question may be one of perception. "As a new direct care nurse, I don't think of myself as a leader, so how is this information applicable?" In reality, even nurses with limited experiences (referred to here as *newly licensed registered nurses [NLRNs]*) are responsible for and thus lead assistive and support personnel. They often lead a team consisting of licensed practical nurses (LPNs)/licensed vocational nurses (LVNs) and unlicensed nursing personnel (UNPs) who are responsible for a group of patients. Nurses may be responsible for including other team members such as housekeeping personnel and allied health professionals (e.g., respiratory therapists, pharmacists, dietitians, and physical therapists) in providing excellent quality care for patients. The NLRN must know how to handle difficult situations, including the decision to involve the unit leadership. Working effectively with people can be quite satisfying. On the other hand, working with people presents some of the greatest challenges in the workplace. Problems such as absenteeism, uncooperative or unproductive employees, clinical incompetence, employees with emotional problems, and employees with substance use issues are only a few. If a nurse or a new leader wants to be successful, these problems must be dealt with in ways to minimize their effects on patient care and on staff morale. Just as documentation of patient care is critical, documentation of performance problems is critical. Overall goals are to assist the employee in the improvement of performance, to maintain the highest standards for the delivery of patient care, and to provide a supportive environment in which all staff members deliver the best care and attain work satisfaction. From this perspective, in this chapter we examine several specific employee problems and address the leader's role and options as well as the responsibilities of the NLRN.

PERSONAL/PERSONNEL PROBLEMS

Absenteeism

One of the most troublesome personnel problems is that of absenteeism (Beesley, 2016). Inadequate staffing adversely affects patient care both directly and indirectly. When an absent caregiver is replaced by another who is unfamiliar with the routines, employee morale suffers and care may not meet established standards. Replacement of absent personnel by temporary personnel or overtime paid to other employees is very costly, and the cost of fringe benefits used by absent workers is quite high. Working with inadequate staffing or working overtime to cover for absent workers creates physical and mental stress. Replacement personnel can also be problematic.

Replacement personnel usually need more supervision, which not only is costly but also may decrease productivity and the quality of patient care. Indirectly, co-workers may become resentful about being forced to assume heavier workloads or being pressured to work extra hours. Chronic absenteeism may lead to increased staff conflicts, to decreased morale, and eventually to increased absenteeism among the entire staff. Given that nurses may prefer to avoid conflict and negative behavior and to accommodate or make excuses for these situations, one way to confront persistent absenteeism is to discuss the situation directly with the employee by verbally using the format in Table 25.1. This same communications format (columns 1 and 2) can be used for many other difficult situations.

Absenteeism also has a deleterious effect on the financial management of a nursing unit. When employee costs are excessive, they compromise the ability to support other creative efforts of the unit such as staff education and new equipment and may affect staff-patient ratios. Also, as care delivery systems become more complex and technically oriented, successful nurse leaders realize that technology is not a replacement for human caregivers. Absent caregivers cannot be replaced with machines.

Absenteeism cannot be totally eliminated. Unplanned illnesses, accidents, bad weather, sick family members, a death in the family, and even jury duty, which are legitimate reasons for missing work and beyond the control of management, will always occur. However, some portion of absenteeism is voluntary and preventable; thus the cause must be identified so that it may be addressed.

TABLE 25.1 Confronting Persistent Absenteeism

Beginning Statement	Decoding the Statement	Statement in Full
"When I observe that……"	Action the person has/has not taken	"When I observe that you have been absent 3 days this month…….
"I feel…."	Your feeling or reaction	"….. I feel concerned and somewhat alarmed….."
"Because….."	Consequences for person, other team members, the unit/the facility	"Because absences have a negative impact on the team, which may have to work shorthanded, and this also can affect the quality of patient care…"
"Can you see how…."	The Tie Down: Seek agreement from the employee concerning outcomes or consequences of behavior	"Can you see how excessive absences affect the smooth functioning of the unit, the workload of other team members, and the safety of patients?"

These stressors lead to a poor work environment and lower the morale of fully engaged nurses. Other members of the team, including NLRNs, have an obligation to identify negative effects of absenteeism.

Absenteeism may also indicate poor work satisfaction. Dissatisfied staff may in fact be completely disengaged, which can lead to increased absences. If the leader believes that the issue is attributable to work dissatisfaction, unit-based discussions may lead to insight about the sources. Such discussions provide an excellent opportunity for the NLRN to listen, to learn, and to speak to issues. If the underlying cause can be identified, the loss of a dissatisfied employee may be preventable if retention is the goal. Some employees who convey that they are never happy with their jobs may continually disrupt the overall unit with their absenteeism and should be terminated.

According to the classic work of Richard Lazarus and Susan Folkman (1984), stress is a state experienced when the demands upon us cannot be balanced by our ability to deal with them. The pace of modern life and the constant increase in the rate of change, especially technologic change, create feelings of inadequacy and an inability to cope. Physical symptoms associated with stress can include chest pain, headaches, indigestion (including nausea and loss of appetite), constipation or diarrhea, stomach cramps, muscle cramps, neck or back pain, or an increase in the frequency of flu and colds. Such symptoms can easily lead to absenteeism and be problematic for the organization.

With role theory as a framework, absenteeism has been linked to role stress and role strain. Absence from work is a way of withdrawing from an undesirable situation short of actually leaving, and many employees increase their absenteeism just before submitting their resignation. If a healthcare worker is experiencing some form of role stress, absenteeism might be used as a strategy. Role strain may be reflected by (1) reduced involvement with colleagues and the organization, (2) decreased commitment to the mission and the team, and (3) job dissatisfaction. All of these could be manifested through absenteeism. With this framework, management of absenteeism is based on the belief that competent role performance requires interpersonal competence. Role competence is demonstrated through the ability of a person to act in a way that honors both the tasks and the interpersonal relationships. Role behavior occurs in a social context rather than in isolation. The theoretical underpinnings of role adaptation and learned behavior are discussed further in the Theory Box. Therefore the nurse leader needs to understand the existing situation, when the situation changed to its current status, when it needs to change further, and how to accomplish such change. People who are more satisfied in their work usually commit to "be there" for their team, which can enhance job satisfaction and may be an effective strategy toward reducing absenteeism.

One model for nonpunitive discipline can be found in Fig. 25.1. This model demonstrates how undesirable behaviors, such as absenteeism, can be successfully altered. Box 25.1 identifies specific steps that are involved in nonpunitive discipline.

THEORY BOX

Social Cognitive Learning Theory

Theory/ Contributor	Key Idea	Application to Practice
Bandura— Social Learning Theory	Bandura's theory served to bridge behaviorists with cognitive learning theorists when he expanded the focus to include memory and motivation. He believed people learn from one another and from their environment via observation, imitation, and modeling.	Nurses learn from other nurses by observation and by modeling their own behavior after what they perceive as successful nursing practice in their peers. Nursing residency programs for new graduates and for experienced nurses transferring to new clinical areas include all of the components of Bandura's theory. Likewise, mentor and preceptor programs use these principles, including learners being highly motivated to learn new skills and to integrate both knowledge and skills into their practice.

Data from McLeod, S. (2016) *Bandura: Social learning theory.* https://simplypsychology.org/bandura.html.

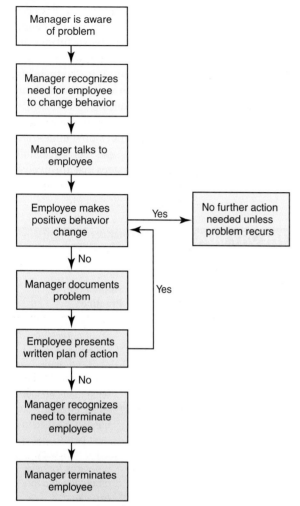

Fig. 25.1 Model for behavioral change.

BOX 25.1 **Steps to Clarify Role Expectations**

Step 1: Remind the employee of the employment policies and procedures of the agency. Sometimes an employee does not know or has forgotten the existing standards, and a reminder with no threats or discipline is all that is needed. The employee must remain ultimately accountable to the organization's policies and procedures.

Step 2: When the oral reminder does not result in a behavior change, put the reminder in writing for the employee and cite the prior oral discussion. These oral and written reminders are simply statements of the problem and the goals to which both the manager and the employee agree. The employee must voluntarily agree with the manager that the behavior in question is not acceptable and must agree to change.

Step 3: If the written reminder fails, only then grant the employee a day of decision, which is a day off with pay, to arrive at a decision about future action. Pay is given for this day so that it is not interpreted as punishment. The employee must return to work with a written decision as to whether or not to accept the standards for work attendance. Remember that this is a voluntary decision on the employee's part. Emphasize to the employee that it is the employee's decision to adhere to the standards.

Step 4: If the employee decides not to adhere to standards, termination results. However, if the employee agrees to adhere to the standards and in the future does not, he or she, in essence, has terminated employment. Keep a copy of the written agreements and give the employee a copy. The manager should be clearly aware of the organization's policy for termination and request assistance from the human resources department as deemed necessary.

This model of nonpunitive discipline allows employees to free themselves from some role stress by clarification of role expectations and assumptions. Employees can receive satisfaction from the realization that a problem may not be inadequate performance caused by personal faults, but rather a lack of clarification of role expectations within the organization. NLRNs may be called on to implement the process described in Box 25.1. For example, the NLRN may be involved with the nurse manager or a support staff member or, in extenuating circumstances, may be directly involved in the process. For example, the NLRN might work with a UNP member who is absent or arrives late. On the other hand, a staff member who is actually quite ill, and even contagious to co-workers and patients, might come to work, infecting everyone. Remember, the focus is on the clear understanding of the situation, the growth of the individual, the smooth and effective functioning of the team, and the safety of the patients.

EXERCISE 25.1 Review the policy manual at a local healthcare organization to determine what constitutes excessive absenteeism. What are the identified consequences?

Uncooperative or Unproductive Employees

The problem of uncooperative or unproductive employees is another area of frustration for the nurse leader. Heitzman (2016) and Markidan (2015) identified two major dimensions of job performance that relate to this problem: motivation and ability. The type and intensity of motivation vary among employees because of differing needs and goals that employees express. The leader can best handle employees with motivation problems by attempting to determine the cause of the problem and by working to provide an environment that is conducive to increased motivation for the employee. If the employee is uncooperative or unproductive because of a lack of ability, education and training are appropriate interventions.

The manager can determine lack of ability on the part of an employee in various ways. Frequent errors in judgment or techniques are often an indication of lack of knowledge, skill, or critical thinking. This illustrates the need for the nurse leader to document all variances or untoward events carefully after discussing them with the employee. When the nurse manager has thorough documentation, trends may be discovered that, in turn, suggest that a specific employee is having problems. The nurse manager can cite problem behaviors and perhaps even trends to the employee. Corrective action is easier to pursue and resolution is more effective with this strategy. When the problem is determined to result from a need for more education or training, the manager can work with the education department or the clinical specialist for the involved unit to help the employee improve his or her skills. Most employees are extremely cooperative in situations such as this because they want to do a good job but sometimes do not know how. Employees may deny they need help or may be too embarrassed to ask for help. When the manager can show an employee concrete evidence of a problem area, cooperation is enhanced.

Immature Employees

Sometimes an unproductive employee simply lacks maturity. This lack of maturity may be described as *emotional intelligence underdevelopment* that results in such problems as being socially inept or unable to control one's impulses. These employees are commonly defensive and emotional or tearful. They lack self-insight into their behavior. Sometimes immaturity in an employee may not be readily apparent to the leader but may be manifested in any of the following actions: defiance, testing of workplace guidelines, passivity or hostility, or little appreciation for any management decisions. The challenge for the nurse leader is not to react in kind, but rather to relate to this employee in a positive and

mature manner. A sense of humor and the ability to ease the employee into a more receptive mood are sometimes helpful. However, the leader needs to determine whether the undesirable behaviors are reflecting a state of being uncomfortable or incompetent. For example, if an employee states, "Administration is always making decisions to make our jobs harder," rather than making a hostile or defensive comment in reply, the manager could take the employee aside and say, "I notice that you seem to be angry about this new policy. Let's talk about it some more." Immature employees either act immaturely all of the time or regress to an immature level when stressed. The nurse leader must recognize immaturity in an employee and react calmly and without anger. The leader must keep in mind that this employee may be displaying dynamics rooted in unresolved personal areas and that the behavior is not a personal attack on the leader. The best way to deal with this behavior is to hold a direct conversation with the employee about the specific problem and define realistic limits of acceptable behavior with consequences for nonadherence. Generally, employees comply with specific limits but will test management in other areas. As this testing occurs, the leader must continue the same limit-setting technique. Remember that the immature employee usually has problems because of a lack of self-worth, power, and self-control. Praise and affirmation are valuable tools that the leader can use to help these employees feel better about themselves. Chapter 28 addresses generational issues if they are factors to consider.

EXERCISE 25.2 A nurse comes to you, the nurse leader, and states that one of the other nurses is tying a knot in the air vent (pigtail) of nasogastric tubes. This nurse does not know how to approach the employee to discuss the problem. What would you do?

Clinical Incompetence

Clinical incompetence is possibly one of the most frustrating problems that the nurse manager faces, although it may be entirely correctable. The problem may surface immediately in a new employee. Despite an effective interview process, a lack of fit may exist between the new nurse's strengths or skill set and the needs of the unit. Such a nurse can be coached and supported to gain competence or to find a different position, one that fully utilizes his or her strengths and skills. At other times, clinical incompetence comes as a surprise if co-workers "cover" for another employee. Some nurses are unwilling to report instances of clinical incompetence because they do not want to feel responsible for getting one of their peers in trouble or because they too may sometimes feel inadequate. When other employees are engaged in enabling behavior by covering for the mistakes of one of their peers, the nurse manager may be surprised to discover that the employee does not know or cannot do what is expected of him or her. Sadly, the employee in question has been able to cover incompetence by hiding behind the performance of another employee. The nurse manager must remind employees that part of professional responsibility is to maintain quality care, and thus they are obligated to report instances of clinical incompetence, even when it means reporting a co-worker. Ignoring violations of a safety rule or poor practice is unprofessional and cannot be tolerated. Additionally some state nursing practice acts make failure to report a violation of a rule or regulation a disciplinary offense.

Most healthcare agencies use skills checklists or a competency evaluation program to ascertain that their employees have and maintain essential skills for the job they are expected to do. A skills checklist is one way to determine basic clinical competency. Box 25.2 presents an example related to a specific competency. This checklist typically contains a number of basic skills along with ones that are essential for safe functioning in the specific area of employment (Dickerson & Chappell, 2016). Any type of skills review should be directly linked to quality improvement indicators. The employee may be asked to do a self-assessment of the listed skills or competencies and then have performance of the skills validated by a peer or co-worker. This is a very effective method for the manager to assess the skill level of employees and to determine where additional education and training may be necessary. In addition, if the manager discovers that an employee cannot perform a skill adequately, the skills list can easily be checked and directly observed behaviors can be assessed to determine at what level the employee is functioning. At the completion of the assessment, a specific plan for remediation can be developed. Sometimes, an employee may be able to perform all of the tasks on a skills checklist but still cannot manage overall patient care effectively. If, in questioning the employee or in evaluating the employee's performance, the manager determines a lack of knowledge or problems with time management exist,

formal education may be the proper course of action. In either event, the manager must establish a written contract containing a plan of action that sets time limits within which certain expectations must be achieved. This ensures compliance on the part of the employee and simultaneously sets a time frame for the manager's action. A more comprehensive program for competency evaluation might include not only the skills checklist but also unit-specific objectives, an overall framework for evaluation, and critical-thinking exercises that are interactive in nature—for example, a complex patient situation such as an assessment in which the nurse is unclear as to what the next step might be. The role of the NLRN leader, particularly with ancillary personnel, is to support the nurse manager as well as to be helpful and supportive of the team members who are striving to improve, to learn, and to grow as healthcare workers.

Emotional Problems

Emotional problems among nursing personnel may affect not only the involved individual but also co-workers and ultimately the delivery of patient care. The nurse manager must be aware that certain behaviors, such as poor judgment, increased errors, increased absenteeism, decreased productivity, and a negative attitude, may be manifestations of emotional problems in employees.

EXERCISE 25.3 A nurse manager began hearing complaints from patients about a nurse named Nancy. Patients were saying that Nancy was abrupt and uncaring with them. The manager had not received any complaints about Nancy before this time, so she questioned Nancy about why this was occurring. Nancy reported that her mother was very ill, and she was so worried about her and so upset that she could not sleep and was tired all of the time. She went on to say that she was having trouble being sympathetic with complaining patients when they did not seem to be as sick as her mother. How would you respond as the nurse manager?

When an employee's behavior changes significantly, personal problems with which the person cannot cope may be the cause. The nurse manager is not and should not be a therapist but must intercede, not only to help the individual with the problems but also to maintain proper functioning of the unit. In dealing with the employee who exhibits behaviors that indicate

BOX 25.2   Example of a Skills Checklist

Purpose

1. The clinical skills inventory is a three-phase tool to enable the newly hired registered nurse (RN) and the nurse manager to determine individual learning needs, verify competency, and plan performance goals.
2. The RN will complete the self-assessment of clinical skills during the first week of employment. The RN will use the appropriate scale to document current knowledge of clinical skills.
3. The nurse manager will document observed competency of the orientee or delegate this to a peer. All columns must be completed on the inventory level.
4. At the end of orientation, the new RN and the manager will use the inventory to identify performance goals on the plan sheet. The skills inventory will be in a specified place on the nursing unit so that it is available to the manager and other RNs. It should be updated at appropriate intervals as specified by the manager.

Scale for Self-Assessment

1 = Unfamiliar/never done
2 = Able to perform with assistance
3 = Can perform with minimal supervision
4 = Independent performance/proficient

Score for Validation of Competency

1 = Unable to perform at present
2 = Able to perform with assistance
3 = Progressing/repeat performance necessary
4 = Able to perform independently

Clinical Skills (Examples)	Self- Assessment		Comment	Validation			Comment
	Scale	Date		Score	Date	Initials	
Epidural catheter care							
NG/Dobbhoff							
Insertion							
Management							
Preoperative care/teaching							
Postoperative care/teaching							

Plan Sheet for Skills Inventory

Name _____

Date _____

Goals	Date to Be Completed

Orientee's signature _____
Manager's signature _____
Date _____

emotional problems, the manager assists the individual to obtain professional help to cope with the problem. The individual's work setting and schedule may need to be adjusted. This may require support from other staff members so no negative patient care results. The manager acknowledges to the employee that he or she is experiencing emotional difficulties, and yet the standards of patient care cannot be compromised. Staff are reassured to witness the care and concern shown a fellow staff member who is in great difficulty. They can interpret that similar support would be given to them if they were in a difficult situation.

The most important approach that the manager can take with an emotionally troubled employee is to provide support and encouragement and to assist the individual to obtain appropriate help. Many organizations have some kind of employee assistance program (EAP) to which the manager should refer any troubled employee. During this process, the manager must remember to check with the human resources department about any implications that may occur because of the Americans with Disabilities Act (ADA). If an employee has a documented mental illness, the employing organization may be under certain legal constraints as specified in the ADA. The nurse manager should always remember that many resources are available to assist with personnel problems including, in some states, services through the professional association. The manager should never feel required to know all of the legal implications regarding employment policies. Rather, the manager must know that help is available and how to access it.

> **EXERCISE 25.4** As a nurse manager in a community health agency, you have just had a meeting that was called by several of your direct care nurses. They expressed concern regarding another nurse colleague who has come to work angry and spiteful during the past week. They state she has made cutting and spiteful remarks to co-workers. Staff are beginning to turn away from her and not help her. She has refused to discuss her distress with her colleagues. These nurses express concern and want you to resolve the situation. What is your response? What would you do?

Substance Use

Substance use, or chemical dependency, among nursing personnel places patients and the organization at risk. Such an employee adversely affects staff morale by increasing stress on other staff members when they have to assume heavier workloads to cover for the chemically dependent employee who is not performing at full capacity or who is often absent. As a result, patient care may be jeopardized because staff are focusing more on the problems of a co-worker than on those of the patients. NLRNs must be aware of the professional responsibilities of reporting incidents in which peers or team members exhibit signs of chemical dependency.

The manager is responsible for early recognition of chemical dependency and referral for treatment when appropriate (National Council of State Boards of Nursing, 2014a, 2014b). State laws vary as to the reportability of chemical dependency. As is true for all nurses, a nurse manager is responsible for upholding the nurse practice act and should be familiar with the legal aspects of chemical dependency in the state in which he or she is employed. As with the employee with emotional problems, the nurse manager should be aware of ADA issues and check with the human resource department for help with how to handle the employment of a chemically dependent employee. Most states and agencies have reporting requirements regarding substance use. The state board of nursing is a key place to determine specific details required by a given state. All nurse managers should familiarize themselves with the nurse practice act in the state in which they are employed and with the personnel policies relating to substance use in their employing agency. Furthermore, nurse managers should ensure that staff are familiar with legal requirements.

In the present social climate, more interest exists in helping affected individuals than in punishing them; showing empathy and understanding also facilitates their work. Identification of an employee with a chemical dependency is usually difficult, especially because one of the primary symptoms is denial. The primary clue to which a manager should be alert when chemical dependency is suspected is any behavioral change in an employee. This change could be any deviation from the behaviors the employee normally exhibits. Some specific behaviors to note might be mood swings, a change from a tidy appearance to an untidy one, an unusual interest in patients' pain control, frequent changes in jobs and shifts, or an increase in absenteeism and tardiness.

When a manager suspects that an employee may be chemically dependent, the manager must intervene, because patient care may be jeopardized. A manager facing a problem with an impaired nurse must be compassionate yet therapeutic. Knowing that denial may be one of the primary signs of substance use, the manager must focus on performance problems that the nurse is exhibiting and urge the nurse to seek counseling or treatment voluntarily. Employee Assistance Programs (EAP) always protect the employee's privacy and are usually available free or at a minimal charge to the employee. The manager should strive to refer any troubled employee to the EAP and/or to the state's peer assistance program. This removes the manager from the counseling role and helps employees get the professional help they need without fear of a breach in confidentiality. If a nurse refuses to seek help voluntarily for a substance use problem, the manager is responsible for following the established policy and laws for such employees. The manager must remember that if the employee who uses substances is terminated and not reported to the State Board of Nursing, the manager not only may be violating a law but also may be enabling this employee to obtain employment in another organization and potentially be in a position to harm patients and co-workers.

Many states have rehabilitation programs for chemically impaired nurses so that they may return to nursing if rehabilitated. Nurse managers are sometimes asked to assist with monitoring the progress of a chemically impaired nurse. Specific guidelines are established through the rehabilitation program with the cooperation of the employee, the organization, and the manager. The manager is typically asked to provide feedback about the employee's progress to the employee and to the state or rehabilitation program involved. These programs vary, but, for example, a nurse who has been an admitted user of opioids may be allowed to work in a setting in which this drug is never used, or the nurse may not be permitted to administer any controlled substances to patients. This, of course, puts an added burden on other staff members, but it can be a positive experience for all because nurses face some of their professional responsibility by helping another nurse while upholding patient care. Often, as a part of their therapy, these nurses are required to share openly with other staff members what their problem is and what they are doing to control it. When handled in a positive, professional way, the nurse manager can turn a potentially destructive situation into a positive, constructive one.

Regardless of the type of personnel issue, the manager needs to have a plan in place for ongoing monitoring and follow-up of issues and problems.

Most all health professionals are aware of the national opioid situation in the country, because it has been emphasized politically. Considerable federal funding is used to address this health crisis (see the Literature Perspective).

LITERATURE PERSPECTIVE

Resource: NIH—National Institute on Drug Abuse. (2017). *Opioid crisis.* https://www.drugabuse.gov/drugs-abuse/opioids/opioid-crisis#.WfuWwJWnC98.email

The misuse and addiction to opioids, including presecription pain relievers, heroin, and synthetic opioids such as fentanyl, consititues a national crisis. The total "economic burden" as described by the Centers for Disease Control and Prevention (CDC) is estimated at $78.5 billion/year, which includes healthcare costs, lost productivity, treatment, and the crimial justice involvement. To establish the extent of this problem, in 2015, 33,000 Americans died as a result of an opioid overdose; this breaks down into the following:

- 21%-29% of patients who take opioids for chronic pain misuse them
- 8%-12% who develop an opioid use disorder
- 4%-6% who misuse prescription opioids transition to heroin
- 80% of people who first use heroin misuse perscription opioids

The five major prioities identified by HHS include:
1. Improving access to treatment and recovery services
2. Promoting availablity and access to overdose-reversing drugs
3. Improved public health surveillance to strenthen understanding of the epidemic
4. Support for innovative research on pain and addition
5. Advancing better practices for pain management
Multiple additonal resources are identified in this article.

Implications for Practice

Every nurse has the potential to address this issue, because it is so widespread. Although many of us will not work in formal treatment and recovery services, we all focus on management of pain and what medications are available to patients. Because nurses also learn many non–medication-based interventions, we may need to increase our awareness of which of our patients need that information.

RESEARCH PERSPECTIVE

Resource: Porath, C. (2016). Managing yourself: An antidote to incivility: How to protect yourself from rude colleagues. *Harvard Business Review, April,* 108–111.

The author has polled thousands of employees in her 20-year career seeking to understand workplace incivility. She has found that 98% of employees experienced uncivil behavior. This kind of behavior decreases levels of performance and takes a marked personal toll. Her research has identified some tactics to minimize the effects of incivility on performance and well-being. Direct confrontation usually doesn't work and simply frustrates the person who has been bullied. Instead the author recommends that working to improve one's own well-being in the workplace as opposed to attempting to change the offender is the most effective. In other words, make yourself impervious to the bad behavior, thrive rather than just survive. The keys are to thrive cognitively. Spend only a limited time on anger and hurt, then move to more productive avenues such as areas for development and actively pursue learning opportunities. Thrive affectively by enhancing the same factors as those that prevent illness: good nutrition, exercise, sleep, and stress management. Also focus on purpose and meaning in your work. In addition, flourish in the areas outside of the workplace such as the community, family life with children and animals or causes such as fundraising for a favorite charity. Focus on thriving makes each of us more engaged, productive, and happy.

Implications for Practice

Employees can learn about how to focus on thriving as an antidote to extreme stress in the workplace caused by uncivil behavior on the part of co-workers. A NLRN can focus on how we develop new nurses and teach them to thrive rather than the ways to continue incivility.

EXERCISE 25.5 Review your state's nurse practice act and rules and regulations. What are you required to do if you believe a nurse has a problem with chemical dependency?

Incivility

Incivility or lateral violence in the workplace is disruptive behavior or communication that creates a negative work environment, thus interfering with quality patient care and safety (AACN, 2016). Such behavior is often nurse-to-nurse or provider-to-provider. These behaviors include nonverbal innuendo such as eye-rolling or eyebrow raising, verbal affronts, undermining activities, withholding information, sabotage, infighting, scapegoating, backstabbing, failure to respect privacy, and broken confidences. Uncivil behavior must be addressed. The first step by the manager, or any nurse for that matter, when he or she has observed the unwanted behavior may be a discussion with the nurse. The next step, after a formal discussion by the manager, is written documentation in the personnel file if the behaviors do not abate. This is followed by a stepwise disciplinary action in association with the human resources department. New nurses need to be cognizant of behaviors of incivility and to understand the guidelines and rules relevant to such behavior in the facility. Also, they need to support increased teamwork by behaving in a positive, upbeat manner and to not become enmeshed in negative behavior on the unit. Work done by Porath (2016) emphasizes how to protect yourself from uncivil behavior and to become more resilient. Nurses can choose how they respond or react to uncivil behavior. These choices can mean the difference between thriving and merely surviving (see the Research Perspective).

DOCUMENTATION

Documentation of personnel problems is unquestionably one of the most important but also one of the most onerous aspects of the nurse manager's job (Fig. 25.2). As much as some managers may wish they would, personnel problems probably will not "disappear" and therefore will eventually have to be resolved. Through careful, ongoing documentation of problems, the manager makes the task of identifying and correcting problems much less burdensome.

Documentation cannot be left to memory! At the time that an employee is involved in a problem situation or receives a compliment or does something extremely well, a brief notation to this effect must be placed in the personnel file. This entry includes the date, time, and a brief description of the incident. Adding a small notation as to what was done about a problem when it occurred is also helpful. Along with this, the nurse

Fig. 25.2 Documentation of personnel problems is an important aspect of the nurse manager's job. (Copyright © geotrac/iStock/Thinkstock.)

manager should keep a log or summary sheet of all reported errors, unusual incidents, and accidents. These extremely important data should include the date, time, and names of involved individuals and should be tallied monthly for analysis by the manager. The few extra minutes each day that the manager spends tracking these data provide invaluable information about organizational and individual functioning. This tracking can then be used to pinpoint an individual's problem areas, areas of excellence in individual performance, and overall organizational problem areas. The manager who keeps careful records about organizational functioning has

greater control in the management of personal and personnel problems. Box 25.3 describes content and format for such documentation and provides an example as an illustration.

It can also be valuable for the nurse who is the recipient of uncivil behavior to keep personal notes similar to those described here. This documentation can then be used if she or he is asked to recall specific incidences. These can be kept privately in a journal or in an electronic file.

PROGRESSIVE DISCIPLINE

When an employee's performance falls below the acceptable standard despite corrective measures that have been taken, some form of discipline must be enacted. Most organizations use some form of progressive discipline to correct problem behaviors. When the nurse leader suspects that specific behaviors may lead to progressive discipline, all interactions must be documented and the human resources department must be involved in the process to ensure accurate adherence to all policies. Progressive discipline consists of evaluating performance and providing feedback within a specified structure of increasing sanctions. These sanctions, progressing from least severe to most severe, are described in Box 25.4. Examples of the kind of workplace behavior that usually involves progressive discipline and could even result in immediate termination are harassment and chemical use.

BOX 25.3 Documentation of Problems

- Description of incident: an objective statement of the facts related to the incident
- Actions: statements describing the plan to correct or prevent future problems
- Follow-up: dates and times that the plan is to be carried out, including required meeting with the employee

Example

Several patients reported that Becky Smith, (night-shift RN) was "curt" and "gruff" and seemed uncaring with them. I called Becky into my office and reiterated the complaints that I had received, including the specifics of times and incidents. I reminded Becky about what my expectations were relating to patient care, emphasizing the importance of a caring attitude with all patients. We discussed what the possible cause of Becky's behavior might be, such as problems at home or lack of sleep. Becky denied being curt or gruff but agreed that some of her mannerisms might be

misinterpreted. I suggested to Becky that perhaps she needed to be particularly aware of her body language and to soften her tone of voice. After discussing this incident and reminding Becky of the importance of caring in nursing, I cited the policy regarding behavior and told Becky that this behavior would not be tolerated. I told Becky we needed to meet every Friday morning at the end of Becky's shift to discuss how the week had gone and to determine how she was interacting with the patients assigned to her. I also told Becky I would be checking with patients to see what they had thought of Becky, pointing out that I do this routinely.

These weekly meetings are to be conducted for 6 weeks, followed by monthly meetings for a 3-month period. If problems do not recur, the meetings will be discontinued after this time.

Joseph P. Riley, RN, MSN
Nurse Manager, Hanson Way Hospital

BOX 25.4　Steps in Progressive Discipline

1. Counsel the employee regarding the problem.
2. Reprimand the employee. A verbal reprimand usually precedes a written one, but some organizations issue both a verbal and a written reprimand simultaneously. When the documentation is written, the employee must sign to verify that the problem was discussed. This does not mean that the employee agrees with the reprimand. It means only that he or she is aware of a written reprimand that is to be placed in the employee's personnel file. The employee always receives a copy of a written reprimand.
3. Suspend the employee if the problem persists. He or she will be suspended without pay for a specified period, usually several days or longer according to the agency policy. During this time, the employee may realize the seriousness of the problem based on the resulting discipline.
4. Allow the employee to return to work with written stipulations regarding problem behavior.
5. Terminate the employee if the problem recurs.

BOX 25.5　Guidelines to Effective Termination

1. The manager must be confident that everything possible has been done to help the employee correct the problem behaviors.
2. The manager must recognize that if employment continues, this employee will have a deleterious effect on overall organizational functioning and, more important, on nursing care.
3. The employee must have been made fully aware of the problem performance and of the fact that all of the correct disciplinary steps have been followed.
4. The nurse manager should check with the human resources and legal departments before proceeding to ensure that termination is justifiable legally and that proper steps have been followed.

TERMINATION

At times, even though the manager has done everything possible to gain the cooperation of a problem employee, the problems may persist. In such cases, termination is the only choice. Termination is one of the most difficult things a manager does, so guidelines are needed to be certain a manager can perform this task without contributing to further distress for either party. Additionally, an organization may require that a representative from human resources or security (or both) be present. Specific guidelines should be followed (Box 25.5).

The nurse manager needs to be confident in the knowledge that all policies regarding termination have been followed before having an actual termination meeting with the employee. It is almost always preferable to err on the side of caution when proceeding with termination of an employee. Remember that termination is something that the employee has caused as a result of persistent problem behaviors or certain behaviors for which the organization has zero tolerance. Termination is not done at the whim of management; it results from failure on the part of the employee to change a problem behavior.

Situations that may warrant immediate dismissal include theft, violence in the workplace, and willful abuse of a patient, to name a few. Again, the manager should use the assistance of the human resource department to ensure that all of the organization's policies are being upheld correctly. The following example illustrates that a manager needs to anticipate a termination to ensure ongoing standards:

Michael has gone through all of the steps in the progressive discipline process as a result of his abusive behavior toward his co-workers. He returned to work and seemed to be doing well until about 6 weeks later, when he slammed down his clipboard during report and angrily accused the charge nurse of always giving him the worst assignments. The nurse manager was present and asked Michael to come into her office. At this point, she told Michael she was relieving him of his assignment that day and asked him to go home to cool off. The manager told him that she would call him the following day about what would be done. Michael went home, and the manager reviewed the incident with her nurse administrator. They both agreed that Michael's behavior not only was intolerable but also violated the terms of his probation and therefore he should be terminated. The manager called Michael the following day as she had agreed to do and asked him to come and meet with her. The manager and administrator met with Michael and reviewed the incidents and the disciplinary measures leading up to this incident. The nurse manager asked the administrator to be present at the scheduled meeting, because it is a good practice to have a witness in a confrontational situation such as termination. The manager stated to Michael that she regretted it had come to this but pointed out to him that his behavior had violated all of the agreed-upon stipulations and, as a result, he would be terminated immediately. Michael seemed embarrassed and anxious and had numerous excuses, but the manager remained firm and merely repeated that Michael, in not fulfilling the agreement, had chosen to end his employment.

EXERCISE 25.6 Review a healthcare organization's policies regarding termination. What are the conditions, such as stealing, violence, or coming to work under the influence of alcohol or drugs, that are described as cause for immediate dismissal? Is using substances at work one of those conditions? Consider how you would intervene with a colleague who exhibited one of these behaviors or conditions.

CONCLUSION

Managing personal and personnel issues is a challenge for every manager. The process is time consuming and detail oriented and does not always result in a positive outcome. All employees share a role with managers to prevent and control personal/personnel problems in their work setting. Everyone must be willing to refuse to allow unethical behavior from co-workers and to speak out and act appropriately when problems occur. The focus of all action is the protection of others: patients and employees.

THE SOLUTION

The nurse manager in charge of the resource float pool wanted to assess the float pool nurses' critical-thinking skills and did this through weekly rounding. The charge nurses of each unit also completed a peer assessment form whenever a nurse floated to the unit so that the nurse who floated there could receive feedback. In this manner, if a pattern emerged from either the rounding assessment or the peer reviews, the float nurse could receive immediate coaching. Finally, the nurse manager decided to have the staff review published information about hourly rounding and review the patient fall protocols from the various units where the float nurse worked.

Would this be a suitable approach for you? Why?

Kathleen Bradley

REFLECTIONS

Think about a time when you were "bullied," humiliated, or publicly berated. How did it make you feel? What was your response? How well did your response work? Now that you have read the chapter, what might you do differently than before reading the chapter?

THE EVIDENCE

Davey, Cummings, Newburn-Cook, and Lo (2009) sought to identify predictors of short-term absenteeism in direct care nurses. Such absenteeism contributes to lack of continuity in patient care and decreases staff morale, which is costly to the facility. A systematic review of studies conducted between 1986 and 2006 led to the inclusion of 16 peer-reviewed research studies. Findings were that the individual "nurse's history of prior absences," "work attitudes" (e.g., job satisfaction, organizational commitment, and work involvement), and other "retention factors" such as shared governance reduced absenteeism, whereas poor leadership, "burnout," and "job stress" increased absenteeism. It became clear that the reasons underlying absenteeism are still poorly understood and that a robust theory for nurse absenteeism is lacking. Further theory development and research are needed.

Major, Abderrahman, and Sweeney (2013) have constructed guidelines for new graduates to assist them in having difficult conversations in conflict situations. These new nurses are encouraged to "start with heart," which translates into encouraging a free flow of conversation. "Learn to look" means to be conscious of when a conversation needs to occur, whereas "make it safe" means to be respectful and to value the other person's perspective. "Master your story" translates as being clear about your feelings and why they were evoked. "State your path" indicates that while sharing your perspective, ask the other nurses how they reached their perspectives. "Explore others' paths" requires asking questions to better understand the other nurses. "Move to action" means the nurses together will decide how the issue being discussed will be resolved.

It is most helpful if the new nurse can address issues before the situation becomes a confrontational issue that can escalate into aggressive, undesirable behavior.

■ TIPS IN THE DOCUMENTATION OF PROBLEMS

- Identify the incident and related facts.
- Describe actions taken by the manager when the problem was identified.
- Develop an action plan for everyone involved.
- Schedule a follow-up meeting to evaluate progress of the action plan.
- Remember to document everything objectively and completely!

REFERENCES

American Association of Critical Care Nurses. (2016). *AACN standards for establishing and sustaining health work environments: A journey to excellence* (2nd ed.). Aliso Viejo, CA: Author.

Beesley, C. (2016). Absenteeism in the workplace: 7 ways to resolve this bottom line killer. https://www.sba.gov/blogs/absenteeism-workplace-7-ways-resolve-bottom-line-killer.

Davey, M. M., Cummings, G., Newburn-Cook, C. V., & Lo, E. A. (2009). Predictors of nurse absenteeism in hospitals: A systematic review. *Journal of Nursing Management, 17*(3), 312–330.

Dickerson, P. & Chappell, K. (2016). Principles of Evaluating Nursing Competence. https://www.td.org/Publications/Magazines/TD-Archive/2016/02/Principles-of-Evaluating-Nursing-Competence.

Heitzman, A. (2016). 7 common characteristics of unproductive employees. https://www.inc.com/adam-heitzman/7-common-characteristics-of-unproductive-employees.html.

Lazarus, R., & Folkman, S. (1984). *Stress, appraisal and coping*. New York: Springer Publishing Company.

Major, K., Abderrahman, E. A., & Sweeney, J. I. (2013). Greening the 'Proclamation for change': Healing through sustainable health care environments. *The American Journal of Nursing, 113*(4), 66–70.

Markidan, L. (2015). How to deal with uncooperative co-workers. https://www.groovehq.com/support/dealing-with-uncooperative-coworkers.

National Council of State Boards of Nursing. (2014a). *A nurse manager's guide to substance use disorder in nursing.* Chicago: Author.

National Council of State Boards of Nursing. (2014b). *What you need to know about substance use disorder in nursing.* Chicago: Author.

NIH – National Institute on Drug Abuse (2017). Opioid Crisis. https://www.drugabuse.gov/drugs-abuse/opioids/opioid-crisis#.WfuWwJWnC98.email.

Porath, C. (2016). Managing yourself an antidote to incivility: How to protect yourself from rude colleagues. *Harvard Business Review* (April), 108–111.

26

Role Transition

Diane M. Twedell

LEARNING OUTCOMES

- Describe the phases of role transition by using a life experience.
- Compare and contrast the role transition between a nurse changing specialties to a nurse moving into a nurse leader role.
- Delineate strategies that will assist nurses through a successful role transition.
- Construct the full scope of a manager role by outlining responsibilities, opportunities, lines of communication, expectations, and support.

KEY TERMS

mentor

role internalization

role negotiation

role strain

role stress

role transition

THE CHALLENGE

Assuming a formal leadership opportunity as a nurse leader is a critical step in professional development. Before seeking a nurse manager position, I had taken opportunities as a staff nurse to lead projects and small teams. I felt comfortable setting up timeline and project plans, speaking in front of an audience, and communicating collaboratively with colleagues and leaders in nursing, administration, and physician groups. I had built a credible reputation as a staff nurse; but how was I going to shift to a nurse manager role? How would I meet the expectations I had set for myself? What was my supervisor going to

expect of me? How was I going to lead nurses who were a generation or two older than I am and full of historical knowledge and experience? What about the physicians? I didn't know them. I began to fear the unknown of hiring, firing, and coaching. I would have the final say in time off policies and enforcing dress code. Was I prepared for this??

What would you do if you were this nurse?

Monica Boege, RN, BSN, MBA
Nurse Manager, Mayo Clinic Health System

INTRODUCTION

Role transition involves transforming one's professional identity. A new graduate makes a transition from the student role to the nurse role. Expectations of students are clearly specified in course and clinical objectives. Expectations for a new nurse as an employee may not be so clear. The new graduate nurse faces the first of several professional transitions, some of which will be easier than others. These transitions continue with career growth and development. The Literature Perspective outlines key differences in role transition concepts between novice and experienced nurses.

Consider the direct care nurse who becomes a nurse manager. The direct care nurse performs tasks related to the care of patients. The direct care nurse has accountability and responsibility for the work that is accomplished. A direct care nurse who becomes a nurse manager must transition into the new role as a generalist, orchestrating diverse tasks and getting work done through others. Although expert knowledge of care remains important, the direct care is now done by others. Thus new skills become equally or more important.

A direct care nurse who moves from an acute care setting to a home health agency must also undergo a role transition. Instead of balancing the needs of multiple patients, the home health nurse can focus on one patient at a time. Yet when a collegial opinion is needed during a visit, no peers are there to consult with. Registered nurses who transition to nurse practitioner roles or other advanced practice roles experience this same type of role transition.

Organizations play a key role in assisting employees through role transitions. Changes in roles can be either painful or exciting and depend largely on the work culture and support provided. According to Arrowsmith, Lau-Walker, Norman, and Maben (2016), role transitions "involve a generalized sense of disequilibrium for people deep in the throes of change" (p. 1736).

Knowing what to expect during this transformation can reduce the stress of accepting and transitioning into a new role and result in quality outcomes. After an overview of the roles of leader, manager, and follower, this chapter describes the process of role transition, with an emphasis on strategies that can be used to ease the transition.

TYPES OF ROLES

Accepting a management or formal leadership position dictates accepting three roles that involve complex processes. The roles of leader, manager, and follower are complex because they involve working through and with unique individuals in a rapidly changing environment. Additionally, in any situation a nurse can perform all three roles. Examples of the people with whom you interact and the processes involved in each role are shown in Table 26.1.

Leader

This is a person who demonstrates and exercises power over others. In the evolving healthcare environment, the nurse leader providing direct patient care also must function as a leader, manager, and follower. As *leader,* the nurse leader recognizes the uniqueness of each patient and provides feedback on clinical progress.

LITERATURE PERSPECTIVE

Resource: Arrowsmith, V., Lau-Walker, M., Norman, I., & Maben, J. (2016). Nurses' perceptions and experiences of work role transitions: A mixed methods systematic review of the literature. *Journal of Advanced Nursing, 72* (8), 1735–1750.

This publication aims to understand nurses' perceptions and experiences of work role transitions. Six databases were searched for peer review research based on work role transitions for nurses. Twenty-six papers were found and two major pathways were identified: one group as novice nurses and the other as experienced nurses. Two major concepts were identified within each pathway,

including striving for professional self and "know how." Striving for professional-self had many emotional attachments and feelings associated with it and was noted with novice nurses. "Know how" was focused on competence and boundaries and was noted in experienced nurses.

Implications for Practice

Identifying specific issues faced by novice and experienced nurses can help the role transition process within the patient care area. Orientation, education, and support can assist both groups of nurses in a successful role transition.

Manager

This is a person with accountability for a group of people. As a manager, the nurse links the patient to the resources to achieve clinical outcomes. Medical information is translated into a format that the patient can use to make informed decisions about treatment and self-care. Through referrals, the nurse manager facilitates continuity of care within the larger system.

Follower

This is a person who contributes to a group's outcomes by implementing activities and providing appropriate feedback. As a *follower,* the nurse is accountable to the team and the supervisor for completing the work that is assigned. The nurse as a follower practices within the policies and procedures of the organization and the standards of the profession.

The daily work of a nurse transitions seamlessly through the three roles, and although this may feel very different during role transition, it occurs during that same time. The nurse is assigned to a preceptor whom he or she follows and learns the cultural norms and practices of a patient care unit; the nurse is also a manager in helping patients navigate a complex system of care and a leader in providing individualized assessment and care to every patient.

ROLES: THE ABCs OF UNDERSTANDING ROLES

Another approach to the complexity of role transition is the acronym ROLES, in which each letter represents a component common to roles (Box 26.1):

R stands for responsibilities. What are the specified duties in the position description for the new position? What tasks are to be completed? What decisions must the person in this position make?

O stands for opportunities, which are untapped aspects of the position.

L represents lines of communication, which are the heart of every leadership role. No matter what role an individual is in, multiple relationships exist with supervisors, staff, and peers.

E stands for expectations. Expectations can vary depending on your goals. Colleagues may expect a nurse anesthetist to be on call every weekend. Direct care nurses have specific expectations of their nurse leader. Learning as much about the expectations others hold for a position and for you provides greater clarity about your fit in the role.

TABLE 26.1 Leader, Manager, and Follower Roles: Interactions and Processes Involved in Each Role

Role	People With Whom Interactions Occur	Processes Involved in the Role
Leader	Persons being led Peers "Boss" Regulating agencies	Listening Encouraging Motivating Organizing Problem solving (high level) Developing Supporting

Manager	Persons being
	  supervised
	Administrators
	Supervisors
	Regulating agencies
		Organizing
		Budgeting
		Hiring
		Evaluating
		Reporting
		Disseminating
		Listening
		Problem solving
		  (unit level)

Follower	Supervisor
	Peers
		Conforming
		Implementing
		Contributing
		Completing
		  assignments
		Alerting
		Listening
		Problem solving
		  (patient and team
		  level)
		Questioning

BOX 26.1 Roles Acronym

Responsibilities
Opportunities
Lines of communication
Expectations
Support

S stands for support, which is closely tied to expectations about performance. All roles are shaped to some degree by the support and services others provide. The acute care nurse has peers readily available when a second opinion is needed. The same nurse may feel lost when confronted with questionable findings during a home visit.

ROLE TRANSITION PROCESS

One way to think about transition to a new role is illustrated in Box 26.2 and Table 26.2. Thinking about transitions in terms of a common social perspective may be helpful for some.

Patricia Benner (1982) developed a Novice to Expert concept that provides a framework for the ongoing development of nurses. It is based on five different levels of practice, including novice, advanced beginner, competent, proficient, and expert. Even very experienced nurses become novices again when introduced into a new role. A very savvy and experienced intensive care unit (ICU) nurse becomes an ICU nurse manager, the individual may be expert in the clinical ICU skills and assessment techniques, but the new world of management may be

---

BOX 26.2   Role Transition Process

Moving out of old roles while learning new roles requires an identity adjustment over time. The persons involved must invest themselves in the process. In this way, role transition can be compared with developing a relationship. The process of developing an intimate relationship with another person provides a familiar framework for considering role transition. Relationships typically move through the phases of dating, commitment, honeymoon, disillusionment, resolution, and maturity.

Role Preview

During the dating phase, the interested persons spend structured time together. Both parties present their best characteristics and dedicate much energy to developing the relationship. Although both parties present their best characteristics, both also are alert to clues that the other party cannot meet their expectations. For example, one may consider the financial and emotional resources that the other person would bring to the relationship. The individuals might spend time with each other's families to get a feel for the emotional climate in which the other person grew up.

Interviewing for a management position is similar to dating. An interview involves touring the unit, visiting with people, and attempting to make a good impression. The potential employer is also attempting to make a favorable impression. The interviewee wants to find out whether this is an organization that will support his or her growth as he or she supports the growth of the organization. Questions are asked about the role of the manager, and the potential manager mentally evaluates whether the described role matches personal expectations about management. Both of these examples represent the phase "role preview."

Role Acceptance

Through the dating process, two people may decide that they want to spend the rest of their lives together and commit to the relationship. Sometimes, one or both of the people decide that they do not want to establish a long-term relationship. In a similar way, after the role preview of the interview process, both parties may agree to establish a relationship as employee and employer. Or one or both of the parties may decide not to establish the relationship. In dating, the public decision to leave other similar relationships and establish this new relationship represents a formal commitment. In role transition, the formal commitment of the employment contract implies acceptance of the management role, or "role acceptance."

Role Exploration

In new relationships, a time of dating and commitment is usually followed by a honeymoon. More than a trip to a vacation spot, the honeymoon has become synonymous with excitement, happiness, and confidence. In a new work role, people also experience a honeymoon phase. The new graduate may be relieved that the educational program was successfully completed and now a salary can be earned. When a new manager is hired, the employer is excited that the search is over. The staff is happy to have a leader, especially if staff members had input into the hiring decision. The new manager is happy, excited, and, most of all, confident in exploring the new roles involved in the management position.

Role Discrepancy

Whether by a gradual process or as the result of a particular event that serves as the turning point, eventually the

BOX 26.2   Role Transition Process—cont'd

honeymoon is over and disillusionment about the relationship occurs. For example, one person may make an expensive purchase without consulting the partner. An argument is followed by a period of painful silence. Similarly, the honeymoon phase in a new employment position can be followed by a period of disillusionment.

Role discrepancy, a gap between role expectations and role performance, causes discomfort and frustration. Role discrepancy can be resolved by either dissolving the relationship or by changing expectations and performance. The importance of the relationship and the perceived differences between performance and expectations, the basis of role discrepancy, must be considered in light of personal values. When the relationship is valued and the differences are seen as correctable, the decision is made to stay in the relationship. This decision requires the couple or the manager to develop the role.

Role Development

Choosing to change either role expectations or role performance or to change both is the process of role development. In an intimate relationship, open communication can clarify expectations. Negotiation may result in reasonable expectations. Certain behaviors may be changed to improve role performance. For example, one person in the relationship learns to call home to let the other know about the possibility of being late.

To reduce role discrepancy in a new management position, the same open communication and negotiation must occur. Expectations need to be clarified and stipulated by both parties. New managers evaluate management styles and techniques to determine which ones best fit them and the situation. The personal management style evolves as the individuals develop the management roles in their own unique ways. If role discrepancy can be reduced and the role developed to be satisfactory to both parties, the new manager can focus on developing the roles of the position and proceed to the phase of role internalization.

Role Internalization

Role internalization occurs in relationships as they mature. No longer do the persons in the relationship consciously consider their roles. They have learned the behaviors that maintain and nurture the relationship. The behaviors become second nature. The energy spent on establishing and developing the relationship can be redirected toward achieving mutual goals. In the same way managers who have been in management positions for several years have internalized their roles. Usually they do not consciously consider their roles. Managers know they have reached the stage of role internalization when they focus on accomplishing mutual goals instead of contemplating whether their role performance matches their role expectations. Managers who have internalized their roles have developed their own unique personal style of management. Table 26.2 summarizes the comparison between the phases of developing an intimate relationship and the phases of role transition to a nurse manager.

Unexpected Role Transition

Not every relationship is successful. Some relationships end in an argument, divorce, or death. When a relationship ends unexpectedly, a person goes through a grieving process. In a similar way, when a person is fired, a position is eliminated, or a job description changes dramatically, the person may have to grieve before being able to engage in role transition. Health care is in a tumultuous state. Mergers, acquisitions, and reductions in work force are commonplace. To be successful, workplace restructuring must be undertaken with the same sensitivity afforded a person who has lost a relationship through death or divorce. Role transition takes time, even in reverse.

The initial response to a change in role can be shock and disbelief. The person may feel numb and unable to function. As the numbness wears off, the person may become angry. The anger fuels resistance to the change and may be directed toward those who initiated the role change. The anger may be directed internally, leading to depression. If the person is unable to acknowledge and talk about the loss, the period of grief may be extended, or emotional baggage may be created that is carried into the next role. Grieving can eventually resolve in acceptance. Lessons learned from the experience are identified and internalized. A new role is sought, and the "dating" begins again.

When a relationship is dissolved in the case of death or divorce, a legal document is prepared to formally dissolve the financial and social obligations between the persons involved. The loss of a position as a result of restructuring or a buyout should involve a similar process. The employer may offer the nurse a severance package that includes financial compensation and outplacement services. If the employer does not offer a written agreement, the nurse should formally request and negotiate reasonable compensation and assistance. Similar to signing a prenuptial agreement, a nurse may have signed a contract with the employer when hired. The terms of that agreement may require the employer to buy out (pay the salary and benefits) for the time remaining on the contract.

Jennifer Jackson Gray

TABLE 26.2   Comparison of Phases in Developing an Intimate Relationship and in Undergoing Role Transition as a Nurse Manager

Phase in Developing an Intimate Relationship	Phase in Role Transition as a Nurse Manager	Characteristics of Phase
Dating	Role preview	Presentation of best characteristics to make favorable impression; both parties evaluate each other to determine likelihood of the other being able to fulfill one's expectations
Commitment to relationship	Role acceptance	Public announcement of mutual decision to initiate contract
Honeymoon	Role exploration	Experience of excitement, confidence, and mutual appreciation
Disillusionment	Role discrepancy	Awareness of difference between role expectations and role performance; reconsideration of whether to continue with contract
Resolution	Role development	Negotiation of role expectations; adjustment of role performance to approximate expectations and to find own unique style
Maturation of relationship	Role internalization	Performance of role congruent with own beliefs and individual style; achievement of mutual goals

overwhelming. Therefore the individual would now be a novice again in the new role of nurse manager.

Becoming a manager or assuming a new role requires a transformation—a profound change in identity. Such a transformation invokes stress as the person changes roles to learn the management role. Several strategies can be helpful in easing the strain and speeding the process of role transition (Box 26.3).

EXERCISE 26.1 You have been a direct care nurse on a busy medical-surgical unit for 3 years. You have been successful in both the clinical practice and in being involved with the shared decision-making committee. An assistant nurse manager position has opened on the evening shift full time, and you are considering applying for the position. As you begin to contemplate this position, what thoughts do you have related to moving from a direct care registered nurse (RN) to a leadership position? Detail what you would do to prepare yourself for the question at interview, "how will you prepare to transition from a peer to a supervisor on this patient care area?" Develop two to three interview questions you might anticipate being asked during the interview about your values and how you work with others.

BOX 26.3   Strategies to Promote Role Transition

- Strengthen internal resources.
- Assess the organization's resources, culture, and group dynamics.
- Negotiate the role.
- Grow with a mentor.
- Develop management knowledge and skills.

STRATEGIES TO PROMOTE ROLE TRANSITION

When a transition is likely, nurses can employ specific strategies to enhance the success of that transition.

Internal Resources

A key strategy in promoting role transition is to recognize, use, and strengthen one's values and beliefs. Behavior is influenced by values and beliefs. It is important that new leaders do not lose sight of their own values and beliefs. The role of manager is not for everyone. One must consider whether personal goals and professional fulfillment can best be achieved through management. One's commitment to the challenges of managing can provide the desire to persevere during the process of role transition.

If an individual in transition understands his or her own personal values, these will help the person respond to situations and relationships. A person's value does not depend on the quality or quickness of the adjustment to the management role. An exercise such as writing down short statements of belief or self-affirmations and posting this information may be helpful as a visual reminder.

Changing circumstances in health care raise the need for flexibility. The effective leader must be able to learn and master new skills, translate information for staff, and adapt behavior to the situation. The new leader should also not expect too much of oneself all at once; understanding that this transition takes time will help with flexibility.

Organizational Assessment

A new manager is much like an immigrant in a new country. An immigrant learns how to access the available resources to acclimate to the new environment. Cultural practices of the new country may seem strange or odd. Such differences can be analyzed and decisions made about which aspects to incorporate into one's own culture. Added subtle differences in communication patterns or group dynamics can also be identified. Understanding the nuances of social interactions is often the most difficult aspect of acclimating to a new country. The transition is smoother for an immigrant who understands himself or herself, assesses the new environment, and learns how to communicate within groups.

The new manager must also learn how to access resources in the organization. Approaching the organization as a foreign culture, the new manager can keenly observe the rituals, accepted practices, and patterns of communication within the organization. This ongoing assessment promotes a speedier transition into the role of manager. An immigrant who spends energy bemoaning the difficulties of the new country may fail to enjoy the advantages that were the attractions to the country in the first place. In the same way, the manager who focuses on the weaknesses of the organization may lack the energy to internalize the new role, a step that is critical to being an effective leader. A new manager who feels out of place in the new role may feel similar to the immigrant who wants to go home. The new manager may forget the reasons why he or she took the new position and just want to be comfortable again and return to a direct-care nurse role.

EXERCISE 26.2 You have successfully obtained the position as assistant nurse manager on the evening shift that you applied for. You are encountering many situations that you have never dealt with before and are feeling a bit lost. What strategies could you use to help you negotiate these situations more successfully?

Role Negotiation

A strategy that is helpful during conflicting role expectations is **role negotiation.** The priority of different role expectations may also require role negotiation with the person above you in the line of command. Ask for input as to which expectations have the highest priorities. Explain personal and family expectations and clearly state the priority that meeting those expectations has. The process may have to be repeated several times before agreement on the expectations related to roles and the priority of each expectation is found. Rewriting the unrealistic expectations to be achievable can reduce three common sources of role stress—ambiguity, overload, and conflict. Each person's role contributes to the end result. All individuals must understand their roles, or the team may fail. The Theory Box provides an overview of role theory as applied to healthcare professionals and can be helpful as an overarching conceptual framework.

Mentors

The process of mentoring is not a new concept. This concept has been alive since Homer's *Odyssey*. Odysseus leaves Ithaca to fight in the Trojan War. Before leaving, he entrusts his son to Mentor. Mentor was to develop and prepare this son for his life and duties. Mentors are a tremendous source of guidance and support for direct care nurses and managers, serving both career functions and psychosocial functions. Mentors need training and feedback to become valuable and effective to mentees. Skills such as assessing competence, providing constructive feedback, and goal development are critical to a mentor's success in guiding a mentee. Career functions are possible because the mentor has sufficient professional experience and organizational authority to

THEORY BOX

Theory/Contributor	Key Ideas	Application to Practice
Hardy (1978) is credited with applying role theory to healthcare professionals. Role is the expected and actual behaviors associated with a position. **Role expectations** are the attitudes and behaviors others anticipate that a person in the role will possess or demonstrate. **Role stress** is a social condition in which role demands are conflicting, irritating, difficult, or impossible to fulfill. **Role strain** is the subjective feeling of discomfort experienced as the result of role stress.	Role stress is a precursor to role strain. Role stress is associated with low productivity and performance. Role stress and role strain can lead a person to withdraw psychologically from the role. Clear, realistic role expectations can decrease the role stress for a new nurse manager.	Clear, realistic role expectations can increase productivity.

Data from Hardy, M.E. (1978). Role stress and role strain. In M.E. Hardy & M.E. Conway (Eds.), *Role theory: Perspectives for health professionals.* New York: Appleton-Century-Crofts.

facilitate the career of the "mentee." The mentor may suggest the mentee be appointed to a key nursing committee or volunteer for a special assignment. The mentor can help provide exposure or opportunities for the mentee to build a reputation of competence. With exposure, the mentor provides protection by absorbing negative feedback, sharing responsibility for controversial decisions, and teaching the unwritten rules about "how things are done around here." These unwritten rules may be more important to job success than the written rules.

The Research Perspective illustrates how mentoring can affect retention of nurses in rural healthcare facilities.

Mentors provide information about how to improve performance, including feedback on current performance. Coaching requires frequent contact and willingness on the part of the mentee to accept feedback. Challenging assignments are given to the mentee that will stretch the limits of knowledge and skill. The mentor helps the mentee learn the technical and management skills necessary to accomplish the task, such as which

RESEARCH PERSPECTIVE

Resource: Jones, S. J. (2017). Establishing a nurse mentor program to improve nurse satisfaction and intent to stay. *Journal for Nurses in Professional Development, 33*(2), 76–78.

Retention of nurses in rural healthcare facilities is a challenge. A nurse mentor program 12 months in length was developed and implemented in a rural emergency department with a one-to-one relationship between mentor and mentee. Support sessions were held monthly with mentors and mentees with discussion topics including effective communication, conflict resolution, and time management. A program coordinator facilitated the ongoing work of the mentor-mentee pairs and was essential to the success. The nurse mentees' satisfaction with their job was measured using the McCloskey/Mueller Job Satisfaction Scale at 3-month intervals throughout the program. The nurse mentees' intent to stay in the job was assessed with the Intent to Stay/Leave Diagnostic Survey. Positive outcomes resulted for both mentors and mentees in this program. The program proved to be a nurturing strategy for mentees who felt supported by an experienced trusted nurse who influenced their intent to stay on their specific patient care unit, and the mentors reported enhanced job satisfaction.

Implications for Practice

The mentor-mentee program that allows dedicated time for relationship development, counseling, and coaching can make the difference for nurse retention. Nurse leaders who implement specific programs to onboard staff can reap the benefits of a satisfied nursing staff.

numbers on the budget printout are added to achieve the total expenditures.

Having a blend of complementary personalities between mentor and mentee is essential. The personal and professional connection between the mentor and mentee is powerful; thus having similar interests and motivations is important. The interpersonal relationship between the mentor and the mentee involves mutual positive regard. The mentee identifies with the mentor's example because the mentee respects the career accomplishments of the mentor. This role modeling is both conscious and unconscious. The mentee with character and self-respect will evaluate the behaviors of the mentor and select those behaviors worthy of being emulated.

Counseling, as another psychosocial function of the mentor, allows the mentee to explore personal concerns. Confidentiality is a prerequisite to sharing personal information. Because the opinion of the mentor is respected, the mentor may provide guidance to the mentee. The best mentors can provide guidance while recognizing that the mentee may choose to disregard the advice. Mentors rely heavily on two strategies: asking questions and telling stories. The latter is designed to illustrate a point, and the former is designed to help the mentee explore personal thoughts to reach a decision.

Being mentored is a learning process. Admiration for a mentor and recognition of the mentor's commitment to self-success can provide an environment of trust in which a mentor-mentee relationship begins. Both persons develop positive expectations of the relationship, and both take the initiative to nurture the new relationship. As more of the mentor functions are experienced, the bond between the mentor and mentee grows stronger.

Relationships between mentors and mentees vary because of individual characteristics and the career phase of each. During the early phases of a career, a nurse manager is concerned about competence, and a mentor can provide valuable coaching (Fig. 26.1). As the nurse manager develops, sponsorship by a mentor can prepare the manager for a promotion. A mentor nearing the end of the work career can find fulfillment in sharing knowledge with new managers and at the same time benefit from the counsel of a recently retired colleague.

> **EXERCISE 26.3** Provide an example of how a new direct care nurse in a patient care area can benefit from a mentor-mentee relationship.

Fig. 26.1 Keeping up with current research is an effective management and education strategy and can provide a basis for coaching.

Management Education

Management performance can be hindered by a specific knowledge deficit. For example, the manager may lack business skills or knowledge about legal aspects of supervision. Strickler, Bohling, Kneis, O'Connor, and Yee (2016) note that "leadership development and succession planning is a challenging task for any organization" (p. 49). They also emphasize how in-house educational programs assist novice nurse leaders transitioning into their new roles.

Recommendations for nursing leaders included formal education and orientation to the role, managing performance and development of staff, and developing communication skills. Additional education should be focused on unit finances and patient relations. Leadership support is pivotal for charge nurses to feel successful.

Leadership Certification

Experience and education provide a firm basis for seeking additional credentials. A nurse holding an administrative position at the nurse executive level with a baccalaureate preparation and 24 months of experience can take an examination to become a certified nursing executive. Nursing administrators with master's degrees and experience at the executive level can take an examination to become a certified nurse executive, advanced. The website of the American Nurses Credentialing Center (ANCC, 2017) has more detailed information about certification examinations (www.nursecredentialing.org). A certification credential also was developed by the

American Organization of Nurse Executives (AONE, 2017) exclusively for the nurse executive and the certified nurse manager leader—the Certification in Executive Nursing Practice (CENP) and Certified Nurse Manager Leader (CNML) *(http://www.aone.org/initiatives/certification.shtml).* These credentials are recognized in the profession as designating someone whose knowledge and experience are credible.

CONCLUSION

Transitions from a direct care nurse position to charge nurse or nurse manager pose new challenges. Nurses who make these transitions with minimal discomfort are reflective of role theory in action. Although nurses today are better prepared to take on more formal leadership roles, the roles themselves are more challenging. Charge nurses and managers are responsible for mentoring and coaching new staff as they transition to their new roles. These transition activities take time and effort to achieve the best results possible.

THE SOLUTION

I felt excited and ready when I accepted a manager position, but I was also anxious to learn a new practice, new faces, local politics, and what was expected of me. First impressions are important, so I was mindful of my appearance, body language, and demeanor during initial meetings. I was aware that I was being watched as "the new person" and wanted to start off strong on the right foot.

As a nurse, I wanted to understand the nursing practice and begin to understand how the team worked together. I was able to probe into strengths of the work area as well as ideas for improvement. I spent several weeks working side by side with the nurses. They were surprised by this, but it seemed natural to me. If I was going to be their voice and leader, I needed to know their world.

In addition to spending time with the staff as they were doing their work, I wanted to spend some time without distraction to focus on each nurse individually. I created a template of ideas we could discuss, blocked time on my calendar, and invited the staff to select a time that would work for them to have informal discussions. I concentrated on learning about the nurses, their families, education, work experiences, and goals. I also welcomed this time as an opportunity for them to learn a little more about me and my goals for the team.

A new manager is given a lot of information during the first few weeks and months at a new job. I found it helpful to take notes. I was able to review the notes as needed when topics would resurface to help jog my memory. I noted areas of concern or topics that I wanted to spend more time on. Finding a way to keep your files, calendar, and to-do's organized is necessary for success.

I learned early on to identify colleagues from whom I could ask for feedback. I was fortunate to have a nurse administrator who was supportive and available during my transition. Finding trusted and respected leaders to work through challenging situations with is essential for success.

I also utilized professional journals, leadership websites, and blogs to offer guidance and help me brainstorm solutions. Learning doesn't stop when refocusing from the bedside, but it does change!

Would this be a suitable approach for you? Why?

Monica Boege
Nurse Manager, Mayo Clinic Health System

REFLECTIONS

Consider various role transitions you have experienced personally. What valuable lessons did you learn? What do you wish you had known before or during a role transition? How will you acquire that information for all subsequent transitions?

THE EVIDENCE

Successful role transition takes time and requires support by preceptors, mentors, managers, and colleagues. The literature supports a pivotal relationship to cultivate early in one's career: that of a mentor. Equally important, though less documented in the literature, is leadership coaching as a critical component of developing oneself as a follower and a leader. Nurse residency programs provide an avenue to assist with role transition for new graduates and leadership development programs, and the former is well documented in the literature.

TIPS FOR ROLE TRANSITION

- Role transition is a normal process. Anticipate and prepare for role changes.
- Identify the responsibilities, opportunities, lines of communication, expectations, and support for a role.
- Use your internal resources to negotiate a role that is consistent with your values and life commitments.

REFERENCES

American Nurses Credentialing Center (ANCC). (2017). *Certification eligibility criteria.* www.nursecredentialing. org/Nurse Executive.

American Organization of Nurse Executives (AONE). (2017). *Nurse leader certification.* www.aone.org/initiatives/ certification.shtml.

Arrowsmith, V., Lau-Walker, M., Norman, I., & Maben, J. (2016). Nurses' perceptions and experiences of work role transitions: A mixed methods systematic review of the literature. *Journal of Advanced Nursing, 72*(88), 1735–1750.

Benner, P. (1982). From novice to expert. *American Journal of Nursing, 82*(3), 402–407.

Hardy, M. E. (1978). Role stress and role strain. In M. E. Hardy & M. E. Conway (Eds.), *Role theory: Perspectives for health professionals.* New York: Appleton-Century-Crofts.

Jones, S. J. (2017). Establishing a nurse mentor program to improve nurse satisfaction and intent to stay. *Journal for Nurses in Staff Development, 33*(2), 76–78.

Strickler, J., Bohling, S., Kneis, C., O'Connor, M., & Yee, P. (2016). Developing nurse leaders from within. *Nursing 2016, 46*(5), 49–57.

27

Managing Your Career

Debra Hagler, M. Margaret Calacci

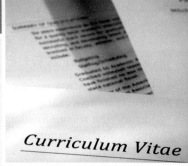

Curriculum Vitae

LEARNING OUTCOMES

- Interpret key concepts in career development.
- Appraise academic programs, continuing education activities, certifications, and organizational involvement to support professional development goals.
- Develop marketing documents to apply for a specific employment position.
- Prepare for an employment interview.

KEY TERMS

branding
career
certification
continuing education

curriculum vitae
licensure
portfolio

professional association (organization)
résumé

THE CHALLENGE

Completing my BSN was not something I had always planned to do. In my previous career, I worked as a forensic interviewer at a children's advocacy center. I was responsible for interviewing children when a report or disclosure of abuse was initiated. I witnessed the compassionate, caring connections the forensic nurses made with these vulnerable children. I came to realize that continuing my education through nursing could support my goals and my passion of advocating for children. This decision presented my first challenge: to be a candidate for forensic nursing certification, I needed to earn a BSN and achieve at least 3 years of nursing experience with additional coursework and precepted training hours in forensics. I would have a long road ahead to land my dream job.

What would you do if you were this nurse?

Cynthia Flores, RN, BSN
Tucson, AZ

INTRODUCTION

The richness and breadth of the nursing profession offers hundreds of career options, including careers not imagined a few decades ago. In fact, a book entitled *301 Careers in Nursing* (Fitzgerald, Ea, & Bai, 2017) includes 100 more options than a previous edition!

Some of these career options are the traditional roles nurses have performed for centuries—providing direct care to patients, leading teams or organizations, teaching, providing public health or school health services, or working in an occupational field. Other roles, such as informatics specialist or educational simulation facilitator, became viable nursing career options more recently. Coordinating preventive care and providing health coaching have been nursing roles for many years and are becoming more common choices for nurses because of soaring public interest in wellness and disease prevention.

Having numerous options creates challenges in determining how to build a career, which educational path best matches the role, which experiences best prepare nurses for advancement in a specific field or role, who might be a willing and helpful mentor, and what new activities and roles need to be developed. Some role options build primarily on experience and others on education and experience. All, however, require that a nurse engage in continued professional development to meet the evolving challenges in health care. How nurses reach their career goals depends on how they manage their career development.

"A career is great when it offers satisfying work, impact on the world, a dependable and adequate income, and personal freedom" (Smith, 2016, p. 172). A career extends beyond employment positions to include the ways an individual engages in activities that provide care to patients, support that care, educate for that care, support the providers of that care, study the ways in which to deliver the care, and engage in the broader perspective of professional and community service. Thinking broadly about a career in a rapidly changing field such as health care is critical to remaining competent and relevant.

Licensure carries certain expectations about maintaining competence and reflecting professional standards. Consumers, insurers, regulatory agencies, and employers expect that nurses will meet professional and legal standards. Nursing has not identified a unified standard for maintaining competence, so requirements for demonstrating continued competency in the United States vary by state. Changing geographic locations during a career may entail meeting different regulatory requirements for continuing professional development.

A CAREER FRAMEWORK

A career, defined as progress throughout an individual's professional life, develops as the individual selects positions that contribute to professional goals. A good position or career fit is built on strong, similar goals and tolerable (or growth-producing) differences. The whole of any work situation is composed of two elements—person and position—interacting in a complex environment. Analyzing position statements and the required skills in light of individual talents can help determine positions that fit your strengths. If gaps occur between the requirements of a "dream" position and your skills, consider whether professional development activities might help improve the match between your current and desired future qualifications. Knowing the structure of the position, the mission and vision of the organization and how they are interpreted through various roles, and a sense of the organization's direction helps in understanding a position's potential fit.

CAREER THEORY

Four major concepts have been used by McDonald and Hite (2015) to explain career development: career success, career competencies, career transitions, and career identity.

Career success refers to a positive outcome over time, beyond a single employment position. Success can be evaluated from an internal focus (whether you have met your own goals) and from an external focus (how your outcomes compare with others on tangible measures such as salary, promotions, and occupational status). Others (parents, spouses, coworkers, friends) may have expectations for you in your career. Understanding the tensions between the expectations of others and your own goals can help clarify how you evaluate your career success.

Career competencies go beyond the direct expertise required for nursing practice in a particular setting. The legal privileges and expectations are listed in state nursing practice acts, rules, and regulations. Licensure is designed to ensure the baseline competencies (i.e., the minimum expectations). However, many additional competencies are important in a successful professional career, such as setting goals, knowing yourself, knowing the position, and engaging in professional development.

Career transitions include changing positions, work descriptions, employers, or roles. Common transitions are making an initial career choice, accepting employment in an organization, seeking promotion, recruitment to a different work setting, involuntary job loss, and retirement.

Career identity is the evolving picture of an individual's vocational role in the world. Career identity is an important part of the overall sense of identity. Observing role models, trying out new behaviors, and reflecting on outcomes of our actions contribute to constructing and reconstructing a sense of career identity.

Individuals influence some aspects of their career development, whereas their employing organizations influence other aspects. Choosing an employment setting and employer is an important decision that goes far beyond the immediate position: employers who promote professional development opportunities for their staff support many more possibilities for individuals throughout their careers. A survey of 871 nurses and nursing employers by Philippou (2015) indicated a sense of shared responsibilities for career management and a time dimension to those responsibilities. Employers reported responsibility for short-term development specific to the employment role, whereas employers and nurse employees shared responsibility for medium-term development activities such as assessing nurses' strengths and weaknesses and identifying education and training needs. Nurse employees perceived a greater responsibility over the long term for their individual careers and future development plans. Employers and individuals who consider their respective and cooperative roles in career development can have useful conversations about meeting the goals of both the individual and the organization.

The Theory Box provides a way of considering a theoretical approach to career development in nursing.

Knowing Yourself

The best opportunity for nurses to manage their careers and for a manager to help nurses gain important experiences is for individuals to know themselves. Knowing what is important, what is valued, and the commitment needed to follow through forms the basis for understanding yourself. Whether positions are plentiful or scarce, knowing yourself can focus the available work or selection process toward capitalizing on one's strengths. Even assessing your strengths through a formal avenue (e.g., StrengthsFinder 2.0 at *www.strengthsfinder.com/home. aspx*) can provide insight. Therefore the beginning of creating a person-position fit is in understanding the person involved. Throughout school and initial experiences in nursing, insight begins to evolve that helps each of us determine our preferences for our life work. Some positions add more to what we want to be able to achieve in the long term than other positions do. As an example, a position that offers educational compensation or flexible scheduling might be preferable when the goal is to return to school and complete advanced education for a specialized role.

Being able to describe yourself from various perspectives is useful. First, knowing your strengths tells what you bring to a position and what you can rely on. When you know your strengths, you can say what they are in a succinct manner and use them as a filter in reading position descriptions to find your fit in an organization. An analysis of your current competencies allows you to see what work needs to be done to meet required or desired standards and competencies. Finally, entering into such analyses can help you see the bigger picture of what you can learn from a particular position that might contribute to your overall goals. The goal of all this work is to know yourself well so that your pursuit of a position or career path fits you and your strengths.

Consideration of a career path such as practitioner, administrator, or educator includes reflection on the most rewarding aspects of prior work. As an example,

THEORY BOX

Career Stages and Mentoring Needs

Theory/ Contributor	Key Ideas	Application to Practice
Angela Barron McBride	**Stages of Career**	**Mentoring Support Needed**
	Preparation: learning and assimilating values	Setting goals and building skills
	Independent Contributions: moving to competence	Networking and opportunities
	Development of Home Setting: moving to expertise	Strategies and sponsorship
	Development of Field/Health Care: authority and vision	External/international opportunities
	The Gadfly Period: shaping the profession without constraints of employment setting	Envisioning postretirement projects

Adapted from McBride, A. B. (2011). *The growth and development of nurse leaders.* New York: Springer Publishing.

RESEARCH PERSPECTIVE

Resource: Helms, M. M., Arfken, D. E., & Bellar, S. (2016). The importance of mentoring and sponsorship in women's career development. *SAM Advanced Management Journal, 81*(3), 4.

Sixteen women acknowledged as business and non-profit organization leaders participated in focus groups to describe their experiences in mentorship and sponsorship. Their discourse with a professional facilitator was transcribed, hand-coded, qualitatively analyzed for content, and developed into themes.

Participants described the mentoring process as a longer-term commitment to helping another person gain confidence and move toward that person's goals, whereas sponsorship was a time-limited relationship of promoting

or advocating for the individual. Although the same pair could be involved in either or both types of relationship, most participants experienced the relationships as distinct from one another. Seeking both mentorship and sponsorship were considered important to professional career development.

Implications for Practice

Consider identifying one or more mentors to help you think about and develop a strategy to meet your long-term career goals. Consider the value of seeking specific sponsors when you want to strengthen support in your application for a new position or role.

---

a nurse who determined that teaching patients, families, and students was the most personally rewarding aspect of practice might plan to develop a career as a nurse educator, whereas someone who finds data fascinating and enjoys seeking answers may pursue a career in nursing informatics.

Core career development strategies are important to success. One key strategy for career development is planning to obtain the right education and experience to meet future goals. Another key strategy is selecting professional peers and mentors to provide good advice. Having a few well-chosen peers, mentors, and role models who respond openly from various perspectives can enrich career planning and development (Fig. 27.1). A mentor can inspire new thinking and new opportunities and steer you toward various roles and clinical areas. That person can also create connections for you and help guide decisions related to timing and context. Mentors might even be able to create opportunities for you to test new approaches to clinical care or to new aspects of a position (see the Research Perspective).

Knowing the Position

Few people, including nurses, hold the same employment position forever. Rapid changes in health care require an evaluation of each employment opportunity through a series of questions. Can the position contribute to increased skills and competencies? Does the position have the potential to recast one's professional profile so that others see the potential for greater contributions? Are the benefits of the position so enticing that they offset limitations of the position? Is the professional practice environment in that organization a safe and

Fig. 27.1 A mentor can inspire new thinking and new opportunities and steer you toward various roles and clinical areas.

collaborative setting for healthcare professionals and patients (American Association of Colleges of Nursing [AACN], n.d.)?

Position assessment begins with understanding the vision and mission of the organization. Assessment also requires finding out specifics of the position, which may be available only through an interview. Many nurse managers look within the organization to hire by transferring someone from a different position in that organization. So one key strategy to use is selecting an organization where you want to work, even if the initial position available is not exactly the best fit for your goals. The potential for inside connections and networking, in addition to knowledge about management styles in the organization and future position openings, can lead you to the position that is the right fit for you. You may find a position that is a good fit for you at one point, but over the course of a career, the position may no longer be a good fit. The position may have changed as much as you did. If the movement was in harmony, the fit remains, but if the position changes in one way and the person in another, the fit devolves.

PROFESSIONAL DEVELOPMENT

One of the keys to maintaining competence and versatility is continuing to learn. "Nursing professional development is a vital phase of lifelong learning in which nurses engage to develop and maintain competence, enhance professional nursing practice, and support achievement of career goals" (American Nurses Association [ANA], 2010, p. 1). Active involvement in education, service, and scholarship opportunities can help prepare you to deal with new roles and challenges in your employment setting and the larger scope of nursing and health care. Engaging in service activities (both community and professional organizations) and sharing your knowledge through research, writing, and speaking (scholarship) allow you to influence others in the profession and through the profession. When positions are scarce or when you are competing for a very desirable position, community and professional service experience and scholarly contributions to nursing may give you the advantage over other candidates. Learning also can occur through informal means: in a conversation with colleagues, by observing leaders in the workplace, through reading an article, or in reflective thought. One way to maximize this learning is to share the idea with others, giving credit to the original source as needed.

Academic Progression

A graduate degree opens the door to numerous career opportunities. Before you make a significant investment in time and money to earn an advanced degree, think carefully about your career goals. Choose a graduate program based on your future career plans (Lindell, Hagler, & Poindexter, 2017). If you dream of conducting clinical research, earning a PhD is likely to be the best preparation for the role. If you want to be a primary care provider in advanced practice, consider earning a DNP. If you want to teach future healthcare professionals, you may be able to prepare for that role in a variety of ways: a master's degree or doctoral degree in nursing or education or a graduate degree in a related field such as public health, sociology, genetics, or informatics. Remember,

however, most teaching positions require a master's degree in nursing as the basic preparation.

Although prior experience can enrich the learning process, the philosophy of delaying entry into graduate education is changing: nurse leaders have identified the profession's need for nurses who have completed graduate degrees earlier in their careers. In addition, the increasing complexity of health care leads to a need for nurses who are also experts in areas outside nursing. Earning a graduate degree in another field may put you in the position of translating advanced knowledge from other disciplines to improve health care. When combined with a graduate degree in nursing, this combination may make you highly sought after.

Admission to graduate programs may require taking a test such as the Graduate Record Examination (GRE), having an above-average grade point average (GPA), and graduating from a professionally accredited school of nursing. Box 27.1 lists some of the factors to consider in selecting a graduate program.

Working while attending a graduate program may be difficult, but it is common among graduate students in nursing. Consider how you learn best. Do you thrive in person-to-person discussions? Do you have need to be face-to-face or are you comfortable with learning via audio or video connection? Do you want some "intense" interactions with others combined with individual activities? Each of these preferences has a solution. For example, distance education online provides an additional option for earning an advanced degree. Flexible scheduling and the convenience of online courses permit many individuals to participate who would not be able to attend traditional programs because of class times or geographic distance. Programs with a combined approach capture the strengths of both approaches. If you learn in interaction with others, actual physical presence with others may be a driving force.

Consider the following example of seeking out a graduate program that fits: You know you want to work with older adult patients. You review the most recent year's online issues of *Journal of Gerontological Nursing* and *Geriatric Nursing* and scan the articles. Are some articles particularly intriguing? Where are those authors affiliated? You can also search online using terms such as "geriatric center of excellence" to find related graduate programs. Do you know any experts in gerontology or geriatrics in your own workplace? Ask those experts for suggestions about academic programs. Review professional organization websites related to gerontology and

---

BOX 27.1   Factors to Consider in Selecting a Graduate Program

Accreditation
- Does the program have national nursing accreditation (master's/doctoral level)?
- Is the institution regionally accredited (e.g., North Central Association of Colleges and Schools)?

Role Preparation
- How closely does the program of study meet your career goals?

Credits
- How many graduate credits are required to complete the degree?
- How many are devoted to clinical or practicum experiences?
- How many relate to classroom experiences?

Thesis/Research
- Is a thesis/dissertation/applied project required?
- If not, what opportunities exist for research development?

Faculty
- What credentials do faculty members hold?
- Are they in leadership positions in the state/national/international scenes?

- Are they competent in your field of interest?
- What is their reputation?

Current Research
- What are the current research, practice, and policy strengths of the institution?

Flexibility
- Do these strengths fit with your interests, or is there flexibility to create your own direction?
- Is flexibility present in scheduling and progress through the program?
- Is classroom attendance required or is online or blended attendance an option?

Admission
- What is required?
- Is the GRE used?
- What is the minimum undergraduate GPA expected?
- Is experience required? What kind? How much?

Costs
- What are the total projected costs?
- What financial aid is available?
- What support is available for graduate students?

GPA, Grade point average; *GRE*, Graduate Record Examination.

---

consider joining to network with other members. These are good starting places for connecting with others who have similar interests and know firsthand about available programs.

EXERCISE 27.1 Assume you are interested in graduate education.
- Use the Internet to locate information about graduate education and financial assistance.
- Determine what specialties exist at the master's/doctoral level.
- Consider doctoral programs permitting entrance from the baccalaureate level.
- Evaluate the clinical interest of the programs of study.
- Decide whether the diverse roles of the advanced practice registered nurse appeal.
- Determine the location of programs nearby and access to distance programs.

EXERCISE 27.2 Imagine you have decided to earn a master's or doctoral degree in nursing. Develop a strategic plan for your graduate education.
- What values do you have that influence your plan?
- Are your interests in primary care, leadership, research, informatics, or education?
- What is your target date for completion of the program?
- What other factors would interfere with beginning or completing your strategic plan?

As one of today's nursing leaders said after earning a doctoral degree: Doors opened up that I didn't even know existed—that is what education can do for you. The point is that we often don't know what we don't know until we learn more. And then we know we must commit to lifelong learning.

BOX 27.2 Factors to Consider in Selecting a Continuing Education Course

Accreditation/Approval
- Is the course accredited and approved? If so, by whom?
- Is that recognition accepted by a certification entity and by the board of nursing (if continuing education is required for reregistration of licensure)?

Credit
- Is the amount of credit appropriate in terms of the expected outcomes?

Course Title
- Does it suggest the type of learner to be involved (e.g., advanced)?
- Does it reflect the expected outcomes?

Speaker(s)
- Is the speaker known as an expert in the field?
- Is the speaker experienced in the field?

Objectives
- Are the objectives logical and attainable?
- Do they reflect knowledge, skills, attitudes, or a combination of these?
- Do they fit a learner's needs?

Content
- Is the content reflective of the objectives?
- Is the content at an appropriate level?

Audience
- Is the audience designed as a general or specific one (e.g., all registered nurses or experienced nurses in state health positions)?

Cost
- What is the direct expense for an individual to attend? Is it affordable?
- Is the cost equitable with that of similar nursing conferences?
- Is travel required?
- Is the program offered online?

Length
- Is the total time frame logical in terms of objectives, personal needs, and time away from work?
- Does the time frame permit breaks from intense learning?

Provider
- Does the provider have an established reputation for quality programs?

Certification

Certification signifies completion of requirements in a particular field beyond basic nursing educational preparation for licensure. Nurses earn certification as recognition of competence in one or more specialty areas. Certification is an expectation in some employment settings for career advancement; in the field of advanced practice nursing, it is a requirement for practice and reimbursement. In many states, certification in advanced practice is the mechanism to achieve recognition as an advanced practice registered nurse from the board of nursing. Consumers, nurses, managers, and administrators value certification as evidence of specific expertise.

Obtaining certification may require testing, continued education, and documented time in a specific practice area. Certification renewal is a process of continued recognition of competence within a defined practice area and may require ongoing participation in continuing education. Certification plays an important part in the advancement of a career and the profession.

In some fields, more than one examination exists; others use an examination in the broad field and numerous options for subspecialties. The American Nurses Credentialing Center (ANCC) *(www.nurse credentialing.org)* offers numerous certification examinations for nurse generalists, nurse practitioners, clinical specialists, nurse administrators, nurse case managers, ambulatory nurses, and informatics nurses. In addition, nursing specialty organizations offer many other certifications through their credentialing organizations.

Continuing Education

Continuing education also contributes to professional growth. Continuing education is defined as "systematic professional learning experiences designed to augment the knowledge, skill, and attitudes of nurses, thereby enriching the nurses' contributions to quality health care and their pursuit of professional career goals" (ANA, 2010, p. 6).

Selecting among the numerous opportunities to pursue for continuing education may be difficult. Box 27.2

lists factors to consider in selecting a continuing education offering. Depending on your particular goal, certain factors may be more influential. For example, if cost is a major factor, program length and speaker credentials may be less influential factors.

In addition to increasing your knowledge base, continuing education provides professional networking opportunities, contributes to meeting certification and licensure requirements, and documents additional efforts in maintaining or developing clinical expertise. Sponsors of continuing education include employers, professional associations, schools, and entrepreneurs.

Professional Associations

The nursing profession embraces the expectation that nurses will belong to professional associations and provide leadership in improving communities. The challenge, of course, is how to incorporate these activities into a busy, committed life!

Belonging to a professional association demonstrates leadership and provides opportunities to meet other leaders, participate in policy formation, continue specialized education, and shape the future. Professional associations (organizations) are groups of people who share a set of professional values and who decide to join their colleagues to effect change. Many nursing associations set standards and objectives to guide the profession and specialty practice. Although associations may have very different agendas and goals related to their specialty areas, many nursing organizations share the long-term goal of uniting and advancing the profession. Those "additional" activities and interests enrich a career and provide for invaluable insight into clinical and professional issues.

Associations represent nurses in particular areas of the profession. Some are clinically focused, such as the American Association of Critical-Care Nurses, the Oncology Nurses Association, and the American Association of Neuroscience Nurses. Others are role-focused, such as the American Organization of Nurse Executives and the National League for Nursing. Still others represent specific groups of nurses, such as the American Assembly for Men in Nursing and the National Black Nurses Association. To attract future members, many specialty organizations offer networking opportunities, informative publications, and discounts on conference rates and liability insurance.

The "umbrella organization" that represents all nurses throughout the United States and its territories is the ANA (www.ana.org). The ANA advances the nursing profession by fostering high standards of nursing practice. Some functions of the ANA include projecting a positive and realistic view of nursing, promoting the economic and general welfare of nurses in the workplace, and lobbying Congress and regulatory agencies on healthcare issues affecting nurses and the public (ANA, 2018). Policymakers look to the ANA for guidance on nursing and health policy issues.

The Honor Society of Nursing, Sigma Theta Tau International, established in 1922, is an example of an invitational association. The organization's mission is to create a global community of nurses who lead in using scholarship, knowledge, and technology to improve the health of the world's people (www.nursingsociety.org). Membership is available to nurses enrolled in baccalaureate, master's, and doctoral education programs and community leaders through a nomination process. This organization provides small grants to aid in beginning research and disseminates research and leadership information through various publications and international meetings.

Connecting With an Organization

The size of an organization is not as important as how the group is organized and who is leading it. Read about the officers and membership composition of the organization before making a commitment through membership. Most associations have a website that lists biographic information about the leaders, locations of upcoming local and national meetings or activities, current policy issues and their positions, election information, and other valuable resource links. Many organizations send regular e-mail newsletters.

Upon joining a nursing organization, you may receive information on the history of the organization, future meetings and current activities, officer contact information, and local contacts. Contact the local office of the organization, if such exists, so that you can immediately begin networking. Most associations are composed of volunteers, all of whom have very busy schedules and different motivations for becoming involved. Taking time to talk to an officer or attend a local meeting and observe the group and the dynamics before making service commitments will help ensure that you make an informed decision. Research the organization, talk to the members, determine the sense of the group dynamics, and assess what you want to derive from the experience and how you can contribute to

---

BOX 27.3   Tangible Benefits from Organizational Involvement

- Substantial discounts on continuing education and professional journals
- Professional standards beyond the individual's workplace
- Resources and discounts for certification
- Quick access to staff experts
- News on legal, legislative, and educational issues
- Group insurance plans for professional liability, health care, and disability
- Travel services, such as auto rentals, hotel stays, and restaurant visits
- Discounted retail services
- A personal sense of advancing the organization's work

BOX 27.4   Skills Developed Through Organizational Involvement

- Conflict management
- Interpersonal communication
- Public speaking
- Mentoring
- Meeting management
- Agenda development
- Facilitation
- Delegation
- Consensus building
- Strategic thinking
- Team building
- Political advocacy
- Legislative work or lobbying
- Problem solving

---

the organization. Look at your strengths and talents to determine whether there is a need or a fit within the organization. Every organization has its struggles, but you can gain tremendous personal and professional benefits from your involvement. Examples of tangible benefits of professional association membership are in Box 27.3.

Reasons for Involvement

Nurses who define themselves as leaders and who want to have influence beyond their workplaces should join at least one professional association. Some reasons for joining organizations include feeling a sense of responsibility to the profession, contributing to the greater good of the profession, enhancing résumé and marketability, supporting particular legislative interests, and social networking. Organizations need all types of members, both active and passive participants, so that they can carry out their missions and conduct activities and business. Organizational involvement is a socialization process that can improve morale—being around others who take pride in and celebrate the nursing profession is contagious. Whatever your preferred level of involvement, you can contribute greatly to your profession by simply becoming a member of a professional association and progressing to active involvement guarantees a world of opportunities.

Some nurses choose to belong to their state nurses' association, whereas others are required to do so. Employment contracts in some states may require nurses to join a union and pay dues to receive pay for employment in those states. In some states, the nurses' associations are also collective bargaining organizations.

Personal and Professional Benefits

Networking and exposure to different opportunities within the nursing profession are two of the most valuable benefits of belonging to an organization. Some nurses may stop working for a time because of family or educational priorities. Organizational membership can help them stay connected to professional issues and colleagues through meetings and publications, smoothing the transition back into practice. In addition to networking, the professional organization can serve as a training ground through which nurses can build skills and gain wonderful leadership experiences. Examples of these skills are in Box 27.4. Furthermore, the Literature Perspective provides a view of a career-long perspective.

All nurses encounter ethical dilemmas and professional challenges. Membership in nursing organizations can provide a continuous source of professional colleagues to draw on for advice and support. Members of a nurses' professional association can be nonbiased, safe colleagues to ask for advice about your situation, especially when you may not want to discuss it with co-workers who could be directly involved. Members may be able to help you connect to the experts in the field.

CONTRIBUTING THROUGH SCHOLARLY ACTIVITIES AND RESEARCH

Nurses and others have contributed over many years to developing the art and science of nursing. Now may be your turn to contribute to improving care. Seek opportunities to learn about areas of particular interest and contribute to healthcare knowledge beyond your own daily assignment. Discuss your areas of interest in health topics with leaders in your workplace. Ask mentors

LITERATURE PERSPECTIVE

Resource: Bleich, M. (2016). Developing a leadership program trajectory. *The Journal of Continuing Education in Nursing, 47*(6), 250–252.

Nurses focus on specific areas of leadership skills development at different points in their careers. Recently graduated nurses in the process of onboarding in a new employment position may focus on their self-awareness as leaders at the point of direct care. Nurses at midcareer explore renewal to expand their leadership potential at the point of care and contribute to the design of care delivery. Nurses late in their careers contribute through role modeling and knowledge transfer for leadership succession.

Healthcare organizations often sponsor educational programs to promote developing future leaders. Programs offered to nursing staff may range from addressing high-stakes communication and improving healthcare safety to extending care delivery models. Administrators and clinical educators who use effective leadership succession planning link their programs into an intentional leadership trajectory and encourage staff at each career point to participate in development initiatives.

Implications for Practice

Nurses interviewing with a potential employer should ask about the leadership development opportunities in an organization. Nurses can prepare for future opportunities by actively seeking leadership development programs rather than waiting to be identified as candidates for available management positions.

---

about opportunities to join projects or committees working on areas important to you (New Careers in Nursing [NCIN], 2015).

For example, perhaps you notice that patient falls are increasing on your unit or that you are seeing more patients who have fallen at home, so you are interested in preventing falls. As a starting point, you could review information about falls prevention on health-related or government websites such as the Agency for Healthcare Research and Quality (AHRQ; *https://www.ahrq. gov/sites/default/files/publications/files/fallpxtoolkit.pdf*) or the Centers for Disease Control and Prevention (CDC, *https://www.cdc.gov/homeandrecreationalsafety/ falls/community_preventfalls.html*). You might join your organization's practice council or evidence-based intervention committee to collaborate on solutions. Your team might seek help from a health librarian to obtain the most pertinent research and other evidence and ask for support from a clinical nurse specialist or health researcher to appraise the evidence about falls and falls prevention. Experienced researchers and leaders can help the team access or collect baseline data for comparison over time and plan how to pilot test an intervention on your unit or in your organization. Those resource persons can also help the team manage the steps for administrative approval and facilitate the process to try out the intervention.

Whether or not you feel the project was successful, knowing what did or did not work helps build knowledge that others can use to move forward. Through professional presentations, your team can share the outcomes and lessons learned with other staff in the organization and to professionals beyond your organization. Through publication in a professional journal, your team can share the knowledge you have gained with professionals worldwide. It may sound daunting at first to think of yourself as a team member doing a presentation at a professional conference or submitting a manuscript for publication. The satisfaction of developing nursing knowledge to improve health begins with taking those first steps to get involved in the issues most important to you and your patients.

EXERCISE 27.3 Think about an experienced nurse who you consider as a role model. Would you want that person as a mentor? If so, how you would enlist that person's assistance in guiding your career?

CAREER MARKETING STRATEGIES

Crafting and Promoting Your Personal Brand

Whether you are an experienced nurse or in transition to a practice area for the first time, being strategic in the evolution and promotion of your personal brand is essential. A personal brand represents the perceptions of others when they see your image or hear your name (Machaz & Shokoofh, 2016). The goal of this section is to design a systematic strategy for documenting professional activities and marketing your personal brand throughout your career. The process begins with personal reflection and self-assessment to convey your identity and professional goals. The ensuing conversations help identify the unique characteristics that define your professional persona. Telling your authentic story sets you apart from other candidates by leveraging your passions, values, experiences, and unique strengths.

Beyond the résumé, curriculum vitae (CV), or digital portfolio, building relationships and networking through social media outlets can either enhance or harm your branding package during the job search process. Your "digital footprint," the evidence available about you through online searches, cannot contain unflattering information that would detract from your marketing goals. Use one or more search engines to discover associations to your name and review the information you find. Remove information that detracts from your professional message on social interaction sites that you can edit. For example, potential employers may interpret a photograph of you drinking what appears to be alcohol in a party setting as evidence of risky health behaviors. A national survey representing a sample of 2186 hiring managers and human resource professionals conducted by the Harris Poll reported that 60% of those surveyed use social media profiles to understand candidates' qualifications and assess their presence on social media. That figure reflects a 500% increase in use of social media profiles by employers over a 10-year period (Careerbuilder.com, 2016).

Data Collection

The reflective task of data collection is to develop a comprehensive view of your professional attributes for your résumé, CV, and portfolio. Together the three documents present the accomplishments that led to your current professional identity as a nurse. Notes of references, recognitions, copies of evaluations, and documents reflecting your successes are examples that help support the CV data. Although this information will take some time to develop and maintain, having it will be beneficial when you prepare for an evaluation, seek promotion, or apply for a new position.

You may have already started a digital portfolio that includes an infographic résumé or sampling of projects and evaluations presented in a visually attractive format (Lee & Cavanaugh, 2016). Some organizations provide electronic portfolios for your professional records so that you can readily access and convert the information into marketing documents as you need them. As an example, the National Student Nurses Association, the ANCC, and The Honor Society of Nursing (Sigma Theta Tau International) each provide access to such a digital

approach. The list in Table 27.1 identifies suggested documents to create or update a CV, résumé, or portfolio. If you do not have any documentation for a specific category, retain the heading as a reminder and think about what you would like to be able to list there in the future.

Depending on your unique background, the extent of data collection varies considerably. If you are new in the profession, analyze any electives, organizational positions, special assignments, or honors you received during school. If you are a second-career nurse, consider relating your previous paid or volunteer work to include relevant skills that demonstrate leadership, financial responsibility, political astuteness, or communication proficiency. If you have a long history as a nurse or a prior relevant career, start with your most recent employment and work backward. Your task may be more challenging because you have to actively think about what you did in the past and determine how to translate those experiences into relevance for nursing (Bolles, 2017).

Curriculum Vitae

A CV is an all-inclusive but superficial record of one's professional life. Typically it begins with your name prominently displayed and centered in bold face font, followed by the contact information in separate lines below. Include applicable contact information such as address with zip code, phone number (identify cell, work, and, if relevant, home), e-mail address, website address, and handles for Twitter, Facebook, or LinkedIn. Avoid casual or personal usernames to ensure you appear professional in your communication. Present information in the body of the CV using reverse chronologic order (most recent information first) with categories such as professional experience, academic and professional preparation, certifications, teaching responsibilities, research, publications, papers/presentations/posters, other creative works, honors, awards, grants, memberships in professional organizations and societies, service, and professional development.

Résumé

Résumés are brief customized documents with examples focused on the qualifications tailored to the position that you seek. A résumé helps the potential employer create an image of a candidate fitting in the organization. Unlike the CV, a résumé provides details. It is presented in sentences or phrases (not both) to share the value of the information. For example, rather than listing years of service in a position by title and organization, a résumé

TABLE 27.1	**Data Collection**
Topics	**Facts Needed**
1. Education	Name of school, address, phone numbers, website, years of attendance, date of graduation, name of degree(s) received, minor earned, honors received (e.g., Dean's List)
2. Professional Development	Dates attended, places, topics and any special outcomes, type and amount of credit earned (e.g., CEUs or contact hours)
3. Experience	Dates of employment, title of position, name of employing agency, location and phone numbers, website, name of chief executive officer, chief nursing officer, immediate supervisor, salary range, typical duties (role description)
4. Community/institutional service	Dates of service, name of committee/task force and the parent organization (e.g., name of hospital or professional organization), your role on the committee (e.g., chairperson, secretary, member), general description of committee's functions, any distinctive accomplishments
5. Publications	Articles: author(s) name(s), year of publication, title, journal, volume, issue, pages; books: author(s), year of publication, title, location, name of publisher, and doi or ISBN number
6. Honors	Date, description of award, special factors related to award (e.g., competitive, community-wide, national)
7. Research	Date, title of research, IRB # (or statement of exemption from consideration), role in research (e.g., principal investigator, coinvestigator, team member), funded/unfunded
8. Speeches/presentations/posters	Date, title of speech presented, place, name of sponsoring organization, nature of the presentation (e.g., keynote, concurrent session), title of presentation; note if refereed
9. Workshops/conferences presented	Date, title of workshop/conference presented, place, name of sponsoring group, nature of the presentation and brief description of the activity
10. Certification	Initial date of certification, expiration date, certifying body, area/type of certification
11. Teaching responsibilities	Date, course title, number of students, ratings if available. Include mentoring and precepting responsibilities.

might include information that you served as the only nurse to provide some distinctive service. For the experienced nurse, a résumé could be used to reflect increasing skills, certifications, and abilities; for the new nurse, it could focus on specific "extra" abilities or competencies that are not normally expected of a new graduate. The résumé is a better choice than a CV for advertising your skills and talents to a prospective employer. Details and action words help the reader view you as accomplishing important work. Verbs that relate to outcomes (produced, created, led) are more powerful in conveying your achievements than process words (participated, attended). Basically, résumés can be produced in two ways: conventional and functional. The *conventional* approach provides chronologic information about positions and activities. The *functional* approach combines multiple positions into role areas you want to highlight as an area of strength that matches a particular position option. Although a conventional résumé emphasizes experience as a heading, the functional résumé headings may relate to implementing evidence-based practice or client education and describe how you achieved results across several positions. A functional approach is best if you are planning a sharp departure from your present position or if you have considerable experience outside of nursing. Be sure to include lessons learned regarding critical thinking, teamwork, conflict management, and communication. Focus on your experience in diverse roles or positions rather than the specific positions held. As with the CV, your résumé should be current, error-free, grammatically correct, accurate, and logical. Documents should be printed on high-quality paper. Electronic résumés are sent as a .pdf file so that no distortion in the design or layout occurs; this is a universally accepted electronic format, so recipients should have no difficulty opening the attachment. Bringing a résumé to an interview is especially useful if you previously provided a CV. In fact, bringing copies of what you already submitted may help a prospective employer who may not have had ready access to your materials earlier.

EXERCISE 27.4 Identify 5 to 10 key search words that would help match employers' positions to your digital résumé.

Professional Letters

During your career, you will need to communicate effectively either through digital or printed correspondence. Every well-designed letter markets you as a professional. The commonly used letters include a cover letter, thank-you letter, and resignation letter. You may also write letters declining positions that you have been offered or recommending others for positions. Professional letters have a similar format, usually three paragraphs: the introduction, body, and conclusion. Just as the résumé and CV, letters should be error-free, grammatically correct, accurate, and logical. Use business formatting on a single page with classic typeface (e.g., Times New Roman), a 10- or 12-point font, and high-quality paper. If sending the letter digitally, create a .pdf file so that the layout will not be distorted. Match your name and contact information as presented on your résumé and CV. This is especially important for the cover letter because it accompanies another document. If any of these documents is sent by e-mail or uploaded to an online portal, you may still choose to follow up by mailing a printed copy. (See Table 27.2 for format and content of professional marketing letters.)

EXERCISE 27.5 Write a cover letter that highlights your personal brand that will persuade an employer to call for an interview.

The Interview

When your career marketing strategy is successful in attracting the interest of an employer, the next step is preparation for the interview (Table 27.3). Your research strategy for the organization includes looking up the website, reviewing press articles, or finding someone in the organization to speak with informally.

Interviewing is a two-way proposition; the interviewee should be gathering as much information as the interviewer. Both should be making judgments throughout the process so that if a position is offered, the interviewee will be prepared to accept, decline, or explore further. In business and healthcare settings, many prospective employers administer basic skills tests. You might ask what to anticipate and, if you have already completed such appraisals, bring the results with you. Applicants to some organizations are interviewed by a panel or participate in a series of interviews that allow fellow employees more say in the hiring process.

To feel more at ease, wear professional but comfortable clothing to the interview. Rehearse possible answers, questions to ask, and points to make so that you are prepared for the interview. Be ready to describe why you want the job; what you know about the company; and how your values, skills, and experience align with the position. Have examples ready that set you apart from the other candidates such as your ability to problem solve, team skills, or work habits. Lastly, research your value to the organization so that when you are given a salary offer you are ready to counteroffer, if necessary, and at the end of the interview ask for the job (Bolles, 2017).

Interview Topics and Questions

During interviews, employers should ask all applicants for a given position the same questions. In addition to providing comparable information as the basis for a decision, the applicant's expectation for equal treatment is upheld. Employers often use behavioral interviewing techniques and ask clinically focused questions to identify the most appropriate applicant for the vacant position. Most likely the first question will be "tell me a little about yourself." The answer should focus on your knowledge, skills, and abilities that make you the best fit for the job. If you have done your homework, you will know what the employer is looking for in your answer. Be prepared to cite how you have faced challenges and dilemmas, because those types of questions are likely to be asked. Rather than being asked, "What are your

TABLE 27.2 Professional Letters

Type of Letter	General Content
General Business Letter Format: Making a good impression	Date and inside address with the name and credentials of the addressee, the person's title, the name of the organization, street address, city, state, and zip code. The typical salutation (greeting) (e.g., "Dear Ms. Smith") is followed by a colon or comma. Between the greeting and the closing are paragraphs conveying the letter's main message. The end of the letter (closing) allows several line spaces between the word (e.g., *Sincerely*) and your printed name followed by your credentials. If your address and other contact information did not appear at the top of the letter, it should appear below your typed name. The space between the closing and your name should allow enough room for your signature. Proofread for layout, typographical errors, spelling, and content.
Cover Letter: The key to getting your curriculum vitae read and entry to the interview process	First paragraph is a brief description of your interest in a specific position and how you learned about it. Second paragraph emphasizes 2-3 unique experiences or strengths on the resume or CV supporting your "fit" to both the position and organization. Closing paragraph conveys enthusiasm about an interview and when you will follow up.
Thank You Letter: Creating a positive impression for present and future interactions	Expresses an appreciation for time and opportunity to interview. The first paragraph identifies what position you interviewed for and a key statement about your discussion to help the interviewer recall the interview. If multiple positions are available prioritize your choice. The middle paragraph reiterates a strength or experience pertinent to the job. You can add a topic you found interesting during the discussion or the reply to an unanswered question in the interview. If you indicated you would provide something to the interviewer, you should reference it here even if it is an attachment. The third paragraph references specific expectation about outcome and when you will follow up.
Resignation Letter: Closure and future reference	Request a meeting with your manager to communicate your resignation in person. A letter should follow your meeting outlining the discussion with manager to include: • Date and if it is negotiable with terms of employment. • Reason for resignation. • Outline of ongoing projects and plan to transfer duties. • Aspects of the employment experience that enhanced your career development. • Major contributions you made to the organization and those the organization helped you gain.

TABLE 27.3	**Interview Goals**
Preparation	Review the organization's mission, vision, and values statements before the interview (via the website or hard copy). Obtain statistics and facts.
	Have 3-5 questions rehearsed and ready to ask about the company or position.
	Recheck your résumé and curriculum vitae for emphasis and new information.
	Print additional copies to bring to the interview.
	Practice using "action" words as you describe your experience.
	Have a story ready that illustrates your brand.
	Plan your transportation, clothing, and accessories, including portfolio and pen.
Appearance	Arrive on time and alone.
	Wear comfortable clothing one step up from usual office attire. If jeans are the norm, wear dress slacks. If business casual is the norm, then wear a suit.
	Make a memorable entrance, make eye contact, shake hands, smile.
	Greet everyone you meet including the receptionist, security guard, or cleaning staff. Say, "Hello, I'm [name]."
	Position yourself with the interviewer so that you are not at "odds" or having to sit in an uncomfortable position to talk.
Personal characteristics	Describe the type of person you are, including personality traits. Be expected to cite examples of when these traits helped or hindered you in previous situations.
	Describe how your education and experience prepared you for this position.
	Describe your skills as a member and leader of a team.
	List situations that characterize your energy, initiative, drive, ambition, and enthusiasm and professional values.
	Accentuate the positive! Appear interested—project competence, confidence, and energy.
	Answer questions directly but know when not to or ask for clarification.
	Say only positive and honest things about your present employer.
The work itself	Discuss the primary position responsibilities.
	Ask about new program directions.
	Prepare to address hypothetical situations that display your problem solving, reasoning, self-confidence, knowledge, and critical thinking. (Creates opportunity to evaluate you in action and under some stress.)
	Ask to speak to current employees.
Organizational fit	Ask intelligent questions that suggest you have prepared for this interview.
	Be clear about what you believe to be distinctive about this organization and how it meets your expectations for a position. Ask hypothetical questions that allow you to learn how the people with whom you are speaking live out the values of the organization.
	Articulate your "fit" with the organization's philosophy, mission, and vision.
Professional opportunities	Keep in mind key points that summarize your experience and its value to the potential employer.
	Inquire about opportunities, educational support, and work-life balance.
	Be clear about what you expect to obtain from any position you consider including advancement opportunities.
	Secure a time frame for notification of an offer.
Follow up	Write a thank-you letter or e-mail message.
	Evaluate your performance: focus on your strengths and weaknesses during the interview and how to manage them in the future.

weaknesses?" you may be asked, "Tell me how you handled the last mistake you made" or "How did your educational program prepare you for critical care nursing?"

Only questions related to the position and its description are legitimate. Employers should not ask other questions (Table 27.4), and applicants should decline to

answer if asked such inappropriate questions (U.S. Equal Employment Opportunity Commission, 2018). If the interviewer asks an inappropriate question, the applicant can choose not to answer the direct question by addressing the content area. For example, if asked about your spouse's employment, you might say, "I believe what you are asking is how long I will be able to be in this position. Let me assure you that I intend to be here for at least 2 years."

Each of the content areas identified in Table 27.4 may be acceptable for an employer to ask, but the questions in column 1 are phrased inappropriately. The second column identifies approaches that are both appropriate and legal. The key to ensuring a fair interviewing process is being prepared, knowing what can be asked legitimately, and knowing how to respond to inappropriate questions.

If you are well prepared, you will know what the organization's stated beliefs are and whether they are compatible with yours. The challenge in an interview is to determine whether those stated beliefs are lived or are merely printed words. If numerous people in the organization can relate how the mission is translated into a specific role, the beliefs are likely lived ones.

TABLE 27.4   Inappropriate and Appropriate Interview Questions

Sample of Inappropriate Questions	Sample of Appropriate and Legal Questions
1. How old are you?	1. Do you know that this position requires someone at least 21 years old?
2. What does your husband (wife) do?	2. This position requires that no one in your immediate family be in the healthcare field or own interests or shares in any healthcare facility. Does this pose a problem?
3. Who takes care of your children?	3. Attendance is important. Are you able to meet this expectation?
4. Are you working "just to help out"?	4. What are your short-term and long-term goals?
5. Do you have any disabilities?	5. Is there anything that would prevent you from performing this work as described?
6. Where were you born?	6. This position requires US citizenship. May I assume you meet this criterion?
7. What are the names of all of the organizations to which you belong?	7. To which professional organizations do you belong?
8. What is your religious preference?	8. We subscribe to a specific religious philosophy and mission. Do you understand that all employees are expected to promote this philosophy and are you able to do so?

EXERCISE 27.6 Select a partner and role-play an interview for a professional nursing position. The potential employer (manager) should focus on competencies of the prospective employee. Include questions and scenarios about common conflicts and challenges seen in the clinical setting. The interviewee (prospective employee) should highlight competencies, decision-making abilities, and critical-thinking abilities when responding to the situation-based questions. Reflect on the process and discuss what learning you can apply to future interviews. You may consider the following questions:

1. Why did you choose to go into nursing? (motivation)
2. Give me an example of a time where you disagreed with a coworker. (conflict management)
3. What was the most useful criticism you ever received? (reflective practice)
4. Please give an example of a time when you had to address an angry client. What was the problem and what was the outcome? (customer service)
5. Everyone has made some poor decisions or has done something that just did not turn out right. Has this happened to you? What happened? What would you do differently in the future? (decision making)

CONCLUSION

A successful career requires strategies designed to lead systematically toward the desired goals. Finding a good fit in a position and a career is important for personal and professional satisfaction. Continued professional development through graduate education, continuing education, certification, service in professional associations, and scholarship is a crucial component of success as a nurse. Involvement in professional associations can open doors to opportunities and skill development. Documenting and representing qualifications through résumés, CVs, and professional letters support employment opportunities and career development.

THE SOLUTION

While I was still in nursing school, my curiosity led me to join the International Association of Forensic Nurses. The networking and connections I established there helped direct me toward my goal of certification. I had plenty of time to explore the expectations and plan ahead for the work and time commitment required.

I decided I would not take a job just to have a job. I was determined not to be distracted by offers that did not align with who I am or what I wanted to accomplish. I started by thinking about my passions, values, and goals. I wanted my career decisions to be meaningful and have a purposeful connection to my overall goals. My employment search led me to a nursing position that aligned with my career objective—working as a nurse in a hospital women's and children's department. The postpartum unit and neonatal intensive care unit provided me experience working with infants, women, and families. Later, when floating to the pediatric floors, I was able to expand my knowledge and experience with a variety of ages and practice numerous nursing skills. For me, this was the right path for learning about caring for different ages of children at varying levels of acuity.

In addition to my full-time hospital job, I started taking the coursework necessary for a career in forensic nursing. I approached a local organization about precepting opportunities. To develop my professional identity, gain leadership experience, and make connections to the greater nursing profession, I sought out colleagues and mentors to talk to about my progress and give me honest feedback. Now, I am almost ready to take my certification examination. I will continue to be a Resource Nurse on several different units in a pediatric hospital until I reach my dream as a pediatric and adult forensic nurse. I keep myself pretty busy between my two jobs, and I absolutely love what I do!

Would this be a suitable approach for you? Why?

Cynthia Flores

REFLECTIONS

Think about what you have done in the name of nursing so far in your life. Consider what the most dramatic example of caring was. What was the most devastating experience? What did you learn from each that helps you be better as a nurse, and maybe even as a person, today?

What are your career goals? What do you need to do to in the next 3 to 5 years to make progress toward those goals? Write a one-paragraph summary.

THE EVIDENCE

Career Builder: Fifty-nine percent of healthcare managers report using social networks to screen candidates. Personal online information that can hurt your chance of being offered employment includes provocative images or information, drinking and using drugs, negative communication about previous employers, and poor communication skills. Online information that managers suggested may support your chance of being hired includes information that supports your qualifications and a good fit with the company, shows a professional image, demonstrates a range of interests, and showcases good communication skills (Careerbuilder.com, 2016).

National Council of State Legislatures: Employers can access information about applicants through Internet or social media accounts that are open to the public.

In some states, laws prohibit employers from requiring applicants to provide passwords or access into the applicants' personal social media accounts (National Conference of State Legislatures, 2017).

Wheatcroft: Employers can be held responsible for negligent hiring. Employers who fail to review social media information on applicants can potentially be found at fault for carelessness if there are bad outcomes later (Wheatcroft, 2016).

TIPS FOR A SUCCESSFUL CAREER

- Find a mentor and be a mentor.
- Keep connected with people and meet new people.
- Learn from what you do each day: what to do differently, how to prevent errors, who to seek as a supporter. Reflect.
- Keep electronic versions of documents related to your accomplishments filed together in an electronic folder.
- Update your CV at least every 6 months so that you always have an accurate, current set of accomplishments and qualifications to share when a special opportunity appears.
- Focus on your strengths and build them into spectacular performances; hone the basics so that you are always prepared.

- Create an individual mission statement.
- Think about what you need to be employable in the face of health system changes.
- Research and create a file of educational programs of interest.
- Join two or more professional organizations: a broad professional group and a specialty.
- Read professional journals and at least one general health/nursing news journal.
- Attend at least one professional meeting each year to network with colleagues. When possible, travel outside of your geographic area.
- Volunteer in your profession and your community.

REFERENCES

American Association of Colleges of Nursing (AACN, n.d.). What every nursing student should know when seeking employment: An interview tip sheet for baccalaureate and higher degree prepared nurses. www.aacn.nche.edu/publications/hallmarks.pdf.

American Nurses Association. (2018). About ANA. https://www.nursingworld.org/ana/about-ana/.

American Nurses Association and National Nursing Staff Development Organization. (2010). *Nursing professional development: Scope and standards of practice.* Silver Spring, MD: Nursesbooks.org.

Bolles, R. N. (2017). *What color is your parachute? A practical manual for job-seekers and career-changers.* New York: Penguin Random House.

Careerbuilder.com. (2016). *Number of employers using social media to screen candidates has increased 500 percent over the last decade.* http://www.careerbuilder.com/share/aboutus/pressreleasesdetail.aspx?ed=12%2F31%2F2016&id=pr945&sd=4%2F28%2F2016.

Fitzgerald, J., Ea, E., & Bai, L. (2017). *301 careers in nursing.* New York: Springer.

Lindell, D., Hagler, D., & Poindexter, K. (2017). PhD or DNP? Defining the path to your career destination. *American Nurse Today, 12*(2), 36–38.

Lee, J. W., & Cavanaugh, T. (2016). Building your brand: The integration of infographic resume as student self-analysis tools and self-branding resources. *Journal of Hospitality, Leisure, Sport & Tourism Education, 18,* 61–68. ISSN 1473-8376. https://doi.org/10.1016/j.jhlste.2016.03.001

Machaz, H., & Shokoofh, K. (2016). Personal branding: An essential choice? *Journal of Multidisciplinary Research, 8* (2), 65–70.

McDonald, K., & Hite, L. (2015). *Career development: A human resource development perspective.* New York: Routledge, Taylor & Francis Group.

National Conference of State Legislatures. (2017). *Access to social media usernames and passwords. Available at* http://www.ncsl.org/research/telecommunications-and-information-technology/employer-access-to-social-media-passwords-2013.aspx.

New Careers in Nursing (NCIN). (2015). *NCIN Scholar Alumni Toolkit: Resources for Successful Transition to Professional Practice.* Washington, DC: Author. Available at *http://www.newcareersinnursing.org/resources/ncin-scholar-alumni-toolkit-resources-successful-transition-professional-practice.*

Philippou, J. (2015). Employers' and employees' views on responsibilities for career management in nursing: A cross-sectional survey. *Journal of Advanced Nursing, 71*(1), 78–89. https://doi.org/10.1111/jan.12473.

Smith, L. (2016). *No fears, no excuses: What you need to do to have a great career.* Boston: Houghton Mifflin Harcourt.

U.S. Equal Employment Opportunity Commission. (2018). Prohibited employment policies/practices. https://www.eeoc.gov/laws/practices/index.cfm.

Wheatcroft, J. (2016). Risks and rewards in the world of social media: Firms – and staff – must tackle the ultimate "double-edged sword." *Human Resource Management International Digest, 24*(5), 16–18. https://doi.org/10.1108/HRMID-04-2016-0056.

28

Developing the Role of Leader

Michael L. Evans

LEARNING OUTCOMES

- Analyze the role of leadership in creating a satisfying working environment for nurses.
- Evaluate transactional and transformational leadership techniques for effectiveness and potential for positive outcomes.
- Value the leadership challenges in dealing with generational differences.
- Compare and contrast leadership and management roles and responsibilities.

- Describe leadership development strategies and how they can promote leadership skills acquisition.
- Analyze leadership opportunities and responsibilities in a variety of venues.
- Explore strategies for making the leadership opportunity positive for both the leader and the followers.

KEY TERMS

leadership
management

mentor
transactional leadership

transformational leadership

THE CHALLENGE

Leadership is occasionally about the heroic moment. More often, it is about the day-to-day efforts to keep your team headed generally the same way, guiding them and making sure they have what they need to do their best work. As a leader, I have found that one of the most important things I can do is to make sure that all members of the team know where we are headed by having a common definition of the terms we are using.

Why would we worry about a common definition for the terms we use? They are all in English, aren't they? They are common and easily understood, aren't they? Maybe yes, but then, maybe no …

The first time I became aware that standard definitions could be a problem was when I was president of a state nurses association. As our board of directors was reviewing the previous board's strategic plan, we saw that one of the main goals was to increase the diversity of our membership. Our board noted that we had failed this one miserably; our members were no more ethnically or racially diverse than they had been before the creation of this goal. We talked about steps we might take to try to achieve this goal, never considering what the word "diversity" meant. Everyone knows, we thought, that diversity is ethnic and racial. No question.

(Continued)

It was more than a year later, when we were still unable to achieve that goal, that we finally talked to some people who had helped write it in the first place. Much to our surprise, their definition of diversity was not based on race or ethnicity. It was based on education and practice setting! The state nurses association membership was primarily made up of direct care nurses, and the former board's goal was to add educators, managers, and others to the demographics of the membership. Without knowing the definition of diversity, our board was unable to create strategies that could help us achieve that goal. We failed before we started.

This experience was put to even greater use a couple of years later. The hospital where I worked had a newly formed patient care delivery committee made up of direct care nurses, managers, and directors, plus human resources representatives. The Vice President of Nursing and I, as a direct care nurse, were cochairs of the committee. Practice changes were to come to our committee for deliberation before implementation. This was shared decision making at a higher level than we had tried before, and making it work was going to take a lot of growing pains.

At one meeting, a discussion about a proposed change turned into a disagreement, then an argument. The meeting ended abruptly, with no solution available. As cochairs, we decided to stop meeting for a while. We needed a "cooling-off" period. This had been a really big disagreement!
What would you do if you were this nurse?

Katheren Koehn, MA, RN
Executive Director, Minnesota Organization of Registered Nurses, Minneapolis, MN

INTRODUCTION

Leadership is a complex, highly important, and challenging skill expected of all nurses. *Leader* refers to performance, not a formal position. We lead when we intervene with courage for a patient. We lead when we organize a group of colleagues to address an organizational problem. We lead when we are formally placed in charge of a project or when we are promoted to a specific management position.

WHAT IS A LEADER?

A leader is an individual who works with others to develop a clear vision of the preferred future and to make that vision happen. According to Grossman and Valiga (2017, p.18), "leadership is not necessarily tied to a position of authority." Leadership is a very important concept in life. Great leaders have been responsible for helping society move forward and for articulating and accomplishing one vision after another throughout time. Dr. Martin Luther King, Jr., called his vision a *dream*, and it was developed because of the input and lived experiences of countless others. Mother Teresa called her vision a *calling*, and it was developed because of the suffering of others. Steven Spielberg calls his vision a *finished motion picture*, and it is developed with the collaboration and inspiration of many other people. Florence Nightingale called her vision *nursing*, and it was developed because people were experiencing a void that was a barrier to their ability to regain or establish health.

Leaders have followers. An individual can have an impressive title, but that title does not make that person a leader. No matter what the person with that title does, he or she can never be successful without having the ability to inspire others to follow. The leader must be able to inspire the commitment of followers.

Leaders are proactive in formulating goals for action, and their efforts are aimed at creating a better world (Grossman & Valiga, 2017). Leaders are involved with formulating and shaping ideas instead of "merely responding to the ideas of others" (p. 19).

Covey (1992), in his classic work, identified eight characteristics of effective leaders (Box 28.1). Effective leaders are continually engaging themselves in lifelong learning. They are service-oriented and concerned with the common good. They radiate positive energy. For people to be inspired and motivated, they must have a positive leader. Effective leaders believe in other people.

BOX 28.1 Covey's Eight Characteristics of Effective Leaders

1. Engage in lifelong learning
2. Are service-oriented
3. Are concerned with the common good
4. Radiate positive energy
5. Believe in other people
6. Lead balanced lives and see life as an adventure
7. Are synergistic; that is, they see things as greater than the sum of the parts
8. Engage themselves in self-renewal

They lead balanced lives and see life as an adventure. Effective leaders are synergistic; that is, they see things as greater than the sum of the parts and they engage themselves in self-renewal.

> **EXERCISE 28.1** List Covey's eight characteristics of effective leaders on the left side of a piece of paper or a word processing document. Next to each characteristic, list any examples of your activities or attributes that reflect the characteristic. Some areas may be blank; others may be full. Think about what this means for you personally.

Healthcare organizations are complex. In fact, health care is complex. Continual learning is essential to stay abreast of new knowledge, to keep the organization moving forward, and to continue delivering the best possible care. An emphasis must be on organizations becoming learning organizations (a concept put forth by Peter Senge in 2006), to provide opportunities and incentives for individuals and groups of individuals to learn continuously over time. A learning organization is one that is continually expanding its capacity to create its future (Senge, 2006). Leaders are responsible for building organizations in which people continually expand their ability to understand complexity and to clarify and improve a shared vision of the future—"that is, they are responsible for learning" (Senge, 2006, p. 340).

The roles of manager and leader are often considered interchangeable, but they are actually quite different. The manager may also be a leader, but the manager is not required to have leadership skills within the context of moving a group of people toward a vision. The term *manager* is a designated leadership position. *Leadership* is an abilities role, and it is most effective if the manager is also a leader. Management can be taught and learned using traditional teaching techniques. Leadership can also be taught, but it is usually a reflection of rich personal experiences. "Although it is desirable for managers to be good leaders, there are leaders who are not managers and, more frequently, managers who are not leaders!" (Wilcox, 2018, p. 205).

Management and leadership are both important in the healthcare environment. Leaders are developed over time and through experience. Thus we must value, support, and provide our leaders with the one thing vital for good leadership—good followership. Leadership is a social process involving leaders and followers interacting. Followers need three qualities from their leaders:

direction, trust, and hope (Bennis, 2009). Trust is reciprocal. Leaders who trust their followers are, in turn, trusted by them. Leaders have learned to be effective leaders from their experience of being effective followers. Followers learn the skills involved in leadership from the follower vantage point. Effective leaders support and nurture their followers in part because they are creating the next generation of leaders.

The manager is concerned with doing things correctly in the present. The role of manager is very important in work organizations, because managers ensure that operations run smoothly and that well-developed formulas are applied to staffing situations, economic decisions, and other daily operations. The manager is not as concerned with developing creative solutions to problems as with using known strategies to address today's issues. A well-managed entity may be proceeding correctly but, without leadership, may be proceeding in the wrong direction (Covey, 1992).

Leadership as an Important Concept for Nurses

Nurses must have leadership to move forward in harmony with changes in society and in health care. Within work organizations, certain nurses are designated as managers. These individuals are important to ensuring that care is delivered in a safe, efficient manner. Nurse leaders are also vital in the workplace to elicit input from others and to formulate a vision for the preferred future.

Moreover, leadership is key for nursing as a profession. "Nurses are increasingly expected to assume the roles of advocate, teacher, caregiver, disseminator of knowledge, manager, contributor to public health policy development, and leader" (Grossman & Valiga, 2017, p. 116). The public depends on nurses to advocate for the public's needs and interests. Nurses must step forward into leadership roles in their workplace, in their professional associations, and in legislative and policy-making arenas. Nurses depend on their leaders to set goals for the future and the pace for achieving them. The public depends on nurse leaders to move the consumer advocacy agenda forward.

Leadership as a Primary Determinant of Workplace Satisfaction

Nurse satisfaction within the workplace is an important construct in nursing administration and healthcare administration. Turnover is extremely costly to any work organization in terms of money, expertise, and knowledge, as well as care quality. Thus being mindful of nurse satisfaction is both an economic and a professional concern.

Followers expect their leaders to provide them with:

- Respect
- A future-focused direction
- Control of the decisions that affect them
- Rewards and recognition
- Balance of life and work
- Professional development guidance

The effective leader in healthcare settings needs to be aware of these important facets of work life that influence followers. The leader should also work with followers to find a way to actualize these important aspects of work life.

A study by Laschinger and Fida (2015) found that leaders identified as authentic leaders created empowering professional practice environments that produce high-quality care and job satisfaction. Authentic leadership was defined as "a positive relational leadership style whereby leaders behave in an authentic manner with their followers and focus on furthering their development" (p. 277). Authentic leadership can be exhibited in any role, including those that are expanding.

An example of an expanding role is that of the clinical nurse leader (CNL). Nurses involved in policy, nurse executives, and education leaders worked together to create the curriculum and end-of-program competencies for CNL education (Bender, 2016). This is a formal role, and CNL graduate educational programs create nurses to fill these positions. The end competencies included an understanding of microsystem dynamics and the need for clinical leadership, interdisciplinary collaboration, teamwork, and process improvement. "There is a growing body of evidence showing improved care environment and patient safety and quality outcomes after redesigning care delivery microsystems to integrate CNL practice" (p. 33).

> **EXERCISE 28.2** Follower behavior nurtures and supports—or deteriorates—leader behavior. Identify the behavior you exhibited during your most recent clinical experience. What was supportive? What did not support the leader?

THE PRACTICE OF LEADERSHIP

Leadership Approaches

How one approaches leadership depends on experience and expectations. Many leadership theories and styles have been described. Two of the most popular theory-based approaches are transactional leadership and transformational leadership. (See the Theory Box.)

Transactional Leadership

A transactional leader is the historical "boss" image. In a transactional leadership environment, employees understand that a superior makes the decisions with little or no input from subordinates. Transactional leadership relies on the power of organizational position and formal authority to reward and punish performance. Followers are fairly secure about what will happen next and how to "play the game" to get where they want to be. A transactional leader uses a *quid pro quo* style to accomplish work (e.g., I'll do *x* in exchange for your doing *y*). Transactional leaders reward employees for high performance and penalize them for poor performance. The leader motivates the self-interest of the employee by offering external rewards that generate conformity with expectations. "The focus of this type of leadership system is the accomplishment of a task, and it is the type often seen in health-care organizations. Some even argue that nurses too often focus on tasks and rewards" (Grossman & Valiga, 2017, p. 110).

Transformational Leadership

Transformational leadership is based on an inspiring vision that changes the framework of the organization for employees. Employees are encouraged to transcend their own self-interest. This style of leadership involves communication that connects with employees' ideals in a way that causes emotional engagement. The transformational leader can motivate employees by articulation of an inspirational vision; by encouragement of novel, innovative thinking; and by individualized consideration of each employee, thus accounting for individual needs and abilities. Bringing people together around an inspiring vision and yet valuing individuals as distinct beings suggests a finely tuned, mindful approach to the role of leader.

Covey (1992) states, "The goal of transformational leadership is to transform people and organizations in a literal sense, to change them in mind and heart; enlarge vision, insight, and understanding; clarify purposes; make behavior congruent with beliefs, principles, or values; and bring about changes that are permanent, self-perpetuating, and momentum-building" (p. 287).

Kouzes and Posner (2012), in their widely-used book, identify five key practices in transformational leadership, as follows:

THEORY BOX

A Comparison of Outcomes in Transactional and Transformational Leadership

Transactional Leadership	Transformational Leadership
Leader Behaviors	**Leader Behaviors**
• Contingent reward *(quid pro quo)*	• Charismatic
• Punitive	• Inspirational and motivational
• Management by exception (active)—monitors performance and takes action to correct	• Intellectually stimulating
• Management by exception (passive)—intervenes only when problems exist	• Individualized consideration
Effect on Follower	**Effect on Follower**
• Fulfills the contract or gets punished	• A shared vision
• Does the work and gets paid	• Increased self-worth
• Corrects errors in a reactive manner	• Challenging and meaningful work
	• Coaching and mentoring happens
	• A sense of being valued
Organizational Outcomes	**Organizational Outcomes**
• Work is supervised and completed according to the rules.	• Increased loyalty
• Deadlines are met.	• Increased commitment
• Limited job satisfaction is evident.	• Increased job satisfaction
• Low to stable levels of commitment are typical.	• Increased morale
	• Increased performance

Modified from McGuire, E., & Kennerly, S. M. (2006). Nurse managers as transformational and transactional leaders. *Nursing Economics, 24*(4), 179–185.

1. Challenging the process, which involves questioning the way things have been done in the past and thinking creatively about new solutions to old problems
2. Inspiring shared vision or bringing everyone together to move toward a goal that all accept as desirable and achievable
3. Enabling others to act, which includes empowering people to believe that their extra effort will have rewards and will make a difference
4. Modeling the way, meaning that the leader must take an active role in the work of change
5. Encouraging the heart by giving attention to those personal things that are important to people, such as saying "thank you" for a job well done and offering praise after a long day

A transformative leader style seems particularly suited to the nursing environment. For example, the Magnet Recognition Program® places great emphasis on this type of leadership to move an organization to high levels of quality. A transformative leader creates a vision of what quality could look like and then provides specific actions that create a sense of community, which supports satisfaction, retention, communication, and interprofessional work. This type of leader listens to the views of others, finds ways to remove barriers, and serves as an advocate for those who care for patients.

Transformational leaders have a vision and are motivated to lead others to follow that vision and make it a reality and "they communicate their values and beliefs to others so that they can achieve a common meaning in their work and realize the vision toward which all are striving" (Grossman & Valiga, 2017, p. 111). Transformational leadership is an effective type of leadership for nurses to lead the changes to meet the needs in the current, complex delivery system (Walters, 2017). "Transformational leaders transform organizations" (p. 49).

Transformational leadership is hard work. Investment of time and energy is required to bring out the best in people. And a leader does not have to be good at everything. A good leader seeks to create a whole from the various members of a team. Transformational leadership is not unique to nursing, as the Research Perspective illustrates.

RESEARCH PERSPECTIVE

Resource: Bulmer, J. (2013). Leadership aspirations of registered nurses: Who wants to follow us? *Journal of Nursing Administration, 43*(3), 130–134.

This descriptive, correlational study measures relationships among perceived support, career stage, educational preparation, and leadership aspiration in registered nurses. The predictors of leadership aspiration were years of experience, educational preparation, and perceived available support.

Overall, fewer than 12.5% of registered nurses aspire to leadership roles. Those newly entering nursing have higher percentages of interest, but the interest wanes over time as nurses become disillusioned with those whom they see as ineffective in leadership roles and with the obstacles they face. Nurses with higher degrees tend to have higher interest in leadership roles. Nurses who perceive that they have support from colleagues, from direct supervisors, and from nonworkplace individuals are more likely to be interested in such formal leadership roles.

Implications for Practice

The estimate is that 75% of current formal nurse leaders plan to leave the workforce by 2020. Therefore more attention must be given to the identification and development of nurse leaders for the future. Because early career nurses and those with higher education are the ones most interested in progressing to formal leadership positions, they should not be overlooked. Past practices of targeting nurses with several years of experience for development should be questioned.

More nurses are graduating from second degree accelerated BSN programs, and many of those already have a wealth of experience outside of health care. Those nurses who are interested in a leadership role should be carefully assessed and formally developed early in their careers while the interest is still high. Nurses who have achieved higher levels of education should also be actively assessed for possible leadership development. Support from the nurse's nurse manager and from having a career coach external to the direct work environment are also correlated with inspiring interest in a formal leadership role.

Because baccalaureate and higher degree programs are expected to provide exposure to content dealing with leadership, these individuals may be ready for career advancement earlier in their careers than has been the case in the past. Actively identifying and developing registered nurses for formal leadership roles is essential in all workplace organizations.

Barriers to Leadership

Leadership demands a commitment of effort and time. Many barriers exist to both leading and following. Good leadership and good followership go hand in hand, and both strengthen the mission of the organization.

False Assumptions

Some people have false assumptions about leaders and leadership. For example, some believe that position and title are equivalent to leadership. Having the title of Chief Executive Officer or Chief Nursing Officer does not guarantee that a person will be a good leader. Consequently, a good executive is not necessarily a good leader. Furthermore, assuming a management or administrative role does not automatically confer the title of leader on an individual. Inspired and forward-moving organizations often select these executives specifically because of their ability to forge a vision and lead others toward it. Leadership is an earned honor and an action-oriented responsibility.

Others believe that workers who do not hold official management positions cannot be leaders. Some nursing units are managed by the nurse manager but led by the unit clerk. Leaders are those who do the best job of sharing their vision of where the followers want to be and how to get there. Many new nurse managers make the mistake of assuming that along with their new job comes the mantle of leadership. Leadership is an earned right and privilege.

Time Constraints

Leadership requires a time commitment; it does not just happen. The leader must fully comprehend the situation at hand, investigate and research options for action, assume the responsibility to communicate the vision to others, and continually reevaluate the organization or the team to ensure that the vision remains relevant and attainable. All of these activities take time. The 21st century has been described as the period of doing more with less. Everyone is busy. Finding time to lead is therefore a barrier for many who have inspirational ideas but lack time to develop the skills needed to lead effectively.

EXERCISE 28.3 Define a clinical or management issue that sparks your passion. Assume you have 6 weeks to make a difference. Create a plan identifying your leadership tasks, the support required from others, and the time frame to move the issue toward resolution. Think about what your message is and how and when you will deliver it. Think about what you would do if no one were responsive to your issue. Think about why the issue may be important for you but not for others.

LEADERSHIP DEVELOPMENT

Leadership effectiveness depends on mastering the art of persuasion and communication. Success depends on persuading followers to accept a vision by using convincing communication techniques and making it possible for the followers to achieve the shared goals. Several important leadership tasks, when used effectively, will help ensure success (Box 28.2). These are discussed in the following sections.

Select a Mentor

A mentor is someone who models behavior, offers advice and criticism, and coaches the novice to develop a personal leadership style. A mentor is a confidante and coach, as well as a cheerleader and teacher. In other words, a mentor is knowledgeable and skilled. Where do you find a mentor? Usually, a mentor is someone who has experience and some success in the leadership realm of interest, such as in a clinical setting or in an organization. A respected faculty member; a nurse manager, director, or clinician; or an organizational officer or active member may be a mentor. Mentorship is a two-way street. The mentor must agree to work with the novice leader and must have some interest in the novice's future development. A mentor can be close enough geographically to allow both observation and practice of leadership behaviors, as well as timely feedback. A mentor may also be geographically remote and yet well connected to the mentee. A mentor should provide advice, feedback, and role modeling. In addition, the mentor has a right to expect assistance with projects, respect, loyalty, and confidentiality. In a mentoring relationship, aspiring leaders soak up knowledge and experience and should expect to return it by serving as a mentor to a young, aspiring leader in the future.

Lead by Example

An effective leader knows that the most effective and visible way to influence people is to lead by example. Desired behavior can be modeled. For example, if an organization has a vision of becoming a political player in the state or community, the leader should be seen engaging in political activities. If the goal is to have improved relationships among followers, the leader must exhibit respect and patience with followers. A key skill to develop is the ability to understand that the leader serves the followers. The effective leader does not send members to do a job but rather leads them toward a mutual goal as a team (Fig. 28.1).

BOX 28.2 Leadership Development Tasks

1. Select a mentor.
2. Lead by example.
3. Accept responsibility.
4. Share the rewards.
5. Have a clear vision.
6. Be willing to grow.

Fig. 28.1 Leading by example helps developing leaders see the mission in action. (Copyright © 2014 Photos.com, a division of Getty Images. All rights reserved.)

Accept Responsibility

Even when the outcome is below expectations, the leader is ultimately responsible for the organization or activity. Effective leaders sometimes react in strange ways when negative outcomes occur. Sometimes these leaders seek to blame others or to make excuses for undesirable or unintended outcomes. Some refuse to accept any responsibility at all. In accepting responsibility, the leader needs to know that there is reward in victory and growth in failure. No one plans to fail, but an effective leader sees failures as opportunities to learn and grow so that previous failures are never repeated. This is called *experience.*

Share the Rewards

An effective leader is as eager to share the glory as to receive it. The more that respect and trust are shared with others, the more they are returned to the leader. Followers who believe their major task is to make the leader look good will soon tire of the task. Empowerment, the act of sharing power with others, is a dynamic process. In essence, sharing power has a synergistic effect that increases power overall. Followers who think the leader is working to make them look good will follow eagerly. Followers form a network and a support base for the leader.

Have a Clear Vision

Leaders see beyond where they are and see where they are going. Strong leaders are proactive and futuristic. The effective leader knows why the journey is necessary and takes the time and energy to inspire others to go along. The ability to communicate and promote the vision is a vital part of achieving it. Effective leaders share their vision and empower followers to come along to achieve it. They also share their leadership skills and successes toward achievement of a goal.

Be Willing to Grow

Thinking that growth for the person or organization is automatic is a misconception. Complacency leads to stagnation. Leaders must continually read about new ideas and approaches, experiment with new concepts, capitalize on a changing world, and seek or create continuing education opportunities to enhance their abilities to lead. Growth takes risk, planning, investment, and work. Setting goals that complement the vision will help the aspiring leader know where to invest time and energy to grow into the desired role.

Leadership development is a lifetime endeavor. Effective leaders are constantly striving to improve their leadership skills. The good news is that leadership skills can be learned and improved. A commitment to improvement strengthens the leader's ability to lead effectively and raises the bar for followers to achieve. As organizations and health care change, the leader is better able to work effectively with an increasingly diverse workforce. The best leaders bring out the best in their followers, as seen in the Literature Perspective.

LEADERSHIP DEVELOPMENT MODEL

The classic novice-to-expert conceptual framework developed by Benner (2001) can serve as a guide for leadership development. The model includes five levels of skill proficiency: novice, advanced beginner, competent, proficient, and expert. This framework is based on skill acquisition, and leadership is a set of skills that can be developed to move along the continuum from novice to expert. The model has been used in many contexts in nursing and has proven to be applicable to different leadership activities, even establishing a collaborative student leadership conference (Ward, Laframboise, & Cosimano, 2016)

Movement from novice to expert in leadership development is a process of leadership skill acquisition over time. The Benner model is appropriate and applicable to leadership development for nurses as they move through the phases of leadership effectiveness.

SURVIVING AND THRIVING AS A LEADER

The keys to leadership are to believe in the vision and to enjoy the journey. The leader has a responsibility to self and to followers to stay healthy and enthusiastic for the mission of the group. Surviving and thriving as a leader are based on the rules in Box 28.3. Each element is discussed in the following sections.

BOX 28.3   The Five Rules of Leaders

1. Maintain balance.
2. Generate self-motivation.
3. Build self-confidence.
4. Listen to constituents.
5. Maintain a positive attitude.

LITERATURE PERSPECTIVE

Resource: Covey, S. M. R. (2012). *Smart trust.* New York: Free Press.

The role of leader includes building trust between the leader and followers and between followers and leaders.

Stephen M. R. Covey, the son of the late Stephen Covey, describes a method for instilling trust in organizations. He describes the dilemma of not knowing whom to trust in an untrusting world. We are born to be very trusting, but as we get older, and after learning many life lessons about trust, we grow less willing to trust.

Smart trust is all about judgment. It enables us to have high trust in a low-trust world. It is how to trust in a low-trust world. It combines the human propensity to want to trust with analysis.

Analysis in smart trust involves assessment of three very important variables:

1. The opportunity or the situation and what you are trusting someone with.
2. Risk or the level of risk involved in the situation.
3. Credibility or the character and competence of the people who are involved.

In the absence of analysis, low propensity to trust produces no trust or indecision, and high propensity to trust produces blind trust or gullibility. In the absence of propensity to trust, low analysis produces distrust or suspicion, and high analysis produces smart trust or judgment. So, Covey posits that application of both propensity to trust and analysis will produce the most positive leadership results.

Smart trust is based on five smart trust actions for leaders to master:

1. Choose to believe in trust. Leaders must create the foundational paradigm out of which all the other trust-building behaviors follow.
2. Start with self. Leaders must focus first on developing character and competence, which is their credibility. This enables leaders to trust themselves and to also give others someone or something in which they can trust.
3. Leaders declare their intent and assume positive intent in others. They signal the goals and intended actions in advance and assume that others also have good intent and want to be trustworthy.
4. Leaders then do what they say they are going to do. They follow through in carrying out the declared intent.
5. They lead out in extending trust to others. These leaders are the first to extend trust to others, which initiates the cycle of mutual trust.

Covey describes the outcome of high levels of mutual trust between leaders and followers. He calls it a *performance multiplier* that can translate directly into greatly improved outcomes, both interpersonally and for productivity of leadership interactions.

Implications for Practice

People notice differences in various workplaces, and they tend to choose the workplace where there is a high level of trust demonstrated between leaders and followers. The culture of the workplace reflects the effectiveness of the leader's ability to create, nurture, and develop relationships based on trust.

The Leader Must Maintain Balance

Time management is essential for an effective leader. Many new leaders, in their zeal to be accessible to their constituents, lose control of their lives. A good strategy for retaining or regaining control is to get control of communication. Good leaders use the simplest and fastest method of communication that makes them accessible but does not tie them down. The keys to success are setting priorities and keeping in control. Effective leaders also maintain work-life balance in their own lives as well as provide time for balance for followers.

The Leader Must Generate Self-Motivation

Leaders who expect their followers to provide them with motivation, to be grateful for the time spent on followers' needs, and to offer frequent and lavish praise are in for a painful awakening. Followers in organizations, work situations, and elected constituencies feel they have

earned the right to criticize the leader by being followers. Followers will have an opinion about everything. Sometimes the comments are favorable, and sometimes they are not. The reason that self-motivation is so essential is because the leader can expect very little external motivation. Most leaders are risk takers and self-starters who are enthused by and believe in the vision they have created. Enthusiasm leads to an energized base, which is a hallmark of a vibrant, healthy organization.

The Leader Must Work to Build Self-Confidence

An effective leader must have self-confidence. This confidence comes from an acceptance of self, despite imperfections. Self-confidence is a self-perpetuating virtue. Effective leaders perform an honest self-appraisal on a regular basis and work to feel good about the job they are doing. A leader who is surrounded by people who enhance the leader's own characteristics makes a formidable leader and strengthens self-confidence in the ability to lead.

The more confident a leader feels, the more likely that success will follow. Success builds self-confidence. Two important factors are related to developing self-confidence. One is avoiding the tendency to become arrogant. The other is maintaining self-confidence despite setbacks.

The Leader Must Listen to His or Her Followers

Followers always have something to say. Leaders must listen to their constituents and determine whether action is indicated. Active listening, which in the US culture includes looking the person in the eye and offering questioning probes, shows an interest in what a person is saying. However, listening does not obligate the leader to any course of action. Clear boundaries must be communicated. A smart leader listens to all sides and makes decisions based on the vision and direction that is best for the group.

The Leader Must Have a Positive Attitude

Positive attitude is vital to leadership success. No one wants to follow a pessimist anywhere. People expect the leader to have the answers, to know where the organization is going, and to take the initiative to get the group to its goal. A positive attitude can be a great ally in sharing and maintaining the vision. Attitude is a choice, not a foregone conclusion. The effective leader uses positive thinking and positive messages to create an environment in which followers believe in the organization, the leader, and themselves. The problems and challenges in health care demand that nurses seek and fill leadership positions in a positive and future-oriented manner.

> **EXERCISE 28.4** Using the five rules for leaders, create a personal description of how you currently maintain balance, generate self-motivation, build self-confidence, listen to constituents, and maintain a positive attitude. Consider what additional strategies could be helpful.

THE NURSE AS LEADER

Nurses in numerous positions and various organizations serve as leaders. Because every nurse has the opportunity to serve as a leader, every nurse can exercise the right to lead.

Leadership Within the Workplace
Nurse Executive as Leader

Leader is a term often used interchangeably with the term *nurse executive*. Although that statement is true, it is also limiting, because many others in any organization can be and are seen as leaders. A primary goal of the nurse executive is leadership within the workplace. The nurse executive has an outstanding opportunity to shape the future of professional practice within a working environment by creating opportunities for direct care nurses and managers to have optimal input into organizational decision making related to the future. The nurse executive thus helps create a shared vision of the preferred future.

The concept of empowerment is important to the role of leadership for the nurse executive in a work organization. Empowerment theory suggests that power must be given away or shared with others in the organization. Direct care nurses may be encouraged to have input into decisions, or they may be given considerable information about how decisions are made. The ability to make or influence changes in the organization is a powerful tool. Nurses must believe that their input and ideas are considered when change occurs. Having input in decisions, having some control over the environment, and receiving feedback about actions taken or not taken all contribute to a feeling of being empowered to have control over one's practice and one's life.

The importance of managers and executives being leaders rather than managers is a recurring theme in the nursing literature. The fact is that both management and leadership skills in the nurse executive are essential. The ability to balance the day-to-day operating knowledge with the ability to lead a nursing service organization into the future is a winning combination.

Nurse Manager as Leader

Management and leadership, although different constructs, can be a strong combination for success. The nurse in the role of manager ensures that the day-to-day elements of the workplace are done correctly. Just as the effective manager pays attention to employee selection, hiring, orientation, continuing employee development, and financial accountability, in the role of leader, the manager raises the level of expectations and helps employees reach their highest level of potential excellence. A primary role of the leader is to inspire. The nurse manager may be seen as the embodiment of leadership in nursing. That person is the "face of leadership" to those in direct care.

Developing with direct care nurses a shared vision of the preferred future is a goal of the nurse manager in the role of leader. Everyone tends to resist change that is thrust upon them. When nurses are active participants in change from its inception, they are far more likely to be invested in outcomes.

An essential element of success for the nurse manager as a leader is the inclusion of direct care nurses in decision making. This contribution can enhance their organizational commitment and create a sense of pride in successful outcomes. The nurse manager inspires staff by involving them in changing the workplace to make it more satisfying. In so doing, the nurse manager also develops personal leadership skills.

A study by Burke, Flanagan, Ditomassi, and Hickey (2017) found that the characteristics of nurse managers most correlated with registered nurse (RN) satisfaction are empowerment, visibility, and role modeling. These characteristics were chosen by groups of nurse managers as well as by groups of RNs. "These findings are significant in that they show a strong correlation between groups. This is different from other studies that have described differing perceptions of staff and leaders" (p. 223).

Another study found a correlation between a nurse manager's emotional intelligence and transformational leadership. That is, a nurse manager with demonstrated emotional intelligence has a predisposition of being a transformational leader. Because the role of nurse manager is so vital, the authors recommended that nurse executives be aware of emotional intelligence before hiring or promoting a nurse to that role (Spano-Szekely, Griffin, Clavelle, & Fitzpatrick, 2016).

Direct Care Nurse as Leader

Workplace leaders create an environment in which others can experience satisfaction and have ideas for increasing the level of workplace satisfaction for nurses on the team. Leaders are those who creatively pose solutions to problems and capitalize on opportunities in the workplace. Furthermore, they support others, who offer numerous ideas about various issues, including patient safety. Nurses who believe that they have good ideas for future improvements should volunteer for opportunities to lead. These opportunities might include practice councils, clinical unit standards committees, or legislative committees to pose new solutions.

They also might include opportunities to be a group spokesperson or team advocate. If the hospital or other workplace has no formalized mechanism for nurse input into organizational decision making, nurses find informal avenues for influence. Those strategies might include asking thought-provoking questions, filing official complaints, creating unit campaigns, or holding informal discussions.

Developing leadership skills for direct care nurses can happen in several ways. Some of these may be employment opportunities (e.g., practice councils), others may be professional opportunities (e.g., a local professional association), and still others may be clinically focused opportunities (e.g., the heart association). Leadership can be developed, and direct care nurse leaders can help establish workplaces that are satisfying and rewarding. Magnet® facilities, for example, depend on direct care nurse leadership to create the intensity of quality work.

Novice leadership skills that contribute to future leadership success involve learning how to work in groups, deal with difficult people, manage conflict, reach consensus on an action, and evaluate actions and outcomes objectively (Fig. 28.2). These opportunities create skills that can lead to some expertise that could transfer to subsequent practice.

The reality of development toward true leadership expertise takes place over a long period and should not be expected during the first year or two of nursing practice. Nevertheless, every leader started somewhere. Movement toward an increasingly complex leadership experience allows the new nurse to move from leading

Fig. 28.2 A leadership trajectory. (From Fagin, C. [2000]. *Essays on nursing leadership.* New York: Springer Publishing.)

and planning with an individual to working with groups, such as families or communities. Further leadership development occurs during interactions with larger groups and through instituting changes in research and application of new techniques and moving toward health policy and political activities. With increasing educational achievement and career experience comes increasing complexity of leadership capabilities.

Leadership Within Professional Organizations

In the United States the best and most important step to take in becoming a leader within the nursing profession is to join a professional organization. Many nurses today take part in several organizations. These associations may be general and broad (e.g., the American Nurses Association), role-based (e.g., the American Organization of Nurse Executives), or clinically focused (e.g., the American Association of Critical-Care Nurses). Volunteering for local or committee memberships is a valued and useful way to learn and to grow within the association.

Many of the professional specialty organizations maintain a national or regional presence rather than having state or local chapters. Some of them have local chapters (e.g., Association of Perioperative Registered Nurses), especially in the larger, more populated areas across the country. The major impact of the professional specialty organization is sharing and dissemination of information, discussion of mutual clinical or role concerns, and education regarding the latest innovations in the field. Leadership opportunities are available to present posters or papers at local, regional, or national conferences, as well as to serve on committees and boards.

After becoming established and known in a local association, running for elected office in the local district or chapter association is a way many leaders within professional associations start their leadership careers. It is not unusual to be unsuccessful in the first attempt at running for an elective office in a professional association, but persistence can do two things: (1) it can help with name recognition, and (2) it can let members know that you are serious about being an association leader.

Leaders, often from local levels, later hold office at the state level. Volunteering for committee assignments and running for elected office in a state-level association establish leadership interest within a professional association. Leadership efforts at the national level are usually more successful after establishing a record of successful leadership at the state level.

This pathway of professional involvement and leadership may seem like a linear progression to more global opportunities for leadership in the profession. However, many successful nursing leaders conceptualize the progression as circular rather than linear. Many well-known leaders who have held high offices at the national or state level take their experience and expertise to return to offices and committee appointments at another level.

Leadership in the Community
Nurses as Community Opinion Leaders

Nurses are valued and respected members of their communities. As trusted professionals, nurses have an opportunity to serve as catalysts in leadership opportunities in the community. In partnership with others in the community, nurses can help build a more just, more peaceful, and healthier society.

Many avenues are available for nurses to serve as community opinion leaders. Attendance at civic gatherings, such as city commission and school board meetings, is an excellent way to be aware of what is happening and to offer input from a nursing perspective. For instance, when the school board begins deliberating whether the budget will accommodate a registered nurse for every school or whether to replace a registered nurse with a trained clerk who can record vaccinations, a nursing voice in the audience could clarify the importance of school nurses to a school population. Writing letters to the editor of a newspaper and participating in public forums give the nurse an avenue to share expertise and mold community opinion.

Nurses as Community Volunteers

Many opportunities exist for volunteer participation in the community. Nurses bring a unique leadership skill set to community activities. The ability to understand complex systems, as well as to understand interpersonal dynamics and communication techniques, constitutes knowledge that is valuable in community volunteer opportunities.

Leadership in mobilizing volunteers for health fairs, screening activities, and educational events is a community need that nurses can and do fill. Such activities promote health and advance the health of the community in important ways. Nurses can also lead efforts to engage others in the community in volunteer activities. In addition, nurses can organize individuals in the community to help develop a vision for the future of the community's health, healthcare opportunities, and healthcare delivery.

From the perspective of the nurse as a community leader, a unique opportunity exists to work with schools, city or county governments, and other community entities to formulate a vision for improving the health of the community through disease prevention and health promotion. The nurse can be a catalyst for a community to recognize present problems and to develop a plan to reach a preferred future.

Leadership Through Appointed and Elected Office

Nurses are valuable leaders in elected and appointed offices at the local, state, and national levels. Because of the trustworthiness of nurses in general, nurses should be able to mobilize resources to raise monies, develop support, and get elected to offices. The potential for nurses in offices at all three levels of government is great. However, the number is small in relation to the percentage of the population nursing represents. In addition to typical sources of campaign support, various healthcare-related political action committees provide assistance to nurses who want to run for office. Nurses who are elected members of governmental bodies can exert their leadership to shape the vision of the government to help meet the health and societal needs of citizens.

Local government opportunities include school boards, city councils, and community boards dealing with various community initiatives.

At the state level, opportunities include serving in the state legislatures; being appointed to state boards, such as the state board of nursing or the state board of health; or serving on special task forces such as those created by the legislature, a state board, or the governor. At the national level, opportunities include being elected as a US representative (nurses are few, but present), being elected as a US senator (no nurse has served in this capacity), being appointed to a federal commission or board, or serving as an expert for a legislator or legislative body.

CONCLUSION

The nurse is in a trusted role as nurturer and provider of care to the most vulnerable in our society. Nurses who choose leadership roles have many of the needed talents to serve their followers and their profession. Visionary and responsible leadership is vital to the future success of nursing as an art and a science. Professional nursing has been blessed with excellent leaders in the past and will continue to be led by the visionary nurse leaders of tomorrow.

THE SOLUTION

After a couple of weeks, we needed to find a way to bring the committee back together. I sat with the Vice President of Nursing (VPN) in her office, considering what our options were. We couldn't just start meeting again without dealing with the issue that had divided us. We had to acknowledge it and work through it before we could move on to other things.

As we were trying to come up with a strategy to bring people together, I remembered the strategic plan definition problem and suggested that we might be having the same sort of problem. We might be fighting over words without a common definition.

It was kind of a funny thing to consider. The words were things like "skill mix," "patient acuity," "hours per patient day," and "assistive personnel." These are common terms; surely we all knew what the words meant. Even so, we decided to test our assumption and see if we

had been using the terms differently from each other. It was risky for both of us. The VPN had to deal with the managers and directors. I had to make it okay for the rest of the nurses.

We brought the committee back together for a meeting in subgroups, making sure that each table had at least one direct care nurse, one manager, one director, and a human resources representative. No one liked the assigned seating, but we were firm that they had to comply with it. Then we gave table assignments to come up with a common definition for certain terms—the ones we were sure they could define. The groups began their assignments and found that they had trouble completing them. It was hard to develop a common definition of these terms that "everyone knows what they mean." After discussion, some groups were able to come up with a definition all could agree to; other groups could not. We discovered that

(Continued)

THE SOLUTION—cont'd

we had actually been fighting different fights. It had been like parallel conversations. We could not come to consensus on practice changes if we were talking about different things, even though we were using the same terms.

Understanding that we had been disagreeing about different things ended the impasse. The practice committee could continue its work. As leaders, we learned that our first job was to make sure everyone understood what

was being talked about, that we were all talking the "same language." The practice committee continued meeting for several years. Debates about practice change were robust—sometimes "spirited." But, we always made sure that we were using our words in the same way so that a lack of definition was never the issue.

Would this be a suitable approach for you? Why?

Katheren Koehn

REFLECTIONS

Consider the various leadership opportunities available to nurses. Ponder what makes sense to you in terms of your involvement to make yourself better, the profession better, and health care better. What will you do?

What specific activities must you engage in? What specific groups must you align with to achieve your expectation of involvement?

THE EVIDENCE

Leadership requires effective communication, responsibility, empowerment, job clarity, continuing of care, and interprofessional collaboration. Enhancing any of those strategies promotes more effective leadership.

In recent years, great emphasis has been placed on transformational leadership. It is closely associated with followers' working conditions—namely involvement, influence, and meaningfulness. Leaders create the workplace environment.

Nurse managers with effective leadership skills are an essential component to addressing the nursing shortage. The manager is the "face" of formal leadership and influences the local workplace environment. When positive places are present, staff turnover is lower.

The presence of a supportive culture in which learning is valued is a key factor in implementing and sustaining best practice guidelines. Transformational leadership creates the supportive culture.

Emerging workforce members have different views of what they seek in their managers and leaders. They want a leader who is receptive to people, who serves as a team player, who is honest, approachable, knowledgeable, motivating, and competent. That person must also be a good communicator and have a positive attitude and good people skills.

TIPS FOR BECOMING A LEADER

- Take advantage of leadership opportunities, and practice your leadership skills.
- Expect to stumble occasionally, but learn from your mistakes and continue.

- Get some help; for example, having a caring mentor is the best way to develop leadership ability.
- Take considered risks.

REFERENCES

Bennis, W. (2009). *On becoming a leader.* New York: Basic Books.

Bender, M. (2016). Clinical nurse leader integration into practice: developing theory to guide best practice. *Journal of Professional Nursing, 32*(1), 32–40.

Benner, P. (2001). *From novice to expert: excellence and power in clinical nursing practice.* Upper Saddle River, NJ: Prentice Hall Health.

Burke, D., Flanagan, J., Ditomassi, M., & Hickey, P. (2017). Characteristics of nurse directors that contribute to registered nurse satisfaction. *Journal of Nursing Administration, 47*(4), 219–223.

Covey, S. R. (1992). *Principle-centered leadership.* New York: Simon & Schuster.

Grossman, S., & Valiga, T. (2017). *The new leadership challenge: creating the future of nursing.* Philadelphia: F.A. Davis Company.

Kouzes, J., & Posner, B. (2012). *The leadership challenge: How to make extraordinary things happen in organizations.* San Francisco: Jossey-Bass.

Laschinger, H., & Fida, R. (2015). Linking nurses' perceptions of patient care quality to job satisfaction. *Journal of Nursing Administration, 45*(5), 276–283.

Senge, P. M. (2006). *The fifth discipline: The art and practice of the learning organization.* New York: Doubleday.

Spano-Szekely, L., Griffin, M., Clavelle, J., & Fitzpatrick, J. (2016). Emotional intelligence and transformational leadership in nurse managers. *Journal of Nursing Administration, 46*(2), 101–108.

Walters, J. (2017). Theories and principles of nursing leadership and management. In E. Murray (Ed.), *Nursing leadership and management.* Philadelphia: F.A. Davis Company.

Ward, J., Laframboise, L., & Cosimano, A. (2016). Collaborative student leadership conference. *Journal of Professional Nursing, 32*(5S), S63–S67.

Wilcox, J. (2018). Challenges of nursing and leadership. In J. Zerwekh & A. Garneau (Eds.), *Nursing today: transitions and trends* (9th ed.). St Louis: Elsevier.

29

Developing the Role of Manager

Jacqueline Gonzalez

LEARNING OUTCOMES

- Value the need for leaders, managers, and followers to focus on patient safety.
- Describe the role of the nurse manager in creating a healthy work environment.
- Apply the concepts of leadership styles and mentoring and their relevance to promoting a

healthy work environment with positive patient outcomes.
- Identify tools to navigate complex systems, using technology and maximizing the use of resources.

KEY TERMS

budget	incivility	organizational culture
bullying	leader	quality indicators
change agent	Magnet®	transformational leadership
dashboards	managed care	value-based purchasing
follower	Maslow's Hierarchy of Needs	
healthy work environment	mentor	

THE CHALLENGE

As a nurse manager, one of the most common and complex challenges I face is making certain that my department/unit is being cost-effective and has the adequate and appropriate staff on duty. In some cases this situation may require a fixed number of staff; in other scenarios the number of staff needed may fluctuate up or down depending on patient volume and meeting patient needs. Having the right number of staff on duty with the appropriate competencies affects patient care as well as employee and physician satisfaction and is critical in leading my unit. Additionally, as

the nurse manager, I must ensure that the right number of staff with the right skill set is available at the right time.

For example, an experience that I have had is that at 9 AM Monday morning on my busy Neurologic Unit and I arrived to discover that there were three sick calls for the day shift. I was immediately faced with the challenge of patients being held in the Post Anesthesia Care Unit awaiting transfer to my unit. The unit requires three more nurses, and I did not have the staff on duty to care for these additional patients at this point in time. I was also fielding

THE CHALLENGE—cont'd

Susan Fornaris, DNP, MHSA, RN, SCRN, CMSRN
Administrative Director, Medical Surgical/Nursing Operations,
Nicklaus Children's Hospital, Miami, FL

calls from the Operating Room (OR), because that staff was upset about the possible delays of their future cases for the day.

What would you do if you were this nurse?

INTRODUCTION

Management can be viewed from different perspectives. The core of role theory began with management theory, a science that has undergone numerous changes in the past century. Since the early 1900s, theories of management have evolved. These include Frederick Winslow Taylor's principles of scientific management; Henry Fayol's general principles of management; and Hawthorne's important findings regarding work environments, productivity, and motivation (Jay, Shafritz, & Ott, 2016). In the mid-1900s, change theory was developed by Kurt Lewin; Peter Drucker established the principle of management by objectives; and McGregor's Theory X and Theory Y, which is based on the idea of two opposing assumptions that people either need to be coerced to perform or they prefer autonomy, evolved (Jang, 2016). All of these theories are based on differing principles designed to depict the management of personnel in achieving organizational goals and objectives. Practice in the 1930s through the 1970s was dominated by participative, humanistic management theories. Although changes in healthcare delivery no doubt are affecting the roles of nurse managers, the relevance of social role theory remains relevant. Newman and Newman (2016) described social role theory as the linkage between social development and personal development. Behaviors include role expectations, the assumption of social roles, and the expected norms of those roles (Newman & Newman, 2016).

Role expectations are the behavioral expectations that are shared or related to each person's role. When a new nurse manager enacts his or her new role, expected behaviors are associated with attaining and delivering results within the role. Importantly, as a nurse manager assumes the social role, the enactment of this role includes the anticipated and predictable qualities of social behavior of the role, such as demonstrating leadership, managing budgets and financial resources, and creating a positive culture within the work environment.

The evolutionary process of management theories has affected how managers address workers' concerns and needs. The beginning management theories discounted concern for workers' psychological needs and focused on productivity and efficiency. When theories relating to human relations evolved from the Hawthorne Corporation's studies of working conditions, workers' social needs and motivations became focal points for the nurse manager. Perhaps often used in nursing, Maslow's (1954) groundbreaking work describing the human Hierarchy of Needs reflects on the needs of human beings that must be satisfied at their most basic level (physiologic, safety) before reaching higher levels (love and self-esteem) to achieve self-actualization. Pontefract (2016) discussed Maslow's hierarchy in relationship to the employee's purpose, belongingness, esteem, and self-actualization. He described the leader's duty of care to help employees feel that they develop purpose at work. Conversely, situational theories, such as the Path-Goal theory, focused on the environment and examine how a leader's behavior affects performance and job satisfaction, clarifying the relationship between the pathway employees take and the outcome or goal they wish to attain.

McGregor's Theory X and Theory Y (see the Theory Box) made two basic opposing assumptions about employees and how the manager should interact with them.

What do all of these theories mean to a manager? Common questions a new manager may ask in self-assessment are: What do I have to do to prepare and educate myself and synthesize this information as I face new challenges ahead? Is it enough to be a clinical expert nurse on my unit as a prerequisite for becoming a nurse manager? What formal and informal educational preparation and experience do I need to prepare myself for this new role? What current and future career goals do I need to identify and map out for my career path to achieve them? What specific knowledge, skills, and personal qualities do I need to have and develop to be most effective in practice? Which mentors and coaches

THEORY BOX

McGregor's Theory X and Theory Y	Style	Implications
Theory X	Authoritarian style, focused on productivity	Management must encourage people to do their work, because there is tendency to avoid working. Assumes that workers must be supervised and reminded and pushed to produce results.
Theory Y	Participative management style, beliefs that people are inherently self-motivated and committed	Management must create an environment where people can be self-directed and achieve satisfying work. Assumes that workers exert self-control and are self-directed in achieving their goals; do not need to be pushed to produce results.

Data from The Economist. (2008). Theories X and Y. http://www.economist.com/node/12370445

will I need to guide me in new skill sets and development in this direction? Will my organization have tools to assist me, such as succession planning, development opportunities, tuition reimbursement, or advanced educational offerings?

Today's fast-paced and changing environment of health care calls for leaders who can lead, manage, and successfully communicate changes and also participate in and drive new initiatives. Innovative and transformational solutions are needed as nurse managers learn to facilitate best practices identified by the frontline staff during this exciting and somewhat turbulent time in health care. Nurse managers must operate and navigate within healthcare agencies and also within the larger social system, including the community they serve. Nurse managers must recognize the need for growth within, which translates into improving one's practice and serving as **mentors** to others. A prerequisite for self-actualization is a bond between the nurse and the community, because the community includes nurse managers' patients and staff.

Nurse managers have many roles in leading their units or departments. Steinhauer (2016) recommends that the role of the nurse manager is and should be as a **change agent** who is described as a transformational leader. Nurse managers have the responsibility of day-to-day decisions for their units, and they must learn to lead and manage change. They must ensure frontline staff buy-in as initiatives evolve that positively affect patient outcomes in the interest of patient quality and safety. To lead through change, nurse managers must identify and develop skill sets that enable them to facilitate others, provide guidance, and inspire those around them to be a part of the change. These essential tools allow nurse managers to not only coach their staff and colleagues but also encourage their leaders in leading by example (Fig. 29.1). These collaborative efforts to bring about change require active listening to understand the viewpoints of others and demonstrating trust and integrity by communicating directly and fairly with teams. The complexity of management is this and much more.

Fig. 29.1 Nurse managers can effectively coach others in their performance. (From Miami Children's Hospital with permission.)

THE DEFINITION OF MANAGEMENT

Management is a generic function that includes focusing on completing the work that must be done. Thus almost every nurse has a vested interest in management. Nurses must manage the care of their patients, and they must also self-manage and manage others for whom they are accountable, even when their titles do not reflect a formal management role. Box 29.1 identifies some key concepts every manager needs to consider.

These concepts are the basis for management. The manager must not only work within these concepts, but also rise to new demands to excel. For example, although managers must manage personnel, they must also lead people and view them as resources in accomplishing today's work. Another example of the role of the manager is in understanding and leveraging the work of people as knowledge workers who use concepts, theories, and thoughts rather than merely relying on everyday skills to complete a task. Turriago-Hoyos, Thoene, and Arjoon (2016) describe Drucker's (1974) classic view of a society as requiring knowledge workers and in fact describe them as knowledge generators. Box 29.2 presents a view of what new views of managers' roles involve.

Drucker's view of management tasks, responsibilities, and practices fits with contemporary thinking about the role of nurse managers. For example, the American Organization of Nurse Executives (AONE) (2016) offers a framework representing three separate domains for the development and learning framework of the nurse

BOX 29.1   Key Concepts Managers Consider

- Hire the right people.
- Create and support active followers and emerging leaders.
- Secure and manage resources (physical, fiscal, and workforce) to support people providing quality care.
- Develop people to their full potential based on qualifications and talent.
- Support decisions closest to the point of care.
- Manage and share data to measure productivity and quality.
- Create collaborative relationships with other disciplines.
- Hold people accountable.

BOX 29.2   New Views of Managers' Roles

- Know yourself.
- Engage people actively in the organization and services.
- Translate the Vision and Mission into actionable plans.
- Create and maintain a healthy, blame-free work environment.
- Incorporate family and significant others in the care of patients.
- Consider new services needed in the community of care.
- Demonstrate and promote interprofessional approaches to care delivery.
- Create a succession plan.

manager. These domains are reviewed in Fig. 29.2 and include the following:

- The science: Managing the business
- The art: Leading the people
- The leader within: Creating the leader in yourself

Nurse managers are responsible for fostering and managing relationships with those they report to, their peers, and frontline staff for whom they are accountable, all the while maintaining the highest level of professionalism and while managing organizational resources. Cox (2016) described management as involving staff and resources to accomplish organizational objectives. She stated that managers must possess primary skills that include human relations, conceptual skills, and technical skills. Nurse managers use such skills as problem solving, motivating, controlling, following through, aligning, and inspiring people. Udod, Cummings, Care, and Jenkins (2017) studied role stressors on the health of 23 nurse managers in a qualitative, exploratory inquiry study. The productivity and health of nurse managers could be adversely affected if they did not possess the coping skills necessary to manage the demands and intensity of the role.

NURSE MANAGER AS CHANGE LEADER

Developing frontline staff today is critical to help them reach their potential. Iacono and Altman (2015) described one organization's journey in reducing catheter-associated urinary tract infection (CAUTI) rate through a leadership program empowering clinicians to improve patient care.

THE NURSE MANAGER

Fig. 29.2 Nurse manager learning domain framework. (From Development and Learning Framework of the Nurse Manager, Copyright © 2016, by the American Organization of Nurse Executives [AONE]. All rights reserved.)

The nurse manager was instrumental in coaching and encouraging the team by providing monthly updates on CAUTI-free days and actions that proved successful. The authors summarized the article by stating the goal of nurse managers is to develop staff "to become the next generation of effective leaders" (p. 43). Morisiani, Bagnasco, and Sasso (2017) presented the results of a convenience sample study of 87 staff nurses to better understand the perceptions that staff nurses have in relationship to their manager's leadership style. This study identified several themes that emerged in relationship to frontline staff satisfaction with their manager, as identified in Table 29.1. When staff feel respected by their leader, they genuinely feel recognized and appreciated. When nurse managers use good listening skills and support and advocate for staff ideas and suggestions, the outcome is the staff feeling cared for by their leader.

Nurse managers must be able to focus on both the individual and the larger goals and outcomes of the department and organization. Their aim is to enable people to develop their abilities and strengths to the fullest and to achieve excellence, thus contributing to the department's overall success. The manager must help people develop realistic, attainable goals that provide an avenue of individual growth that also contributes to the organization's well-being. Active participation, encouragement, and guidance from the manager and from the organization are needed for the individual's developmental efforts to be fully actualized. Nurse managers who are successful in motivating staff often provide an inclusive environment that facilitates clearly set, achievable goals that can result in both team and personal satisfaction.

Nurse managers must possess qualities of a good leader: knowledge, integrity, ambition, good judgment, courage, stamina, enthusiasm, communication skills, planning skills, and administrative abilities. Similarities exist between managers and leaders, and these same

TABLE 29.1 Impact of Style of Leadership on Frontline Staff Satisfaction

Theme	Categories
Respect	Professional recognition
	Fairness
Feeling cared for	Advocacy
	Listening
	Support
Being valued	Personal development
	Team development

From Morsiani, G., Bagnasco, A., & Sasso, L. (2017). How staff nurses perceive the impact of nurse managers' leadership style in terms of job satisfaction: A mixed method study. *Journal of Nursing Management, 25*(2), 119–128.

EXERCISE 29.1 In a small group, discuss the staffing needs of a very busy pediatric hematology and oncology unit for a particular night shift. The patient care staffing needs of this unit are very high, including three new post–bone marrow transplant patients. Today the unit has extra staff on duty, and over the last few days the department has been very busy and short-staffed. Everyone worked together as a team to provide excellent care on these challenging days. Hospital resources are scarce, and if extra staff are left on duty, the unit will be over budget. How does the manager motivate the staff by starting a critical conversation that will engage them in understanding the need to contribute to unit cost-effectiveness? How would you want to hear this conversation? What might make staff be concerned that the message may suggest insincerity in addressing their concerns?

skills, applied differently, are equally important for followers.

Managers address complex issues at the front line by organizing, planning, budgeting, and setting target goals. They meet their goals by planning, organizing, staffing, controlling, following up, and problem solving. By contrast, leaders build a culture of teamwork, setting a broad direction, developing a shared vision, and communicating that direction to staff. Followers collaborate and communicate to translate that direction into action, sharing perceptions about successes and barriers to achieving the vision. Managers address complexity and change, whereas senior leaders primarily set vision and address change. Followers implement patient care change and provide input into organizational change. Successful organizations embrace managers, senior leaders, and follower traits that are relationship based, thus driving change and positive outcomes and providing and ensuring a healthy and effective work environment.

Porter O'Grady (2015b) described the skill of predictive and adaptive capacity as a crucial skill necessary for managers in their role as they are called upon to assist others in coping with change. To enable managers to see the "big picture," several important skills are foundational, such as self-education and reading about environmental influences to understand the broader landscape. Translation of what is learned is also essential so that the message is simple and understandable to those whose role is affected. Finally, nurse managers must be able to engage and empower frontline staff by ensuring that the message is understood on a personal level, with the ultimate outcome being a committed workforce.

NURSE MANAGER ROLE AND THE INTERGENERATIONAL WORKFORCE

Nurse managers face many complexities in the everyday work as they lead their staff. Managing an intergenerational nurse workforce while continuing to ensure the establishment and maintenance of a positive and harmonious workplace environment is certainly a challenge. Each generation has an essential value component as well as a unique style of communication (Smith, 2015). Four generations of the nursing workforce (Generation Y [Millenials], Generation X, Baby Boomers, and veterans) have different beliefs, values, and expectations (Burke, Walker, & Clendon, 2015). These lead to differences that may lead to breakdowns in collaboration or teamwork. Generation Z, the emerging workforce generation, has the highest level of technology usage of any prior generation (Fig. 29.3). Nurse managers must understand what motivates the different generations and use that knowledge to bring together teams to achieve departmental goals. One example is with the implementation of electronic health records where Generation Y nurses may support learning needs of the Baby Boomers. In contrast, the Baby Boomers may provide education, encouragement, and mentorship as the frontline staff gain confidence and learn new skills.

Several benefits are derived for nurse managers and the organization in building intergenerational teams:

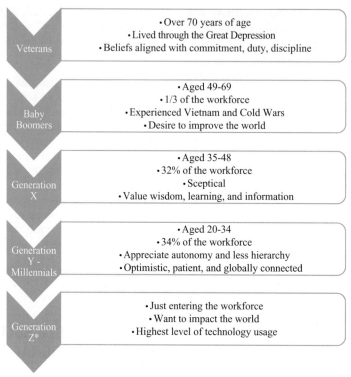

Fig. 29.3 Generational characteristics. (From Burke, A., Walker, L., & Clendon, J. [2015]. Managing intergenerational nursing teams: Evidence from the literature. *Kai Tiaki Nursing Research*, 6[1], 24–27, 2015. Permission: New Zealand Nurses Organization.)

recruitment and retention of nurses, enhanced employee morale and engagement, and a competitive and positive workplace culture (Bursch, 2014). Managing the different groups may require different strategies and words, but the core for all is about safety and quality.

THE NURSE MANAGER AND INTERPROFESSIONAL COLLABORATION

Interprofessional collaboration is described by Sullivan, Kiovsky, Mason, Hill, and Dukes (2015) as essential for nurses to lead change. The National Academy of Medicine's report on *The Future of Nursing: Leading Change, Advancing Health* (2011) recognizes the key importance of building relationships across all disciplines that will enhance quality and accessibility and ultimately provide great value to the patient. The nurse manager's role in fostering true interprofessional collaboration must be a focus to build and create teams

and a workforce that is engaged and committed. Never has it been more essential that departments work together to accomplish departmental and overarching organizational goals. A common example of the importance of interprofessional teamwork is the collaboration and communication that is fundamentally important between the nursing and the pharmacy department to achieve patient safety in medication administration. In-patient settings find this to be a most challenging issue because of the rapidity of change and the availability of new information, such as laboratory results. It is no wonder administering medications is such a challenge.

BUILDING A POSITIVE WORK ENVIRONMENT

Creating a positive work environment includes promoting teamwork and strong collaboration among nurse managers and the frontline staff. Nurses know and appreciate the nurse manager's attention and supportive leadership when the leader's focus is on improving areas that can affect patient care and patient safety. Ma, Shang, and Bott (2015) discussed the importance of developing nurse managers who can build desirable and collaborative unit-level work environments that result in creating a work environment of high-quality care and frontline staff retention. The manager must routinely assess the practice and work environment to ensure a healthy environment, positively impacting staff performance. Nurse managers can create winning situations by building and engaging productive teams as they work toward accomplishing departmental and organizational goals and objectives. They can also motivate their teams by ensuring opportunities for continued growth and development that are directly correlated to a more knowledgeable workforce. The younger generations of staff enjoy working in teams and taking advantage of these developmental opportunities.

Porter-O'Grady (2015a) described the need for leaders to reimagine how work is organized and view health care as "complex adaptive systems" (p. 78). By viewing health care in this manner, the demand for teamwork and managers who provide vision and guide them has never been so important. Porter-O'Grady also described five major components of team dynamics that are essential for the success of a team in a complex adaptive system such as health care. These elements are team purpose, goodness-of-fit (how well the team works together to achieve organizational goals and outcomes), setting the table or preparing for the work ahead, processes that ensure team effectiveness and, finally, evaluation and analysis of the work of the team. Table 29.2 demonstrates the necessary domains of a healthy work environment as classically defined by several leading professional nursing organizations.

Flexibility is key for the leader in striving for win-win solutions. Nurse managers today must serve as leaders who embrace uncertainty and seek to understand behaviors and relationships before attempting to change them. Now, when new nurses enter the workforce with enormous technologic demands for their knowledge and skills, nurse managers need to help support their growth and their comfort while being flexible in managing the unknown. Transformational leadership is significantly correlated with affecting organizational commitment of frontline staff (Brewer et al., 2016). In addition, communicative leadership and support along with organizational commitment are strongly associated as being predictive of voluntary turnover (Nei, Snyder, & Litwiller, 2015).

CONSUMING RESEARCH

Nurse managers' responsibilities are twofold: They must be an advocate for and interpreter of research and they must participate in research. Review of nursing literature, especially in nursing administration journals, reflects the importance of nurse managers to contribute to research either by conducting unit research or participating in large-scale organizational research projects.

Likewise, nurse managers interpret published research findings and support unit-based changes based on this evidence that have implications for the staff or quality of patient care. By implementing best practices that are evidence based, they demonstrate to the frontline nursing team the importance of the benefits from evidence-based care. Nurse managers, as first-line managers, are also in an advantageous position of identifying best nursing practices that can be researched through collaborative efforts of service and educational institutions. Identifying research and practice gaps as well as providing support for frontline nurses in conducting nursing research allows them the opportunity to learn and disseminate their findings of current evidence-based practice in the literature to their colleagues.

The two Research Perspectives identify how managers help produce improved quality. In the first Research Perspective, the power of collaboration when teams work together to improve patient care outcomes is evident. In the second Research Perspective, transformational leadership is shown to have a very substantial impact on the frontline nurse's organizational commitment and intent to stay.

ORGANIZATIONAL CULTURE

In the ever-changing environment of health care, nurse managers need to know the organizational culture at their workplace and how it is integrated with and supports their unit's mission and goals. Clavelle and Porter-O'Grady (2016) performed an in-depth review of the literature and the concepts of shared governance and structural empowerment that have served as a successful framework for creating a positive and involved organizational culture. For many decades, shared

TABLE 29.2 Standards for Creating and Maintaining Healthy Work Environments

Domains of a Healthy Work Environment	AONE (2004)	AACN (2005)	AORN (2015)
Collaboration	A culture that promotes collaboration through trust, diversity, and team orientation	True collaboration encouraged	Collaborative practice culture: all team members are treated respectfully; disruptive behaviors not tolerated
Communication	A culture with clear, respectful, open, and trusting communication	Skilled communication: communication skills equal to clinical skills	Communication-rich culture: clear, respectful, inclusive, timely, open, and trusting communication
Decision making	A structure for participation in shared decision making	Effective decision making: nurses feeling valued in directing and leading care and operations of the organization	Shared decision making: nurses participating in decision making and policy development; responsible for their practice
Staffing	Adequate numbers of qualified staff to meet patient expectations and provide balance to the work and home life of staff	Appropriate staffing: effectively meeting patient needs with matched nurse competencies	Presence of adequate numbers of qualified perioperative registered nurse staff: work and on-call schedules that promote positive work-life balance; quality care provided by adequate staffing
Recognition	Recognition of contributions of nursing staff and recognition by nurses of the contributions they provide to practice	Meaningful recognition: recognize value that every nurse brings to workplace	Recognition of contributions from nursing and their value: recognized by peers and team members for performance; growth options available
Leadership	Presence of a leader who serves as an advocate for nursing, supports empowerment of nurses, and ensures availability of resources	Authentic leadership: authentically embrace healthy work environment and engage team in achieving	Presence of expert, visible, and believable nursing leadership: leadership skills at all levels; nurses as advocates; share decision making
Accountability	A culture in which everyone is accountable and knows what is expected		Accountable for professional practice and to team members: clear role expectations and definitions
Self-actualization	Ongoing education and professional development		Encouragement of professional practice and growth/development: ongoing education, certification and development encouraged and promoted

Data from American Association of Critical-Care Nurses (AACN). (2005). AACN standards for establishing and sustaining healthy work environments. https://www.aacn.org/nursing-excellence/healthy-work-environments; American Organization of Nurse Executives (AONE). (2004). Nursing Organizations Alliance™ Principles & elements of a healthful practice/work environment. http://www.aone.org/resources/healthful-practice-work.pdf; and Association of periOperative Registered Nurses (AORN). (2015). AORN position statement on a healthy perioperative practice environment. https://www.aorn.org/guidelines/clinical-resources/position-statements.

RESEARCH PERSPECTIVE

Resource: Ma, C., Shang, J., & Bott, M. J. (2015). Linking unit collaboration and nursing leadership to nurse outcomes and quality of care. *The Journal of Nursing Administration, 45*(9), 435–442.

This study was conducted as a secondary analysis of 2012 cross-sectional data from the National Database of Nursing Quality Indicators (NDNQI). Survey data from the Job Satisfaction Scale and RN Surveys were analyzed from 237 hospitals, from 73,808 RNs who spent at least 50% of their time in direct care, were not contracted staff, and were employed in their area for at least 3 months. Collaboration was measured using two adapted scales from the Index of Work Satisfaction to better understand teamwork among nurse-nurse interactions as well as nurse-physician interactions. Leadership was also measured with an adapted scale form, the Practice Environment Scales of Nursing Work Index (PES-NWI). Nurse outcomes including job satisfaction and intent to leave were also measured along with nurse-reported quality of care. Quality of care measures were established from the perception of the nurses and included improvement in quality of care and overall quality of care. The following overall hospital covariates were included in the study:

- Bed size
- Magnet® status
- Teaching status
- Geographic location
- Ownership

Nurse unit covariates were unit staffing levels and unit type. Demographics were also controlled, including gender, age, race/ethnicity, unit tenure, education, specialty certification, and status of employment. Study results demonstrated that nursing leadership and improved unit collaboration were associated with higher nurse job satisfaction, a higher retention rate, and nurse-reported improved quality of patient care. In addition, findings indicated that positive nurse-physician collaboration was correlated with improved patient care quality. Importantly, a trusting and supportive environment of leadership and practice led to enhanced nurse outcomes and patient care quality. Magnet® hospitals were cited as best practice in creating an environment of a supportive work environment and collaborative culture.

Implications for Practice

Nurse managers face many challenges, and to manage teams through these challenges, they must possess a strong leadership skill set, including critical thinking at the core. Without critical-thinking skills, success for the nurse manager is uncertain. Nurse managers that lead in creating and supporting a positive work environment that is developed in tandem with the frontline nursing team can create outstanding quality patient outcomes while optimizing nurse retention.

RESEARCH PERSPECTIVE

Resource: Brewer, C. S., Kovner, C. T., Djukic, M., Farehi, F., Greene, W., Chacko, T. & Yang, Y. (2016). Impact of transformational leadership on nurse work outcomes. *Journal of Advanced Nursing, 72*(11), 2879–2893.

This longitudinal cross-sectional study was conducted using an analytical representative sample of 1037 licensed registered nurses from across the nation with 7.5–8.5 years of practice. The aim of this study was to examine the elements of transformational leadership and their associated impact on job satisfaction, nurses' intent to stay, and organizational commitment. Findings demonstrated that transformational leadership had no significant association with job satisfaction or intent to stay; however, it did have a significant association with organizational commitment. Also the intent to stay was positively associated with job satisfaction, organizational commitment, promotional opportunities, age, and mentor support. In contrast, work settings, ethnicity, and nonlocal job opportunities were associated negatively with intent to stay. Conclusions of the authors revealed that although

transformational leadership did not demonstrate a direct correlation with job satisfaction and intent to stay, a positive direct correlation with organizational commitment existed. By creating a positive work environment, nurse managers affect nurse attrition, which could be slowed, and nurse retention could be optimized. Even minimal improvements in organizational commitment and job satisfaction would have a positive effect on increasing nurses' intent to stay.

Implications for Practice

Commitment to the organization has a tremendous impact on the nurse's intent to stay; thus it is essential for nurse managers to proactively work in today's complex healthcare environment in a manner that engages frontline staff. Organizations must invest in helping nurse managers to develop leadership skills that can be fostered to encourage a healthy work environment that encourages mentoring, development, and promotional opportunities, encouraging a culture of collaboration, communication, and growth.

works with. Shared governance has evolved over the years to a new framework of professional governance. Associated attributes comprise such elements as decision making based on evidence, collateral interprofessional relationships, accountability resulting in positive outcomes for all, and finally a professional obligation that is ethical, professional, and legal (Clavelle & Porter-O'Grady, 2016).

Murray et al. (2016) shared an example of the implementation of a shared decision-making (SDM) model in a children's hospital. The overall organizational purpose of the SDM model was to ensure that each employee participated as if he or she had personal ownership in the organization's success. The authors described the evolution of the model over a decade with the aims of organizational consistency and standardization across all settings and the establishment of operational guidelines that supported shared decisions. A key finding was the identification of the need for frontline staff leadership education that assisted council chairs in effectively planning and running meetings. This example of one organization's quest to empower frontline staff to govern their own professional practice demonstrates a move to supporting an organizational culture that can leverage frontline nurses' knowledge and skills in achieving positive outcomes.

MENTORING

Most managers were mentored, formally or informally, at one time in their career by someone of high regard or influence. In turn, a manager should focus attention about preparing future successors. Milton (2017) described the importance of mentoring and the importance of retaining professional nurses in organizational settings. The author further described the relationship of mentor-mentee as one that is personified by living in the moment with a commitment to the success of the other person. The mentor does not insist on his or her own way, but rather the relationship allows for a commitment to a specific purpose. This notion is especially important in terms of nurse manager growth, particularly in the development of moral courage and clinical leadership to manage complex situations and personnel challenges. Having a solid mentor when faced with these situations allows nurse managers to explore options and role-play situations to achieve the best professional outcome. Gopee (2015) defined the mentor role as someone

who supervises, facilitates learning, and assesses. He further explained the mentor's responsibilities to act as a resource and invest in the professional development of mentees, including disseminating best practices and use of evidence-based practice. The role of mentoring is a significant role that nurses in leadership and management positions must embrace. Mentoring is viewed as an interactive, multifaceted role that assists the frontline staff, especially novice nurses, with setting realistic, attainable goals. Through mentoring their staff, nurse managers can help boost staff self-confidence, thereby helping them gain professional satisfaction as they reach their goals. Nurse managers give clinical guidance to their staff, and they can be instrumental in assisting them with their present work and their own professional career development.

DAY-TO-DAY MANAGEMENT CHALLENGES

Nurse managers must be able to balance day-to-day management challenges with three sources of demands: upper management requests, consumer demands, and staff needs. Managers have a pivotal two-way responsibility to ensure that staff members have opportunities for providing input to upper management regarding changes that may affect them and ensure that frontline staff share departmental and practice needs. Many consumers of health services today are well educated and accustomed to providing input into care decisions that affect them, often having reviewed available literature and searched available resources or options for care. Nurse managers need to respect this important perspective of the knowledgeable consumer requests to ensure that care is provided in the broadest context of patient quality, safety, and efficiency. Staff members also may need coaching to achieve recognition and independence when carrying out their roles and responsibilities. Nurse managers must maintain awareness of when to coach and relinquish control, to allow decision making at the point closest to the service. The professional governance model of nursing leadership encourages this transformational approach. Furthermore, the nurse manager is highly influential and critical in creating a practice environment that enhances direct care nurses' satisfaction with the work environment.

Nurse managers also must be authentic clinicians in the areas they manage, and they must "walk the talk" while understanding the perspectives of the frontline staff. Visibility of the nurse manager is essential in building trust and affirming communication with frontline staff. Critically important for being an excellent nurse manager is understanding the correlation between staff satisfaction and engagement and the achievement of optimal patient outcomes, engaging families in the plan of care, and advocating for the allocation of resources and technology in a fair and ethical manner. Nurse managers as clinicians are confronted with complex and ambiguous patient-care situations and must use courage to make decisions to meet one important patient care need at the expense of another. Excellent communication skills are necessary and a must for engaging frontline staff. In understanding and conveying rationale, nurse managers must build consensus in promoting teamwork and successful departmental outcomes.

EXERCISE 29.2 You have learned that employee satisfaction scores are associated with leadership styles. Select a department within an organization that has the highest employee satisfaction scores. Observe the nurse manager of that department over a certain time (e.g., 2 to 4 hours) and note what situations the manager encounters. What is the leadership style that is exhibited? Is power shared or centralized? Are interactions positive or negative? How is the frontline staff engaged? Is the nurse manager engaged in mentoring activities? Provide examples.

Bullying, Incivility, and Workplace Violence

One of the greatest, ongoing challenges a manager faces is supporting staff who may be exposed to bullying, incivility, or actual violence in the workplace. Logan (2016) described the influence of nursing teamwork in relationship to incivility in the workplace. When a bullying environment exists, a greater potential exists for negative outcomes for nurses and patient care. Logan (2016) further posed that a critical need for teamwork as a requirement was essential for hospital-based nurses. With teamwork described as essential for providing high-quality care, other characteristics are critical to teamwork, including leadership, trust, and communication. Nurse managers must create positive work environments where staff feel empowered and encouraged.

Keller, Budin, and Allie (2016) shared one organization's quest and journey to eliminate workplace bullying. As a Magnet® organization, the hospital identified some disruptive and bullying behaviors among the frontline staff. A multidepartmental bullying task force was launched and began a specific approach. A mission statement was established to prevent bullying, and a research study was launched to survey and measure behaviors and characteristics associated with bullying. Of the 707 participating staff members, 58% were staff nurses and 34% were nurse managers. The task force reviewed several studies, including topics such as mentoring, education, aggression management training, and role-playing. The intervention known as the 4Ss was implemented to support the person being bullied: Stand by, Support, Speak up, and Sequester the person who is exhibiting bullying behavior. Houck and Colbert (2017), in their integrative review of the literature, found effects on patient safety such as medication errors, delays in care, patient falls, adverse events, or patient death. Nurse managers must also view patient safety data differently and in relationship to the work environment.

Nurse managers have an added responsibility for the safety of both patients and staff. As the third Research Perspective shows, nurse managers must be sensitive to nurse-to-nurse incivility. High-risk areas, such as the emergency department and psychiatric and intensive care units, require special attention. For nurse managers, "special attention" translates to staff receiving adequate training to prepare for adverse situations that may erupt. Such training may include effective techniques relating to crisis intervention and de-escalation and handling of highly agitated people who may become violent. From the point of hiring through the potential disciplinary process, nurse managers must assess employees and the workplace to help avert bullying, incivility, or violence and the conditions that may lead to it. Top-level administrators are ultimately responsible for employee violence in their organization; however, managers are the first to identify situations that may become out of control. Managers must ensure that their employees receive training and adhere to policies to prevent any increased risk for nonadherence to state and federal employee selection requirements.

Managing Work Complexity and Stress

Managing complexity within healthcare settings is always challenging for nurse managers, including managing personnel diversity. The nursing shortage

RESEARCH PERSPECTIVE

Resource: Kaiser, J. A. (2017). The relationship between leadership style and nurse-to-nurse incivility: Turning the lens inward. *Journal of Nursing Management, 25,* 110–118.

This exploratory study examined reported rates of nursing lateral hostility and the effect of leadership styles. A sample of 237 frontline staff was surveyed investigating nurse-nurse relationships and behavior in relationship to the following leadership styles:

Transactional leadership: focused on managing and task based; little focus on relationship

Laissez-faire leadership: passive and avoidance based; hands off with little direction

Democratic leadership: focused on team and feedback in decision making

Autocratic leadership: hierarchical; minimal leader/subordinate interaction

Transformational leadership: vested, personal interest in followers; team highly engaged and empowered

Study findings concluded that transformational leaders who promoted teamwork and staff empowerment had a profound influence on and were most correlated with low levels of nurse incivility.

Implications for Practice

The findings of the study clearly demonstrate that nurse managers need to promote teamwork and provide a positive workplace environment for employees to eliminate the presence of nurse-to-nurse bullying or incivility. Nurse managers must examine their own behavioral styles and understand the impact of these styles on frontline staff in the workplace. Nurse managers need to avoid the use of transactional or laissez-faire leadership styles that may deter empowerment of the frontline nurse.

---

continues to make this challenge even more difficult. Nurse managers are key persons in creating and maintaining a healthy work setting that keeps stress to a minimum so that the staff can achieve optimal quality of work and job satisfaction. However, before managers can help staff, they must be able to work in a relatively stress-free environment. Lavoie-Tremblay, Fernet, Lavigne, and Austin (2015) found that effective leadership practices were positively correlated with new nurse retention. Avoiding workplace stress by encouraging a nurse-friendly environment of practice along with frontline staff involvement in decision making can help circumvent workplace stress. Improved patient outcomes as well as a positive work environment for everyone is also a probable result. Enhanced or unrealistic performance expectations in the workplace add to the complexity and coping challenges within the healthcare system. Several factors such as experience, a positive organizational environment, and items within the system, such as a realistic span of control and a supportive and empowering leader or chief nursing officer, make a tremendous impact on the perception of stress, support, and coping by the manager. Nurse managers are extremely valuable resources, and mechanisms that reduce the stress in these essential management leaders should be in place.

The seminal work of the Robert Wood Johnson Foundation Initiative on the Future of Nursing by the National Academy of Medicine (Institute of Medicine

[IOM], 2011) recommended that nurses must be ready to assume leadership roles, and new mentoring and leadership development programs must be developed to lead complexity. Professional and personal growth is encouraged and cultivated so that nurses will rise across their profession and be involved in the redesign of healthcare delivery in the United States. Nurse leaders are encouraged to be full partners in developing areas of improvement and new models of care.

A key to successful management is interdependence, and a critical component is collaboration, which optimizes the different strengths of each person. Collaboration requires one to be flexible and broad-minded and to have a strong self-concept. When collaboration is used to solve a conflict or to create new directions, the energies of all parties are focused on solving the problem versus defeating the opposing party and creating the best possible solution rather than one that is just tolerable.

Frontline staff members often look to nurse managers to lead them in addressing workplace issues with higher levels of administration. To do this, nurse managers must possess two sets of skills: (1) the ability to address power sources in the work environment and to define power-based strategies, such as in organizing a following of other nurse managers with similar concerns; and (2) the ability to place pressure on the power holders so that needed changes can occur. Employee "buy-in" to change needs to be thoroughly examined and encouraged.

Staff members look to nurse managers to lead them in ethical, value-based management. No greater stage than the one the manager is on influences frontline staff more, because every employee watches the actions of the manager with keen interest. The manager's commitment to the mission, vision, and values must be demonstrated in everyday behavior, not merely recited on special occasions. This ongoing commitment lends stability in a time of constant change. In other words, although the approach to an issue may change, the core values remain, and the nurse manager is the one who must manage the group through conflict and change to reflect the organization's mission, vision, and values. Without this trust and evidence that is almost palpable, frontline nurses may be skeptical about the manager's commitment to the organization and to them. The nurses will eventually lose faith in the ability of the manager to lead if they do not believe in the authenticity of the manager. The nurse manager then must translate personal commitment to the staff members so that they know they are valued in accomplishing the work of the unit that furthers the mission of the organization.

One way of demonstrating that employees are valued is by recognizing staff through various means. Employees who have gone beyond the scope of their job to meet the needs of the patient, department, or institution deserve recognition. A letter of thanks, a verbal or posted acknowledgment in a departmental meeting, or an award may reflect the institution's philosophy, beliefs, and mission, as exemplified in one institution's "Quality Credo"—communication, competent performance, personal leadership, respect, and teamwork.

EXERCISE 29.3 The Director of Nursing for the local health department has just undergone a tremendous challenge because of a natural disaster of a tornado in the local vicinity. Many staff members, despite their own family needs, are assisting victims with their needs, which range from triaging patients with crisis care to adequate follow-up for chronic disorders such as asthma. The Director of Nursing decides to establish a recognition program for the staff members who have given endless hours to their community. How would you establish this recognition program? Does everyone desire recognition in the same way? If not, how would you determine how different staff would like to be recognized? What resources would you need, and where would you go to seek the needed resources? Would you engage and collaborate with community leaders? How do you want to be recognized?

MANAGING RESOURCES

Each of these concepts inherent in managing resources is addressed in depth elsewhere in this book, but the key point is that the manager must manage all of them, often collaborating and integrating each with others. The practice settings of tomorrow will no doubt continue to include in-hospital care; however, numerous innovative practice models operating from a community-based framework also may be found, as may various models of population health. Nurse managers must create and foster an environment that supports the continual quest to achieve excellent patient outcomes, thus demonstrating the important economic value that nursing brings to health care. The Patient Protection and Affordable Care Act (PPACA) propelled Medicare to reimburse hospitals not on data reporting alone, but on how well the hospital performed or bettered their performance. Value-based purchasing is designed to align the financial incentives of providers with the demonstration of quality outcomes for hospitals (Department of Health and Human Services Centers for Medicare & Medicaid, 2015). Specific quality domains with dimensions and measures are based on hospital performance. Quality domains such as patient care experience, clinical care outcomes, efficiency, and cost-reduction are weighted and measured. Program measures are several and include items such as central line–associated bloodstream infection (CLABSI), catheter-associated urinary tract infection (CAUTI), and influenza immunization (Department of Health and Human Services Centers for Medicare & Medicaid, 2015). Incentives serve as rewards for achieving positive results, and alternatively, penalties are incurred for failing to achieve them.

Nurse managers need to stay abreast of healthcare policy and reimbursement changes that are driven by the value of nursing care in improving patient outcomes. Nurse leaders must not only be aware of these financial changes but also lead and encourage the nursing staff to understand their value in ensuring the achievement of positive patient outcomes.

The manager is responsible for managing all resources designated to the unit of care, including all personnel (professionals and others) under the manager's span of control. The astute manager quickly determines that for a unit to function economically, the ways that nursing care is delivered may have to be altered.

Managed Care

Managed care's goal is to provide needed healthcare services efficiently and at an appropriate cost. In essence, this goal requires nurse managers to know and incorporate business principles into patient-care practices. Nurse managers who know business principles become conduits for ensuring safe, effective, affordable care. Appold (2017) discussed several changes that affect managed care that are on the horizon, including policy, reimbursement, consolidation, and consumer changes. Policy changes center around revision, repeal, or replacement of elements of the Affordable Care Act that will retool Medicaid and Medicare provisions. Reimbursement changes include the pressure for providers working with private and public payers to take on more risk or to expect a lower payment structure. Consolidation will be driven by cost reduction and market competition as mergers may become more common. Finally, consumer changes include more expectations of receiving care and services on demand, streamlining scheduling and registration for a positive patient experience, and continued focus on engaging consumers and the customer experience. Nurse managers need to be aware of the continued review of healthcare costs and the organizational drive toward cost reduction with improvements in quality of care.

Case Management

Case management is a method used for many years to provide care for patients in outpatient service areas. Increasingly, more traditional acute inpatient care is moving to outpatient service areas. The key to effective case management is proactive coordination of care from the point of admission, with identified time frames throughout the patient stay in accomplishing appropriate care outcomes. The nurse manager often provides oversight of or essential collaboration with case managers, and in some settings, the nurse manager is the immediate supervisor of the case managers. Case management involves components of case selection, multidisciplinary assessment, collective planning, coordination of events, negotiation and collaboration, and evaluation and documentation of the outcomes of patient status in measures of cost and quality. Case managers are employed in acute care settings, rehabilitation facilities, subacute care facilities, community-based programs, home care, and insurance companies. These managers must possess a broad range of personal, interpersonal, and management skills.

TECHNOLOGY AND INFORMATICS

Budget and personnel have always been considered critical resources. However, as technology improves, informatics must be integrated with budget and personnel as a critical resource element. The high use and rapid development of technology will continue to modify nurse manager roles. For example, because of the ability to perform more complex surgery through technology such as robotics and microsurgery, nurse managers will find themselves practicing new skills and learning new applications. With the increased expansion of the electronic health record (EHR), nurse managers must continue to encourage the use of clinical information management to assess practice concerns and to advance and standardize care processes. With electronic personnel records and staffing data, tracking individuals' records of work, promotions, and education achievements, to name a few data sets, becomes easier. Informatics in health care is in a stage of constant change and growth. Added to these organizational considerations, nurse managers also need to be aware of what the general public is using to track their health status so that they can help staff be familiar with the common resources people use.

With the groundbreaking implementation of the Health Information Technology for Economic and Clinical Health (HITECH) Act (2009), the federal government committed substantial resources to encourage widespread adoption of EHRs by organizations. The government's goal was to create a seamless flow of information and to transform health care by enabling smart technology such as tablets, smart phones, and web-enabled devices to improve communication. EHRs are designed to do the following:

- Enhance patient engagement in care
- Increase patient convenience and quality
- Enhance coordination of care
- Improve health outcomes and accuracy of diagnoses
- Improve value and practice productivity (Perlin, 2016)

Technology changes abound and are available to organizations to assist in improving patient care and work efficiency. The EHR gives quick and ready access to current and retrospective clinical patient data. These collected data are now being leveraged in clinical informatics to identify information providing trends in care that will improve care of patients and patient populations. The use of electronic patient classification systems allows managers to better measure the acuity of nursing areas, as well as assist in budget planning and in matching patient needs with the right resources. Smart beds are actual patient beds being used in hospital settings that replace the manual process of documenting patients' vital statistics, creating real time for nurses to think critically about what to do regarding the data. Smart beds can actually turn the patient with a prescribed frequency as well as document and collect the information for the nurse. Smart pumps read physician orders and calculate intravenous fluid rates and volume delivery. In-home monitoring and consultation, along with telehealth, change the role of nurses and provide new opportunities for nurse managers to consider services to a population. The accessibility and use of the Internet facilitates the education of staff, patients, and their families. Nurse managers must stay abreast of the changing technology and informatics available in health care and seek ways to leverage it to make improvements. In addition, managers must be early adopters of technology to understand its use and to demonstrate its value in performance to staff and to serve as a change agent in managing generational differences. Older generations of nurses (veterans and many Baby Boomers) did not grow up learning about informatics systems and for most of their careers may have difficulty in adapting to new technology, whereas the Generation X-ers and Generation Y Millenials grew up using technology and would not know how to exist without it.

DASHBOARDS AND DECISION SUPPORT TOOLS

Rome, Nickitas, and Lawrence (2016) advocated for the use of operational and clinical **dashboards** that assist the nurse manager in unit efficiency, effectiveness, and measuring quality of patient care and services. Data that are provided and aggregated electronically can be used by managers in determining variation from standardized quality metrics and intervening as needed. When dashboard information is accessible and transparent to the frontline staff, the nurse manager's use of the information can serve as a catalyst for departmental change and ongoing measurement.

BUDGETS AND FINANCE

Financial skills, including the knowledge of budget as well as the components that comprise the nursing or departmental budget, are a requirement for nurse managers (Rome, 2016). Budgetary allocations, whether they are related to the number of dollars available to manage a unit or related to full-time equivalent employee formulas, are the direct responsibility of nurse managers. For highly centralized organizations, only the administrative group at the executive level decides on the budgetary allocations. "Flat" organizational structures encourage decentralized responsibilities to the patient care areas, and nurse managers must understand, determine, and allocate fiscal resources for their designated unit. In the decentralized organizational model, nurse managers must have the business and financial skills to be able to prepare and justify a detailed budget that reflects the short-term and long-term needs of the unit. Several key concepts are required by nurse managers in areas such as the operating room: Productivity measurement for labor; supply costs; costs and revenues; validation of charge capture; and, importantly, the overall contribution margin (net revenue minus variable costs) (OR Manager, 2015) are examples of what nurse managers need to manage. Position control, building optimal staffing patterns including a patient classification system, is fundamental in maintaining optimal staffing (Hampton, 2017) that flexes with patient acuity and demand allowing for appropriate workforce planning (Kolakowski, 2016). The manager's focus is having the right people, at the right time, and in the right place while maintaining standards of productivity and managing resources (Kolakowski, 2016).

The ability to present a logical position, reinforced with data, is critical for nurse managers to be able to successfully operate their department while gaining the respect of and credibility from financial and operational leaders. Perhaps the most important aspect of a budget is the provision for a mechanism that allows some self-control, such as decision making at the point-of-service (POS), which does not require previous hierarchical approval and a rationale for budgetary spending. Self-scheduling is one way of allowing staff control; however, the nurse manager must set parameters to guide scheduling so that the department remains within the budget.

EXERCISE 29.4 Select and visit a very busy ambulatory surgery or outpatient center. Such places often are an early or late adopter of information technology. Although technology is an enabler of information, it can also feel like a disabler of patient contact. How do patients register? With paper (hard copy) and/or computer? What do you assume about the budget, based on the physical appearance of the setting? What information technology systems are they using? Do the employees seem distracted or motivated? Ask two or three employees to tell you, in a sentence or two, the purpose (vision and mission) of the organization. Can you readily identify the nurse manager? What principles does the manager use to manage the three critical resources of personnel, finances, and technologic access?

QUALITY INDICATORS

The nurse manager and the staff are consistently concerned with the quality of care that is being delivered on their unit. Quality indicators developed by the American Nurses Association (ANA), now managed by Press Ganey (2015), such as the NDNQI, are excellent resources for the nurse manager. The NDNQI measures are specifically concerned with patient safety and aspects of quality of care that may be affected by changes in the delivery of care or staffing resources. The quality indicators address staff mix and nursing hours for acute-care settings, as well as other care components such as nurse satisfaction. NDNQI is designed to assist healthcare organizations in identifying links between nursing care and patient outcomes. Hospitals are compared across the nation in these measurements and others such as core measures developed by The Joint Commission (2017), including care associated with acute myocardial infarctions, congestive heart failure, the treatment of pneumonia, and patient satisfaction. As with the NDNQI measures, the core measures are concerned with level of quality of care and outcomes of care. Organizations may also benchmark within their system or within groups of other organizations to compare outcomes and practices. Nurse managers are constantly concerned with the quality of care that is being delivered on their unit.

PROFESSIONALISM

Nurse managers must set examples of professionalism, which include academic preparation, roles and function, and increasing autonomy. The ANA's classic "Nursing's Social Policy Statement" (ANA, 2011) provides significant ideals for all nurses, specifically autonomy, self-regulation, and accountability. Nurses are guided by a humanistic philosophy that includes the highest regard for self-determination, independence, and choice in decision making, whether for staff or for patients. The policy statement can be used by the nurse manager as a framework for a broader understanding of nursing's connection with society and nursing's accountability to those who receive nursing care that facilitates "health and healing" in a caring relationship. For example, a nurse manager's professional philosophy should include the patient's rights (Fig. 29.4). These rights have traditionally identified such basic elements as human dignity, integrity, honesty, confidentiality, privacy, and informed consent.

EXERCISE 29.5 Nurse Frank Brown has been a nurse in the intensive care unit (ICU) for at least 15 years and is extremely clinically proficient. Today he is caring for Mrs. Gonzalez, a young mother of two who is recovering from injuries sustained in a motor vehicle accident. Mrs. Gonzalez is very anxious about being in the hospital without seeing her children and wants to be able to see them, although they are very young and not typically allowed in the ICU. Mrs. Gonzalez asks Nurse Brown if they can visit. He tells Mrs. Gonzalez that children under the age of 12 years are not permitted by the hospital rules to enter the ICU and exits the bedside. Mrs. Gonzalez begins to cry because she knows her family is worried about her and she knows the children have been crying for her at home. Nurse Brown gives report to the next 12-hour shift and reports that Mrs. Gonzalez is trying to go against hospital policy and that the department needs to be united in adhering to rules. If you were the nurse manager, how would you handle this situation? Was the behavior that Nurse Brown exhibited professional or family-centered behavior? What would be a good solution for Mrs. Gonzalez and her family? How would you demonstrate professionalism in this example? With technology that is available are there additional solutions?

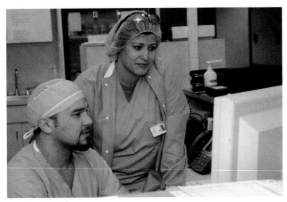

Fig. 29.4 Reviewing unit data and benchmarking it with national data is a source of key information for nurse managers. (From Miami Children's Hospital with permission.)

Professionalism is all encompassing and reflects the manager's professional philosophy as to how he or she interacts with personnel, other disciplines, patients, and families. Professional nurses are ethically and legally accountable to the standards of practice and the accompanying nursing actions delegated to others. Conveying high standards, holding others accountable, and shaping the future of nursing are inherent behaviors of a manager.

The nurse manager is the closest link with the direct care staff, setting the tone, creating a positive work environment, and managing within this context while serving as a professional role model in the development of future managers and leaders. Nurse managers must lead by example because they are highly influential on staff members' decisions to stay or leave. Finally, nurse managers are critical to the success and quality outcomes of any healthcare unit or operation.

CONCLUSION

Nurse managers have a responsibility to the patients they serve by supporting an environment that promotes advocacy for the health and healing of patients within their own emotional and psychosocial support system. By setting the example of professionalism, the manager leads by influence and models the behaviors that the direct care staff can follow. The manager serves a pivotal role in the well-being of a unit and must encourage ethical practice and guide direct care staff in delivering excellent quality care to achieve the desired results and outcomes.

THE SOLUTION

In my career as a nurse manager, patients always come first. Planning for challenging staffing situations starts with assessing the workload and frontline staff skill sets required to meet the care of the patients in the department. I have found that making these decisions about staffing early on as I assess the department's budget is crucial. This begins with hiring new staff with the right talent to provide the care needs required in the department. Importantly, having a trusting and positive working relationships within my team goes a long way in encouraging extra help to arrive. By having and resorting to a staffing contingency plan, I have been able to call staff in and modify the work schedule as needed. By negotiating with frontline staff about their future schedule, I was able to resolve the immediate staffing issue while filling in any future gaps of the schedule. On occasion, if there are relief or per diem staff available, I have also used them as an option. Using resources wisely, including being visible and flexible in directly supporting the immediate team, has been important to my success as a manager. Assessment of the current staffing situation to determine whether nontraditional resources are available to assist, such as an educator or other as-needed resource, is another strategy I have found to ensure that other patients can be received from the operating room (OR). Importantly, communication is key as I inform the OR patient flow coordinator as to present actions and to provide a timely estimate for resolution allowing for patient transfers. Overall, I cannot underscore enough the need for all stakeholders to be made aware of solutions, including the surgeons or anesthesiologist and certified registered nurse anesthetist, so that they are knowledgeable that solutions are in place to be able to receive their patients in a timely manner.

Would this be a suitable approach for you? Why?

Susan Fornaris

REFLECTIONS

Think about the role of the nurse manager from your observations and experience. What do you identify as your opportunities in the role of a nurse manager and how would you proceed in your own development to be prepared to problem solve issues? What is your personal leadership style and how would you strengthen your "tool kit" to successfully manage challenges you may face? Picture a leader whom you admire and reflect upon the person's style of leadership. How does it compare with your own? What skills do you need to further develop to be a more effective leader?

THE EVIDENCE

Older than knowledge about leadership, management views have been documented for decades. Numerous studies repeatedly show the tasks of management are critical to an effective organization. Individuals with both management and leadership skills are more effective than those who have only one set that they execute well. Having a vision is important, and if the nurse manager does not have a road map for how that can be realized on a unit or in a department, it is only an ethereal picture.

TIPS FOR IMPLEMENTING THE ROLE OF NURSE MANAGER

- Be operationally aware.
- Collaborate and communicate with unit staff and other departments on a regular basis.
- Subscribe to a management philosophy that values people.
- Commit to patient-centric, safe, quality care outcomes.
- Learn constantly.
- Know when to take risks.

REFERENCES

American Nurses Association (ANA). (2011). *Nursing's social policy statement (NP-107)*. Washington, DC: American Nurses Publishing.

American Organization of Nurse Executives, (2016). Nurse manager learning domain framework. www.aone.org/resources/leadership%20tools/NMLPframework.shtml.

Appold, K. (2017). Top four healthcare industry changes to watch in 2017. *Managed Healthcare Executive*. http://managedhealthcareexecutive.modernmedicine.com/managed-healthcare-executive/news/top-four-healthcare-industry-changes-watch-2017?page = 0,0.

Brewer, C. S., Kovner, C. T., Djukic, M., Farehi, F., Greene, W., Chacko, T., et al. (2016). Impact of transformational leadership on nurse work outcomes. *Journal of Advanced Nursing, 72*(11), 2879–2893.

Burke, A., Walker, L., & Clendon, J. (2015). Managing intergenerational nursing teams. *Kai Tiaki Nursing Research, 6*(1), 24–27.

Bursch, D. (2014). *Managing the multigenerational workplace*. UNC Kenan-Flagler Business School. http://www.kenan-flagler.unc.edu/~/media/Files/documents/executive-development/managing-the-multigenerational-workplace-white-paper.pdf

Clavelle, J. T., & Porter-O'Grady, T. (2016). Evolution of structural empowerment: Moving from shared to professional governance. *The Journal of Nursing Administration, 46*(6), 308–312.

Cox, J. A. (2016). Leadership and management roles: Challenges and success strategies. *AORN Journal, 104*(2), 155–159.

Department of Health and Human Services Centers for Medicare & Medicaid Services, (2015). Hospital value-Based purchasing. https://www.cms.gov/Outreach-and-Education/Medicare-Learning-Network-MLN/MLNProducts/downloads/Hospital_VBPurchasing_Fact_Sheet_ICN907664.pdf.

Drucker, P. F. (1974). *Management tasks, responsibilities and practices*. New York: Harper & Row.

Gopee, N. (2015). *Mentoring and supervision in healthcare* (pp. 8–222). Thousand Oaks, CA: Sage Publishing.

Hampton, M. (2017). Maintain optimal staffing with position control. *Nursing Management, 48*(1), 7–8.

Health Information Technology for Economic and Clinical Health (HITECH). Act. (2009). www.hhs.gov/ocr/privacy/hipaa/administrative/enforcementrule/hitechenforcementifr.html.

Houck, N. M., & Colbert, A. M. (2017). Patient safety and workplace bullying: An integrative review. *Journal of Nursing Care Quality, 32*(2), 164–171.

Iacono, L., & Altman, M. (2015). Nurses emerge as change leaders. *Nursing Management, 46*(8), 50–53.

Jay, M., Shafritz, J., & Ott, S. (2016). *Classics of organizational theory* (8th ed.). Boston: Cengage Learning.

Kaiser, J. A. (2017). The relationship between leadership style and nurse-to-nurse incivility: Turning the lens inward. *Journal of Nursing Management, 25*(2), 110–118.

Keller, R., Budin, W. C., & Allie, T. (2016). A task force to address bullying: How nurses at one hospital implemented an antibullying program. *American Journal of Nursing, 116*(2), 52–58.

Kolakowski, D. (2016). Constructing a nursing budget using a patient classification system. *Nursing Management, 47*(2), 14–16.

Lavoie-Tremblay, M., Fernet, C., Lavigne, G. L., & Austin, S. (2015). Transformational and abusive leadership practices: Impacts on novice nurses, quality of care and intention to leave. *Journal of Advanced Nursing, 72*(3), 582–592.

Logan, T. R. (2016). Influence of teamwork behaviors on workplace incivility as it applies to nurses. *Creighton Journal of Interdisciplinary Leadership, 2*(1), 47–53.

Ma, C., Shang, J., & Bott, M. J. (2015). Linking unit collaboration and nursing leadership to nurse outcomes and quality of care. *The Journal of Nursing Administration, 45*(9), 435–442.

Maslow, A. (1954). *Motivation and personality.* New York: Harper.

Milton, C. L. (2017). Ethics with mentoring. *Nursing Science Quarterly, 30*(2), 105–106.

Morisiani, G., Bagnasco, A., & Sasso, L. (2017). How staff nurses perceive the impact of nurse managers' leadership style in terms of job satisfaction: A mixed method study. *Journal of Nursing Management, 25*(2), 119–128.

Murray, K., Yasso, S., Schomburg, R., Terhune, M., Beidelschies, M., Bowers, D., et al. (2016). Journey of excellence: Implementing a shared decision-making model: Direct care nurses take ownership of professional practice. *American Journal of Nursing, 116*(4), 50–56.

National Academy of Medicine. (IOM). (2011). *Robert Wood Johnson Foundation's: The future of nursing: Leading change, advancing health.* Washington, DC: The National Academy Press.

Nei, D., Snyder, L. A., & Litwiller, B. J. (2015). Promoting retention of nurses: A meta-analytic examination of causes of nurse turnover. *Health Care Management Review, 40*(3), 237–253.

Newman, B. M., & Newman, P. R. (2016). *Theories of Human Development* (pp. 167–172). New York: Psychology Press.

OR Manager. (2015). Master five key concepts to sharpen financial management skills. *OR Manager, 31*(5), 1–3.

Perlin, J. B. (2016). Health information technology interoperability and use for better care and evidence. *Viewpoint: Vital Directions from the National Academy of Medicine, 316*(16), 1667–1668.

Pontefract, D. (2016). Maybe we need to think about workplace actualization. *Forbes.* https://www.forbes.com/sites/danpontefract/2016/01/26/maybe-we-need-to-think-about-workplace-actualization/#550599f14046.

Porter-O'Grady, T. (2015a). Confluence and convergence: Team effectiveness in complex systems. *Nursing Administration Quarterly, 39*(1), 78–83.

Porter-O'Grady, T. (2015b). The looking glass: Predictive and adaptive capacity in a time of great change. *Nursing Management, 46*(6), 29–30.

Press Ganey. (2015). *Nursing Quality (NDNQI): Improve care quality, prevent adverse events with deep nursing quality insights.* http://www.pressganey.com/solutions/clinical-quality/nursing-quality.

Rome, B., Nickitas, D., & Lawrence, D. A. (2016). The financial landscape and the implications for nursing. *Nurse Leader, 14*(1), 33–37.

Smith, C. (2015). Exemplary leadership: How style and culture predict organizational outcomes. *Nursing Management, 46*(3), 47–51.

Sullivan, M., Kiovsky, R., Mason, D., Hill, C., & Dukes, C. (2015). Interprofessional collaboration and education. *American Journal of Nursing, 115*(3), 47–54.

Steinhauer, R. (2016). *Change agents for good. Reflections on nursing leadership.* https://www.reflectionsonnursingleadership.org/features/more-features/Vol42_4_transformational-leaders-change-agents-for-good.

The Joint Commission. (2017). Joint Commission measures effective January 1, 2017. www.jointcommission.org/joint_commission_measures_effective_january_1_2017.

Turriago-Hoyos, A., Thoene, U., & Arjoon, S. (2016). Knowledge workers and virtues in Peter Drucker's management theory. *SAGE Open, January-March, 2016*, 1–9.

Udod, S. A., Cummings, G., Care, W. D., & Jenkins, M. (2017). Impact of role stressors on the health of nurse managers. *The Journal of Nursing Administration, 47*(3), 159–164.

30

The Strategic Planning Process

Mary Ellen Clyne

LEARNING OUTCOMES

- Explain the purpose of a strategic planning process.
- Understand the strategic planning process.
- Describe the four components of a SWOT analysis.
- Create a S.M.A.R.T. goal.

KEY TERMS

S.M.A.R.T. goal

strategic plan

strategic planning process

SWOT analysis

THE CHALLENGE

A hospital established a strategic plan, and the organization set a goal to be best in class for all quality indicators. This organization was on the Magnet Journey®, and I worked with the Professional Practice Council and Quality Council to incorporate the hospital's strategic plan into a nursing strategic plan. This ensured that the strategic plan and goals would align at the unit level. I noted that a review of the hospital-acquired conditions (HACs) during the Quality Council meeting demonstrated central line–associated bloodstream infections (CLABSIs) in the intensive care unit were above the national benchmark. This deviation was a major concern for me and the Professional Practice Council, because the goal to be best in class for CLABSIs was not achieved.

What would you do if you were this nurse?

Anonymous

INTRODUCTION

A strategic plan is a written plan of action that anticipates the future so that an organization can adapt and survive in a changing and competitive environment. The strategic planning process allows for an organization to take a realistic examination of its current state, where it needs to be, how to get to where it needs to be, and how people know how well they are doing.

Nurse executives are transforming nursing practice by creating a model for intentional improvement and innovation by developing a nursing strategic plan to achieve nursing excellence (Clavelle & Goodwin,

2016). To create this in an effective manner, nurses throughout an organization need to be involved in the process and consider how the overall plan influences the work throughout the organization.

STRATEGIC PLANNING

Strategic planning provides members of the organization with the necessary tactical plans to achieve the organizational goals. The focus of the strategic planning process is designed to encompass the organization's emphasis on the mission, vision, and values; environmental factors affecting the organization (both internally and externally); and the development and execution of new strategies, goals, and tactical plans, which are continuously being evaluated.

The strategic planning process shown in Fig. 30.1 consists of the following steps:

- Phase 1: Environmental Scanning, SWOT Analysis, and Benchmarking—Explore the external, internal, and organizational environment to determine those forces or changes that may affect the work of the organization or that may be crucial to its survival. Analyze the organization's *strengths, weaknesses, opportunities,* and *threats* (SWOT analysis) and its potential for dealing with change. The strengths and weaknesses are analyzed from the current state of the organization, from an internal perspective. The opportunities and threats are external to the organization. Establish and determine your benchmarks.

- Phase 2: Strategic Vision and Mission—Revise, as appropriate, the organization's mission, vision, and values, then select strategic issues.
- Phase 3: Strategic Development—Develop and evaluate the various strategies available to the organization to meet these weaknesses, opportunities, and threats. A plan is developed to guide the organization.
- Phase 4: Implement the Strategy—Select the best strategic option that balances the organization's potential with the challenges of changing conditions, taking into account the values of its management and its social responsibilities. Prepare the strategy and tactical plan to support the strategy. Execute the plan.
- Phase 5: Monitor Progress—Evaluate the strategy. Set up monitoring and plan updating. Revise the plan as appropriate.

REASONS FOR STRATEGIC PLANNING

The healthcare environment is complex and ever changing. To that end, many healthcare organizations can no longer rely on developing a 5- to 10-year strategic plan as was done in the past. Many plans today are based on a 2- to 4-year time frame because of the rapidity of change. Strategic planning for healthcare organizations must be more than an outline of a business plan; it is paramount that the strategic planning process is adaptable, agile, and fluid enough to change course as necessary to meet future changes. The strategic plan becomes the organizational vision for the future (Fig. 30.2).

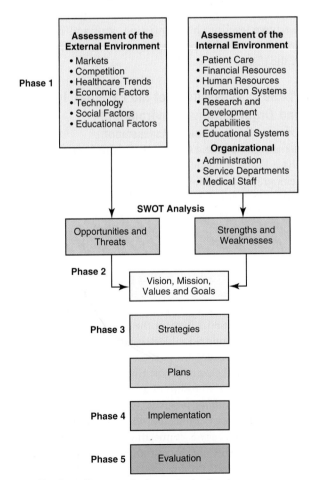

Fig. 30.1 Key steps in the strategic planning process.

Fig. 30.2 A strong and dynamic strategic plan results in efficient and effective use of resources. (Copyright © Sarinyapinngam/iStock/Thinkstock.)

The strategic planning process leads to achievement of goals and objectives, gives meaning to work life, and provides direction and improvement for operational activities of the organization. Furthermore, using a strong and dynamic strategic plan results in efficient and effective use of resources and reflects the organizational culture and customer focus (Strumwasser & Virkstis, 2015). Numerous reasons exist for nurse leaders to plan in a proactive, systematic manner, including: (1) knowledge regarding philosophy, goals, and external and internal operations of the organization and (2) an understanding of the planning process.

The strategic planning process cannot happen in a vacuum, and nurses can be instrumental in this process. The goals of the organization must align with nursing departments so that everyone is working toward those same goals and objectives. An empowered nursing staff can assist in developing a strategic plan for nursing that aligns and emulates with the organization's strategic plan. Nurses are the driving force that can implement and monitor the strategic plan to ensure success that demonstrates an improvement in patient safety, quality outcomes, patient experience, and costs.

PHASES OF THE STRATEGIC PLANNING PROCESS

Strategic planning is a proactive process that is vision-directed, action-oriented, creative, innovative, intentional, and oriented toward positive change for growth (Clavelle & Goodwin, 2016). A successful strategic plan will incorporate the creation of a business plan; this plan is integrated with a financial plan so that resources can be allocated and time can be allotted for implementation. Capital resources required for its realization must also be determined. Execution of the strategic plan is paramount for organizations; failure of focus on execution will paralyze the organization. A strong and dynamic strategic plan results in efficient and effective use of resources.

The term *strategic planning process* is the development of a plan of action covering a defined few years of time, such as 3 to 5 years, although, again, some organizations use a shorter time frame. The initial phase of the strategic planning process is the most difficult and often, when done correctly, the most time consuming.

According to Lowy (2015), a strategic *leader* is someone who can get things accomplished by understanding

> ### BOX 30.1   The Six Core Dilemmas of Implementing Strategic Plans
>
> - Time and resources
> - Integration
> - Leadership
> - Confidence
> - Morale
> - Change

From Lowy, A. (2015). The six dilemmas of strategy execution. *Strategy & Leadership, 43*(6), 18–24.

the dilemmas that are encountered along the way so they can be addressed and is resilient when setbacks transpire. Dilemmas are not to be viewed as negative; instead, dilemmas should be viewed as opportunities. Six core dilemmas comprise the issues a strategic leader must address, as shown in Box 30.1. The strategic leader searches for a new path through purposeful dialogue with various constituents, both internally and externally. Although strategic planning is often achieved at the executive level of an organization, staff and managers provide a valuable perspective and test the feasibility of the plan.

Phase 1: Assessment of the External, Internal, and Organizational Environment
External Environmental Assessment

Assessment of the external environment is the initial phase in the strategic planning process. The economic, demographic, technologic, sociocultural, educational, natural factors (such as natural disasters), and political-legal factors are assessed in terms of their impact on opportunities and threats within the environment. Healthcare leaders can assess the effect of competitors on their environment, and thus plan and monitor their own operations to develop other creative and distinctive programs as they work within the framework of their institutional mission, vision, and goals. An example appears in Box 30.2. One of the current driving forces is the work around Social Determinants of Health.

Another consideration for the external environment is the views of the community. Greater emphasis is being placed on the relationship of a healthcare organization with the community it serves. Often leaders approach this connection by connecting with community leaders. Yet another strategy is connecting with former patients. They are members of the community and have had (or still have) direct experiences with the organization. When considering such involvement, though, specific

BOX 30.2   An Example of Environmental Assessment

A community-based acute care hospital is undertaking a study to examine accessibility, availability, quality, and effectiveness of developing an Orthopedic Center of Excellence. One of the initial steps is to conduct an environmental scan. The factors considered are the following:

- Economic forces and the escalating rates of healthcare costs
- The numbers and types of health professionals, including board-certified orthopedic physicians who are specializing in innovative joint replacement, operating room (OR) orthopedic nurses and OR orthopedic surgical technicians (certified), orthopedic direct care nurses (certified), case managers, social workers, physical and occupational therapists, and pain management specialists
- Cost of orthopedic implants and reimbursement

- The social, political, and regulatory forces, including strategic priorities of the government in health promotion and disease prevention
- The diagnostic services available, including magnetic resonance imaging (MRI) and nuclear diagnostic imaging
- Community outreach and educational opportunities

Patient Trends
- Demographic and population trends (population, employment, socioeconomic indicators, education, ethnicity, and lifestyle issues, with particular emphasis on minority groups)
- Trends in health care (increased emphasis on wellness programs and enhanced technologies)
- Prospective users' input about current and future services
- Social determinants of health

LITERATURE PERSPECTIVE

Resource: Kuucmanic, M., & Sheon, A. R. (2017). What critical ethical values guide strategic planning processes in health care? *AMA Journal of Ethics, 19*(11), 1073–1080.

An ethics case study is presented in which a group of clinicians and former patients disagree on the design of future inpatient units. The authors point out the importance of procedural fairness in the process. Specific steps to ensure everyone is heard, and fairly so, are presented. The group should be encouraged to be honest and open with one another to promote a sense of trust in the process. It is also important for the group to value and

embrace the diverse views that are being shared. Additionally, creating a process for ongoing feedback can be useful in gaining people's commitment to engaging in strategic processes.

Implications for Practice
Finding patients who are articulate and have diverse views is a critical step in gaining patient perspectives. This approach at a service or unit level could be especially effective for both patients and the organization.

attention should be made to the ways to engage these individuals so they feel their input is valued. The Literature Perspective illustrates the potential and the ethical considerations we must make to engage former patients in this process.

EXERCISE 30.1 The Chief Nursing Officer (CNO) of an acute care hospital is interested in becoming a Magnet®-designated hospital. The CNO would like to create a strategic plan for nursing excellence. If you were the CNO, what would the mission statement for nursing say? What would the vision statement for nursing say? What would be the core values of the nursing department?

Internal Environmental Assessment

The internal assessment of the environment relates to the institution of health care and includes a review of the effectiveness of the structure, size, programs, financial resources, human resources, information systems, and research and development capabilities of the organization. In addition, education and training of staff and public demands are reviewed. The management team involves all levels of staff in this process and focuses on the purpose of the organization; the mission and goals; the capabilities, skills, and relationships of various professional and related staff; and the weaknesses and strengths of staff in such areas as leadership, planning, coordination, research, and staff development. The purpose of this assessment is to determine where the organization excels and where it does not.

Organizational Environmental Assessment

The organizational environment assessment relates to the organizational administration, nursing, and service departments. The process is considered an informal evaluation of relationships that define the organizational boundaries to assess for structure and loyalties that may affect the achievement of work. Also, the organizational climate must be assessed because it can shape the strategic direction of the organization. For example, organizations with a culture of engagement are more likely to have nurses in all types of positions actually engaged in this process than are organizations where tensions exist between the organizations' values and how nurses perceive the enactment of those values.

Phase 2: Review of Mission, Vision, and Value Statement, Philosophy, Goals, and Objectives

Mission Statement

A mission statement reflects the purpose and direction of the healthcare organization or a department within it and how it will meet the needs of its internal and external stakeholders. Additionally, a mission statement will support the vision of the organization. A vision statement reflects what the healthcare organization believes in and how it behaves; the vision statement is usually inspirational to impart a mental image of the organization in a futuristic perspective of what the organization wants to achieve. A value statement incorporates the priorities of the organization's culture, with an emotional investment. Normally, four to six core values are defined for a healthcare organization. A statement of philosophy captures the belief system of the organization, which includes its concepts as well as its principles. The content usually specifies organizational beliefs regarding the rights of individuals; beliefs regarding health and nursing; expectations of practitioners; and commitment of the organization to professionalism, education, evaluation, and research. The importance of the mission statement cannot be overstated, yet it is questionable how many individuals in an organization, when questioned directly, can articulate their mission statement or the philosophy. Furthermore, if the mission statement is seen only as an administrative requirement, it is likely a challenge to have nurses articulate how it is lived in patient care.

Classically, Covey (1990) identified that the mission statement is vital to the success of an organization and believes that everyone should participate in the development of the mission statement: "The involvement process is as important as the written product and is the key to its use" (p. 139). "An organizational mission statement, one that truly reflects the deep shared vision and values of everyone within that organization, creates a unity and tremendous commitment" (p. 143). An example of it, along with a vision and philosophy statement, appears in Box 30.3.

EXERCISE 30.2 A Chief Nursing Officer (CNO) is embarking on the Magnet® journey and is working with the nursing leadership team, various professional practice councils, and the frontline nursing staff to create a strategic plan for nursing. The CNO would like to complete an internal environmental assessment regarding the current status of nursing excellence. The nurse leaders and nursing staff are assigned to examine the strengths and weaknesses of the nursing department; examine the quality patient care outcomes indicators; and examine the patient experience scores of a Magnet®-designated organization and review their outcomes on the website *www.hospitalcompare.gov*.

Select a hospital. Evaluate it and determine its strengths and weaknesses. Do the quality scores and patient satisfaction scores demonstrate excellence? Then, find the website of the organization and review the mission, vision, and values, if available. Do these statements make sense given the operational definition for each?

BOX 30.3   Examples of a Mission, Vision, and Philosophy Statement

Mission
The mission of the nursing department is to be the best in class by providing safe, compassionate, quality care while focusing on the individual needs of our patients and their loved ones.

Vision
Clara Maass Medical Center is the best place to give care and the best place to get care.

Philosophy
This organization supports a positive work environment to promote its professional nursing practice and believes in the following principles:

We provide the highest level of quality care while embracing patient safety practices to those whom we serve; nursing care is delivered with respect and dignity by incorporating cultural competency, conscious inclusion, and compassion; we are committed to enhancing the advancement of nursing practice through research and education; and we are driven by our ability to close the gap on healthcare disparities.

Goal Setting

Goal setting is the process of developing, negotiating, and formalizing the targets or objectives of an organization. Goals must be appropriate for the organization. If the goals are not appropriate or not executed, then the plan will most likely fail, which carries negative implications for the organization (Clavelle & Goodwin, 2016; Lowy, 2015; Zwickel, Koppel, Katz, Virkstis, Rothenberger, & Boston-Fleischhauer, 2016).

Below are examples of goals that comprise the nursing strategic plan at the University of California (UC) Irvine Healthcare:

1. Provide high-quality, accessible, patient-centered care.
2. Promote translational research.
3. Provide outstanding educational experiences for new graduate nurses, new hires, and current staff.
4. Establish strong, consistent, and committed leadership.
5. Instill a culture of pride, accountability, and teamwork across nursing.
6. Foster exceptional staff engagement.
7. Create a culture of philanthropy.
8. Develop a sustainable financial future for nursing.
9. Establish strong collaboration and partnerships through Orange County and the region.

EXERCISE 30.3 Review the literature related to a nursing strategic plan. What do the mission statements convey as nursing's mission? What common words and themes are used?

Practical insights that are critical to nurse leaders are that specific goals are more likely to lead to higher performance than are vague or very general goals, such as "try to do your best." Feedback, or knowledge of results, is more likely to motivate individuals toward higher performance levels and commitment to goal achievements. For example, as organizations have become more focused on quality outcomes related to care, they have been able to focus on specific goals and behaviors that result in intentional improvement in quality care.

Four key steps in implementing a goal-setting program are as follows:

1. Set goals that are specific and adhere to a deadline.
2. Promote goal commitment by providing instructions and support to the nursing staff and nurse leaders.
3. Support the achievement of goals with appropriate feedback as soon as possible.
4. Monitor performance at appropriate intervals.

Goals/Objectives

The ability to write clear and concise objectives is an important aspect of nursing leadership. Effective objectives that are *specific, measurable, achievable, relevant,* and *time* bound are known as S.M.A.R.T. goals or objectives, as illustrated in Box 30.4.

S.M.A.R.T objectives are important because they allow for transparency of what is expected so that all stakeholders can be held accountable and are more focused. They also give an organization the purpose to build a culture of success.

BOX 30.4   SMART Goals

Specific: The objective statement is properly constructed and describes exactly what is to be accomplished (it is simple, sensible, and significant).
- It begins with the word *to,* followed by an action verb.
- It specifies a single result to be achieved.
- It specifies a target date for its attainment.

Measurable: The objectives are measurable (it is meaningful and motivating).
- They provide the level of accomplishment of the end result.
- They leave no question as to what is expected.

Achievable: The objectives are agreed on by all parties (it is attainable).
- Mutual agreement is reached by all parties who will be responsible for execution and monitoring.

Relevant: The objectives must be created within the realm of possibility and a challenge (it is reasonable, realistic, resourced, and results based).
- The objectives should not be unrealistic or unattainable.
- They must be written in the span of control for the specific team working toward the goals.
- The team has to be accountable for follow-through.

Time Bound: The objectives should establish a time frame for which the activity or improvement must be achieved (it is time-based).
- Time lines and deadlines are adhered to.
- The time line must be well-defined by avoiding statements such as "in the future."

Phase 3: Identification of Strategies

The third phase of the strategic planning process involves identifying major issues or dilemmas, establishing goals, and developing strategies to meet the goals. The term *strategy* can be defined as an organized and innovative plan that assists an organization to achieve its objectives. All internal stakeholders, including the Chief Nursing Officer and the nursing staff, are involved in this process and are responsible for preparing a detailed plan of action, which may include the following: development of short-term and long-term objectives, formulation of annual department objectives, allocation of resources, and preparation of the budget. Fig. 30.3 shows a portion of a nursing strategic plan for Jersey City Medical Center.

Phase 4: Implementation

The fourth phase of strategic planning is that the specific plan for action is executed in order of priority. This entails open communication with nursing staff (this is paramount) regarding the priorities for the next year and subsequent periods; development of revised policies and procedures regarding the changes; and the creation of departmental and individual- and unit-level objectives related to the plan. The specific plan needs to be focused on marketing, programs, operations, budget, and human resources.

Although the overall strategic plan may be more general in nature, each of the subsequent "drill down" versions applicable to divisions, services, or units should be specific enough that even those not involved in the process have a clear view of what they are to do to contribute to the overall success of the organization. An example of a service-based planning process is addressed in the Literature Perspective. The strategic plan itself may be a few pages in length followed by numerous pages of details to explain what the mission, vision, and values mean in terms of a given area. As a result, if people looked at the plan they would know what clinical services were on growth trajectories, what the marketing services were to do to promote that growth, what recruitment strategies were needed to secure the right people to execute the service, and so forth. A solidly written strategic plan can translate to what an individual could predict for his or her future depending on the clinical area and focus. That

said, a word of caution is needed: in today's rapidly changing healthcare horizon, thinking broadly about the plan is more useful than thinking about this as a definitive word.

When implementing the strategic plan, the plan of action will stipulate the goal(s) to be achieved and what is required to be accomplished, by who, when, and how. Ownership and accountability in seeing this plan through are critical to implementation (Tye & Dent, 2017).

Phase 5: Evaluation

On a consistent basis, at regular intervals, the strategic plan is reviewed to determine whether the execution of goals, objectives, and activities are on target. As stated, a sense of flexibility regarding the objectives is important to consider. Objectives may change as a result of legislation, budget changes, and change in structure or other environmental factors. Therefore alternative activities may need to be adapted for any unforeseen situation.

EXERCISE 30.4 As a nurse in a healthcare organization and chair of the quality council for your unit, you were asked by the Chief Nursing Officer for assistance in developing at least five quality S.M.A.R.T. goals for the nursing strategic plan. Develop a quality goal and list two strategies (actions to be taken) to achieve the goal.

CONCLUSION

Nurses are instrumental in the development of a strategic plan for nursing and for the execution of the strategic planning process. Nurse leaders have business skill competencies, which provide them the opportunity to facilitate the strategic planning process, lending credibility for them to be strategic leaders. Nursing leaders are accountable for setting goals and engaging nurses in those activities. Nurses in direct care need to be engaged in the process to be effective in implementing the plan. A strategic plan is deemed successful when demonstrated intentional improvement in the outcomes is evident.

Plan Summary

JCMC

● Completed	● On Schedule	○ Making Progress
● Behind Schedule	○ Incomplete/Abandoned	○ Not Started

Nursing 2015-2017

Status	Ref #	Goals	Pillar	Council	Leaders	Target Date	Complete
○	1.	NURSING STRATEGIC GOAL: Improve Medication Management Across the Continuum for safe care transition leading to reduced readmissions and improved population health	Quality	Quality & Safety Nursing	Jane Smith	12/31/17	

Status	Ref #	Priority Initiatives			Leaders	Target Date	Complete
○	1.1.	Review literature for evidence based practices for safe care transitions through interdisciplinary medication mngt. Implement the plan in accordance with Organization's Mission, Vision and Magnet standards.			Jane Smith; Mary Jones	3/30/16	3/30/16

Status	Ref #	Tactics	Start Date	As Of	Leaders	Target Date	Complete
○	1.1.1.	Literature review completed	7/1/15	2/29/16	Mary Jones	2/1/16	2/29/16
○	1.1.2.	Present to Barnabas Health Nursing Leadership	1/1/16	2/11/16	Mary Jones; Jane Smith	2/29/16	2/11/16

Status	Ref #	Priority Initiatives			Leaders	Target Date	Complete
○	1.2.	Design and implement the high risk readmission assessment inclusive of the LACE tool and Pharmacy screening for Medical Surgical patients.			Mary Jones	12/31/15	9/28/15

Status	Ref #	Tactics	Start Date	As Of	Leaders	Target Date	Complete
○	1.2.1.	Develop LACE Tool and Pharmacy Screening Form for High Risk Readmission Assessment	6/1/15	9/28/15	Mary Jones	9/28/15	9/28/15
○	1.2.2.	Build High Risk for Readmission Assessment in Soarian	6/1/15	9/1/15	Mary Jones	9/1/15	9/1/15
○	1.2.3.	Professional Practice Council Review and Approval	6/1/15	8/5/15	Mary Jones	8/5/15	8/5/15
○	1.2.4.	P & T Committee Review and Approval	6/1/15	9/24/15	Jane Smith	9/30/15	9/24/15
○	1.2.5.	Implement Training and go live	6/1/15	9/28/15	Mary Jones	9/28/15	9/28/15

Status	Ref #	Priority Initiatives			Leaders	Target Date	Complete
○	1.3.	Review the medication reconciliation process in the outpatient areas and inititate a reconciliation process to empower patients and their caregivers for successful medication management.			Carol Black	12/1/17	6/1/16

Status	Ref #	Tactics	Start Date	As Of	Leaders	Target Date	Complete
○	1.3.1.	Outpatient areas to identify high risk patients for medication reconciliation such as Diabetes patients in Center for Comprehensive Care, Infusion Center, and CHF Clinic	1/1/16	6/1/16	Carol Black	12/1/17	6/1/16

Status	Ref #	Priority Initiatives			Leaders	Target Date	Complete

Plan Summary

JCMC

● Completed	● On Schedule	○ Making Progress
● Behind Schedule	○ Incomplete/Abandoned	○ Not Started

Nursing 2015-2017

Status	Ref #				Leaders	Target Date	Complete
○	1.4.	Implement outreach education to sub-acute facilities on medication management topics			Nancy Frederic; Joanne Reich	12/1/17	

Status	Ref #	Tactics	Start Date	As Of	Leaders	Target Date	Complete
○	1.4.1.	Identify sub acute facility for partnership	1/1/16	3/23/16	Jane Smith	12/1/16	3/23/16
○	1.4.2.	Meet with Nursing Leadership of sub acute facility for joint discussion and agreement	1/1/16	3/23/16	Jane Smith	3/23/16	3/23/16
○	1.4.3.	Conduct educational session with nursing staff at sub acute facility, CEUs provided	3/1/16	9/9/16	Mary Jones; Jane Smith	9/9/16	9/9/16
○	1.4.4.	Repeat Educational Fair in 2017	1/1/17		Jane Smith	11/30/17	

	Note				Posted By		Posted Date
		Michele Lopez and Joanne Reich will schedule a meeting with Nursing Leadership at Alaris Hamilton Park to discuss topics for the 2017 Educational Fair for nursing staff.			Joanne Reich		5/2/17

Status	Ref #	Priority Initiatives			Leaders	Target Date	Complete
○	1.5.	Communicate the plan, provide updates at Nursing Leadership and note progress.			Mary Jones; Jane Smith	12/1/17	

Status	Ref #	Tactics	Start Date	As Of	Leaders	Target Date	Complete
○	1.5.1.	Present Nursing Strategic Plan progess	1/1/16	1/12/17	Jane Smith	12/1/17	1/12/17
○	1.5.2.	Pharmacy notes monthly LACE consults completed	9/1/16	12/31/16	Jane Smith	12/31/16	12/31/16
○	1.5.3.	Care Continuum conducting bedside visits of LACE high risk readmission patients, reported monthly	1/1/16	12/31/16	Jane Smith	12/31/16	12/31/16
○	1.5.4.	Nursing Quality & Safety Council audits Medication Management for completion of home medications list monthly	1/31/16	12/31/16	Jane Smith	12/31/16	12/31/16

Status	Ref #	Goals	Pillar	Council	Leaders	Target Date	Complete
○	2.	NURSING STRATEGIC GOAL: Introduce Motivational Interviewing	Quality	Professional Practice Nursing	Jane Smith	12/31/17	

Status	Ref #	Priority Initiatives			Leaders	Target Date	Complete
○	2.1.	Increase nurses' understanding and increase use of motivational interviewing (MI) techniques across the continuum of care; initiate a pilot introduction of MI.			Jane Smith	4/1/16	12/30/16

Status	Ref #	Tactics	Start Date	As Of	Leaders	Target Date	Complete
○	2.1.1.	Review resources and identify an MI expert to provide introduction to JCMC clinical staff	1/1/16	4/1/16	Jane Smith	4/1/16	4/1/16
○	2.1.2.	Engaged MI Expert, Annie Fahy RN, LCSW, MINT (Motivational Interviewing Network of Trainers)	1/1/16	3/1/16	Jane Smith	3/1/16	3/1/16

Status	Ref #	Priority Initiatives			Leaders	Target Date	Complete

Fig. 30.3 Portion of a nursing strategic plan. (Courtesy Jersey City Medical Center, an affiliate of RWJ Barnabas Health. Jersey City, New Jersey.)

LITERATURE PERSPECTIVE

Resource: Windey, M., Schivinski, E, & Tyrna, J. (2017). Strategic planning: The need to look ahead. *Journal for Nurses in Professional Development, 33*(6), 318–319.

This brief article addresses how one hospital approached the need to ensure adequate staffing. The plan, called *Nurse-Ahead,* allows the nursing department to hire newly licensed nurses without having to request a position or use a position that was posted. The intent was that these individuals would enter into the organization's nurse residency program. This idea was built on a SWOT analysis to create a forecast of how to implement a residency staffing model. The reported turnover rate in the first year was 4%.

Implications for Practice

Not every organization may be able to afford this kind of staffing; however, thinking differently about what is possible created an opportunity for at least one organization to consider how to recruit new graduates and not count them in full staff positions, which in turn allowed for recruitment of more seasoned staff.

THE SOLUTION

Trying to find common ground to achieve the vision of preventing central line–acquired bloodstream infections (CLABSIs) in the intensive care unit (ICU) was of the utmost importance. A shared governance model was developed, and a unit-based quality council was established. I thought this would be a great starting place for the nursing staff to develop a creative way to bring their vision to reality. Specifically, the unit-based quality council could develop a plan to address the eradicate CLABSIs in the ICU by using S.M.A.R.T. objectives to ensure transparency, accountability, and success. Thus the ICU quality council was empowered with decision-making capacity.

The nurses conducted an evidence-based literature review for CLABSIs and disseminated the research studies among the nursing members of the unit-based quality council. Dialogue ensued, and the ICU quality council members were very interested in the findings and wanted to explore ways to become best in class for eradicating CLABSIs in the ICU and to positively affect the overall strategic plan for nursing.

The nurses were engaged and felt empowered to intentionally eradicate CLABSIs. The nurses understood that by embracing the evidence-based practice and adapting their procedures, it would undoubtedly have a profound effect on eradicating CLABSIs. The benefit of being able to eradicate CLABSIs is that it would ultimately demonstrate nursing's commitment to patient safety and delivering the highest quality of care.

The nurses from the quality council reviewed their findings and implications for preventing CLABSIs with the Professional Practice Council. The council fully supported this strategy to achieve the goal. I made sure the nurses on the quality council had all the appropriate resources available to them in making changes to the policies and procedures and empowered the nurses to remove all barriers so they would have success in making their vision come true.

The nurses were fully engaged and invested in eradicating CLABSIs. The nurses were instrumental in making this vision become a reality.

A shared governance model allowed for the nurses to be the change agents of the organization. By establishing various councils, nurses were engaged and empowered to elevate the level of nursing practice and patient outcomes. Nurses were recognized for their expertise and ability to resolve and prevent any potential hospital-acquired conditions or patient safety issues through evidence-based practices. The nurses turned their vision into reality, based on nursing research and best practices. The nursing council members took great pride in their accomplishments, and I recognized them accordingly. The nurses demonstrated their commitment to excellence in patient care, and their efforts did not go unnoticed. I discussed with the hospital leadership, Board of Trustees, and the Medical Staff exactly how the nurses embraced and participated in the strategic planning process to achieve the necessary goals for excellence in patient care.

Would this be a suitable approach for you? Why?

Anonymous

▊ REFLECTIONS

Think back on your experiences thus far. In what way have you been involved with strategic planning? What can you do to convey to others the importance of nurses being engaged in the strategic planning process? What are you willing to commit to in terms of involvement in the future?

▊ THE EVIDENCE

Most organizations have defined mission, vision, and values statements. Bringing those to direct care situations makes the strategic planning process valuable to patients and staff alike. Addressing the dilemmas inherent in strategic planning implementation is a key role nurses can play to make plans effective.

▊ TIPS FOR DEVELOPING AND EXECUTING A STRATEGIC PLAN FOR NURSING

- Be clear about the mission, vision, and values of nursing; ensure they align with the organizational goals and meet the needs of those you serve, and stay true to them.
- Continuously read and listen to wide sources of data to determine any patterns or trends happening that could have an effect on health care as a whole or your organization, and be flexible if changes are imminent.
- Be clear about your role in the organization and its success. Actively participate in the process.
- Think about what messages others need to hear about the intentional improvements being made and tell actual stories that demonstrate the impact of achieving the goals of the nursing strategic plan.

REFERENCES

Clavelle, J., & Goodwin, M. (2016). The center for nursing excellence: A health system model for intentional improvement and innovation. *Journal of Nursing Administration, 46*(11), 613–618.

Covey, S. (1990). *The seven habits of highly effective people.* Toronto: Simon & Schuster.

Lowy, A. (2015). The six dilemmas of strategy execution. *Strategy and Leadership, 43*(6), 18–24. https://doi.org/ 10.1108/SL-07-2015-0062.

Strumwasser, S., & Virkstis, K. (2015). Meaningfully incorporating staff input to enhance frontline engagement. *Journal of Nursing Administration, 45*(4), 179–182.

Tye, J., & Dent, B. (2017). *Building a culture of ownership in healthcare: The invisible architecture of core values, attitude, and self-empowerment.* Indianapolis, IN: Sigma Theta Tau.

University of California (UC) Irvine Healthcare, Nursing Strategic Plan for 2011-2017. Retrieved www. healthsciences.uci.edu/docs/nursing-strategic-plan.pdf.

Zwickel, K., Koppel, J., Katz, M., Virkstis, K., Rothenberger, S., & Boston-Fleischhauer, C. (2016). Translating market forces into frontline terms. *Journal of Nursing Administration, 46*(11), 552–554.

31

The Future
NEXT EXIT

Thriving for the Future

Patricia S. Yoder-Wise

LEARNING OUTCOMES

- Value the need to think about the future while meeting current expectations.
- Ponder two or three projections for the future and what they mean to the practice of nursing.

- Determine three projections for the future that have implications for individual practice.

KEY TERMS

chaos
complexity compression

forecasting
innovation

shared vision
vision

THE CHALLENGE

I had been working for several years and had just accepted a position as a correctional nurse working with high-risk adolescents and adults. I pictured my job of completing physical assessments and managing the medication delivery system. Over time, I learned that I was working with a population who were poor, had high-risk health behaviors, lacked access to health care, and often had physical and mental health problems. They often were returned to the community with many of the same problems. As the only nurse and health advocate in the facility, I realized that I had to search out and develop innovative

solutions to the multitude of unmet health needs. I also knew I didn't have the skills or experiences to develop effective interventions. In addition, I determined that changes in the future that would improve the care for this population were unlikely.

What would you do if you were this nurse?

Sara McCumber, APRN, BC, MSN
Adult/Family Nurse Practitioner, Duluth Clinic, Duluth, Minnesota

INTRODUCTION

Leading and managing in nursing constitute a consistent challenge. One of the biggest challenges is to create a future we wish to see. Even nurses who say they do not want to lead or manage find that the demands of nursing call for continuous leadership and increased

self-management skills. The core point is this: We are all accountable for something, and by virtue of our professional licensure status we must lead when we have the insight, the ability, or the skill needed to move a situation forward. As stated in Chapter 1, every role has expectations associated with it. Thus every nurse has a leadership role to execute in practice.

Changes affecting health care occur rapidly. Even though healthcare changes often happen as a response to something (e.g., a change in funding, a new piece of equipment, a new bundle for care, or new research findings), thinking proactively is useful. In essence, thinking and subsequently acting proactively allows us to shape the future rather than the future simply shaping us.

Just when some stability seems likely, another new project or invention alters the established practice. Today, most people accept apps for phones as standard, yet only a few decades ago a phone was wired and in the house. Two or three generations ago, people received health care (if they sought any) in the home, and if they went to the hospital, it was for weeks—or to die! Today people still tend to seek illness care, and if they are hospitalized, it is for hours or days. Even though little financial reward is associated with wellness, some people and organizations are focusing on prevention and wellness. An example is what the Rosen Hotels in Florida have developed for employee wellness programs. Both owner and employees highly value what they have because it is affordable and proactive.

We see the return of care in the home, but now through remote interactive devices. Robotics have become a necessity in health care. Monitoring our health through apps changes how people are involved in their care. Just think what changes we will experience in our near future! See Fig. 31.1 for a representation of the never-ending cycle of change.

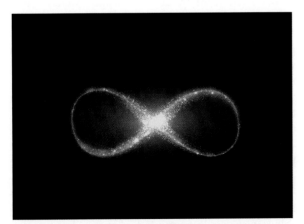

Fig. 31.1 The infinity symbol represents the never-ending cycle of change. (Copyright © Tatianazaets/iStock/Thinkstock.)

LEADERSHIP DEMANDS FOR THE FUTURE

Nurse leaders consistently say that the characteristic they are most seeking in today's professional nurses is leadership. In probing what that means, we often find themes that relate to our activities that may have serendipitous outcomes. We shape the public's view of the profession, the organization in which we work, and health care in general. We influence interprofessional views of what it is to be a professional, and we create the expectations of the nursing profession's potential. Being able to take action when we suspect "something isn't right," whether with the patient or the organization, means that we have different expectations than we did several years ago. All of those examples shape the leadership potential that exists for the future.

If we think about the world as a loose web, we know that every element has the potential to influence every other element. This connectivity with each other, whether within our profession or within the team, means that we influence others all of the time just as others influence us. This influence molds our practices and beliefs as we move health care forward and subsequently changes how we influence others. Thus positions without formal leadership titles contain expectations for leadership, and we must all be prepared and willing to lead whenever the need arises. As an example, this response is exhibited every time a mass casualty occurs. The ability to be bicultural—both leading and following—is crucial to quality care, especially in crisis situations.

> **EXERCISE 31.1** Select two or three well-known community organizations. (They do not even have to be in health care.) Is the official leader always leading, or does that person relinquish that role and take on the role of follower in certain situations? If the leader left, would the organization diminish or suffer its demise, or would the organization thrive? What rationale supports this conclusion?

LEADERSHIP STRENGTHS FOR THE FUTURE

Because so much of nursing's work is accomplished in teams, we have considerable strength in inclusivity (the politics of commonalities). We tend, as do most people, to face our everyday work not capitalizing on thinking long term because we are typically consumed with short-term–focused work. Many efforts for change are slow and cumbersome; the structure of change (the layers in the organization) may be overwhelming and the process detailed. That is the basis of the Institute for Healthcare Improvement *(www.ihi.org)*, which supports small changes and encourages failing fast to determine whether a given small change is worth pursuing. IHI has short-circuited that drawn-out process of formal research studies in an attempt to bring quicker solutions to today's care. Although this rapid change (known as *rapid cycle improvement*) has produced positive results, we may see activities associated with this process as something "layered on" the already full schedule most of us experience at work. However, this emphasis, which is focused on improved care, is critical for safe patient care.

EXERCISE 31.2 Consider a persistent problem in the clinical area. This might relate to the functioning of a team or a clinical care practice. Consider what bothers you about the problem. Then imagine for a moment that you could do something to effect change for this problem. Make a list of "wild" ideas that are not the mainstream responses to such problems.

When we are faced with the pressures of providing care to a patient versus changing the system, we often remain focused on the patient, thus losing the opportunity to change an issue for many patients. To be effective in the future, we must embrace the opportunities to think longer term and more broadly so that more people are affected by our actions. This is the foundation of population health work—affect many. Moving from micromanaging to focusing on establishing expectations for a population, we may feel uncomfortable. However, that movement reinforces our ability to deal with longer-term, larger issues. In addition, the quest for meaning suggests that our actions today create the foundation on which future leaders will build. If we fail to capitalize on today's opportunities, we are diminishing the place at which future leaders will start their careers. Our goal should be to raise expectations about what comprises good, safe, quality care and how nurses contribute to those expectations. This potential is especially critical in times of dramatic, chaotic changes.

How then do today's practitioners know what is expected in the future? The answer may seem trite: Continue to learn and to practice! Our foundation begins with our concern for and advocacy about patient care. That foundation is fairly well engrained in professional nurses' beliefs. The movement from focusing on the nurse-patient relationship to the big picture of nursing (politics and public or health policy activities) may take several years, but the foundation is there. Fagin, in her classic work (2000), identified that we all move from a focus on the nurse-patient relationship, over time and additional preparation, to the higher levels of leadership that focus on larger group changes and policy development. What we do in our professional lives is the legacy we leave for future generations.

EXERCISE 31.3 Think ahead to the time when you might logically die. Rather than being sad that your life has ended, consider all of the good you have done in life and in nursing. Your next of kin is asked to say what he or she believes your nursing legacy to be. What one or two sentences would you want to have said about your contributions to nursing?

One other strength to develop to be successful for the future is considered risk-taking (Crenshaw & Yoder-Wise, 2016). When we think of risks, we tend to hesitate because, like the word, whatever it is sounds risky. Yet the creative ideas, the innovations, the big changes typically derive from a small percentage of people in any group. They operate at the end of a spectrum of risk that is riskier, but the successful ones do so through considered risk, meaning they see an opportunity as risky and have given thought to balancing the risks with the potential gains. This thinking is the basis for the model presented later.

Nurses who seek leadership opportunities will find that many are available—in the employment setting, in professional organizations, and in voluntary community organizations. Balancing the multiple demands in an era of rapid changes and the resultant new expectations becomes an even greater challenge. Merely being employed is no longer sufficient; we must be *employable*. This suggests that we must constantly be focused on competence, on learning, on what the future holds, and on what patients want and need. Failure to do so will make us unemployable and will make the profession undesirable. To be valued in the future we need to know what the future might encompass. An example of being proactively employable is found in the Literature Perspective.

VISIONING, FORECASTING, AND INNOVATION

Whether you are a leader, a follower, or a manager, being able to visualize in your mind what the ideal future is becomes a critical strategy. A **vision** can range from that

LITERATURE PERSPECTIVE

Resource: Boston-Fleischhauer, C. (2017). The explosion of virtual nursing care. *Journal of Nursing Administration,* 47(2), 85–87.

The emergence of the virtual nurses poses exciting opportunities for nurses who can forgo direct patient contact. The author describes how some institutions, including Banner Health and Mercy Health Systems, have developed, and now rely on, intensivists and intensive care (ICU) nurses who can monitor care of remotely located ICU patients. In addition to consulting with local providers and supporting evidence-based practices, they monitor adverse data to intervene before major clinical events occur. Telehealth also is used to provide sitter services, which often are costly to patients and hospitals.

Implications for Practice

This cultural shift requires nurses to think differently about how to provide care. It creates opportunities for new careers, for shaping new practices, and for creating predictive data that can drive additional practice changes.

of an individual to that of a group or to a whole organization. No matter how we engage in this visioning activity, we must be open and honest about what we think for the future. Finding those who do not necessarily think as we do but who are creative thinkers allows us to test ideas so that we enhance our own thinking and performance to higher levels. In the classic book, *The Fifth Discipline: The Art and Practice of the Learning Organization* (2006), Senge said that leadership is really about people working at their best to create the future. And that, in reality, is what we do every day. Forecasting is a specific process whereby we take in information that is current and focused on the future. A subsequent section illustrates some of the current and futuristic thinking that we should consider as we think about the future. Innovation is focused on taking current ideas and resources and creating a better way to provide care or to move a strategy forward more rapidly or see a way for using something for a totally different purpose than intended. An example of what is already innovative is the creation of MakerNurse

(*makernurse.com*). Another example, described in the H & HN publication (Vesley, 2017), is creating innovation teams to compete innovatively to solve problems organizational leaders identify. Using this "reverse pitch" ensures that the innovation projects are aligned with the organizations' current work to be achieved. A study conducted in Pakistan found that when nurses shared knowledge, best practices, mistakes, and problems, they were more likely to be rated as more innovative (see the Research Perspective).

EXERCISE 31.4 Select a group of three or four peers and brainstorm about what you think the future of nursing will be. Consider how technology will affect what we do; consider where our primary place of service will be and how we will deliver care. Think about the changes in society and the political pressures for effective health care and what those might mean for nursing. Think about how you would reform health care. Create a list of ideas to share with others.

RESEARCH PERSPECTIVE

Resource: Masood, M., & Afsar, B. (2017). Transformational leadership and innovative work behavior among nursing staff. *Nursing Inquiry* 24(4). https://doi.org/10.1111/mim12188.

This cross-sectional design used seven tools to measure transformational leadership, psychological empowerment, innovative work behavior, knowledge sharing, intrinsic motivation, empowerment role identity, and trust in leader. Research assistants distributed questionnaires to more than 1400 participants in the public hospitals in Pakistan. A 43% (n = 631) return rate was achieved. After those questionnaires were matched with a survey from a related physician, who rated nurses on innovative behaviors, 587 responses were analyzed. Through structural equation modeling, each of seven hypotheses was verified to determine causal relationships. The researchers found that transformational leadership influences nurses' psychological empowerment, which related to innovation.

Implications for Practice

Although the structure of the workforce in Pakistan differs from that in hospitals in Western healthcare systems, leaders need to create healthy workplaces focused on a blame-free and supportive environment if they wish nurses to be innovative.

Although no one knows the future for certain, many entities engage in formal discussions and predictions. These range from structured groups, such as the World Future Society (*www.wfs.org*) and the Future Today Institute (*https://futuretodayinstitute.com/*), to regular reports and books. Although not everyone is a futurist, each of us needs to be aware of trends. We take for granted that certain practices have remained unchanged. Yet technology *and* creative thinkers and investigators prove us wrong on a regular basis. Our challenge is to think about the future in a way that does not necessarily rely on history and yet builds on today. Converting problems or challenges into opportunities is a skill that opens up opportunities for the future.

THE WISE FORECAST MODEL©

One of the most simplistic models for thinking about the future is the Wise Forecast Model© (Yoder-Wise, 2011). Box 31.1 portrays the three steps.

This three-step model emphasizes what each of us must do proactively to create our own future rather than to passively react to changes as they occur. Either our careers can happen to us or we can prepare for them.

The first step, *learn widely,* means that we must extend our sources of knowledge beyond our role and clinical areas of interest. In fact, we must extend our learning beyond nursing and health care. Widely might encompass another discipline such as architecture or engineering. This extension doesn't mean that someone has to seek a degree in a new field. Learning about the field and how those professionals think might create new ways to think about issues affecting nursing. Just-in-time learning may feel stressful at times, yet it provides new information when it is needed. Thinking about what that learning means beyond the original intent can also create new ways of thinking about an issue. Widely might also include works related to the future-based or general publications, such as *FastCompany* or *Wired.* Subscribing to *Ted Talks'* science newsletter, as an example, provides new ideas too (*http://ted.us1.list-manage.com/subscribe?u=07487d1456302a286cf9c4ccc&id=83c20124eb*).

Initially, this kind of learning may be deliberate; in other words, you might need to set aside specified times to make the effort to garner this diverse information. After a few such sessions, however, information from other fields may pique your interest to the point that you can create a file of "tidbits" of information.

The second step is to *think wildly.* In other words, now we are limited only by our imagination. For example, since they were invented, someone was not satisfied with what we could do with computers. Thus computers evolved from one or two room-sized mainframes to something we could have in a home, to something we could carry in our backpacks, to something we could carry in our hands. Step two is designed to create connections among disparate thoughts. This thinking might be seen as the start of innovations. Thinking wildly includes creating wild questions. Sometimes they are what leads to a wild idea.

Step three, *act wisely,* is designed to draw us back to the reality of what is possible within the organization in which we work, with the funding we have available, and with the amount of time we have to invest in an activity. Acting wisely is, in a sense, a recovery phase to help us balance the wild thinking with reality.

Because the future is about teams and group work, many implications exist for nursing. Developing or strengthening skills related to working with others and facilitating their work and being effective in making decisions about practice and the workplace will be crucial. If the work is team-based, how will evaluations and compensation be structured in the future? Will you receive favorable reviews because the team you work with is productive? Will a team receive a bonus or merit salary increase? If you are not a team player, will you be useful to the organization at all? How will the role of the nurse as a frontline leader and the role of the nurse leader change? These are examples of how to rethink the future.

BOX 31.1	**The Three Steps to the Wise Forecast Model©**

1. Learn widely
2. Think wildly
3. Act wisely

From Yoder-Wise, P. S. (2011). Creating wise forecasts for nursing: The Wise Forecast Model©. *The Journal of Continuing Education in Nursing: Continuing Competence for the Future, 42*(9), 387.

EXERCISE 31.5 Think about the questions just mentioned and suggest how compensation will be formed in the future.

Consider the differences among generations and people. For example, some people are interested in being able to see the world. That used to mean travel abroad. A smart, trendy employer might create an international collaboration that allows nurses to retain their home organization benefits while practicing throughout their home country and the world.

SHARED VISION

The concept of shared vision suggests that several of us buy into a particular view. If we think of a familiar concept, stress, and what Selye (1978) described as *eustress* and *distress,* we have a continuum.

Eustress   Distress

Stress

Again, if you think about stress, you recall that each of us views an event differently and that having no stress results in death. Comparably, we can think about how society is evolving. Stability and total chaos are the ends of a continuum. Moving in some way between those two ends suggests that we live in a constant state of disequilibrium in which we strive toward stability while recognizing we experience chaos. The figure below suggests that in times of great stability, society makes little progress, so life may seem serene. In contrast, society may transform itself during times of great chaos, and life may seem uncontrollable. Thus thinking about the projections for the future becomes more important. For example, think about what people were doing, thinking, believing, and valuing on September 10, 2001. Then think about each in relation to September 11, 2001. We moved from some point on that continuum closer to chaos, no matter where we were in the world or what we were doing. Similarly, several years later when the Boston Marathon was disrupted by bombs exploding near the finish line, we moved closer to the side of chaos. Yet in both circumstances, healthcare professionals responded magnificently and learned from prior, similar events to make their care progressively better.

Stability   Chaos

Society

As we continue to move from "traditional" practices to evidence-based ones and from a heavy focus on tertiary care to one that values primary care, we can assume that we might experience more chaos. The comfort of the known is gone. Rather, practices are evaluated on a regular basis and changes are incorporated so that we are all doing the latest "best" for patients. In our efforts to do the best we can as soon as we can, we have experienced the phenomenon complexity compression, a term that means many changes are happening almost simultaneously, and before one practice can be firmly implanted in our minds, we are already addressing some other new change. This compression can be distracting or useful. As we increase the educational preparation of nurses worldwide, we will be better able to function in this evolving environment.

Our ability to retrieve information and analyze and evaluate it influences our currency with practice expectations. We seem to value the need for shared vision, which includes the idea of operating from a rich database-based approach. To be able to do so, however, we also need to hone our skills in projecting for the future so we know where practice is headed, we need to consider how we interact with our patients, and we need to consider how quickly we can elevate all nursing practitioners to a satisfactory level of working with an evidence-based practice approach.

PROJECTIONS FOR THE FUTURE

If you watch future reports on television or read *Trend Letter* or *The Futurist* (The World Society publication) or books by some classic authors such as Asimov, Clarke, Huxley, Orwell, and Wells, you will find comparable themes about the future. Some ideas that were developed over the past decade have transformed what we do and how we behave. For example:

- Adjustable glasses (creating sharp vision as a person's visual acuity changes), originally created for emerging economies, are available worldwide.
- 3D printers create organs that might not normally be available to those who need them.
- Devices such as the Oculus Rift allow us to experience events we might not want to partake in in real life. (Think how we could learn to interact with highly emotionally disturbed people.)
- Through molecular analysis researchers can swab your mobile phone to determine what you eat and drink, what you wear (clothing and makeup), and what medications you take.
- Temporary tattoos can monitor your health.

The following are some forecasts for the future that will affect nursing. Some are clearly related to health care; others have a tangential impact. In all cases, it is possible to ask the "what if" questions with each (e.g., what if this happens? Or what if more can happen?):

- Knowledge will continue to change dramatically, requiring that we all be dedicated learners. With or without state law, continuing education will be mandatory and essential if we intend to be relevant.
- Knowledge will evolve from the intensity of the current information evolution so that we will access content with meaning and applicability for our work. (The World Future Society [WFS] says by 2025 the intelligent cloud will arrive.)
- As the healthcare system continues to evolve, and as employers limit healthcare coverage and genetics allows us to know more about how an individual would respond to treatment, a shift toward eliminating the current disparities is more likely. Health care also seems to invade one's rights to privacy and choice because, as an example, everyone will have an electronic health record.
- Technology will continue to revolutionize health care. (Robots will provide care and monitor our health; and because they can be "empathetic," people may interact with them in a very personal way. Search for Romotive and Kodomora.)
- Creating a tricorder, the handheld device from Star Trek to assess people's health status, has been a goal that will allow any of us to quickly determine certain data and conditions (http://tricorderproject.org/index.html).
- Increasing diversity will contribute to the following, all of which have major implications for healthcare delivery:
  - More people who are older
  - More people moving to different parts of the country or the world
  - A greater need for speaking two or three languages
  - A view of the glocal community (worldwide diversity in our local communities)
- People will be satisfied with an experience, not simply service.
- Dichotomies will intensify. For example, increased violence and simultaneously an increased expectation for civility will exist.
- Stores will be either very small or huge; and the expansion of those existing only online will continue.

- Macromarketing (targeting masses) will be out; micromarketing (targeting specific populations) will be in; this trend will continue to intensify; and it will intensify applications to health care.
- In most communities, the emergency department will be the primary source of care for persons with mental health disorders.
- We could become narrower in our views of the world, because we can be catered to, based on our distinctive interests. As an example, think about micromarketing where retailers know what brands and sizes of clothing you prefer and send you only information about those products on a regular basis. The danger of this, of course, is that narrow views often lead to intolerance of broader or diverse views.
- Job security will be out; career options will be in.
- Mobile electrocardiograms will allow individuals to run their own ECGs and will allow nurses to have more data in any emergent situation.
- Competition will be out; cooperation will be in.
- Work will be sporadic.
- More people will be living with chronic diseases.
- A focus on prevention and wellness care will include patient accountability expectations with higher insurance rates for those who continue to engage in unhealthy behaviors.
- Water, not oil, will be the scarce resource, according to the World Future Society.
- Robotics will change how chronic diseases can be managed. Being able to have them provide care and monitor specific health indicators will extend nurses' reach.
- Bioengineering will make possible interventions that currently do not exist.
- Emphasis on prevention will redirect care efforts and create new services.
- Work will be accomplished by teams.
- Everyone will need to be a leader. The future explodes with potential.

EXERCISE 31.6 Review the list of projections, and consider how each might affect what you envision as your career. Evaluate each of the items to determine which ones you believe will be most important to you. Rank in order the top five. Compare your list with two or three colleagues' lists, and offer a rationale for your selection. After you hear other viewpoints, consider whether you would change your own rankings.

In nursing, we have issues we can consider in the more narrowed scope of the world; for example:

- How will shared governance continue to enhance the role of clinical nurses?
- How will Magnet® and Pathways to Excellence (ANCC) designations affect where nurses seek employment? (Think wildly!)
- How will continuing competence be measured in the future?
- How will health care emerge over the next several years as a desirable place to work and as a source of help for health-related needs?
- How will the increasing number of men in nursing change the "profile" of the profession?
- Will our profession's ethnic diversity reflect that of the population we serve?
- What can healthcare organizations learn from business, and vice versa?
- Will increasing concern about terrorism affect the flow of nurses across borders?

- Will educational transition move seamlessly across degrees so that we increase our numbers of highly educated nurses by 2020, as the National Academy of Medicine (formerly Institute of Medicine) suggests?

Already numerous opportunities exist for the future. Our task is to determine what best suits what we wish to do in the name of nursing.

CONCLUSION

Numerous changes will occur throughout our lifetimes. How soon will we say (if we haven't already), "When I was young..." Our description might be of something that today is considered fairly advanced. For those who want to thrive, the future forecasts are like the gold ring on the merry-go-round. If you risk and reach far enough, you can grasp it! Lead on … ¡Adelánte!

THE SOLUTION

I joined the professional organization for correctional health professionals and reviewed nursing publications to identify some of the possible options that were viewed as currently successful or likely to happen in the near future. I networked with colleagues at local and state meetings and realized that a graduate degree in public health nursing would help me develop the skills to address the health needs of my population. I also decided to pursue the Clinical Nurse Specialist in Community Health Nursing certification. Clearly, society expected more in the future in both education and credentials. I believed that I had the skills to develop community programs and research studies to help me address the high-risk needs of my client population.

Would this be a suitable approach for you? Why?

Sara McCumber

REFLECTIONS

Too many changes are occurring in the world for us to keep pace. If we participate in actively thinking about the future, however, we are more likely to remain employable and relevant. What two or three ideas have the most relevance for you? How can you use this model to keep your role as nurse relevant and valued? Learning widely, thinking wildly, and acting wisely is a simple process to consider the future.

TIPS FOR THE THRIVING IN THE FUTURE

- Scan literature external to nursing and health care.
- Listen to divergent viewpoints about the economy, federal and state policy, and technology.
- Ask yourself "what if" questions.
- Remember what you find disheartening and use that as a filter for what you learn from numerous fields.

THE EVIDENCE

We know that change is rapid today—our technology outdates rapidly and the latest "new" thing is quickly replaced by something else. In part that is related to how rapidly we disseminate new findings. Equally, if not more, important are financial incentives, such as reimbursement formulas and penalties, associated with the use, or failure of use, of best practices.

REFERENCES

Crenshaw, J.T., & Yoder-Wise, P.S. (2016). Creating an environment of innovation: The risk-taking leadership competency. *Nurse Leader, 11*(1), 24–27. https://doi.org/10/1016/j.mnl.2012.11.001.

Fagin, C. (2000). *Essays on nursing leadership.* New York: Springer.

Selye, H. (1978). *The stress of life.* New York: McGraw-Hill.

Senge, P. (2006). *The fifth discipline: The art and practice of the learning organization.* New York: Doubleday Currency.

Vesely, R. (2017). The reverse pitch. *H&HN* (May), 18-23.

World Future Society Forecasts. http://www.21stcentech.com/world-future-society-20-forecasts-2025.

Yoder-Wise, P. S. (2011). Creating wise forecasts for nursing: The Wise Forecast Model©. *The Journal of Continuing Education in Nursing: Continuing Competence for the Future, 42*(9), 387.

INDEX

Note: Page numbers followed by *f* indicate figures, *t* indicate tables and *b* indicate boxes.